Sociology

Fifth Edition

'There's no one on the planet with such a refined grasp of the practical and political significance of sociology as Anthony Giddens. This new edition of his best-selling textbook is his best yet.'

Anthony Elliott, University of Kent at Canterbury

'I have a high opinion of Giddens's book, which I consider to be a comprehensive and lucid introduction to the major topics, debates and theoretical perspectives in sociology. It combines a detailed overview of the contemporary sociological landscape with sensitivity to the enduring debt that the discipline owes to earlier theorists.

Mike Hawkins, Kingston University

'This new edition is fresh, engaging and topical. One particular feature is worth a mention: a striking introduction that catches the reader's attention right at the start is very effective educationally. I remain a fan of such pedagogical devices. The point is made economically and strikingly at the very beginning and is then carried through the chapter. Some of the chapters do this in an exemplary fashion.'

Nick Abercrombie, University of Lancaster

'The main reason for recommending Giddens's text over many of its competitors lies in the way that the book handles the various sociological specialisms. Although structured through specialist fields such as crime and deviance, families, gender and sexuality and so on, Giddens never loses sight of the general sociological perspective amid the welter of detailed and specialized knowledge. This introductory textbook stands out as a welcome antidote to the impression of fragmentation and diversity of the discipline which students often come away with from textbooks. Giddens still succeeds in demonstrating the continuing intellectual excitement of the sociological enterprise to all new students. For me, this is the foremost consideration when choosing a core introductory textbook and Giddens's *Sociology* is peerless in this regard.'

Phil Sutton, The Robert Gordon University, Aberdeen

'The chapter on theoretical thinking in sociology is clearly written with a strong thread running throughout. Students will like the way in which it brings together many diverse social theories highlighting some of their main similarities and differences in a single chapter. This chapter was towards the end of the book in the fourth edition; moving it nearer to the front of the book in this new edition is an excellent idea and will give students an insight into the theoretical interpretations used by sociologists as they look at the issues discussed in the remaining chapters.'

Steve Williams, University of Glamorgan

'The material on the sociology of everyday life provides an excellent means of encouraging students to examine their own experiences through sociological lenses. The coverage of everyday activities is by far the best offered by any introductory textbook currently available.'

David Inglis, University of Aberdeen

'Chapter 6, "Socialization, the Life-Course and Ageing", provides the reader with a wide-ranging review of social and psychological transitions through the life-course. The text brings together both a discussion of classic studies from Freud onwards as well as an overview of the latest research in the field.'

Chris Phillipson, University of Keele

'Anthony Giddens presents a comprehensive yet accessible account of complex social issues in this book: of changing social institutions, structures and values in society. The text is carefully designed to offer students an insight into current sociological debates and critical thinking, with further reading and glossary. The chapter on "Families and Intimate Relationships" is an authoritative overview of changing family forms and values. It provides a thought-provoking blend of theoretical insights and empirical examples drawn from across the globe. Students will be hooked by questions about love and intimacy at the start of the chapter, since these are issues that touch on all young people's experiences. Yet they will also be challenged by the deconstruction of traditional myths about families, intimacy and sexual relationships in various societies.'

Deborah Chambers, University of Newcastle

'Chapter 7, "Families and Intimate Relationships", is interesting, presenting material in a way currently not available in the market. The text is rich in its engagement with the current diversity of family forms, and presents a clear elaboration of the relevant perspectives for theorizing contemporary family life. The structure of the chapter, divided into short sections with the main concepts clearly explained at the beginning, will be appealing to students.'

Elizabeth Silva, The Open University

'The chapter on health, illness and disability is very clearly written and students will find it very accessible indeed. The accessibility and clarity are especially important for those who have not studied sociology at A-level. The structure works extremely well, and the use of images is especially appealing. I can't think how it could be improved.'

Sarah Nettleton, University of York

'Disability Studies is now an established interdisciplinary field of enquiry within the social sciences. Although the sociology of disability has made a major contribution to this development, it has generally escaped the attention of the majority of mainstream sociologists and particularly those who produce general introductory texts. This book provides the first meaningful and accessible insight into the issues and debates that have emerged from this increasingly important area of sociological analysis.'

Colin Barnes, University of Leeds

'Chapter 9, "Stratificatiom and Class", is engaging and accessible: the captivating "real-life" story in the introduction will quickly catch the attention of readers. The overall structure, which breaks the chapter into sub-sections, is helpful and results in a comprehensive coverage of the subject area.'

Majella Kilkey, University of Hull

'The chapter "Stratification and Class" is well written, clear and well structured. Students are likely to appreciate its clarity, in particular its lucid explanation of what can be quite complex concepts (surplus value, for example) and its succinct discussion of key theorists. It covers the classic debates and studies well, covering Marx and Weber, issues of class schema and key classes, as well as bringing in issues of globalization.'

Tracey Warren, University of Newcastle

'There is a great deal in the chapter on poverty, social exclusion and welfare to engage and challenge readers. The content is comprehensive and succeeds in introducing key debates and conceptual issues relevant to an understanding of poverty. References to up-to-date writings about poverty and the discussion of New Labour welfare reforms make this chapter contemporary and relevant to current debates in the UK.'

Abbey Halcli, Oxford Brookes University

'Chapter 10, "Poverty, Social Exclusion and Welfare", provides the student who is new to the social sciences with a well-evidenced and clearly written introduction to the investigation of poverty and deprivation in Britain. Taking a chronological perspective, Giddens tells the story through the contributions of authors such as Peter Townsend, Joanna Mack and Stewart Lansley, among others, up to the current thinking on social exclusion.'

John Stewart, Lancaster University

'The chapter on global inequality combines sensitivity to national developments, especially the widening economic gaps between the wealthy and the poor in the advanced Anglo-American democracies, with attention paid to international and regional trends, especially those separating the Sub-Saharan Africa, South America and Southern-Central Asia from the developed societies. These trends are not only noted, but also explained in the context of new critical analyses. This is a truly global study of social inequalities.'

Jan Pakulski, University of Tasmania

'Difficult theories and debates are presented logically and mostly chronologically in the chapter on the environment and risk, which is replete with concrete examples that can be used in classroom situations. The language is clear and accessible and concepts are explained in non-technical terminology. Students will appreciate the effective balance between text and graphics and the specific examples that bring environmental debates to life. They are also introduced to environmental issues via an initial discussion of their relevance for sociologists. This tackles their own question (what's it to do with us?) at the outset and is a very helpful chapter introduction.'

Phil Sutton, The Robert Gordon University, Aberdeen

Sociology

Fifth Edition

Anthony Giddens

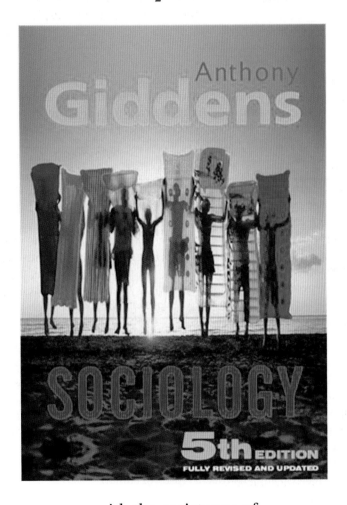

with the assistance of

Simon Griffiths

polity

First published in 2006 by Polity Press

Polity Press
65 Bridge Street
Cambridge CB2 1UR, UK.

Polity Press
350 Main Street
Malden, MA 02148, USA

ISBN 10: 0-7456-3378-1
ISBN 13: 978-07456-3378-7
ISBN 10: 0-7456-3379-x (pb)
ISBN 13: 978-07456-3379-4 (pb)

A catalogue record for this book is available from the British Library.

Typeset in 9.5pt on 13pt Utopia
by Servis Filmsetting Ltd, Manchester
Printed and bound in Italy by Rotolito Lambarda

The publisher has used its best endeavours to ensure that the URLs for external websites referred to in this book are correct and active at the time of going to press. However, the publisher has no responsibility for the websites and can make no guarantee that a site will remain live or that the content is or will remain appropriate.

Every effort has been made to trace all copyright holders, but if any have been inadvertently overlooked the publishers will be pleased to include any necessary credits in any subsequent reprint or edition.

For further information on Polity, visit our website: www.polity.co.uk

Please visit the website dedicated to this book at: www.polity.co.uk/giddens5

Contents

Detailed Contents

Preface to the fifth edition

THE fourth edition of this book was published before the events of 11 September 2001. Keeping pace with the remarkable changes of the contemporary social world, and the years post-9/11, the fifth edition of the text has been rigorously revised and updated, with a substantial amount of new material added. As in previous editions, I have sought to make the book readable and entertaining, but have also tried to keep it at the cutting edge of the discipline. For the first time, the book now includes detailed discussions of global inequality, terrorism, the life-course, ageing and disability, amongst other new topics of current importance. By integrating these new sections with tried and tested parts of the text, I have tried to preserve the reputation of the book as a state-of-the-art introduction to sociology.

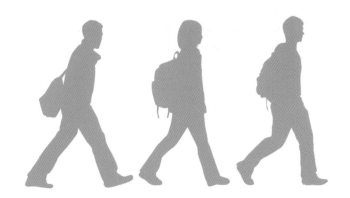

Acknowledgements

THANKS to everyone who helped in the preparation of this book. Many readers of the preceding edition sent useful unsolicited comments, and I am very grateful to them. The preparation of this fifth edition would have been impossible without the active participation of Simon Griffiths, who devoted many months to working on it. Whatever virtues the book may possess are owed as much to him as to me. I am very greatly indebted to him.

I should like to thank all the academics who read drafts of the chapters of the book. There are too many to name individually, but their comments were invaluable. At Polity, I should like to thank the following in particular: John Thompson, David Held, Gill Motley, Neil de Cort and Breffni O'Connor. Emma Longstaff played an absolutely fundamental part in the whole project from beginning to end. She has been marvellous to work with. Sarah Dancy did a wonderful job of copy-editing the text and I am very grateful to her for her careful, meticulous and imaginative work.

Finally, I should like to thank Alena Ledeneva for her consistent help and encouragement.

AG

About this book

THIS book was written in the belief that sociology has a key role to play in modern intellectual culture and a central place within the social sciences. My aim in this fifth edition, as in the previous editions, has been to write a book that combines some originality with an analysis of all the basic issues of interest to sociologists today. The book does not try to introduce overly sophisticated notions; nevertheless, ideas and findings drawn from the cutting edge of the discipline are incorporated throughout. I hope it is not a partisan treatment; I endeavoured to cover the major perspectives in sociology and the major findings of contemporary research in an even-handed, although not indiscriminate, way.

Major themes

The book is constructed around a number of basic themes, each of which helps to give the work a distinctive character. One main theme is that of the *world in change*. Sociology was born of the transformations that wrenched the industrializing social order of the West away from the ways of life characteristic of preceding societies. The world that was created by these changes is the primary object of concern of sociological analysis. The pace of social change has continued to accelerate, and it is possible that we stand on the threshold of transitions as significant as those that occurred in the late eighteenth and nineteenth centuries. Sociology has prime responsibility for charting the transformations that have taken place in the past and for grasping the major lines of development taking place today.

A second fundamental theme of the book is the *globalizing of social life*. For far too long, sociology has been dominated by the view that societies can be studied as independent unities. But even in the past, societies have never really existed in isolation. In current times, we can see a clear acceleration in processes of global integration. This is obvious, for example, in the expansion of international trade across the world. The emphasis on globalization also connects closely with the weight given to the interdependence of the industrialized and the developing worlds today. The first edition, published in 1989, broke new ground in discussing the impact of globalization, an examination of which at that time was only just beginning even in the more technical areas of the discipline. Since then the debate about globalization has vastly intensified, while globalization itself has advanced much further, as have some of the changes in information technology associated with it.

Third, the book takes a strongly *comparative* stance. The study of sociology cannot be taught solely by understanding the institutions of any one particular society. While I have slanted the discussion towards the UK, such discussion is always balanced by a rich variety of materials drawn from other cultures. These include researches carried out in other Western countries, but I also refer often to Russia and the Eastern European societies, which are currently undergoing substantial changes. The book also includes much more material on developing countries than has been usual hitherto in introductions of sociology. In addition, I strongly emphasize the relationship between sociology and anthropology, whose concerns overlap comprehensively. Given the close connections that now mesh societies across the world with one another, and the virtual disappearance of traditional social systems, sociology and anthropology increasingly become indistinguishable.

A fourth theme is the necessity of taking a *historical approach* to sociology. This involves more than just filling in the historical context within which events occur. One of the most important developments in sociology over the past few years has been an increasing emphasis on historical analysis. This should be understood not solely as applying a sociological outlook to the past, but as a way of contributing to our understanding of institutions in the present. Recent work in historical sociology is discussed throughout and provides a framework for the interpretations offered within most of the chapters.

Fifth, particular attention is given throughout the text to *issues of gender*. The study of gender is ordinarily regarded as a specific field within sociology as a whole – and this volume contains a chapter that specifically explores thinking and research on the subject (chapter 12). However, questions about gender relations are so fundamental to sociological analysis that they cannot simply be considered a subdivision. Thus, many chapters contain sections concerned with issues of gender.

A sixth theme is the *micro and macro link*. In many places in the book, I show that interaction in micro-level contexts affects larger social processes and that such macro-level processes influence our day-to-day lives. I emphasize to readers that one can better understand a social situation by analysing it at both the micro and macro levels.

A final theme is the relation between the *social* and the *personal*. Sociological thinking is a vital help to self-understanding, which in turn can be focused back on an improved understanding of the social world. Studying sociology should be a liberating experience: the field enlarges our sympathies and imagination, opens up new perspectives on the sources of our own behaviour and creates an awareness of cultural settings different from our own. In so far as sociological ideas challenge dogma, teach appreciation of cultural variety and allow us insight into the working of social institutions, the practice of sociology enhances the possibilities of human freedom.

Organization of the book

There is not much abstract discussion of basic sociological concepts at the beginning of this book. An expanded and comprehensive glossary at the end provides a useful reference point and collects together important sociological terms used in earlier chapters. Throughout the text, terms found in the glossary are in bold type. I have sought to illustrate ideas, concepts and theories by means of concrete examples. While these are usually taken from sociological research, I have quite often used material from other sources (such as newspaper reports) for illustrative purposes. I have tried to keep the writing style as simple and direct as possible, while endeavouring to make the book lively and 'full of surprises'.

The chapters follow a sequence designed to help achieve a progressive mastery of the different fields of sociology, but I have taken care to ensure that the book can be used flexibly and is easy to adapt to the needs of individual courses. Chapters can be deleted, or studied in a different order, without much loss. Each chapter has been written as a fairly autonomous unit, with substantial cross-referencing to other chapters at relevant points.

There are links at the ends of chapters to offer some starting points to researching the wealth of information about people and about sociology offered by the World Wide Web. The book is also designed to be used in conjunction with the extensive additional material on its own website, available at <http://www.polity.co.uk/giddens>. Both lecturers and students will find a wealth of resources to stimulate critical thinking, and to aid further research into the themes explored by the book. This adds an important new dimension to *Sociology, Fifth edition*, and is designed to benefit both those teaching and those studying in this field.

Sociology

Fifth Edition

Contents

1 What is Sociology?

WE LIVE today – at the beginning of the twenty-first century – in a world that is intensely worrying, yet full of the most extraordinary promise for the future. It is a world awash with change, marked by deep conflicts, tensions and social divisions, as well as by the destructive onslaught of modern technology on the natural environment. Yet we have possibilities of controlling our destiny and shaping our lives for the better that would have been unimaginable to earlier generations.

How did this world come about? Why are our conditions of life so different from those of our parents and grandparents? What directions will change take in the future? These questions are the prime concern of sociology, a field of study that consequently has a fundamental role to play in modern intellectual life.

Sociology is the scientific study of human social life, groups, and societies. It is a dazzling and compelling enterprise, as its subject matter is our own behaviour as social beings. The scope of sociological study is extremely wide, ranging from the analysis of passing encounters between individuals on the street to the investigation of global social processes such as the rise of Islamic fundamentalism.

Most of us see the world in terms of the familiar features of our own lives. Sociology demonstrates the need to take a much broader view of why we are as we are, and why we act as we do. It teaches us that what we regard as natural, inevitable, good or true may not be such, and that the 'givens' of our life are strongly influenced by historical and social forces. Understanding the subtle yet complex and profound ways in which our individual lives reflect the contexts of our social experience is basic to the sociological outlook.

The sociological perspective

Learning to think sociologically – looking, in other words, at the broader view – means cultivating the imagination. Studying sociology cannot be just a routine process of acquiring knowledge. A sociologist is someone who is able to break free from the immediacy of personal circumstances and put things in a wider context. Sociological work depends on what the American author C. Wright Mills, in a famous phrase, called the **sociological imagination** (Mills 1970).

The sociological imagination requires us, above all, to 'think ourselves away' from the familiar routines of our daily lives in order to look at them anew. Consider the simple act of drinking a cup of coffee. What could we find to say, from a sociological point of view, about such an apparently uninteresting piece of behaviour? An enormous amount.

We could point out first of all that coffee is not just a refreshment. It possesses symbolic value as part of our day-to-day social activities. Often the ritual associated with

Getting together with friends for coffee is part of a social ritual.

coffee drinking is much more important than the act of consuming the drink itself. For many Westerners the morning cup of coffee stands at the centre of a personal routine. It is an essential first step to starting the day. Morning coffee is often followed later in the day by coffee with others – the basis of a social ritual. Two people who arrange to meet for coffee are probably more interested in getting together and chatting than in what they actually drink. Drinking and eating in all societies, in fact, provide occasions for social interaction and the enactment of rituals – and these offer a rich subject matter for sociological study.

Second, coffee is a drug, containing caffeine, which has a stimulating effect on the brain. Many people drink coffee for the 'extra lift' it provides. Long days at the office

and late nights studying are made more tolerable by coffee breaks. Coffee is a habit-forming substance, but coffee addicts are not regarded by most people in Western culture as drug users. Like alcohol, coffee is a socially acceptable drug, whereas marijuana, for instance, is not. Yet there are societies that tolerate the consumption of marijuana or even cocaine, but frown on both coffee and alcohol. Sociologists are interested in why these contrasts exist.

Third, an individual who drinks a cup of coffee is caught up in a complicated set of social and economic relationships stretching across the world. Coffee is a product which links people in some of the wealthiest and most impoverished parts of the planet: it is consumed in great quantities in wealthy countries, but is grown primarily in poor ones. Next to oil,

Coffee means their livelihood for these workers sorting beans for a fair trade cooperative in South America.

Coffee houses were centres of gossip and political intrigue for the elite in eighteenth-century Britain.

coffee is the most valuable commodity in international trade; it provides many countries with their largest source of foreign exchange. The production, transportation and distribution of coffee require continuous transactions between people thousands of miles away from the coffee drinker. Studying such global transactions is an important task of sociology, since many aspects of our lives are now affected by worldwide social influences and communications.

Fourth, the act of sipping a coffee presumes a whole process of past social and economic development. Along with other now familiar items of Western diets – like tea, bananas, potatoes and white sugar – coffee became widely consumed only from the late 1800s (although coffee was fashionable amongst the elite before then). Although the drink originated in the Middle East, its mass consumption dates from the period of Western expansion about two centuries ago. Virtually all the coffee we drink today comes from areas (South America and Africa) that were colonized by Europeans; it is in no sense a 'natural' part of the Western diet. The colonial legacy has had an enormous impact on the development of the global coffee trade.

Fifth, coffee is a product that stands at the heart of contemporary debates about globalization, international trade, human rights and environmental destruction. As coffee has grown in popularity, it has become 'branded' and politicized: the decisions that consumers make about what kind of coffee to drink and where to purchase it have become lifestyle choices. Individuals may choose to drink only organic coffee, decaffeinated coffee or coffee that has been 'fairly traded' (through schemes that pay full market prices to small coffee producers in developing countries). They may opt to patronize 'independent' coffee houses, rather than 'corporate' coffee chains such as Starbucks. Coffee drinkers might decide to boycott coffee from certain countries with poor human rights and environmental records. Sociologists are interested to understand how globalization heightens people's awareness of issues occurring in distant corners of the planet and prompts them to act on new knowledge in their own lives.

Studying sociology

The sociological imagination allows us to see that many events that seem to concern only the individual actually reflect larger issues. Divorce, for instance, may be a very difficult process for someone who goes through it – what Mills calls a personal trouble. But divorce, he points out, is also a public issue in a society like present-day Britain, where over a third of all marriages break up within ten years. Unemployment, to take another example, may be a personal tragedy for someone thrown out of a job and unable to find another. Yet it goes far beyond a matter for private despair when millions of people in a society are in the same situation: it is a public issue expressing large social trends.

Try applying this sort of outlook to your own life. It isn't necessary to think only of troubling events. Consider, for instance, why you are turning the pages of this book at all – why you have decided to study sociology. You might be a reluctant sociology student, taking the course only to fulfil a degree requirement. Or you might be enthusiastic to find out more about the subject. Whatever your motivations, you are likely to have a good deal in common, without necessarily knowing it, with others studying sociology. Your private decision reflects your position in the wider society.

Do the following characteristics apply to you? Are you young? White? From a professional or white-collar background? Have you done, or do you still do, some part-time work to boost your income? Do you want to find a good job when you finish your education, but are not especially dedicated to studying? Do you not know really what sociology is but think it has something to do with how people behave in groups? More than three-quarters of you will answer yes to all these questions. University students are not typical of the population as a whole, but tend to be drawn from more privileged backgrounds. And their attitudes usually reflect those held by friends and acquaintances. The social backgrounds from which we come have a great deal to do with what kinds of decisions we think appropriate.

But suppose you answer no to one or more of these questions. You might come from a minority-group background or one of poverty. You may be someone in mid-life or older. All the same, however, further conclusions probably follow. You are likely to have had to struggle to get where you are; you might have had to overcome hostile reactions from friends and others when you told them you were intending to go to college; or you might be combining higher education with full-time parenthood.

Although we are all influenced by the social contexts in which we find ourselves, none of us is simply determined in our behaviour by those contexts. We possess, and create, our own individuality. It is the business of sociology to investigate the connections between what society makes of us and what we make of ourselves. Our activities both structure – give shape to – the social world around us and at the same time are structured by that social world.

The concept of **social structure** is an important one in sociology. It refers to the fact that the social contexts of our lives do not consist just of random assortments of events or actions; they are structured, or patterned, in distinct ways. There are regularities in the ways we behave and in the relationships we have with one another. But social structure is not like a physical structure, such as a building, which exists independently of human actions. Human societies are always in the process of **structuration**. They are reconstructed at every moment by the very 'building blocks' that compose it – human beings like you and me.

As an example, consider again the case of coffee. A cup of coffee does not automatically arrive in your hands. You choose, for example, to go to a particular coffee shop, whether to drink a latte or an espresso. As you make these decisions, along with millions of other people, you shape the market for coffee and affect the lives of coffee producers living perhaps thousands of miles away on the other side of the world.

The development of sociological thinking

When they first start studying sociology, many students are puzzled by the diversity of approaches they encounter. Sociology has never been a discipline in which there is a body of ideas that everyone accepts as valid. Sociologists often quarrel amongst themselves about how to go about studying human behaviour and how research results might best be interpreted. Why should this be so? Why can't sociologists agree with one another more consistently, as natural scientists seem able to do? The answer is bound up with the very nature of the field itself. Sociology is about our own lives and our own behaviour, and studying ourselves is the most complex and difficult endeavour we can undertake.

Theories and theoretical approaches

Trying to understand something as complex as the impact of industrialization on society, for example, raises the importance of theory to sociology. Factual research shows *how* things occur; but sociology does not just consist of collecting **facts**, however important and interesting they may be (for example, it is a fact that I bought a coffee this morning, that it cost a certain amount, that the coffee beans were grown in Central America, etc.). We also want to know *why* things happen, and in order to do so we have to learn to construct explanatory theories. For instance, we know that industrialization has had a major influence on the emergence of modern societies, but what are the origins and preconditions of

In this painting by Brueghel, there are a large number of people engaged in a range of often bizarre activities. The painting at first seems to make little sense. However, the title of the painting, *Netherlandish Proverbs*, helps explain its meaning. The picture actually shows more than a hundred proverbs that were common when it was painted in the sixteenth century. In the same way, sociologists need theory as a context to help make sense of their observations.

industrialization? Why do we find differences between societies in their industrialization processes? Why is industrialization associated with changes in ways of criminal punishment, or in family and marriage systems? To respond to such questions, we have to develop theoretical thinking.

Theories involve constructing abstract interpretations that can be used to explain a wide variety of empirical situations. A **theory** about industrialization, for example, would be concerned with identifying the main features that processes of industrial development share in common and would try to show which of these are most important in explaining such development. Of course, factual research and theories can never completely be separated. We can only develop valid **theoretical approaches** if we are able to test them out by means of factual research.

We need theories to help us make sense of facts. Contrary to popular assertion, facts do not speak for themselves. Many sociologists work primarily on factual research, but unless they are guided by some knowledge of theory, their work is unlikely to explain the complexity of modern societies. This is true even of research carried out with strictly practical objectives.

'Practical people' tend to be suspicious of theorists and may like to see themselves as too 'down to earth' to need to pay attention to more abstract ideas, yet all practical decisions have some theoretical assumptions lying behind them. A manager of a business, for example, might have scant regard for 'theory'. Nonetheless, every approach to business activity involves theoretical assumptions, even if these often remain unstated. Thus, the manager might assume that employees are motivated to work hard mainly by money – the level of wages they receive. This is not only a theoretical interpretation of human behaviour; it is also a mistaken one, as research in industrial sociology tends to demonstrate.

Without a theoretical approach, we would not know what to look for in beginning a study or in interpreting the results of research. However, the illumination of factual evidence is not the only reason for the prime position of theory in sociology. Theoretical thinking must respond to general problems posed by the study of human social life, including issues that are philosophical in nature. Deciding the extent to which sociology should be modelled on the natural sciences and how we should best conceptualize human consciousness, action and institutions are problems that do not have easy solutions.

They have been handled in different ways in the various theoretical approaches that have sprung up in the discipline.

Early theorists

We human beings have always been curious about the sources of our own behaviour, but for thousands of years our attempts to understand ourselves relied on ways of thinking passed down from generation to generation, often expressed in religious terms. (For example, before the rise of modern science, many people believed that gods or spirits were the cause of natural events such as earthquakes.) Although writers from earlier periods provided insights into human behaviour and society, the systematic study of society is a relatively recent development, whose beginnings date back to the late 1700s and early 1800s. The background to the origins of sociology was the series of sweeping changes ushered in by the French Revolution of 1789 and the emergence of the **Industrial Revolution** in Europe. The shattering of traditional ways of life wrought by these changes resulted in the attempts of thinkers to develop a new understanding of both the social and natural worlds.

A key development was the use of science instead of religion to understand the world. The types of questions these nineteenth-century thinkers sought to answer – What is human nature? Why is society structured like it is? How and why do societies change? – are the same questions sociologists try to answer today. Our modern world is radically different from that of the past; it is sociology's task to help us understand this world and what the future is likely to hold.

Auguste Comte

No single individual, of course, can found a whole field of study, and there were many contributors to early sociological thinking. Particular prominence, however, is usually given to the French author Auguste Comte (1798–1857), if only because he actually invented the word 'sociology'. Comte originally used the term 'social physics', but some of his intellectual rivals at the time were also making use of that term. Comte wanted to distinguish his own views from theirs, so he coined the term 'sociology' to describe the subject he wished to establish.

Comte's thinking reflected the turbulent events of his age. The French Revolution had introduced significant changes into society and the growth of industrialization was altering the traditional lives of the French population. Comte sought to create a science of society that could explain the laws of the social world just as natural science explained the functioning of the physical world. Although Comte recognized that each scientific discipline has its own subject matter, he believed that they all share a common logic and scientific method aimed at revealing universal laws. Just as the discovery of laws in the natural world allows us to control and predict events around us, uncovering the laws that govern human society could help us shape our destiny and improve the welfare of humanity. Comte argued that society conforms to invariable laws in much the same way that the physical world does.

Comte's vision for sociology was that of a *positive* science. He believed that sociology should apply the same rigorous scientific methods to the study of society that physics or chemistry use to study the physical world. **Positivism** holds that science should be concerned only with observable entities that are known directly to experience. On the basis of careful sensory observations, one can infer laws that explain the relationship between the observed phenomena. By understanding the causal relationship between events, scientists can then predict how future events will occur. A positivist approach to sociology believes in the production of knowledge about society based on empirical evidence drawn from observation, comparison and experimentation.

Comte's *law of the three stages* claims that human efforts to understand the world have passed through theological, metaphysical and positive stages. In the theological stage, thoughts were guided by religious ideas and the belief that society was an expression of God's will. In the metaphysical stage, which came to the

Auguste Comte (1798–1857)

forefront around the time of the Renaissance, society came to be seen in natural, not supernatural, terms. The positive stage, ushered in by the discoveries and achievements of Copernicus, Galileo and Newton, encouraged the application of scientific techniques to the social world. In keeping with this view, Comte regarded sociology as the last science to develop – following on from physics, chemistry and biology – but as the most significant and complex of all the sciences.

In the later part of his career, Comte drew up ambitious plans for the reconstruction of French society in particular and for human societies in general, based on his sociological viewpoint. He urged the establishment of a 'religion of humanity' that would abandon faith and dogma in favour of a scientific grounding. Sociology would be at the heart of this new religion. Comte was keenly aware of the state of the society in which he lived; he was concerned with the inequalities being produced by industrialization and the threat they posed to social cohesion. The long-term solution, in his view, was the production of a moral consensus that would help to regulate, or hold together, society despite the new patterns of inequality. Although Comte's vision for the reconstruction of society was never realized, his contribution to systematizing and unifying the science of society was important to the later professionalization of sociology as an academic discipline.

Emile Durkheim

The writings of another French author, Emile Durkheim (1858–1917), have had a more lasting impact on modern sociology than those of Comte. Although he drew on

Emile Durkheim (1858–1917)

aspects of Comte's work, Durkheim thought that many of his predecessor's ideas were too speculative and vague and that Comte had not successfully carried out his programme – to establish sociology on a scientific basis. Durkheim saw sociology as a new science that could be used to elucidate traditional philosophical questions by examining them in an empirical manner. Like Comte before him, Durkheim believed that we must study social life with the same objectivity as scientists study the natural world. His famous first principle of sociology was 'Study social facts as *things*!' By this he meant that social life could be analysed as rigorously as objects or events in nature.

Durkheim's writings spanned a broad spectrum of topics. Three of the main themes he addressed were the importance of sociology as an empirical science, the rise of the individual and the formation of a new social order, and the sources and character of moral authority in society. We will encounter Durkheim's ideas again in our discussions of religion, deviance and crime, and work and economic life.

For Durkheim, the main intellectual concern of sociology is the study of **social facts**. Rather than applying sociological methods to the study of individuals, sociologists should instead examine social facts – aspects of social life that shape our actions as individuals, such as the state of the economy or the influence of religion. Durkheim believed that societies have a reality of their own – that is to say that there is more to society than simply the actions and interests of its individual members. According to Durkheim, social facts are ways of acting, thinking or feeling that are *external* to individuals and have their own reality outside the lives and perceptions of individual people. Another attribute of social facts is that they exercise a *coercive power* over individuals. The constraining nature of social facts is often not recognized by people as coercive, however. This is because people generally comply with social facts freely, believing they are acting out of choice. In fact, Durkheim argues, people often simply follow patterns that are general to their society. Social facts can constrain human action in a variety of ways, ranging from outright punishment (in the case of a crime, for example) to social rejection (in the case of unacceptable behaviour) to simple misunderstanding (in the case of the misuse of language).

Durkheim conceded that social facts are difficult to study. Because they are invisible and intangible, social facts cannot be observed directly. Instead, their properties must be revealed indirectly by analysing their effects or by considering attempts that have been made at their expression, such as laws, religious texts or written rules of conduct. In studying social facts, Durkheim stressed the importance of abandoning prejudices and ideology. A scientific attitude demands a mind which is open to the evidence of the senses and free of preconceived ideas which come from outside. Durkheim held that scientific concepts could only be generated through scientific practice. He challenged sociologists to study things as they really are and to construct new concepts that reflect the true nature of social things.

Like the other founders of sociology, Durkheim was preoccupied with the changes transforming society in his own lifetime. He was particularly interested in social and moral solidarity – in other words, what holds society together and keeps it from descending into chaos. Solidarity is maintained when individuals are successfully integrated into social groups and are regulated by a set of shared values and customs. In his first major work, *The Division of Labour in Society*, Durkheim presented an analysis of social change that argued that the advent of the industrial era meant the emergence of a new type of solidarity (Durkheim 1984 [1893]). In making this argument, Durkheim contrasted two types of solidarity, *mechanical* and *organic*, and related them to the **division of labour** – the growth of distinctions between different occupations.

According to Durkheim, traditional cultures with a low division of labour are characterized by mechanical solidarity.

Because most members of the society are involved in similar occupations, they are bound together by common experience and shared beliefs. The strength of these shared beliefs is repressive – the community swiftly punishes anyone who challenges conventional ways of life. In this way, there is little room for individual dissent. Mechanical solidarity, therefore, is grounded in consensus and similarity of belief. The forces of industrialization and urbanization, however, led to a growing division of labour that contributed to the breakdown of this form of solidarity. Durkheim argued that the specialization of tasks and the increasing social differentiation in advanced societies would lead to a new order featuring organic solidarity. Societies characterized by organic solidarity are held together by people's economic interdependence and their recognition of the importance of others' contributions. As the division of labour expands, people become increasingly dependent upon one another, because each person needs goods and services that those in other occupations supply. Relationships of economic reciprocity and mutual dependency come to replace shared beliefs in creating social consensus.

Yet, processes of change in the modern world are so rapid and intense that they give rise to major social difficulties. They can have disruptive effects on traditional lifestyles, morals, religious beliefs and everyday patterns without providing clear new values. Durkheim linked these unsettling conditions to **anomie**, a feeling of aimlessness or despair provoked by modern social life. Traditional moral controls and standards, which used to be supplied by religion, are largely broken down by modern social development, and this leaves many individuals in modern societies feeling that their daily lives lack meaning.

One of Durkheim's most famous studies was concerned with the analysis of suicide (see box). Suicide seems to be a purely personal act, the outcome of extreme personal unhappiness. Durkheim showed, however, that social factors exert a fundamental influence on suicidal behaviour – anomie being one of these influences. Suicide rates show regular patterns from year to year and these patterns must be explained sociologically.

Karl Marx

The ideas of Karl Marx (1818–83) contrast sharply with those of Comte and Durkheim, but, like them, he sought to explain the changes that were taking place in society during the time of the Industrial Revolution. Marx's political activities brought him as a young man into conflict

Karl Marx (1818–83)

Durkheim's study of suicide

One of the classic sociological studies to explore the relationship between the individual and society is Emile Durkheim's analysis of suicide (Durkheim 1952 [1897]). Even though humans see themselves as individuals exercising free will and choice, their behaviours are often socially patterned and shaped. Durkheim's study showed that even a highly personal act like suicide is influenced by the social world.

Research had been conducted on suicide prior to Durkheim's study, but he was the first to insist on a sociological explanation for suicide. Previous writings had acknowledged the influence of social factors on suicide, but looked to considerations such as race, climate or mental disorder to explain an individual's likelihood of committing suicide. According to Durkheim, however, suicide was a *social fact* that could only be explained by other social facts. Suicide was more than simply the aggregate of individual acts – it was a phenomenon that bore patterned properties.

In examining official suicide records in France, Durkheim found that certain categories of people were more likely to commit suicide than others. He discovered, for example, that there were more suicides among men than women, among Protestants as opposed to Catholics, among the wealthy compared to the poor, and among single over married people. Durkheim also noted that suicide rates tended to be lower during times of war and higher during times of economic change or instability.

These findings led Durkheim to conclude that there are social forces external to the individual which affect suicide rates. He related his explanation to the idea of social solidarity and to two types of bonds within society – *social integration* and *social regulation*. Durkheim believed that people who were integrated strongly into social groups, and whose desires and aspirations were regulated by social norms, were less likely to commit suicide. He identified four types of suicide, in accordance with the relative presence or absence of integration and regulation.

Egoistic suicides are marked by low integration in society and occur when an individual is isolated, or when his or her ties to a group are weakened or broken. For example, the low rates of suicide among Catholics might be explained by their strong social community, while the personal and moral freedom of Protestants mean that they 'stand alone' before God. Marriage protects against suicide by integrating the individual into a stable social relationship, while single people remain more isolated within society. The lower suicide rate during wartime, according to Durkheim, can be seen as a sign of heightened social integration.

Anomic suicide is caused by a lack of social regulation. By this, Durkheim referred to the social conditions of *anomie* when people are rendered 'normless' due to rapid change or instability in society. The loss of a fixed point of reference for norms and desires – such as in times of economic upheaval or in personal struggles like divorce – can upset the balance between people's circumstances and their desires.

Altruistic suicide occurs when an individual is 'over-integrated' – social bonds are too strong – and values society more than himself or herself. In such a case, suicide becomes a sacrifice for the 'greater good'. Japanese kamikaze pilots or Islamic 'suicide bombers' are examples of altruistic suicides. Durkheim saw these as characteristic of traditional societies where mechanical solidarity prevails.

The final type of suicide is *fatalistic* suicide. Although Durkheim saw this as of little contemporary relevance, he believed that it results when an individual is over-regulated by society. The oppression of the individual results in a feeling of powerlessness before fate or society.

Suicide rates vary between societies but show regular patterns within societies over time. Durkheim took this as evidence that there are consistent social forces that influence suicide rates. An examination of suicide rates reveals how general social patterns can be detected within individual actions.

Since the publication of *Suicide*, many objections have been raised to the study, particularly about Durkheim's use of official statistics, his dismissal of non-social influences on suicide, and his insistence on classifying all types of suicide together. Nonetheless, the study remains a classic and his fundamental assertion remains: even the seemingly personal act of suicide demands a sociological explanation.

with the German authorities; after a brief stay in France, he settled permanently in exile in Britain. Marx witnessed the growth of factories and industrial production, as well as the inequalities that resulted. His interest in the European labour movement and socialist ideas were reflected in his writings, which covered a diversity of topics. Most of his work concentrated on economic issues, but since he was always concerned to connect economic problems to social institutions, his work was, and is, rich in sociological insights. Even his sternest critics regard his work as important for the development of sociology.

Capitalism and class struggle

Though he wrote about various phases of history, Marx concentrated primarily on change in modern times. For him, the most important changes were bound up with the development of **capitalism**. Capitalism is a system of production that contrasts radically with previous economic systems in history, involving as it does the production of goods and services sold to a wide range of consumers. Marx identified two main elements within capitalist enterprises. The first is *capital* – any asset, including money, machines or even factories, which can be used or invested to make future assets. The accumulation of capital goes hand in hand with the second element, *wage-labour*. Wage-labour refers to the pool of workers who do not own the means of their livelihood but must find employment provided by the owners of capital. Marx believed that those who own capital – **capitalists** – form a ruling class, while the mass of the population make up a class of waged workers, or a working class. As industrialization spread, large numbers of peasants who used to support themselves by working the land moved to the expanding cities and helped to form an urban-based industrial working class. This working class is also referred to as the **proletariat**.

According to Marx, capitalism is inherently a **class** system in which class relations are characterized by conflict. Although owners of capital and workers are each dependent on the other – the capitalists need labour and the workers need wages – the dependency is highly unbalanced. The relationship between classes is an exploitative one, since workers have little or no control over their labour and employers are able to generate profit by appropriating the product of workers' labour. Marx believed that class conflict over economic resources would become more acute with the passing of time.

Social change: the materialist conception of history

Marx's viewpoint was grounded in what he called the **materialist conception of history**. According to this view, it is not the ideas or values which human beings hold that are the main sources of social change. Rather, social change is prompted primarily by economic influences. Conflicts between classes provide the motivation for historical development – they are the 'motor of history'. As Marx wrote at the beginning of *The Communist Manifesto*, 'The history of all hitherto existing society is the history of class struggles' (Marx and Engels 2001 [1848]). Although Marx focused most of his attention on capitalism and modern society, he also examined how societies had developed over the course of history. According to him, social systems make a transition from one mode of production to another – sometimes gradually and sometimes through revolution – as a result of contradictions in their economies. He outlined a progression of historical stages that began with primitive communist societies of hunters and gatherers and passed through ancient slave-owning systems and feudal systems based on the division between landowners and serfs. The emergence of merchants and craftspeople marked the beginning of a commercial or capitalist class that came to displace the landed nobility. In accordance with this view of history, Marx argued that just as the capitalists had united to overthrow the feudal order, so too would the capitalists be supplanted and a new order installed: **communism**.

Marx believed in the inevitability of a workers' revolution which would overthrow the capitalist system and usher in a new society in which there would be no classes – no large-scale divisions between rich and poor. He didn't mean that all inequalities between individuals would disappear. Rather, society would no longer be split into a small class that monopolizes economic and political power and the large mass of people who benefit little from the wealth their work creates. The economic system would come under communal ownership, and a more humane society than we know at present would be established. Marx believed that in the society of the future, production would be more advanced and efficient than production under capitalism.

Marx's work had a far-reaching effect on the twentieth-century world. Until less than two decades ago, more than a third of the earth's population lived in societies, such as the Soviet Union and the countries of Eastern Europe, whose governments claimed to derive their inspiration from Marx's ideas.

Max Weber

Like Marx, Max Weber (pronounced 'veybur') (1864–1920) cannot simply be labelled a sociologist; his interests and concerns ranged across many areas. Born in Germany, where he spent most of his academic career, Weber was an individual of wide learning. His writings covered the fields of economics, law, philosophy and comparative history as well as sociology. Much of his work was also concerned with the development of modern capitalism and the ways in which modern society was different from earlier forms of social organization. Through a series of empirical studies, Weber set forth some of the basic characteristics of modern industrial societies and identified key sociological

Max Weber (1864–1920)

debates that remain central for sociologists today.

In common with other thinkers of his time, Weber sought to understand the nature and causes of social change. He was influenced by Marx but also was strongly critical of some of Marx's major views. He rejected the materialist conception of history and saw class conflict as less significant than did Marx. In Weber's view, economic factors are important, but ideas and values have just as much impact on social change. Weber's celebrated and much discussed work, *The Protestant Ethic and the Spirit of Capitalism* (1976), proposes that religious values – especially those associated with Puritanism – were of fundamental importance in creating a capitalistic outlook. Unlike other early sociological thinkers, Weber believed that sociology should focus on *social action*, not structures. He argued that human motivation and ideas were the forces behind change – ideas, values and beliefs had the power to bring about transformations. According to Weber, individuals have the ability to act freely and to shape the future. He did not believe, as Durkheim and Marx did, that structures existed external to or independent of individuals. Rather, structures in society were formed by a complex interplay of actions. It was the job of sociology to understand the meanings behind those actions.

Some of Weber's most influential writings reflected this concern with social action in analysing the distinctiveness of Western society as compared with other major civilizations. He studied the religions of China, India and the Near East, and in the course of these researches made major contributions to the sociology of religion. Comparing the leading religious systems in China and India with those of the West, Weber concluded that certain aspects of Christian beliefs strongly influenced the rise of capitalism. He argued that the capitalist outlook of Western societies did not emerge, as Marx supposed, only from economic changes. In Weber's view, cultural ideas and values help shape society and our individual actions.

An important element in Weber's sociological perspective was the idea of the **ideal type**. Ideal types are conceptual or analytical models that can be used to understand the world. In the real world, ideal types rarely, if ever, exist – often only some of their attributes will be present. These hypothetical constructions can be very useful, however, as any situation in the real world can be understood by comparing it to an ideal type. In this way, ideal types serve as a fixed point of reference. It is important to point out that by 'ideal' type Weber did not mean that the conception was a perfect or desirable goal. Instead, he meant that it was a 'pure' form of a certain phenomenon. Weber utilized ideal types in his writings on forms of bureaucracy and the market.

Rationalization

In Weber's view, the emergence of modern society was accompanied by important shifts in patterns of social action. He believed that people were moving away from traditional beliefs grounded in superstition, religion, custom and long-standing habit. Instead, individuals were increasingly engaging in rational, instrumental calculations that took into account efficiency and future consequences. In industrial society, there was little room for sentiments and for doing things simply because they had been done that way for generations. The development of science, modern technology and **bureaucracy** was described by Weber collectively as **rationalization** – the organization of social and economic life according to the principles of efficiency and on the basis of technical knowledge. If in traditional societies, religion and long-standing customs largely defined people's attitudes and values, modern society was marked by the rationalization of more and more areas of life, from politics to religion to economic activity.

In Weber's view, the Industrial Revolution and the rise of capitalism were proof of a larger trend towards rationalization. Capitalism is not dominated by class conflict, as Marx believed, but by the rise of *science* and *bureaucracy* – large-scale organizations (for more on bureaucracy see pp. 638–46). Weber saw the scientific character of the West as one of its most distinctive traits. Bureaucracy, the only way of organizing large numbers of people effectively, expands with economic and political growth. Weber used the term *disenchantment* to describe the way in which scientific thinking in the modern world had swept away the forces of sentimentality from the past.

Weber was not entirely optimistic about the outcome of rationalization, however. He was fearful of modern society as a system that would crush the human spirit by attempting to regulate all spheres of social life. He was particularly troubled by the potentially suffocating and dehumanizing effects of bureaucracy and its implications for the fate of **democracy**. The agenda of the eighteenth-century Age of Enlightenment, of advancing progress, wealth and happiness by rejecting custom and superstition in favour of science and technology, produced dangers of its own.

Modern theoretical approaches

The early sociologists were united in their desire to make sense of the changing societies in which they lived. They wanted to do more than simply depict and interpret the momentous events of their time, however. More importantly, they sought to develop ways of studying the social world that could explain the functioning of societies in general and the nature of social change. Yet, as we have seen, Durkheim, Marx and Weber employed very different approaches in their studies of the social world. For example, where Durkheim and Marx focused on the strength of forces external to the individual, Weber took as his point of departure the ability of individuals to act creatively on the outside world. Where Marx pointed to the predominance of economic issues, Weber considered a much wider range of factors to be significant. Such differences in approach have persisted throughout the history of sociology. Even when sociologists agree on the subject of analysis, they often undertake that analysis from different theoretical perspectives.

The three recent theoretical approaches examined below – functionalism, the conflict approach and symbolic interactionism – have connections with Durkheim, Marx and Weber respectively. Throughout this book, you will encounter arguments and ideas that draw upon and illustrate these theoretical approaches.

In chapter 4 we return to the major theoretical approaches to sociology in more detail and examine some of the more recent theoretical developments in sociological thought.

A neglected founder

Although Comte, Durkheim, Marx and Weber are, without doubt, foundational figures in sociology, there were other important thinkers from the same period whose contributions must also be taken into account. Sociology, like many academic fields, has not always lived up to its ideal of acknowledging the importance of every thinker whose work has intrinsic merit. Very few women or members of racial minorities were given the opportunity to become professional sociologists during the 'classical' period of the late nineteenth and early twentieth centuries. In addition, the few that were given the opportunity to do sociological research of lasting importance have frequently been neglected by the field. Individuals like Harriet Martineau deserve the attention of sociologists today.

Harriet Martineau

Harriet Martineau (1802–76) has been called the 'first woman sociologist', but, like Marx and Weber, cannot be thought of simply as a sociologist. She was born and educated in England and was the author of more than fifty books, as well as numerous essays. Martineau is now credited with introducing sociology to Britain through her translation of Comte's founding treatise of the field, *Positive Philosophy* (Rossi 1973). In addition, Martineau conducted a first-hand systematic study of American society during her extensive travels throughout the United States in the 1830s, which is the subject of her book *Society in America* (1962 [1837]). Martineau is significant to sociologists today for several reasons. First, she argued that when one studies a society, one must focus on all its aspects, including key political, religious and social institutions. Second, she insisted that an analysis of a society must include an

understanding of women's lives. Third, she was the first to turn a sociological eye on previously ignored issues, including marriage, children, domestic and religious life, and race relations. As she once wrote, 'The nursery, the boudoir, and the kitchen are all excellent schools in which to learn the morals and manners of a people' (1962 [1837]). Finally, she argued that sociologists should do more than just observe; they should also act in ways to benefit a society. As a result, Martineau was an active proponent of both women's rights and the emancipation of slaves.

Harriet Martineau (1802–76)

Functionalism

Functionalism holds that society is a complex system whose various parts work together to produce stability and solidarity. According to this approach, the disci-

pline of sociology should investigate the relationship of parts of society to each other and to society as a whole. We can analyse the religious beliefs and customs of a society, for example, by showing how they relate to other institutions within it, for the different parts of a society develop in close relation to one another.

To study the function of a social practice or institution is to analyse the contribution which that practice, or institution, makes to the continuation of society. Functionalists, including Comte and Durkheim, have often used an *organic analogy* to compare the operation of society to that of a living organism. They argue that the parts of society work together, just as the various parts of the human body do, for the benefit of society as a whole. To study a bodily organ like the heart, we need to show how it relates to other parts of the body. By pumping blood around the body, the heart plays a vital role in the continuation of the life of the organism. Similarly, analysing the function of a social item means showing the part it plays in the continued existence and health of a society.

Functionalism emphasizes the importance of **moral consensus**, in maintaining order and stability in society. Moral consensus exists when most people in a society share the same values. Functionalists regard order and balance as the normal state of society – this social equilibrium is grounded in the existence of a moral consensus among the members of society. For instance, Durkheim believed that religion reaffirms people's adherence to core social values, thereby contributing to the maintenance of social cohesion.

Until the 1960s, functionalist thought was probably the leading theoretical tradition in sociology, particularly in the United States. Talcott Parsons (1902–79) and Robert K. Merton (1910–2003), who each drew extensively on Durkheim, were two of its most prominent adherents.

Merton's version of functionalism has been particularly influential. Merton distinguished between manifest and latent functions. **Manifest functions** are those known to, and intended by, the participants in a specific type of social activity. **Latent functions** are consequences of that activity of which participants are unaware. To illustrate this distinction, Merton used the example of a rain dance performed by the Hopi Tribe of Arizona and New Mexico. The Hopi believe that the ceremony will bring the rain they need for their crops (manifest function). This is why they organize and participate in it. But the rain dance, Merton argued, using Durkheim's theory of religion, also has the effect of promoting the cohesion of the Hopi society (latent function). A major part of sociological explanation, according to Merton, consists in uncovering the latent functions of social activities and institutions.

Merton also distinguished between functions and **dysfunctions**. To look for the dysfunctional aspects of social behaviour means focusing on features of social life that challenge the existing order of things. For example, it is mistaken to suppose that religion is always functional – that it contributes only to social cohesion. When two groups support different religions or even different versions of the same religion, the result can be major social conflicts, causing widespread social disruption. Thus, wars have often been fought between religious communities – as can be seen in the struggles between Protestants and Catholics in European history.

In recent years, the popularity of functionalism has begun to wane, as its limitations have become apparent. While this was not true of Merton, many functionalist thinkers (Talcott Parsons is an example) unduly stressed factors leading to social cohesion at the expense of those producing division and conflict. The focus on stability and order means that divisions or inequalities in society – based on factors such as class, race and gender – are minimized. There is also less emphasis on the role of creative social action within society. Many critics have argued that functional analysis attributes to societies social qualities that they do not have. Functionalists often wrote as though societies have 'needs' and 'purposes', even though these concepts make sense only when applied to individual human beings.

Conflict perspectives

Like functionalists, sociologists employing **conflict theories** emphasize the importance of structures within society. They also advance a comprehensive 'model' to explain how society works. However, conflict theorists reject functionalism's emphasis on consensus. Instead, they highlight the importance of divisions in society. In doing so, they concentrate on issues of power, inequality and struggle. They tend to see society as composed of distinct groups pursuing their own interests. The existence of separate interests means that the potential for conflict is always present and that certain groups will benefit more than others. Conflict theorists examine the tensions between dominant and disadvantaged groups within society and seek to understand how relationships of control are established and perpetuated.

An influential approach within conflict theory is Marxism, named after Karl Marx, whose work emphasized class conflict.

Numerous interpretations of Marx's major ideas are possible, and there are today schools of Marxist thought that take very different theoretical positions. In all of its versions, Marxism differs from most other traditions of sociology in that its authors see it as a combination of sociological analysis and political reform. Marxism is supposed to generate a programme of radical political change.

However, not all conflict theories take a Marxist approach. Some conflict theorists have also been influenced by Weber. A good example is the contemporary German sociologist Ralf Dahrendorf (1929–). In his now classic work, *Class and Class Conflict in Industrial Society* (1959), Dahrendorf argues that functionalist thinkers only consider one side of society – those aspects of social life where there is harmony and agreement. Just as important, or more so, are areas marked by conflict and division. Conflict, Dahrendorf says, comes mainly from different interests that individuals and groups have. Marx saw differences of interest mainly in terms of classes, but Dahrendorf relates them more broadly to authority and power. In all societies there is a division between those who hold authority and those who are largely excluded from it – between rulers and ruled.

Symbolic interactionism

The work of the American philosopher G. H. Mead (1863–1931) had an important influence on sociological thought, in particular through a perspective called **symbolic interactionism**. Symbolic interactionism springs from a concern with language and meaning. Mead claims that language allows us to become self-conscious beings – aware of our own individuality, and able to see ourselves from the outside as others see us. The key element in this process is the **symbol**. A symbol is something that stands for something else. For example, words that we use to refer to certain objects are in fact symbols which represent what we mean. The word 'spoon' is the symbol we use to describe the utensil that we use to eat soup. Non-verbal gestures or forms of communication are also symbols. Waving at someone or making a rude gesture has symbolic value. Mead argued that humans rely on shared symbols and understandings in their interactions with one another. Because human beings live in a richly symbolic universe, virtually all interactions between human individuals involve an exchange of symbols.

Symbolic interactionism directs our attention to the detail of interpersonal interaction, and how that detail is used to make sense of what others say and do. Sociologists influenced by symbolic interactionism often focus on face-to-face interaction in the contexts of everyday life. They stress the role of such interaction in creating society and its institutions. Max Weber was an important indirect influence on this theoretical approach because, although he acknowledged the existence of social structures – such as classes, parties, status groups and others – he held that these structures were created through the *social actions* of individuals.

While the symbolic interactionist perspective can yield many insights into the nature of our actions in the course of day-to-day social life, it has been criticized for ignoring the larger issues of power and structure within society and how they serve to constrain individual action.

One classic example of symbolic inter-actionism that does take into account the issues of power and structure in our society is Arlie Hochschild's *The Managed Heart: Commercialization of Human Feeling* (1983). Hochschild, a sociology professor at the University of California, observed training sessions and carried out interviews at Delta Airlines' Stewardess Training Centre in Atlanta in the USA. She watched flight attendants being trained to manage their feelings as well as learning other skills. Hochschild recalled the comments of one instructor, a pilot, at the training sessions: 'Now girls, I want you to go out there and really smile', the pilot instructed. 'Your smile is your biggest asset. I want you to go out there and use it. Smile. Really smile. Really lay it on.'

Through her observations and interviews Hochschild found that as Western economies have become increasingly based on the delivery of services, the emotional style of the work we do needs to be understood. Hochschild's study of 'customer service' training amongst flight attendants might feel familiar to anyone who has worked in the service industry before, perhaps in a shop, restaurant or bar. Hochschild calls this training in 'emotional labour' – labour that requires that one manages one's feelings in order to create a publicly observable (and acceptable) facial and body display. According to Hochschild, the companies you work for lay claim not only to your physical movements, but also to your emotions. They own your smile when you are working.

Hochschild's research opened a window on an aspect of life that most people think they understand, but which needed to be understood at a deeper level. She found that service workers – like physical labourers – often feel a sense of distance from the particular aspect of themselves that is given up in work. The physical labourer's arm, for example, might come to feel like a piece of machinery, and only incidentally a part of the person moving it. Likewise, service workers often told Hochschild that their smiles were on them but not of them. In other words, these workers felt a sense of distance from their own emotions. This is interesting when we consider the fact that emotions are usually thought of as a deep and personal part of ourselves.

Hochschild's book is an influential application of symbolic interactionism and many other scholars have built on her ideas since *The Managed Heart* was first published. Although she conducted her research within one of the world's most developed 'service economies' – the United States – Hochschild's findings are applicable to many societies in the present age. Service jobs are expanding rapidly in countries around the world, demanding that more and more people engage in 'emotional labour' at the workplace. In some cultures, such as amongst the Inuit of Greenland, where there isn't the same tradition of public smiling as there is in Western Europe and North America, training in emotional labour has proved to be a somewhat difficult task. In these countries, employees in service jobs are sometimes required to take part in special 'smiling training sessions' – not so different from the ones attended by Delta Airlines stewardesses.

Theoretical thinking in sociology

So far in this chapter we have been concerned with theoretical approaches, which refer to broad, overall orientations to the subject matter of sociology.

However, we can draw a distinction between the *theoretical approaches* discussed above and *theories*. Theories are more narrowly focused and represent attempts to explain particular social conditions or types of event. They are usually formed as part of the process of research and in turn suggest problems to which research investigations should be devoted. An example would be Durkheim's theory of suicide, referred to earlier in this chapter.

Innumerable theories have been developed in the many different areas of research in which sociologists work. Sometimes theories are very precisely set out and are even occasionally expressed in mathematical form – although this is more common in other social sciences (especially economics) than in sociology.

Some theories are also much more encompassing than others. Opinions vary about whether it is desirable or useful for sociologists to concern themselves with very wide-ranging theoretical endeavours. Robert K. Merton (1957), for example, argues forcefully that sociologists should concentrate their attention on what he calls *theories of the middle range*. Rather than attempting to create grand theoretical schemes (in the manner of Marx, for instance), we should be concerned with developing theories that are more modest.

Middle-range theories are specific enough to be directly tested by empirical research, yet sufficiently general to cover a range of different phenomena. A case in point is the theory of *relative deprivation*. This theory holds that the way people evaluate their circumstances depends on whom they compare themselves to. Thus, feelings of deprivation do not conform directly to the level of material poverty that people experience. A family living in a small home in a poor area, where everyone is in more or less similar circumstances, is likely to feel less deprived than a family living in a similar house in a neighbourhood where the majority of the other homes are much larger and the other people more affluent.

It is indeed true that the more wideranging and ambitious a theory is, the more difficult it is to test empirically. Yet, there seems no obvious reason why theoretical thinking in sociology should be confined to the 'middle range'.

Assessing theories, and especially theoretical approaches, in sociology is a challenging and formidable task. Theoretical debates are by definition more abstract than controversies of a more empirical kind. The fact that sociology is not dominated by a single theoretical approach might seem to be a sign of weakness in the subject, but this is not the case. The jostling of rival theoretical approaches and theories is an expression of the vitality of the sociological enterprise. In studying human beings – ourselves – theoretical variety rescues us from dogma. Human behaviour is complicated and many-sided, and it is very unlikely that a single theoretical perspective could cover all of its aspects. Diversity in theoretical thinking provides a rich source of ideas that can be drawn on in research and which stimulates the imaginative capacities so essential to progress in sociological work.

Levels of analysis: microsociology and macrosociology

One important distinction between the different theoretical perspectives we have discussed in this chapter involves the level of analysis each is directed at. The study of everyday behaviour in situations of face-to-face interaction is usually called **micro-sociology**. **Macrosociology** is the analysis of large-scale social systems, like the political system or the economic order. It also includes the analysis of long-term processes of change, such as the development of industrialism. At first glance, it might seem as though micro-analysis and macro-analysis are distinct from one another. In fact, the two are closely connected (Knorr-Cetina and Cicourel 1981; Giddens 1984).

Macro-analysis is essential if we are to understand the institutional background of daily life. The ways in which people live their everyday lives are greatly affected by the broader institutional framework, as is obvious when the daily cycle of activities of a culture like that of the medieval period is compared with life in an industrialized urban environment. In modern societies, we are constantly in contact with strangers. This contact may be indirect and impersonal. However, no matter how many indirect or electronic relations we enter into today, even in the most complex societies, the presence of other people remains crucial. While we may choose just to send an acquaintance an email message, we can also choose to fly thousands of miles to spend the weekend with a friend.

Micro-studies are in turn necessary for illuminating broad institutional patterns. Face-to-face interaction is clearly the main basis of all forms of social organization, no matter how large scale. Suppose we are studying a business corporation. We could understand much about its activities simply by looking at face-to-face behaviour. We could analyse, for example, the interaction of directors in the board-room, people working in the various offices, or the workers on the factory floor. We would not build up a picture of the whole corporation in this way, since some of its business is transacted through printed materials, letters, the telephone and computers. Yet we could certainly contribute significantly to understanding how the organization works.

In later chapters, we will see further examples of how interaction in micro-contexts affects larger social processes, and how macro-systems in turn influence more confined settings of social life.

How can sociology help us in our lives?

Sociology has several practical implications for our lives, as C. Wright Mills emphasized when developing his idea of the sociological imagination, discussed above (p. 4). First, sociology gives us an awareness of cultural differences that allows us to see the social world from many perspectives. Quite often, if we properly understand how others live, we also acquire a better understanding of what their problems are. Practical policies that are not based on an informed aware-ness of the ways of life of people they affect have little chance of success. For example, a white social worker operating in a predominantly Latin American com-munity in South London won't gain the confidence of its members without devel-oping a sensitivity to the differences in social experience between members of different groups in the UK.

Second, sociological research provides

Modern theoretical approaches

Symbolic interactionism stresses the exchange of symbols between individuals in social interaction. Unlike other theories, symbolic interactionism emphasizes the small-scale interactions of individuals, not society as a whole.

Functionalism looks at society as a whole, emphasizing the contribution a social activity makes to society. Merton, whose version of functionalism has been particularly influential, stressed that manifest functions, those intended by the participants in a social activity, are sometimes less important than latent functions, the unintentional consequences of a social act. Merton believed that a major part of sociological explanation is to uncover the latent functions of social acts and institutions.

Many contemporary social theorists are still influenced by Marx and have developed **conflict theories**. The study of inequality using the concept of class is at the heart of Marx's theory.

One way to think about sociology's theoretical approaches is to think in terms of levels of analysis. **Microsociology** is the study of everyday behaviour in situations of face-to-face interaction. **Macrosociology** is the analysis of large-scale social systems. The two are closely connected.

practical help in assessing the results of policy initiatives. A programme of practical reform may simply fail to achieve what its designers sought or may produce unin-tended consequences of an unfortunate kind. For instance, in the years following World War II, large public housing blocks were built in city centres in many coun-tries. These were planned to provide high standards of accommodation for low-income groups from slum areas and offered shopping amenities and other civic services nearby. However, research later showed that many people who had moved from their previous dwellings to large apartment blocks felt isolated and unhappy. High-rise apartment blocks and shopping centres in poorer areas often became dilapidated and provided breeding grounds for muggings and other violent crimes.

Third, and in some ways this is the most important, sociology can provide us with self-enlightenment – increased self-understanding. The more we know about why we act as we do and about the overall workings of our society, the more likely we are to be able to influence our own futures. We should not see sociology as assisting only policy-makers – that is, powerful groups – in making informed decisions. Those in power cannot be assumed always to consider the interests of the less powerful or underprivileged in the policies they pursue. Self-enlightened groups can often benefit from sociological research by using the information gleaned to respond in an effective way to government policies or form policy initiatives of their own. Self-help groups like Alcoholics Anonymous and social movements like the environmental movement are examples of social groups that have directly sought to bring about practical reforms, with some degree of success.

Finally, it should be mentioned that many sociologists concern themselves directly with practical matters as professionals. People trained in sociology are to be found as industrial consultants, urban planners, social workers and personnel managers, as well as in many other jobs. An understanding of society can also help for careers in law, journalism, business and medicine.

There is often a connection between studying sociology and the prompting of social conscience. Should sociologists themselves actively advocate and agitate for programmes of reform or social change? Some argue that sociology can preserve its intellectual independence only if sociologists are studiously neutral in moral and political controversies. Yet are scholars who remain aloof from current debates necessarily more impartial in their assessment of sociological issues than others? No sociologically sophisticated person can be unaware of the inequalities that exist in the world today. It would be strange if sociologists did not take sides on political issues, and it would be illogical to try to ban them from drawing on their expertise in so doing.

In this chapter, we have seen that sociology is a discipline in which we often set aside our personal view of the world to look more carefully at the influences that shape our lives and those of others. Sociology emerged as a distinct intellectual endeavour with the development of modern societies, and the study of such societies remains its principal concern. But sociologists are also preoccupied with a broad range of issues about the nature of social interaction and human societies in general.

Sociology isn't just an abstract intellectual field but has major practical implications for people's lives. Learning to become a sociologist shouldn't be a dull academic endeavour. The best way to make sure it doesn't become so is to approach the subject in an imaginative way and to relate sociological ideas and findings to situations in your own life.

Summary points

1 Sociology can be identified as the systematic study of human societies, giving special emphasis to modern, industrialized systems.

2 The practice of sociology involves the ability to think imaginatively and to detach oneself from preconceived ideas about social life.

3 Sociology came into being as an attempt to understand the far-reaching changes that have occurred in human societies over the past two or three centuries. The changes involved are not just large-scale ones; they also involve shifts in the most intimate and personal characteristics of people's lives.

4 Among the classical founders of sociology, four figures are particularly important: Auguste Comte, Karl Marx, Emile Durkheim and Max Weber. Comte and Marx, working in the mid-nineteenth century, established some of the basic issues of sociology, later elaborated on by Durkheim and Weber. These issues concern the nature of sociology and the impact of the changes brought about by modernization on the social world.

5 A diversity of theoretical approaches is found in sociology. Theoretical disputes are difficult to resolve even in the natural sciences, and in sociology we face special difficulties because of the complex problems involved in subjecting our own behaviour to study.

6 The main theoretical approaches in sociology are functionalism, conflict perspectives and symbolic interactionism. There are some basic differences between each of these approaches, which have strongly influenced the development of the subject in the post-war period.

7 Sociology is a subject with important practical implications. It can contribute to social criticism and practical social reform in several ways. To begin with, the improved understanding of a given set of social circumstances often gives us all a better chance of controlling them. At the same time, sociology provides the means of increasing our cultural sensitivities, allowing policies to be based on an awareness of divergent cultural values. In practical terms, we can investigate the consequences of the adoption of particular policy programmes. Finally, and perhaps most important, sociology provides self-enlightenment, offering groups and individuals an increased opportunity to alter the conditions of their own lives.

Internet links

Extra support and information about this book
http://www.polity.co.uk/giddens5/

New sociology books from Polity
http://www.polity.co.uk/sociology/

The Social Science Information Gateway from Sociology
http://www.sosig.ac.uk/sociology/

The British Sociological Association
http://www.britsoc.co.uk/

Contents

2 Globalization and the Changing World

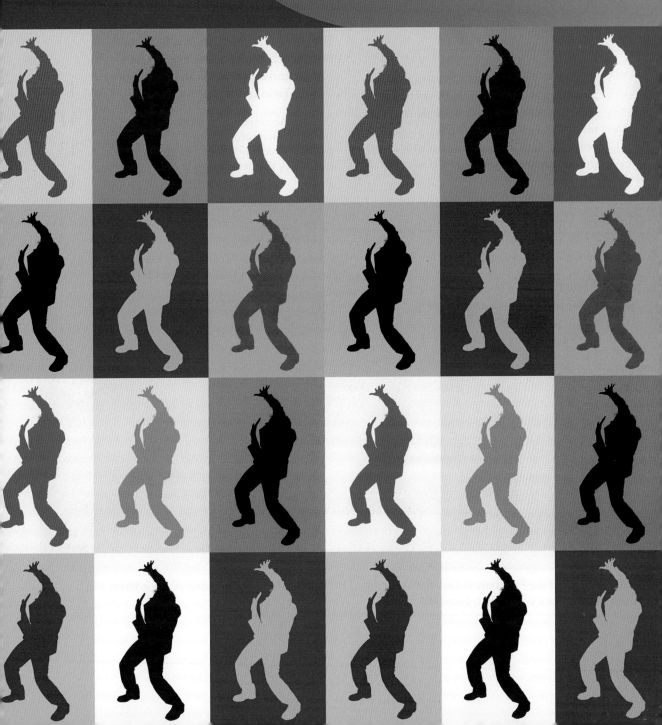

think of the entire span of human existence thus far as a 24-hour day, agriculture would have come into existence at 11.56 p.m. and civilizations at 11.57. The development of modern societies would get under way at only 11.59 and 30 seconds! Yet perhaps as much change has taken place in the last 30 seconds of this human day as in all the time leading up to it.

The pace of change in the modern era is demonstrated if we look at rates of technological development. As the economic historian David Landes has observed:

HUMAN BEINGS have existed on earth for about half a million years. Agriculture, the necessary basis of fixed settlements, is only around twelve thousand years old. Civilizations date back no more than six thousand years or so. If we were to

> Modern technology produces not only more, faster; it turns out objects that could not have been produced under any circumstances by the craft methods of yesterday.

A view of the Pyramids at Giza through a Pizza Hut window, juxtaposing one of the earliest civilizations with twenty-first-century life.

The best Indian hand-spinner could not turn out yarn so fine and regular as that of the [spinning] mule; all the forges in eighteenth century Christendom could not have produced steel sheets so large, smooth and homogeneous as those of a modern strip mill. Most important, modern technology has created things that could scarcely have been conceived in the pre-industrial era: the camera, the motor car, the airplane, the whole array of electronic devices from the radio to the high-speed computer, the nuclear power plant, and so on almost ad infinitum. . . . The result has been an enormous increase in the output and variety of goods and services and this alone has changed man's way of life more than anything since the discovery of fire: the Englishman of 1750 was closer in material things to Caesar's legionnaires than to his own great-grandchildren. (Landes 1969)

The modes of life and social institutions characteristic of the modern world are radically different from those of even the recent past. During a period of only two or three centuries – a minute sliver of time in the context of human history – human social life has been wrenched away from the types of social order in which people lived for thousands of years.

Far more than any generation before us, we face an uncertain future. To be sure, conditions of life for previous generations were always insecure: people were at the mercy of natural disasters, plagues and famines. But though we are largely immune from plague and famine in the industrialized countries today, we must deal now with the social forces we ourselves have unleashed.

Later in this chapter we discuss some of the reasons for the monumental social transformations outlined above and introduce the debate surrounding one of the greatest social changes occurring today:

globalization. First, however, we turn to analysing the main types of society that existed in the past and are still found in the world today. In the present day, we are accustomed to societies that contain many millions of people, many of them living crowded together in urban areas. But for most of human history, the earth was much less densely populated than it is now and it is only over the past hundred years or so that any societies have existed in which the majority of the population are city dwellers. To understand the forms of society that existed prior to modern industrialism, we have to call on the historical dimension of the sociological imagination.

Types of society

A disappearing world: pre-modern societies and their fate

The explorers, traders and missionaries sent out during Europe's great age of discovery met with many different peoples. As the anthropologist Marvin Harris has written in his work *Cannibals and Kings*:

In some regions – Australia, the Arctic, the southern tips of South America and Africa – they found groups still living much like Europe's own long-forgotten stone age ancestors: bands of twenty or thirty people, sprinkled across vast territories, constantly on the move, living entirely by hunting animals and collecting wild plants. These hunter-collectors appeared to be members of a rare and endangered species. In other regions – the forests of eastern North America, the jungles of South America, and East Asia – they found denser populations, inhabiting more or less permanent villages, based on farming and consisting of perhaps one or two large communal structures, but here too the weapons and tools were relics of prehistory. . . . Elsewhere, of course, the explorers encountered fully developed states and empires, headed by despots and ruling classes, and defended by standing armies. It was these great empires, with their cities, monuments, palaces, temples and treasures, that had lured all the Marco Polos and Columbuses across the oceans and deserts in the first place. There was China – the greatest empire in the world, a vast, sophisticated realm whose leaders scorned the 'red-faced barbarians', supplicants from puny kingdoms beyond the pale of the civilised world. And there was India – a land where cows were venerated and the unequal burdens of life were apportioned according to what each soul had merited in its previous incarnation. And then there were the native American states and empires, worlds unto themselves, each with its distinctive arts and religions: the Incas, with their great stone fortresses, suspension bridges, overworked granaries, and state-controlled economy; and the Aztecs, with their bloodthirsty gods fed from human hearts and their incessant search for fresh sacrifices.

(Harris 1978)

This seemingly unlimited variety of premodern societies can actually be grouped into three main categories, each of which is referred to in Harris's description: hunters and gatherers (whom Harris calls 'huntercollectors' in his description above); larger agrarian or pastoral societies (involving agriculture or the tending of domesticated animals); and non-industrial civilizations or traditional states. We shall look at the main characteristics of these in turn (see table 2.1).

Pre-historic cave paintings show us something of the lives of the earliest hunter-gatherers.

Table 2.1   Types of pre-modern human society

Type	Period of Existence	Characteristics
Hunting and gathering societies	50,000 BCE* to the present. Now on the verge of complete disappearance.	Consist of small numbers of people gaining their livelihood from hunting, fishing and the gathering of edible plants. Few inequalities. Differences of rank limited by age and gender.
Agrarian societies	12,000 BCE to the present. Most are now part of larger political entities and are losing their distinct identity.	Based on small rural communities, without towns or cities. Livelihood gained through agriculture, often supplemented by hunting and gathering. Stronger inequalities than among hunters and gatherers. Ruled by chiefs.
Pastoral societies	12,000 BCE to the present. Today mostly part of larger states; their traditional ways of life are being undermined.	Size ranges from a few hundred people to many thousands. Dependent on the tending of domesticated animals for their subsistence. Marked by distinct inequalities. Ruled by chiefs or warrior kings.
Traditional societies or civilizations	6000 BCE to the nineteenth century. All traditional states have disappeared.	Very large in size, some numbering millions of people (though small compared with larger industrialized societies). Some cities exist, in which trade and manufacture are concentrated. Based largely on agriculture. Major inequalities exist among different classes. Distinct apparatus of government headed by a king or emperor.

* Many historians now use BCE (before the Common Era) and CE (Common Era) rather than BC and AD.

The earliest societies: hunters and gatherers

For all but a tiny part of our existence on this planet, human beings have lived in **hunting and gathering societies**. Hunters and gatherers gain their livelihood from hunting, fishing and gathering edible plants growing in the wild. These cultures continue to exist in some parts of the world, such as in a few arid parts of Africa and the jungles of Brazil and New Guinea. Most hunting and gathering cultures, however, have been destroyed or absorbed by the spread of Western culture (the culture of Europe, the United States, Australasia) and those that remain are unlikely to stay intact for much longer. Currently, less than a quarter of a million people in the world support themselves through hunting and gathering – only 0.001 per cent of the world's population (see figure 2.1)

Compared with larger societies – particularly modern societies, such as Britain or the United States – little inequality is found in most hunting and gathering groups. Hunters and gatherers have little interest in developing material wealth beyond what is needed to cater for their basic wants. Their main preoccupations are normally with religious values and with ceremonial and ritual activities. The material goods they need are limited to weapons for hunting, tools for digging and building, traps and cooking utensils. Thus there is little difference among members of the society in the number or kinds of material possessions – there are no divisions of rich and poor. Differences of position or rank tend to be limited to age and sex; men are almost always the hunters, while women gather wild crops, cook and bring up the children. This division of labour between men and women, however, is very important: men tend to dominate public and ceremonial positions.

Hunters and gatherers are not merely 'primitive' peoples whose ways of life no longer hold any interest for us. Studying their cultures allows us to see more clearly that some of our institutions are far from

Only a few hunter-gatherer societies still exist, such as the San bushmen in Botswana.

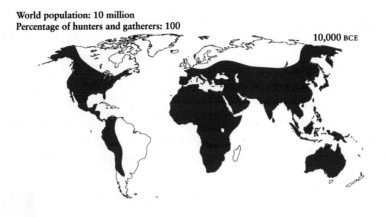

World population: 10 million
Percentage of hunters and gatherers: 100

10,000 BCE

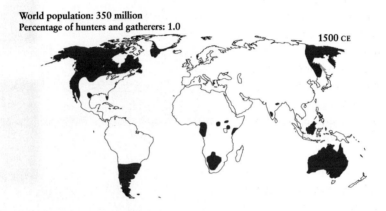

World population: 350 million
Percentage of hunters and gatherers: 1.0

1500 CE

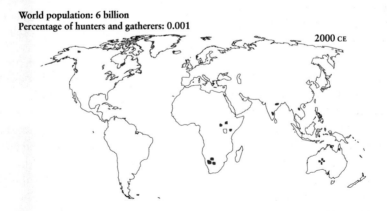

World population: 6 billion
Percentage of hunters and gatherers: 0.001

2000 CE

Figure 2.1   The decline of hunting and gathering societies

Source: Lee and De Vore (1968)

being 'natural' features of human life. Of course, we should not idealize the circumstances in which hunters and gatherers have lived, but nonetheless, the absence of war, the lack of major inequalities of wealth and power and the emphasis on cooperation rather than competition are all instructive reminders that the world created by modern industrial civilization is not necessarily to be equated with 'progress'.

Pastoral and agrarian societies

About twenty thousand years ago, some hunting and gathering groups turned to the raising of domesticated animals and the cultivation of fixed plots of land as their means of livelihood. **Pastoral societies** are those that rely mainly on domesticated livestock, while **agrarian societies** are those that grow crops (practise agriculture). Many societies have had mixed pastoral and agrarian economies.

Depending on the environment in which they live, pastoralists rear and herd animals such as cattle, sheep, goats, camels or horses. Many pastoral societies still exist in the modern world, concentrated especially in areas of Africa, the Middle East and Central Asia. These societies are usually found in regions where there are dense grasslands, or in deserts or mountains. Such regions are not amenable to fruitful agriculture, but may support various kinds of livestock. Pastoral societies usually migrate between different areas according to seasonal changes. Given their nomadic habits, people in pastoral societies do not normally accumulate many material possessions, although their way of life is more complex in material terms than that of hunters and gatherers.

These Masai warriors from Tanzania are amongst some of the few remaining pastoralists in the world today.

At some point, hunting and gathering groups began to sow their own crops rather than simply collect those growing in the wild. This practice first developed as what is usually called 'horticulture', in which small gardens were cultivated by the use of simple hoes or digging instruments. Like pastoralism, horticulture provided for a more assured supply of food than was possible by hunting and gathering and therefore could support larger communities.

Table 2.2   Some agrarian societies still remain

Country	Percentage of workforce in agriculture
Rwanda	90
Uganda	82
Nepal	81
Ethiopia	80
Bangladesh	63
Industrialized societies differ	
Japan	5
Australia	5
Germany	2.8
Canada	3
United States	0.7
United Kingdom	1

Source: CIA World Factbook (2004)

Since they were not on the move, people gaining a livelihood from horticulture could develop larger stocks of material possessions than either hunting and gathering or pastoral communities. Some peoples in the world still rely primarily on horticulture for their livelihood (see table 2.2).

Non-industrial or traditional civilizations

From about 6000 BCE onwards we find evidence of larger societies than ever existed before, which contrast in distinct ways with earlier types (see figure 2.2). These societies were based on the development of cities, showed very pronounced inequalities of wealth and power and were associated with the rule of kings or emperors. Because they involved the use of writing and science and art flourished, they are often called *civilizations*.

The earliest civilizations developed in the Middle East, usually in fertile river areas. The Chinese Empire originated in about 2000 BCE, when powerful states were also founded in what are now India and Pakistan. A number of large civilizations existed in Mexico and Latin America, such as the Aztecs of Mexico, the Mayas of the Yucatan Peninsula and the Incas of Peru.

Most traditional civilizations were also empires; they achieved the size they did through the conquest and incorporation of other peoples (Kautsky 1982). This was true, for instance, of traditional China and Rome. At its height, in the first century CE, the Roman Empire stretched from Britain in north-west Europe to beyond the Middle East. The Chinese empire, which lasted for more than two thousand years, up to the threshold of the twentieth century, covered most of the massive region of eastern Asia now occupied by modern China.

The modern world: the industrialized societies

What has happened to destroy the forms of society which dominated the whole of

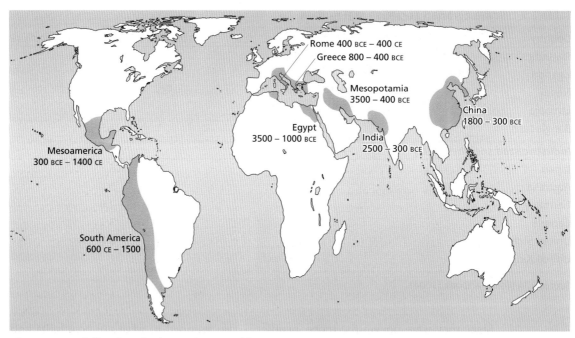

Figure 2.2   Civilizations in the ancient world

history up to two centuries ago? The answer, in a word, is **industrialization** – a term we have already introduced in chapter 1. Industrialization refers to the emergence of machine production, based on the use of inanimate power resources (like steam or electricity). The **industrial societies** (sometimes also called 'modern' or 'developed' societies) are utterly different from any previous type of social order and their development has had consequences stretching far beyond their European origins.

In even the most advanced of traditional civilizations, most people were engaged in working on the land. The relatively low level of technological development did not permit more than a small minority to be freed from the chores of agricultural production. By contrast, a prime feature of industrial societies today is that a large majority of the employed population work in factories, offices or shops rather than in agriculture (as we saw in table 2.2). And over 90 per cent of people live in towns and cities, where most jobs are to be found and new job opportunities are created. The largest cities are vastly greater in size than the urban settlements found in traditional civilizations. In the cities, social life becomes more impersonal and anonymous than before and many of our day-to-day encounters are with strangers rather than with individuals known to us. Large-scale organizations, such as business corporations or government agencies, come to influence the lives of virtually everyone.

The role of cities in the new global order is discussed in chapter 21 in the section 'Cities and globalization' on pp. 921–33.

A further feature of modern societies concerns their political systems, which are more developed and intensive than forms of government in traditional states. In traditional civilizations, the political authorities (monarchs and emperors) had little direct influence on the customs and habits of most of their subjects, who lived in fairly self-contained local villages. With industrialization, transportation and communications became much more rapid, making for a more integrated 'national' community.

The industrial societies were the first nation-states to come into existence. **Nation-states** are political communities, divided from each other by clearly delimited borders rather than the vague frontier areas that used to separate traditional states. National governments have extensive powers over many aspects of citizens' lives, framing laws that apply to all those living within their borders. Britain is a nation-state, as are virtually all other societies in the world today.

The application of industrial technology has by no means been limited to peaceful processes of economic development. From the earliest phases of industrialization, modern production processes have been put to military use and this has radically altered ways of waging war, creating weaponry and modes of military organization much more advanced than those of non-industrial cultures. Together, superior economic strength, political cohesion and military superiority account for the seemingly irresistible spread of Western ways of life across the world over the past two centuries.

Global development

From the seventeenth to the early twentieth century, the Western countries established colonies in numerous areas that were previously occupied by traditional societies, using their superior military strength where necessary. Although virtually all these colonies have now attained their independence, the process of **colonialism** was central to shaping the social map of the globe as we know it today. We have mentioned colonialism earlier, in the previous chapter, in respect of the development of the coffee trade (p. 4–7). In some regions, such as North America, Australia and New Zealand, which were only thinly populated by hunting and gathering communities, Europeans became the majority population. In other areas, including much of Asia, Africa and South America, the local populations remained in the majority.

Societies of the first of these types, including the United States, have become industrialized. Those in the second category are mostly at a much lower level of industrial development and are often referred to as less developed societies, or the *developing world*. Such societies include China, India, most of the African countries (such as Nigeria, Ghana and Algeria) and countries in South America (for example, Brazil, Peru and Venezuela). Since many of these societies are situated south of the United States and Europe, they are sometimes referred to collectively as the South and contrasted to the wealthier, industrialized North.

You may often hear developing countries referred to as part of the Third World. The term **Third World** was originally part of a contrast drawn between three main types of society found in the early twentieth century. **First World** countries were (and are) the industrialized states of Europe, the United States, Canada, Greenland, Australasia (Australia, New Zealand, Tasmania and Melanesia), South Africa and Japan. Nearly all First World societies have multiparty, parliamentary systems of government. **Second World** societies meant the communist countries of what was then the Soviet Union (USSR) and Eastern Europe, including, for example, Czechoslovakia, Poland, East Germany and Hungary. Second World societies were centrally planned economies, which allowed little room for private property or competitive economic enterprise. They were also one-party states: the Communist Party dominated both the political and economic systems. For some seventy-five years, world history was affected by a global rivalry between the Soviet Union and Eastern European countries on the one hand and the capitalistic societies of the West and Japan on the other. Today that rivalry is over. With the ending of the Cold War and the disintegration of communism in the former USSR and Eastern Europe, the Second World has effectively disappeared.

Even though the Three Worlds distinction is still sometimes used in sociology textbooks, today it has outlived whatever usefulness it might once have had as a way of describing the countries of the world. For one thing, the Second World of socialist and communist countries no longer exists and even exceptions such as China are rapidly adopting capitalist economies. It can also be argued that the ranking of First, Second and Third Worlds reflects a value judgement, in which 'first' means 'best' and 'third' means 'worst', and it is therefore best avoided.

The developing world

Many developing societies are in areas that underwent colonial rule in Asia, Africa and South America. A few colonized areas gained independence early, like Haiti, which became the first autonomous black republic in January 1804. The Spanish colonies in South America acquired their freedom in 1810, while Brazil broke away from Portuguese rule in 1822. However, most nations in the developing world have become independent states only since the Second World War, often following bloody anti-colonial struggles. Examples include India, a range of other Asian countries (like Burma, Malaysia and Singapore) and countries in Africa (including, for example, Kenya, Nigeria, Zaire, Tanzania and Algeria).

While they may include peoples living in traditional fashion, developing countries are very different from earlier forms of traditional societies. Their political systems are modelled on systems that were first established in the societies of the West – that is to say, they are nation-states. While most of the population still live in rural areas, many of these societies are experiencing a rapid process of city development. (The growth of cities in the developing world is discussed in chapter 21.) Although agriculture remains the main economic activity, crops are now often produced for sale in world markets rather than for local consumption. Developing countries are not merely societies that have 'lagged behind' the more industrialized areas. They have been in large part created by contact with Western industrialism, which has undermined earlier, more traditional systems.

Conditions in some of the most impoverished of these societies have deteriorated rather than improved over the past few years. There are still around a billion people living on the equivalent of less than one dollar a day.

Global poverty is discussed further in Chapter 11, 'Global Inequality'.

The world's poor are concentrated particularly in South and East Asia and in Africa and Latin America, although there are some important differences between these regions. For example, poverty levels in East Asia and the Pacific have declined over the past decade, while they have risen in the nations of sub-Saharan Africa. During the 1990s, the number of people living on less than one dollar per day in this region has grown from 241 million to 315 million (World Bank 2004). There have also been significant increases in poverty in parts of South Asia, Latin America and the Caribbean. Many of the world's poorest countries also suffer from a serious debt crisis. Payments of interest on loans from foreign lenders can often amount to more than governments' investments in health, welfare and education.

Newly industrializing countries

While the majority of developing countries lag well behind societies of the West, some have now successfully embarked on a process of industrialization. These are sometimes referred to as **newly industrializing countries** (NICs) and they include Brazil and Mexico in Latin America and Hong Kong, South Korea, Singapore and Taiwan in East Asia. The rates of economic growth of the most successful NICs, such as those in East Asia, are several times those of the Western industrial economies. No developing country figured among the top thirty exporters in the world in 1968, but twenty-five years later South Korea was in the top fifteen.

The East Asian NICs have shown the most sustained levels of economic prosperity. They are investing abroad as well as promoting growth at home. South Korea's production of steel has doubled in the last decade and its shipbuilding and electronics industries are among the world's leaders. Singapore is becoming the major financial and commercial centre of Southeast Asia. Taiwan is an important presence in the manufacturing and electronics industries. All these changes in the NICs have directly affected countries such as the United States, whose share of global steel production, for example, has dropped significantly over the past thirty years. (Types of society in the modern world are summarized in table 2.3.)

Social change

We saw at the start of this chapter how the modern world is characterized by modes of life and social institutions that are radically different from those of even the recent past. Social change is difficult to define, because there is a sense in which everything changes, all of the time. Every day is a new day; every moment is a new instant in time. The Greek philosopher Heraclitus pointed out that a person cannot step into the same river twice. On the second occasion, the river is different, since water has flowed along it and the person has

Table 2.3   Societies in the modern world

Type	Period of existence	Characteristics
First World societies	Eighteenth century to the present.	Based on industrial production and generally free enterprise. Majority of people live in towns and cities, a few work in rural agricultural pursuits. Major class inequalities, though less pronounced than in traditional states. Distinct political communities or nation-states, including the nations of the West, Japan, Australia and New Zealand.
Second World societies	Early twentieth century (following the Russian Revolution of 1917) to the early 1990s.	Based on industry, but the economic system is centrally planned. Small proportion of the population work in agriculture; most live in towns and cities. Major class inequalities persist. Distinct political communities or nation-states. Until 1989, composed of the Soviet Union and Eastern Europe, but social and political changes began to transform them into free enterprise economic systems, according to the model of First World societies.
Developing societies ('Third World societies')	Eighteenth century (mostly as colonized areas) to the present.	Majority of the population work in agriculture, using traditional methods of production. Some agricultural produce sold on world markets. Some have free enterprise systems, while others are centrally planned. Distinct political communities or nation-states, including China, India and most African and South American nations.

Table 2.3   (*continued*)

Type	Period of existence	Characteristics
Newly industrializing countries	1970s to the present.	Former developing societies now based on industrial production and generally free enterprise.
		Majority of people live in towns and cities, a few work in agricultural pursuits.
		Major class inequalities, more pronounced than First World societies.
		Average per capita income considerably less than First World societies.
		Include Hong Kong, South Korea, Singapore, Taiwan, Brazil and Mexico.

changed in subtle ways too. While this observation is in a sense correct, we do of course normally want to say that it is the same river and the same person stepping into it on two occasions. There is sufficient continuity in the shape or form of the river and in the physique and personality of the person with wet feet to say that each remains 'the same' through the changes that occur. Given this problem, how do sociologists account for the processes of change that have transformed the way humans lived?

Identifying significant change involves showing how far there are alterations in the *underlying structure* of an object or situation over a period of time. In the case of human societies, to decide how far and in what ways a system is in a process of change we have to show to what degree there is any modification of *basic institutions* during a specific period. All accounts of change also involve showing what remains stable, as a baseline against which to measure alterations. Even in the

rapidly moving world of today there are continuities with the distant past. Major religious systems, for example, such as Christianity or Islam, retain their ties with ideas and practices initiated some two thousand years ago. Yet most institutions in modern societies clearly change much more rapidly than did institutions of the traditional world.

Influences on social change

Social theorists have tried for the past two centuries to develop a grand theory that explains the nature of social change. But no single factor theory has a chance of accounting for the diversity of human social development, from hunting and gathering and pastoral societies to traditional civilizations and finally to the highly complex social systems of today. We can, however, identify the three main factors that have consistently influenced social change: cultural factors, the physical environment and political organization.

Cultural factors

The first main influence on social change consists of cultural factors, which include the effects of religion, communication systems and leadership. Religion may be either a conservative or an innovative force in social life (see chapter 14, 'Religion in Modern Society'). Some forms of religious belief and practice have acted as a brake on change, emphasizing above all the need to adhere to traditional values and rituals. Yet, as Max Weber emphasized, religious convictions frequently play a mobilizing role in pressures for social change.

A particularly important cultural influence that affects the character and pace of change is the nature of communication systems. The invention of writing, for instance, allowed for the keeping of records, making possible increased control of material resources and the development of large-scale organizations. In addition, writing altered people's perception of the relation between past, present and future. Societies that write keep a record of past events and know themselves to have a history. Understanding history can develop a sense of the overall movement or line of development a society is following and people can then actively seek to promote it further.

Under the general heading of cultural factors we should also place *leadership*. Individual leaders have had an enormous influence in world history. We have only to think of great religious figures (like Jesus), political and military leaders (like Julius Caesar), or innovators in science and philosophy (like Isaac Newton) to see that this is the case. A leader capable of pursuing dynamic policies and generating a mass following or radically altering pre-existing modes of thought can overturn a previously established order. The classical sociologist Max Weber examined the role of charismatic leadership in social change.

Weber's conception of leadership is discussed in chapter 14, p. 549.

However, individuals can only reach positions of leadership and become effective if favourable social conditions exist. Adolf Hitler was able to seize power in Germany in the 1930s, for instance, partly as a result of the tensions and crises that beset the country at that time. If those circumstances had not existed, he would probably have remained an obscure figure within a minor political faction. The same was true at a later date of Mahatma Gandhi, the famous pacifist leader in India during the period after the Second World War. Gandhi was able to be effective in securing his country's independence from Britain because the war and other events had unsettled the existing colonial institutions in India.

The physical environment

Second, the physical environment has an effect on the development of human social organization. This is clearest in more extreme environmental conditions, where people must organize their ways of life in relation to weather conditions. Inhabitants of polar regions necessarily develop habits and practices different from those living in subtropical areas. People who live in Alaska, where the winters are long and cold, tend to follow different patterns of social life from people who live in the much warmer Mediterranean countries. Alaskans spend more of their lives indoors and, except for the short period of the summer, plan outdoor activities very care-

Gandhi, shown here on an Indian banknote, helped to bring about India's independence from British rule.

fully, given the inhospitable environment in which they live.

Less extreme physical conditions can also affect society. The native population of Australia has never stopped being hunters and gatherers, since the continent contained hardly any indigenous plants suitable for regular cultivation, or animals that could be domesticated to develop pastoral production. The world's early civilizations mostly originated in areas that contained rich agricultural land – for instance, in river deltas. The ease of communications across land and the availability of sea routes are also important: societies cut off from others by mountain ranges, impassable jungles or deserts often remain relatively unchanged over long periods of time.

Yet the direct influence of the environment on social change is not very great. People are often able to develop considerable productive wealth in relatively inhospitable areas. This is true, for example, of Alaskans, who have been able to develop oil and mineral resources in spite of the harsh nature of their environment. Conversely, hunting and gathering cultures have frequently lived in highly fertile regions without becoming involved in pastoral or agricultural production.

Political organization

A third factor strongly influencing social change is the type of political organization. In hunting and gathering societies, this influence is at a minimum, since there are no political authorities capable of mobilizing the community. In all other types of society, however, the existence of distinct political agencies – chiefs, lords, kings and governments – strongly affects the course of development a society takes. Political systems are not, as Marx believed, direct expressions of underlying economic organization; quite different types of political order may exist in societies that have similar production systems. For instance, some societies based on industrial capitalism have had authoritarian political systems (examples are Nazi Germany and South Africa under apartheid), while others are much more democratic (for example, the United States, Britain or Sweden).

Military power played a fundamental part in the establishment of most traditional states; it influenced their subsequent survival or expansion in an equally basic way. But the connections between the level of production and military strength are again indirect. A ruler may choose to channel resources into building up the military, for example, even when this impoverishes most of the rest of the population – as has happened in North Korea under the rule of Kim Il Sung and his son, Kim Jong Il.

Change in the modern period

What explains why the last two hundred years, the period of modernity, have seen such a tremendous acceleration in the speed of social change? This is a complex issue, but it is not difficult to pinpoint some of the factors involved. Not surprisingly, we can categorize them along lines similar to factors that have influenced social change throughout history, except that we shall subsume the impact of the physical environment within the overall importance of economic factors.

Cultural influences

Among the cultural factors affecting processes of social change in modern times, both the development of science and the secularization of thought have contributed to the *critical* and *innovative* character of the modern outlook. We no longer assume that customs or habits are acceptable merely because they have the age-old authority of tradition. On the contrary, our ways of life increasingly require a 'rational' basis. For instance, a design for a hospital would not be based mainly on traditional tastes, but would consider its capability for serving the purpose of a hospital – effectively caring for the sick.

In addition to *how* we think, the *content* of ideas has also changed. Ideals of self-betterment, freedom, equality and democratic participation are largely creations of the past two or three centuries. Such ideals have served to mobilize processes of social and political change, including revolutions. These ideas cannot be tied to tradition, but rather suggest the constant revision of ways of life in the pursuit of human betterment. Although they were initially developed in the West, such ideals have become genuinely universal in their application, promoting change in most regions of the world.

Economic influences

Of economic influences, the most far-reaching is the impact of industrial capitalism. Capitalism differs in a fundamental way from pre-existing production systems, because it involves the constant expansion of production and the ever-increasing accumulation of wealth. In traditional production systems, levels of production were fairly static, as they were geared to habitual, customary needs. Capitalism promotes the constant revision of the technology of production, a process into which science is increasingly drawn. The rate of technological innovation fostered in modern industry is vastly greater than in any previous type of economic order.

> We look at the influence of economic factors on social change further in chapter 11, in particular by discussing the world-systems theory of Immanuel Wallerstein (pp. 409–11).

Consider the current development of information technology. In recent decades, the power of computers has increased many thousands of times over. A large computer in the 1960s was constructed using thousands of handmade connectors; an equivalent device today is not only much smaller, but requires only a handful of elements in an integrated circuit.

The impact of science and technology on how we live may be largely driven by economic factors, but it also stretches beyond the economic sphere. Science and technology both influence and are influenced by political and cultural factors. Scientific and technological development, for example, helped create modern forms of communication such as radio and television. As we have seen, such electronic forms of communication have produced changes in politics in recent years. Radio, television and the other electronic media have also come to shape how we think and feel about the world.

Political influences

The third major type of influence on change in the modern period consists of political developments. The struggle between nations to expand their power, develop their wealth and triumph militarily over their competitors has been an energizing source of change over the past two or three centuries. Political change in traditional civilizations was normally confined to elites. One aristocratic family, for example, would replace another as rulers, while for the majority of the population life would go on relatively unchanged. This is not true of modern political systems, in which the activities of political leaders and government officials constantly affect the lives of the mass of the population. Both externally and internally, political decision-making promotes and directs social change far more than in previous times.

Political development in the last two or three centuries has certainly influenced economic change as much as economic change has influenced politics. Governments now play a major role in stimulating (and sometimes retarding) rates of economic growth and in all industrial societies there is a high level of state intervention in production, the government being far and away the largest employer.

Military power and war have also been of far-reaching importance. The military strength of the Western nations from the seventeenth century onwards allowed them to influence all quarters of the world – and provided an essential backing to the global spread of Western lifestyles. In the twentieth century, the effects of the two world wars have been profound: the devastation of many countries led to processes of rebuilding that brought about major institutional changes, for example in Germany and Japan after the Second World War. Even those states that were the victors – like the UK – experienced major internal changes as a result of the impact of the war on the economy.

Globalization

The concept of globalization is one that has become widely used in debates in politics, business and the media over the past few years. A decade ago, the term *globalization* was relatively unknown. Today it seems to be on the tip of everyone's tongue. **Globalization** refers to the fact that we all increasingly live in one world, so that individuals, groups and nations become *interdependent*.

Globalization is often portrayed solely as an economic phenomenon. Much is made of the role of transnational corporations whose massive operations stretch across national borders, influencing global production processes and the international distribution of labour. Others point to the electronic integration of global financial markets and the enormous volume of global capital flows. Still others focus on the unprecedented scope of world trade, involving a much broader range of goods and services than ever before.

Although economic forces are an integral part of globalization, it would be wrong to suggest that they alone produce it. Globalization is created by the coming together of political, social, cultural and economic factors. It has been driven forward above all by the development of information and communication technologies that have intensified the speed and scope of interaction between people all over the world. As a simple example, think of the last football World Cup. Because of global television links, some matches are now watched by billions of people across the world.

Factors contributing to globalization

What explains the rise of globalization? As we have seen, explaining all social change is complex, but it is not difficult to pinpoint some of the factors that are contributing to the rise of globalization in contemporary society: these include the rise of information and communications technology, and economic and political factors.

The rise of information and communications technology

The explosion in global communications has been facilitated by a number of important advances in technology and the world's telecommunications infrastructure. In the post-Second World War era, there has been a profound transformation in the scope and intensity of telecommunications flows. Traditional telephonic communication, which depended on analogue signals sent through wires and cables with the help of mechanical crossbar switching, has been replaced by integrated systems in which vast amounts of information are compressed and transferred digitally. Cable technology has become more efficient and less expensive; the development of fibre-optic cables has dramatically expanded the number of channels that can be carried. Where the earliest transatlantic cables laid in the 1950s were capable of carrying fewer than 100 voice paths, by 1997 a single transoceanic cable could carry some 600,000 voice paths (Held 1999). The spread of communications satellites, beginning in the 1960s, has also been significant in expanding international communications. Today a network of more than 200 satellites is in place to facilitate the transfer of information around the globe.

The impact of these communications systems has been staggering. In countries with highly developed telecommunications infrastructures, homes and offices now have multiple links to the outside world, including telephones (both landlines and mobile phones), digital, satellite and cable television, electronic mail and the Internet. The Internet has emerged as the fastest-growing communication tool ever developed – some 140 million people worldwide were using the Internet in mid-1998. Around a billion people were esti-mated to be using the Internet by 2005 (see figure 2.3).

These forms of technology facilitate the compression of time and space: two individuals located on opposite sides of the planet – in Tokyo and London, for example – not only can hold a conversation in real time, but can also send documents and images to one another with the help of satellite technology. Widespread use of the Internet and mobile phones is deepening and accelerating processes of globalization; more and more people are becoming interconnected through the use of these technologies and are doing so in places that have previously been isolated or poorly served by traditional communications (see figure 2.3). Although the telecommunications infrastructure is not

High-street Internet cafés provide online access to those without it at home, or who are away from home.

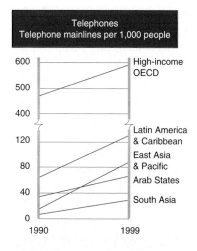

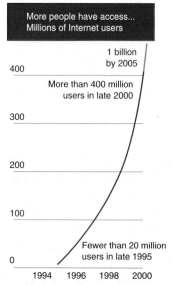

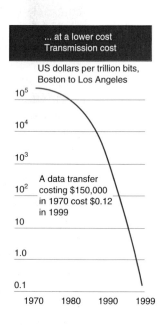

Figure 2.3 The rise of information and communications technology

Source: UNDP (2001), pp. 32 and 41

evenly developed around the world, a growing number of countries can now access international communications networks in a way that was previously impossible.

Information flows

If, as we have seen, the spread of information technology has expanded the pos-

sibilities for contact among people around the globe, it has also facilitated the flow of information about people and events in distant places. Every day, the global media bring news, images and information into people's homes, linking them directly and continuously to the outside world. Some of the most gripping events of the past two decades – such as

The dramatic increase in mobile phone ownership has compressed time and space even further.

the fall of the Berlin Wall, the violent crackdown on democratic protesters in China's Tiananmen Square and the terrorist attacks of 11 September 2001 – have unfolded through the media before a truly global audience. Such events, along with thousands of less dramatic ones, have resulted in a reorientation in people's thinking from the level of the nation-state to the global stage. Individuals are now more aware of their interconnectedness with others and more likely to identify with global issues and processes than was the case in times past.

This shift to a global outlook has two significant dimensions. First, as members of a global community, people increasingly perceive that social responsibility does not stop at national borders but instead extends beyond them. Disasters and injustices facing people on the other side of the globe are not simply misfortunes that must be endured but are legitimate grounds for action and intervention. There is a growing assumption that the international community has an obligation to act in crisis situations to protect the physical well-being or human rights of people whose lives are under threat. In the case of natural disasters, such interventions take the form of humanitarian relief and technical assistance. In recent years, earthquakes in Armenia and Turkey, floods in Mozambique and Bangladesh, famine in Africa and hurricanes in Central America have been rallying points for global assistance.

There have also been stronger calls in recent years for interventions in the case of war, ethnic conflict and the violation of human rights, although such mobilizations are more problematic than in the case of natural disasters. Yet in the case of the first Gulf War in 1991 and the violent conflicts in the former Yugoslavia (Bosnia and Kosovo), military intervention was seen as justified by many people who believed that human rights and national sovereignty had to be defended.

Second, a global outlook means that people are increasingly looking to sources other than the nation-state in formulating their own sense of identity. This is a phenomenon that is both produced by and further accelerates processes of globalization. Local cultural identities in various parts of the world are experiencing powerful revivals at a time when the traditional hold of the nation-state is undergoing profound transformation. In Europe, for example, inhabitants of Scotland and the Basque region of Spain might be more likely to identify themselves as Scottish or Basque – or simply as Europeans – rather than as British or Spanish. The nation-state as a source of identity is waning in many areas, as political shifts at the regional and global levels loosen people's orientations towards the states in which they live.

Economic factors

Globalization is also being driven forward by the integration of the world economy. In contrast to previous eras, the global economy is no longer primarily agricultural or industrial in its basis. Rather, it is increasingly dominated by activity that is weightless and intangible (Quah 1999). This *weightless economy* is one in which products have their base in information, as is the case with computer software, media and entertainment products and Internet-based services. This new economic context has been described using a variety of terms, which we will discuss in more detail in chapter 18, including *post-industrial society*, the *information age* and the *new economy* (pp. 770–2). The emergence of the knowledge society has been linked to the development of a broad base of consumers who are technologically literate and eagerly integrate new advances in computing, entertainment and telecommunications into their everyday lives.

The very operation of the global economy reflects the changes that have occurred in the information age. Many aspects of the economy now work through networks that cross national boundaries, rather than stopping at them (Castells 1996). In order to be competitive in globalizing conditions, businesses and corporations have restructured themselves to be more flexible and less hierarchical in nature. Production practices and organizational patterns have become more flexible, partnering arrangements with other firms have become commonplace and participation in worldwide distribution networks has become essential for doing business in a rapidly changing global market.

Transnational corporations

Among the many economic factors that are driving globalization, the role of transnational corporations is particularly important. **Transnational corporations** are companies that produce goods or market services in more than one country. These may be relatively small firms with one or two factories outside the country in which they are based or gigantic international ventures whose operations criss-cross the globe. Some of the biggest transnational corporations are companies known all

Coca-Cola is a transglobal enterprise, selling its products all over the world. This picture shows Diet Coke on sale in Jordan, in the Middle East.

around the world: Coca-Cola, General Motors, Colgate-Palmolive, Kodak, Mitsubishi and many others. Even when transnational corporations have a clear national base, they are oriented towards global markets and global profits.

Transnational corporations are at the heart of economic globalization. They account for two-thirds of all world trade, they are instrumental in the diffusion of new technology around the globe and they are major actors in international financial markets. As one observer has noted, they are 'the linchpins of the contemporary world economy' (Held 1999). Some five hundred transnational corporations had annual sales of more than 10 billion dollars in 2001, while only seventy-five *countries* could boast gross domestic

products of at least that amount. In other words, the world's leading transnational corporations are larger economically than most of the world's countries (see figure 2.4). In fact, the combined sales of the world's largest five hundred transnational corporations totalled $14.1 trillion – nearly half of the value of goods and services produced by the entire world.

Transnational corporations became a global phenomenon in the years following the Second World War. Expansion in the initial post-war years came from firms based in the United States, but by the 1970s, European and Japanese firms increasingly began to invest abroad. In the late 1980s and 1990s, transnational corporations expanded dramatically with the establishment of three powerful regional markets: Europe (the Single European Market), Asia-Pacific (the Osaka Declaration guaranteed free and open trade by 2010) and North America (the North American Free Trade Agreement). Since the early 1990s, countries in other areas of the world have also liberalized restrictions on foreign investment. By the turn of the twenty-first century, there were few economies in the world that stood beyond the reach of transnational corporations. Over the past decade, transnational corporations based in industrialized economies have been particularly active in expanding their operations in developing countries and in the societies of the former Soviet Union and Eastern Europe.

The argument that manufacturing is becoming increasingly globalized is often expressed in terms of **global commodity chains**, the worldwide networks of labour and production processes yielding a finished product. These networks consist of all pivotal production

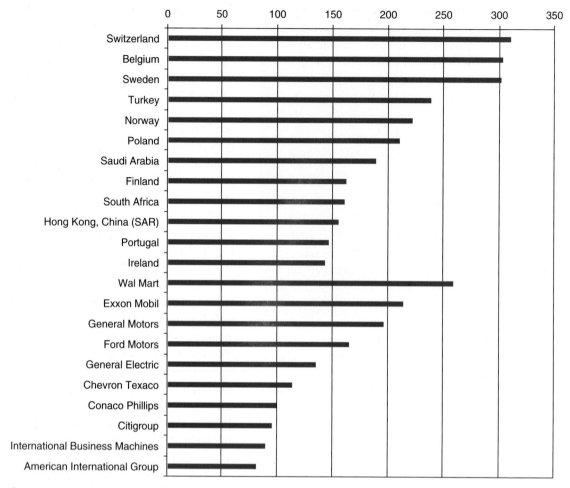

Figure 2.4 Revenue of world's biggest companies compared with GDP of selected countries ($ bn)

Source: *The Economist* (11 September 2003)

activities that form a tightly interlocked 'chain' that extends from the raw materials needed to create the product to its final consumer (Gereffi 1995; Hopkins and Wallerstein 1996; Appelbaum and Christerson 1997).

Manufactures accounted for approximately three-quarters of the world's total economic growth during the period 1990–8. The sharpest growth has been among middle-income countries: manufactures accounted for only 54 per cent of these countries' exports in 1990, compared with 71 per cent just eight years later. China has moved from the ranks of a low- to a middle-income country, largely because of its role as an exporter of manufactured goods, and partly accounts for this trend. Yet the most profitable activities in the commodity chain – engineering, design and advertising – are likely to be found in the core countries, while the least profitable activities, such as factory production, usually are found in peripheral countries. (The use of global commodity chains in the manufacture of the Barbie doll is examined in the box.)

The electronic economy

The 'electronic economy' is another factor that underpins economic globalization. Banks, corporations, fund managers and individual investors are able to shift funds internationally with the click of a mouse. This new ability to move 'electronic money' instantaneously carries with it great risks, however. Transfers of vast amounts of capital can destabilize economies, triggering international financial crises such as the ones that spread from the Asian 'tiger economies' to Russia and beyond in 1998. As the global economy becomes increasingly integrated, a financial collapse in one part of the world can have an enormous effect on distant economies.

The political, economic, social and technological factors described above are joining together to produce a phenomenon that lacks any earlier parallel in terms of its intensity and scope. The consequences of globalization are many and far-reaching, as we shall see later in this chapter. But first we will turn our attention to the main views about globalization that have been expressed in recent years.

Political changes

A third driving force behind contemporary globalization is related to political change. There are several aspects to this: first, the collapse of Soviet-style communism that occurred in a series of dramatic revolutions in Eastern Europe in 1989 and culminated in the dissolution of the Soviet Union itself in 1991. Since the fall of communism, countries in the former Soviet bloc – including Russia, Ukraine, Poland, Hungary, the Czech Republic, the Baltic states, the states of the Caucasus and Central Asia and many others – have been moving towards Western-style political and economic systems. They are no longer isolated from the global community, but are becoming integrated within it. This development has meant the end to the system that existed during the Cold War, when countries of the First World stood apart from those of the Second World. The collapse of communism has hastened processes of globalization but should also be seen as a result of globalization itself. The centrally planned communist economies and the ideological and cultural control of communist political authority were ultimately unable to survive in an era of global media and an electronically integrated world economy.

A second important political factor leading to intensifying globalization is the growth of international and regional mechanisms of government. The United Nations and the European Union are the two most prominent examples of international organizations that bring together nation-states into a common political forum. While the UN does this as an association of individual nation-states, the EU is a more pioneering form of transnational governance in which a certain degree of national sovereignty is relinquished by its member states. The governments of

Barbie and the use of global commodity chains

One illustration of the global commodity chain can be found in the manufacture of the Barbie doll, the most profitable toy in history. The 40-something teenage doll sells at a rate of two per second, bringing the Mattel Corporation, based in Los Angeles, USA, well over a billion dollars in annual revenues. Although she sells mainly in the United States, Europe and Japan, Barbie can also be found in 140 countries around the world. She is a truly global citizen (Tempest 1996). Barbie is global not only in sales, but in terms of her birthplace as well. Barbie was never made in the United States. The first doll was made in Japan in 1959, when that country was still recovering from the Second World War and wages were low. As wages rose in Japan, Barbie moved to other low-wage countries in Asia. Her multiple origins today tell us a great deal about the operation of global commodity chains.

Barbie is designed in the United States, where her marketing and advertising strategies are devised and where most of the profits are made. But the only physical aspect of Barbie that is 'made in the USA' is her cardboard packaging, along with some of the paints and oils that are used to decorate the doll.

Barbie's body and wardrobe span the globe in their origins:

1 Barbie begins her life in Saudi Arabia, where oil is extracted and then refined into the ethylene that is used to create her plastic body.
2 Taiwan's state-owned oil importer, the Chinese Petroleum Corporation, buys the ethylene and sells it to Taiwan's Formosa Plastic Corporation, the world's largest producer of polyvinyl chloride (PVC) plastics, which are used in toys. Formosa Plastics converts the ethylene into the PVC pellets that will be shaped to make Barbie's body.
3 The pellets are then shipped to one of the four Asian factories that make Barbie – two in southern China, one in Indonesia and one in Malaysia. The plastic mould injection machines that shape her body, which are the most expensive part of Barbie's manufacture, are made in the United States and shipped to the factories.
4 Once Barbie's body is moulded, she gets her nylon hair from Japan. Her cotton dresses are made in China, with Chinese cotton – the only raw material in Barbie that actually comes from the country where most Barbies are made.
5 Hong Kong plays a key role in the manufacturing process of the Chinese Barbies. Nearly all the material used in her manufacture is shipped into Hong Kong – one of the world's largest ports – and then trucked to the factories in China. The finished Barbies leave by the same route. Some 23,000 trucks make the daily trip between Hong Kong and southern China's toy factories.

'Global Barbie'.

So where is Barbie actually from? The cardboard and cellophane box containing the 'My First Tea Party' Barbie is labelled 'Made in China', but, as we have seen, almost none of the materials that go into making her actually originates in that country. Out of her $9.99 retail price in the USA (about £6), China gets only about 35 cents, mainly in wages paid to the 11,000 peasant women who assemble her in the two factories. Back in the United States, on the other hand, Mattel makes about $1 in profits.

What about the rest of the money that is made when Barbie is sold for $9.99? Only 65 cents is needed to cover the plastics, cloth, nylon and other materials used in her manufacture. Most of the money goes to pay for machinery and equipment, transoceanic shipping and domestic trucking, advertising and merchandising, retail floor space – and, of course, the profits of Toys 'R' Us and other retailers.

individual EU states are bound by directives, regulations and court judgements from common EU bodies, but they also reap economic, social and political benefits from their participation in the regional union.

Finally, globalization is being driven by international governmental organizations (IGOs) and international non-governmental organizations (INGOs; see also chapter 16, pp. 651–5). An IGO is a body that is established by participating governments and given responsibility for regulating or overseeing a particular domain of activity that is transnational in scope. The first such body, the International Telegraph Union, was founded in 1865. Since that time, a great number of similar bodies have been created to regulate issues ranging from civil aviation to broadcasting to the disposal of hazardous waste. In 1909, there were 37 IGOs in existence to regulate transnational affairs; by 1996, there were 260 (Held et al. 1999).

As the name suggests, international non-governmental organizations differ from IGOs in that they are not affiliated with government institutions. Rather, they are independent organizations that work alongside governmental bodies in making policy decisions and addressing international issues. Some of the best-known INGOs – such as Greenpeace, *Médecins Sans Frontières* (Doctors Without Borders), the Red Cross and Amnesty International – are involved in environmental protection and humanitarian efforts. But the activities of thousands of lesser-known groups also link together countries and communities (see figure 2.5).

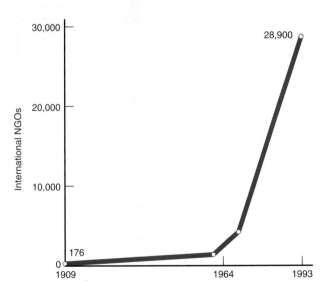

Figure 2.5 The growth in international non-governmental organizations, 1909–93

Source: UNDP (1999)

Table 2.4   Conceptualizing globalization: three tendencies

	Hyperglobalizers	Sceptics	Transformationalists
What's new?	A global age.	Trading blocs, weaker geogovernance than in earlier periods.	Historically unprecedented levels of global inter-connectedness.
Dominant features	Global capitalism, global governance, global civil society.	World less interdependent than in 1890s.	'Thick' (intensive and extensive) globalization.
Power of national governments	Declining or eroding.	Reinforced or enhanced.	Reconstituted, restructured.
Driving forces of globalization	Capitalism and technology.	Governments and markets.	Combined forces of modernity.
Pattern of stratification	Erosion of old hierarchies.	Increased marginalization of South.	New architecture of world order.
Dominant motif	McDonald's, Madonna, etc.	National interest.	Transformation of political community.
Conceptualization of globalization	As a reordering of the framework of human action.	As internationalization and regionalization.	As the reordering of interregional relations and action at a distance.
Historical trajectory	Global civilization.	Regional blocs/clash of civilizations.	Indeterminate: global integration and fragmentation.
Summary argument	The end of the nation-state.	Internationalization depends on government acquiescence and support.	Globalization transforming government power and world politics.

Source: Adapted from Held et al. (1999), p. 10

The globalization debate

In recent years, globalization has become a hotly debated topic. Most people accept that there are important transformations occurring around us, but the extent to which it is valid to explain these as 'globalization' is contested. This is not entirely surprising. As an unpredictable and turbulent process, globalization is seen and understood very differently by observers. David Held and his colleagues (Held 1999) have surveyed the controversy and divided its participants into three schools of thought: *sceptics, hyperglobalizers* and *transformationalists*. These three tendencies within the globalization debate are summarized in table 2.4.

The sceptics

Some thinkers argue that the idea of globalization is overrated – that the debate over globalization is a lot of talk about something that is not new. The sceptics in the globalization controversy believe that present levels of economic interdependence are not unprecedented. Pointing to nineteenth-century statistics on world trade and investment, they contend that modern globalization differs from the past only in the intensity of interaction between nations.

The sceptics agree that there may now be more contact between countries than in previous eras, but in their eyes the current world economy is not sufficiently integrated to constitute a truly globalized economy. This is because the bulk of trade occurs within three regional groups – Europe, Asia-Pacific and North America. The countries of the European Union, for example, trade predominantly among themselves. The same is true of the other regional groups, thereby invalidating the notion of a single global economy (Hirst 1997).

Many sceptics focus on processes of *regionalization* within the world economy – such as the emergence of major financial and trading blocs. To sceptics, the growth of regionalization is evidence that the world economy has become *less* integrated rather than more so (Boyer and Drache 1996; Hirst and Thompson 1999). Compared with the patterns of trade that prevailed a century ago, it is argued that the world economy is less global in its geographical scope and more concentrated on intense pockets of activity.

Sceptics reject the view held by some, such as the hyperglobalizers (see below), that globalization is fundamentally undermining the role of national governments and producing a world order in which they are less central. According to the sceptics, national governments continue to be key players because of their involvement in regulating and coordinating economic activity. Governments, for example, are the driving force behind many trade agreements and policies of economic liberalization.

The hyperglobalizers

The hyperglobalizers take an opposing position to that of the sceptics. They argue that globalization is a very real phenomenon whose consequences can be felt almost everywhere. Globalization is seen as a process that is indifferent to national borders. It is producing a new global order, swept along by powerful flows of cross-border trade and production. One of the best-known hyperglobalizers, the Japanese writer Kenichi Ohmae, sees globalization as leading to a 'borderless world' – a world in which market forces are more powerful than national governments (Ohmae 1990, 1995).

Much of the analysis of globalization offered by hyperglobalizers focuses on the changing role of the nation-state. It is argued that individual countries no longer control their economies because of the vast growth in world trade. National governments and the politicians within them, it is said, are increasingly unable to exercise control over the issues that cross their borders – such as volatile financial markets and environmental threats. Citizens recognize that politicians are limited in their ability to address these problems and, as a result, lose faith in existing systems of governance. Some hyperglobalizers believe that the power of national governments is also being challenged from above – by new regional and international institutions, such as the European Union, the World Trade Organization and others.

Taken together, these shifts signal to the hyperglobalizers the dawning of a global age (Albrow 1997), in which national governments decline in importance and influence.

The transformationalists

The transformationalists take more of a middle position. They see globalization as the central force behind a broad spectrum of changes that are currently shaping modern societies. According to them, the global order is being transformed, but many of the old patterns still remain. Governments, for instance, still retain a good deal of power in spite of the advance of global interdependence. These transformations are not restricted to economics alone, but are equally prominent within the realms of politics, culture and personal life. Transformationalists contend that the current level of globalization is breaking down established boundaries between internal and external, international and domestic. In trying to adjust to this new order, societies, institutions and individuals are being forced to navigate contexts where previous structures have been shaken up.

Unlike hyperglobalizers, transformationalists see globalization as a dynamic and open process that is subject to influence and change. It is developing in a contradictory fashion, encompassing tendencies that frequently operate in opposition to one another. Globalization is not a one-way process, as some claim, but a two-way flow of images, information and influences. Global migration, media and telecommunications are contributing to the diffusion of cultural influences. The world's vibrant 'global cities' are thoroughly multicultural, with ethnic groups and cultures intersecting and living side by side. According to transformationalists, globalization is a decentred and reflexive process characterized by links and cultural flows that work in a multidirectional way. Because globalization is the product of numerous intertwined global networks, it cannot be seen as being driven from one particular part of the world.

Rather than losing sovereignty, as the hyperglobalizers argue, countries are seen by transformationalists as restructuring in response to new forms of economic and social organization that are non-territorial in basis (e.g., corporations, social movements and international bodies). They argue that we are no longer living in a state-centric world; governments are being forced to adopt a more active and outward-looking stance towards governance under the complex conditions of globalization (Rosenau 1997).

Whose view is most nearly correct? Almost certainly that of the transformationalists. The sceptics are mistaken because they underestimate how far the world is changing; world finance markets, for example, are organized on a global level much more than they ever were before. The hyperglobalizers, on the other hand, see globalization too much in economic terms and as too much of a one-way process. In reality, globalization is much more complex.

The impact of globalization

In the first chapter we found that the chief focus of sociology has historically been the study of the industrialized societies. As sociologists, can we thus safely ignore the developing world, leaving this as the domain of anthropology? We certainly cannot. The industrialized and the developing societies have developed in *interconnection* with one another and are today more closely related than ever

Globalization and everyday life: reggae music

When those knowledgeable about popular music listen to a song, they can often pick out the stylistic influences that helped shape it. Each musical style, after all, represents a unique way of combining rhythm, melody, harmony and lyrics. And while it doesn't take a genius to notice the differences between rock, R&B or folk, for example, musicians often combine a number of styles in composing songs. Identifying the components of these combinations can be difficult. But for sociologists, the effort is often rewarding. Different musical styles tend to emerge from different social groups, and studying how styles combine and fuse is a good way to chart the cultural contacts between groups.

Some sociologists have turned their attention to reggae music because it exemplifies the process whereby contacts between social groups result in the creation of new musical forms. Reggae's roots can be traced to West Africa. In the seventeenth century, large numbers of West Africans were enslaved by British colonists and brought by ship to work in the sugar cane fields of the West Indies. Although the British attempted to prevent slaves from playing traditional African music for fear it would serve as a rallying cry to revolt, the slaves managed to keep alive the tradition of African drumming, sometimes by integrating it with the European musical styles imposed by the slave owners. In Jamaica, the drumming of one group of slaves, the Burru, was openly tolerated by slaveholders because it helped meter the pace of work. Slavery was finally abolished in Jamaica in 1834, but the tradition of Burru drumming continued, even as many Burru men migrated from rural areas to the slums of Kingston.

It was in these slums that a new religious cult began to emerge – one that would prove crucial for the development of reggae. In 1930 a man named Haile Selassie was crowned emperor of the African country of Ethiopia. While opponents of European colonialism throughout the world cheered Selassie's ascension to the throne, a number of people in the West Indies came to believe that Selassie was a god, sent to earth to lead the oppressed of Africa to freedom. One of Selassie's names was 'Prince Ras Tafari', and the West Indians who worshipped him called themselves 'Rastafarians'. The Rastafarian cult soon merged with the Burru, and Rastafarian music came to combine Burru styles of drumming with biblical themes of oppression and liberation. In the 1950s, West Indian musicians began mixing Rastafarian rhythms and lyrics with elements of American jazz and black rhythm and blues. These combinations eventually developed into 'ska' music, and then, in the late 1960s, into reggae, with its relatively slow beat, its emphasis on bass, and its stories of urban deprivation and of the power of collective social consciousness. Many reggae artists, such as Bob Marley, became commercial successes, and by the 1970s people the world over were listening to reggae music. In the 1980s and 1990s, reggae was fused with hip-hop (or rap) to produce new sounds (Hebdige 1997), heard in the work of the groups like The Wu-Tang Clan, Shaggy or Sean Paul.

The history of reggae is thus the history of contact between different social groups, and of the meanings – political, spiritual and personal – that those groups expressed through their music. Globalization has increased the intensity of these contacts. It is now possible for a young musician in Scandinavia, for example, to grow up listening to music produced by men and women in the basements of Notting Hill in London, and to be deeply influenced as well by, say, a mariachi performance broadcast live via satellite from Mexico City. If the number of contacts between groups is an important determinant of the pace of musical evolution, it can be predicted that there will be a veritable profusion of new styles in the coming years as the process of globalization continues to unfold.

before. Those of us living in the industrialized societies depend on many raw materials and manufactured products from developing countries to sustain our lives. Conversely, the economies of most developing states depend on trading networks that bind them to the industrialized countries. We can only fully understand the industrialized order against the backdrop of societies in the developing world – in which, in fact, by far the greater proportion of the world's population lives.

Take a close look at the array of products on display the next time you walk into a local shop or supermarket. The diversity of goods we in the West have come to take for granted as available for anyone with the money to buy them depends on amazingly complex economic connections stretching across the world. The store products have been made in, or use ingredients or parts from, a hundred different countries. These parts must be regularly transported across the globe, and constant flows of information are necessary to coordinate the millions of daily transactions.

As the world rapidly moves towards a single, unified economy, businesses and people move about the globe in increasing numbers in search of new markets and economic opportunities. As a result, the cultural map of the world changes: networks of peoples span national borders and even continents, providing cultural connections between their birthplaces and their adoptive countries (Appadurai 1986). A handful of languages comes to dominate, and in some cases replace, the thousands of different languages that were once spoken on the planet.

It is increasingly impossible for cultures to exist as islands. There are few, if any, places on earth so remote as to escape radio, television, air travel – and the throngs of tourists they bring – or the computer. A generation ago, there were still tribes whose way of life was completely untouched by the rest of the world. Today, these peoples use machetes and other tools made in the United States or Japan, wear T-shirts and shorts manufactured in garment factories in the Dominican Republic or Guatemala, and take medicine manufactured in Germany or Switzerland to combat diseases contracted through contact with outsiders. These people also have their stories broadcast to people around the world through satellite television and the Internet. Within a generation or two at the most, all the world's once-isolated cultures will be touched and transformed by global culture, despite their persistent efforts to preserve their age-old ways of life.

The forces that produce a global culture will be discussed throughout this book. These include:

1 Television, which brings British and especially American culture (through networks and programmes such as the BBC, MTV or *Friends*) into homes throughout the world daily, while adapting cultural products from the Netherlands, (such as *Big Brother*) or Sweden (such as *Expedition: Robinson*, which became *Survivor*) for British and American audiences.
2 The emergence of a unified global economy, with business whose factories, management structures and markets often span continents and countries.
3 'Global citizens', such as managers of large corporations, who may spend as

much time criss-crossing the globe as they do at home, identifying with a global, cosmopolitan culture rather than with that of their own nation.

4 A host of international organizations, including United Nations agencies, regional trade and mutual defence associations, multinational banks and other global financial institutions, international labour and health organizations, and global tariff and trade agreements, that are creating a global political, legal and military framework.

5 Electronic communications (telephone, fax, electronic mail, the Internet and the World Wide Web), which makes instantaneous communication with almost any part of the planet an integral part of daily life in the business world.

Does the Internet promote a global culture?

Many believe that the rapid growth of the Internet around the world will hasten the spread of a global culture – one resembling the cultures of Europe and North America, currently home to nearly three-quarters of all Internet users (see figure 2.6). Belief in such values as equality between men and women, the right to speak freely, democratic participation in government and the pursuit of pleasure through consumption are readily diffused throughout the world over the Internet. Moreover, Internet technology itself would seem to foster such values: global communication, seemingly unlimited (and uncensored) information, and instant gratification are all characteristics of the new technology.

Yet it may be premature to conclude that the Internet will sweep aside traditional cultures, replacing them with radi-

cally new cultural values. As the Internet spreads around the world, there is evidence that it is in many ways compatible with traditional cultural values as well, perhaps even a means of strengthening them.

Consider, for example, the Middle Eastern country of Kuwait, a traditional Islamic culture that has recently experienced strong American and European influences. Kuwait, an oil-rich country on the Persian Gulf, has one of the highest average per-person incomes in the world. The government provides free public education through the university level, resulting in high rates of literacy and education for both men and women. Kuwaiti television frequently carries American Football from the USA for example, although broadcasts are regularly interrupted for the traditional Muslim calls to prayer. Half of Kuwait's approximately 2 million people are under the age of 25, and, like their counterparts in Europe and North America, many surf the Internet for new ideas, information and consumer products.

Although Kuwait is in many respects a modern country, cultural norms that treat men and women differently are very strong. Women are generally expected to wear traditional clothing that leaves only the face and hands visible and are forbidden to leave home at night or be seen in public at any time with a man who is not a spouse or relative.

Deborah Wheeler (1998) spent a year studying the impact of the Internet on Kuwaiti culture. The Internet is increasingly popular in Kuwait; half of all Internet users in Middle Eastern Arab countries live in this tiny country. Kuwaiti newspapers frequently carry stories about the Internet

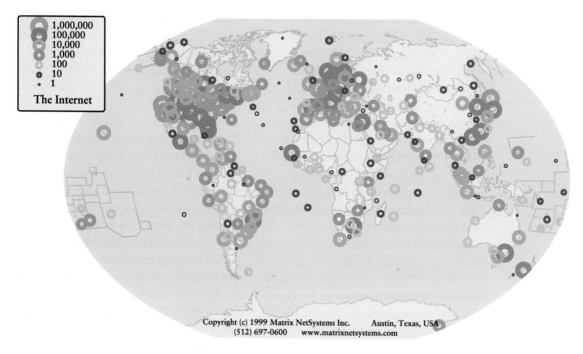

Figure 2.6 Global Internet connectivity: number of Internet servers, January 1999

Source: John Quarterman and colleagues at Matrix Information Directory Services (MIDS), <www.geog.ucl.ac.uk/casa/martin/atlas/mids_intrworld9901_large.gif>

and the Web, and Kuwait University was the first university in the Arab world to hook its students up to the Internet.

Wheeler reports that Kuwaiti teenagers are flocking to Internet cafés, where they spend most of their time in chat rooms or visiting pornographic sites – two activities strongly frowned upon by traditional Islamic culture. According to Wheeler:

> Many young people told me of encounters they were having with the opposite sex in cyberspace. There are even keyboard symbols for kisses (*), kisses on the lips (:*), and embarrassed giggles (LOL) – all those interactions and reactions that make courtship exciting and, in this case, safe. (1998)

The new communications technologies are clearly enabling men and women to talk with one another in a society where such communications outside marriage are extremely limited. Wheeler also notes that, ironically, men and women are segregated in the Internet cafés. Furthermore, she finds that Kuwaitis are extremely reluctant to voice strong opinions or political views online. With the exception of discussing conservative Islamic religious beliefs, which are freely disseminated over the Internet, Kuwaitis are remarkably inhibited online. Wheeler attributes this to the cultural belief that giving out too much information about oneself is dangerous:

In Kuwait, information is more of a potential threat than a means for individual empowerment. It is a weapon to use against your enemies, a tool for keeping conformity, or a reinforcement of regulations of daily life. . . . Kuwait's transition to the information age is influenced by these attitudes and the desire to keep one's reputation protected. This keeps the Internet from registering significant political and social impacts, except for the rise in Kuwaiti Islamist discourses on the Internet. . . . In Kuwait, there is an ethos that states that having and/or pronouncing a political opinion publicly is bad. No one wants to talk on the record or to be quoted. The idea makes people scared or nervous. Only those who are elite feel they can speak freely and openly. (1988)

Wheeler concludes that Kuwaiti culture, which is hundreds of years old, is not likely to be easily transformed by simple exposure to different beliefs and values on the Internet. The fact that a few young people are participating in global chat rooms does not mean that Kuwaiti culture is adopting the sexual attitudes of the United States or even the form of everyday relations found between men and women in the West. The culture that eventually emerges as a result of the new technologies will not be the same as American culture; it will be uniquely Kuwaiti.

The rise of individualism

Although globalization is often associated with changes within big systems – such as the world financial markets, production and trade, and telecommunications – the effects of globalization are felt equally strongly in the private realm. Globalization is not something that is simply out there, operating on a distant plane and not intersecting with individual affairs. Globalization is an 'in here' phenomenon that is affecting our intimate and personal lives in many diverse ways. Inevitably, our personal lives have been altered as globalizing forces enter into our local contexts, our homes and our communities through impersonal sources – such as the media, the Internet and popular culture – as well as through personal contact with individuals from other countries and cultures.

Globalization is fundamentally changing the nature of our everyday experiences. As the societies in which we live undergo profound transformations, the established institutions that used to underpin them have become out of place. This is forcing a redefinition of intimate and personal aspects of our lives, such as the family, gender roles, sexuality, personal identity, our interactions with others and our relationships to work. The way we think of ourselves and our connections with other people is being profoundly altered through globalization.

In our current age, individuals have much more opportunity to shape their own lives than once was the case. At one time, tradition and custom exercised a very strong influence on the path of people's lives. Factors such as social class, gender, ethnicity and even religious affiliation could close off certain avenues for individuals, or open up others. Being born the eldest son of a tailor, for example, would probably ensure that a young man would learn his father's craft and carry on practising that craft throughout his lifetime. Tradition held that a woman's natural sphere was in the home; her life and identity were largely defined by those of her husband or father. In times past, individuals' personal identities were formed in the context of the community into which they were born. The values, lifestyles and ethics prevailing in that community provided relatively fixed guidelines according to which people lived their lives.

Under conditions of globalization, however, we are faced with a move towards a new *individualism*, in which people have actively to construct their own identities. The weight of tradition and established values is retreating, as local communities interact with a new global order. The social codes that formerly guided people's choices and activities have significantly loosened. Today, for example, the eldest son of a tailor could choose any number of paths in constructing his future, women are no longer restricted to the domestic realm and many of the other signposts that shaped people's lives have disappeared. Traditional frameworks of identity are dissolving and new patterns of identity are emerging. Globalization is forcing people to live in a more open, reflexive way. This means that we are constantly responding and adjusting to the changing environment around us; as individuals, we evolve with and within the larger context in which we live. Even the small choices we make in our daily lives – what we wear, how we spend our leisure time and how we take care of our health and our bodies – are part of an ongoing process of creating and re-creating our self-identities.

Conclusion: the need for global governance

As globalization progresses, existing political structures and models appear unequipped to manage a world full of the challenges that transcend national borders. It is not within the capacity of individual governments to control the spread of AIDS, to counter the effects of global warming or to regulate volatile financial markets. Many of the processes affecting societies around the world elude the grasp of current governing mechanisms. In the light of this governing deficit, some have called for new forms of global governance that could address global issues in a global way. As a growing number of challenges operate above the level of individual countries, it is argued that responses to them must also be transnational in scope.

Although it may seem unrealistic to speak of governance above the level of the nation-state, some steps have already been taken towards the creation of a global democratic structure, such as the formation of the United Nations and the European Union. The EU in particular can be seen as an innovative response to globalization and could well become a model for similar organizations in other parts of the world where regional ties are strong. New forms of global governance could help to promote a cosmopolitan world order in which transparent rules and standards for international behaviour, such as the defence of human rights, are established and observed.

The decade that has passed since the end of the Cold War has been marked by violence, internal conflict and chaotic transformations in many areas of the world. While some have taken a pessimistic view, seeing globalization as accelerating crisis and chaos, others see vital opportunities to harness globalizing forces in the pursuit of greater equality, democracy and prosperity. The move towards global governance and more effective regulatory institutions is certainly not misplaced at a time when global interdependence and the rapid pace of change link all of us together more than ever before. It is not beyond our abilities to reassert our will on the social world. Indeed, such a task appears to be both the greatest necessity and the greatest challenge facing human societies at the start of the twenty-first century.

We learn more about global governance in chapter 20, 'Politics, Government and Terrorism'.

Summary points

1   Several types of pre-modern society can be distinguished. In *hunting and gathering societies*, people do not grow crops or keep livestock but gain their livelihood from gathering plants and hunting animals. *Pastoral societies* are those that raise domesticated animals as their major source of subsistence. *Agrarian societies* depend on the cultivation of fixed plots of land. Larger, more developed, urban societies form traditional states or civilizations.

2   The development of industralized societies and the expansion of the West led to the conquest of many parts of the world through the process of *colonialism*, which radically changed long-established social systems and cultures.

3   In industrialized societies, industrial production (whose techniques are also used in the production of food) is the main basis of the economy. Industrialized countries include the nations of the West, plus Japan, Australia and New Zealand. The *developing world*, in which most of the world's population live, are almost all formerly colonized areas. The majority of the population works in agricultural production, some of which is geared to world markets.

4   *Social change* may be defined as the transformation, over time, of the institutions and culture of a society. The modern period, although occupying only a small fraction of human history, has shown rapid and major changes, and the pace of change is accelerating.

5   The development of social organization and institutions, from hunting and gathering to agrarian to modern industrial societies, is far too diverse to be accounted for by any single-factor theory of social change. At least three broad categories of influences can be identified. The physical environment includes such factors as climate or the availability of communication routes (rivers, mountain passes); these are important to consider, especially as they affect early economic development, but should not be overemphasized. Political organization (especially military power) affects all societies, traditional and modern, with the possible exception of hunting and gathering societies. Cultural factors include religion (which can act as a brake on change), communication systems (such as the invention of writing) and individual leadership.

6   The most important economic influence on modern social change is industrial capitalism, which depends on and promotes constant innovation and revision of productive technology. Science and technology also affect (and are affected by)

political factors, the most important of which is the emergence of the modern state with its relatively efficient forms of government. Cultural influences include another effect of science and technology: the critical and innovative character of modern thinking, which constantly challenges tradition and cultural habits.

7   Globalization is often portrayed as an economic phenomenon, but this view is too simplified. Globalization is produced by the coming together of political, economic, cultural and social factors. It is driven forward above all by advances in information and communication technologies that have intensified the speed and scope of interaction between people around the world.

8   Several factors are contributing to increasing globalization. First, the end of the Cold War, the collapse of Soviet-style communism and the growth of international and regional forms of governance have drawn the countries of the world closer together. Second, the spread of information technology has facilitated the flow of information around the globe and has encouraged people to adopt a global outlook. Third, transnational corporations have grown in size and influence, building networks of production and consumption that span the globe and link economic markets.

9   Globalization has become a hotly debated topic. Sceptics believe that the idea of globalization is overrated and that current levels of interconnectedness are not unprecedented. Some sceptics focus instead on processes of regionalization that are intensifying activity within major financial and trade groups. Hyperglobalizers take an opposing position, arguing that globalization is a real and powerful phenomenon that threatens to erode the role of national governments altogether. A third group, the transformationalists, believes that globalization is transforming many aspects of the current global order – including economics, politics and social relations – but that old patterns still remain. According to this view, globalization is a contradictory process, involving a multidirectional flow of influences that sometimes work in opposition.

10   Globalization is producing challenges that cross national borders and elude the reach of existing political structures. Because individual governments are unequipped to handle these transnational issues, there is a need for new forms of global governance that can address global problems in a global way. Reasserting our will on the rapidly changing social world may be the greatest challenge of the twenty-first century.

Questions for further thought

1 How significant are 'great leaders' in processes of social change?

2 How can globalization also be a local phenomenon?

3 Did globalization also cause the downfall of communism?

4 With the growing sense of individualism, are we free to be who we want to be or just spoilt for choice?

5 Are transnational corporations really more powerful than governments?

6 Will globalization lead to a global culture?

Further reading

Ulrich Beck, *What is Globalization?* (Cambridge: Polity, 1999).
R. Cohen and P. Kennedy, *Global Sociology* (London: MacMillan, 2000).
Peter Dicken, *Global Shift: Transforming the World Economy* (New York: Guilford Press, 1998).
John Gray, *False Dawn: The Delusions of Global Capitalism* (London: Granta Books, 1998).
David Held and Anthony McGrew (eds), *The Global Transformations Reader – Second Edition* (Cambridge: Polity, 2003).
Frank J. Lechner and John Boli (eds), *The Globalization Reader* (Oxford: Blackwell, 2000).
Joseph Stiglitz, *Globalization and its Discontents* (London: Allen Lane, 2002).
J. Timmons Roberts and Amy Hite (eds), *From Modernization to Globalization: Perspectives on Development and Social Change* (Oxford: Blackwell, 1999).
Sarah Owen Vandersluis and Paris Yeros (eds), *Poverty in World Politics: Whose Global Era?* (Basingstoke: Macmillan, 1999).

Internet links

Globalization Resource
http://www.polity.co.uk/global

International Forum on Globalization
http://www.ifg.org/

Tradewatch
http://www.tradewatch.org

World Bank Globalization Pages
http://www1.worldbank.org/economicpolicy/globalization

Reith Lectures on Globalization from 1999
http://news.bbc.co.uk/hi/english/static/events/reith_99/default.htm

Contents

3

Asking and Answering Sociological Questions

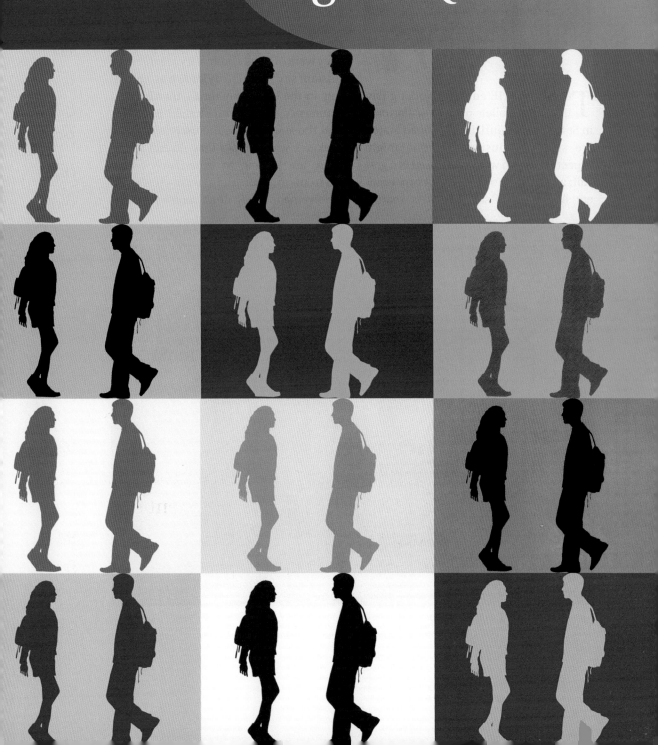

TOWARDS THE end of a working day, the public toilets of a particular park in St Louis, Missouri, in the United States, are suddenly busier than one might expect. One man walks in dressed in a grey suit; another has on a baseball cap, trainers, shorts and a T-shirt; a third is wearing the mechanic's uniform from the garage where he has repaired cars all day. What are these men doing here? Surely other toilets are more conveniently located. Is there some common interest besides the toilets themselves that brings them to this place?

None of these men is visiting the toilets to use them for the purposes for which they were officially built: they are there for 'instant sex' – an activity known as 'cottaging' in the UK. Many men – married and unmarried, those with straight identities and those whose see themselves as gay – seek sex with people they do not know. They are hoping to experience sexual excitement, but they want to avoid involvement. They don't want any com-

Why hang out in public toilets?

mitments that extend beyond the particular encounters they will have in this public convenience.

This kind of search for anonymous, instant sex between men happens all over the world, yet until the late 1960s the phenomenon persisted as a widespread but rarely studied form of human interaction. In the USA, the gay community called the toilets where these activities occur 'tearooms'. Laud Humphreys, a sociologist, visited these public lavatories to conduct research on the participants. He wrote about them in his book *Tearoom Trade* (Humphreys 1970). Unsurprisingly, the book caused widespread controversy when it was published and for some people the issue is still a difficult one to deal with today. Humphreys' research methodology was heavily criticized for being unethical, for example, because his covert fieldwork did not involve seeking the informed consent of the men studied. (The ethics of Humphreys' research are discussed further on pp. 93–4.) However, because of his research in the tearooms, Humphreys was able to cast a new light on the struggles of men who were forced to keep their sexual proclivities secret. He showed that many men who otherwise live 'normal' lives – the people next door – find ways to engage in embarrassing behaviours that will not harm their careers or family lives. Humphreys' research was conducted more than three decades ago, when there was much more stigma associated with gay and lesbian identities and when police were vigilant in enforcing laws against such behaviour. Many lives were ruined in the process of harsh enforcement.

Humphreys spent an extended period of time in such public toilets because an excellent way to understand social pro-cesses is to participate in and observe them. He also conducted survey interviews that enabled him to gather more information than he would have obtained by simply observing the toilets. Humphreys' research opened a window on an aspect of life that many people would be shocked to know existed at all and that certainly needed to be understood at a deeper level. His work was based on systematic research, but it also carried a note of passion.

Humphreys argued that persecution against gay lifestyles leads men to live anguished existences in which they must resort to extreme secrecy and often dangerous activities. His study was conducted before the onset of AIDS; such activity would be much more dangerous today. He argued that tolerance for a gay subculture would put gays in a position where they could provide one another with self-esteem, mutual support and relief from torment.

Sociological questions

The toilets under study in *Tearoom Trade* make a perfect example of a phenomenon that is the subject of many of the kinds of question that sociologists ask. For example, in looking at the surprising activities that occur in public toilets, Humphreys was asking how society works in ways that are different from the official versions of how it should work and how what we take to be natural – a public toilet – is actually *socially constructed* depending on how it is used.

It is also interesting to note that elements of modern theoretical approaches can help us understand the issues addressed by Humphreys' study. An *interactionist* might ask: how does this behaviour take place through processes of interaction? What kinds of interaction take place? Humphreys found that people who go into the tearooms learn from others to be silent. This is a response to the demand for privacy without involvement. Another finding is that men who go into the toilet and do not respond to initial sexual advances will not be approached any further. Each party must collaborate to make a sexual situation occur. A *functionalist* approach might ask: what contribution does the tearoom make to the continuation of society as a whole? The answer is that it provides an outlet for sexual activity that, when carried out in secret, enables the participants and other members of society to carry on as 'normal' people in their everyday lives without challenging the accepted order of things. A *Marxist* approach might ask: is thinking about economic class relations apparent in the tearooms? Humphreys found that the impersonal sex of the tearooms had a democratic quality. Men of all social classes and races would come together in these places for sexual contact. Finally, a *feminist* approach might ask: how can women's lives be considered in this study of an all-male group? This approach was not dominant at the time Humphreys conducted his study, but a feminist today might ask how women's lives – perhaps wives who know nothing about the activity of their male partners – are affected by this secret behaviour in the tearooms. We return to some of these theoretical approaches in the next chapter.

It is now nearly forty years since *Tearoom Trade* was first published, and in the interim society has become more tol-erant of gay identities and gay sex. After the publication of his book, Humphreys became part of the political movement – the gay rights movement – that made this change possible. He used his findings to convince courts and police to ease up on prosecuting men for engaging in gay sex so as to alleviate the damaging side effects of covert sexual activity.

It is the business of sociological research in general to go beyond surface-level understandings of ordinary life, as Humphreys did. Good research should help us understand our social lives in a new way. It should take us by surprise, in the questions that it asks and in the findings it comes up with. The issues that concern sociologists, in both their theorizing and their research, are often similar to those that worry other people. But the results of such research frequently run counter to our common-sense beliefs.

What are the circumstances in which racial or sexual minorities live? How can mass starvation exist in a world that is far wealthier than it has ever been before? What effects will the increasing use of the Internet have on our lives? Is the family beginning to disintegrate as an institution? Sociologists try to provide answers to these and many other questions. Their findings are by no means conclusive. Nevertheless, it is always the aim of sociological theorizing and research to break away from the speculative manner in which the ordinary person usually considers such questions. Good sociological work tries to make the questions as precise as possible and seeks to gather factual evidence before coming to conclusions. To achieve these aims, we must know the most useful **research methods** to apply in a given study and how best to analyse the results.

In their research studies, sociologists will often ask empirical or **factual questions**. For example, many aspects of sexual behaviour, such as those Humphreys studied, need direct and systematic sociological investigation. Thus, we might ask: what kinds of occupation and domestic arrangement are most common among people who go to the tearooms? What proportion of tearoom participants are caught by the police? Factual questions of this kind are often difficult to answer. Official statistics on tearooms would not exist. Even official statistics on crime are of dubious value in revealing the real level of criminal activity. Researchers who have studied crime levels have found that only about half of all serious crimes are reported to the police.

Factual information about one society, of course, will not always tell us whether we are dealing with an unusual case or a general set of influences. Sociologists often want to ask **comparative questions**, relating one social context within a society to another or contrasting examples drawn from different societies. There are significant differences, for example, between the social and legal systems of the USA and the UK. A typical comparative question might be: how much do patterns of criminal behaviour and law enforcement vary between the two countries?

In sociology, we need not only to look at existing societies in relation to one another but also to compare their present and past. The questions sociologists ask in this case are **developmental questions**. To understand the nature of the modern world, we have to look at previous forms of society and also study the main direction that processes of change have taken. Thus, we can investigate, for example, how the first prisons originated and what they are like today.

Factual investigations – or, as sociologists usually prefer to call them, **empirical investigations** – concern how things occur. Yet sociology does not consist of just collecting facts, however important and interesting they may be. We always need to interpret what facts mean, and to do so we must learn to pose **theoretical questions**. Many sociologists work primarily on empirical questions, but unless they are guided in research by some knowledge of theory, their work is unlikely to be illuminating (see table 3.1).

At the same time, sociologists strive not to attain theoretical knowledge for its own sake. A standard view is that while values should not be permitted to bias conclusions, social research should be relevant to real-world concerns. In this chapter, we look further into such issues by asking whether it is possible to produce objective knowledge. We begin by stressing the scientific nature of sociology, before examining the stages involved in sociological research. Some of the most widely used research methods are then compared as we consider some actual investigations. As we shall see, there are often significant differences between the way research should ideally be carried out and real-world studies.

Taking a scientific approach

Durkheim, Marx and the other founders of sociology thought of it as a science; but can we really study human social life in a scientific way? Are Laud Humphreys' observations on 'tearoom trade' really scientific? To answer this question, we must first understand what the word means. What is science?

Table 3.1   A sociologist's line of questioning

Factual question	What happened?	Since the 1980s, girls have been attaining better educational results in school than boys.
Comparative question	Did this happen everywhere?	Was this a global phenomenon, or did it occur just in Britain, or only in a certain region of Britain?
Developmental question	Has this happened over time?	What have been the patterns of girls' educational attainment over time?
Theoretical question	What underlies this phenomenon?	Why are girls now performing better in school? What factors would we look at to explain this change?

Science is the use of systematic methods of empirical investigation, the analysis of data, theoretical thinking and the logical assessment of arguments to develop a body of knowledge about a particular subject matter. Sociology is a scientific endeavour, according to this definition, because it involves systematic methods of empirical investigation, the analysis of data and the assessment of theories in the light of evidence and logical argument.

Studying human beings, however, is different from observing events in the physical world, and sociology shouldn't be seen as directly like a natural science. Unlike objects in nature, humans are self-aware beings who confer sense and purpose on what they do. We can't even describe social life accurately unless we first grasp the concepts that people apply in their behaviour. For instance, to describe a death as a suicide means knowing what the person in question was intending when he died. Suicide can only occur when an individual actively has self-destruction in mind. If he accidentally steps in front of a car and is killed, he cannot be said to have committed suicide.

The fact that we cannot study human beings in exactly the same way as objects in nature is in some ways an advantage to sociology. Sociological researchers profit from being able to pose questions directly to those they study – other human beings. In other respects, sociology creates difficulties not encountered by natural scientists. People who are aware that their activities are being scrutinized frequently will not behave in the same way as they do normally. They may consciously or unconsciously portray themselves in a way that differs from their usual attitudes. They may even try to 'assist' the researcher by giving the responses they believe she wants.

The research process

Let us first look at the stages normally involved in research work. The research process takes in a number of distinct steps, leading from when the investigation is begun to the time its findings are published or made available in written form.

Defining the research problem

All research starts from a research problem. This is sometimes an area of factual ignorance: we may simply wish to

"I'm a social scientist, Michael. That means I can't explain electricity or anything like that, but if you ever want to know about people I'm the man."

improve our knowledge about certain institutions, social processes or cultures. A researcher might set out to answer questions like: what proportion of the population holds strong religious beliefs? Are people today really disaffected with 'big government'? How far does the economic position of women lag behind that of men?

The best sociological research, however, begins with problems that are also puzzles. A puzzle is not just a lack of information, but a *gap in our understanding*. Much of the skill in producing worthwhile sociological research consists in correctly identifying puzzles.

Rather than simply answering the question 'What is going on here?' puzzle-solving research tries to contribute to our understanding of *why* events happen as they do. Thus, we might ask: why are pat-

terns of religious belief changing? What accounts for the decline in the proportions of the population voting in elections in recent years? Why are women poorly represented in high-status jobs?

No piece of research stands alone. Research problems come up as part of ongoing work; one research project may easily lead to another because it raises issues the researcher had not previously considered. A sociologist may discover puzzles by reading the work of other researchers in books and professional journals or by being aware of specific trends in society. For example, over recent years, there have been an increasing number of programmes that seek to treat the mentally ill while they continue to live in the community, rather than confining them in asylums. Sociologists might be prompted to ask: what has given rise to this shift in attitude towards the mentally ill? What are the likely consequences both for the patients themselves and for the rest of the community?

Reviewing the evidence

Once the problem is identified, the next step taken in the research process is usually to review the available evidence in the field; it might be that previous research has already satisfactorily clarified the problem. If not, the sociologist will need to sift through whatever related research does exist to see how useful it is for his purpose. Have previous researchers spotted the same puzzle? How have they tried to resolve it? What aspects of the problem has their research left unanalysed? Drawing upon others' ideas helps the sociologist to clarify the issues that might be raised and the methods that might be used in the research.

Making the problem precise

A third stage involves working out a clear formulation of the research problem. If relevant literature already exists, the researcher might return from the library with a good notion of how the problem should be approached. Hunches about the nature of the problem can sometimes be turned into a definite **hypothesis** – an educated guess about what is going on – at this stage. If the research is to be effective, hypotheses must be formulated in such a way that the factual material gathered will provide evidence either supporting or disproving them.

Working out a design

The researcher must then decide just *how* the research materials are to be collected. A range of different research methods exists, and which one is chosen depends on the overall objectives of the study as well as the aspects of behaviour to be analysed. For some purposes, a survey (in which questionnaires are normally used) might be suitable. In other circumstances, interviews or an observational study, such as that carried out by Laud Humphreys, might be appropriate. We shall learn more about various research methods later in this chapter.

Carrying out the research

At the point of actually proceeding with the research, unforeseen practical difficulties can easily crop up. It might prove impossible to contact some of those to whom questionnaires are to be sent or those whom the researcher wishes to interview. A business firm or government agency may be unwilling to let the researcher carry out the work planned.

Difficulties such as these could potentially **bias** the result of the study and give her a false interpretation. For example, if the researcher is studying how business corporations have complied with equal opportunities programmes for women, then companies that have not complied might not want to be studied. The findings could be biased as a result.

Bias can enter the research process in many ways. For example, if a piece of research is based on surveys of a participant's views, it may be easy for the researcher to push the discussion in a particular way (for example, by asking leading questions that follow her particular prejudices, as the Doonesbury cartoon opposite shows). Alternatively, the interviewee may evade a question that for various reasons he doesn't want to answer. The use of questionnaires with fixed wording can help to reduce *interview bias*, but will not eliminate it. Another source of bias comes when a potential participant in a survey, such as a voluntary questionnaire, decides that she doesn't want to take part. This is known as *non-response bias*, and as a general rule the higher the proportion of non-responses in the sample, the more likely it is that the survey of those who do take part will be biased. Even if every attempt is made to reduce bias in the survey, the observations that sociologists makes in carrying out a piece of research are likely to reflect their own cultural assumptions. This *observer bias* can be difficult, or perhaps even impossible, to eliminate. Later in this chapter we look at some of the other pitfalls and difficulties of sociological research, and discuss how some of these can be avoided (pp. 92–4).

DOONESBURY   by Garry Trudeau

Interpreting the results

Once the material has been gathered together for analysis, the researcher's troubles are not over – they may be just beginning! Working out the implications of the data collected and relating these back to the research problem are rarely easy. While it may be possible to reach a clear answer to the initial questions, many investigations are in the end less than fully conclusive.

Reporting the findings

The research report, usually published as a journal article or book, provides an account of the nature of the research and seeks to justify whatever conclusions are drawn. In Humphreys' case, this report was the book *Tearoom Trade*. This is a final stage only in terms of the individual research project. Most reports indicate questions that remain unanswered and suggest further research that might profitably be done in the future. All individual research investigations are part of the continuing process of research taking place within the sociological community. Other scholars have built on Humphreys' research findings.

Reality intrudes!

The preceding sequence of steps is a simplified version of what happens in actual research projects (see figure 3.1). In real sociological research, these stages rarely succeed each other so neatly, and there is almost always a certain amount of muddling through. The difference is a bit like that between the recipes outlined in a cookbook and the actual process of preparing a meal. People who are experienced cooks often don't work from recipes at all, yet they might cook better than those who do. Following fixed schemes can be unduly restricting; much outstanding sociological research could not in fact be fitted rigidly into this sequence, although most of the steps would be there.

Understanding cause and effect

One of the main problems to be tackled in research methodology is the analysis of cause and effect. A **causal relationship** between two events or situations is an association in which one event or situation produces another. If the handbrake

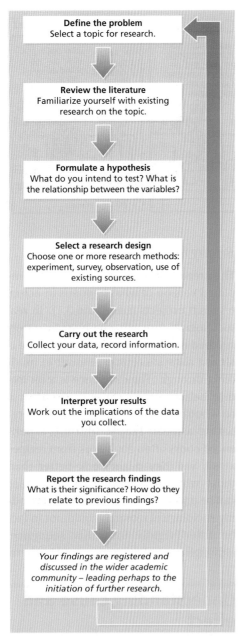

Figure 3.1 Steps in the research process

is released in a car pointing down a hill, the car will roll down the incline, gathering speed progressively as it does so. Taking the brake off *caused* this to

happen; the reasons for this can readily be understood by reference to the physical principles involved. Like natural science, sociology depends on the assumption that all events have causes. Social life is not a random array of occurrences, happening without rhyme or reason. One of the main tasks of sociological research – in combination with theoretical thinking – is to identify causes and effects.

Causation and correlation

Causation cannot be directly inferred from **correlation.** Correlation means the existence of a regular relationship between two sets of occurrences or **variables.** A variable is any dimension along which individuals or groups vary. Age, differences in income, crime rates and social-class differences are among the many variables sociologists study. It might seem as though when two variables are found to be closely correlated, one must be the cause of the other; such is often not the case. There are many correlations without any causal relationship between the variables. For example, over the period since the Second World War, a strong correlation can be found between a decline in pipe-smoking and a decrease in the number of people who regularly go to the cinema. Clearly one change does not cause the other, and we would find it difficult to discover even a remote causal connection between them.

There are many instances, however, in which it is not so obvious that an observed correlation does not imply a causal relationship. Such correlations are traps for the unwary and easily lead to questionable or false conclusions. In his classical work of 1897, *Suicide* (see above, p. 15), Emile Durkheim found a correlation between rates of suicide and the seasons of the year. In the societies that Durkheim studied, levels of suicide increased progressively from January to around June or July. From that time onward they declined over the remainder of the year. It might be supposed that this demonstrates that temperature or climatic change are causally related to the propensity of individuals to kill themselves. Perhaps, as temperatures increase, people become more impulsive and hot-headed. However, the causal relation here has nothing directly to do with temperature or climate at all. In spring and summer most people engage in a more intensive social life than they do in winter. Individuals who are isolated or unhappy tend to experience an intensification of these feelings as the activity level of other people rises. Hence they are likely to experience acute suicidal tendencies more in spring and summer than in autumn and winter, when the pace of social activity slackens. We always have to be on our guard both in assessing whether correlation involves causation and in deciding in which direction causal relations run.

Causal mechanism

Working out causal connections involved in correlations is often a difficult process. There is a strong correlation, for instance, between level of educational achievement and occupational success in modern societies. The better the grades an individual gets in school, the better-paying the job he is likely to get. What explains this correlation? Research tends to show that it is not mainly school experience itself; levels of school attainment are influenced much more by the type of home from which the person comes. Children from better-off homes, whose parents take a strong interest in their learning skills and where books are abundant, are more likely to do well than those coming from homes where these qualities are lacking. The causal mechanisms here are the attitudes of parents towards their children, together with the facilities for learning that a home provides.

Causal connections in sociology should not be understood in too mechanical a way. The attitudes people have and their subjective reasons for acting as they do are causal factors in relationships between variables in social life.

Controls

In assessing the cause or causes that explain a correlation, we need to distinguish **independent variables** from **dependent variables.** An independent variable is one that produces an effect on another variable. The variable affected is the dependent one. In the example just mentioned, academic achievement is the independent variable and occupational income the dependent variable. The distinction refers to the direction of the causal relation we are investigating. The same factor may be an independent variable in one study and a dependent variable in another. It all depends on what causal processes are being analysed. If we were looking at the effects of differences in occupational income on lifestyles, occupational income would then be the independent variable rather than the dependent one.

To find out whether a correlation between variables is a causal connection we use **controls**, which means we hold some variables constant in order to look at the effects of others. By doing this, we are able to judge between explanations of observed correlations, separating causal from non-causal relationships. For example, researchers studying child development have claimed that there is a causal connection between maternal deprivation in infancy and serious personality problems in adulthood. ('Maternal deprivation' means that an infant is separated from its mother for a long period – several months or more – during the early years of its life.) How might we test whether there really is a causal relationship between maternal deprivation and later personality disorders? We would

do so by trying to control, or 'screen out', other possible influences that might explain the correlation.

One source of maternal deprivation is the admission of a child to a hospital for a lengthy period, during which it is separated from its parents. Is it attachment to the mother, however, that really matters? Perhaps if a child receives love and attention from *other* people during infancy, she might subsequently be a stable person. To investigate these possible causal connections, we would have to compare cases where children were deprived of regular care from anyone with other instances in which children were separated from their mothers but received love and care from someone else. If the first group developed severe personality difficulties but the second group did not, we would suspect that regular care from *someone* in infancy is what matters, regardless of whether or not it is the mother. (In fact, children do seem to prosper normally as long as they have a loving, stable relationship with someone looking after them; this person does not have to be the mother herself.)

Identifying causes

There are a large number of possible causes that could be invoked to explain any given correlation. How can we ever be sure that we have covered them all? The answer is that we cannot be sure. We would never be able to carry out and interpret the results of a piece of sociological research satisfactorily if we were compelled to test for the possible influence of every causal factor we could imagine as potentially relevant. Identifying causal relationships is normally guided by previous research into the area in question. If we do not have some reasonable idea beforehand of the causal mechanisms involved in a correlation, we would probably find it very difficult to discover what the real causal connections are. We would not know what to test *for*.

A good example of how difficult it is to be sure of the causal relations involved in a correlation is given by the long history of studies of smoking and lung cancer. Research has consistently demonstrated a strong correlation between the two. Smokers are more likely to contract lung cancer than non-smokers, and very heavy smokers are more likely to do so than light smokers. The correlation can also be expressed the other way around. A high proportion of those who have lung cancer are smokers or have smoked for long periods in their past. There have been so many studies confirming these correlations that it is generally accepted that a causal link is involved, but the exact causal mechanisms are thus far largely unknown.

However much correlational work is done on any issue, there always remains some doubt about possible causal relationships. Other interpretations of the correlation are possible. It has been proposed, for instance, that people who are predisposed to get lung cancer are also predisposed to smoke. In this view, it is not smoking that causes lung cancer, but rather some built-in biological disposition to smoking and cancer.

Research methods

Let's now look at the various research methods sociologists commonly employ in their work (see table 3.2 on p. 86).

Ethnography

Humphreys used **ethnography** (fieldwork, or first-hand studies of people, using **participant observation** or interviewing) as his main research method. Here, the investigator hangs out or works or lives with a group, organization or community, and perhaps takes a direct part in their activities. Where it is successful, ethnography provides information on the behaviour of people in groups, organizations and communities, and also on how those people understand their own behaviour. Once we see how things look from inside a given group, we are likely to develop a better understanding not only of that group, but of social processes that transcend the situation under study.

THE FAR SIDE   By GARY LARSON

"Anthropologists! Anthropologists!"

This cartoon illustrates some of the pitfalls of studying self-conscious subjects.

Table 3.2   Four of the main methods used in sociological research

Research method	Strengths	Limitations
Fieldwork	Usually generates richer and more in-depth information than other methods.	Can only be used to study relatively small groups or communities.
	Ethnography can provide a broader understanding of social processes.	Findings might only apply to the groups or communities studied; it is not easy to generalize on the basis of a single fieldwork study.
Surveys	Make possible the efficient collection of data on large numbers of individuals.	The material gathered may be superficial; where a questionnaire is highly standardized, important differences between respondents' viewpoints may be glossed over.
	Allow for precise comparisons to to made between the answers of respondents.	Responses may be what people profess to believe rather than what they actually believe.
Experiments	The influence of specific variables can be controlled by the investigator.	Many aspects of social life cannot be brought into the laboratory.
	Are usually easier for subsequent researchers to repeat	The responses of those studied may be affected by their experiemntal situation.
Documentary research	Can provide source of in-depth materials as well as data on large numbers, depending on the type of documents studied.	The researcher is dependent on the sources that exist, which may be partial.
	Is often essential when a study is either wholly historical or has a defined historical dimension.	The sources may be difficult to interpret in terms of how far they represent real tendencies – as in the case of some official statistics.

In the traditional works of ethnography, accounts were presented without very much information about the observer. This was because it was believed that an ethnographer could present objective pictures of the things they studied. More recently, ethnographers have increasingly tended to talk about themselves and the nature of their connection to the people under study. Sometimes, for example, it might be a matter of trying to consider how one's race, class or gender affected the work, or how the power differences between observer and observed distorted the dialogue between them.

For a long while, it was usual for research based on participant observation to exclude any account of the hazards or problems that had to be overcome, but more recently the published reminiscences and diaries of fieldworkers have been more open about them. Frequently, feelings of loneliness must be coped with – it isn't easy to fit into a social context or community where you don't really belong. The researcher may be constantly frustrated because the members of the group refuse to talk frankly about themselves; direct queries may be welcomed in some contexts but met with a chilly silence in others. Some types of fieldwork may even be physically dangerous; for instance, a

In fieldwork sociologists have to become close to the communities they are studying, but not so close that they lose their outsider's eye.

researcher studying a delinquent gang might be seen as a police informer or might become unwittingly embroiled in conflicts with rival gangs.

Ethnographic studies also have other major limitations. Only fairly small groups or communities can be studied. And much depends on the skill of the researcher in gaining the confidence of the individuals involved; without this skill,

the research is unlikely to get off the ground at all. The reverse is also possible. A researcher could begin to identify so closely with the group that she becomes too much of an 'insider' and loses the perspective of an outside observer.

Surveys

Interpreting field studies usually involves problems of generalization. Since only a small number of people are under study, we cannot be sure that what is found in one context will apply in other situations as well, or even that two different researchers would come to the same conclusions when studying the same group. This is usually less of a problem in survey research. In a **survey**, questionnaires are either sent or administered directly in interviews to a selected group of people – sometimes as many as several thousand. This group of people is referred to by sociologists as a **population**. Fieldwork is best suited for in-depth studies of small slices of social life; survey research tends to produce information that is less detailed but that can usually be applied over a broad area.

Standardized and open-ended questionnaires

Two sorts of questionnaire are used in surveys. Some contain a standardized, or fixed-choice, set of questions, to which only a fixed range of responses is possible – for instance, '*Yes/No/Don't know*' or '*Very likely/Likely/Unlikely/Very unlikely*'. Such surveys have the advantage that responses are easy to compare and count up, since only a small number of categories are involved. On the other hand, because they do not allow for subtleties of opinion or verbal expression, the information they yield is likely to be restricted in scope, if not misleading.

Other questionnaires are open-ended: respondents have more opportunity to express their views in their own words; they are not limited to making fixed-choice responses. Open-ended questionnaires typically provide more detailed information than standardized ones. The researcher can follow up answers to probe more deeply into what the respondent thinks. On the other hand, the lack of standardization means that responses may be more difficult to compare statistically.

Questionnaire items are normally listed so that a team of interviewers can ask the questions and record responses in the same predetermined order. All the items must be readily understandable to interviewers and interviewees alike. In the large national surveys undertaken regularly by government agencies and research organizations, interviews are carried out more or less simultaneously across the whole country. Those who conduct the interviews and those who analyse the results could not do their work effectively if they constantly had to be checking with each other about ambiguities in the questions or answers.

Questionnaires should also take into consideration the characteristics of respondents. Will they see the point the researcher has in mind in asking a particular question? Have they enough information to answer usefully? Will they answer at all? The terms of a questionnaire might be unfamiliar to the respondents. For instance, the question 'What is your marital status?' might baffle some people. It would be more appropriate to ask, 'Are you single, married, separated, or divorced?' Most surveys are preceded by **pilot studies** in order to pick up problems not anticipated by the investigator. A pilot study is a trial run in which a questionnaire is completed by just a few people. Any difficulties can then be ironed out before the main survey is done.

Sampling

Often sociologists are interested in the characteristics of large numbers of individuals – for example, the political attitudes of the British population as a whole. It would be impossible to study all these people directly, so in such situations researchers engage in **sampling** – they concentrate on a sample, or small proportion of the overall group. One can usually be confident that results from a population sample, as long as it was properly chosen, can be generalized to the total population. Studies of only two to three thousand voters, for instance, can give a very accurate indication of the attitudes and voting intentions of the entire population. But to achieve such accuracy, a sample must be **representative**: the group of individuals studied must be typical of the population as a whole. Sampling is more complex than it might seem, and statisticians have developed rules for working out the correct size and nature of samples.

A particularly important procedure used to ensure that a sample is representative is **random sampling**, in which a sample is chosen so that every member of the population has the same probability of being included. The most sophisticated way of obtaining a random sample is to give each member of the population a number and then use a computer to generate a random list, from which the sample is derived – for instance, by picking every tenth number.

'The people's choice?'

One of the most famous early examples of survey research was 'The people's choice?', a study carried out by Paul Lazarsfeld and a number of colleagues more than half a century ago (Lazarsfeld, Berelson et al. 1948). This study, which investigated the voting intentions of residents of Erie County, Ohio, during the 1940 campaign for the US presidency, pioneered several of the main techniques of survey research in use to this day. In order to probe a little more deeply than a single questionnaire would do, the investigators interviewed each member of a sample of voters on seven separate occasions. The aim was to trace and understand the reasons for changes in voting attitudes.

The research was set up with a number of definite hypotheses in view. One was that relationships and events close to voters in a community influence voting intentions more than distant world affairs, and the findings on the whole confirmed this. The researchers developed sophisticated measurement techniques for analysing political attitudes; yet their work also made significant contributions to theoretical thinking. Among the concepts they helped to introduce were those of 'opinion leaders' and the 'two-step flow of communication'. The study showed that some individuals – opinion leaders – tend to shape the political opinions of those around them. People's views are not formed in a direct fashion, but in a two-step process. In the first step, opinion leaders react to political events; in the second step, those leaders influence people around them – relatives, friends and colleagues. The views expressed by opinion leaders, filtered through personal relationships, then influence the responses of other individuals towards political issues of the day.

Advantages and disadvantages of surveys

Surveys are widely used in sociological research, for several reasons. Responses to questionnaires can be more easily quantified and analysed than material generated by most other research methods; large numbers of people can be studied; and, given sufficient funds, researchers can employ an agency specializing in survey work to collect the responses. The scientific method is the model for this kind of research, as surveys give researchers a statistical measure of what they are studying.

Many sociologists are critical, however, of the survey method. They argue that an appearance of precision can be given to findings whose accuracy may be dubious, given the relatively shallow nature of most survey responses. Levels of non-response are sometimes high, especially when questionnaires are sent and returned through the mail. It is not uncommon for studies to be published based on results derived from little over half of those in a sample, although normally an effort is made to recontact non-respondents or to substitute other people. Little is known about those who choose not to respond to surveys or refuse to be interviewed, but survey research is often experienced as intrusive and time-consuming.

Experiments

An **experiment** can be defined as an attempt to test a hypothesis under highly controlled conditions established by an investigator. Experiments are often used in the natural sciences, as they offer major advantages over other research procedures. In an experimental situation the researcher directly controls the circumstances being studied. As compared with the natural sciences, the scope for experimentation in sociology is quite restricted. Only small groups of individuals can be brought into a laboratory setting, and in such experiments people know that they are being studied and may not behave naturally. Such changes in subject behaviour are referred to as the 'Hawthorne effect'. In the 1930s, researchers conducting a work productivity study at the Western Electric Company's Hawthorne plant near Chicago found to their surprise that worker productivity continued to rise regardless of which experimental conditions were imposed (levels of lighting, break patterns, work team size and so forth). The workers were conscious of being under scrutiny and accelerated their natural work pace.

Nevertheless, experimental methods can occasionally be applied in a helpful way in sociology. An example is the ingenious experiment carried out by Philip Zimbardo, who set up a make-believe jail, assigning some student volunteers to the role of guards and other volunteers to the role of prisoners (Zimbardo 1972). His aim was to see how far playing these different parts led to changes in attitude and behaviour. The results shocked the investigators. Students who played at being guards quickly assumed an authoritarian manner; they displayed real hostility towards the prisoners, ordering them around and verbally abusing and bullying

them. The prisoners, by contrast, showed a mixture of apathy and rebelliousness – a response often noted among inmates in real prisons. These effects were so marked and the level of tension so high that the experiment had to be called off at an early stage. The results, however, were important. Zimbardo concluded that behaviour in prisons is more influenced by the nature of the prison situation itself than by the individual characteristics of those involved.

Life histories

In contrast to experiments, **life histories** belong purely to sociology and the other social sciences; they have no place in natural science. Life histories consist of biographical material assembled about particular individuals – usually as recalled by the individuals themselves. Other procedures of research don't usually yield as much information as the life-history method does about the development of beliefs and attitudes over time. Life-historical studies rarely rely wholly on people's memories, however. Normally, sources such as letters, contemporary reports and newspaper descriptions are used to expand on and check the validity of the information individuals provide. Sociologists' views differ on the value of life histories: some feel they are too unreliable to provide useful information, but others believe they offer sources of insight that few other research methods can match.

Life histories have been successfully employed in studies of major importance. A celebrated early study was *The Polish Peasant in Europe and America*, by W. I. Thomas and Florian Znaniecki, the five volumes of which were first published between 1918 and 1920 (Thomas and Znaniecki 1966). Thomas and Znaniecki were able to provide a more sensitive and subtle account of the experience of migration than would have been possible without the interviews, letters and newspaper articles they collected.

Comparative research

Each of the research methods described above is often applied in a comparative context. **Comparative research** is of central importance in sociology, because making comparisons allows us to clarify what is going on in a particular area of research. Let's take the rate of divorce in Britain – the number of divorces granted each year – as an example. In the early 1960s there were fewer than 30,000 divorces per year in the UK; by the early 1980s this figure had risen to around 160,000 cases per year or more. Do these changes reflect specific features of British society? We can find out by comparing divorce rates in the UK with those of other countries. Such a comparison reveals that compared to most other Western societies the overall trends are similar. Virtually all Western countries have experienced steadily climbing divorce rates over the past half century.

Historical analysis

As was mentioned in chapter 1, a historical perspective is often essential in sociological research. For we frequently need a *time perspective* to make sense of the material we collect about a particular problem.

Sociologists commonly want to investigate past events directly. Some periods of history can be studied in a direct way, while there are still survivors around – such as in the case of the Holocaust in Europe during the Second World War. Research in **oral history** means interviewing people about events they witnessed at some point earlier in their lives. This kind of research work, obviously, can only stretch at the most some sixty or seventy years back in time. For historical research on an earlier period, sociologists are dependent on the use of documents and written records, often contained in the special collections of libraries or the National Archives.

An interesting example of the use of historical documents is sociologist Anthony Ashworth's study of trench warfare during the First World War (Ashworth 1980). Ashworth was concerned with analysing what life was like for men who had to endure being under constant fire, crammed in close proximity for weeks on end. He drew on a diversity of documentary sources: official histories of the war, including those written about different military divisions and battalions; official publications of the time; the notes and records kept informally by individual soldiers; and personal accounts of war experiences. By drawing on such a variety of sources, Ashworth was able to develop a rich and detailed description of life in the trenches. He discovered that most soldiers formed their own ideas about how often they intended to engage in combat with the enemy and often effectively ignored the commands of their officers. For example, on Christmas Day, German and Allied soldiers suspended hostilities, and in one place the two sides even staged an informal soccer match.

Combining comparative and historical research

Ashworth's research concentrated on a relatively short time period. As an example of a study that investigated a much longer one and that also applied comparative research in a historical context, we can take Theda Skocpol's *States and Social Revolutions* (1979), one of the best-known studies of social change. Skocpol set herself an ambitious task: to produce a theory of the origins and nature of revolution grounded in detailed empirical study. She looked at processes of revolution in three different historical contexts: the 1789 revolution in France, the 1917 revolution in Russia (which brought the communists to power and established the Soviet Union, which was eventually dissolved in 1989), and the revolution of 1949 in China (which created communist China).

By analysing a variety of documentary sources, Skocpol was able to develop a powerful explanation of revolutionary change, one that emphasized the underlying social structural conditions. She showed that social revolutions are largely the result of unintended consequences. Before the Russian Revolution, for instance, various political groups were trying to overthrow the pre-existing regime, but none of these – including the Bolsheviks, who eventually came to power – anticipated the revolution that occurred. A series of clashes and confrontations gave rise to a process of social transformation much more radical than anyone had foreseen.

Research in the real world: methods, problems and pitfalls

All research methods, as was stressed earlier, have their advantages and limitations. Hence, it is common to combine several methods in a single piece of research, using each to supplement and check on the others in a process known as **triangulation.** We can see the value of combining methods – and, more generally, the problems and pitfalls of real sociological research – by looking once again at Laud Humphreys' *Tearoom Trade*.

One of the questions that Humphreys wanted to answer was: 'What kinds of men came to the tearooms?' But it was very hard for him to find this out, because all he could really do in the toilets was observe. The norm of silence in the toilets made it difficult to ask any questions, or even to talk. In addition, it would have been very odd if he had begun to ask personal questions of people who basically wanted to be anonymous.

Humphreys' solution was to try to find out more about the men in the tearooms using survey methods. Standing by the door of the toilets, he would write down the car number-plates of people who pulled up to the carpark and went into the toilets for sex. He then gave the numbers to a friend who worked at the Department of Motor Vehicles, securing the addresses of the men.

Months later, Washington University in St Louis, in the United States, where Laud was working, was conducting a door-to-door survey of sexual habits. Humphreys asked the principal investigators in that survey if he could add the names and addresses of his sample of tearoom participants. Humphreys then disguised himself as one of the investigators and went to interview these men at their homes, supposedly just to ask only the survey questions but actually also to learn more about their social backgrounds and lives. He found that most of these men were married and otherwise led very conventional lives. He often interviewed wives and other family members as well.

Human subjects and ethical problems

All research concerned with human beings can pose ethical dilemmas. A key question that sociologists agree must be asked is whether the research poses risks to the subjects that are greater than the risks they face in their everyday lives.

In writing *Tearoom Trade*, Humphreys said he was less than truthful to those whose behaviour he was studying. He said he didn't reveal his identity as a sociologist when observing the tearoom. People who came into the tearoom assumed he was there for the same reasons they were and that his presence could be accepted at face value. While he did not tell any direct lies while observing the tearoom, neither did he reveal the real reason for his presence there. Was this particular aspect of his behaviour ethical? The answer is that, on balance, this particular aspect of his study did not put any of his subjects at risk. On the basis of what he observed in the tearoom, Humphreys did not collect information about the participants that would have identified them. What he knew about them was similar to what all the other people in the tearoom knew. In this way, his presence did not subject

them to any more risk than they already encountered in their everyday lives. At the same time, had Humphreys been completely frank at every stage, the research might not have progressed as far as it did. Indeed, some of the most valuable data that have been collected by sociologists could never have been gathered if the researcher had first explained the project to each person encountered in the research process.

If this were the only dilemma posed by Humphreys' research project, it would not stand out as a notable problem in the ethics of social research. What raised more eyebrows was that Humphreys wrote down the car number-plates of the people who came into the tearooms, obtained their home addresses from a friend who worked at the Department of Motor Vehicles and then visited their homes in the guise of conducting a neutral survey. Even though Humphreys did not reveal to the men's families anything about their activities in the tearooms, and even though he took great pains to keep the data confidential, the knowledge he gained could have been damaging. Since the activity he was documenting was illegal, police officers might have demanded that he release information about the identities of the subjects. It is also possible that a less skilled investigator could have slipped up when interviewing the subjects' families, or that Humphreys could have lost his notes, which could then have been found later by someone else. Considering the number of things that could go wrong in the research process, researchers do not consider projects of this kind to be legitimate. Around the world, government funding bodies for sociological research, such as the Economic and Social Research

Council in the UK, and the professional organizations to which sociologists belong, such as the British Sociological Association, now have much stricter ethical guidelines for researchers engaging in sociological experiments.

Humphreys was one of the first sociologists to study the lives of gay men. His account was a humane treatment that went well beyond the existing stock of knowledge on sexual communities. Although none of his research subjects actually suffered as a result of his book, Humphreys himself later agreed with his critics on the key ethical controversy. He said that were he to do the study again, he would not trace number-plates or go to people's homes. Instead, after gathering his data in the public tearooms, he might try to get to know a subset of the people well enough to inform them of his goals for the study and then ask them to talk about the significance of these activities in their lives.

Is sociology merely a restatement of the obvious?

Because sociologists often study things that we have some personal experience of, one can sometimes wonder if sociology is merely 'a painful elaboration of the obvious' (Wright 2000). Is sociology merely a restatement, in abstract jargon, of things we already know? Is it simply the tedious definition of social phenomena with which we are already familiar? Sociology at its worst can be all of these things, but it is never appropriate to judge any discipline by what its worst practitioners do. In fact, good sociology either sharpens our understanding of the obvious (Berger 1963), or it completely transforms our

common sense. In either event, good sociology is neither tedious nor a restatement of the obvious. Discussions of a new topic in this text sometimes begin with definitions of things that you may already understand. It is necessary for any academic discipline to define its terms. However, when we define a family, for example, as a unit of people who are related to one another, we do so not as an endpoint but instead as a beginning. Often without defining our terms, we cannot move forward to sharper levels of understanding later on – good sociology never defines terms as an end in itself.

The influence of sociology

Sociological research is rarely of interest only to the intellectual community of sociologists. Its results are often disseminated throughout society. Sociology, it must be emphasized, is not just the *study* of modern societies; it is a significant element *in the continuing life* of those societies. Take the transformations taking place in the United Kingdom in marriage, sexuality and the family (discussed in chapters 7 and 12). Few people living in a modern society do not have some knowledge of these changes, as a result of the filtering down of sociological research. Our thinking and behaviour are affected by sociological knowledge in complex and often subtle ways, thus reshaping the very field of sociological investigation. A way of describing this phenomenon, using the technical concepts of sociology, is to say that sociology stands in a reflexive relation to the human beings whose behaviour is studied. **Reflexivity**, as we shall see in chapter 4 (pp. 122–3), describes the interchange between sociological research and

Statistical terms

Research in sociology often makes use of statistical techniques in the analysis of findings. Some are highly sophisticated and complex, but those most often used are easy to understand. The most common are **measures of central tendency** (ways of calculating averages) and **correlation coefficients** (measures of the degree to which one variable relates consistently to another).

There are three methods of calculating averages, each of which has certain advantages and shortcomings. Take as an example the amount of personal wealth (including all assets such as houses, cars, bank accounts and investments) owned by thirteen individuals. Suppose the thirteen own the following amounts:

1 £000 (zero)
2 £5,000
3 £10,000
4 £20,000
5 £40,000
6 £40,000
7 £40,000
8 £80,000
9 £100,000
10 £150,000
11 £200,000
12 £400,000
13 £10,000,000

The **mean** corresponds to the average, arrived at by adding together the personal wealth of all thirteen people and dividing the result by 13. The total is £11,085,000; dividing this by 13, we reach a mean of £852,692.31. This mean is often a useful calculation because it is based on the whole range of data provided. However, it can be misleading where one or a small number of cases are very different from the majority. In the above example, the mean is not in fact an appropriate measure of central tendency, because the presence of one very large figure, £10,000,000, skews the picture. One might get the impression when using the mean to summarize this data that most of the people own far more than they actually do.

In such instances, one of two other measures may be used. The **mode** is the figure that occurs most frequently in a given set of data. In our example, it is £40,000. The problem with the mode is that it doesn't take into account the *overall distribution* of the data, i.e., the range of figures covered. The most frequently occurring case in a set of figures is not necessarily representative of their distribution as a whole and thus may not be a useful average. In this case, £40,000 is too close to the lower end of the figures.

The third measure is the **median**, which is the middle of any set of figures; here, this would be the seventh figure, again £40,000. Our example gives an odd number of figures: thirteen. If there had been an even number – for instance, twelve – the median would be calculated by taking the mean of the two middle cases, figures six and seven. Like the mode, the median gives no idea of the actual *range* of the data measured.

Sometimes a researcher will use more than one measure of central tendency to avoid giving a deceptive picture of the average. More often, he will calculate the **standard deviation** for the data in question. This is a way of calculating the **degree of dispersal**, or the range, of a set of figures – which in this case goes from zero to £10,000,000.

Correlation coefficients offer a useful way of expressing how closely connected two (or more) variables are. Where two variables correlate completely, we can speak of a perfect positive correlation, expressed as 1.0. Where no relation is found between two variables – they have no consistent connection at all – the coefficient is zero. A perfect negative correlation, expressed as 21.0, exists when two variables are in a completely inverse relation to one another. Perfect correlations are never found in the social sciences. Correlations of the order of 0.6 or more, whether positive or negative, are usually regarded as indicating a strong degree of connection between whatever variables are being analysed. Positive correlations on this level might be found between, say, social class background and voting behaviour.

human behaviour. We should not be surprised that sociological findings often correlate closely with common sense. The reason is not simply that sociology comes up with findings we knew already; it is rather that sociological research continually influences what our common-sense knowledge of society actually *is*.

Reading a table

You will often come across tables when reading sociological literature. They sometimes look complex, but are easy to decipher if you follow a few basic steps, listed below; with practice, these will become automatic (see table 3.3 as an example). Do not succumb to the temptation to skip over tables; they contain information in concentrated form, which can be read more quickly than would be possible if the same material were expressed in words. By becoming skilled in the interpretation of tables, you will also be able to check how far the conclusions drawn by a writer actually seem justified.

1 Read the title in full. Tables frequently have longish titles, which represent an attempt by the researcher to state accurately the nature of the information conveyed. The title of table 3.3 gives first the *subject* of the data, second the fact that the table provides material for comparison, and third the fact that data are given only for a limited number of countries.
2 Look for explanatory comments, or *notes*, about the data. Notes may say how the material was collected, or why it is displayed in a particular way. Many of the tables in this book contain explanatory notes. Table 7.2 on p. 225, for example, includes several notes that give more detail about how the numbers given have been reached. If the data have not been gathered by the researcher but are based on findings originally reported elsewhere, a source will be included. The source sometimes gives you some insight into how reliable the information is likely to be, as well as showing where to find the original data. In our table, the source note makes clear that the data have been taken from a publication by the OECD.
3 Read the *headings* along the top and left-hand side of the table. (Sometimes tables are arranged with 'headings' at the foot rather than the top.) These tell you what type of information is contained in each row and column. In reading the table, keep in mind each set of headings as you scan the figures. In our example, the headings on the left give the countries involved, while those at the top refer to the levels of car ownership and the years for which they are given.
4 Identify the units used; the figures in the body of the table may represent cases, percentages, averages or other measures. Sometimes it may be helpful to convert the figures to a form more useful to you: if percentages are not provided, for example, it may be worth calculating them.
5 Consider the conclusions that might be reached from the information in the table. Most tables are discussed by the author, and what she has to say should of course be borne in mind. But you should also ask what further issues or questions could be suggested by the data.

Several interesting trends can be seen in the figures in our table. First, the level of car ownership varies considerably between different countries. The number of cars per 1,000 people was more than five times greater in the United States than in Turkey in 2002. Second, there is a clear connection between car ownership and the level of affluence of a country. In fact, we could probably use car ownership ratios as a rough indicator of differential prosperity. Third, in nearly all countries represented, the level of car ownership increased between 1990 and 2002, but in some the rate of increase has been higher than in others – probably indicating differences in the degree to which countries have successfully generated economic growth or are catching up.

Table 3.3 Number of road motor vehicles per 1,000 inhabitants: comparisons of selected countries

	1990	1991	1992	1993	1994	1995	1996	1997	1998	1999	2000	2001	2002
Austria	462	463	503	515	528	543	495	509	529	544	555	565	537
Belgium	432	442	441	454	464	487	494	482	490	500	511	517	520
Canada	600	619	627	595	569	565	565	564	580	566	569	572	581
Germany	527	527	427	478	523	540	547	551	556	564	570	582	589
Greece	248	246	257	271	283	298	313	328	351	378	406	428	450
Portugal	310	370	407	439	438	501	533	569	610	654	698	711	756
Turkey	57	47	53	61	64	68	97	105	111	116	124	148	148
United Kingdom	443	433	453	441	439	428	448	458	474	486	493	516	533
United States	842	718	779	725	719	771	783	784	792	798	810	816	807

Source: OECD Factbook (2005)

Summary points

1 Sociologists investigate social life by posing distinct questions and trying to find the answers to these by systematic research. These questions may be *factual*, *comparative*, *developmental* or *theoretical*.

2 All research begins from a *research problem*, which interests or puzzles the investigator. Research problems may be suggested by gaps in the existing literature, theoretical debates, or practical issues in the social world. There are a number of clear steps in the development of research strategies – although these are rarely followed exactly in actual research.

3 A *causal relationship* between two events or situations is one in which one event or situation brings about the other. This is more problematic than it seems at first. *Causation* must be distinguished from *correlation*, which refers to the existence of a regular relationship between two *variables*. A variable can be differences in age, income, crime rates, etc. We need to also distinguish *independent variables* from *dependent variables*. An independent variable is a variable that produces an effect on another. Sociologists often use *controls* to ascertain a causal relationship.

4 In fieldwork, or *participant observation*, the researcher spends lengthy periods of time with a group or community being studied. A second method, *survey research*, involves sending or administering questionnaires to samples of a larger *population*. Documentary research uses printed materials, from archives or other resources, as a source for information. Other research methods include *experiments*, the use of *life histories*, historical analysis and *comparative research*.

5   Each of these various methods of research has its limitations. For this reason, researchers will often combine two or more methods in their work, each being used to check or supplement the material obtained from the others. This process is called *triangulation*.

6   Sociological research often poses ethical dilemmas. These may arise either where deception is practised against those who are the subjects of the research, or where the publication of research findings might adversely affect the feelings or lives of those studied. There is no entirely satisfactory way to deal with these issues, but all researchers have to be sensitive to the dilemmas they pose.

Questions for further thought

1 If most research projects start from research problems, who decides what the problems are?

2 Why is it so important to form specific hypotheses that can be supported or disproved?

3 Why does the course of the research process rarely run according to plan?

4 How can the researcher minimize the possibility of error and/or bias?

5 Are some methods of research more scientific than others?

6 Why is it so crucial to distinguish between correlation and causation?

Further reading

Alan Bryman, *Social Research Methods* (Oxford, New York: Oxford University Press, 2001).

Joel Best, *Damned Lies and Statistics: Untangling Numbers from the Media, Politicians, and Activists* (Berkeley: University of California Press, 2001).

Ruth Levitas and Will Guy, *Interpreting Official Statistics* (London: Routledge, 1996).

Martin Hammersley and Paul Atkinson, *Ethnography: Principles in Practice* (London: Routledge, 1995).

Lee Harvey, Morag MacDonald and Anne Devany, *Doing Sociology* (London: Macmillan, 1992).

Tim May, *Social Research: Issues, Methods and Process*, 3rd edn (Buckingham: Open University Press, 2001).

Internet links

Market and Opinion Research International (MORI)
http://www.mori.com

Social Science Information Gateway
http://www.sosig.ac.uk/sociology

Office of National Statistics
http://www.statistics.gov.uk

UK Data Archive
http://www.data-archive.ac.uk/

Contents

4 Theoretical Thinking in Sociology

ASSESSING THEORETICAL perspectives in sociology is a challenging and formidable task. Theoretical debates are by definition more abstract than controversies of a more empirical kind. The fact that there is not a single theoretical position which dominates the whole of sociology might seem to be a sign of weakness in the subject. But this is not so. On the contrary, the jostling of rival theoretical approaches and theories is an expression of the vitality of the sociological enterprise. In studying human beings – ourselves – theoretical variety rescues us from dogma. Human behaviour is complicated and many-sided, and it is very unlikely that a single theoretical outlook could cover all its aspects. Diversity in theoretical thinking provides a rich source of ideas that can be drawn on in research, and stimulates the imaginative capacities so essential to progress in sociological work.

Innumerable theories have been developed in the many different areas of research in which sociologists work. Some are very precisely set out, and even occasionally expressed in mathematical form – although this is more common in other social sciences (especially economics) than in sociology.

Some types of theory attempt to explain much more than others, and opinions vary about how far it is desirable or useful for sociologists to concern themselves with very wide-ranging theoretical efforts. The American sociologist Robert K. Merton, for example, argues forcefully that sociologists should concentrate their attention on what he calls 'theories of middle range' (Merton 1957). Rather than attempting to create grand theoretical schemes, we should be more modest.

Middle-range theories are specific enough to be able to be directly tested by empirical research, yet sufficiently general to cover a range of different phenomena. An example is the theory of relative deprivation. This theory holds that how people evaluate their circumstances depends on whom they compare themselves to. Thus feelings of deprivation do not relate directly to the level of material poverty

Robert K. Merton

that individuals experience (see pp. 343–7). A family living in a small home in a poor area, where everyone is in more or less similar circumstances, is likely to feel less deprived than one living in a similar house in a neighbourhood where the majority of homes are much larger and more affluent.

It is indeed true that the more wide-ranging and ambitious a theory is, the more difficult it is to test it empirically. Yet there seems no obvious reason why theoretical thinking in sociology should be confined to the 'middle range'. To see why this is so, let us take as an example the theory that Max Weber advanced in his study *The Protestant Ethic and the Spirit of Capitalism* (Weber 1976).

Weber's thought was introduced in chapter 1, pp. 17–19, and we will refer to *The Protestant Ethic* again in chapter 14, 'Religion in Modern Society', pp. 539–41.

Max Weber: *The Protestant Ethic*

In *The Protestant Ethic*, Weber set out to tackle a fundamental problem: why did capitalism develop in the West and nowhere else? For some thirteen centuries after the fall of ancient Rome, other civilizations were much more prominent than the West in world history. Europe, in fact, was a rather insignificant area of the globe, while China, India and the Ottoman Empire in the Near East were all major powers. The Chinese in particular were a long way ahead of the West in terms of their level of technological and economic development. What happened to bring about a surge in economic progress in Europe from the seventeenth century onwards?

To answer this question, Weber reasoned, we must show what it is that separates modern industry from earlier types of economic activity. We find the desire to accumulate wealth in many different civilizations, and this is not difficult to explain: people have valued wealth for the comforts, security, power and enjoyment it can bring. They wish to be free of want, and, having accumulated wealth, they use it to make themselves comfortable.

If we look at the economic development of the West, Weber argued, we find something quite different: an attitude towards the accumulation of wealth found nowhere else in history. This attitude is what Weber called the 'spirit of capitalism' – a set of beliefs and values held by the first capitalist merchants and industrialists. These people had a strong drive to accumulate personal wealth. Yet, quite unlike the wealthy elsewhere, they didn't seek to use their accumulated riches to follow a luxurious lifestyle. Their way of life was in fact self-denying and frugal; they lived soberly and quietly, shunning the ordinary manifestations of affluence. This very unusual combination of characteristics, Weber tried to show, was vital to early Western economic development. For unlike the wealthy in previous ages and in other cultures, these groups did not dissipate their wealth. Instead, they reinvested it to promote the further expansion of the enterprises they headed.

The core of Weber's theory is that the attitudes involved in the spirit of capitalism derived from religion. Christianity in general played a part in fostering such an outlook, but the essential motive force was provided by the impact of Protestantism – and especially one variety of

Protestantism, *Puritanism*. The early capitalists were mostly Puritans, and many subscribed to Calvinist views. Weber argued that certain Calvinistic doctrines were the direct source of the spirit of capitalism. One was the idea that human beings are God's instruments on earth, required by the Almighty to work in a *vocation* – an occupation for the greater glory of God.

A second important aspect of Calvinism was the notion of *predestination*, according to which only certain predestined individuals are to be among the 'elect' – to enter heaven in the afterlife. In Calvin's original doctrine, nothing a person does on this earth can alter whether he or she happens to be one of the elect; this is pre-determined by God. However, this belief caused such anxiety among his followers that it was modified to allow believers to recognize certain signs of election.

Success in working in a vocation, indicated by material prosperity, became the main sign that a person was truly one of the elect. A tremendous impetus towards economic success was created among groups influenced by these ideas. Yet this was accompanied by the believer's need to live a sober and frugal life. The Puritans believed luxury to be an evil, so the drive to accumulate wealth became joined to a severe and unadorned lifestyle.

The early entrepreneurs had little awareness that they were helping to produce momentous changes in society; they were impelled above all by religious motives. The ascetic – that is, self-denying – lifestyle of the Puritans has subsequently become an intrinsic part of modern civilization. As Weber wrote:

> The Puritan wanted to work in a calling; we are forced to do so. For when asceticism was carried out of the monastic cells into everyday life, and began to dominate worldly morality, it did its part in building the tremendous cosmos of the modern economic order. ... Since asceticism undertook to remodel the world and to work out its ideals in the world, material goods have gained an increasingly and finally an inexorable power over the lives of men as at no previous period in history. ... The idea of duty in one's calling prowls about in our lives like the ghost of dead religious beliefs. Where the fulfilment of the calling cannot directly be related to the highest spiritual and cultural values, or when, on the other hand, it need not be felt simply as economic compulsion, the individual generally abandons the attempt to justify it at all. In the field of its highest development, in the United States, the pursuit of wealth, stripped of its religious and ethical meaning, tends to become associated with purely mundane passions. (Weber 1976)

Weber's theory has been criticized from many angles. Some have argued, for example, that the outlook he called 'the spirit of capitalism' can be discerned in the early Italian merchant cities in the twelfth century, long before Calvinism was ever heard of. Others have claimed that the key notion of 'working in a vocation', which Weber associated with Protestantism, already existed in Catholic beliefs. Yet the essentials of Weber's account are still accepted by many, and the thesis he advanced remains as bold and illuminating as it did when first formulated. If Weber's thesis is valid, modern economic and social development has been decisively influenced by something that seems at first sight utterly distant from it – a set of religious ideals.

Weber's theory meets several criteria important in theoretical thinking in sociology.

1 It is counterintuitive – it suggests an interpretation that breaks with what common sense would suggest. The theory thus develops a fresh perspective on the issues it covers. Most authors before Weber gave little thought to the possibility that religious ideas could have played a fundamental role in the origins of capitalism.

2 The theory makes sense of something that is otherwise puzzling: why individuals would want to live frugally while making great efforts to accumulate wealth.

3 The theory is capable of illuminating circumstances beyond those it was originally developed to understand. Weber emphasized that he was trying to understand only the early origins of modern capitalism. Nonetheless, it seems reasonable to suppose that parallel values to those instilled by Puritanism might be involved in other situations of successful capitalist development.

4 A good theory is not just one that happens to be valid. It is also one that is *fruitful* in terms of how far it generates new ideas and stimulates further research work. Weber's theory has certainly been highly successful in these respects, providing the springboard for a vast amount of subsequent research and theoretical analysis.

Four theoretical issues

The debate about *The Protestant Ethic* continues today, as do controversies about other aspects of Weber's work. The ideas developed by the classical thinkers, as well as by the later theoretical perspectives discussed in chapter 1, continue to provoke disagreements.

There are several basic theoretical dilemmas – matters of continuing controversy or dispute – which these clashes of viewpoint bring to our attention, some of which concern very general matters to do with how we should interpret human activities and social institutions. We shall discuss four such dilemmas here.

1 One dilemma concerns *human action* and *social structure*. The issue is the following: how far are we creative human actors, actively controlling the conditions of our own lives? Or is most of what we do the result of general social forces outside our control? This issue has always divided, and continues to divide, sociologists. Weber and the symbolic interactionists, for example, stress the active, creative components of human behaviour. Other approaches, such as that of Durkheim, emphasize the constraining nature of social influences of our actions.

2 A second theoretical issue concerns *consensus* and *conflict* in society. Some standpoints in sociology, as we have seen – including functionalism – emphasize the inherent order and harmony of human societies. Those taking this view regard continuity and consensus as the most evident characteristics of societies, however much they may change over time. Other sociologists, on the other hand, accentuate the pervasiveness of social conflict. They see societies as plagued with divisions, tensions and struggles. To them, it is illusory to claim that people tend to live amicably with one another most of the time; even when there are no open confrontations, they say, there remain deep

divisions of interest which at some point are liable to break out into active conflicts.

3 There is a third basic dilemma of theory which hardly figures at all in orthodox traditions of sociology, but which cannot be ignored. This is the problem of how we are to incorporate a satisfactory understanding of *gender* within sociological analysis. The founding figures of sociology were all men, as we saw in chapter 1, and their writings gave virtually no attention to the fact that human beings were gendered. Even those women who were involved in sociology were, until recently, largely neglected (see the box on Harriet Martineau, in chapter 1, p. 20, for example). In the works of the early male sociologists, human individuals appear as if they were 'neuter' – they are abstract 'actors', rather than differentiated women and men. Since we have very little to build on in relating issues of gender to the more established forms of theoretical thinking in sociology, this is perhaps at the current time the most acutely difficult problem of the four to grapple with.

One of the main theoretical dilemmas associated with gender is the following: shall we build 'gender' as a general category into our sociological thinking? Or, alternatively, do we need to analyse gender issues by breaking them down into more specific influences affecting the behaviour of women and men in different contexts? We can put this in another way: are there characteristics that separate men and women, in terms of their identities and social behaviour, in all cultures? Or are gender differences always to be explained mainly in terms

of other differences which divide societies (such as class divisions)?

4 A fourth problem concerns not so much the general characteristics of human behaviour or of societies as a whole, but rather features of *modern social development*. It is to do with the determining influences affecting the origins and nature of modern societies, and derives from the differences between non-Marxist and Marxist approaches. The dilemma centres on the following issue: how far has the modern world been shaped by the economic factors which Marx singled out – in particular, the mechanisms of capitalist economic enterprise? How far, on the other hand, have other influences (such as social, political or cultural factors) shaped social development in the modern era? This is such a fundamental set of questions for sociological theory that we shall consider in some detail the different ideas developed about it.

Structure and action

A major theme pursued by Durkheim, and by many other sociological authors since, is that the societies of which we are members exert **social constraint** over our actions.

Durkheim's thought was introduced in chapter 1, pp. 12–14.

Durkheim argued that society has primacy over the individual person. Society is far more than the sum of individual acts; it has a 'firmness' or 'solidity' comparable to structures in the material environment. Think of a person standing in a room with several doors. The structure of the room constrains the range of her or his possible activities. The siting of the walls and the doors, for example, defines the routes of exit and entry. Social structure, according to Durkheim, constrains our activities in a parallel way, setting limits to what we can do as individuals. It is 'external' to us, just as the walls of the room are.

This point of view is expressed by Durkheim in a famous statement:

> When I perform my duties as a brother, a husband or a citizen and carry out the commitments I have entered into, I fulfil obligations which are defined in law and custom and which are external to myself and my actions. . . . Similarly, the believer has discovered from birth, ready fashioned, the beliefs and practices of his religious life; if they existed before he did, it follows that they exist outside him. The systems of signs that I employ to express my thoughts, the monetary system I use to pay my debts, the credit instruments I utilize in my commercial relationships, the practices I follow in my profession, etc. – all function independently of the use I make of them. (Durkheim 1982)

Although the type of view Durkheim expresses has many adherents, it has also met with sharp criticism. What is 'society', the critics ask, if it is not the composite of many individual actions? If we study a group, we do not see a collective entity, only individuals interacting with one another in various ways. 'Society' is only many individuals behaving in regular ways in relation to each other. According to the critics (who include most sociologists influenced by symbolic interactionism, a theoretical approach introduced in chapter 1, pp. 22–4), as human beings we have reasons for what we do, and we inhabit a social world permeated by cultural meanings. Social phenomena, according to them, are precisely *not* like 'things',

but depend on the symbolic meanings with which we invest what we do. We are not the *creatures* of society, but its *creators*.

Evaluation

It is unlikely that this controversy will ever be fully resolved, since it has existed since modern thinkers first started systematically to try to explain human behaviour. Moreover, it is a debate which is not just confined to sociology, but preoccupies scholars in all fields of the social sciences. You must decide, in the light of your reading of this book, which position you think more nearly correct.

Yet the differences between the two views can be exaggerated. While both cannot be wholly right, we can fairly easily see connections between them. Durkheim's view is clearly in some respects valid. Social institutions do precede the existence of any given individual; it is also evident that they exert constraint over us. Thus, for example, I did not invent the monetary system which exists in Britain. Nor do I have a choice about whether I want to use it or not if I wish to have the goods and services that money can buy. The system of money, like all other established institutions does exist independently of any individual member of society, and constrains that individual's activities.

On the other hand, it is obviously mistaken to suppose that society is 'external' to us in the same way as the physical world is. For the physical world would go on existing whether or not any human beings were alive, whereas it would plainly be nonsensical to say this of society. While society is external to each individual taken singly, by definition it cannot be external to all individuals taken together.

Moreover, although what Durkheim calls 'social facts' might constrain what we do, they do not *determine* what we do. I could choose to live without using money, should I be firmly resolved to do so, even if it might prove very difficult to eke out an existence from day to day. As human beings, we do make choices, and we do not simply respond passively to events around us. The way forward in bridging the gap between 'structure' and 'action' approaches is to recognize that we *actively make and remake* social structure during the course of our everyday activities. For example, the fact that I use the monetary system contributes in a minor, yet necessary, way to the very existence of that system. If everyone, or even the majority of people, at some point decided to avoid using money, the monetary system would dissolve.

As mentioned in chapter 1 (p. 8), a useful term for analysing this process of the active making and remaking of social structure is *structuration*. This is a concept which I (Anthony Giddens) have introduced into sociology in recent years. 'Structure' and 'action' are necessarily related to one another. Societies, communities or groups only have 'structure' in so far as people behave in regular and fairly predictable ways. On the other hand, 'action' is only possible because each of us, as an individual, possesses an enormous amount of socially structured knowledge. The best way to explain this is through the example of language. To exist at all, language must be socially structured – there are properties of language use which every speaker must observe. What someone says in any given context, for instance, wouldn't make sense unless it followed certain grammatical rules. Yet the structu-

ral qualities of language only exist in so far as individual language users actually follow those rules in practice. Language is constantly in the process of structuration.

Erving Goffman and other writers on social interaction (discussed in chapter 5) are quite right to suggest that all human agents are highly knowledgeable. We are what we are as human beings largely because we follow a complex set of conventions – for example, the rituals that strangers observe when passing by on the street. On the other hand, as we apply that knowledge ability in our actions, we give force and content to the very rules and conventions we draw on. Structuration always presumes what the author calls 'the duality of structure'. This means that all social action presumes the existence of structure. But at the same time, structure presumes action, because 'structure'

Erving Goffman

depends on regularities of human behaviour.

Consensus and conflict

It is also useful to begin with Durkheim when contrasting the *consensus* and *conflict* viewpoints. Durkheim sees society as a set of interdependent parts. For most functionalist thinkers, in fact, society is treated as an *integrated whole*, composed of structures which mesh closely with one another. This is very much in accord with Durkheim's emphasis on the constraining, 'external' character of 'social facts'. However, the analogy here is not with the walls of a building, but with the physiology of the body.

A body consists of various specialized parts (such as the brain, heart, lungs, liver and so forth), each of which contributes to sustaining the continuing life of the organism. These necessarily work in harmony with one another; if they do not, the life of the organism is under threat. So it is, according to Durkheim, with society. For a society to have a continuing existence over time, its specialized institutions (such as the political system, religion, the family and the educational system) must work in harmony with one another. The continuation of a society thus depends on cooperation, which in turn presumes a general consensus, or agreement, among its members over basic values.

Those who focus mainly on conflict have a very different outlook. Their guiding assumptions can easily be outlined using Marx's account of class conflict as an example.

Marx's account of class conflict is discussed in chapter 1, pp. 14–17

According to Marx, societies are divided into classes with unequal resources. Since such marked inequalities exist, there are divisions of interest which are 'built into' the social system. These conflicts of interest at some point break out into active change. Not all of those influenced by this viewpoint concentrate on classes to the degree to which Marx did; other divisions are regarded as important in promoting conflict – for example, divisions between racial groups or political factions. Society is seen as essentially *full of tension* regardless of which conflict groups are stronger than others; even the most stable social system represents an uneasy balance of antagonistic groupings.

Evaluation

As with the case of structure and action, it is not likely that this theoretical debate can be completely brought to a close. Yet, once more, the difference between the consensus and conflict standpoints seems wider than it is. The two positions are by no means wholly incompatible. All societies probably involve some kind of general agreement over values, and all certainly involve conflict.

Moreover, as a general rule of sociological analysis we always have to examine the connections *between* consensus and conflict within social systems. The values held by different groups and the goals that their members pursue often reflect a mixture of common and opposed interests. For instance, even in Marx's portrayal of class conflict, different classes share some common interests as well as being pitted against one another. Thus capitalists depend on a labour force to work in their enterprises, just as workers depend on capitalists to provide their wages. Open conflict is not continuous in such circumstances; rather, sometimes what both sides have in common tends to override their differences, while in other situations the reverse is the case.

A useful concept which helps analyse the interrelations of conflict and consensus is that of **ideology** – values and beliefs which help secure the position of more powerful groups at the expense of less powerful ones. Power, ideology and conflict are always closely connected. Many conflicts are *about* power, because of the rewards it can bring. Those who hold most power may depend mainly on the influence of ideology to retain their dominance, but are usually also able to use force if necessary. For instance, in feudal times aristocratic rule was supported by the idea that a minority of people were 'born to govern', but aristocratic rulers often resorted to the use of violence against those who dared to oppose their power.

The issue of gender

Issues of gender are scarcely central in the writings of the major figures who established the framework of modern sociology. The few passages in which they did touch on gender questions, however, allow us at least to specify the outlines of a basic theoretical dilemma – even if there is little in their works to help us try to resolve it. We can best describe this dilemma by contrasting a theme which occasionally occurs in Durkheim's writings with one that appears in those of Marx. Durkheim notes at one point, in the course of his discussion of suicide, that man is 'almost entirely the product of society', while woman is 'to a far greater extent the

product of nature'. Expanding on these observations, he says of man: 'his tastes, aspirations and humour have in large part a collective origin, while his companion's are more directly influenced by her organism. His needs, therefore, are quite different from hers' (1952). In other words, women and men have different identities, tastes and inclinations because women are less socialized and are 'closer to nature' than men.

No one today would accept a view stated in quite this manner. Female identity is as much shaped by socialization as that of males. Yet, when modified somewhat, Durkheim's claim does represent one possible view of the formation and nature of gender. This is that gender differences rest fundamentally on biologically given distinctions between men and women. Such a view does not necessarily mean believing that gender differences are mostly inborn. Rather, it presumes that women's social position and identity are mainly shaped by their involvement in reproduction and child-rearing. If this view is correct, differences of gender are deeply embedded in all societies. The discrepancies in power between women and men reflect the fact that women bear children and are their primary caretakers, whereas men are active in the 'public' spheres of politics, work and war.

Marx's view is substantially at odds with this. For Marx, gender differences in power and status between men and women mainly reflect other divisions – in his eyes, especially class divisions. According to him, in the earliest forms of human society neither gender nor class divisions were present. The power of men over women only came about as class divisions appeared. Women came to be a form of 'private property' owned by men, through the institution of marriage. Women will be freed from their situation of bondage when class divisions are overcome. Again, few if any would accept this analysis today, but we can make it a much more plausible view by generalizing it further. Class is not the only factor shaping social divisions which affect the behaviour of men and women. Other factors include ethnicity and cultural background. For instance, it might be argued that women in a minority group (say, blacks in the United States) have more in common with men in that minority group than they do with women in the majority (that is, white women). Or it may be the case that women from a particular culture (like a small hunting and gathering culture) share more common characteristics with the males of that culture than they do with women in an industrial society.

The rise of the women's movement in recent decades has provoked radical changes within sociology and other disciplines. Feminism has led to a broad-based assault on the perceived male bias both in sociological theory and methodology, and in the very subject matter of sociology. Not only has the male domination of sociology been challenged, but there have also been calls for a comprehensive reconstruction of the discipline itself – both the questions that form its core and the presentation of discussions surrounding them.

Feminist perspectives in sociology emphasize the centrality of gender in analysing the social world. While the diversity of feminist viewpoints makes it difficult to speak in generalities, we can safely say that most feminists agree that knowledge is integrally related to questions of sex and gender. Because men and women have different experiences and view the world from different perspectives, they do not construct their understandings of the world in identical ways. Feminists often charge that traditional sociological theory has denied or ignored the 'gendered' nature of knowledge and has instead projected conceptions of the social world which are male-dominated. Males have traditionally occupied positions of power and authority in society and have an investment in maintaining their privileged roles, according to feminists. Under such conditions, gendered knowledge becomes a vital force in perpetuating established social arrangements and legitimating male domination.

Feminism approaches are discussed further in chapter 12, 'Sexuality and Gender', pp. 469–76.

Some feminist writers have argued that it is a mistake to suppose that either 'men' or 'women' are groups with their own interests or characteristics. Several of these writers, such as Judith Butler (1999), have been influenced by postmodern thinking, which is discussed further below (see pp. 115–17). According to Butler, gender is not a fixed category but a fluid one, exhibited in what people do rather than what they are. If, as Butler argues (2004), gender is something that is 'done', then it is also something that we should fight to 'undo' when it is used by one group to exert power over another. Judith Butler's work and her influence on queer theory are discussed further in chapter 12, p. 458.

Similar themes have been pursued by Susan Faludi. In *Stiffed* (1999), her recent work on masculinity, Faludi shows that the idea that men dominate in all spheres is a myth. On the contrary, there is a crisis of masculinity today in the world men

Judith Butler

supposedly own and run. Some groups of men are still confident and feel in control; many others find themselves marginalized and lacking in self-respect. The success that at least some women have achieved is part of the reason, but so too are changes in the nature of work. The impact of information technology, for example, has made many less-skilled men redundant to society's needs.

> The 'crisis of masculinity' is discussed in relation to education on pp. 712–13.

Evaluation

The issues involved in this third dilemma are highly important, and bear directly on the challenge that feminist authors have thrown down to sociology. No one can seriously dispute that a great deal of sociological analysis in the past has either ignored women or has operated with interpretations of female identity and behaviour that are drastically inadequate. In spite of all the new research on women carried out in sociology over the past twenty years, there are still many areas in which the distinctive activities and con-

cerns of women have been insufficiently studied. But 'bringing the study of women into sociology' is not in and of itself the same as coping with problems of gender, because gender concerns the relations between the identities and behaviour of women *and* men. For the moment, it has to be left as an open question how far gender differences can be illuminated by means of other sociological concepts (class, ethnicity, cultural background and so forth), or how far, on the contrary, other social divisions need to be explained in terms of gender. Certainly some of the major explanatory tasks of sociology in the future will depend on tackling this dilemma effectively.

The shaping of the modern world

The Marxist perspective

Marx's writings threw down a powerful challenge to sociological analysis, one which has not been ignored. From his own time to the present day many sociological debates have centred on Marx's ideas about the development of modern societies. As was mentioned earlier, Marx sees modern societies as *capitalistic*. The driving impulse behind social change in the modern era is the pressure towards constant economic transformation, which is an integral part of capitalist production. Capitalism is a vastly more dynamic economic system than any preceding one. Capitalists compete with one another to sell their goods to consumers, and, in order to survive in a competitive market, firms have to produce their wares as cheaply and efficiently as possible. This leads to constant technological innovation, because increasing the effectiveness of the technology used in a particular production process is one way in which companies can secure an edge over their rivals.

There are also strong incentives to seek out new markets in which to sell goods, acquire cheap raw materials and make use of cheap labour power. Capitalism, therefore, according to Marx, is a restlessly expanding system, pushing outwards across the world. This is how Marx explains the spread of Western industry globally.

Marx's interpretation of the influence of capitalism has found many supporters, and subsequent authors have considerably refined Marx's own portrayal. On the other hand, numerous critics have set out to rebut his view, offering alternative analyses of the influences shaping the modern world. Virtually everyone accepts that capitalism *has* played a major part in creating the world we live in today. But other sociologists have argued both that Marx exaggerated the impact of purely *economic* factors in producing change, and that capitalism is *less central* to modern social development than he claimed. Most of these writers have also been sceptical of Marx's belief that a socialist system would eventually replace capitalism.

The quick collapse of communism in the Soviet Union and Eastern Europe in the years after 1989 led many people to talk of a 'crisis' in Marxist thought that seemed to bear out the scepticism of Marxism's critics (Gamble 1999). Although most Western Marxists had long dismissed what they often described as the 'actually existing socialism' of Russia and elsewhere, the continued survival of Marxism as the official ideology of a large part of the world gave Western Marxists evidence that alternatives to capitalism could succeed.

Weber's view

One of Marx's earliest, and most acute, critics was Max Weber.

> Weber's work was introduced in chapter 1, 'What is Sociology?', pp. 17–19.

Weber's writings, in fact, have been described as involving a lifelong struggle with 'the ghost of Marx' – with the intellectual legacy that Marx left. The alternative position which Weber worked out remains important today. According to him, non-economic factors have played a key role in modern social development. This argument, in fact, is one of the main points of *The Protestant Ethic*. Religious values – especially those associated with Puritanism – were of fundamental importance in creating a capitalistic outlook. This outlook did not emerge, as Marx supposed, from economic changes as such.

Weber's understanding of the nature of modern societies and the reasons for the spread of Western modes of life across the world contrasts substantially with that of Marx. According to Weber, capitalism – a distinct way of organizing economic enterprise – is one among other major factors shaping social development in the modern period. Underlying capitalistic economic mechanisms, and in some ways more fundamental than them, is the impact of *science* and *bureaucracy*. Science has shaped modern technology – and will presumably continue to do so in any future socialist society. Bureaucracy is the only way of organizing large numbers of people effectively, and therefore inevitably expands with economic and political

Marx and Weber compared

Broadly Marxist ideas

1 The main dynamic of modern development is the expansion of capitalistic economic mechanisms.
2 Modern societies are riven with class inequalities, which are basic to their very nature.
3 Major divisions of power, like those affecting the differential position of men and women, derive ultimately from economic inequalities.
4 Modern societies as we know them today (capitalist societies) are of a transitional type – we may expect them to become radically reorganized in the future. Socialism, of one type or another, will eventually replace capitalism.
5 The spread of Western influence across the world is mainly a result of the expansionist tendencies of capitalist enterprise.

Broadly Weberian ideas

1 The main dynamic of modern development is the rationalization of production.
2 Class is one type of inequality among many – such as inequalities between men and women – in modern societies.
3 Power in the economic system is separable from other sources. For instance, male–female inequalities cannot be explained in economic terms.
4 Rationalization is bound to progress further in the future, in all spheres of social life. All modern societies are dependent on the same basic modes of social and economic organization.
5 The global impact of the West comes from its command over industrial resources, together with superior military power.

growth. Weber refers to the development of science, modern technology and bureaucracy collectively as 'rationalization'. Rationalization means the organization of social and economic life according to principles of efficiency, on the basis of technical knowledge.

Evaluation

Which type of interpretation of modern societies, that deriving from Marx or that coming from Weber, is correct? Again, scholars are divided on the issue. The box lists some of these differences. (It must remembered that within each camp there are variations, so not every theorist will agree with all the points.)

The contrasts between Marxist and Weberian standpoints inform many areas of sociology. They influence not only how we analyse the nature of the industrialized societies, but our view of less developed societies also. In addition, the two per-spectives are linked to differing political positions, authors on the left on the whole adopting views on the first side, liberals and conservatives those on the second side. Yet the factors with which this particular dilemma is concerned are of a more directly empirical nature than those involved in the other dilemmas. Factual studies of the paths of evolution of modern societies and less developed countries help us assess how far patterns of change conform to one side or the other.

Recent sociological theory

The dilemmas raised above, over how the modern world was shaped, are still important, but more recent theorists have tried to go beyond both Marx and Weber. With the collapse of communism in Eastern Europe in 1989, Marx's ideas appear less relevant to the contemporary world than many once thought, although a number of scholars continue to use broadly Marxist approaches to tackle the sociological questions that face the modern world (Gamble 1999).

Other sociologists, including some who were originally Marxists, now discount Marx altogether. They believe that his attempt to find general patterns of history was inevitably doomed to failure. For such thinkers, linked to *postmodernism*, sociologists should simply give up on the sorts of theory that both Marx and Weber sought to develop – overall interpretations of social change.

Postmodernism

The advocates of the idea of **postmodernism** claim that the classic social thinkers took their inspiration from the idea that history has a shape – it 'goes somewhere' and leads to progress – and that now this notion has collapsed. There are no longer any 'grand narratives' or **meta-narratives** – overall conceptions of history or society – that make any sense (Lyotard 1985). Not only is there no general notion of progress that can be defended, there is also no such thing as history. The postmodern world is not destined, as Marx hoped, to be a socialist one. Instead, it is one dominated by the new media, which 'take us out' of our past. Postmodern society is highly pluralistic and diverse. In countless films, videos, TV programmes and websites, images circulate around the world. We come into contact with many ideas and values, but these have little connection with the history of the areas in which we live, or indeed with our own personal histories. Everything seems constantly in flux. As one group of authors expressed things:

> Our world is being remade. Mass production, the mass consumer, the big city, big-brother state, the sprawling housing estate, and the nation-state are in decline: flexibility, diversity, differentiation, and mobility, communication, decentralisation and internationalisation are in the ascendant. In the process our own identities, our sense of self, our own subjectivities are being transformed. We are in transition to a new era. (Hall et al. 1988)

One of the important theorists of postmodernity is the French author Jean Baudrillard (whose work is discussed in chapter 15, 'The Media', pp. 601–2). Baudrillard believes that the electronic media have destroyed our relationship to our past and created a chaotic, empty world. He was strongly influenced by Marxism in his early years. However, he argues, the spread of electronic communication and the mass media has reversed the Marxist theorem that economic forces shape society. Instead, social life is influenced above all by signs and images.

In a media-dominated age, Baudrillard says, meaning is created by the flow of images, as in TV programmes. Much of our world has become a sort of make-believe universe in which we are responding to media images rather than to real persons or places. Thus when Diana, Princess of Wales, died in 1997, there was an enormous outpouring of grief, not only in Britain but all over the world. Yet were people mourning a real person? Baudrillard would say not. Princess Diana existed for most people only through the media. Diana's death was more like an event in a soap opera than a real event in the way in which people experienced it; Baudrillard speaks of 'the dissolution of life into TV'.

Jean Baudrillard

Michel Foucault

Although he refused to call himself a post-modernist, Michel Foucault (1926–84) drew heavily on postmodernist thought. In his work, he attempted to illustrate shifts of understanding which separate thinking in our modern world from that of earlier ages. In his writings on crime, the body, madness and sexuality, Foucault analysed the emergence of modern institutions such as prisons, hospitals and schools that have played an increasing role in controlling and monitoring the social population. He wanted to show that there was 'another side' to Enlightenment ideas about individual liberty – one concerned with discipline and surveillance. Foucault advanced important ideas about the relationship between power, ideology and discourse in relation to modern organizational systems.

Michel Foucault

The study of power – how individuals and groups achieve their ends as against those of others – is of fundamental importance in sociology. Marx and Weber, among the classical founders, laid particular emphasis on power; Foucault continued some of the lines of thought they pioneered. The role of discourse is central to his thinking about power and control in society. He used the term to refer to ways of talking or thinking about a particular subject that are united by common assumptions. Foucault demonstrated, for example, the dramatic way in which discourses of madness changed from medieval times until the present day. In the Middle Ages, for example, the insane were generally regarded as harmless; some believed that they may even have possessed a special 'gift' of perception. In modern societies, however, 'madness' has been shaped by a medicalized discourse, which emphasizes illness and treatment. This medicalized discourse is supported and perpetuated by a highly developed and influential network of doctors, medical experts, hospitals, professional associations and medical journals.

Foucault's work is discussed in more detail in chapter 8, 'Health, Illness and Disability', p. 260.

According to Foucault, power works through discourse to shape popular attitudes towards phenomena such as crime, madness or sexuality. Expert discourses established by those with power or authority can often be countered only by competing expert discourses. In such a way, discourses can be used as a powerful tool to restrict alternative ways of thinking or speaking. Knowledge becomes a force of control. A prominent theme through-out Foucault's writings is the way power and knowledge are linked to technologies of surveillance, enforcement and discipline.

Foucault's radical new approach to social theory stands in opposition to the general consensus about the nature of scientific knowledge. This approach, which characterized many of his early works, has become known as Foucault's 'archaeology'. Unlike other social scientists who aim to make sense of the unfamiliar by drawing analogies with that which is familiar, Foucault set about the opposite task: to make sense of the familiar by digging into the past. Foucault energetically attacked the present – the taken-for-granted concepts, beliefs and structures which are largely invisible precisely because they are *familiar*. For example, he explored how the notion of 'sexuality' has not always existed, but has been created through processes of social development. Similar comments can be made about our modern-day conceptions of normal and deviant activity, of sanity and madness, and so forth. Foucault attempted to reveal the assumptions behind our current beliefs and practices and to make the present 'visible' by accessing it from the past. However, we cannot have general theories about society, social development or modernity; we can only understand fragments of them.

Four contemporary sociologists

Many other thinkers have been influenced by Michel Foucault. Surveillance – keeping information about people in order to control their behaviour – is an ever-present phenomenon in a society marked by the rise of mass media. Most contemporary social theorists accept that information technology and new communications systems, together with other technological changes, are producing major social transformations for all of us. However the majority disagree with core ideas of the postmodernists and Foucault. They argue that our attempts to understand general processes in the social world are doomed, as is the notion we can change the world for the better. Manuel Castells, Jürgen Habermas, Ulrich Beck and I (Anthony Giddens) have all claimed that we need as much as ever to develop general theories of the social world and that such theories can help us intervene to shape it in a positive way. Even if one agrees that Marx's dreams of a socialist alternative to capitalism are dead, some of the values which drove the socialist project – those of social community, equality and caring for the weak and vulnerable – are still very much alive.

Jürgen Habermas

Jürgen Habermas: democracy and the public sphere

The German sociologist Jürgen Habermas recognizes that many of Marx's ideas have become obsolete, and looks to Weber as a source of alternative ideas. Yet he also suggests that some of the basic principles which inspired Marx's writing need to be sustained. There is no alternative to capitalism, nor should there be: capitalism has proved capable of generating enormous wealth. Nonetheless, some of the fundamental problems that Marx identified in a capitalistic economy are still there – such as its tendency to produce economic

depressions or crises. We need to re-establish our control over economic processes which have come to control us more than we control them.

One of the main ways of achieving such increased control, Habermas proposes, is by a revival of what he calls the 'public sphere'. The public sphere is essentially the framework of democracy. Orthodox democratic procedures, Habermas argues, involving parliaments and parties, do not provide us with a sufficient basis for collective decision-making. We can renew the public sphere through the reform of democratic procedures and the more consistent involvement of community agencies and other local groups. The modern media of communication do have some of the effects noted by Baudrillard and others. Yet they can also contribute in a fundamental way to the furtherance of democracy. Where television and newspapers, for example, are dominated by commercial interests, they do not provide a focus for democratic discussion. Yet public television and radio, together with the Internet, offer many possibilities for developing open dialogue and discussion.

Habermas has been criticized by feminist authors for not giving due attention to the connections between gender and democracy. Democracy, the critics point out, has often been assumed to be a largely male domain. Habermas, it is argued, should look at the ways in which democracy tends to exclude the full involvement of women. Most parliaments, for instance, only have a minority of women members. Many political debates also tend to downplay issues of specific concern to women. In his major work, *The Theory of Communicative Action* (1986–8), Habermas says virtually nothing about gender. Nancy Fraser (1989) points out that in his discussion of democracy Habermas treats citizenship as gender neutral. But citizenship has typically developed in ways that are much more favourable to men than to women. Women's position in the family, for example, is still largely subordinate to that of men. Inequality in family life is therefore directly relevant to public democracy.

Ulrich Beck

Ulrich Beck: the global risk society

Another German sociologist, Ulrich Beck, also rejects postmodernism. Rather than living in a world 'beyond the modern' we are moving into a phase of what he calls 'the second modernity'. The second modernity refers to the fact that modern institutions are becoming global, while every-day life is breaking free from the hold of tradition and custom. The old industrial society is disappearing and is being replaced by a 'risk society'. What the postmodernists see as chaos, or lack of pattern, Beck sees as risk or uncertainty. The management of risk is the prime feature of the global order.

Beck is not arguing that the contemporary world is more risky than that of previous ages. Rather, it is the nature of the risks we must face that is changing. Risk now derives less from natural dangers or hazards than from uncertainties created by our own social development and by the development of science and technology.

The advance of science and technology creates new risk situations that are very different from those of previous ages. Science and technology obviously provide many benefits for us. Yet they create risks that are hard to measure. Thus no one quite knows, for example, what the risks involved in the development of new technologies, such as genetic modification or nanotechnology, might be. Supporters of genetically modified crops, for example, claim that at best they give us the possibility of ending malnutrition in the world's poorest countries and providing cheap food for everyone. Sceptics claim that they could have dangerous, unintended health consequences.

Beck's ideas on risk are discussed in more detail in chapter 22, 'The Environment and Risk', pp. 965–6.

According to Beck, an important aspect of the risk society is that its hazards are not restricted spatially, temporally or socially. Today's risks affect all countries and all social classes; they have global, not merely personal, consequences. Many forms of manufactured risk, such as those to do with terrorism or pollution for example, cross national boundaries. The explosion at the Chernobyl nuclear power plant in Ukraine in 1986 provides a clear illustration of this point. Everyone living in the immediate vicinity of Chernobyl – regardless of age, class, gender or status – was exposed to dangerous levels of radiation. At the same time, the effects of the accident stretched far beyond Chernobyl itself – throughout Europe and beyond, abnormally high levels of radiation were detected long after the explosion.

Many decisions on the level of everyday life also become infused with risk. Risk and gender relations are actually closely related, for example. Many new uncertainties have entered the relationships between the sexes (as we discuss in chapter 7, 'Families and Intimate Relationships'). One example concerns the areas of love and marriage. A generation ago, in the developed societies, marriage was a fairly straightforward process of life transition – one moved from being unmarried to the status of marriage, and this was assumed to be a fairly permanent situation. Today, many people live together without getting married and divorce rates are high. Anyone contemplating a relationship with another person must take these facts into account, and is therefore involved in risk calculations. The individual must judge his or her likelihood of gaining happiness and security against this uncertain backdrop.

The threat of terrorism provides another example of how risk affects our society. The attacks on New York and Washington on 11 September 2001 changed the extent to which people thought of their communities as at risk from terrorist attack. The fear of terrorism created inertia in economies around the world, particularly in the months after 11 September, as businesses became reluctant to risk large-scale investment. The terrorist attacks also changed the assessment that states made over the balance between the freedom of its citizens and their security.

Beck argues that the nation-state is no longer able to cope in a world of global risk. Instead, there must be transnational cooperation between states. The narrow viewpoint of the nation-state becomes an impediment when it comes to dealing with new risks, such as global warming. When it comes to fighting against international terrorism, Beck argues, we must ask what we are fighting for. His ideal is a cosmopolitan system based on the acknowledgement and acceptance of cultural diversity. Cosmopolitan states do not fight only against terrorism, but also against the causes of terrorism in the world. To Beck, they provide the most positive way to deal with global problems, which appear insoluble at the level of the individual state, but manageable through cooperation.

Beck agrees with Habermas that changes in our society in recent decades do not spell the end of attempts at social and political reform. Rather to the contrary: new forms of activism appear. We see the emergence of a new field of what Beck calls 'sub-politics'. This refers to the activities of groups and agencies operating outside the formal mechanisms of democratic politics, such as ecological, consumer or human rights groups. Responsibility for risk management cannot be left to politicians or scientists alone: other groups of citizens need to be brought in. Groups and movements that develop in the arena of sub-politics, however, can have a big influence on orthodox political mechanisms. For instance, responsibility for the environment, which was previously the province of ecological activists, has now been accepted as part of the conventional political framework.

Manuel Castells: the network economy

Manuel Castells began his academic career as a Marxist. As an expert on urban affairs, he sought to apply Marx's ideas to the study of cities.

> We will see more about Castells's views on urbanism in chapter 21, 'Cities and Urban Spaces', pp. 901–2.

In recent years, however, Castells has moved away from Marxism. Like Baudrillard, he has become concerned with the impact of media and communications

Manuel Castells

technologies. The information society, Castells argues, is marked by the rise of networks and a *network economy*. The new economy, which depends on the connections made possible by global communications, is certainly capitalist. However, the capitalist economy and society of today are quite different from those of the past. The expansion of capitalism is no longer based primarily, as Marx thought it would be, either on the working class or the manufacture of material goods. Instead, telecommunications and computers are the basis of production.

> Castells's ideas on 'the network society' are discussed more fully in chapter 16, 'Organizations and Networks', pp. 671–3.

Castells does not reveal much about how these changes are affecting gender relations. However, he does say a good deal about their effects on personal identity and everyday life. In the network society, personal identity becomes a much more open matter. We don't any longer take our identities from the past; we have actively to make them in interacting with others. This directly affects the sphere of the family and also more generally the structuring of male and female identities. Men and women no longer get their identities from traditional roles. Thus women's 'place' was once in the home, whereas that of men was to be 'out at work'. That division has now broken down.

Castells calls the new global economy the 'automaton' – like Habermas, he thinks that we no longer fully control the world we have created. Castells' statements here echo those made a century earlier by Weber, who thought that the increase in bureaucracy would imprison us all in an 'iron cage'. As Castells puts it, 'humankind's nightmare of seeing our machines taking control of our world seems on the edge of becoming reality – not in the form of robots that eliminate jobs or government computers that police our lives, but as an electronically based system of financial transactions' (2000, p. 56).

Yet Castells has not forgotten his Marxist roots altogether. He thinks that it may be possible to regain more effective control of the global marketplace. This won't come through any sort of revolution, but through the collective efforts of international organizations and countries which have a common interest in regulating international capitalism. Information technology, Castells concludes, can often be a means of local empowerment and community renewal. He quotes as an example the case of Finland. Finland is the most developed information society in the world. All schools in the country have Internet access and most of the population is computer literate. At the same time, Finland has a well-established and effective welfare state which has been adapted to meet the needs of the new economy.

Anthony Giddens: social reflexivity

In my own writings, I also develop a theoretical perspective on the changes happening in the present-day world. We live today in what I call a 'runaway world', a world marked by new risks and uncertainties of the sort Beck diagnoses. But we should place the notion of *trust* alongside that of risk. Trust refers to the confidence we have either in individuals or in institutions.

In a world of rapid transformation, traditional forms of trust tend to become dissolved. Trust in other people used to be based in the local community. Living in a

Anthony Giddens

more globalized society, however, our lives are influenced by people we never see or meet, who may be living on the far side of the world from us. Trust means having confidence in 'abstract systems' – for example, we have to have confidence in agencies for food regulation, the purification of water or the effectiveness of banking systems. Trust and risk are closely bound up with one another. We need to have confidence in such authorities if we are to confront the risks which surround us, and react to them in an effective way.

Living in an information age, in my view, means an increase in social **reflexivity**. Social reflexivity refers to the fact that we have constantly to think about, or reflect upon, the circumstances in which we live our lives. When societies were more geared to custom and tradition, people could follow established ways of doing things in a more unreflective fashion. For us, many aspects of life that for earlier generations were simply taken for granted become matters of open decision-making. For example, for hundreds of years people had no effective ways of limiting the size of their families. With modern forms of contraception, and other forms of technological involvement in reproduction, parents can not only choose how many children they have, but can even decide what sex their children will be. These new possibilities, of course, are fraught with new ethical dilemmas.

We have not inevitably lost control of our own future. In a global age, nations certainly lose some of the power they used to have. For instance, countries have less influence over economic policy than they once had. However, governments retain a good deal of power. Acting collaboratively, nations can get together to reassert their influence over the runaway world. The groups to which Beck points – agencies and movements working outside the formal framework of politics – can have an important role. But they will not supplant orthodox democratic politics. Democracy is still crucial, because groups in the area of 'sub-politics' make divergent claims and have different interests. Such groups may include, for example, those who are actively campaigning in favour of more tolerance of abortion, and those who believe entirely the opposite. Democratic government must assess and react to these varying claims and concerns.

Democracy cannot be limited to the public sphere as defined by Habermas. There is a potential 'democracy of the emotions' emerging in everyday life. A democracy of the emotions refers to the emergence of forms of family life in which men and women participate in an equal fashion. Virtually all forms of traditional family were based on the dominance of men over women, something that was usually sanctioned in law. The increasing equality between the sexes cannot be limited only to the right to vote; it must also involve the personal and intimate sphere. The democratizing of personal life advances to the degree to which relationships are founded on mutual respect, communication and tolerance.

Conclusion

Perhaps today we are at the beginning of a major new phase of development of sociological theory. The ideas of the classic thinkers – Marx, Durkheim and Weber – were formed during times of great social and economic change. We are now living through a period of global transition that is probably just as profound – and is much more widely felt across the world – as any in earlier times. We need to develop new theories to understand the new develop-ments which are transforming our societies today. The theories just analysed are among the most important contributions to this endeavour.

Summary points

1   A diversity of theoretical approaches is found in sociology (and also in the other social sciences). The reason for this is not particularly puzzling: theoretical disputes are difficult to resolve even in the natural sciences, and in sociology we face special difficulties because of the complex problems involved in subjecting our own behaviour to study.

2   Clashes of viewpoint in sociology bring to our attention several basic theoretical dilemmas. An important one concerns how we should relate human action to social structure. Are we the creators of society, or created by it? The choice between these alternatives is not as stark as it may initially appear, and the real problem is how to relate the two aspects of social life to one another.

3   A second dilemma concerns whether societies should be pictured as harmonious and orderly, or whether they should be seen as marked by persistent conflict. Again, the two views are not completely opposed, and we need to show how consensus and conflict interrelate.

4   A third basic dilemma concerns gender, and in particular whether we should build it as a general category into our sociological thinking. Feminist theorists have brought changes both in what sociologists think about, and in the way they think it.

5   A fourth focus of continuing debate in sociology is to do with the analysis of modern social development. Are processes of change in the modern world mainly shaped by capitalist economic development or by other factors, including non-economic ones? Positions taken in this debate are influenced to some extent by the political beliefs and attitudes held by different sociologists.

6   In tackling the issues of social development, more recent theorists have tried to go beyond both Marx and Weber. Postmodern thinkers deny that we can develop any general theories of history or society at all.

7   Other theorists are critical of postmodernism, arguing that we can still develop overall theories of the social world, and in a way that will enable us to intervene to shape it for the better. They include Habermas, with his concept of the 'public sphere'; Beck, and the 'risk society'; Castells, and the 'network society'; and Giddens, in his development of the concept of social reflexivity.

Questions for further thought

1 Why is theoretical thinking so important in sociology?

2 Is Weber's work on the Protestant ethic a single theory or a number of middle-range theories?

3 What does the study of language tell us about the study of society?

4 Can the problem of gender really be incorporated within existing theoretical perspectives?

5 Are the various 'dilemmas' within sociological theory really as difficult to resolve as they appear?

6 How much do recent developments in sociological theory owe to the insights of Marx, Weber and Durkheim?

Further reading

Ulrich Beck, *World Risk Society* (Malden, MA: Polity, 1999).

Judith Butler, *Gender Trouble: Feminism and the Subversion of Identity* (London: Routledge, 1999).

Judith Butler, *Undoing Gender* (London: Routledge, 2004).

Alex Callinicos, *Against Post-Modernism: A Marxist Critique* (Cambridge: Polity, 1989).

Manuel Castells, *End of Millennium*, (Malden, MA: Blackwell Publishers, 1998).

Manuel Castells, *The Rise of the Network Society*, 2nd edn (Oxford: Blackwell, 2000).

Peter Dews (ed.), *Habermas: A Critical Reader* (Oxford: Blackwell, 1999).

Anthony Giddens, *Capitalism and Modern Social Theory*, rev. edn (Cambridge: Cambridge University Press, 1992).

Anthony Giddens, *Runaway World: How Globalisation is Reshaping our Lives* (London: Profile, 2002).

David Harvey, *The Condition of Postmodernity* (Oxford: Blackwell, 1989).

Internet links

Michel Foucault
http://foucault.info/
Judith Butler
http://www.theory.org.uk/ctr-butl.htm
Jürgen Habermas
http://www.habermasonline.org/
Ulrich Beck
http://www.lse.ac.uk/collections/sociology/whoswho/beck.htm
Manuel Castells
http://sociology.berkeley.edu/faculty/castells/
Anthony Giddens
http://old.Ise.ac.uk/collections/meetthedirector/

Contents

5

Social Interaction and Everyday Life

ERIC IS a fitness instructor at an expensive city health club, where he has worked for many years. Over time, he has come to know hundreds of people who exercise at the gym. He worked with some of them when they first joined, explaining to them how to use the equipment. He met many others in his role as an instructor of 'spinning' classes (a group session on exercise bikes). Others he has come to know through casual contact, since many of the same people work out at the same time every week.

The personal space is limited within the gym, due to the proximity of the exercise equipment. For example, in the weight-training circuit, one section contains a number of machines that are very near to each other. Members must work in close proximity to others working out, and they constantly cross one another's paths as they move from machine to machine.

It is almost impossible for Eric to walk

People's behaviour in gyms often provides some good examples of civil inattention.

anywhere in this physical space without making eye contact with someone else he has at least met. He will greet many of these patrons the first time he sees them in the day, but afterwards it is usually understood that they will go about their own business without acknowledging one another in the way they did earlier.

When passers-by quickly glance at one another and then look away again, they demonstrate what Erving Goffman (1967, 1971) calls the **civil inattention** we require of one another in many situations. Civil inattention is not the same as merely ignoring another person. Each individual indicates recognition of the other person's presence, but avoids any gesture that might be taken as too intrusive. Civil inattention to others is something we engage in more or less unconsciously, but it is of fundamental importance to the existence of social life, which must proceed efficiently and, sometimes among total strangers, without fear. When civil inattention occurs among passing strangers, an individual implies to another person that she has no reason to suspect his intentions, be hostile to him or in any other way specifically avoid him.

The best way to see the importance of this is by thinking of examples where it doesn't apply. When a person stares fixedly at another, allowing her face openly to express a particular emotion, it is normally with a lover, family member or close friend. Strangers or chance acquaintances, whether encountered on the street, at work or at a party, virtually never

Sit down next to me at your peril: as bus passengers we try our best to protect our personal space.

hold the gaze of another in this way. To do so may be taken as an indication of hostile intent; for example, racists have been known to give a 'hate stare' to passers-by from other ethnic groups.

Even friends in close conversation need to be careful about how they look at one another. Each individual demonstrates attention and involvement in the conversation by regularly looking at the eyes of the other, but not staring into them. To look too intently might be taken as a sign of mistrust about, or at least failure to understand, what the other is saying. Yet if neither party engages the eyes of the other at all, each is likely to be thought evasive, shifty, or otherwise odd.

The study of daily life

Why should we concern ourselves with such seemingly trivial aspects of social behaviour? Passing someone on the street or exchanging a few words with a friend seem minor and uninteresting activities, things we do countless times a day without giving them any thought. In fact, the study of such apparently insignificant forms of **social interaction** is of major importance in sociology – and, far from being uninteresting, is one of the most absorbing of all areas of sociological investigation. There are three reasons for this.

First, our day-to-day routines, with their almost constant interactions with others, give structure and form to what we do; we can learn a great deal about ourselves as social beings, and about social life itself, from studying them. Our lives are organized around the repetition of similar patterns of behaviour from day to day, week to week, month to month, and year to year. Think of what you did yesterday, for example, and the day before that. If they were both weekdays, in all probability you got up at about the same time each day (an important routine in itself). If you are a student, you may have gone off to a class fairly early in the morning, perhaps making the journey from home to campus that you make virtually every weekday. You perhaps met some friends for lunch, returning to classes or private study in the afternoon. Later, you retraced your steps back home, possibly going out in the evening with other friends.

Of course, the routines we follow from day to day are not identical, and our patterns of activity at weekends usually contrast with those on weekdays. And if we make a major change in our life, like leaving college to take up a job, alterations in our daily routines are usually necessary; but then we establish a new and fairly regular set of habits again.

Second, the study of everyday life reveals to us how humans can act creatively to shape reality. Although social behaviour is guided to some extent by forces such as roles, norms and shared expectations, individuals perceive reality differently according to their backgrounds, interests and motivations. Because individuals are capable of creative action, they continuously shape reality through the decisions and actions they take. In other words, reality is not fixed or static – it is created through human interactions. This notion of *the social construction of reality* lies at the heart of the symbolic interactionist perspective introduced in chapter 1, and is discussed further below (pp. 152–4).

Third, studying social interaction in

everyday life sheds light on larger social systems and institutions. All large-scale social systems, in fact, depend on the patterns of social interaction we engage in daily. This is easy to demonstrate. Consider again the case of two strangers passing in the street. Such an event may seem to have little direct relevance to large-scale, more permanent forms of social organization. But when we take into account many such interactions, this is no longer so. In modern societies, most people live in towns and cities and constantly interact with others whom they do not know personally. Civil inattention is one among other mechanisms that give city life, with its bustling crowds and fleeting, impersonal contacts, the character it has.

In this chapter, we shall discuss the non-verbal cues (the facial expressions and bodily gestures) which we all use when interacting with others. We will then move on to analyse everyday speech – how we use language to communicate to others the meanings we wish to get across. Finally, we will focus on the ways in which our lives are structured by daily routines, paying particular attention to how we coordinate our actions across space and time. In this chapter we also find that the study of the small, everyday practices that sociologists of social interaction study are not separate from any of the large-scale issues examined in the later chapters of this book, such as gender or class; instead, we find that they are intimately linked. We look at two specific examples of the link between micro- and macrosociology in the boxes on pages 134 and 140–1.

We examined the link between everyday social interactions and larger social structures from a theoretical standpoint in chapter 4, 'Theoretical Thinking in Sociology', pp. 122–3.

Non-verbal communication

Social interaction requires numerous forms of **non-verbal communication** – the exchange of information and meaning through facial expressions, gestures and movements of the body. Non-verbal communication is sometimes referred to as 'body language', but this is misleading because we characteristically use such non-verbal cues to eliminate or expand on what is said with words.

'Face', gestures and emotion

One major aspect of non-verbal communication is the facial expression of emotion. Paul Ekman and his colleagues have developed what they call the Facial Action Coding System (FACS) for describing movements of the facial muscles that give rise to particular expressions (Ekman and Friesen 1978). By this means, they have tried to inject some precision into an area notoriously open to inconsistent or contradictory interpretations – for there is little agreement about how emotions are to be identified and classified. Charles Darwin, the originator of evolutionary theory, claimed that basic modes of emotional expression are the same in all human beings. Although some have disputed the claim, Ekman's research among people from widely different cultural backgrounds seems to confirm this. Ekman and Friesen carried out a study of an isolated community in New Guinea, whose members had previously had

These photographs by Paul Ekman of facial expression from a tribesman in an isolated community in New Guinea helped to test the idea that basic modes of emotional expression are the same among all people. Here the instructions were to show how your face would look if you were a person in a story and (A) your friend had come and you were happy; (B) your child had died; (C) you were angry and about to fight; and (D) you saw a dead pig that had been lying there a long time.

virtually no contact with outsiders. When they were shown pictures of facial expressions expressing six emotions (happiness, sadness, anger, disgust, fear, surprise), the New Guineans were able to identify these emotions.

According to Ekman, the results of his own and similar studies of different peoples support the view that the facial expression of emotion and its interpretation are innate in human beings. He acknowledges that his evidence does not conclusively demonstrate this, and it may be that widely shared cultural learning experiences are involved; however, his conclusions are supported by other types of research. I. Eibl-Eibesfeldt (1973) studied six children born deaf and blind to see how far their facial expressions were the same as those of sighted, hearing individuals in particular emotional situations. He found that the children smiled when

engaged in obviously pleasurable activities, raised their eyebrows in surprise when sniffing at an object with an unaccustomed smell and frowned when repeatedly offered a disliked object. Since they could not have seen other people behaving in these ways, it seems that these responses must have been innately determined. Using the FACS, Ekman and Friesen identified a number of the discrete facial muscle actions in newborn infants that are also found in adult expressions of emotion. Infants seem, for example, to produce facial expressions similar to the adult expression of disgust (pursing the lips and frowning) in response to sour tastes.

But although the facial expression of emotion seems to be partly innate, individual and cultural factors influence what exact form facial movements take and the contexts in which they are deemed appropriate. How people smile, for example, the precise movement of the lips and other facial muscles, and how fleeting the smile is all vary between cultures.

There are no gestures or bodily postures that have been shown to characterize all, or even most, cultures. In some societies, for instance, people nod when they mean no, the opposite of Anglo-American practice. Gestures that Europeans and Americans tend to use a great deal, such as pointing, seem not to exist among certain peoples (Bull 1983). Similarly, a straightened forefinger placed at the centre of the cheek and rotated is used in parts of Italy as a gesture of praise, but appears to be unknown elsewhere. Like facial expressions, gestures and bodily posture are continually used to fill out utterances, as well as conveying meanings when nothing is actually said. All three can be used to joke, show irony or show scepticism.

The non-verbal impressions that we convey often inadvertently indicate that what we say is not quite what we mean. Blushing is perhaps the most obvious example of how physical indicators can contradict our stated meanings. But there are many more subtle signs that can be picked up by other people. As an example, a trained eye can often detect deceit by studying non-verbal cues. Sweating, fidgeting, staring or shifting eyes, and facial expressions held for a long time (genuine facial expressions tend to evaporate after four or five seconds) could indicate that a person is being deceptive. Thus, we use facial expressions and bodily gestures of other people to add to what they communicate verbally and to check how far they are sincere in what they say and whether we can trust them.

Non-verbal communication and gender

Is there a gender dimension to everyday social interaction? There are reasons to believe that there is. Because interactions are shaped by the larger social context, it is not surprising that both verbal and non-verbal communication may be perceived and expressed differently by men and women. Understandings of gender and gender roles are greatly influenced by social factors and are related broadly to issues of power and status in society. These dynamics are evident even in standard interactions in daily life. Take as an example one of the most common non-verbal expressions – eye contact. Individuals use eye contact in a wide variety of ways, often to catch someone's attention or to begin a social interaction. In societies where men on the whole dominate women in both public and private life, men may feel more free than women to make eye contact with strangers.

A particular form of eye contact – staring – illustrates the contrasts in meaning between men and women of identical forms of non-verbal communication. A man who stares at a woman can be seen as acting in a 'natural' or 'innocent' way; if the woman is uncomfortable, she can evade the gaze by looking away or choosing not to sustain the interaction. On the other hand, a woman who stares at a man is often regarded as behaving in a suggestive or sexually leading manner. Taken individually, such cases may seem inconsequential; when viewed collectively, they help reinforce patterns of gender inequality (Burgoon et al. 1996).

There are other gender differences in non-verbal communication as well. Studies have shown that the way that men tend to sit is more relaxed than women. Men tend to lean back with their legs open, whereas women tend to have a more closed body position, sitting upright, with their hands in their lap and their legs crossed. Women tend to stand closer to the person they are talking to than men; and men make physical contact with women during conversation far more often than the other way around (women are generally expected to view this as normal). Studies have also shown that women tend to show their emotions more obviously (through facial expressions), and that they seek and break eye contact more often than men. Sociolo-gists have argued that these seemingly small-scale micro-level interactions rein-force the wider macro-level inequality in our society. Men control more space when standing and sitting than women because they tend to stand further away from the person they are talking to, and because they tend to sprawl when sitting, and they dem-onstrate control through more frequent physical contact. Women, it has been argued, seek approval through eye contact and facial expression; when men make eye contact, a woman is more likely to look away than another man. Thus, it is argued, micro-level studies of non-verbal forms of communication provide subtle cues which demonstrate men's power over women in wider society (Young 1990).

Women and men in public

As we saw in chapter 1, *microsociology*, the study of everyday behaviour in situations of face-to-face interaction, and *macrosociology*, the study of the broader features of society like class or gender hierarchies, are closely connected (Knorr-Cetina and Cicourel 1981; Giddens 1984). In this box we look at an example of how an event that may seem to be a prime example of microsociology – a woman walking down the street is verbally harassed by a group of men – is linked to the bigger issues that make up macrosociology.

In her study, *Passing By: Gender and Public Harassment* (1995), Carol Brooks Gardner found that in various settings – most famously, the edge of construction sites – these types of unwanted interaction occur as something women frequently experience as abusive.

Although the harassment of a single woman might be analysed in micro-sociological terms by looking at a single interaction, it is not fruitful to view it that simply. Such harassment is typical of street talk involving men and women who are strangers (Gardner 1995). And these kinds of interaction cannot simply be understood without also looking at the larger background of gender hierarchy in society. In this way we can see how micro- and macro-analysis are connected. For example, Gardner linked the harassment of women by men to the larger system of gender inequality, represented by male privilege in public spaces, women's physical vulnerability and the omnipresent threat of rape.

Without making this link between micro- and macrosociology, we can only have a limited understanding of these interactions. It might seem as though these types of interaction are isolated instances or that they could be eliminated by teaching people good manners. Understanding the link between micro and macro helps us see that in order to attack the problem at its root cause, one would need to focus on eliminating the forms of gender inequality that give rise to such interactions.

The social rules of interaction

Although we routinely use non-verbal cues in our own behaviour and in making sense of the behaviour of others, much of our interaction is done through talk – casual verbal exchange – carried on in informal conversations with others. It has always been accepted by sociologists that language is fundamental to social life. Recently, however, an approach has been developed that is specifically concerned with how people use language in the ordinary contexts of everyday life.

Ethnomethodology is the study of the 'ethnomethods' – the folk, or lay, methods – people use to *make sense* of what others do, and particularly of what they say. This term was coined by Harold Garfinkel, whose work is discussed below. We all apply these methods, normally without having to give any conscious attention to them. Often we can only make sense of what is said in conversation if we know the social context, which does not appear in the words themselves. Take the following conversation (Heritage 1985):

> A: I have a 14-year-old son.
> B: Well, that's all right.
> A: I also have a dog.
> B: Oh, I'm sorry.

What do you think is happening here? What is the relation between the speakers? What if you were told that this is a conversation between a prospective tenant and a landlord? The conversation then becomes sensible: some landlords accept children but don't permit their tenants to keep pets. Yet if we don't know the social context, the responses of individual B seem to bear no relation to the statements of A. *Part* of the sense is in the words, and *part* is in the way in which the meaning emerges from the social context.

Shared understandings

The most inconsequential forms of daily talk presume complicated, shared knowledge brought into play by those speaking. In fact, our small talk is so complex that it has so far proved impossible to programme even the most sophisticated computers to converse convincingly with human beings for very long. The words used in ordinary talk do not always have precise meanings, and we 'fix' what we want to say through the unstated assumptions that back it up. If Maria asks Tom: 'What did you do yesterday?' there is no obvious answer suggested by the words in the question themselves. A day is a long time, and it would be logical for Tom to answer: 'Well, at 7:16, I woke up. At 7:18, I got out of bed, went to the bathroom and started to brush my teeth. At 7:19, I turned on the shower . . . '. We understand the type of response the question calls for by knowing Maria, what sort of activities she and Tom consider relevant, and what Tom usually does on a particular day of the week, among other things.

Garfinkel's experiments

The 'background expectancies' with which we organize ordinary conversations were highlighted by some experiments Harold Garfinkel (1963) undertook with student volunteers. The students were asked to engage a friend or relative in conversation and to insist that casual remarks or general comments be actively pursued to make their meaning precise. If someone said, 'Have a nice day', the student was to respond, 'Nice in what sense, exactly?' 'Which part of the day do you mean?' and so forth. One of the exchanges that resulted ran as follows (S is the friend, E the student volunteer):

S: How are you?
E: How am I in regard to what? My health, my finance, my school work, my peace of mind, my . . . ?
S: [red in the face and suddenly out of control]: Look! I was just trying to be polite. Frankly, I don't give a damn how you are.

Why do people get so upset when apparently minor conventions of talk are not followed? The answer is that the stability and meaningfulness of our daily social lives depend on the sharing of unstated cultural assumptions about what is said and why. If we weren't able to take these for granted, meaningful communication would be impossible. Any question or contribution to a conversation would have to be followed by a massive 'search procedure' of the sort Garfinkel's subjects were told to initiate, and interaction would simply break down. What seem at first sight to be unimportant conventions of talk, therefore, turn out to be fundamental to the very fabric of social life, which is why their breach is so serious.

Note that in everyday life, people on occasion deliberately feign ignorance of unstated knowledge. This may be done to rebuff the others, poke fun at them, cause embarrassment or call attention to a double meaning in what was said. Consider, for example, this classic exchange between parent and teenager:

P: Where are you going?
T: Out.
P: What are you going to do?
T: Nothing.

The responses of the teenager are effectively the opposite of those of the volunteers in Garfinkel's experiments. Rather than pursuing enquiries where this is not normally done, the teenager declines to provide appropriate answers at all – essentially saying, 'Mind your own business!'

The first question might elicit a different response from another person in another context:

A: Where are you going?
B: I'm going quietly round the bend.

B deliberately misreads A's question in order ironically to convey worry or frustration. Comedy and joking thrive on such deliberate misunderstandings of the unstated assumptions involved in talk. There is nothing threatening about this so long as the parties concerned recognize that the intent is to provoke laughter.

'Interactional vandalism'

We have already seen that conversations are one of the main ways in which our daily lives are maintained in a stable and coherent manner. We feel most comfortable when the tacit conventions of small talk are adhered to; when they are breached, we can feel threatened, confused and insecure. In most everyday talk, conversants are carefully attuned to the cues being given by others – such as changes in intonation, slight pauses or gestures – in order to facilitate conversation smoothly. By being mutually aware, conversants 'cooperate' in opening and closing interactions, and in taking turns to speak. Interactions in which one party is conversationally 'uncooperative', however, can give rise to tensions.

Garfinkel's students created tense

Hallo, I'm Jeff... I'm your customer today... we'd both like mineral water to start and a menu. My particular special is coq au vin and we will not be needing a wine list. We certainly hope to enjoy our meal and should we need anything, we'll certainly let you know.

5.4 Many of the 'rules' of everyday conversation become obvious only when someone breaks them.

situations by intentionally undermining conversational rules as part of a sociological experiment. But what about situations in the real world in which people 'make trouble' through their conversational practices? One US study investigated verbal interchanges between pedestrians and street people in New York City to understand why such interactions are often seen as problematic by passers-by. The researchers used a technique called **conversation analysis** to compare a selection of street interchanges with samples of everyday talk. Conversation analysis is a methodology that examines all facets of a conversation for meaning – from the smallest filler words (such as 'um' and 'ah') to the precise timing of interchanges (including pauses, interruptions and overlaps).

The study looked at interactions between black men – many of whom were homeless, alcoholic or drug-addicted – and white women who passed by them on the street. The men would often try to initiate conversations with passing women by calling out to them, paying them compliments or asking them questions. But something 'goes wrong' in these conversations, because the women rarely respond as they would in a normal interaction. Even though the men's comments are seldom hostile in tone, the women tend to quicken their step and stare fixedly ahead. The following shows attempts by Mudrick, a black man in his late fifties, to engage women in conversation (Duneier and Molotch 1999):

> [Mudrick] begins this interaction as a white woman, who looks about 25, approaches at a steady pace:
> 1   *Mudrick*: I love you baby.
>   *She crosses her arms and quickens her walk, ignoring the comment.*
> 2   *Mudrick*: Marry me.
>   *Next, it is two white women, also probably in their mid-twenties:*
> 3   *Mudrick*: Hi girls, you all look very nice today. You have some money? Buy some books.
>   *They ignore him. Next, it is a young black woman:*
> 4   *Mudrick*: Hey pretty. Hey pretty.
>   *She keeps walking without acknowledging him.*
> 5   *Mudrick*: 'Scuse me. 'Scuse me. I know you hear me.
>   *Then he addresses a white woman in her thirties:*
> 6   *Mudrick*: I'm watching you. You look nice, you know.
>   *She ignores him.*

Negotiating smooth 'openings' and 'closings' to conversations is a fundamental requirement for urban civility. These crucial aspects of conversation were highly problematic between the men and women. When the women resisted the men's attempts at opening a conversation, the men ignored the women's resistance and persisted. Similarly, if the men succeeded in opening a conversation, they often refused to respond to cues from the women to close the conversation once it had got under way:

1 *Mudrick*: Hey pretty.
2 *Woman*: Hi how you doin'.
3 *Mudrick*: You alright?
4 *Mudrick*: You look very nice you know. I like how you have your hair pinned.
5 *Mudrick*: You married?
6 *Woman*: Yeah.
7 *Mudrick*: Huh?
8 *Woman*: Yeah.
9 *Mudrick*: Where the rings at?
10 *Woman*: I have it home.
11 *Mudrick*: Y'have it home?
12 *Woman*: Yeah.
13 *Mudrick*: Can I get your name?
14 *Mudrick:* My name is Mudrick, what's yours?
She does not answer and walks on.
(Duneier and Molotch 1999)

In this instance, Mudrick made nine out of the fourteen utterances that comprised the interaction to initiate the conversation and to elicit further responses from the woman. From the transcript alone, it is quite evident that the woman is not interested in talking, but when conversation analysis is applied to the tape recording, her reluctance becomes even clearer. The woman delays all of her responses – even when she does give them, while Mudrick replies immediately, his comments sometimes overlapping hers. Timing in conversations is a very precise indicator; delaying a response by even a fraction of a second is adequate in most everyday interactions to signal the desire to change the course of a conversation. By betraying these tacit rules of sociability, Mudrick was practising conversation in a way that was 'technically rude'. The woman, in return, was also 'technically rude' in ignoring Mudrick's repeated attempts to engage her in talk. It is the 'technically rude' nature of these street interchanges that make them problematic for passers-by to handle. When standard cues for opening and closing conversations are not adhered to, individuals feel a sense of profound and inexplicable insecurity.

The term **interactional vandalism** describes cases like these, in which a subordinate person breaks the tacit rules of everyday interaction that are of value to the more powerful. The men on the street often conform to everyday forms of speech in their interactions with one another, local shopkeepers, the police, relatives and acquaintances. But when they choose to, they subvert the tacit conventions for everyday talk in a way that leaves passers-by disoriented. Even more than physical assaults or vulgar verbal abuse, interactional vandalism leaves victims unable to articulate what has happened.

This study of interactional vandalism provides another example of the two-way links between micro-level interactions and forces that operate on the macro-level. To the men on the street, the white women who ignore their attempts at conversation appear distant, cold and bereft of sympathy – legitimate 'targets' for such interactions. The women, meanwhile, may often take the men's behaviour as proof that they are indeed dangerous and best avoided. Interactional vandalism is closely tied up with overarching class, gender and racial structures. The fear and anxiety generated in such mundane interactions help to constitute the outside statuses and forces that, in turn, influence the interactions themselves. Interactional vandalism is part of a self-reinforcing system of mutual suspicion and incivility.

Response cries

Some kinds of utterance are not talk but consist of muttered exclamations, or what Goffman (1981) has called **response cries**. Consider Lucy, who exclaims, 'Oops!' after knocking over a glass of water. 'Oops!' seems to be merely an uninteresting reflex response to a mishap, rather like blinking your eye when a person moves a hand sharply towards your face. It is not a reflex, however, as shown by the fact that people do not usually make the exclamation when alone. 'Oops!' is normally directed towards others present. The exclamation demonstrates to witnesses that the lapse is only minor and momentary, not something that should cast doubt on Lucy's command of her actions.

'Oops!' is used only in situations of minor failure, rather than in major accidents or calamities – which also demonstrates that the exclamation is part of our controlled management of the details of social life. Moreover, the word may be used by someone observing Lucy, rather than by Lucy herself, or it may be used to sound a warning to another. 'Oops!' is normally a curt sound, but the 'oo' may be prolonged in some situations. Thus, someone might extend the sound to cover a critical moment in performing a task. For instance, a parent may utter an extended 'Oops!' or 'Oopsadaisy!' when playfully tossing a child in the air. The sound covers the brief phase when the child may feel a loss of control, reassuring him and probably at the same time developing his understanding of response cries.

This may all sound very contrived and exaggerated. Why should we bother to analyse such an inconsequential utterance in this detail? Surely we don't pay as much attention to what we say as this example suggests? Of course we don't – on a conscious level. The crucial point, however, is that we take for granted an immensely complicated, continuous control of our appearance and actions. In situations of interaction, we are never expected just to be present on the scene. Others expect, as we expect of them, that we will display what Goffman calls 'controlled alertness'. A fundamental part of being human is continually demonstrating to others our competence in the routines of daily life.

THE FAR SIDE   By GARY LARSON

Basic lives

Ordinary life would be impossible if we had to think consciously about every daily routine.

Streetwise

Have you ever crossed to the other side of the street when you felt threatened by someone behind you or someone coming towards you? One sociologist who tried to understand simple interactions of this kind is Elijah Anderson. Anderson began by describing social interaction on the streets of two adjacent urban neighbourhoods in the United States. His book, *Streetwise: Race, Class, and Change in an Urban Community* (1990), found that studying everyday life sheds light on how social order is created by the individual building blocks of infinite micro-level interactions. He was particularly interested in understanding interactions when at least one party was viewed as threatening. Anderson showed that the ways many blacks and whites interact on the streets had a great deal to do with the structure of racial stereotypes, which is itself linked to the economic structure of society. In this way, he showed the link between micro-interactions and the larger macro-structures of society.

Anderson began by recalling Erving Goffman's description of how social roles and statuses come into existence in particular contexts or locations. Goffman (1959) wrote:

> When an individual enters the presence of others, they commonly seek to acquire information about him or bring into play information already possessed. . . . Information about the individual helps to define the situation, enabling others to know in advance what he will expect of them and they may expect of him.

Following Goffman's lead, Anderson (1990) asked what types of behavioural cues and signs make up the vocabulary of public interaction? He concluded:

Skin colour, gender, age, companions, clothing, jewellery, and the objects people carry help identify them, so that assumptions are formed and communication can occur. Movements (quick or slow, false or sincere, comprehensible or incomprehensible) further refine this public communication. Factors like time of day or an activity that 'explains' a person's presence can also affect in what way and how quickly the image of 'stranger' is neutralized. If a stranger cannot pass inspection and be assessed as 'safe', the image of predator may arise, and fellow pedestrians may try to maintain a distance consistent with that image.

Anderson showed that the people most likely to pass inspection are those who do not fall into commonly accepted stereotypes of dangerous persons: 'Children readily pass inspection, while women and white men do so more slowly, black women, black men, and black male teenagers most slowly of all.' In showing that interactional tensions derive from outside statuses such as race, class and gender, Anderson shows that we cannot develop a full understanding of the situation by looking at the micro-interactions themselves. This is how he makes the link between micro-interactions and macro-processes.

Anderson argues that people are 'streetwise' when they develop skills such as 'the art of avoidance' to deal with their felt vulnerability towards violence and crime. According to Anderson, whites who are not streetwise do not recognize the difference between different kinds of black men (e.g., between middle-class youths and gang members). They may also not know how to alter the number of paces to walk behind a 'suspicious' person or how to bypass 'bad blocks' at various times of day.

Studies such as Anderson's and Carol Brooks Gardner's (on p. 134) demonstrate how microsociology is useful in illuminating the broad institutional patterns that are the content of macrosociology. Face-to-face interaction is clearly the main basis of all forms of social organization, no matter how large-scale. We could not build up a full account of gender and race in our society from these studies alone, yet we could certainly contribute significantly to understanding these issues better. In later chapters, we will see further examples of how interaction in micro-contexts affects larger social processes, and how macro-systems in turn influence more confined settings of social life.

Face, body and speech in interaction

Let us summarize at this point what we have learned so far. Everyday interaction depends on subtle relationships between what we convey with our faces and bodies and what we express in words. We use the facial expressions and bodily gestures of other people to fill in what they communicate verbally and to check if they are sincere in what they say. Mostly without realizing it, each of us keeps a tight and continuous control over facial expression, bodily posture and movement in the course of our daily interaction with others.

Face, bodily management and speech, then, are used to convey certain meanings and to hide others. We also organize our activities in the *contexts* of social life to achieve the same ends, as we shall now see.

Encounters

In many social situations, we engage in what Goffman calls **unfocused interaction** with others. Unfocused interaction takes place whenever individuals exhibit mutual awareness of one another's presence. This is usually the case anywhere that large numbers of people are assembled together, as on a busy street, in a theatre crowd or at a party. When people are in the presence of others, even if they do not directly talk to them, they continually communicate non-verbally through their posture and facial and physical gestures.

Focused interaction occurs when individuals directly attend to what others say or do. Social interaction will often involve both focused and unfocused exchanges. Goffman calls an instance of focused interaction an **encounter**, and much of our day-to-day life consists of encounters with other people – family, friends, colleagues – frequently occurring against the background of unfocused interaction with others present on the scene. Small talk, seminar discussions, games and routine face-to-face contacts (with ticket attendants, waiters, shop assistants and so forth) are all examples of encounters.

Encounters always need 'openings', which indicate that civil inattention is being discarded. When strangers meet and begin to talk at a party, the moment of ceasing civil inattention is always risky, since misunderstandings can easily occur about the nature of the encounter being established (Goffman 1971). Hence, the making of eye contact may first be ambiguous and tentative. The person who is looking to make eye contact can then act as though he had made no direct move if the overture is not accepted. In focused interaction, each person communicates as much by facial expression and gesture as by the words actually exchanged. Goffman distinguishes between the expressions individuals 'give' and those they 'give off'. The first are the words and facial expressions people use to produce certain impressions on others. The second are the clues that others may spot to

check their sincerity or truthfulness. For instance, a restaurant owner listens with a polite smile to the statements that customers give about how much they enjoyed their meals. At the same time, she is noting the signals the customers give off – how pleased they seemed to be while eating the food, whether a lot was left over, and the tone of voice they use to express their satisfaction, for example.

Waiters and other workers in the service industries are, of course, told to smile and be polite in their social interaction with customers. In a famous study of the airline industry, Arlie Hochschild describes this 'emotional labour'.

> Arlie Hochschild's account of how air stewardesses are trained to interact with passengers was discussed in chapter 1, 'What is Sociology?', pp. 23–4.

Impression management

Goffman and other writers on social interaction often use notions from the theatre in their analyses. The concept of **social role**, for example, originated in a theatrical setting. Roles are socially defined expectations that a person in a given **status**, or **social position**, follows. To be a teacher is to hold a specific position; the teacher's role consists of acting in specified ways towards her pupils. Goffman sees social life as though played out by actors on a stage – or on many stages, because how we act depends on the roles we are playing at a particular time. People are sensitive to how they are seen by others and use many forms of **impression management** to compel others to react to them in the ways they wish. Although we may sometimes do this in a calculated way, usually it is among the things we do without conscious attention. When Philip attends a business meeting, he wears a suit and tie and is on his best behaviour; that evening, when relaxing with friends at a football game, he wears jeans and a sweatshirt and tells a lot of jokes. This is impression management.

As we just noted above, the social roles that we adopt are highly dependent on our social status. A person's social status can be different depending on the social context. For instance, as a 'student', you have a certain status and are expected to act a certain way when you are around your professors. As a 'son or daughter', you have a different status from a student, and society (especially your parents) has different expectations for you. Likewise, as a 'friend', you have an entirely different position in the social order, and the roles you adopt would change accordingly. Obviously, a person has many statuses at the same time. Sociologists refer to the group of statuses that you occupy as a **status set**.

Sociologists also like to distinguish between ascribed status and achieved status. An **ascribed status** is one that you are 'assigned' based on biological factors such as race, sex or age. Thus, your ascribed statuses could be 'white', 'female' and 'teenager'. An **achieved status** is one that is earned through an individual's own effort. Your achieved statuses could be 'graduate', 'athlete' or 'employee'. While we may like to believe that it is our achieved statuses that are most important, society may not agree. In any society, some statuses have priority over all other statuses and generally determine a person's overall position in society. Sociologists refer to this as a **master status** (Hughes 1945;

Becker 1963). The most common master statuses are those based on gender and race. Sociologists have shown that in an encounter, one of the first things that people notice about one another is gender and race (Omi and Winant 1994). As we shall see shortly, both race and gender strongly shape our social interactions.

Front and back regions

Much of social life, Goffman suggested, can be divided into front regions and back regions. **Front regions** are social occasions or encounters in which individuals act out formal roles; they are 'onstage performances'. Teamwork is often involved in creating front-region performances. Two prominent politicians in the same party may put on an elaborate show of unity and friendship before the television cameras, even though each privately detests the other. A wife and husband may take care to conceal their quarrels from their children, preserving a front of harmony, only to fight bitterly once the children are safely tucked up in bed.

The **back regions** are where people assemble the props and prepare themselves for interaction in the more formal settings. Back regions resemble the backstage of a theatre or the off-camera activities of filmmaking. When they are safely behind the scenes, people can relax and give vent to feelings and styles of behaviour they keep in check when on front stage. (In the box on p. 146–7 we look at how the sociologist Spencer Cahill applied Goffman's dramaturgical analysis to study back-region social interaction in public toilets.) Back regions permit 'profanity, open sexual remarks, elaborate griping . . . rough informal dress, "sloppy" sitting and standing posture, use of dialect or substandard speech, mumbling and shouting, playful aggressiveness and "kidding," inconsiderateness for the other in minor but potentially symbolic acts, minor self-involvement such as humming, whistling, chewing, nibbling, belching and flatulence' (Goffman 1973). Thus, a waitress may be the soul of quiet courtesy when serving a customer, but become loud and aggressive once behind the swing doors of the kitchen. Probably few people would continue to patronize restaurants if they could see all that goes on in the kitchens.

> Goffman has made many important contributions to the study of social interaction. His writings on stigma and spoiled identities are discussed in chapter 8, p. 269.

"Hmmm... what shall I wear today...?"

Adopting roles: intimate examinations

For an example of collaboration in impression management that also borrows from the theatre, let's look at one particular study in some detail. James Henslin and Mae Biggs studied a specific, highly delicate type of encounter: a woman's visit to a gynaecologist (1971, 1997). At the time of the study most pelvic examinations were carried out by male doctors, and hence the experience was (and sometimes still is) fraught with potential ambiguities and embarrassment for both parties. Men and women in the West are socialized to think of the genitals as the most private part of the body, and seeing, and particularly touching, the genitals of another person is ordinarily associated with intimate sexual encounters. Some women feel so worried by the prospect of a pelvic examination that they refuse to visit the doctor, male or female, even when they suspect there is a strong medical reason to do so.

Henslin and Biggs analysed material collected by Biggs, a trained nurse, from a large number of gynaecological examinations. They interpreted what they found as having several typical stages. Adopting a dramaturgical metaphor, they suggested that each phase could be treated as a distinct scene, in which the parts played by the actors alter as the episode unfolds. In the prologue, the woman enters the waiting room preparing to assume the role of patient and temporarily discarding her outside identity. Called into the consulting room, she adopts the 'patient' role, and the first scene opens. The doctor assumes a business-like, professional manner and treats the patient as a proper and competent person, maintaining eye contact and listening politely to what she has to say. If he decides an examination is called for, he tells her so and leaves the room; scene one is over.

As he leaves, the nurse comes in. She is an important stagehand in the main scene shortly to begin. She soothes any worries that the patient might have, acting as both a confidante – knowing some of the 'things women have to put up with' – and a collaborator in what is to follow. Crucially, the nurse helps alter the patient from a person to a 'non-person' for the vital scene – which features a body, part of which is to be scrutinized, rather than a complete human being. In Henslin and Biggs's study, the nurse not only supervises the patient's undressing, but takes over aspects that normally the patient would control. Thus, she takes the patient's clothes and folds them. Most women wish their underwear to be out of sight when the doctor returns, and the nurse makes sure that this is so. She guides the patient to the examining table and covers most of her body with a sheet before the physician returns.

The central scene now opens, with the nurse as well as the doctor taking part. The presence of the nurse helps ensure that the interaction between the doctor and the patient is free of sexual overtones and also provides a legal witness should the physician be charged with unprofessional conduct. The examination proceeds as though the personality of the patient were absent; the sheet across her separates the genital area from the rest of her body, and her position does not allow her to watch the examination itself. Apart from any specific medical queries, the doctor ignores her, sitting on a low stool, out of her line of vision. The patient collaborates in becoming a temporary non-person, not initiating conversation and keeping any movements to a minimum.

In the interval between this and the final scene, the nurse again plays the role of stagehand, helping the patient to become a full person once more. After the doctor has left the room, the two may again engage in conversation, the patient expressing relief that the examination is over. Having dressed and re-groomed herself, the patient is ready to face the concluding scene. The doctor re-enters the room and, in discussing the results of the examination, again treats the patient as a complete and responsible person. Resuming his polite, professional manner, he conveys that his reactions to her are in no way altered by the intimate contact with her body. The epilogue is played out when she leaves the doctor's surgery, taking up again her identity in the outside world. The patient and the doctor have thus collaborated in such a way as to manage the interaction and the impression each participant forms of the other.

Personal space

There are cultural differences in the definition of **personal space.** In Western culture, people usually maintain a distance of at least three feet when engaged in focused interaction with others; when standing side by side, they may stand more closely together. In the Middle East, people often stand closer to one another than is thought acceptable in the West. Westerners visiting that part of the world are likely to find themselves disconcerted by this unexpected physical proximity.

Edward T. Hall, who has worked extensively on non-verbal communication, distinguishes four zones of personal space.

Intimate distance, of up to one and a half feet, is reserved for very few social contacts. Only those involved in relationships in which regular bodily touching is permitted, such as lovers or parents and children, operate within this zone of private space. *Personal distance*, from one and a half to four feet, is the normal spacing for encounters with friends and close acquaintances. Some intimacy of contact is permitted, but this tends to be strictly limited. *Social distance*, from four to twelve feet, is the zone usually maintained in formal settings such as interviews. The fourth zone is that of *public distance*, beyond twelve feet, preserved by those who are performing to an audience.

In ordinary interaction, the most fraught zones are those of intimate and personal distance. If these zones are invaded, people try to recapture their space. We may stare at the intruder as if to say, 'Move away!' or elbow him aside. When people are forced into proximity closer than they deem desirable, they might create a kind of physical boundary; a reader at a crowded library desk might physically demarcate a private space by stacking books around its edges (Hall 1969, 1973).

Here, gender issues also play a role, in much the same way as in other forms of non-verbal communication. Men have traditionally enjoyed greater freedom than women in the use of space, including movement into the personal space of women who may not necessarily be intimates or even close acquaintances. A man who guides a woman by the arm when they walk together, or who places a hand on her lower back when showing her through a door, may be doing so as a gesture of friendly care or politeness. The reverse phenomenon, however – a woman entering a man's personal space – is often construed as flirtation or a sexual advance. New laws and standards regarding sexual harassment in many Western countries seek to protect people's personal space – both men and women – from unwanted touching or contact by others.

Many of the issues discussed in this chapter relate to the way in which our bodies are shaped by the society we live in. The relationship between sociology and the body is discussed in chapter 8, 'Health, Illness and Disability'.

Using your sociological imagination: backstage behaviour in public toilets

The American sociologist Spencer Cahill led a research team which studied social interaction in the public toilets (or 'bathrooms') of shopping centres, college campuses, bars and restaurants. Here, we look at how Cahill uses Goffman's description of front and back regions in his study. Cahill found that what Goffman (1959) called entire 'performance teams' would sometimes retreat into public toilets to conceal embarrassment when a collective performance goes wrong.

The following conversation between three young women was recorded in the bathroom of a student centre on a college campus. Although the incident that led to this conversation was not observed, it obviously resulted in such paralysing embarrassment.

A: That was sooo embarrassing! I can't believe that just happened. [general laughter]

B: He must think we are the biggest bunch of losers.

A: I can't believe I just screamed loud enough for everyone to hear.

C: It really wasn't all that loud. I'm sure he didn't hear you.

B: ___, we didn't see him right away, and I did try to tell you but you were so busy talking that I . . .

A: I can't believe that just happened. I feel like such an asshole.

B: Don't worry 'bout it. At least he knows who you are now. Are you ready?

A: I'm so embarrassed. What if he's still out there?

B: You're going to have to see him at some point.

In addition to concealing temporary loss of control, these defensive strategies also buy individuals and performance teams time, as this example illustrates, in which to gather themselves together before once again facing the front stage audience. . .

As Goffman (1959) observed, performance teams routinely use backstage regions to gather themselves together [and] discuss . . . problems involved in the staging of a collective performance: 'Here the team can run through its performance, checking for offending expressions when no audience is present to be affronted by them; here poor members of the team . . . can be schooled or dropped from the performance.'

In the conversation reproduced above, for example, B and C not only attempt to belittle the discrediting implications of A's earlier actions, but B also schools A in the art of staging collective performances. If, according to B, A had paid more attention to the other team members' directional cues, she could have avoided this embarrassing incident.

In addition to retreating into public bathrooms after the failure of a collective performance, performance teams also retire to public bathrooms in order to take preventive measures against such an occurrence. Here the team may agree upon collusive signals, rehearse their planned performance and exchange strategic information. In bathrooms in bars, for example, performance teams were sometimes overheard discussing the planned targets of members' erotic overtures, the overtures they had received, the source of such overtures, and their likely responses. By providing other members of a performance team with such strategic information, of course, an individual may prevent them from interfering with his or her personal project and may even enlist their aid in accomplishing it.

Sometimes, moreover, the backstage discussions that occur in public bathrooms are at least partially concerned with a team member's morale or that of the entire team. In the previously discussed conversation between the three young women, for example, B and C attempt to boost A's moral by both belittling the discrediting implications of her earlier actions and encouraging her to 'go on with the show'.

Source: Cahill et al. (1985)

Questions

1 Why is Goffman's dramaturgical account useful in analysing social interaction in public bathrooms?
2 Are the concepts of role adoption, civil inattention and personal space useful in studying social interaction in the public toilets of bars and restaurants?
3 What backstage areas do you regularly experience?

Interaction in time and space

Understanding how activities are distributed in time and space is fundamental to analysing encounters, and also to understanding social life in general. All interaction is situated – it occurs in a particular place and has a specific duration in time. Our actions over the course of a day tend to be 'zoned' in time as well as in space.

Thus, for example, most people spend a zone – say, from 9:00 a.m. to 5:00 p.m. – of their daily time working. Their weekly time is also zoned: They are likely to work on weekdays and spend weekends at home, altering the pattern of their activities on the weekend days. As we move through the temporal zones of the day, we are also often moving across space as well: to get to work, we may take a bus from one area of a city to another or perhaps commute in from the suburbs. When we analyse the contexts of social interaction, therefore, it is often useful to look at people's movements across *time-space*.

The concept of **regionalization** will help us understand how social life is zoned in time-space. Take the example of a private house. A modern house is regionalized into rooms, hallways and floors if there is more than one storey. These spaces are not just physically separate areas, but are zoned in time as well. The living rooms and kitchen are used most in the daylight hours, the bedrooms at night. The interaction that occurs in these regions is bound by both spatial and temporal divisions. Some areas of the house form back regions, with 'performances' taking place in the others. At times, the whole house can become a back region. Once again, this idea is beautifully captured by Goffman:

> Of a Sunday morning, a whole household can use the wall around its domestic establishment to conceal a relaxing slovenliness in dress and civil endeavor, extending to all rooms the informality that is usually restricted to kitchen and bedrooms. So, too, in American middle-class neighborhoods, on afternoons the line between children's playground and home may be defined as backstage by mothers, who pass along it wearing jeans, loafers, and a minimum of make-up. . . . And, of course, a region that is thoroughly established as a front region for the regular performance of a particular routine often functions as a back region before and after each performance, for at these times the permanent fixtures may undergo repairs, restoration, and rearrangement, or the performers may hold dress rehearsals. To see this we need only glance into a restaurant, or store, or home, a few minutes before these establishments are opened to us for the day. (Goffman 1973)

Clock time

In modern societies, the zoning of our activities is strongly influenced by **clock time.** Without clocks and the precise timing of activities, and thereby their coordination across space, industrialized societies could not exist (Mumford 1973). The measuring of time by clocks is today standardized across the globe, making possible the complex international transport systems and communications we now depend on. World standard time was first introduced in 1884 at a conference of nations held in Washington. The globe was then partitioned into twenty-four time zones, each one hour apart, and an exact beginning of the universal day was fixed.

Fourteenth-century monasteries were the first organizations to try to schedule the activities of their inmates precisely across the day and week. Today, there is virtually no group or organization that does not do so – the greater the number of people and resources involved, the more precise the scheduling must be. Eviatar Zerubavel (1979, 1982) demonstrated this in his study of the temporal structure of a large modern hospital. A hospital must operate on a 24-hour basis, and coordinating the staff and resources is a highly complex matter. For instance, the nurses work for one time period in ward A, another time period in ward B, and so on, and are also called on to alternate between day- and night-shift work. Nurses, doctors and other staff, plus the resources they need, must be integrated together both in time and in space.

Social life and the ordering of space and time

The Internet is another example of how closely forms of social life are bound up with our control of space and time. The Internet makes it possible for us to interact with people we never see or meet, in any corner of the world. Such technological change 'rearranges' space – we can interact with anyone without moving from our chair. It also alters our experience of time, because communication on the electronic highway is almost immediate. Until about fifty years ago, most communication across space required a duration of time. If you sent a letter to someone abroad, there was a time gap while the letter was carried by ship, train, truck or plane to the person to whom it was written.

People still write letters by hand today, of course, but instantaneous communication has become basic to our social world. Our lives would be almost unimaginable without it. We are so used to being able to switch on the TV and watch the news or make a phone call or send an email to a friend in another part of the world that it is hard for us to imagine what life would be like otherwise.

Everyday life in cultural and historical perspective

Some of the mechanisms of social interaction analysed by Goffman, Garfinkel and others seem to be universal. But much of Goffman's discussion of civil inattention and other kinds of interaction primarily concerns societies in which contact with strangers is commonplace. What about very small traditional societies, where there are no strangers and few settings in which more than a handful of people are together at any one time?

To see some of the contrasts between social interaction in modern and traditional societies, let's take as an example one of the least developed cultures in terms of technology remaining in the world: the !Kung (sometimes known as the Bushmen), who live in the Kalahari Desert area of Botswana and Namibia, in southern Africa (Lee 1968, 1969; the exclamation mark refers to a click sound one makes before pronouncing the name). Although their way of life is changing because of outside influences, their traditional patterns of social life are still evident.

The !Kung live in groups of some thirty or forty people, in temporary settlements near water holes. Food is scarce in their environment, and they must walk far and wide to find it. Such roaming takes up most of the average day. Women and children often stay back in the camp, but equally often the whole group spends the day walking. Members of the community will sometimes fan out over an area of up to a hundred square miles in the course of a day, returning to the camp at night to eat and sleep. The men may be alone or in groups of two or three for much of the day. There is one period of the year, however, when the routines of their daily activities change: the winter rainy season, when water is abundant and food much easier to come by. The everyday life of the !Kung during this period is centred around ritual and ceremonial activities, the preparation for and enactment of which is very time-consuming.

The members of most !Kung groups never see anyone they don't know reasonably well. Until contacts with the outside became more common in recent years, they had no word for 'stranger'. While the !Kung, particularly the males, may spend long periods of the day out of contact with others, in the community itself there is little opportunity for privacy. Families sleep in flimsy, open dwellings, with virtually all activities open to public view. No one has studied the !Kung with Goffman's observations on everyday life in mind, but it is easy to see that some aspects of his work have limited application to !Kung social life. There are few opportunities, for example, to create front and back regions. The closing off of different gatherings and encounters by the walls of rooms, separate buildings and the various neighbourhoods of cities common in modern societies are remote from the activities of the !Kung.

The form of social interaction of the !Kung is very different from the interaction that takes place in the modern city. City life forces us to interact almost constantly with strangers.

A famous account of social interaction in the city was given by one of the early founders of sociology, Georg Simmel, whose work is discussed in chapter 21, 'Cities and Urban Spaces', p. 896.

Globalization and everyday life: international tourism

Have you ever had a face-to-face conversation with someone from another country? Or connected to an overseas website? Have you ever travelled to another part of the world? If you answered 'yes' to any of these questions, you have witnessed the effects of globalization on social interaction. Globalization – a relatively recent phenomenon – has changed both the frequency and the nature of interactions between people of different nations. The historical sociologist Charles Tilly, in fact, defines globalization in terms of these changes. According to Tilly, 'globalization means an increase in the geographic range of locally consequential social interactions' (Tilly 1995). In other words, with globalization, a greater proportion of our interactions come to involve, directly or indirectly, people from other countries.

What are the characteristics of social interactions that take place between individuals of different nations? Important contributions to the study of this problem have been made by those working in the area of the sociology of tourism. Sociologists of tourism note that globalization has greatly expanded the possibilities for international travel, both by encouraging an interest in other countries and by facilitating the movement of tourists across international borders. Between 1982 and 2002, the number of visits to the UK made by overseas residents doubled and spending on these visits more than tripled. These visitors now pump almost £12 billion a year into the UK economy. Britons are also travelling the world in record numbers (Office of National Statistics 2004b).

High levels of international tourism, of course, translate into an increase in the number of face-to-face interactions between people of different countries. The sociologist John Urry (1990,

2001) argues that the 'tourist gaze' – the expectation on the part of the tourist that he or she will have 'exotic' experiences while travelling abroad – shapes many of these interactions. Urry compares the tourist gaze to Foucault's conception of the medical gaze (discussed in chapter 8, pp. 260–1). Urry argues that the tourist gaze is just as socially organized by professional experts, systematic in its application and as detached as the medical gaze, but this time it is organized in its search for 'exotic' experiences. These are experiences that violate our everyday expectations about how social interaction and interaction with the physical environment are supposed to proceed.

Britons travelling in the United States, for example, may delight in the fact that the Americans drive on the right-hand side of the road. At the same time, such behaviour is disconcerting to drivers from the UK. Our rules of the road are so ingrained that we experience systematic violations of those rules as strange, weird and exotic. Yet, as tourists, we take pleasure in this strangeness. In a sense, it is what we have paid money to see – along with the Empire State Building or the Eiffel Tower. Imagine how disappointed you would be if you were to travel to a different country only to find that it was almost exactly the same as the city or town in which you grew up.

Yet most tourists do not want their experiences to be *too* exotic. A popular destination for young, particularly US, travellers in Paris, for example, is a McDonald's restaurant. Some go to see if there is any truth to the line from Quentin Tarantino's movie *Pulp Fiction* that because the French use the metric system, McDonald's 'quarter pounder with cheese'

Brits abroad seeking out the familiar pleasures of burger and chips, or an all-day breakfast.

hamburgers are called 'Royales with cheese' (it is true, by the way). Britons travelling abroad often cannot resist eating and drinking in British- and Irish-style pubs. Sometimes such diversions are the result of curiosity, but often people enjoy the comfort of eating familiar food in a familiar setting. The contradictory demands for the exotic and the familiar are at the heart of the tourist gaze.

The tourist gaze may put strains on face-to-face interactions between tourists and locals. Locals who are part of the tourist industry may appreciate overseas travellers for the economic benefits they bring to the places they visit. Other locals may resent tourists for their demanding attitudes or for the overdevelopment that often occurs in popular tourist destinations. Tourists may interrogate locals about aspects of their everyday lives, such as their food, work and recreational habits; they may do this either to enhance their understanding of other cultures or to judge negatively those who are different from themselves.

As tourism increases with the march of globalization, sociologists will have to watch carefully to see what dominant patterns of interaction emerge between tourists and locals, and to determine, among other things, whether these interactions tend to be friendly or antagonistic.

The social construction of reality: the sociological debate

Within sociology, many different theoretical frameworks are used to explain social reality. These theories differ in their explanations of social phenomena, yet they share the assumption that social reality exists independently of people's talking about it or living in it. This assumption has been challenged by a broad body of sociological thought known as **social constructionism**.

Social constructivists believe that what individuals and society perceive and understand as reality is itself a *construction*, a creation of the social interaction of individuals and groups. Trying to 'explain' social reality is to overlook and to reify (regard as a given truth) the processes through which such reality is constructed. Therefore, social constructivists argue that sociologists need to document and analyse these processes and not simply be concerned with the concept of social reality they give rise to. Social constructionism has been seen as an important influence on the postmodern school of thought in sociology.

For more on postmodernism, see chapter 4, 'Theoretical Thinking in Sociology', pp. 114–17.

In their 1966 classic study, *The Social Construction of Reality*, sociologists Peter Berger and Thomas Luckmann examine common-sense knowledge – those things that individuals take for granted as real. They emphasize that these 'obvious' facts of social reality may differ among people from different cultures, and even among different people within the same culture. The task becomes an analysis of the *processes* by which individuals come to perceive what is 'real' to them as real.

Social constructivists apply the ideas of Berger and Luckmann to the investigation of social phenomena, to illuminate the ways in which members of society come to know and simultaneously create what is real. While social constructivists have examined such diverse topics as medicine and medical treatment, gender relations and emotions, much of their work has focused on social problems, such as the crime 'problem'.

The work of Aaron Cicourel (1968) provides an example of social constructionist research in the area of youth crime. Sometimes, data regarding rates and cases of youth crime are taken as given (i.e., real), and theories are created to explain the patterns observed in the data. For example, at first glance arrest and court data would seem to indicate that young people from single-parent families are more likely to commit delinquent acts than those from two-parent homes. Some sociologists have therefore developed explanations for this observed relationship: perhaps children from single-parent homes have less supervision, or perhaps they lack appropriate role models.

By contrast, Cicourel observed the *processes* involved in the arrest and classification of youths suspected of committing crimes; that is, he observed the creation of the 'official' crime data. He discovered that police procedures in the handling of young offenders rely on common-sense understandings of what young offenders are 'really like'.

For example, when youths from lower-class families were arrested, police were more likely to view their offences as results of poor supervision or a lack of proper role models, and would retain the young people in custody. Offenders from upper-class homes, however, were more likely to be released to their parents' care, where police and parents believed the young person could receive proper discipline. Thus, the practices of police serve formally to assign the label of 'young offender' more often to those from lower-class homes than to those from upper-class homes – even when the youths have committed similar offences. This assignment produces the very data which in turn confirm the relationships held by the common-sense views; for example, that young people from poor families are more likely to engage in crime. Cicourel's study shows that through interacting with other people in society, we transform our common-sense notions of reality into independent, 'objective' proof of their own validity.

> You will find more discussion of the construction of the crime 'problem' in chapter 19, 'Crime and Deviance'.

Social constructionism is not without its critics. Sociologists Steve Woolgar and Dorothy Pawluch argue that social constructivists aim to show the subjective creation of social reality, yet in doing so selectively view certain features as objective and others as constructed. For example, in analyses examining which young people become labelled as delinquent, social constructivists often argue that the initial behaviours reported for the young people are identical; therefore, any differences between those labelled as criminals and those avoiding such a label must be due to the construction of the label itself. Critics argue that social constructionism inconsistently presents the initial behaviours as objective, while arguing that the labelling process is subjective (Woolgar and Pawluch 1985).

Other sociologists have criticized social constructionism for its unwillingness to accept broader social forces as powerful influences on observable social outcomes. For example, some critics have argued that while reality may be a constructed perpetuation of common-sense beliefs, these beliefs themselves may be caused by existing social factors such as capitalism or patriarchy.

Ultimately, social constructionism offers a theoretical approach to understanding social reality that radically differs from most other sociological approaches. Rather than assuming that social reality objectively exists, social constructivists work to document and analyse the processes through which social reality is constructed, such that the construction then serves to confirm its own status as social reality.

Social interaction in cyberspace

In modern societies, in complete contrast to the !Kung, discussed on pp. 149–50 – as will be explored in the chapters that follow – we constantly interact with others whom we may never see or meet. Almost all of our everyday transactions, such as buying groceries or making a bank deposit, bring us into contact – but *indirect* contact – with people who may live thousands of miles away.

Now that email, instant messaging, online communities and chat rooms have become facts of life for many people in industrialized countries, what is the nature of these interactions, and what new complexities are emerging from them? Sceptics argue that indirect communication through email and the Internet contains a wealth of problems not found in face-to-face social interaction. As Katz et al. put it: 'To type is not to be human, to be in cyberspace is not to be real; all is pretence and alienation, a poor substitute for the real thing' (2001). In particular, supporters of this view argue that computer-mediated communication technology is too limited to prevent users hiding behind false identities (see box opposite). This also allows trickery, lechery, manipulation, emotional swindles and so on:

The problem lies in the nature of human communication. We think of it as a product of the mind, but it's done by bodies: faces move, voices intone, bodies sway, hands gesture. . . . On the Internet, the mind is present but the body is gone. Recipients get few clues to the personality and mood of the person, can only guess why messages are sent, what they mean, what responses to make. Trust is virtually out the window. It's a risky business. (Locke 2000)

Yet defenders of new technology argue that there are ways in which good or bad reputations can be built and trust can be established, so reducing the risks of online communication. One of the best known, and much discussed, trust systems in an online community is used by the auction site eBay (see box on p. 156).

Furthermore Internet enthusiasts argue that online communication has many inherent advantages that cannot be claimed by more traditional forms of interaction such as the telephone and face-to-face meetings. The human voice, for example, may be far superior in terms of expressing emotion and subtleties of meaning, but it can also convey information about the speaker's age, gender, ethnicity or social position – information that could be used to the speaker's disadvantage. Electronic communication, it is noted, masks all these identifying markers and ensures that attention focuses strictly on the content of the message. This can be a great advantage for women or other traditionally disadvantaged groups whose opinions are sometimes devalued in other settings (Pascoe 2000). Electronic interaction is often presented as liberating and empowering, since people can create their own online identities and speak more freely than they would elsewhere.

Using your sociological imagination: the problems of social interaction in cyberspace

The section below was taken from an article written in the early days of the Internet, but it reflects problems and raises questions that are still relevant today.

I 'met' Joan in the late spring of 1983, shortly after I first hooked my personal computer up to a modem and entered the strange new world of online communications. . . . Her 'handle' was 'Talkin' Lady'. According to the conventions of the medium, people have a (usually frivolous) handle when they're on 'open' channels with many users, but when two people choose to enter a private talk mode, they'll often exchange real information about themselves. I soon learned that her real name was Joan Sue Greene, and that she was a New York neuropsychologist in her late twenties, who had been severely disfigured in a car accident that was the fault of a drunken driver. The accident had killed her boyfriend. Joan herself spent a year in the hospital, being treated for brain damage, which affected both her speech and her ability to walk. Mute, confined to a wheelchair, and frequently suffering intense back and leg pain, Joan had at first been so embittered about her disabilities that she literally didn't want to live.

Then her mentor, a former professor at Johns Hopkins [University], presented her with a computer, a modem, and a year's subscription to CompuServe [the first online service to offer real-time chat] to be used specifically doing what Joan was doing – making friends online. At first, her handle had been 'Quiet Lady', in reference to her muteness. But Joan could type – which is, after all, how one 'talks' on a computer – and she had a sassy, bright, generous personality that blossomed in a medium where physicalness doesn't count. Joan became enormously popular, and her new handle, 'Talkin' Lady', was a reflection of her new sense of self. Over the next two years, she became a monumental online presence who served both as a support for other disabled women and as an inspiring stereotype-smasher to the able-bodied. Through her many intense friendships and (in some cases) her online romances, she changed the lives of dozens of women.

Thus it was a huge shock early this year when, through a complicated series of events, Joan was revealed as being not disabled at all. More to the point, Joan, in fact, was not a woman. She was really a man we'll call Alex – a prominent New York psychiatrist in his early fifties who was engaged in a bizarre, all-consuming experiment to see what it felt like to be female, and to experience the intimacy of female friendship.

Even those who barely knew Joan felt implicated – and somehow betrayed – by Alex's deception. Many of us online like to believe that we're a utopian community of the future, and Alex's experiment proved to us all that technology is no shield against deceit. We lost our innocence, if not our faith.

To some of Alex's victims – including a women who had an affair with the real-life Alex, after being introduced to him by Joan – the experiment was a 'mind rape', pure and simple. (Several people, in fact have tentatively explored the possibility of bringing charges against Alex as a psychiatrist, although the case is without precedent, to put it mildly.) To some other victims, Alex was not so much an impostor as a seeker whose search went out of control. (Several of those are attempting to continue a friendship with Alex – and, as one woman put it, 'to relate to the soul, not the sex of the person. The soul is the same as before.') Either way, this is a peculiarly modern story about a man who used some of our most up-to-date technology to play out some of our oldest assumptions about gender roles.

Source: Gelder (1996)

Questions

1 Are there important differences between social interactions in cyberspace compared with face-to-face meetings?
2 What are the advantages and disadvantages of online interaction compared with meeting people face to face?

Establishing trust in cyberspace: the eBay feedback system

Currently the largest, and one of the oldest (launched September 1995), person-to-person auction houses is eBay. By 2005 eBay was made up of more than 100 million people around the world who buy and sell products on the eBay websites. Remarkably, eBay offers no warranties or guarantees for any of the goods that are auctioned off – buyers and sellers assume all risks for the transaction, with eBay serving as a listing agency. It would seem to be a market ripe with the possibility of large-scale fraud and deceit, and yet the default rate for trades conducted through eBay is remarkably small. Both eBay and the participants in its market credit an institutionalized reputation system at the site – known as the Feedback Forum – for the very high rate of successful trades.

After every seller's or bidder's name is a number in parenthesis. In the case of a seller, the information is displayed as follows:

Seller name (265☆)

The number is a summary measure of a person's reputation in the eBay market. Registered users are allowed to post positive, negative and neutral comments about users with whom they have traded. Each positive comment is given a score of +1, each negative comment is given a score of −1, with neutral comments not affecting one's score in either direction. At certain levels, market participants are also awarded a colour star which marks the number of net positive comments they have received. . . .

One is able to contact the person via email by

clicking on the name; clicking on the number following someone's name leads to their full feedback profile. There one finds the full list of comments, with email links and ratings numbers for every evaluator as well (thus, one can explore the reputation of the evaluators just as one can for the evaluated). A typical positive comment might be 'Well packaged, fast delivery. Highly recommended. A+.' . . .

A high feedback rating is an extremely valuable asset. Many participants report that they are more willing to trade with someone with a high rating, or even that they will only trade with individuals with high ratings. In that sense, some traders are able to create a brand identity that increases their volume of sales or even the price at which they are able to sell items. . . . Even a few negative ratings can seriously damage a reputation, and so frequent traders are very careful about nurturing their rating by providing swift execution of honest trades. The potential damage of a negative comment is a subject of great concern among frequent participants. . . . One can choose to make one's entire feedback profile private, but this is a huge disadvantage in a market which relies on these reputations.

Source: Kollock (1999)

Internet sceptics have also argued that indirect, online communication encourages isolation and prevents real friendships from forming, but this does not seem to reflect the reality. A survey of Internet users carried out between 1995 and 2000 showed that, far from increasing social isolation, Internet usage is associated with significant and increased online and offline social interactions. The survey found that Internet users tend to communicate with others through other media – especially by the telephone – more than non-users do, meet face-to-face with friends more than non-users and interact with others more in general (Katz et al. 2001).

Conclusion: the compulsion of proximity?

Despite the rise in indirect communication, however, it seems that humans still value direct contact. People in business, for instance, continue to attend meetings, sometimes flying halfway around the world to do so, when it would seem much cheaper and more efficient to transact business through a conference call or video link. Family members could arrange 'virtual' reunions or holiday gatherings using electronic real-time communications, but we all recognize that they would lack the warmth and intimacy of face-to-face celebrations.

An explanation for this phenomenon comes from Deidre Boden and Harvey Molotch, who have studied what they call the **compulsion of proximity**: the need of individuals to meet with one another in situations of *co-presence*, or face-to-face interaction. People put themselves out to attend meetings, Boden and Molotch suggest, because situations of co-presence, for reasons documented by Goffman in his studies of interaction, supply much richer information about how other people think and feel, and about their sincerity, than any form of electronic communication. Only by actually being in the presence of people who make decisions affecting us in important ways do we feel able to learn what is going on and feel confident that we can impress them with our own views and our own sincerity. 'Co-presence', Boden and Molotch (1994) say, 'affects access to the body part that "never lies", the eyes – the "windows on the soul". Eye contact itself signals a degree of intimacy and trust; copresent interactants continuously monitor the subtle movements of this most subtle body part'.

Summary points

1   Many apparently trivial aspects of our day-to-day behaviour turn out on close examination to be both complex and important aspects of *social interaction*. An example is the gaze – looking at other people. In most interactions, eye contact is fairly fleeting. To stare at another person could be taken as a sign of hostility – or on some occasions, of love. The study of social interaction is a fundamental area in sociology, illuminating many aspects of social life.

2   Many different expressions are conveyed by the human face. It is widely held that basic aspects of the facial expressions of emotion are innate. Cross-cultural studies demonstrate quite close similarities between members of different cultures both in facial expression and in the interpretation of emotions registered on the human face.

3   The study of ordinary talk and conversation has come to be called *ethnomethodology*, a term first coined by Harold Garfinkel. Ethnomethodology is the analysis of the ways in which we actively – although usually in a taken-for-granted way – make sense of what others mean by what they say and do.

4   We can learn a great deal about the nature of talk by studying *response cries* (exclamations).

5   *Unfocused interaction* is the mutual awareness individuals have of one another in large gatherings when not directly in conversation together. *Focused interaction*, which can be divided up into distinct *encounters*, or episodes of interaction, is when two or more individuals are directly attending to what the other or others are saying and doing.

6   Social interaction can often be illuminatingly studied by applying the dramaturgical model – studying social interaction as if those involved were actors on a stage, having a set and props. As in the theatre, in the various contexts of social life there tend to be clear distinctions between *front regions* (the stage itself) and *back regions,* where the actors prepare themselves for the performance and relax afterwards.

7   All social interaction is situated in time and space. We can analyse how our daily lives are 'zoned' in both time and space combined by looking at how activities occur during definite durations and at the same time involve spatial movement.

8   Some mechanisms of social interaction may be universal, but many are not. The !Kung of southern Africa, for example, live in small mobile bands, where there is little privacy and thus little opportunity to create front and back regions.

9   Modern societies are characterized largely by indirect interpersonal transactions (such as making bank deposits), which lack any co-presence. This leads to what has been called the *compulsion of proximity*, the tendency to want to meet in person whenever possible, perhaps because this makes it easier to gather information about how others think and feel, and to accomplish *impression management.*

Questions for further thought

1 Would social life be possible without shared background assumptions among members of a society?

2 How might a tourist view your home town or city differently from you?

3 How easy would it be to conduct 'interactional vandalism' in the classroom?

4 How do you 'look confident'?

5 What strategies do women on their own use in bars and cafés to indicate that they want to be left alone?

6 Can electronic communication substitute for face-to-face interaction?

Further reading

Peter Berger and Thomas Luckmann, *The Social Construction of Reality: A Treatise in the Sociology of Knowledge* (Garden City, NY: Doubleday, 1966).

Stanley Cohen and Laurie Taylor, *Escape Attempts: The Theory and Practice of Resistance to Everyday Life*, 2nd edn (London: Routledge, 1995).

Erving Goffman, *Behaviour in Public Places* (New York: Free Press, 1963).

Erving Goffman, *The Presentation of the Self in Everyday Life* (Harmondsworth: Penguin, 1969).

Phil Manning, *Erving Goffman and Modern Sociology* (Cambridge: Polity, 1992).

Internet links

Nonverbal Communication Pages
http://www.natcom.org/ctronline/nonverb.htm

Introduction to symbolic interactionism
http://web.grinnell.edu/courses/soc/s00/soc111-01/IntroTheories/Symbolic.html

Ethno/CA News (online resource for ethnomethodology and conversation analysis)
http://www2.fmg.uva.nl/emca/

Erving Goffman Website
http://people.brandeis.edu/~teuber/goffmanbio.html

Contents

6 Socialization, The Life-Course and Ageing

AT THE start of J. K. Rowling's first Harry Potter adventure, *Harry Potter and the Philosopher's Stone*, the shrewd wizard Albus Dumbledore leaves Harry, a newly orphaned infant, at the doorstep of his non-magician (or 'Muggle') uncle and aunt's house. Harry has already shown himself to have unique powers, but Dumbledore is concerned that if left in the wizard world, Harry won't mature healthily. 'It would be enough to turn any boy's head', he says. 'Famous before he can walk and talk! Famous for something he won't even remember. Can't you see how much better off he'll be, growing up away from all that until he's ready to take it?' (Rowling 1998).

The Harry Potter novels, each of which follows Harry through a single school year, are based on the principle that there is no adventure greater than that of growing up. Although Harry attends the Hogwarts School of Witchcraft and Wizardry, it's still a school, because everyone, even a young wizard with limitless power, needs help developing a set of values. We all pass through important life stages: the passage from childhood to adolescence, and then to adulthood. So, for example, as the Harry Potter series progresses, Harry feels the onset of sexual urges, to which he responds with an entirely common awkwardness. Since sports are an important place for many children to learn about camaraderie and ambition, Harry plays

the wizard sport Quidditch. Rowling loves to use the paranormal to help us see the enchanting complexities behind the fundamentals of everyday life. In her universe, owls unerringly deliver letters; is this really any stranger than the postal system or email? The function of all classic children's stories is to make the process of growing up more understandable, whether they're set in a fairy-tale universe, our own world, or – as with the innovation of the Harry Potter series – both.

Socialization is the process whereby the helpless infant gradually becomes a self-aware, knowledgeable person, skilled in the ways of the culture into which he or she was born. Socialization among the young allows for the more general phenomenon of social reproduction – the process whereby societies have structural continuity over time. During the course of socialization, especially in the early years of life, children learn the ways of their elders, thereby perpetuating their values, norms, and social practices. All societies have characteristics that endure over long stretches of time, even though their members change as individuals are born and die. British society, for example, has many distinctive social and cultural characteristics that have persisted for generations – such as the fact that English is the main language spoken.

As we'll see in this chapter, socialization connects the different generations to one another. The birth of a child alters the lives of those who are responsible for its upbringing – who themselves therefore undergo new learning experiences. Parenting usually ties the activities of adults to children for the remainder of their lives. Older people still remain parents when they become grandparents, of course, thus forging another set of relationships connecting the different generations with each other. Although the process of cultural learning is much more intense in infancy and early childhood than later, learning and adjustment go on through the whole life cycle.

The sections that follow deal with the theme of 'nature versus nurture', a common debate in sociology. We shall first examine the main theoretical interpretations put forward by different writers about how and why children develop as they do, including theories that explain how we develop gender identities. Then we shall move on to discuss the main groups and social contexts that influence socialization during the course of individuals' lives, from childhood to later life. Last we shall look at some of the most important of the sociological issues surrounding ageing.

Culture, society and child socialization

Theories of child development

One of the most distinctive features of human beings, compared to other animals, is that humans are *self-aware*. How should we understand the emergence of a sense of self – the awareness that the individual has a distinct identity separate from others? During the first months of his life, the infant possesses little or no understanding of differences between human beings and material objects in his environment, and has no awareness of self. Children do not begin to use concepts like 'I', 'me' and 'you' until the age of two or after. Only gradually do they then come to understand that others have distinct identities, consciousness and needs separate from their own.

The problem of the emergence of self is a much-debated one and is viewed rather differently in contrasting theoretical perspectives. To some extent, this is because the most prominent theories about child development emphasize different aspects of socialization. The American philosopher and sociologist George Herbert Mead gives attention mainly to how children learn to use the concepts of 'I' and 'me'. The Swiss student of child behaviour, Jean Piaget, worked on many aspects of child development, but his most well-known writings concern **cognition** – the ways in which children learn to *think* about themselves and their environment.

G. H. Mead and the development of self

Since Mead's ideas form the main basis of a general tradition of theoretical thinking, **symbolic interactionism**, they have had a very broad impact in sociology. Symbolic interactionism emphasizes that interaction between human beings takes place through symbols and the interpretation of meanings (see chapter 1). But in addition, Mead's work provides an account of the main phases of child development, giving particular attention to the emergence of a sense of self.

According to Mead, infants and young children first of all develop as social beings by imitating the actions of those around them. Play is one way in which this takes place, and in their play small children often imitate what adults do. A small child will make mud pies, having seen an adult cooking, or dig with a spoon, having observed someone gardening. Children's play evolves from simple imitation to more complicated games in which a child of four or five years old will act out an adult role. Mead called this 'taking the role of the other' – learning what it is like to be in the shoes of another person. It is only at this stage that children acquire a developed sense of self. Children achieve an understanding of themselves as separate agents – as a 'me' – by seeing themselves through the eyes of others.

We achieve self-awareness, according to Mead, when we learn to distinguish the 'me' from the 'I'. The 'I' is the unsocialized infant, a bundle of spontaneous wants and desires. The 'me', as Mead used the term, is the **social self**. Individuals develop **self-consciousness**, Mead argued, by coming to see themselves as others see them. A further stage of child development, according to Mead, occurs when the child is about eight or nine years old. This is the age at which children tend to take part in organized games, rather than unsystematic play. It is at this period that they begin to understand the overall **values** and *morality* according to which social life is conducted. To learn organized games, children must understand the rules of play and notions of fairness and equal participation. Children at this stage learn to grasp what Mead termed the **generalized other** – the general values and moral rules of the culture in which they are developing.

Jean Piaget and the stages of cognitive development

Piaget placed great emphasis on the child's active capability to make sense of the world. Children do not passively soak up information, but instead select and interpret what they see, hear and feel in the world around them. Piaget described several distinct stages of cognitive development during which children learn to think about themselves and their environment. Each stage involves the acquisition of new skills and depends on the successful completion of the preceding one.

Piaget called the first stage, which lasts from birth up to about the age of two, the **sensorimotor stage**, because infants learn mainly by touching objects, manipulating them, and physically exploring their environment. Until the age of about four months or so, infants cannot differentiate themselves from their environment. For example, a child will not realize that her own movements cause the sides of her crib to rattle. Objects are not differentiated from persons, and the infant is unaware that anything exists outside her range of vision. Infants gradually learn to distinguish people from objects, coming to see that both have an existence independent of their immediate perceptions. The main accomplishment of this stage is that by its close children understand their environment to have distinct and stable properties.

The next phase, called the **preoperational stage**, is the one to which Piaget devoted the bulk of his research. This stage lasts from the age of two to seven. During the course of it, children acquire a mastery of language and become able to use words to represent objects and images in a symbolic fashion. A four-year-old might use a sweeping hand, for example, to represent the concept 'aeroplane'. Piaget termed the stage 'preoperational' because children are not yet able to use their developing mental capabilities systematically. Children in this stage are **egocentric**. As Piaget used it, this concept does not refer to selfishness, but to the tendency of the child to interpret the world exclusively in terms of his own position. A child during this period does not understand, for instance, that others see objects from a different perspective from his own. Holding a book upright, the child may ask about a picture in it, not realizing that the other person sitting opposite can only see the back of the book.

Children at the preoperational stage are not able to hold connected conversations with another. In egocentric speech, what each child says is more or less unrelated to what the other speaker said. Children talk together, but not *to* one another in the same sense as adults. During this phase of development, children have no general understanding of categories of thought that adults tend to take for granted: concepts such as causality, speed, weight or number. Even if the child sees water poured from a tall, thin container into a shorter, wider one, she will not understand that the volume of water remains the same – and concludes rather that there is less water because the water level is lower.

A third period, the **concrete operational stage**, lasts from the age of seven to eleven. During this phase, children master abstract, logical notions. They are able to handle ideas such as causality without much difficulty. A child at this stage of development will recognize the false reasoning involved in the idea that the wide container holds less water than the thin, narrow one, even though the water levels are different. She becomes capable of carrying out the mathematical operations of multiplying, dividing and subtracting. Children by this stage are much less egocentric. In the preoperational stage, if a girl is asked, 'How many sisters do you have?' she may correctly answer 'one'. But if asked, 'How many sisters does your sister have?' she will probably answer 'none', because she cannot see herself from the point of view of her sister. The concrete operational child is able to answer such a question with ease.

The years from eleven to fifteen cover what Piaget called the **formal operational stage**. During adolescence, the developing child becomes able to grasp highly abstract and hypothetical ideas. When faced with a problem, children at this stage are able to review all the possible ways of solving it and go through them theoretically in order to reach a solution. The young person at the formal operational stage is able to understand why some questions are trick ones. To the question, 'What creatures are both poodles and dogs?' the individual might not be able to give the correct reply but will understand why the answer 'poodles' is right and appreciate the humour in it.

According to Piaget, the first three stages of development are universal; but not all adults reach the third, formal operational stage. The development of formal operational thought depends in part on processes of schooling. Adults of limited educational attainment tend to continue to think in more concrete terms and retain large traces of egocentrism.

Agencies of socialization

Sociologists often speak of socialization as occurring in two broad phases, involving a number of different agencies of socialization. **Agencies of socialization** are groups or social contexts in which significant processes of socialization occur. Primary socialization occurs in infancy and childhood and is the most intense period of cultural learning. It is the time when children learn language and basic behavioural patterns that form the foundation for later learning. The family is the main agent of socialization during this phase. Secondary socialization takes place later in childhood and into maturity. In this phase, other agents of socialization take over some of the responsibility from the family. Schools, peer groups, organizations, the media and eventually the workplace become socializing forces for individuals. Social interactions in these contexts help people learn the values, norms and beliefs that make up the patterns of their culture.

The family

Since family systems vary widely, the range of family contacts that the infant experiences is by no means standard across cultures. The mother everywhere is normally the most important individual in the child's early life, but the nature of the relationships established between mothers and their children is influenced by the form and regularity of their contact. This is, in turn, conditioned by the character of family institutions and their relation to other groups in society.

In modern societies, most early socialization occurs within a small-scale family context. The majority of British children spend their early years within a domestic unit containing mother, father and perhaps one or two other children. In many other cultures, by contrast, aunts, uncles and grandparents are often part of a single household and serve as caretakers even for very young infants. Yet even within British society there are many variations in the nature of family contexts.

Some children are brought up in single-parent households; some are cared for by two mothering and fathering agents (divorced parents and step-parents). A high proportion of women with families are now employed outside the home and return to their paid work relatively soon after the births of their children. In spite of these variations, the family normally remains the major agency of socialization from infancy to adolescence and beyond – in a sequence of development connecting the generations.

> We look at issues concerning families in more detail in chapter 7, 'Families and Intimate Relationships'.

Families have varying 'locations' within the overall institutions of a society. In most traditional societies, the family into which a person was born largely determined the individual's social position for the rest of his or her life. In modern societies, social position is not inherited at birth in this way, yet the region and social class of the family into which an individual is born affects patterns of socialization quite distinctly. Children pick up ways of behaviour characteristic of their parents or others in their neighbourhood or community.

> We look at issues of class in more depth in chapter 9 on 'Stratification and Class'.

Varying patterns of child-rearing and discipline, together with contrasting values and expectations, are found in different sectors of large-scale societies. It is easy to understand the influence of different types of family background if we think of what life is like, say, for a child growing up in a poor ethnic-minority family living in a run-down area of a city compared to one born into an affluent white family in the suburbs (Kohn 1977).

Of course, few if any children simply take over unquestioningly the outlook of their parents. This is especially true in the modern world, in which change is so pervasive. Moreover, the very existence of a range of socializing agencies in modern societies leads to many divergences between the outlooks of children, adolescents and the parental generation.

Schools

Another important socializing agency is the school. Schooling is a formal process: students pursue a definite curriculum of subjects. Yet schools are agencies of socialization in more subtle respects. Children are expected to be quiet in class, be punctual at lessons and observe rules of school discipline. They are required to accept and respond to the authority of the teaching staff. Reactions of teachers also affect the expectations children have of themselves. These expectations in turn become linked to their job experience when they leave school. Peer groups are often formed at school, and the system of keeping children in classes according to age reinforces their impact.

> We discuss socialization in education in more detail in chapter 17, 'Education.

Peer relationships

Another socializing agency is the **peer group**. Peer groups consist of children of a similar age. In some cultures, particularly small traditional societies, peer groups are formalized as **age-grades** (normally confined to males). There are often specific ceremonies or rites that mark the transition of men from one age-grade to another.

Those within a particular age-grade generally maintain close and friendly connections throughout their lives. A typical set of age-grades consists of childhood, junior warriorhood, senior warriorhood, junior elderhood and senior elderhood. Men move through these grades not as individuals, but as whole groups.

The family's importance in socialization is obvious, since the experience of the infant and young child is shaped more or less exclusively within it. It is less apparent, especially to those of us living in Western societies, how significant peer groups are. Yet even without formal age-grades, children over the age of four or five usually spend a great deal of time in the company of friends the same age. Given the high proportion of women now in the workforce, whose young children play together in day-care centres, peer relations are even more important today than they were before (Corsaro 1997; Harris 1998).

In her book *Gender Play* (Thorne 1993), the sociologist Barrie Thorne looked at socialization in this way. As others had before her, she wanted to understand how children come to know what it means to be male and female (you will learn three classic theories of gender socialization later in this chapter, pp. 172–5). Rather than seeing children as passively learning the meaning of gender from their parents and teachers, she looked at the way in which children actively create and recreate the meaning of gender in their interactions with each other. The social activities that schoolchildren do together can be as important as other agents for their socialization.

Thorne spent two years observing fourth and fifth graders at two schools in Michigan and California, sitting in the classroom with them and observing their activities outside the classroom. She watched games such as 'chase and kiss' – known by names such as 'kiss-catch' in the UK – so as to learn how children construct and experience gender meanings in the classroom and on the playground.

Thorne found that peer groups have a great influence on gender socialization, particularly as children talk about their changing bodies, a subject of great fascination. The social context created by these children determined whether a child's bodily change was experienced with embarrassment or worn with pride. As Thorne (1993) observed:

> If the most popular women started menstruating or wearing bras (even if they didn't need to), then other girls wanted these changes too. But if the popular didn't wear bras and hadn't . . . gotten their periods, then these developments were viewed as less desirable.

Thorne's research is a powerful reminder that children are social actors who help create their social world and influence their own socialization. Still, the impact of societal and cultural influences is tremendous, since the activities that children pursue and the values they hold are determined by influences such as their families and the media.

Peer relations are likely to have a significant impact beyond childhood and adolescence. Informal groups of people of similar ages, at work and in other situations, are usually of enduring importance in shaping individuals' attitudes and behaviour.

The mass media

Newspapers, periodicals and journals flourished in the West from the early 1800s onward, but they were confined to a fairly small readership. It was not until a century later that such printed materials became part of the daily experience of millions of people, influencing their attitudes and opinions. The spread of **mass media** involving printed documents was soon accompanied by electronic communication – radio, television, records and videos. Recent surveys have found that men and women in the UK spend, on average, 2.41 and 2.17 hours respectively every day watching television, videos or DVDs (Office for National Statistics 2005). The media plays an enormous role in shaping our understanding of the world.

Much research has been done to assess the effects of television programmes on the audiences they reach, particularly children. Perhaps the most commonly researched topic is the impact of television on propensities to crime and violence. The most extensive studies are those carried out by George Gerbner and his collaborators, who have analysed samples of prime-time and weekend daytime TV for all the major American networks each year since 1967. The number and frequency of violent acts and episodes are charted for a range of programmes. Violence is defined as physical force directed against the self or others, in which physical harm or death occurs. Television drama emerges as highly violent in character. On average, 80 per cent of programmes contain violence, with a rate of 7.5 violent episodes per hour. Children's programmes show even higher levels of violence, although killing is less commonly portrayed. Cartoons depict the highest number of violent acts and episodes of any type of television programme (Gerbner 1979).

In general, research on the effects of television on audiences has tended to treat children as passive and undiscriminating in their reactions to what they see. Robert Hodge and David Tripp (1986) emphasized that children's responses to TV involve interpreting, or 'reading', what they see, not just registering the content of programmes. They suggested that most research has not taken account of the complexity of children's mental processes. Watching television, even trivial programmes, is not an inherently low-level intellectual activity; children read programmes by relating them to other systems of meaning in their everyday lives. According to Hodge and Tripp, it is not the violence alone that has effects on behaviour, but rather the general framework of attitudes within which it is both presented and read.

Audience responses to the media are discussed in chapter 15, 'The Media', pp. 608–13.

Gender socialization

Agencies of socialization play an important role in how children learn **gender roles.** Let's now turn to the study of **gender socialization,** the learning of gender roles through social factors such as the family and the media.

Reactions of parents and adults

Many studies have been carried out on the degree to which gender differences are the result of social influences. Studies of mother–infant interaction show differences in the treatment of boys and girls even when parents believe their reactions to both are the same. Adults asked to assess the personality of a baby give different answers according to whether or not they believe the child to be a girl or a boy. In one experiment, five young mothers were observed in interaction with a six-month-old called Beth. They tended to smile at her often and offer her dolls to play with. She was seen as 'sweet', having a 'soft cry'. The reaction of a second group of mothers to a child the same age, named Adam, was noticeably different. The baby was likely to be offered a train or other 'male toys' to play with. Beth and Adam were actually the same child, dressed in different clothes (Will et al. 1976).

Gender learning

Gender learning by infants is almost certainly unconscious. Before children can accurately label themselves as either a boy or a girl, they receive a range of pre-verbal cues. For instance, male and female adults usually handle infants differently. The cosmetics women use contain scents different from those the baby might learn to associate with males. Systematic differences in dress, hairstyle and so on provide visual cues for the infant in the learning process. By the age of two, children have a partial understanding of what gender is. They know whether they are a boy or a girl, and they can usually categorize others accurately. Not until the age of five or six, however, does a child know that a person's gender does not change, that everyone has gender and that sex differences between girls and boys are anatomically based.

The toys, picture books and television programmes with which young children come into contact all tend to emphasize differences between male and female attributes. Toy stores and mail-order catalogues usually categorize their products by gender. Even some toys that seem neutral in terms of gender are not so in practice. For example, toy kittens and rabbits are recommended for girls, while lions and tigers are seen as more appropriate for boys.

Vanda Lucia Zammuner (1986) studied the toy preferences of children aged between seven and ten in Italy and Holland. Children's attitudes towards a variety of toys were analysed; stereotypically masculine and feminine toys, as well as toys presumed not to be gender-typed, were included. Both the children and their parents were asked to assess which toys were suitable for boys and which for girls. There was close agreement between the adults and the children. On average, the Italian children chose gender-differentiated toys to play with more often than the Dutch children – a finding that conformed to expectations, since Italian culture tends to hold a more traditional view of gender divisions than does Dutch society. As in other studies, girls from both societies chose gender-neutral or boys' toys to play with far more than boys chose girls' toys.

Storybooks and television

More than thirty years ago, Lenore Weitzman and her colleagues (1972) carried out an analysis of gender roles in some of the most widely used pre-school children's books and found several clear differences in gender roles. Males played a much larger part in the stories and pictures than females did, outnumbering females by a ratio of 11 to 1. When animals with gender identities were included, the ratio was 95 to 1. The activities of males and females also differed. The males engaged in adventurous pursuits and outdoor activities that demanded independence and strength. Where girls did appear, they were portrayed as passive and were confined mostly to indoor activities. Girls cooked and cleaned for the males or awaited their return. Much the same was true of the adult men and women represented in the storybooks. Women who were not wives and mothers were imaginary creatures like witches or fairy godmothers. There was not a single woman in all the books analysed who held an occupation outside the home. By contrast, the men were depicted as fighters, policemen, judges, kings and so forth.

More recent research suggests that things have changed somewhat but that the large bulk of children's literature nevertheless remains much the same (Davies 1991). Fairy tales, for example, embody traditional attitudes towards gender and towards the sorts of aims and ambitions that girls and boys are expected to have. 'Some day my prince will come' – in versions of fairy tales from several centuries ago, this usually implied that a girl from a poor family might dream of wealth and fortune. Today, its meaning has become more closely tied to the ideals of romantic love. Some feminists have tried to rewrite some of the most celebrated fairy tales, reversing their usual emphases: 'I really didn't notice that he had a funny nose. And he certainly looked better all dressed up in fancy clothes. He's not nearly as attractive as he seemed the other night. So I think I'll just pretend that this glass slipper feels too tight' (Viorst 1986). Like this version of *Cinderella*, however, these rewrites are found mainly in books directed to adult audiences, and have hardly affected the tales told in innumerable children's books.

Although there are some notable exceptions, analyses of television programmes designed for children conform to the findings about children's books. Studies of the most frequently watched cartoons show that most of the leading figures are male and that males dominate the active pursuits. Similar images are found in the commercials that appear throughout the programmes.

The difficulty of non-sexist child-rearing

June Statham (1986) studied the experiences of a group of parents committed to non-sexist child-rearing. Thirty adults in eighteen families were involved in the research, which included children aged between six months and twelve years. The parents were of middle-class background, mostly involved in academic work as teachers or professors. Statham found that most of the parents did not simply try to modify traditional gender roles by seeking to make girls more like boys; they wanted to foster new combinations of the feminine and masculine. They wished boys to be more sensitive to others' feelings and capable of expressing warmth, while girls were encouraged to seek opportunities for learning and self-advancement. All the parents found existing patterns of gender learning difficult to combat. They were reasonably successful at persuading the children to play with non-gender-typed toys, but even this proved more difficult than many of them had expected. One mother commented to the researcher:

If you walk into a toy shop, it's full of war toys for boys and domestic toys for girls, and it sums up society the way it is. This is the way children are being socialized: it's all right for boys to be taught to kill and hurt, and I think it's terrible, it makes me feel sick. I try not to go into toy shops, I feel so angry.

Practically all the children in fact possessed, and played with, gender-typed toys, given to them by relatives.

There are now some storybooks available with strong, independent girls as the main characters, but few depict boys in non-traditional roles. A mother of a five-year-old boy told of her son's reaction when she reversed the sexes of the characters in a story she read to him:

> In fact he was a bit upset when I went through a book which has a boy and a girl in very traditional roles, and changed all the he's to she's and she's to he's. When I first started doing that, he was inclined to say 'you don't like boys, you only like girls'. I had to explain that that wasn't true at all, it's just that there's not enough written about girls. (Statham 1986)

The novelist and critic Allison Pearson (2002) also found how powerful gender socialization could be when she tried to present her daughter with a less anatomically improbable doll than the Barbies she loved:

> One day, in an attempt to stem the toxic tide, I brought home a Scandinavian doll which looked like a Barbie designed by a feminist committee: a wholesome small-breasted individual wearing khaki, she clearly worked at something useful in developing countries. Alas, this poor social democrat never got to meet the Barbies. 'It's a boy!' my daughter yelled in horror, before dropping the liberal compromise in the bucket her baby brother reserved for drowning snails.

Clearly, gender socialization is very powerful, and challenges to it can be upsetting. Once a gender is 'assigned', society expects individuals to act like 'females' and 'males'. It is in the practices of everyday life that these expectations are fulfilled and reproduced (Bourdieu 1990; Lorber 1994).

The sociological debate

Freud's theory

Perhaps the most influential – and controversial – theory of the emergence of gender identity is that of Sigmund Freud (1856–1939). According to Freud, the learning of gender differences in infants and young children is centred on the possession or absence of the penis. 'I have a penis' is equivalent to 'I am a boy', while 'I am a girl' is equivalent to 'I lack a penis'. Freud is careful to say that it is not just the anatomical distinctions that matter here; the possession or absence of the penis is symbolic of masculinity and femininity.

At around the age of four or five, the theory goes, a boy feels threatened by the discipline and autonomy his father demands of him, fantasizing that the father wishes to remove his penis. Partly consciously, but mostly on an unconscious level, the boy recognizes the father as a rival for the affections of his mother. In repressing erotic feelings towards the mother and accepting the father as a superior being, the boy identifies with the father and becomes aware of his male identity. The boy gives up his love for his mother out of an unconscious fear of castration by his father. Girls, on the other hand, supposedly suffer from 'penis envy' because they do not possess the visible organ that distinguishes boys. The mother becomes devalued in the little girl's eyes, because she is also seen to lack a penis and to be unable to provide one. When the girl identifies with the mother, she takes over the submissive attitude involved in the recognition of being 'second best'.

Once this phase is over, the child has learned to repress his erotic feelings. The period from about the age of five to puberty, according to Freud, is one of latency – sexual activities tend to be suspended until the biological changes involved in puberty reactivate erotic desires in a direct way. The latency period, covering the early and middle years of school, is the time at which same-gender peer groups are most important in the child's life.

Major objections have been raised to Freud's views, particularly by feminists, but also by many other authors (Mitchell 1975; Coward 1984). First, Freud seems to identify gender identity too closely with genital awareness; other more subtle factors are surely involved. Second, the theory seems to depend on the notion that the penis is superior to the vagina, which is thought of as just a lack of the male organ. Yet why shouldn't the female genitals be considered superior to those of the male? Third, Freud treats the father as the primary disciplining agent, whereas in many cultures the mother plays the more significant part in the imposition of discipline. Fourth, Freud believes that gender learning is concentrated at the age of four or five. Most later authors have emphasized the importance of earlier learning, beginning in infancy.

Chodorow's theory

While many writers have made use of Freud's approach in studying gender development, they have usually modified it in major respects. An important example is the sociologist Nancy Chodorow (1978, 1988). She argues that learning to feel male or female derives from the infant's attachment to his parents from an early age. She places much more emphasis than Freud does on the importance of the mother rather than the father. Children tend to become emotionally involved with the mother, since she is easily the most dominant influence in their early lives. This attachment has at some point to be broken in order for the child to achieve a separate sense of self – the child is required to become less closely dependent.

Chodorow argues that the breaking process occurs in a different way for boys and girls. Girls remain closer to the mother – able, for example, to go on hugging and kissing her and imitating what she does. Because there is no sharp break from the mother, the girl, and later the adult woman, develops a sense of self that is more continuous with other people. Her identity is more likely to be merged with or dependent on another's: first her mother, later a man. In Chodorow's view, this tends to produce characteristics of sensitivity and emotional compassion in women.

Boys gain a sense of self via a more radical rejection of their original closeness to the mother, forging their understanding of masculinity from what is not feminine. They learn not to be 'sissies' or 'mummy's boys'. As a result, boys are relatively unskilled in relating closely to others; they develop more analytical ways of looking at the world. They take a more active view of their lives, emphasizing achievement, but they have repressed their ability to understand their own feelings and those of others.

To some extent, Chodorow reverses Freud's emphasis. Masculinity, rather than femininity, is defined by a loss, the forfeit-ing of continued close attachment to the mother. Male identity is formed through separation; thus, men later in life uncon-sciously feel that their identity is endan-gered if they become involved in close emotional relationships with others. Women, on the other hand, feel that the absence of a close relation to another person threatens their self-esteem. These patterns are passed on from generation to generation, because of the primary role women play in the early socialization of children. Women express and define themselves mainly in terms of relation-ships. Men have repressed these needs and adopt a more manipulative stance towards the world.

Chodorow's work has met with various criticisms. Janet Sayers (1986), for example, has suggested that Chodorow does not explain the struggle of women, particularly in current times, to become autonomous, independent beings. Women (and men), she points out, are more contradictory in their psychological make-up than Chodorow's theory suggests. Femininity may conceal feelings of aggressiveness or assertiveness, which are revealed only obliquely or in certain contexts (Brennan 1988). Chodorow has also been criticized for her narrow conception of the family, one based on a white, middle-class model. What happens, for example, in one-parent households or, as in many Chicano com-munities, families where children are cared for by more than one adult (Segura and Pierce 1993)?

These criticisms don't undermine Chodorow's ideas, which remain impor-tant. They teach us a good deal about the nature of femininity, and they help us to understand the origins of what has been called 'male inexpressiveness' – the diffi-culty men have in revealing their feelings to others (Balswick 1983).

Gilligan's theory

Carol Gilligan (1982) has further devel-oped Chodorow's analysis. Her work con-centrates on the images that adult women and men have of themselves and their attainments. Women, she agrees with Chodorow, define themselves in terms of personal relationships and judge their achievements by reference to the ability to care for others. Women's place in the lives of men is traditionally that of caretaker and helpmate. But the qualities developed in these tasks are frequently devalued by men, who see their own emphasis on indi-vidual achievement as the only form of 'success'. Concern with relationships on the part of women appears to them as a weakness rather than as the strength that in fact it is.

Gilligan carried out intensive interviews with about two hundred American women and men of varying ages and social backgrounds. She asked all the interviewees a range of questions con-cerning their moral outlook and concep-tions of self. Consistent differences emerged between the views of the women and the men. For instance, the interview-ees were asked: 'What does it mean to say something is morally right or wrong?' Whereas the men tended to respond to this question by mentioning abstract ideals of duty, justice and individual freedom, the women persistently raised the theme of helping others. Thus a female college student answered the question in the following way:

> 'It [morality] has to do with responsibilities
> and obligations and values, mainly values.

. . . In my life situation I relate morality with interpersonal relationships that have to do with respect for the other person and myself.' The interviewer then asked: 'Why respect other people?' receiving the answer, 'Because they have a consciousness or feelings that can be hurt, an awareness that can be hurt.' (Gilligan 1982)

The women were more tentative in their moral judgements than the men, seeing possible contradictions between following a strict moral code and avoiding harming others. Gilligan suggests that this outlook reflects the traditional situation of women, anchored in caring relationships, rather than the 'outward-looking' attitudes of men. Women have in the past deferred to the judgements of men, while being aware that they have qualities that most men lack. Their views of themselves are based on successfully fulfilling the needs of others, rather than on pride in individual achievement (Gilligan 1982).

Socialization through the life-course

The various transitions through which individuals pass during their lives seem at first sight to be biologically fixed – from childhood to adulthood and eventually to death. But the stages of the human **life-course** are social as well as biological in nature (Vincent 2003). They are influenced by cultural differences and also by the material circumstances of people's lives in given types of society. For example, in the modern West, death is usually thought of in relation to elderly people, because most people live to be over seventy. In traditional societies of the past, however, more people died at a younger age than survived to old age.

Childhood

To people living in modern societies, childhood is a clear and distinct stage of life. Children are distinct from babies or toddlers; childhood intervenes between infancy and the teen years. Yet the concept of childhood, like so many other aspects of social life today, has only come into being over the past two or three centuries. In earlier societies, the young moved directly from a lengthy infancy into working roles within the community. The French historian Philippe Ariès (1965) has argued that 'childhood', conceived of as a separate phase of development, did not exist in medieval times. In the paintings of medieval Europe, children are portrayed as little adults, with mature faces and the same style of dress as their elders. Children took part in the same work and play activities as adults, rather than in the childhood games we now take for granted.

Right up to the twentieth century, in most Western countries, children were put to work at what now seems a very early age. There are countries in the world today, in fact, in which young children are engaged in full-time work, sometimes in physically demanding circumstances (e.g., in coal mines). The ideas that children have distinctive rights and that the use of child labour is morally repugnant are quite recent developments.

The issue of child labour is discussed in chapter 11 on 'Global Inequality', pp. 400–1.

Because of the long period of childhood that we recognize today, societies now are in some respects more child-centred than traditional ones. But a child-centred society, it must be emphasized, is not one in which all children experience love and care from parents or other adults. The physical and sexual abuse of children is a commonplace feature of family life in present-day society, although the full extent of such abuse has only recently come to light. Child abuse has clear connections with what seems to us today like the frequent mistreatment of children in pre-modern Europe.

It seems possible that, as a result of changes currently occurring in modern societies, the separate character of childhood is diminishing once more. Some observers have suggested that children now grow up so fast that this is in fact the case. They point out that even small children may watch the same television programmes as adults, thereby becoming much more familiar early on with the adult world than did preceding generations.

The teenager

The idea of the 'teenager', so familiar to us today, also didn't exist until recently. The biological changes involved in puberty (the point at which a person becomes capable of adult sexual activity and reproduction) are universal. Yet in many cultures these do not produce the degree of turmoil and uncertainty often found among young people in modern societies. In cultures that foster age-grades, for example, with distinct ceremonials that signal a person's transition to adulthood, the process of psycho-sexual development generally seems easier to negotiate. Adolescents in such societies have less to 'unlearn' since the pace of change is slower. There is a time when children in Western societies are required to be chil-

In modern Western societies young teenagers hover between childhood and adulthood.

dren no longer: to put away their toys and break with childish pursuits. In traditional cultures, where children are already working alongside adults, this process of unlearning is normally much less jarring.

In Western societies, teenagers are betwixt and between: they often try to follow adult ways, but they are treated in law as children. They may wish to go to work, but they are constrained to stay in school. Teenagers in the West live in between childhood and adulthood, growing up in a society subject to continuous change.

Young adulthood

Young adulthood seems increasingly to be a specific stage in personal and sexual development in modern societies (Goldscheider and Waite 1991). Particularly among more affluent groups, people in their early twenties are taking the time to travel and explore sexual, political and religious affiliations. The importance of this postponement of the responsibilities of full adulthood is likely to grow, given the extended period of education many people now undergo.

Mature adulthood

Most young adults in the West today can look forward to a life stretching right through to old age. In pre-modern times, few could anticipate such a future with much confidence. Death through sickness or injury was much more frequent among all age groups than it is today, and women in particular were at great risk because of the high rate of mortality in childbirth.

On the other hand, some of the strains we experience now were less pronounced in previous times. People usually maintained a closer connection with their parents and other kin than in today's more mobile populations, and the routines of work they followed were the same as those of their forebears. In current times, major uncertainties must be resolved in marriage, family life and other social contexts. We have to 'make' our own lives more than people did in the past. The creation of sexual and marital ties, for instance, now depends on individual initiative and selection, rather than being fixed by parents. This represents greater freedom for the individual, but the responsibility can also impose difficulties.

Keeping a forward-looking outlook in middle age has taken on a particular importance in modern societies. Most people do not expect to be doing the same thing all their lives, as was the case for the majority in traditional cultures. Individuals who have spent their lives in one career may find the level they have reached in middle age unsatisfying and further opportunities blocked. Women who have spent their early adulthood raising a family and whose children have left home may feel themselves to be without any social value. The phenomenon of a 'midlife crisis' is very real for many middle-aged people. A person may feel she has thrown away the opportunities that life had to offer, or she will never attain goals cherished since childhood. Yet growing older need not lead to resignation or bleak despair; a release from childhood dreams can be liberating.

Old age

In traditional societies, older people were often accorded a great deal of respect. Among cultures that included age-grades, the elders usually had a major – often the final – say over matters of importance to the community. Within families, the authority of both men and women mostly increased with age. In industrialized societies, by contrast, older people tend to lack authority within both the family and the wider social community. Having retired from the labour force, they may be poorer than ever before in their lives. At the same time, there has been a great increase in the proportion of the population aged over sixty-five, as we see in the next section.

Transition to the age-grade of elder in a traditional culture often marked the pinnacle of the status an individual could achieve. In modern societies, retirement tends to bring the opposite consequences. No longer living with their children and often having retired from paid work, older people may find it difficult to make the final period of their life rewarding. It used to be thought that those who successfully cope with old age do so by turning to their inner resources, becoming less interested in the material rewards that social life has to offer. While this may often be true, it seems likely that in a society in which many are physically healthy in old age, an outward-looking view will become more and more prevalent. Those in retirement might find renewal in what has been called the 'third age', in which a new phase of education begins (see also the discussion in chapter 17 on lifelong learning, pp. 696–7). In the section below we look at the sociological issues surrounding ageing in more detail.

Ageing

Fauja Singh ran his first London marathon in 2000, at the age of eighty-nine. It took him 6 hours and 54 minutes. He had last run seriously fifty-three years earlier. When he recorded a near-identical marathon time in 2001, he found he had knocked almost an hour off the world record for the over-nineties. In 2002 he trimmed his time down to 6 hours and 45 minutes. That year, 407 runners took longer than Singh to complete the London marathon; many were in their thirties. When Singh was that age he was running cross-country races in his native India. By the time India gained independence in 1947, new priorities had led Singh to hang up his running shoes at the age of thirty-six. A lifetime later – widowed and living in Ilford, East London – Singh has four children, thirteen grandchildren and five great-grandchildren scattered across three continents; he began looking for

Fauja Singh was still running marathons in his nineties.

new challenges. He started to punctuate his daily walks with bursts of jogging. His legs soon regained their lost strength. Then Singh saw a television programme about the marathon and was inspired. He has since run marathons all over the world and raised thousands of pounds for charity (Askwith 2003).

People, especially in the richer countries, are leading longer, healthier and more productive lives than ever before. During 1952, when she came to the throne, the Queen sent 273 birthday telegrams to congratulate centenarians on their birthday. Now that figure is more than 3,000 per year (Cayton, quoted by Kingshill Research Centre 2002). Growing old can be a fulfilling and rewarding experience, as it was with the people just described; or it can be filled with physical distress and social isolation. For most older people the experience of ageing lies somewhere in between.

In this section, we shall examine the nature of ageing, exploring what it means to grow old in a world that is rapidly changing. We begin with a brief snapshot of how the British population is growing older, before examining biological, psychological and social aspects of ageing. We then look at the ways in which people adapt to growing old, at least in the eyes of sociologists. This will lead us to a discussion of ageing in the United Kingdom, focusing on some of the special challenges and problems that older people face. We also discuss political issues surrounding the ageing of the British population, issues that assume increasing importance given the growing numbers of older people. We conclude with a discussion of the greying of the world population.

The greying of UK society

Throughout the world, societies are ageing. A growing proportion of the Earth's population is living into its sixties, seventies and beyond and this process is likely to continue during the twenty-first century (Lloyd-Sherlock 2004). Britain's population is no exception. As figure 6.1 shows, the proportion of Britons aged over 65 was around 5 per cent in all the population Censuses taken between 1851 and 1911, before tripling during the twentieth century. These changes are due to many factors. Modern agriculture, sanitation systems, epidemic control and medicine have all contributed to a decline in mortality throughout the world. In most societies

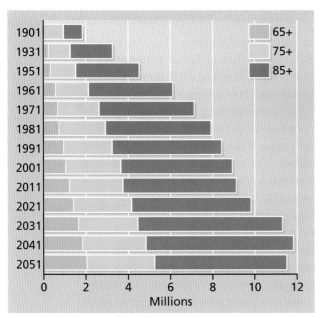

Figure 6.1 Elderly population in the UK, 1901–2051

Source: OPCS. From *Sociology Review* 8.2 (Nov. 1998), back cover. Crown copyright

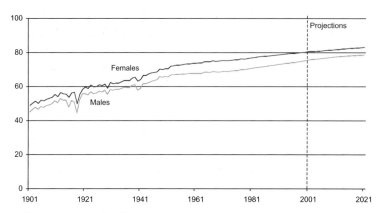

Figure 6.2   Life expectancy in the UK

Source: http://www.statistics.gov.uk/STATBASE/ssdataset.asp?vlnk=7420

today, fewer children die in infancy, and more adults survive to old age.

Looking at the changing demographic statistics, some sociologists and gerontologists refer to the '**greying**' of the population (Peterson 1999). 'Greying' is the result of two long-term trends in industrial societies: the tendency of families to have fewer children (discussed in chapter 7), and the fact that people are living longer. The average life expectancy at birth for British men increased from forty-five years for someone born in 1900 to seventy-six years for someone born today. For a woman in Britain, life expectancy rose from forty-eight to eighty in the same period (see figure 6.2). Most of these gains occurred in the first half of the twentieth century and were largely due to the improved chances for survival among the young. In 1921, 84.0 infants in 1,000 live births died before the age of one in the United Kingdom; by 2002 the rate was just 4.8 deaths for every 1,000 live births (HMSO 2004). By 2003 average life expectancy had risen to 80.5 (HMSO 2005).

These trends have enormous importance for the future of British society.

How do people age?

In examining the nature of ageing we will draw on studies of **social gerontology**, a discipline concerned with the study of the social aspects of ageing. Studying ageing is a bit like examining a moving target. As people grow older, society itself changes at the same time, and so does the very meaning of being 'old' (Riley et al. 1988). For Britons born in the first quarter of the twentieth century, a secondary education was regarded as more than sufficient for most of the available jobs, and most people did not expect to live much past their fifties – and then only at the cost of suffering a variety of disabilities. Today, those very same people find themselves in their seventies and eighties; many are relatively healthy, unwilling to disengage from work and social life, and in need of more schooling than they ever dreamed would be necessary.

What does it mean to age? **Ageing** can be sociologically defined as the combination of biological, psychological and social processes that affect people as they grow older (Abeles and Riley 1987; Atchley 2000). These processes suggest the metaphor of three different, although interrelated, developmental 'clocks': (1) a biological one, which refers to the physical body; (2) a psychological one, which refers to the mind and mental capabilities; and (3) a social one, which refers to cultural norms, values and role expectations having to do with age. There is an enormous range of variation in all three of these processes, as will be shown below. Our notions about the meaning of age are rapidly changing, both because recent research is dispelling many myths about ageing and because advances in nutrition and health have enabled many people to live longer, healthier lives than ever before.

Biological ageing

There are well-established biological effects of ageing, although the exact chronological age at which they occur varies greatly from individual to individual, depending on genetics and lifestyle. In general, for men and women alike, biological ageing typically means:

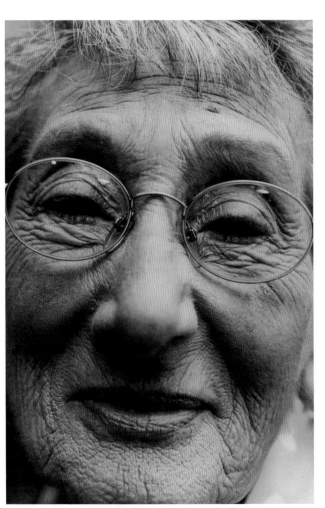

Ultimately, the impact of biological ageing is unavoidable.

- declining vision, as the eye lens loses its elasticity (small type is the bane of most people over fifty);
- hearing loss, first of higher-pitched tones, then of lower-pitched ones;
- wrinkles, as the skin's underlying structure becomes more and more brittle (millions of pounds invested in skin lotion and increasingly common surgical face-lifts only delay the inevitable);
- a decline of muscle mass and an accompanying accumulation of fat, especially around the middle (eating habits that were offset by exercise when you were twenty-five come back to haunt you when you are fifty); and
- a drop in cardiovascular efficiency, as less oxygen can be inhaled and utilized during exercise (lifelong runners who ran six-minute miles at the age of thirty are happy to break an eight-minute mile once they turn sixty).

The normal processes of ageing cannot be avoided, but they can be partly compensated for and offset by good health, proper diet and nutrition, and a reasonable amount of exercise (John 1988). Lifestyle can make a significant health difference for people of all ages. For many people, the physical changes of ageing do not significantly prevent them from leading active, independent lives well into their eighties. Some scientists have even argued that with a proper lifestyle and advances in medical technology, more and more people will be able to live relatively illness-free lives until they reach their biological maximum, experiencing only a brief period of sickness just before death (Fries 1980). There is a debate about when, or even if, we are genetically programmed to die (Kirkwood 2001). About ninety to one hundred years seems to be the upper end of the genetically determined age distribution for most human beings, although some have argued that it may be as high as 120 (Fries 1980; Rusting 1992; Treas 1995; Atchley 2000). When the world's oldest officially recorded person, the French-woman Jeanne Calment, died in 1997, she was 122. She rode a bicycle until the age of 100 and had met Vincent van Gogh as a child. Other people have claimed to be even older, though their ages cannot be verified.

Even though the majority of older people in the UK suffer no significant physical impairment and remain physically active, unfortunate stereotypes about the 'weak and frail elderly' continue to exist (Heise 1987). These stereotypes have more to do with the social than the biological meaning of ageing in Western culture, which is preoccupied with youthfulness and fears of growing old and dying.

Psychological ageing

The psychological effects of ageing are much less well established than the physical effects, although research into the psychology of ageing is continuing at an expanding pace. Even though such things as memory, learning, intelligence, skills and motivation to learn are widely assumed to decline with age, research into the psychology of ageing suggests a much more complicated process (Birren and Schaie 2001).

Memory and learning ability, for example, do not decline significantly until very late in life for most people, although the speed with which one recalls or analyses information may slow down somewhat, giving the false impression of mental impairment. For most older people whose lives are stimulating and rich, such mental abilities as motivation to learn, clarity of thought, and problem-solving capacity do not appear to decline significantly until very late in life (Baltes and Schaie 1977; Schaie 1979; Atchley 2000).

Current research has focused on the extent to which memory loss relates to other variables, such as health, personality and social structures. Scientists and psychologists argue that intellectual decline is not necessarily irreversible, and are working on ways to identify older people at risk so that medical intervention may be taken which will allow longer maintenance of higher levels of intellectual function (Schaie 1990).

Even Alzheimer's disease, the progressive deterioration of brain cells which is the primary cause of dementia in old age, is relatively rare in non-institutionalized persons under seventy-five, although it may afflict as many as half of all people over eighty-five. Recent research, particularly in the controversial area of stem cells, has created the hope that the treatment of Alzheimer's disease may one day be possible. Former US President Ronald Reagan, who died in 2004, is perhaps the most famous recent example of someone suffering from Alzheimer's. His wife, Nancy Reagan, has publicly supported stem-cell research.

Social ageing

Social age consists of the norms, values and roles that are culturally associated with a particular chronological age. Ideas about social age differ from one society to another and, at least in modern industrial societies, change over time as well. Societies such as Japan and China have traditionally revered older people, regarding them as a source of historical memory and wisdom. Societies such as the UK and the USA are more likely to dismiss them as non-productive, dependent people who are out of step with the times – both because they are less likely to have the high-tech skills so valued by young people and because of their culture's obsession with youthfulness. A fortune is now being spent on prescription drugs, plastic surgery and home remedies that promise eternal youth. These include such things as tummy-tucks and face-lifts, antibaldness pills and lotions, and pills that claim to increase memory and concentration. In the USA, three weeks after it hit the market in 1998, the anti-impotence drug Viagra accounted for 94 per cent of all prescription drug sales (Hotz 1998).

Role expectations are extremely important sources of one's personal identity. Some of the roles associated with ageing in British society are generally positive: lord, senior adviser, doting grandparent, religious elder, wise spiritual teacher. Other roles may be damaging, leading to lowered self-esteem and isolation. Highly stigmatizing stereotypical roles for older people in British culture exist; think of phrases like 'grumpy old', 'silly old', 'boring old' and 'dirty old' man or woman (Kirkwood 2001). In fact, like all people, older people do not simply passively play out assigned social roles; they actively shape and redefine them (Riley et al. 1988). We discuss discrimination against older people below (pp. 196–7).

"We rarely watch television. Most of our free time is devoted to sex."

Growing old: competing sociological explanations

Social gerontologists have offered a number of theories regarding the nature of ageing in British society. Some of the earliest theories emphasized individual adaptation to changing social roles as a person grows older. Later theories focused on how social structures shape the lives of older people and on the concept of the life-course. The most recent theories have been more multifaceted, focusing on the ways in which older people actively create their lives within specific institutional contexts.

The first generation of theories: functionalism

The earliest theories of ageing reflected the functionalist approach that was dominant in sociology during the 1950s and 1960s. They emphasized how individuals adjusted to changing social roles as they aged and how those roles were useful to society. The earliest theories often assumed that ageing brings with it physical and psychological decline and that changing social roles have to take this decline into account (Hendricks 1992).

The American sociologist Talcott Parsons, one of the most influential functionalist theorists of the 1950s, argued that society needs to find roles for older people consistent with advanced age. He expressed concern that the USA, in particular, with its emphasis on youth and its avoidance of death, had failed to provide roles that adequately drew on the potential wisdom and maturity of its older citizens. Moreover, given the greying of society that was evident even in Parsons's

time, he argued that this failure could well lead to older people's becoming discouraged and alienated from society. In order to achieve a 'healthy maturity', Parsons (1960) argued, older people need to adjust psychologically to their changed circumstances, while society needs to redefine the social roles older people have. Old roles (such as work) have to be abandoned, while new forms of productive activity (such as volunteer service) need to be identified.

Parsons's ideas anticipated those of **disengagement theory**, the notion that it is functional for society to remove people from their traditional roles when they grow older, thereby freeing up those roles for others (Cumming and Henry 1961; Estes et al. 1992). According to this perspective, given the increasing frailty, illness and dependency of older people, it becomes increasingly dysfunctional for them to occupy traditional social roles they are no longer capable of adequately fulfilling. Older people therefore should retire from their jobs, pull back from civic life and eventually withdraw from other activities as well. Disengagement is assumed to be functional for the larger society because it opens up roles formerly filled by older people for younger ones, who presumably will carry them out with fresh energy and new skills. Disengagement is also assumed to be functional for older people because it enables them to take on less taxing roles consistent with their advancing age and declining health. A number of studies of older adults indeed report that the large majority feel good about retiring, which they claim has improved their morale and increased their happiness (Palmore 1985; Howard 1986).

While there is obviously some truth to disengagement theory, the idea that older people should completely disengage from the larger society takes for granted the prevailing stereotype that old age necessarily involves frailty and dependence. Critics of functionalist theories of ageing argue that these theories emphasize the need for older people to adapt to existing conditions, but that they do not question whether or not the circumstances faced by older people are just. In reaction, another group of theorists arose – those growing out of the social conflict tradition (Hendricks 1992).

The second generation of theories: age stratification theory and life-course theory

From the mid-1970s a new range of theories was introduced into gerontology (Estes et al. 2003). Two of the most important contributions were *age stratification theory* and the *life-course model*. Age stratification theory looks at the role and influence of social structures, such as retirement policy, on the process of individual ageing and on the wider stratification of older people in society. One important aspect of age stratification theory is the concept of *structural lag* (Riley et al. 1994). This provides an account of how structures do not keep pace with changes in the population and in individuals' lives. For example, in the UK, when the retirement age was set at 65 soon after the Second World War, life expectancy and quality of life for older people was considerably lower than it is today (see figure 6.2, p. 180).

Like the age stratification approach, the life-course perspective also moved beyond looking at ageing in terms of individual adjustment. (The idea of the life-course was introduced on p. 175 above.) This perspective views ageing as one phase of a lifetime shaped by the historical, social, economic and environmental factors that occurred at earlier ages in the life-course. Thus the life-course model views ageing as a process that continues from birth to death. In this, it contrasts with earlier theories that focus solely on the elderly as a distinctive group. The theory bridges micro- and macrosociology in examining the relationships between psychological states, social structures and social processes (Elder 1974).

The third generation of theories: political economy theory

One of the most important strands in the study of ageing in recent years has been the *political economy perspective* pioneered by Carroll Estes. Political economy theory provides an account of the role of the state and capitalism as contributing to systems of domination and marginalization of older people.

Political economy theory focuses on the role of economic and political systems in shaping and reproducing the prevailing power arrangements and inequalities in society. Social policy – in income, health or social security, for example – is understood as the result of social struggles, conflicts and the dominant power relations of the time. Policy affecting older people reflects the stratification of society by gender, race and class. As such, the phenomena of ageing and old age are directly related to the larger society in which they are situated and cannot be considered in isolation from the other social forces (Estes and Minkler 1991; Estes et al. 2003).

Aspects of ageing in the UK

Although ageing is a process which presents new possibilities, it is also accompanied by a set of unfamiliar challenges. As people age, they face a combination of physical, emotional and material problems that can be difficult to negotiate. One challenge that marks a significant transition is retirement. For most people, work does not just pay the bills, it also contributes to their sense of personal identity. In this case, retirement does not only lead to a loss of income; it can also lead to a loss of status to which many people find it difficult to adjust. Another significant transition that many older people face is the loss of a spouse. Widowhood can represent the loss of a partner of forty or fifty years, and someone who has been the main source of companionship and support. The Hollywood film *About Schmidt* (2002) stars Jack Nicholson in the title role as a man coming to terms with changes in his own life.

The older population reflects the diversity of UK society discussed throughout this book. Older people are rich, poor and in between; they belong to all ethnic groups; they live alone and in families of various sorts; they vary in their political values and preferences; and they are gay and lesbian as well as heterosexual. Furthermore, like other people in Britain, they are diverse with respect to health. These differences can influence the ability of older people to maintain their autonomy and overall well-being.

As well as the diversity of the older population noted above, 'old age' now covers a wide and increasing age span. A distinc-

tion is often drawn between the third and fourth ages of life. The third age covers the years from fifty to seventy-four when people are able to lead active independent lives, increasingly free from day-to-day parenting responsibilities and the labour market. Many in this group have the time and money to fund an expanding consumer market and culture. The success of Saga in the UK, a company that aims its tours, and other products, solely at the over-fifties market is evidence of the increasing power of the 'grey pound'. In contrast, the fourth age refers to the years of life when people's independence and ability to care fully for themselves is more seriously challenged.

In this section, we look at the affect of inequality, gender and ethnicity on the experience of ageing in the UK.

Inequality and older people

Overall, in the UK, older people tend to be more materially disadvantaged than other segments of the population. This picture is repeated across other European Union countries, as we see in figure 6.3. However, older people's subjective feelings about their standard of living are not solely based on material factors, but draw on other reference groups to which they compare themselves. Comparisons are possible with their memories of earlier life. In this, they are likely to compare themselves positively with the past in material terms (although not necessarily in moral or social ones). However, they are also likely to compare themselves with the standard of living that they enjoyed before retirement, which is likely to be materially better than their current position. Older people may also compare themselves with the

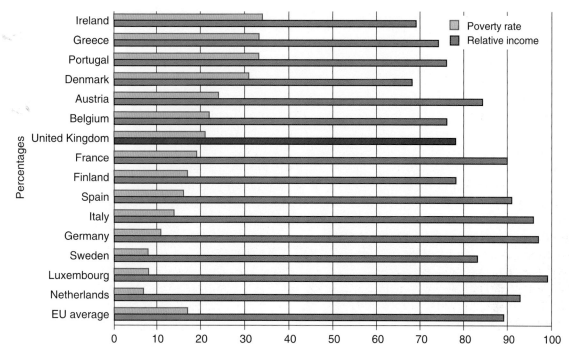

Figure 6.3 Poverty rate[a] and relative income[b] of people aged 65 and over: EU comparison, 1998

[a] Percentage with income below 60 per cent of the median equivalized income of the national population
[b] Median equivalized income of those aged 65 and over as a percentage of the population aged 0 to 64

Source: *Social Trends* 34 (2004), p. 7

average living conditions of society as a whole or of other retirees. Thus there is no common subjective experience of inequality amongst older people (Vincent 1999).

The inequalities of class, race and gender are often exacerbated when a person stops paid work, so the added inequality of old age means that older women, minorities and manual workers are poorer than peer equivalents in middle age. Retirement can result in a loss of income that may cause a significant drop in an older person's standard of living. The ability to build up a private occupational or personal pension during working life is one of the key determinants of income inequality between pensioners. Consequently, it is older men who were previously employed as professionals or managers who tend to have the highest gross weekly income in later life.

We look at poverty amongst older people in more detail in chapter 10, 'Poverty, Social Inclusion and Welfare', pp. 351–2.

A survey of the lifestyles of 1,317 older people in Britain, carried out by the

For some, old age is a time of acute poverty, ill health, depression and loneliness.

University of Kent (Milne and Harding 1999), found evidence of two distinct 'worlds'. In one world, composed of individuals in the early years of retirement who live in a shared household with an occupational pension, there is a reasonably comfortable lifestyle. In the second world, made up of those over the age of eighty who live alone and with few savings, people can suffer from acute poverty. Anxiety about money was second only to declining health as the main concern among the survey respondents.

The feminization of later life

Women tend to live longer than men. In the UK, life expectancy at birth for women in 2003 was almost five years longer than for men (National Office of Statistics 2004a). Because of this, widowhood is the norm for older women. Nearly half of women aged sixty-five and over, and four-fifths of women aged eighty-five and over, are widowed. By contrast, more than three-quarters of men aged between sixty-five and sixty-nine are married, falling to 60 per cent by their early eighties (HMSO 2004). This numerical predominance of women has been described as the 'feminization of later life'.

Although later life was disproportionately female throughout the latter half of the twentieth century in the UK, the proportion of women to men has fluctuated and is now declining somewhat. There are currently more than three times as many women as men over the age of ninety in the UK, but this figure is predicted to fall to twice as many by 2021. One reason for the decline in the number of women to men is the death of so many young men who fought in the First World War. This genera-

England and Wales
Number of females for every 100 males

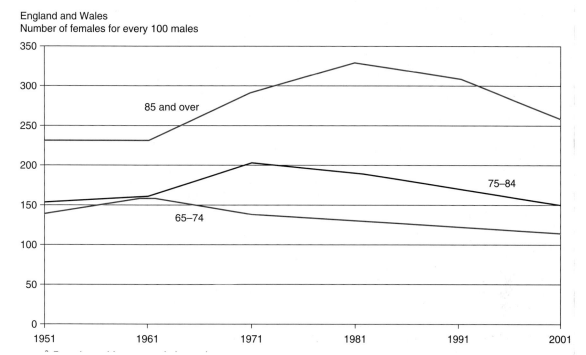

Figure 6.4 Sex ratios among older people: by age, 1951–2001[a]

[a] Based on mid-year population estimates

Source: Social Trends 34 (2004), p. 7

tion of women first reached retirement age in the 1961 Census, which began a sharp rise in the sex ratio imbalance. A second reason for the declining imbalance between older men and women is the more rapid fall in male, rather than female, mortality over the age of sixty-five during the second half of the twentieth century. Figure 6.4 shows how the sex ratio among older people has fluctuated since 1951.

Older women are more likely to be poor than their male contemporaries. We saw above that the ability to build private pension entitlements is one of the main causes of inequalities in wealth between

older people. Women are far less likely to have the same pension entitlements as men because of the gender gap in pay and also the loss of lifetime earnings associated with having children. Only 43 per cent of older women had any income from private pensions (including widows' pensions based on their late husbands' private pensions), compared to 71 per cent of men (HMSO 2004). Figure 6.5 shows the proportion of men and women over the age of sixty-five who receive private pensions and the median amounts for those with this source of income.

Studies reveal that as well as lower personal income than men, older women also

Great Britain					Percentages
	Percentage receiving		Median amount for those with private pension (£ per week)		Ratio of females' to males' private pension income (percentages)
	Males	Females	Males	Females	
Marital status					
Married/cohabiting	74	28	92	34	37
Single	52	61	65	70	108
Widowed	70	56	61	46	75
Divorced/separated	57	36	78	48	62
Socio-economic group					
Professional/managerial	90	64	172	95	55
Intermediate	60	51	84	43	51
Routine and manual	62	34	50	28	56
All	71	43	83	44	53

Figure 6.5   Private pensions[a] receipt among those aged 65 and over: by marital status and socio-economic group,[b] 2001/2

[a] Occupational or personal pension, including survivor pensions
[b] Based on own occupation and classified according to the National Statistics Socio-economic Classification (NS-SeC). See Appendix, Part 1: NS-SeC. The data are unweighted

Source: Social Trends 34 (2004), p. 11

suffer inequalities in other resources such as car ownership. Only 42 per cent of women aged between the ages of seventy-five and eighty-four have a car, compared to 66 per cent of men. The discrepancy in car ownership may not seem a major concern, but it can significantly restrict women's overall mobility and their access to healthcare, shopping and contact with others.

With increasing age, women suffer more than men from disability. This means that they require more assistance and support simply to carry out everyday tasks and personal care routines, such as bathing and getting in and out of bed. Approximately half of Britain's older women live alone, compared to only a fifth of older men. Thus, there are specific gender implications for patterns of care that need to be made available to the older population (Arber et al. 2003).

Age and ethnicity

The income of older people in the UK from ethnic minorities also tends to be lower than that of their white counterparts, and reliance on means-tested benefits is greater (Berthoud 1998). Older people from ethnic minorities groups are also disadvantaged in other measures of wealth such as car ownership and housing tenure (although certain groups such as Indians and Chinese have rates of home ownership comparable to that of white people). In general, Pakistanis and Bangladeshis in the UK have high rates of poverty compared to other groups and this pattern is continued into later life.

Ginn and Arber (2000) have examined ethnic and gender differences in the income of individuals amongst the older population. They found that older Asian women tend to be particularly disadvan-taged. Retired ethnic minorities are often unable to supplement their state pension with an occupational or private one. The lack of a private pension reflects shorter employment records in Britain for the largely migrant older ethnic population, discrimination in the labour market, the limited availability and type of jobs found in the areas where minorities have settled and sometimes a lack of fluency in English. For older women in some specific minority groups, economic disadvantage may also result from cultural norms acting as a barrier to employment earlier in life.

Using your sociological imagination: an ageless future?

Mike Hepworth, in his book Stories of Ageing (2000), uses literature to encourage his readers to 'explore fiction as an imaginative resource for understanding variations in the meaning of the experience of ageing in society'. In the section below, Hepworth discusses how science and technology could radically alter how we understand ageing:

For centuries in Western culture ageing has been imagined as a condition of existence from which human beings can only be rescued by supernatural forces. True, there has always been the quest to prolong active life, but until very recently the search has been a dream rather than a reality. And when people have experienced eternal life it has more often than not been a curse rather than a blessing, as in the legend of The Wandering Jew and The Flying Dutchman. [In literature, sometimes] supernatural forces do intervene in the apparently natural order of things to arrest the normal processes of physical ageing, as happens in the case of Faust (Fielder 1946), who makes a pact with the Devil and sells his own soul, and in Oscar Wilde's novel about moral corruption *The Picture of Dorian Gray*. Dorian Gray is an aesthete with wondrous good looks whose face and body remain mysteriously unmarked by his excessive indulgence in immoral practices; all external signs of his debauchery (in this story a form of premature ageing) are mysteriously transferred to his portrait. When he finally attacks the painting with a knife in an attempt to destroy the evidence of his past he succeeds only in destroying himself, so close has the affinity between the portrait and himself become. On his death the portrait reverts back to the original image of youth – 'all the wonder of his exquisite youth and beauty' (1960: 167) – leaving the dead body unrecognisably that of an old man, 'withered, wrinkled, and loathsome of visage' (p. 167).

Outside the realms of legend and the romantic imagination there was until very recently only one future of ageing in Western culture if one was lucky to live long enough to grow older: the Christian vision of the inevitable decline of the human body, death and an afterlife of either Heaven or Hell. The dualistic separation of the body from the soul in Christian thought regards the ageing of the body in the temporal world as a brief testing ground for eternal spiritual life beyond the veil. The corruption of the flesh frees the soul or essential self for an other-worldly existence out of time. Heaven is the compensation for graceful or virtuous ageing and not looking for pacts with the Devil to prolong a youthfully active life.

But times are rapidly changing and the emergence of modern scientific medicine and technology has offered an alternative promise to release from the ageing body in this world rather than the next (Katz 1996). One of the interesting features of this development is that contemporary models of an ageless future have become predominantly biological rather than essentially spiritual (Cole 1992). The prevailing belief now is that it is the science of the biological body, and not the religion of the eternal immaterial soul, which will arrest the process of ageing and extend the period of youthful life. The prominent social gerontologist Jabber F. Gubrium (Gubrium 1986) has commented on our reluctance in contemporary society to accept the 'normality' of a biologically limited life span. The widespread faith in the limitless potential of science to solve human problems encourages us to turn expectantly to medical science to transform ageing from the natural termination of the life-course into a disease which is potentially curable. In this optimistic vision of the future of ageing the biological risks associated with later life will be curable and the human life span extended well beyond the biblical three score years and ten. One of these days ageing will disappear from the human agenda when cures for the illnesses associated with growing older have been found and ailing and malfunctioning body parts can be replaced.

One way of defeating the ageing process is for humans to become cyborgs or to assume the 'post-human' bodies of partly biological and partly technological beings (Featherstone 1995). [Unlike Drew Leder's idea of the 'dys-appearing body' (1990), which makes its presence felt as pain, disease and dysfunction], this vision of the future is one where the dys-appearing body literally *disappears*. Any part of the internal body which causes distress in later life will be removed and replaced with a genetically engineered or transplanted substitute. The story of the ageing body will thus become not a story of how individuals cope or come to terms with its limitations but science fiction come true. The body will be a machine and the meaning of ageing may cease to be a matter of concern.

Source: Hepworth (2000), pp. 124–5

Questions

1 Is the desire for eternal youthfulness the product of an ageist society?
2 If we can eliminate the effects of ageing on the body does it make sense to talk about ageing at all?
3 Do you agree with the claim of some sociologists that we can look forward to an ageless future?

The politics of ageing

'The global ageing crisis'?

In Britain in 1850, the proportion of the population over the age of sixty-five was around 5 per cent. The figure today is over 15 per cent, and it will continue to grow. This significant shift in age distribution within the population presents specific challenges for Britain and many other industrialized countries. One way of understanding why is by thinking about the **dependency ratio** – the relationship between the number of young children and retired individuals, on the one hand, and people of working age, on the other. (The increasing dependency ratio in several countries in the UK is shown in figure 6.6.) As the proportion of older people continues to grow, the demands on social services and health systems will increase as well. The growth in life expectancy means that pensions will need to be paid for more years than they are at present (see figure 6.7).

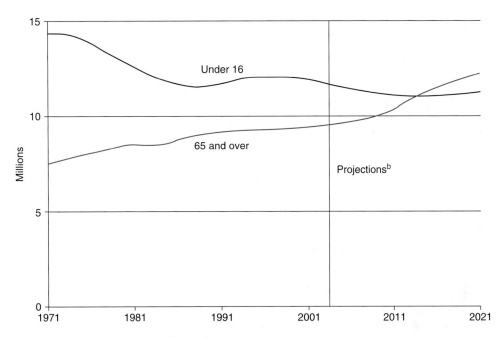

Figure 6.6 Dependent population by age, UK, 1971–2021[a]

[a] Population estimates for 2001 and 2002 include provisional results from the Manchester matching exercise
[b] 2001-based projections

Source: *Social Trends* 34 (2004), p. 17

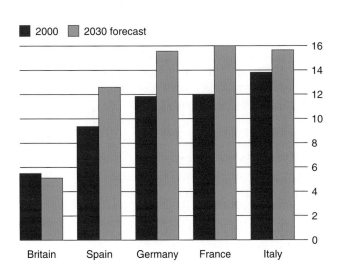

However, the working population funds the programmes that support the older population. As the old-age dependency ratio grows, some argue that increasing strain will be placed on available resources. In the light of demographic projections, governments, interest groups

Figure 6.7 Pension funding as a percentage of GDP in selected countries, 2000 and 2030

Source: 'The Crumbling Pillars of Old Age', *The Economist* (27 September 2003)

and policy-makers are being forced to look ahead and to develop proposals for meeting the needs of a changing population. Some pension associations are now warning that the current pension payment scheme is not sustainable indefinitely. They have called for an increase in the minimum pension age for both women (now sixty, rising to sixty-five) and men (now sixty-five) to seventy, in order to compensate for increased longevity. (The debate about the ageing population and welfare spending is discussed in the box below.)

Ageing and the welfare state: a ticking time bomb?

What does an ageing population mean for the welfare state? In *Averting the Old Age Crisis* (1994), the World Bank argued that the dramatic rise in the proportion of older people would mean that welfare spending on pensions and medical care would become increasingly difficult to finance. This was true for both the developed and the developing worlds, but the rich countries would get into trouble sooner. There, the ratio of people of working age to those over sixty-five, currently about four to one, would halve to two to one by 2030. The working population would have to carry a huge tax burden to support the increasing numbers of people claiming pensions. In the years since, there has been a torrent of books, conferences and policy initiatives about how to deal with this problem (*The Economist* 2000).

Several recent writers have contested this view. In a study of the American pension system, Dean Baker and Mark Weisbrot, *Social Security: The Phony Crisis* (1999), have demonstrated that even on highly conservative assumptions about economic growth, the forecast insolvency of the social security system in the USA within thirty years is highly unlikely to happen. They argue that much of the pressure to privatize the system has come from Wall Street. This is because if a state paid system of social security were to be replaced with individual private pensions, America's financial-services industry would stand to gain 130 million new investment accounts.

Similarly, in his historical survey of pension provision around the world, *Banking on Death* (2002), the British sociologist Robin Blackburn has argued that fears that an ageing population will lead to a pension crisis have been spread by financial interests and the political right in order to push for free market alternatives to the state pension. This has, in the process, spread widespread unease about people's financial security after retirement. Blackburn is also critical of the way in which private companies have run pension funds – the world of 'grey capitalism' as he calls it – where employees' savings are handed over to the managers of pension funds, looking for maximum short-term returns on their investments rather than long-term security for pension holders.

In his book, *The Imaginary Time Bomb* (2002), the British sociologist Phil Mullan has argued that those who believe that the ageing population is a ticking time bomb about to bring about a series of devastating social problems are falling for a series of myths that he seeks to defuse. For example, on healthcare Mullan argues that it is a myth that an ageing population will mean an exponential rise in ill health and dependency. He responds that ageing is not an illness, and most elderly people are neither ill nor disabled. One of the reasons that people are living longer is the improvement in living conditions over the last century, and he argues that if this improvement continues elderly people will be fitter and healthier than their predecessors. A second 'myth' that Mullan attacks is the belief that ageing populations will bankrupt the state pension scheme, so that pensions need to be reformed away from state pay-as-you-go systems to private schemes. Mullan points out that state provision of pensions tends to be much more efficient than private schemes, so there are no grounds for this reform.

Recently, the concept of older people as a 'dependent population' has been criticized; depicting a group as 'dependent' implies that they are in some way a problem for society. Chris Gilleard and Paul Higgs (2005) have argued that a new affluence has spread across society and across the life-course. Although they accept that not all older people are uniformly fit and financially secure, they say that for many people looking forward to retirement, later life has changed for the better. Many of the concepts that have conventionally been applied to the position of people in later life – for example, that they are socially disengaged or dependent upon the state – nowadays seem insufficient. For example, the generation of adults now reaching retirement age grew up in the post-war years of the 1950s and 1960s, when youth culture became dominated by 'conspicuous consumption' of fashion, music and so on. As

"Hello, we're new age pensioners"

older people, maintaining the habits they picked up as younger people, they continue to be important consumers, and enjoy an independent lifestyle.

Arber and Ginn (HMSO 2004) also argue that the idea of dependency now needs reconsidering. First, the age ranges used to define dependency (under sixteen and over sixty-four) no longer reflect the actual patterns of employment in this country. Fewer young people now enter the labour market full time at the age of sixteen, tending instead to stay in formal education for longer, and most workers leave the labour market years before the age of sixty-five. At the same time more women than ever before are in paid employment off-setting the shorter duration of employment amongst men.

Second, Arber and Ginn argue, activity that benefits the economy is not confined to active participation in the labour market. Evidence shows that, rather than being a burden, older people make many productive economic and social contributions. Older people are often involved in providing unpaid and informal care to less able partners, drastically reducing the cost to the state of provision of health and personal care. They are also a major source of care provision for grandchildren, allowing daughters and daughters-in-law to enter the labour market. Older people are also active in voluntary organizations. Arber and Ginn suggest that older people may also be an important source of financial support for their grown-up children – for example, providing them with loans, educational fees, gifts and help for housing. Many studies have also found that older parents continue to provide emotional support for their adult children, particularly during times of difficulty, such as divorce.

Ageism

Activist groups have started to fight against **ageism** – discrimination against people on the basis of their age – seeking to encourage a positive view of old age and older people. Ageism is an ideology just as sexism and racism are. There are as many false stereotypes of older people as there are in other areas. For instance, it is often believed that older workers are less competent than younger ones, that most people over sixty-five are in hospitals or homes for the elderly, and that a high proportion are senile. All these beliefs are erroneous. The productivity and attendance records of workers over sixty are superior on average to those of younger age groups; 95 per cent of people over sixty-five live in private dwellings; and only about 7 per cent of those between sixty-five and eighty show pronounced symptoms of senile decay. In the UK, the government has put forward proposals to ban age discrimination, which could cover recruitment, training (including entry to higher education), promotion, pay, job-retention and – importantly – retirement.

In one study (Levin 1988), college students were shown a photograph of the same man at ages twenty-five, fifty-two and seventy-three, and were asked to rate him in terms of a variety of personality characteristics. The ratings were significantly more negative for the man depicted at the age of seventy-three. When he looked old in his photograph, the students were more likely to perceive him negatively, even though they knew absolutely nothing about him. The mere fact that he was older was sufficient to trigger a negative cultural stereotype. Widely shared cultural stereotypes of 'grumpy old men' can lead to private opinions that are hurtful to older people.

Older people often provide much-needed help to their communities, for example by looking after grandchildren.

The sociologist Bill Bytheway has provided a theoretical account of ageism that draws on social constructionism (an approach introduced in chapter 5, pp. 152–4). Bytheway (1995) begins by questioning the reality of the terms 'old age' and 'elderly'. He argues that we presume that these terms have some kind of universal reality that they do not have. He demonstrates by asking what we mean by the term 'old age': 'Is it a condition, a period of life, a state of mind, or what?' Is there any scientific evidence that something exists that can be called old age? If it exists, how do people enter it and become elderly? To Bytheway, the categories we use to describe ageing – such as 'the elderly' and 'the old' – are themselves ageist. They are socially constructed in order to legitimize the separation and management of people on the basis of their chronological age by dominant groups with something to gain from the inequalities associated with ageism.

The greying of the world population

An 'elder explosion' is sweeping the world today. The 1998 report of the United Nations Population Fund (UNFPA 1998)

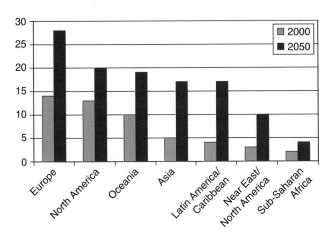

Figure 6.8 Proportion of population over the age of 65 by region, 2000 and 2050 (projected)

Source: UNFPA (2004)

notes that the sixty-five-and-older population worldwide grew by about 9 million in 1998. By 2010, this population will grow by 14.5 million; by 2050, 21 million. The most rapid growth of the sixty-five-and-older group will take place in the industrialized nations of the world, where families have fewer children and people live longer than in poorer countries. In the industrialized countries, the percentage of the older population grew from 8 per cent in 1950 to 14 per cent in 1998, and it is projected to reach 25 per cent by 2050. After the middle of the century, the developing nations will follow suit, as they experience their own elder explosion.

The populations of most of the world's societies are ageing as the result of a decline in both birth and death rates, although the populations of the poorer countries continue to have shorter life spans because of poverty, malnutrition and disease (see chapter 11). According to United Nations estimates (UNFPA 1998), the world's average life expectancy grew from forty-six in 1950 to fifty in 1985 and will reach seventy-one by 2025. At that time, some 800 million people will be over the age of sixty-five, nearly a three-fold increase in numbers from 1990 (see figure 6.8). Among the very old (those over eighty-five), whose medical and service needs are the greatest, the number will increase by half in North America, while it will double in China and grow nearly one and a half times in West Africa (Sokolovsky 1990). (The issues that an ageing population creates for China are discussed on p. 198.) This growth will place increasing demands on the resources of many countries that are already too poor to support their populations adequately.

Globalization and everyday life: China's ageing population

China has 130 million elderly residents, who make up just over 10 per cent of the population. But with the changing balance of young and old that figure is predicted to rise more than 31 per cent by the year 2050. This is as a result of the strict one-child policy, introduced in 1979 in an attempt to control China's booming population. Under the law, each couple living in the cities is allowed only one child, unless one or both partners are from an ethnic minority or they are both only children.

China's population growth
1950   563m
1960   650m
1970   820m
1980   985m
1990   1.14bn
2000   1.26bn
Source: US Census Bureau

In most rural areas, a couple may have a second child after a break of several years. The law is particularly strict in cities, where forced sterilizations, late abortions and punishment of couples who break the rules have often triggered international criticism. But the policy has badly backfired, leaving the working population struggling to provide for those who have retired.

Resentment

A growing number of single young people are finding themselves faced with the daunting prospect of caring for parents and four grandparents – a phenomenon known as a 4–2–1 family. But this does not change the fact that with the communist welfare system fast disintegrating under the pressure of economic reforms, many people are finding it increasingly hard to provide care for their elders. Those who can afford it have begun to transfer their traditional responsibilities of looking after their relatives at home to private nursing homes – a move which has itself sparked some resentment. Elderly people in China were traditionally venerated and today's elderly population expects to be looked after. Some people have even sued their families for neglect.

By the year 2030 officials estimate that care for an estimated 300 million elderly will consume a full 10 per cent of national income. Unless further action is taken, experts say the burden of caring for a greying population could begin to have a major impact on the speed of China's development.

Source: BBC (1 September 2000)

This explosion has enormous implications for social policy. More than 150 nations currently provide public assistance for people who are elderly or disabled, or for their survivors when they die. Older people are especially likely to require costly healthcare services. Their rapid growth in numbers threatens to strain the medical systems in many industrial nations, where the cost of providing healthcare to older people is likely to overwhelm government budgets.

Countries vary widely in what they are doing to cope with their growing numbers of older people. As we have seen already, the United Kingdom relies primarily on the state pension and the National Health Service to provide a safety net to serve the financial and health needs of older people. Other industrial nations provide a much broader array of services. In Japan, for example, men and women remain active well into old age because the Japanese culture encourages this activity and because business policies often support post-retirement work with the same company the person worked for before retirement. A number of national laws in Japan support the employment and training of older workers, and private businesses also support retraining.

The combination of greying and globalization will shape the lives of older people throughout the world well into this century. Traditional patterns of family care will be challenged, as family-based economies continue to give way to labour on the farms and in the offices and factories of global businesses. (Family patterns are already changing in the West, as we see in our discussion of 'the beanpole family', chapter 7, p. 233.) Like the industrial nations early in the twentieth century, all societies will be challenged to find roles for their ageing citizens. This challenge will include identifying new means of economic support, often financed by government programmes. It will also entail identifying ways to incorporate rather than isolate older people, by drawing on their considerable reserves of experience and talents.

Summary points

1   *Socialization* is the process whereby, through contact with other human beings, the helpless infant gradually becomes a self-aware, knowledgeable human being, skilled in the ways of the given culture and environment.

2   According to G. H. Mead, the child achieves an understanding of being a separate agent by seeing how others behave towards him or her in social contexts. At a later stage, entering into organized games, learning the rules of play, the child comes to understand 'the *generalized other*' – general values and cultural rules.

3   Jean Piaget distinguishes several main stages in the development of the child's capability to make sense of the world. Each stage involves the acquisition of new cognitive skills and depends on the successful completion of the preceding one. According to Piaget these stages of cognitive development are universal features of socialization.

4   *Agencies of socialization* are structured groups or contexts within which significant processes of socialization occur. In all cultures, the family is the principal socializing agency of the child during infancy. Other influences include *peer groups*, schools, and the *mass media*.

5   The development of mass communications has enlarged the range of socializing agencies. The spread of mass printed media was later accompanied by the use of electronic communication. TV exerts a particularly powerful influence, reaching people of all ages at regular intervals every day.

6   *Gender socialization* begins virtually as soon as an infant is born. Even parents who believe they treat children equally tend to produce different responses to boys and girls. These differences are reinforced by many other cultural influences.

7   Socialization continues throughout the life cycle. At each distinct phase of life there are transitions to be made or crises to be overcome. This includes facing death as the termination of physical existence.

8   Biological, psychological and social *ageing* are not the same and may vary considerably within and across cultures. It is important not to confuse a person's *social age* with his or

her chronological age. Physical ageing is inevitable, but for most people, proper nutrition, diet and exercise can preserve a high level of health well into old age.

9 Because of low mortality and fertility rates, Western societies are rapidly greying or ageing. The older population constitutes a large and rapidly growing category that is extremely diverse economically, socially and politically. However, it is possible to divide a third and a fourth age representing the 'young-old' and the 'old-old'.

10 Functionalist theories of ageing originally argued that the disengagement of older people from society was desirable. *Disengagement theory* held that older people should pull back from their traditional social roles as younger people move into them. *Activity theory*, on the other hand, soon came to emphasize the importance of being engaged and busy as a source of vitality. Conflict theorists of ageing have focused on how the routine operation of social institutions produces various forms of inequality among older people. The most recent theories regard older people as capable of taking control over their own lives and playing an active role in politics and the economy.

11 Older people are more likely to be materially disadvantaged than other groups. Older women are also more likely to suffer from poverty than their male counterparts, and older members of ethnic minorities are more likely to suffer poverty than older white people. There are considerably more older women than men, although this imbalance is declining somewhat.

12 The greying of the population has resulted in a greater 'dependency ratio'. This has led to new debates about the funding of services for older people.

13 Globalization threatens the traditional roles of older people in many societies. The role of older people throughout the world is in a rapid state of transition.

Questions for further thought

1 In what ways does socialization differ from indoctrination or brainwashing?

2 What is the relationship between self-identity and our social identities?

3 How significant is primary socialization in complex and rapidly changing societies?

4 How is a person's ageing shaped by social factors?

5 Aside from physical characteristics are boys and girls naturally different?

6 Is there a 'global ageing crisis'?

7 Have you witnessed examples of ageism in your everyday life?

Further reading

Simon Biggs, *Understanding Ageing* (Buckingham: Open University Press, 1993).

R. Blackburn, *Banking on Death, or Investing in Life* (London: Verso, 2002).

B. Bytheway, *Ageism* (Buckingham: Open University Press, 1999).

Chris Gilleard and Paul Higgs, *Contexts of Ageing: Class, Cohort and Community* (Cambridge: Polity, 2005).

Phil Mullan, *The Imaginary Time Bomb: Why an Ageing Population is Not a Social Problem* (London: A. B. Taurus, 2000).

P. Laslett, *The Third Age* (London: Weidenfeld & Nicolson, 1989).

Peter G. Peterson, *Gray Dawn: How the Coming Age Wave Will Transform America – and the World* (New York: Random House, 1999).

John Vincent, *Old Age* (London: Routledge, 2003).

Internet links

The Centre for Policy on Ageing
http://www.cpa.org.uk/ageinfo/ageinfo.html

OECD – international work on ageing
http://www.oecd.org/topic/0,2686,en_2649_37435_1_1_1_1_37457,00.html

United Nations Programme on Ageing
http://www.un.org/esa/socdev/ageing/

World Heath Organization on Ageing and the Life-Course
http://www.who. int/ageing/en/

Contents

7 Families and Intimate Relationships

HAVE YOU ever been in love? Almost certainly you have. Most people from their teens on know what being in love is like. Love and romance provide, for many of us, some of the most intense feelings we ever experience. Why do people fall in love? The answer at first sight seems obvious. Love expresses a mutual and physical attachment two individuals feel for one another. These days, we might be sceptical of the idea that love is 'for ever', but falling in love, we tend to think, is an experience arising from universal human emotions. It seems natural for a couple who fall in love to want personal and sexual fulfilment in their relationship, perhaps by marrying and/or starting a family.

Yet this situation, which may appear to be 'natural' to us today, is in fact very unusual. Beginning a long-term partnership, or starting a family, with someone who you have fallen in love with is *not* an experience most people across the world have. Amongst certain Asian communities in the UK, for example, arranged marriages remain the norm. In these cases, falling in love is rarely thought of as having any connection to marriage or to starting a new family. The idea of basing a long-term partnership on romantic love did not become widespread until fairly recently in our society and has never even existed in most other cultures.

Only in modern times have love and sexuality come to be seen as closely connected in Western industrialized societies. John Boswell, a historian of medieval Europe, has remarked on how unusual are our modern ideas about romantic love. In Europe of the Middle Ages, virtually no one married for love. There was in fact a medieval saying: 'To love one's wife with one's emotions is adultery.' In those days and for centuries afterwards, men and

women married mainly in order to keep property in the hands of family or to raise children to work in the family farm. Once married, they may have become close companions; this happened after marriage, however, rather than before. People sometimes had sexual affairs outside marriage, but these inspired few of the emotions we currently associate with love. Romantic love was regarded as at best a weakness and at worst a kind of sickness.

Our attitudes today are almost completely the opposite. Boswell quite rightly speaks of a 'virtual obsession of modern industrial culture' with romantic love:

> Those immersed in this 'sea of love' tend to take it for granted. . . . Very few premodern or non-industrialized contemporary cultures would agree with the contention – uncontroversial in the West – that 'the purpose of a man is to love a woman, and the purpose of a woman is to love a man.' Most human beings in most times and places would find this a very meagre measure of human value! (Boswell 1995: xix)

It was only in the late eighteenth century that the concept of romantic love began to make its presence felt. Romantic love – as distinct from the more or less universal compulsions of passionate love – involved idealizing its object. The idea of romantic love more or less coincided with the emergence of the novel as a literary form, and the spread of romantic novels played a vital part in spreading the idea of romantic love (Radway 1984). For women, in particular, romantic love involved telling oneself stories about how the relationship could lead to personal fulfilment.

Romantic love, therefore, cannot be understood as a natural part of human life; rather, it has been shaped by broad social and historical influences. For most people in the UK today, the couple, married or unmarried, is at the core of what the family is. The couple came to be at the centre of family life as the economic role of the family dwindled, and love, or love and sexual attraction, became the basis of forming marriage ties (although, as we shall see later in this chapter, the term 'family' should by no means only be understood as involving a heterosexual couple and their children).

Most people in our society believe that a good relationship is based on emotional communication or intimacy. The idea of intimacy, like so many other familiar notions we've discussed in this book, is a recent one. As we have seen, marriage was never in the past based on intimacy and emotional communication. No doubt this was important to a good marriage, but it was not the foundation of it. For the modern couple it is. Communication is the means of establishing a good relationship in the first place, and it is the chief rationale for its continuation. A good relationship is a relationship of equals, where each party has equal rights and obligations. In such a relationship, each person has respect, and wants the best, for the other. Talk, or dialogue, is the basis of making the relationship work. Relationships function best if people don't hide too much from each other – there has to be mutual trust. And trust has to be worked at; it can't just be taken for granted. Finally, a good relationship is one free from arbitrary power, coercion or violence (Giddens 1993).

The theme of much of this book has been social change. We live in a turbulent, difficult and unfamiliar world today. Whether we like it or not, we all must come to terms with the mixture of opportunity

The BBC's production of Jane Austen's novel *Pride and Prejudice* tells a classic story of romantic love championing against adversity.

and risk it presents. The discussion above, on romantic love, shows that nowhere is this observation truer than in the domain of personal and emotional life.

How do we begin to understand the nature of these changes and their impact on our lives? It's only possible to understand what is going on with our intimate relationships and with the family as a social institution today if we know something about how people lived in the past and how people currently live in other societies. So in this chapter, we look at the historical development of marriage and the family. We then examine families and intimate relationships in Britain today. The final section of the chapter looks at some of the theoretical perspectives that

attempt to explain the family and intimate relationships, before concluding by turning to the current debate over 'family values'.

Basic concepts

We need first of all to define some basic concepts, particularly those of family, kinship and marriage. A **family** is a group of persons directly linked by kin connections, the adult members of which assume responsibility for caring for children. **Kinship** ties are connections between individuals, established either through marriage or through the lines of descent that connect blood relatives (mothers, fathers, siblings, offspring, etc.). **Marriage** can be defined as a socially acknowledged and approved sexual union between two adult individuals. When two people marry, they become kin to one another; the marriage bond also, however, connects together a wider range of kinspeople. Parents, brothers, sisters and other blood relatives become relatives of the partner through marriage.

Family relationships are always recognized within wider kinship groups. In virtually all societies we can identify what sociologists and anthropologists call the **nuclear family**, two adults living together in a household with their own or adopted children. In most traditional societies, the nuclear family was part of a larger kinship network of some type. When close relatives other than a married couple and children live either in the same household or in a close and continuous relationship with one another, we speak of an extended family. An **extended family** may include grandparents, brothers and their wives, sisters and their husbands, aunts and nephews.

In most Western societies, marriage, and therefore the family, are associated with **monogamy**. It is illegal for a man or woman to be married to more than one spouse at any one time. This is not the case everywhere, however. In a famous comparison of several hundred societies in the mid-twentieth century, George Murdock (1949) found that **polygamy**, which allows a husband or wife to have more than one spouse, was permitted in more than 80 per cent of them. There are two types of polygamy: **polygyny**, in which a man may be married to more than one woman at the same time, and **polyandry**, much less

An unusual family photograph, showing Utah polygamist Tom Green with his five wives and some of his twenty-nine children.

common, in which a woman may have two or more husbands simultaneously. The best-known group to practise polygamy in the West are the Fundamentalist Mormons, based largely in Utah, in the United States, where the practice is illegal, but prosecutions are rare. The practice of having many wives was abandoned by mainstream Mormons a century ago as a condition of Utah becoming part of the United States. It is estimated that 30,000 fundamentalists still practise polygamy in Utah.

Many sociologists believe that we cannot speak about 'the family' as if there is one model of family life that is more or less universal. As we shall see in this chapter, there are many different family forms: two-parent families, step-families, lone-parent families and so on. The sociologist Diana Gittins (1993) has argued that it seems more appropriate to speak of 'families' rather than 'the family'. Referring to 'families' emphasizes the diversity of family forms. While as a shorthand term we may often speak of 'the family', it is vital to remember what a variety this covers.

The family in history

Sociologists once thought that prior to the modern period, the predominant form of family in Western Europe was of the extended type. Research has shown this view to be mistaken. The nuclear family, consisting of a father, mother and dependent children, seems long to have been pre-eminent. Pre-modern household size was larger than it is today, but the difference is not especially great. In England, for example, throughout the seventeenth, eighteenth and nineteenth centuries, the average household size was 4.75 persons. The current average in the UK is 2.4 (HMSO 2004). Since the earlier figure includes domestic servants, the difference in family size is small.

Children in pre-modern Europe were often working – helping their parents on the farm – from the age of seven or eight. Those who did not remain in the family enterprise frequently left the parental household at an early age to do domestic work in the houses of others or to follow apprenticeships. Children who went away to work in other households would rarely see their parents again.

Other factors made family groups then even more impermanent than they are now, in spite of the high rates of divorce in current times. Rates of mortality (the number of deaths per thousand of the population in any one year) for people of all ages were much higher. A quarter or more of all infants in early modern Europe did not survive beyond the first year of life (in contrast to well under 1 per cent today), and women frequently died in childbirth. The death of children or of one or both spouses often shattered family relations.

The development of family life

The historical sociologist Lawrence Stone has charted some of the changes leading from pre-modern to modern forms of family life in Europe. Stone distinguished three phases in the development of the family from the 1500s to the 1800s:

1 In the early part of this period, the main family form was a type of nuclear family that lived in fairly small households but maintained deeply embedded relationships within the community, including

with other kin. This family structure was not clearly separated from the community. According to Stone (although some historians have challenged this), the family at that time was not a major focus of emotional attachment or dependence for its members. People didn't experience, or look for, the emotional intimacies we associate with family life today.

Sex within marriage was not regarded as a source of pleasure but as a necessity to propagate children. Individual freedom of choice in marriage and other matters of family life were subordinated to the interests of parents, other kin or the community. Outside aristocratic circles, where it was sometimes actively encouraged, erotic or romantic love was regarded by moralists and theologians as a sickness. As Stone puts it, the family during this period 'was an open-ended, low-keyed, unemotional, authoritarian institution. ... It was also very short-lived, being frequently dissolved by the death of the husband or wife or the death or very early departure from the home of the children' (1980).

2 This type of family was succeeded by a transitional form that lasted from the early seventeenth century to the beginning of the eighteenth. This later type was largely confined to the upper reaches of society, but it was nevertheless very important because from it spread attitudes that have since become almost universal. The nuclear family became a more separate entity, distinct from ties to other kin and to the local community. There was a growing stress on the importance of marital and parental love, although there was also an increase in the authoritarian power of fathers.

3 In the third phase, the type of family system we are most familiar with in the West today gradually evolved. This family is a group tied by close emotional bonds, enjoying a high degree of domestic privacy and preoccupied with the rearing of children. It is marked by the rise of **affective individualism**, the formation of marriage ties on the basis of personal selection, guided by sexual attraction or romantic love. Sexual aspects of love began to be glorified within marriage instead of in extramarital relationships. The family became geared to consumption rather than production, as a result of the increasing spread of workplaces separate from the home. Women became associated with domesticity and men with being the breadwinner. In recent decades the idea of the male breadwinner 'heading' the family is being increasingly challenged, as increasing numbers of women enter the workplace, and family structures continue to diversify. (We examine these changes further later in this chapter.)

The historian John Boswell, who was mentioned at the start of this chapter, has noted:

> In premodern Europe marriage usually began as a property arrangement, was in its middle mostly about raising children, and ended about love. Few couples in fact married 'for love', but many grew to love each other in time as they jointly managed their household, reared their offspring, and shared life's experiences. Nearly all surviving epitaphs to spouses evince profound affection. By contrast, in most of the modern West, marriage *begins* about love, in its middle is still mostly about raising children (if there are children), and ends – often – about property, by which point love is absent or a distant memory. (1995: xxi)

Was the nuclear family ever really the norm?

The way we never were: myths of the traditional family

Many people, generally writing from a conservative point of view, argue that family life is becoming dangerously undermined (we examine the current debate about family values at the end of this chapter, pp. 245–6). They contrast what they see as the decline of the family with more traditional forms of family life. Was the family of the past as peaceful and harmonious as many people recall it, or is this simply an idealized fiction? As Stephanie Coontz points out in her book *The Way We Never Were* (1992), as with other visions of a golden age of the past, the rosy light shed on the 'traditional family' dissolves when we look back to previous times to see what things really were like.

Many admire the apparent discipline and stability of the Victorian family. However, because families at this time suffered especially high death rates, the average length of marriages was less than twelve years, and more than half of all children saw the death of at least one parent by the time they were twenty-one. The admired discipline of the Victorian family was rooted in the strict authority of parents over their children. The way in which this authority was exercised would be considered exceedingly harsh by today's standards.

If we consider the Victorian family of the 1850s, the ideal family still eludes us.

In this period, wives were more or less forcibly confined to the home. According to Victorian morality, women were supposed to be strictly virtuous, while men were sexually licentious: many visited prostitutes and paid regular visits to brothels. In fact, wives and husbands often had little to do with one another, communicating only through their children. Moreover, domesticity wasn't even an option for poorer groups of this period. In factories and workshops families worked long hours with little time for home life. Child labour was also rampant in these groups.

Our most recent memory draws us to the 1950s as the time of the ideal family. This was a period when women worked only in the home, while men were responsible for earning the family wage. Yet large numbers of women didn't actually *want* to retreat to a purely domestic role, and felt miserable and trapped in it. Many women had held paid jobs during the Second World War as part of the war effort. They lost these jobs when men returned home. Moreover, men were still emotionally removed from their wives and often observed a strong sexual double standard, seeking sexual adventures for themselves but setting a strict code for their spouse.

The American author Betty Friedan wrote a best-selling book, *The Feminine Mystique*, which first appeared in 1963, although its research referred to the decade of the 1950s. Friedan struck a chord in the hearts of thousands of women when she spoke of the 'problem with no name': the oppressive nature of a domestic life bound up with child care, domestic drudgery and a husband who only occasionally put in an appearance and with whom little emotional communication was possible. Even more severe than the oppressive home life endured by many women were the alcoholism and violence suffered within many families during a time when society was not fully prepared to confront these issues.

Changes in family patterns worldwide

There is a diversity of family forms today in different societies across the world. In some areas, such as more remote regions in Asia, Africa and the Pacific Rim, traditional family systems are little altered. In most developing countries, however, widespread changes are occurring. The origins of these changes are complex, but several factors can be picked out as especially important. One is the spread of Western culture. Western ideals of romantic love, for example, have spread to societies in which they were previously unknown. Another factor is the development of centralized government in areas previously composed of autonomous smaller societies. People's lives become influenced by their involvement in a national political system; moreover, governments make active attempts to alter traditional ways of behaviour. Because of the problem of rapidly expanding population growth, for example in China (discussed below on pp. 245–6), states frequently introduce programmes that advocate smaller families, the use of contraception, and so forth. A further influence is the large-scale migration from rural to urban areas. Often men go to work in towns or cities, leaving family members in the home village. Alternatively, a nuclear family group will move as a unit to the city. In both cases, traditional family forms and kinship systems may become weakened.

Finally, and perhaps most important, employment opportunities away from the land and in such organizations as government bureaucracies, mines, plantations and – where they exist – industrial firms tend to have disruptive consequences for family systems previously centred on landed production in the local community.

In general, these changes are creating a worldwide movement towards the breaking down of the extended family systems and other types of kinship groups. This was first documented by William J. Goode in his book *World Revolution in Family Patterns* (1963) and has been borne out by subsequent research.

Recent developments

The most important changes occurring worldwide are the following:

1 Clans and other kin groups are declining in their influence.
2 There is a general trend towards the free selection of a spouse.
3 The rights of women are becoming more widely recognized, in respect to both the initiation of marriage and decision-making within the family.
4 Arranged marriages are becoming less common.
5 Higher levels of sexual freedom, for men and women, are developing in societies that were very restrictive.
6 There is a general trend towards the extension of children's rights.
7 There is an increased acceptance of same-sex partnerships.

It would be a mistake to exaggerate these trends, or to presume that they have occurred uniformly around the world – many of them are still being fought for and are bitterly contested. (The suppression of women's rights in Afghanistan under the Taliban from 1996 to 2001 – discussed in chapter 20, p. 852 – provides one example of how these trends are not uniform.) Similarly it would be a mistake to suppose that the extended family is everywhere in decline. In most societies today, extended families are still the norm, and traditional family practices continue. Moreover, there are differences in the speed at which change is occurring, and there are reversals and countertrends.

Families and intimate relationships in the UK

Given the culturally diverse character of the United Kingdom today, there are considerable variations in family and marriage within the country. Some of the most striking include differences between family patterns of white and non-white people, and we need to consider why this is so. We will then move on to examine issues surrounding divorce and remarriage in relation to contemporary patterns of family life. Let us first, however, describe some basic characteristics which nearly all families in Britain share.

Overall characteristics

Features of the family as a whole in the UK are the following:

1 Like other Western families, the British family is monogamous, monogamy being established in law. Given the high rate of divorce that now exists in the United Kingdom, however, some observers have suggested that the British marriage pattern should be

called serial monogamy. That is to say, individuals are permitted to have a number of spouses in sequence, although no one may have more than one wife or husband at any one time. It is misleading, though, to muddle legal monogamy with sexual practice. It is obvious that a high proportion of Britons engage in sexual relations with individuals other than their spouses.

2 British marriage is based on the idea of romantic love. Affective individualism has become the major influence. Couples are expected to develop mutual affection, based on personal attraction and compatibility, as a basis for contracting marriage relationships. Romantic love as part of marriage has become 'naturalized' in contemporary Britain; it seems to be a normal part of human existence, rather than a distinctive feature of modern culture. Of course, the reality is divergent from the ideology. The emphasis on personal satisfaction in marriage has raised expectations which sometimes cannot be met, and this is one factor involved in increasing rates of divorce.

3 The British family is patrilineal and neolocal. **Patrilineal** inheritance involves children taking the surname of the father. In the past it also meant that property would usually pass down the male line, although this is far less common today. (Many societies in the world are **matrilineal** – surnames, and often property, pass down the female line.) A **neolocal residence** pattern involves a married couple moving into a dwelling away from both of their families. Neolocalism, however, is not an absolutely fixed trait of the British family. Many families in the UK, particularly in poorer, working-class or Asian neighbourhoods, are **matrilocal** – the newly-weds settle in an area close to where the bride's parents live. (If the couple lives near or with the groom's parents, it is called **patrilocal**.)

4 The British family is often described as nuclear, consisting of one or two parents living in a household with their children, although nuclear family units are by no means completely isolated from other kin ties. However, the dominance of the nuclear family is being eroded, as we see below.

Development and diversity in family patterns

According to Rapoport et al., 'families in Britain today are in transition from coping in a society in which there was a single overriding norm of what a family should be like to a society in which a plurality of norms are recognised as legitimate and, indeed, desirable' (1982: 476). Substantiating this argument, they identify five types of diversity: *organizational, cultural, class, life course* and *cohort*. We could add to this list *sexual* diversity. The diversity of family forms that the Rapoports identify is more obvious today than when she first wrote more than twenty years ago.

> The life-course is also discussed in chapter 6, 'Socialization, the Life-Course and Ageing', pp. 175–8.

Families *organize* their respective individual domestic duties and their links with the wider social environment in a variety of ways. The contrast between 'orthodox' families – the woman as 'housewife', the husband as 'breadwinner' – and dual-career or one-parent families illustrate this diversity. *Culturally,* there is greater diversity of family benefits and values than used to be the case. The presence of ethnic minorities (such as families of Asian or West Indian origin, which are discussed below) and the influence of movements such as feminism have produced considerable cultural variety in family forms. Persistent *class* divisions between the poor, the skilled working classes and the various groupings within the middle and upper classes sustain major variations in family structure. Variations in family experience during the *life course* are fairly obvious. For instance, one individual might come into a family in which both parents had stayed together, and herself or himself go on to marry and then divorce. Another person might be brought up in a single-parent family, be multiply married and have children by each marriage.

The term *cohort* refers to generations within families. Connections between parents and grandparents, for example, have probably now become weaker than they were. On the other hand, more people now live into old age, and three 'ongoing' families might exist in close relation to one another: married grandchildren, their parents and the grandparents. There is also greater *sexual* diversity in family organizations than ever before. As homosexuality becomes increasingly accepted in many Western societies, partnerships and families are formed based on partnerships between homosexual as well as heterosexual couples.

Gay marriage is discussed in chapter 12, 'Sexuality and Gender', pp. 434–6.

South Asian families

Among the variety of British family types, there is one pattern distinctively different from most others – that associated with South Asian groups. The South Asian population in the UK numbers more than a million people. Migration began in the 1950s from three main areas of the Indian subcontinent: Punjab, Gujarat and Bengal. In Britain, these migrants formed

Extended Asian families often show strong familial bonds.

communities based on religion, area of origin, caste and, most importantly, kinship. Many migrants found their ideas of honour and family loyalty almost entirely absent among the indigenous British population. They tried to maintain family unity, but housing proved a problem. Large old houses were available in run-down areas; moving up-market usually meant moving into smaller houses and breaking up the extended family.

South Asian children born in the UK today are often exposed to two very different cultures. At home, their parents expect or demand conformity to the norms of cooperation, respect and family loyalty. At school, they are expected to pursue academic success in a competitive and individualistic social environment. Most choose to organize their domestic and personal lives in terms of the ethnic sub-culture, as they value the close relationships associated with traditional family life. Yet involvement with British culture has brought changes. The Western tradition of marrying 'for love' frequently comes into conflict with the practice of arranged marriages within Asian communities. Such unions, arranged by parents and family members, are predicated on the belief that love comes from within marriage. Young people of both sexes are demanding greater consultation in the arrangement of their marriages.

Statistical findings from the Policy Study Institute's fourth national survey of ethnic minorities (Modood et al. 1997) indicate that Indians, Pakistanis, Bangladeshis and African-Asians were the ethnic groups most likely to be married. Among all families with dependent children in 2001, 65 per cent of Asian or Asian British one-family households consisted of a married couple, while among whites and African-Caribbeans the percentages were somewhat lower. Cohabitation was proportionately smaller amongst Asian and Asian British couples with children than it was amongst other ethnic groups (see table 7.1). Although there appear to be some signs of change among South Asian families in Britain – such as young people wanting a greater say in marriages and a slight rise in divorces and lone-parent households – on the whole South Asian ethnic groups in the UK continue to have remarkably strong familial bonds.

Black families

Families of African-Caribbean origin in Britain have a different structure again. There are far fewer black women aged between twenty and forty-four living with a husband than there are white women in the same age group. Rates of divorce and separation are higher among African-Caribbeans than among other ethnic groups in Britain. Lone-parent households are more common among African-Caribbeans than among any other ethnic minority; yet unlike other groups, single African-Caribbean mothers are more likely to be employed (Modood et al. 1997). The high proportion of lone-parent families (the vast majority of which are headed by the mother) amongst the black or black British population compared to other ethnic groups can be seen in table 7.1 below.

In the UK, the same factors seem to be at work among black families in the poorer neighbourhoods of London and other cities. Many discussions of black families concentrate on the low rates of formal marriage, but some observers believe that this emphasis is misplaced. The marriage relationship does not necessarily form the

Table 7.1   British families with dependent children: by ethnic group,[a] 2001 (%)

	One family households			Other households with dependent children	All
	Married couple families	Cohabiting couple families	Lone-parent families		
White	60	12	22	6	100
Mixed	38	11	39	12	100
Asian or Asian British					
Indian	68	2	10	21	100
Pakistani	61	2	13	24	100
Bangladeshi	63	2	12	23	100
Other Asian	66	3	12	19	100
All Asian or Asian British	65	2	11	22	100
Black or black British					
Black Caribbean	29	11	48	12	100
Black African	38	7	36	19	100
Other Black	24	9	52	15	100
All black or black British	32	9	43	15	100
Chinese	69	3	15	13	100
Other ethnic group	67	3	18	12	100
All ethnic groups	60	11	22	7	100

[a] Of household reference person

Source: *Social Trends* 34 (2004), p. 28

structure of the black family as it does for the family in other groups. Extended kinship networks are important in West Indian groups – much more significant, relative to marital ties, than in most white communities in the UK. A mother heading a lone-parent family is likely to have a close and supportive network of relatives to depend on. Siblings also play an important role in many African-Caribbean families by helping to raise younger children (Chamberlain 1999). This contradicts the idea that black single parents and their children necessarily form unstable families.

Inequality within the family

Balancing work and care

One of the major factors affecting women's careers is the male perception that for female employees, work comes second to having children. One study carried out in Britain in the mid-1980s (Homans 1987) investigated the views of managers interviewing female applicants for positions as technical staff in the health services. The researchers found that the interviewers always asked the women about whether or

There is a high proportion of lone parents amongst the UK's African-Caribbean population.

not they had, or intended to have, children (this is now illegal in both the UK and the USA). They virtually never followed this practice with male applicants. When asked why, two themes ran through their answers: women with children may require extra time off for school holidays or if a child falls sick, and responsibility for child care is a mother's problem rather than a parental one.

Some managers thought their questions indicated an attitude of 'caring' towards female employees. But most saw such a line of questioning as part of their task to assess how far a female applicant would prove a reliable colleague. Thus, one manager remarked:

> It's a bit of a personal question, I appreciate that, but I think it's something that has to be considered. It's something that can't happen to a man really, but I suppose in a sense it's unfair – it's not equal opportunity because the man could never find himself having a family as such. (Homans 1987)

While men cannot biologically 'have a family' in the sense of bearing children,

they can be fully involved in and responsible for child care. Such a possibility was not taken into account by any of the managers studied. The same attitudes were held about the promotion of women. Women were seen as likely to interrupt their careers to care for young children, no matter how senior a position they might have reached. The few women in this study who held senior management positions were all without children, and several of those who planned to have children in the future said they intended to leave their jobs and would perhaps retrain for other positions subsequently.

How should we interpret these findings? Are women's job opportunities hampered mainly by male prejudices? Some managers expressed the view that women with children should *not* work, but should occupy themselves with child care and the home. Most, however, accepted the principle that women should have the same career opportunities as men. The bias in their attitudes had less to do with the workplace itself than with the domestic responsibilities of parenting. So long as most of the population take it for granted that parenting cannot be shared on an equal basis by both women and men, the problems facing women employees will persist. It will remain a fact of life, as one of the managers put it, that women are disadvantaged, compared with men, in their career opportunities.

In addition, as we saw earlier, the average wage of employed women is well below that of men, although the difference has narrowed somewhat over the past thirty years. Even within the same occupational categories, women on average earn lower salaries than men.

In her book *Working Women Don't Have*

Wives (1994), Terri Apter argues that women find themselves struggling with two contradictory forces. They want and need economic independence, but at the same time they want to be mothers to their children. Both goals are reasonable, but while men with wives who take prime responsibility for domestic work can achieve them, women cannot do likewise. Greater flexibility in working life is one partial solution. Much more difficult is getting men to alter their attitudes.

Housework

Although there have been revolutionary changes in women's status in recent decades in the UK, including the entry of women into male-dominated professions, one area of work has lagged far behind: **housework**. Because of the increase in the number of married women in the workforce and their resulting change in status, it was presumed that men would contribute more to housework. On the whole, this has not been the case. Although men now do more housework than they did three decades ago and women do slightly less, the balance is still unequal. Recent surveys in the UK have found that women still do the majority of housework and child care, on average spending 4 hours 3 minutes a day on these activities compared to 2 hours 17 minutes for men (HMSO 2005). Some sociologists have argued that where women are already working in the paid sector, this extra work, in effect, amounts to a 'second shift' (Hochschild 1989; Shelton 1992). In the late 1980s findings like these led Arlie Hochschild to call the state of relations between women and men a 'stalled revolution'. Why does housework remain women's work? This

question has been the focus of a good deal of research in recent years.

Some sociologists have suggested that this phenomenon is best explained as a result of economic forces: household work is exchanged for economic support. Because women earn less than men, they are more likely to remain economically dependent on their husbands and thus perform the bulk of the housework. Until the earnings gap is narrowed, women are likely to remain in their dependent position. Hochschild has suggested that women are thus doubly oppressed by men: once during the 'first shift' and then again during the 'second shift'. But while this dependency model contributes to our understanding of the gendered aspects of housework, it breaks down when applied to situations where the wife earns more than her husband. For instance, of the husbands whom Hochschild studied who earned less than their wives, none shared in the housework.

Some sociologists approach the problem from a symbolic interactionist perspective, asking how the performance or non-performance of housework is related to the gender roles created by society. For example, through interviews and participant observation, Hochschild found that the assignment of household tasks falls clearly along gendered lines. Wives do most of the daily chores, such as cooking and routine cleaning, while husbands tend to take on more occasional tasks, such as mowing the lawn or doing home repairs. The major difference between these two types of task is the amount of control the individual has over when they do the work. The jobs done by women in the home are those that tend to bind them to a fixed schedule, whereas men's household tasks are done less regularly and are more discretionary.

In her book *Feeding the Family* (1991), the sociologist Marjorie Devault looked at how the caring activities within a household are socially constructed as women's work. She argues that women perform the bulk of the housework because the family 'incorporates a strong and relatively enduring association of caring activity with the woman's position in the household'. Observing the division of responsibility for cooking, Devault remarks that the gendered relations of feeding and eating 'convey the message that giving service is part of being a woman, and receiving it is fundamentally part of being a man'. Even in households where men contribute, an egalitarian division of household labour between spouses is greatly impeded when the couple have children – children require constant attention, and their care schedules are often unpredictable. Mothers overwhelmingly spend more time with child-rearing tasks than do their spouses (Shelton 1992).

Sociologists argue that underlying this inequitable distribution of tasks is the implicit understanding that men and women are responsible for, and should operate in, different spheres. Men are expected to be providers, while women are expected to tend to their families – even if they are breadwinners as well as mothers. Expectations like this reinforce traditional gender roles learned during childhood socialization. By reproducing these roles in everyday life, men and women 'do gender' and reinforce gender as a means for society to differentiate between men and women.

Intimate violence

Since family or kin relations form part of everyone's existence, family life encompasses virtually the whole range of emotional experience. Family relationships – between wife and husband, parents and children, brothers and sisters, or between distant relatives – can be warm and fulfilling. But they can equally well contain the most pronounced tensions, driving people to despair or filling them with a deep sense of anxiety and guilt. This side of family life belies the rosy images of harmony that are quite often emphasized in TV commercials and elsewhere in the popular media. Domestic violence and the abuse of children are two of the most disturbing aspects.

Sexual abuse of children

The sexual abuse of children can most easily be defined as the carrying out of sexual acts by adults with children below the age of consent (sixteen years old in Britain). **Incest** refers to sexual relations between close kin. Not all incest counts as child sexual abuse. For example, sexual intercourse between brother and sister is incestuous, but does not fit the definition of abuse. In child sexual abuse, an adult is essentially exploiting an infant or child for sexual purposes. Nevertheless, the most common form of incest is one that is also child sexual abuse – incestuous relations between fathers and young daughters.

Incest, and child sexual abuse more generally, are phenomena that have been 'discovered' only in the past few decades. Of course it has long been known that such sexual acts occur, but it was assumed by most social observers that the strong taboos that exist against this behaviour meant that it was extremely uncommon. This is not the case. Child sexual abuse has proved to be disturbingly commonplace. It is probably found more often among poorer families, but exists at all levels of the social hierarchy – as well as in institutions, as we shall see below.

Although in its more obvious versions its nature is plain, the full extent of child sexual abuse is difficult, if not impossible, to calculate because of the many forms it can assume. No fully agreed definitions of either child abuse in general, or child sexual abuse in particular have been arrived at, either by researchers or in the courts. A section of the Children Act of 1989 speaks of 'significant harm' being caused by lack of reasonable care – but what is 'significant' is left quite vague. The National Society for the Protection of Cruelty to Children (NSPCC) defines four categories of abuse: 'neglect', 'physical abuse', 'emotional abuse' and 'sexual abuse'. Sexual abuse is defined as 'sexual contact between a child and adult for the purpose of the adult's sexual gratification' (Lyon and de Cruz 1993).

Force or the threat of violence is involved in many cases of incest. In some instances children are more or less willing participants, but this seems quite rare. Children are sexual beings, of course, and quite often engage in mild sexual play or exploration with one another. But most of the children subjected to sexual contact with adult family members find the experience repugnant, shameful or disturbing. There is now considerable material to indicate that child sexual abuse may have long-term consequences for its sufferers. Studies of prostitutes, juvenile offenders, adolescent runaways and drug users show

that a high proportion have a history of child sexual abuse. Of course, correlation is not causation. Demonstrating that people in these categories have been sexually abused as children does not show that such abuse was a causal influence over their later behaviour. Probably a range of factors is involved, such as family conflicts, parental neglect and physical violence.

Domestic violence

We may define domestic violence as physical abuse directed by one member of the family against another or others. Studies show that the prime targets of physical abuse are children, especially small children. The horrific murder of an eight-year-old girl, Victoria Climbié, in February 2000 brought extreme forms of domestic violence against children to the public's attention. Victoria, who came to Europe from West Africa, died of hypothermia after months of torture and neglect inflicted by her great-aunt, Marie Therese Kouao, and the woman's boyfriend, Carl Manning. Her abusers were jailed for life in November 2000. During their trial, police and health and social services were all criticized for missing opportunities to save the girl. The government ordered an inquiry, chaired by Lord Laming, which examined the role of the professionals and made recommendations to the government on how to prevent such a tragedy from happening again (Laming 2003).

Violence by men against their female partners is the second most common type of domestic violence. Two women each week in the UK are killed by their partners. At any one time 10 per cent of women are experiencing domestic violence, and it affects between a third and a quarter of women at some point in their lives. Domestic violence is the most common crime against women, who are at greater risk of violence from men in their own families or from close acquaintances than they are from strangers (Rawstorne 2002).

The issue of domestic violence attracted popular and academic attention during the 1970s as a result of the work undertaken by feminist groups with refuge centres for 'battered women'. Before that time, domestic violence, like child abuse, was a phenomenon which was tactfully ignored. Feminist studies of domestic violence drew attention to the prevalence and severity of violence against women in the home. Most violent episodes between spouses reported to the police involve violence by husbands against their wives. There are far fewer reported cases of women using physical force against their husbands. Feminists have pointed to such statistics to support their claims that domestic violence is a major form of male control over women.

> For perspectives on patriarchy and domination, see the section 'Radical feminism' in chapter 12, 'Sexuality and Gender', pp. 471–2.

In a backlash against feminist arguments, conservative commentators have claimed that violence in the family is not about patriarchal male power, as feminists contend, but about 'dysfunctional families'. Violence against women is a reflection of the growing crisis of the family and the erosion of standards of morality. They question the finding that violence from wives towards husbands is rare, and suggest that men are less lively to report instances of violence against them from their wives than vice versa (Straus and Gelles 1986).

Such assertions have been strongly criticized by feminists and by other scholars who argue that violence by females is in any case more restrained and episodic than that of men, and much less likely to cause enduring physical harm. They argue that it is not sufficient to look at the 'number' of violent incidents within families. Instead it is essential to look at the meaning, context and effect of violence. 'Wife battering' – the regular physical brutalizing of wives by husbands – has no real equivalent the other way round. Research found that violence by women against their male partners is often defensive rather than offensive, with women resorting to violence only after suffering repeated attacks over time (Rawstorne 2002). Men who physically abuse children are also much more likely to do so in a consistent way, causing long-standing injuries, than are women.

Why is domestic violence relatively commonplace? Several sets of factors are involved. One is the combination of emotional intensity and personal intimacy characteristic of family life. Family ties are normally charged with strong emotions, often mixing love and hate. Quarrels which break out in the domestic setting can unleash antagonisms that would not be felt in the same way in other social contexts. What seems only a minor incident can precipitate full-scale hostilities between partners or between parents and children. A man tolerant towards eccentricities in the behaviour of other women may become furious if his wife talks too much at a dinner party or reveals intimacies he wishes to keep secret.

A second influence is the fact that a

good deal of violence within the family is actually tolerated, and even approved of. Although socially sanctioned family violence is relatively confined in nature, it can easily spill over into more severe forms of assault. Many children in Britain have at some time been slapped or hit, if only in a minor way, by one of their parents. Such actions quite often meet with general approval on the part of others, and they are probably not even thought of as 'violence' – although there is increasing pressure from some groups for the UK to follow many of the other European countries, which have legislation outlawing the physical punishment of children.

Social Class

While no social class is immune to spousal abuse, several studies indicate that it is more common among low-income couples (Cherlin 1999). More than three decades ago, William Goode (1971) suggested that low-income men may be more prone to violence because they have few other means with which to control their wives, such as a higher income or level of education. In addition, the high levels of stress induced by poverty and unemployment may lead to more violence within families. In support of these assertions, Gelles and Cornell (1990) found that unemployed men are nearly twice as likely as employed men to assault their wives.

Divorce and separation

The rise of divorce

For many centuries in the West, marriage was regarded as virtually indissoluble. Divorces were granted only in very limited cases, such as non-consummation of marriage. One or two industrial countries

still do not recognize divorce. Yet these are now isolated examples. Most countries have moved rapidly towards making divorce more easily available. The so-called adversarial system used to be characteristic of virtually all industrialized countries. For a divorce to be granted, one spouse had to bring charges (for example, cruelty, desertion or adultery) against the other. The first 'no fault' divorce laws were introduced in some countries in the mid-1960s. Since then, many Western states have followed suit, although the details vary. In the UK, the Divorce Reform Act, which made it easier for couples to obtain a divorce and contained 'no fault' provisions, was passed in 1969 and came into effect in 1971. The 'no fault' principle was further consolidated in a new bill passed in 1996.

Between 1960 and 1970 the divorce rate in Britain grew by a steady 9 per cent each year, doubling within that decade. By 1972 it had doubled again, partly as a result of the 1969 Act, which made it easier for many in marriages that had long been 'dead' to get a divorce. Since 1980 the divorce rate has stabilized to some degree, but remains at a very high level compared to any previous period. Around two-fifths of all marriages in the UK now end in divorce. The fall in the number of marriages each year and the rise in the number of divorces are shown in figure 7.1.

Divorce rates are obviously not a direct index of marital unhappiness. For one thing, rates of divorce do not include people who are separated but not legally divorced. Moreover, people who are unhappily married may choose to stay together – because they believe in the sanctity of marriage, or worry about the finan-

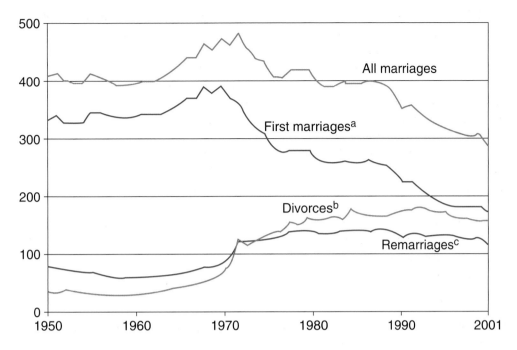

a   For both partners
b   Includes annulments. Data for 1950 to 1970 are for Great Britain only
c   For one or both partners

Figure 7.1 Marriages and divorces, UK (thousands)

Source: Social Trends 34 (2004), p. 31

cial or emotional consequences of a break-up, or wish to remain with one another to give their children a 'family' home.

Why is divorce becoming more common? Several factors are involved, to do with wider social changes. Except for a very small proportion of wealthy people, marriage today no longer has much connection with the desire to perpetuate property and status from generation to generation. As women become more economically independent, marriage is less of a necessary economic partnership than it used to be. Greater overall prosperity means that it is easier to establish a separate household, if there is marital disaffec-tion, than used to be the case. The fact that little stigma now attaches to divorce is in some part the result of these developments, but also adds momentum to them. A further important factor is the growing tendency to evaluate marriage in terms of the levels of personal satisfaction it offers. Rising rates of divorce do not seem to indicate a deep dissatisfaction with marriage as such, but an increased determination to make it a rewarding and satisfying relationship.

Lone-parent households

Lone-parent households have become increasingly common in recent decades.

Diane Vaughan on 'uncoupling': the experience of breaking up

It is extremely difficult to draw up a balance sheet of the social advantages and costs of high levels of divorce. More tolerant attitudes mean that couples can terminate an unrewarding relationship without incurring social ostracism. On the other hand, the break-up of a marriage is almost always emotionally stressful for both the couple and their children, and may create financial hardship for one or both parties. (In the box below, pp. 228–9, we look at Carol Smart and Bren Neale's work on the experience of raising a family after divorce.)

In her book, *Uncoupling: The Turning Points in Intimate Relationships* (1990), Diane Vaughan has analysed the relationships between partners during the course of separation or divorce. She carried out a series of interviews with more than a hundred recently separated or divorced people (mainly from middle-class backgrounds) to chart the transition from living together to living apart. The notion of *uncoupling* refers to the break-up of a long-term intimate relationship. She found that in many cases, before the physical parting, there had been a *social separation* – at least one of the partners developed a new pattern of life, becoming interested in new pursuits and making new friends in contexts in which the other was not present. This usually meant keeping secrets from the other – especially, of course, when a relationship with a lover was involved.

According to Vaughan's research, uncoupling is often unintentional at first. One individual – whom she called the *initiator* – becomes less satisfied with the relationship than the other, and creates a 'territory' independent of the activities in which the couple engages together.

For some time before this, the initiator may have been trying unsuccessfully to change the partner, to get him or her to behave in more acceptable ways, foster shared interests and so forth. At some point, the initiator feels that the attempt has failed and that the relationship is fundamentally flawed. From then onwards, he or she becomes preoccupied with the ways in which the relationship or the partner is defective. Vaughan suggests this is the opposite of the process of 'falling in love' at the beginning of a relationship, when an individual focuses on the attractive features of the other, ignoring those that might be less acceptable.

Initiators seriously considering a break notably discuss their relationship extensively with others, 'comparing notes'. In doing so, they weigh the costs and benefits of separation. Can I survive on my own? How will friends and parents react? Will the children suffer? Will I be financially solvent? Having thought about these and other problems, some decide to try again to make the relationship work. For those who proceed with a separation, these discussions and enquiries help make the break less intimidating, building confidence that they are doing the right thing. Most initiators become convinced that a responsibility for their own self-development takes priority over commitment to the other.

Of course, uncoupling is not always wholly led by one individual. The other partner may also have decided that the relationship cannot be saved. In some situations, an abrupt reversal of roles occurs. The person who previously wanted to save the relationship becomes determined to end it, whilst the erstwhile initiator wishes to carry on.

In the UK, the proportion of people in lone-parent, one-family households increased from 4 per cent in 1971 to 12 per cent in 2003 (see table 7.2). It is important to note that lone parenthood is an overwhelmingly female category. On average, they are among the poorest groups in contemporary society. Many lone parents, whether they have ever been married or not, still face social disapproval as well as economic insecurity. Earlier and more judgemental terms such as 'deserted wives', 'fatherless families' and 'broken homes' are tending to disappear, however.

The category of lone-parent household is an internally diverse one. For instance,

Table 7.2   UK households: by type of household and family, 1971–2003 (%)

	1971	1981	1991	2001[a]	2003[a]
One family households					
Living alone	6	8	11	12	13
Couple					
No children	19	20	23	25	25
Dependent children[b]	52	47	41	39	38
Non-dependent children only	10	10	11	8	8
Lone parent	4	6	10	12	12
Other households	9	9	4	4	5
All people in private households (=100%) (millions)	53.4	53.9	55.4	–	–
People not in private households (millions)	0.9	0.8	0.8	–	–
Total population (millions)[c]	54.4	54.8	56.2	57.4	57.6

[a] At spring. These estimates are not seasonally adjusted and have not been adjusted to take account of the Census 2001 results

[b] May also include non-dependent children

[c] Data for 1971 to 1991 are Census enumerated. Data for 2001 and 2002 are mid-year estimates

Source: Social Trends 34 (2004), p. 31

more than half of widowed mothers are owner-occupiers, but the vast majority of never-married lone mothers live in rented accommodation. Lone parenthood tends to be a changing state, and its boundaries are rather blurred: there are multiple paths entering into lone parenthood and exiting from it. In the case of a person whose spouse dies, the break is obviously clear-cut – although even here a person might have been living on his or her own in practical terms if the partner was in hospital for some while before they died. About 60 per cent of lone-parent households today, however, are brought about by separation or divorce.

Among the lone-parent families in the UK, the fastest growing category is that of single, never-married mothers. By the late 1990s, they constituted 9 per cent of the total number of families with dependent children (see table 7.3). Of these, it is difficult to know how many have deliberately opted to raise children alone. Most people do not wish to be lone parents. The ongoing Millennium Cohort Study, which is currently following the lives of children born in the first few years of this century, has found that younger women are more likely to become solo mothers, and that the more educated the woman, the more likely she is to have a baby within marriage. The research also revealed that for 85 per cent of solo mothers their pregnancy was unplanned, in contrast to 52 per cent of cohabiting couples and 18 per cent of married women. For the majority of unmarried or never-married mothers, there is also a high correlation between the rate of births outside marriage and indicators of poverty and social deprivation. As we saw earlier, these influences are very important in explaining the high proportion of lone-parent households among families of West Indian background in the UK. However, a growing minority of women are now choosing to have a child or children without the support of a spouse or partner. 'Single mothers by choice' is an apt description of some lone parents, normally those who possess sufficient resources to manage satisfactorily as a single-parent household.

Crow and Hardey (1992) argue that the great diversity of 'pathways' into and out of lone-parent families means that lone parents as a whole are not a uniform or cohesive group. Although lone-parent families may share certain material and social disadvantages in common, they have little collective identity. The plurality of routes means that, for the purposes of social policy, the boundaries of lone parenthood are difficult to define and its needs difficult to target.

The 'absent father'

The time from the late 1930s up to the 1970s has sometimes been called the period of the 'absent father'. During the Second World War, many fathers rarely saw their children because of their war service. In the period following the war, in a high proportion of families women were not in the paid labour force and stayed at home to look after the children. The father was the main breadwinner and consequently was out at work all day; he would see his children only in the evenings and at weekends.

With rising divorce rates in more recent years, and the increasing number of lone-parent households, the theme of the **absent father** has come to mean something different. It has come to refer to

Table 7.3 Families in Great Britain headed by lone parents as a percentage[a] of all families with dependent children: by marital status

	1971	1976	1981	1986	1991–2	1996–7	1998–9
Lone mother							
Single	1	2	2	3	6	7	9
Widowed	2	2	2	1	1	1	1
Divorced	2	3	4	6	6	6	8
Separated	2	2	2	3	4	5	5
All lone mothers	7	9	11	13	18	20	22
Lone father	1	2	2	1	1	2	2
Married/cohabiting couple[b]	92	89	87	86	81	79	75
All families with dependent children	100	100	100	100	100	100	100

[a] Dependent children are persons under 16 or aged 16 to 18 and in full-time education, in the family unit and living in the household

[b] Includes married women whose husband are not defined as resident in the household

Source: Social Trends 30 (2000), p. 37

fathers who, as a result of separation or divorce, have only infrequent contact with their children or lose touch with them altogether. In both Britain and the United States, which have among the highest divorce rates in the world, this situation has provoked intense debate. Some have proclaimed the 'death of the dad'.

Writing from contrasting perspectives, sociologists and commentators have seized on the increasing proportion of fatherless families as the key to a whole diversity of social problems, from rising crime to mushrooming welfare costs for child support. Some have argued that children will never become effective members of a social group unless they are exposed to constant examples of negotiation, cooperation and compromise between adults in their immediate environment (Dennis and Erdos 1992). Boys who grow up without a father will struggle to be successful parents themselves, according to such arguments.

American authors who have figured prominently in the debate have had a great deal of influence over discussions of the issue in the UK. In his book *Fatherless America* (1995) David Blankenhorn argues that societies with high divorce rates are facing not just the loss of fathers but the very erosion of the idea of fatherhood – with lethal social consequences, because many children are growing up now without an authority figure to turn to in times of need. Marriage and fatherhood in all societies up to the present provided a means of channelling men's sexual and aggressive energies. Without them, these energies are likely to be expressed in criminality and violence. As one reviewer of Blankenhorn's book put it, 'better to have a dad who comes home from a nasty job to drink beer in front of the television than no dad at all' (*The Economist* 1995).

Yet, is it? The issue of absent fathers overlaps with that of the more general question of the effects of divorce on children – and there, as we saw, the implications of the available evidence are far from clear. As the same reviewer put it: 'Does not a yobbish father spawn yobbish sons? Are not some fathers bad for the family?' Some scholars have suggested that the key question is not whether the father is present, but how engaged he is in family life and parenting. In other words, the make-up of the household may not be as important as the quality of care, attention and support that children receive from its members.

The issue of fatherlessness has recently gained a lot of media attention in the UK from the high-profile stunts of the pressure group *Fathers 4 Justice*, whose members, amongst other things, threw a condom filled with purple flour at the Prime Minister in the House of Commons in May 2004 and scaled the walls of Buckingham Palace dressed as Batman in September 2004. The group claims that British law, which aims to serve 'the best interests' of the child, is biased in favour of the mother when couples split up by making it difficult for fathers to stay in contact with their children.

Changing attitudes to family life

There seem to be substantial class differences affecting reactions to the changing character of family life and the existence of high levels of divorce. In her book *Families on the Fault Line* (1994), Lillian Rubin interviewed the members of thirty-two working-class families in depth. She

High-profile stunts such as this draw attention to fathers' feelings of marginalization in the family, the courts and in government policy.

Carol Smart and Bren Neale: *Family Fragments?*

Between 1994 and 1996, Carol Smart and Bren Neale carried out two rounds of interviews with a group of sixty parents from West Yorkshire who had either separated or divorced after the passage of the 1989 Children Act. This Act altered the situation facing parents and children on divorce by abolishing the old notions of 'custody' and 'access' so that parents would no longer feel that they had to fight over their children. The Act meant that the legal relationship between children and their parents was not changed by divorce; it also encouraged parents to share child-rearing and required judges and others to listen more to the views of children. Smart and Neale were interested to know how patterns of parenting were initially

formed after divorce and how they changed over time. In their investigation, they compared parents' expectations about post-divorce parenting at the point of separation with the 'reality' of their circumstances one year later.

Smart and Neale found that parenting after divorce involved a process of constant adjustment that many parents had not anticipated and were ill-prepared for. Parenting skills which worked as part of a two-parent team were not necessarily successful in a lone-parent household. Parents were forced to re-evaluate continuously their approaches to parenting, not only in terms of 'big decisions' affecting their children, but in regard to the everyday aspects of child-rearing that were now occurring across two households instead of one. Following a divorce, parents faced two opposing demands – their own needs for separation and distance from their former spouse, and the need to remain connected as part of co-parenting responsibilities.

Smart and Neale found that the lived experience of post-divorce parenting was extremely fluid and changed over time. When interviewed a year after their separation, many parents were able to look back at the initial stages of lone parenting and assess the parenting decisions they had made. Often parents re-evaluated their behaviour and actions in the light of their changing understandings. For example, many parents were worried about the harm that their children would suffer as a result of the divorce, but were unsure how to transform their fears and sense of guilt into constructive action. This led some parents to hold on too tightly to their children or to treat them like 'adult' confidantes. In other cases it led to alienation, distance and the loss of meaningful connections.

In the media and certain political contexts, according to the authors, there is an implicit – and sometimes explicit – assumption that after divorce, adults abandon morality and begin to act selfishly and in their own interests. All of a sudden, flexibility, generosity, compromise and sensitivity disappear; the moral framework in which decisions about family and welfare were previously made gets discarded. Smart and Neale's interviews with divorced parents led them to reject this argument. They claim that parents do operate within a moral framework when parenting, but that it is perhaps best understood as a morality of care rather than an unambiguous moral reasoning based on set principles or beliefs. Smart and Neale argue that as parents care for their children, decisions emerge about 'the proper thing to do'. These decisions are highly contextual; parents must weigh a large number of considerations, including the effects of the decision on the children, whether it is the appropriate time to act and what harmful implications it might have on the co-parenting relationship. Consider the following from a lone mother whose ex-husband requested custody of their children:

I said, 'Look, if you really, really feel that you can look after these kids on a full-time basis, don't you think you ought to give yourself a weekend with them and then just see how it feels and then maybe after a weekend maybe progress to say you're having them for a full week and see how you cope with them.' He just absolutely hit the roof because he's got this thing in his head that he'd be baby-sitting for me, so he said 'No.' I said, 'Look, in that case I'm not even prepared to discuss it with you because I feel you just don't know how hard it is, you haven't had the children on a full-time basis for three years, I do feel that you're just out of it a little. [I feel you should have them] in a normal everyday routine, bringing them to school, picking them up from school, cooking, cleaning, washing and ironing for them, helping them with their homework, if they're sick, nursing them. And then we will rediscuss, reassess the situation.'

(Smart and Neale 1999)

Here the mother was trying to determine the 'right thing to do' while balancing multiple factors. In the context of a difficult relationship with her former spouse and the need to defend the progress she had made in her own self-development, she was still attempting to work constructively with him in the interests of the children.

Smart and Neale conclude that divorce unleashes changes in circumstances which can rarely be 'put straight' once and for all. Successful post-divorce parenting demands constant negotiation and communication. While the 1989 Children's Act has added necessary flexibility to contemporary post-divorce parenting arrangements, its emphasis on the welfare of the child may overlook the crucial role played by the quality of the relationship between divorced parents.

concluded that, compared to middle-class families, working-class parents tend to be more traditional. The norms that many middle-class parents have accepted, such as the open expression of pre-marital sex, are more widely disapproved of by working-class people, even where they are not particularly religious. In working-class households there tends therefore to be more of a conflict between the generations.

The young people in Rubin's study agree that their attitudes towards sexual behaviour, marriage and gender divisions are distinct from those of their parents. But they insist that they are not just concerned with pleasure seeking. They simply hold to different values from those of the older generation.

Rubin found the young women she interviewed to be much more ambivalent about marriage than were their parents' generation. They were keenly aware of the imperfections of men and spoke of exploring the options available and of living life more fully and openly than was possible for their mothers. The generational shift in men's attitudes was not as great.

Rubin's research was done in the United States, but her findings accord closely with those of researchers in Britain and other European countries. Helen Wilkinson and Geoff Mulgan carried out two large-scale studies of men and women aged between eighteen and thirty-four in the UK (Wilkinson 1994; Wilkinson and Mulgan 1995). They found major changes happening in the outlook of young women in particular; and that the values of this age group contrasted in a general way with those of the older generations in Britain.

Among young women there is 'a desire for autonomy and self-fulfilment, through work as much as family' and 'the valuing of risk, excitement and change'. In these terms there is a growing convergence between the traditional values of men and the newer values of women. The values of the younger generation, Wilkinson and Mulgan suggest, have been shaped by their inheritance of freedoms largely unavailable to earlier generations – freedom for women to work and control their own reproduction, freedom of mobility for both sexes and freedom to define one's own style of life. Such freedoms lead to greater openness, generosity and tolerance; but they can also produce a narrow, selfish individualism and a lack of trust in others. Of those in the sample, 29 per cent of women and 51 per cent of men wanted to 'delay having children as long as possible'. Of women in the sixty to twenty-four age group, 75 per cent believed that single parents can bring up children as well as a couple can. The study found that marriage was losing its appeal for both women and men in this age group.

New partnerships and step-families

Remarriage

Remarriage can involve various circumstances. Some remarried couples are in their early twenties, neither of them bringing a child to the new relationship. A couple who remarry in their late twenties, their thirties or early forties might each take one or more children from the first marriage to live with them. Those who remarry at later ages might have adult children who never live in the new homes that the parents establish. There may also be children within the new marriage itself. Either partner of the new couple may previously have been single, divorced or

Prince Charles's marriage to Camilla Parker-Bowles is testament to the enduring importance of marriage in UK society. They are perhaps the most famous step-parents in Britain today.

widowed, adding up to eight possible combinations. Generalizations about remarriage therefore have to be made with considerable caution, although some general points are worth making.

In 1900 about nine-tenths of all marriages in the United Kingdom were first marriages. Most remarriages involved at least one widowed person. With the rise in the divorce rate, the level of remarriage also began to climb, and an increasing proportion of remarriages began to involve divorced people. In 1971, 20 per cent of marriages were remarriages (for at least one partner); by 2001 that number was more than 40 per cent (as figure 7.1 on p. 223 shows).

Odd though it might seem, the best way to maximize the chances of getting married, for both sexes, is to have been married before! People who have been married and divorced are more likely to marry again than single people in comparable age groups are to marry for the first time. At all age levels, divorced men are more likely to remarry than divorced women: three in every four divorced women, but five in every six divorced men, remarry. In statistical terms, at least, remarriages are less successful than first marriages. Rates of divorce from second marriages are higher than those from first marriages.

This does not show that second marriages are doomed to fail. People who have been divorced may have higher expectations of marriage than those who have not. Hence they may be more ready to dissolve new marriages than those only married once. It is possible that the second marriages which endure might be more satisfying, on average, than first marriages.

Step-families

The term *step-family* refers to a family in which at least one of the adults has children from a previous marriage or relationship. Sociologists often refer to such groups as **reconstituted families**. There are clearly joys and benefits associated with reconstituted families and with the growth of extended families which results. But certain difficulties also tend to arise. In the first place, there is usually a biological parent living elsewhere whose influence over the child or children is likely to remain powerful.

Second, cooperative relations between divorced individuals are often strained when one or both remarries. Take the case of a woman with two children who marries a man who also has two, and all live together. If the 'outside' parents insist that children visit them at the same times as before, the major tensions involved in melding such a newly established family together will be exacerbated. For example, it may prove impossible ever to have the new family together at weekends.

Third, reconstituted families merge children from different backgrounds, who may have varying expectations of appropriate behaviour within the family. Since most step-children 'belong' to two households, the likelihood of clashes in habits and outlook is considerable. Here is a step-mother describing her experience, after the problems she faced led to separation:

> There's a lot of guilt. You cannot do what you would normally do with your own child, so you feel guilty, but if you do have a normal reaction and get angry, you feel guilty about that, too. You are always so afraid you will be unfair. Her [step-daughter's] father and I did not agree and he would say I nagged if I disciplined her. The more he did nothing to structure her, the more I seemed to nag . . . I wanted to provide something for her, to be an element of her life which was missing, but perhaps I am not flexible enough.
>
> (Smith 1990)

There are few established norms which define the relationship between step-parent and step-child. Should a child call a new step-parent by name, or is 'Dad' or 'Mum' more appropriate? Should the step-parent discipline the children as a natural parent would? How should a step-parent treat the new spouse of his or her previous partner when collecting the children?

Reconstituted families are developing types of kinship connection which are quite recent additions to modern Western societies; the difficulties created by remarriage *after divorce* are also new. Members of these families are developing their own ways of adjusting to the relatively uncharted circumstances in which they find themselves. Some authors today speak of **binuclear families**, meaning that the two households which form after a divorce still comprise one family system where there are children involved.

In the face of such rich and confusing transformations, perhaps the most appropriate conclusion to be drawn is a simple one: while marriages are broken up by divorce, families on the whole are not. Especially where children are involved, many ties persist despite the reconstructed family connections brought into being through remarriage.

Bean-pole families

Julia Brannen (2003) argues that, in the UK, we are now living in the age of the 'bean-pole family'. Brannen argues that the family household is just one part of a network of kin relations that, increasingly, consists of several generations. This is largely because people are living longer. She notes that at the age of fifty, three-fifths of the UK population have at least one parent still alive, and just over a third are grandparents. There is also a rise in the number of four generation families – families that include great-grandchildren.

Whilst the 'vertical' links between generations of the family are strengthened by increasing life expectancy, the 'horizontal' links within generations are weakening, as divorce rates rise, fertility rates fall and people have fewer children. Brannen therefore characterizes contemporary families as long and thin 'bean-pole structures' (see figure 7.2).

Brannen found that grandparents are increasingly providing intergenerational services, particularly informal child care for their grandchildren. Demand for intergenerational support is particularly high amongst single-parent families, where older generations can also often provide emotional support in times of need, such as during a divorce. In turn, the 'pivot generation', sandwiched between older and younger generations, will often become a carer for their parents (as they become elderly), their children and perhaps even grandchildren.

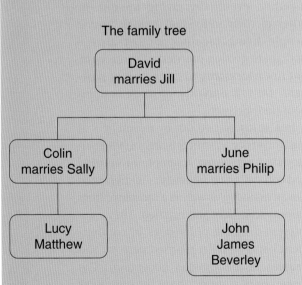

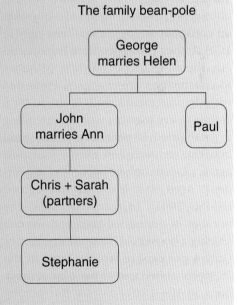

Figure 7.2   The family tree and the family bean-pole.

Source: Sociology Review 13/1 (September 2003)

Alternatives to traditional forms of marriage and family life

Cohabitation

Cohabitation – where a couple live together in a sexual relationship without being married – has become increasingly widespread in most Western societies. If previously marriage was the defining basis of a union between two people, it can no longer be regarded as such. Today it may be more appropriate to speak of *coupling* and *uncoupling*, as we do when discussing the experience of divorce above. A growing number of couples in committed long-term relationships choose not to marry, but reside together and raise children together.

In Britain until very recently, cohabitation was generally regarded as somewhat scandalous. The General Household Survey, the main source of data on British household patterns, included a question on cohabitation for the first time only in 1979. Among young people in Britain, and elsewhere in Europe, however, attitudes to cohabitation are changing. Presented with the statement that 'It is alright for a couple to live together without intending to get married', 88 per cent of people aged between eighteen and twenty-four now agree, whereas only 40 per cent of respondents aged sixty-five and over agreed (HMSO 2004). In recent decades, the number of unmarried men and women sharing a household has gone up sharply. Only 4 per cent of women born in the 1920s cohabited and 19 per cent of those born in the 1940s did so. But among women born in the 1960s, the percentage is nearly half. By 2001/2, the proportion of cohabiting unmarried women under the age of sixty was 28 per cent; for men the figure was 25 per cent (HMSO 2004). The prevalence of cohabitation was highest for women aged between twenty-five and twenty-nine and for men aged between thirty and thirty-four (see figure 7.3). Although cohabitation has become increasingly popular, research suggests that marriage is still more stable. Unmarried couples who live together are three to four times more likely to split up than those who are married.

Cohabitation in Britain today seems to be for the most part an experimental stage before marriage, although the length of cohabitation prior to marriage is increasing and more and more couples are choosing it as an alternative to marriage. Young people often find themselves living together by drifting into it, rather than through calculated planning. A couple who are already having a sexual relationship spend more and more time together, eventually giving up one or other of their individual homes. Young people living together almost always anticipate getting married at some date, but not necessarily to their current partners. Only a minority of such couples pool their finances.

In a study carried out by researchers at the University of Nottingham in 1999, sociologists interviewed a sample of married and cohabiting couples with children aged eleven or under, as well as a sample of their parents who were still married. They were interested in the differences in commitment between older married persons and couples in the younger generation. The researchers found that the younger married and cohabiting couples had more in common with each other than with their parents. While the older generation saw

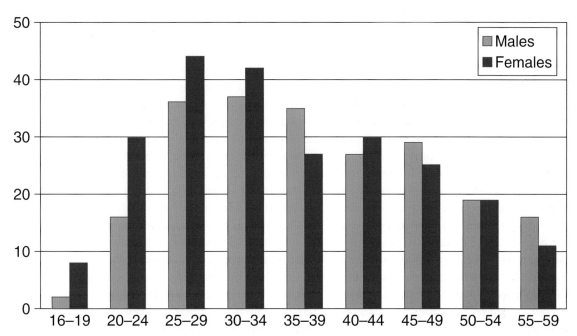

Figure 7.3 Non-married people cohabiting: Great Britain, by sex and age, 2001/2ᵃ (%)

ᵃ Males and females aged 16–59. Includes those respondents describing themselves as separated

Source: *Social Trends* 34 (2004), p. 33

marriage in terms of obligations and duties, the younger generation emphasized freely given commitments. The main difference between the younger respondents was that some of them preferred to have their commitment recognized publicly through marriage (Dyer 1999).

Gay and lesbian partnerships

Many homosexual men and women now live in stable relationships as couples. But because most countries still do not sanction marriage between homosexuals, relationships between gay men and between lesbians are grounded in personal commitment and mutual trust rather than in law. The term 'families of choice' has sometimes been applied to gay partnerships to

reflect the positive and creative forms of everyday life that homosexual couples are increasingly able to pursue together. Many traditional features of heterosexual partnerships – such as mutual support, care and responsibility in illness, the joining of finances, and so forth – are becoming integrated into gay and lesbian families in ways that were not possible earlier.

Homosexuality is discussed further in chapter 12 'Sexuality and Gender', and gay marriage on pp. 434–6.

Since the 1980s there has been a growing academic interest in gay and lesbian partnerships. Sociologists have seen homosexual relationships as displaying forms of intimacy and equality quite different from those common in hetero-sexual couples. Because gays and lesbians have been excluded from the institution of marriage and because traditional gender roles are not easily applicable to same-sex couples, homosexual partnerships must be constructed and negotiated outside the norms and guidelines that govern many heterosexual unions. Some have suggested that the AIDS epidemic was an important factor in the development of a distinctive culture of care and commitment among homosexual partners.

Weeks et al. (1999) point to three significant patterns within gay and lesbian partnerships. First, there is more opportunity for *equality between partners* because they are not guided by the cultural and social assumptions that underpin heterosexual relationships. Gay and lesbian couples may choose to shape their relationships deliberately so that they avoid the types of inequalities and power imbalances that are characteristic of many heterosexual couples. Second, homosexual partners *negotiate* the parameters and inner workings of their relationships. If heterosexual couples are influenced by socially embedded gender roles, same-sex couples face fewer expectations about who should do what within the relationship. For example, if women tend to do more of the housework and child care in heterosexual marriages, there are no such expectations within homosexual partnerships. Everything becomes a matter for negotiation; this may result in a more equal sharing of responsibilities. Third, gay and lesbian partnerships demonstrate a particular form of *commitment* that lacks an institutional backing. Mutual trust, the willingness to work at difficulties and a shared responsibility for 'emotional labour' seem to be the hallmarks of homosexual partnerships (Weeks et al. 1999).

Relaxation of previously intolerant attitudes towards homosexuality has been accompanied by a growing willingness by the courts to allocate custody of children to mothers living in lesbian relationships. Techniques of artificial insemination mean that lesbians may have children and become gay-parent families without any heterosexual contacts. While virtually every homosexual family with children in Britain involves two women, for a period in the late 1960s and early 1970s social welfare agencies in several cities in the USA placed homeless gay teenage boys in the custody of gay male couples. The practice was discontinued, largely because of adverse public reaction.

A number of recent legal victories for homosexual couples indicate that their rights are gradually becoming enshrined in law.

New legal rights of homosexual couples are discussed further in chapter 12, 'Sexuality and Gender', pp. 434–6.

In Britain, a landmark 1999 ruling declared that a homosexual couple in a stable relationship could be defined as a family. This classification of homosexual partners as 'members of the family' will affect legal categories such as immigration, social security, taxation, inheritance and child support.

In 1999 a US court upheld the paternal rights of a gay male couple to be named jointly on the birth certificate of their children born to a surrogate mother. One of the men who brought the case said, 'We are celebrating a legal victory. The nuclear family as we know it is evolving. The emphasis should not be on it being a

Changing social norms mean that same-sex couples are now openly bringing up their children together in some countries.

Table 7.4   Average age at marriage: England and Wales, 1971–2001

	First marriage	
	Males	Females
1971	24.6	22.6
1981	25.4	23.1
1991	27.5	25.5
2001	30.6	28.4

Source: *Social Trends* 34 (2004), p. 32

father and a mother but on loving, nurturing parents, whether that be a single mother or a gay couple living in a committed relationship' (Hartley-Brewer 1999).

Staying single

Recent trends in household composition raise the question: are we becoming a nation of singles? The proportion of one-person households in the UK increased from 18 per cent in 1971 to 29 per cent in 2003 (HMSO 2004). Several factors have combined to increase the numbers of people living alone in modern Western societies. One is a trend towards later marriages – in 2001 people in the UK were marrying on average about six years later than was the case in the early 1970s (as table 7.4 shows); another, as we have seen, is the rising rate of divorce. Yet another is the growing number of older people in the population whose partners have died (discussed in chapter 6, pp. 188–90). Nearly half of the one-person households in the UK are one-pensioner-only households.

Being single means different things at different periods of the **life-course**. A larger proportion of people in their twenties are unmarried than used to be the case. By their mid-thirties, however, only a small minority of men and women have never been married. The majority of single people aged thirty to fifty are divorced and 'in between' marriages. Most single people over fifty are widowed.

The concept of the life-course were discussed in chapter 6, 'Socialization, the Life-Course and Ageing', pp. 175–8.

More than ever before, young people are leaving home simply to start an independent life rather than to get married (which had been one of the most common paths out of the home in the past). Hence it seems that the trend of 'staying single' or living on one's own may be part of the societal trend towards valuing independence at the expense of family life. Still, while independence or 'staying single' may be an increasingly common path out of the parental home, most people do eventually marry.

Theoretical perspectives on the family and intimate relationships

The study of the family and family life has been taken up differently by sociologists of contrasting persuasions. Many of the perspectives adopted even a few decades ago now seem much less convincing in the light of recent research and important changes in the social world. Nevertheless, it is valuable to trace briefly the evolution of sociological thinking before turning to contemporary approaches to the study of the family.

Functionalism

The functionalist perspective sees society as a set of social institutions that perform specific functions to ensure continuity and consensus. According to this perspective, the family performs important tasks that contribute to society's basic needs and helps to perpetuate social order. Sociologists working in the functionalist tradition have regarded the nuclear family as fulfilling certain specialized roles in modern societies. With the advent of industrialization, the family became less important as a unit of economic production and more focused on reproduction, child-rearing and socialization.

According to the American sociologist Talcott Parsons, the family's two main functions are *primary socialization* and *personality stabilization* (Parsons and Bales 1956). **Primary socialization** is the process by which children learn the cultural norms of the society into which they are born. Because this happens during the early years of childhood, the family is the most important arena for the development of the human personality. **Personality stabilization** refers to the role that the family plays in assisting adult family members emotionally. Marriage between adult men and women is the arrangement through which adult personalities are supported and kept healthy. In industrial society the role of the family in stabilizing adult personalities is said to be critical. This is because the nuclear family is often distanced from its extended kin and is unable to draw on larger kinship ties as families could do before industrialization.

Parsons regarded the nuclear family as the unit best equipped to handle the demands of industrial society. In the 'conventional family', one adult can work outside the home while the second adult cares for the home and children. In practical terms, this specialization of roles within the nuclear family involved the husband adopting the 'instrumental' role as breadwinner, and the wife assuming the 'affective', emotional role in domestic settings.

In our present age, Parsons's view of the family comes across as inadequate and outdated. Functionalist theories of the family have come under heavy criticism for justifying the domestic division of labour between men and women as something natural and unproblematic. Yet viewed in their own historical context, the theories are somewhat more understandable. The immediate post-war years saw women returning to their traditional domestic roles and men reassuming positions as sole breadwinners. We can criticize functionalist views of the family on other grounds, however. In emphasizing the importance of the family in performing certain functions, both theorists neglect the role that other social institutions, such as government, media and schools, play in socializing children. The theories also neglect variations in family forms that do not correspond to the model of the nuclear family. Families that did not conform to the white, suburban, middle-class 'ideal' were seen as deviant.

Feminist approaches

For many people, the family provides a vital source of solace and comfort, love and companionship. Yet as we saw above, it can also be a locus for exploitation, loneliness and profound inequality. Feminism has had a great impact on sociology by challenging the vision of the family as a harmonious and egalitarian realm. During the 1970s and 1980s, feminist perspectives dominated most debates and research on the family. If previously the sociology of the family had focused on family structures, the historical development of the nuclear and extended family and the importance of kinship ties, feminism succeeded in directing attention inside families to examine the experiences of women in the domestic sphere. Many feminist writers have questioned the vision that the family is a cooperative unit based on common interests and mutual support. They have sought to show that the presence of unequal power relationships within the family means that certain family members tend to benefit more than others.

Feminist writings have emphasized a broad spectrum of topics, but three main themes are of particular importance. One of the central concerns, which we will explore in greater depth in chapter 18, 'Work and Economic Life', is the *domestic division of labour* – the way in which tasks are allocated between members of a household. Among feminists there are differing opinions about the historical emergence of this division. While some feminists see it as an outcome of industrial capitalism, others claim that it is linked to patriarchy, and thus predates industrialization. There is reason to believe that a domestic division of labour existed prior to industrialization, but it seems clear that capitalist production brought about a much sharper distinction between the domestic and work realms. This process resulted in the crystallization of 'male spheres' and 'female spheres' and power relationships which are felt to this day. Until recently, the **male breadwinner** model has been widespread in most industrialized societies.

Feminist sociologists have undertaken studies on the way domestic tasks, such as child care and housework, are shared between men and women. They have investigated the validity of claims such as that of the 'symmetrical family' (Young and Willmott 1973) – the belief that, over time, families are becoming more egalitarian in the distribution of roles and responsibilities. Findings have shown that women continue to bear the main responsibility for domestic tasks and enjoy less leisure time than men, despite the fact that more women are working in paid employment outside the home than ever before (Hochschild 1989; Gershuny 1994; Sullivan 1997). Pursuing a related theme, some sociologists have examined the contrasting realms of paid and unpaid work, focusing on the contribution that women's unpaid domestic labour makes to the overall economy (Oakley 1974). Others have investigated the way in which resources are distributed among family members and the patterns of access to and control over household finances (Pahl 1989).

Second, feminists have drawn attention to the *unequal power relationships* that exist within many families. One topic which has received increased attention as a result of this is the phenomenon of domestic violence. 'Wife battering', marital rape, incest and the sexual abuse of children have all received more public attention as a result of feminists' claims that the violent and abusive sides of family life have long been ignored in both academic contexts and legal and policy circles (see pp. 219–22 below). Feminist sociologists have sought to understand how the family serves as an arena for gender oppression and even physical abuse.

The study of *caring activities* is a third area where feminists have made important contributions. This is a broad realm which encompasses a variety of processes, from attending to a family member who is ill to looking after an elderly relative over a long period of time. Sometimes caring means simply being attuned to someone else's psychological well-being – several feminist writers have been interested in 'emotion work' within relationships. Not only do women tend to shoulder concrete tasks such as cleaning and child care, but they also invest large amounts of emotional labour in maintaining personal relationships (Duncombe and Marsden 1993). While caring activities are grounded in love and deep emotion, they are also a form of work which demands an ability to listen, perceive, negotiate and act creatively.

Recent perspectives

Theoretical and empirical studies conducted from a feminist perspective during the last few decades have generated increased interest in the family and intimate relationships among both academics and the general population. Terms such as the 'second shift' – referring to women's dual roles at work and at home – have entered our everyday vocabulary. But because they often focused on specific issues within the domestic realm, feminist studies of the family did not always reflect larger trends and influences taking place outside the home.

In the past decade an important body of sociological literature on the family has emerged which draws on feminist perspectives, but is not strictly informed by them. Of primary concern are the larger transformations which are taking place in family forms – the formation and dissolution of families and households, and the evolving expectations within individuals' personal relationships. The rise in divorce and lone parenting, the emergence of 'reconstituted families' and gay families, and the popularity of cohabitation are all subjects of concern. Yet these transformations cannot be understood apart from the larger changes occurring in our late modern age. Attention must be paid to the shifts occurring at the societal, and even global, level if we are to grasp the link between personal transformations and larger patterns of change.

Anthony Giddens: The Transformation of Intimacy

In my own work, particularly *The Transformation of Intimacy* (1993), I looked at how intimate relationships are changing in modern society. The introduction to this chapter shows that marriage in pre-modern society was not generally based on sexual attraction or romantic love; instead, it was more often linked to the economic context in which to create a family or to enable the inheritance of property. For the peasantry, a life characterized by unremitting hard labour was unlikely to be conducive to sexual passion – although opportunities for men to engage in extramarital liaisons were numerous.

Romantic love, as distinct from the more or less universal compulsions of passionate love, developed in the late eighteenth century (as we saw on pp. 204–6). Despite its promise of an equal relationship based on mutual attraction, romantic love has in practice tended to lead to the dominance of men over women. For many men, the tensions between the respectability of romantic love and the compulsions of passionate love were dealt with by separating the comfort of the wife and home from the sexuality of the mistress or prostitute. The double standard here was that a woman should remain a virgin until the right man arrives; whereas no such norm applied to the men.

I argue that the most recent phase of modernity has seen another transformation in the nature of intimate relationships. There has been the development of **plastic sexuality**. For people in modern societies there is a much greater choice over when, how often and with whom they have sex than ever before (as we will see in chapter 12, 'Sexuality and Gender'). With plastic sexuality, sex can be untied from reproduction. This is partly due to improved methods of contraception, which have largely freed women from the fear of repetitive (and life-threatening) pregnancies and childbirths. However, it is not only technological developments that led to the emergence of plastic sexuality, but crucially the development of a sense of the self that could be actively chosen. This process can be described as the growth of social reflexivity, and is discussed in more detail in chapter 4 on pp. 122–3.

With the emergence of plastic sexuality, there is a change in the nature of love. I argued that the ideals of romantic love are fragmenting and being replaced by **confluent love**. Confluent love is active and contingent. It jars with the forever, one-and-only qualities of romantic love. The emergence of confluent love goes some way towards explaining the rise of separation and divorce discussed earlier in this chapter. Romantic love meant that once people had married they were usually stuck with one another, no matter how the relationship developed. Now people have more choice: whereas divorce was previously difficult or impossible to obtain, married people are now no longer bound to stay together if the relationship doesn't work.

Rather than basing relationships on romantic passion, people are increasingly pursuing the ideal of the **pure relationship**, in which couples remain because they choose to do so. As the idea of confluent love becomes consolidated as a real possibility, the more the idea of finding the Mr or Mrs Right recedes and the more the idea of finding the right relationship becomes crucial. The pure relationship is held together by the acceptance on the part of each partner that, 'until further notice', each gains sufficient benefits from the relationship to make its continuance worthwhile. Love is based upon emotional intimacy that generates trust. Love develops depending on how much each partner is prepared to reveal concerns and needs and to be vulnerable to the other. Each partner in the relationship constantly monitors their concerns to see if they are deriving sufficient satisfaction from the relationship for it to go on.

There is a diversity of forms of pure relationship. Marriage can be one, though it is increasingly an expression of such a relationship once it already exists (as the number of couples cohabiting rises) rather than a way of achieving it. However, pure relationships are certainly not limited to marriage or indeed to heterosexual couples. In some forms, same-sex relationships, because of their open and negotiated status, come closer to the ideal of pure relationships than do heterosexual ones.

Some critics have argued that the instability of the pure relationship, which was thought of as a relationship between adults, contrasts with the complexities of family practices which also include children, and neglects the different experiences which men and women tend to have when a (heterosexual) relationship ends. By focusing on relationships between adults, critics have noted, the idea of a pure relationship reflects the marginaliza-

tion of children and childhood in sociological thought (Smart and Neale 1999).

Many of the ideas found in *The Transformation of Intimacy* are also found in the writings of the husband-and-wife team of Beck and Beck-Gernsheim. They too argue that modern life, and in particular the spread of individual choice, has led to enormous transformations in the way we conduct out intimate relationships. Below, we look at their thought in more detail.

Ulrich Beck and Elizabeth Beck-Gernsheim: The Normal Chaos of Love

In *The Normal Chaos of Love* (1995), Beck and Beck-Gernsheim examine the tumultuous nature of personal relationships, marriages and family patterns against the backdrop of a rapidly changing world. The traditions, rules and guidelines which used to govern personal relationships no longer apply, they argue, and individuals are now confronted with an endless series of choices as part of constructing, adjusting, improving or dissolving the unions they form with others. The fact that marriages are now entered into voluntarily, rather than for economic purposes or at the urging of family, brings both freedoms and new strains. In fact, the authors conclude, they demand a great deal of hard work and effort.

Beck and Beck-Gernsheim see our age as one filled with colliding interests between family, work, love and the freedom to pursue individual goals. This collision is felt acutely within personal relationships, particularly when there are two 'labour market biographies' to juggle instead of one. By this the authors mean that a growing number of women in addition to men are pursuing careers over the course of their lifetimes. Previously women were more likely to work part time outside the home, or to take significant time away from their careers to raise children. These patterns are less fixed than they once were; both men and women now place emphasis on their professional and personal needs. Beck and Beck-Gernsheim conclude that relationships in our modern age are about much more than relationships, so to speak. Not only are love, sex, children, marriage and domestic duties topics for negotiation, but relationships are now also about work, politics, economics, professions and inequality. A diverse selection of problems – from the mundane to the profound – now confront modern couples.

Perhaps it is not surprising, then, that antagonisms between men and women are on the rise. Beck and Beck-Gernsheim claim that the 'battle between the sexes' is the 'central drama of our times', as evidenced in the growth of the marriage counselling industry, family courts, marital self-help groups and divorce rates. But even though marriage and family life seem to be more 'flimsy' than ever before, they still remain very important to people. Divorce is increasingly common, but rates of remarriage are high. The birth rate may be declining, but there is a huge demand for fertility treatment. Fewer people may choose to get married, but the desire to live with someone as part of a couple is certainly holding steady. What can explain these competing tendencies?

According to the authors, the answer is simple: love. They claim that today's 'battle of the sexes' is the clearest possible indication of people's 'hunger for love'. People marry for the sake of love and divorce for the sake of love; they engage in an endless cycle of hoping, regretting and trying again. While on the one hand the tensions between men and women are high, there remains a deep hope and faith in the possibility of finding true love and fulfilment.

You might think that 'love' is too simplistic an answer for the complexities of our current age. But Beck and Beck-Gernsheim argue that it is precisely because our world is so overwhelming, impersonal, abstract and rapidly changing that love has become increasingly important. According to the authors, love is the only place where people can truly find themselves and connect with others. In our world of uncertainty and risk, they write, love is real:

> Love is a search for oneself, a craving to really get in contact with me and you, sharing bodies, sharing thoughts, encountering one another with nothing held back, making confessions and being forgiven, understanding, confirming and supporting what was and what is, longing for a home and trust to counteract the doubts and anxieties modern life generates. If nothing seems certain or safe, if even breathing is risky in a polluted world, then people chase after the misleading dreams of love until they suddenly turn into nightmares. (1995: 175–6)

Love is at once desperate and soothing, they argue. It is a 'powerful force obeying rules of its own and inscribing its messages into people's expectations, anxieties and behaviour patterns'. In our fluctuating world it has become a new source of faith. Critics have attacked Beck and Beck-Gernsheim's exclusive focus on heterosexuality – they argued that the battle between the sexes is the 'central drama of our times' – which, they have argued, marginalizes homosexual relationships (Smart and Neale 1999).

Zygmunt Bauman: Liquid Love

In his book, *Liquid Love* (2003) the sociologist Zygmunt Bauman argues that nowadays relationships are 'the hottest talk of the town and ostensibly the sole game worth playing, despite their notorious risks'. His book is about the 'frailty of human bonds', the feeling of insecurity that this frailty leads to and our responses to it.

Bauman writes that the hero of his book is 'the man without bonds' (of, for example, family, class, religion or marriage) or at least the man without fixed, unbreakable ties. Those ties that Bauman's hero does have are loosely knotted, so that they can be released again, with little delay if the circumstances change. To Bauman, the circumstances will change often – he uses the metaphor 'liquid' to describe modern society, which he sees as characterized by constant change and a lack of lasting bonds.

Bauman argues that in a world of rampant 'individualization', relationships are a mixed blessing; they are filled with conflicting desires, which pull in different ways. On the one hand, there is the desire for freedom, for loose bonds that we can escape from if we so choose and for individualism. On the other hand, there is the desire for greater security that is gained by tightening the bonds between ourselves and our partners. As it is, Bauman argues, we swing back and forth between the two polarities of security and freedom. Often we run to experts – therapists or columnists, for example – for advice on how we can combine the two. To Bauman, this is attempting 'to have the cake and eat it, to cream off the sweet delights of relationship while omitting its better and tougher bits'.

The result is a society of 'semi-detached couples' in 'top pocket relationships'. By the phrase 'top pocket relationships', Bauman means something that can be pulled out when needed, but pushed deep inside the pocket the moment they are not. Bauman even compares people's attitudes to the relationship in 'liquid modern' society to the drink Ribena – in a concentrated form it is nauseating, and is best consumed diluted.

Our response to the 'frailty of human bonds' is to replace quality in our relationships for quantity. It is not the depth of our relationships, but the number of contacts that we have which becomes important to us. That is partly why, Bauman argues, we are always talking on mobile phones and texting one another (and even typing text messages in truncated sentences to increase the speed we can send them). It is not the message itself that is important, but the constant circulation of messages, without which we feel excluded.

Bauman notes that people now speak more of connections and networks and less of relationships. Whereas to be in a relationship means to be mutually engaged, networks suggest moments of being in touch. In a network, connections can be made on demand and broken at will. Connections are virtual, not real relationships. What really symbolizes the liquid modern relationship for Bauman is computer dating. He cites an interview with a twenty-eight-year-old man who notes the one decisive advantage of electronic relations: 'You can always press delete.'

Bauman is often accused of being too pessimistic about the transformations to our intimate relationships that have occurred in recent times. Is he right in his assessment? The view we take over these changes affects some of the big social and political questions of recent times. Below, we turn to the ongoing debate about the decline, or otherwise, of family values.

Conclusion: the debate about family values

'The family is collapsing!' cry the advocates of family values, surveying the changes of the past few decades – a more liberal and open attitude towards sexuality, steeply climbing divorce rates and a general seeking for personal happiness at the expense of older conceptions of family duty. We must recover a moral sense of family life, they argue. We must reinstate the traditional family, which was much more stable and ordered than the tangled web of relationships in which most of us find ourselves now (O'Neill 2002).

These arguments are not only heard in Europe and the United States. Changes affecting the personal and emotional spheres go far beyond the borders of any particular country. We find the same issues almost everywhere, differing only in degree and according to the cultural context in which they take place. In China, for example, the state is considering making divorce more difficult to obtain. In the late 1960s, very liberal marriage laws were passed. Marriage is a working contract that can be dissolved 'when husband and wife both desire it'. Even if one partner objects, divorce can be granted when 'mutual affection' has gone from the marriage. Only a two-week wait is required, after which the two pay a few pounds and are henceforth independent. The Chinese divorce rate is still low compared with Western countries, but it is rising rapidly – as is true in the other developing Asian societies. In Chinese cities, not only divorce, but also cohabitation is becoming more frequent. In the vast Chinese countryside, by contrast, everything is different. Marriage and the family are much more traditional – in spite of the official policy of limiting childbirth through a mixture of incentives and punishment. Marriage is an arrangement between two families, fixed by the parents rather than the individuals concerned. A recent study in the province of Gansu, which has only a low level of economic development, found that 60 per cent of marriages are still arranged by parents. As a Chinese saying has it: 'Meet once, nod your head and marry.' There is a twist in the story in modernizing China. Many of those currently divorcing in the urban centres were married in the traditional manner in the country.

In China, there is much talk of protecting the 'traditional' family. In many Western countries, the debate is even more intense and divisive. Defenders of the traditional family form argue that the emphasis on relationships comes at the expense of the family as a basic institution of society. Many of these critics now speak of the breakdown of the family. If such a breakdown is occurring, it is extremely significant. The family is the meeting point of a range of trends affecting society as a whole – increasing equality between the sexes, the widespread entry of women into the labour force, changes in sexual behaviour and expectations, the changing relationship between home and work. Among all the changes going on today, none is more important than those happening in our personal lives – in sexuality, emotional life, marriage and the family. There is a global revolution going on in how we think of ourselves and how we form ties and connections with others. It is a revolution advancing unevenly in different parts of the world, with much resistance.

'Rubbish!' others reply. The family is not collapsing; it is merely diversifying. They argue that we should actively encourage a variety of family forms and sexual life, rather than supposing that everyone has to be compressed into the same mould (Hite 1994).

Which side is right? We should probably be critical of both views. A return to the traditional family isn't a possibility. This is not only because, as we saw above (pp. 210–11), the traditional family as it is usually thought of never existed, or because there were too many oppressive facets to families in the past to make them a model for today. It is also because the social changes that have transformed earlier forms of marriage and the family are mostly irreversible. Women won't return in large numbers to a domestic situation from which they have painfully managed to extricate themselves. Sexual partnerships and marriage today, for better or worse, can't be like they used to be. Emotional communication – more precisely, the active creation and sustaining of relationships – has become central to our lives in the personal and family domain.

What will be the result? The divorce rate may have levelled off from its previous steep increase, but it is not dropping. All measures of divorce are to some extent estimates, but on the basis of past trends, we can guess that some 60 per cent of all marriages contracted now might end in divorce within ten years.

Divorce, as we've seen, is not always a reflection of unhappiness. People who may in former times have felt constrained to remain in miserable marriages can make a fresh start. But there can be no doubt that the trends affecting sexuality, marriage and the family create deep anxieties for some people at the same time as they generate new possibilities for satisfaction and self-fulfilment for others.

Those who argue that the great diversity in family forms that exists today is to be welcomed, as freeing us from the limitations and sufferings of the past, surely have a certain amount of right on their side. Men and women can remain single if they wish, without having to face the social disapproval that once came from being a bachelor or, even more, a spinster. Couples in live-in relationships no longer face social rejection by their more 'respectable' married friends. Gay couples can set up house together and bring up children without facing the same level of hostility they would have in the past.

These things having been said, it is difficult to resist the conclusion that we stand at a crossroads. Will the future bring about the further decay of long-term marriages or partnerships? Will we more and more inhabit an emotional and sexual landscape scarred by bitterness and violence? None can say for certain. But such a sociological analysis of marriage and the family as we have just concluded strongly suggests that we won't resolve our problems by looking to the past. We must try to reconcile the individual freedoms most of us have come to value in our personal lives with the need to form stable and lasting relations with other people.

Summary points

1 *Kinship*, *family* and *marriage* are closely related terms of key significance for sociology and anthropology. Kinship comprises either genetic ties or ties initiated by marriage. A family is a group of kin having responsibility for the upbringing of children. Marriage is a bond between two people living together in a socially approved sexual relationship.

2 A *nuclear family* is a household in which a married couple (or single parent) lives together with their own or adopted children. Where kin other than a married couple and children live in the same household, or are involved in close and continuous relationships, we speak of the existence of an *extended family*.

3 In Western societies, marriage, and therefore the family, are associated with *monogamy* (a culturally approved sexual relationship between one woman and one man). Many other cultures tolerate or encourage *polygamy*, in which an individual may be married to two or more spouses at the same time.

4 During the twentieth century, the predominance of the traditional nuclear family has been steadily eroded in most industrialized societies. A great diversity of family forms currently exists.

5 There is considerable diversity in family forms among ethnic minority groups. In Britain, families of South Asian and African-Caribbean origin differ from the dominant family types.

6 Divorce rates have been rising in the post-war years, and the number of first marriages has declined. As a result, a growing proportion of the population lives in lone-parent households.

7 Rates of remarriage are quite high. Remarriage can lead to the formation of a *reconstituted family* – a family in which at least one of the adults has children from a previous marriage or relationship. The term 'absent father' refers to fathers who have infrequent contact with their children (or no contact at all) following a separation or divorce.

8 Marriage is no longer the defining basis for a union between two people. *Cohabitation* (where a couple lives together in a sexual relationship outside marriage) has become more widespread in many industrial countries. Gay men and lesbians are increasingly able to live together as couples as attitudes to homosexuality become more relaxed. In some instances, homosexual couples have gained the legal right to be defined as a family.

9 Family life is by no means always a picture of harmony and happiness; sexual abuse and domestic violence sometimes occur within it. Most sexual abuse of children and domestic violence is carried out by males, and seems to connect with other types of violent behaviour in which some men are involved.

10 Marriage has ceased to be the condition for regular sexual experience, for either sex; it is no longer the basis of economic activity. It seems certain that varying forms of social and sexual relationships will flourish still further. Marriage and the family remain firmly established institutions, yet are undergoing major stresses and strains.

Questions for further thought

1 Are all family forms equally acceptable in contemporary societies?

2 How can rising divorce rates indicate that the marriage relationship has become more rather than less important?

3 With the decline of the male breadwinner, what new roles are there for men within families?

4 Is love enough to secure the institution of the family?

5 Are family values in decline? And does this matter?

Further reading

G. Allan and G. Crow, *Families, Households and Society* (New York: Palgrave, 2001).

Linda Hantrais and Marlene Lohkamp-Himminghofen (eds), *Changing Family Forms, Law and Policy* (Loughborough: Cross-National Research Group, European Research Centre, Loughborough University, 1999).

Gordon Hughes and Ross Ferguson (eds), *Ordering Lives: Family, Work and Welfare* (London: Routledge, 2000).

Richard M. Lerner and Domini R. Castellino (eds), *Adolescents and their Families: Structure, Function and Parent–Youth Relationships* (New York: Garland, 1999).

Jane Lewis, *End of Marriage: Individualism and Intimate Relations* (Cheltenham: E. Elgar, 2001).

D. Newman and E. Grauerholz, *Sociology of Families*, 2nd edn (London: Sage, 2002).

E. B. Silva and C. Smart (eds), *The 'New' Family* (London: Sage, 1999).

L. Steel and W. Kidd, *The Family* (Palgrave Macmillan, 2001).

Helen Wilkinson (ed.), *Family Business* (London: Demos, 2000).

Internet links

Centre for Policy Studies – a think-tank created to foster the family, enterprise, individualism and liberty
http://www.cps.org.uk

Civitas
http://www.civitas.org.uk/

Clearinghouse on International Developments in Child, Youth and Family Policies
http://www.childpolicyintl.org/

Demos – a think-tank covering research on social exclusion, the family and poverty
http://www.demos.co.uk

Family Research Council
http://www.frc.org/

Contents

8 Health, Illness and Disability

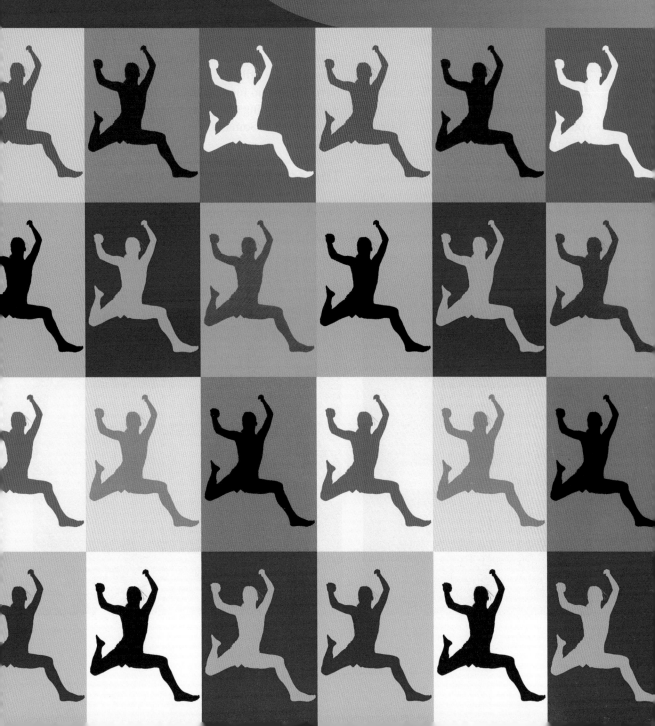

LOOK AT the two photographs below. The images of a sunken face and an emaciated body are almost identical. The young African girl on the left is dying from a simple lack of food. The young woman on the right is a British teenager, dying because, in a society with a superabundance of food, she chose not to eat or to eat so sparingly that her life was endangered.

The social dynamics involved in each case are utterly different. Starvation from lack of food is caused by factors outside people's control and affects only the very poor. The British teenager, living in one of the wealthiest countries in the world, is suffering from anorexia, an illness with no known physical origin. Obsessed with the ideal of achieving a slim body, she has eventually given up eating altogether. Anorexia and other eating disorders are illnesses of the affluent, not of those who have little or no food. They are unknown in the developing countries where food is scarce, such as Somalia.

The sociology of the body

Throughout much of human history, a few people – saints or mystics, for example –

have deliberately chosen to starve them-selves for religious reasons. Anorexia on the other hand, has no specific connection to religious beliefs, and it primarily affects women. It is an illness of the body, and thus we might think that we would have to look to biological or physical factors to explain it. But health and illness, like other topics we've studied, are also affected by social and cultural influences, such as the pressure to achieve a slim body.

Although it is an illness that expresses itself in physical symptoms, anorexia is closely related to the idea of being on a diet, which in turn is connected with

This painting by Rubens, completed around 1613, depicts Venus, the goddess of love and beauty.

changing views of physical attractiveness, particularly of women, in modern society. In most pre-modern societies, the ideal female shape was a fleshy one. Thinness was not regarded as desirable at all – partly because it was associated with lack of food and therefore with poverty. Even in Europe in the 1600s and 1700s, the ideal female shape was well proportioned. Anyone who has seen paintings of the period, such as those by Rubens (shown below), will have noticed how curvaceous (even plump) the women depicted in them are. The notion of slimness as the desirable feminine shape originated among some middle-class groups in the late nineteenth century, but it has become generalized as an ideal for most women only recently.

Anorexia thus has its origins in the changing body image of women in the recent history of modern societies. It was first identified as a disorder in France in 1874, but it remained obscure until the past thirty or forty years (Brown and Jasper 1993). Since then, it has become increas-ingly common among young women. So has bulimia – bingeing on food, followed by self-induced vomiting. Anorexia and bulimia are often found together in the same individual. Someone may become extremely thin through a starvation diet and then enter a phase of eating enor-mous amounts and purging in order to maintain a normal weight, followed by a period of again becoming very thin.

Anorexia and other eating disorders are no longer obscure forms of illness in modern societies. A survey of women in the UK aged between 18 and 24 showed that only a quarter of them were happy with their weight; 39 per cent said that they thought about their weight every day and one in ten said that they regularly starved themselves of food (Flour Advisory Bureau 1998). The Eating Disorders Association has estimated that the combined total in the UK for males and females diagnosed and undiagnosed with an eating disorder is 1.15 million.

Nor is obsession with slenderness – and the resulting eating disorders – limited to women in Europe and the United States. As Western images of feminine beauty have spread to the rest of the world, so too have their associated illnesses. Eating disorders were first documented in Japan, for example, in the 1960s, a consequence of that county's rapid economic growth and incorporation into the global economy. Anorexia is now found among 1 per cent of young Japanese women, roughly the same percentage as that found in the United States. During the 1980s and 1990s, eating problems surfaced among young, primarily affluent women in Hong Kong and Singapore, as well as in urban areas in Taiwan, China, the Philippines, India and Pakistan (Efron 1997). In a study reported by Medscape's *General Medicine* (2004), the prevelance of bulimia nervosa in female subjects in Western countries ranged from 0.3 to 7.3 per cent, compared to 0.46 to 3.2 per cent in the non-Western world (ANFED 2005).

Once again, something that may seem to be a purely personal trouble – difficulties with food and despair over one's appearance – turns out to be a public issue. If we include not just life-threatening forms of anorexia but also obsessive concern with dieting and bodily appearance, eating disorders are now part of the lives of millions of people; today they are found not only in the UK but in all the industrial countries.

The spread of eating disorders is astonishing, and brings home clearly the influence of social factors on our health and capacity for social interaction. The field known as **sociology of the body** investigates the ways in which our bodies are affected by these social influences. As human beings, we obviously all possess a body, but this is not something we just have and it is not something physical that exits outside of society. Our bodies are deeply affected by our social experiences, as well as by the norms and values of the groups to which we belong.

One major theme in this chapter is the increasing separation of the body from 'nature' – from our surrounding environment and our biological rhythms. Our bodies are being invaded by the influence of science and **technology**, ranging from machines to diets, and this is creating new dilemmas. The increasing prevalence of forms of plastic surgery, for example, has introduced new options but has also generated intense social controversies. We shall look at one such controversy, plastic surgery for people with facial disfigurements, later in the chapter.

The term 'technology' should not be understood in too narrow a way here. In its most basic sense, it refers to material technologies such as those involved in modern medicine – for example, the scanning machine that allows a doctor to chart a baby's development prior to birth. But we must take account of what Michel Foucault (1988) called 'social technologies' affecting the body. By this phrase, he means that the body is increasingly something we have to 'create' rather than simply accept. A social technology is any kind of regular intervention we make into the functioning of our bodies in order to alter them in specific ways. An example is dieting, so central to anorexia.

A bewildering array of foods from around the globe is now available on every high street in the UK and other wealthy countries.

In what follows, we will first analyse why eating disorders have become so common. From there, we will study the wider social dimensions of health. Then we turn to the sociology of disability, and look, in particular, at the social and cultural construction of disablement.

The sociology of health and illness

To understand why eating disorders have become so commonplace in current times, we should think back to the social changes analysed earlier in the book. So another major theme of this chapter is the effect of social change on the body. Anorexia actually reflects certain kinds of social change, including the impact of globalization.

The rise of eating disorders in Western societies coincides directly with the globalization of food production, which has increased greatly in the last three or four decades. The invention of new modes of refrigeration plus the use of container transportation have allowed food to be stored for long periods and to be delivered from one side of the world to the other. Since the 1950s, supermarkets have stocked foods from all over the world (for those who can afford it – now the majority of the population in Western societies). Most of them are available all the time, not just, as was true previously, when they are in season locally.

Over the past decade or so, people in the

UK and in other developed countries have begun to think more carefully about their diet. This does not mean that everyone is desperately trying to get thin. Rather, when all foods are available more or less all the time, we must *decide* what to eat – in other words, construct a diet, where 'diet' means the foods we habitually consume. To construct out diet we have to decide what to eat in relation to the many sorts of new medical information with which science now bombards us – for instance, that cholesterol levels are a factor in causing heart disease. In a society in which food is abundant, we are able for the first time to design our bodies in relation to our lifestyle habits (such as jogging, bicycling, swimming and yoga) and what we eat. Eating disorders have their origins in the opportunities, but also the profound strains and tensions, this situation produces.

Why do eating disorders affect women in particular and young women most acutely? To begin with, it should be pointed out that not all those suffering from eating disorders are women; about 10 per cent are men (Eating Disorders Association 2000). But men don't suffer from anorexia or bulimia as often as women, partly because widely held social norms stress the importance of physical attractiveness more for women than for men and partly because desirable body images of men differ from those of women. Drawing on the diaries of American girls over the last two centuries, Joan Jacobs Brumberg (1997) argues that nowadays when adolescent girls in the USA ask themselves the questions 'Who am I?' and 'Who do I want to be?' the answer, far more than it was a century ago, is likely to revolve around the body. Brumberg argues that 'commercial interests' increasingly play on the body angst of young girls. She concludes that the body is now so central to American girls' sense of self that it has become their central project.

Anorexia and other eating disorders reflect the current situation in which women play a much larger part in the wider society than they used to but are still judged as much by their appearance as by their attainments. Eating disorders are rooted in feelings of shame about the body. The individual feels herself to be inadequate and imperfect, and her anxieties about how others perceive her become focused through her feelings about her body. Ideals of slimness at that point become obsessive – shedding weight becomes the means of making everything all right in her world. Once she starts to diet and exercise compulsively, she can become locked into a pattern of refusing food altogether or of vomiting up what she has eaten. If the pattern is not broken (and some forms of psychotherapy and medical treatment have proved effective here), the sufferer can actually starve herself to death.

The spread of eating disorders reflects the influence of science and technology on our ways of life today: calorie-counting has only been possible with the advance of technology. But the impact of technology is always conditioned by social factors. We have much more autonomy over the body than ever before, a situation that creates new possibilities of a positive kind as well as new anxieties and problems. What is happening is part of what sociologists call the **socialization of nature**. This phrase refers to the fact that phenomena that used to be 'natural', or given in nature, have now become social – they depend on our own social decisions.

Using your sociological imagination: alternative medicine

Earlier in her life Jan Mason enjoyed vibrant health. But when she began experiencing extreme tiredness and depression, she found that her regular doctor was unable to provide her with much relief:

> Before, I was a very fit person. I could swim, play squash, run, and suddenly I just keeled over. I went to the doctor but nobody could tell me what it was. My GP said it was glandular fever and gave me antibiotics which gave me terrible thrush. Then he kept saying that he did not know what it was either. . . . I went through all the tests. I was really very poorly. It went on for six months. I was still ill and they still did not know what it was.
>
> (Quoted in Sharma 1992: 37)

Jan's doctor suggested that she try anti-depressants, concluding that she was suffering from the effects of stress. Jan knew that anti-depressants were not the answer for her, even though she acknowledged that her undiagnosed condition had become a great stress in her life. After listening to a radio programme, she suspected that her lethargy might be a result of post-viral fatigue syndrome. On the advice of a friend, she sought out the assistance of a homeopath – an alternative medical practitioner who assesses the state of the whole body and then, using minuscule doses of substances, treats 'like with like', on the assumption that the symptoms of a disease are part of a body's self-healing process. On finding a homeopath whose approach she was comfortable with, Jan was pleased with the treatment she received (Sharma 1992).

Jan is one of a growing number of people who are incorporating non-orthodox medical practices into their health routines. In many industrialized societies over the last decade, there has been a surge of interest in the potential of **alternative medicine**. The number of alternative medical practitioners is expanding, as are the forms of healing which are available. From herbal remedies to acupuncture, from reflexology to chiropractic treatments, modern society is witnessing an explosion of healthcare alternatives which lie outside, or overlap with, the 'official' medical system. It has been estimated that as many as one in four Britons

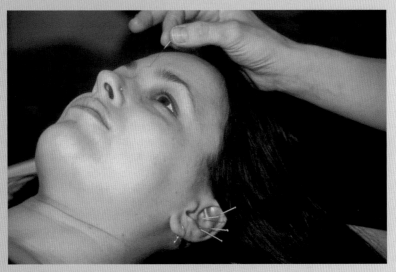

Acupuncture is one of the many strands of complementary medicine being chosen by people who are taking a more active interest in their treatment and questioning the biomedical model of health.

have consulted an alternative practitioner. The profile of the typical individual who seeks out alternative forms of healing is female, young to middle-aged, and middle class.

Industrialized countries have some of the most well-developed, well-resourced medical facilities in the world. Why, then, are a growing number of people choosing to abandon the healthcare system for 'unscientific' treatments such as aromatherapy and hypnotherapy? First, it is important to stress that not everyone who uses alternative medicine does so as a substitute for orthodox treatment (although some alternative approaches, such as homeopathy, reject the basis of orthodox medicine entirely). Many people combine elements of both approaches. For this reason, some scholars prefer to call non-orthodox techniques complementary medicine rather than alternative medicine (Saks 1992).

There are a number of reasons why individuals might seek the services of an alternative practitioner. Some people perceive orthodox medicine as deficient, or incapable of relieving chronic, nagging pains or symptoms of stress and anxiety. Others are dissatisfied with the way modern healthcare systems function – long waiting lists, referrals through chains of specialists, financial restrictions and so forth. Connected to this are concerns about the harmful side-effects of medication and the intrusiveness of surgery – both techniques favoured by modern healthcare systems. The asymmetrical power relationship between doctors and patients is at the heart of some people's choice to avail themselves of alternative medicine. They feel that the role of the 'passive patient' does not grant them enough input into their own treatment and healing. Finally, some individuals profess religious or philosophical objections to orthodox medicine, which tends to treat the mind and body separately. They believe that the spiritual and psychological dimensions of health and illness are often not taken into account in the practice of orthodox medicine.

The growth of alternative medicine presents a number of interesting questions for sociologists to consider. First and foremost, it is a fascinating reflection of the transformations occurring within modern societies. We are living in an age where more and more information is available – from a variety of sources – to draw on in making choices about our lives. Healthcare is no exception in this regard. Individuals are increasingly becoming 'health consumers' – adopting an active stance towards their own health and well-being. Not only are we able to make choices about the type of practitioners to consult, but we are also demanding more involvement in our own care and treatment. In this way, the growth of alternative medicine is linked to the expansion of the self-help movement, which involves support groups, learning circles and self-help books. People are now more likely than ever before to seize control of their lives and actively reshape them, rather than to rely on the instructions or opinions of others.

Another issue of interest to sociologists relates to the changing nature of health and illness in the late modern period. Many of the conditions and illnesses for which individuals seek alternative medical treatment seem to be products of the modern age itself. Insomnia, anxiety, stress, depression, fatigue and chronic pain (caused by arthritis, cancer and other diseases) are all on the rise in industrialized societies. While these conditions have long existed, they appear to be causing greater distress and disruption to people's health than ever before. Recent surveys have revealed that stress has now surpassed the common cold as the biggest cause of absence from work. The World Health Organization predicts that within twenty years depression will be the most debilitating disease in the world. Ironically, it seems that these consequences of modernity are ones which orthodox medicine has great difficulty in addressing. While alternative medicine is unlikely to overtake 'official' healthcare altogether, indications are that its role will continue to grow.

Questions

1 Why has there been such a rise in alternative medicines and treatments in recent years?
2 How do the assumptions that underlie the biomedical model of health (see pp. 260–4) differ from those found in alternative medicine?

Sociological perspectives on medicine

The rise of the biomedical model of health

Like many of the ideas we explore in this book, 'health' and 'illness' are terms that are culturally and socially defined. Cultures differ in what they consider to be healthy and normal. All cultures have known concepts of physical health and illness, but most of what we now recognize as medicine is a consequence of developments in Western society over the past three centuries. In pre-modern cultures, the family was the main institution coping with sickness or affliction. There have always been individuals who specialized as healers, using a mixture of physical and magical remedies, and many of these traditional systems of treatment survive today in non-Western cultures throughout the world. A large number of them belong to the category of alternative medicines discussed above.

For approximately two hundred years now, the dominant Western ideas about medicine have been expressed in the **biomedical model of health**. This understanding of health and illness developed along with the growth of modern societies. In fact, it can be seen as one of the main features of such societies. Its emergence was closely linked to the triumph of science and reason over traditional or religious-based explanations of the world (see the discussion of Weber and rationalization in chapter 1, pp. 18–19). Before looking at the biomedical model in more depth, let us briefly consider the social and historical context in which it arose.

Public health

We saw above how members of traditional societies relied largely on folk remedies, treatments and healing techniques which were passed down from generation to generation. Illnesses were frequently regarded in magical or religious terms and were attributed to the presence of evil spirits or 'sin'. For peasants and average town-dwellers, there was no outside authority that was concerned with their health in the way that states and public health systems are today. Health was a private matter, not a public concern.

The rise of both the nation-state and industrialization brought about drastic changes in this situation, however. The emergence of nation-states with defined territories produced a shift in attitudes towards local people, who were no longer simply inhabitants of the land, but were a population falling under the rule of a central authority. The human population was seen as a resource to be monitored and regulated as part of the process of maximizing national wealth and power. The state began to take a heightened interest in the health of its population, as the well-being of its members affected the nation's productivity, level of prosperity, defensive capabilities and rate of growth. The study of **demography** – the size, composition and dynamics of human populations – assumed much greater importance. The Census was introduced in order to record and monitor changes occurring in the population. Statistics of all sorts were collected and calculated: birth rates, mortality rates, average ages of marriage and child-bearing, suicide rates, life expectancy, diet, common illnesses, causes of death and so forth.

Michel Foucault (1926–1984) has made an influential contribution to our understanding of the rise of modern medicine by drawing attention to the regulation and disciplining of bodies by the state (1973). He argues that sexuality and sexual behaviour were of central importance to this process. Sex was both the way in which the population could reproduce and grow, and a potential threat to its health and well-being. Sexuality not linked to reproduction was something to be repressed and controlled. This monitoring of sexuality by the state occurred in part through the collection of data about marriage, sexual behaviour, legitimacy and illegitimacy, the use of contraception and abortions. This surveillance went hand in hand with the promotion of strong public norms about sexual morality and acceptable sexual activity. For example, sexual 'perversions' such as homosexuality, masturbation and sex outside marriage were all labelled and condemned (see chapter 12, 'Sexuality and Gender').

The idea of public health took shape in an attempt to eradicate '**pathologies**' from the population – the 'social body'. The state began to assume responsibility for improving the conditions in which the population lived. Sanitation and water systems were developed to protect against disease. Roads were paved and attention was devoted to housing. Regulations were gradually imposed on slaughterhouses and facilities for food processing. Burial practices were monitored to ensure that they did not pose a health threat to the population. A whole series of institutions, such as prisons, asylums, workhouses, schools and hospitals emerged as part of the move towards monitoring, controlling and reforming the people.

The biomedical model

Medical practices were closely intertwined with the social changes described above. The application of science to medical diagnosis and cure was the major feature of the development of modern healthcare systems. Disease came to be defined objectively, in terms of identifiable objective 'signs' located in the body, as opposed to symptoms experienced by the patient. Formal medical care by trained 'experts' became the accepted way of treating both physical and mental illnesses. Medicine became a tool of reform for behaviours or conditions perceived as 'deviant' – from crime to homosexuality to mental illness.

There are three main assumptions on which the biomedical model of health is predicated. First, disease is viewed as a breakdown within the human body that diverts it from its 'normal' state of being. The germ theory of disease, developed in the late 1800s, holds that there is a specific identifiable agent behind every disease. In order to restore the body to health, the cause of the disease must be isolated and treated.

Second, the mind and body can be treated separately. The patient represents a *sick body* – a pathology – rather than a whole individual. The emphasis is on curing the disease, rather than on the individual's well-being. The biomedical model holds that the sick body can be manipulated, investigated and treated in isolation, without considering other factors. Medical specialists adopt a 'medical gaze', a detached approach in viewing and treating the sick patient. The treatment is to be carried out in a neutral, value-free manner, with information collected and

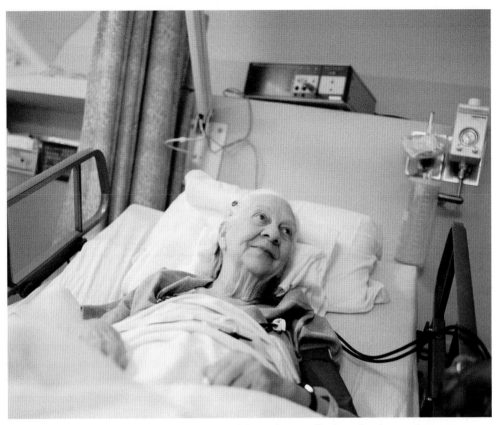

According to the biomedical model of health, to the medical profession patients represent only 'sick bodies'.

compiled, in clinical terms, in a patient's official file.

Third, trained *medical specialists* are considered the only experts in the treatment of disease. The medical profession as a body adheres to a recognized code of ethics and is made up of accredited individuals who have successfully completed long-term training. There is no room for self-taught healers or 'non-scientific' medical practices. The hospital represents the appropriate environment in which to treat serious illnesses; these treatments often rely on some combination of technology, medication or surgery. The main

assumptions and critiques of the biomedical model are summarized in table 8.1.

Criticisms of the biomedical model

Over the past few decades, the biomedical model of illness described above has been the object of growing criticism. First, some scholars have claimed that the effectiveness of scientific medicine is 'overrated'. In spite of the prestige that modern medicine has acquired, improvements in overall health can be attributed far more to social and environmental changes than to medical skill. Effective sanitation, better nutrition and improved

Table 8.1   Assumptions and critiques of the biomedical model

Assumptions	Critiques
Disease is a breakdown of the human body caused by a specific biological agent.	Disease is socially constructed, not something that can be revealed through 'scientific truth'.
The patient is a passive being whose 'sick body' can be treated separately from his or her mind.	The patient's opinions and experience of illness is crucial to the treatment. The patient is an active, 'whole' being whose overall well-being – not just physical health – is important.
Medical specialists possess 'expert knowledge' and offer the only valid treatment of disease.	Medical experts are not the only source of knowledge about health and illness. Alternative forms of knowledge are equally valid.
The appropriate arena for treatment is the hospital, where medical technology is concentrated and best employed.	Healing does not need to take place in a hospital. Treatments utilizing technology, medication and surgery are not necessarily superior.

sewerage and hygiene were more influential, particularly in reducing the infant mortality rates and deaths of young children (McKeown 1979). Drugs, advances in surgery, and antibiotics did not significantly decrease death rates until well into the twentieth century. Antibiotics used to treat bacterial infections first became available in the 1930s and 1940s, while immunizations (against diseases such as polio) were developed later. Ivan Illich (1975) has even suggested that modern medicine has done more harm than good because of *iatrogenesis*, or 'self-caused' disease. Illich argued that there are three types: clinical, social and cultural iatrogenesis. Clinical iatrogenesis is where medical treatment makes the patient worse or creates new conditions. Social iatrogenesis is where medicine expands into more and more areas, creating an artificial demand for its services. Social iatrogenesis, Illich argued, leads to cultural iatrogenesis, where the ability to cope with the challenges of everyday life is progressively reduced by medical explanations and alternatives. To critics like Illich,

the scope of modern medicine should be dramatically reduced.

Second, modern medicine has been accused of discounting the opinions and experiences of the patients it seeks to treat. Because medicine is supposedly based on objective, scientific understandings of the causes and cures of specific physical ailments, there is little perceived need to listen to the individual interpretations that patients give to their conditions. Each patient is a 'sick body' to be treated and cured. Critics argue, however, that effective treatment can only take place when the patient is treated as a thinking, capable being with their own valid understandings and interpretations.

Third, critics argue that scientific medicine posits itself as superior to any alternative form of medicine or healing. A belief has been perpetuated that anything that is 'unscientific' is necessarily inferior. As we have already seen, the assertion that modern medicine is somehow a more valid form of knowledge is being undermined by the growing popularity of alternative forms of medicine, such as homeopathy and acupuncture.

Fourth, some sociologists have argued that the medical profession wields enormous power in defining what does and does not constitute illness. It is able to use its position as the arbiter of 'scientific truth' to bring more and more realms of human life under medical control. Some of the strongest criticisms along these lines have come from women who argue that the processes of pregnancy and childbirth have been appropriated and 'medicalized' by modern medicine. Rather than remaining in the hands of women – with the help of midwives in the home – childbirth now occurs in hospitals under the direction of predominantly male specialists. Pregnancy, a common and natural phenomenon, is treated as an 'illness' laden with risks and danger. Feminists argue that women have lost control over this process, as their opinions and knowledge are deemed irrelevant by the 'experts' who now oversee reproductive processes (Oakley 1984). Similar concerns about the medicalization of 'normal' conditions have been raised in relation to hyperactivity in children (see box on p. 265), unhappiness or mild depression (commonly regulated with the help of medications like Prozac), and tiredness (frequently labelled Chronic Fatigue Syndrome). Many of the assumptions of the biomedical model are being increasingly questioned, as the world in which it developed changes.

Fifth, critics have argued that the assumptions underlying the biomedical model of health have lent themselves to gross political manipulation, in particular through **eugenics**, the attempt to genetically 'improve' the human race through 'good breeding'. Scientific and medical 'experts' in Nazi Germany took these policies to their most extreme, by claiming that they had identified a racially superior, light-skinned 'Aryan' race. Their eugenic programmes led to the genocide of millions of people who belonged to groups the Nazis saw as biologically inferior, such as Jews and gypsies, as well as the systematic murder of more than 250,000 disabled people (Burleigh 1994).

Although Nazi Germany made by far the most murderous use of eugenic policies, it should be remembered that in the twentieth century, eugenics – often described as 'population policies' – were also used in several other European countries and the USA against particular sections of the population, notably the disabled. These policies mostly took the form of the compulsory sterilization of 'feeble-minded' women. Racism led to black women being grossly over-represented among the 60,000 people forcibly sterilized in several US states between 1907 and 1960. In Scandinavia, political leaders and geneticists adopted policies for compulsory sterilization because they were concerned that the emerging welfare state would encourage the 'unfit' to reproduce and would therefore reduce the quality of the 'national stock'. In Sweden alone, 63,000 people, 90 per cent of them women, were sterilized between 1934 and 1975. Norway, a much smaller country, sterilized 48,000 people in the same period. British and Dutch medical experts and policy-makers, by contrast, adopted voluntary sterilization, together with the mass institutionalization and segregation of the 'feeble-minded' (Rose 1999).

Today, the rapid development of medical technology is raising new and difficult questions for critics of the biomedical model. A great deal of scientific endeavour is now being devoted to the expansion of genetic engineering, which makes it possible to intervene in the genetic make-up of the foetus so as to influence its subsequent development. The debate about genetic engineering is often polarized between critics, who see it as fatally corrupted by the history of eugenics in the twentieth century discussed above, and supporters who argue it is separate from these events (Kerr and Shakespeare 2002). According to its supporters, genetic engineering will create enormous opportunities. It is possible, for example, to identify the genetic factors that make some people vulnerable to certain diseases. Genetic reprogramming will ensure that these illnesses are no longer passed on from generation to generation. In 2004 a group of people in the UK with a particular form of inherited bowel cancer were granted the right by the government's Human Fertilization and Embryology Authority to select embryos free from genes that might trigger the disease in future generations. The decision means that only those embryos free of the gene that could cause the cancer will be implanted into the mother's womb. Without the screening process, infants would have a 50 per cent chance of inheriting the disease (*The Times*, 1 November 2004). The selection of embryos was previously approved only for childhood or untreatable disorders such as cystic fibrosis and Huntington's disease (*The Times*, 6 November 2004). On the other hand, the ruling by the Human Fertilization and Embryology Authority deepens the controversy over 'designer babies'. It sets a precedent that will allow doctors to 'cherry-pick' embryos for a much wider range of traits than at present. It is now scientifically possible, for example, to 'design' bodies before birth in terms of colour of skin, hair and eyes, weight and so forth.

Several of the criticisms of the biomedical model, discussed above, apply also to the genetic engineering debate. Many of those with concerns about the biomedical model will question the role of medical experts in exerting their authority over the technology. Will there be unintended consequences of medical intervention? What role will parents-to-be have in making decisions about the selection of embryos? Is this another case of (traditionally male) medical experts giving authoritative medical advice to (obviously female) future mothers? What safeguards should be present to prevent sexism, racism or disablism in embryo selection? And how are these categories defined? Genetic engineering is unlikely to be cheap. Will this mean that those who can afford to pay will be able to programme out from their children any traits they see as socially undesirable? What will happen to the children of more deprived groups, who will continue to be born naturally? Some sociologists have argued that differential access to genetic engineering might lead to the emergence of a 'biological underclass'. Those who don't have the physical advantages genetic engineering can bring might be subject to prejudice and discrimination by those who do enjoy these advantages. They might have difficulty finding employment and life or health insurance (Duster 1990). For sociologists, the rapid pace in which new medical technologies are advancing raises an increasing number of new and difficult questions.

The 'medicalization' of hyperactivity

In the past decade, the number of prescriptions written for the drug Ritalin has grown exponentially. In the United States, nearly 3 per cent of children between the ages of five and eighteen are on Ritalin. In Britain in 1998, more than 125,000 prescriptions for Ritalin were issued – up from only 3,500 in 1993. By 2007 experts predict that one in seven children will be taking the drug (*Observer*, May 2003). What is Ritalin and why should sociologists be concerned with it? Ritalin is a drug prescribed to children and adolescents with Attention Deficit Hyperactive Disorder (ADHD) – a psychological disorder which, according to many physicians and psychiatrists, accounts for children's inattentiveness, difficulty in concentrating and inability to learn in school. Ritalin has been described as 'the magic pill'. It helps children to focus, it calms them down and it helps them to learn more effectively. Children who were once disruptive and problematic in the classroom become 'angelic' students, say some teachers, once they begin taking Ritalin.

Critics of Ritalin, however, argue that the drug is far from the harmless 'magic pill' which it is often made out to be. Despite the fact that it has been prescribed in growing quantities in the USA and UK over recent years, no comprehensive research has been carried out on its possible long-term effects on children's brains and bodies. Perhaps more worrying is the claim that Ritalin has become a convenient 'solution' to what is in fact not even a physical problem. Opponents of Ritalin argue that the 'symptoms' of ADHD are in fact reflections of the growing pressure and stress on modern children – an increasingly fast pace of life, the overwhelming effect of information technology, lack of exercise, high-sugar diets and the fraying of family life. Through the use of Ritalin, it is claimed, the medical profession has succeeded in 'medicalizing' child hyperactivity and inattentiveness, rather than drawing attention to the social causes of the observed symptoms.

Medicine and health in a changing world

There is a growing realization that it is not only medical experts who possess knowledge and understanding about health and illness. All of us are in a position to interpret and shape our own well-being through our understanding of our bodies, and through choices in our everyday lives about diet, exercise, consumption patterns and general lifestyle. These new directions in popular thinking about health, along with the other criticisms of modern medicine outlined above, are contributing to some profound transformations within healthcare systems in modern societies (see figure 8.1). They also explain the rise in alternative or complementary medicine, discussed above.

Yet other factors are relevant here as well: the nature and scale of disease itself have been changing. In earlier times, the major illnesses were infectious diseases such as tuberculosis, cholera, malaria and polio. They often took on epidemic proportions and could threaten a whole population. In industrialized countries today, such acute infectious diseases have become a minor cause of death; some of them have been substantially eradicated. The most common causes of death in industrialized countries are now non-infectious chronic diseases such as cancer, heart disease, diabetes or circulatory diseases. This shift is referred to as the 'health transition'. Whereas in pre-modern societies the highest rates of death were among infants and young children, today death rates rise with increasing age. Because people are living longer and suffering predominantly from

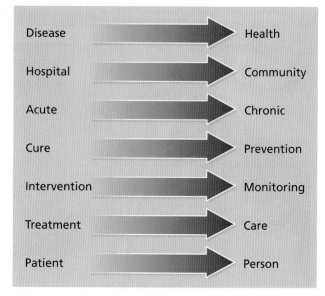

Figure 8.1   Contemporary transformations in health and medicine

Source: Nettleton (2006)

chronic degenerative diseases, there is the need for a new approach to health and caring. There is also increased emphasis on 'lifestyle choices' – such as smoking, exercise and diet – which are seen to influence the onset of many chronic illnesses.

Whether these contemporary transformations in healthcare will result in a new 'health paradigm' to replace the biomedical model, as some scholars have suggested, is unclear. But it is certain that we are witnessing a period of significant and rapid reform in modern medicine and in people's attitudes towards it.

Sociological perspectives on health and illness

One of the main concerns of sociologists is to examine the experience of illness.

Sociologists ask how illness, such as anorexia discussed above, is experienced and interpreted by the sick person and by those with whom she comes into contact. If you have ever been ill, even for a short period of time, you know that patterns in everyday life are temporarily modified and your interactions with others become transformed. This is because the 'normal' functioning of the body is a vital, but often unnoticed, part of our lives. We depend on our bodies to operate as they should; our very sense of self is predicated on the expectation that our bodies will facilitate, not impede, our social interactions and daily activities.

Illness has both personal and public dimensions. When we become ill, not only do we experience pain, discomfort, confusion and other challenges, but others are affected as well. People in close contact with us may extend sympathy, care and support. They may struggle to make sense of the fact of our illness or to find ways to incorporate it into the patterns of their own lives. Others with whom we come into contact may also react to illness; these reactions in turn help to shape our own interpretations and can pose challenges to our sense of self.

Two ways of understanding the experience of illness have been particularly influential in sociological thought. The first, associated with the functionalist school, sets forth the norms of behaviour which individuals are thought to adopt when sick. The second view, favoured by symbolic interactionists, is a broader attempt to reveal the interpretations which are ascribed to illness and how these meanings influence people's actions and behaviour.

The sick role

The prominent functionalist thinker Talcott Parsons (1952) advanced the notion of the **sick role** in order to describe the patterns of behaviour which the sick person adopts in order to minimize the disruptive impact of illness. Functionalist thought holds that society usually operates in a smooth and consensual manner. Illness is therefore seen as a dysfunction which can disrupt the flow of this normal state of being. A sick individual, for example, might not be able to perform all of his or her standard responsibilities or might be less reliable and efficient than usual. Because sick people are not able to carry out their normal roles, the lives of people around them are disrupted: assignments at work go unfinished and cause stress for co-workers, responsibilities at home are not fulfilled, and so forth.

For more on functionalism see chapter 1, 'What is Sociology?' pp. 20–2.

According to Parsons, people learn the sick role through socialization and enact it

"We're running a little behind, so I'd like each of you to ask yourself, 'Am I really that sick, or would I just be wasting the doctor's valuable time?'"

– with the cooperation of others – when they fall ill. There are three pillars of the sick role:

1 *The sick person is not personally responsible for being sick.* Illness is seen as the result of physical causes beyond the individual's control. The onset of illness is unrelated to the individual's behaviour or actions.

2 *The sick person is entitled to certain rights and privileges, including a withdrawal from normal responsibilities.* Since the sick person bears no responsibility for the illness, he or she is exempted from certain duties, roles and behaviours which otherwise apply. For example, the sick person might be 'released' from normal duties around the home. Behaviour that is not as polite or thoughtful as usual might be excused. The sick person gains the right to stay in bed, for example, or to take time off from work.

3 *The sick person must work to regain health by consulting a medical expert and agreeing to become a 'patient'.* The sick role is a temporary and 'conditional' one which is contingent on the sick person actively trying to get well. In order to occupy the sick role, the sick person must receive the sanction of a medical professional who legitimates the person's claim of illness. Confirmation of illness via an expert opinion allows those surrounding the sick person to accept the validity of his or her claims. The patient is expected to cooperate in his or her own recovery by following the 'doctor's orders'. A sick person who refuses to consult a doctor, or who does not heed the advice of a medical authority, puts his or her sick role status in jeopardy.

Parsons's sick role has been refined by other sociologists, who suggest that all illnesses are not 'the same' as far as the sick role is concerned. They argue that the experience of the sick role varies with the type of illness, since people's reactions to a sick person are influenced by the severity of the illness and by their perception of it. Thus, the added rights and privileges which are part of the sick role may not be uniformly experienced. Freidson (1970) identified three versions of the sick role which correspond with different types and degrees of illness. The *conditional* sick role applies to individuals who are suffering from a temporary condition from which they can recover. The sick person is expected to 'get well' and receives some rights and privileges according to the severity of the illness. For example, someone suffering from bronchitis would reap more benefits than the sufferer of a common cold. The *unconditionally legitimate* sick role refers to individuals who are suffering from incurable illnesses. Because the sick person cannot 'do' anything to get well, he or she is automatically entitled to occupy the sick role. The unconditionally legitimate role might apply to individuals suffering from alopecia (total hair loss) or severe acne (in both cases there are no special privileges, but rather an acknowledgement that the individual is not responsible for the illness), or from cancer or Parkinson's disease – which result in important privileges and the right to abandon many or most duties. The final sick role is the *illegitimate* role. The illegitimate role obtains when an individual suffers from a disease or condition that is stigmatized by others. In such cases, there is a sense that the individual might somehow bear responsibility for the illness; additional rights and privileges are not necessarily granted. Alcoholism is one example of a stigmatized illness which affects a sufferer's right to assume the sick role.

Erving Goffman (1963) argued that **stigma** is a relationship of devaluation in which one individual is disqualified from full social acceptance. Stigma can take many forms – for example, physical (see Paul Hunt's discussion of disability below – p. 281), biographical (such as the possession of a criminal record) or contextual (for example 'hanging out with the wrong crowd'). Stigmas are rarely based on valid understandings. They spring from stereotypes or perceptions which may be false, or only partially correct. Stigmatization often appears in the medical context (see the case study on facial disfigurement on pp. 285–6). Goffman argued that inherent in the process of stigmatization is social control. Stigmatizing groups is one way in which society controls their behaviour. In some cases, the stigma is never removed and the person is never fully accepted into society. (This was true of people afflicted with leprosy in the Middle Ages, who were popularly disowned and forced to live in separate leper colonies. It has been true more recently with AIDS patients.) Within medical institutions stigma can play a role in determining the attitude of the medical expert towards the patient. Stigmatized patients (drug addicts, for example) might be ignored when asking questions or seeking to clarify information about their treatment. The result is medical dominance by doctors and other staff over patients.

Critiques of the 'sick role'

The sick role model has been an influential theory which reveals clearly how the ill person is an integral part of a larger social context. But there are a number of criticisms which can be levied against it. Some writers have argued that the sick role 'formula' is unable to capture the *experience* of illness. Others point out that it cannot be applied universally. For example, the sick role theory does not account for instances when doctors and patients disagree about a diagnosis, or have opposing interests. Furthermore, assuming the sick role is not always a straightforward process. Some individuals suffer for years from chronic pain or from symptoms that are repeatedly misdiagnosed. They are denied the sick role until a clear diagnosis of their condition is made. In other cases, social factors such as race, class and gender can affect whether, and how readily, the sick role is granted. The sick role cannot be divorced from the social, cultural and economic influences which surround it.

The realities of life and illness are more complex than the sick role suggests. The increasing emphasis on lifestyle and health in our modern age means that individuals are seen as bearing ever greater responsibility for their own well-being. This contradicts the first premise of the sick role – that the individual is not to blame for his or her illness. Moreover, in modern societies the shift away from acute infectious disease towards chronic illness has made the sick role less applicable. Whereas the sick role might be useful in understanding acute illness, it is less useful in the case of chronic illness: there is no one formula for chronically ill or disabled people to follow. Living with illness is experienced and interpreted in a multiplicity of ways by sick people – and by those who surround them.

We shall now turn to some of the ways that sociologists of the symbolic interactionist school have attempted to understand the experience of illness.

Illness as 'lived experience'

Symbolic interactionists are interested in the ways people interpret the social world and the meanings they ascribe to it. Many sociologists have applied this approach to the realm of health and illness in order to understand how people experience being ill or perceive the illness of others. How do people react and adjust to news about a serious illness? How does illness shape individuals' daily lives? How does living with a chronic illness affect an individual's self-identity?

As we saw in our discussion of ageing (chapter 6) people in industrialized societies are now living longer, but suffering later in life from chronic illnesses. Medicine is able to relieve the pain and discomfort associated with some of these conditions, but a growing number of people are faced with the prospect of living with illness over a long period of time. Sociologists are concerned with how illness in such cases becomes incorporated in an individual's personal 'biography'.

One theme that sociologists have explored is how chronically ill individuals learn to cope with the practical and emotional implications of their illness. Certain illnesses demand regular treatments or maintenance which can affect people's daily routines. Dialysis, insulin injections or taking large numbers of pills demand that individuals adjust their schedules in response to illness. Other illnesses can have unpredictable effects on the body, such as the sudden loss of bowel or bladder control, or violent nausea. Individuals suffering from such conditions are forced to develop strategies for managing their illness in day-to-day life. These include both practical considerations – such as always noting the location of the toilet when in an unfamiliar place – as well as skills for managing interpersonal relations, both intimate and commonplace. Although the symptoms of the illness can be embarrassing and disruptive, people develop coping strategies to live life as normally as possible (Kelly 1992).

At the same time, the experience of illness can pose challenges to and bring about transformations in people's sense of self. These develop both through the actual reactions of others to the illness, and through imagined or perceived reactions. For the chronically ill or disabled, social interactions which are routine for many people become tinged with risk or uncertainty. The shared understandings that underpin standard everyday interactions are not always present when illness or disability is a factor, and interpretations of common situations may differ substantially. An ill person may be in need of assistance but not want to appear dependent, for example. An individual may feel sympathy for someone who has been diagnosed with an illness, but be unsure whether to address the subject directly. The changed context of social interactions can precipitate transformations in self-identity.

Some sociologists have investigated how chronically ill individuals manage their illnesses within the overall context of their lives (Jobling 1988; Williams 1993). Illness can place enormous demands on people's time, energy, strength and emotional reserves. Corbin and Strauss (1985) studied the regimes of health which the chronically ill develop in order to organize their daily lives. They identified three types of 'work' contained in people's everyday strategies. Illness work refers to those activities involved in managing their condition, such as treating pain, doing diagnostic tests or undergoing physical therapy. Everyday work pertains to the management of daily life – maintaining relationships with others, running the household affairs and pursuing professional or personal interests. Biographical work involves those activities that the ill person does as part of building or reconstructing their personal narrative. In other words, it is the process of incorporating the illness into one's life, making sense of it and developing ways of explaining it to others. Such a process can help people restore meaning and order to their lives after coming to terms with the knowledge of chronic illness. From studying how illness affects the individual, we now turn to examine patterns of illness and health within society, and discuss how health outcomes differ between social groups.

The social basis of health

The twentieth century witnessed a significant overall rise in life expectancy for people who live in industrialized countries. In the UK life expectancy at birth rose from around the age of forty-five for men and forty-nine for women in 1901, to over seventy-five for men and eighty for women, by 2003. Diseases such as polio, scarlet fever and tuberculosis have virtually been eradicated. Compared to other parts of the world, standards of health and well-being are relatively high. Many of these advances in public health have been attributed to the power of modern medicine. There is a commonly held assumption that medical research has been – and will continue to be – successful in uncovering the biological causes of disease and in developing effective treatments to control them. As medical knowledge and expertise grow, the argument runs, we can expect to see sustained and steady improvements in public health.

Although this approach to health and disease has been extremely influential, it is somewhat unsatisfactory for sociologists. This is because it ignores the important role of social and environmental influences on patterns of health and illness. The improvements in overall public health over the past century cannot conceal the fact that health and illness are not distributed evenly throughout the population. Research has shown that certain groups of people tend to enjoy much better health than others. These health inequalities appear to be tied to larger socio-economic patterns.

Sociologists and specialists in social **epidemiology** – scientists who study the distribution and incidence of disease and illness within the population – have attempted to explain the link between health and variables such as social class, gender, race, age and geography. While most scholars acknowledge the correlation between health and social inequalities, there is no agreement about the nature of the connection or about how health inequalities should be addressed. One of the main areas of debate concentrates on the relative importance of individual variables (such as lifestyle, behaviour, diet and cultural patterns) versus environmental or structural factors (such as income distribution and poverty). In this section we will look at variations in health patterns in Britain according to social class, gender and ethnicity and review some of the competing explanations for their persistence.

Class and health

Research on health and class has revealed a clear relationship between patterns of mortality and morbidity (illness) and an individual's social class. In Britain, the Black Report – a major nationwide study (DHSS 1980) – was important in publicizing the extent of class-based health inequalities. Many people found the results shocking. Although there was found to be a trend towards better health in society as a whole, significant disparities were seen to exist between various classes, affecting health indicators from birth weight to blood pressure to risk of chronic illness. Individuals from higher socio-economic positions are on average healthier, taller and stronger, and live longer than those lower down the social scale. Differences are greatest in respect to infant mortality (children dying in the first year of life) and child death, but poorer people are at greater risk of dying at all ages than more affluent people.

Some of the main class-based inequalities in health have been summarized by Browne and Bottrill (1999). They include:

1 Unskilled manual workers in the lowest occupational class are twice as likely to die before retirement age than professional white-collar workers in the top occupational class.
2 Twice as many babies are stillborn or die within the first week of life in unskilled families than in professional families (see table 8.2).
3 An individual born into the highest occupational class (professional white-collar workers) is likely to live on average seven years longer than someone born into the lowest occupational class (unskilled manual workers).
4 Some 90 per cent of the major causes of death are more common in the two lowest occupational classes than the three higher occupational classes (see figure 8.2).

Table 8.2   Infant mortality: by social class in England and Wales (per 1,000 live births)[a]

	Inside marriage		Outside marriage	
	1991	2001	1991	2001
Professional	5.1	3.6	4.2	4.5
Managerial and technical	5.3	3.6	6.6	4.0
Skilled non-manual	6.1	4.5	8.5	5.3
Skilled manual	6.2	5.0	7.7	5.8
Semi-skilled manual	7.1	6.2	9.6	6.7
Unskilled manual	8.2	7.2	11.0	7.5
Other	11.6	6.7	21.2	10.8
All	6.3	4.6	8.8	6.1

[a] Infant mortality is deaths within one year of birth; social class is based on occupation of father at death registration

Source: Social Trends 34 (2004)

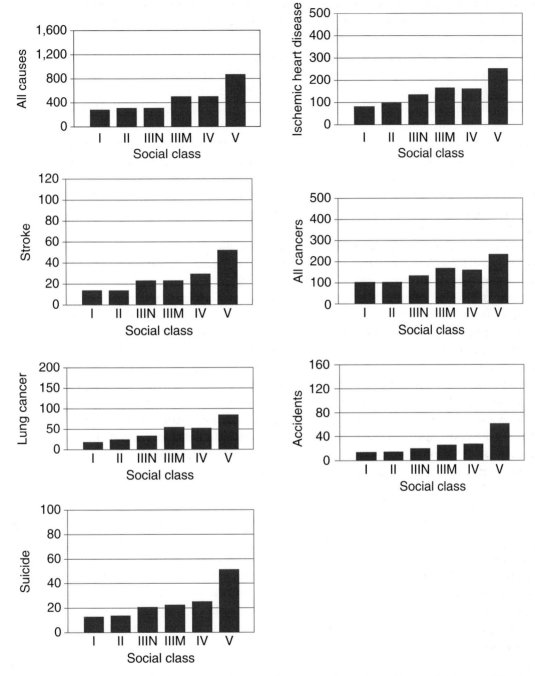

Figure 8.2 Mortality of men in the UK aged 20–64, by cause of death and by social class, 1991–3 (rates per 100,000)

Source: ONS (2001)

5 Working-class people visit their doctors more often and for a wider range of ailments than people in professional occupations; long-standing illness is 50 per cent higher among unskilled manual workers than among professionals.
6 Class-based health inequalities are even more pronounced among the long-term unemployed; people in work tend to live longer than those who are without work.

Studies conducted in other industrialized countries have confirmed that there is a clear class gradient to health. Some scholars believe that the relative health inequality between the richest and poorest members of society is widening. Yet despite a growing amount of research aimed at revealing the link between health inequality and social class, scholars have been unsuccessful in locating the actual mechanisms which connect the two. Several competing explanations have been advanced for the causes behind the correlation.

The Black Report, which was commissioned by the government to review data on health inequalities and to make recommendations for policy and further research, concentrated most heavily on materialist explanations of health inequality. Materialist or environmental explanations see the cause of health inequalities in large social structures such as poverty, wealth and income distribution, unemployment, housing, pollution and poor working conditions. The patterns in health inequalities between classes are seen as the result of material deprivation. Reducing inequalities in health can only be done by addressing the root causes of social inequalities in general. While not discounting the possible validity of other arguments, the Black Report stressed the need for a comprehensive anti-poverty strategy and for improvements in education in order to combat health inequalities.

The Conservative government headed by Margaret Thatcher was dismissive of the Black Report's findings, pronouncing the public expenditure required by the report to be both unrealistic and unforeseeable. Thatcher's government (1979–90) tended to focus on cultural and behavioural explanations for health inequalities. Cultural and behavioural explanations emphasize the importance of individual lifestyles on health. Lower social classes tend to engage in certain activities – such as smoking, poor diet and higher consumption of alcohol – which are detrimental to good health. This argument sees individuals as bearing primary responsibility for poor health, as many lifestyle choices are freely made. Some proponents of this approach argue that such behaviours are embedded within the social class context, rather than under the exclusive control of individuals. Nevertheless, they also identify lifestyle and consumption patterns as the main causes of poor health. Subsequent governments have continued to place emphasis on public health campaigns to influence individuals' lifestyle choices. Anti-smoking initiatives, healthy eating and exercise programmes are examples of two such efforts to shape public behaviour. Campaigns like this exhort individuals to take responsibility for their own well-being; they pay less attention to the way social position can constrain people's choices and possibilities. As an example, fresh fruit and vegetables that are central to a good diet are much more expensive than many

Poor diet is just one of the factors associated with ill health amongst Britain's most deprived people.

foods high in fat and cholesterol. Studies show that the greatest consumption of healthy food is among high-income groups.

The Labour government elected in 1997 has taken a broader approach to health inequalities, acknowledging the importance of both cultural and material factors on people's health. They commissioned an independent inquiry into inequalities in health, chaired by Sir Donald Acheson. The Acheson Report was published in November 1998 and confirmed that for many aspects of health, inequality has generally worsened in the last few decades, especially in the 1980s and early 1990s. Building on evidence from the Acheson Report, the government published a White Paper, *Our Healthier Nation*, in July 1999 that emphasized the many diverse influences – social, economic, environmental and cultural – which work together to produce ill health (some of these are illustrated in figure 8.3). It also proposed a set of government initiatives linking health with, for example, unemployment, substandard housing and education, to address not only the symptoms of poor health, but its causes as well.

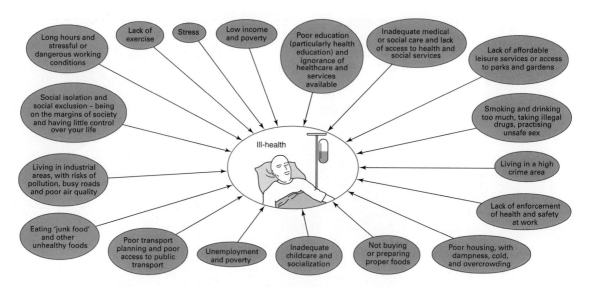

Figure 8.3   Cultural and material influences on health

Source: Browne (2005), p. 410

Gender and health

Disparities in health between men and women have also been noted in research. Women enjoy a longer life expectancy than men in almost every country in the world (UNDP 2004). In the UK, causes of death and patterns of illness show some differences between men and women (see figure 8.4). Although heart disease affects men more than women, it is still the most frequent killer of both men and women under the age of sixty-five. Men, however, suffer from higher rates of death from accidents and violence and are also more prone to drug and alcohol dependency.

Material circumstances appear to influence women's health status, but this has traditionally been a difficult factor to gauge. Many studies have tended to classify women according to the social class of their husbands, producing a distorted picture of women's health (see chapter 9, 'Stratification and Class'). We do know, however, that women are more likely to seek medical attention and have higher rates of self-reported illness than men.

Women in industrialized countries report twice as much anxiety and depression as men. According to some observers, the multiple roles which women tend to perform – domestic work, child care, professional responsibilities – may increase the stress on women and contribute to higher rates of illness. Lesley Doyal (1995) has suggested that patterns of women's health and sickness may best be explained in relation to the main areas of activities which constitute their lives. Women's lives are inherently different from men's in terms of the roles and tasks that are commonly performed – domestic work, sexual reproduction, childbearing and mother-

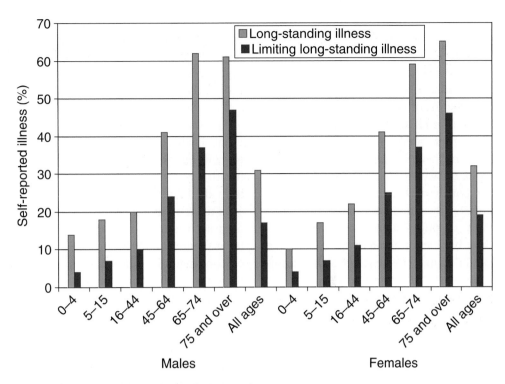

Figure 8.4 Self-reported illness: by sex and age, 2003–4

Source: *Social Trends* 35 (2005)

ing, regulating fertility through birth control, and so forth. (Although it could be argued that this is decreasingly true as more women enter the workplace.) According to Doyal, 'it is the cumulative effects of these various labours that are the major determinants of women's states of health'. Therefore, any analysis of women's health should consider the interaction between social, psychological and biological influences.

Heather Graham has studied the effects of stress on the health of white working-class women. She has highlighted the fact that women at the lower socio-economic end of the spectrum have less access to support networks in times of life crisis

than do middle-class women. Working-class women, she notes, tend to encounter life crises (such as job loss, divorce, eviction from housing or the death of a child) more often than other groups, but generally have weaker coping skills and fewer outlets for anxiety. Not only is the resulting stress harmful both physically and psychologically, but some of the coping strategies which are turned to – such as smoking – are also damaging. Graham argues that smoking is a way of reducing tension when personal and material resources are stretched to breaking point. Thus it occupies a paradoxical position in women's lives – increasing the health risk for women and their children, while simultaneously allowing them to cope under difficult circumstances (Graham 1987, 1994).

Ann Oakley and her colleagues (1994) have studied the role of social support in the health of socially disadvantaged women and children in four English cities. She argues that the relationship between stress and health applies both to major life crises and smaller problems, and that it is felt particularly acutely in the lives of working-class people. Oakley notes that social support – such as counselling services, hotlines or home visits – can act as a 'buffer' against the negative health consequences of stress commonly experienced by women. Other studies have shown that social support is an important factor that can help people in adjusting to disease and illness (Ell 1996).

Ethnicity and health

Although health in industrial societies is ethnically patterned, our understanding of the relationship between ethnicity and health is partial at best. An increasing number of sociological studies are being conducted in this area, but the evidence remains inconclusive. In some cases, trends that have been attributed to membership of an ethnic group may have ignored other factors, such as class or gender, which may also be significant.

Nevertheless, the incidence of certain illnesses is higher among individuals from African-Caribbean and Asian backgrounds. In the UK, mortality from liver cancer, tuberculosis and diabetes are higher among these populations than among whites. African-Caribbeans suffer from higher than average rates of hypertension and sickle-cell anaemia (an inher-

ited disorder affecting red blood cells) than the average for the UK. People from the Indian subcontinent experience higher mortality from heart disease than the average for the UK.

Some scholars have turned to cultural and behavioural accounts to explain ethnic health patterning. In a similar way to cultural explanations of class-based health inequalities, emphasis is placed on individual and group lifestyles which are seen to result in poorer health. These are often seen as linked to religious or cultural beliefs, such as dietary and cooking habits or consanguinity (the practice of inter-marriage within families at the level of second cousins). Critics argue that cultural explanations have failed to identify the real problem – the structural inequalities which affect ethnic groups and the racism and discrimination they encounter in the healthcare system.

Social-structural explanations for ethnic patterning in health focus on the social context in which African-Caribbeans and Asians live in the UK. African-Caribbeans and Asians frequently experience multiple disadvantages which can be harmful to their health. These might include poor or overcrowded housing conditions, high rates of unemployment and over-representation in hazardous, low-paying occupations. Such material factors are then compounded by the effects of racism, either experienced directly in the form of violence, threats or discrimination, or in 'institutionalized' forms.

Institutional racism has been noted in the provision of healthcare (Alexander 1999). Ethnic groups may experience unequal or problematic access to health services. Language barriers can present difficulties if information cannot be relayed effectively; culturally specific understandings of illness and treatment are often not considered by professionals within the health service. The National Health Service has been criticized for not requiring more awareness of cultural and religious beliefs among its staff and for paying less attention to diseases which occur predominantly in the non-white population.

> Institutional racism is discussed in more detail in chapter 13, 'Race, Ethnicity and Migration', pp. 493–4.

There is no consensus on the connection between ethnicity and health inequalities. Indeed, much research still remains to be done. Yet it is clear that the question of ethnicity and health inequalities must be considered in relation to larger social, economic and political factors which affect the experience of ethnic minority groups in Britain.

Health and social cohesion

In trying to unravel the causes of health inequalities, a growing number of sociologists are turning their attention to the role of social support and social cohesion in promoting good health. As you may recall from our discussion of Durkheim in chapter 1 ('What is Sociology?'), social solidarity is one of the most important concepts in sociology. Durkheim saw the degree and type of solidarity within a culture as one of its most critical features. In his study of suicide, for example, he found that individuals and groups that were well integrated into society were less likely to take their own lives than others.

In several articles, and in his book

Unhealthy Societies: The Afflictions of Inequality (1996), Richard Wilkinson argues that the healthiest societies in the world are not the richest countries, but those in which income is distributed most evenly and levels of social integration are highest. High levels of national wealth, according to Wilkinson, do not necessarily translate into better health for the population. In surveying empirical data from countries around the world, Wilkinson notes a clear relationship between mortality rates and patterns of income distribution. Inhabitants of countries such as Japan and Sweden, which are regarded as some of the most egalitarian societies in the world, enjoy better levels of health on average than do citizens of countries where the gap between the rich and the poor is more pronounced, such as the United States.

In Wilkinson's view, the widening gap in income distribution undermines social cohesion and makes it more difficult for people to manage risks and challenges. Heightened social isolation and the failure to cope with stress are reflected in health indicators. Wilkinson argues that social factors – the strength of social contacts, ties within communities, availability of social support, a sense of security – are the main determinants of the relative health of a society.

Wilkinson's thesis has provoked energetic responses. Some claim that his work should become required reading for policy-makers and politicians. They agree with Wilkinson that too much emphasis has been placed on market relations and the drive towards prosperity. This approach has failed many members of society, they argue; it is time to consider more humane and socially responsible policies to support those who are disadvantaged. Others criticize his study on methodological grounds and argue that he has failed to show a clear causal relationship between income inequality and poor health (Judge 1995). Illness, critics contend, could be caused by any number of other mediating factors. They argue that the empirical evidence for his claims remains suggestive at best.

Earlier in this chapter we examined some of the assumptions that have historically provided the foundations for the orthodox, biomedical model of health. Many of these assumptions were also found in the way that disability has conventionally been understood in the UK and in other developed countries. Similarly the recent trends that we discussed above as a reaction to the biomedical model of health – such as scepticism that the medical expert always knows best and the moves to take greater account of the opinions and experiences of patients – have formed part of a more recent rejection of this conventional understanding of disability. It is to a discussion of some of the issues surrounding disability that we now turn.

The sociology of disability

The poet Simon Brisenden neatly summarizes the sense of exclusion that many disabled people feel from orthodox medicine and medical practitioners in his book *Poems for Perfect People*, when he asked: 'The man who cut your skin / and delved within / has he got any scars?' Brisenden was one of many disabled people whose work has led to a re-evaluation of the conventional understanding of disability in the UK and other developed countries.

Much of this discussion is taking place in the new field of **disability studies**. In this section, we examine the dominant understanding of disability by discussing what has become known as the individual model. We then turn to look at how this model has been challenged, notably by disabled people themselves, by a social model of disability, and offer a brief evaluation of this challenge. Lastly we look briefly at the level and background of impairment in the UK and globally. We begin, however, by discussing the language of disability.

Sociologists argue that our awareness and understanding of social issues is, at least partly, shaped by the words we use. In recent decades a critique of the terms which people have historically drawn upon to discuss disability has become increasingly important to those writing in this area. The word 'handicapped', for example, has largely fallen out of use because it was thought to be associated with 'cap in hand', charity and begging. Other terms, originally used to describe certain impairments, are rejected because they are now used mainly as insults – terms such as 'spastic' or 'cripple' are examples. Some metaphors, which are still in everyday use, like 'turning a blind eye' or 'a deaf ear', have been criticized because they imply a sense of exclusion. As we shall see, even the way in which we understand the term 'disability' is subject to much debate.

The individual model of disability

Historically, in Western societies such as Britain, an individual model of disability has been dominant. This model contends that individual limitations are the main cause of the problems experienced by disabled people. In the **individual model of disability**, bodily 'abnormality' is seen as causing some degree of 'disability' or functional limitation – an individual 'suffering' from quadriplegia is incapable of walking, for example. This functional limitation is seen as the basis for a wider classification of an individual as 'an invalid'. Underpinning the individual model is a 'personal tragedy approach' to disability. The disabled individual is regarded as an unfortunate victim of a chance event. Medical specialists play a central role in the individual model because it is their job to offer curative and rehabilitative diagnosis to the 'problems' suffered by the disabled individual. For this reason the individual model is often described as the 'medical model'. It is the power of the medical expert over disabled people's lives that Simon Brisenden attacked in the poem that started this section. In recent decades, this individual model of disability has been increasingly questioned, as we find below.

The social model of disability

An important early challenge to the individual model of disability was a collection edited by Paul Hunt entitled *Stigma: The Experience of Disability* (1966) (see p. 269 for a discussion of Goffman's account of stigma). Hunt argued that 'the problem of disability lies not only in the impairment of function and its effects on us individually, but also, more importantly, in the area of our relationship with "normal" people'. Hunt was a leading activist in the early years of the disability movement in Britain and became a founding member of the Union of Physically Impaired Against Segregation (UPIAS). In its manifesto, *Fundamental Principles of Disability* (1976), UPIAS developed a radical alternative to the individual model by arguing that there was a crucial distinction between 'impairment' and 'disability' (the full UPIAS definitions can be seen in the box).

UPIAS largely accepted the definition of physical 'impairment' as a biomedical property of *individuals* (although they subsequently extended it to include non-physical, sensory and intellectual forms of impairment). 'Disability', however, was defined in *social* terms. This challenged conventional understandings of the term. Disability was no longer understood as the problem of an individual, but in terms of the social barriers that people with impairments faced in participating fully in society. In the box on p. 283 we look at how Mike Oliver turns the assumptions in the individual model of disability around by rewriting the questions that the UK Office of Population, Censuses and Surveys (OPCS) used to assess 'disability' in the 1980s. Oliver (1983) was the first theorist to make the distinction between the individual and the **social model of disability** explicit (these distinctions are usefully summarized in table 8.3 overleaf). The social model of disability was given

---

UPIAS definitions of impairment and disability

Impairment
'Lacking part or all of a limb, or having a defective limb, organ or mechanism of the body.'

Disability
'The disadvantage or restriction of activity caused by a contemporary social organization which takes no or little account of people who have physical impairments and thus excludes them from participation in the mainstream of social activities.'

Table 8.3   Two models of disability

Individual model	Social model
Personal tragedy model	Social oppression theory
Personal problem	Social problem
Individual treatment	Social action
Medicalization	Self-help
Professional dominance	Individual and collective responsibility
Expertise	Experience
Individual identity	Collective identity
Prejudice	Discrimination
Care	Rights
Control	Choice
Policy	Politics
Individual adjustment	Social change

Source: Adapted from Oliver (1996), p. 34

further academic credibility by the work of Vic Finkelstein (1980, 1981), Colin Barnes (1991) and Oliver himself (1990, 1996).

Social model theorists need to give an explanation of why the social, cultural or historical barriers against disabled people have developed. Some advocates of the social model, influenced by Marx, have argued that a materialist understanding of disability is needed (see pp. 16–17 for more on materialism). Oliver (1996), for example, argues that, historically, barriers were erected against disabled people's full participation in society during the Industrial Revolution when they were excluded from the labour market, as the first capitalist factories began to base employment on individual waged labour. As this historical process developed, Oliver argues, 'so many [disabled people] were unable to keep or retain jobs that they became a social problem for the capitalist state whose initial response to all social problems was harsh deterrence and institu-

tionalization'. Even today disabled people's presence in the workforce is still relatively small (as we shall see on pp. 287–8).

Evaluation of the social model

The social model has been enormously influential in shaping the way that we think about disability today. Although it originated in the UK, the social model is gaining global influence. It has been described as 'the big idea' of the British disability movement (Hasler 1993). In focusing on the removal of social barriers to full participation, the social model allows disabled people to focus on a political strategy. This has led some to argue that in accepting the social model disabled people have formed 'a new social movement' (Oliver and Zarb 1989). In replacing the individual model, which identifies the 'invalidity' of the individual as the cause of disability, with a model in which disability is the result of oppression, the social model has been seen as

Turning the assumptions in the OPCS questions around with the social model

OPCS question	Oliver's question
'Can you tell what is wrong with you?'	'Can you tell me what is wrong with society?'
'What complaint causes your difficulty in holding, gripping or turning things?'	'What defects in the design of everyday equipment like jars, bottles and tins causes you difficulty in holding them?'
'Are your difficulties in understanding people mainly due to a hearing problem?'	'Are your difficulties in understanding people mainly due to their inability to communicate with you?'
'Do you have a scar blemish or deformity which limits your daily activities?'	'Do other people's reactions to any scar blemish or deformity you may have limit your daily activities?'
'Have you attended a special school because of a long-term health problem or disability?'	'Have you attended a special school because of your education authority's policy of sending people with your health problem/disability to such places?'
'Does your health problem/disability prevent you from going out as often or as far as you would like?'	What is it about the local environment that makes it difficult for you to get about in your neighbourhood?'
'Does your health problem/disability make it difficult for you to travel by bus?'	'Are there any transport or financial problems which prevent you from going out as often or as far as you would like?'
'Does your health problem/disability affect your work in any way at present?'	'Do you have problems at work because of the physical environment or the attitudes of others?'
'Does your health problem/disability mean that you need to live with relatives or someone else who can help or look after you?'	'Are community services so poor that you need to rely on relatives or someone else to provide you with the right level of personal assistance?'
'Does your present accommodation have any adaptations because of your health problem/disability?'	'Did the poor design of your house mean that you had to have it adapted to suit your needs?'

Source: Oliver (1990)

'liberating' by some disabled people (Beresford and Wallcraft 1997).

Since the late 1980s, however, several lines of criticism have been developed against the social model. First, it is argued that it neglects the often painful or uncomfortable experiences of impairment, which are central to many disabled people's lives. Shakespeare and Watson argue that: 'We are not just disabled people, we are also people with impairments, and to pretend otherwise is to ignore a major part of our biographies' (2002). Against this accusation, defenders of the social model have argued that rather than denying everyday experiences of impairment, the social model merely seeks to focus attention on the *social* barriers to full participation in society that are raised against disabled people.

Is this paralympic swimmer disabled?

Second, many people accept that they have impairments, but do not wish to be labelled as 'disabled'. In a recent survey of people claiming government benefits for disability, fewer than half chose to define themselves as disabled. Many people rejected the term because they saw their health problems related to illness rather than disability or because they did not believe that they were ill enough to be so categorized (Department for Work and Pensions 2002). However, Barnes (2003) has pointed out that in a society where disability is too often still associated with abnormality, it is not surprising that some people with impairments chose to reject the label 'disabled'.

Lastly, medical sociologists in particular tend to reject the social model by arguing that the division between impairment and disability, on which it rests, is false. These critics argue that the social model separates impairment, which is defined biomedically, from disability, which is defined socially. Medical sociologists have tended to argue that both disability and impairment are socially structured and are closely interrelated. Shakespeare and Watson argue that the division between impairment and disability collapses when one asks, 'Where does impairment end and disability start?' In some cases the division is straightforward – a failure to design suitable wheelchair access in a building clearly creates a socially constructed disabling barrier to wheelchair users. However, there are many more cases where it is impossible to remove all the sources of disability because they are not caused by oppressive conditions in society. Medical sociologists critical of the social model might argue that to be impaired by constant pain or by significant intellectual limitations, for example, disables the individual from full participation in society in a way that cannot be removed by social change. These critics would argue that a full account of disability must also take into account disability caused by impairments and not just those caused by society.

Supporters of the social model have argued that this last claim is based on a blurring of the distinction between disability and impairment, which they argue is rooted in the biomedical model of thinking that underlies the individual model of disability. They respond that the social model certainly does not deny that an impairment can be the cause of pain or that there are things that an individual might not be able to do solely because of a particular impairment. Indeed, Carol Thomas (1999, 2002), an advocate of the social model of disability, uses the phrase 'impairment effects' to take into account the ensuing psycho-emotional implications of impairment for disabled people.

Given the contested nature of the term 'disability' and the variety of impairments linked to disability, an account of the numbers of disabled people in the UK and globally is difficult. However, it is to these issues that we turn below.

Using your sociological imagination: why I want you to look me in the face

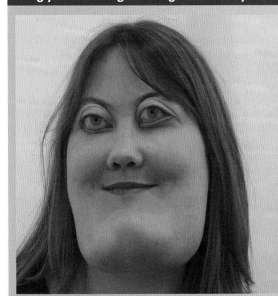

Instead of people looking away, gasping or shuddering, Vicky Lucas wants them to know that her face is integral to who she is. And, as she explains here, she likes who she is.

I have a rare genetic disorder called Cherubism, which affects my face. I was diagnosed when I was about four years old. I was too young to remember what happened, but visiting hospitals became a regular part of my life.

Although it was only when I was about six that my face started to really change shape, I don't remember a time when I didn't look different.

Growing up with a facial disfigurement wasn't easy. When puberty kicked in, it included all the usual developments with a little bit extra – my face became very large and my eyes were more affected too.

Double take

My teenage years were difficult. People would sometimes stare or do a double take. Some people would be downright nasty and call me names.

Even when people said 'Oh you poor thing!' their pity also hurt me and that hurt would stay with me for a long time. I became very withdrawn, afraid of how I might be treated if I went out.

But over time, I gradually started to develop my self-esteem and self-confidence and I started to feel that I shouldn't waste my life just because of other people's attitudes towards me.

At the age of sixteen I went to college and studied subjects such as film, media studies and photography. I started to research the representation of disfigured people in the media.

When I looked at how people with facial disfigurements are portrayed in films, well, no wonder people don't know how to react to us! Freddy Krueger in Nightmare on Elm Street, the Joker in Batman, the various scarred villains in gangster films . . . the list is endless.

Bad assumption

With stereotypes like that, it's hardly surprising that people assume that if you have a facial difference, there must be something 'different' or 'bad' about you in the inside too.

This was a huge turning point for me because I realized that facial disfigurement was not just a medical issue, but a social issue as well.

I realized that the reason why I was so unhappy was not because of my face, but the way some people would react to it. I decided that it wasn't my face that I wanted to change, but social attitudes. I'm not against plastic surgery. It's just that my personal choice is to not have it.

Now, at the age of twenty-four, I'm used to seeing my face reflected back at me in the mirror and I'm okay with it. Though I could quite happily do without the headaches and double vision. I also dislike being physically unable to wink, but I've overcome this particular disability by doing a nice line in fluttering and blinking.

But my face is integral to who I am. The way people treat me and the way I've had to learn to live my life has created the person I am today.

Lack of imagination

I love the good genuine friends my face has brought me and I appreciate the way it's made me want to be a better person. I also have a boyfriend who thinks I look like a cat. I'm not quite sure if I agree with him, but I'm certainly not complaining!

Now, whenever a person says I'm ugly, I just pity them for their lack of imagination. For every person who calls me fat chin, I think 'Nah! It's just that you've got a really small weak one. Talk about chin envy!'

For every naturally curious stare I get, I give a friendly smile. And if they don't smile back within my 10-second time limit, I give them a very effective scowl.

Last week, walking in the street with my boyfriend, a man walked towards me and went 'Urghhhhhooooooh!'

Confrontation

It wasn't so much a word as a strange guttural sound, and the kind that only funny looking people could understand the subtext to. I was so angry that I confronted him.

I won't go into details of what I did but let's just say it's probably the last time he ever gives a strange guttural sound to a funny looking woman in the street ever again.

Two minutes later, as we were walking home, a homeless man came up to me asking for change. He asked me how I was. 'Fine', I said and I told him what had just happened. There was a short pause. Then he smiled and said 'I hope you hurt him!' We all laughed.

It's funny how some strangers can be so cruel and hurtful, and yet others, the ones you'd least expect, the ones you would usually ignore and think nothing of, can be so warm and kind.

That pretty much sums up my life. I go from experiencing the worst in people to the very best, and often within the same five minutes! It makes my life more challenging, but also very interesting. I wouldn't want to change that for the world.

Source: *BBC News Magazine* (6 August 2003)

Questions

1 Are people with facial disfigurements disabled?
2 Does this news story tell you anything about a distinction between impairment and disability or not?
3 Does this news story tell you anything about the social model of disability?

Disability in the UK and globally

In the UK, the Disability Discrimination Act (DDA) was passed in 1995 and gave disabled people certain legal protection from discrimination in several areas, including employment and access to goods and services. Further legislation was introduced in 1999 that led to the creation of the Disability Rights Commission, set up to work towards 'the elimination of discrimination against disabled people'. The DDA defined a disabled person as 'anyone with a physical or mental impairment, which has a substantial and long-term adverse effect upon their ability to carry out normal day-to-day activities'. This definition of disability includes, for example, people with mental health problems as well as people with facial disfigurements and avoids the common misconception that disability mainly concerns mobility impairments or is largely congenital. In fact, around 77 per cent of disabled people became disabled after the age of sixteen (Employers' Forum on Disability 2003) and the percentage of the population who are disabled continues to increase with age (see figure 8.5).

Under the DDA definition, at least 8.5 million people in the UK (approximately 10 per cent of the population) are disabled, of whom 6.8 million are of working age (Office of National Statistics 2002). Of this latter group, only around 3 million people are employed (Disability Rights Commission 2002). However, a recent survey shows that 93 per cent of people who conformed to the DDA definition of

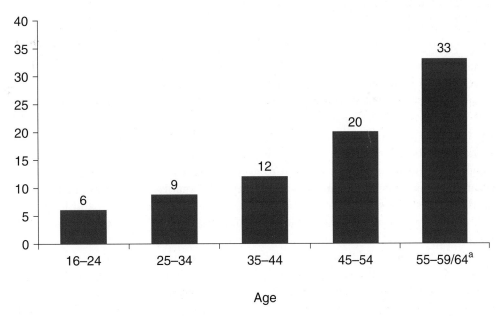

Figure 8.5   Disabled people in the UK: by age (% of age group)

[a] Statutory pension age

Source: 'From Exclusion to Inclusion', Final Report of the Disability Rights Task Force (1999)

Disabled protesters campaigning for their rights.

disability agreed that getting a job was important to them. People with impairments linked to disability still belong to one of the most disadvantaged groups in the UK. They are more likely to be out of work than the able-bodied, and those people who have impairments linked to disability who are in employment tend to earn less. In 1998 the average take-home pay of disabled employees was £196 per week, compared to £212 for non-disabled workers (NOP 1998). Yet disability-related expenditure by governments is high compared to many other areas of spending – the UK government spends more than £19 billion a year on incapacity and disability benefits (BBC, 9 April 2002). By 1999, the wealthiest countries spent at least twice as much on disability-related programmes as they did on unemployment compensation (OECD 2003).

It is estimated that there are nearly 500 million 'disabled' people in the world, 80 per cent of them living in developing countries such as India or China (The World Bank Group 2002). The World Health Organization argues that the main cause of 'chronic disease and long-term impairments' in developing countries is poverty, inadequate sanitation, poor diet and bad housing. Injuries, such as broken bones, will often result in long-term impairment in developing countries that would not occur if treatment and rehabilitation facilities had been available, as they generally are in the West. Iron deficiency, 'anaemia' and chronic infections of the pelvis (sometimes caused by female circumcision) are major causes of impairment leading to disability in women in many developing countries. It is estimated that around 250,000 children lose their sight each year because their diet lacks Vitamin A, which is found in green vegetables. It has been suggested that up to half of the world's impairment could be preventable by improving policies to confront poverty, malnutrition, sanitation, drinking water and employment conditions to reduce accidents (Charlton 1998). War and its aftermath (such as uncleared landmines) is another major cause of impairment. Furthermore, in poorer countries disabled children are far less likely to receive the same level of education as other children, which exacerbates their poverty later in life. From the evidence, we can see that in the developing world poverty creates impairments and shapes disability in the developing world in ways that can make it very different from that experienced in the West.

The very different experiences of impairment and disability which people around the world have illustrate a wider idea reflected in this chapter: that our experience of our own bodies and our interactions with others – whether able-bodied or disabled, sick or healthy – are shaped by the changing social contexts in which we find ourselves. In order to develop a sociological perspective on illness, health and disability, we need to examine the social and technological changes that shape our understanding of these aspects of human life.

Summary points

1. Western medicine is based on the biomedical model of health – the belief that disease can be defined in objective terms and that the sick body can be restored to health through scientifically based medical treatment. The biomedical model of health emerged alongside modern societies. It was linked to the rise of demographics – the study of the size, composition and dynamics of human populations – and the growing interest of states in promoting public health. Modern healthcare systems were greatly influenced by the application of science to medical diagnosis and cure.

2. The biomedical model of health has come under increasing criticism. It has been argued that scientific medicine is not as effective as it is made out to be, that medical professionals do not value the opinions of the patients being treated, and that the medical profession considers itself superior to any alternative forms of healing that do not subscribe to orthodox approaches.

3. Sociologists are interested in the experience of illness – how being sick, chronically ill or disabled is experienced by the sick person and by those nearby. The idea of the sick role, developed by Talcott Parsons, suggests that a sick person adopts certain forms of behaviour in order to minimize the disruptive impact of illness. A sick individual is granted certain privileges, such as the right to withdraw from normal responsibilities, but in return must work actively to regain health by agreeing to follow medical advice.

4. Symbolic interactionists have investigated how people cope with disease and chronic illness in their daily lives. The experience of illness can provoke changes in individuals'

self-identity and in their daily routines. This sociological dimension of the body is becoming increasingly relevant for many societies; people are now living longer than ever before and tend to suffer more from chronic debilitating conditions than from acute illnesses.

5. Sociological research reveals close connections between illness and inequality. Within industrial countries, poorer groups have a shorter average life expectancy, and are more susceptible to disease, than more affluent strata. Richer countries also have higher average life expectancies than poorer ones. Some people believe that class-based health inequalities can be explained by cultural and behavioural factors, such as diet and lifestyle. Others place emphasis on structural influences, such as unemployment, sub-standard housing and poor working conditions.

6. Patterns of health and illness have gender and racial dimensions as well. Women on the whole live longer than men in almost every country of the world, yet they experience a higher incidence of illness than men. Certain illnesses are more common among ethnic minority groups than among the white population. Genetic explanations have been advanced to account for gender and racial differences in health, yet these alone cannot explain the inequalities. While there may be some biological basis to certain health conditions, overall patterns of health and illness must also take into account social factors and differences in material conditions between groups.

7. The individual model of disability holds individual limitations to be the main cause of the problems experienced by disabled people. In the individual model, bodily 'abnormality' is seen as causing some degree of 'disability' or functional limitation. This functional limitation is seen as the basis for a wider classification of an individual as 'an invalid'. Underpinning the individual model is a 'personal tragedy approach' to disability.

8. The social model of disability locates the cause of disability within society, rather than the individual. It is not the individual's limitations that causes disability but the barriers that society places in the way of full participation for disabled people.

9. In most wealthy countries government expenditure on disability-related programmes is much higher than on unemployment compensation. Despite this, disabled people are one of the most socially disadvantaged groups in developed countries. Most people with impairments live in the developing world.

Questions for further thought

1 What could be done to reduce inequalities in healthcare?

2 How can the differences in the lives of women and men account for their different experiences of ill health?

3 What policies would you recommend to make the NHS more responsive to the cultural backgrounds of patients?

4 Does the medicalization of conditions such as pregnancy and unhappiness increase the power of the medical establishment while disempowering the patient?

5 In what ways are people disabled in your community or educational institution?

Further reading

Lesley Doyal, *What Makes Women Sick* (London: Macmillan, 1995).

Jenny Morris, *Pride Against Prejudice: A Personal Politics of Disablility* (London: Women's Press, 1991).

Sarah Nettleton, *The Sociology of Health and Illness* (Cambridge: Polity, 1995).

C. Barnes, G. Mercer and T. Shakespeare, *Exploring Disability: A Sociological Introduction* (Cambridge: Polity, 1999).

C. Barnes, M. Oliver and L. Barton (eds), *Disability Studies Today* (Cambridge: Polity, 2002).

C. Barnes and G. Mercer, *Disability* (Cambridge: Polity, 2003).

Internet links

European Observatory on Health Systems and Policies
http://www.euro.who.int/observatory

International Public Health
http://www.ldb.org/iphw/

Wellcome Library on the History and Understanding of Medicine
http://www.wellcome.ac.uk/knowledgecentre/wellcomesites/

World Health Organization
http://www.who.int

Leeds University Disability Archive
http://www.leeds.ac.uk/disability-studies/archiveuk/index.html

BBC Disabilities Magazine
http://www.bbc.co.uk/ouch/

Contents

9 Stratification and Class

HAVE YOU ever bought an Indian meal in a British supermarket? If you have, there's a strong chance that it was made by Noon Products. The company specializes in supplying Indian food to the big supermarket chains and has an annual turnover of around £90 million. Its founder, Sir Gulam Noon, was estimated to have amassed a fortune of £50 million according to the 2004 *Sunday Times Rich List*.

Gulam Noon was born in India. His family owned a sweet shop in Bombay, 'Royal Sweets'. They were not particularly well off, but managed to get by until their father's death when Gulam was seven. After that it was a struggle, and, as a young teenager, Gulam would combine school with work in the shop. Having completed school, he joined the family business full time. He soon changed the way the business was marketed, expanded the shop and built a factory. His ambitions, however, were not limited to 'Royal Sweets', and other ventures quickly followed, including printing and construction ventures.

Prince Charles and Sir Gulam Noon

Not satisfied with his successes in India, Gulam looked to England to further his experience. He established 'Royal Sweets' in Southall, London and brought chefs with him from India to get the business going. Within the year there were nine shops, built around the Asian communities of London and Leicester. Today the 'Royal Sweets' chain has forty shops and an annual turnover of £9 million.

Other commercial ventures followed the success of 'Royal Sweets', and in 1989 Noon Products was established. Gulam spotted a niche in the market: 'All the pre-packaged Indian ready meals available from the supermarkets were insipid and frankly unacceptable. I thought I could do better.' The business began with just eleven employees, but soon they were selling authentic Indian foods to the frozen food company Birds Eye, and then to the supermarket chains Waitrose and Sainsbury's.

There are now more than a hundred different Noon dishes, produced in three plants, operated by 1,100 employees. Between 250,000 and 300,000 meals are made every day. The produce range has been expanded from Indian food to include Thai and Mexican dishes, amongst others. In 2002 Gulam was knighted for his services to the food industry. Reflecting on what has inspired him during his life, Sir Gulam concludes: 'I'm a self-made man and a quick learner! Nothing comes easily, you've just got to work at it.'

Few of us can expect the kind of wealth that Sir Gulam now possesses. But his rags-to-riches life history raises interesting questions for sociologists. Is it just an isolated incident or is his story being repeated, although perhaps less spectacularly, across the UK? How much chance does someone from a poor background have of reaching the top of the economic ladder? For every Gulam Noon in our society, how many people slide down the economic ladder from wealth to poverty? The issues of wealth and poverty which Sir Gulam's life story raises lead us to broader questions. Why do economic inequalities exist in our society? How unequal are modern societies? What social factors will influence your economic position in society? Are your chances any different if you are a woman? How does the globalization of the economy affect your life chances? These are just a few of the sorts of question that sociologists ask and try to answer, and they are the focus of this chapter. The study of inequalities in society is one of the most important areas of sociology, because our material resources determine a great deal about our lives. Here, we begin by looking at what sociologists mean when they talk about stratification and class. We then look at some of the most influential theories of class, and attempts to measure it, in sociological thought, after which we take a more detailed look at social class in Western society today. We close with a discussion of social mobility and conclude by briefly considering the continuing importance of social class in helping us to understand the world around us.

Systems of stratification

Sociologists speak of **social stratification** to describe inequalities that exist between individuals and groups within human societies. Often we think of stratification in terms of assets or property, but it can also occur because of other attributes, such as gender, age, religious affiliation or military rank.

Individuals and groups enjoy differential (unequal) access to rewards based on their position within the stratification scheme. Thus, stratification can most simply be defined as structured inequalities between different groupings of people. It is useful to think of stratification as rather like the geological layering of rock in the earth's surface. Societies can be seen as consisting of 'strata' in a hierarchy, with the more favoured at the top and the less privileged nearer the bottom.

All socially stratified systems share three characteristics:

1 *The rankings apply to social categories of people who share a common characteristic without necessarily interacting or identifying with one another.* For example, women may be ranked differently from men or wealthy people differently from the poor. This does not mean that individuals from a particular category cannot change their rank; however, it does mean that the category continues to exist even if individuals move out of it and into another category.
2 *People's life experiences and opportunities depend heavily on how their social category is ranked.* Being male or female, black or white, upper class or working class makes a big difference in terms of your life chances – often as big a difference as personal effort or good fortune (such as winning a lottery).
3 *The ranks of different social categories tend to change very slowly over time.* In British society, for example, only recently have women as a whole begun to achieve equality with men.

See more about equality between men and women in chapter 12, 'Sexuality and Gender'.

As we saw in chapter 2, stratified societies have changed throughout human history. In the earliest human societies, which were based on hunting and gathering, there was very little social stratification – mainly because there was very little by way of wealth or other resources to be divided up. The development of agriculture produced considerably more wealth and, as a result, a great increase in stratification. Social stratification in agricultural societies increasingly came to resemble a pyramid, with a large number of people at the bottom and a successively smaller number of people as you move towards the top. Today, industrial and post-industrial societies are extremely complex; their stratification is more likely to resemble a teardrop, with a large number of people in the middle and lower-middle ranks (the so-called middle class), a slightly smaller number of people at the bottom, and very few people as one moves towards the top.

Historically, four basic systems of stratification can be distinguished: *slavery, caste, estates* and *class.* These are sometimes found in conjunction with one another: slavery, for instance, existed alongside classes in ancient Greece and Rome, and in the Southern United States before the Civil War of the 1860s.

Slavery

Slavery is an extreme form of inequality, in which certain people are owned as property by others. The legal conditions of slave ownership have varied considerably among different societies. Sometimes slaves were deprived of almost all rights by law – as was the case on Southern plantations in the United States – while in other societies, their position was more akin to that of servants. For example, in the ancient Greek city-state of Athens, some slaves occupied positions of great responsibility. They were excluded from political positions and from the military, but were accepted in most other types of occupation. Some were literate and worked as government administrators; many were trained in craft skills. Even so, not all slaves could count on such good luck. For the less fortunate, their days began and ended in hard labour in the mines.

Throughout history, slaves have often fought back against their subjection; the slave rebellions in the American South before the Civil War are one example. Because of such resistance, systems of slave labour have tended to be unstable. High productivity could only be achieved through constant supervision and brutal punishment. Slave-labour systems eventually broke down, partly because of the struggles they provoked and partly because economic or other incentives motivate people to produce more effectively than does direct compulsion. Slavery is simply not economically efficient. Moreover, from about the eighteenth century on, many people in Europe and America came to see slavery as morally wrong. Today, slavery is illegal in every country of the world, but it still exists in some places. Recent research has documented that people are taken by force and held against their will. From enslaved brick-makers in Pakistan to sex slaves in Thailand and domestic slaves in relatively wealthy countries like the UK and France, slavery remains a significant human rights violation in the world today (Bales 1999).

Caste

A **caste** system is a social system in which one's social status is given for life. In caste societies, therefore, different social levels are closed, so that all individuals must remain at the social level of their birth throughout life. Everyone's social status is based on personal characteristics – such as perceived race or ethnicity (often based on such physical characteristics as skin colour), parental religion or parental caste – that are accidents of birth and are therefore believed to be unchangeable. A person is born into a caste and remains there for life. In a sense, caste societies can be seen as a special type of class society – in which class position is ascribed at birth. They have typically been found in agricultural societies that have not yet developed industrial capitalist economies, such as rural India or South Africa prior to the end of white rule in 1992.

Prior to modern times, caste systems were found throughout the world. In Europe, for example, Jews were frequently treated as a separate caste, forced to live in restricted neighbourhoods and barred from intermarrying (and in some instances even interacting) with non-Jews. The term 'ghetto' is said to derive from the Venetian word for 'foundry', the site of one of Europe's first official Jewish ghettos, established by the government of Venice in 1516. The term eventually came to refer to those sections of European towns where Jews were legally compelled to live, long before it was used to describe minority neighbourhoods in US cities, with their castelike qualities of racial and ethnic segregation.

In caste systems, intimate contact with members of other castes is strongly discouraged. Such 'purity' of a caste is often maintained by rules of **endogamy**, marriage within one's social group as required by custom or law.

Caste in India and South Africa

The few remaining caste systems in the world are being seriously challenged by globalization. The Indian caste system, for example, reflects Hindu religious beliefs and is more than two thousand years old. According to Hindu beliefs, there are four major castes, each roughly associated with broad occupational groupings. The four castes consist of the *Brahmins* (scholars and spiritual leaders) on top, followed by the *Ksyatriyas* (soldiers and rulers), the *Vaisyas* (farmers and merchants) and the *Shudras* (labourers and artisans). Beneath the four castes are those known as the 'untouchables' or *Dalits* ('oppressed people'), who – as their name suggests – are to be avoided at all costs. Untouchables are limited to the worst jobs in society such as removing human waste, and they often resort to begging and searching in garbage for their food. In traditional areas of India, some members of higher castes still regard physical contact with untouchables to be so contaminating that a mere touch requires cleansing rituals. India made it illegal to discriminate on the basis of caste in 1949, but aspects of the system remain in full force today, particularly in rural areas.

As India's modern capitalist economy brings people of different castes together, whether it be in the same workplace, aeroplane or restaurant, it is increasingly difficult to maintain the rigid barriers required to sustain the caste system. As more and more of India is touched by globalization, it seems reasonable to assume that its caste system will weaken still further.

Before its abolition in 1992, the South African caste system, termed **apartheid**, rigidly separated black Africans, Indians, 'coloureds' (people of mixed races) and Asians from whites. In this case, caste was based entirely on race. Whites, who made up only 15 per cent of the total population, controlled virtually all of the country's wealth, owned most of the usable land, ran the principal businesses and industries and had a monopoly on political power, since blacks lacked the right to vote. Blacks – who made up three-quarters of the population – were segregated into impoverished *bantustans* ('homelands') and were allowed out only to work for the white minority.

Apartheid, widespread discrimination and oppression created intense conflict between the white minority and the black, mixed-race and Asian majority. Decades of often violent struggle against apartheid finally proved successful in the 1990s. The most powerful black organization, the African National Congress (ANC), mobilized an economically devastating global boycott of South African businesses, forcing South Africa's white leaders to dismantle apartheid, which was abolished by popular vote among South African whites in 1992. In 1994, in the country's first ever multiracial elections, the black majority won control of the government, and Nelson Mandela – the black leader of the ANC, who had spent twenty-seven years imprisoned by the white government – was elected president.

Under apartheid in South Africa, black and white people were socially segregated.

Estates

Estates were part of European feudalism, but also existed in many other traditional civilizations. The feudal estates consisted of strata with differing obligations and rights towards each other, some of these differences being established in law. In Europe, the highest estate was composed of the aristocracy and gentry. The clergy formed another estate, having lower status but possessing various distinctive privileges. Those in what came to be called the 'third estate' were the commoners – serfs, free peasants, merchants and artisans. In contrast to castes, a certain degree of intermarriage and mobility was tolerated between the estates. Commoners

might be knighted, for example, in payment for special services given to the monarch; merchants could sometimes purchase titles. A remnant of the system persists in Britain, where hereditary titles are still recognized (though since 1999 peers are no longer automatically entitled to vote in the House of Lords), and business leaders, civil servants and others may be honoured with a knighthood for their services.

Estates have tended to develop in the past wherever there was a traditional aristocracy based on noble birth. In feudal systems, such as in medieval Europe, estates were closely bound up with the manorial community: they formed a local, rather than a national, system of stratification. In more centralized traditional empires, such as China or Japan, they were organized on a more national basis. Sometimes the differences between the estates were justified by religious beliefs, although rarely in as strict a way as in the Hindu caste system.

Class

Class systems differ in many respects from slavery, castes or estates. We can define a class as a large-scale grouping of people who share common economic resources, which strongly influence the type of lifestyle they are able to lead. Ownership of wealth, together with occupation, are the chief bases of class differences. Classes differ from earlier forms of stratification in four main respects:

1 *Class systems are fluid.* Unlike the other types of strata, classes are not established by legal or religious provisions. The boundaries between classes are never clear-cut. There are no formal restrictions on intermarriage between people from different classes.
2 *Class positions are in some part achieved.* An individual's class is not simply given at birth, as is the case in the other types of stratification systems. Social mobility – movement upward and downward in the class structure – is more common than in the other types.
3 *Class is economically based.* Classes depend on economic differences between groups of individuals – inequalities in the possession of material resources. In the other types of stratification systems, non-economic factors (such as race in the former South African caste system) are generally most important.

4 *Class systems are large scale and impersonal.* In the other types of stratification systems, inequalities are expressed primarily in personal relationships of duty or obligation – between slave and master or lower- and higher-caste individuals. Class systems, by contrast, operate mainly through large-scale, impersonal associations. For instance, one major basis of class differences is in inequalities of pay and working conditions.

Will caste give way to class?

There is some evidence that globalization will hasten the end of legally sanctioned caste systems throughout the world. Most official caste systems have already given way to class-based ones in industrial capitalist societies; South Africa, mentioned earlier, is the most prominent recent example (Berger 1986). Modern industrial production requires that people move about freely, work at whatever jobs they are suited or able to do, and change jobs frequently according to economic conditions. The rigid restrictions found in caste systems interfere with this necessary freedom. Furthermore, as the world increasingly becomes a single economic unit, caste-like relationships will become increasingly vulnerable to economic pressures. Nonetheless, elements of caste persist even in post-industrial societies. For example, some Indian immigrants to the West seek to arrange traditional marriages for their children along caste lines.

Theories of class and stratification

The theories developed by Karl Marx and Max Weber form the basis of most sociological analysis of class and stratification.

> Chapter 1 contains an introduction to the thought of Marx and Weber as well as a discussion of what 'theories' set out to do.

Scholars working in the Marxist tradition have further developed the ideas Marx himself set out; others have tried to elaborate Weber's concepts. We shall begin by examining the theories set forth by Marx and Weber before analysing the neo-Marxist approach put forth by Erik Olin Wright.

Karl Marx's theory

Most of Marx's works were concerned with stratification and, above all, with social class, yet surprisingly he failed to provide a systematic analysis of the concept of class. The manuscript Marx was working on at the time of his death (subsequently published as part of his major work, *Capital*) breaks off just at the point where he posed the question 'What constitutes a class?' Marx's concept of class has thus to be reconstructed from the body of his writings as a whole. Since the various passages where he discussed class are not always fully consistent, there have been many disputes between scholars about 'what Marx really meant'. The main outlines of his views, however, are fairly clear.

The nature of class

For Marx a class is a group of people who stand in a common relationship to the means of production – the means by which they gain a livelihood. Before the rise of modern industry, the means of production consisted primarily of land and the instruments used to tend crops or pastoral animals. In pre-industrial societies, therefore, the two main classes consisted of those who owned the land (aristocrats, gentry or slave-holders) and those actively engaged in producing from it (serfs, slaves and free peasantry). In modern industrial societies, factories, offices, machinery and the wealth or capital needed to buy them have become more important. The two main classes consist of those who own these new means of production – industrialists or capitalists – and those who earn their living by selling their labour to them – the working class or, in the now somewhat archaic term Marx sometimes favoured, the **proletariat**.

According to Marx, the relationship between classes is an exploitative one. In feudal societies, exploitation often took the form of the direct transfer of produce from the peasantry to the aristocracy. Serfs were compelled to give a certain proportion of their production to their aristocratic master, or had to work for a number of days each month in his fields to produce crops to be consumed by him and his retinue. In modern capitalist societies, the source of exploitation is less obvious, and Marx devoted much attention to trying to clarify its nature. In the course of the working day, Marx reasoned, workers produce more than is actually needed by employers to repay the cost of hiring them. This surplus value is the source of profit, which capitalists are able to put to their own use. A group of workers in a clothing factory, say, might be able to produce a hundred suits a day. Selling 75 per cent of the suits provides enough income for the manufacturer to pay the workers' wages and for the cost of plant and equipment. Income from the sale of the remainder of the garments is taken as profit.

Marx was struck by the inequalities created by the capitalist system. Although in earlier times aristocrats lived a life of luxury, completely different from that of the peasantry, agrarian societies were relatively poor. Even if there had been no aristocracy, standards of living would inevitably have been meagre. With the development of modern industry, however, wealth is produced on a scale far beyond anything seen before, but workers have little access to the wealth that their labour creates. They remain relatively poor, while the wealth accumulated by the propertied class grows. Marx used the term **pauperization** to describe the process by which the working class grows increasingly impoverished in relation to the capitalist class. Even if workers become more affluent in absolute terms, the gap separating them from the capitalist class continues to stretch ever wider. These inequalities between the capitalist and the working class were not strictly economic in nature. Marx noted how the development of modern factories and the mechanization of production means that work frequently becomes dull and oppressive in the extreme. The labour which is the source of our wealth is often both physically wearing and mentally tedious – as in the case of a factory hand whose job consists of routine tasks carried on day in, day out, in an unchanging environment.

Max Weber's theory

Weber's approach to stratification was built on the analysis developed by Marx, but he modified and elaborated it. Like Marx, Weber regarded society as charac-terized by conflicts over power and resources. Yet where Marx saw polarized class relations and economic issues at the heart of all social conflict, Weber developed a more complex, multidimensional view of society. Social stratification is not simply a matter of class, according to Weber, but is shaped by two further aspects: **status** and **party**. These three overlapping elements of stratification produce an enormous number of possible positions within society, rather than the more rigid bipolar model which Marx proposed.

Although Weber accepted Marx's view that class is founded on objectively given economic conditions, he saw a greater variety of economic factors as important in class formation than were recognized by Marx. According to Weber, class divisions derive not only from control or lack of control of the means of production, but from economic differences which have nothing directly to do with property. Such resources include especially the skills and credentials, or qualifications, which affect the types of job people are able to obtain. Weber believed that an individual's *market position* strongly influences his or her overall life chances. Those in managerial or professional occupations earn more and have more favourable conditions of work, for example, than people in blue-collar jobs. The qualifications they possess, such as degrees, diplomas and the skills they have acquired, make them more 'marketable' than others without such qualifications. At a lower level, among blue-collar workers, skilled craftsmen are able to secure higher wages than the semi- or unskilled.

Status in Weber's theory refers to differences between social groups in the social honour or prestige they are accorded by others. In traditional societies, status was often determined on the basis of first-hand knowledge of a person gained through multiple interactions in different contexts over a period of years. Yet as societies grew more complex, it became impossible for status always to be accorded in this way. Instead, according to Weber, status came to be expressed through people's *styles of life*. Markers and symbols of status – such as housing, dress, manner of speech and occupation – all help to shape an individual's social standing in the eyes of others. People sharing the same status form a community in which there is a sense of shared identity.

While Marx believed that status distinctions are the result of class divisions in society, Weber argued that status often varies independently of class divisions. Possession of wealth normally tends to confer high status, but there are many exceptions. The term 'genteel poverty' refers to one example. In Britain, individuals from aristocratic families continue to enjoy considerable social esteem even when their fortunes have been lost. Conversely, 'new money' is often looked on with some scorn by the well-established wealthy.

In modern societies, Weber pointed out, party formation is an important aspect of *power*, and can influence stratification independently of class and status. Party defines a group of individuals who work together because they have common backgrounds, aims or interests. Often a party works in an organized fashion towards a specific goal which is in the interest of the party membership. Marx tended to explain both status differences and party organization in terms of class.

Neither, in fact, can be reduced to class divisions, Weber argued, even though each is influenced by them; both can in turn influence the economic circumstances of individuals and groups, thereby affecting class. Parties may appeal to concerns cutting across class differences; for example, parties may be based on religious affiliation or nationalist ideals. A Marxist might attempt to explain the conflicts between Catholics and Protestants in Northern Ireland in class terms, since more Catholics than Protestants are in working-class jobs. A follower of Weber would argue that such an explanation is ineffective, because many Protestants are also working class in background. The parties to which people are affiliated express religious as well as class differences.

Weber's writings on stratification are important, because they show that other dimensions of stratification besides class strongly influence people's lives. While Marx tried to reduce social stratification to class divisions alone, Weber drew attention to the complex interplay of class, status and party as separate aspects of social stratification creating a more flexible basis for analysing stratification than that provided by Marx.

Erik Olin Wright's theory of class

The American sociologist Erik Olin Wright has developed an influential theory of class which combines aspects of both Marx's and Weber's approaches (Wright 1978, 1985, 1997). According to Wright, there are three dimensions of control over economic resources in modern capitalist production, and these allow us to identify the major classes which exist.

1 Control over investments or money capital.
2 Control over the physical means of production (land or factories and offices).
3 Control over labour power.

Those who belong to the capitalist class have control over each of these dimensions in the production system. Members of the working class have control over none of them. In between these two main classes, however, are the groups whose position is more ambiguous – the managers and white-collar workers mentioned above. These people are in what Wright calls contradictory class locations, because they are able to influence some aspects of production, but are denied control over others. White-collar and professional employees, for example, have to contract their labour power to employers in order to make a living in the same way as manual workers do. But at the same time they have a greater degree of control over the work setting than most people in blue-collar jobs. Wright terms the class position of such workers 'contradictory' because they are neither capitalists nor manual workers, yet they share certain common features with each.

A large segment of the population – 85 to 90 per cent, according to Wright (1997) – fall into the category of those who are forced to sell their labour because they do not control the means of production. Yet within this population there is a great deal of diversity, ranging from the traditional manual working class to white-collar workers. In order to differentiate class locations within this large population, Wright takes two factors into account: the relationship to authority, and the possession of skills or expertise. First, Wright

argues that many middle-class workers, such as managers and supervisors, enjoy *relationships towards authority* that are more privileged than those of the working class. Such individuals are called on by capitalists to assist in controlling the working class – for example, by monitoring an employee's work or by conducting personnel reviews and evaluations – and are rewarded for their 'loyalty' by earning higher wages and receiving regular promotions. Yet, at the same time, these individuals remain under the control of the capitalist owners. In other words, they are both exploiters and exploited.

The second factor which differentiates class locations within the middle classes is the *possession of skills and expertise*. According to Wright, middle-class employees possessing skills which are in demand in the labour market are able to exercise a specific form of power in the capitalist system. Given that their expertise is in short supply, they are able to earn a higher wage. The lucrative positions available to information technology specialists in the emerging knowledge economy illustrate this point. Moreover, Wright argues, because employees with knowledge and skills are more difficult to monitor and control, employers are obliged to secure their loyalty and cooperation by rewarding them accordingly.

Measuring class

Both theoretical and empirical studies have investigated the link between class standing and other dimensions of social life, such as voting patterns, educational attainment and physical health. Yet, as we have seen, the concept of class is far from clear-cut. Both in academic circles and in common usage, the term 'class' is understood and used in a wide variety of ways. How, then, can sociologists and researchers measure an imprecise concept such as class for the purpose of empirical studies?

The linkages between social class and other issues are discussed at various points throughout this book, as a glance at the index will show. Some important discussions can be found on:

- social class and health, pp. 272–6
- social class and gender, pp. 324–7
- social class and ethnicity, pp. 509–15
- social class and domestic violence, p. 222
- social class and higher education, p. 699
- social class and religion, p. 562
- social class and unemployment, p. 784

When an abstract concept such as class is transformed into a measurable variable in a study, we say that the concept has been *operationalized*. This means that it has been defined clearly and concretely enough to be tested through empirical research. Sociologists have operationalized class through a variety of schemes which attempt to map the class structure of society. Such schemes provide a theoretical framework by which individuals are allocated to social class categories.

A common feature of most class schemes is that they are based on the occupational structure. Sociologists have seen class divisions as corresponding generally with material and social inequalities that are linked to types of employment. The development of capitalism and industrialism has been marked by a growing division of labour and an increasingly complicated occupational structure. Although no longer as true as it once was,

occupation is one of the most critical factors in an individual's social standing, life chances and level of material comfort. Social scientists have used occupation extensively as an indicator of social class because of the belief that individuals in the same occupation tend to experience similar degrees of social advantage or disadvantage, maintain comparable lifestyles, and share similar opportunities in life.

Class schemes based on the occupational structure take a number of different forms. Some schemes are largely descriptive in nature – they reflect the shape of the occupational and class structure in society without addressing the relations between social classes. Such models have been favoured by scholars who see stratification as unproblematic and part of the natural social order, such as those working in the functionalist tradition.

Functionalism was introduced in chapter 1, 'What is Sociology?', pp. 20–2.

Other schemes are more theoretically informed – often drawing on the ideas of Marx or Weber – and concern themselves with explaining the relations *between* classes in society. 'Relational' class schemes tend to be favoured by sociologists working within conflict paradigms in order to demonstrate the divisions and tensions within society. Erik Olin Wright's theory of class (see pp. 303–4) is an example of a relational class scheme, because it seeks to depict the processes of class exploitation from a Marxist perspective.

John Goldthorpe: class and occupation

Some sociologists have been dissatisfied with descriptive class schemes, claiming that they merely reflect social and material inequalities between classes rather than seeking to explain the class processes which give birth to them. With such concerns in mind, sociologist John Goldthorpe created a scheme for use in empirical research on social mobility. The *Goldthorpe class scheme* was designed not as a hierarchy, but as a representation of the 'relational' nature of contemporary class structure.

Goldthorpe's theories have been highly influential. His account of class is discussed in this section. His writings on social mobility are examined below on pp. 330–1.

Although Goldthorpe now underplays any explicit theoretical influence on his scheme (Erikson and Goldthorpe 1993), sociologists have often pointed to the Goldthorpe classification as an example of a neo-Weberian class scheme. This is because Goldthorpe's original scheme identified class locations on the basis of two main factors: market situation and work situation. An individual's *market situation* concerns his or her level of pay, job security and prospects for advancement; it emphasizes material rewards and general life chances. The *work situation*, by contrast, focuses on questions of control, power and authority within the occupation. An individual's work situation is concerned with the degree of autonomy in the workplace and the overall relations of control affecting an employee.

Goldthorpe devised his scheme by evaluating occupations on the basis of their

Table 9.1   Goldthorpe's class scheme

Class			Employment relation
Service	I	Higher-grade professionals, administrators and officials. Large managers and proprietors.	Employer or service relationship.
	II	Lower-grade professionals, administrators and officials. Small managers and proprietors.	Service relationship.
Intermediate	III	Routine non-manual employees in administration and commerce (largely clerical). Rank and file employees in service industries.	Intermediate.
	IIIb	Routine non-manual employees, lower grade (sales and services).	Intermediate (men), labour contract (women).
	IV	Small proprietors and self-employed artisans.	Employer.
	IVb	Small proprietors and artisans without employees.	Self-employed.
	IVc	Farmers and smallholders, other self-employed agricultural.	Employer or self-employed.
	V	Lower-grade technicians, supervisors of manual workers.	Intermediate.
Working	VI	Skilled manual workers.	Labour contract.
	VII	Semi-skilled and unskilled manual workers.	Labour contract.
	VIIb	Agricultural workers.	Labour contract.

Source: Adapted from Crompton (1998), p. 67

relative market and work situations. The resulting classification is shown in table 9.1. Encompassing eleven class locations, Goldthorpe's scheme is more detailed than many others. Yet in common usage the class locations are compressed into three main class strata: a 'service' class (classes I and II), an 'intermediate class' (classes III and IV) and a 'working class' (classes V, VI and VII). Goldthorpe also acknowledges the presence of an elite class of property holders at the very top of the scheme, but argues that it is such a small segment of society that it is not meaningful as a category in empirical studies.

In recent writings Goldthorpe has emphasized *employment relations* within his scheme, rather than the notion of work situation described above (Goldthorpe and Marshall 1992). By this, Goldthorpe draws attention to different types of employment contract. A labour contract supposes an exchange of wages and effort which is specifically defined and delimited, while a service contract has a 'prospective' element such as the possibility of salary growth or promotion. According to Goldthorpe, the working class is characterized by labour contracts and the service class by service contracts; the intermediate class locations experience intermediate types of employment relations.

Evaluating Goldthorpe's class scheme

Goldthorpe's class scheme has been used widely in empirical research. It has been useful in highlighting class-based inequalities, such as those related to health and education, as well as reflecting class-based dimensions in voting patterns, political outlooks and general social attitudes. Yet it

is important to note several significant limitations to schemes such as Goldthorpe's which should caution us against applying them uncritically.

Occupational class schemes are difficult to apply to the *economically inactive*, such as the unemployed, students, pensioners and children. Unemployed and retired individuals are often classified on the basis of their previous work activity, although this can be problematic in the case of the long-term unemployed or people with sporadic work histories. Students can sometimes be classified according to their discipline, but this is more likely to be successful in cases where the field of study correlates closely to a specific occupation (such as engineering or medicine).

Class schemes based on occupational distinctions are also unable to reflect the importance of *property ownership* and *wealth* to social class. Occupational titles alone are not sufficient indicators of an individual's wealth and overall assets. This is particularly true among the richest members of society, including entrepreneurs, financiers and the 'old rich', whose occupational titles of 'director' or 'executive' place them in the same category as many professionals of much more limited means. In other words, class schemes derived from occupational categories do not accurately reflect the enormous concentration of wealth among the 'economic elite'. By classifying such individuals alongside other upper-class professionals, the occupational class schemes dilute the relative weight of property relations in social stratification.

John Westergaard is one sociologist who has disputed Goldthorpe's view that because the rich are so few in number they can be excluded from schemes detailing class structure. As Westergaard argues:

> It is the intense concentration of power and privilege in so few hands that makes these people top. Their socio-structural weight overall, immensely disproportionate to their small numbers, makes the society they top a class society, whatever may be the pattern of divisions beneath them. (1995: 127)

As we have seen, there are a number of complexities involved in devising class schemes that can reliably 'map' the class structure of society. Even within a relatively 'stable' occupational structure, measuring and mapping social class is fraught with diffi-culty. Yet the rapid economic transformations occurring in industrial societies have made the measurement of class even more problematic, and have even led some to question the usefulness of class as a concept. New categories of occupations are emerging, there has been a general shift away from industrial production towards service and knowledge work, and an enormous number of women have entered the workforce in recent decades. Occupational class schemes are not necessarily well suited to capturing the dynamic processes of class formation, mobility and change that are provoked by such social transformations.

Using your sociological imagination: the death of class?

In recent years there has been a vigorous debate within sociology about the usefulness of 'class'. Some sociologists, such as Ray Pahl, have even questioned whether it is still a useful concept in attempting to understand contemporary societies. Australian academics Jan Pakulski and Malcolm Waters have been prominent amongst those who argue that class is no longer the key to understanding contemporary societies. In their book, *The Death of Class* [1996], they argue that contemporary societies have undergone profound social changes and are no longer to be accurately seen as 'class societies'.

A time of social change

Pakulski and Waters argue that industrial societies are now undergoing a period of tremendous social change. We are witnessing a period when the political, social and economic importance of class is in decline. Industrial societies have changed from being organized class societies to a new stage, which Pakulski and Waters call 'status conventionalism'. Pakulski and Waters use this term to indicate that inequalities, although they remain, are the result of differences in status (prestige) and in the lifestyle and consumption patterns favoured by such status groups. Class is no longer an important factor in a person's identity, and the class communities exemplified by Young and Willmott's study of Bethnal Green [1973] are a thing of the past. These changes in turn mean that attempts to explain political and social behaviour by reference to class are also out of date. Class, it seems, is well and truly dead.

Property ownership

One of the reasons for this huge shift is that there have been important changes in property ownership. Property ownership, it is claimed, is now less restricted. This means that there is both more competition amongst firms, since there are more of them, and less opportunity for a dominant capitalist or managerial class to reproduce and pass on its own privilege to the next generation of capitalists. Inequality, however, remains and, where it does arise, is the result of the failure of groups to achieve a high status, not their class position (their position in a division of labour).

Increase in consumer power

These changes have been accompanied by an increase in consumer power. In ever more competitive and diverse markets, firms have to be much more sensitive in heeding the wishes of consumers. There has thus been a shift in the balance of power in advanced industrial societies. What marks out the underprivileged in contemporary society, what Pakulski and Waters refer to as an 'ascriptively disprivileged underclass', is their inability to engage in 'status consumption', which is to say, their inability to buy cars, clothes, houses, holidays and other consumer goods.

For Pakulski and Waters, contemporary societies are stratified, but this stratification is achieved through cultural consumption, not class position in the division of labour. It seems that they are claiming that the differences between, say, a skilled worker from Luton, who drives a Ford Escort, lives in semi-detached house worth between about £80,000 and £100,000 and who goes on package holidays to Spain, and an Oxbridge-educated lawyer living in Hampstead, who drives a Mercedes, has a house worth £200,000 and who holidays in private rented villas in Tuscany, are purely issues of status: it is not that they are members of different classes. It is all a matter of style, taste and status (prestige), not of location in the division of labour.

Processes of globalization

The shift from organized class society to status conventionalism is explained as being the result of processes of globalization, changes in the economy, technology and politics. Pakulski and Waters argue that globalization has led to a new international division of labour, in which the 'first world' is increasingly post-industrial – there are simply fewer of the sort of manual working-class occupations which characterized the previous era of 'organized class society'. At the same time, in a globalized world, nation-states are less self-contained and are less able to govern either their population or market forces than they once were. Stratification and inequality still exist, but they exist more on a global than a national basis; we see more significant inequalities between different nations than we do within a nation-state.

Economic organization in 'first world' societies, powered by technological change, has become far less reliant on unskilled manual labour. Work requires increasing levels of skill and knowledge. Production techniques reflect post-Fordist explanations, which emphasize the need for a highly skilled and flexible labour force, producing customized goods for niche markets. As the skilled manual labour force has declined, there has been an increase in the service sector and a shift to the 'knowledge economy'.

The political and social implications

These changes have had profound political and social implications. As mentioned above, collective class-based communities have collapsed. In the case of the UK this has occurred as old industries, such as coal mining, have 'down-sized' and populations have shifted to the more affluent urbanized areas in the south. Greater geographical mobility has led to changes in family structure – single-person households are on the increase in the UK. Pakulski and Waters argue that, in the context of greater geographical mobility, the importance of the family as a site of class reproduction (as in Young and Willmott) is now very much in decline.

Drawing on the work of Ulrich Beck, Pakulski and Waters claim that we now live in an 'individualized' society. Rather than see themselves as members of a social class, people nowadays tend to see themselves simply as individuals. Their identity will be more influenced by their status, through their consumption patterns and through factors such as their race, gender, age or regional/national identity.

Nothing but a theory?

These are substantial claims – and Pakulski and Waters seem happy to make them with little in the way of empirical evidence; their book presents what is almost exclusively a theoretical argument. Many sociologists would agree that we are living through a period of tremendous social change, but have Pakulski and Waters portrayed the changes accurately?

Criticism of Pakulski and Waters has tended to focus on the way they have defined class. Rosemary Crompton has argued that, while traditional definitions of class have tended to neglect cultural factors such as gender, race and status differences, the Pakulski and Waters definition is unhelpful and confuses class and status. John Scott and Lydia Morris also argue for a need to make distinctions between the class positions of individuals – their location in a division of labour – and the collective phenomena of social class through which people express a sense of belonging to a group and have a shared sense of identity and values. This last sense of class (a more subjective and collective sense) may or may not exist in a society at a particular time – it will depend on many social, economic and political factors.

It is this last aspect of class that appears to have diminished in recent years. This does not mean that status and the cultural aspects of

stratification are now so dominant that the economic aspects of class are of no significance; indeed, mobility studies and inequalities of wealth indicate the opposite. Class is not dead – it is just becoming that bit more complex!

Source: Abbott (2001)

Questions

1 Is social class, as Pakulski and Waters argue, 'dead'?
2 Do you see yourself as a member of a particular class? If so, how has it affected your life?

Social class divisions in Western society today

The question of the upper class

Who is right, Westergaard or Goldthorpe? Is there still a distinctive **upper class**, founded on ownership of wealth and property? Or should we be talking more of a wider service class, as Goldthorpe suggests? One way of approaching these issues is to look at how far wealth and income are concentrated in the hands of a few.

Reliable information about the distribution of wealth is difficult to obtain. Some countries keep more accurate statistics than others, but there is always a considerable amount of guesswork involved. The affluent do not usually publicize the full range of their assets; it has often been remarked that we know far more about the poor than we do about the wealthy. What is certain is that wealth is indeed concentrated in the hands of a small minority. In Britain the top 1 per cent own some 23 per

cent of all marketable wealth. The most wealthy 10 per cent of the population own well over half the total marketable wealth, while the least wealthy half of the population own only 5 per cent of the total wealth (see table 9.2).

Ownership of stocks and bonds is more unequal than holdings of wealth as a whole. The top 1 per cent in the UK own some 75 per cent of privately held corporate shares; the top 5 per cent own over 90 per cent of the total. But there has also been more change in this respect. Some 25 per cent of the population own shares, which compares with 14 per cent in 1986 – many people bought shares for the first time during the privatization programme of the Conservative government that came to power in 1979. The increase is even more dramatic when looked at over a longer period, for in 1979 only 5 per cent of the population held shares. Most of these holdings are small (worth less than £1,000 at 1991 prices), and institutional share ownership – shares held by companies in other firms – is growing faster than individual share ownership.

Table 9.2   Distribution of wealth in the UK, 1991–2002[a] (%)

	1991	1996	2000	2001	2002
Marketable wealth					
Percentage of wealth owned by[b]					
Most wealthy 1%	17	20	23	22	23
Most wealthy 5%	35	40	44	42	43
Most wealthy 10%	47	52	56	54	56
Most wealthy 25%	71	74	75	72	74
Most wealthy 50%	92	93	95	94	94
Total marketable wealth (£ billion)	1,711	2,092	3,131	3,477	3,464
Marketable wealth less value of dwellings					
Percentage of wealth owned by[b]					
Most wealthy 1%	29	26	33	34	35
Most wealthy 5%	51	49	59	58	62
Most wealthy 10%	64	63	73	72	75
Most wealthy 25%	80	81	89	88	88
Most wealthy 50%	93	94	98	98	98

[a] Estimates for individual years should be treated with caution as they are affected by sampling error and the particular pattern of deaths in that year
[b] Adults aged 18 and over

Source: Social Trends 35 (2004), p. 80

'The rich' do not constitute a homogeneous group. Neither do they form a static category: individuals follow varying trajectories into and out of wealth. Some rich people were born into families of 'old money' – an expression which refers to long-standing wealth that has been passed down through generations. Other affluent individuals are 'self-made', having successfully built up wealth from more humble beginnings. Profiles of the richest members of society vary enormously. Next to members of long-standing affluent families are music and film celebrities, athletes and representatives of the 'new elite' who have made millions through the development and promotion of computers, telecommunications and the Internet. Like poverty, wealth must be regarded in the context of life cycles. Some individuals become wealthy very quickly, only to lose much or all of it; others may experience a gradual growth or decline in assets over time.

While it is difficult to collect precise information about the assets and lives of the rich, it is possible to trace broad shifts in the composition of the wealthiest segment of society. Some noteworthy trends have arisen in Britain in recent years. First, 'self-made millionaires', like Sir Gulam Noon who we discussed at the start of this chapter, appear to be making up a greater proportion of the wealthiest individuals. More than 75 per cent of the 1,000 richest Britons in 2004 made their own wealth, rather than inheriting it. Second, a small but growing number of

Table 9.3   Britain's ten richest individuals

	Name	Worth (millions)	Industry
1	Roman Abramovich	£7,500	Oil, football and investments
2	The Duke of Westminster	£5,500	Property
3	Hans Rausing and family	£5,000	Food packaging
4	Philip Green	£3,610	Retailing
5	Lakshmi Mittal	£3,500	Steel
6	Sir Richard Branson	£2,600	Transport and mobile phones
7	Kirsten and Jorn Rausing	£2,575	Inheritance, bloodstock and investments
8	Bernie and Slavica Ecclestone	£2,323	Motor racing
9	Charlene and Michel de Carvalho	£2,260	Inheritance, brewing and banking
10	David and Simon Reuben	£2,200	Property and metal trading

Source: *Sunday Times Rich List* (2004)

women are entering the ranks of the rich. In 1989 only six women were represented among the wealthiest Britons; by 2004 the number had risen to seventy-eight. Third, in recent years many of the wealthiest members of society are quite young – in their twenties or thirties. In 2000, seventeen Britons under the age of thirty were worth more than £30 million. Fourth, ethnic minorities, particularly those of Asian origin, have been increasing their presence among the super-rich (*Sunday Times Rich List*, 2000). Finally, many of the richest people in Britain – including the richest, Roman Abramovich – were not born in the country, but decided to make it their place of residence for a variety of reasons, including the relatively low rates of tax for the super-rich. Britain's richest individuals, as listed in 2004, are shown in table 9.3.

Although the composition of the rich is certainly changing, the view that there is no longer a distinguishable upper class is questionable. John Scott (1991) has argued that the upper class today has changed shape but retains its distinctive position.

He points to three distinctive groups who together form a *constellation of interests* in controlling – and profiting from – big business. *Senior executives* in large corporations may not own their companies, but they are often able to accumulate shareholdings, and these connect them both to old-style *industrial entrepreneurs* and to '*finance capitalists*'. Finance capitalists, a category that includes the people who run the insurance companies, banks, investment funds and other organizations that are large institutional shareholders, are in Scott's view at the core of the upper class today.

Policies encouraging entrepreneurship during the 1980s and the information technology boom of the 1990s have led to a new wave of entry into the upper class of people who have made a fortune from business and technological advances. At the same time, the growth of corporate shareholding among middle-class households has broadened the profile of corporate ownership. Yet the concentration of power and wealth in the upper class remains intact. While corporate owner-

Few people today have the aristocratic prestige and wealth of the recently deceased Duke of Devonshire. In this photograph, his house and grounds staff are seen watching the funeral cortege.

ship patterns may be more diffuse than in earlier times, it is still a small minority who benefit substantially from share-holding.

We can conclude from this that we need a concept both of the *upper class* and the *service class*. The **upper class** consists of a small minority of individuals who have both wealth and power, and are able to transmit their privileges to their children. The upper class can be roughly identified as the top 1 per cent of wealth-holders. Below that class is the **service class**, made up, as Goldthorpe says, of professionals, managers and top administrators. They make up some 5 per cent of the popula-tion. Those whom Goldthorpe calls the 'intermediate class' are perhaps more simply called the *middle class*. Let us look in more detail at this class.

The middle class

The phrase the **middle class** covers a broad spectrum of people working in many different occupations, from employees in the service industry to school teachers to medical professionals. Some authors prefer to speak of the 'middle classes' to draw attention to the diversity of occupa-tions, class and status situations, and life chances that characterize its members. According to most observers, the middle class now encompasses the majority of the population in Britain and most other industrialized countries. This is because the proportion of white-collar jobs has risen markedly relative to blue-collar ones over the course of the century (see chapter 18, 'Work and Economic Life').

Members of the middle class, by merit of their educational credentials or technical qualifications, occupy positions that provide them with greater material and cultural advantages than those enjoyed by manual workers. Unlike the working class, members of the middle class can sell their mental *and* their physical labour power in order to earn a living. While this distinction is useful in forming a rough division between the middle and working classes, the dynamic nature of the occupational structure and the possibility of upward and downward social mobility make it difficult to define the boundaries of the middle class with great precision.

The middle class is not internally cohesive and is unlikely to become so, given the diversity of its members and their differing interests (Butler and Savage 1995). It is true that the middle class is not as homogeneous as the working class; nor do its members share a common social background or cultural outlook, as is largely the case with the top layers of the upper class. The 'loose' composition of the middle class is not a new phenomenon, however; it has been an abiding feature of the middle class since its emergence in the early nineteenth century.

Professional, managerial and administrative occupations have been among the fastest growing sectors of the middle class. There are several reasons why this is so. The first is related to the importance of large-scale organizations in modern societies (see chapter 16, 'Organizations and Networks'). The spread of bureaucracies has created opportunities and a demand for employees to work within institutional settings. Individuals such as doctors and lawyers who might have been self-employed in earlier times now tend to work in institutional environments. Second, the growth of professionals is a reflection of the expanding number of people who work in sectors of the economy where the government plays a major role. The creation of the welfare state led to an enormous growth in many professions involved in carrying out its mandate, such as social workers, teachers and healthcare professionals. Finally, with the deepening of economic and industrial development, there has been an ever-growing demand for the services of experts in the fields of law, finance, accounting, technology and information systems. In this sense, professions can be seen as both a product of the modern era and a central contributor to its evolution and expansion.

Professionals, managers and higher-level administrators gain their position largely from their possession of *credentials* – degrees, diplomas and other qualifications. As a whole, they enjoy relatively secure and remunerative careers, and their separation from people in more routine non-manual jobs has probably grown more pronounced in recent years. Some authors have seen professionals and other higher white-collar groups as forming a specific class – the 'professional/managerial class' (Ehrenreich and Ehrenreich 1979). The degree of division between them and white-collar workers, however, does not seem either deep or clear-cut enough to make such a position defensible.

Other authors have examined the ways in which white-collar professionals join together to maximize their own interests and to secure high levels of material reward and prestige. The case of the medical profession illustrates this point clearly (Parry and Parry 1976). Some groups within the medical profession, such as doctors, have successfully organized themselves to protect their standing in society and to ensure a high level of material reward. Three main dimensions of *professionalism* have enabled this to happen: entry into the profession is restricted to those who meet a strict set of defined criteria (qualifications); a professional association monitors and disciplines the conduct and performance of its members; and it is generally accepted that only members of the profession are qualified to practise medicine. Through such channels, self-governing professional associations are able to exclude unwanted individuals from the profession and to enhance the market position of their own members.

The changing nature of the working class

Marx believed that the **working class** – people working in manufacture as blue-collar labour – would become progressively larger and larger. That was the basis for his view that the working class would create the momentum for a revolutionary transformation of society. In fact, the working class has got smaller and smaller. Only a quarter of a century ago, some 40 per cent of the working population was in blue-collar work. Now, in the UK, only about 18 per cent is, and this proportion is still dropping. Moreover, the conditions under which working-class people are living, and the styles of life they are following, are altering.

British society, in common with most other industrialized countries, has considerable numbers of poor people. However, the majority of individuals working in blue-collar occupations no longer live in poverty. As was mentioned earlier, the income of manual workers has increased considerably since the turn of the century. This rising standard of living is expressed in the increased availability of consumer goods to all classes. About 50 per cent of blue-collar workers now own their own homes. Cars, washing machines, televisions and telephones are owned by a very high proportion of households.

We examine this issue more closely in chapter 10, 'Poverty, Social Exclusion and Welfare'.

The phenomenon of working-class affluence suggests yet another possible route towards a more 'middle-class society'. Perhaps, as blue-collar workers grow more prosperous, they become more middle class. This idea, with the sociologist's characteristic fondness for cumbersome names, came to be known as the **embourgeoisement thesis**. Embourgeoisement means 'becoming more bourgeois', a Marx-style term for 'becoming more middle class'. In the 1950s, when the thesis was first advanced, its supporters argued that many blue-collar workers earning middle-class wages would adopt middle-class values, outlooks and lifestyles as well. There was a widely held belief that progress within industrial society was having a powerful effect on the shape of social stratification.

In the 1960s, John Goldthorpe and his colleagues carried out what came to be a very well-known study in order to test the embourgeoisement hypothesis. In undertaking the study, they argued that if the embourgeoisement thesis was true, affluent blue-collar employees should be virtually indistinguishable from white-collar employees in terms of their attitudes to work, lifestyle and politics. Based on interviews with workers in the car and chemical industries in Luton, the research was published in three volumes. It is often referred to as the *Affluent Worker* study (Goldthorpe 1968–9). A total of 229 manual workers were studied, together with 54 white-collar workers for purposes of comparison. Many of the blue-collar workers had migrated to the area in search of well-paid jobs; compared to most other manual workers, they were in fact highly paid and earned more than most lower-level white-collar workers.

Goldthorpe and his colleagues focused on three dimensions of working-class attitudes and found very little support for the embourgeoisement thesis. In terms of economic outlooks and attitudes to work, the authors agreed that many workers had acquired a middle-class standard of living on the basis of their income and ownership of consumer goods. Yet this relative affluence was attained through positions characterized by poor benefits, low chances for promotion and little intrinsic job satisfaction. The authors of the study found that affluent workers had an *instrumental orientation* to their work: they saw it as a means to an end, the end of gaining good wages. Their work was mostly repetitive and uninteresting, and they had little direct commitment to it.

Despite levels of affluence comparable with those of white-collar employees, the workers in the study did not associate with white-collar workers in their leisure time, and did not aspire to rise up the class ladder. Goldthorpe and his colleagues found that most socializing was done at home with immediate family members or kin, or with other working-class neighbours. There was little indication that the workers were moving towards middle-class norms and values. In terms of political outlooks, the authors found that there was a negative correlation between working-class affluence and support for the Conservative Party. Supporters of the embourgeoisement thesis had predicted that growing affluence among the working class would weaken traditional support for the Labour Party.

The results of the study, in the eyes of its authors, were clear-cut: the embourgeoisement thesis was false. These workers were not in the process of becoming more middle class. However, Goldthorpe and his colleagues did concede the possibility of some convergence between the lower-middle class and upper-working class on certain points. Affluent workers shared with their white-collar counterparts similar patterns of economic consumption, a privatized home-centred outlook and support for *instrumental collectivism* (collective action through unions to improve wages and conditions) at the workplace.

No strictly comparable research has been carried out in the intervening years, and it is not clear how far, if the conclusions reached by Goldthorpe et al. were valid at the time, they remain true now. It is generally agreed that the old, traditional working-class communities have tended to become fragmented, or have broken down altogether, with the decline of manufacturing industry and the impact of consumerism. Just how far such fragmentation has proceeded, however, remains open to dispute.

The underclass?

The term '**underclass**' is often used to describe the segment of the population located at the very bottom of the class structure. Members of the underclass have living standards that are significantly lower than the majority of people in society. It is a group characterized by multiple disadvantages. Many are among the long-term unemployed, or drift in and out of jobs. Some are homeless, or have no permanent place in which to live. Members of the underclass may spend long periods of time dependent on state welfare benefits. The underclass is frequently described as 'marginalized' or 'excluded' from the way of life that is maintained by the bulk of the population.

The underclass is often associated with underprivileged ethnic minority groups. Much of the debate about the underclass originated in the United States, where the preponderance of poor blacks living in inner-city areas prompted talk of a 'black underclass' (Wilson 1978; Murray 1984; Murray 1990; Lister 1996). This is not simply an American phenomenon, however. In Britain, blacks and Asians are disproportionately represented in the underclass. In some European countries, migrant workers who found jobs in times of greater prosperity twenty years ago now make up a large part of this sector. This is true, for instance, of Algerians in France and Turkish immigrants in Germany.

The term 'underclass' is a contested one at the centre of a furious sociological debate. Although the term has now entered everyday speech, many scholars and commentators are wary of using it at all. It is a concept that encompasses a broad spec-trum of meanings, some of which are seen as politically charged and negative in connotation. Most researchers in Europe prefer the notion of '**social exclusion**'.

> Social exclusion is discussed in detail in chapter 10, 'Poverty, Social Exclusion and Welfare', pp. 356–65.

Social exclusion is a broader concept than that of underclass, and has the advantage that it emphasizes *processes* – mechanisms of exclusion – rather than simply states.

The concept of an underclass has a long history. Marx wrote of a 'lumpenproletariat' composed of individuals located persistently outside the dominant forms of economic production and exchange. In later years, the notion was applied to the 'dangerous classes' of paupers, thieves and vagabonds who refused to work and instead survived on the margins of society as 'social parasites'. In more recent years, the idea of an underclass that is dependent on welfare benefits and bereft of initiative has enjoyed a renaissance, again due largely to the writings of Charles Murray, to whose views on this issue we shall turn shortly.

Background to the underclass debate

Recent debates over the underclass have been prompted by several important works published by American sociologists about the position of poor blacks living in inner-city areas. In *The Declining Significance of Race* (1978), drawing on research done in Chicago, William Julius Wilson argued that a substantial black middle class – white-collar workers and professionals – has emerged over the past three or four decades in the United States. Not all African-Americans still live in city ghettos, and those who remain are kept there, Wilson maintained, not so much by active discrimination as by economic factors – in other words, by class rather than by race. The old racist barriers are disappearing; blacks are stuck in the ghetto as a result of economic disadvantages.

Charles Murray agreed about the existence of a black underclass in most big cities. According to Murray (1984), however, African-Americans find themselves at the bottom of society as a result of the very welfare policies designed to help improve their position. This is a reiteration of the 'culture of poverty' thesis, where, it is argued, people become dependent on welfare handouts and then have little incentive to find jobs, build solid communities or make stable marriages.

The idea of welfare dependency is discussed further in chapter 10, 'Poverty, Society Exclusion and Welfare', p. 372

In reply to Murray's claims, Wilson repeated and extended his previous arguments, again using research carried out in Chicago. The movement of many whites from the cities to the suburbs, the decline of urban industries, and other urban economic problems, he suggested, led to high rates of joblessness among African-American men. The forms of social disintegration to which Murray pointed, including the high proportion of unmarried black mothers, Wilson explained in terms of the shrinking of the available pool of 'marriageable' (employed) men.

In more recent work, Wilson has examined the role of such social processes in creating spatially concentrated pockets of urban deprivation populated by a so-

called 'ghetto poor'. Members of the ghetto poor – predominantly African-American and Hispanic – experience multiple deprivations, from low educational qualifications and standards of health to high levels of criminal victimization. They are also disadvantaged by a weak urban infrastructure – including inadequate public transportation, community facilities and educational institutions – which further reduces their chances of integrating into society socially, politically and economically (Wilson 1999).

The underclass, the EU and migration

Much debate over the underclass in the United States centres around its ethnic dimension. Increasingly, this is the case in Europe as well; the tendencies towards economic division and social exclusion now characteristic of America seem to be hardening both in Britain and other countries in Western Europe. The underclass is closely linked to questions of race, ethnicity and migration. In cities such as London, Manchester, Rotterdam, Frankfurt, Paris and Naples, there are neighbourhoods marked by severe economic deprivation. Hamburg is Europe's richest city, as measured by average personal income, and has the highest proportion of millionaires in Germany; it also has the highest proportion of people on welfare and unemployment – 40 per cent above the national average.

The majority of poor and unemployed people in West European countries are native to their countries, but there are also many first- and second-generation immigrants in poverty and trapped in deteriorating city neighbourhoods. Sizeable populations of Turks in Germany, Algerians in France and Albanians in Italy, for example, have grown up in each of these countries. Migrants in search of a better standard of living are often relegated to casual jobs that offer low wages and few career prospects. Furthermore, migrants' earnings are frequently sent home in order to support family members who have remained behind. The standard of living for recent immigrants can be precariously low.

In cases where family members attempt to join a migrant illegally so that the family can be reunited, the potential for exclusion and marginalization is particularly high. Ineligible for state welfare benefits, migrants lacking official status are unable to draw on support from the state in order to maintain a minimum standard of living. Such individuals are extremely vulnerable, trapped in highly constrained conditions with few channels of recourse in the event of crisis or misfortune.

Is there an underclass in Britain?

Since his initial writings about the United States, Charles Murray has subsequently applied his arguments to the UK (1990). According to him, the UK also has an underclass and, although it is not on the same scale as the one found in the USA, it is rapidly 'deepening' (1994). The underclass in the UK will include not only members of ethnic minorities, but also whites from impoverished areas where social disintegration is advancing. Murray's work found favour with the political right, including many in the Conservative Party, and debates about his theory are highly politicized.

Murray focuses on three areas to support his claims for the existence of an underclass in the UK: unemployment, crime and rising illegitimacy (Murray 1990; Herrnstein and Murray 1994). Murray does not believe that high unemployment as such is a problem. The problem, as he sees it, is with people's (particularly young men's) refusal to take difficult jobs. He contrasts the attitudes of the generation who lived through the Great Depression of the early 1930s with the unemployed youth of Britain in the 1980s. Whilst the older generation was keen to avoid what Murray sees as the disgrace of unemployment, the current generation is not. The reasons for this lie in the perverse incentives of the welfare state which provides benefit to the unemployed, effectively paying people not to work. Murray believes too that rising crime rates have also contributed to an underclass. As crime rates soar, the informal social controls that existed within communities break down and the community becomes weaker and more fragmented.

A more balanced picture of the crime rate is discussed in chapter 19, 'Crime and Deviance'.

Last, and in his 1994 account of the deepening the underclass in the UK he suggests most importantly, the rising levels of illegitimacy (children born outside of marriage) produces children with no sense of discipline and no family or father to control them.

Changing family structure was discussed in chapter 7, 'Families and Intimate Relationships', and the rise in births outside of marriage on pp. 225–6.

Again, Murray attributes the rise in illegitimacy to the perverse incentives of the welfare state, which he accuses of paying more to single mothers than to families, and believes that the deepening of the underclass can be attributed to the immorality of those who pursue those incentives.

Murray's work has been sharply criticized, however, by other sociologists working in this country, and most reject the concept of the underclass, as least as he has described it. Duncan Gallie is one sociologist who argues that there is little basis for the idea of an underclass with a distinct culture. In his analysis of data from the Social Change and Economic Life Initiative, Gallie (1994) asserts that there is little difference between working-class individuals and the long-term unemployed in terms of their political outlooks or work histories. In his view, the long-term unemployed may experience greater isolation and impoverishment, but they continue to identify with the wider working class. He found that people who have been unemployed for long periods of time are more committed to the concept of work than are others.

Lydia Morris has examined the spatial dimensions of poverty in Hartlepool, in the north-east of England. It is in areas like Hartlepool, where there has been a decline in manufacturing industry and a large-scale rise in unemployment, that an underclass is likely to emerge. Yet Morris's research did not confirm the emergence of a distinct underclass. In her estimation, the concept of underclass is too simplistic (and politicized) to reflect the complexity of poverty and social disadvantage in contemporary society. Morris studied three groups of unemployed workers: first, couples in which the man had been unemployed for at least twelve months; second, couples in which the man had held the same job for the last twelve

months; and third, couples in which the man had started a new job within the last twelve months.

In terms of whether individuals and families have networks of support on which they can rely, Morris found little difference between the three groups. Those who had been unemployed for more than a year were still concerned with the search for work; they had not yet adopted an anti-work culture. The situation of these men resulted from the long-term economic decline of the area, lack of skills and a relative absence of work-based informal contacts who might have helped them to find local employment. Morris did find, however, that most of the long-term unemployed had partners who were also unemployed, and that they had the highest proportion of unemployed friends. Nevertheless, she concluded that 'there is no direct evidence in my study of a distinctive culture of the "underclass"' (1993: 410).

Morris's research is by no means conclusive. It was conducted in only one part of the country, and that was an area where ethnic minorities were not heavily represented. West Indian and Asian men are more concentrated in semi-skilled work and have higher average rates of unemployment than white males.

Evaluation

How can we make sense of these contrasting approaches to the underclass? Does sociological research support the idea of a distinct class of disadvantaged people who are united by similar life chances?

The idea of the underclass was introduced from the United States and continues to make the most sense there. In the USA, extremes of rich and poor are more marked than in Western Europe. Particularly where economic and social deprivation converge with racial divisions, groups of the underprivileged tend to find themselves locked out of the wider society.

Whilst the concept of the underclass in these circumstances appears useful, in the European countries its use is more questionable. While similar conditions of disadvantage exist in Europe, they seem less pronounced than in the USA. There isn't the same level of separation between those who live in conditions of marked deprivation and the rest of the society.

However, even in the USA, recent studies have suggested that, although the urban poor is an immobile stratum, accounts of a 'defeated and disconnected underclass' are exaggerated. Thus, recent studies of fast food workers and homeless street traders have argued that the separations between the urban poor and the rest of society are not as great as scholars of the underclass believe (Duneier 1999; Newman 2000).

Class and lifestyle

In analysing class location, sociologists have traditionally relied on conventional indicators of class location such as market position, relations to the means of production and occupation. Some recent authors, however, argue that we should evaluate individuals' class location not only, or even mainly, in terms of economics and employment, but in relation also to cultural factors such as lifestyle and consumption patterns. According to this approach, our current age is one in which

Is Britain a meritocracy? Both Tony Blair and Conservative leader David Cameron went to expensive public schools and Oxford University.

'symbols' and markers related to *consumption* are playing an ever greater role in daily life. Individual identities are structured to a greater extent around lifestyle choices – such as how to dress, what to eat, how to care for one's body and where to relax – and less around more traditional class indicators such as employment.

The French sociologist Pierre Bourdieu (1930–2002) supports the view that lifestyle choices are an important indicator of class. Bourdieu argued that economic capital – which consists of material goods such as property, wealth and income – was important, but he believed it only provided a partial understanding of class. Bourdieu's conception of social class is extremely general (see Crompton 1993). He identifies four forms of 'capital' that characterize class position, of which *economic capital* is only one: the others are *cultural, social* and *symbolic* (Bourdieu 1986). Bourdieu argues that individuals increasingly distinguish themselves from others, not according to economic factors, but on the basis of *cultural capital* – which includes education, appreciation of the arts, consumption and leisure pursuits. People are aided in the process of accumulating cultural capital by the proliferation of 'need merchants' selling goods and services – either symbolic or actual – for consumption within the capitalist system. Advertisers, marketers, fashion designers, style consultants, interior designers, personal trainers, therapists, web designers and many others are all involved in influencing cultural tastes and promoting lifestyle choices among an ever-widening community of consumers.

Also important in Bourdieu's analysis of class is *social capital* – one's networks of friends and contacts. Bourdieu defined social capital as the resources that individuals or groups gain 'by virtue of possessing a durable network of more or less institutionalized relationships of mutual acquaintance and recognition' (1992). The concept of social capital is an important tool in contemporary sociology, and Bourdieu's discussion of the term marked an important step in the current proliferation of the idea, which is now often associated with the American political scientist Robert Putnam.

> Putnam's studies on social capital are discussed in chapter 16, 'Organization and Networks', pp. 675–77

Last, Bourdieu argues that *symbolic capital* – which includes possessing a good reputation – is a final important indication of social class. The idea of symbolic capital is similar to that of status.

Each type of capital in Bourdieu's account is related and, to an extent, being in possession of one can help in the pursuit of the others. For example, a businessman who makes a large amount of money (economic capital) might not have particularly fine tastes in the arts, but can pay for his children to attend private schools where these pursuits are encouraged (and so his children gain cultural capital). The businessman's money might lead him to make new contacts with senior people in the business world, and his children will meet the children of other wealthy families, so he, and they, will gain social capital. Similarly someone with a large group of well-connected friends (social capital) might be quickly promoted to a senior position in her company, where she does well, and gains in economic and symbolic capital.

Beverley Skeggs and the formation of class and gender

Bourdieu's work on class (see pp. 322–4) has been highly influential and has been applied to many sociologists' studies on class. The British sociologist Beverley Skeggs used Bourdieu's account of class and culture to examine the formation of class and gender in her study of women in northwest England. Skeggs (1997) followed the lives of eighty-three working-class women over a twelve-year period, who had all enrolled, at one point, in a course for carers at a local further education college. Following Bourdieu's terminology, Skeggs found that the women she studied possessed low economic, cultural, social and symbolic capital. They were poorly paid, had limited success in formal education, few relationships that they could draw on with people in powerful positions and they possessed low status in the eyes of higher social classes. Skeggs claims that the lack of various forms of capital amongst the group of women in her study reflects the wider lack of positive identities for working-class women in the UK. (Working-class men, by contrast, do not have the same difficulty gaining a positive identity, Skeggs believes, and it has often been provided through participation in the trade union movement.) For women, therefore, to be called 'working class' Skeggs argues, is to be labelled dirty, valueless and dangerous.

It is this theoretical background, Skeggs argues, that explains why the women in her study were so reluctant to describe themselves as working class. They were well aware of cultural jibes aimed at working-class women about 'white stilettos', 'Sharons' and 'Traceys'. In interviews Skeggs found that the women tended to 'disidentify' with a perception of themselves as working class. When discussing sexuality for example, the women were keen to avoid the accusation that they were 'tarty' and thus devaluing the limited capital that they did possess as young, marriageable women. It was important amongst the group that they were sexually desirable and that they could 'get a man' if they so wanted. Weddings and marriage offered the chance of respectability and responsibility. The choice to pursue a course in caring emphasized these concerns: training to be a carer taught the women good parenting and offered the possibility of respectable paid work over unemployment after qualification.

Although the group of women tried to disidentify with a view of themselves as working class, and often saw class as of marginal importance in their own lives, Skeggs argues that it is actually fundamental to the way that they lived, and their attempts to distance themselves from a working-class identity made it even more so. Skeggs's account of the lives of a group of women in the northwest of England shows how class is closely interlinked with other forms of identity, in this case gender.

Other scholars have agreed with Bourdieu that class divisions can be linked to distinctive lifestyle and consumption patterns. Thus, speaking of groupings within the middle class, Savage et al. (1992) identify three sectors based on cultural tastes and 'assets'. Professionals in public service, who are high in cultural capital and low in economic capital, tend to pursue healthy, active lifestyles involving exercise, low alcohol consumption and participation in cultural and community activities. Managers and bureaucrats, by contrast, are typified by 'undistinctive' patterns of consumption, which involve average or low levels of exercise, little engagement with cultural activities, and a preference for traditional styles in home furnishings and fashion. The third grouping, the 'postmoderns', pursue a lifestyle that is lacking in any defining principle and may contain elements not traditionally enjoyed alongside each other. Thus, horseback riding and an interest in classical literature may be accompanied by a fascination with extreme sports like rock climbing and a love of raves and Ecstasy.

In general it would be difficult to dispute that stratification within classes, as well as between classes, has come to depend not only on occupational differences but also on differences in consumption and lifestyle. This is borne out by looking at trends in society as a whole. The rapid expansion of the service economy and the entertainment and leisure industry, for example, reflect an increasing emphasis on consumption within industrialized countries. Modern societies have become consumer societies, geared to the acquisition of material goods. In some respects a consumer society is a 'mass society', where class differences are to a degree overridden; thus people from different class backgrounds may all watch similar television programmes or shop for clothing in the same high street shops. Yet class differences can also become *intensified* through variations in lifestyle and 'taste' (Bourdieu 1986).

While bearing these shifts in mind, however, it is impossible to ignore the critical role played by economic factors in the reproduction of social inequalities. For the most part, individuals experiencing extreme social and material deprivations are not doing so as part of a lifestyle choice. Rather, their circumstances are constrained by factors relating to the economic and occupational structure (Crompton 1998).

Gender and stratification

For many years research on stratification was 'gender-blind' – it was written as though women did not exist, or as though, for purposes of analysing divisions of power, wealth and prestige, women were unimportant and uninteresting. Yet gender itself is one of the most profound examples of stratification. There are no societies in which men do not, in some aspects of social life, have more wealth, status and influence than women.

One of the main problems posed by the study of gender and stratification in modern societies sounds simple, but turns out to be difficult to resolve. This is the question of how far we can understand gender inequalities in modern times mainly in terms of class divisions. Inequalities of gender are more deep-rooted historically than class systems; men have superior standing to women even in hunter-gatherer societies, where there are no classes. Yet class divisions are so marked in modern societies that there is no doubt that they 'overlap' substantially with gender inequalities. The material position of most women tends to reflect that of their fathers or husbands; hence it can be argued that we have to explain gender inequalities mainly in class terms.

Determining women's class position

The view that class inequalities largely govern gender stratification was often an unstated assumption until quite recently. However, feminist critiques and the undeniable changes in women's economic role in many Western societies have broken this issue open for debate.

The 'conventional position' in class analysis was that the paid work of women is relatively insignificant compared to that of men, and that therefore women can be regarded as being in the same class as their husbands (Goldthorpe 1983). According to Goldthorpe, whose own class

Is inequality declining in class-based societies?

There is some evidence that at least until recently, the class systems in mature capitalist societies became increasingly open to movement between classes, thereby reducing the level of inequality. In 1955, the Nobel Prize-winning economist Simon Kuznets proposed a hypothesis that has since been called the **Kuznets Curve**: a formula showing that inequality increases during the early stages of capitalist development, then declines, and eventually stabilizes at a relatively low level (Kuznets 1955; see also figure 9.1). Studies of European countries, the United States and Canada suggested that inequality peaked in these places before the Second World War,

declined through the 1950s and remained roughly the same through the 1970s (Berger 1986; Nielsen 1994). Lowered post-war inequality was due in part to economic expansion in industrial societies, which created opportunities for people at the bottom to move up, and also because of government health insurance, welfare and other programmes aimed at reducing inequality. However, Kuznets's prediction may well turn out to apply only to industrial societies. The emergence of *post*-industrial society has brought with it an increase in inequality in many developed nations since the 1970s (see chapter 10), which calls into question Kuznet's theory.

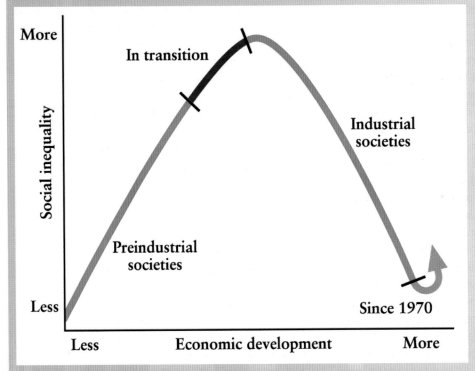

Figure 9.1   The Kuznets Curve

Source: Nielsen (1994), pp. 654–77

scheme was originally predicated on this belief, this is not a view based on an ideology of sexism. On the contrary, it recognizes the subordinate position in which most women find themselves in the labour force. Women are more likely to have part-time jobs than men, and tend to have more intermittent experience of paid employment because they may withdraw for lengthy periods to bear and care for children (see chapter 18, 'Work and Economic Life'). Since the majority of women have traditionally been in a position of economic dependence on their husbands, it follows that their class position is most often governed by the husband's class situation.

Goldthorpe's argument has been criticized in several ways. First, in a substantial proportion of households the income of women is essential to maintaining the family's economic position and mode of life. In these circumstances women's paid employment in some part determines the class position of households. Second, a wife's occupation may sometimes set the standard of the position of the family as a whole. Even where a woman earns less than her husband, her working situation may still be the 'lead' factor in influencing the class of her husband. This could be the case, for instance, if the husband is an unskilled or semi-skilled blue-collar worker and the wife, say, the manager of a shop. Third, where 'cross-class' households exist – in which the work of the husband is in a different category from that of the wife – there may be some purposes for which it is more realistic to treat men and women, even within the same households, as being in different class positions. Fourth, the proportion of households in which women are the sole

Assessing a woman's class position on the basis of her husband's class has been criticized, since not all women are economically dependent on their husbands, as was traditionally often the case.

breadwinners is increasing. The growing numbers of lone mothers and childless working women are testament to this fact. Such women are by definition the determining influence on the class positions of their own households, except in cases where alimony payments put a woman on the same economic level as her ex-husband (Stanworth 1984; Walby 1986).

Goldthorpe and others have defended the conventional position, yet some important changes have also been incorporated into his scheme. For research purposes, the partner of the higher class can be used to classify a household, whether that person be a man or a woman. Rather than classification based on the 'male breadwinner', household classification is now determined by the 'dominant breadwinner'. Furthermore, class III in Goldthorpe's scheme has been divided into two subcategories to reflect the preponderance of women in low-level white-collar work. When the scheme is applied to women, class IIIb (non-manual workers in sales and services) is treated as class VII. This is seen as a more accurate representation of the position of unskilled and semi-skilled women in the labour market.

Beyond the household?

Developing the debate over the assignment of class positions, some authors have suggested that the class position of an individual should be determined without reference to the household. Social class, in other words, would be assessed from occupation independently for each individual, without specific reference to that person's domestic circumstances. This approach was taken, for example, in the work of Gordon Marshall and his colleagues in a study of the class system of the UK (Marshall 1988).

Such a perspective, however, also has its difficulties. It leaves on one side those who are not in paid employment, including not only full-time housewives, but also retired people and the unemployed. The latter two groups can be categorized in terms of the last occupations they held, but this can be problematic if they have not worked for some while. Moreover, it seems potentially very misleading to ignore the household altogether. Whether individuals are single or in a domestic partnership can make a large difference in the opportunities open to them.

The impact of women's employment on class divisions

The entry of women into paid employment has had a significant impact on household incomes. But this impact has been experienced unevenly and may be leading to an accentuation of class divisions between households. A growing number of women are moving into professional and managerial positions and earning high salaries. This is contributing to a polarization between high-income 'dual-earner households', on the one hand, and 'single-earner' or 'no-earner' households on the other (see chapter 18, 'Work and Economic Life').

Research has shown that high-earning women tend to have high-earning partners, and that the wives of men in professional and managerial occupations have higher earnings than other employed female partners. Marriage tends to produce partnerships where both individuals are relatively privileged or disadvantaged in terms of occupational attainment (Bonney 1992).

The impact of such dual-earner partnerships is heightened by the fact that the average childbearing age is rising, particularly among professional women. The growing number of dual-earner childless couples is helping to fuel the widening gap between the highest and lowest paid households.

Social mobility

In studying stratification, we have to consider not only the differences between economic positions or occupations, but also what happens to the individuals who occupy them. The term 'social mobility' refers to the movement of individuals and groups between different socio-economic positions. Vertical mobility means movement up or down the socio-economic scale. Those who gain in property, income or status are said to be *upwardly mobile* – like Sir Gulam Noon whose life history was summarized at the start of this chapter – while those who move in the opposite direction are *downwardly mobile*. In modern societies there is also a great deal of lateral mobility, which refers to geographical movement between neighbourhoods, towns or regions. Vertical and lateral mobility are often combined. For instance, someone working in a company in one city might be promoted to a higher position in a branch of the firm located in another town, or even in a different country.

There are two ways of studying social mobility. First, we can look at individuals' own careers – how far they move up or down the social scale in the course of their working lives. This is usually called intra-generational mobility. Alternatively, we can analyse how far children enter the same type of occupation as their parents or grandparents. Mobility across the generations is called intergenerational mobility.

Comparative mobility studies

The amount of vertical mobility in a society is a major index of the degree of its 'openness', indicating how far talented individuals born into lower strata can move up the socio-economic ladder. In this respect, social mobility is an important political issue, particularly in states committed to the liberal vision of equality of opportunity for all citizens. How 'open' are the industrialized countries in terms of social mobility? Is there more equality of opportunity in Britain than elsewhere?

Studies of social mobility have been carried on for a period of more than fifty years and frequently involve international comparisons. An important early study was conducted by Peter Blau and Otis Dudley Duncan in the 1960s (1967). Their investigation remains the most detailed study of social mobility yet carried out in any single country. (Wide-ranging though it may have been, like most other studies of mobility it bears out the points made previously – all those studied were men.) Blau and Duncan collected information on a national sample of 20,000 males. They concluded that there was much vertical mobility in the United States, but nearly all of this was between occupational positions quite close to one another. 'Long-range' mobility was found to be rare. Although downward movement did occur, both within the careers of individuals and intergenerationally, it was much less common than upward mobility. The reason for this is that white-collar and professional jobs have grown much more rapidly than blue-collar ones, a shift that created openings for sons of blue-collar workers to move into white-collar positions. Blau and Duncan emphasized the importance of education and training on an individual's chances for success. In their view, upward social mobility is generally characteristic of industrial societies as a whole and contributes to social stability and integration.

Perhaps the most celebrated international study of social mobility was that carried out by Seymour Martin Lipset and Reinhard Bendix (1959). They analysed data from nine industrialized societies – Britain, France, West Germany, Sweden, Switzerland, Japan, Denmark, Italy and the United States, concentrating on mobility of men from blue-collar to white-collar work. Contrary to their expectations, they discovered no evidence that the United States was more open than the European societies. Total vertical mobility across the blue-collar/white-collar line was 30 per cent in the United States, with the other societies varying between 27 and 31 per cent. Lipset and Bendix concluded that all the industrialized countries were experiencing similar changes in respect of the expansion of white-collar jobs. This led to an 'upward surge of mobility' of comparable dimensions in all of them. Others have questioned their findings, arguing that significant differences between countries are found if more attention is given to downward mobility, and if long-range mobility is also brought into consideration (Heath 1981; Grusky and Hauser 1984).

Most studies of social mobility, such as the ones described here, have focused upon 'objective' dimensions of mobility – that is to say, how much mobility seems to exist, in which directions and for what parts of the population. Gordon Marshall and David Firth (Marshall and Firth 1999) have taken a different approach in their comparative study of social mobility; they have investigated people's 'subjective' feelings about changing class positions. The authors designed their research in response to what they term 'unsubstantiated speculation' among sociologists about the likely effects of social mobility on individuals' sense of well-being. While some have argued that social mobility produces a sense of disequilibrium, isola-

tion and unrootedness, others have taken a more optimistic view, suggesting that a gradual process of adaptation to a new class inevitably takes place.

Using survey data from ten countries – Bulgaria, the Czech Republic, Slovakia, Estonia, Germany, Poland, Russia, Slovenia, the USA and the UK – Marshall and Firth examined whether class mobility was linked to a heightened sense of satisfaction or dissatisfaction with aspects of everyday life such as family, community, work, income and politics. The authors on the whole found little evidence of an association between respondents' class experiences and their overall life satisfaction. This was as true for individuals who had moved from working-class origins to middle-class positions as it was for those who had been downwardly mobile.

Downward mobility

Although downward mobility is less common than upward mobility, it is still a widespread phenomenon. Downward intragenerational mobility is also common. Mobility of this type is quite often associated with psychological problems and anxieties, where individuals become unable to sustain the lifestyles to which they have become accustomed. Redundancy is another of the main sources of downward mobility. Middle-aged people who lose their jobs, for example, either find it hard to gain new employment at all, or can only obtain work at a lower level of income than before.

Thus far, there have been very few studies of downward mobility in the UK. It is probable, however, that downward mobility, in inter- and intragenerational terms, is on the increase in Britain as it is in the United States. In the USA there have been several recent studies of the phenomenon. Over the 1980s and early 1990s, for the first time since the Second World War, there was a general downturn in the average real earnings (earnings after adjusting for inflation) of people in middle-level white-collar jobs in the USA. Thus, even if such jobs continue to expand relative to others, they may not support the lifestyle aspirations they once did.

Corporate restructuring and 'downsizing' are the main reasons why these changes are happening. In the face of increasing global competition, many companies have trimmed their workforces. White-collar as well as full-time blue-collar jobs have been lost – to be replaced by poorly paid, part-time occupations.

Studies have shown that in the USA downward mobility is particularly common among divorced or separated women with children. Women who enjoyed a moderately comfortable middle-class way of life when they were married often find themselves living 'hand-to-mouth' after getting divorced. In many cases, alimony payments are meagre or non-existent; women attempting to juggle work, child care and domestic responsibilities find it difficult to make ends meet (Schwarz and Volgy 1992).

Social mobility in Britain

Overall levels of mobility have been extensively studied in Britain over the post-war period – although, again, virtually all the research has concentrated on men. An early study was directed by David Glass (1954). Glass's work analysed intergenera-

tional mobility for a longish period up to the 1950s. His findings correspond to those noted above in respect of international data (around 30 per cent mobility from blue-collar to white-collar jobs). Glass's research was in fact widely drawn on by those making international comparisons. On the whole, Glass concluded that Britain was not a particularly 'open' society. While a good deal of mobility occurred, most of this was short range. Upward mobility was much more common than downward mobility, and was mostly concentrated at the middle levels of the class structure. People right at the bottom tended to stay there; almost 50 per cent of sons of workers in professional and managerial jobs were themselves in similar occupations. Glass also found a high degree of 'self-recruitment' of this sort into elite positions within society.

Another important piece of research, known as the Oxford Mobility Study, was carried out by John Goldthorpe and his colleagues, based on the findings from a 1972 survey (Goldthorpe et al. 1980). They sought to investigate how far patterns of social mobility had altered since the time of Glass's work, and concluded that the overall level of mobility of men was in fact higher than in the previous period, with rather more long-range movement being noted. The main reason for this, however, was once again not that the occupational system had become more egalitarian. Rather, the origin of the changes was the continued acceleration in the growth of higher white-collar jobs relative to blue-collar ones. The researchers found that two-thirds of the sons of unskilled or semi-skilled manual workers were themselves in manual occupations. About 30 per cent of professionals and managers were of working-class origins, while some 4 per cent of men in blue-collar work were from professional or managerial backgrounds.

Despite finding evidence of higher rates of absolute social mobility, the Oxford Mobility Study concluded that the relative chances for mobility among different segments of the population in Britain remained highly unequal, and that inequalities of opportunity remained squarely grounded within the class structure.

The original Oxford Mobility Study was updated on the basis of new material collected about ten years later (Goldthorpe and Payne 1986). The major findings of the earlier work were corroborated, but some further developments were found. The chances of men from blue-collar backgrounds getting professional or managerial jobs, for example, had increased. Once again, this was traced to changes in the occupational structure, producing a reduction of blue-collar occupations relative to higher white-collar jobs.

Marshall et al. produced results in the 1980s which largely corroborated the findings of Goldthorpe and others. In the Essex Mobility Study, the authors found that about a third of people in higher white-collar or professional jobs were from blue-collar backgrounds. Findings such as these demonstrate a substantial amount of fluidity in British society: for many people, it is indeed possible to move up the social hierarchy, in terms of both intragenerational and intergenerational mobility. Yet the scales are still biased against women whose mobility chances are hampered by their over-representation in routine non-manual jobs. The fluid character of modern society derives mostly from its propensity to upgrade

occupations. Marshall and his co-workers conclude: 'More "room at the top" has not been accompanied by great equality in the opportunities to get there' (1988, p. 138). However, one should bear in mind a point made earlier: mobility is a long-term process, and if the society is becoming more 'open', the full effects will not be seen for a generation.

However, in a study by Jo Blanden, Alissa Goodman, Paul Gregg and Stephen Machin at the London School of Economics, published in 2002, the authors found a reversal of this process. They compared intergenerational mobility in Britain between two groups, the first all born in March 1958 and the second in April 1970. Even though these groups are only twelve years different in age, the study documented a sharp fall in intergenerational mobility of economic status between them. The study found that the economic status of the group born in 1970 was much more strongly connected to the economic status of their parents than the group born in 1958. The authors suggested that one of the reasons for the fall in intergenerational mobility from the earlier to the later groups was that the rise in education attainment from the late 1970s onwards benefited children of the wealthy more than children of the less well-off.

Is Britain a meritocracy?

Peter Saunders (1990, 1996) has been one of the most vocal critics of the British tradition of social mobility research encompassing studies such as those done by Glass and Goldthorpe. According to Saunders, Britain is a true meritocracy because rewards go naturally to those who are best able to 'perform' and achieve. In his view, ability and effort are the key factors in occupational success, not class background. Saunders uses empirical data from the National Child Development Study to show that children who are bright and hard-working will succeed regardless of the social advantages or disadvantages they may experience. In his estimation, Britain may be an unequal society, but it is a fair one.

In response to such claims, Richard Breen and John Goldthorpe criticize Saunders on both theoretical and methodological grounds (Breen and Goldthorpe 1999). They accuse Saunders of introducing biases into his analysis of the survey data, such as excluding respondents who were unemployed. Breen and Goldthorpe provide an alternative analysis of the same data used by Saunders and produce radically different findings which substantiate their own belief in the importance of class barriers to social mobility. The authors conclude that individual merit is certainly a contributing factor in determining individuals' class positions, but that 'class of origin' remains a powerful influence. According to Breen and Goldthorpe, children from disadvantaged backgrounds must show more merit than those who are advantaged to acquire similar class positions.

Gender and social mobility

Although so much research into social mobility has focused on men, in recent years more attention has begun to be paid to patterns of mobility among women. At a time when girls are 'outperforming' boys in school and females are outnumbering males in higher education, it is tempting to conclude that long-standing gender inequalities in society may be relaxing their hold (for more on this see chapter 17, 'Education', pp. 715–19). Has the occupational structure become more 'open' to women, or are their mobility chances still guided largely by family and social background?

A cohort study by the Economic and Social Research Council, *Twenty-Something in the 1990s*, has traced the lives of 9,000 Britons born during the same week in 1970. In the most recent survey of the respondents, at the age of twenty-six, it was found that for both men and women family background and class of origin remain powerful influences. The study concluded that the young people who are coping best with the transition to adulthood were those who had obtained a better education, postponed children and marriage, and had fathers in professional occupations. Individuals who had come from disadvantaged backgrounds had a greater tendency to remain there.

The study found that, on the whole, women today are experiencing much greater opportunity than their counterparts in the previous generation. Middle-class women have benefited the most from the shifts mentioned above: they were just as likely as their male peers to go to university and to move into well-paid jobs on graduation. This trend towards greater equality was also reflected in women's heightened confidence and sense of self-esteem, compared with a similar cohort of women born just twelve years earlier.

Women's chances of entering a good career are improving, but two major obstacles remain. Male managers and employers still discriminate against women applicants. They do so at least partly because of their belief that 'women are not really interested in careers', and that they are likely to leave the workforce when they begin a family. Having children does indeed still have a very substantial effect on the career chances of women. This is less because they are uninterested in a career than because they are often effectively forced to choose between advancement at work and having children. Men are rarely willing to share full responsibility for domestic work and child care. Although many more women than before are organizing their domestic lives in order to pursue a career, there are still major barriers in their way.

Conclusion: the importance of class

Although the traditional hold of class is most certainly weakening in some ways, particularly in terms of people's identities, class divisions remain at the heart of core economic inequalities in modern societies. Class continues to exert a great influence on our lives, and class membership is correlated with a variety of inequalities from life expectancy and overall physical health to access to education and well-paid jobs.

Inequalities between the poor and the more affluent have expanded in Britain over the last three decades. Is growing class inequality a price that has to be paid to secure economic development? This assumption was particularly prominent during the period of the Thatcher government after 1979. The pursuit of wealth, the reasoning was, creates economic development because it is a motivating force encouraging innovation and drive. Many argue that in the present day, globalization and the deregulation of economic markets are leading to a widening of the gap between rich and poor and a 'hardening' of class inequalities.

Yet it is important to remember that our activities are never completely determined by class divisions: many people experience social mobility. The entrepreneur Gulam Noon, whose life story we began this chapter with, provides a particularly vivid example of social mobility. The expansion of higher education, the growing accessibility of professional qualifications and the emergence of the Internet and the 'new economy' are all also presenting important new channels for upward mobility. Such developments are further eroding old class and stratification patterns and are contributing to a more fluid, meritocratic order.

Summary points

1 Social stratification refers to the division of society into layers or strata. When we talk of social stratification, we draw attention to the unequal positions occupied by individuals in society. Stratification by gender and age is found in all societies. In the larger traditional societies and in industrialized countries today, there is stratification in terms of wealth, property and access to material goods and cultural products.

2 Four major types of stratification system can be distinguished: slavery, caste, estates and class. Whereas the first three depend on legal or religiously sanctioned inequalities, class divisions are not 'officially' recognized, but stem from economic factors affecting the material circumstances of people's lives.

3 The most prominent and influential theories of stratification are those developed by Marx and Weber. Marx placed primary emphasis on class, which he saw as an objectively given characteristic of the economic structure of society. He saw a fundamental split between the owners of capital and the workers who do not own capital. Weber accepted a similar view, but distinguished two other aspects of stratification – status and party. Status refers to the esteem or 'social honour' given to individuals or groups; party refers to the active mobilizing of groups to secure definite ends.

4   Occupation is frequently used as an indicator of social class. Individuals in the same occupation tend to experience similar degrees of social advantage or disadvantage, and to enjoy similar life chances. Sociologists have traditionally used occupational class schemes to map the class structure of society. Class schemes are valuable for tracing broad class-based inequalities and patterns, but are limited in other ways. For example, class schemes are difficult to apply to the economically inactive and do not reflect the importance of property ownership and wealth to social class.

5   Most people in modern societies are more affluent today than was the case several generations ago, yet wealth remains highly concentrated in a relatively small number of hands. The upper class consists of a small minority of people who have both wealth and power, and the chance of passing on their privileges to the next generation. The rich are a diverse and changing group; self-made millionaires, women and young people have been entering the ranks of the rich in greater numbers in recent years.

6   The middle class is composed broadly of those working in white-collar occupations, such as teachers, medical professionals and employees in the service industry. In most industrialized countries, the middle class now encompasses the majority of the population; this is due in large part to the growth of professional, managerial and administrative occupations. Unlike the working class, members of the middle class generally possess educational credentials or technical qualifications which allow them to sell their mental as well as their physical labour in order to earn a living.

7   The working class is composed of people working in blue-collar or manual occupations. The working class has shrunk significantly during the twentieth century, with the decline in manufacturing work. Members of the working class are more affluent than they were a century ago.

8   The underclass is a segment of the population that lives in severely disadvantaged conditions at the margins of society. The idea of the underclass was first developed in the United States to describe the position of poor ethnic minorities in urban areas. Although the notion of the underclass has been applied to Britain, the concept is perhaps more useful in the US context, where there is a greater separation between those who are heavily deprived and the rest of society, although, even in the USA, it is a highly controversial issue.

9   Some authors have more recently suggested that cultural factors such as lifestyle and consumption patterns are important influences on class position. According to such a view, individual identities are now more structured around lifestyle choices than they are around traditional class indicators such as occupation.

10 Analyses of stratification have traditionally been written from a male point of view. This is partly because of the assumption that gender inequalities reflect class differences; this assumption is highly questionable. Gender influences stratification in modern societies to some degree independently of class.

11 An individual's class position is at least in some part achieved; it is not simply 'given' from birth. Social mobility, both upwards and

downwards in the class structure, is a fairly common feature.

12 In the study of social mobility, a distinction is made between intragenerational and intergenerational mobility. The first of these refers to movement up or down the social scale within an individual's working life. The second concerns movement across the generations, as when a daughter or son from a blue-collar background becomes a professional. Social mobility is mostly of limited range. Most people remain close to the level of the families from which they came, although the expansion of white-collar jobs in the last few decades has provided the opportunity for considerable short-range upward mobility.

13 *Social capital* refers to the knowledge and connections that enable people to cooperate with one another for mutual benefit and extend their influence. Some social scientists have argued that social capital has declined in the United States during the last quarter century, a process they worry indicates a decline in America's commitment to civic engagement.

Questions for further thought

1 Which of the theoretical approaches to stratification seem most relevant to your everyday experiences?

2 Why do so many sociologists use occupation as a measure of social class?

3 Why is downward mobility less common than upward mobility in modern societies?

4 What do sociologists mean by 'relational' class schemes?

5 Which is the most appropriate unit for class analysis: the individual or the household?

6 Is inequality in society a bad thing as long as everyone is adequately fed and clothed?

Further reading

Rosemary Crompton, *Class and Stratification: An Introduction to Current Debates* (Cambridge: Polity, 1998).

Michael Lavalette and Gerry Mooney (eds), *Class Struggle and Social Welfare* (New York: Routledge, 2000).

Charles Murray et al., *Charles Murray and the Underclass: The Developing Debate* (London: IEA Health and Welfare Unit in association with *The Sunday Times*, 1996).

Sally R. Munt (ed.), *Cultural Studies and the Working Class* (London: Cassell, 2000).

Christine Zmroczek and Pat Mahony (eds), *Women and Social Class: International Feminist Perspectives* (London: UCL Press, 1999).

Internet links

Bibliography on social class (University of Amsterdam)
http://www.pscw.uva.nl/sociosite/CLASS/bibA.html

Explorations in Social Inequalities
http://www.trinity.edu/mkearl/strat.html

Marxists Internet Archive
http://www.marxists.org

Multidisciplinary Program in Inequality and Social Policy at the Kennedy School of
    Government
http://www.ksg.harvard.edu/inequality/

The Progress of Nations 2000 Unicef Report
http://www.unicef.org/pon00/

Contents

10 Poverty, Social Exclusion and Welfare

CAROL IS a woman of twenty-four who works at a telephone call centre, providing information and customer service to people who want to make travel arrangements over the telephone. She works long hours, often late into the evening. The people who work alongside her at the call centre are all women. They sit in a large room in long rows, separated from one another by grey partitions. The women speak into telephone headsets while entering and retrieving information from the computer terminals in front of them.

Like many of her co-workers, Carol is a lone mother. She supports her two small children on her low wages. Most months she receives a small amount of child support from her ex-husband, but it never seems to be enough to cover expenses, and she has spent many hours in communication with the Child Support Agency to try and regularize the payments. Carol rarely manages to save money. Three mornings a week she takes on extra work as a cleaner at an office building near her flat. The money she is able to earn from this additional work allows her to pay most of her bills on time, to buy clothes for her children, repay a loan she took out to furnish her flat, and to cover the cost of child care. Carol's income is also supple-

mented by benefits given to her as a resident of a council-owned flat, a single mother and a low earner. Despite these payments and working extra hours, Carol struggles each month to make ends meet. Her prime goal is to save up enough to move herself and her children from the council-owned flat on a housing estate into a safer, more desirable area.

On the evenings when Carol works late at the call centre, she rushes from work to fetch her two children from her mother, who cares for them after the day-care

centre closes each afternoon. Carol is often late because the bus she takes to and from work doesn't arrive on time. If she is lucky, the children fall back to sleep as soon as she takes them home, but on many nights it is a struggle to get them to bed. By the time the children are asleep, Carol is too exhausted to do anything but switch on the television. She has little time to shop for food or to cook proper meals, so she and the children eat a lot of frozen foods. She does most of her shopping at the nearest cheap supermarket, but the store is still a bus journey and a difficult walk away with heavy bags, and she is normally exhausted by the time she returns home. She knows that her children would all benefit from a more balanced diet, but there are no shops close by on the council estate and, in any case, she can't afford to buy many fresh products.

Carol worries about spending too much time away from her children, but she doesn't see any way around her dilemma. After she and her husband divorced, she spent the first eighteen months at home with the children, living off government benefits. Although she is struggling to cope with her present situation, she does not want to become dependent on welfare. Carol hopes that after some years of experience at the call centre, she might be able to rise into a more responsible and better-paid position.

Many people who encounter someone like Carol might make certain assumptions about her life. They might conclude that Carol's poverty and low position in society are a result of her natural abilities or a consequence of her own personal upbringing. Others might blame Carol for not working hard enough to overcome her difficult situation. How does sociology help us to judge which of these views is most accurate? It is the job of sociology to analyse these assumptions and to develop a broader view of our society that can make sense of the experiences of people like Carol.

Carol and her children are only one example of the many households in the United Kingdom that exist in conditions of poverty. According to the Organization for Economic Cooperation and Development (OECD), Britain has one of the worst poverty records in the developed world. Many people might be shocked to learn that Britain holds such a dubious distinction. More affluent people often have little accurate knowledge about the extent of the poverty in their midst. In this chapter we examine the concept and experience of poverty more closely. We also look at the wider concept of social exclusion. In the final section we look at how the welfare state has grown in response to poverty, and we examine some of the recent attempts to reform it. (This chapter focuses on poverty in the UK. Chapter 11 looks at the issue of poverty and inequality in a global context.)

Poverty

What is poverty?

What is poverty and how should it be defined? Two different approaches to poverty have been favoured by sociologists and researchers: **absolute poverty** and **relative poverty**. The concept of absolute poverty is grounded in the idea of subsistence – the basic conditions that must be met in order to sustain a physically healthy existence. People who lack these fundamental requirements for human existence – such as sufficient food, shelter and clothing – are said to live in poverty. The concept of absolute poverty is seen as universally applicable. It is held that standards for human subsistence are more or less the same for all people of an equivalent age and physique, regardless of where they live. Any individual, anywhere in the world, can be said to live in poverty if he or she falls below this universal standard. As we will see in chapter 11, 'Global Inequality', many people in the world today still live and die in absolute poverty.

Not everyone accepts that it is possible to identify such a standard, however. It is more appropriate, they argue, to use the concept of relative poverty, which relates poverty to the overall standard of living that prevails in a particular society. Advocates of the concept of relative poverty hold that poverty is culturally defined and should not be measured according to some universal standard of deprivation. It is wrong to assume that human needs are everywhere identical – in fact, they differ both within and across societies. Things that are seen as essential in one society might be regarded as luxuries in another. For example, in most industrialized countries, running water, flush toilets and the regular consumption of fruit and vegetables are regarded as basic necessities for a healthy life; people who live without them could be said to live in poverty. Yet in many developing societies, such items are not standard among the bulk of the population and it would not make sense to measure poverty according to their presence or absence.

There are difficulties in the formulations of both absolute and relative poverty. One common technique for measuring absolute poverty is to determine a **poverty line**, based on the price of the basic goods needed for human survival in a particular society. Individuals or households whose income falls below the poverty line are said to live in poverty. Yet using a single criterion of poverty can be problematic, because such definitions fail to take into account variations in human needs within and between societies. It is much more expensive, for example, to live in some areas of the country than others; the cost of basic necessities will differ from region to region. As another example, individuals who are engaged in physical labour outdoors will be likely to have greater nutritional needs than, say, office workers who spend their days sitting inside. A single criterion of poverty tends to mean that some individuals are assessed as above the poverty line when in fact their income does not even meet their basic subsistence needs.

The concept of relative poverty presents its own complexities, however. One of the main ones is the fact that, as societies develop, understandings of relative poverty must also change. As societies become more affluent, standards for relative poverty are gradually adjusted upwards. At one time, for example, refrigerators, central heating and telephones were considered to be luxury goods. Yet in most industrialized societies today, they are seen as necessities for leading a full and active life. Some critics have cautioned that the use of the concept of relative poverty tends to deflect attention away from the fact that even the least affluent members of society are now considerably better off than in earlier times. They question whether 'true' poverty can be said to exist in a society, such as

Who is poor? This child in a refugee camp? ...

present-day Britain, where consumer goods like televisions and washing machines now sit in practically every home. Defenders of relative conceptions of poverty point out that access to consumer goods is valueless if an individual or group is unable to access more basic goods, such as nutritious food and good healthcare.

In the next section we examine some of the main methods used to measure poverty that have been used in the UK.

Measuring poverty

Official measurements of poverty

In contrast to the United States and many other countries, where there is an official 'poverty line', interpretations of poverty as such in Britain are not provided by the government. Because of the absence of an official definition of poverty, researchers in the UK have relied on other statistical indicators, such as benefit provision, to measure poverty levels. From the mid-1960s onwards researchers have followed

... or these children from a dilapidated housing estate?

Abel-Smith and Townsend in defining anyone having an income at or below the level of supplementary benefit as living 'in poverty'. Supplementary benefit was a means-tested cash benefit paid by the state to people whose income did not reach a level deemed appropriate by Parliament for subsistence. In the UK, supplementary benefit was replaced by income support in 1988, and across much of Europe poverty is now most commonly measured using income inequality, where poverty is defined as the number of households living on or below 60 per cent (or in earlier measures 50 per cent) of median income. Under this measure, the number of people living in poverty increased dramatically throughout the 1980s, peaking in 1991/2, before falling from the mid-1990s onwards (see table

10.1). In 2004, the Department Work and Pensions calculated that 9.5 million people were living in poverty according to this measure, representing 16 per cent of the total population.

Peter Townsend: relative deprivation

Some researchers believe that official measures, of the kind discussed above, do not give a true picture of poverty. Several important studies have been carried out that define poverty as deprivation. One pioneer in this approach is Peter Townsend, whose work since the late 1950s increased public awareness of poverty in the UK. Rather than relying on income statistics, Townsend's studies have concentrated on people's subjective understanding of poverty. In his classic study, *Poverty in the United Kingdom* (1979), Townsend

Table 10.1   Number and percentage of individuals living in households with below 60 per cent of median income (before housing costs)

Year	Number (millions)	Percentage
1979	6.5	12
1981	6.9	13
1987	9.3	17
1988/9	10.9	19
1990/1	11.4	20
1991/2	11.7	21
1992/3	11.4	20
1993/4	10.5	18
1994/5	9.8	18
1995/6	9.4	17
1996/7	10.3	18
1997/8	10.3	18
1998/9	10.2	18
1999/2000	10.0	18
2000/1	9.7	17
2001/2	9.7	17

Source: Department for Work and Pensions, *Households Below Average Income 1994/5–2001/2*, in Flaherty et al. (2004), p. 43

Table 10.2   Townsend's deprivation index (1979)

Characteristics	Percentage of the population
1 Has not had a holiday away from home in the last 12 months.	53.6
2 Adults only. Has not had a relative or a friend to the home for a meal or snack in the last four weeks.	33.4
3 Adults only. Has not been out in the last four weeks to a relative or friend for a meal or snack.	45.1
4 Children only (under 15). Has not had a friend to play or to tea in the last four weeks.	36.3
5 Children only. Did not have a party on last birthday.	56.6
6 Has not had an afternoon or evening out for entertainment in the last two weeks.	47.0
7 Does not have fresh meat (including meals out) as many as four days a week.	19.3
8 Has gone through one or more days in the past fortnight without a cooked meal.	7.0
9 Has not had a cooked breakfast most days of the week.	67.3
10 Household does not have a refrigerator.	45.1
11 Household does not usually have a Sunday joint (three in four times).	25.9
12 Household does not have sole use of four amenities (flush WC; sink or washbasin and cold water tap; fixed bath or shower and gas/electric cooker).	21.4

Source: Townsend (1979), p. 250

examined the responses to more than two thousand questionnaires filled in by households across the UK during the late 1960s. Respondents provided detailed information about their lifestyles, including their living conditions, eating habits, leisure and civic activities, as well as their income. From this information Townsend selected twelve items he believed would be relevant to the whole population rather than to particular groups, and calculated the proportion of the population deprived of them. (The results can be seen in table 10.2.)

Townsend gave each household a score on a *deprivation index* – the higher the score, the more deprived the household was. He then compared the position of households on the index to their total income, making allowances for the number of people in each household, whether the adults were working, the ages of the children and whether any members of the house were disabled. Townsend concluded that his survey revealed a threshold for levels of income under which levels of deprivation rose rapidly. It was these households which Townsend described as suffering from poverty. He calculated that these households formed 22.9 per cent of the population, far higher than previous figures had suggested. Based on these findings, he concluded that government rates for means-tested benefits were more that 50 per cent too low, falling well short of the minimum need by a household to participate fully and meaningfully in society. Townsend's work shows that as income falls, families appear to withdraw from taking part in quite ordinary family-type things: they become 'socially excluded', a concept which we discuss further below (pp. 356–65).

Although Townsend's approach has proved to be influential, as we shall see below, it has been criticized by some commentators. David Piachaud, for example, has argued that the items that Townsend selected for his deprivation index (shown in table 10.2) have an arbitrary quality: 'It is not clear what they have to do with poverty, nor how they were selected' (1987). Several of the categories in Townsend's deprivation index could be more to do with social or cultural decisions than with poverty. If someone chooses not to eat meat or cooked breakfast, or decides not to socialize regularly or holiday away, it is not obvious that that person is suffering from poverty.

Joanna Mack and Stewart Lansley: Breadline Britain

Building on Townsend's definition of poverty as deprivation, Joanna Mack and Stewart Lansley have carried out two important studies on relative poverty in Britain, the first in 1983 and a second in 1990. For a television programme called *Breadline Britain*, Mack and Lansley conducted an opinion poll to determine what people considered to be 'necessities' for an 'acceptable' standard of living. On the basis of these responses, they created a list of twenty-two basic necessities that more than 50 per cent of respondents considered important for a normal life. They defined poverty as the condition in which three or more items from that list were lacking.

By asking respondents what *they* thought to be necessities, rather than choosing the necessities themselves, Mack and Lansley avoided the criticism Piachaud and others had directed against Townsend's original survey – namely, that his choice of those items that made up the deprivation index was arbitrary. Mack and Lansley also included a question in their survey asking whether items which respondents lacked were a matter of personal choice or one of necessity. If the respondents answered that it was a matter of choice, then they were not classified as being deprived of that item.

In their first survey in 1983 Mack and Lansley estimated that there were around 7.5 million people in the UK living in poverty – around 14 per cent of the population. The different method of calculation they used gave them a far lower, but still a substantial, figure than Townsend's study did for the extent of poverty in the UK. Mack and Lansley then repeated the exercise in 1990. Their results revealed a significant growth in poverty during the 1980s, with the number of people living in poverty (in the 1990 study defined as a lack of three or more of twenty-six necessities) rising to 11 million, and the number living in severe poverty (a lack of seven or more necessities) rising from 2.6 to 3.5 million (Mack and Lansley 1985, 1992).

David Gordon: Poverty and Social Exclusion in Britain

Drawing on the earlier *Breadline Britain* survey and the pioneering work of Peter Townsend (who also contributed to this study), David Gordon and his colleagues carried out a similar survey in 2000 called *Poverty and Social Exclusion in Britain* (generally known as the PSE survey). Like

Mack and Lansley, Gordon and his team used a questionnaire to determine what people considered to be 'necessities' for an acceptable standard of life in modern Britain. Based on these responses, they created a list of thirty-five items that more than 50 per cent of the population considered important for a normal life. The list of those items that over half the survey deemed 'necessary' can be seen in table 10.3.

From this list the team found that six of the items – a TV, a fridge, beds and bedding for everyone, a washing machine, medicines prescribed by a doctor and a deep freezer/fridge freezer – did not add to the reliability or validity of the definition of deprivation of necessities in terms of distinguishing between rich and poor, so these were dropped from the analysis. Gordon and his colleagues then set a threshold for deprivation, based on an enforced lack of two or more necessities combined with a low income.

Based on possession of necessities, the PSE survey found that around 72 per cent of people lacked just one or none of the items on the list because they couldn't afford them, although further analysis showed that this figure included approximately 10 per cent of people whose incomes suggested that they were vulnerable to poverty. This left 28 per cent of the sample who lacked two or more necessities, although the surveyors found that this included around 2 per cent whose incomes were high enough to suggest that they had now risen out of poverty, leaving 26 per cent of the population who could be classified as poor. (The results of the survey are summarized in table 10.4.)

Because Gordon and his colleagues followed a similar method to that of Mack and Lansley's two earlier *Breadline Britain* surveys, discussed above, they were also able to use their data to compare how the level of poverty in the UK had changed over time. Comparing the PSE survey, published in 2000, with the two *Breadline Britain* surveys, Gordon et al. found that the number of households that lacked three or more socially perceived necessities (the number set as the poverty threshold in Mack and Lansley's studies) increased substantially over time, from 14 per cent in 1983 to 21 per cent by 1990 and to 24 per cent by 1999. Thus, the PSE survey found that whilst the British population had, as a whole, become much richer since the early 1980s, by 2000, in terms of enforced lack of necessities, there had been a dramatic rise in poverty for those at the bottom. (Later in this chapter we look at the progress made on poverty by the Labour administration, see pp. 374–6.)

Who are the poor?

The face of poverty is diverse and ever-changing, so it is difficult to present a profile of 'the poor'. Yet in the UK as a whole people in certain categories are more likely than others to be living in poverty. In particular, people who are disadvantaged or discriminated against in other aspects of life have an increased chance of being poor. In this section we look at how poverty is patterned in the UK by focusing briefly on several groups that suffer poverty disproportionately compared to the population as a whole: children, women, ethnic minorities and older people. We begin, however, by looking at the regional dimension to poverty.

In the UK, some regions are poorer than others, but as a government report in

Table 10.3   Perception of adult necessities and how many people lack them (all figures show % of adult population)

	Items considered:		Items that respondents:	
	Necessary	Not necessary	Don't have, don't want	Don't have, can't afford
Beds and bedding for everyone	95	4	0.2	1
Heating to warm living areas of the home	94	5	0.4	1
Damp-free home	93	6	3	6
Visiting friends or family in hospital	92	7	8	3
Two meals a day	91	9	3	1
Medicines prescribed by doctor	90	9	5	1
Refrigerator	89	11	1	0.1
Fresh fruit and vegetables daily	86	13	7	4
Warm, waterproof coat	85	14	2	4
Replace or repair broken electrical goods	85	14	6	12
Visits to friends or family	84	15	3	2
Celebrations on special occasions such as Christmas	83	16	2	2
Money to keep home in a decent state of decoration	82	17	2	14
Visits to school, e.g. sports day	81	17	33	2
Attending weddings, funerals	80	19	3	3
Meat, fish or vegetarian equivalent every other day	79	19	4	3
Insurance of contents of dwelling	79	20	5	8
Hobby or leisure activity	78	20	12	7
Washing machine	76	22	3	1
Collect children from school	75	23	36	2
Telephone	71	28	1	1
Appropriate clothes for job interviews	69	28	13	4
Deep freezer/fridge freezer	68	30	3	2
Carpets in living rooms and bedrooms	67	31	2	3
Regular savings (of £10 per month) for rainy days or retirement	66	32	7	25
Two pairs of all-weather shoes	64	34	4	5
Friends or family round for a meal	64	34	10	6
A small amount of money to spend on self weekly, not on family	59	39	3	13
Television	56	43	1	1
Roast joint/vegetarian equivalent once a week	56	41	11	3
Presents for friends/family once a year	56	42	1	3

Table 10.3 *continued*

	Items considered:		Items that respondents:	
	Necessary	Not necessary	Don't have, don't want	Don't have, can't afford
A holiday away from home once a year not with relatives	55	43	14	18
Replace worn-out furniture	54	43	6	12
Dictionary	53	44	6	5
An outfit for social occasions	51	46	4	4

Source: Gordon et al. (2000), p. 14

Table 10.4 Results of the Poverty and Social Exclusion Survey, 2000

Poverty classifications	Percentage (to the nearest whole per cent)
Poor	26
Vulnerable to poverty	10
Risen out of poverty	2
Not poor	62

Source: Gordon et al. (2000), p. 18

December 1999 stressed, the 'disparity within regions is at least as great as that between them' (Cabinet Office 1999). In a recent account of life in 'low-pay Britain' the journalist Polly Toynbee provided an account of the pockets of poverty amongst the wealthy. Leaving an expensive home in Clapham, South London, she moved into a flat in one of the UK's poorest estates, and took a succession of poorly paid jobs. The flat was less than ten minutes' walk from her own front door. She chose to stay close to her home because '[p]overty is not somewhere else, up north in Barrow or Jarrow, it is in the next street, intricately interwoven with wealth. ... There is a far less deep North/South or regional wealth-gap than

the great social divide to be found within each area' (Toynbee 2003).

The proportion of children living in households with an income below 60 per cent of the national average more than doubled between 1979 and 1996/7, from 14 to 34 per cent. The ending of child poverty by 2020 was one of the most ambitious pledges made after Labour came to office in 1997, and they have had some success (see 'New Labour and welfare reform', pp. 374–6 below). In various ways children living in poverty tend to have worse health than those who do not. They are more likely to have a low birth weight, be injured (and killed) in a road accident (because they are more likely to be pedestrians and less likely to have access to a safe play area or garden), suffer abuse, self-harm and attempt suicide. Poorer children are also less likely to do well at school and are far more likely to become poor adults (Flaherty et al., 2004).

Women are more likely to be poor than men, although their poverty has often been masked behind studies that focused on 'male-headed households' (Ruspini, 2000).

The PSE survey carried out by Gordon and his colleagues (2000) found that women comprised 58 per cent of those adults living in poverty. The causes of women's poverty are complex. One important element concerns the gendered division of labour both inside and outside the home. The burden of domestic labour and the responsibility of caring for children and relatives still falls disproportionately on women. This has an important affect on their ambitions and ability to work outside the home. It means that they are far more likely than men to be in part-time, rather than full-time, paid employment and earn less as a result. Although more women are entering paid work in the UK than ever before, amongst the labour force occupational segregation between 'a man's job' and 'women's work' remains entrenched. Women are disproportionately represented in less well-paid industries (Flaherty et al., 2004).

Members of ethnic minority groups are also disproportionately represented among the poor. Pakistani and Bangladeshi individuals, in particular, are far more likely to have an income of less than 60 per cent of the average than individuals of other ethnicities (see table 10.5). Part of the reason for this are the high unemployment and low employment rates for all ethnic minorities in the UK. The unemployment rate for African and Pakistani/Bangladeshi people in 2002, for example, was three times higher than for

Ethnic minority people are amongst the poorest in Western societies, often as a result of high unemployment.

Table 10.5 Percentage of individuals in income fifths, after housing costs, by ethnic group, Great Britain, 2001/2

	Percentage					'000s
	5 (bottom)	4	3	2	1	
White	18	20	20	21	21	52.1
Black Caribbean	34	21	17	13	16	0.8
Black non-Caribbean	43	22	14	12	9	0.6
Indian	26	15	26	16	17	1.0
Pakistani/Bangladeshi	61	20	11	6	3	1.0
Other	37	18	15	12	18	1.5
All individuals	20	20	20	20	20	57.0

Source: Department for Work and Pensions, *Households Below Average Income 1994/5–2001/2*, in Flaherty et al. (2004), p. 188

whites. In the winter of 2002/3, only 58 per cent of people from an ethnic minority were in employment, compared to 76 per cent of the white population. There is also a high degree of labour market segregation. Pakistani groups are heavily concentrated in the former heavy-manufacturing and textile industry areas, such as Yorkshire and Birmingham – industries which fell into recession in the late 1970s and 1980s. Black Caribbean men are over-represented in manual occupations, particularly within the transport and communications industries. Chinese and Bangladeshis are particularly concentrated in the catering industry. There is some evidence to show that some occupational segregation has occurred because ethnic minorities perceive certain industries or employers as 'white', whereas some employers see ethnic minorities as 'outside their recruitment pool' (Performance and Innovation Unit 2002; Flaherty et al. 2004). Ethnic minorities in the UK are also more likely to have poorly paid jobs, struggle at school, live in deprived areas and in poor quality

housing and to suffer health problems (Flaherty et al. 2004).

Many people who may have been reasonably paid during their working lives experience a sharp reduction in income (and status) upon retirement, especially if they did not, or could not afford to, invest in a private pension whilst working. The ageing of the population is putting increasing strain on state pension provision. As life expectancy increases, so does the number of older people in the population. Between 1961 and 2001 the number of people in the UK aged 65 and over more than doubled to 9.4 million. At the age of 65 men can now expect to live, on average, a further 15 years and women a further 20 years.

Life expectancy in the UK is discussed in more detail in chapter 6, 'Socialization, the Life-Course and Ageing', pp. 179–80.

In recent years studies have shown that pensioners are far more likely than the working population to experience persistent poverty. Between 1998 and 2001, 18 per cent of pensioners experienced persistent poverty, compared to 7 per cent of the working population. The number of pensioners with low incomes also increases with age. Studies have also found that in recent decades older women and those from ethnic minorities are more likely to experience poverty then other pensioners

Findings of this kind led the Chancellor of the Exchequer, Gordon Brown, to state in 2002: 'Our aim is to end pensioner poverty in our country.' The introduction of a pension credit in October 2003, which guaranteed a minimum income for people over 60, and promised to raise the income of half of all those people in this age group in the UK, went some way towards meeting this goal. The success of this policy depends, of course, on all of those entitled to claim the benefit actually doing so (Flaherty et al. 2004).

Explaining poverty

Explanations of poverty can be grouped under two main headings: theories that see poor individuals as responsible for their own poverty, and theories that view poverty as produced and reproduced by structural forces in society. These competing approaches are sometimes described as 'blame the victim' and 'blame the system' theories respectively. We shall briefly examine each in turn.

There is a long history of attitudes that hold the poor as responsible for their own disadvantaged positions. Early efforts to address the effects of poverty, such as the poorhouses of the nineteenth century, were grounded in a belief that poverty was the result of an inadequacy or pathology of individuals. The poor were seen as those who were unable – due to lack of

skills, moral or physical weakness, absence of motivation, or below average ability – to succeed in society. Social standing was taken as a reflection of a person's talent and effort; those who deserved to succeed did so, while others less capable were doomed to fail. The existence of 'winners' and 'losers' was regarded as a fact of life.

As we see in our discussion of the rise of the welfare state below (pp. 365–76), accounts of poverty that explain it as primarily an individual failing lost popularity during the mid-twentieth century, but beginning in the 1970s and 1980s they enjoyed a renaissance, as the political emphasis on entrepreneurship and individual ambition rewarded those who 'succeeded' in society, and held those who did not responsible for the circumstances in which they found themselves. Often, explanations for poverty were sought in the lifestyles of poor people, along with the attitudes and outlooks they supposedly espoused. One influential version of this thesis was put forward by the American sociologist Charles Murray (whose work was examined in more detail in chapter 9, pp. 317–21). Murray (1984) argues that there is an underclass of individual who must take personal responsibility for their poverty. This group forms part of a **dependency culture** (see the box on '**welfare dependency**' below, p. 372). By this term, Murray refers to poor people who rely on government welfare provision rather than entering the labour market. He argues that the growth of the welfare state has created a sub-culture that undermines personal ambition and the capacity for self-help. Rather than looking to the future and striving to achieve a better life, the welfare dependent are content to accept handouts. Welfare, Murray argues, has eroded people's incentive to work. Murray does contrast those individuals who must take personal responsibility for their poverty with those who are poor through 'no fault of their own' – such as widows, orphans or people who are disabled, for example.

Theories such as these seem to resonate among the British population. Surveys have shown that the majority of Britons regard the poor as responsible for their own poverty and are suspicious of those who live 'for free' on 'government handouts'. Many believe that people on welfare could find work if they were determined to do so. Yet these views are out of line with the realities of poverty. About a quarter of those living in poverty in the UK are in work anyway, but earn too little to bring them over the poverty threshold. Of the remainder, the majority are children under fourteen, those aged sixty-five and over, and the ill or disabled. In spite of popular views about the high level of welfare cheating, fewer than 1 per cent of welfare applications involve fraudulent claims – much lower than is the case for income tax returns, where it is estimated that more than 10 per cent of tax is lost through misreporting or evasion.

The second approach to explaining poverty emphasizes larger social processes that produce conditions of poverty that are difficult for individuals to overcome. According to such a view, structural forces within society – factors like class, gender, ethnicity, occupational position, educational attainment and so forth – shape the way in which resources are distributed. Writers who advocate structural explanations for poverty argue that the lack of ambition among the poor, which is

often taken for the 'dependency culture', is in fact a consequence of their constrained situations, not a cause of it. Reducing poverty is not a matter of changing individual outlooks, they claim, but requires policy measures aimed at distributing income and resources more equally throughout society. Child care subsidies, a minimum hourly wage and guaranteed income levels for families are examples of policy measures that have sought to redress persistent social inequalities.

The American sociologist William Julius Wilson put forward one important and quite recent version of this 'structural' argument in his book *When Work Disappears: The World of the New Urban Poor* (1996). Wilson's position can be described as the 'economic restructuring' hypothesis. He argues (1987, 1996) that persistent urban poverty stems primarily from the structural transformation of the inner-city economy. The decline of manufacturing industries, the 'suburbanization' of employment and the rise of a low-wage service sector have dramatically reduced the number of jobs available for those immediately leaving education that pay wages sufficient to support a family. The high rate of joblessness resulting from economic shifts has led to a shrinking pool of 'marriageable' men (those financially able to support a family). Thus, marriage has become less attractive to poor women, the number of children born out of wedlock has increased and female-headed families have proliferated. New generations of children are born into poverty, and the vicious cycle is perpetuated. Wilson argues that black Americans suffer disproportionately because of past discrimination and because they are concentrated in locations and occupations particularly affected by economic restructuring.

Wilson argued that these economic changes were accompanied by an increase in the spatial concentration of poverty within black neighbourhoods in the USA. This new geography of poverty, he felt, was due in part to the civil rights movement of the 1960s, which provided middle-class blacks with new opportunities outside the ghetto. The out-migration of middle-class families from ghetto areas left behind a destitute community that lacked the institutions, resources and values necessary for success in post-industrial society. Wilson also acknowledges that such neighbourhoods lack locally available training and education and have suffered from the dissolution of government and private support of local organizations that once supplied job information as well as employment opportunities. Thus, the urban underclass arose from a complex interplay of civil rights policy, economic restructuring and a historical legacy of discrimination.

Evaluation

Both explanations of poverty, as outlined above, have enjoyed broad support, and variations of each view are consistently encountered in public debates about poverty. Critics of the culture of poverty view accuse its advocates of 'individualizing' poverty and blaming the poor for circumstances largely beyond their control. They see the poor as victims, not as freeloaders who are abusing the system. Yet we should be cautious about accepting uncritically the arguments of those who see the causes of poverty as lying exclusively in the structure of society itself. Such an approach implies that the poor simply passively accept the difficult situations in which they find themselves. This is far from the truth, as we shall see below.

Poverty and social mobility

Most research into poverty in the past has focused on people's entry into poverty and has measured aggregate levels of poverty year by year. Less attention has traditionally been paid to the 'life cycle' of poverty – people's trajectories out of (and often back into) poverty over time.

A widely held view of poverty is that it is a permanent condition. Yet being poor does not necessarily mean being mired in poverty. A substantial proportion of people in poverty at any one time have either enjoyed superior conditions of life previously or can be expected to climb out of poverty at some time in the future. Recent research has revealed a significant amount of mobility into and out of poverty: a surprising number of people are successful in escaping poverty, and at the same time a larger number than previously realized live in poverty at some point during their lives.

Statistical findings from the British Household Panel Survey (BHPS) show that just over half of the individuals who were in the bottom fifth (quintile) by income in 1991 were in the same category in 1996 (see table 10.6). This does not necessarily mean that these people remained consistently in the same position over the five-year period, however. While some of them may have done so, others are likely to have risen out of the bottom quintile and returned to it again during that time. The BHPS also reveals that one in ten adults remained consistently in the poorest 20 per cent (bottom quintile) during five out

Table 10.6   Adults moving within the income distribution between 1991 and 1996, Great Britain (%)

	1996 income grouping					
	Bottom fifth	Next fifth	Middle fifth	Next fifth	Top fifth	All adults
1991 income grouping						
Bottom fifth	52	26	12	7	4	100
Next fifth	25	35	22	12	6	100
Middle fifth	11	21	33	23	12	100
Next fifth	7	12	20	37	23	100
Top fifth	4	6	11	21	59	100

Sources: British Household Panel Survey, Institute for Social and Economic Research. From *Social Trends* 29 (1999), p. 98. Crown copyright

of the six years in which the survey was administered, and that over the full period 60 per cent of adults were never in the bottom quintile. On the whole, these findings suggest that about half of the adults in the bottom quintile at any given time are suffering from a constant state of low income, while the other half are moving in and out of the poorest group from year to year (HMSO 1999).

Data on German income patterns between 1984 and 1994 have also revealed significant mobility into and out of poverty. Over 30 per cent of Germans were poor (earning less than half the average, i.e. half the median, income) for at least one year during the decade under review; this represents a figure more than three times higher than the maximum number of poor in any given year (Leisering and Leibfried 1999). Among those who 'escaped' poverty, the average income level attained was about 30 per cent above the poverty line. Yet more than half of those individuals fell back into poverty for at least one year during the ten-year period.

Using data from the UK's New Earnings Survey Panel Dataset and other sources,

Abigail McKnight (2000) has analysed trends in *earnings* mobility in Britain between 1977 and 1997. By tracking groups of low-paid workers, McKnight found a significant amount of persistence in low pay. Her survey showed that around a fifth of employees in the lowest earnings quartile (quarter) are still there six years later. McKnight also found that people who are unemployed, who are amongst the poorest group in Britain, are most likely to gain employment in the lowest-paid sections when they do find work; and that low-paid employees are more likely to go on to experience unemployment than are higher-paid employees.

Scholars have stressed that we should interpret such findings carefully, as they can easily be used by those who wish to scale back on welfare provisions or avoid poverty as a political and social issue altogether. John Hills at the Centre for Analysis of Social Exclusion has cautioned against accepting a 'lottery model' view of income determination. By this he means that we should be sceptical of arguments which present poverty as a 'one-off' outcome that is experienced by people more or less randomly as they move through the income hierarchy. This view suggests that the inequalities between the wealthy and poor in society are not terribly critical; everyone has a chance of being a winner or a loser at some point, so the idea of poverty is no longer a cause for serious concern. Some unlucky individuals may end up having low incomes for several years in a row, the argument goes, but essentially, low income is a random phenomenon.

As Hills points out (1998), the BHPS does reveal a fair amount of short-range mobility on the part of those living in poverty. For example, among individuals in the poorest decile (tenth), 46 per cent were still there the following year. This suggests that more than half of the people in the lowest decile managed to escape from poverty. Yet a closer look shows that 67 per cent of the individuals remain within the bottom two deciles; only one-third progress further than this. Among the bottom fifth of the population by income, 65 per cent were still in the same position a year later; meanwhile, 85 per cent remained in the bottom two-fifths. Such findings suggest that about one-third of low income is 'transient' in nature, while the other two-thirds are not. According to Hills, it is misleading to think that over time the population gradually 'mingles' throughout the income deciles. Rather, many of those who move out of poverty do not advance far, and eventually drift back in again; the 'escape rates' for those who remain at the bottom for more than a year get progressively lower (Hills 1998).

While climbing out of poverty is surely fraught with challenges and obstacles, research findings indicate that movement into and out of poverty is more fluid than is often thought. Poverty is not simply the result of social forces acting on a passive population. Even individuals in severely disadvantaged positions can seize on opportunities to better their positions; the power of human agency to bring about change should not be underestimated. Social policy can play an important role in maximizing the action potential of disadvantaged individuals and communities. In our discussion of welfare later in this chapter, we will draw attention to policy measures designed to relieve poverty by strengthening the labour market, education and training opportunities, and social cohesion.

> Social mobility is also discussed in chapter 9, 'Stratification and Class', pp. 327–32

Social exclusion

What is social exclusion?

The idea of **social exclusion** has been taken up by politicians, but was first introduced by sociological writers to refer to new sources of inequality. Social exclusion refers to ways in which individuals may become cut off from full involvement in the wider society. For instance, people who live in a dilapidated housing estate, with poor schools and few employment opportunities in the area, may effectively be denied opportunities for self-betterment that most people in society have.

The concept of social exclusion raises the question of personal responsibility. After all, the word 'exclusion' implies that someone or something is being shut out by another. Certainly, there are instances in which individuals are excluded through decisions which lie outside their own control. Banks might refuse to grant a current account or credit cards to individuals living in a certain postal code area. Insurance companies might reject an application for a policy on the basis of an applicant's personal history and background. An employee made redundant later in life may be refused further jobs on the basis of his or her age.

But social exclusion is not only the result of people being excluded – it can also result from people excluding themselves from aspects of mainstream society. Individuals can choose to drop out of education, to turn down a job opportunity and become economically inactive, or to abstain from voting in political elections. In considering the phenomenon of social exclusion, we must once again be conscious of the interaction between human agency and responsibility on the one hand, and the role of social forces in shaping people's circumstances on the other.

> The idea that individuals exclude themselves from full participation in society has been developed by Charles Murray in his theory of the underclass, discussed in detail in chapter 9, 'Stratification and Class', pp. 317–21.

Social exclusion is a broader concept than poverty, though it does include it. It focuses attention on a broad range of factors that prevent individuals or groups from having opportunities open to the majority of the population. The PSE survey by David Gordon and his colleagues (see pp. 346–7) distinguishes four dimensions to social exclusion: poverty or exclusion from adequate income or resources (which we have discussed above); labour

market exclusion, service exclusion and exclusion from social relations (Gordon et al. 2000). Below we look at the last three elements of social exclusion.

Labour market exclusion

For the individual, work is important, not just because it provides an adequate income, but also because involvement in the labour market is an important arena for social interaction. Thus, labour market exclusion can lead to the other forms of social exclusion – poverty, service exclusion and exclusion from social relations. Consequently, increasing the number of people in paid work has been seen as an important way to reduce social exclusion by politicians concerned about the issue (see below, pp. 374–6).

To be in a 'jobless household', however, should not necessarily be associated with unemployment. The PSE survey found that 43 per cent of adults (50 per cent of women and 37 per cent of men) are not in paid work. By far the largest group of those who are not active in the labour market are retired (24 per cent of all adults). Other groups who are inactive in the labour market include people involved in domestic and caring activities, those unable to work, perhaps because of disability, and students. Overall, we should be cautious about claiming that labour market inactivity is a sign of social exclusion in itself, because of the high proportion of the population that this involves, but we can say that exclusion from the labour market significantly increases the risk of social exclusion.

Service exclusion

An important aspect of social exclusion is lack of access to basic services, whether these are in the home (such as power and water supplies) or outside it (for example, access to transport, shops or financial services). Service exclusion can involve individual exclusion (when an individual cannot use a service because they cannot afford to do so) or collective exclusion (when a service is unavailable to the community). The PSE survey found that almost a quarter of people are excluded from two or more basic services (see the list in table 10.7) and only just over a half of people had access to the full range of publicly and privately provided services. Table 10.6 shows the levels of collective and individual exclusion from each of the various services.

Exclusion from social relations

There are many ways in which people can be excluded from social relations. First,

Table 10.7   Public and private services used by respondents (%)

	Collective exclusion			Individual exclusion	
	Use – adequate	Use – inadequate	Don't use – unavailable or unsuitable	Don't use – can't afford	Don't use – don't want or not relevant
Public services					
Libraries	55	6	3	0	36
Public sports facilities	39	7	5	1	48
Museums and galleries	29	4	13	1	52
Evening classes	17	2	5	3	73
A public or community village hall	31	3	9	0	56
A hospital with accident/ emergency unit	75	13	2	0	10
Doctor	92	6	0	0	2
Dentist	83	5	1	0	11
Optician	78	3	1	1	17
Post office	93	4	0	0	2
Private services					
Places of worship	30	1	2	0	66
Bus services	38	15	6	0	41
Train or tube station	37	10	10	1	41
Petrol stations	75	2	2	1	21
Chemist	93	3	1	0	3
Corner shop	73	7	8	0	12
Medium to large supermarket	92	4	2	0	2
Banks or building societies	87	7	1	0	4
Pub	53	4	2	2	37
Cinema or theatre	45	6	10	5	33

Source: Gordon et al. (2000), p. 58

this type of exclusion can mean that individuals are unable to participate in common social activities, such as visiting friends and family, celebrating special occasions, spending time on hobbies, having friends round for a meal and taking holidays. Second, people are excluded from social relations if they are isolated from friends and family – the PSE survey found that 2 per cent of people had no contact with either a family member or a friend outside their own house even a few times a year. A third aspect of exclusion from social relations involves a lack of practical and emotional support in times of need – someone to help with heavy jobs around the house or in the garden or to talk to when depressed or to get advice from about important life changes. Fourth, people are excluded from social relations through a lack of civic engagement. Civic engagement includes voting, getting involved in local or national politics, writing a letter to a newspaper or campaigning on an issue one feels strongly about. Lastly, some people are excluded from social relations because they are confined to their home, perhaps due to disability, caring responsibilities or because they feel unsafe on the streets.

Examples of social exclusion

Sociologists have conducted research into the different ways that individuals and communities experience exclusion. Investigations have focused on topics as diverse as housing, education, the labour market, crime, young people and the elderly. We shall now look briefly at three examples of exclusion that have attracted attention in Britain, as well as in other industrialized societies.

Housing and neighbourhoods

The nature of social exclusion can be seen clearly within the housing sector. While many people in industrialized societies live in comfortable, spacious housing, others reside in dwellings that are overcrowded, inadequately heated or structurally unsound. When entering the housing market, individuals are able to secure housing on the basis of their existing and projected resources. Thus, a dual-earning childless couple will have a greater chance of obtaining a mortgage for a home in an attractive area. In recent decades house prices have risen considerably faster than inflation in much of the UK (particularly in the south-east), ensuring that owner-occupiers realize large profits on their property. By contrast, a household whose adults are unemployed or in low-paying jobs may be restricted to less desirable options in the rented or public housing sector.

Stratification within the housing market occurs at both the household and community level. Just as disadvantaged individuals are excluded from desirable housing options, so whole communities can be excluded from opportunities and activities that are norms for the rest of society. Exclusion can take on a spatial dimension: neighbourhoods vary greatly in terms of safety, environmental conditions and the availability of services and public facilities. For example, low-demand neighbourhoods tend to have fewer basic services such as banks, food shops and post offices than do more desirable areas. Community spaces such as parks, sports grounds and libraries may also be limited. Yet people living in disadvantaged places are often dependent on

Run-down housing estates can be sites of intense social exclusion, where many factors combine to prevent full social participation.

what few facilities are available. Unlike residents of more affluent areas, they may not have access to transport (or funds) which would allow them to shop and use services elsewhere.

In deprived communities, it can be difficult for people to overcome exclusion and to take steps to engage more fully in society. Social networks may be weak; this reduces the circulation of information about jobs, political activities and community events. High unemployment and low income levels place strains on family life; crime and juvenile delinquency undermine the overall quality of life in the neighbourhood. Low-demand housing areas often experience high household turnover rates as many residents seek to move on to more desirable housing, while new, disadvantaged entrants to the housing market continue to arrive.

Rural areas

Although much attention is paid to social exclusion in urban settings, people living in rural regions can also experience exclusion. Some social workers and care-givers believe that the challenges of exclusion in the countryside are as large, if not larger, than those in cities. In small villages and sparsely populated areas, access to goods, services and facilities is not as extensive as in more settled areas. In most industrial societies, proximity to basic services such as doctors, schools and government services is considered a necessity for leading an active, full and healthy life. But rural residents often have limited access to such services and are dependent on the facilities available within their local community.

Access to transport is one of the biggest factors affecting rural exclusion. If a household owns or has access to a car, it is easier to remain integrated in society. For example, family members can consider taking jobs in other towns, periodic shopping trips can be arranged to areas that have a larger selection of shops, and visits to friends or family in other areas can be organized more readily. Young people can be fetched home from parties. People who do not have access to their own transport, however, are dependent on public transport, and in country areas such services are limited in scope. Some villages, for example, might be serviced by bus only a few times a day or week, with reduced schedules on weekends and holidays, and none later in the evening.

Homelessness

Homelessness is one of the most extreme forms of exclusion. People lacking a permanent residence may be shut out of many of the everyday activities which others take for granted, such as going to work, keeping a bank account, entertaining friends and even getting letters in the post.

Most homeless people are in some form of temporary accommodation, although there are still many people who sleep rough on the street. Some homeless people deliberately choose to roam the streets, sleeping rough, free from the constraints of property and possessions. But the large majority have no such wish at all; they have been pushed over the edge into homelessness by factors beyond their control. Once they find themselves without a permanent dwelling, their lives sometimes deteriorate into a spiral of hardship and deprivation.

Who sleeps on the streets in Britain? The answer is very complicated. For example, from the 1960s onwards, people with mental health problems and learning difficulties were discharged from institutions as a result of changes in healthcare policy. Before that, these people would have spent years in what used to be called long-stay psychiatric or mental subnormality hospitals. This process of deinstitutionalization was prompted by several factors. One was the desire of the government to save money – the cost of residential care in mental health institutions is high. Another, more praiseworthy motive was the belief on the part of leaders of the psychiatric profession that long-term hospitalization often did more harm than good. Anyone who could be cared for on an out-patient basis therefore should be. The results have not borne out the hopes of those who saw deinstitutionalization as a positive step. Some hospitals discharged people who had nowhere to go and who perhaps had not lived in the outside world for years. Often, little concrete provision for proper out-patient care was in fact made (SEU 1998).

Surveys consistently show that about a quarter of people who sleep rough have spent time in mental health institutions, or have had a diagnosis of mental illness. Hence changes in relevant healthcare policy are likely to have a disproportionate effect on the incidence of homelessness. Most people who are homeless, however,

Homelessness is one of the most complicated, and extreme, forms of social exclusion.

have not suffered mental health problems; nor are they alcoholics or regular consumers of illegal drugs. They are people who find themselves on the streets because they have experienced personal disasters, often several at a time. Becoming homeless is rarely the outcome of a direct 'cause–effect' sequence. A number of misfortunes may occur in quick succession, resulting in a powerful downward spiral. A woman may get divorced, for instance, and at the same time lose not only her home but also her job. A young person may have trouble at home and make for the big city without any means of support. Research has indicated that those who are most vulnerable to home-

lessness are people from lower working-class backgrounds who have no specific job skills and very low incomes. Long-term joblessness is a major indicator. Family and relationship breakdowns also appear to be key influences.

Although the vast majority of people who are homeless manage to sleep in shelters or receive temporary accommodation, those who find themselves sleeping rough are often in danger. Research by the Institute for Public Policy Research (IPPR) into homelessness and street crime in London, Glasgow and Swansea provides the first indication of the extent of victimization suffered by homeless people on the streets. The British Crime Survey, the leading statistical indicator of crime in Britain, does not include homeless people among its respondents. In *Unsafe Streets* (1999), the IPPR revealed that four out of five rough sleepers have been the victims of crime at least once. Almost half of them have been assaulted, yet only one-fifth chose to report the crimes to the police. The picture that emerges is one of homeless people who are victims of high levels of violence on the streets, but who are also excluded from the systems of legal and police protection that might possibly offer some assistance.

While making homelessness a top priority has been universally praised, there is little consensus on how to get people off the streets into permanent housing and leading more stable lives. Advocates for homeless people agree that a more long-term approach – including counselling, mediation services, job training and befriending schemes – is needed. Yet, in the meantime, many charity groups are loath to suspend short-term measures such as delivering soup, sleeping bags and warm clothing to homeless people on the streets. The issue is a controversial one. In trying to shift attention towards the need for permanent solutions, the government's 'homelessness tsar' Louise Casey remarked that 'well-meaning people are spending money servicing the problem on the streets and keeping it there' (quoted in Gillan 1999). Many housing action groups agree. Yet charity and outreach groups such as the Salvation Army take a different approach: as long as there are people living on the streets, they will continue to go to them and offer what assistance they can.

Even though it is not the whole answer, most sociologists who have studied the issue agree that the provision of more adequate forms of housing is of key importance in tackling the multiple problems of facing people who are homeless, whether the housing is directly sponsored by the government or not. As Christopher Jencks concludes in his book *The Homeless* (1994): 'Regardless of why people are on the streets, giving them a place to live that offers a modicum of privacy and stability is usually the most important thing we can do to improve their lives. Without stable housing, nothing else is likely to work.'

Others disagree, stressing that homelessness is only 20 per cent about 'bricks and mortar' and 80 per cent about social work and outreach to counter the effects of family breakdown, violence and abuse, drug and alcohol addictions and depression. Mike, a homeless man in his late fifties, concurs: 'I think that for most people the situation is much more complicated than it seems. Often the problem is about their own belief in themselves, their self worth. A lot of people on the street have low self esteem. They don't believe they can do anything better' (quoted in Bamforth 1999).

Crime and social exclusion

Some sociologists have argued that in industrialized societies such as Britain and the United States there are strong links between crime and social exclusion. There is a trend in modern societies, they argue, away from inclusive goals (based on citizenship rights) and towards arrangements which accept and even promote the exclusion of some citizens (Young 1998, 1999). Crime rates may be reflecting the fact that a growing number of people do not feel valued by – or feel

Social exclusion at the top

The examples of exclusion that we have considered thus far all concern individuals or groups who, for whatever reason, are unable to participate fully in institutions and activities used by the majority of the population. Yet not all cases of exclusion occur among those who are disadvantaged at the bottom of society. In recent years, new dynamics of 'social exclusion at the top' have been emerging. By this, it is meant that a minority of individuals at the very top of society can 'opt out' of participation in mainstream institutions by merit of their affluence, influence and connections.

Exclusion at the top can take a number of forms. The wealthy might retreat fully from the realm of public education and healthcare services, preferring to pay for private services and attention. Affluent residential communities are increasingly closed off from the rest of society – the so-called 'gated communities' located behind tall walls and security checkpoints. Tax payments and financial obligations can be drastically reduced through careful management and the help of private financial planners. Particularly in the United States, active political participation among the elite is often replaced by large donations to political candidates who are seen to represent their interests. In a number of ways, the very wealthy are able to escape from their social and financial responsibilities into a closed, private realm largely separate from the rest of society. Just as social exclusion at the 'bottom' undermines social solidarity and cohesion, exclusion at the 'top' is similarly detrimental to an integrated society.

The very wealthy, including celebrities such as Jennifer Lopez, practise their own form of social exclusion, which can also have detrimental effects.

they have an investment in – the societies in which they live.

Elliott Currie is an American sociologist who has investigated the connections between social exclusion and crime in the United States, particularly among young people. Currie argues that American society is a 'natural laboratory' that is already demonstrating the 'ominous underside' of market-driven social policy: rising poverty and homelessness, drug abuse and sharp increases in violent crime. He notes that young people are increasingly growing up on their own without the guidance and support they need from the adult population. While faced by the seductive lure of the market and consumer goods, young people are also confronted by diminishing opportunities in the labour market to sustain a livelihood. This can result in a profound sense of relative deprivation, and a willingness to turn to illegitimate means of sustaining a desired lifestyle.

According to Currie there are several main links between the growth of crime and social exclusion. First, shifts in the labour market and government taxation and minimum wage policies have led to an enormous growth in both relative and absolute poverty within the American population. Second, this rise in social exclusion is felt in local communities, which suffer from a loss of stable livelihoods, transient populations, increasingly expensive housing and a weakening of social cohesion. Third, economic deprivation and community fragmentation strain family life. Adults in many poor families are forced to take on several jobs in order to survive – a situation which produces perpetual stress, anxiety and absence from home. The socialization and nurturing of children is, as a result, weakened; the overall 'social impoverishment' of the community means that there is little opportunity for parents to turn to other families or relatives for support. Fourth, the state has 'rolled back' many of the programmes and public services that could 'reincorporate' the socially excluded, such as early childhood intervention, child care and mental healthcare.

Finally, the standards of economic status and consumption that are promoted within society cannot be met through legitimate means by the socially excluded population. According to Currie, who echoes Merton's earlier ideas about 'strain' (see chapter 19, p. 797), one of the most troublesome dimensions to this connection between social exclusion and crime is that legitimate channels for change are bypassed in favour of illegal ones. Crime is favoured over alternative means, such as the political system or community organization (Currie 1998).

The welfare state

In most industrialized societies, poverty and social exclusion at the bottom are alleviated to some degree by the **welfare state**. Why is it that welfare states have developed in most industrialized countries? How can we explain the variations in the welfare models favoured by different states? The face of welfare is different from country to country, yet on the whole industrial societies have devoted a large share of their resources to addressing public needs.

Theories of the welfare state

Most industrialized and industrializing countries in the world today are welfare states. By this, it is meant that the state plays a central role in the provision of welfare, which it does through a system that offers services and benefits that meet people's basic needs for things such as healthcare, education, housing and income. An important role of the welfare state is managing the risks faced by people over the course of their lives: sickness, disability, job loss and old age. The services provided by the welfare state and the levels of spending on it vary from country to country. Some countries have highly developed welfare systems and devote a large proportion of the national budget to them. In Sweden, for example, tax revenues represent around 53 per cent of the gross domestic product (GDP). By comparison, other Western nations take far less in tax. In the UK, tax revenues represent around 38 per cent of GDP and in the USA just under 30 per cent (Townsend 2002). In this chapter, we have focused on the role of the welfare state in alleviating poverty. However, the role of the welfare state in providing these services and benefits is discussed throughout the book. Chapter 8 looks at the welfare state and the provision of healthcare, chapter 17 looks at the role of the welfare state in providing education, and chapter 6 looks at the welfare state and the provision of services and benefits for older people.

Many theories have been advanced to explain the evolution of the welfare state. Marxists have seen welfare as necessary for sustaining a capitalist system, while functionalist theorists held that welfare systems helped to integrate society in an orderly way under the conditions of advanced industrialization. While these and other views have enjoyed support over the years, the writings of T. H. Marshall and Gøsta Esping-Andersen have been perhaps the most influential contributions to theories of the welfare state.

T. H. Marshall: citizenship rights

Writing in the 1960s, T. H. Marshall saw welfare as an outcome of the progressive development of citizenship rights alongside the growth of industrial societies. Taking an historical approach, Marshall traced the evolution of citizenship in Britain and identified three key stages. The eighteenth century, according to Marshall, was the time when civil rights were obtained. These included important personal liberties such as freedom of speech, thought and religion, the right to own property, and the right to fair legal treatment. In the nineteenth century, political rights were gained: the right to vote, to hold office and to participate in the political process. The third set of rights – social rights – were obtained in the twentieth century. The right of citizens to economic and social security through education, healthcare, housing, pensions and other services became enshrined in the welfare state. The incorporation of social rights into the notion of citizenship meant that everyone was entitled to live a full and active life and had a right to a reasonable income, regardless of their position in society. In this respect, the rights associated with social citizenship greatly advanced the ideal of equality for all (Marshall 1973).

Marshall's views have been influential in sociological debates over the nature of citizenship and questions of social inclusion and exclusion. The concept of rights and responsibilities is tightly intertwined with the notion of citizenship; these ideas are enjoying popularity in current discussions about how to promote 'active citizenship'. Yet although Marshall's work on citizenship rights remains relevant to contemporary discussions, it is of limited usefulness. Critics have noted that Marshall focused exclusively on the UK in developing his views on citizenship rights; it is not clear that the evolution to welfare has occurred in the same way in other societies.

Gøsta Esping-Andersen: three worlds of welfare

The Danish writer Gøsta Esping-Andersen's *The Three Worlds of Welfare Capitalism* (1990) is a later addition to theories of the welfare state. In this important work, he compares Western welfare systems and presents a three-part typology of 'welfare regimes'. In creating this typology, Esping-Andersen evaluated the level of welfare **decommodification** – a term which simply means the degree to which welfare services are free from the market. In a system with high decommodification, welfare is provided publicly and is not in any way linked to one's income or economic resources. In a commodified system, welfare services are treated more like commodities – that is, they are sold on the market like any other good or service. By comparing policies on pensions, unemployment and income support among countries, Esping-Andersen identified the following three types of welfare regime:

1 *Social democratic* Social democratic welfare regimes are highly decommodified. Welfare services are subsidized by the state and available to all citizens (universal benefits). Most Scandinavian states are examples of a social democratic welfare regime.
2 *Conservative-corporatist* In conservative-corporatist states, such as France and Germany, welfare services may be highly decommodified, but they are not necessarily universal. The amount of benefits to which a citizen is entitled depends on their position in society. This type of welfare regime may not be aimed at eliminating inequalities, but at maintaining social stability, strong families and loyalty to the state.
3 *Liberal* The United States is an example of a liberal welfare regime. Welfare is highly commodified and sold through the market. **Means-tested benefits** are available to the very needy, but become highly stigmatized. This is because the majority of the population is expected to purchase its own welfare through the market.

The United Kingdom does not fall cleanly into any of these three 'ideal types'. Formerly, it was closer to a social democratic model, but welfare reforms since the 1970s have been bringing it closer to a liberal welfare regime with higher levels of commodification.

The welfare state in the UK

One of the main differences between welfare models is the availability of benefits to the population. In welfare systems providing universal benefits, welfare when it is needed is a right to be enjoyed equally by all, regardless of their economic status. An example of this in the UK is the provision of child benefit which goes to the parents or guardians of children under the age of sixteen regardless of their income or savings. Welfare systems predicated on universal benefits are designed to ensure that all citizens' basic welfare needs are met on an ongoing basis. The Swedish system has a higher proportion of universal benefits than the UK one, which depends more on means-tested benefits. 'Means-testing' refers to an administrative process by which the state assesses the actual income (or resources) of an applicant for welfare against its standardized rate, and, if there is a shortfall, makes up the difference as a social security benefit, or provides the service. Examples of means-tested benefits in the UK are Income Support, Housing Benefit and Working Family Tax Credit. Examples of means-tested services are those provided by local authority social services departments as residential care, or part of community care, packages.

This distinction between universal and means-tested benefits is expressed at a policy level in two contrasting approaches to welfare. Supporters of an *institutional* view of welfare argue that access to welfare services should be provided as a right for everyone. Those taking a *residualist* view believe that welfare should only be available to members of society who truly need help and are unable to meet their own welfare needs.

The debate between those who believe in an institutional view of welfare and those who believe in a residualist view is often presented as a dispute about taxation. Welfare services have to be funded through tax. Advocates of the 'safety-net welfare state' approach stress that only the most in need – as demonstrated through means-testing – should be the recipients of welfare benefits. Supporters of a residual view of welfare see the welfare state as expensive, ineffective and too bureaucratic. On the other hand, some feel that tax levels should be high, because the welfare state needs to be well funded. They argue that the welfare state must be maintained and even expanded in order for the state to limit the harsh polarizing effects of the market, even though this means a large tax burden. They claim that it is the responsibility of any civilized state to provide for and protect its citizens. The former Minister for Welfare Reform, Frank Field, whose discussion paper *New Ambitions for Our Country* (1998) is discussed below (p. 374), is a strong critic of means-testing and residualist approaches to welfare. Field resigned from the government in 1998 after a dispute with the Chancellor Gordon Brown, who, Field believed, blocked his proposals for welfare reform and was too sympathetic to the idea of means-testing as a way of regulating delivery of benefits.

This difference of opinion over institutional and residual welfare models is at the heart of current debates over welfare reform. In all industrialized countries, the future of the welfare state is under intense examination. As the face of society changes – through globalization, migration, changes in the family and work, and other fundamental shifts – the nature of welfare must also change. In the next section we shall examine the formation of the welfare state in Britain, the challenges it currently faces and attempts to reform it.

The formation of the British welfare state

The welfare state as we currently know it was created during the twentieth century, yet its roots stretch back to the Poor Laws of 1601 and the dissolution of the monasteries. The monasteries had provided for the poor; without this provision, abject poverty and a near complete absence of care for the sick resulted, leading to the creation of the Poor Laws. With the development of industrial capitalism and the transition from an agricultural to an industrial society, traditional forms of informal support within families and communities began to break down. In order to maintain social order and reduce the new inequalities brought about by capitalism, it was necessary to offer assistance to those members of society who found themselves on the periphery of the market economy. This resulted in 1834 in the Poor Law Amendment Act. Under the

Act, workhouses were built, offering a lower standard of living than anything available outside. The idea was that the living conditions in the poorhouses would make people do all they could to avoid poverty. With time, as part of the process of nation-building, the state came to play a more central role in administering to the needy. Legislation which established the national administration of education and

The introduction in the 1940s of the National Health Service in the UK aimed to improve the health and well-being of the nation.

public health in the late 1800s was a precursor of the more extensive programmes which would come into being in the twentieth century.

The welfare state expanded further under the pre-First World War Liberal government, which introduced, amongst other policies, pensions, health and unemployment insurance. The years following the Second World War witnessed a further powerful drive for the reform and expansion of the welfare system. Rather than concentrating solely on the destitute and ill, the focus of welfare was broadened to include all members of society. The war had been an intense and traumatic experience for the entire nation – rich and poor. It produced a sense of solidarity and the realization that misfortune and tragedy were not restricted to the disadvantaged alone.

This shift from a selective to a universalist vision of welfare had been encapsulated in the Beveridge Report of 1942, often regarded as the blueprint for the modern welfare state. The Beveridge Report was aimed at eradicating the five great evils: Want, Disease, Ignorance, Squalor and Idleness. A series of legislative measures under the post-war Labour government began to translate this vision into concrete action. Several main acts lay at the core of the new universalist welfare state. The wartime National government had already introduced the Education Act in 1944, which tackled lack of schooling, while the 1946 National Health Act was concerned with improving the quality of health among the population. 'Want' was addressed through the 1946 National Insurance Act, which set up a scheme to protect against loss of earnings due to unemployment, ill-health, retirement or widowhood. The 1948 National Assistance Act provided means-tested support for those who were not covered under the National Insurance Act, and finally abolished the old Poor Laws. Other legislation addressed the needs of families (1945 Family Allowances Act) and the demand for improved housing conditions (1946 New Towns Act).

The British welfare state came into being under a set of specific conditions and alongside certain prevailing notions about the nature of society. The premises on which the welfare state was built were threefold. First, it equated work with paid labour and was grounded in a belief in the possibility of full employment. The ultimate goal was a society in which paid work played a central role for most people, but where welfare would meet the needs of those who were located outside the market economy through the mischance of unemployment or disability. Connected to this, the vision for the welfare state was predicated on a patriarchal conception of families – the male breadwinner was to support the family, while his wife tended to the home. Welfare programmes were designed around this traditional family model, with a second tier of services aimed at those families in which a male breadwinner was absent.

Second, the welfare state was seen as promoting national solidarity. It would integrate the nation by involving the entire population in a common set of services. Welfare was a way of strengthening the connection between the state and the population. Third, the welfare state was concerned with managing risks that occurred as a natural part of the life course. In this sense, welfare was viewed as a type of insurance that could be employed against the potential troubles of an unpredictable future. Unemployment, illness and other misfortunes in the country's social and economic life could be managed through the welfare state.

These principles underpinned the enormous expansion of the welfare state in the three decades following the war. As the manufacturing economy grew, the welfare state represented a successful class 'bargain' that met the needs of the working class as well as those of the economic elite who depended on a healthy, high-performing workforce. Yet, as we shall see in the next sections, beginning in the 1970s the splintering of political opinion into institutional and residualist welfare camps became increasingly pronounced. By the 1990s both the left and the right had acknowledged that the conditions under which the welfare state was formed had changed, rendering the Beveridge vision for welfare outmoded and in need of significant reform.

Reforming the welfare state: the Conservative 'roll-back'

The political consensus about the purposes of the welfare state began to break down in the 1970s and intensified during the 1980s when the administrations of Margaret Thatcher in the UK and Ronald Reagan in the USA attempted to 'roll back' the welfare state. Several main criticisms were at the heart of attempts to reduce welfare. The first concerned the mounting financial costs. General economic recession, growing unemployment and the emergence of enormous welfare bureaucracies meant that expenditure continued to increase steadily – and at a rate greater than that of overall economic expansion. A debate over welfare spending ensued, with advocates of a roll-back pointing to the ballooning financial pressure on the welfare system. Policy-makers emphasized the potentially overwhelming impact of the 'demographic time bomb' on the welfare system: the number of people dependent on welfare services was growing as the population aged, yet the number of young people of working age paying into the system was declining. This signalled a potential financial crisis.

The 'greying' of the population is discussed in chapter 6, 'Socialization, the Life-Course and Ageing', pp. 179–80.

A second line of criticism was related to the notion of welfare dependency. Critics of existing welfare institutions argued that people become dependent on the very programmes that are supposed to allow them to forge an independent and meaningful life. They become not just materially dependent, but psychologically dependent on the arrival of the welfare payment. Instead of taking an active attitude towards their lives, they tend to adopt a resigned and passive one, looking to the welfare system to support them (see box on p. 372).

In Britain, the debate over welfare dependency was linked to criticisms of the

Margaret Thatcher's Conservative government (1979–90) heavily criticized the UK's so-called 'dependency culture'.

'nanny state', a phrase suggesting that the government dutifully (but unnecessarily) took care of citizens' every need. The Conservative government under the leadership of Margaret Thatcher promoted individual initiative and self-sufficiency as core values. As part of the turn towards a fully free market economy, reliance on what were described as 'handouts from the state' was discouraged through a series of welfare reforms. Only those who were unable to pay for their own welfare were to receive assistance from the state. The 1988 Social Security Act allowed the state to cut back on welfare expenditures by raising the eligibility criteria for income support, family credit and housing benefit.

The Conservative government implemented a number of welfare reforms that began to shift responsibility for public welfare away from the state towards the private sector, the voluntary sector and local communities. Services which were formerly provided by the state at highly subsidized rates were privatized or made subject to more stringent means-testing. One example of this can be seen in the privatization of council housing in the 1980s. The 1980 Housing Act allowed rents for council housing to be raised significantly, laying the groundwork for a large-scale sell-off of council housing stock. This move towards residualism in housing provision was particularly harmful to those located just above the means-tested eligibility line for housing benefit, as they could no longer get access to public housing, but could ill-afford to rent accommodation at market rates. (Residu-

Welfare dependency

The idea of welfare dependency is a controversial one and some deny that such dependency is widespread. 'Being on welfare' is commonly regarded as a source of shame, they say, and most people who are in such a position probably strive actively to escape from it as far as possible.

Carol Walker has analysed research into how people living on income support manage to organize their lives. She found a picture very different from that painted by those who argue that living on welfare is an easy option. Of unemployed respondents in one study, 80 per cent had experienced a deterioration in their living standards since living on welfare. For nearly all, life became much more of a struggle. For a minority, on the other hand, social assistance can bring improvements in living standards. For instance, someone who is unemployed and reaches the age of sixty is relabelled a 'pensioner claimant' and can claim benefits 30 per cent higher than those previously obtained.

The category of those whose circumstances may improve does in fact include single parents. Research indicates that as many as a third of single parents – almost all of them women – were better off after the break-up of their marriage than they were before. The large majority, however, became worse off.

Only 12 per cent of people living on social assistance in the 1990s said they were 'managing quite well'. Most said they were 'just getting by' or 'getting into difficulties'. Planning ahead is difficult. Money cannot be put aside for the future, and bills are a matter of constant concern. In spite of its importance, food is often treated as an item which can be cut back on when money is short. Walker concludes: 'Despite sensational newspaper headlines, living on social assistance is not an option most people would choose if they were offered a genuine alternative. Most find themselves in that position because of some traumatic event in their lives: loss of a job, loss of a partner or the onset of ill health' (Walker 1994: 9).

alist welfare models were introduced on p. 368.) Critics argue that the privatization of council housing contributed significantly to the growth of homelessness in the 1980s and 1990s.

Another attempt to reduce welfare expenditure and increase its efficiency came through the introduction of market principles in the provision of public services. The Conservative government argued that injecting a degree of competition into welfare services such as healthcare and education would provide the public with greater choice and ensure high-quality service. Consumers could, in effect, 'vote with their feet' by choosing among schools or healthcare providers. Institutions providing substandard services would be obliged to improve or be forced to close down, just like a business. This is because funding for an institution would be based on the number of students, or patients, who chose to use its services. Critics charged that 'internal markets' within public services would lead to lower-quality services and a stratified system of service provision, rather than protecting the value of equal service for all citizens.

Evaluating the Conservative roll-back

To what extent did the Conservative governments of the 1980s succeed in rolling back the welfare state? In *Dismantling the Welfare State?* (1994), Christopher Pierson compares the process of welfare 'retrenchment' in Britain and the USA under the Thatcher and Reagan administrations and concludes that the welfare states emerged from the Conservative era relatively intact. Although both administrations came into office with the express intent of slashing welfare expendi-

ture, Pierson argues that the obstacles to rolling back welfare were ultimately more than either government could overcome. The reason for this lies in the way in which social policy had unfolded over time: since its inception the welfare state and its institutions had given rise to specific constituencies that actively defended the benefits they received against political efforts to reduce them. From organized labour unions to associations of retired persons, an intricate network of interest groups mobilized in support of welfare.

According to Pierson, decisions about welfare retrenchment were guided primarily by a fear of public outcry and backlash. Politicians found that rolling back the welfare state was far from the mirror opposite of welfare expansion. As a result, a new brand of political activity emerged: attempts were made to minimize opposition by compensating 'losing' groups or working to prevent alliances from forming between interest groups. 'Far more than in the era of welfare state expansion,' Pierson writes, 'struggles over social policy become struggles over information about the causes and consequences of policy change' (1994: 8). Those social programmes in which retrenchment did occur, such as unemployment benefit, were generally those in which interest groups were successfully prevented from mobilizing.

Pierson sees the welfare state as under severe strain, but rejects the notion that it is 'in crisis'. Social spending has held fairly constant, he argues, and all the core components of the welfare state remain in place. While not denying the great rise in inequalities as a result of welfare reform in the 1980s, he points out that social policy on the whole was not reformed to the extent that industrial relations or regulatory policy were. In Britain a huge majority of the population continues to rely on public health and education services, while in the United States welfare services are more residualized.

New Labour and welfare reform

Welfare reform remained a top priority for the New Labour government which came to office in the UK in 1997. Agreeing in some respects with Conservative critics of welfare (and breaking with traditional left politics), New Labour argued that new welfare policies are needed to cope with poverty and inequality as well as to improve health and education. The welfare state itself is often part of the problem, creating dependencies and offering a 'hand-out' instead of a 'hand up'. This has resulted in huge bureaucracies that now struggle to manage social problems in their full-blown form, rather than dealing with them pre-emptively at their origin. Such an approach has not proved to be successful in reducing poverty or redistributing income throughout the population. Most of the reduction in poverty, it is argued, is the result of overall increases in wealth rather than social policy.

One of the main difficulties with the welfare system is that the conditions under which it was created have changed significantly. The welfare state was created at a time of full employment. Changes in family structure rendered the patriarchal view of the male breadwinner inapplicable. An enormous number of women had entered the workforce and the growth of lone-parent households has placed new demands on the welfare state. There has also been a distinct shift in the types of risk

that the welfare state needs to contend with.

> The idea of the state as a means of pooling risk was introduced above, p. 365. The concept of the risk society, and its implications for the welfare state, is discussed in chapter 4, 'Theoretical Thinking in Sociology', pp. 119–21.

As an example, the welfare state proved to be an inadequate tool for dealing with the harmful consequences of environmental pollution or lifestyle choices such as smoking.

Soon after arriving in office the government published a discussion paper, *New Ambitions for Our Country: A New Contract for Welfare* (1998), which provided an evaluation of the welfare state and described a vision of 'active welfare' aimed at empowering people in both their careers and personal lives. The paper was largely the work of the then Minister for Welfare Reform, Frank Field, whose opposition to residualist welfare was discussed above (p. 368). Arguing that old solutions to poverty and inequality no longer applied, New Labour advanced the idea of a welfare contract between the state and citizens based on both rights and responsibilities. The role of the state is to help people into work and stable income, not simply to assist them when they are located outside the labour market. At the same time, citizens must build on their action potential in order to change their circumstances, rather than waiting for welfare benefits to be dispensed.

Employment became one of the cornerstones of New Labour social policy and great attention has been paid to the role of dynamic labour markets in welfare reform. The aim to increase the number of people participating in the labour market has been largely successful so far. The employment rate for people of working age in the three months to June 2003 was 75 per cent, the highest for 13 years. The idea behind this approach is that the market not only creates inequalities, but can be part of reducing them as well. Getting people into work and income into households is one of the main steps that can be taken in reducing poverty. Among the most significant welfare reforms introduced under New Labour are the welfare-to-work programmes (see box), whose driving intention is to move recipients from welfare into paid jobs. Welfare-to-work benefits are directed towards encouraging a variety of groups to enter the labour market. Young

Evaluating welfare-to-work programmes

Since 1997 the Labour government has put forward a number of policies and targets to move people from welfare into work. 'New Deal' programmes have been set up for certain groups such as the disabled, the long-term unemployed, young people and those aged over 50. Similar programmes have existed for some time in the United States, and there has been some opportunity there to study their implications. Daniel Friedlander and Gary Burtless studied four different government-initiated programmes designed to encourage welfare recipients to find paid work. The programmes were roughly similar. They provided financial benefits for welfare recipients who actively searched for jobs, as well as guidance in job-hunting techniques and opportunities for education and training. The target populations were mainly single-parent heads of households who were recipients of Aid to Families with Dependent Children, the largest cash welfare programme in the country. Friedlander and Burtless found that the programmes did achieve results. People involved in them were able either to enter employment or to start working sooner than others who didn't participate. In all four programmes, the earnings produced were several times greater than the net cost of the programme. They were least effective, however, in helping those who needed them the most – those who had been out of work for a lengthy period, the long-term unemployed (Friedlander and Burtless 1994).

Although welfare-to-work programmes have succeeded in reducing American welfare claims by approximately 40 per cent, some statistics suggest that the outcomes are not entirely positive. In the USA, approximately 20 per cent of those who cease to receive welfare do not work and have no source of independent income; nearly one-third who do get jobs return to claim welfare again within a year. Between a third and a half of welfare leavers who are in work find that their incomes are less than their previous benefit levels. In Wisconsin, the US state which was one of the first to introduce welfare-to-work programmes, two-thirds of welfare leavers live below the poverty line (Evans 2000). Pointing to such findings, critics argue that the apparent success of welfare-to-work initiatives in reducing the absolute number of welfare cases conceals some troublesome patterns in the actual experiences of those who lose their welfare.

Others question the effectiveness of local empowerment 'zones' for combating social exclusion. They argue that poverty and deprivation are not concentrated in those designated areas alone, yet the programmes are targeted as if all the poor live together. In the UK, the findings of the government's own Social Exclusion Unit back this claim: in 1997, when Labour came to power, two-thirds of all unemployed people lived in areas outside the forty-four most deprived boroughs of the country. Localized initiatives, sceptics point out, cannot replace a nation-wide anti-poverty strategy, because too many people fall outside the boundaries of the designated empowerment zones.

people under the age of twenty-five are offered training and job opportunities instead of receiving state income support; lone parents are granted a tax credit to assist with child care costs; and the long-term unemployed are offered lessons on how to present themselves to employers during job interviews.

As well as the welfare-to-work programmes discussed above, New Labour has also used the welfare state to raise the income of those in low-paid jobs. A minimum wage was introduced in 1999. There have also been reductions in the basic rate of income tax and, in 2003, the introduction of a working tax credit directed at low earners without children. In 1999 a commitment was made to abolish child poverty by 2020. In addition to the changes above, increases in child benefit and means-tested benefit rates for children under the age of eleven were targeted more directly at ending child poverty. The latest assessments show that the government has had some success in its aim, with child poverty falling by a million by 2002 (Piachaud and Sutherland 2002). However, it has been pointed out that even if the ten-year target of halving child poverty by 2010 is met, levels will still be higher than in 1979 when Margaret Thatcher became Prime Minister (Flaherty et al. 2004).

New Labour has also undertaken to improve the social capacity of individuals and communities to 'help themselves' by supporting local initiatives aimed at reducing poverty. Community empowerment zones in health action, employment and education have been created across the country, allowing local policy-makers to design solutions appropriate for the needs of local residents. Such an approach has several benefits. Assistance is targeted in a more direct way, small-scale innovative schemes can be introduced and local participation in decision-making is enhanced. Such programmes promote a more active form of welfare in which citizens are integrally involved in building better lives for themselves in partnership with the state.

The debate over welfare reform has not subsided, although there is a general consensus that change is necessary. The New Labour approach is not without its critics. Some see welfare-to-work programmes as a ruthless way of cutting social expenditure. People unable to enter the labour market, despite training and child-care incentives, risk losing their welfare benefits. Although the programmes are aimed at cutting the conditions for welfare dependency, they can end up forcing those who lose benefits into a life of crime, prostitution or homelessness.

Conclusion: poverty and welfare in a changing world

The theory underlying the policies of Margaret Thatcher's and John Major's governments (1979–97) was that cutting tax rates for individuals and corporations would generate high levels of economic growth, the fruits of which would 'trickle down' to the poor. Similar policies were implemented in the USA during Ronald Reagan's and George Bush Senior's presidencies (1980–92) and again under George Bush Junior (2000–), with comparable results. The evidence does not support the 'trickle-down' thesis. Such an economic policy may or may not generate acceleration of economic development, but the result tends to expand the differentials between the poor and the wealthy, and increase the numbers living in poverty. Both income-based measures of poverty and those based on the deprivation of necessities increased significantly from the late 1970s.

Changes in the occupational structure and the global economy have also contributed to the trend towards inequality in Britain, the United States and elsewhere. A decline in the manual workforce had an important effect both on patterns of income distribution and unemployment. It is often the case that workers in unskilled or semi-skilled jobs have found it difficult to re-enter a rapidly changing labour market where educational qualifications and technological competence are in increasing demand. Although there has been a marked expansion of opportunities in the service sector, much of this has been for positions that are low-paid and with little prospect for advancement.

Politicians on the left have traditionally been intent on eradicating poverty (and increasing equality of outcome) by redistributing wealth from the affluent to the needy. The welfare state and high levels of taxation were two ways in which this was attempted. Such approaches have failed to eradicate poverty, however, and often generated unintended consequences. The large council estates constructed in post-war Britain, sometimes built to rehouse slum-dwellers, became some of the most socially excluded areas in the UK. Similarly, the expansion of the welfare state after 1945 led to a degree of welfare dependency.

Increasingly, new visions of equality are being advanced which diverge from earlier 'left' and 'right' agendas for social policy. The concept of equality is being revised in a more dynamic manner, emphasizing equality of opportunity and the importance of pluralism and lifestyle diversity. Our understandings of inequality are also beginning to change. Although economic inequalities persist, our society is becoming more egalitarian in other ways.

Women are much more equal in economic, social and cultural terms than in previous generations, and significant legal and social advances are being made among minorities. The entry of women into the labour market has meant a growing divide between 'work-rich' households, characterized by dual earners, and 'work-poor' households where no one is active in the labour market. Women's earnings have become more critical to household income than they were in earlier times, and with women occupying influential and highly paid positions in greater numbers than before, the impact of their earnings can carry enormous weight. Indeed, the success of dual-earner households, particularly those without children, is one of the most important factors in the shifting pattern of income distribution. The differences between two-earner, one-earner and no-earner households are becoming increasingly apparent.

Against this backdrop, however, there are new risks and threats facing our societies. These risks do not discriminate between the affluent and the poor. Pollution, destruction to the environment, and the runaway growth of urban areas are problems that we have manufactured ourselves. They are threats for which we are all responsible and which demand lifestyle changes from everyone if they are to be managed.

As we begin to address these new challenges, the role of the state and welfare services is necessarily coming under review. Welfare is not simply about material prosperity, but about the overall well-being of the population. Social policy is concerning itself with promoting social cohesion, fostering networks of interdependence and maximizing people's abilities to help themselves. Rights and responsibilities are taking on new importance – not only for those at the bottom attempting to move off welfare into work, but also for those at the top whose wealth does not entitle them to evade civic, social and fiscal duties.

Summary points

1   There are two different ways of understanding poverty. Absolute poverty refers to a lack of the basic resources needed to maintain health and effective bodily functioning. Relative poverty involves assessing the gaps between the living conditions of some groups and those enjoyed by the majority of the population.

2   In many countries official measurements of poverty are made in relation to a poverty line, a level below which people are said to live in poverty. Subjective measurements of poverty are based on people's own understandings of what is required for an acceptable standard of living.

3   Poverty is widespread in the affluent countries. In the 1980s and 1990s Britain gained one of the worst poverty records in the developed world. Inequalities between the rich and poor widened dramatically as a result of government policies, changes in the occupational structure and unemployment.

4   The poor are a diverse group, but individuals who are disadvantaged or discriminated against in other aspects of life (such as older people, children, women and ethnic minorities) have an increased chance of being poor.

5   Two main approaches have been taken to explain poverty. The 'culture of poverty' and 'dependency culture' arguments claim that the poor are responsible for their own disadvantages. Due to a lack of skills, an absence of motivation or a moral weakness, the poor are unable to succeed in society. Some of them become dependent on outside assistance, such as welfare provision, rather than helping themselves. The second approach argues that poverty results from larger social processes, which are both reinforced and influenced by the action of individuals.

6   Social exclusion refers to processes by which individuals may become cut off from full involvement in the wider society. Social exclusion is a wider term than poverty, though lack of resources and income is one dimension of social exclusion. Other aspects of social exclusion include exclusion from the labour market, services and social relations. Homelessness is one of the most extreme forms of social exclusion. Homeless people lacking a permanent residence may be shut out of many everyday activities which most people take for granted.

7   Welfare states are those in which the government plays a central role in reducing inequalities in the population through the provision or subsidization of certain goods and services. Welfare services vary from country to country, but often include education, healthcare, housing, income

support, disability, unemployment and pensions.

8 In welfare states that provide universal benefits, welfare at times of need is a right to be equally enjoyed by all, regardless of income level or economic status. Means-tested benefits, by contrast, are made available only to some individuals, whose eligibility is determined on the basis of low income and little or no savings. The future of welfare provision is being debated in most industrialized countries. On the one side are those who believe that welfare should be well funded and universal; on the other are people who believe it should serve only as a safety net for those who truly cannot otherwise get help.

9 The present British welfare state developed in the twentieth century, undergoing periods of expansion during the pre-First World War Liberal government and the post-war Labour government. It was oriented to a broad vision of welfare that included all members of society. By the 1970s the welfare state was being criticized as ineffective, bureaucratic and too expensive. There was concern over welfare dependency – when people become dependent on the very programmes that are supposed to help them to lead an independent life.

10 Margaret Thatcher's Conservative government attempted to roll back the welfare state by shifting responsibility for public welfare away from the state to the private sector, the voluntary sector and local communities. Deinstitutionalization is the process by which individuals cared for by the state (in institutions) are returned to their families and communities.

11 The New Labour government has carried out a raft of measures on welfare reform, including welfare-to-work programmes aimed at moving welfare recipients into paid jobs and reducing child poverty.

Questions for further thought

1 Look again at the opening paragraphs of this chapter: why is Carol poor?

2 What level of income would you need in order to participate 'fully and meaningfully' in society?

3 Why did rates of poverty increase in the UK from the mid-1970s?

4 Does welfare dependency provide an explanation for the persistence of poverty?

5 What are the causes of homelessness and how best can it be tackled?

6 Why have efforts to reduce welfare spending largely failed?

Further reading

Jet Bussemaker (ed.), *Citizenship and Welfare State Reform in Europe* (London: Routledge, 1999).

H. Dean, *Welfare Rights and Social Policy* (Harlow: Prentice Hall, 2002).

Jan Flaherty, John Veit-Wilson and Paul Dornan, *Poverty: The Facts*, 5th edn (London: CPAG, 2004).

Gordon Hughes and Ross Ferguson (eds), *Ordering Lives: Family, Work and Welfare* (London: Routledge, 2000).

Ruth Lister, *Poverty* (Cambridge: Polity, 2004).

T. H. Marshall, *Citizenship and Social Class, and Other Essays* (Cambridge: Cambridge University Press, 1950).

J. Pierson, *Tackling Social Exclusion* (London: Routledge, 2001).

T. Ridge, *Childhood Poverty and Social Exclusion* (Bristol: Policy Press, 2002).

Robert Walker (ed.), *Ending Child Poverty: Popular Welfare for the Twenty-First Century?* (Bristol: Policy Press, 1999).

Internet links

Social Exclusion Unit
http://www.socialexclusion.unit.gov.uk

Child Poverty Action Group
http://www.cpag.org.uk/

Monitoring Poverty and Social Exclusion
http://www.poverty.org.uk/

Opportunity for All
http://www.dwp.gov.uk/ofa/

The Social Market Foundation
http://www.smf.co.uk/

Contents

11 Global Inequality

THE PAST quarter of a century has seen the appearance of more global billionaires than ever before in history. By the beginning of the twenty-first century there were 573 billionaires worldwide – 308 in the United States, 114 in Europe, 88 in Asia, 32 in Latin America, 15 in Canada, 13 in the Middle East, and 3 in Australia (Forbes 2000) (here, a billionaire is defined as someone with wealth of at least a thousand million $US). Their combined assets in mid-2000 were estimated at $1.1 trillion – greater than the total gross national products of eighty-seven countries representing more than a third of the world's population (calculated from World Bank 2000–1).

In 2004, the wealthiest individual in the world was Microsoft Corporation's founder Bill Gates, with a net worth of £25.3 billion (see table 11.1). Gates, whose fortune is based largely on ownership of his company's stock, would seem the personification of the entrepreneurial spirit: a computer nerd turned capitalist whose software provides the operating system for nearly all personal computers. During the late 1990s, Gates had a net worth of around $100 billion. Shortly after reaching this peak, the lofty value of Microsoft's stock began to decline, leaving Gates's fortune greatly reduced but still sufficient

for him to rank as the wealthiest individual in the world (Forbes 2004).

The wealthiest individual in the UK in 2004, with £7.5 billion was Roman Abramovich, best known in Britain as owner of Chelsea Football Club. Abramovich comes from a poor background in Russia, was orphaned at the age of four and at one time sold car tyres to supplement his income. After the collapse of the Soviet Union in the early 1990s, he made a fortune from the privatization of the Russian oil industry. The Duke of Westminster, who came second on the UK list, with £5.5 billion, is the owner of large chunks of property in Mayfair and Belgravia – two of the most expensive locations in London. Others in the top ten include Philip Green, the owner of the Arcadia retailing group, in fourth place with $3.6 billion, which includes the high street outlets British Home Stores, Top Man, Top Shop and Miss Selfridges; and Sir Richard Branson, in sixth place, whose Virgin group has made money from music, trains, planes, mortgages, mobile phones and even bridal gowns, giving him a personal fortune of £2.6 billion (see table 9.3 on p. 312).

Among the world's top forty richest individuals and families in 2004, sixteen were from North America, fifteen were from Europe (including Russia), six were from the Middle East, two were from Hong Kong and one was from Mexico (Forbes 2004). If Bill Gates typifies the Western, high-tech entrepreneur, Hong Kong's Li Ka-shing – who was number 25 on the list – is the hero in a rags-to-riches story that characterizes the success of many Asian businessmen. Li (his surname) began his career by making plastic flowers; in 2004, his $6.7 billion in personal wealth derived from a wide range of real estate and other

Table 11.1   The 40 richest individuals and families in the world, 2004

	Name	Country	Business	Wealth
1	Robson Walton and family	America	Retail (Wal-Mart)	£54.2bn
2	Bill Gates	America	Software (Microsoft)	£25.3bn
3	Warren Buffett	America	Investments	£23.3bn
4	Karl & Theo Albrecht and family	Germany	Supermarkets	£22.3bn
5	Forrest Jr & John Mars and family	America	Confectionery	£16.9bn
6	King Fahd and family	Saudi Arabia	Oil	£13.5bn
7	Barbara Cox Anthony and Anne Cox Chambers	America	Media	£12.1bn
8	Prince Alwaleed	Saudi Arabia	Investments	£11.6bn
9	Paul Allen	America	Software (Microsoft)	£11.4bn
10=	Sheikh of Abu Dhabi	Abu Dhabi	Oil, investments	£10.8bn
10=	Johanna Quandt and family	Germany	Cars (BMW)	£10.8bn
12	Liliane Bettencourt	France	Cosmetics	£10.2bn
13	Larry Ellison	America	Computers (Oracle)	£10.1bn
14	Ingvar Kamprad	Sweden	Retail (Ikea)	£10bn
15	Kenneth Thomson	Canada	Media, oil	£9.3bn
16	Samuel & Donald Newhouse	America	Publishing	£8.3bn
17	Robert & Thomas Pritzker	America	Hotels, investments	£8.2bn
18=	Emir of Kuwait	Kuwait	Oil	£8.1bn
18=	Mikhail Khodorkovsky	Russia	Oil	£8.1bn
20	Abigail & Edward Johnson	America	Investments	£8bn
21	Sultan of Brunei	Brunei	Oil	£7.7bn
22=	Roman Abramovich	UK	Oil, investments	£7.5bn
22=	Carlos Slim Helu	Mexico	Telecoms	£7.5bn
24	Michael Dell	America	Computers (Dell)	£7bn
25=	Steve Ballmer	America	Software (Microsoft)	£6.7bn
25=	The Brenninkmeyer family	Holland	Retail	£6.7bn
25=	Li Ka-shing	Hong Kong	Industry	£6.7bn
28	Bernard Arnault	France	Luxury goods	£6.6bn
29	The Kwok brothers	Hong Kong	Property	£6.2bn
30	John Kluge	America	Media, phones	£5.7bn
31=	Silvio Berlusconi	Italy	Media	£5.4bn
31=	Sheikh Makhtoum	UAE	Oil, financial services	£5.4bn
33=	Birgit Rausing and family	Sweden	Packaging	£5bn
33=	The Duke of Westminster	UK	Property	£5bn
35=	Charles Ergen	America	Satellite TV	£4.9bn
35=	Amancio Ortega	Spain	Fashion	£4.9bn
35=	Hans Rausing and family	UK	Packaging	£4.9bn
38	Sumner Redstone	America	Media	£4.8bn
39=	The Oeri/Hoffmann family	Switzerland	Pharmaceuticals	£4.7bn
39=	Stefan Persson	Sweden	Retail	£4.7bn

Source: *Sunday Times* (18 April 2004)

investments throughout Asia, including family ownership of STAR TV, a television-transmission satellite whose broadcasts reach half the world.

Globalization, the increased economic, political, social and cultural interconnect-edness of the world, has produced the opportunities for unthinkable wealth. A glance at the lists of the wealthiest people in the UK and around the world shows that most of them could describe their riches as 'new entrepreneurial wealth', rapidly made during the course of one individual's life. (Fewer people on the lists are rich because of inherited wealth, passed down from one generation to the next, although there are exceptions, such as the (sixth) Duke of Westminster – the second richest person in the UK.) Both Roman Abramovich, the richest person in the UK, and Bill Gates, the world's richest individual, exemplify this kind of new entrepreneurial wealth. Both of these multi-billionaires were born into relatively modest backgrounds in their respective countries before gaining fantastic economic success. Both men benefited from globalization: Abramovich

Sir Richard Branson is one of the wealthiest people in the UK, although his fortune is dwarfed by figures such as Bill Gates.

Many millions of workers are employed in 'sweatshops' across the globe, working long hours in poor conditions for little financial reward.

through buying up sections of the Russian oil industry in the 1990s as the country sold its nationalized industries on the global market, and Gates through his involvement with some of the new information and communication technologies that drive globalization. (The idea of globalization was introduced in chapter 2.)

Yet the benefits of globalization have been uneven, and are not enjoyed by all. Consider, for example, Wirat Tasago, a twenty-four-year-old garment worker in Bangkok, Thailand. Tasago – along with more than a million other Thai garment workers, most of whom are women – labours from 8 a.m. until about 11 p.m. six days a week, earning little more than the equivalent of £2 pounds an hour (Dahlburg 1995). Billions of workers such as Tasago are being drawn into the global labour force, many working in oppressive conditions that would be unacceptable, if not unimaginable, under UK employment laws, such as the minimum wage. And these are the fortunate ones: although many countries, such as Russia, have found engagement in the global economy socially and economically difficult, especially initially, the populations of those societies that have remained outside the world economy, such as North Korea, have typically fared far worse.

In the previous chapter, we examined poverty and social exclusion in the UK, noting large differences among individuals' income, wealth, work and quality of life. The same is true to an even greater scale in the world as a whole. Just as we can speak of rich or poor individuals within a country, so we can talk about rich or poor people or countries in the world system. In this chapter, we look at global inequality in the late twentieth and early twenty-first centuries. We begin with a brief discussion of what is understood by the term 'global inequality', and how our definition of the term changes how we think about it. We examine what differences in economic standards of living mean for people throughout the world. We then turn to the newly industrializing countries of the world to understand which countries are improving their fortunes and why. This will lead us to a discussion of different theories that attempt to explain why global inequality exists and what can be done about it. We conclude this section by speculating on the future of economic inequality in a global world. From an examination of global inequality, we then move to an account of global population growth, a trend occurring at its greatest pace in some of the poorest countries in the world.

Economic inequality is only one form of global social inequalities. Because of the gross economic inequalities in the world today, and because space is necessarily limited in a book of this kind, this chapter focuses on economic inequality rather than other forms. Inequalities of status, such as those associated with stigmatization and exclusion are examined in other chapters. (The concept of stigmatization, for example, is discussed in chapter 8, p. 269.) The world is also characterized by enormous inequalities of power, particularly within dictatorial regimes. This inequality of power exists both between and within states and is an important source of many of the world's most entrenched conflicts. (We discuss political power and inequality in chapter 20.)

Global economic inequality

Global economic inequality refers primarily to the systematic differences in wealth, incomes and working conditions that exist between countries. These differences between countries exist alongside differences within countries: even the wealthiest countries today have growing numbers of poor people, while less wealthy nations are producing many of the world's super-rich. Sociology's challenge is not merely to identify all such differences, but to explain why they occur – and how they might be overcome.

One way to classify countries in terms of global inequality is to compare their economic productivity. One important measure of economic productivity is **Gross Domestic Product** or GDP. A country's GDP is made up of all the goods and services on record as being produced by a country's economy in a particular year. Income earned abroad by individuals or corporations is not included in GDP. An important alternative measure is Gross **National Income** or GNI. (GNI was formally referred to as Gross National Product or GNP). Unlike GDP, GNI *includes* income earned by individuals or corporations outside the country. Measures of economic activity, such as GDP or GNI, are often given per person; this allows us to compare the wealth of an average inhabitant of a country. In order to compare different countries, we need to use a common currency. Most international institutions, such as the World Bank, use the US dollar.

The World Bank is an international lending organization that provides loans for development projects in poorer countries. It uses per person GNI to classify countries as high-income, upper-middle-income, lower-middle-income or low-income. This system of classification will help us to understand more easily why there are such vast differences in living standards between countries.

The World Bank (2003) divides 132 countries, containing nearly 6 billion people, into the three economic classes. (There are 74 other economies in the world, encompassing about 178 million people, for whom the World Bank did not provide data, either because the data were lacking or because the economies had fewer than 1.5 million people.) While 40 per cent of the world's population lives in low-income countries, only 15 per cent live in high-income countries. Bear in mind that this classification is based on *average* income for each country; it therefore masks income inequality *within* each country. Such differences can be significant, although we do not focus on them in this chapter. For example, the World Bank classifies India as a low-income country, since its per-person GNI in 1999 was only $450. Yet despite widespread poverty,

India also boasts a large and growing middle class. China, on the other hand, was reclassified in 1999 from low- to middle-income, since its GNI per capita in that year was $780 (recall the World Bank's lower limit for a middle-income country is $756). Yet even though its average income now confers middle-class status on China, it nonetheless has hundreds of millions of people living in poverty.

Comparing countries on the basis of income alone, however, may be misleading, since GNI includes only goods and services that are produced for cash sale. Many people in low-income countries are farmers or herders who produce for their own families or for barter, involving non-cash transactions. The value of their crops and animals is not taken into account in the statistics. Further, economic output is not a country's whole story. Countries possess unique and widely differing languages and traditions. Poor countries are no less rich in history and culture than their wealthier neighbours, even though the lives of their people are much harsher.

Even if we do compare countries solely on the basis of economic statistics, the statistics that we choose for our comparisons are likely to make a difference to our conclusions. For example, if we choose to study global inequality by comparing levels of *household consumption* (of, say, food, medicine or other products) rather than GNI, we might reach a different conclusion on global inequality. We could also choose to take into account other factors. A comparison of the GNI of several countries is all very well, but it doesn't take into account how much things actually cost in a country. For example, if two countries have a more or less equal GNI, but in the first an average meal costs a family just a few cents, whereas in the second a meal costs a few dollars, then we might conclude that it is misleading to argue that they are equally wealthy – after all, in the first country one gets considerably more for one's money (in practice, the difference is unlikely to be this exaggerated). Instead, the surveyor might choose to compare *purchasing power parities* (PPP) that eliminate the difference in prices between two countries. *The Economist* magazine uses a famous measure of PPP with its light-hearted Big Mac Index, which compares the cost of the hamburger – made with identical ingredients, as we will see in chapter 16, pp. 636–7 – in different countries. In this chapter we concentrate on comparisons of GNI between countries, but you should always be aware that several other measures are also commonly used.

High-income countries

The *high-income countries* are generally those that were the first to industrialize, a process that began in England some 250 years ago and then spread to Europe, the United States and Canada. It was only about thirty years ago that Japan joined the ranks of high-income, industrialized nations, while Singapore, Hong Kong and Taiwan moved into this category during the 1980s and 1990s. The reasons for the success of these Asian latecomers to industrialization are much debated by sociologists and economists. We will look at these reasons later in the chapter.

High-income countries account for only 15 per cent of the world's population (roughly 891 million people) – yet lay claim to 79 per cent of the world's annual output of wealth (derived from World Bank 2000–1). High-income countries

offer decent housing, adequate food, drinkable water and other comforts unknown in many parts of the world. Although these countries often have large numbers of poor people, most of their inhabitants enjoy a standard of living unimaginable by the majority of the world's people.

Middle-income countries

The *middle-income countries* are primarily found in East and Southeast Asia, the oil-rich countries of the Middle East and North Africa, the Americas (Mexico, Central America, Cuba and other countries in the Caribbean, and South America), and the once Communist republics that formerly made up the Soviet Union and its East European allies. Most of these countries began to industrialize relatively late in the twentieth century and therefore are not yet as industrially developed (nor as wealthy) as the high-income countries. The countries that once comprised the Soviet Union, on the other hand, are highly industrialized, although their living standards have been eroded since the collapse of communism and the move to capitalist economies. In Russia, for example, the wages of ordinary people dropped by nearly a third between 1998 and 1999, while retirement pensions dropped by nearly half: millions of people, many of them elderly, suddenly found themselves destitute (CIA 2000).

In 1999, middle-income countries included 45 per cent of the world's population (2.7 billion people) but accounted for only 18 per cent of the wealth produced in that year. Although many people in these countries are substantially better off than their neighbours in low-income countries, most do not enjoy anything resembling the standard of living common in high-income countries. The ranks of the world's middle-income countries expanded between 1999 and 2000, at least according to the World Bank's system of classification, when China – with 1.3 billion people (22 per cent of the world's population) – was reclassified from low- to middle-income because of its economic growth. This reclassification is somewhat misleading, however. China's average per person income of $1,100 per year in 2003 is quite close to the cut-off for low-income countries (at $766), and a large majority of its population in fact are in the low-income category by World Bank standards.

Low-income countries

Finally, the *low-income countries* include much of eastern, western and sub-Saharan Africa; Vietnam, Cambodia, Indonesia and a few other East Asian countries; India, Nepal, Bangladesh and Pakistan in South Asia; East and Central European countries such as Georgia and Ukraine; and Haiti and Nicaragua in the Western Hemisphere. These countries mostly have agricultural economies and are only recently beginning to industrialize. Scholars debate the reasons for their late industrialization and widespread poverty, as we will see later in this chapter.

In 1999, the low-income countries included 40 per cent of the world's population (2.4 billion people) yet produced only 3 per cent of the world's yearly output of wealth. What is more, this inequality is increasing. Fertility is much higher in low-income countries than elsewhere, where large families provide additional farm labour or otherwise contribute to family income. (In wealthy industrial societies, where children are more likely to be in school than on the farm, the economic benefit of large families declines, and so people tend to have fewer children.) Because of this, the populations of low-income countries (with the principal exception of India) are growing more than three times as fast as those of high-income countries (World Bank 2003). (Global population growth is discussed in detail on pp. 418–28.) In many of these low-income countries, people struggle with poverty, malnutrition and even starvation. Most people live in rural areas, although this is rapidly changing. Hundreds of millions of people are moving to huge, densely populated cities, where they live either in dilapidated housing or on the open streets (see chapter 21, 'Cities and Urban Spaces').

Is global economic inequality increasing?

The question of whether global inequality is rising or falling has polarized opinion in recent years. Protesters have argued that globalization creates inequality, whilst its defenders argue that globalization is a great levelling force between the world's rich and poor. The first dramatic changes in global inequality occurred more than two centuries ago with the Industrial Revolution, as Europe, and then other regions, underwent rapid economic expansion, leaving the rest of the world far behind in terms of wealth.

Those who believe that global inequality is expanding argue that in the last few decades globalization has exacerbated the trend towards inequality that began with industrialization. Globalization's critics cite statistics of the kind used in the UN Human Development Report (UNDP 1999), which noted that in 1960, 20 per cent of the world's people in the rich countries had thirty times the income of the poorest 20 per cent; by 1997, they had seventy-four times the income of the poorest 20 per cent (quoted in *The Economist*, 18 July 2002).

By contrast, others have pointed out that over the last few decades the overall standard of living in the world has slowly risen. Many indicators that measure the living standards of the world's poorest people show improvements. Illiteracy is down, infant death rates and malnutrition are falling, people are living longer, and poverty (often defined as the number of people living on less than either one or two dollars a day) is down.

However, there are substantial differences between countries. Many of these gains have been in the high- and middle-income countries, while living standards in many of the poorest countries have declined. Indeed, whilst the 1990s was a time of economic boom for the world's richest country, the United States, the UN Human Development Report for 2003 found that more than fifty countries, located mainly in sub-Saharan Africa, suffered falling living standards during the decade as a result of famine, the global AIDS epidemic, conflict and failed economic policies.

As the above disputes show, the way we chose to measure global inequality makes a big difference to the conclusions that we reach on the issue. The economist Stanley Fischer compared two ways of looking at global income inequality: the first simply compares income inequality between countries; the second takes into account

the number of people living in those countries as well. The first way of looking at global inequality is shown in figure 11.1a. It shows the average income of a selection of poor and rich countries between 1980 and 2000, with each country represented on the graph by a uniform dot. The figure shows that during this period the average income of the poorest nations grew much more slowly than the average income of the world's richest nations. Hence, the trend (shown by the black line) appears to show inequality increasing as the economies of the richer countries on the right of the graph grow more quickly than those of the poorer countries (on the left). (If the poorest countries had grown faster than the richest, the black trends line would slope down from left to right.) The gap between the richest and the poorest of the world's countries therefore appears to be growing.

The second chart, which takes into account the population size of the countries, presents a rather different view on global inequality. Figure 11.1b shows the same chart, but this time the dots that represent each country have been drawn in proportion to the size of the number of people living in that country. What is particularly noticeable about this graph is that two of the world's biggest countries – India and China, which between them account for well over one-third of the world's population – have increased the sizes of their economies considerably since 1980. Because of the size of these two countries, a population-weighted line of best fit drawn through the second chart would slope downwards, implying that global inequality is falling, as, on average, the populations of the poorest countries catch up.

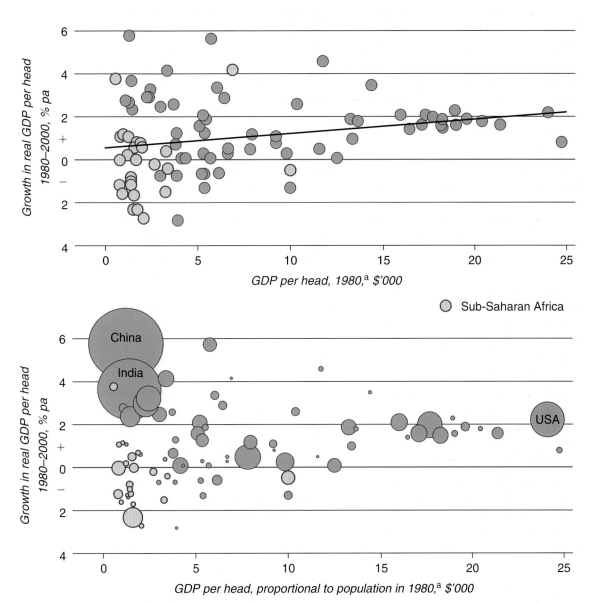

Figure 11.1 Two ways of looking at global income inequality

[a] 1996 prices

Source: *The Economist* (11 March 2004)

Once we take account of the fact that China and India have performed so well economically since 1980, and especially since 1990, together with the fact that these two countries account for such a big share of the world's poorest people, global poverty appears to be relatively stable. Those countries that have done best economically in the period since 1980 – like India, China and Vietnam, for example – also tend to be those countries that have integrated most successfully into the global economy. The enormous inequality still found *within* those countries that have grown economically in recent decades means that some critics have asked at what price integration into the global economy comes.

Life in rich and poor countries

An enormous gulf in living standards separates most people in rich countries from their counterparts in poor ones (Harvard Magazine 2000). Wealth and poverty make life different in a host of ways. For instance, about one-third of the world's poor are undernourished, and almost all are illiterate and lack access to even primary school education. While most of the world is still rural, within a decade there are likely to be more urban than rural poor.

> Urbanization in developing countries is discussed in more detail in chapter 21, 'Cities and Urban Spaces', pp. 918–21.

Many of the poor come from tribes or racial and ethnic groups that differ from the dominant groups of their countries, and their poverty is at least in part the result of discrimination.

Here we look at differences between high- and low-income countries in terms of health, starvation and famine, and education and literacy.

Health

People in high-income countries are far healthier than their counterparts in low-income countries. Low-income countries generally suffer from inadequate health facilities, and when they do have hospitals or clinics, these seldom serve the poorest people. People living in low-income countries also lack proper sanitation, drink polluted water and run a much greater risk of contracting infectious diseases. They are more likely to suffer malnourishment, starvation and famine. These factors all contribute to physical weakness and poor health, making people in low-income countries susceptible to illness and disease. There is growing evidence that high rates of HIV/AIDS infection found in many African countries are due in part to the weakened health of impoverished people (Stillwagon 2001).

Because of poor health conditions, people in low-income countries are more likely to die in infancy and less likely to live to old age than people in high-income countries. Infants are eleven times more likely to die at birth in low-income countries than they are in high-income countries, and – if they survive birth – they are likely to live on average eighteen years fewer (see table 11.3). Children often die of illnesses that are readily treated in wealthier countries, such as measles or diarrhoea. In some parts of the world, such as sub-Saharan Africa, a child is more likely to die before the age of five than to enter secondary school (World Bank 1996). Still,

Table 11.2   The global quality of life has risen during the past 30 years

Quality of life indicator	1968	1998
Percentage illiterate	53	30
Average number of children per woman	6	3
Number of children who die in first year	1 in 4	1 in 8
Number of infants who die each year	12 million	7 million
Number of people suffering from malnutrition	4 out of 10	2 out of 10
Life expectancy at birth	50 years	61 years
Annual per person income	roughly $700	roughly $1,100
Percentage living on less than $1/day	roughly 50	roughly 25

Source: Salter (1998)

conditions have improved in low- and middle-income countries: between 1980 and 1998, for example, the infant mortality rate dropped from 97 (per thousand live births) to 68 in low-income countries and from 60 to 31 in middle-income countries.

During the past three decades, some improvements have occurred in most of the middle-income countries of the world and in some of the low-income countries as well. Throughout the world, infant mortality has been cut in half, and average life expectancy has increased by ten years or more. The wider availability of modern medical technology, improved sanitation and rising incomes account for these changes.

Hunger, malnutrition and famine

Hunger, malnutrition and famine are major global sources of poor health. These problems are nothing new. What seems to be new is their extent – the fact that so many people in the world today appear to be on the brink of starvation (see figure 11.2). A study by the United Nations World Food Program (UNWFP 2001) estimated that 830 million people go hungry every day, 95 per cent of them in developing countries. The programme defines 'hunger' as a diet of 1,800 or fewer calories a day – an amount insufficient to provide adults with the nutrients required for active, healthy lives.

According to the World Food Programme study, 200 million of the world's hungry are children under the age of five, who are underweight because they lack adequate food. Every year hunger kills an estimated 12 million children. As one ten-year-old child from the west African country of Gabon told researchers from the World Bank: 'When I leave for school in the mornings I don't have any breakfast. At noon there is no lunch, in the evening I get a little supper, and that is not enough. So when I see another child eating, I watch him, and if he doesn't give me something I think I'm going to die of hunger' (Narayan 1999). Yet more than three-quarters of all malnourished children under the age of five in the world's low- and middle-income countries live in countries that actually produce a food surplus (Lappe 1998). It has been estimated that the amount the population of the United States spends on pet food each year ($13 billion) would eradicate much of the

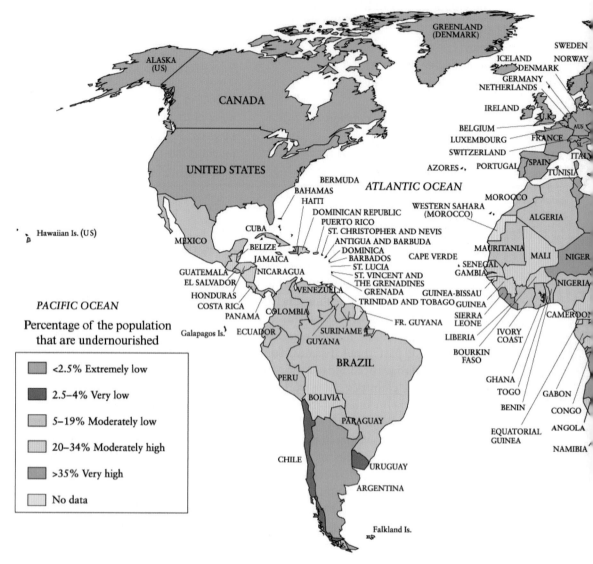

Figure 11.2 Hunger is a global problem

Source: UNWFP (2001)

world's human hunger (*Bread for the World Institute* 2005).

Most famine and hunger today are the result of a combination of natural and social forces. Drought alone affects an estimated 100 million people in the world today. In countries such as Sudan, Ethiopia, Eritrea, Indonesia, Afghanistan, Sierra Leone, Guinea and Tajikistan, the combination of drought and internal warfare has devastated food production, resulting in starvation and death for millions of people.

In Latin America and the Caribbean, 53 million people (11 per cent of the population) are malnourished – a number that rises to 180 million (33 per cent) in sub-Saharan Africa, and 525 million (17 per cent) in Asia (UNWFP 2001).

The AIDS epidemic has also contributed to the problem of food shortages and hunger, killing many working-age adults. A study by the United Nations Food and Agricultural Association (FAO) has predicted that HIV/AIDS-caused deaths in

Every year hunger, resulting from both natural and social causes, kills about 12 million children.

the ten African countries most afflicted by the epidemic will reduce the labour force by 26 per cent by the year 2020. Of the estimated 26 million people worldwide infected with HIV, 95 per cent live in developing countries. According to the FAO, the epidemic can be devastating to nutrition, food security and agricultural production, affecting 'the entire society's ability to maintain and reproduce itself' (UN FAO 2001).

The countries affected by famine and starvation are for the most part too poor to pay for new technologies that would increase their food production. Nor can they afford to purchase sufficient food imports from elsewhere in the world. At the same time, paradoxically, as world hunger grows, food production continues to increase. Between 1965 and 1999, for example, world production of grain doubled. Even allowing for the substantial world population increase over this period, the global production of grain per person was 15 per cent higher in 1999 than it was thirty-four years earlier. This growth, however, is not evenly distributed around the world. In much of Africa, for example, food production per person declined in recent years. Surplus food produced in high-income countries such as the United States is seldom affordable to the countries that need it most.

Education and literacy

Education and literacy are important routes to economic development. Here, again, lower-income countries are disadvantaged, since they can seldom afford

Table 11.3   Differences in education and literacy: low-, middle- and high-income countries

	Income level		
	Low	Middle	High
Percentage of children of official secondary school age (as defined in each country) enrolled in full-time education, 1997	51	71	96
Public expenditure on education as percentage of GNP, 1997	3.3	4.8	5.4
Percentage of males over the age of 15, illiterate, 1998	30	10	0
Percentage of females over the age of 15, illiterate, 1998	49	20	0

Source: World Bank (2000–1)

high-quality public education systems. As a consequence, children in high-income countries are much more likely to get schooling than are children in low-income countries, and adults in high-income countries are much more likely to be able to read and write (see table 11.4). While virtually all secondary school-aged males and females are still in full-time education in high-income countries, in 1997, only 71 per cent are in middle-income countries and only 51 per cent in low-income countries. In low-income countries, 30 per cent of male adults and almost half of female

Education plays a crucial role in countries' economic development, but low-income nations' schools are often underfunded.

adults are unable to read and write. One reason for these differences is a sizeable gap in public expenditures on education: high-income countries spend a much larger percentage of their gross domestic product on education than do low-income countries (World Bank 2000–1).

Education is important for several reasons. First, as noted, it contributes to economic growth, since people with advanced schooling provide the skilled work necessary for high-wage industries. Second, education offers the only hope for escaping from the cycle of harsh working conditions and poverty, since poorly educated people are condemned to low-wage, unskilled jobs. Finally, educated people are less likely to have large numbers of children, thus slowing the global population explosion that contributes to global poverty.

Child labour

Does child labour still exist in the world today? According to the United Nations International Labour Organization (UNILO), more than 250 million boys and girls between the ages of five and fourteen are working in developing countries, about one out of every four children in the world. Some 50–60 million children between the ages of five and eleven work under hazardous conditions. Child labour is found throughout the developing world – in Asia (61 per cent of the children are engaged in labour), Africa (32 per cent), and Latin America (7 per cent). They are forced to work because of a combination of family poverty, lack of education and traditional indifference among some people in many countries to the plight of those who are poor or who are ethnic minorities (ILO 2000; UNICEF 2000).

Two-thirds of working children labour in agriculture, with the rest in manufacturing, wholesale and retail trade, restaurants and hotels, and a variety of services, including working as servants in wealthy households. At best, these children work for long hours with little pay and are therefore unable to go to school and develop the skills that might eventually enable them to escape their lives of poverty. However, simply enforcing an immediate ban on all child labour, even if it were possible, might be counter-productive. Child labour is a better alternative to child prostitution or starvation, for example. The challenge is not just to end child labour, but also to move children from work into education, and to ensure that they are properly provided for during their school years. Child labour must be fought in a way that does not cause more harm to the children.

The worst forms of child labour are hazardous and exploitative. Work is carried out under slave-like conditions, and children suffer a variety of illnesses and injuries. The UNILO provides a grisly summary: 'Wounds, broken or complete loss of body parts, burns and skin diseases, eye and hearing impairment, respiratory and gastro-intestinal illnesses, fever, headaches from excessive heat in the fields or factories' (ILO 2000).

A United Nations report provides several examples:

In Malaysia, children may work up to 17-hour days on rubber plantations, exposed to insect and snake bites. In the United Republic of Tanzania, they pick coffee, inhaling pesticides. In Portugal, children as young as twelve are subject to the heavy labour and myriad dangers of the construction industry. In Morocco, they hunch at looms for long hours and little pay, knotting the strands of luxury carpets for export. In the United States, children are exploited in garment industry sweatshops. In the Philippines, young boys dive in dangerous conditions to help set nets for deep-sea fishing.

Conditions in many factories are horrible:

Dust from the chemical powders and strong vapours in both the storeroom and the boiler room were obvious. . . . We found 250 children, mostly below ten years of age, working in a long hall filling in a slotted frame with sticks. Row upon row of children, some barely five years old, were involved in the work. (UNICEF 1997)

One form of child labour that is close to slavery is 'bonded labour'. In this system children as young as eight or nine are pledged by their parents to factory owners in exchange for small loans. These children are paid so little that they never manage to reduce the debt, condemning them to a lifetime of bondage. One case of bonded labour that attracted international attention was that of Iqbal Masih, a Pakistani child who, at the age of four, was sold into slavery by his father in order to borrow 600 rupees (roughly $16) for the wedding of his first-born son. For six years, Iqbal spent most of his time chained to a carpet-weaving loom, tying tiny knots for hours on end. After fleeing the factory at the age of ten, he began speaking to labour organizations and schools about his experience. Iqbal paid a bitter price for his outspokenness: when he was thirteen, while riding his bicycle in his hometown, he was gunned down by agents believed to be working for the carpet industry (www.freethechildren.org; Bobak 1996).

Abolishing exploitative child labour will require countries around the world to enact strong laws against the practice and be willing to enforce them. International organizations, such as the UNILO, have outlined a set of standards for such laws to follow. In June 1999, the UNILO adopted Convention 182, calling for the abolition of the 'Worst Forms of Child Labour'. These are defined as including:

- all forms of slavery or practices similar to slavery, such as the sale and trafficking of children, debt bondage and serfdom, and forced or compulsory labour, including forced or compulsory recruitment of children for use in armed conflict;
- the use, procuring or offering of a child for prostitution, for the production of pornography, or for pornographic performances;
- the use, procuring or offering of a child for illicit activities, in particular for the production and trafficking of drugs as defined in the relevant international treaties; and
- work that, by its nature or the circumstances in which it is carried out, is likely to harm the health, safety, or morals of children. (ILO 1999)

Countries must also provide free public education and require that children attend school full time (UNICEF 2000). But at least part of the responsibility for solving the problem lies with the global corporations that manufacture goods using child labour – and, ultimately, with the consumers who buy those goods.

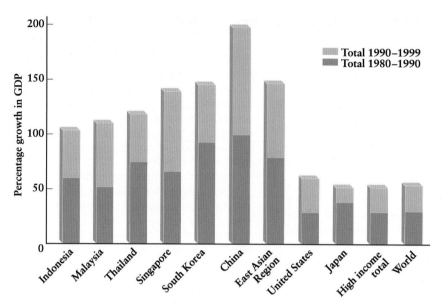

Figure 11.3   Percentage growth in GDP in selected East Asian countries, the United States and the world as a whole, 1980–1990 and 1990–1999

Source: World Bank (2000–1); World Development Indicators (2003)

Can poor countries become rich?

As we saw in chapter 2, by the mid-1970s, a number of low-income countries in East Asia were undergoing a process of industrialization that appeared to threaten the global economic dominance of the United States and Europe (Amsden 1989). This process began with Japan in the 1950s but quickly extended to the **newly industrializing countries** (NICs), that is, the rapidly growing economies of the world, particularly in East Asia but also in Latin America. The East Asian NICs included Hong Kong in the 1960s and Taiwan, South Korea and Singapore in the 1970s and 1980s. Other Asian countries began to follow in the 1980s and the early 1990s, most notably

China, but also including Malaysia, Thailand and Indonesia. Today, most are middle-income, and some – such as Hong Kong, South Korea, Taiwan, and Singapore – have moved up to the high-income category.

Figure 11.3 compares the economic growth of seven East Asian countries (including Japan) with the United States, from 1980 to 1999. These are all places that were poor only two generations ago. The low- and middle-income economies of the East Asian region as a whole averaged 7.7 per cent growth a year during that period, a rate that is extraordinary by world standards (World Bank 2000–1). By 1999, the gross domestic product per person in Singapore was virtually the same as that in the United States. China, the world's most populous country, has one of the most rapidly growing economies on the planet. At an average annual growth rate of 10 per cent between 1980 and 1999, the Chinese economy doubled in size.

Economic growth in East Asia has not been without its costs. These have included the sometimes violent repression of labour and civil rights, terrible factory conditions, the exploitation of an increasingly female workforce, the exploitation of immigrant workers from impoverished neighbouring countries and widespread environmental degradation. Nonetheless, thanks to the sacrifices of past generations of workers, large numbers of people in these countries are prospering.

How do social scientists account for the rapid economic growth in the East Asian NICs, especially from the mid-1970s through to the mid-1990s? The answer to this question may hold some crucial lessons for those low-income countries elsewhere that hope to follow in the steps of the NICs. Although the NICs' success is partly due to historically unique factors, it is also due to factors that could lead to a rethinking about the causes of global inequality. To understand the rapid development of this region, we need to view these countries both historically and within the context of the world economic system today.

The economic success of the East Asian NICs can be attributed to a combination of factors. Some of these are historical, including those that stem from world political and economic shifts. Some are cultural. Still others have to do with the ways these countries have pursued economic growth. Some of the factors that aided their success are as follows:

1 *Historically, Taiwan, South Korea, Hong Kong and Singapore were once part of colonial situations that, while imposing many hardships, also helped to pave the way for economic growth.* Taiwan and Korea were tied to the Japanese Empire; Hong Kong and Singapore were former British colonies. Japan eliminated large landowners who opposed industrialization, and both Britain and Japan encouraged industrial development, constructed roads and other transportation systems, and built relatively efficient governmental bureaucracies in these particular colonies. Britain also actively developed both Hong Kong and Singapore as trading centres (Gold 1986; Cumings 1987). Elsewhere in the world – for example, in Latin America and Africa – countries that are today poor did not fare so well in their dealings with richer, more powerful nations.

2 *The East Asian region benefited from a long period of world economic growth.* Between the 1950s and the mid-1970s, the growing economies of Europe and the United States provided a substantial market for the clothing, footwear and electronics that were increasingly being made in East Asia, creating a 'window of opportunity' for economic development. Furthermore, periodic economic slowdowns in the United States and Europe forced businesses to cut their labour costs and spurred the relocation of factories to low-wage East Asian countries (Henderson and Appelbaum 1992). One World Bank study (World Bank 1995) found that between 1970 and 1990, wage increases averaged 3 per cent yearly in developing countries where economic growth was led by exports to wealthier countries, while

wages failed to increase elsewhere in the developing world.

3 *Economic growth in this region took off at the high point of the Cold War, when the United States and its allies, in erecting a defence against Communist China, provided generous economic and military aid.* Direct aid and loans fuelled investment in such new technologies as transistors, semiconductors and other electronics, contributing to the development of local industries. Military assistance frequently favoured strong (often military) governments that were willing to use repression to keep labour costs low (Mirza 1986; Cumings 1987, 1997; Castells 1992).

4 *Some sociologists argue that the economic success of Japan and the East Asian NICs is due in part to their cultural traditions, in particular, their shared Confucian philosophy.* Nearly a century ago, Max Weber (1977) argued that the Protestant belief in thrift, frugality and hard work partly explained the rise of capitalism in Western Europe. Weber's argument has been applied to Asian economic history. Confucianism, it is argued, inculcates respect for one's elders and superiors, education, hard work and proven accomplishments as the key to advancement as well as a willingness to sacrifice today to earn a greater reward tomorrow. As a result of these values, the Weberian argument goes, Asian workers and managers are highly loyal to their companies, submissive to authority, hardworking and success-oriented. Workers and capitalists alike are said to be frugal. Instead of living lavishly, they are likely to reinvest their wealth in further economic growth (Berger 1986; Wong 1986).

This explanation has some merit, but it overlooks the fact that businesses are not always revered and respected in Asia. During the late 1950s, pitched battles occurred between workers and capitalists in Japan – as they did in South Korea in the late 1980s. Students and workers throughout the East Asian NICs have opposed business and governmental policies they felt to be unfair, often at the risk of imprisonment and sometimes even their lives (Deyo 1989; Ho 1990). Furthermore, such central Confucian cultural values as thrift appear to be on the decline in Japan and the NICs, as young people – raised in the booming prosperity of recent years – increasingly value conspicuous consumption over austerity and investment (Helm 1992).

5 *Many of the East Asian governments followed strong policies that favoured economic growth.* Their governments played active roles in keeping labour costs low, encouraged economic development through tax breaks and other economic policies and offered free public education. We shall discuss the role of East Asian government policies later in this chapter.

Whether the growth of these economies will continue is unclear. In 1997–8, a combination of poor investment decisions, corruption and world economic conditions brought these countries' economic expansion to an abrupt halt. Their stock markets collapsed, their currencies fell and the entire global economy was threatened. The experience of Hong Kong was typical: after thirty-seven years of continuous growth, the economy stalled and its stock market lost more than half its value. It remains to be seen whether the 'Asian meltdown', as the newspapers called it in early 1998, will have a long-term effect on the region or is merely a blip in its recent growth. Once their current economic problems are solved, many economists believe, the newly industrializing Asian economies will resume their growth, although perhaps not at the meteoric rates of the past.

Theories of development

What causes global inequality? How can it be overcome? In the box on pp. 406–7, we look at some of the issues facing poor countries. In this section, we shall examine four different kinds of theory that have been advanced over the years to explain development: market-oriented, dependency, world systems and state-centred theories. These theories have strengths and weaknesses. One shortcoming of all of them is that they frequently give short shrift to the role of women in economic development. By putting the theories together, however, we should be able to answer a key question facing the 85 per cent of the world's population living outside high-income countries: how can they move up in the world economy?

Market-oriented theories

Forty years ago, the most influential theories of global inequality advanced by British and American economists and sociologists were **market-oriented theories**. These theories assume that the best possible economic consequences will result if individuals are free – uninhibited by any form of governmental constraint – to make their own economic decisions. Unrestricted capitalism, if it is allowed to

develop fully, is said to be the avenue to economic growth. Government bureaucracy should not dictate which goods to produce, what prices to charge or how much workers should be paid. According to market-oriented theorists, governmental direction of the economies of low-income countries results in blockages to economic development. In this view, local governments should get out of the way of development (Rostow 1961; Warren 1980; Ranis 1996).

One of the most influential early proponents of such theories was W. W. Rostow, an economic adviser to former US President John F. Kennedy, whose ideas helped shape US foreign policy towards Latin America during the 1960s. Rostow's explanation is one version of a market-oriented approach, termed 'modernization theory'. **Modernization theory** argues that low-income societies can develop economically only if they give up their traditional ways and adopt modern economic institutions, technologies and cultural values that emphasize savings and productive investment.

According to Rostow (1961), the traditional cultural values and social institutions of low-income countries impede their economic effectiveness. For example, many people in low-income countries, in Rostow's view, lack a strong work ethic; they would sooner consume today than invest for the future. Large families are also seen as partly responsible for 'economic backwardness', since a breadwinner with many mouths to feed can hardly be expected to save money for investment purposes.

But to modernization theorists, the problems in low-income countries run even deeper. The cultures of such countries, according to the theory, tend to

Issues in global inequality

Poverty

Most of sub-Saharan Africa is in the World Bank's lowest income category of less than $765 Gross National Income (GNI) per person per year. Ethiopia and Burundi are the worst off with just $90 GNI per person.

Even middle-income countries like Gabon and Botswana have sizeable sections of the population living in poverty.

North Africa generally fares better than sub-Saharan Africa. Here, the economies are more stable, trade and tourism are relatively high and AIDS is less prevalent.

Development campaigners are urging the G8 to reform the rules on debt, aid and trade to help lift more African nations out of poverty.

Debt

The Heavily Indebted Poor Countries initiative (HIPC) was set up in 1996 to reduce the debt of the poorest countries.

Poor countries are eligible for the scheme if they face unsustainable debt that cannot be reduced by traditional methods. They also have to agree to follow certain policies of good governance as defined by the World Bank and the IMF.

Once these are established the country is at 'decision point' and the amount of debt relief is established.

Critics of the scheme say the parameters are too strict and more countries should be eligible for HIPC debt relief.

This map shows how much 'decision point' HIPC countries spend on repaying debts and interest.

Fourteen African HIPC countries will have their debts totally written off under a new plan drawn up by the G8 finance ministers.

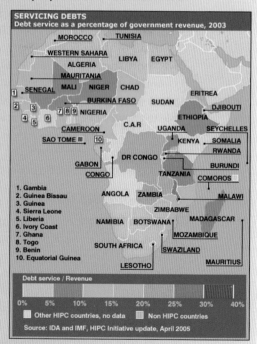

AFRICA'S INCOME
Gross National Income per capita, 2003

1. Gambia
2. Guinea Bissau
3. Guinea
4. Sierra Leone
5. Liberia
6. Ivory Coast
7. Ghana
8. Togo
9. Benin
10. Equatorial Guinea

WORLD BANK CATEGORY:

LOW INCOME	LOWER MIDDLE INCOME	UPPER MIDDLE INCOME
<$250	$766-$1,500	$3,036 - $5,000
$251-$500	$1,501-$2,500	$5,001-$7,500
$501-$765	$2,501-$3,035	$7,501-$9,385
No available data		

Source: World Bank - World Development Indicators database 2005

SERVICING DEBTS
Debt service as a percentage of government revenue, 2003

1. Gambia
2. Guinea Bissau
3. Guinea
4. Sierra Leone
5. Liberia
6. Ivory Coast
7. Ghana
8. Togo
9. Benin
10. Equatorial Guinea

Debt service / Revenue

0%   5%   10%   15%   20%   25%   30%   40%

Other HIPC countries, no data   Non HIPC countries

Source: IDA and IMF, HIPC Initiative update, April 2005

Sources: http://news.bbc.co.uk/l/shared/spl/hi/africa/05/africa_economy/html/poverty.stm
http://news.bbc.co.uk/l/shared/spl/hi/africa/05/africa_economy/html/debt.stm

Aid

Africa receives about a third of the total aid given by governments around the world, according to the Organization for Economic Co-operation and Development.

Much of this has conditions attached, meaning governments must implement certain policies to receive the aid or must spend the money on goods and services from the donor country.

The World Bank, which is reviewing its conditionality policies, argues that aid is far more effective, and less vulnerable to corruption, when coupled with improved governance.

There was a sharp drop in rich countries' relative spending on aid in the late 1990s.

The Make Poverty History campaign is urging the G8 to raise an extra $50bn more in aid per year and to enforce earlier pledges for developed countries to give 0.70% of their annual GDP in aid.

Trade

Africa is rich in natural resources such as minerals, timber and oil but trade with the rest of the world is often difficult.

Factors include poor infrastructure, government instability, corruption and the impact of AIDS on the population of working age.

Poorer countries and agencies such as Oxfam also argue that international trade rules are unfair and favour the developed world.

They say rich countries 'dump' subsidized products on developing nations by undercutting local producers.

And they accuse the World Trade Organization (WTO) of forcing developing nations to open their markets to the rest of the world but failing to lower rich countries' tariff barriers in return.

But the WTO says that low-income countries receive special treatment, including exemption from some regulations that apply to richer nations.

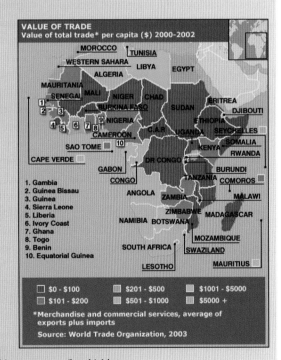

Sources: http://news.bbc.co.uk/l/shared/spl/hi/africa/05/africa_economy/html/aid.stm
http://news.bbc.co.uk/l/shared/spl/hi/africa/05/africa_economy/html/trade.stm

support 'fatalism' – a value system that views hardship and suffering as the unavoidable plight of life. Acceptance of one's lot in life thus discourages people from working hard and being thrifty in order to overcome their fate. In this view, then, a country's poverty is due largely to the cultural failings of the people themselves. Such failings are reinforced by government policies that set wages and control prices and generally interfere in the operation of the economy. How can low-income countries break out of their poverty? Rostow viewed economic growth as going through several stages, which he likened to the journey of an aeroplane:

1 *The traditional stage.* This is the stage just described. It is characterized by low rates of savings, the supposed lack of a work ethic, and the so-called fatalistic value system. The aeroplane is not yet off the ground.

2 *Take-off to economic growth.* The traditional stage, Rostow argued, can give way to a second one: economic take-off. This occurs when poor countries begin to jettison their traditional values and institutions and start to save and invest money for the future. The role of wealthy countries, like the United States, is to facilitate this growth. They can do this by financing birth control programmes or providing low-cost loans for electrification, road and airport construction, and starting new industries.

3 *Drive to technological maturity.* According to Rostow, with the help of money and advice from high-income countries, the aeroplane of economic growth would taxi down the runway, pick up speed and become airborne. The country would then approach technological maturity. In the aeronautical metaphor, the plane would slowly climb to cruising altitude, improving its technology, reinvesting its recently acquired wealth in new industries and adopting the institutions and values of the high-income countries.

4 *High mass consumption.* Finally, the country would reach the phase of high mass consumption. Now people are able to enjoy the fruits of their labour by achieving a high standard of living. The aeroplane (country) cruises along on automatic pilot, having entered the ranks of high-income countries.

Rostow's ideas remain influential. Indeed, perhaps the prevailing view among economists today, **neo-liberalism**, argues that free-market forces, achieved by minimizing governmental restrictions on business, provide the only route to economic growth. Neo-liberalism holds that global free trade will enable all countries of the world to prosper; eliminating governmental regulation is seen as necessary for economic growth to occur. Neo-liberal economists therefore call for an end to restrictions on trade and often challenge minimum wage and other labour laws, as well as environmental restrictions on business.

Sociologists, on the other hand, focus on the cultural aspects of Rostow's theory: whether and how certain beliefs and institutions hinder development (Davis 1987; So 1990). These include religious values, moral beliefs, belief in magic, and folk traditions and practices. Sociologists also examine other conditions that resist change; particularly the belief local cultures have that moral decay and social unrest accompany business and trade.

Dependency and world system theories

During the 1960s, a number of theorists questioned market-oriented explanations of global inequality such as modernization theory. Many of these critics were sociologists and economists from the low-income countries of Latin America and Africa, who drew on Marxist ideas to reject the idea that their countries' economic underdevelopment was due to their own cultural or institutional faults. Instead, they build on the theories of Karl Marx, who argued that world capitalism would create a class of countries manipulated by more powerful countries, just as capitalism within countries leads to the exploitation of workers. The **dependency theorists**, as they are called, argue that the poverty of low-income countries stems from their exploitation by wealthy countries and the multinational corporations that are based in wealthy countries. In their view, global capitalism locked their countries into a downward spiral of exploitation and poverty.

According to dependency theories, this exploitation began with **colonialism**, a political-economic system under which powerful countries established, for their own profit, rule over weaker peoples or countries. Powerful nations have colonized other countries usually to procure the raw materials needed for their factories and to control markets for the products manufactured in those factories. Under colonial rule, for example, the petroleum, copper, iron and food products required by industrial economies are extracted from low-income countries by businesses based in high-income countries. Although colonialism typically involved European countries establishing colonies in North and South America, Africa and Asia, some Asian countries (such as Japan) had colonies as well.

Even though colonialism ended throughout most of the world after the Second World War, the exploitation did not: transnational corporations continued to reap enormous profits from their branches in low-income countries. According to dependency theory, these global companies, often with the support of the powerful banks and governments of rich countries, established factories in poor countries, using cheap labour and raw materials to maximize production costs without governmental interference. In turn, the low prices set for labour and raw materials prevented poor countries from accumulating the profit necessary to industrialize themselves. Local businesses that might compete with foreign corporations were prevented from doing so. In this view, poor countries are forced to borrow from rich countries, thus increasing their economic dependency.

Low-income countries are thus seen not as underdeveloped, but rather as mis-developed (Frank 1966; Emmanuel 1972). With the exception of a handful of local politicians and businesspeople who serve the interests of the foreign corporations, people fall into poverty. Peasants are forced to choose between starvation and working at near-starvation wages on foreign-controlled plantations and in foreign-controlled mines and factories. Since dependency theorists believe that such exploitation has kept their countries from achieving economic growth, they typically call for revolutionary changes that would push foreign corporations out of their countries altogether (e.g. Frank 1969).

While political and military power is usually ignored by market-oriented theorists, dependency theorists regard the exercise of power as central to enforcing unequal economic relationships. According to this theory, whenever local leaders question such unequal arrangements, their voices are quickly suppressed. Unionization is usually outlawed, and labour organizers are jailed and sometimes killed. When people elect a government opposing these policies, that government is likely to be overthrown by the country's military, often backed by the armed forces of the industrialized countries themselves. Dependency theorists point to many examples: the role of the CIA in overthrowing the Marxist governments of Guatemala in 1954 and Chile in 1973 and in undermining support for the leftist government in Nicaragua in the 1980s. In the view of dependency theory, global economic inequality is thus backed up by force: economic elites in poor countries, backed by their counterparts in wealthy ones, use police and military power to keep the local population under control.

Brazilian sociologist Enrique Fernando Cardoso, once a prominent dependency theorist, argued more than twenty-five years ago that some degree of dependent development was nonetheless possible – that under certain circumstances, poor countries can still develop economically, although only in ways shaped by their reliance on the wealthier countries (Cardoso and Faletto 1979). In particular, the governments of these countries could play a key role in steering a course between dependency and development (Evans 1979). As President of Brazil from 1995 to 2003, Cardoso changed his thinking, calling for greater integration of Brazil into the global economy.

During the last quarter of a century, sociologists have increasingly seen the world as a single (although often conflict-ridden) economic system. Although dependency theories hold that individual countries are economically tied to one another, **world-systems theory**, which is strongly influenced by dependency theory, argues that the world capitalist economic system is not merely a collection of independent countries engaged in diplomatic and economic relations with one another, but must instead be understood as a single unit. The world-systems approach is most closely identified with the work of Immanuel Wallerstein and his colleagues (Wallerstein 1974, 1990 and elsewhere). Wallerstein showed that capitalism has long existed as a global economic system, beginning with the extension of markets and trade in Europe in the fifteenth and sixteenth centuries. The world system is seen as comprising four overlapping elements (Chase-Dunn 1989):

- a world market for goods and labour;
- the division of the population into different economic classes, particularly capitalists and workers;
- an international system of formal and informal political relations among the most powerful countries, whose competition with one another helps shape the world economy; and
- the carving up of the world into three unequal economic zones, with the wealthier zones exploiting the poorer ones.

World-systems theorists term these three economic zones 'core', 'periphery' and 'semi-periphery'. All countries in the world system are said to fall into one of the three categories. **Core countries** are the most advanced industrial countries, taking the lion's share of profits in the world economic system. These include Japan, the United States and the countries of Western Europe. **Peripheral countries** comprise low-income, largely agricultural countries that are often manipulated by core countries for their own economic advantage. Examples of peripheral countries are found throughout Africa and to a lesser extent in Latin America and Asia. Natural resources, such as agricultural products, minerals and other raw materials, flow from periphery to core – as do the profits. The core, in turn, sells finished goods to the periphery, also at a profit. World-systems theorists argue that core countries have made themselves wealthy with this unequal trade, while at the same time limiting the economic development of peripheral countries. Finally, the **semi-peripheral countries** occupy an intermediate position: these are semi-industrialized, middle-income countries that extract profits from the more peripheral countries and in turn yield profits to the core countries. Examples of semi-peripheral countries include Mexico in North America; Brazil, Argentina and Chile in South America; and the newly industrializing economies of East Asia. The semi-periphery, though to some degree controlled by the core, is thus also able to exploit the periphery. Moreover, the greater economic success of the semi-periphery holds out to the periphery the promise of similar development.

Although the world system tends to change very slowly, once-powerful countries eventually lose their economic power and others then take their place. For example, some five centuries ago the Italian city-states of Venice and Genoa dominated the world capitalist economy. They were superseded by the Dutch, then the British and currently the United States. Today, in the view of some world-systems theorists, American dominance is giving way to a more 'multi-polar' world where economic power will be shared between the United States, Europe and Asia (Arrighi 1994).

State-centred theories

Some of the most recent explanations of successful economic development emphasize the role of state policy in promoting growth. Differing sharply from market-oriented theories, **state-centred theories** argue that appropriate government policies do not interfere with economic development but rather can play a key role in bringing it about. A large body of research now suggests that in some regions of the world, such as East Asia, successful economic development has been state-led. Even the World Bank, long a strong proponent of free-market theories of development, has changed its thinking about the role of the state. In its 1997 report *The State in a Changing World*, the World Bank concluded that without an effective state, 'sustainable development, both economic and social, is impossible'.

Strong governments contributed in various ways to economic growth in the East Asian NICs during the 1980s and 1990s (Appelbaum and Henderson 1992; Amsden, Kochanowicz et al. 1994; World Bank 1997):

1 *East Asian governments have sometimes aggressively acted to ensure political stability, while keeping labour costs low.* This has been accomplished by acts of repression, such as outlawing trade unions, banning strikes, jailing labour leaders and, in general, silencing the voices of workers. The governments of Taiwan, South Korea and Singapore in particular have engaged in such practices.

2 *East Asian governments have frequently sought to steer economic development in desired directions.* For example, state agencies have often provided cheap loans and tax breaks to businesses that invest in industries favoured by the government. Sometimes this strategy has backfired, resulting in bad loans held by the government (one of the causes of the region's economic problems during the late 1990s). Some governments have prevented businesses from investing their profits in other countries, forcing them to invest in economic growth at home. Sometimes governments have owned and therefore controlled key industries. For example, the Japanese government has owned railways, the steel industry and banks; the South Korean government has owned banks; and the government of Singapore has owned airlines and the armaments and ship-repair industries.

3 *East Asian governments have often been heavily involved in social programmes such as low-cost housing and universal education.* The world's largest public housing systems (outside socialist or formerly socialist countries) have been in Hong Kong and Singapore, where government subsidies keep rents extremely low. As a result, workers don't require high wages to pay for their housing, so they can compete better with American and European workers in the emerging global labour market. In Singapore, which has an extremely strong central government, well-funded public education and training help to provide workers with the skills they need to compete effectively in the emerging global labour market. The Singaporean government also requires businesses and individual citizen alike to save a large percentage of their income for investment in future growth.

Evaluating theories of development

Each of the four sets of theories of global inequality just discussed has its strengths and weaknesses. Together they enable us to better understand the causes and cures for global inequality.

Market-oriented theories recommend the adoption of modern capitalist institutions to promote economic development, as the recent example of East Asia attests. They further argue that countries can develop economically only if they open their borders to trade, and they can cite evidence in support of this argument. But market-oriented theories also fail to take into account the various economic ties between poor countries and wealthy ones – ties that can impede economic growth under some conditions and enhance it under others. They tend to blame low-income countries themselves for their poverty rather than looking to the influence of outside factors, such as the business operations of more powerful nations. Market-oriented theories also ignore the ways government can work with the private sector to spur economic development. Finally, they fail to explain why some countries manage to take off economically while others remain grounded in poverty and underdevelopment.

Dependency theories address the market-oriented theories' neglect in considering poor countries' ties with wealthy countries by focusing on how wealthy nations have economically exploited poor ones. However, while dependency theories help to account for much of the economic backwardness in Latin America and Africa, they are unable to explain the occasional success story among such low-income countries as Brazil, Argentina and Mexico or the rapidly expanding economies of East Asia. In fact, some countries, once in the low-income category, have risen economically even in the presence of multinational corporations. Even some former colonies, such as Hong Kong and Singapore, both once dependent on Great Britain, count among the success stories. World-systems theory sought to overcome the shortcomings of dependency theories by analysing the world economy as a whole. Rather than beginning with individual countries, world-systems theorists look at the complex global web of political and economic relationships that influence development and inequality in poor and rich nations alike.

State-centred theories stress the governmental role in fostering economic growth. They thus offer a useful alternative to both the prevailing market-oriented theories, with their emphasis on states as economic hindrances, and dependency theories, which view states as allies of global business elites in exploiting poor countries. When combined with the other theories – particularly world-systems theory – state-centred theories can explain the radical changes now transforming the world economy.

The role of international organizations and global inequality

There are a number of international organizations whose work impacts on global poverty. The International Monetary Fund (IMF) and the World Bank – together known as the Bretton Woods Institutions – were established during the Second World War. They are based in Washington, in the United States, and their membership is made up of governments from across the world. The IMF is an organization of 184 countries. The main work of the IMF is in maintaining stability in the international financial system – most noticeably when it is called in to sort out a large debt crisis, for example in Argentina from 2001 to 2003. It also works with governments across the world to improve their economic management, but it is precisely that advice which is often criticized as causing some of the problems that poorer countries face (e.g. Stiglitz 2002).

The World Bank Group's mission is to fight poverty and improve the living standards of people in the developing world. It is a development bank which provides loans, policy advice, technical assistance and knowledge-sharing services to low- and middle-income countries to reduce poverty. The World Bank is made up of a number of accounts providing relatively cheap finance – mainly loans – for its member governments. Recently, the Bank has also started giving governments grants for specific programmes. It also provides technical expertise alongside its loans and grants. Both the World Bank and the IMF have been accused of promoting market-driven reforms to the detriment of poor countries and people, and both have made an effort in recent years to concentrate more on the elimination of poverty.

One example of the new approach taken by the World Bank and IMF in recent years has been the initiative (known as HIPC – Heavily Indebted Poor Countries Initiative) to grant debt relief to many of the poorest countries. Some countries had taken on so many loans over a number of decades, which had attracted so much interest, that they could not afford to pay them back. If they were to pay them back in full, it would probably have wiped out the resources that the countries' governments had available for education, health and other basic services. The HIPC Initiative was launched in 1996 to give those countries sufficient relief – funded by governments of rich countries, including the UK – that they could deal with their debt burden as well as tackle poverty. A key element of this Initiative was the requirement for all countries involved to produce and implement a Poverty Reduction Strategy Paper. By 2004, twenty-five countries had taken part in the HIPC process.

The United Nations, perhaps the best known of the international organizations, includes a series of funds and programmes, which work across the world to tackle the causes and effects of poverty. Examples include the United Nations Development Programme and United Nations Children's Fund, both based in New York, the World Food Programme in Rome and the World Health Organization (WHO) in Geneva. All have country offices across the world. Each aims to tackle diff-erent aspects of poverty. UNICEF's work is focused on girls' education, protection of children and immunization, as well as provision of clean water and sanitation. UNDP works with governments in poor countries to improve governance, including the rule of law, justice, state provision of basic services and tackling corruption. Add perhaps another ten UN organizations in any one country and there is likely to be a complicated mix of organizations covering a number of interrelated issues. One key concern is the spread of HIV and its effects on economic, health, institutional capacity, family and social spheres. At least four UN organizations are therefore involved in tackling this problem. UN organizations generally suffer from low levels of core funding compared to their Bretton Woods cousins. Some UN organizations, like the WHO, are also involved in setting international standards and undertaking research.

One member of the UN family that has been under the spotlight in recent years is the World Trade Organization. Based in Geneva, it regulates international trade through negotiations between its 148 member governments and a mechanism for resolving trade disputes. The current round of negotiations, launched in Doha in Qatar in 2001, is referred to by some as a 'development round'. There is a widespread view that the current international trading system is not fair to poorer countries and is constraining their economic development. A prime aim of these negotiations is to rectify this through, for example, improved access for these countries goods and services to others' markets.

The organizations above are described as multilateral organizations, as they involve many, indeed the majority of, countries. So-called bilateral donors are also involved in the reduction of global poverty. In the UK, the government's Department for International Development (DfID), works with specific poor countries to meet the Millennium Development Goals. These goals were set out by the international community in the late 1990s. They include a series of targets, of which two of the most important are halving, between 1990 and 2015, the proportion of people whose income is less than $1 a day and ensuring that, by 2015, all children will be able to complete a full course of primary schooling. Several of these targets are unlikely to be met. In the UK, the work of DfID includes the provision of grants and expertise in the country, as well as policy and advocacy at the international level to remove some of the structural barriers to the reduction of poverty (for example debt, trade rules and exploitation of resources).

Global economic inequality in a changing world

Today the social and economic forces leading to a single global capitalist economy appear to be irresistible. The principal challenge to this outcome – socialism – ended with the collapse of the Soviet Union in 1991. The largest remaining socialist country in the world today, the People's Republic of China, is rapidly adopting many capitalist economic institutions and is the fastest-growing economy in the world. It is too soon to tell how far the future leaders of China will move down the capitalist road. Will they eventually adopt a complete market-oriented economy or some combination of state controls and capitalist institutions?

Most China experts agree on one thing: when China, with its 1.2 billion people, fully enters the global capitalist system, its impact will be felt around the world. China has an enormous workforce, much of which is well trained and educated and now receives extremely low wages – sometimes less than one-twentieth of what UK workers earn in comparable jobs. Such a workforce will be extremely competitive in a global economy and will force wages down from Los Angeles to London.

What does rapid globalization mean for the future of global inequality? No sociologist knows for certain, but many possible scenarios exist. For one, our world might be dominated by large, global corporations, with workers everywhere competing with one another at a global wage. Such a scenario might predict falling wages for large numbers of people in today's high-income countries and rising wages for a few in low-income countries. There might be a general levelling out of average income around the world, although at a level much lower than that currently enjoyed in the United Kingdom and other industrialized nations. In this scenario, the polarization between the haves and the have-nots within countries would grow, as the whole world would be increasingly divided into those who benefit from the global economy and those who do not. Such polarization could fuel conflict between ethnic groups, and even nations, as those suffering from economic globalization would blame others for their plight (Hirst and Thompson 1992; Wagar 1992).

On the other hand, a global economy could mean greater opportunity for everyone, as the benefits of modern technology stimulate worldwide economic growth.

According to this more optimistic scenario, the more successful East Asian NICs, such as Hong Kong, Taiwan, South Korea and Singapore, are only a sign of things to come. Other NICs such as Malaysia and Thailand will soon follow, along with China, Indonesia, Vietnam and other Asian countries. India, the world's second most populous country, already boasts a middle class of around 200 million people, about a quarter of its total population (although roughly the same number live in poverty) (Kulkarni 1993).

A countervailing trend, however, is the technology gap that divides rich and poor countries, which today appears to be widening, making it even more difficult for poor countries to catch up. The global technology gap is a result of the disparity in wealth between nations, but it also reinforces those disparities, widening the gap between rich and poor countries. Poor countries cannot easily afford modern technology – yet, in the absence of modern technology, they face major barriers to overcoming poverty. They are caught in a vicious downward spiral from which it is difficult to escape.

Jeffrey Sachs, Director of the Earth Institute at Columbia University in New York, and a prominent adviser to many East European and developing countries, claims that the world is divided into three classes: technology innovators, technology adopters and the technologically disconnected (Sachs 2000).

Technology innovators are those regions that provide nearly all of the world's technological inventions; they account for no more than 15 per cent of the world's population. *Technology adopters* are those regions that are able to adopt technologies invented elsewhere, applying them to production and consumption; they account for 50 per cent of the world's population. Finally, the *technologically disconnected* are those regions that neither innovate nor adopt technologies developed elsewhere; they account for 35 per cent of the world's population. Note that Sachs speaks of regions rather than countries. In today's increasingly borderless world, technology use (or exclusion) does not always respect national frontiers. For example, Sachs notes that technologically disconnected regions include 'southern Mexico and pockets of tropical Central America; the Andean countries; most of tropical Brazil; tropical sub-Saharan Africa; most of the former Soviet Union aside from the areas nearest to European and Asian markets; landlocked parts of Asia such as the Ganges valley states of India; landlocked Laos and Cambodia; and the deep-interior states of China' (Sachs 2000). These are impoverished regions that lack access to markets or major ocean trading routes. They are caught in what Sachs terms a 'poverty trap', plagued by 'tropical infectious disease, low agricultural productivity and environmental degradation – all requiring technological solutions beyond their means' (Sachs 2000).

Innovation requires a critical mass of ideas and technology to become self-sustaining. 'Silicon Valley', near San Francisco in the United States, provides one example of how technological innovation tends to be concentrated in regions rich in universities and high-tech firms. Silicon Valley grew up around Stanford University and other educational and research institutions located south of San Francisco. Poor countries are ill-equipped to develop such high-tech regions. Sachs calculates that forty-eight tropical or partly tropical countries, whose combined population totalled 750 million, accounted for only forty-seven of the 51,000 patents granted in the USA to foreign inventors in 1997. Most poor countries lack even a science adviser to their government. Moreover, these countries are too poor to import computers, mobile phones, fax machines, computerized factory machinery or other kinds of high technology. Nor can they afford to license technology from the foreign companies that hold the patents.

What can be done to overcome the technological abyss that divides rich and poor countries? Sachs calls on wealthy, high-technology countries to provide much greater financial and technical assistance to poor countries than they now do. For example, lethal infectious diseases such as malaria, measles and diarrhoea claim million of lives each year in poor countries. The modern medical technology necessary to eradicate these illnesses would cost only $10 billion a year – less than $15 from every person who lives in a high-income country, if the cost were shared equally.

Sachs urges the governments of wealthy countries, along with international lending institutions, to provide loans and grants for scientific and technological development. Sachs notes that very little money is available to support research and development in poor countries. The World Bank, a major source of funding for development projects in poor countries, spends only $60 million a year supporting tropical, agricultural or health research and development. By way of comparison, Merck, the giant pharmaceutical corporation, spends thirty-five times that much ($2.1 billion) for research and development for its own products. Even universities in wealthy nations could play a role, establishing overseas research and training institutes that would foster collaborative research projects. From computers and the Internet to biotechnology, the 'wealth of nations' increasingly depends on modern information technology. As long as major regions of the world remain technologically disconnected, it seems unlikely that global poverty will be eradicated.

Russian society now displays striking contrasts between rich and poor.

In the most optimistic view, the republics of the former Soviet Union, as well as the formerly socialist countries of Eastern Europe, will eventually advance into the ranks of the high-income countries. Economic growth will spread to Latin America, Africa and the rest of the world. Because capitalism requires that workers be mobile, the remaining caste societies around the world will be replaced by class-based societies. These societies will experience enhanced opportunities for upward mobility.

What is the future of global inequality? It is difficult to be entirely optimistic for now. Global economic growth has slowed, and many of the once promising economies of Asia now seem to be in trouble. The Russian economy, in its move from socialism to capitalism, has encountered many pitfalls, leaving many Russians much poorer than ever. It remains to be seen whether the countries of the world will learn from one another and work together to create better lives for their peoples. What is certain is that the past quarter of a century has witnessed a global economic transformation of unprecedented magnitude. The effects of this transformation in the next twenty-five years will leave few lives on the planet untouched.

If global inequality is one of the most important issues facing the earth today, another is the dramatic increase in the globe's population in recent decades. Global poverty and population growth are tied together, for it is in some of the world's poorest countries that population growth is greatest. It is to a discussion of this phenomenon that we now turn.

World population growth

It was estimated that the Earth's six-billionth inhabitant was born on 12 October 1999. The world's population is booming – it has doubled since 1960. An American expert on population studies, Paul Ehrlich, calculated in the 1960s that if the rate of population growth at that time were to continue, nine hundred years from now (not a long period in world history as a whole) there would be 60,000,000,000,000,000 (60 quadrillion) people on the face of the earth. There would be one hundred people for every square yard of the Earth's surface, including both land and water.

The physicist J. H. Fremlin worked out that housing such a population would require a continuous two-thousand-storey building covering the entire planet. Even in such a stupendous structure there would only be three or four yards of floor space per person (Fremlin 1964).

Such a picture, of course, is nothing more than nightmarish fiction designed to drive home how cataclysmic the consequences of continued population growth would be. The real issue is what will happen over the next thirty or forty years. Partly because governments and other agencies heeded the warnings of Ehrlich and others, by introducing population control programmes, there are grounds for supposing that world population growth is beginning to trail off (see figure 11.4). Estimates calculated in the 1960s of the likely world population by the year 2000 turned out to be inaccurate. The World Bank estimated the

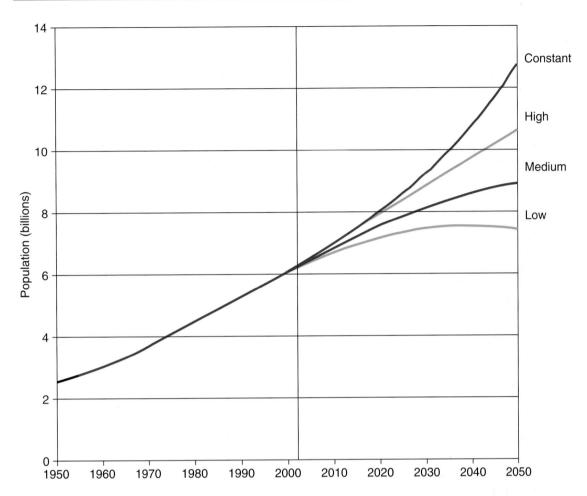

Figure 11.4 Estimated and projected population of the world by projection variant, 1950–2050

Source: UN (2003a)

world population to be just over 6 billion in 2000, compared to some earlier estimates of over 8 billion. Nevertheless, considering that a century ago there were only 1.5 billion people in the world, this still represents growth of staggering proportions. Moreover, the factors underlying population growth are by no means completely predictable, and all estimates have to be interpreted with caution.

Population analysis: demography

The study of population is referred to as **demography**. The term was invented about a century and a half ago, at a time when nations were beginning to keep official statistics on the nature and distribution of their populations. Demography is concerned with measuring the size of populations and explaining their rise or decline. Population patterns are governed by three factors: births, deaths and migrations. Demography is customarily treated as a branch of sociology, because the factors that influence the level of births and deaths in a given group or society, as well as migrations of population, are largely social and cultural.

Demographic work tends to be statistical. All the developed nations today gather and analyse basic statistics on their populations by carrying out censuses (systematic surveys designed to find out about the whole population of a given country). Rigorous as the modes of data collection now are, even in these nations demographic statistics are not wholly accurate. In the United Kingdom, there has been a population Census every ten years since 1801. The Census aims to be as accurate as possible, but for various reasons some people might not be registered in the official population statistics, for example illegal immigrants, homeless people, transients and others who for one reason or another avoided registration. In many developing countries, particularly those with recent high rates of population growth, demographic statistics are much more unreliable.

Dynamics of population change

Rates of population growth or decline are measured by subtracting the number of deaths per thousand over a given period from the number of births per thousand – this is usually calculated annually. Some European countries have negative growth rates – in other words, their populations are declining. Virtually all of the industrialized countries have growth rates of less than 0.5 per cent. Rates of population growth were high in the eighteenth and nineteenth centuries in Europe and the United States, but have since levelled off. Many developing countries today have rates of between 2 and 3 per cent (see figure 11.6 on p. 424). These may not seem very different from the rates of the industrialized countries, but in fact, the difference is enormous.

The reason for this is that growth in population is exponential. There is an ancient Persian myth that helps to illustrate this. A courtier asked a ruler to reward him for his services by giving him twice as many grains of rice for each service than he had given him the time before, starting with a single grain on the first square of a chess board. Believing that he was onto a good thing, the king commanded grain to be brought up from his storehouse. By the twenty-first square, the storehouse was empty; the fortieth square required ten billion grains of rice (Meadows 1972). In other words, starting with one item and doubling it, doubling the result, and so on, rapidly leads to huge figures – 1:2:4:8:16:32:64:128, and so on. In seven operations, the figure has grown by 128 times. Exactly the same principle applies to population growth. We can

Demography: key concepts

Among the basic concepts used by demographers, the most important are crude birth rates, fertility, fecundity and crude death rates. **Crude birth rates** are expressed as the number of live births per year per thousand of the population. They are called 'crude' rates because of their very general character. Crude birth rates, for example, do not tell us what proportion of a population are male or female, or what the age distribution of a population is (the relative proportions of young and old people in the population). Where statistics are collected that relate birth or death rates to such categories, demographers speak of 'specific' rather than 'crude' rates. For instance, an age-specific birth rate might specify the number of births per thousand women in different age groups.

If we wish to understand population patterns in any detail, the information provided by specific birth rates is normally necessary. Crude birth rates, however, are useful for making overall comparisons between different groups, societies and regions. Thus the crude birth rate in the United Kingdom in 2002 was eleven per thousand. Other industrialized countries have lower rates, such as nine per thousand in Germany, Russia and Italy. In many other parts of the world, crude birth rates are much higher. In India, for instance, the crude birth rate is twenty-four per thousand; in Ethiopia it is forty-three per thousand (<http://www.unicef.org/infobycountry/ index.html>).

Birth rates are an expression of the fertility of women. **Fertility** refers to how many live-born children the average woman has. A fertility rate is usually calculated as the average number of births per thousand women of childbearing age.

Fertility is distinguished from **fecundity**, which means the potential number of children women are biologically capable of bearing. It is physically possible for a normal woman to bear a child every year during the period when she is capable of conception. There are variations in fecundity according to the age at which women reach puberty and menopause, both of which differ among countries as well as among individuals. While there may be families in which a woman bears twenty or more children,

fertility rates in practice are always much lower than fecundity rates, because social and cultural factors limit breeding.

Crude death rates (also called 'mortality rates') are calculated in the same way as birth rates – the number of deaths per thousand of population per year. Again, there are major variations among countries, but death rates in many societies in the developing world are falling to levels comparable to those in developed nations. The death rate in the United Kingdom in 2002 was ten per thousand. In India it was nine per thousand; in Ethiopia it was eighteen per thousand. A few countries have much higher death rates. In Sierra Leone, for example, the death rate is thirty per thousand. Like crude birth rates, crude death rates only provide a very general index of **mortality** (the number of deaths in a population). Specific death rates give more precise information. A particularly important specific death rate is the **infant mortality rate**: the number of babies per thousand births in any year who die before reaching the age of one. One of the key factors underlying the population explosion has been reductions in infant mortality rates.

Declining rates of infant mortality are the most important influence on increasing **life expectancy** – that is, the number of years the average person can expect to live. In 2003, life expectancy at birth for women born in the UK was almost 81 years, compared with 76 years for men. This contrasts with 49 and 45 years respectively at the turn of the last century in 1901. This does not mean, however, that most people born in 1901 died when they were in their forties. When there is a high infant mortality rate, as there is in many developing nations, the average life expectancy – which is a statistical average – is brought down. Illness, nutrition and the influence of natural disasters are other factors that influence life expectancy. Life expectancy has to be distinguished from **life span**, which is the maximum number of years that an individual could live. While life expectancy has increased in most societies in the world, life span has remained unaltered. Only a small proportion of people live to be one hundred or more.

Many of the poorest countries in the world are experiencing massive population growth.

measure this effect by means of the **doubling time**, the period of time it takes for the population to double. A population growth of 1 per cent will produce a doubling of numbers in seventy years. At 2 per cent growth, a population will double in thirty-five years, while at 3 per cent it will double in twenty-three years. Paul Ehrlich, who was mentioned at the start of this section, was so concerned about population growth precisely because the doubling time of the world population had been decreasing at an accelerating rate. It took until 1850 for the population to reach one billion. During the next eighty years, by 1930, it doubled to two billion. He predicted correctly that the next doubling, to four billion, would occur by 1975.

Malthusianism

In pre-modern societies, birth rates were very high by the standards of the industrialized world today. Nonetheless, population growth remained low until the eighteenth century because there was a rough overall balance between births and deaths. The general trend of numbers was upward, and there were sometimes periods of more marked population increase, but these were followed by increases in death rates. In medieval Europe, for example, when harvests were bad, marriages tended to be postponed and the number of conceptions fell, while deaths increased. These complementary trends reduced the number of mouths to be fed. No pre-industrial society was able to escape from this self-regulating rhythm (Wrigley 1968).

During the period of the rise of industrialism, many looked forward to a new age in which scarcity would be a phenomenon of the past. The development of modern industry, it was widely supposed, would create a new era of abundance. In his celebrated work *Essay on the Principle of Population* (Malthus 1976; orig. 1798), Thomas Malthus criticized these ideas and initiated a debate about the connection between population and food resources that continues to this day. At the time Malthus wrote, the population in Europe was growing rapidly. Malthus pointed out that while population increase is exponential, food supply depends on fixed resources that can be expanded only by developing new land for cultivation. Population growth therefore tends to outstrip the means of support available. The inevitable outcome is famine, which, combined with the influence of war and plagues, acts as a natural limit to population increase. Malthus predicted that human beings would always live in circumstances of misery and starvation, unless they practised what he called 'moral restraint'. His cure for excessive population growth was for people strictly to limit their frequency of sexual intercourse. (The use of contraception he proclaimed to be a 'vice'.)

For a while, **Malthusianism** was ignored,

since the population development of the Western countries followed a quite different pattern from that which he had anticipated – as we shall see below. Rates of population growth trailed off in the nineteenth and twentieth centuries. Indeed, in the 1930s there were major worries about population decline in many industrialized countries, including the United Kingdom. The upsurge in world population growth in the twentieth century has again lent some credence to Malthus's views, although few support them in their original version. Population expansion in developing countries seems to be outstripping the resources that those countries can generate to feed their citizenry.

The demographic transition

Demographers often refer to the changes in the ratio of births to deaths in the industrialized countries from the nineteenth century onward as the **demographic transition**. The notion was first explored by Warren S. Thompson, who described a three-stage process in which one type of population stability would be eventually replaced by another as a society reached an advanced level of economic development (Thompson 1929).

Stage one refers to the conditions characteristic of most traditional societies, in which both birth and death rates are high and the infant mortality rate is especially large. Population grows little, if at all, as the high number of births is more or less balanced by the level of deaths. *Stage two*, which began in Europe and the United States in the early part of the nineteenth century – with wide regional variations – occurs when death rates fall while fertility

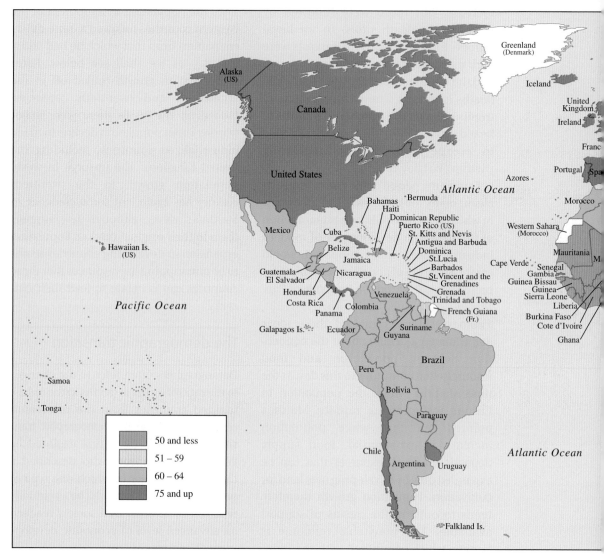

Figure 11.6   Life expectancies in global perspective, 2002

Source: World Bank (2003)

remains high. This is therefore a phase of marked population growth. It is subsequently replaced by *stage three*, in which, with industrial development, birth rates drop to a level such that population is again fairly stable.

Demographers do not fully agree about how this sequence of change should be interpreted, or how long-lasting stage three is likely to be. Fertility in the Western countries has not been completely stable over the past century or so and there

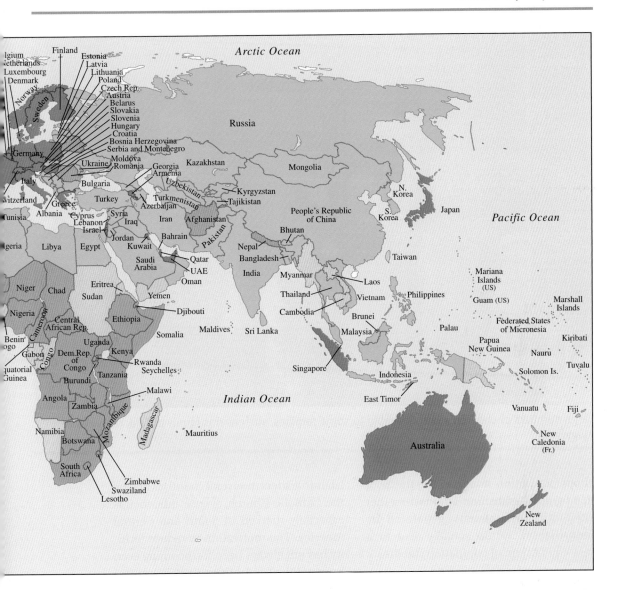

remain considerable differences in fertility between the industrialized nations, as well as between classes or regions within them. Nevertheless, it is generally accepted that this sequence accurately describes a major transformation in the demographic character of modern societies.

The theory of demographic transition directly opposes the ideas of Thomas Malthus. Whereas for Malthus, increasing prosperity would automatically bring

Large numbers of children seem desirable to some families, such as this family of Tajik refugees in Kyrgyzstan

about population increase, the thesis of demographic transition emphasizes that economic development, generated by industrialism, would actually lead to a new equilibrium of population stability.

Prospects for change

Fertility remains high in developing world societies because traditional attitudes to family size have been maintained. Having large numbers of children is often still regarded as desirable, providing a source of labour on family-run farms. Some religions are either opposed to birth control or affirm the desirability of having many children. Contraception is opposed by

Islamic leaders in several countries and by the Catholic Church, whose influence is especially marked in South and Central America. The motivation to reduce fertility has not always been forthcoming even from political authorities. In 1974, contraceptives were banned in Argentina as part of a programme to double the population of the country as fast as possible; this was seen as a means of developing its economic and military strength.

Yet a decline in fertility levels has at last occurred in some large developing countries. An example is China, which currently has a population of about 1.3 billion people – almost a quarter of the world's population as a whole. The Chinese government established one of the most extensive programmes of population control that any country has undertaken, with the object of stabilizing the country's numbers at close to their current level. The government instituted incentives (such as better housing and free healthcare and education) to promote single-child families, while families with more than one child face special hardships (wages are cut for those who have a third child). In some cases the Chinese government's policy has had horrific unintended consequences. A traditional preference for boys, and a belief that males will look after their parents in their old age whereas females, once married, 'belong to' someone else, has led to some newborn girls being killed by their families in preference to facing the penalties of having a second child. However, there is evidence that China's antenatal policies, however harsh they may appear, have had a substantial impact on limiting its population growth.

China's programme demands a degree of centralized government control that is either unacceptable or unavailable in most other developing countries. In India, for instance, many schemes for promoting family planning and the use of contraceptives have been tried, but with only relatively small success. In 1988 India had a population of 789 million. By 2000, its population just topped a billion. And even if its population growth rate does diminish, by 2050 India will be the most populous country in the world, with more than 1.5 billion people.

It is claimed that the demographic changes that will occur over the next hundred years will be greater than any that have taken place in all of human history. It is difficult to predict with any precision the rate at which the world population will rise, but the United Nations has several fertility scenarios. The 'high' scenario places the world's population at more than 25 billion people by 2150. The 'medium' fertility scenario, which the UN deems most likely, assumes that fertility levels will stabilize at just over two children per woman, resulting in a world population of 11.8 billion people by 2150.

This overall population increase conceals two distinct trends. First, most developing countries will undergo the process of demographic transition described above. This will result in a substantial surge in the population, as death rates fall. India and China are each likely to see their populations reach 1.5 billion people. Areas in Asia, Africa and Latin America will similarly experience rapid growth before the population eventually stabilizes.

The second trend concerns the developed countries that have already undergone demographic transition. These societies will experience very slight population growth, if any at all. Instead, a process of ageing will occur in which the number of young people will decline in absolute terms and the older segment of the population will increase markedly. This will have widespread economic and social implications for developed countries: as the dependency ratio increases, pressure will mount on health and social services. Yet, as their numbers grow, older people will also have more political weight and may be able to push for higher expenditures on programmes and services of importance to them.

The ageing of the population is discussed in chapter 6, 'Socialization, the Life-Course and Ageing', pp. 178–99.

What will be the consequences of these demographic changes? Some observers see the makings of widespread social upheaval – particularly in the developing countries undergoing demographic transition. Changes in the economy and labour markets may prompt widespread internal migration as people in rural areas search for work. The rapid growth of cities is likely to lead to environmental damage, new public health risks, overloaded infrastructures, rising crime and impoverished squatter settlements.

Famine and food shortages are another serious concern. As we saw in our discussion of global inequality (above) there are around 830 million people in the world suffering from hunger or under-nourishment. As the population rises, levels of food output will need to rise accordingly to avoid widespread scarcity. Yet it is difficult to see how this can happen; many of the world's poorest areas are particularly affected by water shortages, shrinking farmland and soil degradation – processes that reduce, rather than enhance, agricultural productivity. It is almost certain that food production will not occur at a level to ensure self-sufficiency. Large amounts of food and grain will need to be imported from areas where there are surpluses. According to the Food and Agricultural Organization (FAO), by 2010 industrialized countries will be producing 1,614 pounds of grain per person, compared to only 507 pounds per head in the developing world.

Technological advances in agriculture and industry are unpredictable, so no one can be sure how large a population the world might eventually be able to support. Yet even at current population levels, global resources may already be well below those required to create living standards in the less developed world comparable to those of the industrialized countries.

Summary points

1 The countries of the world can be stratified according to their per-person gross national income. Currently, 40 per cent of the world's population live in low-income countries, compared with only 16 per cent in high-income countries.

2 An estimated 1.3 billion people in the world, or nearly one in four people, live in poverty today, an increase since the early 1980s. Many are the victims of discrimination based on race, ethnicity or tribal affiliation.

3 In general, people in high-income countries enjoy a far higher standard of living than their counterparts in low-income countries. They are likely to have more food to eat, less likely to starve or suffer from malnutrition and likely to live longer. They are far more likely to be literate and educated and therefore have higher-skilled, higher-paying jobs. Additionally, they are less likely to have large families, and their children are much less likely to die in infancy of malnutrition or childhood diseases.

4 Such newly industrializing countries as Hong Kong, Singapore, Taiwan and South Korea have experienced explosive economic growth since the mid-1970s. This growth is due partly to historical circumstances, to a lesser degree to the cultural characteristics of these countries, and most important, to the central role played by their governments.

Whether this growth will continue is now in question, given the economic difficulties some of these countries currently face.

5   *Market-oriented theories* of *global inequality*, such as *modernization theory*, claim that cultural and institutional barriers to development explain the poverty of low-income societies. In this view, to eliminate poverty, fatalistic attitudes must be overcome, government meddling in economic affairs ended, and a high rate of savings and investment encouraged.

6   *Dependency theories* claim that global poverty is the result of the exploitation of poor countries by wealthy ones. *Dependent development theory* argues that even though the economic fate of poor countries is ultimately determined by wealthy ones, some development is possible within dependent capitalistic relations. *World-systems theory* argues that the capitalist world system as a whole – not just individual countries – must be understood if we hope to make sense of global inequality. World-systems theory focuses on the relationships of *core, peripheral* and *semi-peripheral countries* in the global economy and on long-term trends in the global economy.

7   *State-centred theories* emphasize the role that governments can play in fostering economic development. These theories draw on the experience of the rapidly growing East Asian newly industrializing economies as an example.

8   No one can say for sure whether global inequality will increase or decrease in the future. It is possible that some levelling out of wages will occur worldwide, as wages decline in wealthy countries and rise in poor countries. It is also possible that all countries will some day prosper as the result of a unified global economy.

9   Population growth is one of the most significant global problems currently faced by humanity. *Malthusianism* is the idea, first advanced by Thomas Malthus two centuries ago, that population growth tends to outstrip the resources available to support it. Unless people limited their frequency of sexual intercourse, he argued, excessive population growth would ensure a future of misery and starvation.

10 The study of population growth is called *demography*. Much demographic work is statistical, but demographers are also concerned with trying to explain why population patterns take the form they do. The most important concepts in population analysis are birth rates, death rates, fertility and fecundity.

11 The changes in population patterns are usually analysed in terms of a process of *demographic transition*. Prior to industrialization, both birth and death rates were high. During the beginning of industrialization, there was population growth, because death rates were reduced while birth rates took longer to decline. Finally a new equilibrium was reached with low birth rates balancing low death rates.

12 World population is projected to grow to over 10 billion people by 2150. Most of this growth will occur in the developing world, where countries will undergo demographic transition and experience rapid growth before the population stabilizes. In the

developed world, population will grow only slightly. Instead, a process of ageing will occur and the number of young people will decline in absolute terms. These population trends will have far-reaching implications for labour markets, welfare systems, food and water supplies, the natural environment and the conditions in urban areas.

Questions for further thought

1 If people in the poorest countries were freed from absolute poverty, would it matter that there are global billionaires?

2 Can poor countries become rich? If so, how? What, if anything, is preventing them?

3 Does responsibility for ending global poverty lie with people in the rich countries or the poor?

4 Why is the study of demography sociological?

5 Was Malthus right after all?

Further reading

Titus Alexander, *Unravelling Global Apartheid: An Overview of World Politics* (Cambridge: Polity, 1996).

Vic George and Robert Page (eds), *Global Social Problems* (Cambridge: Polity, 2004).

Jorge Larrain, *Theories of Development: Capitalism, Colonialism and Dependency* (Cambridge: Polity, 1989).

Geoffrey McNicoll, *Population Weights in the International Order* (New York: Population Council, 1999).

Internet links

Economist Inequality papers
http://www.economist.com/inequalitypapers

The Global Site
http://www.theglobalsite.ac.uk

The IMF
http://www.imf.org

Make Poverty History
http://www.makepovertyhistory.org

The United Nations
http://www.un.org

The World Bank Globalization Homepage
http://www.worldbank.org/economicpolicy/globalization/

Contents

12 Sexuality and Gender

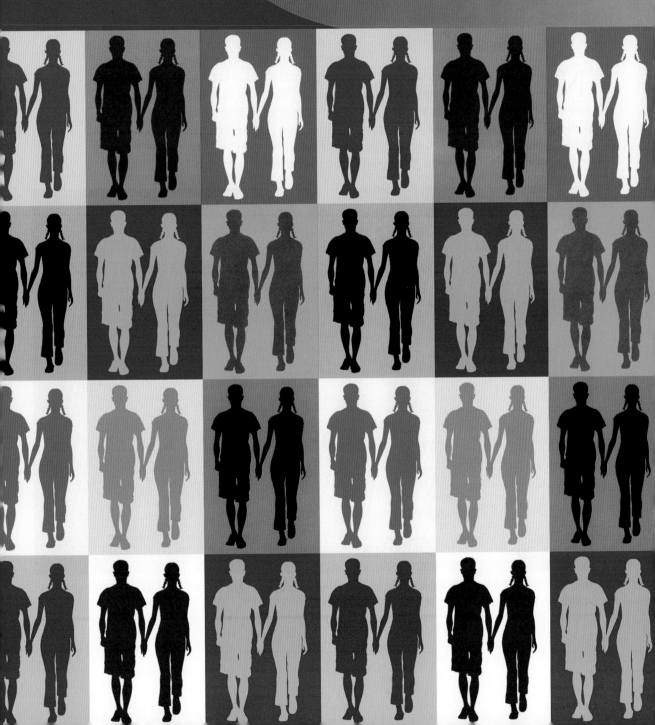

'NOW BY the power vested in me by the state of Massachusetts as a justice of the peace, and most of all by the power of your own love, I now pronounce you married under the laws of Massachusetts', intoned the City clerk, Margaret Drury, shortly after 9 a.m. on 17 May 2004. 'You may seal this marriage with a kiss.' The couple embraced. Marcia Kadish, who had married her partner of eighteen years, was overjoyed: 'I feel all tingly and wonderful', she said. 'So much love. Can't you see it is just bursting out of me?' Her partner said it felt like 'winning the lottery'.

Yet the marriage caused great controversy in the United States. 'The documents being issued across Massachusetts may say "marriage licence" at the top but they are really death certificates for the institution of marriage', said James Dobson, head of Christian group 'Focus on the Family'. The reason for the contro-

This was the very first same-sex couple to be issued with a marriage licence in Massachusetts, after waiting in front of the town hall building for 24 hours.

versy was that Marcia Kadish's long-term partner was also a woman – Tanya McCloskey. The couple was amongst the first same-sex couples to be married under new laws in the US state of Massachusetts. Throughout the day, one gay couple after another filed out of the local town hall clutching the newly issued papers that would allow them to get married. Outside, thousands of people had gathered to applaud the couples, and to celebrate a right that many of them regarded as self-evident.

The state of Massachusetts has often been at the cusp of liberal reforms in the USA. In May 2004, after months of battles in and out of the state Supreme Court and legislature, it became the first state to legalize gay marriage. Although increasing numbers of people in the USA do accept that marriages between homosexuals should be recognized as valid by the law, the majority (55 per cent in May 2004) has consistently been against it (Gallup 2004). Massachusetts joined the Netherlands, Belgium and large parts of Canada as one of the few places in the world where gay marriages are legally recognized.

In many ways, homosexuality has become more normalized – more of an accepted part of everyday society. Several countries have passed legislation to protect the rights of homosexuals. When South Africa adopted its new constitution in 1996, it became one of the only countries in the world constitutionally to guarantee the rights of homosexuals. Many countries in Europe, including Denmark, the Netherlands and Spain, now permit homosexual partners to register with the state and to claim most of the prerogatives of marriage. The UK government passed similar legislation in November 2004,

giving gay and lesbian couples the chance to receive similar legal rights as married couples if they chose to register their partnership at a civil ceremony. This includes social security and pension benefits, tenancy rights, possible parental responsibility for a partner's children, full recognition for life assurance, responsibility to provide reasonable maintenance for partners and children, the same tax treatment as married couples and visiting rights in hospitals.

More and more gay activists in Europe, the USA and elsewhere are pushing for homosexual marriage to be fully legalized. Why do they care? After all, as we discuss in chapter 7, marriage between heterosexual couples appears to be in decline. Activists care because they want the same status, rights and obligations as anyone else. Marriage today is above all an emotional commitment, but as recognized by the state it also has definite legal implications. It gives to partners important rights and responsibilities, of the kind given by civil partnerships in the UK. 'Ceremonies of commitment' – non-legal marriages – have also become popular among both homosexuals and heterosexuals in America, but don't confer these rights and obligations. Conversely, of course, these legal rights and obligations are one reason why many heterosexual couples now decide either to defer marriage or not to get married at all.

Opponents of homosexual marriage condemn it as either frivolous or unnatural. They see it as legitimating a sexual orientation which the state should be doing its best to curb. There are pressure groups in America dedicated to getting homosexuals to change their ways and marry people of the opposite sex. Some still see homosexuality as a perversion and are violently opposed to any provisions that might normalize it.

Yet the majority of gay people simply want to be seen as ordinary. They point out that homosexuals need economic and emotional security as much as others do. In his book *Virtually Normal* (1995), Andrew Sullivan argues forcefully for the virtues of homosexual marriage. As a Catholic and a homosexual, Sullivan has agonized over how his religious beliefs can be reconciled with his sexuality. He argues that homosexuality is at least in part given in nature – it is not usually something that is simply 'chosen'. To ask that someone renounce homosexuality is to ask that he or she give up the chance of loving, and being loved, by another. That love should be capable of expression inside marriage. If homosexuals are not to become an alienated minority, he concludes, gay marriage must be legalized.

The possibility of legal gay marriage demonstrates how radically ideas about sexuality have changed in recent decades. After all, it was only in 1967 that male homosexuality was legalized in the UK. Gay marriage also raises questions about sexual orientation: to what extent is sexual orientation inborn and to what extent is it learned? Many of the themes that we examine in this chapter overlap with the questions raised in chapter 7, 'Families and Intimate Relationships'. Human sexuality is tied up with our ideas about love and the question of what makes a good relationship. Increasingly, people argue that a good relationship must be one between equals. Gay marriage has only become possible through a struggle against discrimination and inequality that is still continuing.

We begin this chapter by discussing human sexuality and examine how sexual behaviour is changing in Western society. We then look more specifically at sexual orientation, and particularly at issues surrounding homosexuality in the West. This leads us to the broader issue of gender, and raises questions of what it means to be a man or a woman in modern society. We close with a discussion of gender inequality and look at how women's equality is increasingly finding a global expression.

Human sexuality

Ideas about **sexuality** are undergoing dramatic changes. Over the last few decades in Western countries, important aspects of people's sexual lives have been altered in a fundamental way. In traditional societies, sexuality was tied tightly to the process of reproduction, but in our current age, it has been separated from it. Sexuality has become a dimension of life for each individual to explore and shape. If sexuality once was 'defined' in terms of heterosexuality and monogamy in the context of marital relations, there is now a growing acceptance of diverse forms of sexual behaviour and orientations in a broad variety of contexts, as we saw in the discussion of gay marriage above.

In this section, we explore some of the issues surrounding human sexual behaviour: the importance of biological versus social influences, how society shapes sexual activity and the influence of procreative technology. We then examine some of the recent trends in human sexual behaviour in Western society.

Biology and sexual behaviour

Sexuality has long been considered a highly personal subject. For this reason it is a challenging area for sociologists to study. Until recently, much of what we have known about sexuality came from biologists, medical researchers and sexologists. Scholars have also looked to the animal world in an attempt to understand more about human sexual behaviour.

There is clearly a biological basis to sexuality, because female anatomy differs from that of the male. There also exists a biological imperative to reproduce; otherwise, the human species would become extinct. Some sociobiologists, such as David Barash (1979), have argued that there is an evolutionary explanation for why men tend to be more sexually promiscuous than women. His argument is that men are biologically disposed to impregnate as many women as possible, while women want stable partners to protect the biological inheritance invested in their children. This is because, while men produce millions of sperm during a lifetime, women only produce a few hundred eggs and have to carry the foetus within their body for nine months. His argument is supported by studies of the sexual behaviour of animals which claim to show that males are normally more promiscuous than females of the same species.

Many commentators are dismissive of this evolutionary approach. Steven Rose, for example, has argued that, unlike most animals, human behaviour is shaped more by the environment than determined by genetically programmed instincts: 'The human infant is born with relatively few of its neural pathways already committed' (Rose et al. 1984). Rose argues that humans have an exceptionally long infancy relative to other animals, which gives them far more time than other species to learn from their experiences.

The claims of the sociobiologists such as Barash are fiercely contested, especially as regards any implications for human sexual behaviour. One thing clearly distinguishes humans from animals, however. Human sexual behaviour is meaningful – that is, humans use and express their sexuality in a variety of ways. For humans, sexual activity is much more than biological. It is symbolic, reflecting who we are and the emotions we are experiencing. As we shall see, sexuality is far too complicated to be wholly attributable to biological traits. It must be understood in terms of the social meanings which humans ascribe to it.

Social influences on sexual behaviour

Most people, in all societies, are heterosexual – they look to the other sex for emotional involvement and sexual pleasure. Heterosexuality in every society has historically been the basis of marriage and family. Yet there are many minority sexual tastes and inclinations too. Judith Lorber (1994) distinguishes as many as ten different sexual identities: straight (heterosexual) woman, straight man, lesbian woman, gay man, bisexual woman, bisexual man, transvestite woman (a woman who regularly dresses as a man), transvestite man (a man who regularly dresses as a woman), transsexual woman (a man who becomes a woman), and transsexual man (a woman who becomes a man). Sexual practices themselves are even more diverse.

Among possible sexual practices are the following. A man or woman can have sexual relations with women, men or both. This can happen one at a time or with three or more participating. One can have sex with oneself (masturbation) or with no one (celibacy). Someone can have sexual relations with trans-sexuals or with people who erotically cross-dress, use pornography or sexual devices, practise sado-masochism (the erotic use of bondage and the inflicting of pain), have sex with animals and so on (Lorber 1994).

In all societies there are sexual norms that approve of some practices while discouraging or condemning others. Members of a society learn these norms through socialization. Over the last few decades, for example, sexual norms in Western cultures have been linked to ideas of romantic love and family relationships. Such norms, however, vary widely between different cultures. Homosexuality is a case in point. Some cultures have either tolerated or actively encouraged homosexuality in certain contexts. Among the ancient Greeks, for instance, the love of men for boys was idealized as the highest form of sexual love.

Sexual norms differ across time and space. In Ancient Greece, relationships between men and boys were an accepted norm.

Accepted types of sexual behaviour also vary between different cultures, which is one way we know that most sexual responses are learned rather than innate. The most extensive study was carried out fifty years ago by Clellan Ford and Frank Beach (1951), who surveyed anthropological evidence from more than two hundred societies. Striking variations were found in what is regarded as 'natural' sexual behaviour and in norms of sexual attractiveness. For example, in some cultures, extended foreplay, perhaps lasting hours, is thought desirable and even necessary prior to intercourse; in others, foreplay is virtually non-existent. In some

Whose body is the most attractive? In some cultures, a curvy rather than a skinny female body shape is thought to be more appealing.

societies, it is believed that overly frequent intercourse leads to physical debilitation or illness. Among the Seniang of the South Pacific, advice on the desirability of spacing out love-making is given by the elders of the village – who also believe that a person with white hair may legitimately copulate every night.

In most cultures, norms of sexual attractiveness (held by both females and males) focus more on physical looks for women than for men, a situation that seems to be gradually changing in the West as women increasingly become active in spheres outside the home. The traits seen as most important in female beauty, however, differ greatly. In the modern West, a slim, small body is admired, while in other cultures a much more generous shape is regarded as most attractive (as we saw in chapter 8, 'Health, Illness and Disability'). Sometimes the breasts are not seen as a source of sexual stimulus, whereas in some societies great erotic significance is attached to them. Some societies place great store on the shape of the face, while others emphasize the shape and colour of the eyes or the size and form of the nose and lips.

Whilst sexuality is shaped by the society in which we live, it is also shaped by the technologies available within that society. Below, we examine some of the ways in which technological change affects sexual behaviour.

Sexuality and procreative technology

For hundreds of years, childbirth and child-rearing dominated the lives of most women. In traditional societies,

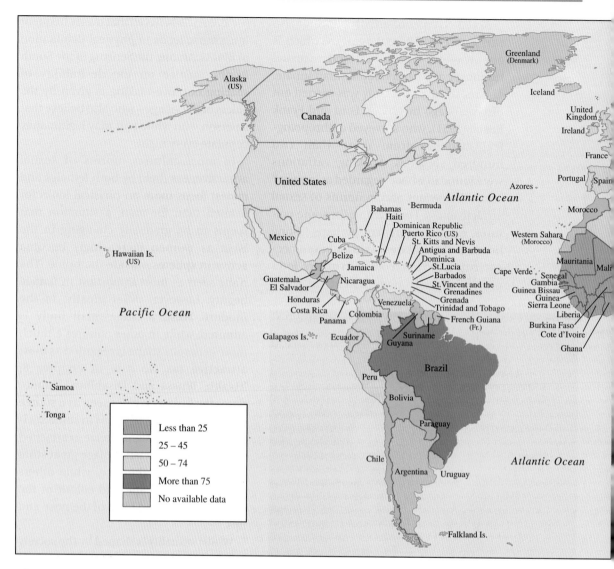

Figure 12.1   Percentage of married women using contraception

Source: UN Statistics Division (2003)

contraception was ineffective or, in some societies, unknown. Even in Europe and the United States as late as the eighteenth century, it was common for women to experience as many as twenty pregnancies (often involving miscar- riages and infant deaths). Improved methods of contraception have helped alter this situation in a fundamental way. Far from any longer being natural, it is almost unknown in the industrial countries for women to undergo so many

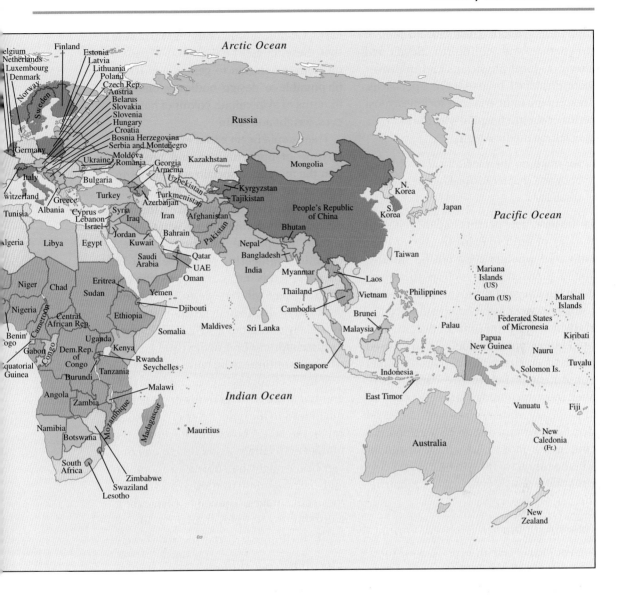

pregnancies. Advances in contraceptive technology enable most women and men to control whether and when they choose to have children (see figure 12.1).

Contraception is only one example of a **procreative technology**. Some of the other areas in which natural processes have become social are described below.

Childbirth

Medical science has not always been involved with the major life transitions from birth to death. The medicalization of pregnancy and childbirth developed slowly, as local physicians and midwives were displaced by paediatric specialists. Today in the industrialized societies, most births occur in a hospital with the help of a specialized medical team.

For more on the medicalization of the body see chapter 8, 'Health, Illness and Disability'.

In the past, new parents had to wait until the day of birth to learn the sex of their baby and whether it would be healthy. Today, prenatal tests such as the sonogram (an image of the foetus produced by using ultrasonic waves) and amniocentesis (which draws off some of the amniotic fluid from around the foetus) can be used to discover structural or chromosomal abnormalities before the baby's birth. Such new technology presents couples and society with new ethical and legal decisions. When a disorder is detected, the couple are faced with the decision of whether or not to have the baby, knowing it may be seriously disabled throughout its life.

Genetic engineering: designer babies

A great deal of scientific endeavour these days is being devoted to the expansion of genetic engineering; that is, intervening in the genetic make-up of the foetus so as to influence its subsequent development. The likely social impact of genetic engineering is starting to provoke debates almost as intense as those that surround the issue of abortion. According to its supporters, genetic engineering will bring us many benefits. It is possible, for example, to identify the genetic factors that make some people vulnerable to certain dis-

eases. Genetic reprogramming will ensure that these illnesses are no longer passed on from generation to generation. It will be possible to 'design' bodies before birth in terms of skin colour, colour of hair and eyes, weight and so on.

There could be no better example of the mixture of opportunities and problems that the increasing socialization of nature creates for us than genetic engineering. What choices will parents make if they can design their babies, and what limits should be placed on those choices? Genetic engineering is unlikely to be cheap. Will this mean that those who can afford to pay will be able to programme out from their children any traits they see as socially undesirable? What will happen to the children of more deprived groups, who will continue to be born naturally?

Some sociologists have argued that differential access to genetic engineering might lead to the emergence of a 'biological underclass'. Those who don't have the physical advantages genetic engineering can bring might be subject to prejudice and discrimination by those who do enjoy these advantages. They might have difficulty finding employment and life or health insurance (Duster 1990).

The abortion debate

Perhaps the most controversial ethical dilemma created by modern reproductive technologies in modern societies is this: under what conditions should abortion be available to women? The abortion debate has become so intense, particularly in the United States, precisely because it centres on basic ethical issues to which there are no easy solutions. Those who are 'pro-life' believe that abortion is always wrong except in extreme circumstances, because it is equivalent to murder. For them, ethical issues are above all subject to the value that must be placed on human life. Those who are 'pro-choice' argue that the mother's control over her own body – her own right to live a rewarding life – must be the primary consideration.

The debate has led to numerous episodes of violence. Can it ever be resolved? At least one prominent social and legal theorist, Ronald Dworkin (1993), has suggested that it can. The intense divisions between those who are pro-life and those who are pro-choice, he argues, hide deeper sources of agreement between the two sides, and in this there is a source of hope. At previous periods of history, life was often relatively cheap. In current times, however, we have come to place a high value on the sanctity of human life. Each side agrees with this value, but they interpret it differently, the one emphasizing the interests of the child, the other the interests of the mother. If the two sides can be persuaded that they share a common ethical value, Dworkin suggests, a more constructive dialogue may be possible.

Sexuality in Western culture

Western attitudes towards sexual behaviour were for nearly two thousand years moulded primarily by Christianity. Although different Christian sects and denominations have held divergent views about the proper place of sexuality in life, the dominant view of the Christian Church has been that all sexual behaviour is suspect except what is needed for reproduction. At some periods, this view produced an extreme prudishness in society at large. But at other times, many people ignored or reacted against the Church's teachings, commonly engaging in practices (such as adultery) forbidden by religious authorities. The idea that sexual fulfilment can and should be sought only through marriage was rare.

In the nineteenth century, religious presumptions about sexuality became partly replaced by medical ones. Most of the early writings by doctors about sexual behaviour, however, were as stern as the views of the Church. Some argued that any type of sexual activity unconnected with reproduction causes serious physical harm. Masturbation was said to bring on blindness, insanity, heart disease and other ailments, while oral sex was claimed to cause cancer. In Victorian times, sexual hypocrisy abounded. Virtuous women were believed to be indifferent to sexuality, accepting the attentions of their husbands only as a duty. Yet in the expanding towns and cities, where prostitution was rife and often openly tolerated, 'loose' women were seen in an entirely different category from their respectable sisters.

Many Victorian men who were on the face of things sober, well-behaved citizens, devoted to their wives, regularly visited prostitutes or kept mistresses. Such behaviour was treated leniently, whereas 'respectable' women who took lovers were regarded as scandalous and were shunned in public society if their behaviour came to light. The different attitudes towards the sexual activities of men and women formed a double standard, which has long existed and whose residues still linger on today (Barret-Ducrocq, 1992).

In current times, traditional attitudes exist alongside much more liberal attitudes towards sexuality, which developed particularly strongly in the 1960s. Some people, particularly those influenced by

INTERIOR OF A WEST-END BROTHEL.

In Victorian times, a man could keep a mistress or visit a prostitute with impunity. A woman who did the same would be considered totally unacceptable.

Christian teachings, believe that pre-marital sex is wrong, and generally frown on all forms of sexual behaviour except heterosexual activity within the confines of marriage – although it is now much more commonly accepted that sexual pleasure is a desirable and important feature. Others, by contrast, condone or actively approve of pre-marital sex and hold tolerant attitudes towards different sexual practices (see table 12.1). Sexual attitudes have undoubtedly become more permissive over the past thirty years in most Western countries. In films and plays,

scenes are shown that previously would have been completely unacceptable, while pornographic material is readily available to most adults who want it.

Sexual behaviour: Kinsey's studies

We can speak much more confidently about public values concerning sexuality than we can about private practices, for by their nature such practices go mostly undocumented. When Alfred Kinsey began his research in the United States in the 1940s and 1950s, it was the first time a major investigation of actual sexual

Table 12.1 Attitudes towards sexual relations, Great Britain, 1998 (%)[a]

	Always wrong	Mostly wrong	Sometimes wrong	Rarely wrong	Not wrong at all	Other[b]	All
A man and a woman having sexual relations before marriage	8	8	12	10	58	5	100
A married person having sexual relations with someone other than their spouse	52	29	13	1	2	4	100
A boy and a girl having sexual relations aged under 16	56	24	11	3	3	3	100
Sexual relations between two adults of the same sex	39	12	11	8	23	8	100

[a] People aged 18 and over were asked whether they thought different types of sexual relations were wrong, on a five-point scale ranging from 'Always wrong' to 'Not wrong at all'.

[b] Includes those who did not reply, those who replied 'Don't know', and those responding 'Depends' or 'Varies'.

Source: Social Trends 30 (2000)

behaviour had been undertaken. Kinsey and his co-researchers faced condemnation from religious organizations, and his work was denounced as immoral in the newspapers and in Congress. But he persisted, and eventually obtained sexual life histories of 18,000 people, a reasonably representative sample of the white American population (Kinsey 1948, 1953).

Kinsey's results were surprising to most and shocking to many, because they revealed a great difference between the public expectations of sexual behaviour prevailing at that time and actual sexual conduct. He found that almost 70 per cent of men had visited a prostitute, and 84 per cent had had pre-marital sexual experience. Yet, following the double standard, 40 per cent of men expected their wives to be virgins at the time of marriage. More than 90 per cent of males had engaged in masturbation and nearly 60 per cent in

some form of oral sexual activity. Among women, around 50 per cent had had pre-marital sexual experience, although mostly with their prospective husbands. Some 60 per cent had masturbated, and the same percentage had engaged in oral-genital contacts.

The gap between publicly accepted attitudes and actual behaviour that Kinsey's findings demonstrated was probably especially great at that particular period, just after the Second World War. A phase of sexual liberalization had begun rather earlier, in the 1920s, when many younger people felt freed from the strict moral codes that had governed earlier generations. Sexual behaviour probably changed a good deal, but issues concerning sexuality were not openly discussed in the way that has become familiar now. People participating in sexual activities that were still strongly disapproved of on a public level concealed them, not realizing the full extent to which others were engaging in similar practices. The more permissive era of the 1960s brought openly declared attitudes more into line with the realities of behaviour. Kinsey died in 1956, but the Institute for Sex Research which he headed continues its research to this day. It was renamed the Kinsey Institute for Research in Sex, Gender and Reproduction in 1981 to celebrate his contribution to research.

Prostitution

Prostitution can be defined as the granting of sexual favours for monetary gain. The word 'prostitute' began to come into common usage in the late eighteenth century. In the ancient world, most purveyors of sexuality for economic reward were courtesans, concubines (kept mistresses) or slaves. Courtesans and concubines often had a high position in traditional societies.

A key aspect of modern prostitution is that women and their clients are generally unknown to one another. Although men may become 'regular customers', the relationship is not initially established on the basis of personal acquaintance. This was not true of most forms of the dispensing of sexual favours for material gain in earlier times. Prostitution is directly connected to the break-up of small-scale communities, the development of large impersonal urban areas and the commercializing of social relations. In small-scale traditional communities, sexual relations were controlled by their very visibility. In newly developed urban areas, more anonymous social connections were easily established.

Prostitution today

Prostitutes in the UK today come mainly from poorer social backgrounds, as they did in the past, but they have been joined by considerable numbers of middle-class women. The increasing divorce rate has tempted some newly impoverished women into prostitution. In addition, some women unable to find jobs after graduation work in massage parlours, or in call-girl networks, while looking for other employment opportunities.

A United Nations resolution passed in 1951 condemns those who organize prostitution or profit from the activities of prostitutes, but does not ban prostitution as such. A total of fifty-three member states, including the UK, have formally accepted the resolution, although their legislation on prostitution varies widely. In some countries prostitution itself is illegal. Other countries, like Britain, prohibit only certain types, such as street soliciting or child prostitution. Some national or local governments license officially recognized brothels or sex parlours – such as the 'Eros centres' in Germany or the sex houses in Amsterdam. In October 1999 the Dutch Parliament turned prostitution into an official profession for the estimated 30,000 women who work in the sex industry. All venues where sex is sold will now be regulated, licensed and inspected by local authorities. Only a few countries license male prostitutes.

Legislation against prostitution rarely punishes clients. Those who purchase sexual services are not arrested or prosecuted, and in court procedures their identities may be kept hidden. There are far fewer studies of clients than of those selling sex, and it is rare for anyone to suggest – as is often stated or implied about prostitutes – that the clients are psychologically disturbed. The imbalance in research surely expresses an uncritical acceptance of orthodox stereotypes of sexuality according to which it is 'normal' for men to actively seek a variety of sexual outlets, while those who cater for these needs are condemned.

The global 'sex industry'

Prostitution is part of the **sex tourism** industry in several areas of the world – for instance, in Thailand and the Philippines. Package tours, oriented towards prostitution, draw men to these areas from Europe, the United States and Japan, often in search of sex with minors – although these tours are illegal in the United Kingdom.

Sex tourism in the Far East has its origins in the provision of prostitutes for American troops during the Korean and Vietnam wars. 'Rest and recreation' centres were built in Thailand, the Philippines, Vietnam, Korea and Taiwan. Some still remain, particularly in the Philippines, catering to regular shipments of tourists as well as to the military stationed in the region.

A report published in 1998 by the International Labour Organization (ILO) found that prostitution and the sex industry in Southeast Asia have taken on the dimensions of a fully fledged commercial sector, having grown rapidly over recent decades. Cheaper global travel and the large differential in the exchange rate between Asian and international currencies have made sex tourism more affordable and attractive to foreigners. Furthermore, the sex industry is linked to economic hardship. Some desperate families force their own children into prostitution; other young people are unwittingly lured into the sex trade by responding innocently to advertisements for 'entertainers' or 'dancers'. Migration patterns from rural to urban areas are an important factor in the growth of the sex industry, as many women eager to leave their traditional and constraining home towns grasp at any opportunity to do so.

The ILO report warns that many of the countries in which the sex industry is particularly widespread do not have a legal framework or social policies for handling its many consequences. Prostitution bears serious implications for the spread of AIDS and sexually transmitted diseases. It is also often associated with violence, criminality, the drug trade, exploitation and violations of human rights (Lim 1998).

Explaining prostitution

Why does prostitution exist? Certainly it is an enduring phenomenon, which resists the attempts of governments to eliminate it. It is also almost always a matter of women selling sexual favours to men, rather than the reverse – although there are some instances, as in Hamburg, in Germany, where 'houses of pleasure' exist to provide male sexual services to women. Of course, boys or men also prostitute themselves with other men.

No single factor can explain prostitution. It might seem that men simply have stronger, or more persistent, sexual needs than women, and therefore require the outlets that prostitution provides. But this explanation is implausible. Most women seem capable of developing their sexuality in a more intense fashion than men of comparable age. Moreover, if prostitution existed simply to serve sexual needs, there would surely be many male prostitutes catering for women.

The most persuasive general conclusion to be drawn is that prostitution expresses, and to some extent helps perpetuate, the tendency of men to treat women as objects who can be 'used' for sexual purposes. Prostitution expresses in a particular context the inequalities of power between men and women. Of course, many other elements are also involved. Prostitution offers a means of obtaining sexual satisfaction for people who, because of their physical shortcomings or the existence of restrictive moral codes, cannot find other sexual partners. Prostitutes cater for men who are away from home, desire sexual encounters without commitment or have unusual sexual tastes that other women will not accept. But these factors are relevant to the extent of the occurrence of prostitution rather than to its overall nature.

Sexual behaviour after Kinsey

In the 1960s, the social movements that challenged the existing order of things, like those associated with countercultural or 'hippy' lifestyles, also broke with existing sexual norms. These movements preached sexual freedom, and the invention of the contraceptive pill for women allowed sexual pleasure to be clearly separated from reproduction. Women's groups also started pressing for greater independence from male sexual values, the rejection of the double standard and recognition of the need for women to achieve greater sexual satisfaction in their relationships.

Until recently it was difficult to know with accuracy how much sexual behaviour had changed since the time of Kinsey's research. In the late 1980s, Lillian Rubin interviewed a thousand Americans between the ages of thirteen and forty-eight to try to discover what changes had occurred in sexual behaviour and attitudes over the preceding thirty years or so. According to her findings, there were indeed significant developments. Sexual activity was typically beginning at a younger age than was characteristic of the previous generation; moreover, the sexual practices of teenagers tended to be as varied and comprehensive as those of adults. There was still a double standard, but it was not as powerful as it had been. One of the most important changes was that women had come to expect, and actively pursue, sexual pleasure in relationships. They were expecting to receive, not only to provide, sexual satisfaction – a phenomenon that Rubin argues (1990) has major consequences for both sexes.

Women are more sexually liberated than was once the case; but along with this development, which most men applaud, has come a new assertiveness that many men find difficult to accept. The men Rubin talked to often said they 'felt inadequate', were afraid they could 'never do anything right' and found it 'impossible to satisfy women these days' (Rubin 1990).

Men feel inadequate? Doesn't this contradict all that we have come to expect? For in modern society, men continue to dominate in most spheres, and they are in general much more violent towards women than the other way round. Such violence is substantially aimed at the control and continuing subordination of women. Yet a number of authors – as we see below in our study of Bob Connell and the gender order (pp. 462–7) – have begun to argue that masculinity is a burden as much as a source of reward. Much male sexuality, some add, is compulsive rather than satisfying. If men were to stop using sexuality as a means of control, not only women but they themselves would gain.

Theorizing sexuality

Two researchers at the Kinsey Institute, John Gagnon and William Simon, began to take a more theoretical interest in the data that they were dealing with. In their highly influential book *Sexual Conduct* (1973), the authors suggested the metaphor of a script was helpful in understanding human sexual behaviour.

The metaphor of a script builds on the metaphor of a drama to explain everyday social interaction, introduced by Erving Goffman. (In chapter 5 we examined Goffman's dramaturgical analysis and looked at various examples of social interaction where the metaphor is appropriate.) Sex, argued Gagnon and Simon, is also usefully analysed through the metaphor of a drama. There are elaborate rules, rituals and a metaphorical script to tell us the 'who, what, where and when and even why we have sex'.

As Kinsey and his team showed, sexual behaviour includes an enormous diversity of possible activities: fleeting hetero- or homosexual encounters, prostitution, sex with a long-term partner and so on. For humans, none of these sex acts occurs without forethought or preparation. Each sexual act involves a sexual script to make it comprehensible. Take a meeting between a man and a female prostitute for example. The sexual encounters will involve finding a suitable partner (*who*), negotiation over the sexual act and the price (*what*), the finding of a location, such as a hotel or a brothel (*where*), the agreement to meet (*when*) and, perhaps, some explanation or justification of the action – loneliness, relationship problems or companionship, for example (*why*). This example uses a man's sexual encounter with a prostitute, but any sexual act could have been applied.

To Gagnon and Simon, a reading of the sexual script is crucial if we want to understand human sexuality. The authors argue that these scripts take three important forms: 'personal scripts' are carried within an individual's head and provide information about their own sexual desires; 'interactive scripts' are negotiated between sexual partners and involve explanation of roles; 'historical-cultural scripts' exist within a wider culture and provide (often unconscious) information on a person's role and the sexual expectations that exist within that culture.

The work of Gagnon and Simon is seen as the foundation of the 'social-constructivist' approach to sexuality. Social constructionism was discussed in more detail in chapter 5 on pp. 152–4.

A new fidelity?

In 1994 a team of researchers published *The Social Organization of Sexuality: Sexual Practices in the United States*, the most comprehensive study of sexual behaviour in any country since Kinsey. To the surprise of many, their findings suggested an essential sexual conservatism among Americans. For instance, 83 per cent of their subjects had had only one partner (or no partner at all) in the preceding year and among married people the figure rises to 96 per cent. Fidelity to one's spouse is also quite common: only 10 per cent of women and fewer than 25 per cent of men reported having an extramarital affair during their lifetime. According to the study, Americans average only three partners during their entire lifetime. Despite the apparently settled nature of behaviour, some distinct changes emerge from this study, the most significant being a progressive increase in the level of pre-marital sexual experience, particularly among women. In fact, more than 95 per cent of Americans getting married today are sexually experienced (Laumann 1994).

The support for sexual fidelity which the researchers found in the USA also seems to be found in the UK. A poll carried out in 2000 showed that 72 per cent of people considered it 'very wrong' and 21 per cent 'fairly wrong' to have sex with someone other than their partner. Perhaps not surprisingly, people who were religiously devout, and those who were widowed, considered it more wrong than the non-religious and the single. Interestingly, it was the youngest group (those aged between fifteen and twenty-four) who were most likely to agree that life in Britain would be improved if people were more sexually faithful (MORI, 2000). Intimate relationships are discussed in more detail in chapter 7.

Surveys of sexual behaviour are fraught with difficulties. We simply don't know how far people tell the truth about their sexual lives when asked by a researcher. *The Social Organization of Sexuality* seems to show that Americans are less adventurous in their sexual lives than they used to be at the time of the Kinsey reports. It may be that the Kinsey reports themselves were inaccurate. Perhaps the fear of AIDS has led many people to restrict the range of their sexual activities. Or perhaps for some reason people are more prone today to hide aspects of their sexual activities. We cannot be sure.

The validity of surveys of sexual behaviour became the focus of intense debate (Lewontin 1995). Critics of the research just discussed have asserted that such surveys do not generate reliable information about sexual practices. Part of the controversy centred on replies from older people questioned. The researchers reported that 45 per cent of men aged between eighty and eighty-five years old say they have sex with their partner. The critics feel that this is so obviously untrue that it calls into doubt the findings of the whole survey. The researchers defended themselves against the charge, and received some support from specialists in the study of older people, who accused the critics of having negative stereotypes of ageing. They pointed out that in one study of older men living outside institutions, 74 per cent were sexually active. One study in fact found that most men even in their nineties sustained an interest in sex.

In the section below we focus our discussion more specifically on sexual orientation, particularly on homosexuality, and examine some of the key debates, issues and theories in this area on which sociologists are working.

Sexual orientation

Sexual orientation concerns the direction of one's sexual or romantic attraction. The term 'sexual preference', which is sometimes incorrectly used instead of sexual orientation, is misleading and is to be avoided, since it implies that one's sexual or romantic attraction is entirely a matter of personal choice. As you will see below, sexual orientation in all cultures results from a complex interplay of biological and social factors not yet fully understood.

The most commonly found sexual orientation in all cultures, including the United Kingdom, is **heterosexuality**, a sexual or romantic attraction for persons of the opposite sex (*hetero* comes from the Greek word meaning 'other' or 'different'). **Homosexuality** involves the sexual or romantic attraction for persons of one's own sex. Today, the term *gay* is used to refer to male homosexuals, **lesbian** for female homosexuals, and *bi* as shorthand for **bisexuals**, people who experience sexual or romantic attraction for persons of either sex.

Orientation of sexual activities or feelings towards others of the same sex exists in all cultures. In some non-Western cultures, homosexual relations are accepted or even encouraged among certain groups. The Batak people of northern Sumatra, for example, permit male homosexual relations before marriage. Boys leave the parental home at puberty and sleep in a dwelling with a dozen or so older males who initiate the newcomers into homosexual practices. In many societies, however, homosexuality is not accepted in such an open way. In the Western world, for example, the prevailing idea of the homosexual is of an individual clearly marked off in terms of his or her sexual tastes from the majority of the population.

In his studies of sexuality, Michel Foucault has shown that before the eighteenth century, the notion of a homosexual person seems barely to have existed (Foucault 1978). The act of sodomy was denounced by Church authorities and by the law; in England and several other European countries, it was punishable by death. However, sodomy was not defined specifically as a homosexual offence. It applied to relations between men and women, men and animals, as well as men among themselves. The term 'homosexuality' was coined in the 1860s, and from then on, homosexuals were increasingly regarded as being a separate type of people with a particular sexual aberration (Weeks 1986). Homosexuality became part of a 'medicalized' discourse; it was spoken of in clinical terms as a psychiatric disorder or a perversion, rather than a religious 'sin'. Homosexuals, along with other 'deviants' such as paedophiles and transvestites, were seen as suffering from a biological pathology that threatened the wholesomeness of mainstream society.

> For more on medicalized perspectives see chapter 8, 'Health, Illness and Disability', p. 263.

The death penalty for 'unnatural acts' was abolished in the United States after independence, and in European countries in the late eighteenth and early nineteenth centuries. Until just a few decades ago, however, homosexuality remained a criminal activity in virtually all Western countries. The shift of homosexuals from the margins of society to the mainstream is not yet complete, but rapid progress has been seen over recent years, as the discussion of gay marriage that opens this chapter shows.

Is sexual orientation inborn or learned?

Most sociologists currently believe that one's sexual orientation – whether homosexual, heterosexual or something else – results from a complex interplay between biological factors and social learning. Since heterosexuality is the norm for most people, a great deal of research has focused on why some people become homosexual. Some scholars argue that biological influences are the most important, predisposing certain people to become homosexual from birth (Bell et al. 1981). Biological explanations for homosexuality have included differences in such things as brain characteristics of homosexuals (Maugh and Zamichow 1991) and the impact on foetal development of the mother's in utero hormone production during pregnancy (McFadden and Champlin 2000). Such studies, which are based on small numbers of cases, give highly inconclusive (and highly controversial) results (Healy 2001). It is virtually impossible to separate biological from early social influences in determining a person's sexual orientation.

Studies of twins hold some promise for understanding if there is any genetic basis for homosexuality, since identical twins share identical genes. In two related studies, Bailey and Pillard (Bailey and Pillard 1991; Bailey 1993) examined 167 pairs of brothers and 143 pairs of sisters, with each pair of siblings raised in the same family, in which at least one sibling defined him- or herself as homosexual. Some of these pairs were identical twins (who share all genes), some were fraternal twins (who share some genes) and some were adoptive brothers or sisters (who share no genes). The researchers reasoned that if sexual orientation is determined entirely by biology, then all of the identical twins should be homosexual, since their genetic make-up is identical. Among the fraternal twins, some pairs would be homosexual, since some genes are shared. The lowest rates of homosexuality were predicted for the adoptive brothers and sisters.

The results of this study seem to show that homosexuality results from a combination of biological and social factors. Among both the men and the women studied, roughly one out of every two identical twins was homosexual, compared with one out of every five fraternal twins, and one out of every ten adoptive brothers and sisters. In other words, a woman or man is five times more likely to be lesbian or gay if her or his identical twin is lesbian or gay than if his or her sibling is lesbian or gay but related only through adoption. These results offer some support for the importance of biological factors, since the higher the percentage of shared genes, the greater the percentage of cases in which both siblings were homosexual. However, since approximately half of the identical twin brothers and sisters of homosexuals were not themselves homosexual, a great deal of social learning must also be involved; otherwise one would expect *all* identical twin siblings of homosexuals to be homosexual as well.

It's clear that even studies of identical twins cannot fully isolate biological from social factors. It is often the case that even in infancy, identical twins are treated more like one another by parents, peers and teachers than are fraternal twins, who in turn are treated more like one another than are adoptive siblings. Thus, identical twins may have more than genes in common: they may share a higher proportion of similar socializing experiences as well.

Homosexuality in Western culture

Kenneth Plummer, in a classic study, distinguished four types of homosexuality within modern Western culture. *Casual homosexuality* (1975) is a passing homosexual encounter that does not substantially structure a person's overall sexual life. Schoolboy crushes and mutual masturbation are examples. *Situated activities* refer to circumstances in which homosexual acts are regularly carried out but do not become an individual's overriding

"We're not doing anything for Gay Pride this year. We're here, we're queer, we're used to it."

preference. In settings such as prisons or military camps, where men live without women, homosexual behaviour of this kind is common, regarded as a substitute for heterosexual behaviour rather than as preferable.

Personalized homosexuality refers to individuals who have a preference for homosexual activities but who are isolated from groups in which this is easily accepted. Homosexuality here is a furtive activity, hidden away from friends and colleagues. *Homosexuality as a way of life* refers to individuals who have 'come out' and have made associations with others of similar sexual tastes a key part of their lives. Such people usually belong to gay subcultures, in which homosexual activities are integrated into a distinct lifestyle. Such communities often provide the possibility of collective political action to advance the rights and interests of homosexuals.

The proportion of the population (both male and female) who have had homosexual experiences or experienced strong inclinations towards homosexuality is probably much larger than those who follow an openly gay lifestyle. The probable extent of homosexuality in Western cultures first became known with the publication of Alfred Kinsey's research. According to his findings, no more than half of all American men are completely heterosexual, judged by their sexual activities and inclinations after puberty. Of Kinsey's sample, 8 per cent had been involved in exclusively homosexual relationships for periods of three years or more. A further 10 per cent had engaged in homosexual and heterosexual activities more or less equally. Kinsey's most striking finding was that 37 per cent of men had had at least one homosexual experience to

the level of orgasm. An additional 13 per cent had felt homosexual desires but had not acted on them.

Rates of homosexuality among women indicated by the Kinsey researches were lower. About 2 per cent of females were exclusively homosexual. Homosexual experiences were reported by 13 per cent, while a further 15 per cent admitted they had felt homosexual desires without acting on them. Kinsey and his colleagues were startled by the level of homosexuality their studies revealed, so the results were rechecked using different methods, but the conclusions remained the same (Kinsey 1948, 1953).

The results from *The Social Organization of Sexuality* (Laumann 1994) call into question the findings of Kinsey's study on the prevalence of homosexuality. In contrast to Kinsey's 37 per cent, only 9 per cent of men in the later study reported having had a homosexual encounter to the level of orgasm, only about 8 per cent of men reported having homosexual desires (compared to 13 per cent) and just under 3 per cent reported a sexual encounter with another man in the preceding year. As the authors of this later study acknowledged, the stigma that remains attached to homosexuality probably contributed to a general underreporting of homosexual behaviour. And, as one critic noted, the authors' random sample failed to address the geographical concentration of homosexuals in large cities, where they probably constitute close to 10 per cent of the overall population (Laumann 1994).

Lesbianism

Male homosexuality generally receives more attention than **lesbianism** – homosexual attachment or activities among women. Lesbian groups tend to be less highly organized than male gay subcultures and include a lower proportion of casual relationships. In campaigns for homosexual rights, lesbian activist groups are often treated as if their interests were identical to those of male organizations. But while there is sometimes close cooperation between male gays and lesbians, there are also differences, particularly where lesbians are actively involved in feminism. Some lesbian women came to feel that the gay liberation movement reflected the interests of men, while liberal and radical feminists were concerned exclusively with the concerns of middle-class, heterosexual women. Thus, a distinctive brand of lesbian feminism emerged which promoted the spread of 'female values' and challenged the established, dominant institution of male heterosexuality (Rich 1981). Many gay women view lesbianism less as a sexual orientation and more as a commitment to and form of solidarity with other women – politically, socially and personally (Seidman 1997).

Attitudes towards homosexuality

Attitudes of intolerance towards homosexuality have been so pronounced in the past that it is only during recent years that some of the myths surrounding the subject have been dispelled. Homosexuality has long been stigmatized in the United Kingdom and around the world. (The concept of 'stigma' is discussed on p. 269) **Homophobia**, a term coined in the late 1960s, refers to an aversion or hatred of homosexuals and their lifestyles, along with behaviour based on such aversion. Homophobia is a form of prejudice that is

reflected not only in overt acts of hostility and violence towards lesbians and gays, but also in various forms of verbal abuse that are widespread in British culture – for example, using terms like 'fag' or 'queer' to insult a heterosexual male, or using female-related offensive terms like 'sissy' or 'pansy' to put down gay men. Although homosexuality is becoming more accepted, homophobia remains ingrained in many realms of Western society; antagonism towards homosexuals persists in many people's emotional attitudes. Instances of violent assault and murder of homosexuals remain all too common.

See the issues raised in the section 'Crimes against homosexuals', in chapter 19, pp. 819–20.

Some kinds of male gay behaviour might be seen as attempts to alter the usual connections of masculinity and power – one reason, perhaps, why the heterosexual community so often finds them threatening. Gay men tend to reject the image of the effeminacy popularly associated with them, and they deviate from this in two ways. One is through cultivating outrageous effeminacy – a 'camp' masculinity that parodies the stereotype. The other is by developing a 'macho' image. This also is not conventionally masculine; men dressed as motorcyclists or cowboys are again parodying masculinity, by exaggerating it – think of the 1970s band The Village People singing *YMCA*, for example (Bertelson 1986).

Some sociologists have investigated the effect of the AIDS epidemic on popular attitudes to homosexuality. They suggest that the epidemic has challenged some of

The Village People demonstrate a particularly extreme parody of 'macho' forms of masculinity.

the main ideological foundations of heterosexual masculinity. Sexuality and sexual behaviour, for example, have become topics of public discussion, from safe sex campaigns backed by government funds to media coverage of the spread of the epidemic. The epidemic has threatened the legitimacy of traditional ideas of morality by drawing public attention to the prevalence of pre-marital sex, extramarital affairs and non-heterosexual relations in society. But most of all, in increasing the visibility of homosexuals, the epidemic has called the 'universality' of heterosexuality into question and has demonstrated that alternatives exist to the traditional nuclear family (Redman 1996). The response has sometimes taken hysterical and paranoid forms, however. Homosexuals are depicted as a deviant threat to the moral well-being of 'normal society'. In order to preserve heterosexual masculinity as the 'norm', it becomes necessary to marginalize and vilify the perceived threat (Rutherford and Chapman 1988).

The movement for gay and lesbian civil rights

Until recently, most homosexuals hid their sexual orientation, for fear that 'coming out of the closet' would cost them their jobs, families and friends, and leave them open to verbal and physical abuse. Yet, since the late 1960s, many homosexuals have acknowledged their homosexuality openly, and as we saw in the discussion of gay marriage that started this chapter, in some areas the lives of homosexual men and women have to a large extent been normalized (Seidman et al. 1999). London, New York, San Francisco, Sydney and many other large metropolitan areas around the world have thriving gay and lesbian communities. 'Coming out' may be important not only for the person who does so, but for others in the larger society; previously 'closeted' lesbians and gays come to realize they are not alone, while heterosexuals are forced to recognize that people whom they have admired and respected are homosexual.

The current global wave of gay and lesbian civil rights movements began partly as an outgrowth of the social movements of the 1960s, which emphasized pride in racial and ethnic identity. One pivotal event was the Stonewall Riots in June 1969 in the United States, when New York City's gay community – angered by continual police harassment – fought the New York Police Department for two days, a public action that for most people (gay or not) was practically unthinkable (Weeks 1977; D'Emilio 1983). The Stonewall Riots became a symbol of gay pride, heralding

the 'coming out' of gays and lesbians, who insisted not only on equal treatment under the law, but also on a complete end to the stigmatization of their lifestyle. In 1994, on the twenty-fifth anniversary of the Stonewall Riots, 100,000 people attended the International March on the United Nations to Affirm the Human Rights of Lesbian and Gay People. It is clear that significant strides have been made, although discrimination and outright homophobia remain serious problems for many lesbian, gay and bisexual people.

There are enormous differences between countries in the degree to which homosexuality is legally punishable (see figure 12.2). In Africa, for example, male homosexual acts have been legalized in only a handful of countries, while female homosexuality is seldom mentioned in the law at all. In South Africa, the official policy of the former white government was to regard homosexuality as a psychiatric problem that threatened national security. Once it took power, however, the black government legislated full equality. In Asia and the Middle East, the situation is similar: male homosexuality is banned in the vast majority of countries, including all those that are predominantly Islamic. Europe, meanwhile, has some of the most liberal laws in the world: homosexuality has been legalized in nearly all countries, and, as we saw above, several countries legally recognize same-sex marriages.

Today there is a growing movement around the world for the rights of homosexuals. The International Lesbian and Gay Association (ILGA), which was founded in 1978, today has more than 400 member organizations in around ninety countries (ILGA 2004). It holds international conferences, supports lesbian and

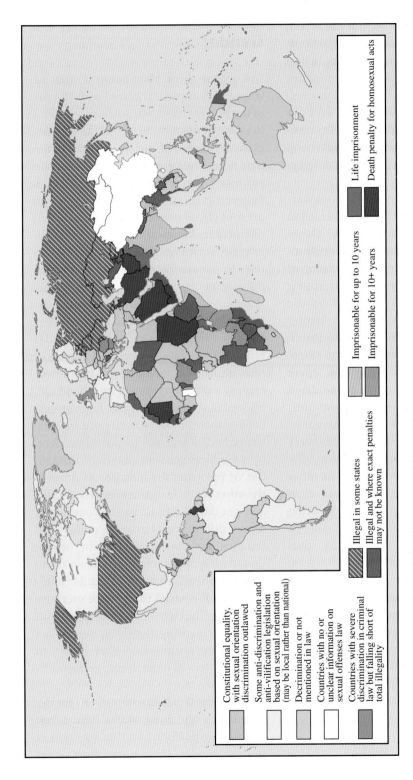

Figure 12.2 Sexual minorities and the law across the world

Source: New Internationalist 326 (October 2000)

Constitutional equality, with sexual orientation discrimination outlawed

Some anti-discrimination and anti-vilification legislation based on sexual orientation (may be local rather than national)

Decrimination or not mentioned in law

Countries with no or unclear information on sexual offenses law

Countries with severe discrimination in criminal law but falling short of total illegality

Illegal in some states

Illegal and where exact penalties may not be known

Imprisonable for up to 10 years

Imprisonable for 10+ years

Life imprisonment

Death penalty for homosexual acts

gay social movements around the world, and lobbies international organizations. For example, it convinced the Council of Europe to require all of its member nations to repeal laws banning homosexuality. In general, active lesbian and gay social movements tend to thrive in countries that emphasize individual rights and liberal state policies (Frank and McEneaney 1999).

The advance in the rights of homosexuals in many parts of the world has led to the emergence of **queer theory**. Queer theory builds upon the social constructionist approach to sexuality developed by Gagnon and Simon (see above, pp. 448–9), and is partly based on the work of Judith Butler discussed in chapter 4. The term 'queer', previously an insult, emerged as a self-characterization of lesbians and gay men in the 1980s. Queer theory argues that sociology is prejudiced towards heterosexuals and that non-heterosexual voices must be brought to the fore. Queer theorists argue that every major sociological topic (religion, the body, globalization, etc), as well as other subjects, including literature and even lesbian and gay studies, should bring queer voices to the centre to challenge the heterosexual assumptions that underlie much contemporary thinking (Epstein 2002).

So far, we have discussed men's and women's sexualities, but we haven't asked what *being a man*, or *being a woman* means. It is to a discussion of gender that we now turn to look at some of the answers to this, and other, questions.

Gender

You might think that being a man or woman is simply associated with the sex of the physical body we are born with. But like many questions of interest to sociologists, the nature of maleness and femaleness is not so easily classified. This section examines the origins of the differences between men and women. Before we go on, though, we need to make an important distinction, between **sex** and **gender**. In general, sociologists use the term *sex* to refer to the anatomical and physiological differences that define male and female bodies. *Gender*, by contrast, concerns the psychological, social and cultural differences between males and females. Gender is linked to socially constructed notions of masculinity and femininity; it is not necessarily a direct product of an individual's biological sex. Some people, for example, believe that they have been born into the wrong bodies and seek to 'put things right' by switching genders part way through life, or following the lifestyles or dress of the other sex. The distinction between sex and gender is a fundamental one, since many differences between males and females are not biological in origin. Contrasting approaches have been taken to explain the formation of gender identities and the social roles based on those identities. The debate is really one about how much learning there is: some scholars allow more prominence than others to social influences in analysing gender differences.

Sociological interpretations of gender differences and inequalities have taken contrasting positions on this question of sex and gender. Three broad approaches will be explored below. First we shall look at arguments for a biological basis to behavioural differences between men and women. Next, attention will turn to theories placing central importance on socialization and the learning of gender roles. Finally, we shall consider the ideas of scholars who believe that both gender and sex have no biological basis, but are entirely socially constructed.

Gender and biology: natural differences?

How far are differences in the behaviour of women and men the result of sex rather than gender? In other words, how much are they the result of biological differences? As we saw above in the section 'Biology and sexual behaviour' (p. 437), some authors hold that aspects of human biology – ranging from hormones to chromosomes to brain size to genetics – are responsible for innate differences in behaviour between men and women. These differences, they claim, can be seen in some form across all cultures, implying that natural factors are responsible for the inequalities between genders which characterize most societies. Such researchers are likely to draw attention to the fact, for example, that in almost all cultures, men rather than women take part in hunting and warfare. Surely, they argue, this indicates that men possess biologically based tendencies towards aggression that women lack?

Many researchers remain unconvinced by this argument. The level of aggressiveness of males, they say, varies widely between different cultures, and women are expected to be more passive or gentle in some cultures than in others (Elshtain 1987). Critics point out that theories of 'natural difference' are often grounded in data on animal behaviour rather than in anthropological or historical evidence about human behaviour, which reveal variation over time and place. Moreover, they add, because a trait is more or less universal, it does not follow that it is biological in origin; there may be cultural factors of a general kind that produce such characteristics. For instance, in the majority of cultures, most women spend a significant part of their lives caring for children and could not readily take part in hunting or war.

Although the hypothesis that biological factors determine behaviour patterns in men and women cannot be dismissed out of hand, nearly a century of research to identify the physiological origins of such an influence has been unsuccessful. There is no evidence of the mechanisms which would link such biological forces with the complex social behaviour exhibited by human men and women (Connell 1987). Theories which see individuals as complying with some kind of innate predisposition neglect the vital role of social interaction in shaping human behaviour.

Gender socialization

Another route to take in understanding the origins of gender differences is the study of **gender socialization**, the learning of gender roles with the help of social agencies such as the family and the media. Such an approach makes a distinction between biological sex and social gender – an infant is born with the first and develops the second. Through contact with various agencies of socialization, both primary and secondary, children gradually internalize the social norms and expectations which are seen to correspond with their sex. Gender differences are not biologically determined, they are culturally produced. According to this view, gender inequalities result because men and women are socialized into different roles.

Theories of gender socialization have been favoured by functionalists who see boys and girls as learning 'sex roles' and the male and female identities – masculinity and femininity – which accompany them (see below, pp. 467–9, 'Functionalist approaches'). They are guided in this process by positive and negative **sanctions**, socially applied forces which reward or restrain behaviour. For example, a small boy could be positively sanctioned in his behaviour ('What a brave boy you are!'), or be the recipient of negative sanction ('Boys don't play with dolls'). These positive and negative reinforcements aid boys and girls in learning and conforming to expected sex roles. If an individual develops gender practices which do not correspond to his or her biological sex – that is, they are deviant – the explanation is seen to reside in inadequate or irregular socialization. According to this functionalist view, socializing agencies contribute to the maintenance of social order by overseeing the smooth gender socialization of new generations.

This rigid interpretation of sex roles and socialization has been criticized on a number of fronts. Many writers argue that gender socialization is not an inherently smooth process; different 'agencies' such as the family, schools and peer groups may be at odds with one another. Moreover, socialization theories ignore the ability of individuals to reject, or modify, the social expectations surrounding sex roles. As Connell has argued:

'Agencies of socialization' cannot produce mechanical effects in a growing person. What they do is invite the child to participate in social practice on given terms. The invitation may be, and often is, coercive – accompanied by heavy pressure to accept and no mention of an alternative . . . Yet children do decline, or more exactly start making their own moves on the terrain of gender. They may refuse heterosexuality . . . they may set about blending masculine and feminine elements, for example girls insisting on competitive sport at school. They may start a split in their own lives, for example boys dressing in drag when by themselves. They may construct a fantasy life at odds with their actual practice, which is perhaps the commonest move of all. (1987)

It is important to remember that humans are not passive objects or unquestioning recipients of gender 'programming', as some sociologists have suggested. People are active agents who create and modify roles for themselves. While we should be sceptical of any wholesale adoption of the sex roles approach, many studies have shown that to some degree gender identities are a result of social influences.

Social influences on gender identity flow through many diverse channels; even parents committed to raising their children in a 'non-sexist' way find existing patterns of gender learning difficult to combat (Statham 1986). Studies of parent–child interactions, for example, have shown distinct differences in the treatment of boys and girls even when the parents believe their reactions to both are the same. The toys, picture books and television programmes experienced by young children all tend to emphasize differences between male and female attributes. Although the situation is changing somewhat, male characters generally outnumber females in most children's books, television programmes and films. Male characters tend to play more active, adventurous roles, while females are portrayed as passive, expectant and domestically oriented (Weitzman 1972; Zammuner 1987; Davies 1991). Feminist researchers have demonstrated how cultural and media products marketed to young audiences embody traditional attitudes towards gender and towards the sorts of aims and ambitions girls and boys are expected to have.

Clearly, gender socialization is very powerful, and challenges to it can be upsetting. Once a gender is 'assigned', society expects individuals to act like 'females' or 'males'. It is in the practices of everyday life that these expectations are fulfilled and reproduced (Bourdieu 1990; Lorber 1994).

For more discussion of gender socialization, see chapter 6, 'Socialization, the Life-course and Ageing', pp. 469–72.

The social construction of gender and sex

In recent years, socialization and gender role theories have been criticized by a growing number of sociologists. Rather than seeing sex as biologically determined and gender as culturally learned, they argue that we should view *both* sex and gender as socially constructed products. Not only is gender a purely social creation that lacks a fixed 'essence', but the human body itself is subject to social forces which shape and alter it in various ways. We can give our bodies meanings which challenge what is usually thought of as 'natural'. Individuals can choose to construct and reconstruct their bodies as they please – ranging from exercise, dieting, piercing and personal fashion, to plastic surgery and sex-change operations.

12.7 This young Wodaabe man, from the Gerewol in Niger, is taking part in a formal dance. The kohl on his lips and eyes, and his eye-rolling and grinning are thought to give him extra sex appeal to the young women of the Wodaabe.

For more on how individuals increasingly chose to construct their bodies, see chapter 8, 'Health, Illness and Disability'.

Technology is blurring the boundaries of our physical bodies. Thus, the argument goes, the human body and biology are not 'givens', but are subject to human agency and personal choice within different social contexts.

According to such a perspective, writers who focus on gender roles and role learning implicitly accept that there *is* a biological basis to gender differences. In the socialization approach, a biological distinction between the sexes provides a framework which becomes 'culturally elaborated' in society itself. In contrast to this, theorists who believe in the social construction of sex and gender reject all biological basis for gender differences. Gender identities emerge, they argue, in relation to perceived sex differences in society and in turn help to shape those differences. For example, a society in which ideas of masculinity are characterized by physical strength and 'tough' attitudes will encourage men to cultivate a specific body image and set of mannerisms. In other words, gender identities and sex differences are inextricably linked within individual human bodies (Connell 1987; Scott and Morgan 1993; Butler 1999).

Femininities, masculinities and gender relations

Considering feminists' concern with women's subordination in society, it is perhaps not surprising that most early research on gender concerned itself almost exclusively with women and concepts of femininity. Men and masculinity were regarded as relatively straightforward and unproblematic. Little effort was made to examine masculinity, the experience of being a man, or the formation of male identities. Sociologists were more concerned with understanding men's oppression of women and their role in maintaining patriarchy.

Since the late 1980s, however, greater attention has been devoted to critical studies of men and masculinity. The fundamental changes affecting the role of women and family patterns in industrialized societies have raised questions about the nature of masculinity and its changing role in society. What does it mean to be a man in late modern society? How are the traditional expectations and pressures on men being transformed in a rapidly changing age? Is masculinity in crisis?

In recent years, sociologists have become increasingly interested in the positions and experience of men within the larger order that shapes them. This shift within the sociology of gender and sexuality has led to new emphasis on the study of men and masculinity within the overarching context of **gender relations**, the societally patterned interactions between men and women. Sociologists are interested to grasp how male identities are constructed and what impact socially prescribed roles have on men's behaviour.

R. W. Connell: the gender order

In *Gender and Power* (1987), *The Men and the Boys* (2001) and *Masculinities* (2005), Bob Connell sets forth one of the most complete theoretical accounts of gender. His approach has been particularly influential in sociology because he has integrated the concepts of patriarchy and masculinity into an overarching theory of gender relations. According to Connell, masculinities are a critical part of the gender order and cannot be understood separate from it, or from the femininities which accompany them.

Connell is concerned with how the social power held by men creates and sustains gender inequality. He stresses that empirical evidence on gender inequality is not simply a 'shapeless heap of data', but reveals the basis of an 'organized field of human practice and social relations' through which women are kept in subordinate positions to men (Connell 1987). In Western capitalist societies, he claims, gender relations are still defined by patriarchal power. From the individual to the institutional level, various types of masculinity and femininity are all arranged around a central premise: the dominance of men over women.

According to Connell, gender relations are the product of everyday interactions and practices. The actions and behaviour of average people in their personal lives are directly linked to collective social arrangements in society. These arrangements are continuously reproduced over lifetimes and generations, but are also subject to change.

Connell sets forth three aspects of society which interact to form a society's **gender order** – patterns of power relations between masculinities and femininities that are widespread throughout society. According to Connell, *labour, power* and *cathexis* (personal/sexual relationships) are distinct but interrelated parts of society that work together and change in relation to one other. These three realms represent the main sites in which gender relations are constituted and constrained. *Labour* refers to the sexual division of labour both within the home (such as domestic responsibilities and child care) and in the labour market (issues like occu-

pational segregation and unequal pay). *Power* operates through social relations such as authority, violence and ideology in institutions, the state, the military and domestic life. *Cathexis* concerns dynamics within intimate, emotional and personal relationships, including marriage, sexuality and child-rearing.

Gender relations, as they are enacted in these three areas of society, are structured on a societal level in a particular gender order. Connell uses the term **gender regime** to refer to the play of gender relations in smaller settings, such as a specific institution. Thus, a family, a neighbourhood and a state all have their own gender regimes. Máirtín Mac an Ghaill has conducted an important study on the formation of masculinities in one such gender regime – the school (see box).

The gender hierarchy

Connell believes that there are many different expressions of masculinity and femininity. At the level of society, these contrasting versions are ordered in a hierarchy which is oriented around one defining premise – the domination of men over women (see figure 12.3 on p. 465). Connell uses stylized 'ideal types' of masculinities and femininities in his hierarchy. At the top of the hierarchy is **hegemonic masculinity**, which is dominant over all other masculinities and femininities in society. Hegemonic refers to the concept of *hegemony* – the social dominance of a certain group, exercised not through brute force, but through a cultural dynamic which extends into private life and social realms. Thus, the media, education and ideology can all be channels through which hegemony is established. According to Connell, hegemonic masculinity is

Máirtín Mac an Ghaill: education and the formation of masculinities and sexualities

Máirtín Mac an Ghaill carried out ethnographic research at a British state secondary school to explore its 'gender regime' – the way gender relations play out within the confines of the school.

Drawing on Connell's work, Mac an Ghaill was interested in how schools actively create a range of masculinities and femininities among students. Although he was particularly curious about the formation of heterosexual masculinities, he also investigated the experiences of a group of gay male students. Mac an Ghaill's findings, published in *The Making of Men* (1994), revealed that the school itself is an institution characterized by gendered and heterosexual patterns.

The prevailing 'regime' encourages the construction of gender relations among students which coincide with the larger gender order – that is, a hierarchy of dominant and subordinate masculinities and femininities could be detected within the confines of the school. Social influences and practices as diverse as disciplinary procedures, subject allocation, teacher–student and student–teacher interactions, and surveillance all contribute to the formation of heterosexual masculinities.

Mac an Ghaill notes four emergent types of masculinity in the school setting. The macho lads are a group of white, working-class boys who are defiant of school authority and disdainful of the learning process and student achievers (see also chapter 17, 'Education', p. 818). Mac an Ghaill concludes that the macho lads are undergoing a 'crisis of masculinity', as the manual and unskilled/semi-skilled jobs which they once saw as defining their future identities are no longer available. This leaves the lads in a psychological and practical dilemma about their futures which is difficult for them to comprehend and even harder to resolve.

The second group is made up of academic achievers who see themselves as future professionals. These boys are stereotyped by the 'macho lads' (and teachers) as effeminate, 'dickhead achievers'. The most common route taken by the achievers in handling the vicious stereotyping, according to Mac an Ghaill, is to retain confidence that their hard work and academic credentials will grant them a secure future. This forms the basis of their masculine identities.

The third group, the new enterprisers, are boys who gravitate towards subjects in the new vocational curriculum, such as computer science and business studies. Mac an Ghaill sees them as children of the new 'enterprise culture' which was cultivated during the Thatcher years. For these boys, success in A-level exams is relatively useless for their emphasis on the market and their instrumental planning for the future.

The real Englishmen compose the final group. They are the most troublesome of the middle-class groups as they maintain an ambivalent attitude towards academic learning, but see themselves as 'arbiters of culture', superior to anything their teachers can offer. Because they are oriented towards entry into a career, masculinity for the 'real Englishmen' involves the appearance of effortless academic achievement.

In his study of homosexual male students, Mac an Ghaill found that a distinctly heterosexual set of norms and values – based on traditional relationships and nuclear families – is taken for granted in all classroom discussions that touch on gender or sexuality. This leads to difficult 'confusions and contradictions' in the construction of gender and sexual identities for young gay men, who can simultaneously feel ignored and categorized by others.

associated first and foremost with hetero-sexuality and marriage, but also with authority, paid work, strength and physical toughness. Examples of men who embody hegemonic masculinity include the action picture star, and now Governor of California, Arnold Schwarzenegger, rappers like 50 Cent and the entrepreneur Donald Trump.

Although hegemonic masculinity is held up as an ideal form of masculinity, only a few men in society can live up to it. A large number of men, however, still gain advantage from hegemonic masculinity's dominant position in the patriarchal order. Connell refers to this as the 'patriarchal dividend' and to those who benefit from it as embodying **complicit masculinity**.

Existing in a subordinated relationship

to hegemonic masculinity are a number of subordinated masculinities and femininities. Among subordinated masculinities, the most important is that of **homosexual masculinity**. In a gender order dominated by hegemonic masculinity, the homosexual is seen as the opposite of the 'real man'; he does not measure up to the hegemonic masculine ideal and often embodies many of the 'cast off' traits of hegemonic masculinity. Homosexual masculinity is stigmatized, and ranks at the bottom of the gender hierarchy for men.

Connell argues that femininities are all formed in positions of subordination to hegemonic masculinity. One form of femininity – **emphasized femininity** – is an important complement to hegemonic masculinity. It is oriented to accommodating the interests and desires of men and is characterized by 'compliance, nurturance and empathy'. Among young women it is associated with sexual receptivity, while among older women it implies motherhood. Connell refers to Marilyn Monroe as both 'archetype and satirist' of emphasized femininity. He stresses that images of emphasized femininity remain highly prevalent in the media, advertising and marketing campaigns.

Finally, there are subordinated femininities which reject the version of emphasized femininity outlined above. But on the whole, the overwhelming attention devoted to maintaining emphasized femininity as the conventional norm in society means that other subordinated femininities which resist convention are not given voice. Women who have developed non-subordinated identities and lifestyles include feminists, lesbians, spinsters, midwives, witches, prostitutes and manual workers. The experiences of these

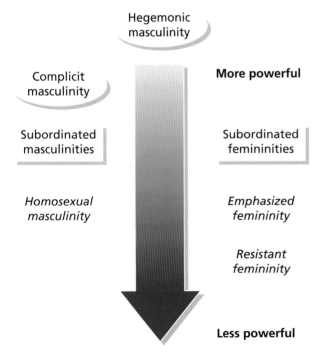

Figure 12.3 The gender hierarchy

resistant femininities, however, are largely 'hidden from history'.

Change in the gender order: crisis tendencies

Although Connell has set forth a clearly organized gender hierarchy, he rejects the view that gender relations are fixed or static. On the contrary, he believes that they are the outcome of an ongoing process and are therefore open to change and challenge. He sees the gender order in dynamic terms. Because he believes that sex and gender are socially constructed, he argues that people can change their gender orientations. By this he does not necessarily mean that people can switch their sexualities from homosexual to heterosexual and vice versa, although this does occur in some cases, but that people's gender identities and outlooks are constantly being adjusted. Women who once subscribed to 'emphasized femininity' might develop a feminist consciousness, for example. This constant possibility of change makes patterns of gender relations open to disruption and subject to the power of human agency.

While some sociologists suggest that Western society is undergoing a 'gender crisis', Connell suggests that we are simply in the presence of powerful tendencies towards crisis. These crisis tendencies take three forms. First, there is the *crisis of institutionalization*. By this, Connell means that institutions which have traditionally supported men's power – the family and the state – are gradually being undermined. The legitimacy of men's domination over women is being weakened through legislation on divorce, domestic violence and rape, and economic questions such as taxation and

pensions. Second, there is a *crisis of sexuality*, in which hegemonic heterosexuality is less dominant than it once was. The growing strength of women's sexuality and gay sexuality puts traditional hegemonic masculinity under pressure. Finally, there is a *crisis of interest formation*. Connell argues that there are new foundations for social interests which contradict the existing gender order. Married women's rights, gay movements and the growth of 'anti-sexist' attitudes among men all pose threats to the current order. Connell argues that the actions of individuals and groups can bring about change in the gender order. The crisis tendencies already in evidence within the existing order could be exploited in order to bring about the eradication of gender inequality (Connell 1987, 2005).

More recently, Connell has begun to examine the affect of globalization on the gender order. He argues that gender itself has become globalized. This involves interaction between previously distinct, local gender orders as well as the creation of new arenas of gender relations beyond individual localities.

Connell argues that there are several crucial new arenas of gender relations that play a part in the globalization of gender: transnational and multinational corporations, which tend to have a strong gender division of labour and a masculine management culture; international non-governmental organizations, such as the UN agencies, which are also gendered and mainly run by men; the international media, which again has a strong gender division of labour and disseminates particular understandings of gender through its output; and, lastly, global markets (in capital, commodities, services and labour) which tend to be strongly gender-structured and can increasingly reach into local economies.

To Connell the globalization of gender has resulted in interaction between local gender orders and the new arenas of gender relations discussed above, so that it is now possible to talk of a 'world gender order'. He argues that globalization provides the context in which we must now think about the lives of men and the construction and enactment of masculinities in the future.

Perspectives on gender inequality

We have seen that gender is a socially created concept which attributes differing social roles and identities to men and women. Yet as the work of Bob Connell and Máirtín Mac an Ghaill have shown, gender differences are rarely neutral – in almost all societies, gender is a significant form of social stratification. Gender is a critical factor in structuring the types of opportunities and life chances faced by individuals and groups, and strongly influences the roles they play within social institutions from the household to the state. Although the roles of men and women vary from culture to culture, there is no known instance of a society in which females are more powerful than males. Men's roles are generally more highly valued and rewarded than women's roles: in almost every culture, women bear the primary responsibility for child care and domestic work, while men have traditionally borne responsibility for providing the family livelihood. The prevailing division of labour between the sexes has led to

men and women assuming unequal positions in terms of power, prestige and wealth.

Despite the advances that women have made in countries around the world, gender differences continue to serve as the basis for social inequalities. Investigating and accounting for **gender inequality** has become a central concern of sociologists. Many theoretical perspectives have been advanced to explain men's enduring dominance over women – in the realm of economics, politics, the family and elsewhere. In this section we shall review the main theoretical approaches to explaining the nature of gender inequality at the level of society, leaving our discussion of gender inequality in specific settings and institutions to other chapters of the book (see box).

Functionalist approaches

As we saw in chapter 1 ('What is Sociology?'), the functional approach sees society as a system of interlinked parts which, when in balance, operate smoothly to produce social solidarity. Thus, functionalist and functionalist-inspired perspectives on gender seek to show that gender differences contribute to social stability and integration. While such views once commanded great support, they have been heavily criticized for neglecting social tensions at the expense of consensus and for promulgating a conservative view of the social world.

Writers who subscribe to the 'natural differences' school of thought tend to argue that the division of labour between men and women is biologically based. Women and men perform those tasks for which they are biologically best suited.

Thus, the anthropologist George Murdock saw it as both practical and convenient that women should concentrate on domestic and family responsibilities while men work outside the home. On the basis of a cross-cultural study of more than two hundred societies, Murdock (1949) concluded that the sexual division of labour is present in all cultures. While this is not the result of biological 'programming', it is the most logical basis for the organization of society.

Talcott Parsons, a leading functionalist thinker, concerned himself with the role of the family in industrial societies (Parsons and Bales 1956). He was particularly interested in the socialization of children, and believed that stable, supportive families are the key to successful socialization. In Parsons's view, the family operates most efficiently with a clear-cut sexual division of labour in which females act in *expressive* roles, providing care and security to children and offering them emotional support. Men, on the other hand, should perform *instrumental* roles – namely, being the breadwinner in the family. Because of the stressful nature of this role, women's expressive and nurturing tendencies should also be used to stabilize and comfort men. This complementary division of labour, springing from a biological distinction between the sexes, would ensure the solidarity of the family.

Another functionalist perspective on child-rearing was advanced by John Bowlby (1953), who argued that the mother is crucial to the primary socialization of children. If the mother is absent, or if a child is separated from the mother at a young age – a state referred to as **maternal**

Exploring gender inequalities

Sociologists define gender inequality as the difference in the status, power and prestige women and men have in groups, collectivities and societies. In thinking about gender inequality between men and women, one can ask the following questions: do women and men have equal access to valued societal resources – for example, food, money, power and time? Do women and men have similar life options? Are women's and men's roles and activities valued similarly? These fundamental questions are raised at many points throughout the text, as we make our way through the main themes that have attracted the interest of sociologists. You can find detailed discussions about gender issues in the following places:

- gender in sociological theory: chapter 4, pp. 110–12
- non-verbal communication and gender: chapter 5, pp. 133–4
- gender socialization: chapter 6, pp. 169–72
- gender and health: chapter 8, pp. 276–8
- gender and class: chapter 9, pp. 324–7
- religion and gender: chapter 14, pp. 552–3
- gender and achievement in school: chapter 17, pp. 715–20
- gender and crime: chapter 19, pp. 815–20

Gender and gender inequality are also central issues throughout chapter 7, 'Family and Intimate Relationships'.

deprivation – the child runs a high risk of being inadequately socialized. This can lead to serious social and psychological difficulties later in life, including anti-social and psychopathic tendencies. Bowlby argued that a child's well-being and mental health can be best guaranteed through a close, personal and continuous relationship with its mother. He did concede that an absent mother can be replaced by a 'mother-substitute', but suggested that such a substitute should also be a woman – leaving little doubt about his view that the mothering role is a distinctly female one. Bowlby's maternal deprivation thesis has been used by some to argue that working mothers are neglectful of their children.

Evaluation

Feminists have sharply criticized claims to a biological basis to the sexual division of labour, arguing that there is nothing natural or inevitable about the allocation of tasks in society. Women are not prevented from pursuing occupations on the basis of any biological features; rather, humans are socialized into roles that are culturally expected of them.

There is a steady stream of evidence to suggest that the maternal deprivation thesis is questionable – studies have shown that children's educational performance and personal development are in fact enhanced when both parents are employed at least part of the time outside the home. Parsons's view on the 'expressive' female has similarly been attacked by feminists and other sociologists who see such views as condoning the domination of women in the home. There is no basis to the belief that the 'expressive' female is necessary for the smooth operation of the family – rather, it is a role which is promoted largely for the convenience of men.

Feminist approaches

The feminist movement has given rise to a large body of theory which attempts to explain gender inequalities and set forth agendas for overcoming those inequal-

ities. **Feminist theories** in relation to gender inequality contrast markedly with one another. Competing schools of feminism have sought to explain gender inequalities through a variety of deeply embedded social processes, such as sexism, patriarchy and capitalism. We begin by looking at the major strands of feminism in the UK during the twentieth century: liberal, socialist (or Marxist) and radical feminism. The distinction between the different strands of feminism has never been clear-cut, although it provides a useful introduction. The tripartite categorization has become less useful in recent decades with the introduction of new forms of feminism that draw upon, and cut across, the earlier strands (Barker 1997). We will conclude this section with a brief examination of two important newer theories: black and postmodern feminism.

Liberal feminism

Liberal feminism looks for explanations of gender inequalities in social and cultural attitudes. An important early contribution to liberal feminism came from the English philosopher John Stuart Mill in his essay *The Subjection of Women* (1869), which called for legal and political equality between the sexes, including the right to vote. Unlike radical and socialist feminists, whose work we examine below, liberal feminists do not see women's subordination as part of a larger system or structure. Instead, they draw attention to many separate factors which contribute to inequalities between men and women. For example, in recent decades liberal feminists have campaigned against sexism and discrimination against women in the workplace, educational institutions and the media. They tend to focus their energies on establishing and protecting equal opportunities for women through legislation and other democratic means. In the UK, legal advances such as the Equal Pay Act (1970) and the Sex Discrimination Act (1975) were actively supported by liberal feminists, who argued that enshrining equality in law is important to eliminating discrimination against women. Liberal feminists seek to work through the existing system to bring about reforms in a gradual way. In this respect, they are more moderate in their aims and methods than many radical and socialist feminists, who call for an overthrow of the existing system.

While liberal feminists have contributed greatly to the advancement of women over the past century, critics charge that they are unsuccessful in dealing with the root causes of gender inequality and do not acknowledge the systemic nature of women's oppression in society. By focusing on the independent deprivations which women suffer – sexism, discrimination, the 'glass ceiling', unequal pay – liberal feminists draw only a partial picture of gender inequality. Radical feminists accuse liberal feminists of encouraging women to accept an unequal society and its competitive character.

Socialist and Marxist feminism

Socialist feminism developed from Marx's conflict theory (introduced in chapter 1, pp. 14–17), although Marx himself had little to say about gender inequality. It has been critical of liberal feminism for its perceived inability to see that there are powerful interests in society hostile to equality for women (Bryson 1993). Socialist feminists have sought to defeat both patriarchy and capitalism (Mitchell 1966). It was Marx's friend and collaborator Friedrich Engels who did more than Marx to provide an account of gender equality from a Marxist perspective.

Engels argued that under capitalism, material and economic factors underlay women's subservience to men, because **patriarchy** (like class oppression) has its roots in private property. Engels argued that capitalism intensifies patriarchy – men's domination over women – by concentrating wealth and power in the hands of a small number of men. Capitalism intensifies patriarchy more than earlier social systems because it creates enormous wealth compared to previous eras which confers power on men as wage-earners as well as possessors and inheritors of property. Second, for the capitalist economy to succeed, it must define people – in particular women – as consumers, persuading them that their needs will only be met through ever-increasing consumption of goods and products. Last, capitalism relies on women to labour for free in the home, caring and cleaning. To Engels, capitalism exploited men by paying low wages and women by paying no wages. Payment for housework is an important component of many feminists' belief, and is discussed further in chapter 18, 'Work and Economic Life'.

Socialist feminists have argued that the reformist goals of liberal feminism are inadequate. They have called for the restructuring of the family, the end of 'domestic slavery' and the introduction of some collective means of carrying out child-rearing, caring and household maintenance. Following Marx, many argued that these ends would be achieved through a socialist revolution, which would produce true equality under a state-centred economy designed to meet the needs of all.

Radical feminism

At the heart of **radical feminism** is the belief that men are responsible for and benefit from the exploitation of women. The analysis of patriarchy – the systematic domination of females by males – is of central concern to this branch of feminism. Patriarchy is viewed as a universal phenomenon that has existed across time and cultures. Radical feminists often concentrate on the family as one of the primary sources of women's oppression in society. They argue that men exploit women by relying on the free domestic labour that women provide in the home. As a group, men also deny women access to positions of power and influence in society.

Radical feminists differ in their interpretations of the basis of patriarchy, but most agree that it involves the appropriation of women's bodies and sexuality in some form. Shulamith Firestone (1971), an early radical feminist writer, argues that men control women's roles in reproduction and child-rearing. Because women are biologically able to give birth to children, they become dependent materially on men for protection and livelihood. This 'biological inequality' is socially organized in the nuclear family. Firestone speaks of a 'sex class' to describe women's social position and argues that women can be emancipated only through the abolition of the family and the power relations which characterize it.

Other radical feminists point to male violence against women as central to male supremacy. According to such a view, domestic violence, rape and sexual harassment are all part of the systematic oppression of women, rather than isolated cases with their own psychological or criminal roots. Even interactions in daily life – such as non-verbal communication, patterns of listening and interrupting, and women's sense of comfort in public – contribute to gender inequality. Moreover, the argument goes, popular conceptions of beauty and sexuality are imposed by men on women in order to produce a certain type of femininity. For example, social and cultural norms that emphasize a slim body and a caring, nurturing attitude towards men help to perpetuate women's subordination. The 'objectification' of women through the media, fashion and advertising turns women into sexual objects whose main role is to please and entertain men. Radical feminists do not believe that women can be liberated from sexual oppression through reforms or gradual change. Because patriarchy is a systemic phenomenon, they argue, gender equality can only be attained by overthrowing the patriarchal order.

The use of patriarchy as a concept for explaining gender inequality has been popular with many feminist theorists. In asserting that 'the personal is political', radical feminists have drawn widespread attention to the many linked dimensions of women's oppression. Their emphasis on male violence and the objectification of women has brought these issues into the heart of mainstream debates about women's subordination.

Many objections can be raised, however, to radical feminist views. The

Many radical and socialist feminists argue that 'lads' mags' such as these, as well as harder-core pornography, perpetuate women's subordination to men.

main one, perhaps, is that the concept of patriarchy as it has been used is inadequate as a general explanation for women's oppression. Radical feminists have tended to claim that patriarchy has existed throughout history and across cultures – that it is a universal phenomenon. Critics argue, however, that such a conception of patriarchy does not leave room for historical or cultural variations. It also ignores the important influence that race, class or ethnicity may have on the nature of women's subordination. In other words, it is not possible to see patriarchy as a universal phenomenon; doing so risks *biological reductionism* – attributing all the complexities of gender inequal-ity to a simple distinction between men and women.

Sylvia Walby has advanced an important reconceptualization of patriarchy (see box). Walby argues that the notion of patriarchy remains a valuable and useful explanatory tool, providing that it is used in certain ways.

Black feminism

Do the versions of feminism outlined above apply equally to the experiences of both white and non-white women? Many **black feminists**, and feminists from developing countries, claim they do not. They argue that ethnic divisions among women are not considered by the main feminist schools of thought, which are oriented to the dilemmas of white, predominantly middle-class women living in industrialized societies. It is not valid, they claim, to generalize theories about women's subordination as a whole from the experience of a specific group of women. Moreover, the very idea that there is a 'unified' form of gender oppression that is experienced equally by all women is problematic.

Dissatisfaction with existing forms of feminism has led to the emergence of a strand of thought which concentrates on the particular problems facing black women. In the foreword to her personal

Sylvia Walby: theorizing patriarchy

The idea of patriarchy has been central to many feminist interpretations of gender inequality. But as an analytical tool, it has also been criticized for failing to explain changes and diversity in gender inequality. Surely, critics argue, we cannot speak of one uniform and unchanging system of oppression for all of history? Sylvia Walby is one theorist who believes that the concept of patriarchy is essential to any analysis of gender inequality. But she agrees that many criticisms of it are valid. In *Theorizing Patriarchy* (1990), Walby presents a way of understanding patriarchy that is more flexible than its predecessors. It allows room for change over historical time, and for consideration of ethnic and class differences.

For Walby, patriarchy is 'a system of social structures and practices in which men dominate, oppress and exploit women' (1990: 20). She sees patriarchy and capitalism as distinct systems which interact in different ways – sometimes harmoniously, sometimes in tension – depending on historical conditions. Capitalism, she argues, has generally benefited from patriarchy through the sexual division of labour. But at other times, capitalism and patriarchy have been at odds with one another. For example, in wartime, when women have entered the labour market in great numbers, the interests of capitalism and patriarchy have not been aligned.

Walby identifies six structures through which patriarchy operates. She recognizes that a weakness of early feminist theory was the tendency to focus on one 'essential' cause of women's oppression, such as male violence or women's role in reproduction. Because Walby is concerned with the depth and interconnectedness of gender inequality, she sees patriarchy as composed of six structures that are independent, but interact with one another.

1   *Production relations in the household* Women's unpaid domestic labour, such as housework and child care, is expropriated by her husband (or cohabitee).
2   *Paid work* Women in the labour market are excluded from certain types of work, receive lower pay, and are segregated in less skilled jobs.
3   *The patriarchal state* In its policies and priorities, the state has a systematic bias towards patriarchal interests.
4   *Male violence* Although male violence is often seen as composed of individualistic acts, it is patterned and systematic. Women routinely experience this violence, and are affected by it in standard ways. The state effectively condones the violence with its refusal to intervene, except in exceptional cases.
5   *Patriarchal relations in sexuality* This is manifested in 'compulsory heterosexuality' and in the sexual double standard between men and women (in which different 'rules' for sexual behaviour apply).
6   *Patriarchal cultural institutions* A variety of institutions and practices – including media, religion and education – produce representations of women 'within a patriarchal gaze'. These representations influence women's identities and prescribe acceptable standards of behaviour and action.

Walby distinguishes two distinct forms of patriarchy. Private patriarchy is domination of women which occurs within the household at the hands of an individual patriarch. It is an exclusionary strategy, because women are essentially prevented from taking part in public life. Public patriarchy, on the other hand, is more collective in form. Women are involved in public realms, such as politics and the labour market, but remain segregated from wealth, power and status.

Walby contends that at least in Britain, there has been a shift in patriarchy – both in degree and form – from the Victorian era to present day. She notes that the narrowing of the wage gap and the gains in women's education demonstrate a shift in the degree of patriarchy, but do not signal its defeat. If at one time women's oppression was found chiefly in the home, it is now located throughout society as a whole – women are now segregated and subordinated in all areas of the public realm. In other words, patriarchy has shifted in form from private to public. As Walby quips: liberated from the home, women now have the whole of society in which to be exploited.

memoirs, American black feminist bell hooks (always written with lower case letters) argues:

> Many feminist thinkers writing and talking about girlhood right now like to suggest that black girls have better self-esteem than their white counterparts. The measurement of this difference is often that black girls are more assertive, speak more, appear more confident. Yet in traditional southern-based black life, it was and is expected of girls to be articulate, to hold ourselves with dignity. Our parents and teachers were always urging us to stand up right and speak clearly. These traits were meant to uplift the race. They were not necessarily traits associated with building female self-esteem. An out-spoken girl might still feel that she was worthless because her skin was not light enough or her hair the right texture. These are the variables that white researchers often do not consider when they measure the self-esteem of black females with a yard-stick that was designed based on values emerging from white experience. (hooks 1997)

Black feminist writings tend to emphasize history – aspects of the past which inform the current problems facing black women. The writings of American black feminists emphasize the influence of the powerful legacy of slavery, segregation and the civil rights movement on gender inequalities in the black community. They point out that early black suffragettes supported the campaign for women's rights, but realized that the question of race could not be ignored: black women were discriminated against on the basis of their race and gender. In recent years, black women have not been central to the women's liberation movement in part because 'womanhood' dominated their identities much less than concepts of race did.

hooks has argued that explanatory frameworks favoured by white feminists – for example, the view of the family as a mainstay of patriarchy – may not be applicable in black communities, where the family represents a main point of solidarity against racism. In other words, the oppression of black women may be found in different locations compared with that of white women.

Black feminists contend, therefore, that any theory of gender equality which does not take racism into account cannot be expected to explain black women's oppression adequately. Class dimensions are another factor which cannot be neglected in the case of many black women. Some black feminists have held that the strength of black feminist theory is its focus on the interplay between race, class and gender concerns. Black women are multiply disadvantaged, they argue, on the basis of their colour, their sex and their class position. When these three factors interact, they reinforce and intensify one another (Brewer 1993).

Postmodern feminism

Like black feminism, **postmodern feminism** challenges the idea that there is a unitary basis of identity and experience shared by all women.

> Postmodern approaches in sociology were introduced in chapter 4, pp. 115–17.

This strand of feminism draws on the cultural phenomenon of postmodernism in the arts, architecture, philosophy and economics. Some of the roots of postmodern feminism are found in the work of Continental theorists like Derrida (1978, 1981), Lacan (1995) and de Beauvoir (1949). Postmodern feminists reject the claim that there is a grand theory that can explain the position of women in society, or that there is any single, universal essence or category of 'woman'. Consequently, these feminists reject the accounts given by others to explain gender inequality – such as patriarchy, race or class – as 'essentialist' (Beasley 1999).

Instead, postmodernism encourages the acceptances of many different standpoints as equally valid. Rather than there existing an essential core to womanhood, there are many individuals and groups, all of whom have very different experiences (heterosexuals, lesbians, black women,

working-class women, etc.). The 'otherness' of different groups and individuals is celebrated in all its diverse forms. Emphasis on the positive side of 'otherness' is a major theme in postmodern feminism, and symbolizes plurality, diversity, difference and openness: there are many truths, roles and constructions of reality. Hence, the recognition of difference (of sexuality, age and race, for example) is central to postmodern feminism.

As well as the recognition of difference between groups and individuals, postmodern feminists have stressed the importance of 'deconstruction'. In particular, they have sought to deconstruct male language and a masculine view of the world. In its place, postmodern feminists have attempted to create fluid, open terms and language which more closely reflect women's experiences. For many postmodern feminists, men see the world in terms of pairs or binary distinctions ('good versus bad', 'right versus wrong', 'beautiful versus ugly', for example). Men, they argue, have cast the male as normal, and female as a deviation from it. The founder of modern psychiatry Sigmund Freud, for example, saw women as men who lacked a penis and argued that they envied males for possessing one. In this masculine world-view, the female is always cast in the role of the 'other'. Deconstruction involves attacking binary concepts and recasting their opposites in a new and positive manner.

> For Freud's views on gender socialization, see chapter 5, pp.172–3.

Postmodern feminism is said to have the most difficult relationship with the previous strands of feminism discussed above (Carrington 1995, 1998). This is largely because of its belief that many feminists may be misled in assuming that it is possible to provide overarching explanations for women's oppression and to find steps towards its resolution.

The influence of feminist movements has had a profound effect on Western societies, but increasingly, it is challenging gender inequality in other areas of the world. We conclude with a brief discussion of gender in an increasingly globalized world.

Conclusion: gender and globalization

In this chapter, most of our discussion has focused on notions of gender within Western industrialized societies. We have seen how the women's movement has given rise to a powerful body of sociological theory to make sense of persistent gender inequalities and to advance agendas for overcoming them. Feminism is not merely an academic exercise, however; nor is it restricted to Western Europe and North America. In today's increasingly globalized world, there is a good chance that those who become active in the British women's movement will come into contact with women pursuing other feminist struggles overseas.

The women's movement, of course, is not simply a Western European or American phenomenon. In China, for example, women are working to secure 'equal rights, employment, women's role in production, and women's participation in politics' (Zhang and Xu 1995). In South Africa, women played a pivotal role in the battle against apartheid and are fighting in the post-apartheid era to improve 'the material conditions of the oppressed majority; those who have been denied

access to education, decent homes, health facilities, and jobs' (Kemp et al. 1995). In Peru, activists have been working for decades to give women a greater 'opportunity to participate in public life' (Blondet 1995), while 'in Russia, women's protest was responsible for blocking the passage of legislation that the Russian parliament considered in 1992 that encouraged women to stay home and perform "socially necessary labour" ' (Basu 1995).

Although participants in women's movements have, for many years, cultivated ties to activists in other countries, the number and importance of such contacts has increased with globalization. A prime forum for the establishment of cross-national contacts has been the United Nation's Conference on Women, held four times since 1975. (There are now proposals for a fifth conference to be held before 2010.) Approximately 50,000 people – of whom more than two-thirds were women – attended the most recent conference, held in Beijing, China, in 1995. Delegates from 181 nations attended, along with representatives from thousands of non-governmental organizations. Seeking ways to 'ensure women's equal access to economic resources including land, credit, science and technology, vocational training, information, communication and markets', conference participants spent ten days listening to presentations on the state of women worldwide, debating ways to improve their condition, and building professional and personal ties to one another. Mallika Dutt, one of the attendees, wrote in the journal *Feminist Studies* that 'for most women from the United States, Beijing was an eye-opening, humbling, and transformative experience. US women were startled by the sophisticated analysis and well-organized and powerful voices of women from other parts of the world' (Dutt 1996). At the same time, according to Dutt, many of the conference participants left Beijing with a 'sense of global solidarity, pride, and affirmation' (1996).

The Platform for Action finally agreed to by the conference participants called on the countries of the world to address such issues as:

- the persistent and increasing burden of poverty on women;
- violence against women;
- the effects of armed or other kinds of conflict on women;

- inequality between men and women in the sharing of power and decision-making;
- stereotyping of women;
- gender inequalities in the management of natural resources;
- persistent discrimination against and violation of the rights of the girl child.

Must women's movements have an international orientation to be effective? Are women's interests essentially the same throughout the world? What might feminism mean to women in the developing world? These and many other questions are being hotly debated as the process of globalization continues apace.

Summary points

1 While there is clearly a biological basis to human sexuality, most sexual behaviour seems to be learned rather than innate. Sexual practices vary widely between and within cultures. In the West, Christianity has been important in shaping sexual attitudes. In societies with rigid sexual codes, double standards and hypocrisy are common. The gulf between norms and actual practice can be tremendous, as studies of sexual behaviour have shown. In the West, repressive attitudes to sexuality gave way to a more permissive outlook in the 1960s, the effects of which are still obvious today.

2 Most people in the world are heterosexual, yet there are also many minority sexual tastes and inclinations. Homosexuality seems to exist in all cultures, and in recent years attitudes towards homosexuals have become more relaxed. In some countries

laws have been passed that recognize homosexual unions and grant gay couples the same rights as married people.

3 Sociologists distinguish between sex and gender. Sex refers to the biological differences between male and female bodies, while gender concerns the psychological, social and cultural differences between men and women.

4 Some people argue that differences between men and women are genetically determined. However, there is no conclusive evidence to suggest a biological basis to gender differences.

5 Gender socialization refers to the learning of gender roles with the help of agencies such as the family and the media. Gender socialization is thought to begin as soon as an infant is born. Children learn and internalize the norms and expectations that are seen to correspond to their biological sex. In such a way, they adopt 'sex roles' and

the male and female identities (masculinity and femininity) that accompany them.

6   Some sociologists believe that both sex and gender are socially constructed products that can be shaped and altered in various ways. Not only does gender lack a fixed 'essence', but the very substratum of the human body can be changed through social influences and technological interventions.

7   Gender inequality refers to the differences in status, power and prestige enjoyed by women and men in various contexts. In explaining gender inequality, functionalists have emphasized that gender differences and the sexual division of labour contribute to social stability and integration. Feminist approaches reject the idea that gender inequality is somehow natural. Liberal feminists have explained gender inequality in terms of social and cultural attitudes, such as sexism and discrimination. Radical feminists argue that men are responsible for the exploitation of women through patriarchy – the systematic domination of females by males. Black feminists have seen factors such as class and ethnicity, in addition to gender, as essential for understanding the oppression experienced by non-white women.

8   Gender relations refer to societally patterned interactions between men and women in society. Some sociologists have argued that a gender order exists in which expressions of masculinity and femininity are organized in a hierarchy that promotes the domination of men over women.

9   In recent years more attention has been paid to the nature of masculinity. Some observers believe that wide economic and social transformations are provoking a crisis of masculinity in which men's traditional roles are being eroded.

Questions for further thought

1   Would it be either possible or desirable to eliminate gender differences in society?

2   Is it possible to retain gender differences whilst eliminating gender inequalities?

3   How do factors such as class, ethnicity and sexual orientation shape our experience of gender?

4   What new kinds of masculinities and femininities are likely to emerge in the next few decades in response to broader processes of social change?

5   In what ways is social interaction structured around an assumed heterosexual norm?

Further reading

Joe Bristow, *Sexuality* (London, New York: Routledge, 1997).

R. W. Connell, *Gender* (Cambridge: Polity, 2002).

John Horton and Sue Mendus (eds), *Toleration, Identity, and Difference* (Basingstoke: Macmillan, 1999).

Michael S. Kimmel and Michael A. Messner, *Men's Lives* (Boston, MA: Allyn and Bacon, 1998).

Lynne Segal, *Why Feminism?* (Cambridge: Polity, 1999).

A. Stein and C. Williams, *Sexuality and Gender* (Malden, MA: Blackwell, 2002).

Internet links

Social Science Information Gateway on Gender and Sexuality
http://www.sosig.ac.uk/roads/subject-listing/World-cat/socgend.html

Fawcett Library, now known as The Women's Library
http://www.thewomenslibrary.ac.uk/

Queer Resource Directory
http://www.qrd.org/

Voice of the Shuttle
http://vos.ucsb.edu/browse.asp?id=2711

BBC Debate on Gay Marriage
http://www.bbc.co.uk/religion/ethics/samesexmarriage/index.shtml

Contents

13 Race, Ethnicity and Migration

UNTIL JUST over a decade ago, South Africa was governed by apartheid – a system of forced racial segregation. Under apartheid, every South African was classified into one of four categories: white (descendants of European immigrants), 'coloured' (people whose descent is traced from members of more than one 'race'), Asian and black. The white South African minority, comprising some 13 per cent of the population, ruled over the non-white majority. Non-whites had no vote and no representation in the central government. Segregation was enforced at all levels of society, from public places like washrooms and railway carriages, to residential neighbourhoods and schools. Millions of blacks were herded into so-called 'homelands', well away from the main cities, and worked as migrant labourers in gold and diamond mines.

Apartheid was encoded in law, but enforced through violence and brutality.

Townships like this were home to millions of black South Africans under apartheid.

The National Party, which formalized apartheid after coming to power in 1948, used law-enforcement and security organs to suppress all resistance to the apartheid regime. Opposition groups were outlawed and political dissidents were detained without trial and often tortured. Peaceful demonstrations frequently ended in violence. After years of international condemnation, economic and cultural sanctions, and growing domestic resistance, the apartheid regime began to weaken. When F. W. de Klerk became President of South Africa in 1989, he inherited a country that was deep in crisis and virtually ungovernable.

In 1990, de Klerk lifted the ban on the African National Congress (ANC), the main opposition party, and freed its leader, Nelson Mandela, after twenty-seven years of imprisonment. A series of complex negotiations followed, paving the way for South Africa's first national election involving both whites and non-whites. On 27 April 1994 the ANC received an overwhelming 62 per cent of the vote and Nelson Mandela became South Africa's first post-apartheid president.

The task facing Mandela and the ANC was enormous. In a country of thirty-eight million people, nine million were impoverished and twenty million lived without electricity. Unemployment was widespread. More than half the black population was illiterate and infant mortality rates were more than ten times higher among blacks than among whites. But besides being a profoundly unequal society in material terms, South Africa was also a highly divided one. Decades of ideological rule premised on a belief in racial superiority left the country scarred and in desperate need of reconciliation. The

atrocities of the apartheid regime demanded redress, and the culture of racial oppression had to be dismantled. Ethnic tensions within the African population flared up in violent outbreaks and threatened to lead to civil war.

During his presidency, which ended in 1999, Mandela diligently laid the groundwork for the emergence of an equitable, multi-ethnic society. The constitution adopted in 1996 is one of the most progressive in the world, outlawing all discrimination on the basis of race, or ethnic or social origin, or religion and belief, alongside sexual orientation, disability and pregnancy. Mandela's repeated calls for a 'new patriotism' sought to rally both 'nervous whites' and 'impatient blacks' into a common nation-building project. Dissenting political groups, such as the Zulu-based Inkatha Freedom Party (IFP), were brought into government in order to reduce ethnic and political tensions that could lead to violence.

One of the most notable events to occur during Mandela's presidency was aimed at addressing the legacy of the apartheid past. Beginning in April 1996 and ending in July 1998, the Truth and Reconciliation Commission (TRC) held hearings in communities across South Africa to examine the abuses of human rights which had occurred under apartheid. The Nobel laureate Archbishop Desmond Tutu led the TRC in investigating acts and abuses committed between 1960 and 1994. More than 21,000 testimonies were given and recorded; sessions were open to the public and covered extensively in the media. The TRC hearings were designed to uncover the realities of the apartheid era – from the most horrific to the most banal – for all to see; they were not intended to serve as

Nelson Mandela being sworn in as President of South Africa in 1994, after twenty-seven years in prison.

trials or to mete out punishments. Those who committed crimes under apartheid, including policemen and security authorities, were offered amnesty in return for their honest testimonies and the 'full disclosure' of all relevant information.

The Truth and Reconciliation Commission published a 3,500-page report of its findings in 1998. Not surprisingly, the apartheid government was identified as the main perpetrator of human rights abuses, although transgressions committed by other organizations, including the ANC, were also noted. Some have criticized the TRC as little more than an archive of apartheid-era crimes, unable to

'right the wrongs' that had occurred. But many others believe that the very process of gathering testimonies – from those who committed abuses and from those who were abused – brought into focus the injustices of the apartheid era.

Certainly the TRC could not overcome single-handedly the decades of racial division and discrimination. South Africa remains a fractured society and continues to struggle against bigotry and intolerance. A series of 'transformation bills' passed in 2000 outlawed hate speech and established a series of 'equality courts' to hear charges of racial discrimination. Yet the TRC hearings were a powerful episode in South Africa's post-apartheid history and established a new standard for openness and honesty in addressing racial divisions. The TRC forced attention to be paid to the dangerous consequences of racial hatred and, through its own example, demonstrated the power of communication and dialogue in the process of reconciliation.

In this chapter we shall investigate the notions of 'race' and ethnicity and question why racial and ethnic divisions so frequently produce social conflicts – as they have done in South Africa and many other societies. After considering the ways that social scientists understand and use the concepts of race and ethnicity, we shall turn to the topics of prejudice, discrimination and racism and discuss sociological interpretations that help to explain their persistence. From there, we will address models of ethnic integration and explore examples of ethnic conflict. In the final sections of the chapter, we will turn to ethnic diversity and ethnic relations in the United Kingdom and Europe, paying particular attention to trends in immigration and patterns of ethnic inequality, before examining migration on a global level.

Key concepts

Race

Race is one of the most complex concepts in sociology, not least because of the contradiction between its everyday usage and its scientific basis (or absence thereof). Many people today believe, mistakenly, that humans can be readily separated into biologically different races. This is not surprising considering the numerous attempts by scholars and governments, like that of South Africa (discussed above) before the ending of apartheid, to establish racial categorizations of the peoples of the world. Some authors have distinguished four or five major races, while others have recognized as many as three dozen.

Scientific theories of race arose in the late eighteenth and early nineteenth centuries. They were used to justify the emerging social order, as England and other European nations became imperial powers ruling over subject territories and populations. Count Joseph Arthur de Gobineau (1816–82), who is sometimes called the father of modern racism, proposed the existence of three races: white (*Caucasian*), black (*Negroid*) and yellow (*Mongoloid*). According to de Gobineau, the white race possesses superior intelligence, morality and will-power; it is these inherited qualities that underlie the spread of Western influence across the world. The blacks, by contrast, are the least capable, marked by an animal nature, a lack of morality and emotional instability. The ideas of de Gobineau and fellow proponents of scientific racism later influenced Adolf Hitler, who transformed them into the ideology of the Nazi party, and other white supremacist groups such as the Ku-Klux-Klan in the United States and the architects of apartheid in South Africa.

In the years following the Second World War, 'race science' has been thoroughly discredited. In biological terms there are no clear-cut 'races', only a range of physical variations in human beings. Differences in physical type between groups of human beings arise from population inbreeding, which varies according to the degree of contact between different social or cultural groups. Human population groups are a continuum. The genetic diversity within populations that share visible physical traits is as great as the diversity between them. By virtue of these facts, the scientific community has virtually abandoned the concept of race. Many social scientists concur, arguing that race is nothing more than an ideological construct whose use in academic circles only perpetuates the commonly held belief that it has a biological grounding (Miles 1993). Other social scientists disagree, claiming that race as a concept has meaning to many people, even if its biological basis has been discredited. For sociological analysis, they argue, race remains a vital, if highly contested concept. Some scholars therefore choose to use the word 'race' in inverted commas to reflect its misleading, but commonplace, usage.

What is race, then, if it does not refer to biological categories? There are clear physical differences between human beings, and some of these differences are inherited. But the question of why some differences and not others become matters for social discrimination and prejudice has nothing to do with biology. Racial differences, therefore, should be understood as physical variations singled out by the members of a community or society as socially significant. Differences in skin colour, for example, are treated as significant, whereas differences in colour of hair are not. Race can be understood as a set of social relationships which allow individuals and groups to be located, and various attributes or competencies assigned, on the basis of biologically grounded features.

This photograph of former US Secretary of State Colin Powell and former Kenyan President Daniel arap Moi illustrates the huge variation in actual skin tone of people described as 'black'.

Racial distinctions are more than ways of describing human differences – they are also important factors in the reproduction of patterns of power and inequality within society.

The process by which understandings of race are used to classify individuals or groups of people is called **racialization**. Historically, racialization meant that certain groups of people came to be labelled as constituting distinct biological groups on the basis of naturally occurring physical features (as in the ideas set forth by de Gobineau). During the period of history from the fifteenth century onwards, as Europeans came into increased contact with people from different regions of the world, attempts were made to systematize knowledge by categorizing and explaining both natural and social phenomena. Non-European populations were 'racialized' in opposition to the European 'white race'. In some instances this racialization took on 'codified' institutional forms, as in the case of slavery in the American colonies and apartheid in South Africa. More commonly, however, everyday social institutions became racialized in a de facto manner. Within a racialized system, aspects of individuals' daily lives – including employment, personal relations, housing, healthcare, education and legal representation – are shaped and constrained by their own racialized positions within that system.

Ethnicity

While the idea of race mistakenly implies something fixed and biological, the concept of **ethnicity** is an idea that is purely social in meaning. Ethnicity refers to the cultural practices and outlooks of a given community of people that set them apart from others. Members of ethnic groups see themselves as culturally distinct from other groups in a society, and are seen by those other groups to be so in return. Different characteristics may serve to distinguish ethnic groups from one another, but the most usual are language, history or ancestry (real or imagined), religion and styles of dress or adornment.

Ethnic differences are wholly learned, a point that seems self-evident until we remember how often some groups have been regarded as 'born to rule' or 'shiftless', 'unintelligent' and so forth. In fact, there is nothing innate about ethnicity; it is a purely social phenomenon that is produced and reproduced over time. Through socialization, young people assimilate the lifestyles, norms and beliefs of their communities.

For many people, ethnicity is central to individual and group identity, but its significance can vary among individuals. It can provide an important thread of continuity with the past and is often kept alive through the practice of cultural traditions. Every year, for instance, the excitement and virtuoso displays of Carnival evoke the Caribbean on the streets of Notting Hill, in London. As another example, third-generation Americans of Irish descent may proudly identify themselves as Irish-American, despite having lived their entire lives in the United States. Irish traditions and customs are often passed down through generations of families and in the larger Irish community. Although it is maintained within tradition, ethnicity is not static and unchanging. Rather, it is fluid and adaptable to changing circumstances. In the case of Irish-Americans, for instance, it is possible to see how popular customs from Ireland have been maintained but transformed in the context of American society. The boisterous St Patrick's Day parades in many US cities are one example of how Irish heritage has been recast with a distinctly American flair. Similar examples can be found around the globe in cases where populations – as a result of migration, war, shifting labour markets or other factors – have

488 RACE, ETHNICITY AND MIGRATION

'Black' identity

The use of the term 'black' to describe individuals and populations has undergone fundamental transformations over the years and remains highly contested. For a long time, 'black' was a derogatory label assigned by whites. Only in the 1960s did Americans and Britons of African descent 'reclaim' the term and apply it to themselves in a positive way. 'Black' became a source of pride and identity, rather than a racial slur. The slogan 'black is beautiful' and the motivational concept of 'black power' were central to the black liberation movement. These ideas were used to counter the symbolic domination of 'whiteness' over 'blackness'. As the term 'black' became more accepted within British society, it began to be applied to non-whites who were not of African descent – particularly Asians. The term 'black' was more than simply a label, however; it also contained an underlying political message. Because 'black' people had all experienced racism and exclusion at the hands of the white population, there was a call for them to mobilize around their common black identity in pushing for change.

In the late 1980s some scholars and members of ethnic minority groups began to challenge the use of the term 'black' to refer to the non-white population as a whole. While acknowledging that non-whites have shared a common oppression, they argue that the term 'black' obscures the differences between ethnic groups.

According to opponents of the term, more attention should be paid to the distinctive experiences of individual ethnic minority groups, rather than presuming a shared experience. Tariq Modood has been one of the leading critics, arguing that the term 'black' is used too loosely – sometimes meaning only people of African descent, and other times referring collectively to Asians as well. He believes that the term over-emphasizes oppression based on skin colour and neglects the large amount of racism that is culturally based. According to Modood, Asians tend not to see themselves as 'black' because of the powerful connotations between the term 'black' and the experience of people of African origin. Finally, Modood points out that 'black' implies an essential identity which is inherently false. Non-white populations possess many diverse identities, just as do groups within the so-called 'white' population (Modood 1994).

There is no clear consensus about the use of the term 'black' in sociology. While the criticisms raised by Modood and others are surely valid, the term 'black' remains a useful way to speak about the shared experience of white racism that most non-whites have encountered. Recent

---

mixed to produce ethnically diverse communities.

Sociologists often favour the term 'ethnicity' over the term 'race' (discussed above), because it is a concept that is completely social in meaning. However, references to ethnicity and ethnic differences can be problematic, especially if they suggest contrast with a 'non-ethnic' norm. In Britain, for example, ethnicity is commonly used to refer to cultural practices and traditions that differ from 'indigenous' British practices. The term 'ethnic' is applied to realms as diverse as cuisine, clothing, music and neighbourhoods to designate practices that are 'non-British'. Using ethnic labels in this collective manner risks producing divisions between 'us' and 'them', where certain parts of the population are seen as 'ethnic' and others are not. In fact, ethnicity is an attribute possessed by all members of a population, not merely certain segments of it. Yet, as we shall see, in practice ethnicity is most often associated with minority groups within a population.

trends within sociology, however, seem to support Modood's concerns. Writers associated with the postmodern school tend to highlight the differences between various ethnic minority groups, rather than dwell on the significance of a collective 'black' identity.

US athletes highlighted awareness of black identity and caused controversy with their black power salutes on the medals rostrum of the 1968 Olympic Games in Mexico City.

Minority groups

The notion of **minority groups** (often **ethnic minorities**) is widely used in sociology and is more than a merely numerical distinction. There are many minorities in a statistical sense, such as people over six feet tall or wearing shoes bigger than size 12, but these are not minorities according to the sociological concept. In sociology, members of a minority group are disad-vantaged when compared with the dominant group (a group possessing more wealth, power and prestige) and have some sense of *group solidarity*, of belonging together. The experience of being the subject of prejudice and discrimination usually heightens feelings of common loyalty and interests.

Thus sociologists frequently use the term 'minority' in a non-literal way to refer to a group's subordinate position within society, rather than its numerical representation. There are many cases in which a 'minority' is in fact in the majority. In some geographical areas such as inner cities, ethnic minority groups make up the majority of the population, but are nonetheless referred to as 'minorities'. This is because the term 'minority' captures their disadvantaged positions. Women are sometimes described as a minority group, while in many countries of the world they form the numerical majority. Yet because women tend to be disadvantaged in comparison with men (the 'majority'), the term is applied to them as well.

Members of minority groups often tend to see themselves as a people apart from the majority. They are usually physically and socially isolated from the larger community. They tend to be concentrated in certain neighbourhoods, cities or regions of a country. There is little intermarriage between those in the majority and members of the minority group, or between minority groups. People within the minority sometimes actively promote **endogamy** (marriage within the group) in order to keep alive their cultural distinctiveness.

Some scholars have favoured speaking of 'minorities' to refer collectively to groups that have experienced prejudice at the hands of the 'majority' society. The term 'minorities' draws attention to the pervasiveness of discrimination by highlighting the commonalities between experiences of various subordinate groups within society. As an example, disablist attitudes, anti-Semitism, homophobia and racism share many features in common and reveal how oppression against different groups can take similar forms. At the same time, however, speaking collectively of 'minorities' can result in generalizations about discrimination and oppression that do not accurately reflect the experiences of specific groups. Although homosexuals and Pakistanis are both minority groups in London, the way in which they experience subordination in society is far from identical.

Many minorities are both ethnically and physically distinct from the rest of the population. This is the case with West Indians and Asians in Britain, for example, and with African-Americans, Chinese and other groups in the United States. As we noted above, in practice the designation of a group or a set of traditions as 'ethnic' occurs somewhat selectively. While West Indians in Britain and African-Americans in the United States are clear examples of ethnic minorities, Britons and Americans of Italian or Polish descent are less likely to be considered ethnic minorities. Frequently, physical differences such as skin colour are the defining factor in designating an ethnic minority. As we shall see in this chapter, ethnic distinctions are rarely neutral, but are commonly associated with inequalities of wealth and power, as well as with antagonisms between groups.

Prejudice and discrimination

The concept of race is modern, but prejudice and discrimination have been widespread in human history, and we must first clearly distinguish between them. **Prejudice** refers to opinions or attitudes held by members of one group towards another. A prejudiced person's preconceived views are often based on hearsay rather than on direct evidence, and are resistant to

Sudanese model Alex Wek is a rare black face in the Western fashion industry.

stereotypes contain a grain of truth; others are simply a mechanism of **displacement**, in which feelings of hostility or anger are directed against objects that are not the real origin of those feelings. Stereotypes become embedded in cultural understandings and are difficult to erode, even when they are gross distortions of reality. The belief that single mothers are dependent on welfare and refuse to work is an example of a persistent stereotype that lacks basis in fact. A great number of single mothers do work, and many who receive welfare benefits would prefer to work but have no access to child care. **Scapegoating** is common when two deprived ethnic groups come into competition with one another for economic rewards. People who direct racial attacks against ethnic minorities, for example, are often in an economic position similar to theirs. A recent poll found that half of all people who felt 'hard done by' believed that immigrants and ethnic minorities were getting priority over them (MORI, 2003; *The Economist*, 26 February 2004). They blame ethnic minorities for grievances whose real causes lie elsewhere.

Scapegoating is normally directed against groups that are distinctive and relatively powerless, because they make an easy target. Protestants, Catholics, Jews, Italians, black Africans, Muslims, gypsies and others have played the unwilling role of scapegoat at various times throughout Western history. Scapegoating frequently involves projection, the unconscious attribution to others of one's own desires or characteristics. Research has consistently demonstrated that when the members of a dominant group practice violence against a minority and exploit it sexually, they are likely to believe that the

change even in the face of new information. People may harbour favourable prejudices about groups with which they identify and negative prejudices against others. Someone who is prejudiced against a particular group will not deal with its members impartially.

Prejudices are often grounded in **stereotypes**, fixed and inflexible characterizations of a group of people. Stereotypes are often applied to ethnic minority groups, such as the notion that all black men are naturally athletic or that all East Asians are hardworking, diligent students. Some minority group itself displays these traits of sexual violence. For instance, in apartheid South Africa, the belief that black males are exceptionally potent sexually and that black women are promiscuous was widespread among whites. Black males were thought to be highly dangerous sexually to white women – while in fact, virtually all criminal sexual contact was initiated by white men against black women (Simpson and Yinger 1986).

If prejudice describes attitudes and opinions, **discrimination** refers to actual behaviour towards another group or individual. Discrimination can be seen in activities that disqualify members of one group from opportunities open to others, as when a black Briton is refused a job made available to a white person. Although prejudice is often the basis of discrimination, the two may exist separately. People may have prejudiced attitudes that they do not act on. Equally important, discrimination does not necessarily derive directly from prejudice. For example, white house-buyers might steer away from purchasing properties in predominantly black neighbourhoods not because of attitudes of hostility they might have towards those who live there, but because of worries about declining property values. Prejudiced attitudes in this case influence discrimination, but in an indirect fashion.

An anti-Semitic attack on a Jewish cemetery in Germany.

Racism

One widespread form of prejudice is **racism** – prejudice based on socially significant physical distinctions. A racist is someone who believes that some individuals are superior or inferior to others on the basis of racialized differences. Racism is commonly thought of as behaviour or attitudes held by certain individuals or groups. An individual may profess racist beliefs or may join in with a group, such as a white supremacist organization, which promotes a racist agenda. Yet many have argued that racism is more than simply the ideas held by a small number of bigoted individuals. Rather, racism is embedded in the very structure and oper-ation of society. The idea of **institutional racism** suggests that racism pervades all of society's structures in a systematic manner. According to this view, institutions such as the police, the health service and the educational system all promote policies that favour certain groups while discriminating against others.

The idea of institutional racism was developed in the United States in the late 1960s by civil rights campaigners who believed that racism underpins the very fabric of society, rather than merely representing the opinions of a small minority (Omi and Winant 1994). In subsequent years, the existence of institutional racism came to be widely accepted and openly acknowledged in many settings. An important investigation into the practices of the

The persistence of racism

Why has racism flourished? There are several reasons. One important factor leading to modern racism was simply the invention and diffusion of the concept of race itself. Quasi-racist attitudes have been known to exist for hundreds of years. But the notion of race as a set of fixed traits emerged with the rise of 'race science', which we have discussed. The notion of the superiority of the white race, although completely without value factually, remains a key element of white racism.

A second reason for the rise of modern racism lies in the exploitative relations that Europeans established with non-white peoples. The slave trade could not have been carried on had it not been widely believed by Europeans that blacks belonged to an inferior, even subhuman, race. Racism helped justify colonial rule over non-white peoples and denied them the rights of political participation that were being won by whites in their European homelands. Some sociologists argue that exclusion from citizenship remains a central feature of modern-day racism as well.

A third reason concerns the large-scale migration of ethnic minorities to Britain, Europe and North America – regions which were previously predominantly white (with the exception of indigenous people of North America). As the post-war economic boom faltered in the mid-1970s, and most Western economies moved from being short of labour (and having relatively open borders) to having large numbers of people unemployed, some members of the native population began to believe that immigrants were filling limited jobs and claiming welfare that they believed they were entitled to. Immigrants became an easy scapegoat for dissatisfied natives, often encouraged by the media. In practice, this widely held fear is largely a myth. Immigrant workers tend not to displace local workers, but are more likely to complement them by doing the work that local people reject, by providing valuable additional skills or creating jobs. Similarly once they are allowed to work, immigrants are likely to make a net contribution to the government budget as taxpayers.

London Metropolitan Police Service, in the light of the murder of Stephen Lawrence (see box below), found institutional racism to be pervasive within the police force and criminal justice system (Macpherson 1999). In culture and the arts, institutional racism has been revealed in spheres such as television broadcasting (negative or limited portrayal of ethnic minorities in programming) and the international modelling industry (industry-wide bias against non-white fashion models).

The murder of Stephen Lawrence and the Macpherson Report

In 1993, a black teenager, Stephen Lawrence, was killed in a racially motivated attack at the hands of five white youths as he was waiting at a bus stop with a friend in south-east London. Unprovoked, the young men fell on Lawrence, stabbed him twice and left him on the pavement to die. That no one has been convicted of his murder has been seen as a gross miscarriage of justice and a testimony to the pervasive racism in the law enforcement and criminal justice systems.

The commission which inquired into the case concluded that the investigation into Lawrence's murder was mishandled from the very start (Macpherson 1999). Police arriving on the scene made little effort to pursue Lawrence's attackers and displayed a lack of respect for his parents, denying them access to information about the case to which they were entitled. An erroneous assumption was made that Lawrence had been involved in a street brawl, rather than being an innocent victim of an unprovoked racist attack. Police surveillance of the suspects was poorly organized and conducted with a 'lack of urgency'; searches of the suspects' dwellings, for example, were not performed thoroughly, despite tips describing where weapons might be concealed. Senior officers who were in a position to intervene in the case to correct such mistakes failed to do so. During the course of the investigation and subsequent inquiries into it, police withheld vital information, protected one another and refused to take responsibility for mistakes.

Due to the perseverance of Lawrence's parents, three of the suspects were brought to trial in 1996, but the case collapsed when a judge ruled that the evidence presented by one witness was inadmissible. Jack Straw, who was then Home Secretary, announced a full inquiry into the Lawrence case in 1997; the findings of the inquiry were published in 1999 in the Macpherson Report. The authors of the report were unequivocal in their findings: 'The conclusions to be drawn from all the evidence in connection with the investigation of Stephen Lawrence's racist murder are clear. There is no doubt but that there were fundamental errors. The investigation was marred by a combination of professional incompetence, institutional racism and a failure of leadership by senior officers.'

The charge of *institutional racism* (discussed on p. 493) was one of the most important outcomes of the inquiry. The authors of the report concluded that not only the Metropolitan Police, but many other institutions including the criminal justice system, are implicated in a 'collective failure . . . to provide an appropriate and professional service to people because of their colour, culture or ethnic origin. It can be seen or detected in processes, attitudes and behaviour which amount to discrimination through unwitting prejudice, ignorance, thoughtlessness, and racist stereotyping which disadvantage minority ethnic people' (Macpherson 1999). The Macpherson Report concluded that 'it is incumbent upon every institution to examine their policies and the outcome of their policies' to ensure that no segment of the population be disadvantaged. Seventy recommendations were set forth for improving the way in which racist crimes are policed. These included race-awareness training for police officers, stronger disciplinary powers to remove racist officers, clearer definitions of what constitutes a racist incident, and a commitment to increasing the total number of black and Asian officers in the police force.

From 'old racism' to 'new racism'

Just as the concept of biological race has been discredited, old-style 'biological' racism based on differences in physical traits is rarely openly expressed in society today. The end to legalized segregation in the United States and the collapse of apartheid in South Africa were important turning points in the rejection of biological racism. In both of these cases, racist attitudes were proclaimed by directly associating physical traits with biological inferiority. Such blatantly racist ideas are rarely heard today, except in the cases of violent hate crimes or the platforms of certain extremist groups. But this is not to say that racist attitudes have disappeared from modern societies. Rather, as some scholars argue, they have been replaced by a more sophisticated **new racism** (or *cultural racism*), which uses the idea of cultural differences to exclude certain groups (Barker 1981).

Those who argue that a 'new racism' has emerged claim that cultural arguments are now employed instead of biological ones in order to discriminate against certain segments of the population. According to this view, hierarchies of superiority and inferiority are constructed according to the values of the majority culture. Those groups that stand apart from the majority can become marginalized or vilified for their refusal to assimilate. It is alleged that new racism has a clear political dimension. Prominent examples of new racism can be seen in the efforts by some American politicians to enact official English-only language policies and in the conflicts in France over girls who wish to wear Islamic headscarves to school (see chapter 14, p. 558 for more on this controversy). The fact that racism is increasingly exercised on cultural rather than biological grounds has led some scholars to suggest that we live in an age of 'multiple racisms', where discrimination is experienced differently across segments of the population (Back 1995).

Sociological interpretations of racism

Some of the concepts that are discussed above – such as stereotypical thinking, displacement and projection – help explain prejudice and discrimination through psychological mechanisms. They provide an account of the nature of prejudiced and racist attitudes and why ethnic differences matter so much to people, but they tell us little about the social processes involved in racism. To study such processes, we must call on sociological ideas.

Ethnocentrism, group closure and allocation of resources

Sociological concepts relevant to ethnic conflicts on a general level are those of ethnocentrism, ethnic group closure and resource allocation. **Ethnocentrism** is a suspicion of outsiders combined with a tendency to evaluate the culture of others in terms of one's own culture. Virtually all cultures have been ethnocentric to some degree, and it is easy to see how ethnocentrism combines with stereotypical thought discussed above (p. 491). Outsiders are thought of as aliens, barbarians or morally and mentally inferior. This was how most civilizations viewed the members of smaller cultures, for example, and the attitude has fuelled innumerable ethnic clashes in history.

Ethnocentrism and **group closure**, or ethnic group closure, frequently go together. 'Closure' refers to the process whereby groups maintain boundaries separating themselves from others. These boundaries are formed by means of exclusion devices, which sharpen the divisions between one ethnic group and another (Barth 1969). Such devices include limiting or prohibiting intermarriage between the groups, restrictions on social contact or economic relationships like trading, and the physical separation of groups (as in the case of ethnic ghettos). Black Americans have experienced all three exclusion devices: racial intermarriage has been illegal in some states, economic and social segregation was enforced by law in the South, and segregated black ghettos still exist in most major cities.

Sometimes groups of equal power mutually enforce lines of closure: their members keep separate from each other, but neither group dominates the other. More commonly, however, one ethnic group occupies a position of power over another. In these circumstances, group closure coincides with **resource allocation**, instituting inequalities in the distribution of wealth and material goods.

Some of the fiercest conflicts between ethnic groups centre on the lines of closure between them precisely because these lines signal inequalities in wealth, power or social standing. The concept of ethnic group closure helps us understand both the dramatic and the more insidious differences that separate communities of people from one another – not just why the members of some groups get shot, lynched, beaten up or harassed, but also why they don't get good jobs, a good education or a desirable place to live. Wealth, power and social status are scarce resources – some groups have more of them than others. To hold on to their distinctive positions, privileged groups sometimes undertake extreme acts of violence against others. Similarly, members of underprivileged groups may also turn to violence as a means of trying to improve their own situation.

Conflict theories

Conflict theories, by contrast, are concerned with the links between racism and prejudice on the one hand and relationships of power and inequality on the other. Early conflict approaches to racism were heavily influenced by Marxist ideas, which saw the economic system as the determining factor for all other aspects of society. Some Marxist theorists held that racism was a product of the capitalist system, arguing that the ruling class used slavery, colonization and racism as tools for exploiting labour (Cox 1959).

Later, neo-Marxist scholars saw these early formulations as too rigid and simplistic and suggested that racism was not the product of economic forces alone. A set of articles published in 1982 by the Birmingham Centre for Contemporary Cultural Studies, *The Empire Strikes Back*, takes a broader view of the rise of racism. While agreeing that the capitalist exploitation of labour is one factor, John Solomos, Paul Gilroy and others point to a variety of historical and political influences which led to the emergence of a specific brand of racism in Britain in the 1970s and 1980s. They argue that racism is a complex and multifaceted phenomenon involving the interplay of ethnic minority and working-class identities and beliefs. In their eyes, racism is much more than simply a set of oppressive ideas enacted against the non-white population by powerful elites (Hall 1982).

Ethnic integration and conflict

Many states in the world today are characterized by multi-ethnic populations. Often they have evolved in this way over the course of centuries. Some Middle Eastern and Central European states, for example, like Turkey or Hungary, are ethnically diverse as a result of long histories of changing borders, occupations by foreign powers and regional migration. Other societies have become multi-ethnic more rapidly, as a result of deliberate policies encouraging migration, or by way of colonial and imperial legacies.

In an age of globalization and rapid social change, the rich benefits and complex challenges of ethnic diversity are confronting a growing number of states. International migration is accelerating with the further integration of the global economy; the movement and mixing of human populations seems sure to intensify in years to come. Meanwhile, ethnic tensions and conflicts continue to flare in societies around the world, threatening to lead to the disintegration of some multi-ethnic states and hinting at protracted violence in others. How can ethnic diversity be accommodated and the outbreak of ethnic conflict averted? Within multi-ethnic societies, what should be the relation between ethnic minority groups and the majority population? There are three primary models of ethnic integration that have been adopted by multi-ethnic societies in relation to these challenges:

assimilation, the 'melting pot' and, finally, cultural pluralism or multiculturalism. It is important to realize that these three models are ideal types, and in practice are not easy to achieve.

Ideal types were discussed in chapter 1, 'What is Sociology?', p. 18.

Models of ethnic integration

The first avenue is **assimilation**, meaning that immigrants abandon their original customs and practices, moulding their behaviour to the values and norms of the majority. An assimilationist approach demands that immigrants change their language, dress, lifestyles and cultural outlooks as part of integrating into a new social order. In the United States, which was formed as a 'nation of immigrants', generations of immigrants were subjected to pressure to become 'assimilated' in this way, and many of their children became more or less completely 'American' as a result. Most official policies in the UK have been aimed at assimilating immigrants into British society. Of course, even if minorities try to assimilate, many are unable to do so if they are racialized or if their attempts are rebuffed – whether it be in employment or dating or any other context.

A second model is that of the **melting pot**. Rather than the traditions of the immigrants being dissolved in favour of those dominant among the pre-existing population, they become blended to form new, evolving cultural patterns. Not only are differing cultural values and norms 'brought in' to a society from the outside, but diversity is also created as ethnic groups adapt to the wider social environments in which they find themselves. One

Britain's favourite dish: a symbol of its 'melting-pot' culture?

often-cited literal example of a melting-pot culture is the chicken tikka masala, a meal invented in Indian restaurants in the UK. The chicken tikka is an Indian dish, and the masala sauce was added to satisfy the desire of British people to have gravy served on their meat. In 2001 the meal was famously described by the former Foreign Secretary Robin Cook (1946–2005), as a 'British national dish' (Cook 2001).

Many have believed that the melting-pot model is the most desirable outcome of ethnic diversity. Traditions and customs of immigrant populations are not abandoned, but contribute to and shape a constantly transforming social milieu. Hybrid forms of cuisine, fashion, music and architecture are manifestations of the melting-pot approach. To a limited degree, this model is an accurate expression of aspects of American cultural development. Although the 'Anglo' culture has remained the pre-eminent one, its character in some part reflects the impact of the many different groups that now compose the American population.

The third model is that of **cultural pluralism**, in which ethnic cultures are given full validity to exist separately, yet participate in the larger society's economic and political life. A recent outgrowth of pluralism is **multiculturalism**, in which ethnic groups exist separately and *equally*. The United States and other Western countries are pluralistic in many senses, but ethnic differences have for the most part been associated with inequalities rather than equal but independent membership in the national community. It does seem at least possible to create a society in which ethnic groups are separate but equal, as is demonstrated by Switzerland, where French, German and Italian groups coexist in the same society.

In Britain and elsewhere in Europe, the leaders of most ethnic minority groups have increasingly emphasized the path of pluralism. To achieve 'distinct but equal' status will demand major struggles, and as yet this is a very distant option. Ethnic minorities are still perceived by many people as a threat: to their job, their safety and the 'national culture'. The scapegoating of ethnic minorities is a persistent tendency. With the young in Western Europe quite often still holding similar prejudices to those of older generations, ethnic minorities in most countries face a future of continued discrimination, in a social climate characterized by tension and anxiety.

Ethnic conflict

Ethnic diversity can greatly enrich societies. Multi-ethnic states are often vibrant and dynamic places that are strengthened by the varied contributions of their inhabitants. But such states can also be fragile, especially in the face of internal upheaval or external threat. Differing linguistic, religious and cultural backgrounds can become fault-lines that result in open antagonism between ethnic groups. Sometimes societies with long histories of ethnic tolerance and integration can rapidly become engulfed in *ethnic conflict* – hostilities between different ethnic groups or communities.

This was the case in the former Yugoslavia in the 1990s, a region renowned for its rich multi-ethnic heritage. The Balkans have long been the crossroads of Europe. Centuries of migration and the rule of successive empires have produced a diverse, intermixed population composed predominantly of Slavs (such as the Eastern Orthodox Serbs), Croats (Catholic), Muslims and Jews. After 1991, alongside major political and social transformations following the fall of communism, deadly conflicts broke out between ethnic groups in several areas of the former Yugoslavia.

The conflicts in the former Yugoslavia involved attempts at **ethnic cleansing**, the creation of ethnically homogeneous areas through the mass expulsion of other ethnic populations. Croatia, for example, has become an independent 'mono-ethnic' state after a costly war in which thousands of Serbs were expelled from the country. A war which broke out in Bosnia in 1992 between Serbs, Croats and Muslims involved the ethnic cleansing of the Bosnian Muslim population at the hands of the Serbs. Thousands of Muslim men were forced into internment camps and a campaign of systematic rape was carried out against Muslim women. The war in Kosovo in 1999 was prompted by charges that Serbian forces were ethnically cleansing the Kosovar Albanian (Muslim) population from the province.

In both Bosnia and Kosovo, ethnic conflict became internationalized. Hundreds of thousands of refugees spilled over into neighbouring areas, further destabilizing the region. Western states intervened both diplomatically and militarily to protect the human rights of ethnic groups which had become targets of ethnic cleansing. In the short term, such interventions succeeded in quelling the systematic violence. Yet they had unintended consequences as well. The fragile peace in Bosnia was maintained, but only through the presence of peacekeeping troops and the partitioning of the country into separate ethnic enclaves. In Kosovo, a process of 'reverse ethnic cleansing' ensued after the NATO bombing campaign in 1999. Ethnic Albanian Kosovars began to drive the local Serb population out of Kosovo; the presence of UN-led 'Kfor' troops proved to be inadequate to prevent ethnic tensions from reigniting.

Ethnic cleansing involves the forced relocation of ethnic populations through targeted violence, harassment, threats and campaigns of terror. **Genocide**, by contrast, describes the systematic elimination of one ethnic group at the hands of another. The term 'genocide' has often been used to describe the process by which indigenous populations in North and South America were decimated after the arrival of European explorers and settlers. Disease, forced relocation and campaigns of violence destroyed many native populations, although the extent to which this was systematically planned remains contested.

The twentieth century witnessed the

emergence of 'organized' genocide and carries the dubious distinction of being the most 'genocidal' century in history. In the Armenian genocide of 1915–23, more than a million Armenians were killed at the hands of the Ottoman Turks. The Nazi Holocaust resulted in the death of more than six million Jews and remains the most horrific example of the planned extermination of one ethnic group by another. The ethnic Hutu majority in Rwanda launched a genocidal campaign against the ethnic Tutsi minority in 1994, claiming the lives of more than 800,000 individuals within a span of three months. More than two million Rwandan refugees spilled over into neighbouring states, heightening ethnic tensions in countries such as Burundi and Zaire (now Congo). More recently, government backed Arab militia have been accused of ethnic cleansing in Sudan after an uprising by the some of the black population of the Western region of Darfur in 2003. Reprisals by the militia led to the loss of at least 70,000 lives and left around two million people homeless (United Nations figures, BBC News, 2005).

It has been noted that violent conflicts around the globe are increasingly based on ethnic divisions, as the examples of Rwanda and Sudan show. Only a tiny proportion of wars now occur between states; the vast majority of conflicts are civil wars with ethnic dimensions. In a world of increasing interdependence and competition, international factors become even more important in shaping ethnic relations, while the effects of 'internal' ethnic conflicts are felt well outside national borders. As we have seen, ethnic conflicts attract international attention and have sometimes provoked physical intervention. International war crimes tribunals have been convened to investigate and try those responsible for the ethnic cleansing and genocide in Yugoslavia and Rwanda. Responding to and preventing ethnic conflict has become one of the key challenges facing both individual states and international political structures. Although ethnic tensions are often experienced, interpreted and described at the local level, they are increasingly taking on national and international dimensions.

Migration and ethnic diversity in the UK

Immigration

While we may think of immigration to Britain as a phenomenon of the twentieth century, it is a process whose roots stretch back to the earliest stages of written history and beyond. The considerable number of Irish, Welsh and Scottish names scattered among the English people today is a reminder of the traditional flow of people from the 'Celtic fringes' to the urban centres of England. In the early nineteenth century, long before the advent of major immigration from distant colonies, developing English cities attracted migrants from the less prosperous areas of the British Isles.

The spread of industrialization, however, was drastically to transform migration patterns within the country as well as international immigration to England. The growth of opportunities for work in urban areas coupled with the decline of household production in the countryside encouraged the trend towards rural–urban migration. Demands within the labour market also gave new impetus to

The ethnic Hutu majority in Rwanda claimed the lives of more than 800,000 Tutsis during the genocide of 1994.

immigration from abroad. Although Irish, Jewish and black communities existed in Britain long before to the Industrial Revolution, the surge of opportunity radically altered the scale and scope of international immigration. New waves of Dutch, Chinese, Irish and black immigrants helped to transform the socio-economic climate in England.

A more recent large wave of immigration to Britain occurred when the Nazi persecutions of the early 1930s sent a generation of European Jews fleeing westwards to safety. One survey estimated that 60,000 Jews settled in the UK between 1933 and 1939, but the real figure may well have been higher. Between 1933 and 1939 some 80,000 refugees arrived from Central

Europe, and a further 70,000 came during the war itself. By May 1945, Europe faced an unprecedented refugee problem: millions of people had become refugees. Several hundred thousand of these settled in Britain.

In the period after the Second World War Britain experienced immigration on a vast scale – most of the new residents came from the Commonwealth countries in response to job opportunities. There was a marked shortage of labour in postwar Britain; for a while, employers were keen to attract immigrant labour. In addition to rebuilding the country and economy following the destruction of the war, industrial expansion was providing British workers with unprecedented mobility and creating a need for labour in unskilled and manual positions. Those in governing circles were influenced by the notion of Britain's great imperial heritage, and therefore felt that people from the West Indies, India, Pakistan and the former colonies in Africa were all British subjects and entitled to settle in Britain. The influx of immigrants was aided by the adoption of the 1948 British Nationality Act, which granted favourable immigration rights to citizens of Commonwealth countries.

With each wave of immigration, ethnic minorities radically changed the religious make-up of the UK. British cities, in particular, are now multi-ethnic and religiously diverse. In the nineteenth century immigrants from Ireland swelled the number of Catholics in the UK, particularly in cities such as Liverpool or Glasgow, where many of them settled. In the postwar period large-scale immigration from Asia increased the number of Muslims (many of whom originate from the largely

Immigration brings about new ideas of what it means to be British, at all levels of society, as this image of a black Queen Elizabeth suggests.

Muslim countries of Pakistan and Bangladesh) and Hindus (most of whom have originated from India) in the UK. Immigration has created new questions about what it means to be British and how ethnic and religious minorities can integrate fully in British society.

Religious diversity in the UK is discussed in more detail in chapter 14, 'Religion in Modern Society'.

Immigration policy in Britain since the 1960s

The 1960s marked the start of a gradual rolling back of the notion that inhabitants of the British Empire had the right to immigrate to Britain and claim citizenship. Although the changing contours of the labour market may have played some role in the new restrictions on immigration, it was also a response to the backlash against the influx of immigrants on the part of many white Britons. In particular, working people living in the poorer areas to which the new immigrants gravitated were sensitive to the disruptions that immigration caused to their own everyday lives. Attitudes to the newcomers were often hostile. The 1958 Notting Hill riots in which white residents attacked black immigrants were a testament to the strength of racist attitudes.

For more on urban riots, see chapter 21, 'Cities and Urban Spaces', pp. 912–14.

The growing chorus of calls for immigration control were echoed in a famous phrase from Enoch Powell, a Conservative front-bench minister at the time. In a 1962

There was a rise in Commonwealth immigrants coming to Britain after the Second World War in response to a national labour shortage, but they often faced racism. Immigration was later restricted.

speech in Birmingham, Powell envisaged an extraordinary growth in the non-white population in Britain: 'Like the Romans, I seem to see "the River Tiber flowing with much blood".' A Gallup poll showed that 75 per cent of the population were broadly sympathetic to Powell's views.

Anti-racist campaigners and writers have argued that British immigration policy is racist and discriminatory against non-whites. Beginning in 1962 with the Commonwealth Immigrants Act, a series of measures were passed which restricted entry and settlement rights for non-whites, while protecting the ability of whites to enter Britain relatively freely. Even among citizens of Commonwealth states, immigration laws discriminated against inhabitants of the predominantly non-white 'New Commonwealth' states, while preserving the rights of immigrants from 'old Commonwealth' countries such as Canada and Australia. The introduction of the 'patriality principle' in the 1968 Commonwealth Immigrants Act meant that in order to claim British citizenship, a citizen of a Commonwealth country must have been born, adopted or naturalized in the UK, or have a parent or grandparent who met those criteria. On the whole, such requirements made immigration much more possible for whites than for non-whites.

A British Nationality Act passed in 1981 tightened up the conditions under which people from former or existing dependent territories could enter the UK. British citizenship was separated from citizenship of British dependent territories. A category of 'British Overseas Citizens' was created, referring mainly to people living in Hong Kong, Malaysia and Singapore; they were not entitled to settle in the UK, and their children could not inherit their citizenship. Commonwealth citizens, who could previously register as British citizens after living in the country for five years, now had to apply for naturalization under the same conditions as people from anywhere else in the world. Other restrictions on entry and right of residence were also added. Legislation introduced in 1988 and 1996 increased these restrictions even further.

As opportunities for immigrants to enter the country have declined, Britain has also reduced the possibilities for **asylum-seekers** to enter the country. To be granted asylum, an individual must claim that being forced to leave the country would break obligations that the government has to them under the United Nations 'Convention and Protocol relating to the Status of Refugees'. Under this agreement, signed in 1951, nations are obliged to protect refugees who are fleeing persecution in their own country and treat them at least as well as other foreign nationals on their territory. Legislation on asylum was passed in 1991 introducing stringent checks on people claiming refugee status, including fingerprinting, a reduction in access to free legal advice and the doubling of fines levied on airlines which bring in passengers not holding valid visas. The 1993 Asylum and Immigration Appeals Act has led to an increased number of refusals and to an escalation of the number of asylum-seekers held in detention centres for long periods of time. The BBC reported a 61 per cent decrease in immigration in the period 2003–5.

In recent years the issues of ethnicity and immigration have moved up the political agenda considerably in the UK (and other rich nations, see below). Surveys have shown that the proportion of Britons

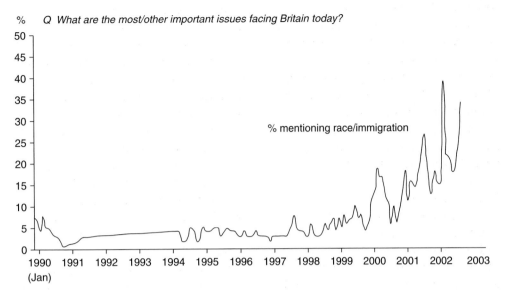

%   *Q What are the most/other important issues facing Britain today?*

% mentioning race/immigration

Figure 13.1   The rise in public concern about race and immigration (base: *c.* 2,000 British adults)

Source: MORI (10 February 2003)

who see 'race' or 'immigration' as the most important issue facing the country rose from around 5 per cent for most of the 1990s, to 39 per cent during a peak in public concern in May 2002 (see figure 13.1). This placed race and immigration second only to the NHS as the most important issue of the time. As opportunities for people able to enter the UK as immigrants were cut off, there was a sharp rise in the number of people seeking asylum. Depictions, particularly in tabloid newspapers, of 'bogus' asylum-seekers 'swamping' the UK have helped to create a distorted image of immigration and asylum. Surveys have found that, although the UK hosts just 1.98 per cent of the world's asylum-seekers and refugees, the public estimated a number ten times higher, believing, on average, that Britain hosts nearly a quarter (23 per cent) of the

world's refugees and asylum-seekers (MORI, 17 June 2002). Surveys also found that respondents grossly overvalued the financial aid that people looking for asylum in the UK receive, estimating that an asylum-seeker receives £113 a week to live on. In fact, when that survey was carried out in 2000, a single adult seeking asylum received £36.54 a week (then in vouchers) to be spent at designated stores (MORI, 23 October 2000).

New Labour has introduced three new pieces of legislation covering immigration and asylum since their election in 1997. The 1998 Immigration and Asylum Act tightened the criteria used to decide whether asylum-seekers were allowed to remain in the country and attempted to streamline the asylum process. The 2002 Nationality, Immigration and Asylum Act, which built on the government's White Paper *Secure*

Borders, Safe Haven: Integration with Diversity (2002), set new requirements for people wanting British citizenship, including a basic knowledge of life in the UK, citizenship ceremonies and a pledge of allegiance. The Act also provided for the housing of asylum-seekers in specially built accommodation centres dispersed around the country, a measure widely criticized by refugee groups. The voucher system, under which asylum-seekers were given vouchers rather than cash, was also brought to an end by the Act. The system had been widely condemned as stigmatizing refugees.

The concept of stigmatization is discussed in chapter 8, 'Health, Illness and Disability', p. 269.

A further piece of legislation, the 2004 Asylum and Immigration Act, made asylum still more difficult to claim, again attempted to streamline the system and introduced new penalties for those involved in people trafficking. Immigration control became an important issue in the run-up to the 2005 general election.

Ethnic diversity

Ethnic minority groups now make up almost 8 per cent of the overall British population (HMSO 2004). As we have seen, immigration has been a significant factor in shaping the country's ethnic composition. But it is important to note that in our current age immigration is now responsible for a declining proportion of the minority ethnic population. For every ethnic group, children are much more likely to have been born in Britain than older members. This marks an important

shift away from an 'immigrant population' to a non-white British population with full citizenship rights.

The 1991 Census marked the first time that respondents were asked to classify themselves in ethnic terms. Prior to this, data about the ethnic composition of the population had been determined according to information on the place of birth of the 'head of the household'. Yet, as a growing percentage of the ethnic minority population came to be born in Britain, this approach was deemed inadequate. 'Self-classification' measures of ethnic group membership have now become standard for most official surveys and studies, such as the Labour Force Survey (LFS). Yet because the ethnic classifications used in studies do not always correspond with one another, comparing data across studies can be difficult (Mason 1995). The number of people belonging to the largest ethnic minority groups, according to the 2001 Census, is shown in figure 13.2. As always, it is necessary to be cautious about the accuracy of official statistics. For example, respondents' understandings of their own ethnicity may be more complex than the stated 'options' or categories on a survey (Moore 1995). This is particularly true in the case of individuals of mixed ethnic backgrounds.

The 2001 Census showed that Britain's ethnic minority population, now numbering more than 4.6 million people, is concentrated primarily in the most densely populated urban areas of England (see figure 13.3). More than 75 per cent of ethnic minorities live in Greater London, the West Midlands, Yorkshire and Humberside, and the North-West and Merseyside (Strategy Unit 2003). In London, 29 per cent of all residents are non-white. By

David Goodhart: ethnic diversity versus the welfare state?

In a controversial article published in February 2004, David Goodhart, the editor of *Prospect* magazine, argued that there is a trade-off between an ethnically *diverse* society and one that has the *solidarity* between citizens that allows it to have a decent welfare system to protect those in need. To Goodhart, people are willing to pay taxes – to go towards pensions or unemployment benefit, for example – if they believe that they are paying to help people who are in some way like themselves; people who share at least common values and assumptions. Goodhart called this trade-off 'the progressive dilemma' which faces all those who want both a diverse and a solidaristic society.

As evidence of this trade-off, Goodhart pointed to the Scandinavian countries, such as Sweden and Denmark, which historically have the world's most generous welfare states. He argued that it has been possible to build large welfare systems in these countries because they are fairly socially and ethnically homogeneous, so people are prepared to pay more in taxes. In contrast, welfare states have been weaker in ethnically more divided countries such as the United States.

Goodhart asked if there is a 'tipping point' that occurs somewhere between the proportion of the population in Britain who belong to an ethnic minority group (fewer than one in ten people) and that of United States (which is nearer one in three), where a wholly different US-style society is created; that is, one with sharp ethnic divisions and a weak welfare state. He suggested that for this tipping point to be avoided and for feelings of solidarity towards incomers not to be overstretched, it is important that there are limits to the number of people allowed to enter the country and that the process of asylum and immigration is seen to be transparent and under control (Goodhart 2004).

Goodhart's thesis has been heavily criticized. The sociologist Saskia Sassen has argued that in the long run, integration of immigrants does happen, and that, broadly speaking, immigrants face the same sort of difficulties in becoming accepted today as they did in previous centuries. Historically, all European societies have over time incorporated many, if not all, the major foreign immigrant groups. Past experience shows that it has often taken no more than a couple of generations to turn 'them' into 'us' – the community that can experience solidarity in Goodhart's analysis (Sassen 2004).

The political theorist Bhikhu Parekh has also attacked Goodhart's thesis. One of the arguments that Parekh put forward is that Goodhart gets the relationship between solidarity and the redistribution of the welfare state the wrong way round. Goodhart is convinced that solidarity is a necessary precondition of redistribution. That is a half truth, argued Parekh; one could just as plausibly say that redistribution generates loyalty, creates common life experiences and so on, and therefore paves the way for solidarity. The relation between the two is far more complex than Goodhart suggests in his article (Parekh 2004).

Bernard Crick, another political theorist and an adviser to the former Home Secretary David Blunkett, asked Goodhart, 'Solidarity of what?' Goodhart discusses solidarity in Britain, but, Crick noted, if Goodhart had talked of the United Kingdom (instead of Britain), it might have reminded him that we have been a multinational and a multi-ethnic state for a long time. Dual identities are something many of us are used to living with. Nowadays, the dual status of being British and Scottish, Welsh, Irish or English is fully accepted. The question does not concern either solidarity or loss of identity: our identity lies partly in being a member of more than one group – Britishness can accept more diversity than Goodhart realizes (Crick 2004).

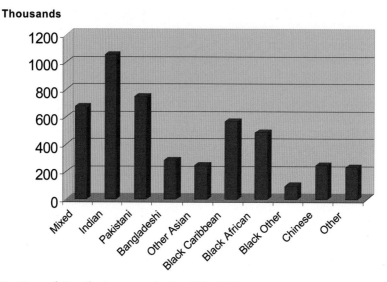

Figure 13.2 Non-white ethnic groups in the UK, 2001

Source: Census 2001: ONS (2003a)

contrast, the more rural regions such as the North-East and South-West have an ethnic minority population of less than 2 per cent (Office of National Statistics 2002b). Many members of ethnic minorities do not live in the inner city by choice; they moved there because such areas were least favoured by the white population. In many cities a process of suburbanization occurred, and empty properties became available as whites moved out.

For more on suburbanization, see chapter 21, 'Cities and Urban Spaces', pp. 908–9.

The 2001 Census also showed that people from the non-white ethnic groups had a younger age structure than the white population in the UK. The 'Mixed' group were the youngest, with half under the age of sixteen. The 'Bangladeshi', 'Other Black' and 'Pakistani' groups also had young age struc-

tures, with more than a third of each of these groups under sixteen years old (ONS 2003a). In terms of gender, the composition of most ethnic minority groups is more balanced between the sexes than in previous times. In earlier years, the bulk of immigrants, particularly from New Commonwealth countries, such as India and the Caribbean, were men. Later policies favoured immigration for the purpose of family reunification, a shift which helped to equalize the proportions of men and women in many ethnic minority groups.

The above descriptions of ethnic diversity in Britain can be taken as only the broadest indicators of extremely complex and diversified patterns within the population. Increasingly, sociologists and scholars from other disciplines are emphasizing the need to focus on differences between Britain's ethnic minority groups, rather than speaking generally

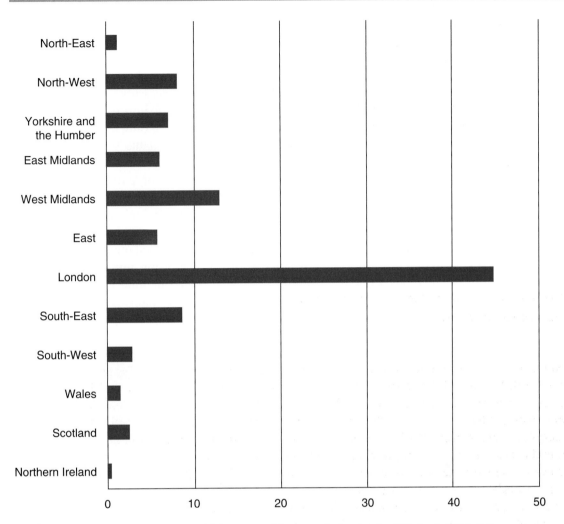

Figure 13.3 Regional distribution of the non-white population in the UK, April 2001 (%)

Source: ONS (2002b)

about the experience of ethnic minorities. As we shall see in the following section on race and inequality, black and Asian people in Britain are disadvantaged as a whole in comparison with the white population, but there is much differentiation among ethnic minority groups that bears close examination.

Ethnic minorities and the labour market

Employment is a crucial area for monitoring the effects of social and economic disadvantages due to factors such as gender, age, class and ethnicity. Studies on the position of ethnic minorities in the labour market have revealed patterns of disadvantage in terms of occupational distribution, wage levels, discrimination in hiring and promotional practices, and unemployment rates. We shall consider some of these themes in this section.

Trends in occupational patterns since 1960

The earliest national survey of ethnic minorities in Britain, which was conducted by the Policy Studies Institute (PSI) in the 1960s, found that most recent immigrants were clustered disproportionately in manual occupations within a small number of industries. Even those recent arrivals who possessed qualifica-

tions from their countries of origin tended to work in jobs incommensurate with their abilities. Discrimination on the basis of ethnic background was a common and overt practice, with some employers refusing to hire non-white workers, or agreeing to do so only when there was a shortage of suitable white workers.

By the 1970s, employment patterns had shifted slightly. The second PSI report in 1974 showed that members of ethnic minority groups continued to occupy semi-skilled or unskilled manual positions, although a growing number were employed in skilled manual jobs. Few ethnic minorities were represented in professional and managerial posi-

A large proportion of the UK's ethnic minorities are under the age of 16.

tions. Regardless of changes in legislation to prevent racial discrimination in hiring practices, research found that whites were consistently offered interviews and job opportunities in preference to equally qualified non-white applicants.

The third PSI national survey of ethnic minorities, in 1982, found that, with the exception of African-Asian and Indian men, ethnic minorities were suffering rates of unemployment that were twice as high as for whites due to the general economic recession, which had a strong impact on the manufacturing sector. Qualified non-whites with fluent English, however, were increasingly entering white-collar positions, and on the whole there was a narrowing in the wage gap between ethnic minorities and whites. Starting in the late 1970s a growing number of ethnic minorities took up self-employment, contributing to higher earnings and lower levels of unemployment, especially among Indians and African Asians.

Globalization and everyday life: ethnic minorities and the 'new economy'

Because of the high concentration of ethnic minority workers in manufacturing and industry, many observers have suggested that the decline of the industrial economy has had a disproportionate impact on this segment of the population. Higher rates of unemployment, they argue, are a reflection of the effects of economic restructuring on ethnic minority workers, since they are less skilled and more vulnerable. The shift of the British economy from one based on industry to one driven by technology and the service sector (the 'new economy') has been harmful to ethnic minority workers who are less well equipped to make the transition into new occupations.

This conventional view has been challenged, however, by findings such as those of the PSI surveys and comparisons of Labour Force Survey and Census statistics (Iganski and Payne 1999). These studies have demonstrated that certain non-white groups have in fact attained high levels of economic and occupational success in recent decades, in much the same way as successful white workers. The process of economic restructuring, they argue, has actually contributed to reducing the gap between ethnic minority and white populations in the labour market. This is because large-scale transformations within the economy have tended to embrace both ethnic minority and white populations.

Using data from three decades of Labour Force Surveys and Censuses (1971, 1981 and 1991), Paul Iganski and Geoff Payne found that, as a whole, ethnic minority groups experienced lower levels of job loss than did the rest of the industrial labour force. Between 1971 and 1991 the manufacturing jobs that were lost by non-whites accounted for 12 per cent of those economically active in 1971, while among the overall workforce the figure was 14.4 per cent. Iganski and Payne note that there were significant disparities within this overall trend – for example, between men and women and also across industrial sectors. But on the whole, they found that the move to the 'new economy' tended to sweep up non-whites and whites alike in a way that narrowed the gap between them. According to Iganski and Payne, there is now a substantial non-white population in Britain whose occupational structure is changing in ways that are indistinguishable from that of the majority white population.

Iganski and Payne (1999) are careful to point out that the substantial gains made by certain ethnic minority groups should not be mistaken for the end of occupational disadvantage. Rather, they contend, this 'collective social mobility' demonstrates that the forces of post-industrial restructuring are stronger than those of racial discrimination and persistent disadvantage.

Recent findings

Recent investigations of ethnic minorities in the UK have revealed more than ever before the divergent employment trajectories of different ethnic groups. For example, the government's Strategy Unit found that Indians and Chinese are, on average, out-performing whites in the labour market. However, other groups are doing less well: Pakistanis, Bangladeshis and black Caribbeans experience, on average, significantly higher unemployment and lower earnings than whites (Strategy Unit 2003).

As well as noting the diversity in employment statistics between ethnic minority groups, the fourth PSI survey, published in 1997, also found that among non-white women, employment patterns vary strongly. Caribbean women are much less likely to be in manual work than are white women, while Indian women, like Pakistanis, tend to occupy primarily manual jobs. There is a much higher level of economic activity among Caribbean and Indian women, while Pakistani and Bangladeshi women are less active in the labour market. On average Caribbean and Indian women tend to have slightly higher full-time earnings than do white women, although among Indian women there is a sharp polarization between those on relatively high incomes and those who are on low incomes (Modood et al. 1997). Figure 13.4 shows how much unemployment rates for men and women vary across different ethnic backgrounds.

The most successful non-whites, as measured in terms of level of income, are those South Asians who are self-employed or small employers. The proportion of people in this category has risen steadily over the past twenty years: Indian men and women are now more than twice as likely to be self-employed than whites. Studies indicate that discrimination among wage and salary employers is one reason for the overrepresentation of ethnic minorities in self-employment (Clark and Drinkwater 1998). Asian corner shops and other forms of Asian-run business have become such a prominent aspect of British society that some have suggested that they could lead an economic revival of inner-city areas. Tariq Modood has explained the 'Indian economic success' as the result of hard work, community and family support, and the high priority granted to education (Modood 1991).

It is important not to overstate the prosperity and potential impact of South Asian small businesses, however. Many self-employed Asians work extremely long hours – up to sixty or eighty hours per week – for relatively low levels of overall income. They are registered as self-employed, but are in effect employed by other members of the family who run the business; and they do not have the usual advantages that employees enjoy of sick pay, paid holidays and employer contributions to National Insurance.

Advances within the occupational structure are not always matched by increased representation at the top levels of power. Despite the fact that a higher number of ethnic minorities occupy white-collar professional positions than was the case previously, there appears to be a 'glass ceiling' which prevents all but a few people from the ethnic minorities from advancing to the top positions within large companies and organizations. In general, ethnic minority men – even the most highly qualified – are only

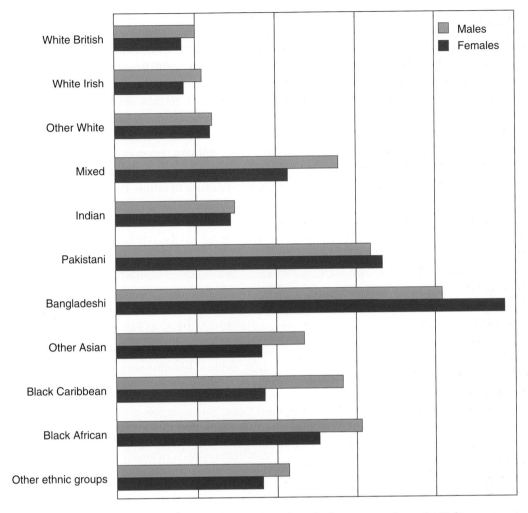

Figure 13.4 Unemployment rates in Great Britain: by ethnic group and sex, 2001/2

Source: ONS (2002b), p. 12

half as likely as white men to be represented among the top 10 per cent of jobs by power, status and earnings (Modood et al. 1997).

Housing

Ethnic minorities in Britain tend to experience discrimination, harassment and material deprivation in the housing market. Since the early calls for immigration controls, housing has been at the forefront of struggles over resources between groups and tendencies towards ethnic closure. One reason for this may be that housing is a highly symbolic matter – it indicates status, provides security and interweaves with overall livelihood. As with employment patterns, differentials in the quality and type of housing vary across ethnic groups. Although the non-white population as a whole is more disadvantaged than whites in terms of housing, this is far from a unified picture. Certain groups, such as those of Indian origin, have attained very high levels of home ownership, while others are clustered disproportionately in substandard accommodation or the social housing sector (Ratcliffe 1999).

A number of factors contribute to housing differentials between non-white and white populations, and among non-white groups. Racial harassment or violent attacks, which are still frequent not only in Britain but across Europe, are likely to encourage a certain degree of ethnic segregation in housing patterns. Non-white families with the means to move into more affluent, predominantly white neighbourhoods may be dissuaded from doing so because of ethnic hostility. Another factor relates to the physical condition of housing. In general, housing

Social capital and ethnic minority employment

A recent way of thinking about the way that groups relate to wider communities has developd from the concept of social capital.

The idea of social capital is discussed in more depth in chapter 16, 'Organizations and Networks', pp. 675–9.

Broadly speaking, social capital metrics attempt to measure how well connected individuals are to their communities, and to their society more broadly. Measures of social capital are divided into two types, 'bridging' and 'bonding'. Bridging social capital consists of networks that link the members of a given social group with the wider society, whereas bonding social capital links members of the social group with each other (Putnam 2000).

The distinction between bridging and bonding social capital may be important in understanding the labour market fortunes of ethnic minorities. Bridging social capital is likely to be of considerable importance in the process of a job search, particularly for employment fields such as the media where recruitment is principally by word of mouth. An ethnic minority individual who is socially isolated will, almost by definition, lack this bridging social capital and therefore lack access to some employment opportunities. It is quite possible that a lack of these bridging social networks will limit the chances of obtaining work with white employers.

On the other hand, geographically concentrated ethnic minorities, such as the Pakistanis and Bangladeshis, may develop higher levels of bonding social capital. This may provide a basis for a successful local economy and may lead to group economic success via that route. The members of these minorities may thus gain opportunities with co-ethnic employers that they lack with white employers. Entrepreneurship is relatively high among Pakistanis and Bangladeshis. Bonding social capital may thus compensate, in part, for lack of bridging social capital.

However, the correlation between social isolation and geographical concentration on the one hand and labour market performance on the other is not always precise. Whilst lack of bridging social capital might perhaps help to explain the large disadvantages for Pakistanis and Bangladeshis, it is not clear how it can explain the fact that disadvantages are also quite large for black Caribbeans, who are socially perhaps the most integrated of all the visible ethnic minorities (as indexed, for example, by their rates of intermarriage with white people). Chinese relative economic success is also quite hard to explain by this kind of argument.

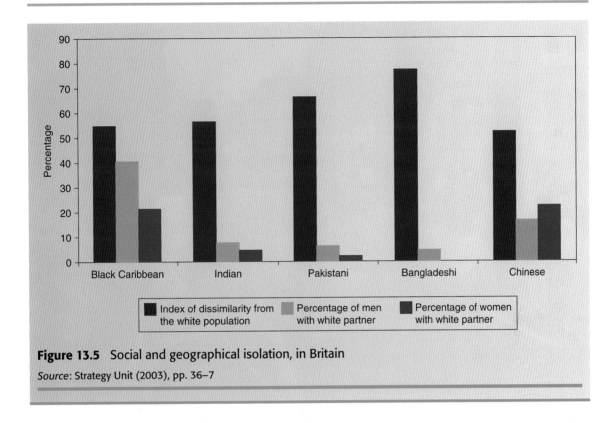

Figure 13.5 Social and geographical isolation, in Britain
Source: Strategy Unit (2003), pp. 36–7

occupied by ethnic minority groups tends to be in greater disrepair than that of the white population. A high proportion of Pakistanis and Bangladeshis live in accommodation that is overcrowded (because of the large average size of their households); their housing also tends to be more susceptible to damp and more likely to lack central heating.

People of Indian origin, by contrast, are as likely as whites to occupy detached or semi-detached homes and are less likely than other ethnic groups to reside in inner-city neighbourhoods. African-Caribbean households, on the other hand, are much more likely to rent accommodation in the social housing sector, rather than become home-owners. This may be related to the high proportion of lone-parent families within this ethnic group.

How can ethnic differentials in housing be understood? Some sociologists have argued that as a result of the competitive processes in the housing market, ethnic minorities have emerged as a distinct 'housing class' (Rex and Moore 1967). According to such an approach, the challenges facing minority groups – from economic disadvantage to racial discrimination – mean that they have few options and little chance to exert control over their housing position. Ethnic minorities are essentially forced to make do with inadequate housing because they have few or no choices in the matter. While there are certainly many constraining circumstances which disadvantage ethnic

The Notting Hill Carnival takes place in an area of London that became home to large numbers of West Indian immigrants when they first settled in Britain. The rising cost of housing in Notting Hill means that many African-Caribbean people have now moved out of the area.

minorities in the housing market, it would be wrong to imply that they are simply passive victims of discriminatory or racist forces. Patterns and practices change over time through the choices made by social actors. Discrimination can also become an impetus for creative action.

The criminal justice system

Since the 1960s members of ethnic minority groups have been represented in ever greater numbers within the criminal justice system, both as offenders and victims. Compared to their distribution in the overall population, ethnic minorities are overrepresented in prisons. In 2002, 16 per cent of male prisoners in England and Wales were from an ethnic minority group (HMSO 2004).

There is reason to believe that members of ethnic minority groups suffer from discriminatory treatment once they are within the criminal justice system. There is a higher rate of custodial sentencing among non-whites, even in cases where there are few or no previous convictions. Ethnic minorities are also more likely to experience discrimination or racial attacks once imprisoned. Some scholars have pointed out that the administration of the criminal justice system is over-whelmingly dominated by whites. A small percentage of practising lawyers are black, and blacks compose less than 2 per cent of the police force (Denney 1998).

Non-white groups are all vulnerable to racism of one kind or another – including racially motivated attacks. Most escape such treatment, but for a minority the experience can be disturbing and brutal. It has been estimated that racially motivated incidents represented 12 per cent of all crime against minority ethnic people (compared with 2 per cent for white people) (Office of National Statistics 2002b). According to the British Crime Survey, the estimated number of racially motivated offences in England and Wales fell from 390,000 in 1995 to 280,000 in 1999. The number of racially motivated incidents against black, Indian, Pakistani and Bangladeshi people also fell, from 145,000 in 1995 to 98,000 in 1999 (ibid.).

The British Crime Survey also found that emotional reactions to racially motivated incidents were generally more severe than for non-racially motivated incidents. In 1999, 42 per cent of victims of racially motivated crime said that they had been 'very much affected' by the incident, compared with 19 per cent of victims of other sorts of crime. Black victims were most likely to report being 'very much affected', 55 per cent compared with 41 per cent for both Asian and white victims (ibid.).

How can we account for these patterns of crime and victimization? As we will see in chapter 19 ('Crime and Deviance'), crime is not evenly distributed among the population. There appears to be a distinct spatial element to patterns of crime and victimization. Areas that suffer from material deprivation generally have higher crime rates and individuals living in such regions run a greater risk of falling victim to crime.

The deprivations to which people exposed to racism are subject both help to produce, and are produced by, the decaying environment of the inner cities (see also chapter 21, 'Cities and Urban Spaces'). Here, there are clear correlations between race, unemployment and crime, which tend to centre particularly on the position of young males from ethnic minority backgrounds. Through the political and media creations of 'moral panics' about crime, a public link has been established between race and crime.

> The idea of a 'moral panic' is discussed in chapter 19, 'Crime and Deviance', p. 802.

Yet the experience of many people from ethnic minorities, and particularly young men, is that it is precisely they who are the 'objects of violent exploitation' in their encounters with whites and to some extent also, unfortunately, the police.

Police racism

Sociological studies have been instrumental in revealing racist attitudes among police officers. In the 1980s, a study of police by Roger Graef (1989) concluded that police were 'actively hostile to all minority groups'. He noted the frequency with which officers would use stereotypes and racial slurs when speaking about ethnic minorities. During the 1990s, several high-profile incidents in Britain and the United States raised awareness about police racism in ways that no study ever could. The racist murder of Stephen Lawrence in 1993 (see the box above, p. 494) has significantly altered the nature of the debate over racism in Britain by demonstrating that it is not restricted to certain individuals, but can pervade entire institutions.

Following the publication of the Macpherson Report into the Stephen Lawrence murder in 1999, Jack Straw, the then Home Secretary, challenged police to become 'champions of a multicultural society'. Many of the report's seventy recommendations were acted on within a year of its publication, although critics have claimed that change is not occurring quickly enough. In the first year after the report, more than one-third of police forces had not hired any additional black or Asian officers and the number of ethnic minority officers had fallen in nine out of forty-three forces in England and Wales. There have also been indications of an 'anti-Macpherson backlash' among some segments of the law-enforcement community, who believe that the report unfairly targeted police (Fitzgerald 2001).

In the light of incidents like the murder of Stephen Lawrence, it is hardly surprising that research confirms that hostility to the police is a common phenomenon among ethnic minorities (Keith 1993). To some extent, such attitudes are simply the result of direct experience; the attitudes of young blacks in particular are shaped by the policing strategies they encounter. The fourth PSI survey (discussed on pp. 512–13), found that only a quarter of the respondents who had been racially attacked in the previous year chose to report the attack to the police. Half of those who did turn to the police were dissatisfied with the treatment they received. Many felt that the police response showed that they had no real interest in knowing about or investigating the incident (Modood et al. 1997).

Ethnic minorities are in the greatest need of protection by police and the criminal justice system because they are more likely to be victims of crime than whites, but there are some indications that law-enforcement policies seem to have a racial character that targets non-whites: so-called 'stop-and-search' policies, for example, tend to target non-whites disproportionately. The number of 'stop-and-search' procedures against ethnic minorities fell after the publication of the Macpherson Report in 1999, but has since risen as police forces became more sensitive to the risk of terrorism. This has led to a rise in the number of cases where British Asians, some of whom are Muslim, have been stopped and searched, with police using new powers granted to them under the 2000 Terrorism Act.

In London, a recent report found that black people were eight times and Asian people were five times more likely to be stopped and searched than white people (Metropolitan Police 2004).

Other aspects of ethnic minority life in the UK are discussed elsewhere in the book. Ethnicity and ageing is discussed in chapter 5, pp. 190–1; ethnicity and health in chapter 8, pp. 278–9; and ethnicity and education in chapter 17, pp. 721–3.

Immigration and ethnic relations in Continental Europe

Like Britain, most other European countries have been profoundly transformed by migration during the twentieth century.

Large-scale migrations took place in Europe during the first two decades after the Second World War. The Mediterranean countries provided the nations in the North and West with cheap labour. Migrants moving from areas like Turkey, North Africa, Greece and southern Spain and Italy were for a period actively encouraged by host countries facing acute shortages of labour. Switzerland, Germany, Belgium and Sweden all have considerable populations of migrant workers. At the same time, countries that used to be colonial powers experienced an influx of immigrants from their former colonies: this applied primarily to France (Algerians) and the Netherlands (Indonesians), as well as the UK.

Labour migration into and within Western Europe slowed down appreciably as the post-war boom turned into a recession in the late 1970s. But since the fall of the Berlin Wall in 1989 and the transformations occurring in the countries of Eastern Europe and the former Soviet Union, Europe has witnessed the birth of what has been termed the **new migration**. This 'new migration' has been marked by two main events. First, the opening of borders between East and West led to the migration of some five million people in Europe between 1989 and 1994. Second, war and ethnic strife in the former Yugoslavia has resulted in a surge of approximately five million refugees into other regions of Europe (Koser and Lutz 1998). The geographical patterns of European migration have also shifted, with the lines between countries of origin and countries of destination becoming increasingly blurred. Countries in Southern and Central Europe have become destinations for many

migrants, a notable departure from earlier immigration trends.

Another feature of the 'new migration' is that of ethnic 'unmixing'. In the former Soviet Union, the former Yugoslavia and in some Central European states, shifting borders, changing political regimes or the outbreak of conflict have led to migrations on the principle of 'ethnic affinity'. A clear illustration of this can be seen in the case of the thousands of ethnic Russians who found themselves living in newly independent countries – such as Latvia, Kazakhstan and Ukraine – following the break-up of the Soviet Union. Many of them are choosing to migrate back to Russia as part of a process of ethnic unmixing (Brubaker 1998).

Migration and the European Union

As part of the move towards European integration, many of the earlier barriers to the free movement of commodities, capital and employees have been removed. This has led to a dramatic increase in regional migration among European countries. Citizens of countries in the European Union – including the ten new member states, largely from East Europe, that joined the EU in May 2004 – now have the right to work in any other EU country. Professionals with highly developed skills and qualifications have joined the ranks of asylum-seekers and economic migrants as the largest groups of European migrants. With this shift, scholars have noted a growing polarization within the migrant population between the 'haves' and the 'have-nots'.

Migration into the EU from non-EU countries has become one of the most pressing issues on the political agenda in a number of European states. As the process of European integration continues, a number of countries have dissolved internal border controls with neighbouring states as part of the Schengen agreement, which came into force in 1995. Fifteen countries have now signed up to the agreement, which means that they now only monitor their external borders and allow free entry from neighbouring member states (see figure 13.6). This reconfiguration of European border controls has had an enormous impact on illegal immigration into the EU and on cross-border crime. Illegal immigrants able to gain access to a Schengen state can move unimpeded throughout the entire Schengen zone.

Since most EU states have now limited legal immigration to cases of family reunification, instances of illegal immigration have been on the increase. Some illegal migrants enter the EU legally as students or visitors and overstay their visas, but a growing number of illegal immigrants are smuggled across borders. The International Centre for Migration Policy Development estimates that 400,000 people are smuggled into the EU annually. Italy's long coastal border has been considered one of the most porous in Europe, attracting illegal immigrants from nearby Albania, the former Yugoslavia, Turkey and Iraq. Since joining the Schengen agreement, Italy has tightened its external border significantly. Germany, which receives a disproportionate share of illegal immigrants and applications from asylum-seekers, has been working with the governments in Poland and the Czech Republic to strengthen controls on their eastern borders.

The racism that is associated with anti-immigration sentiment has produced some explosive incidents in Europe and the 1990s saw a revival in the electoral fortunes of far-right parties in several European countries, including France, Switzerland, Italy, Austria, Denmark and the Netherlands. In the UK, the first-past-the-post system to elect Members of Parliament, where only one candidate is returned in each constituency, prevents minor parties from winning seats in the House of Commons. However, support for the far-right British National Party is at its highest point since the 1970s, and the party has several seats on local councils. The anti-immigration UK Independence Party has also seen a surge in popular support, winning 12 seats in the 2004 elections for the European Parliament.

The tightening of control over the 'new migrants' is not taking place in a vacuum, however. Informal responses to changes in immigration policies occur in the trafficking and smuggling networks. Trade in human migrants has become one of the fastest growing categories of organized crime in Europe. Just as such criminal groupings manage to shuttle drugs, weapons and stolen goods across borders, they are also capable of smuggling illegal immigrants by various means. Migrants and smugglers join together in drawing on the knowledge and experience of other migrants in making choices about their own movements. In this sense, policy restrictions seem to be provoking new forms of resistance (Koser and Lutz 1998).

The risks that migrants take in search of a better life often have tragic consequences, for example when fifty-eight

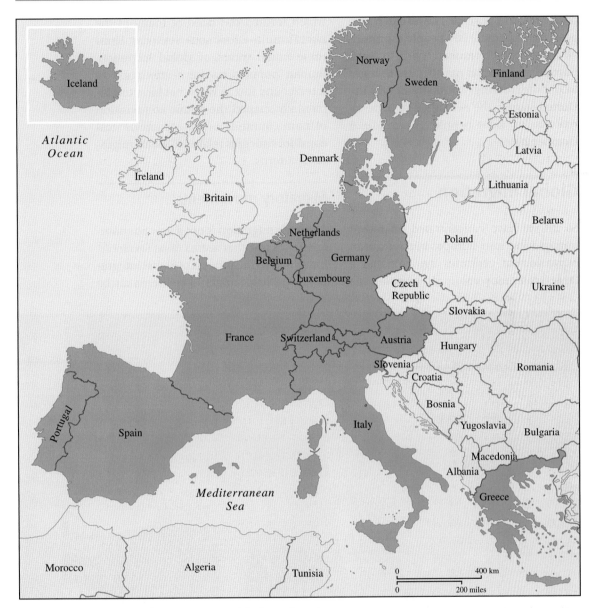

Figure 13.6 The Schengen zone countries (in red)

Chinese people suffocated in a lorry in Dover off the English coast in June 2000, or when at least twenty-six people died on an overcrowded Libyan boat attempting to land in Sicily, off the coast of southern Italy, in August 2004. Because of the illegal nature of most of this migration, the number of people who actually die attempting to enter the West is difficult to gauge, but one recent survey estimated that up to 4,000 migrants drown at sea every year as they attempt to flee persecution or poverty. The research suggests that around 2,000 people die annually in the Mediterranean trying to reach Europe, and similar number are thought to die on crossings to Australia and the United States – the two other main destinations for 'boat people' (*Guardian*, 9 October 2004).

which formed the basis of many of the world's multi-ethnic societies today. Since these initial waves of global migration, human populations have continued to interact and mix in ways that have fundamentally shaped the ethnic composition of many countries. In this section we shall consider concepts related to global migration patterns.

Global migration

So far we have concentrated on recent immigration into Europe, but European expansionism centuries ago initiated a large-scale movement of populations

Migratory movements

Although migration is not a new phenomenon, it is one that seems to be accelerating as part of the process of global integration. Worldwide migration patterns can be

In the UK, fears about 'bogus asylum-seekers' have been linked to concerns about national security, especially in the years after 11 September 2001. This picture shows immigrants who have been smuggled illegaly into the UK.

seen as one reflection of the rapidly changing economic, political and cultural ties between countries. It has been estimated that around 175 million people currently reside in a country other than where they were born, equivalent to around 3 per cent of the world's population (*International Migration Report* 2002), prompting some scholars to label this the 'age of migration' (Castles and Miller 1993).

Immigration, the movement of people into a country to settle, and **emigration**, the process by which people leave a country to settle in another, combine to produce global migration patterns linking countries of origin and countries of destination. Migratory movements add to ethnic and cultural diversity in many societies and help to shape demographic, economic and social dynamics. The intensification of global migration since the Second World War, and particularly in more recent decades, has transformed immigration into an important political issue in many countries. Rising immigration rates in many Western societies have challenged commonly held notions of national identity and have forced a re-examination of concepts of citizenship.

Scholars have identified four models of migration to describe the main global population movements since 1945. The *classic model* of migration applies to countries such as Canada, the United States and Australia, which have developed as 'nations of immigrants'. In such cases, immigration has been largely encouraged and the promise of citizenship has been extended to newcomers, although restrictions and quotas help to limit the annual intake of immigrants. The *colonial model* of immigration, pursued by countries such as France and the United Kingdom, tends to favour immigrants from former colonies over those from other countries. The large number of immigrants to Britain in the years after the Second World War from Commonwealth countries, such as India or Jamaica, reflected this tendency.

Countries such as Germany, Switzerland and Belgium have followed a third policy – the *guest workers model*. Under such a scheme, immigrants are admitted into the country on a temporary basis, often in order to fulfil demands within the labour market, but do not receive citizenship rights even after long periods of settlement.

Finally, *illegal forms* of immigration are becoming increasingly common as a result of tightening immigration laws in many industrialized countries. Immigrants who are able to gain entry into a country either secretly or under a 'non-immigration' pretence are often able to live illegally outside the realm of official society. Examples of this can be seen in the large number of Mexican 'illegal aliens' in many Southern American states, or in the growing international business of smuggling refugees across national borders (as we saw above).

In examining recent trends in global migration, Stephen Castles and Mark Miller (1993) identified four tendencies that they claim will characterize migration patterns in coming years:

1 *Acceleration* Migration across borders is occurring in greater numbers than ever before.
2 *Diversification* Most countries now receive immigrants of many different types, in contrast with earlier times

when particular forms of immigration, such as labour immigration or refugees, were predominant.

3 *Globalization*   Migration has become more global in nature, involving a greater number of countries as both senders and recipients (see figures 13.7 and 13.8).

4 *Feminization*   A growing number of migrants are women, making contemporary migration much less male-dominated than in previous times. The increase in female migrants is closely related to changes in the global labour market, including the growing demand for domestic workers, the expansion of sex tourism and 'trafficking' in women (see chapter 12, 'Sexuality and Gender', pp. 446–7), and the 'mail-order brides' phenomenon.

Globalization and migration

What are the forces behind global migration and how are they changing as a result of globalization? Many early theories about migration focused on so-called **push and pull factors**. 'Push factors' referred to dynamics within a country of origin which forced people to emigrate, such as war, famine, political oppression or population pressures. 'Pull factors', by contrast, were those features of destination countries which attracted immigrants: prosperous labour markets, better overall living conditions and lower population density, for example, could 'pull' immigrants from other regions.

More recently 'push and pull' theories of migration have been criticized for offering overly simplistic explanations of a complex and multifaceted process. Instead, scholars of migration are increas-ingly looking at global migration patterns as 'systems' which are produced through interactions between macro-level and micro-level processes. While this idea may sound complicated, it is actually quite simple. Macro-level factors refer to over-arching issues such as the political situation in an area, the laws and regulations controlling immigration and emigration, or changes in the international economy. Micro-level factors, on the other hand, are concerned with the resources, knowledge and understandings that the migrant populations themselves possess.

The intersection of macro- and micro-processes can be seen in the case of Germany's large Turkish immigrant community. On the macro-level are factors such as Germany's economic need for labour, its policy of accepting foreign 'guest workers' and the state of the Turkish economy which prevents many Turks from earning at the level they would wish. At the micro-level are the informal networks and channels of mutual support within the Turkish community in Germany and the strong links to family and friends who have remained in Turkey. Among potential Turkish migrants, knowledge about Germany and 'social capital' – human or community resources that can be drawn on – help to make Germany one of the most popular destination countries. Supporters of the migration systems approach emphasize that no one factor can explain the process of migration. Rather, each particular migratory movement, like that between Turkey and Germany, is the product of an interaction of macro- and micro-level processes.

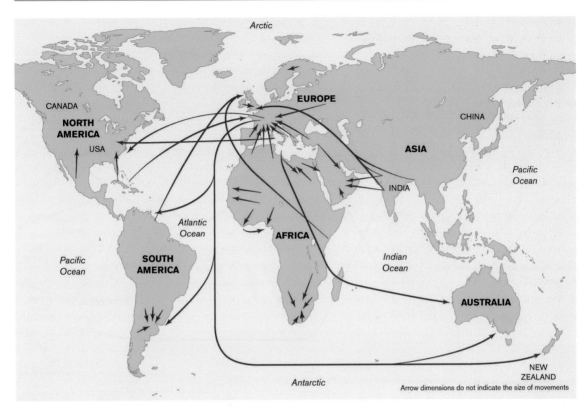

Figure 13.7 Global migrations, 1945–73

Source: Castles (1993), p. 67

Global diasporas

Another way to understand global migration patterns is through the study of **diasporas**. This term refers to the dispersal of an ethnic population from an original homeland into foreign areas, often in a forced manner or under traumatic circumstances. References are often made to the Jewish and African diasporas to describe the way in which these populations have become redistributed across the globe as a result of slavery and genocide. Although members of a diaspora are by definition scattered geographically,

they are held together by factors such as shared history, a collective memory of the original homeland or a common ethnic identity which is nurtured and preserved.

Robin Cohen has argued that diasporas occur in a number of diverse forms, although the most commonly cited examples are those which occurred involuntarily as a result of persecution and violence. In *Global Diasporas* (1997), Cohen adopts a historical approach and identifies five different categories of diaspora according to the forces underlying the original population dispersion: *victim* (for example, African, Jewish and Armenian); *imperial* (British); *labour* (Indian); *trade* (Chinese);

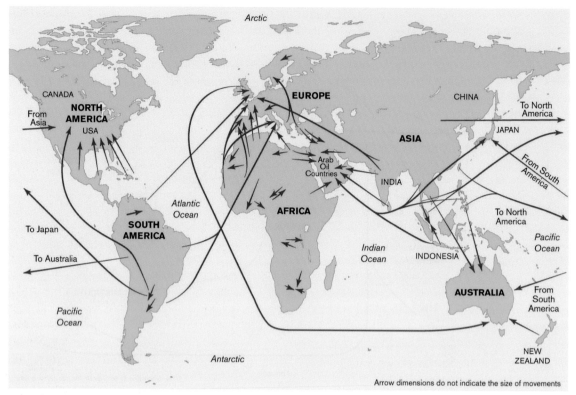

Figure 13.8 Global migratory movements from 1973

Source: Castles and Miller (1993), p. 6

and *cultural* (Caribbean). In certain of these cases, such as that of the Chinese, large-scale population movements occurred on a voluntary basis, not as the result of a defining traumatic event. In reality, as Cohen admits, these categories are overlapping and diasporas occur for a variety of reasons.

Despite the diversity of forms, however, all diasporas share certain key features. Cohen suggests that all diasporas meet the following criteria:

• a forced or voluntary movement from an original homeland to a new region or regions;

• a shared memory about the original homeland, a commitment to its preservation and belief in the possibility of eventual return;

• a strong ethnic identity sustained over time and distance;

• a sense of solidarity with members of the same ethnic group also living in areas of the diaspora;

• a degree of tension in relation to the host societies;

• the potential for valuable and creative contributions to pluralistic host societies.

Some scholars have accused Cohen of trying to simplify complex and distinctive migration experiences into a narrow typology, by associating 'categories' of diasporas with particular ethnic groups. Others argue that his conceptualization of diaspora is not sufficiently precise for the analysis he undertakes. Yet despite these critiques, Cohen's study is valuable for demonstrating that diasporas are not static, but are ongoing processes of maintaining collective identity and preserving ethnic culture in a rapidly globalizing world.

Conclusion

In our globalizing world, ideas – and people – are flowing across borders in greater volumes than ever before in history. These processes are profoundly altering the societies in which we live. Many societies are becoming ethnically diverse for the first time; others are finding that existing patterns of multi-ethnicity are being transformed or intensified. In all societies, however, individuals are coming into regular contact with people who think differently, look different and live differently from themselves. These interactions are happening in person, as a result of global migration, as well as through the images that are transmitted through the media and Internet.

Some welcome this new ethnic and cultural complexity as a vital component of a cosmopolitan society. Others find it dangerous and threatening. Those who maintain a fundamentalist outlook on the world seek refuge in established tradition, and reject dialogue with those who are different (see chapter 14, 'Religion'). Many of the ethnic conflicts that are raging across the globe today can be seen as expressions of this kind of fundamentalist approach. One of the main challenges facing our globalizing world is how to generate a society that is more cosmopolitan in nature. As the patient efforts of the Truth and Reconciliation Commission in South Africa have shown, creating a forum for open and respectful communication is a difficult, but effective, first step in initiating racial reconciliation.

Summary points

1   Race refers to physical and other characteristics, such as skin colour and intelligence, treated by members of a community or society as socially significant. Many popular beliefs about race are mythical. There are no clear-cut characteristics by means of which human beings can be allocated to different races.

2   Sections of a population form ethnic groups by virtue of sharing common cultural characteristics which separate them from others in that population. Ethnicity refers to cultural differences that set one group apart from another. The main distinguishing characteristics of an ethnic group are language, history or ancestry, religion and styles of dress or adornment. Ethnic differences are wholly learned, although they are sometimes thought of as 'natural'.

3   A minority group is one whose members are discriminated against by the majority population in a society. Members of minority groups often have a strong sense of group solidarity, deriving in part from the collective experience of exclusion.

4   Racism means falsely ascribing inherited characteristics of personality or behaviour to individuals of a particular physical appearance. A racist is someone who believes that a biological explanation can be given for characteristics of inferiority supposedly possessed by people of one physical stock or another.

5   Institutional racism refers to patterns of discrimination that have become structured into existing social institutions.

6   New racism describes racist attitudes that are expressed through notions of cultural difference, rather than biological inferiority.

7   Three models of ethnic integration have been adopted by multi-ethnic societies. In the model of assimilation, new immigrant groups adopt the attitudes and language of the dominant community. In a melting pot, the different cultures and outlooks of the ethnic groups in a society are merged together. Pluralism means that ethnic groups exist separately and are seen as equal participants in economic and political life.

8   Multi-ethnic states can be fragile and sometimes experience episodes of ethnic conflict. Ethnic cleansing is a form of ethnic conflict in which ethnically homogeneous areas are created through the mass expulsion of other ethnic groups. Genocide describes the systematic elimination of one ethnic group at the hands of another.

9   Immigration has led to the existence of numerous different ethnic groups within Britain, the USA and other industrial countries. In Britain, ethnic minority groups as a whole experience disadvantages in relation to the white population – in areas such as employment, income, housing and crime. However, patterns of inequality have been shifting and there are now many differences between ethnic minority groups, with some groups having largely attained parity with the white population.

10 The new migration refers to altered patterns of migration in Europe that have resulted from the end of the Cold War, prolonged ethnic conflict in the former Yugoslavia, and the deepening of European integration. Illegal immigration has been increasing as opportunities for legal immigration into the EU have gradually been limited.

11 Migration is the movement of people from one region or society to another for the purpose of settlement. Global migration, the movement of individuals across national borders, has increased in the years following the Second World War and is further intensifying with globalization. Diaspora refers to the dispersal of an ethnic population from an original homeland into foreign areas, often in a forced manner or under traumatic circumstances.

Questions for further thought

1 Should the concept of race be discarded in sociology?

2 Why is racism so difficult to define?

3 Why do some people in the UK still hold racist attitudes to this day?

4 How might an unprejudiced person find himself or herself acting in a discriminatory way?

5 Is it possible for all ethnic groups to be equal participants in social and political life? Why or why not?

6 Is a 'melting-pot' culture possible in Britain?

7 Should you be able to live and work anywhere in the world?

Further reading

Michael Banton, *Ethnic and Racial Consciousness*, 2nd edn (Harlow, New York: Longman, 1997).

Martin Bulmer and John Solomos (eds), *Ethnic and Racial Studies Today* (New York: Routledge, 1999).

Stephen Cornell and Douglas Hartmann, *Ethnicity and Race: Making Identities in a Changing World* (Thousand Oaks, CA: Pine Forge Press, 1998).

Philomena Essed, *Everyday Racism* (Claremont, CA: Hunter House, 1990).

Liz Fawcett, *Religion, Ethnicity and Social Change* (Basingstoke: Macmillan, 2000).

David Mason, *Race and Ethnicity in Modern Britain* (Oxford: Oxford University Press, 2000).

Michael Omi and Howard Winant, *Racial Formation in the United States*, rev. edn (New York: Routledge, 1994).

Will Kymlicka, *The New Debate over Minority Rights* (Toronto: University of Toronto, 1997).

Miri Song, *Choosing Ethnic Identity* (Cambridge: Polity, 2003).

Internet links

Black and Asian History Map
http://www.blackhistorymap.com

Centre for Research in Ethnic Relations, Warwick University
http://www.csv.warwick.ac.uk/fac/soc/CRER_RC

Commission for Racial Equality
http://www.cre.gov.uk

SOSIG on the Sociology of Race and Ethnicity
http://www.sosig.ac.uk/roads/subject-listing/World-cat/socrace.html

United Nations Commissioner for Refugees
http://www.ohchr.org/english/

Contents

14 Religion in Modern Society

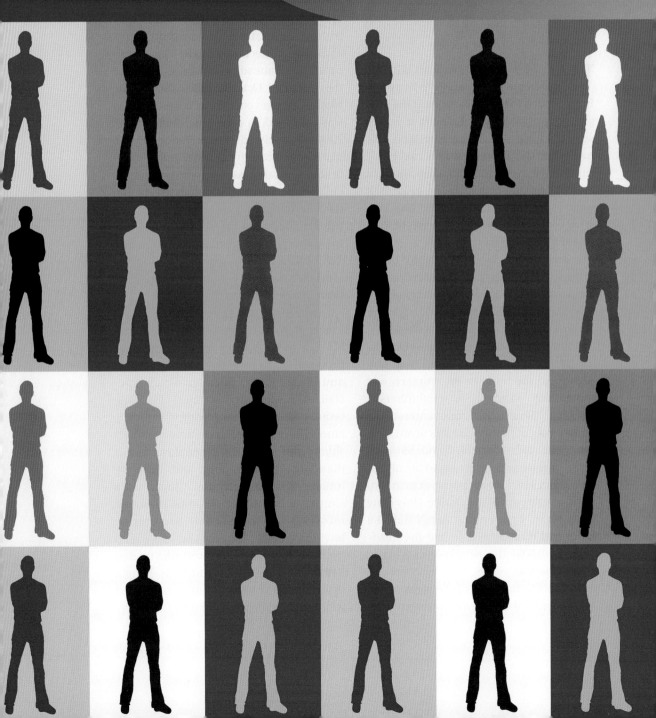

WHEN MONICA Besara, an illiterate mother of five from North Bengal in India, visited the Catholic nuns at the Missionaries of Charity in Calcutta it was to seek their blessing before she died. She had what she thought was a malignant tumour in her stomach that modern medical treatment had failed to cure. It was 5 September 1998, exactly one year after the death of Mother Teresa, the nun awarded the Nobel Prize for her work with the sick and poor and the founder of the Missionaries of Charity. The nuns prayed for Besara and placed a medallion on her stomach that had been blessed by Mother Teresa. The lump disappeared overnight.

Besara recalls that she had been suffering with a 'splitting headache, day and night, and the lump in the stomach was unbearably painful'. She remembers a service at the church to commemorate the anniversary of Mother Teresa's death. 'It is there' she said; 'I had the vision. Mother's death-picture was lying next to the altar. I saw a light like this [she points at a camera flash] coming out of the picture. Only I saw it. At 1 a.m. I got up and found that the lump had disappeared as had the headache. I walked the next morning like a normal person.'

To Monica Besara and the nuns at the Missionaries of Charity, this was a miracle.

A medical team sent out by the Catholic Church to investigate agreed. The nuns issued a statement saying that 'God has worked his miracle through Mother [Teresa] and we are so very happy'. The Pope, as head of the Catholic Church, accepted that a miracle had taken place and ordered the beatification of Mother Teresa, the final step before sainthood – normally attained after the Pope's approval of a second miracle. The beatification went ahead to celebrations around the world in October 2003. In Albania, Mother Teresa's country of origin, the day was observed as a national holiday and 2004 was declared Mother Teresa Year. In her adopted country of India, priests celebrated special Masses across the country, children paraded on Calcutta's streets, and the ceremony, held at the Vatican in Italy, was broadcast live on national television. In Rome, films, musicals, cartoons and exhibitions were shown celebrating Mother Teresa's life, and her relics have been put on display.

Despite the Catholic Church's insistence, not everyone is convinced that Monica Besara's recovery was a miracle. Probir Ghosh is founder of India's Science and Rationalists' Society, which specializes in exposing holy men who dupe ordinary Indians into paying for miracle cures. His organization claims a membership of more than 20,000 people and has a mandate to 'free poor and illiterate Indians from superstition'. Ghosh has a simple solution for Besara's dramatic recovery: 'the medication had started having effect, when the so-called "miracle" happened.' Doctors who treated Besara at various hospitals in Bengal made similar statements, and questioned whether the growth was actually a cancer-

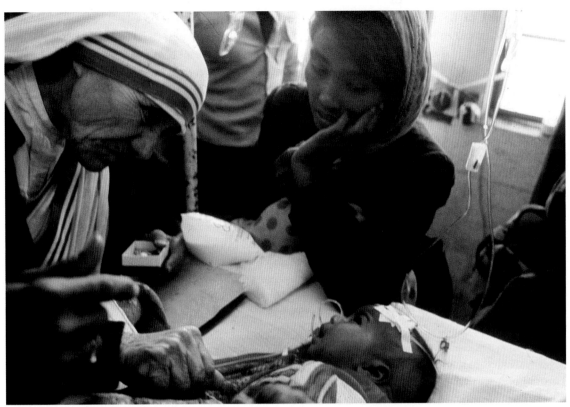

Mother Teresa became famous for her work amongst India's poorest people.

ous tumour or something more benign. Ghosh argued that 'Mother Teresa was a great soul and I think it is an insult to her legacy to make her sainthood dependent on bogus miracles. It should be linked to her great work among the poor.'

At times, religion and science seem to be at odds with one another. The debate around the miracle of Monica Besara shows that a religious outlook and modern rationalist thought exist in an uneasy state of tension. With the deepening of modernity, a rationalist perspective has conquered many aspects of our existence; its hold seems unlikely to be weakened in the foreseeable future. Yet there will always be reactions against science

and rationalist thought, for they remain silent on such fundamental questions as the meaning and purpose of life. It is these matters which have always been at the core of religion and have fuelled the idea of faith, an emotional leap into belief.

Religion has had a strong hold over the lives of human beings for thousands of years. In one form or another, religion is found in all known human societies. The earliest societies on record, of which we have evidence only through archaeological remains, show clear traces of religious symbols and ceremonies. Cave drawings suggest that religious beliefs and practices existed more than 40,000 years ago. Throughout subsequent history, religion has continued to be a central part of human experience, influencing how we perceive and react to the environments in which we live.

Why has religion been such a pervasive aspect of human societies? How is its role changing in late modern societies? Under what conditions does religion unite communities, and under what conditions does it divide them? How can religion have such a purchase on individuals' lives that they are prepared to sacrifice themselves for its ideals? These are the questions that we shall try to answer in this chapter. In order to do so, we shall have to ask what religion actually is, and look at some of the different forms that religious beliefs and practices take. We shall also consider the main sociological theories of religion and analyse the various types of religious organization that can be distinguished. Throughout, we will consider the fate of religion in the modern world; for it has seemed to many observers that, with the rise of science and modern industry, religion today has become a less central force in social life than it was prior to the modern age.

Sociological theories and ideas

The sociological study of religion

The study of religion is a challenging enterprise which places quite special demands on the sociological imagination. In analysing religious practices, we have to make sense of the many different beliefs and rituals found in the various human cultures. We must be sensitive to ideals that inspire profound conviction in believers, yet at the same time take a balanced view of them. We have to confront ideas that seek the eternal, while recognizing that religious groups also promote quite mundane goals – such as acquiring finance or soliciting for followers. We need to recognize the diversity of religious beliefs and modes of conduct, but also probe into the nature of religion as a general phenomenon.

Sociologists define **religion** as a cultural system of commonly shared beliefs and rituals that provides a sense of ultimate meaning and purpose by creating an idea of reality that is sacred, all-encompassing and supernatural (Durkheim 1965; Berger 1967; Wuthnow 1988). There are three key elements in this definition:

1 *Religion is a form of culture.* Culture consists of the shared beliefs, values, norms and ideas that create a common identity among a group of people. Religion shares all of these characteristics.

2 *Religion involves beliefs that take the form of ritualized practices.* All religions thus have a behavioural aspect – special activities in which believers take part and that identify them as members of the religious community.

3 *Perhaps most important, religion provides a sense of purpose* – a feeling that life is ultimately meaningful. It does so by explaining coherently and compellingly what transcends or overshadows everyday life, in ways that other aspects of culture (such as an educational system or a belief in democracy) typically cannot (Geertz 1973; Wuthnow 1988).

What is absent from the sociological definition of religion is as important as what is included: nowhere is there mention of

God. We often think of **theism**, a belief in one or more supernatural deities (the term originates from the Greek word for God), as basic to religion, but this is not necessarily the case. As we shall see later, some religions, such as Buddhism, believe in the existence of spiritual forces rather than a particular God.

How sociologists think about religion

When sociologists study religion, they do so as sociologists and not as believers (or disbelievers) in any particular faith. This stance has several implications for the sociological study of religion:

1 *Sociologists are not concerned with whether religious beliefs are true or false.* From a sociological perspective, religions are regarded not as being decreed by God but as being socially constructed by human beings. As a result, sociologists put aside their personal beliefs when they study religion. They are concerned with the human rather than the divine aspects of religion. Sociologists ask: How is the religion organized? What are its principal beliefs and values? How is it related to the larger society? What explains its success or failure in recruiting and retaining believers? The question of whether a particular belief is 'good' or 'true', however important it may be to the believers of the religion under study, is not something that sociologists are able to address as sociologists. (As individuals, they may have strong opinions on the matter, but one hopes that as sociologists they can keep these opinions from biasing their research.)

2 *Sociologists are especially concerned with the social organization of religion.*

Religions are among the most important institutions in society. They are a primary source of the most deep-seated norms and values. At the same time, religions are typically practised through an enormous variety of social forms. Within Christianity and Judaism, for example, religious practice often occurs in formal organizations, such as churches or synagogues. Yet this is not necessarily true of such Asian religions as Hinduism and Buddhism, where religious practices are likely to occur in the home or some other natural setting. The sociology of religion is concerned with how different religious institutions and organizations actually function. The earliest European religions were often indistinguishable from the larger society, as religious beliefs and practices were incorporated into daily life. This is still true in many parts of the world today. In modern industrial society, however, religions have become established in separate, often bureaucratic, organizations, and so sociologists focus on the organizations through which religions must operate in order to survive (Hammond 1992). As we shall see below, this institutionalization has even led some sociologists to view religions in the United States and Europe as similar to business organizations, competing with one another for members (Warner 1993).

3 *Sociologists often view religions as a major source of social solidarity.* To the extent that religions provide believers with a common set of norms and values, they are an important source of social solidarity. Religious beliefs, rituals and bonds help to create a 'moral community' in which all members

know how to behave towards one another (Wuthnow 1988). If a single religion dominates a society, it may be an important source of social stability. If a society's members adhere to numerous competing religions, however, religious differences may lead to destabilizing social conflicts. Recent examples of religious conflict within a society include struggles between Sikhs, Hindus and Muslims in India; clashes between Muslims and Christians in Bosnia and other parts of the former Yugoslavia; and 'hate crimes' against Jews, Muslims and other religious minorities in the United States.

4 *Sociologists tend to explain the appeal of religion in terms of social forces rather than in terms of purely personal, spiritual or psychological factors.* For many people, religious beliefs are a deeply personal experience, involving a strong sense of connection with forces that transcend everyday reality. Sociologists do not question the depth of such feelings and experiences, but they are unlikely to limit themselves to a purely spiritual explanation of religious commitment. A person may claim that he or she became religious when God suddenly appeared in a vision, but sociologists are likely to look for more earthly explanations. Some researchers argue that people often 'get religion' when their fundamental sense of a social order is threatened by economic hardship, loneliness, loss or grief, physical suffering, or poor health (Berger 1967; Schwartz 1970; Glock 1976; Stark and Bainbridge 1980). In explaining the appeal of religious movements, sociologists are more likely to focus on the problems of the social order than on the psychological response of the individual.

Theories of religion

Sociological approaches to religion are still strongly influenced by the ideas of the three 'classical' sociological theorists: Marx, Durkheim and Weber. None of the three was himself religious, and all thought that the significance of religion would decrease in modern times. Each believed that religion is in a fundamental sense an illusion. The advocates of different faiths may be wholly persuaded of the validity of the beliefs they hold and the rituals in which they participate, yet the very diversity of religions and their obvious connection to different types of society, the three thinkers held, make these claims inherently implausible. An individual born into an Australian society of hunters and gatherers would plainly have different religious beliefs from someone born into the caste system of India or the Catholic Church of medieval Europe. However, as we shall see below, although the classical sociologists agreed in this respect, they developed very different theories when it came to studying the role of religion in society.

Marx: religion and inequality

In spite of his influence on the subject, Karl Marx never studied religion in any detail. His ideas mostly derived from the writings of several early nineteenth-century theological and philosophical authors. One of these was Ludwig Feuerbach, who wrote a famous work called *The Essence of Christianity* (1957). According to Feuerbach, religion consists of ideas and values produced by human beings in the course of their cultural development, but mistakenly projected on to divine forces or gods. Because human beings do not fully understand their own history, they tend to attribute socially created values and norms to the activities of gods. Thus the story of the ten commandments given to Moses by God is a mythical version of the origin of the moral precepts which govern the lives of Jewish and Christian believers.

So long as we do not understand the nature of the religious symbols we ourselves have created, Feuerbach argues, we are condemned to be prisoners of forces of history we cannot control. Feuerbach uses the term '**alienation**' to refer to the establishing of gods or divine forces distinct from human beings. Humanly created values and ideas come to be seen as the product of *alien* or separate beings – religious forces and gods. While the effects of alienation have in the past been negative, the understanding of religion as alienation, according to Feuerbach, promises great hope for the future. Once human beings realize that the values projected on to religion are really their own, those values become capable of realization on this earth, rather than being deferred to an afterlife. The powers believed to be possessed by God in Christianity can be appropriated by human beings themselves. Christians believe that while God is all-powerful and all-loving, human beings themselves are imperfect and flawed. However, the potential for love and goodness and the power to control our own lives, Feuerbach believed, are present in human social institutions and can be brought to fruition once we understand their true nature.

Marx accepted the view that religion represents human self-alienation. It is often believed that Marx was dismissive of religion, but this is far from true. Religion, he writes, is the 'heart of a heartless world' – a haven from the harshness of daily reality. In Marx's view, religion in its traditional form will, and should, disappear; yet this is because the positive values embodied in religion can become guiding ideals for improving the lot of humanity on this earth, *not* because these ideals and values themselves are mistaken. We should not fear the gods we ourselves have created, and we should cease endowing them with values we ourselves can realize.

Marx declared, in a famous phrase, that religion has been the 'opium of the people'. Religion defers happiness and rewards to the afterlife, teaching the resigned acceptance of existing conditions in this life. Attention is thus diverted away from inequalities and injustices in this world by the promise of what is to come in the next. Religion has a strong ideological element: religious beliefs and values often provide justifications of inequalities of wealth and power. For example, the teaching that 'the meek shall inherit the earth' suggests attitudes of humility and non-resistance to oppression.

Durkheim: functionalism and religious ritual

In contrast to Marx, Emile Durkheim spent a good part of his intellectual career studying religion, concentrating particularly on religion in small-scale, traditional societies. Durkheim's work, *The Elementary Forms of the Religious Life* (1976 [1912]), is one of the most influential studies in the sociology of religion. Durkheim does not connect religion primarily with social inequalities or power, but relates it to the overall nature of the institutions of a society. He bases his work on a study of totemism as practised by Australian Aboriginal societies, and he argues that **totemism** represents religion in its most 'elementary' or simple form – hence the title of his book.

A totem was originally an animal or plant taken as having particular symbolic significance for a group. It is a *sacred* object, regarded with veneration and surrounded by various ritual activities. Durkheim defines religion in terms of a distinction between the **sacred** and the **profane**. Sacred objects and symbols, he holds, are treated as *apart* from the routine aspects of existence, which are the realm of the profane. Eating the totemic animal or plant, except on special ceremonial occasions, is usually forbidden, and as a sacred object the totem is believed to have divine properties which separate it completely from other animals that might be hunted, or crops gathered and consumed.

Why is the totem sacred? According to Durkheim, it is because it is the symbol of the group itself; it stands for the values central to the group or community. The reverence which people feel for the totem actually derives from the respect they hold for central social values. In religion, the object of worship is actually society itself.

Durkheim strongly emphasized that religions are never just a matter of belief. All religion involves regular ceremonial and ritual activities in which a group of believers meets together. In collective ceremonials, a sense of group solidarity is affirmed and heightened. Ceremonials take individuals away from the concerns of profane social life into an elevated

Durkheim argues that rituals like the Puja ceremonies in Calcutta mark out the spiritual from the ordinary, but in doing so reinforce key social values.

sphere, in which they feel in contact with higher forces. These higher forces, attributed to totems, divine influences or gods, are really the expression of the influence of the collectivity over the individual.

Ceremony and ritual, in Durkheim's view, are essential to binding the members of groups together. This is why they are found not only in regular situations of worship, but also in the various life crises when major social transitions are experienced – for example, birth, marriage and death. In virtually all societies, ritual and ceremonial procedures are observed on such occasions. Durkheim reasons that collective ceremonials reaffirm group solidarity at a time when people are forced to adjust to major changes in their lives. Funeral rituals demonstrate that the values of the group outlive the passing of particular individuals, and so provide a means for bereaved people to adjust to their altered circumstances. Mourning is not the spontaneous expression of grief – or, at least, it is only so for those personally affected by the death. Mourning is a duty imposed by the group.

In small traditional cultures, Durkheim argued, almost all aspects of life are permeated by religion. Religious ceremonials both originate new ideas and categories of thought, and reaffirm existing values. Religion is not just a series of sentiments and activities; it actually conditions the *modes of thinking* of individuals in traditional cultures. Even the most basic categories of thought, including how time and space are thought of, were first framed in religious terms. The concept of 'time', for instance, was originally derived from counting the intervals involved in religious ceremonials.

With the development of modern societies, Durkheim believed, the influence of religion wanes. Scientific thinking increasingly replaces religious explanation, and ceremonial and ritual activities come to occupy only a small part of individuals' lives. Durkheim agrees with Marx that traditional religion – that is, religion involving divine forces or gods – is on the verge of disappearing. 'The old gods are

dead', Durkheim writes. Yet he says that there is a sense in which religion, in altered forms, is likely to continue. Even modern societies depend for their cohesion on rituals that reaffirm their values; new ceremonial activities can thus be expected to emerge to replace the old. Durkheim is vague about what these might be, but it seems that he has in mind the celebration of humanist and political values such as freedom, equality and social cooperation.

Weber: world religions and social change

Durkheim based his arguments on a very small range of examples, even though he claims his ideas apply to religion in general. Max Weber, by contrast, embarked on a massive study of religions worldwide. No scholar before or since has undertaken a task of such scope. Most of his attention was concentrated on what he called the *world religions* – those that have attracted large numbers of believers and decisively affected the course of global history. He made detailed studies of Hinduism, Buddhism, Taoism and ancient Judaism (Weber 1951, 1952, 1958, 1963), and in *The Protestant Ethic and the Spirit of Capitalism* (1976) and elsewhere, he wrote extensively about the impact of Christianity on the history of the West. He did not, however, complete his projected study of Islam.

Weber's writings on religion differ from those of Durkheim in that they concentrate on the connection between religion and social change, something to which Durkheim gave little attention. They contrast with the work of Marx because Weber argues that religion is not necessarily a conservative force; on the contrary, religiously inspired movements have often produced dramatic social transformations. Thus Protestantism – particularly Puritanism – was the source of the capitalistic outlook found in the modern West. The early entrepreneurs were mostly Calvinists. Their drive to succeed, which helped initiate Western economic development, was originally prompted by a desire to serve God. Material success was for them a sign of divine favour.

Weber saw his research on the world religions as a single project. His discussion of the impact of Protestantism on the development of the West is part of a comprehensive attempt to understand the influence of religion on social and economic life in varying cultures. Analysing the Eastern religions, Weber concluded that they provided insuperable barriers to the development of industrial capitalism, such as took place in the West. This is not because the non-Western civilizations are backward; they have simply accepted values different from those which came to predominate in Europe.

In traditional China and India, Weber pointed out, there was at certain periods a significant development of commerce, manufacture and urbanism, but these did not generate the radical patterns of social change involved in the rise of industrial capitalism in the West. Religion was a major influence in inhibiting such change. For example, Hinduism is what Weber called an 'other-worldly' religion. That is to say, its highest values stress escape from the toils of the material world to a higher plane of spiritual existence. The religious feelings and motivations produced by Hinduism do not focus on controlling or shaping the material world. On the contrary, Hinduism sees material reality as a

veil hiding the true concerns to which humankind should be oriented. Confucianism also acted to direct effort away from economic development, as this came to be understood in the West, emphasizing harmony with the world rather than promoting active mastery of it. Although China was for a long while the most powerful and culturally most developed civilization in the world, its dominant religious values acted as a brake on a strong commitment to economic development for its own sake.

Weber regarded Christianity as a *salvation religion*, involving the belief that human beings can be 'saved' if they adopt the beliefs of the religion and follow its moral tenets. The notions of sin and of being rescued from sinfulness by God's grace are important here. They generate a tension and an emotional dynamism essentially absent from the Eastern religions. Salvation religions have a 'revolutionary' aspect. While the religions of the East cultivate an attitude of passivity in the believer towards the existing order, Christianity involves a constant struggle against sin, and hence can stimulate revolt against the existing order of things. Religious leaders – like Jesus – arise, who reinterpret existing doctrines in such a way as to challenge the prevailing power structure.

Critical assessment of the classical views

Marx, Durkheim and Weber each identified some important general characteristics of religion, and in some ways their views complement one another. Marx was right to claim that religion often has ideological implications, serving to justify the interests of ruling groups at the expense of others: there are innumerable instances of this in history. Take as an example the influence of Christianity on the European colonialists' efforts to subject other cultures to their rule. The missionaries who sought to convert 'heathen' peoples to Christian beliefs were no doubt sincere, yet the effect of their teachings was to reinforce the destruction of traditional cultures and the imposition of white domination. The various Christian denominations almost all tolerated, or endorsed, slavery in the United States and other parts of the world up to the nineteenth century. Doctrines were developed that claimed slavery was based on divine law, disobedient slaves being guilty of an offence against God as well as their masters.

Yet Weber was certainly correct to emphasize the unsettling, and often revolutionary, impact of religious ideals on pre-established social orders. Despite the churches' early support for slavery in the United States, many church leaders later played a key role in the fight to abolish it. Religious beliefs have prompted many social movements seeking to overthrow unjust systems of authority, playing a prominent part, for instance, in the civil rights movements of the 1960s in the United States. Religion has also influenced social change – often provoking much bloodshed – through the armed clashes and wars fought for religious motives.

These divisive influences of religion, so prominent in history, find little mention in Durkheim's work. Durkheim emphasized above all the role of religion in promoting social cohesion. Yet it is not difficult to redirect his ideas towards explaining religious division, conflict and change as well as solidarity. After all, much of the strength

of feeling which may be generated *against* other religious groups derives from the commitment to religious values generated *within* each community of believers.

Among the most valuable aspects of Durkheim's writings is his stress on ritual and ceremony. All religions involve regular assemblies of believers, at which ritual prescriptions are observed. As he rightly points out, ritual activities also mark the major transitions of life – birth, entry to adulthood (rituals associated with puberty are found in many cultures), marriage and death (van Gennep 1977).

In the rest of this chapter we shall make use of ideas developed by all three authors. First, we shall outline the major world religions and the different types of religious organization. Then we will go on to discuss the sociological debate over secularization, the idea that religion is becoming less significant in industrial societies. From there we will then consider some of the developments in world religion which challenge the idea of secularization – namely the rise of new religious movements and the power of religious fundamentalism.

Real world religions

In traditional societies, religion usually plays a central part in social life. Religious symbols and rituals are often integrated with the material and artistic culture of the society – music, painting or carving, dance, storytelling and literature. In small cultures, there is no professional priesthood, but there are always certain individuals who specialize in knowledge of religious (and often magical) practices. Although there are various sorts of such specialists, one common type is the **shaman** (a word originating among North American Indians). A shaman is an individual believed to be able to direct spirits or non-natural forces through ritual means. Shamans are sometimes essentially magicians rather than religious leaders, however, and are often consulted by individuals dissatisfied with what is offered in the religious rituals of the community.

Totemism and animism

Two forms of religion found frequently in smaller cultures are **totemism** and **animism**. The word 'totem' originated among North American Indian tribes, but has been widely used to refer to species of animals or plants believed to have supernatural powers. Usually each kinship group or clan within a society has its own particular totem, with which various ritual activities are associated. Totemic beliefs might seem alien to those living in industrialized societies, yet in certain relatively minor contexts, symbols similar to those of totemism are familiar – as when a sports team has an animal or plant for its emblem: mascots are totems.

Animism is a belief in spirits or ghosts, thought to populate the same world as human beings. Such spirits may be seen as either benign or malevolent, and may influence human behaviour in numerous respects. In some cultures, for example, spirits are believed to cause illness or madness, and may also possess or take over individuals in such a way as to control their behaviour. Animistic beliefs are not confined to small cultures, but are found to some degree in many religious settings. In medieval Europe, those believed to be possessed by evil spirits were frequently persecuted as sorcerers or witches.

Small, seemingly 'simple' societies frequently have complex systems of religious belief. Totemism and animism are more common among these societies than in larger ones, but some small societies have far more complex religions. The Nuer of southern Sudan, for instance, described by E. E. Evans-Pritchard (1956), have an elaborate set of theological ideas centred on a 'high god' or 'sky spirit'. Religions which incline towards **monotheism** (belief in one god), however, are found relatively infrequently among smaller traditional cultures. Most are **polytheistic** – there is a belief in many gods.

Judaism, Christianity and Islam

The three most influential monotheistic religions in world history are *Judaism*, *Christianity* and *Islam*. All originated in the Middle East and each has influenced the others.

Judaism

Judaism is the oldest of the three religions, dating from about 1000 BCE. The early Hebrews were nomads, living in and around ancient Egypt. Their **prophets**, or religious leaders, partly drew their ideas from existing religious beliefs in the region, but differed in their commitment to a single, almighty God. Most of their neighbours were polytheistic. The Hebrews believed that God demands obedience to strict moral codes, and insisted on their claim to a monopoly of truth, seeing their beliefs as the only true religion (Zeitlin 1984, 1988).

Until the creation of Israel, not long after the end of the Second World War, as the *Messiah* – a Hebrew word meaning 'the anointed', the Greek term for which was 'Christ' – awaited by the Jews. Paul, a Greek-speaking Roman citizen, was a major initiator of the spread of Christianity, preaching extensively in Asia Minor and Greece. Although the Christians were at first savagely persecuted, the Emperor Constantine eventually adopted Christianity as the official religion of the Roman Empire. Christianity spread to become a dominant force in Western culture for the next two thousand years.

Christianity today commands a greater number of adherents, and is more generally spread across the world, than any other religion (see figure 14.1). Over a thousand million individuals regard themselves as Christians, but there are many divisions in terms of theology and church organization, the main branches being Roman Catholicism, Protestantism and Eastern Orthodoxy.

Islam

The origins of Islam, today the second largest religion in the world (see figure 14.1), overlap with those of Christianity. Islam derives from the teachings of the prophet Muhammad in the seventh century CE. The single God of Islam, Allah, is believed to hold sway over all human and natural life. The *Pillars of Islam* are the five essential religious duties of Muslims (as believers in Islam are called). The first is the recitation of the Islamic creed: 'There is no god but Allah, and Muhammad is the apostle of Allah.' The second is the saying of formal prayers five times each day, preceded by ceremonial washing. The worshipper at these prayers must always face towards the holy city of Mecca in Saudi Arabia, no matter how far

A devout Jew reads the Torah.

there was no state of which Judaism was the official religion. Jewish communities survived in Europe, North Africa and Asia, although they were frequently persecuted – culminating in the murder of millions of Jews by the Nazis in concentration camps during the war.

Christianity

Many Judaic views were taken over and incorporated as part of Christianity. Jesus was an Orthodox Jew, and Christianity began as a sect of Judaism; it is not clear that Jesus wished to found a distinctive religion. His disciples came to think of him

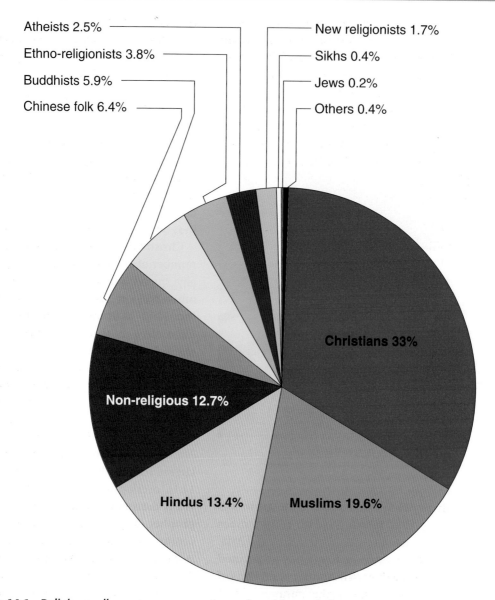

Atheists 2.5%
Ethno-religionists 3.8%
Buddhists 5.9%
Chinese folk 6.4%

New religionists 1.7%
Sikhs 0.4%
Jews 0.2%
Others 0.4%

Christians 33%

Non-religious 12.7%

Hindus 13.4%   Muslims 19.6%

Figure 14.1   Religious adherents as a percentage of world population, 2000

Source: Barrett, Kurian and Johnson, *World Christian Encyclopedia* (Oxford University Press, 2001), p. 4

away that is. The third pillar is the giving of alms (money to the poor), set out in Islamic law, which has often been used as a source of taxation by the state. The fourth is the observance of Ramadan, a month of fasting during which no food or drink may be taken during daylight. Finally, there is the expectation that every believer will attempt, at least once, to make a pilgrimage to Mecca.

Muslims believe that Allah spoke through earlier prophets – including Moses and Jesus – before Muhammad, whose teachings most directly express his will. Islam has come to be very widespread, having some thousand million adherents throughout the world. The majority are concentrated in North and East Africa, the Middle East and Pakistan.

The religions of the Far East

Hinduism

There are major contrasts between Judaism, Christianity and Islam, and the religions of the Far East. The oldest of all the great religions still prominent in the world today is *Hinduism*, the core beliefs of which date back some six thousand years. Hinduism is a polytheistic religion. It is so internally diverse that some scholars have suggested that it should be regarded as a cluster of related religions rather than a single religious orientation; many local cults and religious practices are linked by a few generally held beliefs.

Most Hindus accept the doctrine of the cycle of **reincarnation** – the belief that all living beings are part of an eternal process of birth, death and rebirth. A second key feature is the caste system, based on the belief that individuals are born into a particular position in a social and ritual hierarchy, according to the nature of their activities in previous incarnations. A different set of duties and rituals exists for each caste, and one's fate in the next life is governed mainly by how well these duties are performed in this one. Hinduism accepts the possibility of numerous different religious standpoints, not drawing a clear line between believers and non-believers. There are more than 750 million

Hindus, virtually all living on the Indian subcontinent. Hinduism does not seek to convert others into 'true believers', unlike Christianity and Islam.

Buddhism, Confucianism, Taoism

The **ethical religions** of the East encompass *Buddhism, Confucianism* and *Taoism*. These religions have no gods. Rather, they emphasize ethical ideals that relate the believer to the natural cohesion and unity of the universe.

Buddhism derives from the teachings of Siddhartha Gautama, the Buddha ('enlightened one'), who was a Hindu prince in a small kingdom in south Nepal in the sixth century BCE. According to the Buddha, human beings can escape the reincarnation cycle by the renunciation of desire. The path of salvation lies in a life of self-discipline and meditation, separated from the tasks of the mundane world. The overall objective of Buddhism is the attainment of *Nirvana*, complete spiritual fulfilment. The Buddha rejected Hindu ritual and the authority of the castes. Like Hinduism, Buddhism tolerates many local variations, including belief in local deities, not insisting on a single view. Buddhism today is a major influence in several states in the Far East, including Thailand, Burma, Sri Lanka, China, Japan and Korea.

Confucianism was the basis of the culture of the ruling groups in traditional China. 'Confucius' (the Latinized form of the name K'ung Fu-tzu), lived in the sixth century BCE, the same period as Buddha. Confucius was a teacher, not a religious prophet in the manner of the Middle Eastern religious leaders. Confucius is not seen by his followers as a god, but as 'the wisest of wise men'. Confucianism seeks to adjust human life to the inner harmony of nature, emphasizing the veneration of ancestors.

Taoism shares similar principles, stressing meditation and non-violence as means to the higher life. Like Confucius, Lao-tzu, the founder of Taoism, was a teacher rather than a religious prophet. Although some elements survive in the beliefs and practices of many Chinese, both Confucianism and Taoism have lost much of their influence in China as a result of determined opposition from the government.

Religious organizations

The sociology of religion has concerned itself with non-European religions since its origins in the writings of Durkheim and Weber. Nonetheless, there has frequently been a tendency to view all religions through concepts and theories that grew out of the European experience. For example, notions like *denomination* or *sect* presuppose the existence of formally organized religious institutions; they are of questionable utility in the study of religions that emphasize ongoing spiritual practice as a part of daily life or that pursue the complete integration of religion with civic and political life. In recent decades, there has been an effort to create a more comparative sociology of religion, one that seeks to understand religious traditions from within their own frames of reference (Wilson 1982; Van der Veer 1994).

Early theorists such as Max Weber (Weber 1963), Ernst Troeltsch (Troeltsch 1931) and Richard Niebuhr (Niebuhr 1929) described religious organizations as falling along a continuum, based on the degree to which they are well established and conventional: churches lie at one end

(they are conventional and well established), cults lie at the other (they are neither) and sects fall somewhere in the middle. These distinctions were based on the study of European and US religions. There is much debate over how well they apply to the non-Christian world.

Today, sociologists are aware that the terms *sect* and *cult* have negative connotations, and this is something they wish to avoid. For this reason, contemporary sociologists of religion sometimes use the phrase *new religious movements* to characterize novel religious organizations that lack the respectability that comes with being well established for a long period of time (Hexham and Poewe 1997; Hadden 1997).

Churches and sects

All religions involve communities of believers, but there are many different ways in which such communities are organized. One mode of classifying religious organizations was first put forward by Max Weber and his colleague, the religious historian Ernst Troeltsch (Troeltsch 1981). Weber and Troeltsch distinguished between churches and sects. A **church** is a large, well-established religious body – like the Catholic Church or the Church of England. A **sect** is a smaller, less highly organized grouping of committed believers, usually setting itself up in protest against what a church has become – as Calvinists or Methodists did. Churches normally have a formal, bureaucratic structure, with a hierarchy of religious officials, and tend to represent the conservative face of religion, since they are integrated into the existing institutional order. Most of their adherents are like their parents in being church members.

Sects are comparatively small; they usually aim at discovering and following 'the true way', and tend to withdraw from the surrounding society into communities of their own. The members of sects regard established churches as corrupt. Most have few or no officials, all members being regarded as equal participants. A small proportion of people are born into sects, but most actively join them in order to further their beliefs.

Denominations and cults

Other authors have further developed the church/sect typology as originally set out by Weber and Troeltsch. One of these is Howard Becker (1950), who added two further types: the **denomination** and the **cult**. A denomination is a sect which has 'cooled down' and become an institutionalized body rather than an active protest group. Sects which survive over any period of time inevitably become denominations. Thus Calvinism and Methodism were sects during their early formation, when they generated great fervour among their members; but over the years they have become more 'respectable'. Denominations are recognized as more or less legitimate by churches and exist alongside them, quite often cooperating harmoniously with them.

Cults resemble sects, but have different emphases. They are the most loosely knit and transient of all religious organizations, being composed of individuals who reject what they see as the values of the outside society. Their focus is on individual experience, bringing like-minded individuals together. People do not formally join a cult, but rather follow particular theories or prescribed ways of behaviour. Members are usually allowed to maintain other religious connections. Like sects, cults quite often form around an inspirational leader. Instances of cults in the West today would include groups of believers in spiritualism, astrology or transcendental meditation.

A tragic example of a cult built around an inspirational leader came to light in the USA in 1993. David Koresh, who led the Branch Davidian religious cult, claimed to be a messiah. He was also allegedly stockpiling illegal weapons, practising polygyny and having sex with some of the children living in the group's compound in Waco, Texas. Up to eighty members of the cult (including nineteen children) burned to death as a fire engulfed their complex when it came under assault by officials from the US government after a lengthy armed stand-off. Controversy remains over whether the fire was ordered by Koresh, who reportedly preferred mass suicide to surrender, or whether the actions of the federal authorities caused the tragedy.

It should be obvious that what is a cult in one country may well be an established religious practice in another. When Indian gurus (religious teachers) bring their beliefs into the United Kingdom, what might be considered an established religion in India is regarded as a cult in the UK. Christianity began as an indigenous cult in ancient Jerusalem, and in many Asian countries today Evangelical Protestantism is regarded as a cult imported from the West, and particularly the United States. Thus, cults should not be thought of as 'weird'. A leading sociologist of religion, Jeffrey K. Hadden, points out (1997) that all the approximately 100,000 religions that humans have devised were once new; most if not all were initially despised cults from the standpoint of

David Koresh, shown here in a video still, was a mesmeric leader of the Branch Davidian religious cult. Many of its followers died in tragic circumstances.

respectable religious belief of the times. Jesus was crucified because his ideas were so threatening to the established order of the Roman-dominated religious establishment of ancient Judaea.

Movements

Religious movements represent a subtype of social movement in general.

> Social movements are discussed in more detail in chapter 20, 'Politics, Government and Terrorism', pp. 867–71.

A religious movement is an association of people who join together to spread a new religion or to promote a new interpretation of an existing religion. Religious movements are larger than sects and less exclusivist in their membership – although like churches and sects, movements and sects (or cults) are not always clearly distinct from one another. In fact, all sects and cults can be classified as religious movements. Examples of religious movements include the groups that originally founded and spread Christianity in the first century, the Lutheran movement that split Christianity in Europe about 1,500 years later and the groups involved in the more recent Islamic Revolution (discussed in more detail later in the chapter).

Religious movements tend to pass through certain definite phases of development. In the first phase, the movement usually derives its life and cohesion from a powerful leader. Max Weber classified such leaders as **charismatic**, that is, having inspirational qualities capable of capturing the imagination and devotion of a mass of followers. (Charismatic leaders in Weber's formulation could include political as well as religious figures – revolutionary China's Mao Tse-tung for example, as well as Jesus and Muhammad.) The leaders of religious movements are usually critical of the religious establishment and seek to proclaim a new message. In their early years, religious movements are fluid; they do not have an established authority system. Their members are normally in direct contact with the charismatic leader, and together they spread the new teachings.

The second phase of development occurs following the death of the leader. Rarely does a new charismatic leader arise from the masses, so this phase is crucial. The movement is now faced with what Weber termed the 'routinization of charisma'. To survive, it has to create formalized rules and procedures, since it can no longer depend on the central role of the leader in organizing the followers. Many movements fade away when their leaders die or lose their influence. A movement that survives and takes on a permanent character becomes a church. In other words, it becomes a formal organization of believers with an established authority system and established symbols and rituals. The church might itself at some later point become the origin of other

movements that question its teachings and either set themselves up in opposition or break away completely.

New religious movements

Although traditional churches have been experiencing a decline in membership in recent decades, we see below in figures 14.3 and 14.4 (p. 563) that other forms of religious activity have been on the rise. Sociologists use the term **new religious movements** to refer collectively to the broad range of religious and spiritual groups, cults and sects that have emerged in Western countries, including the United Kingdom, alongside mainstream religions. New religious movements encompass an enormous diversity of groups, from spiritual and self-help groups within the **New Age movement** to exclusive sects such as the Hare Krishnas (International Society for Krishna Consciousness).

Many new religious movements are derived from the major religious traditions which we discussed above, Hinduism, Christianity and Buddhism, while others have emerged from traditions that were almost unknown in the West until recently. Some new religious movements are essentially new creations of the charismatic leaders who head their activities. This is the case, for example, with the Unification Church led by the Reverend Sun Myung Moon, who is seen by his supporters as a messiah, and whose church claims 4.5 million members. Membership in new religious movements mostly consists of converts rather than individuals brought up in a particular faith. Members more often than not are well educated and from middle-class backgrounds.

Most new religious movements in Britain originated in the United States or the East, although a few, such as the Aetherius Society (founded in 1955) and the Emin Foundation (founded in 1971), were established in Britain. Since the Second World War, the United States has witnessed a far greater proliferation of religious movements than at any previous time in its history, including an unprecedented series of mergers and divisions between denominations. Most have been short-lived, but a few have achieved remarkable followings.

Various theories to explain the popularity of new religious movements have been advanced. Some observers have argued that they should be seen as a response to the process of liberalization and secularization within society and even within traditional churches. People who feel that traditional religions have become ritualistic and devoid of spiritual meaning may find comfort and a greater sense of community in smaller, less impersonal new religious movements.

Others have pointed to new religious movements as an outcome of rapid social change (Wilson 1982). As traditional social norms are disrupted, people search for both explanations and reassurance. The rise of groups and sects that emphasize personal spirituality, for example, suggest that many individuals feel a need to reconnect with their own values or beliefs in the face of instability and uncertainty.

A further factor may be that new religious movements appeal to people who feel alienated from mainstream society. The collective, communal approaches of sects and cults, some authors argue, can offer support and a sense of belonging. For example, middle-class youths are not marginalized from society in a material

sense, but they may feel isolated emotionally and spiritually. Membership in a cult can help to overcome this feeling of alienation (Wallis 1984).

New religious movements can be understood as falling into three broad categories: *world-affirming, world-rejecting* and *world-accommodating* movements. Each is based on the relationship of the individual group to the larger social world.

World-affirming movements

World-affirming movements are more akin to self-help or therapy groups than to conventional religious groups. They are movements that often lack rituals, churches and formal theologies, turning their focus on members' spiritual well-being. As the name suggests, world-affirming movements do not reject the outside world or its values. Rather, they seek to enhance their followers' abilities to perform and succeed in that world by unlocking human potential.

The Church of Scientology is one example of such a group. Founded by L. Ron Hubbard, the Church of Scientology has grown from its original base in California to include a large membership in countries around the world. Scientologists believe we are all spiritual beings, but have neglected our spiritual nature. Through training that makes them aware of their real spiritual capacities, people can recover forgotten supernatural powers, clear their minds and reveal their full potential.

Many strands of the so-called **New Age movement** fall under the category of world-affirming movements. The New Age movement emerged from the counterculture of the 1960s and 1970s and encompasses a broad spectrum of beliefs, practices and ways of life. Pagan teachings (Celtic, Druidic, Native American and others), shamanism, forms of Asian mysticism, Wiccan rituals and Zen meditation are only a few of the activities that are thought of as 'New Age'.

On the surface, the mysticism of the New Age movement appears to stand in stark contrast to the modern societies in which it is favoured. Followers of New Age movements seek out and develop alternative ways of life in order to cope with the challenges of modernity. Yet New Age activities should not be interpreted as simply a radical break with the present. They should also be seen as part of a larger cultural trajectory that *exemplifies* aspects of mainstream culture. In late modern societies, individuals possess unparalleled degrees of autonomy and freedom to chart their own lives. In this respect, the aims of the New Age movement coincide closely with the modern age: people are encouraged to move beyond traditional values and expectations and to live their lives actively and reflexively.

World-rejecting movements

As opposed to world-affirming groups, **world-rejecting movements** are highly critical of the outside world. They often demand significant lifestyle changes from their followers – members may be expected to live ascetically, to change their dress or hairstyle, or to follow a certain diet. World-rejecting movements are frequently exclusive, in contrast to world-affirming movements, which tend to be inclusive in nature. Some world-rejecting movements display characteristics of *total institutions*; members are expected to subsume their individual identities in that of the group, to adhere to strict ethical codes or rules and to withdraw from activity in the outside world.

Most of the world-rejecting movements place far more demands on their members, in terms of time and commitment, than do older established religions. Some groups have been known to use the technique of 'love bombing' to gain the individual's total adherence. A potential convert is overwhelmed by attention and constant displays of instant affection until he or she is drawn emotionally into the group. Some new movements, in fact, have been accused of brainwashing their adherents – seeking to control their minds in such a way as to rob them of the capacity for independent decision-making.

Many world-rejecting cults and sects have come under the intense scrutiny of state authorities, the media and the public. Certain extreme cases of world-rejecting cults have attracted much concern. For example, the Japanese group Aum Shinrikyo released deadly sarin gas into the Tokyo subway system in 1995, injuring thousands of commuters and killing twelve people. (The cult's leader, Shoko Asahara, was sentenced to death for ordering the attacks by the Japanese courts in February 2004.) The Branch Davidian cult in the United States (discussed above, p. 547) also grabbed the world media's attention when it became embroiled in a deadly confrontation with US authorities in 1993 after accusations of child abuse and weapons stock-piling.

World-accommodating movements

The third type of new religious movement is the one most like traditional religions. **World-accommodating movements** tend to emphasize the importance of inner religious life over more worldly concerns.

Members of such groups seek to reclaim the spiritual purity that they believe has been lost in traditional religious settings. Where followers of world-rejecting and world-affirming groups often alter their lifestyles in accordance with their religious activity, many adherents of world-accommodating movements carry on in their everyday lives and careers with little visible change. One example of a world-accommodating movement is Pentecostalism. Pentecostalists believe that the Holy Spirit can be heard through individuals who are granted the gift of 'speaking in tongues'.

Christianity, gender and sexuality

Churches and denominations, as the preceding discussion has indicated, are religious organizations with defined systems of authority. In these hierarchies, as in other areas of social life, women are mostly excluded from power. This is very clear in Christianity, but it is also characteristic of all the major religions.

More than a hundred years ago, Elizabeth Cady Stanton, an American campaigner for women's rights, published a series of commentaries on the Scriptures, entitled *The Woman's Bible*. In her view, the deity had created women and men as beings of equal value, and the Bible should fully reflect this fact. Its 'masculinist' character, she believed, reflected not the authentic word of God, but the fact that the Bible was written by men. In 1870, the Church of England established a Revising Committee to revise and update the biblical texts; but as Stanton pointed out, the committee contained not a single woman. She asserted that there was no reason to suppose that God is a man, since it was clear in the Scriptures that all human beings were fashioned in the image of God. When a colleague opened a women's rights conference with a prayer to 'God, our Mother', there was a virulent reaction from the church authorities. Yet Stanton pressed ahead, organizing a Women's Revising Committee in America, composed of twenty-three women, to advise her in preparing *The Woman's Bible*, which was published in 1895.

A century later the Anglican Church is still largely dominated by men, although recently this has begun to change. In the Church of England between 1987 and 1992 women were allowed to be deaconesses, but not permitted to be priests. Although they were officially part of the laity, they were not allowed to conduct certain basic religious rituals, like pronouncing blessings or solemnizing marriages. In 1992, after increasing pressure, particularly from women inside the Church of England, the Synod (governing assembly) voted to make the priesthood open to women. The decision is still opposed by many conservatives in the Anglican Church, who argue that the full acceptance of women is a blasphemous deviation from revealed biblical truth and a move away from eventual reunification with the Catholic Church. As a result of the decision to allow women priests, some people decided to withdraw from the Church of England, often converting to Catholicism. Ten years later around a fifth of priests in the Church of England are women, and it is expected that there will soon be more women priests than men priests. In July 2005, the Church of England voted to begin the process that would allow women to become bishops, a decision strongly opposed by several senior figures in the Church.

The Catholic Church has been more conservative in its attitude to women than the Church of England, and persists in formally supporting inequalities of gender. Calls for the ordination of women have been consistently turned down by the Catholic authorities. In 1977 the Sacred Congregation for the Doctrine of the Faith, in Rome, declared formally that women were not admissible to the Catholic priesthood. The reason given was that Jesus did not call a woman to be one of his disciples. In January 2004 seven women, who had been ordained as priests by rebel Argentinean Bishop, Romulo Antonio Braschi, were excommunicated from the Church and their ordinations overturned by the Vatican. Pope John Paul II (1920–2005) encouraged women to recall their roles as wives and mothers, attacked feminist ideologies which assert that men and women are fundamentally the same and supported policies prohibiting abortion and the use of contraception which place further limitations on women's freedom (Vatican 2004).

Controversy in the Anglican Church in recent years has shifted away from gender to the issue of homosexuality and the priesthood. Homosexuals have long served in the Christian Church, but with their sexual inclinations either suppressed, ignored or unobserved. (The Catholic Church still holds to the position set out in 1961 that those 'affected by the perverse inclination' towards homosexuality must be barred from taking religious vows or being ordained.) Other Protestant denominations have introduced liberal policies towards homosexuals and openly gay clergy have been admitted to the priesthood in some of the smaller denominations. The Evangelical Lutheran Church

in the Netherlands was the first European Christian denomination to decide that lesbians and gays could serve as pastors in 1972. Other denominations, such as the United Church of Canada (in 1988) and the Norwegian Church (in 2000), have also followed suit.

The controversy over the admission of homosexuals to the priesthood came to the fore in the UK in June 2003 when Dr Jeffrey John, an acknowledged homosexual living a celibate life, was appointed Bishop of Reading. He eventually declined to take the post after his appointment caused a bitter row within the international Anglican Church. In August 2003 the rank and file of the Anglican Church in America voted to elect an openly gay bishop, Reverend Canon Gene Robinson of New Hampshire. A conservative lobby group, Anglican Mainstream, has now been created to lobby against the appointment of gay clergy and the issue remains unresolved.

Secularization and religious revival

Secularization

As we have seen, one view shared by early sociological thinkers was that traditional religion would become more and more marginal to the modern world. Marx, Durkheim and Weber all believed that a process of secularization was bound to occur as societies modernized and became more reliant on science and technology to control and explain the social world. **Secularization** describes the process whereby religion loses its influence over the various spheres of social life.

Many places of worship have now been put to different use, such as this discount carpet store in Armley in the north of England.

The debate over the *secularization thesis* is one of the most complex areas in the sociology of religion. In the most basic terms, there is disagreement between supporters of the secularization thesis – who agree with sociology's founding fathers and see religion as diminishing in power and importance in the modern world – and opponents of the concept, who argue that religion remains a significant force, albeit often in new and unfamiliar forms.

The enduring popularity of new religious movements presents a challenge to the secularization thesis. Opponents of the thesis point to the diversity and dynamism of new religious movements and argue that religion and spirituality remain a central facet of modern life. As traditional religions lose their hold, religion is not disappearing, but is being channelled in new directions. Not all scholars agree, however. Proponents of the idea of secularization point out that these movements remain peripheral to society as a whole, even if they make a profound impact on the lives of their individual followers. New religious movements are fragmented and relatively unorganized; they also suffer from high turnover rates as people are attracted to a movement for some time and then move on to something new. Compared to a serious religious commitment, they argue, participation in a new religious movement appears little more than a hobby or lifestyle choice.

The sociological debate

Secularization is a complex sociological concept, in part because there is little consensus about how the process should be measured. Moreover, many sociologists employ definitions of religion which do not coincide – while some argue that religion is best understood in terms of the traditional church, others argue that a much broader view must be taken to include dimensions such as personal spirituality and deep commitment to certain values. These differences in perception will necessarily influence arguments for or against secularization.

Secularization can be evaluated according to a number of aspects or dimensions. Some of them are objective in nature, such as the level of membership of religious organizations. Statistics and official records can show how many people belong to a church or other religious body and are active in attending services or other ceremonies. As we shall see, with the exception of the USA, the industrialized countries have all experienced considerable secularization according to this index. The pattern of religious decline seen in Britain is found in most of Western Europe, including Catholic countries such as France or Italy. More Italians than French attend church regularly and participate in the major rituals (such as Easter communion), but the overall pattern of declining religious observance is similar in both cases.

A second dimension of secularization concerns how far churches and other religious organizations maintain their

social influence, wealth and *prestige.* In earlier times, religious organizations could wield considerable influence over governments and social agencies, and commanded high respect in the community. How far is this still the case? The answer to the question is clear. Even if we confine ourselves to the last century, we see that religious organizations have progressively lost much of the social and political influence they previously had – and the trend is worldwide, although there are some exceptions. Church leaders can no longer automatically expect to be influential with the powerful. While some established churches remain very wealthy by any standards, and new religious movements may rapidly build up fortunes, the material circumstances of many long-standing religious organizations are insecure. Churches and temples have to be sold off, or are in a state of disrepair.

The third dimension of secularization concerns beliefs and values. We can call this the dimension of *religiosity.* Levels of church-going and the degree of social influence of churches are obviously not necessarily a direct expression of the beliefs or ideals people hold. Many who have religious beliefs do not regularly attend services or take part in public ceremonies; conversely, regularity of such attendance or participation does not always imply the holding of strong religious views – people may attend out of habit or because it is expected of them in their community.

As in the other dimensions of secularization, we need an accurate understanding of the past to see how far religiosity has declined today. Supporters of the secularization thesis argue that, in the past, religion was far more important to people's daily lives than it is today. The church was

In the UK, church attendance has dropped dramatically over the last hundred years or so, and the average age of the congregation has risen considerably. More recently, however, some denominations have reported a rise in attendance.

at the heart of local affairs and was a strong influence within family and personal life. Yet critics of the thesis contest this idea, arguing that just because people attended church more regularly does not necessarily prove that they were more religious. In many traditional societies, including medieval Europe, commitment to religious belief was less strong and less important in day-to-day life than might be supposed. Research into English history, for example, shows that lukewarm commitment to religious beliefs was common among the ordinary people. Religious sceptics seem to have been found in most cultures, particularly in the larger traditional societies (Ginzburg 1980).

Yet there can be no doubt at all that the hold of religious ideas today is less than was generally the case in the traditional world – particularly if we include under the term 'religion' the whole range of the supernatural in which people believed. Most of us simply do not any longer experience our environment as permeated by divine or spiritual entities. Some of the major tensions in the world today – like those afflict-ing the Middle East, Chechnya and Sudan – derive primarily, or in some part, from religious differences. But the majority of conflicts and wars are now mainly secular in nature – concerned with divergent polit-ical creeds or material interests.

Bearing in mind these three dimensions of secularization, let us review some recent trends in religion in Britain and the United States and consider how they support or contradict the idea of secular-ization. We begin though with a brief account of the development of religion in Europe.

Religion in Europe

The influence of Christianity was a crucial element in the evolution of Europe as a political unit. One possible border to what we now define as Europe is down the line of the first great split in European Chris-tian thought in the eleventh century, between Catholic and Eastern Orthodox forms of Christianity. Orthodox Christian-ity is still the dominant religion in many East European countries, including Bul-garia, Belarus, Cyprus, Georgia, Greece, Romania, Russia, Serbia and Ukraine.

In Western Europe the division of the continent into Catholic and Protestant in the sixteenth century marked a second great rupture in Christian thought. This process, known as the Reformation, is inseparable from the division of Western Europe into the relatively stable patch-work of modern nation-states that we still see on the map today. Very broadly, Western Europe divided itself into a Prot-estant North (Scandinavia and Scotland); a Catholic South (which includes Spain, Portugal, Italy and France, as well as

Belgium and Ireland further north) and several more or less denominationally mixed countries (including Britain and Northern Ireland, the Netherlands and Germany).

The Reformation took different forms in different countries, but was unified by the attempt to escape the influence of the Pope and the Catholic Church. A variety of denominations of Protestantism, and relations between Church and State, emerged in Europe. Below we give a brief sketch of religion in some of the major Western European nations.

The Nordic countries (Sweden, Norway, Denmark, Finland and Iceland) have a state church (the Lutheran State Church of Northern Europe). The population is char-acterized by a high rate of church mem-bership, but a low level of both religious practice and acceptance of Christian beliefs. These countries have been described as 'belonging without believing' (as table 14.1 shows). Particularly in Sweden the close relationship between Church and State is now being ques-tioned. Many people find the idea of a church that is specially privileged by the state inappropriate in an increasingly eth-nically and culturally diverse country.

Germany can still be characterized as being divided between Catholicism and Protestantism. However, this is now chal-lenged, first, by a growing Muslim popula-tion (see below, figure 14.2) and second, by an increase in the number of people who claim no religious allegiance. This second point is partly explained by the reunifica-tion of East and West Germany after the fall of the Berlin Wall in 1989, and the suppres-sion of Christianity in the former Commu-nist countries of Eastern Europe, including East Germany.

Table 14.1   Frequency of church attendance in Western Europe, 1990 (%)

	At least once a week	Once a month or more	Once a month	Christmas, Easter, etc.	Once a year	Never
European average	29		10	8	5	40
Catholic countries						
Belgium	23		8	13	4	52
France	10		7	17	7	59
Ireland	81		7	6	1	5
Italy	40		13	23	4	19
Portugal	33		8	8	4	47
Spain	33		10	15	4	38
Mixed countries						
Great Britain	13		10	12	8	56
Netherlands	21		10	16	5	47
Northern Ireland	49		18	6	7	18
West Germany	19		15	16	9	41
Lutheran countries						
Denmark		11				
Finland		—				
Iceland		9				
Norway		10				
Sweden		10				

Source: Ashford and Timms (1992); reproduced in Davie (2000), p. 9

France is largely a Catholic country, but it is far more like the Protestant countries of Northern Europe in demonstrating low levels of religious belief and practices (see table 14.1). Of all the countries of Western Europe, France has the strictest separation between Church and State. The French state is strictly secular and refuses to privilege any religion or denomination. This takes in the exclusion of discussion of religion in all state institutions, including a ban on religious education in state-run schools. This strict separation between Church and State also led to the controversial ban on 'conspicuous' religious items in French school which came into place in September 2004, and particularly affected those Muslim girls who wore headscarves.

Italy, Spain and Portugal are largely Catholic. They demonstrate higher levels of religious belief and practice than most other European countries, especially those in the north (see table 14.1). The Catholic Church, based inside Italy, enjoys a high level of influence in all of these countries. In Italy, Catholicism is privileged above other denominations and religions. In Spain, the Catholic Church was instrumental in supporting the political right in the civil war which led to General Franco's dictatorship between 1939 and 1975. There is no official link between State and Church in Spain, although the Catholic Church is privileged by its dominance in terms of numbers. In Portugal, despite some constitutional reform in the 1970s, the Catholic Church still has a degree of influence in law (Davie 2000).

Religious minorities

Europe is also home to sizeable non-Christian religious minorities. Although Jews have been present in Europe for centuries, their recent history has been bound up with anti-Semitic discrimination and genocide.

Racism and discrimination are discussed in more detail in chapter 13.

In the years after the Second Word War, many Jews who had survived the holocaust left Europe for the newly created state of Israel. These factors meant that the number of Jews living in Europe fell dramatically during the twentieth century from 9.6 million in 1937 to fewer than 2 million by the mid-1990s (as table 14.2 shows).

In the twentieth century global migration, partly shaped by Europe's colonial history, has also led to the development of sizeable non-Judeo-Christian minorities across the whole of the European continent for the first time. Of these, Islam is by far the largest non-Christian faith, with at least six million members in Europe, making up around 3 per cent of its population. (Figure 14.2 shows the migration of Muslims into Europe and their country of origin.) The colonial links between France and North Africa account for a sizeable French Muslim population of three to four million. Germany, by contrast, has large numbers of Muslim migrant workers from Turkey and South-East Europe. Britain's Muslim population, as we shall see below, comes largely from the former British Empire countries of the Indian subcontinent (Davie 2000). Below we develop a wider picture of religion in the UK.

Religion in the United Kingdom

Before 2001, questions about religion had not been included in the Census for 150 years. The most recent Census therefore provides a much more accurate portrait of religion in Britain than earlier assessments, which had been based on surveys of public opinion and reports from individual denominations. The 2001 Census found that around 78 per cent of the UK population reported having a religion, and almost 72 per cent of people described themselves as Christian. Other religions in the UK have far fewer adherents than Christianity. Islam is the next most common faith – almost 3 per cent of the population describe themselves as Muslim. Other significant groups include Hindus, Sikhs, Jews and Buddhists, each accounting for less than 1 per cent of the total population (see table 14.3).

The extent to which people identified with a religion varied around the UK. Perhaps unsurprisingly, given its history as a site of religious conflict, people in Northern Ireland were more likely to say that they identified with a religion (86 per cent) than those in England and Wales (77 per cent) and in Scotland (67 per cent). About 16 per cent of the UK population stated that they had no religion. This category included agnostics and atheists. (It also included the 390,000 people – less than 1 per cent – who described their religion as 'Jedi', inspired by a hoax email campaign, reported in the media, which falsely claimed that the belief system at the centre of the Star Wars films would receive official government recognition if enough people cited it on their Census forms.)

Table 14.2   Jewish populations in Europe, 1937–94

	1937	1946	1967	1994
Austria	191,000	31,000[a]	12,500	7,000
Belgium	65,000	45,000	40,500	31,800
Bulgaria	49,000	44,200	5,000	1,900
Czechoslovakia	357,000	55,000	15,000	7,600[b]
Denmark	8,500	5,500	6,000	6,400
Estonia[c]	4,600	—	—	3,500
Finland	2,000	2,000	1,750	1,300
France	300,000	225,000	535,000	530,000
Germany	500,000	153,000[a]	30,000	55,000
Great Britain	330,000	370,000	400,000	295,000
Greece	77,000	10,000	6,500	4,800
Hungary	400,000	145,000	80,000	56,000
Ireland (Republic)	5,000	3,900	2,900	1,200
Italy	48,000	53,000[a]	35,000	31,000
Latvia[c]	95,000	—	—	18,000
Lithuania[c]	155,000	—	—	6,500
Luxembourg	3,500	500	500	600
Netherlands	140,000	28,000	30,000	25,000
Norway	2,000	750	1,000	1,000
Poland	3,250,000	215,000	21,000	6,000
Portugal	n/a	4,000	1,000	300
Romania	850,000	420,000	100,000	10,000
Spain	n/a	6,000	6,000	12,000
Sweden	7,500	15,500	13,000	16,500
Switzerland	18,000	35,000	20,000	19,000
Turkey[d]	50,000	48,000	35,000	18,000
USSR/CIS[d]	2,669,000	1,971,000	1,715,000	812,000
Yugoslavia	71,000	12,000	7,000	3,500[e]
Total	9,648,100	3,898,350	3,119,650	1,980,900

Note: These figures, collated from many sources, are of varying reliability and in some cases are subject to a wide margin of error and interpretation. This warning applies particularly to the figures for 1946, a year in which there was considerable Jewish population movement. It must also be borne in mind that the boundaries of many European countries changed between 1937 and 1946.

n/a = not available.

[a] Includes 'Displaced Persons'. [b] Total for Czech Republic and Slovakia. [c] Baltic States included in USSR between 1941 and 1991. [d] Excludes Asiatic regions. [e] Total for former Yugoslavia.

Source: Wasserstein (1996); reproduced in Davie (2000), p. 123

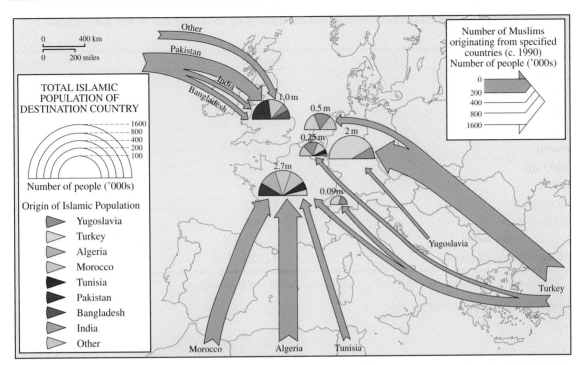

Figure 14.2 Number of European Muslims originating from specifies countries and total Islamic population of European destination countries, *c.*1900

Source: Vertovec and Peach (1997); reproduced in Davie (2000), p .128

Although over 70 per cent of the UK population describe themselves as Christian, a far smaller figure regularly go to church. According to the 1851 Census of religion, about 40 per cent of adults in England and Wales attended church each Sunday; by 1900 this had dropped to 35 per cent, by 1950 to 20 per cent and by 2000 to 8 per cent. (The decline in Anglican church membership is shown in figure 14.3.) The main British denominations lost an average 5 per cent of churchgoers during the 1980s, with the most substantial decline (of 8 per cent) among Roman Catholics. There are now some signs that this trend is slowing. In Greater London, for example, attendance at Anglican churches fell by 30 per cent during the 1980s, but rose by 3 per cent between 1989 and 1998. Outside the Church of England, Baptists increased their attendance figures by 11 per cent between 1989 and 1998 – see figure 14.4 (The *Economist*, 21 December 2000).

The general trend in decline in church attendance, however, is somewhat uneven. A difference exists, for example between Trinitarian and non-Trinitarian churches. Trinitarian churches, which include Anglicans, Catholics, Methodists and Presbyterians, among others, are those that believe in the unity of the Trinity

Table 14.3   Those who described themselves as 'Belonging to a religion' in the 2001 Census, England and Wales[a]

	Thousands	Percentages
Christian	37,338	71.7
Muslim	1,547	3.0
Hindu	552	1.1
Sikh	329	0.6
Jewish	260	0.5
Buddhist	144	0.3
Other	151	0.3
All religions	40,322	77.5
No religion	7,709	14.8
Religion not stated	4,011	7.7
All no religion/not stated	11,720	22.5

[a] The question was voluntary, with tick box options, and asked 'What is your religion?'

Source: Social Trends 34 (2004), p. 209

in one God. Membership of Trinitarian churches fell from 8.8 million in 1970 to 6.5 million in 1994. However, there was an increase in the membership of some non-Trinitarian churches, such as the Mormons and the Jehovah's Witnesses, over the same period (see table 14.4). Among ethnic minority populations, attendance at church and religious services has also been rising. A number of 'new religious movements' (see above, pp. 549–52) have also attracted followers in Britain.

There is a discernible pattern to religion in the UK in terms of age, sex, class and geography. Generally, older people are more religious than those in younger age groups. Church-going among young people reaches a peak at the age of fifteen, after which average levels of attendance slump until people reach their thirties and forties and enthusiasm is revived; church-going thereafter rises with increasing age.

Women are more likely to be involved in organized religion than men. In Anglican churches this is only marginally the case, but in Christian Science churches, for example, women outnumber men by four to one.

In general, church attendance and professed religious belief are higher among more affluent than among poorer groups. The Church of England has been called 'the Conservative Party at prayer', and there is still some truth in this. Catholics are more likely to be working class. This class orientation shows itself in voting patterns: Anglicans tend to vote Conservative and Catholics to vote Labour, as do many Methodists, Methodism having originally been closely connected with the rise of the Labour Party. Religious participation also varies widely according to where people live: 35 per cent of adults in Merseyside and 32 per cent in Lancashire are church members,

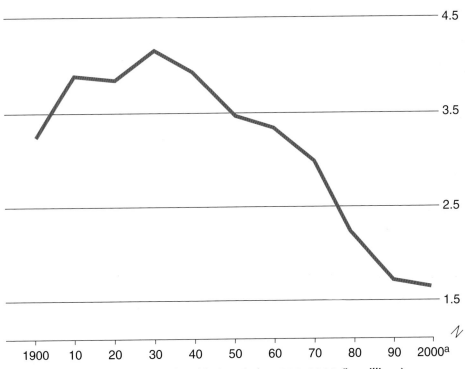

Figure 14.3 Total Anglican membership in Britain, 1900–2000 (in millions)

ª Estimate

Source: *The Economist* (21 December 2000)

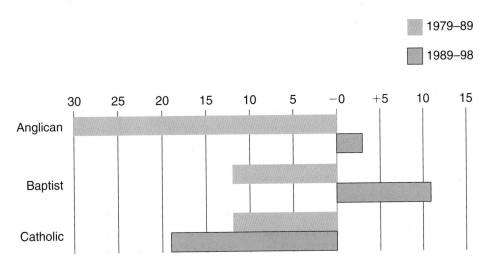

Figure 14.4 Percentage change in church attendance in Greater London, 1979–98

Source: *The Economist* (21 December 2000)

Table 14.4   UK religious communities, 1975–2005 (in millions)

Denominational group	1975	1980	1985	1990	1995	2000	2005
Anglican	29.3[2]	29.0[2]	28.8[2]	28.6[3]	28.4[2]	28.3[2]	28.2[2]
Roman Catholic	5.6	5.7	5.7	5.7	5.9	5.8	5.8
Orthodox	0.4	0.4	0.4	0.5	0.5	0.5	0.6
Presbyterian	3.4[2]	3.3[2]	3.2[2]	3.2[2]	3.1[2]	2.9[2]	2.9[2]
Baptist	0.5[2]	0.5[2]	0.5[2]	0.5[2]	0.5[2]	0.5[2]	0.5[2]
Methodist	1.7[2]	1.6[2]	1.5[2]	1.5[2]	1.4[2]	1.3[2]	1.2[2]
All other churches	1.0	1.2	1.3	1.2	1.3	1.4	1.3
Total Trinitarian	*41.9*	*41.7*	*41.4*	*41.2*	*40.9*	*40.7*	*40.5*
Non-Trinitarian	0.7	0.8	1.0	1.1	1.3	1.4	1.4
Total Christian	*42.6*	*42.5*	*42.4*	*42.3*	*42.2*	*42.1*	*41.9*
Muslim	0.4	0.7[2]	1.0[2]	1.3[2]	1.4[2]	1.6[2]	1.7[2]
Hindu	0.4[2]	0.5[2]	0.5[2]	0.5[2]	0.5[2]	0.6[2]	0.6[2]
Sikh	0.1[2]	0.1[2]	0.2[2]	0.2[2]	0.3[2]	0.3[2]	0.4[2]
Jew	0.4	0.3	0.3	0.3	0.3	0.3	0.3
Buddhist	0.0	0.1	0.1	0.1	0.1	0.2	0.2
Other religions	0.1	0.1	0.1	0.1	0.2	0.2	0.2
Total all religions	*44.0*	*44.3*	*44.6*	*44.8*	*45.0*	*45.2*	*45.3*
Percentage of population:							
Christian	76	76	74	74	73	72	70
Muslim	1	1	2	2	2	3	3
All other religions	1	2	2	2	2	2	3
Total all religions	*78*	*79*	*78*	*78*	*77*	*77*	*76*

[a] Estimate   [b] Revised figure   [c] Previously included Buddhists

Source: UKCH Religious Trends 4 (2003/4), p. 2.2

compared with only 9 per cent in Humberside and 11 per cent in Nottinghamshire. One reason for this is immigration – Liverpool has a large population of Irish Catholics, just as North London is a focus for Jews and Bradford for Muslims and Sikhs.

In terms of their consequences for day-to-day behaviour, religious differences are much more marked in Northern Ireland than anywhere else in Britain. The clashes between Protestants and Catholics which occur there involve only a minority from either faith, but are often acute and violent. The influence of religion in Northern Ireland is not easy to disentangle from other factors involved in the antagonisms; the belief there in a 'united Ireland', in which Eire and Northern Ireland would become one state, is generally held among Catholics and rejected by Protestants. But political considerations and ideas of nationalism play an important role alongside religious beliefs.

Religion in the United States

Compared to the citizens of other industrial nations, Americans are unusually religious. With few exceptions, 'the United States has been the most God-believing and religion-adhering, fundamentalist, and religiously traditional country in Christendom [where] more new religions have been born . . . than any other country' (Lipset 1991). According to public opinion polls, around three out of every five Americans say that religion is 'very important' in their own life and at any given time around 40 per cent will have been to church in the previous week (Gallup 2004). The overwhelming majority of Americans reportedly believe in God and claim they regularly pray, the majority one or more times a day (Center 1994, 1998). Seven out of ten Americans report that they believe in an afterlife (Roof and McKinney 1990; Warner 1993).

The US government does not officially collect data on religious affiliation, but a picture can be drawn from occasional government surveys, public opinion polls and church records. These show that the United States is the most religiously diverse country in the world, with more than 1,500 distinct religions (Melton 1989). Despite this variety, surveys also reveal that the majority of Americans define themselves as Christian and belong to a relatively small number of religious denominations.

About 52 per cent of Americans identify themselves as Protestants and 24 per cent as Catholics. Other significant religious groups include Mormons, Muslims and Jews (Pew 2002). The Catholic Church has shown by far the largest increase in membership, partly because of the immigration of Catholics from Mexico and Central and South America. Yet the growth in Catholic Church membership has also slowed in recent years, as some followers have drifted away, either ceasing to identify themselves as Catholics or shifting to Protestantism.

Although Catholics continue to grow in number, the percentages who attend church have shown a sharp decline over the past few decades, beginning in the 1960s and levelling off in the mid-1970s. One of the main reasons was the papal encyclical of 1968, which reaffirmed the ban on the use of contraceptives among Catholics. The encyclical offered no leeway for people whose conscience allowed for the use of contraceptives. They were faced with disobeying the church, and many Catholics did just that. A survey in the USA found that three-quarters of Catholic women of child-bearing age use contraception and 96 per cent of all Catholic women who have ever had sex have used contraception at some point in their lives (National Survey of Family Growth 1995). In addition, a recent poll found that 50 per cent of American Catholics reject the notion that the Pope is infallible when he teaches on matters of morals, such as birth control and abortion (Gallup 2003). A large proportion of Catholics have therefore come to doubt or defy the Church's authority over various areas of their lives.

A clearer picture of religious life in the USA can be obtained if we break down the large Protestant category into major subgroups. According to surveys, the largest Protestant denomination in the USA is made up of Baptists, who account for around 16 per cent of the population – about a third of all Protestants. Other significant Protestant groups include

Contemporary approaches: 'religious economy'

One of the most recent and influential approaches to the sociology of religion is tailored to Western societies, and particularly the United States, which offers many different faiths from which to pick and choose. Taking their cue from economic theory, sociologists who favour the **religious economy** approach argue that religions can be fruitfully understood as organizations in competition with one another for followers (Stark and Bainbridge 1987; Finke and Stark 1988, 1992; Moore 1994).

Like contemporary economists who study businesses, these sociologists argue that competition is preferable to monopoly when it comes to ensuring religious vitality. This position is exactly opposite to those of the classical theorists. Marx, Durkheim and Weber assumed that religion weakens when it is challenged by different religious or secular viewpoints, whereas the religious economists argue that competition increases the overall level of religious involvement in modern society. Religious economists believe this to be true for two reasons. First, competition makes each religious group try that much harder to win followers. Second, the presence of numerous religions means that there is likely to be something for just about everyone. In culturally diverse societies a single religion will probably appeal to only a limited range of followers, while the presence of Indian gurus and fundamentalist preachers, in addition to more traditional churches, is likely to encourage a high level of religious participation.

This analysis is adapted from the business world, in which competition presumably encourages the emergence of highly specialized products that appeal to the very specific markets. In fact, the religious economists borrow the language of business in describing the conditions that lead to the success or failure of a particular religious organization. According to Roger Finke and Rodney Stark (1992), a successful religious group must be well organized for competition, have eloquent preachers who are effective 'sales reps' in spreading the word, offer beliefs and rituals that are packaged as an appealing product, and develop effective marketing techniques. Religion, in this view, is a business much like any other. Television evangelists have been especially good businesspeople in selling their religious products.

Thus religious economists such as Finke and Stark do not see competition as undermining religious beliefs and thus contributing to secularization. Rather, they argue that modern religion is constantly renewing itself through active marketing and recruitment. Although there is a growing body of research that supports the notion that competition is good for religion (Stark and Bainbridge 1980, 1985; Finke and Stark 1992), not all research comes to this conclusion (Land et al. 1991).

The religious economy approach overestimates the extent to which people rationally pick and choose among different religions, as if they were shopping around for a new car or a pair of shoes. Among deeply committed believers, particularly in societies that lack religious pluralism, it is not obvious that religion is a matter of rational choice. In such societies, even when people are allowed to choose among different religions, most are likely to practise their childhood religion without ever questioning whether or not there are more appealing alternatives. Even in the United States, where the religious economy approach originated, sociologists may overlook the spiritual aspects of religion if they simply assume that religious buyers are always on spiritual shopping sprees. A study of baby boomers in the USA (the generation born in the two decades after the end of the Second World War) found that a third had remained loyal to their childhood faith, while another third had continued to profess their childhood beliefs although they no longer belonged to a religious organization. Thus only a third were actively looking around for a new religion, making the sorts of choice presumed by the religious economy approach (Roof 1993).

Methodists (7 per cent), Lutherans (5 per cent) Presbyterians (3 per cent), Pentecostalists (2 per cent), Episcopalians (2 per cent) and Mormons and Latter-Day Saints (1 per cent) (ARIS 2001).

Several studies have noted that a change has taken place in recent decades in the composition of the Protestant Church in America. Membership of the liberal, or mainstream, American churches, such as the Lutherans, Episcopalians (Anglicans), Methodists and Presbyterians, is in decline. However, there has been an increase in the membership of conservative, or non-traditional, Protestant churches such as the Pentecostalists and the Southern Baptists (Roof and McKinney 1990; Jones et al. 2002).

These figures are important because they indicate the growing strength of conservative Protestants in the United States. Conservative Protestants emphasize a literal interpretation of the Bible, morality in daily life and conversion through evangelizing. They can be contrasted with the more historically established liberal Protestants, who tend to adopt a more flexible, humanistic approach to their religious practices. Somewhere in between are moderate Protestants.

The conservative denominations inspire deep loyalty and commitment, and they are highly effective in recruiting new members, particularly young people. Twice as many people belong to conservative Protestant groups as liberal ones, and conservative Protestants may soon outnumber moderates as well (Roof and McKinney 1990). Liberal Protestantism in particular has suffered. The ageing members of the liberal Protestant denominations have not been replaced by new young followers, commitment is low and some current members are switching to other faiths. Black Protestant churches also continue to thrive in the United States, as their members move into the middle class and a degree of economic and political prominence (Roof and McKinney 1990; Finke and Stark 1992).

The Protestant Church in the USA has also seen a huge rise in **evangelicalism**, the belief in spiritual rebirth (being 'born again'). Evangelicalism can be seen in part as a response to growing secularism, religious diversity and, in general, the decline of once core Protestant values in American life (Wuthnow 1988). In recent years, there has been an enormous growth in evangelical denominations, paralleled by a decline in the more mainstream Protestant religious affiliations. Many Protestants are clearly seeking the more direct, personal and emotional religious experience promised by evangelical denominations.

The US President, George W. Bush, is a born-again Christian, and has said that his faith helped him to overcome a drink problem earlier in life and to start afresh. He has likened America's international role after the terrorist attacks on the USA on 11 September 2001 to a battle against forces of evil. Bush's born-again Christianity is reflected in his conservative views on gay marriage and abortion. His evangelical religious values were vital in helping him to win a second term as President in November 2004, when he gained the support of the vast majority of evangelical Christians in the USA who saw these moral issues as crucial.

The controversy surrounding gay marriage in the States is discussed in chapter 12, 'Sexuality and Gender', pp. 434–6.

Evangelical organizations are good at mobilizing resources to help achieve their religious and political objectives, as the

The USA has witnessed a dramatic growth in evangelicalism. The support of evangelical Christians helped George W. Bush into power.

2004 presidential election demonstrated. In the business-like language used by the religious economists (see box on p. 566), they have proved to be extremely competitive 'spiritual entrepreneurs' in the 'religious marketplace' (Hatch 1989). Radio and television have provided important new marketing technologies, used by some evangelicals to reach a much wider audience than was previously possible. Called 'televangelists' because they conduct their evangelical ministries on the television, these ministers depart from many earlier evangelicals by preaching a 'gospel of prosperity': the belief that God wants the faithful to be financially prosperous and satisfied, rather than to sacrifice and suffer. This approach differs considerably from the austere emphasis on hard work and self-denial ordinarily associated with traditional conservative Protestant beliefs (Hadden and Shupe 1987; Bruce 1990). Luxurious houses of worship, epitomized by Robert H. Schuller's Crystal Cathedral in Garden Grove, California, provide the televised settings for electronic churches, whose congregants are geographically dispersed and are united primarily by means of electronic technology. Theology and fund-raising are the staples of televangelism, which must support not only the television ministries themselves, but also schools, universities, theme parks and sometimes the lavish lifestyles of its preachers.

The electronic preaching of religion has

become particularly prevalent in Latin America, where North American television programmes are shown. As a result, Protestant movements, most of them of the Pentecostal kind, have made a dramatic impact on such countries as Chile and Brazil, which are predominantly Catholic (Martin 1990).

Although some evangelicals combine a thoroughly modern lifestyle with traditional religious beliefs, others strongly reject many contemporary beliefs and practices. Fundamentalists are evangelicals who are anti-modern in many of their beliefs, calling for strict codes of morality and conduct. These frequently include taboos against drinking, smoking and other 'worldly evils', a belief in biblical infallibility and a strong emphasis on Christ's impending return to earth (Balmer 1989). Their 'old-time religion' clearly distinguishes good from evil and right from wrong (Roof and McKinney 1990). The rise in Christian fundamentalism is discussed below (pp. 575–7).

In the debate over secularization, the United States represents an important exception to the view that religion is declining in Western societies. While on the one hand the USA is one of the most thoroughly 'modernized' countries, it is also characterized by some of the highest levels of popular religious belief and membership in the world. Steve Bruce, one of the leading advocates of the secularization thesis, has argued that the persistence of religion in the USA can be understood in terms of *cultural transition* (Bruce 1996). In cases where societies undergo rapid and profound demographic or economic change, Bruce suggests, religion can play a critical role in helping people adjust to new conditions

and survive instability. Industrialization came relatively late to the United States and proceeded very quickly, he argues, among a population that was composed of a great diversity of ethnic groups. In the USA, religion was important in stabilizing people's identities and allowed a smoother cultural transition into the American 'melting pot'. The USA is by no means alone in placing a great deal of emphasis on the importance of religion, as figure 14.5 illustrates.

Evaluating the secularization thesis

There is little question among sociologists that, considered as a long-term trend, religion in the traditional church has declined in most Western countries – with the notable exception of the USA. The influence of religion has diminished along each of the three dimensions of secularization, much as nineteenth-century sociologists predicted it would. Should we conclude that they and later proponents of the secularization thesis were correct? Has the appeal of religion lost its grasp with the deepening of modernity? Such a conclusion would be questionable for a number of reasons.

First, the present position of religion in Britain and other Western countries is much more complex than supporters of the secularization thesis suggest. Religious and spiritual belief remain powerful and motivating forces in many people's lives, even if they do not choose to worship formally through the framework of the traditional church. Some scholars have suggested that there has been a move towards 'believing without belonging' (Davie 1994) – as we have seen in our discussion of

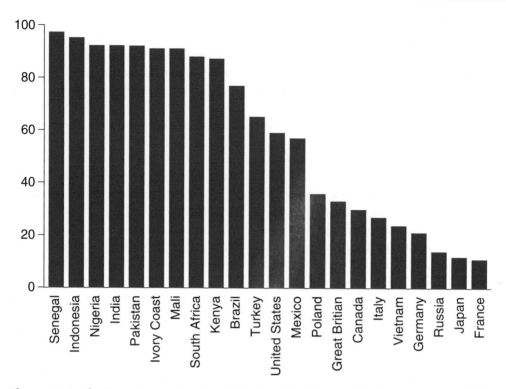

Figure 14.5 The importance given to religion in selected countries (percentage of adult population saying religion is 'very important' in their lives)

Source: Pew Research Centre (2002)

religious belief in the UK, people maintain a belief in God or a higher force, but practise and develop their faith outside institutionalized forms of religion.

Second, secularization cannot be measured according to membership in mainstream Trinitarian churches alone. To do so discounts the growing role of non-Western faiths and new religious movements, both internationally and within industrialized societies. In Britain, for example, active membership within traditional churches is falling, yet participation among Muslims, Hindus, Sikhs, Jews, evangelical 'born-again' believers and Orthodox Christians remains dynamic.

Third, there seems to be little evidence of secularization in non-Western societies. In many areas of the Middle East, Asia, Africa and India, a vital and dynamic Islamic fundamentalism challenges Westernization. When the Pope toured South America, millions of Catholics there enthusiastically followed his progress. Eastern Orthodoxy has been enthusiastically re-embraced by citizens in parts of the former Soviet Union after decades of repression of the Church by the Communist leadership. This enthusiastic support for religion around the globe is, unfortunately, mirrored by religiously inspired conflicts as well. Just as religion can be a source of solace and support, it has also been and continues to be at the origin of intense social struggles and conflicts.

One can point to evidence both in favour of and against the idea of secularization. It seems clear that secularization as a concept is most useful in explaining changes that are occurring within the traditional churches today – both in terms of declining power and influence and in regard to internal secularizing processes affecting, for example, the role of women and gays. Modernizing forces in society at large are being felt within many traditional religious institutions.

Above all, however, religion in the late modern world should be evaluated against a backdrop of rapid change, instability and diversity. Even if traditional forms of religion are receding to a degree, religion still remains a critical force in our social world. The appeal of religion, in its traditional and novel forms, is likely to be long-lasting. Religion provides many people with insights into complex questions about life and meaning that cannot be answered satisfactorily with rationalist perspectives.

It is not surprising then, that during these times of rapid change, many people look for – and find – answers and calm in religion. Fundamentalism is perhaps the clearest example of this phenomenon. Yet, increasingly, religious responses to change are occurring in new and unfamiliar forms: new religious movements, cults, sects and 'New Age' activities. While these groups may not 'look like' forms of religion on the surface, many critics of the secularization hypothesis believe that they represent transformations of religious belief in the face of profound social change.

Religious fundamentalism

The strength of religious fundamentalism is another indication that secularization has not triumphed in the modern world. The term **fundamentalism** can be applied in many different contexts to describe strict adherence to a set of principles or beliefs. *Religious fundamentalism* describes the approach taken by religious groups which call for the literal interpretation of basic scriptures or texts and believe that the doctrines which emerge from such readings should be applied to all aspects of social, economic and political life.

Religious fundamentalists believe that only one view – their own – of the world is possible and that this view is the correct one: there is no room for ambiguity or multiple interpretations. Within religious fundamentalist movements, access to the exact meanings of scriptures is restricted to a set of privileged 'interpreters' – such as priests, clergy or other religious leaders. This gives these leaders a great amount of authority – not only in religious matters, but in secular ones as well. Religious fundamentalists have become powerful political figures in opposition movements, within mainstream political parties (including in the United States) and as heads of state (for example in Iran, see chapter 20, p. 853).

Religious fundamentalism is a relatively new phenomenon – it is only in the last two to three decades that the term has entered common usage. It has arisen largely in response to globalization. As the forces of modernization progressively undermine traditional elements of the social world – such as the nuclear family and the domination of women by men – fundamentalism has arisen in defence of traditional beliefs. In a globalizing world which demands rational reasons, fundamentalism insists on faith-based answers and references to ritual truth: fundamentalism is tradition defended in a traditional way. Fundamentalism has more to do with how beliefs are defended and justified than with the content of the beliefs themselves.

Although fundamentalism sets itself in opposition to modernity, it also employs modern approaches in asserting its beliefs. Christian fundamentalists in the United States, for example, were among the first to use television as a medium for spreading their doctrines; Islamic fundamentalists fighting Russian forces in Chechnya have developed websites to set forth their views; Hindutva militants in India have used the Internet and email to promote a feeling of 'Hindu identity'.

In this section we shall examine two of the most prominent forms of religious fundamentalism. In the last thirty years, Islamic and Christian fundamentalism have both grown in strength, shaping the contours of both national and international politics.

Islamic fundamentalism

Of the early sociological thinkers, only Weber might have suspected that a traditional religious system like Islam could undergo a major revival and become the basis of important political developments in the late twentieth century; yet this is exactly what occurred in the 1980s in Iran. In recent years, Islamic revivalism has spread, with a significant impact on other countries, including Egypt, Syria, Lebanon, Algeria, Afghanistan and Nigeria. What explains this large-scale renewal of Islam?

To understand the phenomenon, we have to look both to aspects of Islam as a traditional religion and to secular changes that have affected modern states where its influence is pervasive. Islam, like Christianity, is a religion that has continually stimulated activism: the Koran – the Islamic holy scripture – is full of instructions to believers to 'struggle in the way of God'. This struggle is against both unbelievers and those who introduce corruption into the Muslim community. Over the centuries there have been successive generations of Muslim reformers, and Islam has become as internally divided as Christianity.

Shiism split from the main body of orthodox Islam early in its history and has remained influential. Shiism has been the official religion of Iran (earlier known as Persia) since the sixteenth century and was the source of the ideas behind the Iranian revolution. The Shiites trace their beginnings to Imam Ali, a seventh-century religious and political leader who is believed to have shown qualities of personal devotion to God and virtue outstanding among the worldly rulers of the time. Ali's descendants came to be seen as the rightful leaders of Islam, since they were held to belong to the prophet Muhammad's family, unlike the dynasties actually in power. The Shiites believed that the rule of Muhammad's rightful heir would eventually be instituted, doing away with the tyrannies and injustices associated with existing regimes. Muhammad's heir would be a leader directly guided by God, governing in accordance with the Koran.

There are large Shiite populations in other Middle Eastern countries, including Iraq, Turkey and Saudi Arabia, as well as in India and Pakistan. Islamic leadership in these countries, however, is in the hands

The three most prominent leaders of the Islamic revolution in Iran – Ayatollah Khomeini (in the foreground), Ayatollah Ali Khamenei and then President Hashemi Rafsanjani – look down from a poster over a street in Tehran.

Islam and the West

During the Middle Ages, there was a more or less constant struggle between Christian Europe and the Muslim states, which controlled large sections of what became Spain, Greece, Yugoslavia, Bulgaria and Romania. Most of the lands conquered by the Muslims were reclaimed by the Europeans, and many of their possessions in North Africa were in fact colonized as Western power grew in the eighteenth and nineteenth centuries. These reverses were catastrophic for Muslim religion and civilization, which Islamic believers held to be the highest and most advanced possible, transcending all others. In the late nineteenth century, the inability of the Muslim world effectively to resist the spread of Western culture led to reform movements seeking to restore Islam to its original purity and strength. A key idea was that Islam should respond to the Western challenge by affirming the identity of its own beliefs and practices.

This idea has been developed in various ways in the twentieth century, and formed a backdrop to the Islamic revolution in Iran of 1978–9. The revolution was fuelled initially by internal opposition to the Shah of Iran, who had accepted and tried to promote forms of modernization modelled on the West – for example, land reform, extending the vote to women and developing secular education. The movement that overthrew the Shah brought together people of diverse interests, by no means all of whom were attached to Islamic fundamentalism, but a dominant figure was the Ayatollah Khomeini, who provided a radical reinterpretation of Shiite ideas.

Following the revolution, Khomeini established a government organized

of the majority, the Sunni. The Sunni Muslims follow the 'Beaten Path', a series of traditions deriving from the Koran which tolerate a considerable diversity of opinion, in contrast to the more rigidly defined views of the Shiites.

according to traditional Islamic law. Religion, as specified in the Koran, became the direct basis of all political and economic life. Under Islamic law – *sharia* – as it was revived, men and women are kept rigorously segregated, women are obliged to cover their bodies and heads in public, practising homosexuals are sent to the firing squad and adulterers are stoned to death. The strict code is accompanied by a very nationalistic outlook, which sets itself especially against Western influences.

The aim of the Islamic Republic in Iran was to Islamicize the state – to organize government and society so that Islamic teachings would become dominant in all spheres. The process was by no means completed, however, and there forces emerged to act against it. Zubaida (1996) has distinguished three sets of groups now engaged in struggle with one another. The *radicals* want to carry on with and deepen the Islamic revolution. They also believe that the revolution should be actively exported to other Islamic countries. The *conservatives* are made up mostly of religious functionaries, who think that the revolution has gone far enough. It has given them a position of power in society which they wish to hold on to. The *pragmatists* favour market reforms and the opening up of the economy to foreign investment and trade. They oppose the strict imposition of Islamic codes on women, the family and the legal system.

The death of the Ayatollah Khomeini in 1989 was a blow to radical and conservative elements in Iran; his successor, Ayatollah Ali Khamenei, retains the loyalty of Iran's powerful mullahs (religious leaders), but is increasingly unpopular with average Iranian citizens, who resent the repressive regime and persistent social ills. The fault-lines within Iranian society between pragmatists and others came to the surface quite clearly under the reform-minded presidency of Mohammad Khatami (1997–2005). Khatami's administration was characterized by disputes with conservatives who largely managed to hamper Khatami's attempts at reform of Iranian society. The election of Tehran's deeply conservative mayor Mahmond Ahmadinejad, as President in 2005, decreased tensions between the country's religious and political leadership, but increased tensions with the West.

The spread of Islamic revivalism

Although the ideas underlying the Iranian revolution were supposed to unite the whole of the Islamic world against the West, governments of countries where the Shiites are in a minority have not aligned themselves closely with the situation in Iran. Yet Islamic fundamentalism has achieved significant popularity in most of these other states, and various forms of Islamic revivalism elsewhere have been stimulated by it.

Although Islamic fundamentalist movements have gained influence in many countries in North Africa, the Middle East and South Asia over the past ten to fifteen years, they have succeeded in coming to power in only two other states. Sudan has been ruled since 1989 by Hassan al-Turabi's National Salvation Front. The fundamentalist Taliban regime consolidated its hold on the fragmented state of Afghanistan in 1996 but was ousted from power at the end of 2001 by Afghan opposition forces and the US military. In many other states, Islamic fundamentalist groups have gained influence but have been prevented from rising to power. In Egypt, Turkey and Algeria, for example, Islamic fundamentalist uprisings have been suppressed by the state or the military.

Many have worried that the Islamic world is heading for a confrontation with those parts of the world that do not share its beliefs. The political scientist Samuel Huntington (1996) has argued that struggles between Western and Islamic views might become part of a worldwide 'clash of civilizations' with the ending of the Cold War and with increasing globalization. According to Huntington, the nation-state is no longer the main influence in international relations; rivalries and conflicts will therefore occur between larger cultures or civilizations.

We saw examples of such conflicts during the 1990s in the former Yugoslavia, in Bosnia and in Kosovo, where the Bosnian Muslims and Albanian Kosovars fought against the Serbs, who represent an Orthodox Christian culture. Such events have heightened awareness of Muslims as a world community; as observers have noted: 'Bosnia has become a rallying point for Muslims throughout the Muslim world. . . . [It] has created and sharpened the sense of polarization and radicalization in Muslim societies, while at the same time increasing the sense of being a Muslim' (Ahmed and Donnan 1994).

The wars in the former Yugoslavia are discussed in more detail in chapter 13, 'Race, Ethnicity and Migration', p. 499.

In the same way, the American-led war in Iraq became a rallying point for radical Muslims after the invasion in 2003. As an explanation of the causes of the terrorist attacks on New York and Washington on 11 September 2001, the American decision to oust the Islamic regime in Afghanistan and the revival of religious resistance to the US presence in Iraq after 2003, Huntington's thesis gained widespread media attention.

At the start of the twenty-first century, Islamic opposition is still building up in states such as Malaysia and Indonesia, several provinces within Nigeria have recently implemented *sharia* law, and the war in Chechnya has attracted the participation of Islamic militants who support the establishment of an Islamic state in the Caucasus. Members of Osama bin Laden's al-Qaeda terrorist network come from all over the Muslim world. Islamic symbolism and forms of dress have become important markers of identity for the growing number of Muslims living outside the Islamic world. Events such as the Gulf War and the 9/11 terrorist attacks in New York and Washington have provoked variable but intense reactions within the Islamic world either against or in response to the West.

Islamic revivalism plainly cannot be understood wholly in religious terms; it represents in part a reaction against the impact of the West and is a movement of national or cultural assertion. It is doubtful whether Islamic revivalism, even in its most fundamentalist forms, should be seen only as a renewal of traditionally held ideas. What has occurred is something more complex. Traditional practices and modes of life have been revived, but they have also been combined with concerns that relate specifically to modern times.

Christian fundamentalism

The growth of Christian fundamentalist religious organizations in the UK and

Europe, but particularly marked in the United States, is one of the most notable features of the past few decades. Fundamentalists believe that 'the Bible, quite bluntly, is a workable guidebook for politics, government, business, families, and all of the affairs of mankind' (Capps 1990). The Bible is taken as infallible by fundamentalists – its contents are expressions of the Divine Truth. Fundamentalist Christians believe in the divinity of Christ and in the possibility of the salvation of one's soul through the acceptance of Christ as personal saviour. Fundamentalist Christians are committed to spreading their message and converting those who have not yet adopted the same beliefs.

Christian fundamentalism is a reaction against liberal theology and supporters of 'secular humanism' – those who 'favour the emancipation of reason, desires and instincts in opposition to faith and obedience to God's command' (Kepel 1994). Christian fundamentalism sets itself against the 'moral crisis' wrought by modernization – the decline of the traditional family, the threat to individual morality and the weakening relationship between man and God.

In the United States, beginning with the Reverend Jerry Falwell's Moral Majority in the 1970s, some fundamentalist groups became increasingly involved in what has been termed the 'New Christian Right' in national politics, particularly in the conservative wing of the Republican Party (Simpson 1985; Woodrum 1988; Kiecolt and Nelson 1991). Falwell noted 'five major problems that have political consequences, that moral Americans should be ready to face: abortion, homosexuality, pornography, humanism, the fractured family' (in Kepel 1994). Taking concrete

In 2005, a number of Christian groups protested in an attempt to prevent the feeding and hydration tubes from being removed from Terri Schiavo, a badly brain-damaged Florida woman.

action, the New Christian Right aimed first at the nation's schools, lobbying lawmakers on the content of school curricula and trying to overturn the ban on prayer in school, and moved quickly to support Operation Rescue, the militant organization which blockades abortion clinics. Fundamentalist religious organizations are a powerful force in the USA and have helped to shape Republican Party policies and rhetoric during the Reagan and both Bush administrations.

Jerry Falwell initially blamed the 9/11 terrorist attacks on New York and Washington on 'sinners' in the USA. He commented on live television: 'I really believe that the pagans, and the abortionists, and the feminists, and the gays and the lesbians who are actively trying to make that an alternative lifestyle, the [American Civil Liberties Union], People For the American Way [both liberal organizations], all of them who have tried to secularize America. I point the finger in their face and say "you helped this happen"' (CNN, 14 September 2001). Although he later apologized for these remarks, he caused further controversy by stating that 'Mohammad was a terrorist. I read enough by both Muslims and non-Muslims [to decide] that he was a violent man, a man of war' (BBC, 13 October 2002). Again, he apologized for the remark, but it was too late to stop sectarian rioting between Hindus and Muslims reacting against his claims in Solapur, Western India, which left at least eight people dead. Not surprisingly, his comments led to widespread condemnation from Islamic leaders around the world.

Prominent preachers on the New Christian Right have founded a number of universities to produce a new generation of 'counter-elite' schooled in fundamentalist Christian beliefs and able to take up prominent positions in the media, academia, politics and the arts. Liberty University (founded by Jerry Falwell), Oral Roberts University, Bob Jones University and others confer degrees in standard academic disciplines, taught within the framework of biblical infallibility. On campus, strict ethical standards are maintained within students' private lives and sexuality is channelled towards marriage alone:

> To anybody who has spent some time on the Liberty campus, it is a striking spectacle. The dormitories are single-sex, and strict surveillance, a mixture of coercion and self-discipline, is practised. French kissing is forbidden, and any sexual relations between unmarried students are punished by expulsion. (Married couples live in town.) But kissing on the cheek is permitted, and couples are free to hold hands, though not to put an arm round the partner's waist. Students willingly defend this sexual self-discipline when questioned about it by a visiting stranger; they maintain total repression would be bound to lead to deviant practices, in particular to homosexuality, which (they say) is rife in a rival Fundamentalist university in which all flirting is forbidden. On the other hand, the expression of sexual desire would go against the spirit of the educational aims of the university.
>
> (Kepel 1994)

The Christian fundamentalist movement in the United States draws support from across the country, but there is a strong regional element. The American South has become known as the 'Bible Belt' – a swath of land located below the agricultural 'cattle belt', 'maize belt' and 'cotton belt'. Many of America's best-known and most influential evangelists are based in the southern and mid-western states of Virginia, Oklahoma and North Carolina. The most influential fundamentalist groups in the United States are the Southern Baptist Convention, the Assemblies of God, and the Seventh-Day Adventists.

Conclusion

In a globalizing age that is in desperate need of mutual understanding and dialogue, religious fundamentalism can be a destructive force. Fundamentalism is edged with the possibility of violence – in the cases of Islamic and Christian fundamentalism, examples of violence inspired by religious allegiance are not uncommon. There have been a number of violent clashes over the past few years between Islamic and Christian groups in Lebanon, Indonesia and other countries. Yet in an increasingly cosmopolitan world, people of contrasting traditions and beliefs are coming into contact with one another more than ever before. As the unquestioning acceptance of traditional ideas declines, we must all live in a more open and reflective way – discussion and dialogue are essential between people of differing beliefs. They are the main way in which violence can be controlled or dissolved.

Summary points

1 Religion exists in all known societies, although religious beliefs and practices vary from culture to culture. All religions involve a set of symbols, involving feelings of reverence, linked to rituals practised by a community of believers.

2 Sociological approaches to religion have been most influenced by the ideas of the three 'classical' thinkers: Marx, Durkheim and Weber. All held that religion is in a fundamental sense an illusion and that the 'other' world which religion creates is our world, distorted through the lens of religious symbolism. However, each viewed the role of religion in society very differently:

   • to Marx, religion contains a strong ideological element: religion provides justification for the inequalities of wealth and power found in society;

   • to Durkheim, religion is important because of the cohesive functions it serves, especially in ensuring that people meet regularly to affirm common beliefs and values;

   • to Weber, religion is important because of the role it plays in social change, particularly the development of Western capitalism.

3 Totemism and animism are common types of religion in smaller cultures. In totemism, a species of animal or plant is perceived as possessing supernatural powers. Animism means a belief in spirits or ghosts, populating the same world as human beings, sometimes possessing them.

4 The three most influential monotheistic religions (religions in which there is only one God) in world history are Judaism, Christianity and Islam. Polytheism (belief in several or many gods) is common in other religions. In some religions, like Confucianism, there are no gods or supernatural beings.

5 Churches are large and established religious bodies, normally with a formal bureaucratic structure and a hierarchy of religious officials. Sects are smaller, less formal groups of believers, usually set up to revive an established church. If a sect survives over a period of time and becomes institutionalized, it is called a denomination. Cults resemble sects, but are more loosely knit groups, which follow similar practices, but not within formal organizations.

6 Secularization refers to the declining influence of religion. Measuring the level of

secularization is complicated, because several dimensions of change are involved: level of membership of religious organizations, their social status, and people's personal religiosity. Although the influence of religion has definitely declined, religion is certainly not on the verge of disappearing, and continues to unite as well as to divide people in the modern world.

7 Rates of regular church attendance in the UK and most other European countries are low. In the United States, by contrast, a much higher proportion of the population goes to church regularly. Far more people in the UK, Europe and the USA say they believe in God than attend church regularly.

8 Although traditional churches have been experiencing a decline in membership in recent decades, many new religious movements have emerged alongside mainstream religions. New religious movements encompass a broad range of religious and spiritual groups, cults and sects. They can be broadly divided into world-affirming movements, which are akin to self-help groups; world-rejecting movements, which withdraw from and criticize the outside world; and world-accommodating movements, which emphasize inner religious life over worldly concerns.

9 Fundamentalism has become common among some believers in different religious groups across the world. 'Fundamentalists' are called this because they believe in returning to the fundamentals of their religious doctrines. Islamic fundamentalism has affected many countries in the Middle East following the 1979 Islamic revolution in Iran which set up a religiously inspired government. Christian fundamentalism in the United States is a reaction against secular values and a perceived moral crisis in American society. In their efforts to convert non-believers, fundamentalist Christians have pioneered the 'electronic church' – the use of television, radio and new technologies to build a following.

Questions for further thought

1 Can miracles happen in the modern world?

2 How can a religion be distinguished from a political or moral belief system?

3 Is religion likely to mean something different to women than it does to men?

4 In what ways can religion be a force for both social stability and social change?

5 How reasonable is it to characterize religiosity in Britain or the United States as 'believing without belonging'?

6 What is it about the modern world which has given rise to the growth of new religious movements?

Further reading

Alan Aldridge, *Religion in the Contemporary World: A Sociological Introduction* (Cambridge: Polity, 2000).

Eileen Barker and Margit Warburg (eds), *New Religions and New Religiosity* (Aarhus: Aarhus University Press, 1998).

Grace Davie, *Religion in Modern Europe: A Memory Mutates* (New York: Oxford University Press, 2000).

Malcolm Hamilton, *The Sociology of Religion: Theoretical and Comparative Perspectives* (London: Routledge, 2001).

Stephen J. Hunt, *Religion in Western Society* (New York: Palgrave, 2002).

Hugh McLeod, *Religion and the People of Western Europe, 1789–1989* (Oxford: Oxford University Press, 1997).

Phillip Sutton and Stephen Vertigans, *Resurgent Islam: A Sociological Approach* (Cambridge: Polity, 2005).

David Westerlund (ed.), *Questioning the Secular State: The Worldwide Resurgence of Religion in Politics* (London: C. Hurst, 1996).

Internet links

Academic Info Religion Gateway
http://www.academicinfo.net/religindex.html

American Religion Data Archive
http://www.thearda.com/

Journal for Cultural and Religious Theory (online)
http://www.jcrt.org

BBC Religion Pages
http://www.bbc.co.uk/religion

Religious Tolerance
http://www.religioustolerance.org

Contents

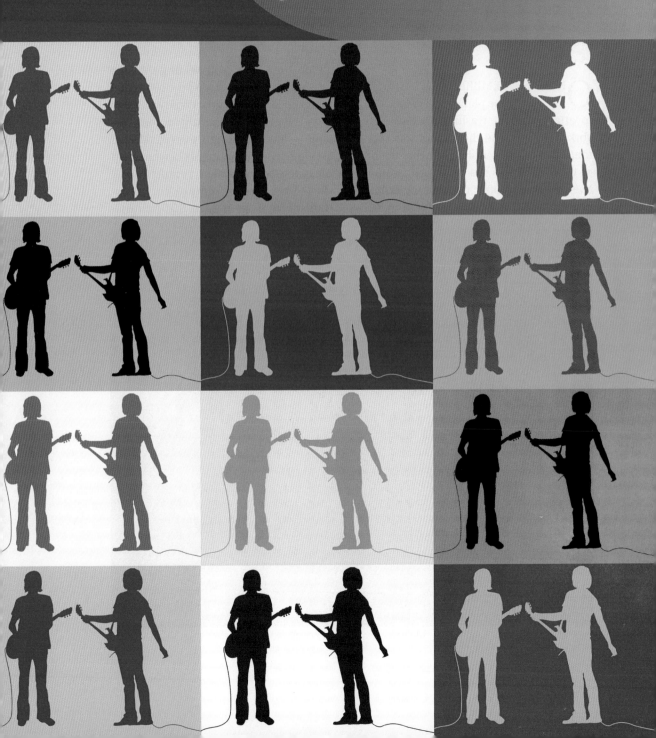

15 The Media

ON 11 SEPTEMBER 2001, terrorists hijacked three planes and used them to attack sites in Washington and New York. The timing of the attacks was such that when a plane crashed into the second of the Twin Towers in New York, around twenty minutes after the first tower had been struck, it is estimated that a global audience of two billion watched the incident on television in real time. Almost 140 years earlier, in 1865, the actor John Wilkes Booth assassinated US President Abraham Lincoln in a Washington theatre. It took twelve days before the news reached London. The ship carrying the message from the United States was met by a smaller boat off the south coast of Ireland and the news was telegraphed to London from Cork, still beating the ship by three days. (It wasn't until the 1950s that a dedicated trans-oceanic cable existed to carry telegraphs instantly across the Atlantic – although long-wave radio trans-mission between continents became pos-sible in the early twentieth century.)

In the twenty-first century, communi-cations technology is such that informa-

Do you know Osama Bin Laden's face better than that of your next-door neighbour?

more by the type of the media than by the content, or the messages, which the media convey. A society in which satellite television plays an important part, for example, is obviously a very different medium from one that relies on the printed word carried aboard an ocean liner. Everyday life is experienced differently in a society in which the television, relaying news instantaneously from one side of the globe to the other, plays an important role to one that relies on horses, ships or the telegraph wire, for example. The electronic media, according to McLuhan, are creating a **global village** – people throughout the world see major events unfold and hence participate in them together. For billions of people around the world the image of Osama Bin Laden, the man blamed for masterminding the terrorist attacks on New York and Washington, is more instantly recognizable to them than their next-door neighbour.

We live today in an interconnected world in which people experience the same events from many different places. Thanks to globalization and the power of communications technology, people from Caracas to Cairo are able to receive the same popular music, news, films and television programmes. Twenty-four-hour news channels report on stories as they occur and broadcast coverage of the unfolding events for the rest of the world to see. Films made in Hollywood or Hong Kong reach audiences around the world, while celebrities such as David Beckham and Tiger Woods have become household names on every continent.

For several decades, we have been witnessing a process of convergence in the production, distribution and consumption of information. Whereas at one time

tion can be shared instantaneously, and by millions of people simultaneously, almost anywhere around the world. **Communication** – the transfer of information from one individual or group to another, whether in speech or through the mass media of modern times – is crucial to any society. One influential early theorist of communication media was the Canadian author Marshall McLuhan. According to McLuhan, 'the medium is the message'. That is to say, society is influenced much ways of communicating, such as print, television and film, were relatively self-contained spheres, they have now become intertwined to a remarkable degree. The divisions between forms of communication are no longer as dramatic as they once were: television, radio, newspapers and telephones are undergoing profound transformations as a result of advances in technology and the rapid spread of the Internet. While newspapers remain central to our lives, the ways they are organized and deliver their services are changing. Newspapers can be read online, mobile telephone use is exploding, and digital television and satellite broadcasting services allow an unprecedented diversity of choice for viewing audiences. It is the Internet, however, that is at the heart of this communications revolution. With the expansion of technologies such as voice recognition, broadband transmission, web casting and cable links, the Internet threatens to erase the distinctions between traditional forms of media and to become the conduit for the delivery of information, entertainment, advertising and commerce to media audiences.

In this chapter, we'll study the transformations affecting mass media and communications as part of globalization. The **mass media** include a wide variety of forms, including television, newspapers, films, magazines, radio, advertisements, video games and CDs. These are referred to as 'mass' media because they reach mass audiences – audiences comprised of very large numbers of people.

We begin the study of the mass media by considering some of the forms it can take. We discuss older, more traditional forms of media, such as the press, cinema, radio and television, before looking at the recent development of new forms of media like the Internet. Second, we shall explore some of the key theoretical perspectives on the media. Next, we look at the some of the issues surrounding mass media and society, such as bias, the effects of the media and audiences. Last, we look at the development of the mass media in a global age.

Traditional and new media

An important precursor to the mass media was the invention of the printing press in the mid-fifteenth century, which made the high-speed reproduction of texts possible for the first time. Yet, although technological advances played a crucial part in the development of the mass media, the influence of social, cultural and economic factors must also be taken into account. The mass media could only develop in societies with a relatively free press and an educated and wealthy enough population to take advantage of it. In the last few years, new technologies, such as the Internet, have revolutionized the mass media and wider society too. In the next section we look at the development of new forms of media; first, we examine the rise of the mass media in the UK, by looking at briefly at the press, film, radio and television.

Traditional media

The press

The development of the press in Britain during the nineteenth century occurred at a time of political and social unrest. The government exerted its control over the emerging newspaper industry through strict laws on libel and sedition, which prevented political agitation; at the same time, a stamp tax was imposed to ensure that newspapers were only affordable by the well-off. The stamp tax had unintended consequences, as illegal and inexpensive pamphlets emerged, spreading radical views amongst the newly industrial working class. The biggest of these pamphlets, such as William Cobbett's weekly *Political Register*, outsold the official, 'stamped' press many times over (Hall 1982).

The stamp tax – condemned by its opponents as a 'tax on knowledge' – was finally repealed in 1855 after a series of reductions, leading many writers to hail a golden era of British journalism marked by a 'transition from official to popular control' (Koss 1973). An alternative view was put forward by James Curran and Jean Seaton challenged this view in their historical account of the British press, *Power Without Responsibility* (2003). They saw the repeal of the stamp tax as an attempt to break the popularity of the radical press and to boost the sales of more 'respectable' newspapers. For Curran and Seaton the repeal of the stamp tax did not introduce a new era of press freedom, but a time of repression and ideological control, this time by market forces rather than government. (The issue of media control is discussed below, pp. 615–20.)

The newspaper was a fundamentally important development in the history of modern media, because it packaged many different types of information in a limited and easily reproducible format. Newspapers contained in a single package information on current affairs, entertainment and consumer goods. The cheap daily press was pioneered in the United States.

The one-cent daily paper was originally established in New York and then copied in other major eastern US cities. By the early 1900s there were city or regional newspapers covering most of the American states; in contrast to the smaller countries of Europe, national newspapers did not develop. The invention of cheap newsprint was the key to the mass diffusion of newspapers from the late nineteenth century onwards.

Curran and Seaton have noted that extra revenue from advertising enabled the cover prices to fall dramatically during this period, making the newspaper affordable for all. They also argue that advertising undermined the radical press as advertisers tended to place announcements in papers to which they were politically sympathetic, and to select papers with a smaller circulation and a wealthy readership, rather than radical papers with a higher circulation which sold to readers who would be unlikely to afford the product advertised (Curran and Seaton 2003).

By the early twentieth century new types of national newspaper had emerged in the UK, such as the *Daily Mail*, *Daily Express, Mirror* and the *News of the World*, selling a mixture of news, entertainment and patriotism to a largely working-class readership. *The Times* and *Daily Telegraph* provided more serious news analysis for wealthier readers. Ownership of much of the news media by this stage was concentrated amongst a handful of rich entrepreneurs. By the 1930s Lords Beaverbrook, Camrose, Kemsley and Rothermere owned 50 per cent of British national and local daily papers and 30 per cent of the Sunday papers. Critics have argued that the 'press barons', as they became known, used their ownership of national newspapers to promote their own political causes and ambitions (Curran and Seaton 2003). (We discuss the issue of media ownership further below: see pp. 599–601.)

For half a century or more, newspapers were the chief way of conveying information quickly and comprehensively to a mass public. Their influence has waned with the rise of radio, cinema and – much more important – television and, increasingly, the Internet. Figures for newspaper readership suggest that the proportion of people who read a national daily paper in Britain has declined since the early 1980s. Among men, the proportion of daily newspaper readers dropped from 76 per cent in 1981 to 60 per cent in 1998–9; readership levels are somewhat lower among women, but a similar drop – from 68 per cent to 51 per cent – has taken place (HMSO 2000).

Online communication might well bite further into newspaper circulation. News information is now available online almost instantaneously and is constantly updated during the course of the day. Many newspapers can also be accessed and read online free of charge.

Film

The first film to be shown to paying customers was in 1895 in Paris, France, where the Lumière brothers' *Arrival of the Train in La Ciotat Station* caused viewers to flee from their seats as the screen slowly filled with an oncoming steam engine. Whilst the print media in the UK developed slowly over many decades, film and the cinema arrived much faster. The first cinema in the UK opened in 1896 and by 1914 there were more than five hundred in London alone. Cinema tickets could be afforded by all classes and the decline in working hours and rise in unemployment in the late 1920s meant the cinema-goers soon formed a mass audience.

Audience demands were soon leading cinemas to screen two new programmes a week, each consisting of two films, a B-movie and the main feature. The demand for new films led studios to churn out productions to tight schedules. These films tended to be formulaic and created by bureaucratic organizations with a high degree of specialization and division of labour.

Bureaucracy is further discussed in chapter 16, 'Organizations and Networks', pp. 638–46.)

As the industry became more commercialized a 'star system' emerged, with studios encouraging interest in the personal lives of actors like Mary Pickford and Rudolf Valentino, whose appearance in a film would ensure a box-office hit.

By 1925, 95 per cent of the films shown in the UK were American. Cinemas were increasingly controlled by the American studios which owned the distribution rights to films. The studios could oblige cinemas to bulk-buy future productions, effectively freezing out competitors. As with the print media, ownership had become largely concentrated amongst a few large corporations. The American production of the films raises questions about cultural imperialism and the mass media, which we return to below (see pp. 626–30).

Radio and television

As audiences, we interact differently with the radio and television from how we do with the cinema. Radio and television

Paul Julius Reuter initiated a prototype news service in Paris in 1849, using carrier pigeons as well as the electric telegraph in his network. By 1923, the company he founded, Reuters, was transmitting news by radio.

enters the household in a way that the cinema cannot. Neither do these media demand the attention that film does. Listening to the radio, in particular, is com-bined with other activities in the everyday lives of its audience – most radio is listened to in the morning as part of the ritual of preparation for the day. Television and radio also have an immediacy which film does not: they can report events, as they did the terrorist attacks in the USA in September 2001, from almost anywhere in the world to a mass audience as they happen.

In the UK, radio was quickly taken under the control of a public monopoly, which by 1926 had become known as the British Broadcasting Corporation (BBC). Radio provided the organizational model for television broadcasting in the UK, and the BBC remains a public organization to this day, funded by licence fees charged to every household that owns a television set. For some years the BBC was the only organization permitted to broadcast either radio or television programmes in the UK. This policy was relaxed with the introduction of commercial television in the 1950s – dependent on advertising for its revenue, rather than the licence fee – and later a host of commercial radio stations.

The first Director-General of the BBC, John Reith (later Lord Reith), a strict Presbyterian Christian, imposed his values rigidily on the organization. To Reith the purpose of the BBC was to 'inform, educate and entertain'; it could be added, in that order. As the historian A. J. P. Taylor has written, Reith used 'the brute force of monopoly to stamp Christian morality on the British people' (cited in Curran and Seaton 2003). It was during this period that the distinctive role of the BBC as a public-service broadcaster developed. (The future of public service broadcasting in the UK is discussed further on p. 614.)

The number of television sets in the UK

and the amount of time that people spend viewing them increased dramatically from the 1950s onwards. Television now dominates the other media. If the current trends in TV watching continue, by the age of eighteen the average child born today will have spent more time watching television than in any other activity except sleep. Virtually every household now possesses a TV set. In the UK, every day around 85 per cent of adults watch television (HMSO 2004), and the average set is switched on for between three and six hours per day. Much the same is true in other West European countries and in the USA. Individuals aged four and over in the UK watch an average of twenty-five hours of television a week. Older people watch twice as much television as children, perhaps because they are not in school and go to bed later in the evening, and people from lower social classes watch more than those from the top three social classes (see figure 15.1).

Television and social life

Several media theorists have been highly sceptical about the effects that a seemingly ever-increasing diet of television has had on the population: two well-known accounts have been provided by Robert Putnam in his recent works on social capital and Neil Postman (1931–2003) in his tellingly titled book, *Amusing Ourselves to Death: Public Discourse in the Age of Show Business* (1985).

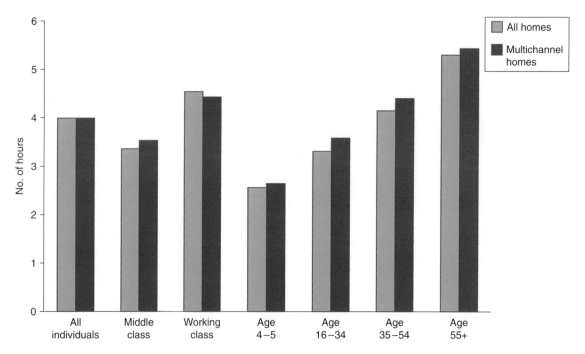

Figure 15.1   Number of hours of television viewed per household per day, by age and social class, January–March 2003

Source: Adapted from Ofcom (2003), p. 32

To Postman, television presents serious issues as entertainment because, in his phrase, 'the form excludes the content'. By this, he means that television as 'the form' is a medium that is incapable of sustaining serious 'content'. For Postman, rational argument is best carried on in the form of the printed word, which is capable of sustaining complex and serious content. He harks back to the nineteenth century as an 'age of reason', when the written word was dominant. Postman's argument contains some similarities with Marshall McLuhan's claim that 'the medium is the message' (see p. 585), although Postman is much more sceptical than McLuhan about the benefits of electronic media. To Postman, the medium of print creates a rational population, whereas the medium of television creates an entertained one. In a society dominated by the television, news, education and politics are all reduced to entertainment, so that we are, as the title of his book indicates, doing nothing more than 'amusing ourselves to death'.

Although Postman's book is fiercely argued, it has been criticized as being based on impression rather than empirical research. This criticism cannot be levelled at the work of the American political theorist Robert Putnam.

Putnam's thesis on the decline of 'social capital' is examined in more detail in chapter 16, 'Organizations and Networks', pp. 675–9.

By **social capital**, as we have seen, Putnam is referring to useful social networks, a sense of mutual obligation and trustworthiness, an understanding of the norms that govern effective behaviour and, in general, other social resources that enable people to act effectively. Putnam's account, put forward in his book *Bowling Alone* (2000) and elsewhere, is based on research in the United States, where he finds significant decline in social capital over the last few decades. Putnam (1996) suggests a culprit for that decline: television.

Putnam points out that in 1950, around the time measures of social capital peaked, barely 10 per cent of Americans had a television set in their homes; by 1959, this figure had risen to 90 per cent. Studies estimate that the average American now watches roughly four hours of TV every day (not including periods when television is merely playing in the background). A conservative estimate of television viewing in the USA means that this one activity now absorbs around 40 per cent of the average American's free time. Putnam notes that this massive change in the way Americans spend their lives coincided precisely with the years of declining social capital.

Putnam argues that the link between mass television watching and the erosion of social capital is not merely circumstantial. Taking other facts into consideration, such as education, age and gender, TV viewing is strongly and negatively related to social trust and group membership. Using the same criteria, the correlation of newspaper reading to social trust and group membership is positive.

One reason Putnam suggests for why TV viewing erodes social capital is the effect of programme content on viewers. For example, studies suggest that heavy watchers of TV are unusually sceptical about the benevolence of other people – by overestimating crime rates for example. Putnam concludes: 'Just as the erosion of the ozone layer was detected only many years after the proliferation of the chlorofluorocarbons that caused it, so too the erosion of America's social capital became visible only several decades after the underlying process had begun.' Although Putnam warns against nostalgia for the 1950s, he argues that it is time for critical reflection on the effects of technologies on our lives (Putnam 1995).

New media

In his book *Being Digital* (1995), the founder of the media laboratory at the Massachusetts Institute of Technology, Nicholas Negroponte, analyses the profound importance of digital data in current communications technologies. Any piece of information, including pictures, moving images and sounds, can be translated through a binary system into 'bits'. A bit is either 1 or 0. For instance, the digital representation of 1, 2, 3, 4, 5, is 1, 10, 11, 100, 101, etc. Digitization – and speed – is at the origin of the development of multimedia: what used to be different media needing different technologies (such as visuals and sound) can now be combined on a single medium (DVD and PCs, etc.). In recent years the processing power of computers has doubled every eighteen months. This means, for example, that it is now possible to watch films and listen to music via the Internet. Digitization also permits the development of interactive media, allowing individuals actively to participate in, or structure, what they see or hear. In this section we examine the profound impact that digitization has had on the media.

Digital television

Since the beginning of the twenty-first century, television broadcasting technology has been undergoing a revolution, with the transfer of programme transmission from analogue to digital. Analogue TV is the 'old' system of broadcasting that has been used to transmit signals to television sets around the country since the 1940s. It converts sound and pictures into waves, which are transmitted through the air and picked up by the aerial on the roof of the house or on top of the television.

Digital TV works by transforming pictures and sound into information that is understood by a computer. Digital transmissions are received in three ways: through the TV aerial and a decoder (often a set-top box), via a satellite dish or via cable. The television acts like a computer and converts this information back into pictures and sound. Broadcasters and service providers argue that digital television not only means more channels, but also a better quality of sound and pictures and additional services. Digital TV offers the possibility of, for instance, interactive television, the Internet, home shopping and home banking. The arrival of digital TV has also created the possibility of single units that merge the personal computer with the television, although these are not yet widely in use.

In the UK, the government hopes that all viewers will have transferred from analogue to digital television by 2012, when the transmission of television on analogue frequencies is expected to stop. All transmissions from then on will be digital. By 2004, one-third of UK households had already switched to digital television.

The number of television channels available to British audiences has been increasing as a result of advances in satellite, cable and digital technology. In 2003, one service provider, Sky, offered a

Digital and satellite television gives viewers a seemingly endless choice of viewing.

monthly subscription package that gave the viewer a choice of 187 channels. The introduction of digital television on to the UK commercial market in 1998 greatly increased the proportion of viewers subscribing to pay television. In 2003, 26 per cent of British households subscribed to satellite television, while 9 per cent subscribed to cable television (Ofcom 2003)

The Internet

Although we have concentrated so far on newspapers, film and television, the media cannot be thought of only in those terms. One of the most fundamental aspects of the media concerns the very infrastructure through which information is communicated and exchanged. Some important technological advances during the second half of the twentieth century have completely transformed the face of **telecommunications** – the communication of information, sounds or images at a distance through a technological medium.

New communications technologies stand, for example, behind profound changes in the world's money systems and stock markets. Money is no longer gold, or the cash in your pocket. More and more, money has become electronic, stored in computers in the world's banks. The value of whatever cash you do happen to have in your pocket is determined by the activities of traders on electronically linked money markets. Such markets have been created only over the last few decades: they are the product of a marriage between computers and satellite communication technology. 'Technology', it has been said, 'is rapidly turning the stock exchange into a seamless global market, open 24 hours a day' (Gibbons 1990).

Four technological trends have contributed to these developments: first, the constant improvement in the capabilities of computers, together with declining costs; second, digitization of data (discussed in relation to television on pp. 494–5), making possible the integration of computer and telecommunications technologies; third, satellite communications development; and fourth, fibre optics, which allow many different messages to travel down a single small cable. The dramatic communications explosion of recent years shows no signs of slowing down.

The origins of the Internet

By the early 1990s, it was becoming clear that the future lay not with the individual personal computer (PC) but with a global system of interconnected computers – the **Internet**. Although many computer users may not have realized it at the time, the PC was quickly to become little more than a point of access to events happening elsewhere – events happening on a network stretching across the planet, a network that is not owned by any individual or company.

> The potential of the Internet for the growth of international activism is explored in chapter 20, 'Politics, Government and Terrorism', pp. 870–1.

The Internet originated during the Cold War period that preceded 1989. The 'Net' developed out of a system used in the Pen-

tagon, the headquarters of the American military, from 1969. This system was first of all named the ARPA net, after the Pentagon's Advanced Research Projects Agency. The aim was limited. The ARPA sought to allow scientists working on military contracts in different parts of America to pool their resources and to share the expensive equipment they were using. Almost as an afterthought, its originators thought up a way of sending messages too – thus electronic mail, 'email', was born.

The Pentagon Internet consisted of five hundred computers until the early 1980s, all located in military laboratories and university computer science departments. Other people in universities then started catching on, and began using the system for their own purposes. By 1987 the Internet had expanded to include 28,000 host computers, at many different universities and research labs.

The spread of commercial Internet service providers (ISPs) that offer dial-up, and later broadband, access through modems has fuelled the growing proportion of households with online capabilities. Online services, electronic bulletin boards, chat-rooms and software libraries were put onto the net by a bewildering variety of people, initially mainly situated in the United States, but now all over the world. Corporations also got in on the act. In 1994 companies overtook universities as the dominant users of the network.

The best-known use of the Internet is the World Wide Web (www). Indeed, like a cuckoo in a nest, it threatens to take over its host. The web is in effect a global multimedia library. It was invented by a software engineer at a Swiss physics lab in 1990; the software that popularized it across the world was written by an under-

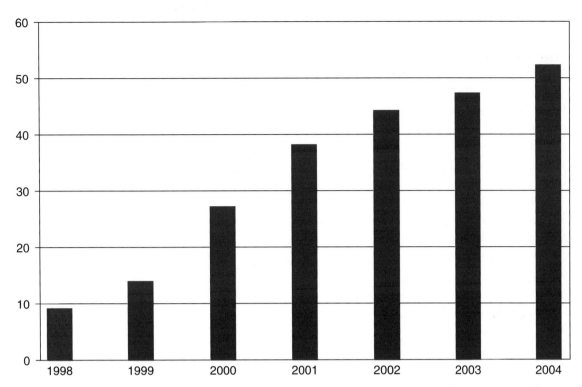

Figure 15.2 Households in the UK with home Internet access, 1998–2004 (%)

Source: National Statistics Online (2004)

graduate at the University of Illinois. Users generally navigate the web with the help of an Internet 'browser' – a software program that allows individuals to search for information, locate particular sites or web pages, and mark those pages for future reference. Through the web, it is possible to download a wide variety of documents and programs, from government policy papers to anti-virus software to computer games. As websites have grown in sophistication, they have become a feast for the senses. Many are adorned with intricate graphics and photographs, or contain video and audio files. The web also serves as the main interface for 'e-commerce' – business transactions conducted online.

With the spread of home-based personal computers access to the Internet in the UK has grown considerably in recent years. By the second quarter of 2004, 52 per cent of households in the UK (12.8 million) could access the Internet from home, compared with just 9 per cent (2.2 million) in the same quarter of 1998 – see figure 15.2.

According to a survey by the National Office of Statistics, the most common use of the Internet among UK adults who had used it during the previous three months was email (85 per cent) and finding information about goods or services (82 per cent). The most frequent place of access was the person's own home (82 per cent), followed by their workplace (42 per cent).

Table 15.1   Internet users around the world: per 1,000 people (2002)

All developing countries	40.9
Least developed countries	2.8
Arab States	28.0
East Asia and the Pacific	60.9
Latin America and the Caribbean	81.2
South Asia	14.9
Sub-Saharan Africa	9.6
Central and Eastern Europe and the CIS	71.8
OECD	383.1
High-income OECD	450.5
High human development	382.6
Medium human development	37.3
Low human development	5.9
High income	445.8
Middle income	59.5
Low income	13.0
World	99.4

Source: UNDP (2004)

In July 2004, 37 per cent of adults had never used the Internet (HMSO 2004).

How many people are actually connected to the Internet globally is unknown, but the United Nations estimates that by 2000 around 10 per cent of the world's population were Internet users – and that number is rising fast. However, this access to the Internet is highly uneven (see table 15.1). In 2002, although 45 per cent of people in high-income countries, such as those in Western Europe or North America, were classed as Internet users, only around 1.3 per cent of people in low-income countries, which includes much of Africa, were classified as such.

The impact of the Internet

In a world of quite stunning technological change, no one can be sure what the future holds. Many see the Internet as exemplifying the new global order emerging at the close of the twentieth century. Exchanges on the Internet take place in cyberspace. **Cyberspace** means the space of interaction formed by the global network of computers that compose the Internet. In cyberspace, we are no longer 'people', but messages on one another's screens. The Internet provides no certainty about other people's identity, whether they are male or female, or where they are. There is a famous cartoon about the Internet, which has a dog sitting in front of a computer. The caption reads: 'The great thing about the Internet is that no one knows you are a dog.'

The spread of the Internet across the globe has raised important questions for sociologists. The Internet is transforming the contours of daily life – blurring the boundaries between the global and local, presenting new channels for communication and interaction, and allowing more and more everyday tasks to be carried out online. Yet at the same time as it provides exciting new opportunities to explore the social world, the Internet also threatens to undermine human relationships and communities. Although the 'information age' is still in its early stages, many sociologists are already debating the complex implications of the Internet for late modern societies.

Opinions on the effects of the Internet on social interaction fall into two broad categories. On the one hand are those observers who see the online world as fostering new forms of electronic relationship that either enhance or supplement existing face-to-face interactions. While travelling or working abroad, individuals can use the Internet to communicate regularly with friends and relatives at home. Distance and separation become more tolerable. The Internet also allows the formation of new types of relationship: 'anonymous' online users can meet in 'chat-rooms' and discuss topics of mutual interest. These cyber contacts sometimes evolve into fully fledged electronic friendships or even result in face-to-face meetings. Many Internet users become part of lively online communities that are qualitatively different from those they inhabit in the physical world. Scholars who see the Internet as a positive addition to human interaction argue that it expands and enriches people's social networks.

On the other hand, not everyone takes such an enthusiastic outlook. As people spend more and more time communicating online and handling their daily tasks in cyberspace, it may be that they spend less time interacting with one another in the physical world. Some sociologists fear that the spread of Internet technology will lead to increased social isolation and atomization. They argue that one effect of increasing Internet access in households is that people are spending less 'quality time' with their families and friends. The Internet is encroaching on domestic life as the lines between work and home are blurred: many employees continue to work at home after hours – checking email or finishing tasks that they were unable to complete during the day. Human contact is reduced, personal relationships suffer, traditional forms of entertainment such as the theatre and books fall by the wayside, and the fabric of social life is weakened.

The Internet also raises challenging questions about personal identity, creates new forms of community and new possibilities for democratic participation. These issues are discussed in chapter 5, 'Social Interaction and Everyday Life', pp. 154–7.

How are we to evaluate these contrasting positions? Most certainly, there are elements of truth on both sides of the debate. The Internet is undoubtedly broadening our horizons and presents unprecedented opportunities for making contact with others. Yet the frenzied pace at which it is expanding also presents challenges and threats to traditional forms of human interaction. Will the Internet radically transform society into a fragmented, impersonal realm where humans rarely venture out of their homes and lose their ability to communicate? It seems unlikely. About fifty years ago, very similar fears were expressed as television burst onto the media scene. In *The Lonely Crowd* (1961), an influential sociological analysis of American society in the 1950s, David Riesman and his colleagues expressed concern about the effects of TV on family and community life. While some of their fears were well placed, television and the mass media have also enriched the social world in many ways.

Just as with television before it, the Internet has aroused both hopes and the fears. Will we lose our identities in cyberspace? Will computerized technology dominate us, rather than the reverse? Will human beings retreat into an anti-social online world? The answer to each of these questions, fortunately, is almost certainly 'no'. As we saw earlier in the discussion on the 'compulsion of proximity' in chapter 5 (pp. 157–8), people don't use video conferencing if they can get together with others in an ordinary way. Business executives have far more forms of electronic communication available to them than ever before. At the same time, the number of face-to-face business conferences has shot up.

The sociologist Manuel Castells argues that the Internet will continue to grow because it allows networks to flourish. For Castells, networks are the defining organizational structure of our age.

> Castells' work is discussed in more detail in chapter 16, 'Organizations and Networks', pp. 671–3.

The inherent flexibility and adaptability of networks give them enormous advantages over older types of rational, hierarchical organizations. Castells argues that the Internet gives businesses the capability for global coordination of decentralized and highly complex activities. For individuals, the Internet will enable new combinations of work and self-employment, individual expression, collaboration and sociability, and for political activists it will make it possible for networks of individuals to combine and co-operate and spread their message around the world. Playing on McLuhan's idea that 'the medium is the message', Castells argues that now, 'the network is the message' (2001).

Theoretical perspectives on the media

In this section we examine two of the most influential theoretical approaches to the study of the mass media – functionalism and conflict theory – and introduce some of the important recent contributions to the debate.

Functionalism

In the mid-twentieth century, functionalist theorists such as Charles Wright and Harold Laswell focused on the ways in which the media function in integrating society (Wright 1960; Laswell 1960).

> Functionalist thought was introduced in chapter 1, 'What is Sociology?', pp. 20–2.

Following the media theorist Denis McQuail (2000), several of the most important social functions of the media are reviewed below:

1 *Information*   The media provides us with a continuous flow of information about the world, from webcams and radio reports that alert us to traffic jams, to rolling weather reports, the stock market and news stories about issues that affect us personally.

2 *Correlation*   The media explains, and helps us to understand the meaning of the information it gives us. It provides support for established social norms and has an important role in the socialization of children. (Socialization is discussed further in chapter 6.)

3 *Continuity*   The media has a function in expressing the dominant culture, recognizing new social developments and forging common values.

4 *Entertainment*   The media provides amusement, diversion and reduces social tension.

5 *Mobilization*   To encourage economic development, work, religion or support in times of war, the media can campaign to mobilize society to meet these objectives.

In recent decades functionalist theories of the media have fallen into decline. In particular, they were criticized for viewing the audience as passive recipients rather than active interpreters of a media message. (More recent and sophisticated accounts of audience response are discussed below, pp. 608–10.) Furthermore, functionalism has been dismissed for doing nothing more than describing the media, rather than explaining it. As functionalist theories of the media declined in popularity, other forms of analysis came to the fore, in particular conflict approaches influenced by Marxism.

Conflict theories

In Europe, conflict approaches to the mass media have been popular. Below, we look at two of the most important theories of the media from a broadly Marxist standpoint: the political economy approach and the cultural industry approach. Other approaches that have been influential within this framework include the work of the Glasgow Media Group (which we examine on pp. 606–8).

Political economy approaches

Political economy approaches view the media as an industry, and examine the way in which the major means of communication have come to be owned by private interests. The ownership of the media has often been concentrated in the hands of a few wealthy media magnates – the dominance of the press barons in the pre-war British press (discussed on pp. 587–8) provides one example. In the global age, the ownership of the media crosses national borders. Below, we profile the Australian-born media mogul Rupert Murdoch, the owner of Sky and other media institutions (pp. 627–8).

Advocates of a political economy view argue that economic interests work to exclude those voices that lack economic power. Moreover, the voices that do survive are those that are least likely to criticize the prevailing distribution of wealth (Golding and Murdock 1997). This view was famously advanced by the American radical Noam Chomsky, in *Media Control: The Spectacular Achievement of Propaganda* (1991). Chomsky is highly critical of the dominance of large corporations over the American and global media. For Chomsky, their dominance

Rupert Murdoch's company, News Corporation, operates on six continents. Its holdings include the *News of the World*, the *Sun*, part of Twentieth Century Fox, HarperCollins and Sky – amongst many other major media.

results in the tight control of information given to the public. During the Cold War, these corporations controlled information to create a climate of fear of the Soviet Union. Since the collapse of the USSR in 1991, Chomsky argues that the corporately owned media have created new fears, such as global terrorism, and that these fears have prevented real issues, such as the unaccountability of corporations or the lack of democracy in the USA, from being discussed.

The cultural industry

Members of the Frankfurt School, such as Theodore Adorno (1903–69), were highly critical of the effect of mass media on the mass population. The Frankfurt School (established in the 1920s) consisted of a loose group of theorists inspired by Marx who nevertheless argued that Marx's views needed radical revision. Among other things, they held that Marx had not given enough attention to the influence of culture in modern capitalist society.

Members of the Frankfurt School argued that leisure time had been industrialized. They made an extensive study of what they called the 'culture industry', meaning the entertainment industries of film, TV, popular music, radio, newspapers and magazines (Horkheimer and Adorno 2002). They argued that the production of culture had become just as standardized and dominated by the desire for profit as other industries. In a mass society, the leisure industry was used to induce appropriate values amongst the public: leisure was no longer a break form work, but a preparation for it.

Members of the Frankfurt School argued that the spread of the culture industry, with its undemanding and standardized products, undermined the capacity of individuals for critical and independent thought. Art disappears, swamped by commercialization – 'Mozart's Greatest Hits' – and culture is replaced by entertainment. As Lazarsfeld and Merton commented on the USA in the 1950s: 'Economic power seems to have reduced direct exploitation and to have turned to a subtler type of psychological exploitation' (cited in Curran and Seaton 2003).

Recent theories

Jürgen Habermas: the public sphere

The German philosopher and sociologist Jürgen Habermas is linked to the Frankfurt School of social thought. Habermas took up some of these themes initiated by the Frankfurt School, but developed them in a different way. He has analysed the evolution of the media from the early eighteenth century up to the present day, tracing the emergence – and subsequent decay – of the 'public sphere' (1989). The **public sphere** is an arena of public debate in which issues of general concern can be discussed and opinions formed.

According to Habermas, the public sphere developed first in the salons and coffee houses of London, Paris and other European cities (one of these salons is depicted in chapter 1 on p. 6). People used to meet to discuss issues of the moment. Political debate became a matter of particular importance. Although only small numbers of the population were involved, Habermas argues that the salons were vital to the early development of democracy, for they introduced the idea of resolving political problems through public discussion. The public sphere – at least in principle – involves individuals coming together as equals in a forum for public debate.

However, the promise offered by the early development of the public sphere, Habermas concluded, has not been fully realized. Democratic debate in modern societies is stifled by the development of the culture industry. The spread of mass media and mass entertainment causes the public sphere to become largely a sham. Politics is stage-managed in Parliament and the media, while commercial interests triumph over those of the public. 'Public opinion' is not formed through open, rational discussion, but through manipulation and control – as, for example, in advertising.

Habermas's writing is discussed in more detail in chapter 4, 'Theoretical Thinking in Sociology', pp. 118–19.

Jean Baudrillard: the world of hyperreality

One of the most influential current theorists of the media is the postmodernist French author Jean Baudrillard, whose work has been strongly influenced by the ideas of McLuhan, who was discussed earlier this chapter (p. 585). Baudrillard regards the impact of modern mass media as being quite different from, and very much more profound than, that of any technology. The coming of the mass media, particularly electronic media such as television, has transformed the very nature of our lives. TV does not just 'represent' the world to us; it increasingly defines what the world in which we live actually *is*.

Consider as an example the trial of O. J. Simpson, a celebrated court case that unfolded in Los Angeles in 1994–5. Simpson originally became famous as an American football star, but later became known around the world as a result of appearing in several popular films, including the *Naked Gun* series. He was accused of the murder of his wife Nicole, and after a very long trial was acquitted.

The case became compulsive TV viewing for 95 million Americans, who watched Simpson evade arrest as his car sped along a California highway for sixty miles. Not only was his arrest televised, his trial was also broadcast live on US television, and watched around the globe, including in Britain. In America, six television channels showed continuous coverage of the trial. More than 90 per cent of the US television audience claimed to have watched the trial, and 142 million people heard the 'not guilty' verdict delivered on 3 October 1995. More than 2,000 reporters covered the trial, and more than 80 books have been written about it.

In media terms, it was the trial of the century. The trial was not confined to the courtroom; it was also a televisual event linking millions of viewers and commentators in the media. It is an illustration of what Baudrillard calls '**hyperreality**'. There is no longer a 'reality' (the events in the courtroom) which television allows us to see; the 'reality' is actually the string of images on the TV screens of the world, which defined the trial as a global event.

Just before the outbreak of hostilities in the first Gulf War in 1991, Baudrillard wrote a newspaper article entitled 'The Gulf War cannot happen'. When war was declared and a bloody conflict took place, it might seem obvious that Baudrillard had been wrong. Not a bit of it. After the end of the war, Baudrillard wrote a second article: 'The Gulf War did not happen'. What did he mean? He meant that the war was not like other wars that have happened in history. It was a war of the media age, a televisual spectacle, in which, along with other viewers throughout the world, George Bush Senior and former President of Iraq Saddam Hussein watched the coverage by CNN to see what was actually 'happening'.

Baudrillard argues that, in an age where the mass media are everywhere, in effect a new reality – hyperreality – is created, composed of the intermingling of people's behaviour and media images. The world of hyperreality is constructed of **simulacra** – images which only get their meaning from other images and hence have no grounding in an 'external reality'. A famous series of advertisements for Silk Cut cigarettes, for example, didn't refer to the cigarettes at all, but only to previous ads which had appeared in a long series. No political leader today can win an election who doesn't appear constantly on television: the TV image of the leader is the 'person' most viewers know.

John Thompson: the media and modern society

Drawing in some part on the writings of Habermas, John Thompson has analysed the relation between the media and the development of industrial societies (1990, 1995). From early forms of print

Most of what we know about politicians comes from the television, or what we read in the newspapers.

through to electronic communication, Thompson argues, the media have played a central role in the development of modern institutions. The main founders of sociology, including Marx, Weber and Durkheim, Thompson believes, gave too little attention to the role of media in shaping even the early development of modern society.

Sympathetic to some of the ideas of Habermas, Thompson is also critical of him, as he is of the Frankfurt School and of Baudrillard. The Frankfurt School's attitude to the culture industry was too negative. The modern mass media, Thompson thinks, do not deny us the possibility of

critical thought; in fact, they provide us with many forms of information to which we couldn't have had access before. In common with the Frankfurt School, Habermas treats us too much as the passive recipients of media messages. In Thompson's words:

Media messages are commonly discussed by individuals in the course of reception and subsequent to it. . . . [They] are transformed through an ongoing process of telling and retelling, interpretation and reinterpretation, commentary, laughter and criticism. . . . By taking hold of messages and routinely incorporating them into our lives . . . we are constantly shaping and

reshaping our skills and stocks of knowledge, testing our feelings and tastes, and expanding the horizons of our experience. (1995: 42–3)

Thompson's theory of the media depends on a distinction between three types of interaction (see table 15.2). *Face-to-face interaction*, such as people talking at a party, is rich in clues used by individuals to make sense of what others say (see chapter 5, 'Social Interaction and Everyday Life'). *Mediated interaction* involves the use of a media technology – paper, electrical connections, electronic impulses. Characteristic of mediated interaction is that it is stretched out in time and space – it goes well beyond the contexts of ordinary face-to-face interaction. Mediated interaction takes place

between individuals in a direct way – for instance, two people talking on the telephone – but there isn't an opportunity for the same variety of clues.

A third type of interaction is *mediated quasi-interaction*. This refers to the sort of social relations created by the mass media. Such interaction is stretched across time and space, but it doesn't link individuals directly: hence the term 'quasi-interaction'. The two previous types are 'dialogical': individuals communicate in a direct way. Mediated quasi-interaction is 'monological': a TV programme, for example, is a one-way form of communication. People watching the programme may discuss it, and perhaps address some remarks to the TV set – but, of course, it doesn't answer back.

Table 15.2 Types of interaction

Interactional characteristics	Face-to-face interaction	Mediated interaction	Mediated quasi-interaction
Space–time constitution	Context of co-presence; shared spatial-temporal reference system	Separation of contexts; extended availability in time and space	Separation of contexts; extended availability in time and space
Range of symbolic cues	Multiplicity of symbolic cues	Narrowing of the range of symbolic cues	Narrowing of the range of symbolic cues
Action orientation	Oriented towards specific others	Oriented towards specific others	Oriented towards an indefinite range of potential recipients
Dialogical/ monological	Dialogical	Dialogical	Monological

Source: Thompson (1995), p. 465

Thompson's point is not that the third type comes to dominate the other two – essentially the view taken by Baudrillard. Rather, all three types intermingle in our lives today. The mass media, Thompson suggests, change the balance between the public and the private in our lives, bringing more into the public domain than before, and often leading to debate and controversy.

Ideology and the media

The study of the media is closely related to the impact of *ideology* in society. **Ideology** refers to the influence of ideas on people's beliefs and actions. The concept has been widely used in media studies, as well as in other areas of sociology, but it has also long been controversial. The word was first coined by a French writer, Destutt de Tracy, in the late 1700s. He used it to mean a 'science of ideas'.

In the hands of later authors, however, the term became used in a more critical way. Marx, for example, regarded ideology as 'false consciousness'. Powerful groups

are able to control the dominant ideas circulating in a society so as to justify their own position. Thus, according to Marx, religion is often ideological: it teaches the poor to be content with their lot. The social analyst should uncover the distortions of ideology so as to allow the powerless to gain a true perspective on their lives – and take action to improve their conditions of life.

Thompson calls de Tracy's view the *neutral* conception of ideology and Marx's view the *critical* conception of ideology. Neutral conceptions 'characterize phenomena as ideology or ideological without implying that these phenomena are necessarily misleading, illusory or aligned with the interests of any particular group'. Critical notions of ideology 'convey a negative, critical or pejorative sense' and carry with them 'an implicit criticism or condemnation' (1990: 53–4).

Thompson argues that the critical notion is to be preferred, because it links ideology with power. Ideology is about the exercise of symbolic power – how ideas are used to hide, justify or legitimate the interests of dominant groups in the social order.

In their studies, members of the Glasgow Media Group, discussed below, were in effect analysing ideological aspects of TV news reporting and how it biased covered. They found that news tended to favour the government and management at the expense of the strikers. In general, Thompson believes, mass media – including not only the news but all varieties of programme content and genre – greatly expand the scope of ideology in modern societies. They reach mass audiences and are, in his terms, based on 'quasi-interaction' – audiences cannot answer back in a direct way.

Bias and the media: the Glasgow University Research Group

TV news

Sociological studies of television have given a good deal of attention to its coverage of the news. A substantial proportion of the population no longer reads newspapers; TV news is thus a key source of information about what goes on in the world. Some of the best-known – and most controversial – research studies concerned with television news have been those carried out by the Glasgow University Media Group. Over the last three decades, the group has published a series of works critical of the presentation of the news, including *Bad News, More Bad News, Really Bad News* and *War and Peace News*. They followed similar research strategies in each of these books, although they altered the focus of their investigations.

Bad News (Glasgow Media Group 1976), their first and most influential book, was based on an analysis of TV news broadcasts on the three UK terrestrial channels available at that time between January and June 1975. The objective was to provide a systematic and dispassionate analysis of the content of the news and the ways in which it was presented. *Bad News* concentrated on the portrayal of industrial disputes. The later books concentrated more on political coverage and on the Falklands War of 1982.

The conclusion of *Bad News* was that news about industrial relations was typically presented in a selective and slanted fashion. Terms like 'trouble', 'radical' and 'pointless strike' suggested anti-union views. The effects of strikes, causing disruption for the public, were much more likely to be reported on than their causes. Film material that was used very often made the activities of protesters appear irrational and aggressive. For example, film of strikers stopping people entering a factory would focus on any confrontations that occurred, even if they were very infrequent.

Bad News also pointed out that those who construct the news act as 'gatekeepers' for what gets on the agenda – in other words, what the public hears about at all. Strikes in which there were active confrontations between workers and management, for instance, might get widely reported. More consequential and long-lasting industrial disputes of a different sort might be largely ignored. The view of news journalists, the Glasgow Media Group suggested, tends to reflect their middle-class backgrounds and supports the views of the dominant groups in society, who inevitably see strikers as dangerous and irresponsible.

The works of the Glasgow Media Group were much discussed in media circles as well as in the academic community. Some news producers accused the researchers of simply exercising their own biases, which they thought lay with the strikers. They pointed out that, while *Bad News* contained a chapter on 'The trade unions and the media', there was no chapter on 'Management and the media'. This should have been discussed, critics of the Glasgow Media Group argued, because news journalists are often accused by management of organizations facing strikes of bias against them, rather than against the strikers.

Academic critics made similar points. Martin Harrison (1985) gained access to transcripts of ITN news broadcasts for the period covered by the original study. On this basis he argued that the five months analysed in the study were not typical. There was an abnormal number of days lost because of industrial action over the period. It would have been impossible for the news to report all of these, and therefore the tendency to focus on the more colourful episodes was understandable.

In Harrison's view, the Glasgow Media Group was wrong to claim that news broadcasts concentrated too much on the effects of strikes. After all, many more people are normally affected by strikes than take part in them. Sometimes millions of people find their lives disrupted by the actions of just a handful of people. Finally, according to Harrison's analysis, some of the assertions made by the Media Group were simply false. For example, contrary to what the Group stated, the news did normally name the unions involved in disputes and did say whether or not the strikes were official or unofficial.

In replying to such criticism, members of the Group noted that Harrison's research had been partly sponsored by ITN, possibly compromising his academic impartiality. The transcripts scrutinized by Harrison were not complete and some passages were included that ITN did not in fact broadcast at all.

In recent years, members of the Glasgow Media Group have carried out a range of further research studies. The latest edition of the *Bad News* series, *Bad News from Israel* (Philo and Berry 2004), examined television news reporting of the Israeli-Palestinian conflict. The study was carried out over a two-year period and was supported by several senior television news broadcasters and journalists who were involved in panel discussions with members of an 800-person sample audience. As well as looking at the television coverage of the conflict, the authors were interested in how the coverage related to the understanding, beliefs and attitudes of the audience.

The study concluded that the television news coverage of the conflict confused viewers and substantially featured Israeli government views. The study found a bias towards official 'Israeli perspectives', particularly on BBC 1, where Israelis were interviewed or reported more than twice as much as Palestinians. In addition, American politicians who supported Israel were often featured. The study also found that the news gave a strong emphasis to Israeli casualties, relative to Palestinians (although two to three times more Palestinians than Israelis died). There were also differences in the language used by journalists to describe Israeli and Palestinian attacks. For example, journalists would often describe Palestinian acts as 'terrorism', but when an Israeli group was reported as trying to bomb a Palestinian school, they were referred to as 'extremists' or 'vigilantes' (Philo and Berry 2004).

Bad News from Israel also argued that there was little coverage devoted to the history or origins of the conflict. The great majority of viewers depended on this news as their main source of information. The gaps in their knowledge closely paralleled the 'gaps' in the news. The survey argued that, again, this worked against the Palestinians, by giving the impression that the problems 'started' with Palestinian action (Philo and Berry 2004).

In their earlier volume, *Getting the Message*, the Glasgow Media Group collected together recent research on news broadcasting. The editor of the volume, John Eldridge, points out that the debate provoked by the original work of the Glasgow Media Group still continues (1993). To say what would count as objectivity in news reporting will always be difficult. As against those who say that the idea of objectivity makes no sense (see 'Baudrillard: the world of hyperreality', pp. 601–2 above), Eldridge affirms the importance of continuing to look at media products with a critical eye. Accuracy in news reporting can and must be studied. After all, when the football results are reported, we expect them to be accurate. A simple example like this, Eldridge argues, reminds us that issues of truth are always involved in news reporting.

Yet the point holds that the news is never just a 'description' of what 'actually happened' on a given day or in a given week. The 'news' is a complex construction that regularly influences what it is 'about'. For example, when a politician appears on a news programme and makes a comment about a controversial issue – say, the state of the economy and what should be done about it – that comment itself becomes 'news' in subsequent programmes.

Audiences and media effects

The effect that ideological bias has on the audience depends upon the theoretical position one takes over the role of the audience in the mass media. Here, we turn to the question through a brief analysis of audience studies.

Audience studies

One of the earliest, and the most straightforward, models of audience response is the *hypodermic model*. This compares the media message to a drug injected by syringe. The model is based on the assumption that the audience (patient) passively and directly accepts the message and does not critically engage with it in any way. The hypodermic model also assumes that the message is received and interpreted in more or less the same way by all members of society. The concept of *narcotization*, associated with the Frankfurt School (see pp. 600–1), draws on the hypodermic model. Under this view, the media is seen as 'drugging' the audience, destroying its ability to think critically about the wider world (Marcuse 1964). The hypodermic model is now out of fashion, and was often little more than an unstated assumption in the works of early writers on the mass media. However, the model's assumptions about the media can still be found in the works of contempo-

The hypodermic model assumes that media messages are passively received by viewers. Such ideas are often implicit in arguments about the effects of television on children.

rary writers who are sceptical about the effects of the mass media on modern society.

Critics of the hypodermic model have pointed out that it takes no account of the very different responses that different audiences have to the media, treating them as homogenous and passive. Most theorists now argue that audience responses go through various stages. In their work on audience response, Katz and Lazarsfeld drew on studies of political broadcasts during US presidential elections, and argued that audience response is formed through a *two-step flow*: the first step is when the media reaches the audi-ence; the second comes when the audience interprets the media through their social interaction with influential people – 'opinion leaders' – who further shape audience response (Katz and Lazarsfeld 1955).

Later models assume a more active role for an audience in response to the media. The *gratification model* looks at the ways in which different audiences use the media to meet their own needs (Lull 1990). Audiences may use the media to learn more about the world they live in – finding out about the weather or stock market for example. Others may use the media to help with their relationships, to feel part of a fictional community (from watching TV soaps, for example), or to get on with friends and colleagues who also watch the same programme. (We discuss soap operas in the box opposite) Critics of this model have argued that it assumes that audience needs already exist, not that they are created by the media.

Later theories of audience response have looked at the ways in which people actively interpret the media. Stuart Hall's account of *reception theory* focuses on the way in which an audience's class and cultural background affects that way in which it makes sense of different media 'texts' – a term that is used to encompass various forms of media from books and newspapers to films and CDs. Some members of an audience may simply accept the preferred reading 'encoded' in a text – such as a news bulletin – by its producer. This preferred reading, Hall argues, is likely to reflect the dominant or mainstream ideology (as the Glasgow Media Group, whose work is discussed above on pp. 606–8, found). However, Hall argues that the understanding of a text also depends on the cultural and class background of the person interpreting it. Other members of an audience may take an 'oppositional' reading of a text, because their social position places them in conflict with the preferred reading. For example, a worker involved in strike action or a member of an ethnic minority is likely to take an oppositional reading of a text such as a news story on industrial or race relations, rather than accept the dominant reading encoded in the text by its producer (Hall 1980).

Following Hall, recent theories have focused on the way in which audiences filter information through their own experience (Halloran 1970). The audience may link different media 'texts' (programmes or genres, for example) or use one type of media to engage with another – questioning what they are told on the television compared to the newspaper (Fiske 1988). Here the audience has a powerful role, far removed from the hypodermic model. The *interpretative model* views audience response as shaping the media through its engagement or rejection of its output.

Media effects

The perceived effects of the media are manifold. The media has been blamed for alienation, copy-cat killings, producing apathy amongst the population, reinforcing prejudices and trivializing important issues (Watson 2003). Of course, the extent to which we blame the media for negative effects depends upon the view taken of how active or passive an audience is, as we have seen above. In this section we look at two areas in which the media is said to have a negative effect: violence and pornography.

The media and violence

The incidence of violence in television programmes is well documented. The most extensive studies have been carried out by Gerbner and his collaborators, who analysed samples of prime-time and weekend day-time television for all the major American networks each year after 1967. The number and frequency of violent acts and episodes of violence were charted for a range of types of programme. Violence is defined in the research as the threat or use of physical force, directed against the self or others, in which physical harm or death is involved. Television

Genres, audience response and soap operas

A genre created by radio and television came to be called 'soap opera' – now TV's most popular type of programme. Of the most watched TV shows in Britain each week, almost all are soaps – *EastEnders*, *Coronation Street* and many others. Soap operas fall into various different types, or subgenres, at least as represented on British TV. Soaps produced in the UK, like *Coronation Street*, tend to be gritty and down to earth, often concerned with the lives of poorer people. Second, there are American imports, many of which, like *Dallas* or *Dynasty* in the 1980s, portray individuals leading more glamorous lives. A third category is made up of Australian imports, such as *Neighbours*. These tend to be low-budget productions, featuring middle-class homes and lifestyles.

Soaps are like TV as a whole: continuous. Individual stories may come to an end, and different characters appear and disappear, but the soap itself has no ending until it is taken off the air completely. Tension is created between episodes by so-called 'cliff-hangers'. The episode stops abruptly just before some key event happens and the viewer has to wait until the next episode to see how things turn out.

A basic part of the genre of soap opera is that it demands regular viewing on the part of whoever watches it. A single episode makes very little sense. Soap operas presume a history, which the regular viewer knows – he or she becomes familiar with the characters, with their personalities and their life experiences. The threads, which are linked to create such a history, are above all personal and emotional – soaps for the most part do not look at larger social or economic frameworks, which impinge only from the outside.

Sociologists have put differing views forward as to why soap operas are so popular – and they are popular across the world, not only in Britain or America, but also in Africa, Asia and Latin America. Some think that they provide a means of *escape*, particularly where women (who watch soaps in greater numbers than men) find their own lives dull or oppressive. Such a view is not particularly convincing, though, given that many soaps feature people whose lives are just as problematic. More plausible is the idea that soap operas address universal properties of personal and emotional life. They explore dilemmas anyone may face, and perhaps they even help some viewers to think more creatively about their own lives. The sociologist Dorothy Hobson, in her book *Soap Opera*, has written that soaps work not because they are escapist, but 'because the audience has intimate familiarity with the characters and their lives. Through its characters the soap opera must connect with the experience of its audience, and its content must be stories of the ordinary' (Hobson 2002).

Questions

1 Do you watch soap operas? Explain why or why not from a sociological perspective.
2 How do functionalist and conflict theories explain the popularity of soap operas?

drama emerged as highly violent in character: on average, 80 per cent of such programmes contained violence, with a rate of 7.5 violent episodes per hour. Children's programmes showed even higher levels of violence, although killing was less commonly portrayed. Cartoons contained the highest number of violent acts and episodes of any type of television programme (Gerbner 1979, 1980; Gunter 1985).

In what ways, if at all, does the depiction of violence influence the audience? F. S. Anderson collected the findings of sixty-seven studies conducted over the twenty years from 1956 to 1976 investigating the influence of TV violence on tendencies to aggression among children. About three-quarters of the studies claimed to find some such association. In 20 per cent of cases there were no clear-cut results, while in 3 per cent of the researches the investigators concluded that watching television violence actually decreases aggression (Anderson 1977; Liebert et al. 1982).

The studies Anderson surveyed, however, differ widely in the methods used, the strength of the association supposedly revealed and the definition of 'aggressive behaviour'. In crime dramas featuring violence (and in many children's cartoons) there are underlying themes of justice and retribution. A far higher proportion of miscreants are brought to justice in crime dramas than happens with police investigations in real life, and in cartoons harmful or threatening characters usually tend to get their 'just deserts'. It does not necessarily follow that high levels of the portrayal of violence create directly imitative patterns among those watching, who are perhaps more influenced by the underlying moral themes. In general, research on the effects of television on audiences has tended to treat viewers – children and adults – as passive and undiscriminating in their reactions to what they see.

Although most studies have not found a link between television violence and violence in real life, the issue has remained a controversial one. In the USA, an amendment to the 1996 Telecommunications Act forced almost all televisions made after 1999 to have a built-in 'V-Chip' (the V stands for 'violence'), an electronic device that enables parents to filter violent and sexually explicit material from the programmes their children watch on TV. The television industry was asked to develop a rating system, similar to one used in films, to use with the V-Chip (Signorielli 2003). Studies have found, however, that although parents express strong concerns about what their children watch on television, few bother to turn on their television's V-chip (Annenberg Center 2003). There was a joke that the parents would be unable to work out how to turn the V-chip on or off without their young son or daughter showing them how.

Pornography

The debate about the effects of pornography has many similarities to discussions about the media effects of violence. Legal regulation of sexually explicit pictures has a long history. In the USA legislation, known as the Comstock laws, was passed in the late nineteenth century, banning sexually explicit material, which it defined as material that would offend the sensibility of a young girl (Grossberg et al. 1998).

From the late 1970s the links between pornography and sexual violence against women began to be increasingly debated, especially amongst feminists. The argument was put forward that pornography objectifies women and users of pornography are more likely than non-users to be sexually violent towards women. The feminist writer Robin Morgan summed this up concisely with the comment: 'Pornography is the theory, and rape the practice' (Morgan 1994).

> See chapter 12, 'Sexuality and Gender', pp. 471–2, for more about radical feminists' views.

Sociological research into this area has generally attempted to assess if a causal link exists between the use of pornography and sexual aggression. A report for the American Psychological Association found that, amongst adults, whilst there are no antisocial effects to viewing erotica, or sexually explicit materials that are not violent or degrading to women, repeated exposure to sexualized violence does desensitize users to the severity of rape and reduce emotional reaction to the depicted victim (Huston et al. 1992). As the expansion of the Internet makes pornographic and violent materials ever more easily available, questions about audience responses and media effects are increasingly important.

The control of the media

Political control

Public broadcasting and the BBC

In most countries the state has been directly involved with the administration of television broadcasting. In Britain the British Broadcasting Corporation, which initiated the first television programmes ever produced, is a public organization, funded, as we have already seen, by licence fees paid by every household that owns a set. For some years the BBC was the only organization permitted to broadcast either radio or television programmes in Britain, but today, alongside the two terrestrial BBC TV stations, BBC 1 and 2, there exist three terrestrial commercial television channels (ITV, Channel 4 and 5). Only the BBC is funded by the licence fee; the commercial channels rely on revenue generated by advertising. The frequency and duration of advertising is controlled by law, with a maximum of six minutes per hour. These regulations also apply to satellite channels, which became widely available to subscribers in the 1980s. (The future of the BBC is discussed in the box on p. 614.)

In the USA the three leading television organizations are all commercial networks – the American Broadcasting Company (ABC), Columbia Broadcasting System (CBS) and the National Broadcasting Company (NBC). Networks are limited by law to owning no more than five licensed stations, which in the case of these three organizations are in the biggest cities. The 'big three' together reach over a quarter of all households through their own stations. Some two hundred affiliated stations are also attached to each network, comprising 90 per cent of the seven hundred or so TV stations in the country. The networks depend for their income on selling advertising time. The National Association of Broadcasters, a private body, lays down guidelines about the proportion of viewing time per hour to be devoted to advertising: 9.5 minutes per hour during 'prime time' and 16 per hour at other periods. TV companies use regularly collected statistics (ratings) of how many people watch specific programmes in setting advertising fees. The ratings also, of course, strongly influence decisions on which programmes to continue to show.

The power of publicly run television stations has been reduced since the advent of multi-channel TV, DVD and video, and the arrival of services such as Sky+ (which combines a digital video recorder and satellite receiver to find and record programmes the viewer has expressed an interest in, effectively creating a personalized channel). In return for a subscription fee or one-off payment for a digital set-top box, today's television watcher can select from a multiplicity of channels and programmes. In such circumstances people increasingly do their own 'programming', constructing personal viewing schedules rather than depending on the presupplied network scheduling.

Digital, satellite and cable are altering the nature of television almost everywhere. As these make inroads into the domains of the orthodox terrestrial television channels, it will become yet more difficult for governments to control the

The future of the BBC

The position of the BBC – like that of public broadcasters in most other countries – is under strain and has been the subject of much controversy. The future of the BBC has become problematic because of the fragmentation of its audience. The development of digital technology has meant that literally hundreds of commercial cable and satellite channels have become available which threaten the dominance of the BBC. From having a monopoly of the British television audience until the launch of commercial television in the mid-1950s the BBC's share of the terrestrial television audience had fallen to around 36 per cent by 2003. As the number of BBC viewers falls, more people have started to question why they have to pay the licence fee – particularly if they do not watch BBC television or listen to BBC radio stations.

During the 1990s the BBC, along with other public monopolies such as the National Health Service, was put under considerable pressure to become more efficient and market-orientated. Sir John Birt, Director-General from 1992 to 1999, introduced an internal market giving programme-makers freedom to buy resources like camera crews from outside the BBC; he also developed the BBC's commercial activities and dramatically cut the costs of programme-making, often through job cuts (Born 2004).

Critics of public monopolies have suggested that this does not go far enough and have pushed for the BBC to be privatized. For example, David Elstein, the former chief executive of Channel 5, argued in a recent report commissioned by the Conservative Party that the BBC should become a subscription service to those who wish to use it and the licence fee should be abolished (2004). So far, the idea of wholesale privatization has been resisted.

Many people believe that it is important for the BBC to stay in public ownership. Yet, as some commentators have noted, the effects of deregulation in the environment in which it operates, as well as financial pressures, have turned the BBC into a commercial system which preserves part of its original public service element. Supporters of the BBC argue that as the television sector is deregulated, the role of the BBC becomes ever more important, particularly in keeping programme standards high, and – now that people over the age of seventy-five get free TV licences – reaching socially excluded portions of the population. As a former Director of Policy and Planning for the BBC commented:

> There are real fears that more will mean worse, that competition will fragment audiences and investment across multiple outlets, leading to tabloid values and to a nation divided between those who embrace the new services and those who either cannot afford to or do not wish to do so. The challenge for public policy is to deliver the best of both worlds; to drive growth and to sustain quality. (Currie and Siner 1999)

Despite the fallout from the Hutton Inquiry in 2004 (see box opposite), which caused the resignation of several senior figures in the organization, the government has guaranteed the future of the BBC, at least in the short term. A report from Ofcom, the government's media industry regulator, stressed the importance of the BBC in providing programming that is 'high quality, original, innovative, challenging, engaging and widely available', and have recommended that the license fee survives until at least 2016 (Ofcom 2003).

content of TV, as they have characteristically done in the past. For example, the reach of Western media seems to have played a part in the circumstances that produced the revolutions of 1989 in Eastern Europe.

For more about the effects of a globalized media, see chapter 20 'Politics, Government and Terrorism', pp. 618–30.

The Iraq dossier row

To rally support for war, the Prime Minister's office published a dossier of charges against Iraq in September 2002. It claimed, among other things, that Iraq could deploy weapons of mass destruction (WMD) within 45 minutes.

Yet with no WMD used by Iraqi forces in the ensuing war and none found, the dossier's veracity came under suspicion. One of its allegations, which George Bush made part of his 2003 state-of-the-union address, was discredited by intelligence sources. Then, in June 2003, a BBC journalist accused Alistair Campbell, Tony Blair's chief spin-doctor, of having 'sexed up' the dossier against the wishes of Britain's security services (in particular, inserting the '45-minute' claim).

A parliamentary investigation cleared Mr Campbell of this charge (he resigned in August 2003). But the BBC refused to back down, sparking a furious row with the government. This took a tragic turn when a government scientist [Dr David Kelly], who'd been exposed as the main source of the BBC's story, committed suicide. An inquiry into his death, which reported in January 2004, cleared the government of 'sexing up' the dossier and largely — but not wholly — vindicated the scientist's employers, the Defence Ministry. Criticism was instead heaped on the BBC, prompting the resignations of its director-general and chairman of governors.

A related inquiry into intelligence failures, headed by Lord Butler, in July 2004 cleared the government of any deliberate attempt to mislead Parliament. But it did suggest that Mr Blair was prepared to exaggerate what turned out to be fairly thin evidence to bolster the case for a war.

Source: *The Economist* (5 April 2005)

Anti-monopoly measures

As the authors of *Bad News* pointed out, (see above, pp. 606–8) those who construct the news act as 'gatekeepers' for what gets on the agenda. News stories that are successfully broadcast or published are not always chosen according to some simple criterion of newsworthy-ness. Journalists are well aware that they must find stories that fit with the agenda of the organization they work for, and these news organizations may have political agendas of their own – they are not just in the business of selling goods but of influencing opinions. For this reason the rise and influence of the media entrepreneurs and the large media companies worries many. The proprietors of such corporations, like Rupert Murdoch (see box on pp. 627–8), make no secret of their political views, which inevitably are a cause of concern to political parties and other groups holding different political positions.

Recognizing this, all countries have provisions that seek to control media ownership. But how tight should these be? And given the global character of media enterprises, can national governments in any case have much hope of controlling them?

The issue of **media regulation** is more complex than might appear at first sight. It seems obvious that it is in the public interest that there should be a diversity of media organizations, since this is likely to ensure that many different groups and political perspectives can be listened to. Yet placing limits on who can own what, and what forms of media technology they can use, might affect the economic prosperity of the media sector. A country that is too restrictive might find itself left behind – the media industries are one of the fastest growing sectors of the modern economy.

Critics of media concentration say that the large media companies wield excessive power. Businesses, on the other hand, argue that if they are subject to regulation they cannot make effective commercial decisions and will lose out in global competition. Moreover, they ask, who is to do the regulating? Who is to regulate the regulators?

One guiding thread of media regulation policy might be the recognition that market dominance by two or three large media companies simultaneously threatens both proper economic competition and democracy – since the media owners are unelected. Existing anti-monopoly legislation can be brought into play here, although it differs widely across Europe and other industrial countries.

Competitiveness means pluralism, or should do – and presumably pluralism is good for democracy. Yet is pluralism enough? Many point to the USA in arguing that having a plurality of media channels does not guarantee quality and accuracy of content (as Chomsky's criticisms, discussed above, demonstrate). Some see the maintenance of a strong public broadcasting sector as of key importance in blocking the dominance of the large media companies. Yet public broadcasting systems, which in Britain are led by the BBC, create their own problems. In most countries they themselves used to be a monopoly and in many countries were effectively used as a means of government propaganda. The question of who is to regulate the regulators comes up here with particular force. (The issue of government attempts to control the mass media and democratization in China is discussed in the box.)

Globalization and everyday life: censorship and the media in China

The contradictory nature of globalization is illustrated clearly in China, a country that is undergoing rapid cultural and economic transformation under the watchful eye of the Chinese Communist Party.

In the 1980s, the Chinese government oversaw the expansion of a national television system and encouraged the purchase of televisions by its citizens. The government saw television broadcasting as a means of uniting the country and promoting party authority. Television, however, can be a volatile medium. Not only is it not possible for television broadcasting to be tightly controlled in an age of satellite based channels, but Chinese audiences have demonstrated their willingness to interpret TV content in ways that run contrary to government intentions (Lull 1997).

In interviews with a hundred Chinese families, James Lull found that Chinese audiences, like other populations under Communist regimes, were 'masters of interpretation, reading between the lines in order to pick up the less obvious messages'. In his interviews, Lull noted that his respondents would not only describe what they watched, but how they watched it: 'Because viewers know that the government often bends and exaggerates its reports, they become skilled at imagining the true situation. What is presented, what is left out, what is given priority, how things are said – all these modes are noticed and interpreted sensitively.'

Lull concluded that many of the messages seen by Chinese audiences on TV – primarily in imported films and commercials – run contrary to the way of life and opportunities available in their own society. Seeing television content emphasizing individuality and the consumer society, many Chinese viewers felt their own options were constrained in real life. Television conveyed to Chinese audiences that other social systems seemed to function more smoothly and offer greater freedom than their own.

More recently, the Internet and other new communication technologies have posed fresh *challenges for the Chinese government. While some people contend that these new media will help people circumvent state controls, others maintain that the state censors are likely to keep pace with technological advances.*

'The Great Firewall of China'

The Chinese effort to censor the Internet is a feat of technology, legislation and manpower. According to the BBC, which is almost completely blocked within the 'great firewall of China' (as it is known among techies), 50,000 different Chinese authorities 'do nothing but monitor traffic on the internet'. No single law exists to permit this mass invasion of privacy and proscription of free speech. Rather, hundreds of articles in dozens of pieces of legislation work to obfuscate the mandate of the government to maintain political order through censorship.

According to *Internet Filtering in China in 2004–2005: A Country Study*, the most rigorous survey of Chinese internet filtering to date, China's censorship regime extends from the fatpipe backbone to the street cyber-café. Chinese communications infrastructure allows packets of data to be filtered at 'choke points' designed into the network, while on the street liability for prohibited content is extended onto multiple parties – author, host, reader – to chilling effect. All this takes place under the watchful eye of machine and human censors, the latter often volunteers.

The ramifications of this system, as the Open Net Initiative's John Parley stressed when he delivered a report to the US-China Economic and Security Review Commission in April, 'should be of concern to anyone who believes in participatory democracy'. The ONI found that 60 per cent of sites relating to opposition political parties were blocked, as were 90 per cent of sites detailing the Nine Commentaries, a series of columns about the Chinese Communist Party published by the Hong Kong-based Epoch Times and associated by some with the banned spiritual movement Falun Gong.

The censorship does not end at the World Wide Web. New internet-based technologies, which looked to lend hope to free speech when ONI filed its last report on China in 2002, are also being targeted. Although email censorship is not as rampant as many (including the Chinese themselves) believe, blogs, discussion forums and bulletin boards have all been targeted through various measures of state control.

What then, of China's 94 million web surfers? One discussion thread at Slashdot, the well-respected and popular discussion forum for techno-libertarians, is telling. When a well-meaning Westerner offered a list of links prefaced with 'assuming that you can read Slashdot, here are a few web pages that your government would probably prefer you not to read', one poster, Hung Wei Lo responded: 'I have traveled to China many times and work with many H1-B's [temporary workers from outside US] from all parts of China. All of them are already quite knowledgeable about all the information provided in the links above, and most do not hesitate to engage in discussions about such topics over lunch. The fact that you feel all 1.6 billion Chinese are most certainly blind to these pieces of information is a direct result of years of indoctrination of Western (I'm assuming American) propaganda.'

Indeed, anti-Japanese protests [in 2005] have been cited by some as an example of how the Chinese people circumvent their state's diligent censorship regime using networked technologies such as mobile text messages (SMS), instant messaging, emails, bulletin boards and blogs to communicate and organize. The argument here of course is that the authorities were ambivalent towards these protests – one blogger reports that the state sent its own SMS during the disturbances: 'We ask the people to express your patriotic passion through the right channel, following the law and maintaining order.'

China will have to keep up with the slew of emerging technologies making untapped networked communication more sophisticated by the day. . . . Judging by the past record, it cannot be assumed that the state censorship machinery will not be able to meet these future challenges.

Source: Hogge (2005). This article was originally published on the independent online magazine <http://www/opendemocracy.net/>. Reprinted by permission of openDemocracy

One issue that complicates the question of media regulation is the very rapid rate of technological change. The media are constantly being transformed by technical innovations, and forms of technology, which were once distinct, are now fusing together. If television programmes are watched via the Internet, for example, what type of media regulation applies? Among member states of the European Union the question of media and telecommunications convergence is at the forefront of debate. While some see the need for coordinated legislation that would harmonize telecommunications, broadcasting and information technology across Europe, this has been difficult to bring about. The role of the EU in media regulation remains weak. The current policy document 'Television without frontiers' was originally due to be revised again in 2002, but has since been postponed as debate continues.

The global media and democracy

In their work on the global media, Edward Herman and Robert McChesney (1997) explore the effects of international media on the workings of democratic states. On the one hand, the spread of global media sources can successfully put pressure on authoritarian governments to loosen their hold over state-controlled broadcasting outlets. As it becomes increasingly difficult to contain media products within national borders, many 'closed' societies are discovering that the media can become a powerful force in support of democracy (see box about China). Even in a multiparty political system like that of India, we saw that commercialization of television allowed more prominence for the views of opposition politicians. The global media have allowed for the widespread dissemination of viewpoints such as individualism, the respect for human rights and promoting the rights of minorities.

Yet Herman and McChesney also stress the dangers of the global media order and the threat it poses to the healthy functioning of democracy. As the global media become increasingly concentrated and commercialized, they encroach on the functioning of the important 'public sphere' in the way described by Habermas (see p. 601 above). Commercialized media, they claim, are beholden to the power of advertising revenue and are compelled to favour content that guarantees high ratings and sales. As a result, entertainment will necessarily triumph over controversy and debate. This form of self-censorship by the media weakens citizen participation in public affairs and undermines people's understandings of public issues. According to Herman and McChesney, the global media are little more than the 'new missionaries of global capitalism': non-commercial media space is steadily being taken over by those who are eager to put it to the 'best economic use' (Herman 1998). In their eyes, the 'culture of entertainment' promoted by media institutions is steadily shrinking the public sphere and undermining the workings of democracy.

The media in a global age

As we have seen throughout this book, the Internet is one of the main contributors to – and manifestations of – current processes of globalization. Yet globalization is also transforming the international reach and impact of other forms of media as well. In this section we will consider some of the changes affecting the mass media under conditions of globalization.

Although the media have always had international dimensions – such as the gathering of news stories and the distribution of films overseas – until the 1970s most media companies operated within specific domestic markets in accordance with regulations from national governments. The media industry was also differentiated into distinct sectors – for the most part, cinema, print media, radio and television broadcasting all operated independently of one another.

In the past three or four decades, however, profound transformations have taken place within the media industry. National markets have given way to a fluid global market, while new technologies have led to the fusion of forms of media that were once distinct. By the start of the twenty-first century, the global media market was dominated by a group of about twenty multinational corporations whose role in the production, distribution and marketing of news and entertainment could be felt in almost every country in the world.

In their work on globalization, David Held and his colleagues (1999) point to five major shifts that have contributed to bringing about the global media order:

1 *Increasing concentration of ownership* The global media is now dominated by a small number of powerful corporations. The small-scale, independent media companies have gradually been incorporated into highly centralized media conglomerates.

2 *A shift from public to private ownership* Traditionally, media and telecommunications companies in almost all countries were partially or fully owned by the state. In the past few decades, the liberalization of the business environment and the relaxing of regulations have led to the privatization (and commercialization) of media companies in many countries.

3 *Transnational corporate structures* Media companies no longer operate strictly within national boundaries. Likewise, media ownership rules have been loosened to allow cross-border investment and acquisition.

4 *Diversification over a variety of media products* The media industry has diversified and is much less segmented than in previous times. Enormous media conglomerates, such as AOL-Time Warner (profiled below), produce and distribute a mix of media content, including music, news, print media and television programming.

5 *A growing number of corporate media mergers* There has been a distinctive trend towards alliances between companies in different segments of the media industry. Telecommunications firms, computer hardware and software manufacturers, and media 'content' producers are increasingly involved in corporate mergers as media forms become increasingly integrated.

The globalization of the media has thrust 'horizontal' forms of communications to centre stage. If traditional media forms ensured that communication occurred within the boundaries of nation-states in a 'vertical' fashion, globalization is leading to the horizontal integration of communications. Not only are people making connections with one another at a grass-roots level, but also media products are being disseminated widely due to new harmonized regulatory frameworks, ownership policies and transnational marketing strategies. Communications and media can now more readily extend themselves beyond the confines of individual countries (Srebrenny-Mohammadi et al. 1997).

Yet like other aspects of global society, the new information order has developed unevenly and reflects divisions between the developed societies and less developed countries. In this section we shall explore the dimensions of media globalization before considering arguments by some commentators that the new global media order would be better described as 'media imperialism'.

Music

As David Held and his colleagues have noted in their investigation into the globalization of media and communications, 'the musical form is one that lends itself to globalization more effectively than any other' (1999: 351). This is because music is able to transcend the limitations of written and spoken language to reach and appeal to a mass audience. The global music industry, dominated by a small number of multinational corporations, has been built on its ability to find, produce, market and distribute the musical abilities of thousands of artists to audiences around the world. The growth of technology – from personal stereo systems to music television (such as MTV) to the compact disc – have provided newer, more sophisticated ways for music to be distributed globally. Over recent decades, an 'institutional complex' of companies has developed as part of the global marketing and distribution of music.

The global industry in recorded music is one of the most concentrated. The five largest firms – Universal (which absorbed PolyGram in 1998), Time Warner (discussed on pp. 623–5 below), Sony, EMI and Bertelsmann – control between 80 and 90 per cent of all music sales internationally (Herman and McChesney 1997). Until January 2000, when it announced a merger with Time Warner, EMI was the only company among the top five that was not part of a larger media conglomerate. The global music industry experienced substantial growth during the mid-1990s, with sales in developing countries particularly strong, prompting many of the top companies to sign more local artists in anticipation of further market growth. However, as we shall see below the music industry has been challenged by the arrival of the Internet, which allows users to illegally share music for free more easily and extensively than before.

The growth of the global music industry in the post-war period has been due primarily to the success of popular music – originating mainly in America and Britain – and the spread of the youth cultures and subcultures that identify with it (Held et al. 1999). The globalization of music, therefore, has been one of the main forces in the diffusion of American and British styles and music genres to international audiences. The USA and the UK are the world leaders in the export of popular music, with other countries having much lower levels of domestic music production. While some critics argue that the domination of the music industry by these two countries undermines the success of local musical sounds and traditions, it is important to remember that globalization is a two-way street. The growing popularity of 'world music' – such as the phenomenal success of Latin-inspired sounds in the United States – is testimony to the fact that globalization leads to cultural diffusion in all directions.

The Internet and the music industry

The Internet has changed many aspects of our daily lives; from our leisure pursuits to the way business is conducted. For 'traditional' media companies, such as the music industry, the Internet presents both an enormous opportunity and a serious threat.

Although the music industry is becoming ever more concentrated in the hands of a few international conglomerates, some observers believe that it is the most vulnerable link within the 'culture industry'. This is because the Internet allows music to be shared and downloaded digitally, rather than purchased from local music stores. The global music industry is currently mainly comprised of a complex network of factories, distribution chains, music shops and sales staff. If the Internet removes the need for all these elements by allowing music to be marketed and downloaded directly, what will be left of the music industry?

The music industry is now attempting to come to terms with the effects of digitalization. Global music sales have been falling, with annual record sales down from $40 billion (£22 billion) to $30 billion (£17 billion) between 2000 and 2004. The sector has undergone large-scale redundancies and has been forced to restructure. Many in the music industry claim that the illegal swapping of music files, such as MP3s, over the Internet is one of the major causes of this loss of revenue. Research by the British Phonographic Industry (BPI) found that eight million people in the UK claim to be downloading music, 92 per cent of them using illegal sites (BBC, 7 October 2004). Although attempts are being made to impose tight controls on the replication of legally purchased music, the pace of technological change is eclipsing the ability of the industry to curtail piracy.

One case that attracted much attention in 2000 was the Napster case. Napster is a software program that allows people to trade files over the Internet – including music copied to files on other sharers' computers. The record industry filed several lawsuits against the small company behind Napster, eventually forcing it to stop providing the file-sharing software. However, since the victory over Napster the music industry has had mixed fortunes in its court actions against the companies that support file-swapping on the Internet. In 2003, a US judge ruled that two file-swapping networks, Grokster and Morpheus, were not responsible for the legal status of files traded on their systems, but the legal battle continues.

As well as attacking the companies that create file-sharing software the music industry has gone after individual computer users who illegally share music files. In 2004, the BPI issued a statement claiming it would sue individual music fans who swapped song files over the Internet. This follows similar action by the Recording Industry Association of America (RIAA), which by 2004 had sued more than 5,700 downloaders. In 2003, the RIAA took action against a college student in Michigan,

USA, who ran a network offering more than 650,000 files – the equivalent of more than 43,000 albums (BBC, 7 October 2004).

As well as attacking illegal file sharing, the music industry has begun to adapt to the challenges of the Internet by offering legal download services. The downloading is legal because royalties are paid on the songs to record labels and artists. The Internet has seen a large increase, catalysed by the advent of the portable MP3 player, particularly Apple's iPod, and by the rise in the number of online companies offering songs that can be legally purchased and downloaded. By the end of 2004, more than 125 million legal downloads of songs had been purchased and an official 'music download chart' had been established. After initial rejection of the Internet by the music industry, by the mid-2000s its successful adaptation to selling music through legal downloading was perceived by many in the industry to be crucial to its future (BBC, 28 June 2004).

Cinema

There are different ways to assess the globalization of cinema. One way is to consider where films are produced and the sources of financing that support them. By such criteria, there has unquestionably been a process of globalization in the cinema industry. According to studies by the United Nations Educational, Scientific and Cultural Organization (UNESCO), many nations possess the capacity to produce films. In the 1980s approximately twenty-five countries were producing fifty or more films a year, while a small handful of countries – the United States, Japan, South Korea, Hong Kong and India – led all the others in producing more than 150 films a year (Held et al. 1999).

Another way to assess the globalization of cinema is to consider the extent to which nationally produced films are exported to other countries. In the 1920s, when feature films first saw the light of day, Hollywood made four-fifths of all films screened in the world; today, the United States continues to be the largest influence in the cinema industry. (After the United States, the next largest exporters of films are India, France and Italy.) The governments of many countries provide subsidies to aid their own film industries, but no other country rivals the United States as an exporter of feature films. As figure 15.3 shows, the top-grossing films of all time at the international (non-US) box office were all US films. In 2003, for instance, American films dominated the UK box office, accounting for almost 62 per cent of takings; films solely originating in the UK, by contrast, accounted for just 2.5 per cent of money taken (UK Film Council, 2003).

Hollywood studios generate well over half of their revenues from the overseas distribution of films. In an effort to increase the size of foreign audiences further, these studios are involved in building multiplex cinemas around the world. Global box office revenues are forecast to rise to $25.6 billion (£14 billion) by 2010, nearly double the 1995 total, as the audiences increase. The spread of video and more recently DVD players globally has also increased the number of people who are now able regularly to watch Hollywood films.

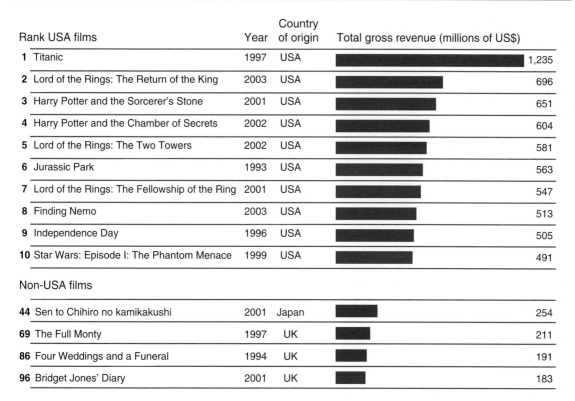

Rank	USA films	Year	Country of origin	Total gross revenue (millions of US$)
1	Titanic	1997	USA	1,235
2	Lord of the Rings: The Return of the King	2003	USA	696
3	Harry Potter and the Sorcerer's Stone	2001	USA	651
4	Harry Potter and the Chamber of Secrets	2002	USA	604
5	Lord of the Rings: The Two Towers	2002	USA	581
6	Jurassic Park	1993	USA	563
7	Lord of the Rings: The Fellowship of the Ring	2001	USA	547
8	Finding Nemo	2003	USA	513
9	Independence Day	1996	USA	505
10	Star Wars: Episode I: The Phantom Menace	1999	USA	491
	Non-USA films			
44	Sen to Chihiro no kamikakushi	2001	Japan	254
69	The Full Monty	1997	UK	211
86	Four Weddings and a Funeral	1994	UK	191
96	Bridget Jones' Diary	2001	UK	183

Figure 15.3 Top-grossing films of all time at the international (non-US) box office, April 2004

Source: Internet Movie Database <http://www.imdb.com/Top/>; UNDP (2004), p. 97

Media 'supercompanies'

In January 2000 two of the world's most influential media companies joined together in what was the largest corporate merger the world had ever seen. In a deal worth $337 billion, the world's biggest media company, Time Warner, and the world's largest Internet service provider, America Online (AOL), announced their intention to create the 'world's first fully integrated media and communications company for the Internet Century'. The merger brought together the enormous media 'content' owned by Time Warner – including newspapers and magazines, film studios and TV stations – with the powerful Internet distribution capabilities of AOL, whose subscription base exceeded twenty-five million people in fifteen countries at the time of the merger.

The merger generated enormous excitement in financial markets, as it created the world's fourth largest company. But even more than its size, the deal attracted great attention as the first major union between 'old media' and 'new media'. The origins of Time Warner date back to 1923 when Henry Luce founded *Time* magazine, a weekly publication that summarized and interpreted the voluminous amount of information contained in daily newspapers. The overwhelming success of *Time* was soon followed by the creation of the business magazine *Fortune* in 1930 and the photographic magazine *Life* in 1936. Over the course of the twentieth century, Time Inc. grew into a media corporation embracing TV and radio stations, the music industry, the vast Warner Brothers movie and cartoon empire, and the world's first twenty-four-hour news channel, CNN. At the time of the merger, Time Warner's annual turnover was $26 billion; 120 million readers read its magazines each month and the company owned the rights to an archive of 5,700 films, as well as some of the most popular network television programmes.

If the history of Time Warner closely mirrored the general development of communications in the twenty-first century, the rise of America Online is typical of the 'new media' of the information age. Founded in 1982, AOL initially offered dial-up Internet access charged at an hourly rate. By 1994 it had 1 million subscribed users; after introducing unlimited Internet use for a standard monthly fee in 1996, its membership soared to 4.5 million. As the number of users continued to grow – 8 million people were using AOL by 1997 – the company embarked on a series of mergers, acquisitions and alliances, which consolidated its position as the pre-eminent Internet service provider. CompuServe and Netscape were both purchased by AOL, a joint venture with the German company Bertelsmann in 1995 led to the creation of AOL Europe, and an alliance with Sun Microsystems has allowed AOL to enter the realm of e-commerce.

The merger between the two companies was set to create a $350 billon multinational, AOL-Time Warner, bringing 24 million AOL subscribers, 120 million magazine readers and the television channels CNN, HBO and Warner Brothers all under one corporate roof. Yet the merger has, so far, suffered grave difficulties. In particular, AOL was never able to meet its ambitious subscriber or revenue targets and the technological spin-offs from combining film and Internet technologies were slow to materialize. As investors adjusted their expectations of what the corporation could achieve, the media giant looked in imminent danger of being forced into a break-up. In 2002, the company posted a loss of almost $100 billion. That loss resulted in the company dropping AOL from the company name in 2003.

The decline of AOL is now believed to be stabilizing and the company is claiming success in more traditional media such as cable and films. Yet much of the company's immediate accomplishments after 2002 relied upon the success of *The Lord of the Rings* film trilogy. With no guaranteed blockbuster films in the production pipeline at Time Warner, and the Internet service provider industry becoming increasingly competitive, some analysts are wondering how certain the future is for the world's largest media company.

The implications of the AOL/Time Warner merger will not be clear for some time, yet already the lines have been drawn between those who see the deal as unleashing exciting new technological potentials and those who are concerned about the domination of the media by large corporations. The enthusiasts see the merger as an important step towards the creation of media 'supercompanies' that can deliver direct to people's homes, through the Internet, all the news shows, TV programmes, films and music they want, when they want them.

Not everyone agrees, however, that the idea of media supercompanies is one that should be aspired to. Where enthusiasts see a dream, critics sense a nightmare. As media corporations become ever more concentrated, centralized and global in their reach, there is reason to be concerned that the important role of the media as a forum for free speech, expression and debate will be curtailed. A single company that controls both the content – TV programmes, music, films, news sources – *and* the means of distribution is in a position of great power. It can promote its own material (the singers and celebrities it has made famous), it can exercise self-censorship (omitting news stories that might cast its holdings or corporate supporters in a negative light), and it can 'cross-endorse' products within its own empire at the expense of those outside it.

The vision of the Internet in the hands of several media conglomerates stands in stark contrast to the idea of a free and unrestricted electronic realm held out by Internet enthusiasts just a few years ago. In its early years, the Internet was viewed by many as an individualistic realm where users could roam freely, searching for and sharing information, making connections, and interacting outside the realm of corporate power. The looming presence of corporate media giants and advertisers has threatened this, however. Critics worry that the rise of corporate power on the Internet will drown out everything but the 'corporate message' and may lead to the Internet becoming a restricted domain accessible only to subscribers.

It is difficult to assess these competing opinions; almost certainly there is truth in both perspectives. Media mergers and technological advance are sure to expand the way communications and entertainment are organized and delivered. Just as early media pioneers in film and music were influenced by the rise of TV networks and the music industry, so the Internet age will provoke more dramatic changes in the mass media: in coming years, audiences will have much greater choice about what they consume and when. But concerns about corporate domination of the media are not misplaced. Already there are accounts of media conglomerates avoiding coverage of unfavourable news stories relating to partner companies. Arguments for keeping the Internet free and open are grounded in important convictions about the value of an unrestricted public space where ideas can be shared and debated.

It is important to remember that there are few inevitabilities in the social world. Attempts at total control of information sources and distribution channels rarely succeed, either because of anti-trust legislation aimed at preventing monopolies, or through the persistent and creative responses of media users who seek out alternative information routes. Media consumers are not 'cultural dopes' who can be manipulated effortlessly by corporate interests; as the scope and volume of media forms and content expand, individuals are becoming more, not less, skilled in interpreting and evaluating the messages and material they encounter.

Media imperialism?

The paramount position of the industrialized countries, above all the United States, in the production and diffusion of media has led many observers to speak of **media imperialism** (e.g. Herman and McChesney 2003). According to this view, a cultural empire has been established. Less developed countries are held to be especially vulnerable, because they lack the resources to maintain their own cultural independence.

The headquarters of the world's twenty largest media conglomerates are all located in industrialized nations; the majority of them are in the United States. Media empires such as AOL-Time Warner, Disney/ABC and Viacom are all US-based. Other large media corporations – apart from the Murdoch empire profiled in the box – include the Japanese Sony Corporation, which owns CBS Records and Columbia Pictures; the German Bertelsmann group, owner of RCA Records and a large US-based set of publishing companies; and the Mondadori, a publishing house controlled by the television corporation owned by Silvio Berlusconi, the Italian Prime Minister (and one of the world's forty richest individuals – see chapter 11, p. 385).

Through the electronic media, Western cultural products have certainly become widely diffused round the globe. As we have seen, American films are available around the world, as is Western popular music. Plans to build a Disney theme park in Hong Kong were announced in 1999. The park, expected to cost $3.5 billion, is due to open in early 2006 and will largely replicate American attractions, rather than reflect local culture. As the chairman of Disney theme parks indicated, this may be just the beginning: 'If there is only one Disney theme park in a country with 1.3 billion people, that doesn't compare very well to five theme parks in the US with only a population of 280 million' (quoted in Gittings 1999).

It is not only the more popular entertainment forms that are at issue, however. Control of the world's news by the major Western agencies, it has been suggested, means the predominance of a 'First World outlook' in the information conveyed. Thus it has been claimed that attention is given to the developing world in news broadcasts mainly in times of disaster, crisis or military confrontation, and that the daily files of other types of news kept on the industrialized world are not maintained for developing world coverage.

The global spread of Western, and especially American, culture has led to resentment in some regions and has contributed to a surge in anti-American sentiment in many parts of the world.

Resistance and alternatives to the global media

While the power and reach of the global media are undeniable, there are forces within all countries that can serve to slow the media onslaught and shape the nature of media products in a way that reflects local traditions, cultures and priorities. Religion, tradition and popular outlooks are all strong brakes on media globalization, while local regulations and domestic media institutions can also play a role in limiting the impact of global media sources.

Media entrepreneurs: Rupert Murdoch

Rupert Murdoch is an Australian-born entrepreneur who is the head of one of the world's largest media empires. News Corporation's holdings include nine different media operating on six continents. By 2001 News Corporation's turnover was £16.5 billion and it employed 34,000 staff (BBC, 16 July 2001). In October 2004, ABC News reported the annual turnover as £29 billion.

Murdoch established News Corporation in Australia before moving into the British and American markets in the 1960s. His initial purchases of the *News of the World* and the *Sun* in Britain in 1969 and the *New York Post* in the mid-1970s paved the way for a dramatic expansion in later acquisitions. In the USA alone, News Corporation's holdings now include more than 130 newspapers. Murdoch turned many of these newspapers towards sensationalistic journalism, building on the three themes of sex, crime and sport. The *Sun*, for example, became highly successful, with the highest circulation of any daily English-language newspaper in the world, standing at around 3.4 million copies daily in mid-2004.

In the 1980s Murdoch started to expand into television, establishing Sky TV, a satellite and cable chain that, after initial reverses, proved commercially successful. He also owns 64 per cent of the Star TV network based in Hong Kong. Its declared strategy is to 'control the skies' in satellite transmission over an area from Japan to Turkey, taking in the gigantic markets of India and China. It transmits five channels, one of which is BBC World News.

In 1985, Murdoch bought a half interest in Twentieth Century Fox, a film company that owns the rights to more than 2,000 films. His Fox Broadcasting Company started up in 1987 and has become the fourth major television network in the United States after ABC, CBS and NBC. Murdoch now owns twenty-two US television stations, which account for over 40 per cent of TV households in the United States. He controls twenty-five magazines, including the popular TV Guide, and acquired the US-based publishers, Harper and Row – now renamed HarperCollins – in 1987.

In recent years Murdoch has invested heavily in the profitable digital satellite television industry, particularly through his ownership of Sky and coverage of live sporting events such as basketball and live premiership football. According to Murdoch, sports coverage is News Corporation's 'battering ram' for entering new media markets (Herman and McChesney 1997). Because sporting events are best viewed live, they lend themselves to the 'pay-per-view' format that is profitable both for Murdoch and for advertisers. Competition for broadcasting rights to key fixtures is intense between News Corporation and other media empires as the

global demand for sport eclipses other kinds of events.

Governments can cause trouble for Murdoch, because, at least within their own boundaries, they can introduce legislation limiting media cross-ownership – that is, a situation where the same firm owns several newspapers and TV stations. The European Union has also expressed concern about the dominant position of very large media companies. Yet Murdoch's power is not easily contained, given its global spread. He is weighty enough to influence governments, but it is in the nature of the telecommunications business that it is everywhere and nowhere. Murdoch's power base is very large, but also elusive.

In a speech given in October 1994, Murdoch took on those who see his media empire as a threat to democracy and freedom of debate. 'Because capitalists are always trying to stab each other in the back,' Murdoch argued, 'free markets do not lead to monopolies. Essentially, monopolies can only exist when governments support them.' 'We at News Corporation', he went on to say, 'are enlightened.' He discovered that in India, where Star television

transmissions could be picked up, thousands of private operators had invested in satellite dishes and were selling Star programming illegally. Well, what we should do, Murdoch argued, is applaud! News Corporation, he concluded, looks forward to 'a long partnership with these splendid entrepreneurs' (Murdoch 1994).

Murdoch was for a while the head of the largest media organization the world has known. In 1995, however, he was overtaken when the Disney Company and ABC merged. The Disney Chairman at the time, Michael Eisner, made it clear that he wanted to compete with Murdoch in the rapidly expanding markets of Asia. Murdoch's response to the merger was, 'They are twice as big as me now.' Then he added: 'A bigger target.' The merger of AOL and Time Warner presented another target for Murdoch, but it seems clear that he will not shrink from the challenge. The chief executives of Disney, Time Warner and Viacom have all noted that Murdoch is the media executive they respect and fear the most – and whose moves they study most carefully (Herman and McChesney 1997).

Ali Mohammadi (1998) investigated the response of Islamic countries to the forces of media globalization. The rise of international electronic empires that operate across state borders is perceived as a threat to the cultural identity and national interests of many Islamic states. According to Mohammadi, resistance against the incursion of outside media forms has ranged from muted criticism to the outright banning of Western satellites. The reaction to media globalization and the action taken by individual countries in large part reflect their overall responses towards the legacy of Western colonialism and the encroachment of modernity. In analysing Islamic responses to media globalization, Mohammadi divides states

into three broad categories: modernist, mixed and traditional.

Until the mid-1980s, most television programming in the Islamic world was produced and distributed within national borders or through Arabsat – the pan-Arab satellite broadcasting network composed of twenty-one states. The liberalization of broadcasting and the power of global satellite TV have transformed the contours of television in the Islamic world. The events of the 1991 Gulf War made the Middle East a centre of attention for the global media industry and significantly affected television broadcasting and consumption within the region as well. Satellites spread rapidly, with Bahrain, Egypt, Saudi Arabia, Kuwait, Dubai, Tunisia and Jordan all

خاص الجزيرة
aljazeera exclusive

جماعة تسمي نفسها كتائب المجاهدين تعلن
أنها تحتجز أربعة إيطاليين

خبر عاجل

وارئ لتأمين إجلاء من يرغب من الرعايا الروس من العراق

كبر

Aljazeera has become one of the most popular channels in the Middle East.

launching satellite channels by 1993. By the end of the decade, most Islamic states had established their own satellite channels, as well as accessing global media programmes.

Aljazeera is the largest and most controversial Arabic news channel in the Middle East, offering news coverage twenty-four hours a day. Founded in 1996, and based in Qatar, the Aljazeera news network is the fastest growing network among Arab communities and Arabic-speaking people around the world. Some critics have argued that Aljazeera is overly sensational, and shows too much violent and emotion-

ally charged footage from war zones, as well as giving disproportionate coverage to fundamentalist and extremist groups. Its political programmes are most popular, but other shows covering culture, sport and health help to increase the channel's audience share.

In some Islamic states, the themes and material dealt with on Western television have created tension. Programmes relating to gender and human rights issues are particularly controversial; Saudi Arabia, for example, no longer supports BBC Arabic because of concerns over its coverage of human rights issues. Three Islamic states – Iran, Saudi Arabia and Malaysia – have banned satellite access to Western television. Iran has been the staunchest opponent of the Western media, branding it a source of 'cultural pollution' and the promotion of Western consumer values.

Such strong responses are in the minority, however. Mohammadi concluded that, although Islamic countries have responded to media globalization by attempting to resist or provide an alternative, most have found it necessary to accept certain modifications to their culture in order to maintain their own cultural identity. In his eyes, the 'traditionalist approach', such as that favoured by Iran and Saudi Arabia, is losing ground to responses based on adaptation and modernization (Mohammadi 1998).

Conclusion

As individuals, we don't control technological change, and the sheer pace of such change threatens to swamp our lives. The often cited notion of an 'information superhighway' suggests an orderly road map, whereas the impact of the new technologies often feels chaotic and disruptive.

Yet the arrival of the wired-up world, thus far at any rate, hasn't produced any of the overwhelmingly negative scenarios predicted by some sceptics. 'Big Brother' has not emerged as a result of the Internet: rather to the contrary, it has promoted decentralization and individualism. In spite of the enormous hype surrounding the potential collapse of the global computer infrastructure at the turn of the millennium – from the so-called 'Y2K bug' – the moment passed relatively uneventfully. Finally, books and other 'pre-electronic' media look unlikely to disappear. Bulky as it is, this book is handier to use than a computerized version would be. Even Bill Gates has found it necessary to write a book to describe the new high-tech world he anticipates.

Summary points

1   The mass media have come to play a fundamental role in modern society. The mass media are media of communication – newspapers, magazines, television, radio, cinema, videos, CDs and other forms – which reach mass audiences, and their influence on our lives is profound. The media not only provide entertainment, but provide and shape much of the information we act on in our daily lives.

2   The newspapers were among the most important of early mass media. They continue to be significant, but other, newer media, particularly television and the Internet, have supplemented them.

3   Next to the Internet, television is the most important development in the media over the past forty years. In most countries the state has been directly involved in the administration of television broadcasting. Satellite and cable technology are altering the nature of television in fundamental ways; public television broadcasting is losing audience share as a multiplicity of channels become available, and governments have less control over the content of television programmes.

4   In recent years, advances in new communications technology have transformed telecommunications – the communication of text, sounds or images at a distance through a technological medium. Digitization, fibre optics and satellite systems work together to facilitate multimedia – the combination of several media forms in a single medium – and interactive media, which allow individuals actively to participate in what they see or hear. Mobile telephones are currently at the forefront of innovations in telecommunications.

5   The Internet is allowing unprecedented levels of interconnectedness and interactivity. The number of worldwide Internet users has been growing rapidly and the range of activities that can be completed online continues to expand. The Internet is providing exciting new possibilities, but some worry that it may undermine human relationships and communities by encouraging social isolation and anonymity.

6   The media industry has become globalized over the past three decades. Several trends can be noted: the ownership of media is increasingly concentrated in the hands of large media conglomerates; private ownership of media is eclipsing public ownership; media companies operate across national borders; media companies have diversified their activities; and media mergers have become more frequent. The global media industry – music, television, cinema and news – is dominated by a small number of multinational corporations.

7   The sense today of inhabiting one world is in large part a result of the international scope of media and communications. A world information order – an international system of the production, distribution and consumption of informational goods – has come into being. Given the paramount position of the industrial countries in the world information order, many argue that developing countries are subject to a new form of media imperialism. Many critics worry that concentration of media power in the hands of a few companies or powerful individuals undermines the workings of democracy.

8   A range of different theories of the media have been developed. Innis and McLuhan argued that the media influence society more in terms of how they communicate than in what they communicate. In McLuhan's words, 'the medium is the message': TV, for example, influences people's behaviour and attitudes because it is so different in nature from other media, such as newspapers or books.

9   Other important theorists include Habermas, Baudrillard and Thompson. Habermas points to the role of the media in creating a 'public sphere' – a sphere of public opinion and public debate. Baudrillard has been strongly influenced by McLuhan. He argued that the new media, particularly television, actually change the 'reality' we experience. Thompson argues that the mass media have created a new form of social interaction – 'mediated quasi-interaction' – that is more limited, narrow and one-way than everyday social interaction.

Questions for further thought

1 Should governments seek to protect national cultures by limiting the spread of satellite and cable TV?

2 Does the Internet undermine authoritarian governments? Is it different from older media in this?

3 If your only source of information was soap operas, in what ways would your view of your country be distorted or incomplete?

4 Has the concentration of ownership in the music industry led to a reduction in consumer choice?

5 Will the globalization of communication improve our understanding of cultural differences or annihilate those differences?

Further reading

Chris Barker, *Television, Globalization and Cultural Identities* (Buckingham: Open University Press, 1999).

Timothy E. Cook, *Governing with the News: The News Media as a Political Institution* (Chicago: The University of Chicago Press, 1998).

David Croteau and William Hoynes, *Media Society*, 3rd edn (London: Sage, 2003).

David Deacon, Michael Pickering, Peter Golding and Graham Murdock, *Researching Communications: A Practical Guide to Methods in Media and Cultural Analysis* (London: Arnold, 1999).

Lawrence Grossberg, Ellen Wartella and D. Charles Whitney, *Mediamaking: Mass Media in a Popular Culure* (London: Sage, 1998).

Denis McQuail, *Mass Communication Theory*, 4th edn (London: Sage, 2000).

James Slevin, *The Internet and Society* (Cambridge: Polity, 2000).

John Thompson, *The Media and Modernity* (Cambridge: Polity, 1995).

James Watson, *Media Communication*, 3rd edn (Basingstoke: Macmillan, 2003).

Internet links

Foundation for Information Policy Research (UK)
http://www.fipr.org

The Modernist Journals Project
http://www.modjourn.brown.edu

News Watch
http://www.newswatch.org

OECD ICT Homepage
http://www.oecd.org/topic/0,2686,en_2649_37409_1_1_1_1_37409,00.html

Theory.org
http://www.theory.org.uk

Contents

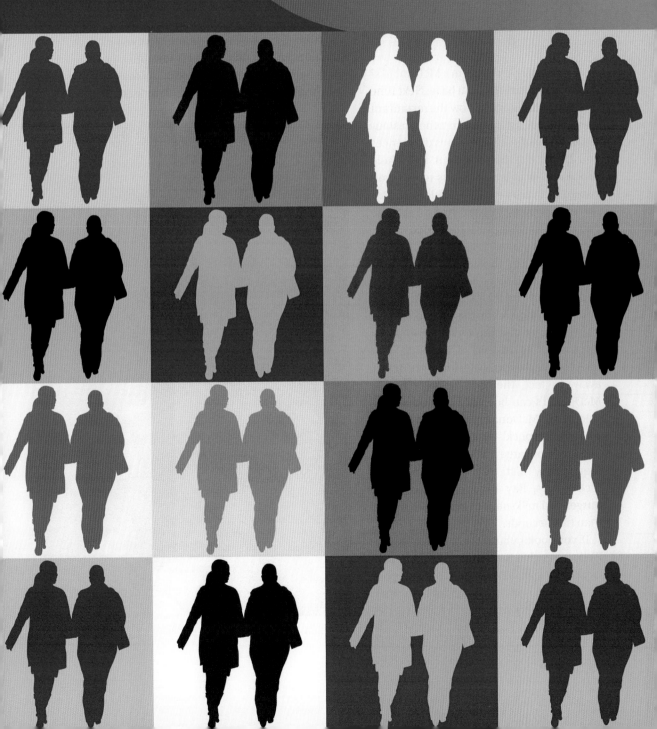

16 Organizations and Networks

HAVE YOU ever eaten in a McDonald's? Chances are that you have. Next time that you're there, study how the restaurant is organized. Compared to other restaurants, one of the most obvious differences you'll notice is how efficient the whole process is, or at least appears to be – you can go in hungry and leave full in almost no time at all. You go straight to the counter and get given your food there, instead of a waiter showing you to your table and taking your order. If you chose to eat in, there are no tablecloths and only a minimum of cutlery. Aside from the tray, anything you need to eat your food, and the wrapping that the food arrives in, is disposable. At the end of the meal, you take your packaging to the bin and throw it away. In fact, the food and service at McDonald's can be easily quantified and calculated. McDonald's aims to give 'more bang for the buck' – you buy 'value meals', 'Big Macs' or 'large fries'. And the service is measurably fast too. The founder of McDonald's, Ray Kroc, aimed to get a burger and milkshake to customers in less than fifty seconds.

If you look behind the counter, you're likely to see that the members of staff each work on a specialized and quite straight-forward job: one makes the fries, another flips the burgers, a third puts the burger in a bun and adds the salad. You might also notice how much of the process is automated – milkshakes are made at the press of a button, the deep fryers work at set temperatures and timers let the staff know when the food is ready; even the tills have buttons for each item, so staff do not have to learn prices.

If you have visited a McDonald's restaurant abroad, as well as at home, you will have noticed that there are very few differences between them. The interior decoration may vary slightly, the language

spoken will differ from country to country, but the layout, the menu, the procedure for ordering, the staff uniforms, the tables, the packaging and the 'service with a smile' are virtually identical. The McDonald's experience is designed to be *uniform and predictable* whether you are in London or Lima. No matter where they are located, visitors to McDonald's know that they can expect quick service and a product that is filling and consistent in any of the more than 30,000 restaurants in 119 countries worldwide (McDonald's 2004).

The American sociologist George Ritzer (1983, 1993, 1998) argues that McDonald's provides a vivid metaphor of the transformations taking place in industrialized societies. He argues that what we are witnessing is the 'McDonaldization' of society. According to Ritzer, McDonaldization is 'the process by which the principles of the fast-food restaurants are coming to dominate more and more sectors of American society as well as the rest of the world'. Ritzer uses the four guiding principles for McDonald's restaurants – *efficiency, calculability, uniformity* and *control through automation* – to show that our society is becoming ever more 'rationalized' with time. (Ritzer's argument is strongly influenced by Max Weber, whose theory of rationalization is discussed further on pp. 18–19.) Ritzer is keen to point out that he has no special desire to pick on McDonald's. McDonald's is simply the most obvious example of this process – and besides, he notes, 'McDonaldization' is more catchy than 'Burger Kingization' or 'Starbuckization'.

Ritzer, like the classical sociologist Max Weber before him, is fearful of the harmful effects of rationalization. He argues that McDonaldization spawns a series of irrationalities – which he calls the 'irrationality of rationality'. These irrationalities include damage to our health (from a 'high calorie, fat, cholesterol, salt, and sugar content' diet) and to the environment – think of all the packaging that is thrown away with each meal. Most of all, Ritzer argues, McDonaldization is 'dehumanizing'. We file forward in queues to get a burger as if on a conveyer belt, whilst staff on the other side of the counter repeat the same specialized task again and again like robots on an assembly line.

The study and theory of organizations is an important aspect of sociology. It was a central concern of the classical sociologist Max Weber (whose ideas Ritzer drew upon). In this chapter, we examine what sociologists say about organization, and ask whether theories like Weber's still hold true in a world characterized by loose networks.

Organizations

People frequently band together to pursue activities that they could otherwise not readily accomplish by themselves. A principal means for accomplishing such cooperative actions is the **organization**, a group with an identifiable membership that engages in concerted collective actions to achieve a common purpose (Aldrich and Marsden 1988). An organization can be a small group of people who know each other face to face, but it is more likely to be a larger, impersonal one: universities, religious bodies and business corporations (like McDonald's discussed at the start of this chapter) are all examples of organizations. Such organizations are a central feature of all societies, and their study is a core concern of sociology today.

Organizations tend to be highly formal in modern industrial and post-industrial societies. A formal organization is one that is rationally designed to achieve its objectives, often by means of explicit rules, regulations and procedures. The modern bureaucratic organization, discussed later in this chapter, is a prime example of a formal organization. As Max Weber first recognized in the 1920s (see Weber 1979), there has been a long-term rising trend in Europe and North America towards formal organizations. This is in part the result of the fact that formality is often a requirement for legal standing. For a college or university to be legally accredited, for example, it must satisfy explicit written standards governing everything from grading policy to faculty performance to fire safety. Today, formal organizations are the dominant form of organization throughout the entire world.

Most social systems in the traditional world developed over lengthy periods as a result of custom and habit. Organizations, on the other hand, are mostly designed – established with definite aims in view and housed in buildings or physical settings specifically constructed to help realize those aims. The edifices in which hospitals, colleges or business firms carry on their activities are mostly custom built.

In current times, organizations play a much more important part in our everyday lives than was ever true previously. Besides delivering us into this world, they also mark our progress through it and see us out of it when we die. Even before we are born, our mothers, and probably our fathers too, are involved in classes, pregnancy check-ups and so forth, carried out within hospitals and other medical organizations. Every child born today is registered by a government organization, which collects information on us from birth to death. Most people today die in a hospital – not at home, as was once the case – and each death must be formally registered with the government too.

It is easy to see why organizations are so important to us today. In the pre-modern world, families, close relatives and neighbours provided for most needs – food, the instruction of children, work and leisure-time activities. In modern times, the mass of the population is much more *interdependent* than was ever the case before. Many of our requirements are supplied by people we never meet and who indeed might live many thousands of miles away. A tremendous amount of coordination of activities and resources – which organizations provide – is needed in such circumstances.

The tremendous influence organizations have come to exert over our lives cannot be seen as wholly beneficial. Organizations often have the effect of taking things out of our own hands and putting them under the control of officials or experts over whom we have little influence. For instance, we are all *required* to do certain things the government tells us to do – pay taxes, abide by laws, go off to fight wars – or face punishment. As sources of social power, organizations can thus subject the individual to dictates she or he may be powerless to resist.

Organizations as bureaucracies

Max Weber developed the first systematic interpretation of the rise of modern organizations. Organizations, he argued, are ways of coordinating the activities of human beings, or the goods they produce, in a stable way across space and time. Weber emphasized that the development of organizations depends on the control of information, and he stressed the central importance of writing in this process: an organization needs written rules for its functioning, and files in which its 'memory' is stored. Weber saw organizations as strongly hierarchical, with power tending to be concentrated at the top. Was Weber right? If he was, it matters a great deal to us all. For Weber detected a clash as well as a connection between modern organizations and democracy that he believed had far-reaching consequences for social life.

All large-scale organizations, according to Weber, tend to be bureaucratic in nature. The word '*bureaucracy*' was coined by a Monsieur de Gournay in 1745, who added the word *bureau*, meaning both an office and a writing table, to *cracy*, a term derived from the Greek verb meaning 'to rule'. **Bureaucracy** is thus the rule of officials. The term was first applied only to government officials, but it was gradually extended to refer to large organizations in general.

From the beginning, the concept was used in a disparaging way. De Gournay spoke of the developing power of officials as 'an illness called bureaumania'. The French novelist Honoré de Balzac saw bureaucracy as 'the giant power wielded by pygmies'. The Czech author Franz Kafka gave a nightmarish depiction of an impersonal and unintelligible bureaucracy in his novel *The Trial*, first published in 1925. This sort of view has persisted into current times: bureaucracy is frequently associated with red tape, inefficiency and wastefulness. Other writers, however, have seen bureaucracy in a different light – as a model of carefulness, precision and effective administration. Bureaucracy, they argue, is in fact the most efficient form of organization human beings have devised, because in bureaucracies all tasks are regulated by strict rules of procedure. Weber's account of bureaucracy steers a way between these two extremes. A limited number of bureaucratic organizations, he pointed out, existed in the traditional civilizations. For example, a bureaucratic officialdom in imperial China was responsible for the overall affairs of government.

Bureaucracy – the giant power wielded by pygmies?

But it is only in modern times that bureaucracies have developed fully.

According to Weber, the expansion of bureaucracy is inevitable in modern societies; bureaucratic authority is the only way of coping with the administrative requirements of large-scale social systems. However, Weber also believed that bureaucracy exhibits a number of major failings, as we will see, which have important implications for the nature of modern social life.

In order to study the origins and nature of the expansion of bureaucratic organizations, Weber constructed an ideal type of bureaucracy. (*Ideal* here refers not to what is most desirable, but to a pure form of bureaucratic organization. An **ideal type** is an abstract description constructed by accentuating certain features of real cases so as to pinpoint their most essential characteristics.) Weber (1979) listed several characteristics of the ideal type of bureaucracy:

1 There is a clear-cut hierarchy of authority, such that tasks in the organization are distributed as 'official duties'. A bureaucracy looks like a pyramid, with the positions of highest authority at the top. There is a chain of command stretching from top to bottom, thus making coordinated decision-making possible. Each higher office controls and supervises the one below it in the hierarchy.

2 Written rules govern the conduct of officials at all levels of the organization. This does not mean that bureaucratic duties are just a matter of routine. The higher the office, the more the rules tend to encompass a wide variety of cases and demand flexibility in their interpretation.

3 Officials are full time and salaried. Each job in the hierarchy has a definite and

In the business world, and in other organizations, informal networks may be created by people who get together during out-of-work hours.

fixed salary attached to it. Individuals are expected to make a career within the organization. Promotion is possible based on capability, seniority or a mixture of the two.

4 There is a separation between the tasks of an official within the organization and his life outside. The home life of the

official is distinct from his activities in the workplace and is also physically separated from it.

5 No members of the organization own the material resources with which they operate. The development of bureaucracy, according to Weber, separates workers from the control of their means of production. In traditional communities, farmers and craft workers usually had control over their processes of production and owned the tools they used. In bureaucracies, officials do not own the offices they work in, the desks they sit at, or the office machinery they use.

Weber believed that the more an organization approaches the ideal type of bureaucracy, the more effective it will be in pursuing the objectives for which it was established. He often likened bureaucracies to sophisticated machines operating by the principle of **rationality** (see chapter 1). Yet he recognized that bureaucracy could be inefficient and accepted that many bureaucratic jobs are dull, offering little opportunity for the exercise of creative capabilities. While Weber feared that the rationalization of society could have negative consequences, he concluded that bureaucratic routine and the authority of officialdom over our lives are prices we pay for the technical effectiveness of bureaucratic organizations. Since Weber's time, the rationalization of society has become more widespread. Critics of this development who share Weber's initial concerns, such as George Ritzer, whose account of the McDonaldization of society was discussed in the introduction to this chapter, have questioned whether the efficiency of rational organizations comes

at a price greater than Weber could have imagined.

Formal and informal relations within bureaucracies

Weber's analysis of bureaucracy gave prime place to **formal relations** within organizations, the relations between people as stated in the rules of the organization. Weber had little to say about the informal connections and small-group relations that may exist in all organizations. But in bureaucracies, informal ways of doing things often allow for a flexibility that couldn't otherwise be achieved.

In a classic study, Peter Blau (1963) looked at **informal relations** in a government agency whose task was to investigate possible income-tax violations. Agents who came across problems they were unsure how to deal with were supposed to discuss them with their immediate supervisor; the rules of procedure stated that they should not consult colleagues working at the same level as themselves. Most officials were wary of approaching their supervisors, however, because they felt this might suggest a lack of competence on their part and could reduce their promotion chances. Hence, they usually consulted one another, violating the official rules. This not only helped to provide concrete advice; it also reduced the anxieties involved in working alone. A cohesive set of loyalties often found in small groups developed among those working at the same level. The problems these workers faced, Blau concludes, were probably coped with much more effectively as a result. The group was able to evolve informal procedures allowing for more initiative and responsibility than was provided for by the formal rules of the organization.

Informal networks tend to develop at all levels of organizations. At the very top, personal ties and connections may be more important than the formal situations in which decisions are supposed to be made. For example, meetings of boards of directors and shareholders supposedly determine the policies of business corporations. In practice, a few members of the board often really run the corporation, making their decisions informally and expecting the board to approve them. Informal networks of this sort can also stretch across different corporations. Business leaders from different firms frequently consult one another in an informal way and may belong to the same clubs and leisure-time associations. Informal networks are discussed later in this chapter in more detail, on pp. 670–3.

John Meyer and Brian Rowan (1977) argue that formal rules and procedures in organizations are usually quite distant from the practices actually adopted by the organizations' members. Formal rules, in their view, are often 'myths' that people profess to follow but that have little substance in reality. They serve to legitimate – to justify – ways in which tasks are carried out, even while these ways may diverge greatly from how things are 'supposed to be done' according to the rules.

Formal procedures, Meyer and Rowan point out, often have a ceremonial or ritual character. People will make a show of conforming to them in order to get on with their real work using other, more informal procedures. For example, rules governing ward procedure in a hospital help justify how nurses act towards patients. For example, a nurse will faithfully fill in a patient's chart hanging at the end of the bed, but will check the patient's progress by means of other, informal criteria – how well the person is looking and whether he or she seems alert and lively. Rigorously keeping up the charts impresses the patients and keeps the doctors happy, but is not always essential to the nurse's assessments.

Deciding how far informal procedures generally help or hinder the effectiveness of organizations is not a simple matter. Systems that resemble Weber's ideal type tend to give rise to a forest of unofficial ways of doing things. This is partly because the flexibility that is lacking ends up being achieved by unofficial tinkering with formal rules. For those in dull jobs, informal procedures often also help to create a more satisfying work environment. Informal connections between officials in higher positions may be effective in ways that aid the organization as a whole. On the other hand, these officials may be more concerned about advancing or protecting their own interests than furthering those of the overall organization.

The dysfunctions of bureaucracy

Robert Merton, a functionalist scholar, examined Weber's bureaucratic ideal type and concluded that several elements inherent in bureaucracy could lead to harmful consequences for the smooth functioning of the bureaucracy itself (Merton 1957). He referred to these as 'dysfunctions of bureaucracy'.

> For more on functionalism, see chapter 1, 'What is Sociology?', pp. 20–2.

First, Merton noted that bureaucrats are trained to rely strictly on written rules and procedures. They are not encouraged to be flexible, to use their own judgement in making decisions or to seek creative solutions; bureaucracy is about managing cases according to a set of objective criteria. Merton feared that this rigidity could lead to *bureaucratic ritualism*, a situation in which the rules are upheld at any cost, even in cases where another solution might be a better one for the organization as a whole.

A second concern of Merton's is that adherence to the bureaucratic rules could eventually take precedence over the underlying organizational goals. Because so much emphasis is placed on the correct procedure, it is possible to lose sight of the big picture. A bureaucrat responsible for processing insurance claims, for example, might refuse to compensate a policy-holder for legitimate damages, citing the absence or incorrect completion of a form. In other words, processing the claim correctly could come to take precedence over the needs of the client who has suffered a loss.

Merton foresaw the possibility of tension between the public and bureaucracy in such cases. This concern was not entirely misplaced. Most of us interact with large bureaucracies on a regular basis – from insurance companies to local government to the Inland Revenue. Not infrequently, we encounter situations in which public servants and bureaucrats seem to be unconcerned with our needs. One of the major weaknesses of bureaucracy is the difficulty it has in addressing cases that need special treatment and consideration.

Organizations as mechanistic and organic systems

Can bureaucratic procedures be applied effectively to all types of work? Some scholars have suggested that bureaucracy makes logical sense for carrying out routine tasks but that it can be problematic in contexts where the demands of work change unpredictably. In their research on innovation and change in electronics companies, Tom Burns and G. M. Stalker (1996) found that bureaucracies are of limited effectiveness in industries where flexibility and being on the cutting edge are prime concerns.

Burns and Stalker distinguished between two types of organization: *mechanistic* and *organic*. Mechanistic organizations are bureaucratic systems in which there is a hierarchical chain of command, with communication flowing vertically through clear channels. Each employee is responsible for a particular task; once the task is completed, responsibility passes onto the next employee. Work within such a system is anonymous, with people at the top and those at the bottom rarely in communication with one another.

Organic organizations, by contrast, are characterized by a looser structure in which the overall goals of the organization take precedence over narrowly defined responsibilities. Communication flows and directives are more diffuse, moving along many trajectories, not simply vertical ones. Everyone involved in the organization is seen as possessing legitimate knowledge and input that can be drawn on in solving problems; decisions are not the exclusive domain of people at the top.

According to Burns and Stalker, organic organizations are much better equipped to handle the changing demands of an innovative market, such as telecommunications, computer software or biotechnology. The more fluid internal structure means that they can respond more quickly and appropriately to shifts in the market and can come up with solutions more creatively and rapidly. Mechanistic organizations are better suited to more traditional, stable forms of production that are less susceptible to swings in the market. Although their study was first published forty years ago, it is highly relevant to present-day discussions of organizational change (see the section 'Beyond bureaucracy?' below, pp. 664–9). Burns and Stalker foreshadowed many of the issues that have taken centre stage in recent debates over globalization, flexible specialization and debureaucratization.

Bureaucracy versus democracy?

Even in democracies like the UK, government organizations hold enormous amounts of information about us, from records of our dates of birth, schools and universities attended and jobs held, to data on income used for tax collecting, and information used for issuing drivers' licences and allocating National Insurance numbers. Since we don't always know what information is held on us, and which agencies are holding it, people fear that such surveillance activities can infringe on the principle of democracy. These fears formed the basis of George Orwell's famous novel, *1984*, in which the state, 'Big Brother', uses surveillance of its citizens to suppress internal criticism and the difference of opinion normal in any democracy.

Recent proposals to introduce identity cards in the UK from 2008, and make them compulsory after 2013, have focused these concerns. The new cards are likely to contain a photograph of the card-holder, their name, address, gender, date of birth and a microchip which would hold biometric information, such as the person's fingerprints, iris image or facial dimensions. Critics have expressed concerns that a national central database which contains information about people's identity will not be secure and will pose a threat to people's rights to privacy and freedom from discrimination. Supporters of identity cards argue that some types of surveillance may actually protect the principle of democracy. Proponents of identity cards argue that their introduction will make it easier to carry out surveillance for terrorists, for example, which will protect democracy and enable it to function.

The diminishing of democracy with the advance of modern forms of organization was something that worried Weber a great deal. What especially disturbed him was the prospect of rule by faceless bureaucrats. How can democracy be anything other than a meaningless slogan in the face of the increasing power that bureaucratic organizations are wielding over us? After all, Weber reasoned, bureaucracies are necessarily specialized and hierarchical. Those near the bottom of the organization inevitably find themselves reduced to carrying out mundane tasks and have no power over what they do; power passes to those at the top. Weber's student Robert Michels (1967) invented a phrase, which has since become famous, to refer to this loss of power: in large-scale organizations, and more generally a society dominated by organizations, he argued, there is an **iron law of oligarchy** (oligarchy means rule by the few). According to Michels, the flow of power towards the top is simply an inevitable part of an increasingly bureaucratized world – hence the term 'iron law'.

Was Michels right? It surely is correct to

Is bureaucracy really that bad?

As the sociologist Paul du Gay admits, 'These are not the best days for bureaucracy'. As we have seen, since the term 'bureaucracy' was coined, it has been used in a negative way. In an influential recent book, *In Praise of Bureaucracy* (2000), du Gay resists this attack. Whilst recognizing that bureaucracies can and do, of course, have flaws, he seeks to defend bureaucracy against the most common lines of criticism directed against it.

First, du Gay argues against the claim that there are ethical problems with the idea of bureaucracy. He singles out the sociologist Zygmunt Bauman's book on the holocaust as an important account of this view. Bauman believes that it was only with the development of the bureaucratic institutions associated with modern society that horrendous acts like the holocaust in the Second World War became possible. The planned genocide of millions of people by the Nazis in the Final Solution could only happen

once institutions were in place that distanced people from taking moral responsibility for their actions. Rather than being a barbaric explosion of violence, Bauman argues, the holocaust could happen because rational bureaucratic institutions had emerged that separated discrete tasks from their consequences. German bureaucrats, and particularly the SS, would focus on carrying out their allotted tasks to the best of their abilities, and on following orders – for example, making sure that a railway line had been built, or that a group of people was moved from one part of the country to another – rather than questioning the whole rationale behind mass murder (Bauman 1989).

As we have seen, Bauman believes that responsibility is diluted in a bureaucracy. Du Gay believes quite the opposite. For the holocaust to happen, du Gay contends, the Nazis had to overcome the legitimate and ethical procedures integral to bureaucracy. Du Gay argues that

Was Auschwitz the ultimate expression of bureaucratic organization?

bureaucracies have an important ethos, which includes the equal and impartial treatment of all citizens regardless of their values. To du Gay the holocaust came about when the racist convictions of Nazis overcame the impartial application of rules that is essential to a bureaucracy.

Du Gay also seeks to defend bureaucracy against a second line of attack, by rejecting what he sees as the current fashionable talk of the need for entrepreneurial reform of bureaucracies, especially public services. He stresses that the ethos of bureaucratic impartiality is being undermined by an increasingly politicized civil service, enthusiastic to get the job done in the way that pleases politicians, rather than following a bureaucratic framework that ensures administrative responsibility for the public interest and constitutional legitimacy (du Gay 2000).

say that large-scale organizations involve the centralizing of power. Yet there is good reason to suppose that the 'iron law of oligarchy' is not quite so hard and fast as Michels claimed. The connections between oligarchy and bureaucratic centralization are more ambiguous than he supposed.

We should recognize first that unequal power is not just a function of size, as Michels presumed. In modest-sized groups there can also be very marked differences of power. In a small business, for instance, where the activities of employees are directly visible to the directors, much tighter control might be exerted than in offices in larger organizations. As organizations expand in size, power relationships often in fact become looser. Those at the middle and lower levels may have little influence over general policies forged at the top. On the other hand, because of the specialization and expertise involved in bureaucracy, people at the top also lose control over many administrative decisions, which are handled by those lower down.

In many modern organizations, power is also quite often openly delegated downward from superiors to subordinates. In many large companies, corporate heads are so busy coordinating different depart-ments, coping with crises, and analysing budget and forecast figures that they have little time for original thinking. They hand over consideration of policy issues to others below them, whose task is to develop proposals about them. Many corporate leaders frankly admit that for the most part they simply accept the conclusions given to them.

The physical setting of organizations

Most modern organizations function in specially designed physical settings. A building that houses a particular organization possesses specific features relevant to the organization's activities, but it also shares important architectural characteristics with buildings of other organizations. The architecture of a hospital, for instance, differs in some respects from that of a business firm or a school. The hospital's separate wards, consulting rooms, operating rooms and offices give the overall building a definite layout, while a school may consist of classrooms, laboratories and a gymnasium. Yet there is a general resemblance: both are likely to contain hallways with doors leading off and to use standard decoration and furnishings throughout. Apart from the differing dress of the people moving through the corridors, the buildings in which modern organizations are usually housed have a definite sameness to them. And they often look similar from the outside as well as within their interiors. It would not be unusual to ask, on driving past a building, 'Is that a school?' and receive the response, 'No, it's a hospital.'

Michel Foucault's theory of organizations: the control of time and space

Michel Foucault showed that the architecture of an organization is directly involved with its social make-up and system of authority (Foucault 1971, 1979). By studying the physical characteristics of organizations, we can shed new light on the problems Weber analysed. The offices Weber discussed abstractly are also architectural settings – rooms, separated by corridors. The buildings of large firms are sometimes actually constructed physically as a hierarchy, in which the more elevated one's position in the hierarchy of authority, the nearer to the top of the building one's office is; the phrase 'the top floor' is sometimes used to mean those who hold ultimate power in the organization.

The physical organization of this 1940s typing pool means that the workers are kept under close surveillance. In modern organizations, surveillance tends to take new forms.

In many other ways, the geography of an organization will affect its functioning, especially in cases where systems rely heavily on informal relationships. Physical proximity makes forming groups easier, while physical distance can polarize groups, resulting in a 'them' and 'us' attitude between departments.

Surveillance in organizations

The arrangement of rooms, hallways and open spaces in an organization's buildings can provide basic clues to how its system of authority operates. In some organizations, groups of people work collectively in open settings. Because of the dull, repetitive nature of certain kinds of industrial work, like assembly-line production, regular supervision is needed to ensure that workers sustain the pace of labour. The same is often true of other types of routine work, such as that carried out by customer service operators in call centres, who often have their calls and activities monitored by their supervisors. Foucault laid great emphasis on how visibility, or lack of it, in the architectural settings of modern organizations influences and expresses patterns of authority. Their level of visibility determines how easily subordinates can be subject to what Foucault calls **surveillance**, the supervision of activities in organizations. In modern organizations, everyone, even in relatively high positions of authority, is subject to surveillance; but the more lowly a person is, the more his or her behaviour tends to be closely scrutinized.

Surveillance takes several forms. One is the direct supervision of the work of subordinates by superiors. Consider the example of a school classroom. Pupils sit at tables or desks, often arranged in rows, all in view of the teacher. Children are supposed to look alert or otherwise be absorbed in their work. Of course, how far this actually happens in practice depends on the abilities of the teacher and the inclinations of the children to conform to what is expected of them.

A second type of surveillance is more subtle but equally important. It consists of keeping files, records, and case histories about people's work lives. Weber saw the importance of written records (nowadays often computerized) in modern organizations but did not fully explore how they can be used to regulate behaviour.

Employee records usually provide complete work histories, registering personal details and often giving character evaluations. Such records are used to monitor employees' behaviour and assess recommendations for promotion. In many business firms, individuals at each level in the organization prepare annual reports on the performance of those in the levels just below them. School records and college transcripts are also used to monitor individuals' performance as they move through the organization. Records are kept on file for academic staff, too.

Lastly, there is self-surveillance, where *assumptions* about the surveillance by others change ones behaviour and limit what one does. Think of the example used above of the telephone operator in a call centre. The operator will often have no way of knowing whether calls are being monitored, or how often supervisors listen in to phone conversations. Yet, operators are likely to assume that they are under surveillance from management and

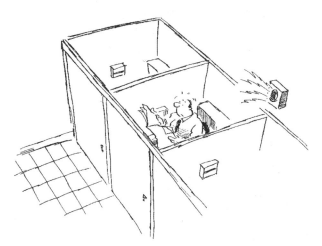

'Sensors indicate that No. 2 cubicle has been occupied for eighteen minutes. Do you require assistance?'

so keep calls short, efficient and formal, in line with the company guidelines.

Organizations cannot operate effectively if employees' work is haphazard. In business firms, as Weber pointed out, people are expected to work regular hours. Activities must be consistently coordinated in time and space, something promoted both by the physical settings of organizations and by the precise scheduling of detailed timetables. Timetables regularize activities across time and space – in Foucault's words, they 'efficiently distribute bodies' around the organization. Timetables are a condition of organizational discipline, because they slot the activities of large numbers of people together. If a university did not strictly observe a lecture timetable, for example, it would soon collapse into complete chaos. A timetable makes possible the intensive use of time and space: each can be packed with many people and many activities.

Under surveillance: the prison

Foucault paid a great deal of attention to organizations, like prisons, in which individuals are physically separated for long periods from the outside world. In such organizations, people are incarcerated – kept hidden away – from the external social environment. A prison illustrates in clear detail the nature of surveillance because it seeks to maximize control over inmates' behaviour. Foucault asks: 'Is it surprising that prisons resemble factories, schools, barracks, hospitals, which all resemble prisons?' (Foucault 1979).

According to Foucault, the modern prison has its origins in the Panopticon, an organization planned by the philosopher and social thinker Jeremy Bentham in the nineteenth century. 'Panopticon' was the name Bentham gave to an ideal prison he designed, which he tried on various occasions to sell to the British government. The design was never fully implemented, but some of its main principles were incorporated into prisons built in the nineteenth century in Europe and the United States. The Panopticon was circular in shape, with the cells built around the outside edge. In the centre was an inspection tower. Two windows were placed in every cell, one facing the inspection tower and the other facing outside. The aim of the design was to make prisoners visible to guards at all times. The windows in the tower itself were equipped with Venetian blinds, so that while the prison staff could keep the prisoners under constant observation, they themselves could be invisible.

The limits of surveillance

Foucault was right about prisons. Even today, most prisons look remarkably like the Panopticon. He was also right about the central role of surveillance in modern societies, an issue that has become even more important now because of the growing impact of information and communications technologies. We live in what some have called the **surveillance society** (Lyon 1994) – a society in which information about our lives is gathered by all types of organizations.

But Weber's and Foucault's arguments that the most effective way to run an organization is to maximize surveillance – to have clear and consistent divisions of authority – is a mistake, at least if we apply it to business firms, which don't (as prisons do) exert total control over people's lives in closed settings. Prisons do

A prison built following Bentham's model of the Panopticon.

not actually make a good model for organizations as a whole. Direct supervision may work tolerably well when the people involved, as in prisons, are basically hostile to those in authority over them and do not want to be where they are. But in organizations where managers desire others to cooperate with them in reaching common goals, the situation is different. Too much direct supervision alienates employees, who feel they are denied any opportunities for involvement in the work they do (Sabel 1982; Grint 2005).

This is one main reason why organizations founded on the sorts of principle formulated by Weber and Foucault, such as large factories involving assembly-line production and rigid authority hierarchies, eventually ran into great difficulties. Workers were not inclined to devote themselves to their work in such settings; continuous supervision was in fact *required* to get them to work reasonably hard at all, but it promoted resentment and antagonism.

People are also prone to resist high levels of surveillance in the second sense mentioned by Foucault: the collection of written information about them. That was one of the main reasons why the Soviet-style communist societies broke down. In these societies, people were spied on regularly either by the secret police or by others in the pay of the secret police – even including relatives and neighbours. The government also kept detailed information on its citizenry in order to clamp down on possible opposition to their rule. The result was a form of society that was politically authoritarian and, towards the end, economically inefficient. The whole society did indeed come almost to resemble a gigantic prison, with all the discontents, conflicts, and modes of opposition prisons generate – and from which, in the end, the population broke free.

Organizations that span the world

For the first time in history, organizations have become truly global in scale. Information technologies have rendered national borders less meaningful, since they can no longer contain key economic, cultural and environmental activities. As a consequence, international organizations

are expected to continue to grow in number and importance, providing a measure of predictability and stability in a world where nations are no longer the all-powerful actors they once were (Union of International Associations 1996–7).

Sociologists therefore study international organizations in order to understand better how it is possible to create institutions that span national borders and what their effects will be. Some sociologists even argue that global organizations will push the world's countries to become more and more alike (Thomas 1987; Scott and Meyer 1994; McNeely 1995).

International organizations are not new, however. For example, organizations concerned with managing trade across borders have existed for centuries. The Hanseatic League, a business alliance among German merchants and cities, was one such organization, dominating trade in the North and Baltic Seas from the middle of the thirteenth century to the middle of the seventeenth century. But it was not until the creation of the short-lived League of Nations in 1919 that truly global organizations, with elaborate bureaucracies and member nations around the world, were formed. The United Nations, created in 1945, is perhaps the most prominent modern example of a global organization.

Sociologists have divided international organizations into two principal types: *international governmental organizations* comprise national governments, while *international non-governmental organizations* comprise private organizations. We will consider each of these separately.

International governmental organizations

The first type of global organization is the **international governmental organization** (IGO), a type of international organization established by treaties between governments for purposes of conducting business between the nations making up its membership. Such organizations emerge for reasons of national security (both the League of Nations and the United Nations were created after highly destructive world wars), the regulation of trade (for example, by the World Trade Organization), social welfare or human rights or, increasingly, environmental protection.

Some of the most powerful IGOs today were created to unify national economies into large and powerful trading blocks. One of the most advanced IGOs is the European Union (EU), whose rules since May 2004 have governed twenty-five European member states. The EU was formed to create a single European economy, in which businesses could operate freely across borders in search of markets and labour and workers could move freely in search of jobs. EU members have common economic policies and, since 2002, twelve of them even share a single currency (the euro). Not all Europeans welcome this development, however, arguing that it means that member countries will eventually surrender most of their economic decision-making to the EU as a whole.

IGOs can also wield considerable military power, provided that their member nations are willing to do so. The North Atlantic Treaty Organization (NATO) and the UN, for example, used the full weight of their members' combined military might against Iraq during the first Gulf

War in 1991, and again in Kosovo, in the former Yugoslavia, in 1999. Yet since nations ultimately control their own use of military force, there are limits to the authority of even the most powerful military IGOs, whose strength derives from the voluntary participation of their member nations. In the face of violent civil strife in Bosnia and the African countries of Somalia and Rwanda, for example, UN peacekeeping efforts have proved largely ineffective.

IGOs often tend to reflect inequalities in power among their member nations. For example, the UN Security Council is responsible for maintaining international peace and security and is therefore the most powerful organization within the UN. Its five permanent members include Britain, the United States, China, France and Russia, giving these countries significant control over the Security Council's actions. The remaining ten countries are elected by the UN General Assembly for two-year terms and therefore have less ongoing power than the permanent members.

At the beginning of the twentieth century, there were only about three dozen IGOs in the world, although data for that time are sketchy. By 1981, when consistent reporting criteria were adopted, there were 1,039; by 1996, there were 1,830 (Union of International Associations 1996–7). Today it is estimated that there are as many as 5,500 international governmental organizations (Union of International Organizations 2002).

International non-governmental organizations

The second type of global organization is the **international non-governmental organization** (INGO), which consists of international organizations established by agreements between the individuals or private organizations making up their membership. Examples include the International Sociological Association, the International Council of Women and the environmental group Greenpeace. As with IGOs, the number of INGOs has increased explosively in recent years – from fewer than two hundred near the beginning of the twentieth century to about 15,000 in the mid-1990s (Union of International Associations 1996–7). Today there are an estimated 31,100 international non-governmental organizations (Union of International Organizations 2002).

In general, INGOs are primarily concerned with promoting the global interests of their members, largely through influencing the UN, other INGOs or individual governments. They also engage in research and education and spread information by means of international conferences, meetings and journals. INGOs have succeeded in shaping the policies of powerful nations.

Using your sociological imagination: a company of the past or future?

'The world has changed. Our customers have changed. We have to change, too.' Brave words from Jim Cantalupo, [former] chairman and chief executive of McDonald's . . . [who died in 2004. He] promised investors . . . that the world's biggest fast-food chain no longer wanted to be bigger than everybody else, just better.

It is a promise the company will struggle to keep. In January [2003] McDonald's announced its first quarterly loss since going public in 1965. Comparable store sales in America, stagnant for the past decade, have been falling for 12 months. McDonald's, once a byword for good service, has been ranked the worst company for customer satisfaction in America for nearly a decade – below even health insurers and banks. The group's share price has slumped from more than $48 in 1999, to hover around a ten-year low of $12 . . .

Even more damning, Mr Cantalupo and Charlie Bell [Cantalupo's successor until his own early death from cancer in 2005], his number two and heir-apparent, spent much of their presentation promising improvements in the basics of restaurant management – cleanliness, service and staff productivity – just to keep customers coming back. Under Mr Greenberg, McDonald's did not even have a system for monitoring standards, so as to avoid trouble with franchisees. A grading system and 'mystery shopper' policy are now in place, and the group promises to get tougher on its owner-operators.

The menu too has been a mess. It will be slimmed, so to speak. There will be fewer confusing meal choices and more healthier, premium products such as salads, yoghurts and sliced fruit. Although it has long denied that its food is linked to obesity, McDonald's, a firm that is all about image, has finally twigged that its brand is under threat from its unhealthy reputation. In a confusing attempt to be all things to all people (something Mr Cantalupo said he wants to avoid) the group plans to offer 'champagne taste on a beer budget', with new premium-priced foods, even as it declares value 'part of the brand heritage'. Advertising and store ambience are getting an overhaul too; the group's classier French stores may be a model. Less classy is Mr Bell's idea to aim Ronald McDonald, the group mascot (and apparently the second most-recognized icon in America after Santa Claus) at young adults, a 'key demographic' after children.

All this leaves many investors wondering whether McDonald's really 'gets it', as Mr Cantalupo kept insisting in his presentation. With the rise of 'fast casual' restaurants such as gourmet sandwich shops, the McDonald's offering looks increasingly outdated. The group's most recent genuine menu hit was the introduction of Chicken McNuggets in 1983.

Franchisees, used to 10–15% annual growth and fat margins, have seen their profits come under pressure and have been alienated by poorly executed initiatives from headquarters, such as the expensive new 'Made for You' kitchens that they had to buy . . .

Ironically, Ray Kroc, who founded and then expanded McDonald's as much by buying and renting property as by selling hamburgers, has left the group a gold mine to exploit. Peter Oakes, an analyst at Merrill Lynch, notes that the group owns 75% of the buildings and 40% of the land at its 30,000 locations. He calculates that the land alone, which has a book value of $4 billion, would fetch $12 billion (before tax) today. That value could be exploited through a sale-and-leaseback programme . . .

Add it all up and McDonald's could easily hand several billion dollars back to its investors. Given the looming danger of obesity litigation and a backlash against marketing 'unhealthy' food to children, returning supersized lumps of money to shareholders now could come to look farsighted. Alas, it may take more change at the top to milk this particular cash cow.

'Did somebody say a loss?' *The Economist*
(10 April 2003)

Questions

1 Is a process of 'deMcDonaldization' under way in favour of more adaptable network enterprises?
2 Is McDonald's neglecting its 'guiding principles': efficiency, calculability, uniformity and control through automation?

McDonald's has been trying to reinvent itself in recent years, following a fall in sales. This new-look London branch is now virtually indistinguishable from a bar or coffee shop.

One prominent (and highly successful) example of an INGO is the International Campaign to Ban Landmines (ICBL). The campaign, along with its founder Jody Williams, was awarded the Nobel Peace Prize in 1997 for its success in getting a majority of the world's countries to agree to a treaty banning the devastating use of landmines. The Nobel Prize committee commended the campaign for changing 'a vision to a feasible reality', adding that 'this work has grown into a convincing example of an effective policy for peace that could prove decisive in the international effort for disarmament' (ICBL 2001).

The ICBL is affiliated with more than a thousand other INGOs in some sixty countries. Together they have focused public attention on the dangers posed to civilians of the more than 100 million anti-personnel mines that are a deadly legacy of former wars fought in Europe, Asia and Africa. These mines are unlike other weapons. They can remain active for decades after a war, terrorizing and trapping whole populations. In Cambodia, for example, fertile croplands have been mined, threatening with starvation farmers who are not willing to risk action that could reduce them or their families to a shower of scraps. The campaign's efforts resulted in a treaty banning the use, production, stock-piling and transfer of anti-personnel landmines. The treaty, which became international law in March 1999, is supported by 150 countries.

Although they are far more numerous than IGOs and have achieved some successes, INGOs have far less influence, since legal power (including enforcement) ultimately lies with governments. In the effort to ban landmines, for instance, although most of the major powers in the world signed the treaty, the United States, citing security concerns in Korea, refused to do so, as did Russia. Some INGOs, like Amnesty International and Greenpeace, have nonetheless achieved considerable influence.

Economic organizations

Modern societies are, in Marx's term, capitalistic. **Capitalism** is a way of organizing economic life that is distinguished by the following important features: private ownership of the means of production; profit as incentive; free competition for markets to sell goods, acquire cheap materials and utilize cheap labour; and restless expansion and investment to accumulate capital. Capitalism, which began to spread with the growth of the Industrial Revolution in the early nineteenth century, is a vastly more dynamic economic system than any other that preceded it in history. While the system has had many critics, like Marx, it is now the most widespread form of economic organization in the world.

So far in this chapter, we have been looking at work mostly from the perspective of occupations and employees. We have studied patterns of work and the factors influencing the development of trade unions. Here, we concern ourselves with the nature of the business firms in which the workforce is employed. (It should, however, also be recognized that many people today are employees of government organizations, although we shall not consider these here.) What is happening to business corporations today, and how are they run?

Corporations and corporate power

Since the turn of the twentieth century, modern capitalist economies have been increasingly influenced by the rise of large business **corporations**. A recent survey of the world's top two hundred corporations showed that between 1983 and 1999 their combined sales grew from the equivalent of 25 per cent to 27.5 per cent of world GDP. During the same period, the profits of these corporations grew 362.4 per cent, while the number of people they employ grew by only 14.4 per cent (Anderson and Cavanagh 2000).

Of course, there still exist thousands of smaller firms and enterprises within the British economy. In these companies, the image of the **entrepreneur** – the boss who owns and runs the firm – is by no means obsolete. The large corporations are a different matter. Ever since Adolf Berle and Gardiner Means published their celebrated study *The Modern Corporation and Private Property* in the 1930s, it has been accepted that most of the largest firms are not run by those who own them (see Berle and Means 1997). In theory, the large corporations are the property of their shareholders, who have the right to make all important decisions. But Berle and Means argued that since share ownership is so dispersed, actual control has passed into the hands of the managers who run firms on a day-to-day basis. *Ownership* of the corporations is thus separated from their *control.*

Whether run by owners or managers, the power of the major corporations is very extensive. When one or a handful of firms dominate in a given industry, they often cooperate in setting prices rather than freely competing with one another.

Thus, the giant oil companies normally follow one another's lead in the price charged for gasoline. When one firm occupies a commanding position in a given industry, it is said to be in a **monopoly** position. More common is a situation of **oligopoly**, in which a small group of giant corporations predominate. In situations of oligopoly, firms are able more or less to dictate the terms on which they buy goods and services from the smaller firms that are their suppliers.

Types of corporate capitalism

There have been three general stages in the development of business corporations, although each overlaps with the others and all continue to coexist today. The first stage, characteristic of the nineteenth and early twentieth centuries, was dominated by **family capitalism**. Large firms were run either by individual entrepreneurs or by members of the same family and then passed on to their descendants. The famous corporate dynasties, such as the Sainsburys in the UK or the Rockefellers in the USA, belong in this category. These individuals and families did not just own a single large corporation, but held a diversity of economic interests and stood at the apex of economic empires.

Most of the big firms founded by entrepreneurial families have since become public companies – that is, shares of their stock are traded on the open market – and have passed into managerial control. But important elements of family capitalism remain, even within some of the word's largest corporations, such as the Ford car company, whose Chief Executive is William Clay Ford, Jr., the great-grandson of Henry Ford who founded the company.

Among small firms, such as local shops run by their owners, small plumbing and house-painting businesses and so forth, family capitalism continues to dominate. Some of these firms, such as shops that remain in the hands of the same family for two or more generations, are also dynasties on a minor scale. However, the small business sector is a highly unstable one, and economic failure is very common; the proportion of firms owned by members of the same family for extended periods is minuscule.

In the large corporate sector, family capitalism was increasingly succeeded by **managerial capitalism**. As managers came to have more and more influence through the growth of very large firms, the entrepreneurial families were displaced. The result has been described as the replacement of the family in the company by the company itself. The corporation emerged as a more defined economic entity. In studying the two hundred largest manufacturing corporations in the United States, Michael Allen found that in cases where profit showed a decline, family-controlled enterprises were unlikely to replace their chief executive, but manager-controlled firms did so rapidly (Allen 1981).

There is no question that managerial capitalism has left an indelible imprint on modern society. The large corporation drives not only patterns of consumption but also the experience of employment in contemporary society – it is difficult to imagine how different the work lives of many Britons would be in the absence of large factories or corporate bureaucracies. Sociologists have identified another area in which the large corporation has left a mark on modern institutions. **Welfare cap-**

italism refers to a practice that sought to make the corporation – rather than the state or trade unions – the primary shelter from the uncertainties of the market in modern industrial life. Beginning at the end of the nineteenth century, large firms began to provide certain services to their employees, including child care, recreational facilities, profit-sharing plans, paid holidays, unemployment insurance and life insurance. These programmes often had a paternalistic bent, such as that sponsoring 'home visits' for the 'moral education' of employees. Viewed in less benevolent terms, a major objective of welfare capitalism was coercion, as employers deployed all manner of tactics – including violence – to avoid unionization.

In his study of the US labour movement, Sanford Jacoby (1997) argues that conventional histories typically suggest that welfare capitalism met its demise in the Depression years of the 1930s, as trade unions achieved unprecedented levels of influence and as President Franklin Roosevelt's New Deal administration began to guarantee many of the benefits provided by firms. In contrast to this standard interpretation, Jacoby argues that welfare capitalism did not die but instead went underground during the apex of the labour movement. In firms that avoided unionization during the period between the 1930s and 1960s – like the US-based companies Kodak, Sears and Thompson Products – welfare capitalism was modernized, shedding blatantly paternalistic aspects and routinizing benefit programmes. When the union movement began to weaken after 1970, these companies offered a model to many other firms, which were now able to press their advantage against flanking unions, reasserting the role of the firm as 'industrial manor'.

Despite the overwhelming importance of managerial capitalism in shaping the modern economy, many scholars now see emerging the contours of a third, different phase in the evolution of the corporation. They argue that managerial capitalism has today partly ceded place to **institutional capitalism**. This term refers to the emergence of a consolidated network of business leadership, concerned not only with decision-making within single firms, but also with the development of corporate power beyond them. Institutional capitalism is based on the practice of corporations holding shares in other firms. In effect, interlocking boards of directors exercise control over much of the corporate landscape. This reverses the process of increasing managerial control, since the managers' shareholdings are dwarfed by the large blocks of shares owned by other corporations. One of the main reasons for the spread of institutional capitalism is the shift in patterns of investment that has occurred over the past thirty years. Rather than investing directly by buying shares in a business, individuals now invest in money market, trust, insurance and pension funds that are controlled by large financial organizations, which in turn invest these grouped savings in industrial corporations.

Transnational corporations

With the intensifying of globalization, most large corporations now operate in an international economic context. When they establish branches in two or several countries, they are referred to as multinational or **transnational corporations**. *Transnational* is the preferred term, indicating that these companies operate across many different national boundaries.

The largest transnationals are gigantic; their wealth outstrips that of many countries. Half of the hundred largest economic units in the world today are nations; the other half are transnational corporations. The scope of these companies' operations is staggering. The six hundred largest transnationals account for more than one-fifth of the total industrial and agricultural production in the global economy; about seventy are responsible for half of total global sales (Dicken 1992). The revenues of the largest two hundred companies rose tenfold between the mid-1970s and the 1990s, reaching $9.5 trillion in 2001. In 2003 it was estimated that the world's top ten pharmaceutical companies controlled over 53 per cent of the global market share. Over the past twenty years, the transnationals' activities have become increasingly global: only three of the world's largest companies in 1950 had manufacturing subsidiaries in more than twenty countries; some fifty do so today. These are still a small minority; most of the transnationals have subsidiaries in two to five countries.

Of the top two hundred companies in the year 2000, US corporations dominated the list, with 82 slots (41 per cent of the total); Japanese firms came second, with 41 slots (Anderson and Cavanagh 2000). However, the proportion of American companies in the top two hundred has fallen significantly since 1960, when just five Japanese corporations were included in that list. Contrary to common belief, three-quarters of all foreign direct investment is between the industrialized countries. Nevertheless, the involvements of transnationals in developing world countries are extensive, with Brazil, Mexico and India showing the highest levels of foreign investment. The most rapid rate of increase in corporate investment by far has been in the Asian newly industrializing countries (NICs) of Singapore, Taiwan, Hong Kong, South Korea and Malaysia.

The reach of the transnationals in recent decades would not have been possible without advances in transport and communications. Air travel now allows people to move around the world at a speed that would have seemed inconceivable even sixty years ago. The development of extremely large ocean-going vessels (superfreighters), together with containers that can be shifted directly from one type of carrier to another, makes possible the easy transport of bulk materials.

Telecommunications technologies now permit more or less instantaneous communication from one part of the world to another. Satellites have been used for commercial telecommunications since 1965, when the first one in use could carry 240 telephone conversations at once. Current satellites can carry at least 12,000 simultaneous conversations! The larger transnationals now have their own satellite-based communications systems. The Mitsubishi corporation, for instance, has a massive network, across which 5 million words are transmitted to and from its headquarters in Tokyo each day.

Types of transnational corporations

The transnationals came to assume an increasingly important place in the world economy over the course of the twentieth century. They are of key importance in the international **division of labour** – the specialization in producing goods for the world market that divides regions into zones of industrial or agricultural production or high- or low-skilled labour (Fröbel, Heinrichs et al. 1979; McMichael 1996). Just as national economies have become increasingly *concentrated* – dominated by a limited number of very large companies – so too has the world economy. In the case of the United Kingdom and several of the other leading industrialized countries, the firms that dominate nationally also have a very wide-ranging international presence. Many sectors of world production (such as agribusiness) are *oligopolies* – production is controlled by three or four corporations that dominate the market. Over the past two or three decades, international oligopolies have developed in the automobile, microprocessor and electronics industries, and in the production of some other goods marketed worldwide.

H. V. Perlmutter (1972) divided transnational corporations into three types. One consists of **ethnocentric transnationals**, in which company policy is set and, as far as possible, put into practice from a headquarters in the country of origin. Companies and plants that the parent corporation owns around the world are cultural extensions of the originating company – its practices are standardized across the globe. A second category is that of **polycentric transnationals**, where overseas subsidiaries are managed by local firms in each country. The headquarters in the country or countries of origin of the main company establish broad guidelines within which local companies manage their own affairs. Finally, there are **geocentric transnationals**, which are international in their management structure. Managerial systems are integrated on a global basis, and higher managers are very mobile, moving from country to country as needs dictate.

Of all transnationals, Japanese companies tend to be the most strongly ethnocentric in Perlmutter's terms. Their worldwide operations are usually controlled tightly from the parent corporation, sometimes with the close involvement of the Japanese government. The Japanese Ministry of International Trade and Industry (MITI) plays a much more direct part in the overseeing of Japanese-based foreign enterprise than Western governments do. MITI has produced a series of development plans coordinating the overseas spread of Japanese firms over the past two decades. One distinctive Japanese type of transnational consists of the giant trading companies or *sogo shosha*. These are colossal conglomerates whose main concern is with the financing and support of trade. They provide financial, organizational and information services to other companies. About half of Japanese exports and imports are routed through the ten largest *sogo shosha*. Some, like Mitsubishi, also have large manufacturing interests of their own. (Japanese corporations are discussed further on pp. 665–6 below.)

Planning on a world scale

The global corporations have become the first organizations able to plan on a truly world scale. Pepsi and Coca-Cola adverts, for example, reach billions of people across the globe. A few companies with developed global networks are able to shape the commercial activities of diverse nations. Richard Barnet and John Cavanagh (1994) argue that there are four webs of interconnecting commercial activity in the new world economy: the Global Cultural Bazaar, the Global Shopping Mall, the Global Workplace and the Global Financial Network. The Global Cultural Bazaar is the newest of the four, but is already the most extensive. Global images and global dreams are diffused through movies, TV programmes, music, videos, games, toys and T-shirts, sold on a worldwide basis. All over the earth, even in the poorest developing world countries, people are using the same electronic devices to see or listen to the same commercially produced songs and shows.

The Global Shopping Mall is a 'planetary supermarket with a dazzling spread of things to eat, drink, wear and enjoy', according to Barnet and Cavanagh. It is more exclusive than the Cultural Bazaar because the poor haven't the resources to participate – they have the status only of window shoppers. Of the 5.5 billion people who make up the world's population, 3.5 billion lack the cash or credit to purchase any consumer goods.

The third global web, the Global Workplace, is the increasingly complex global division of labour that affects all of us. It consists of the massive array of offices, factories, restaurants and millions of other places where goods are produced and consumed or information is exchanged. This web is closely bound up with the Global Financial Network, which it fuels and is financed by. The Global Financial Network consists of billions of bits of information stored in computers and portrayed on computer screens. It entails almost endless currency exchanges, credit card transactions, insurance plans, and the buying and selling of stocks and shares.

Advertising for Pepsi and Coca-Cola in Tripoli, Lebanon.

The large corporation: the same, but different

There are big differences between the large corporation of the first decade of the twenty-first century and its counterpart of the mid-twentieth century. Many of the names are the same – General Motors, Ford and IBM for example – but these have been joined by other giant firms, largely unknown in the 1950s, such as Microsoft and Intel. They all wield great power, and their top executives still inhabit the large buildings that dominate so many city centres.

But below the surface of similarities between today and half a century ago, some profound transformations have taken place. The origin of these transformations lies in that process we have encountered often in this book: globalization. Over the past fifty years, the giant corporations have become more and more caught up in global competition; as a result, their internal composition, and in a way their very nature, has altered.

Former US Labour Secretary Robert Reich has written:

> Underneath, all is changing. America's core corporation no longer plans and implements the production of a large volume of

goods and services; it no longer invests in a vast array of factories, machinery, laboratories, inventories, and other tangible assets; it no longer employs armies of production workers and middle-level managers. . . . In fact, the core corporation is no longer even American. It is, increasingly, a façade, behind which teems an array of decentralised groups and subgroups continuously contracting with similarly diffuse working units all over the world. (Reich 1991)

The large corporation is less and less a big business and more an 'enterprise web' – a central organization that links smaller firms together. IBM, for example, which used to be one of the most jealously self-sufficient of all large corporations, in the 1980s and early 1990s joined with dozens of US-based companies and more than eighty foreign-based firms to share strategic planning and cope with production problems.

Some corporations remain strongly bureaucratic and are often centred in the country in which they first became established. However, most are no longer so clearly located anywhere. The old transnational corporation used to work mainly from its national headquarters, from where its overseas production plants and subsidiaries were controlled. Now, with the transformation of space and time (discussed in chapter 5, 'Social Interaction and Everyday Life', pp. 147–50), groups situated in any region of the world are able, via telecommunications and computers, to work with others. Nations still try to influence flows of information, resources and money across their borders. But modern communications technologies make this increasingly difficult, if not impossible. Knowledge and finances can be transferred across the world as electronic blips moving at the speed of light.

The products of the transnational companies similarly have an international character. When is something 'Made in Britain' or any other country and when is it not? There is no longer any clear answer.

In chapter 2, 'Globalization and the Changing World' (pp. 67–8), we looked at the example of Barbie, the all-American doll.

Barbie's packaging says that she is 'Made in China', but as that chapter showed, her body and wardrobe span the globe in their origins, from the Middle to the Far East, before she is eventually sold in the United States, or shipped on again for sale elsewhere.

Women and the corporation

Until two or three decades ago, organizational studies did not devote very much attention to the question of gender. Weber's theory of bureaucracy and many of the influential responses to Weber that came in subsequent years were written by men and presumed a model of organizations that placed men squarely at the centre. The rise of feminist scholarship in the 1970s, however, led to examinations of gender relations in all the main institutions in society, including organizations and bureaucracy. Feminist sociologists not only focused on the imbalance of gender roles within organizations, they also explored the ways in which modern organizations themselves had developed in a specifically gendered way.

Feminists have argued that the emergence of the modern organization and the bureaucratic career was dependent on a particular gender configuration. They point to two main ways in which gender is embedded in the very structure of modern

"*That was a fine report, Barbara. But since the sexes speak different languages, I probably didn't understand a word of it.*"

organizations. First, bureaucracies are characterized by occupational gender segregation. As women began to enter the labour market in greater numbers, they tended to be segregated into categories of occupations that were low paying and involved routine work. These positions were subordinate to those occupied by men and did not provide opportunities for women to be promoted. Women were used as a source of cheap, reliable labour, but were not granted the same opportunities as men to build careers.

Second, the idea of a bureaucratic career was in fact a *male* career in which women played a crucial supporting role. At the workplace, women performed the routine tasks – as clerks, secretaries and office managers – thereby freeing up men to advance their careers. Men could concentrate on obtaining promotions or landing big accounts because the female support staff handled much of the busy work. In the domestic sphere, women also supported the bureaucratic career by

caring for the home, the children and the man's day-to-day well-being. Women serviced the needs of the male bureaucrat by allowing him to work long hours, travel and focus solely on his work without concerning himself with personal or domestic issues.

As a result of these two tendencies, early feminist writers argued, modern organizations have developed as male-dominated preserves in which women are excluded from power, denied opportunities to advance their careers and victimized on the basis of their gender through sexual harassment and discrimination. Although most early feminist analysis focused on a common set of concerns – unequal pay, discrimination, and the male hold on power – there was no consensus about the best approach to take in working for women's equality. Two of the leading feminist works on women and organizations exemplified the split between liberal and radical feminist perspectives.

One important liberal perspective was Rosabeth Moss Kanter's *Men and Women of the Corporation* (1977), one of the earliest examinations of women in bureaucratic settings. Kanter investigated the position of women in corporations and analysed the ways in which they were excluded from gaining power. She focused on 'male homosociability' – the way in which men successfully kept power within a closed circle and allowed access only to those who were part of the same close group. Women and ethnic minorities were effectively denied opportunities for advancement and were shut out of the social networks and personal relationships that were crucial for promotions.

Although Kanter was critical of these

gender imbalances within modern corporations, she was not entirely pessimistic about the future. In her eyes, the problem was one of *power*, not gender. Women were in a disadvantaged position, not because they were women per se, but because they did not wield sufficient power within organizations. As greater numbers of women came to assume powerful roles, according to Kanter, the imbalances would be swept away. Her analysis can be described as a liberal feminist approach because she is primarily concerned with equality of opportunity and ensuring that women are permitted to attain positions comparable with those of men.

An alternative approach was presented by the radical feminist Kathy Ferguson in *The Feminist Case Against Bureaucracy* (1984), which differs greatly from that of Kanter. Ferguson did not see the gender imbalance within organizations as something that could be resolved with the promotion of more women to positions of power. In Ferguson's view, modern organizations were fundamentally tainted by male values and patterns of domination. Women would always be relegated to subordinate roles within such structures, she argued. The only true solution was for women to build their own organizations on principles very different from those designed by and for men. Women, she argued, have the capacity to organize in a way that is more democratic, participatory and cooperative than men, who are prone to authoritarian tactics, inflexible procedures and an insensitive management style.

Debates about conflict and power within organizations are an important issue in the sociology of organizations.

In chapter 18 (pp.756–62) we discuss one aspect of this, gender in equality in the workplace, in more detail.

Beyond bureaucracy?

Bureaucracies still exist aplenty in the West, and sociologists such as George Ritzer, whose thesis on the 'McDonaldization' of society we looked at the start of this chapter argue that bureaucracy still characterizes organizations in Western societies. However, others believe that although Weber's model of bureaucracy, mirrored by that of Foucault, may once have held good, it is now starting to look archaic. Numerous organizations are overhauling themselves to become less, rather than more, hierarchical.

In the 1960s, Burns and Stalker concluded that traditional bureaucratic structures can stifle innovation and creativity in cutting-edge industries (see pp. 643–4); in today's electronic economy, few would dispute the importance of these findings. Departing from rigid vertical command structures, many organizations are turning to 'horizontal', collaborative models in order to become more flexible and responsive to fluctuating markets. In this section, we shall examine some of the main forces behind these shifts, including globalization and the growth of information technology, and consider some of the ways in which late modern organizations are reinventing themselves in the light of the changing circumstances.

Organizational change: the Japanese model

Many of the changes that can now be witnessed in organizations around the world were first pioneered amongst some of the large Japanese manufacturing corporations, such as Nissan and Panasonic. Although the Japanese economy suffered in the 1990s, it has been phenomenally successful during most of the post-war period. This economic success was often attributed to the distinctive characteristics of large Japanese corporations – which differed substantially from most business firms in the West. As we shall see, many of the organizational characteristics associated with Japanese corporations have been adapted and modified in other countries in recent years.

> The organization of Japanese business contains important overlaps with the move to post-Fordism, discussed in chapter 18, 'Work and Economic Life', pp. 762–6.

Japanese companies have diverged from the characteristics that Weber associated with bureaucracy in several ways:

1 *Bottom-up decision-making* The big Japanese corporations do not form a pyramid of authority as Weber portrayed it, with each level being responsible only to the one above. Rather, workers low down in the organization are consulted about policies being considered by management, and even the top executives regularly meet them.

2 *Less specialization* In Japanese organizations, employees specialize much less than their counterparts in the West.

Young workers entering a firm in a management training position will spend the first year learning generally how the various departments of the firm operate. They will then rotate through a variety of positions in both local branches and national headquarters in order to gain experience in the many dimensions of the company's activities. By the time employees reach the peak of their careers, some thirty years after having begun as a trainee, they will have mastered all the important tasks.

3 *Job security* The large corporations in Japan are committed to the lifetime employment of those they hire; the employee is guaranteed a job. Pay and responsibility are geared to seniority – how many years a worker has been with the firm – rather than to a competitive struggle for promotion.

4 *Group-oriented production* At all levels of the corporation, people are involved in small cooperative 'teams', or work groups. The groups, rather than individual members, are evaluated in terms of their performance. Unlike their Western counterparts, the 'organization charts' of Japanese companies – maps of the authority system – show only groups, not individual positions.

5 *Merging of work and private lives* In Weber's depiction of bureaucracy, there is a clear division between the work of people within the organization and their activities outside. This is in fact true of most Western corporations, in which the relation between firm and employee is an economic one. Japanese corporations, by contrast, provide for many of their employees' needs, expecting in return a high level of loyalty to the firm. Workers receive material benefits

from the company over and above their salaries. The electrical firm Hitachi, for example, studied by Ronald Dore (1973), provided housing for all unmarried workers and nearly half of its married male employees. Company loans were available for the education of children and to help with the cost of weddings and funerals.

Studies of Japanese-run plants in Britain and the United States indicate that 'bottom-up' decision-making does work outside Japan. Workers seem to respond positively to the greater level of involvement these plants provide (White and Trevor 1983). It seems reasonable to conclude, therefore, that the Japanese model does carry some lessons relevant to the Weberian conception of bureaucracy. Organizations that closely resemble Weber's ideal type are probably much less effective than they appear on paper, because they do not permit lower-level employees to develop a sense of involvement and autonomy in relation to their work tasks.

Until recently, many British and US business writers looked to the Japanese corporation as a model that Anglo-American companies should follow (Hutton 1995). The slowdown in the Japanese economy during the 1990s has led many experts to question this assumption. The commitment and sense of obligation that many Japanese companies traditionally had towards their staff may have encouraged loyalty, but it has also been criticized as inflexible and uncompetitive. As we have seen, during much of the post-war period core workers in Japanese companies could expect to be with the same company their entire working lives, dismissals or redundancies were rare

and ambition for promotion was not particularly encouraged. The economic problems facing the country from the early 1990s, which only now appear to be easing, have meant that the future of Japanese business is torn between traditionalists, seeking to preserve the old system, and radical capitalists supporting reform towards a more competitive, individualistic model of business (Freedman 2001).

The transformation of management

Most of the components of the 'Japanese model' described above come down to issues of management. While it is impossible to ignore specific production-level practices developed by the Japanese, a large part of the Japanese approach focused on management–worker relations and ensured that employees at all levels felt a personal attachment to the company. The emphasis on teamwork, consensus-building approaches and broad-based employee participation were in stark contrast to traditional Western forms of management that were more hierarchical and authoritarian.

In the 1980s, many Western organizations introduced new management techniques in order to boost productivity and competitiveness. Two popular branches of management theory – *human resource management* and the *corporate culture approach* – indicated that the Japanese model had not gone unnoticed in the West. The first of these, **human resource management** (HRM), is a style of management which regards a company's workforce as vital to economic competitiveness: if the employees are not completely dedicated to the firm and its product, the firm will never be a leader in its field. In order to generate employee enthusiasm and commitment, the entire organizational culture must be retooled so that workers feel they have an investment in the workplace and in the work process. According to HRM, human resources issues should not be the exclusive domain of designated 'personnel officers', but should be a top priority for all members of company management.

HRM is based on the assumption that there is no serious conflict within the company between workers and employers and there is therefore little need for trade unions to represent the workforce. Instead, HRM presents the company as an integrated whole, the only rivalry being that with its competitor firms. Instead of dealing with its workers through negotiation with trade unions, companies using

Globalization and everyday life: the computerization of the workplace

For businesses competing in the global economy, investment in information technology – computer and communications equipment – is a necessity. Firms in the financial sector rely heavily on computers to engage in transactions in international financial markets; manufacturing firms depend on communications equipment to coordinate global production processes; and the customers of consumer services firms demand twenty-four-hour-a-day access to their accounts by telephone or the Internet. In short, information technology has become part of the basic infrastructure of business.

While some of these technologies have made workers' lives easier, there is reason to worry that the new high-tech workplace may erode their power and rights. First, business reliance on information technology may undermine coalitions among workers. There is great demand today for employees with high-tech skills, whereas those who finish school or further education with few such skills find themselves eligible only for a limited number of positions. Increasingly, there are coming to be two 'classes' of employees in firms: a privileged class with high-tech skills and another class relegated to lower-status work. But when employees negotiate with management over such issues as wages, hours and benefits, employee unity is essential for securing concessions. Will high-tech workers side with lower-skilled employees in workplace disputes, or will they be more likely to side with

management? The status of worker rights and benefits in the future may well hinge on the answer to this question.

Second, in part because new communications technologies allow the branch offices and production facilities of multinational firms to communicate easily with one another, a higher proportion of manufactured goods is coming to be produced on a transnational basis – a situation that may make individual workers more easily replaceable. Robert Reich, who served as US Labour Secretary under President Clinton, provides the following example of a global production process:

> Precision ice-hockey equipment is designed in Sweden, financed in Canada, and assembled in Cleveland and Denmark for distribution in North America and Europe, respectively, out of alloys whose molecular structure was researched and patented in Delaware and fabricated in Japan. An advertising campaign is conceived in Britain; film footage is shot in Canada, dubbed in Britain, and edited in New York. (Reich 1991)

Although high-tech, high-skilled workers will be needed to carry out many aspects of the production process, these skills may no longer give workers the same bargaining power vis-à-vis management that skilled craftsmanship carried with it in previous eras. Because the manufacturing process has now been broken down into many small components, and because each of these components is carried out at a different production facility, the number of skills that any one worker must have is more limited than was the case in previous eras, making it easier for companies to replace contentious workers. Communications technologies thus arguably further the process that the Marxist scholar Harry Braverman (1974) called 'the deskilling of labour'.

Third, the nature of workplace surveillance is likely to change substantially as information technology becomes even more important for business. Employers have always watched their employees closely, monitoring performance, seeking to improve efficiency, checking to make sure they do not steal. But as a greater proportion of work comes to be done by

computer, the capacity of managers to scrutinize the behaviour of their employees increases. Computerized performance evaluations, scrutiny of employee email and enhanced management access to personal employee information – such an Orwellian scenario becomes ever more likely as the role of information technology in the workplace expands.

Questions

1   Do you think these dangers are real, or is the impact of information technology on organizations essentially benign for employees?
2   What steps, if any, do you think can be taken to counter these trends?

In modern open-plan offices like these, employers can still keep workers under close surveillance.

the techniques of HRM seek to individualize their workforce by providing individual contracts and perforce-related pay. Recent studies have shown that whilst workers may comply with the dictates of HRM at work, many are privately cynical about the assumption of corporate unity that underlies it (Thompson and Findlay, 1999).

The second management trend – creating a distinctive **corporate culture** – is closely related to human resource management. In order to promote loyalty to the company and pride in its work, the company's management works with employees to build an organizational culture involving rituals, events or traditions unique to that company alone. These cultural activities are designed to draw all members of the firm – from the most senior managers to the newest employee – together so that they make common cause with each other and strengthen group solidarity. Company picnics or 'fun days', 'casual Fridays' (days on which employees can 'dress down') and company-sponsored community service projects are examples of techniques for building a corporate culture.

In recent years, a number of Western companies have been founded according to the management principles described above. Rather than constructing themselves according to a traditional bureaucratic model, companies like the Saturn car company in the United States have organized themselves along these new managerial lines. At Saturn, for example, employees at all levels have the opportunity to have spells in positions in other areas of the company in order to gain a better sense of the operation of the firm as a whole. Shopfloor workers spend time

with the marketing team, sharing insights into the way in which the vehicles are made. Sales staff rotate through the servicing department to become more aware of common maintenance problems that might concern prospective buyers. Representatives from both sales and the shopfloor are involved in product design teams in order to discuss shortcomings which the management may not have been aware of in earlier models. A corporate culture focused on friendly and knowledgeable customer service unifies company employees and enhances the sense of company pride.

The study of networks

Social networks

There is an old saying that 'it's not *what* you know, it's *who* you know'. This adage expresses the value of having 'good connections'. Sociologists refer to such connections as **networks** – all the direct and indirect connections that link a person or a group with other people or groups. Your personal networks thus include people you know directly (such as your friends) as well as people you know indirectly (such as your friends' friends). Personal networks often include people of similar race, class, ethnicity and other types of social background, although there are exceptions. For example, if you subscribe to an online mailing list, you are part of a network that consists of all the people on the list, who may be of different racial or ethnic backgrounds and genders. Because groups and organizations can also be networked – for example, all the alumni of a particular university – belonging to such groups can greatly extend your reach and influence.

A business meeting?

Social groups are an important source for acquiring networks; but not all networks are social groups. Many networks lack the shared expectations and common sense of identity that are the hallmark of social groups. For example, you are not likely to share a sense of identity with the subscribers to an online mailing list, nor will you probably even know the neighbours of most of your co-workers at the office, even though they would form part of your social network.

Networks serve us in many ways. Sociologist Mark Granovetter (1973) demonstrated that there can be enormous strength in weak ties, particularly among higher socio-economic groups. Granovetter showed that upper-level professional and managerial employees are likely to hear about new jobs through connections such as distant relatives or remote acquaintances. Such weak ties can be of great benefit because relatives or acquaintances tend to have very different sets of connections from those of closer friends, whose social contacts are likely to be similar to one's own. Among lower socio-economic groups, Granovetter argued, weak ties are not necessarily bridges to other networks and so do not really widen opportunities (Marsden and Lin 1982; Wellman et al. 1988; Knoke 1990). After graduation from college, you may rely on a good degree and a strong CV to find a job. But it may prove more beneficial if it happens that your friend at college went to school with the interviewer in the organization where you are seeking work.

Most people rely on their personal networks in order to gain advantages, but not everyone has equal access to powerful networks. Some sociologists argue, for example, that women's business and political networks are weaker than men's, so that women's power in these spheres is reduced (Brass 1985). Several of the best-known public schools in the UK, such as Eton and Harrow, only admit boys, thereby denying women access to powerful connections formed by pupils during their school years. In general, sociologists have found that when women look for work, their job market networks comprise fewer ties than do men's, meaning that women know fewer people in fewer occupations (Marsden 1987; Moore 1990). Meagre networks tend to channel women into female-typical jobs, which usually offer less pay and fewer opportunities for advancement (Ross and Reskin 1992; Drentea 1998). Still, as more and more women move up into higher-level positions, the resulting networks can foster further advancement. One study found that women are more likely to be hired or promoted into job levels that already have a high proportion of women (Cohen et al. 1998).

Networks confer more than economic advantage. You are likely to rely on your networks for a broad range of contacts, from obtaining access to your Member of Parliament to finding a date. Similarly, when you visit another country your friends, school or religious organization may steer you to their overseas connections, who can then help you find your way around in the unfamiliar environment. When you graduate from school or

further education, your alumni group can further extend your network of social support.

Networks and information technology

As we have seen, networks are very old forms of human practice. But for the sociologist Manuel Castells, networks, powered by the development of **information technology** and particularly of the Internet, are the defining organizational structure of our age. The inherent flexibility and adaptability of networks gives them enormous advantages over older types of organization. In the past, rational, hierarchical bureaucracies of the kind Weber described proved to be highly successful at using resources to meet the organization's goals. Networks, in contrast, were unable to coordinate functions, focus on specific goals or accomplish given tasks as successfully as bureaucracies. To Castells, the enormous advances in computing and technology during the last quarter of the twentieth century, which created what he calls the 'Internet Galaxy' (2001), changed all that. The arrival of the Internet means that data can now be processed instantaneously in almost any part of the world; there is no need for physical proximity between those involved. As a result, the introduction of new technology has allowed many companies to 're-engineer' their organizational structure, becoming more decentralized, and reinforcing the tendency towards smaller, more flexible types of enterprises. (These changes have also led to a rise in homeworking, as we will see on pp. 773–4.)

Traditionally, identifying the boundaries of organizations has been fairly

The global Benetton operation is based on a network principle.

straightforward. Organizations were generally located in defined physical spaces, such as an office building, a suite of rooms or, in the case of a hospital or university, a whole campus. The mission or tasks an organization aimed to fulfil were also usually clear-cut. A central feature of bureaucracies, for example, was adherment to a defined set of responsibilities, and procedures for carrying them out. Weber's view of bureaucracy was that of a self-contained unit that intersected with outside entities at limited and designated points.

We have already seen how the physical boundaries of organizations are being worn away by the capacity of new information technology to transcend countries and time zones. But the same process is also affecting the work that organizations do and the way in which it is coordinated. Many organizations no longer operate as independent units, as they once did. A growing number are finding that their operations run more effectively when they are linked into a web of complex relationships with other organizations and companies. No longer is there a clear dividing line between the organization and outside groups. Globalization, information technology and trends in occupational patterns all mean that organizational boundaries are more open and fluid than they once were.

In *The Rise of the Network Society* (1996), Castells argues that the 'network enterprise' is the organizational form best suited to a global, information economy. By this, he means that it is increasingly impossible for organizations – be they large corporations or small businesses – to survive if they are not part of a network. What enables the process of networking to occur is the growth of information technology: organizations around the world are able to locate each other, enter readily into contact and coordinate joint activities through an electronic medium. Castells cites several examples of organizational networking and emphasizes that they have originated in diverse cultural and institutional contexts. According to Castells, however, they all represent 'different dimensions of a fundamental process' – the disintegration of the traditional, rational bureaucracy.

Although there are many examples of organizations as networks, let us consider an illustrative case. The sociologist Stewart Clegg studied the clothing retailers Benetton. At first glance, you might not think that Benetton, with its 5,000 outlets around the world, is particularly different from any other global fashion brand. But in fact Benetton is an example of a particular type of network organization that is made possible by advances in information technology. The Benetton outlets around the world are licensed franchises run by individuals who are not employed by Benetton directly, but who are part of a larger complex devoted to making and selling Benetton products.

The entire operation is based on a network principle: the central Benetton firm in Italy subcontracts orders for products to a variety of manufacturers based on demand from its franchises round the globe. Computers link the various parts of the network, so that, at the touch of a till button at, for example, the Moscow outlet, information is relayed back to the headquarters in Italy about the shipments it needs. Whereas other international fashion retailers introduce identical sets of products into all their shops worldwide, Benetton's structure allows it to customize orders for individual franchises. Rather than entering into regular contracts with suppliers, Benetton can react to the market and call on its loose network of collaborating partners to provide services when needed (Clegg 1990).

Is the combination of information technology with networks taking us completely away from Weber's pessimistic vision of the future of bureaucracy? We should be cautious about such a view. Bureaucratic systems are more internally fluid than Weber believed and are increasingly being challenged by other, less hierarchical forms of organization. But, as Ritzer shows in his thesis on the McDonaldization of society they probably won't disappear altogether, like the dinosaurs. In the near future, there is likely to be a continuing push and pull between tendencies towards large size, impersonality and hierarchy in organizations on the one hand, and opposing influences on the other.

How do organizations and networks affect your life?

Social capital: the ties that bind

One of the principal reasons people join organizations is to gain connections and increase their influence. The time and energy invested in an organization can bring welcome returns. Parents who belong to a Parent-Teacher Association, for example, are more likely to be able to influence school policy than those who do not belong. The members know whom to call, what to say and how to exert pressure on school officials.

Sociologists call these fruits of organizational membership **social capital**, the social knowledge and connections that enable people to accomplish their goals and extend their influence. Although the idea of social capital can be traced back to antiquity, the expression entered mainstream academic discussion in the late 1980s. In Europe, the concept was particularly associated with the French sociologist Pierre Bourdieu (whose use of the term is discussed in chapter 9, pp. 321–4). The last decade has seen an explosion in the use of the term 'social capital', sparked by the influential work of the American political scientist Robert Putnam (1995, 2000).

Social capital includes useful social networks, a sense of mutual obligation and trustworthiness, an understanding of the norms that govern effective behaviour and, in general, other social resources that enable people to act effectively. For example, university students often become active in the student union or newspaper partly because they hope to learn social skills and make connections that will pay off when they graduate. They may, for example, get to interact with lecturers and administrators, who then will support them when they are looking for a job or applying for postgraduate courses.

Differences in social capital mirror larger social inequalities. In general, for example, men have more capital than women, whites more than non-whites, the wealthy more than the poor. The social capital gained from being educated at a public school, such as Eton or Harrow in the UK, is an important reason why many parents send their children there, but, as in these cases the schools are single-sex and fee-paying, capital is limited to wealthy males. Attendance at these schools gives the pupils access to powerful social, political and business resources later in life, helping to extend their wealth and influence. Differences in social capital can also be found among countries. According to the World Bank (2001), countries with high levels of social capital, where businesspeople can effectively develop the 'networks of trust' that foster healthy economies, are more likely to experience economic growth. An example is the rapid growth experienced by many East Asian economies in the 1980s, a growth some sociologists have argued was fuelled by strong business networks.

Robert Putnam completed an extensive study of social capital in the United States and distinguished two types of social capital: *bridging social capital*, which is outward-looking and inclusive, and *bonding social capital*, which is inward-looking and exclusive. Bridging social capital unifies people across social cleavages. The capacity to unify people can be seen in such examples as the civil rights movement, which brought blacks and whites together in the struggle for racial equality, and inter-faith religious organizations. Bonding social capital reinforces exclusive identities and homogeneous groups; it can be found in ethnic fraternal organizations, church-based women's reading groups and fashionable country clubs (Putnam 2000).

People who actively belong to organizations are more likely to feel 'connected';

they feel engaged, able to 'make a difference'. From the standpoint of the larger society, social capital, the bridging form in particular, provides people with a feeling that they are part of a wider community, and one that includes people who are different from themselves. Democracy flourishes when social capital is strong. Indeed, cross-national survey evidence suggests that levels of civic engagement in the United States, where Putnam's research was based, are among the highest in the world (Putnam 1993, 2000). But there is equally strong evidence that during the past thirty or so years, the ties of political involvement, club membership and other forms of social and civic engagement that bind Americans to one another have significantly diminished. Could it be that democracy is being eroded as a result?

Bowling alone: an example of declining social capital?

Putnam argued that participation in organizations provides many Americans with such social capital as the ability to cooperate with others for mutual benefit, a sense of trust and a feeling of belonging to the larger society. This kind of social capital is essential for effective citizenship. Yet, according to Putnam, these social ties are rapidly lessening in American society (see table 16.1). One subtle but significant sign of this decline (Putnam 1995, 2000), is seen in American bowling alleys: more and more people are bowling alone these days. Putnam points out that league bowlers consume three times as much beer and pizza as solo bowlers, a fact which suggests to him that the former spend more time socializing, perhaps even discussing civic issues. Bowling alone, according to

Putnam (2000), is symptomatic of the loss of community today:

> The most whimsical yet discomfiting evidence of social disengagement in contemporary America that I have discovered is this: more Americans are bowling today than ever before, but bowling in organized leagues has plummeted in the last decade or so. Between 1980 and 1993 the total number of bowlers in America increased by 10 percent, while league bowling decreased by 40 percent. (Lest this be thought a wholly trivial example, I should note that nearly 80 million Americans went bowling at least once in 1993, nearly a third more than voted in the 1994 Congressional elections and roughly the same number as claim to attend church regularly. . . .)
>
> For the first two-thirds of the twentieth century a powerful tide bore Americans into ever deeper engagement in the life of their communities, but a few decades ago – silently, without warning – that tide reversed and we were overtaken by a treacherous rip current. Without at first noticing, we have been pulled apart from one another and from our communities over the last third of the century.

Putnam points out that not only has bowling in organized leagues declined, but organizational memberships of all sorts have dropped by as much as 25 per cent since the 1970s. In the USA, parent-teacher associations, the National Federation of Women's Clubs, the League of Women Voters and the Red Cross have all experienced membership declines of roughly 50 per cent since the 1960s. Putnam reports that in 1974, about one in four adults regularly volunteered his or her time to such associations; today, the number is closer to one in five. Social organizations such as the Lions Club and Masons have also experienced membership declines. Along with these organizational declines, fewer people in the USA

Table 16.1   Twenty-year declines in political and community participation, 1973/4–1993/4

Activity	Percentage decline
Service as an officer of some club or organization	42
Work for a political party	42
Service on a committee for some local organization	39
Attendance at a public meeting on town or school affairs	35
Attendance at a political rally or speech	34
Delivery of a speech	24
Writing to a congressman or senator	23
Signing a petition	22
Membership in a 'better government' group	19
Holding or running for political office	16
Writing a letter to the newspaper	14
Writing an article for a magazine or newspaper	10
Participation in at least one of these 12 activities	25

Source: Putnam (2000), p. 45

report that they socialize with their neighbours or feel that most people can be trusted.

Such declines in organizational membership, neighbourliness and trust in general have been paralleled by a decline in democratic participation. Voter turnout in presidential and parliamentary elections in the USA fell considerably since its peak in the late 1960s (although it rose again during the highly polarized presidential election between George Bush Junior and John Kerry in 2004). Similarly, attendance at public meetings concerning education or civic affairs has dropped sharply since the 1970s, and three out of four Americans today tell pollsters that they either 'never' trust the government or do so only 'sometimes' (Putnam 1995).

Putnam argues that even in those organizations with increased membership, such as the American Association of Retired Persons (AARP, with 33 million members), the statistics are deceiving: the vast majority of these organizations' members simply pay their annual dues and receive a newsletter. Very few members actively participate, failing to develop the social capital Putnam regards as an important underpinning of democracy. Many of the most popular organizations today, such as keep fit programmes or weight watchers' groups, emphasize personal growth and health rather than collective goals to benefit society as a whole.

There are undoubtedly many reasons for these declines. For one thing, women, who were traditionally active in voluntary organizations, are more likely to hold a job than ever before. For another, people are increasingly disillusioned with government and less likely to think that their vote counts. Furthermore, people now spend more time commuting and so use up time and energy that might have been available for civic activities. But the principal source of declining civic participation, according to Putnam, is simple: television. The many hours people spend at home alone in the USA watching TV has replaced social engagement in the community.

Is Europe also suffering the same decline in social capital? In a survey of the literature on social capital (2000), David Halpern, at the time an adviser to the British Prime Minister Tony Blair, argued that it would be wrong to assume that all countries are following America's declining levels of social capital. Halpern stressed that trends in social capital differ between countries and that different indicators give a different picture. In general, Halpern found, Sweden, the Netherlands and Japan show stable or rising levels of social capital, whereas for Germany and France the indicators are more mixed. However, Halpern concludes that social capital in the UK, along with Australia and the USA, has declined significantly in the last few decades.

Evidence for a fall in social capital in the UK is manifold. In recent decades the membership of several important associations in Britain has fallen dramatically. In particular, trades unions, traditional women's organizations – such as the Women's Institute – churches, youth groups and service organizations have all seen their memberships fall. There is also evidence that there is a steady decline in political engagement. Voter turnout in general elections fell from a peak of 82 per cent in 1951 to just 58 per cent in 2001 (before rising slightly in 2005). Only 46 per cent of eligible voters turned out for the 2004 European elections. As Halpern (2005) has noted, people in the UK are also less likely to give money to charity than in the past, and less likely to trust their neighbours. The proportion of people describing their neighbourhood as one where 'people do things together and try to help each other' fell from 43 per cent in 1984 to just 28 per cent in 1996.

Looking at Europe as a whole, the evidence for a decline in social capital is far more mixed than in the USA. Robert Putnam, the most influential of the theorists on social capital, is not particularly hopeful. He writes: 'Some evidence suggests that Europe is about to follow the American pattern with a lag of a few decades. Europe may have a social capital "cold", but not yet the full-blown American "pneumonia".'

Conclusion

The organizations and networks that people belong to exert an enormous influence over their lives. As we have seen in this chapter, conventional groups appear to be losing ground in people's daily lives. For example, today's students are less likely to join civic groups and organizations – or even vote – then were their parents, a decline that may well signal a lower commitment to their communities. Some sociologists worry that this signals a weakening of society itself, which could bring about social instability.

As we have also seen, the global economy and information technology are redefining group life in ways that are now beginning to be felt. For instance, the older generation of workers is likely to spend much of their careers in a relatively small handful of long-lasting, bureaucratic organizations; the younger generation is much more likely to be part of a larger number of networked, 'flexible' ones. Many of today's group affiliations will be created through the Internet or through other forms of communication that are developing all the time. It will become increasingly easy to connect with like-minded people anywhere on the planet, creating geographically dispersed groups around the world, whose members may never meet each other face-to-face.

How will these trends affect the quality of social relationships? For nearly all of human history, most people have inter-acted exclusively with others who are close at hand. The Industrial Revolution, which facilitated the rise of large, impersonal bureaucracies where people knew one another poorly if at all, changed the nature of social interaction. Today, the information revolution is once again changing human interaction. Tomorrow's groups and organizations could provide a renewed sense of communication and social intimacy – or they could spell further isolation and social distance.

Summary points

1   All modern organizations are in some degree bureaucratic in nature. Bureaucracy is characterized by a clearly defined hierarchy of authority; written rules governing the conduct of officials (who work full time for a salary); and a separation between the tasks of the official within the organization and life outside it. Members of the organization do not own the material resources with which they operate. Max Weber argued that modern bureaucracy is a highly effective means of organizing large numbers of people, ensuring that decisions are made according to general criteria.

2   Informal networks tend to develop at all levels both within and between organizations. The study of these informal ties is as important as the more formal characteristics on which Weber concentrated his attention.

3   The physical settings of organizations strongly influence their social features. The architecture of modern organizations is closely connected to surveillance as a means of securing obedience to those in authority. Surveillance refers to the supervision of people's activities, as well as to the keeping of files and records about them. Self-surveillance refers to the way people limit their behaviour because of the assumption that they are under surveillance.

4   The work of Weber and Michels identifies a tension between bureaucracy and democracy. On the one hand, there are long-term processes of the centralization of decision-making associated with the development of modern societies. On the other, one of the main features of the past two centuries has been expanding pressures towards democracy. The trends conflict, with neither one in a position of dominance.

5   Modern organizations have evolved as gendered institutions. Women have traditionally been segregated into certain occupational categories that support the ability of men to advance their careers. In recent years, women have been entering professional and managerial positions in greater numbers, but some believe that women have to adopt a traditionally male management style on order to succeed at top levels.

6 Large organizations have started to restructure themselves over recent years to become less bureaucratic and more flexible. Many Western firms have adopted aspects of Japanese management systems: more consultation of lower-level workers by managerial executives; pay and responsibility linked to seniority; and groups, rather than individuals, evaluated for their performance.

7. Two important forms of global organization are international governmental organizations (IGOs) and international non-governmental organizations (INGOs). Both play an increasingly important role in the world today, and IGOs – particularly the United Nations – may become key organizational actors as the pace of globalization increases.

8 The modern economy is dominated by the large corporations. When one firm has a commanding influence in a given industry, it is in a monopoly position. When a cluster of firms wields such influence, a situation of oligopoly exists. Through their influence on government policy and on the consumption of goods, the giant corporations have a profound effect on people's lives.

9 Corporations have undergone profound transformations in recent years because of increasing world interdependence, or globalization. The modern corporation is increasingly an enterprise web of many smaller firms linked together, rather than a single big business.

10 Multinational or transnational corporations operate across different national boundaries. The largest of them exercise tremendous economic power. Half of the one hundred largest economic units are not countries, but privately owned companies.

11 New information technology is changing the way in which organizations work. Many tasks can now be completed electronically, a fact that allows organizations to transcend time and space. The physical boundaries of organizations are being eroded by the capabilities of new technology. Many organizations now work as loose networks, rather than as self-contained independent units.

12 Networks constitute a broad source of relationships, direct and indirect, including connections that may be extremely important in business and politics. Women, ethnic minorities and lower-income people typically have less access to the most influential economic and political networks than do men in the UK.

13 Social capital refers to the knowledge and connections that enable people to cooperate with one another for mutual benefit and extend their influence. Some social scientists, who have focused their studies on the USA, have argued that social capital has declined since the 1970s, a process they worry indicates a decline in commitment to civic engagement.

Questions for further thought

1 What are the advantages of being dealt with in a bureaucratic manner?

2 Why do people in organizations so frequently depart from formal procedures?

3 What do schools, hospitals and prisons have in common?

4 Are large organizations 'fundamentally tainted' by male values?

5 How do network organizations manage to be everywhere and nowhere?

6 Why is there such a complex relationship between bureaucracy and democracy?

Further reading

Zygmunt Bauman, *Modernity and the Holocaust* (Cambridge: Polity, 2003).

Manuel Castells, *The Rise of the Network Society* (Oxford: Blackwell, 1996).

Stuart Clegg, *Modern Organizations: Organization Studies in the Postmodern World* (London: Sage, 1990).

Paul Du Gay, *In Praise of Democracy: Weber, Organization, Ethics* (London: Sage, 2000).

David Lyon, *The Electronic Eye: The Rise of Surveillance Society* (Cambridge: Polity, 1994).

Internet links

Center for the Sociology of Organizations (CNRS, Paris)
http://www.cso.edu

Electronic Journal of Radical Organization Theory, including back issues online
http://www.mngt.waikato.ac.nz/research/ejrot/

Foucault site
http://www.qut.edu.au/edu/cpol/foucault/links.htm

Social Capital Gateway
http://www.socialcapitalgateway.org/

Contents

17 Education

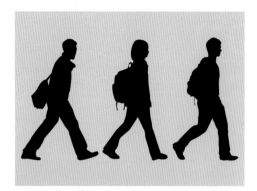

IN 1998 Shaun had two years left at primary school. He was hard-working, poor, white and working class and had clear ideas about his secondary education: 'I'm gonna go to Westbury because my mate Mark's going there and my girlfriend . . . Sutton Boys' is like one of the worst schools around here, only tramps go there.' A year later, Shaun was not so certain: 'I might not get into Westbury 'cos it's siblings and how far away you live and I haven't got any siblings there and I live a little way out so I might have to go on a waiting list. . . . I might go to Sutton Boys' instead 'cos all my mates are going there.'

Shaun's headteacher, Mrs Whitticker, had told him that Westbury would be far too risky a choice as he lived on the edge of its catchment area. Shaun and his mother resigned themselves to applying to Sutton Boys'. Shaun's mother was bitterly disappointed, but she accepted the advice: 'I could have wept at the thought of him going to Sutton, but what choice did we have 'cos Mrs Whitticker said we didn't have any?' Shaun and his mother worried about the reputation of Sutton Boys'. As

Shaun said: 'My mum and I think the standards might be too low because people just bunk and everything at Sutton.'

Before he began secondary school, Shaun and his mother had 'lots of serious discussions' about how Shaun could still do well at Sutton Boys' despite its poor reputation. Maura, his mother, said: 'We've had some real heart to hearts. He's putting a brave face on it but I can see how worried he is. I've said you just have to work twice as hard to do well if you go to a school like that rather than somewhere like Westbury where the kids expect to get on with their work instead of mucking about all the time.' Shaun too, is determined not 'to get dragged down' and will 'work much harder because like it's secondary and the most important school days of your life because that's when you're coming up to your GCSEs'.

Over the next few years Shaun faced constant tension between being tough in the playground and hardworking in the classroom. Just before the move to secondary school, Shaun's main rationale for accepting that Sutton Boys' might be a reasonable school for him was that lots of his friends were also going there. At the end of his first term in secondary school Shaun says that his friendships with some people had changed. He says that he could no longer be friends with David, his best friend from primary school, because whereas, before:

> Whenever David was in trouble with a fight I was always there to help him. We always helped each other or if someone needed us for a fight. But here now I'm not really into fighting. Fighting ain't nothing but trouble so I try and keep out of it. . . . Fighting is for the kids who don't want to learn and don't want to do well at school and I don't want to be like that.

Shaun was suspended twice from his primary school for fighting, and had a local reputation for being 'tough', which he saw as vital to sustain if he was to survive in Sutton Boys'. Yet in order to succeed academically, Shaun had deliberately to set himself apart from the rest of his peer group: 'All the other kids were spitting spit balls out of paper at the teacher and I just sat down and tried to take no notice.' The only other two boys 'to keep their heads down and try and get on with their work' were 'outsiders' to the local male working-class culture. One was American and, in Shaun's words, 'dead clever'. The other was Portuguese and his parents were actively looking to place him in another school. Shaun had continually to prove to his peers that he was still really 'a lad' and to avoid being reclassified as a 'geek'.

As a result, on the estate and in the playground, Shaun resurrected his old self, in contrast to his displays of hard-working, non-conformity in the classroom. He reclaimed a very different identity as 'tough' and as 'a skilful footballer', which redeemed – most of the time – his 'geekiness' in the classroom. This brought Shaun into conflict with his mother, who worried about him hanging out with the wrong crowd. At secondary school, the tension between academic work and being one of the lads grew and Shaun would sometimes wish he was younger:

> It's getting harder because like some boys, yeah, like a couple of my friends, yeah, they go 'Oh, you are teacher's pet' and all that. Right? What? Am I teacher's pet because I do my work and tell you lot to shut up when you are talking and miss is trying to talk? And they go, 'yeah so you're still a teacher's pet'. Well, if you don't like it go away, innit.

Shaun's story, told in a series of interviews with the sociologist Diane Reay between 1997 and 2001, raises many issues that preoccupy us in this chapter and we return to Shaun at several points over the coming pages. In particular, Shaun's account of the transition from primary to secondary school raises questions about the links between education and wider social structures, such as class and gender (Reay 2002).

We begin this chapter with the wider question: 'What is education for?' before investigating the origins and development of the educational system in Britain and considering the recent political debates to which education has given rise, including several of the issues that affected Shaun, such as parental 'choice' in secondary schools, school standards and how to cope with failing schools. We then review some of the main theoretical approaches to education before addressing the question of inequalities in education, considering its intersection with gender, ethnicity and class. We also examine some of the ways in which education is being transformed through changes in technology and the new demands of the global knowledge economy. The chapter will conclude with some thoughts on the nature of intelligence and the importance of lifelong learning.

The importance of education

Why is education an important issue for sociologists? For Durkheim, one of sociology's founding figures, education played an important role in the socialization of children.

Durkheim's functionalist approach to sociology was introduced in chapter 1, 'What is Sociology?', pp. 12–14

Most importantly, for Durkheim, through education, and particularly by learning history, children gain an understanding of the common values in society, uniting a multitude of separate individuals. These common values will include religious and moral beliefs, and a sense of self-discipline. Durkheim believes that education enables children to internalize the social rules that contribute to the functioning of society.

In industrial societies, Durkheim argues (1925), education also has another function in the socialization of children: it teaches the skills needed to perform specialist occupations. In traditional societies, occupational skills could be learnt within the family. As society became more complicated and a division of labour emerged in the production of goods, an education system developed that could pass on the skills needed to fill the various specialized, occupational roles.

A different functionalist approach to education is found in the works of the American sociologist Talcott Parsons. Whereas Durkheim was concerned with the way in which nineteenth-century French society was becoming increasingly individualistic and argued that education created social solidarity, in the mid-twentieth century Parsons believed that the function of education was to instil the value of individual achievement in a child. This value was crucial to the functioning of industrialized societies, but it could not be learnt in the family. Families treat children in a *particular* way.

A child's status in the family is *ascribed*; it is largely fixed from birth. By contrast, a child's status in school is largely *achieved*. In schools, children are assessed according to *universal* standards, such as exams. For Parsons, the function of education is to enable children to move from the particularistic standards of the family to the universal standards needed in modern, adult society. According to Parsons, schools, like wider society, largely operate on a **meritocratic** basis: children achieve their status according to merit (or worth) rather than according to their sex, race or class (Parsons and Bales 1956). However, as we shall see, Parsons's view that schools operate on meritocratic principles has been subject to much criticism. Sociologists influenced by social conflict theories have highlighted the ways in which *ascribed* inequalities are reproduced in the education system.

The importance of education and peer relations in socialization is discussed further in chapter 6, 'Socialization, the Life-Course and Ageing', pp. 167–8.

Education in the UK

Until a century and a half ago, and even more recently, the children of the wealthy were educated by private tutors. Most of the population had no schooling whatsoever until the first few decades of the nineteenth century, when in European countries and the United States, systems of primary schools began to be constructed.

The process of industrialization and the expansion of the cities served to increase demands for specialized schooling.

People now work in many different occupations, and work skills can no longer be passed on directly from parents to children. The acquisition of knowledge becomes increasingly based on abstract learning (of subjects like maths, science, history, literature and so forth), rather than on the practical transmission of specific skills. In a modern society people have to be furnished with basic skills, such as reading, writing and calculating and a general knowledge of their physical, social and economic environment; and it is also important that they know how to learn, so that they are able to master new, sometimes very technical, forms of information.

Origins and development

Although the modern educational system first took shape in most Western societies in the early part of the nineteenth century, Britain was much more reluctant than most other countries to establish an integrated national system. By the mid-1800s, Holland, Switzerland and the German states had achieved more or less universal enrolment in elementary schools, but England and Wales fell far short of such a target. Education in Scotland was somewhat more developed.

Between 1870 (when compulsory education was first established in Britain) and the Second World War, successive governments increased expenditure on education. The minimum school-leaving age rose from ten to fourteen, and more and more schools were built, but education was not really considered to be a major area for government intervention. Most schools were run by private or church authorities under the supervision of local government boards. The Second World War changed this attitude. Recruits to the armed forces were given ability and learning tests; the results startled the authorities by showing a low level of educational skills. Concerned about prospects for post-war recovery, the government began to rethink the existing educational system (Halsey 1997).

In the years before 1944, the vast majority of British children attended a single free school, the elementary school, until the age of fourteen. Secondary schools existed alongside the elementary system, but parents had to pay. This system divided children clearly along lines of social class – children from poorer backgrounds were almost all confined to elementary schooling. Less than 2 per cent of the population attended university. The Education Act of 1944 initiated several major changes, including free secondary education for all, the raising of the school-leaving age to fifteen and a commitment to equality of opportunity in education. Education became a major responsibility of elected local government.

As a result of the 1944 Act, the majority of local education authorities adopted academic selection as a means of providing secondary education tailored to children's needs. Selection at the age of eleven – the age of transition from primary to secondary school – was supposed to sort out the more able children from the others, regardless of social background. For most pupils, results in the so-called 'eleven-plus' examination determined whether they went on to grammar schools (which provided a highly academic curriculum) or to secondary modern schools (which had a mix of general and vocational learning). A minority of children also went either to technical schools or to special schools. The option of staying on at school until seventeen was available for all those who were regarded as qualified and who wanted to continue their education.

By the 1960s – partly as a result of sociological research – it had become clear that the results of the eleven-plus system had not come up to expectations. The Crowther Report of 1959 showed that only 12 per cent of pupils continued in school until the age of seventeen, and early leaving was shown to be more closely related to class background than to academic performance. The Labour government that was returned to power in 1964 was committed to establishing comprehensive schools and to abolishing the division between grammar and secondary modern, thereby also putting an end to the eleven-plus examination. The schools would thus mix together children of diverse class backgrounds. However, there was confusion over what the comprehensive school should offer: 'grammar schools for all' or a completely new type of education? No one solution was found to the problem, and different schools and regions developed their own approaches. Some local authorities resisted the change, and in a few areas grammar schools still exist.

Since the early 1970s state education has been strongly affected by the jolting transition from a situation in which labour power was in short supply and there were demands on the schools to provide the skills the economy needed, to one in which there was too much – leading to a time of rising unemployment and reduced government revenue. Educational expan-

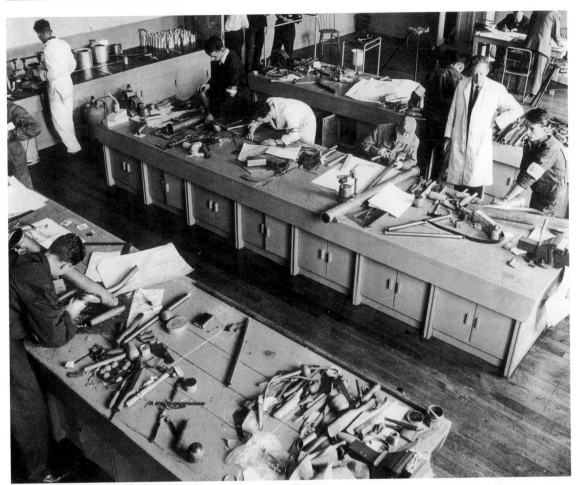

At secondary modern schools, the levels of vocational training offered differed for boys and girls.

sion, which had characterized the whole of the post-war period, was suddenly replaced by contraction and attempts at a reduction in government expenditure. The percentage of general government expenditure on education rose steadily from 7.3 per cent in 1953 to 13.3 per cent by 1973. But by 1979 this figure had fallen to 12.2 per cent, and, with the exception of a drop to 11 per cent in the mid-1980s, education spending as a share of the government total has remained at around 12 per cent ever since. (This figure, however, disguises the increases in expenditure on education in recent years as total welfare spending increases: see pp. 693–5 below.)

Secondary education and politics

Education has long been a political battleground and continues to be so to this day. A protracted debate has centred on the impact of comprehensive schooling – on

The 'public' schools

The public schools in Britain are an oddity in more ways than one. They are not 'public' at all but, on the contrary, private, fee-paying institutions. The degree of independence they have from the rest of the education system and the key role they play in the society at large marks them out from the systems of other countries. There are some private schools, often linked to religious denominations, in all Western societies, but in no other society are private schools either so exclusive or so important as in the UK.

The public schools are nominally subject to state supervision, but in fact few major pieces of educational legislation have affected them. They were left untouched by the 1944 Act, as they were by the setting up of the comprehensive schools; and the large majority stayed single-sex schools until relatively recently. There are about 2,300 fee-paying schools in England, educating some 6 per cent of the population. They include a diversity of different organizations, from prestigious establishments such as Eton, Rugby or Charterhouse, through to so-called minor public schools whose names would be unknown to most people.

The term 'public school' is limited by some educationalists to a group of the major fee-paying schools. These include those schools which are members of the Headmasters' Conference (HMC), originally formed in 1871. Initially there were only fifty schools in the Conference. The number has now expanded to more than 240. Schools like those listed above – Eton, Rugby and the rest – are members. Individuals who have attended HMC schools tend to dominate the higher positions in British society. A study by Ivan Reid and others, for example, published in 1991, showed that 84 per cent of judges, 70 per cent of bank directors and 49 per cent of top civil servants had attended an HMC school (Reid 1991).

As a result of the 1988 Education Reform Act, all state schools have to follow a standard national curriculum, which involves testing pupils at the ages of seven, eleven, fourteen and sixteen. Representatives from the fee-paying schools were involved in the creation of the national curriculum. Yet these schools do not have to follow it. The fee-paying schools can teach whatever they wish and have no obligation to test children. Most have opted to follow the national curriculum, but some have simply ignored it.

Eton College schoolboys in their very traditional school uniform.

educational standards and on inequalities in the wider society. Originally, comprehensive education attracted support from both ends of the political spectrum. However, it was the Labour government, as mentioned, which set the system into motion and therefore support for comprehensive education has tended to be associated much more with the political left than with the right. The architects of comprehensive education believed that the new schools would provide for greater equality of opportunity than was possible in selective education. They did not give much thought to the curriculum as such, being more concerned with equality of access.

Education policy under the Conservatives, 1979–97

When Margaret Thatcher became Prime Minister in 1979, the Conservatives became more vocal in their criticisms of comprehensive schooling. They believed that grammar schools should not have been allowed more or less to disappear, as had happened with the introduction of the comprehensive system. Whilst many in the Labour Party during the post-war period had argued that grammar schools were socially divisive, Conservatives were determined to create a greater variety of schools at the secondary level, with a correspondingly greater scope for parents to choose the nature of their children's education.

In the late 1980s, Margaret Thatcher started speaking of creating a 'revolution' in the running of schools. Such a revolution was due to dismantle the giant comprehensive system and reduce the power of the local education authorities that were responsible for running them. The

Thatcher 'revolution' in education can be understood in the context of what she, and many of her supporters, saw as a wider economic and moral decline in British life that was evident by the 1970s. She believed that the comprehensive system was failing to encourage 'family' values and was producing students without the skills needed to create a vibrant and internationally competitive economy. She also believed that the comprehensive system was often run inefficiently by unnecessarily large government bureaucracies.

The 1988 Education Act introduced significant reforms – some of which met with great opposition. A national curriculum was established which specified a universal framework of teaching for the state sector. The introduction of the national curriculum was strongly resisted by some groups in the teaching profession, who were opposed to such standardized testing and who felt the curriculum to be unnecessarily confining. Teachers took strike action against the tests in the summer of 1993.

The 1988 Education Act also introduced a new system of school management, called the 'local management of schools'. The devolution of the administration of schools was to balance the inevitable centralization involved in the national curriculum. A new group of City Technology Colleges (CTCs) and grant-maintained schools was also to be established. Grant-maintained schools would have the choice to 'opt out' of local authority control and receive funding directly from the state – effectively becoming a business funded from central government. They would also have the right to select up to 50 per cent of their student intake on the basis of ability. Critics claimed that this would exaggerate existing inequality among schools and undermine the egalitarian principle of comprehensive schools. In 1992 a new funding agency was established which was gradually to take over the provision of places in schools that opted out. In the White Paper detailing the tasks of the agency, the government said that it hoped 'that over time all schools will have become grant-maintained' – in other words, would have opted out. By 1995, however, only 1,000 schools had done so out of a total number of 23,000 state schools.

Evaluation

With the 1988 Act, the Conservative government sought to introduce an element of market competition into education, as it had done in other spheres (see chapter 10, pp. 370–4). Schools would become subject to the rules of supply and demand, competition and consumer choice. In general, the changes aimed to empower the 'consumers' of education (parents and children) over the 'producers' (the teachers). School heads were given greater financial responsibilities, and schools were permitted to 'opt out' from the control of local education authorities to become 'independent state schools'. League tables were introduced, ranking the performance of schools, in the belief that this would instil competition, and allow parents to make an informed decision in choosing schools for their children.

Gewirtz et al. (1995) examined the marketization of the education system in a range of fifteen schools in three neighbouring Local Education Authorities (LEAs) in London. They found that the Conservative government's educational reforms were creating a shift from comprehensive to market values within the education system. For example they argued that schools were particularly keen to attract children who were likely to do well in their GCSE exams, boosting the school's overall ranking in the league tables. Schools also increased their efforts at marketing, for example by producing glossy brochures, even when this meant that funding had to be transferred from less profitable areas, such as the teaching of children with Special Educational Needs (SEN).

Gewirtz et al. focused their research on the issue of parental choice over which school their children went to. The research found that, contrary to Parsons's understanding of the education system as a meritocracy (examined above, pp. 686–7), for many parents the choice over which school their child attended was severely limited, as we saw with Shaun's mother in the introduction to this chapter. The researchers argued that the extent of school choice largely depends upon parents' social class and cultural capital.

> The term 'cultural capital' was introduced in chapter 9, 'Stratification and Class', p. 322.

They argued that it was possible to distinguish three broad groups of parents from their ability to choose schools:

1 *Privileged/skilled choosers* are able to spend time looking at and researching the different options, and consulting widely with teachers and other parents. These parents are also confident in using the appeals system if their child is not accepted at his or her first-choice

school. This group would sometimes plan ahead, and make sure their child attends a primary school that is a feeder for a successful secondary school.

2 *Semi-skilled choosers* are also engaged in actively selecting a school, but are unable to engage in the market to the extent of the previous group. They don't have the same cultural resources, such as informed friends with knowledge of how the system works, to draw upon and are therefore less confident about the process. As a group, they are less likely to appeal if their first choice is rejected and more likely to accept news stories and hearsay about a school than the first group.

3 *Disconnected choosers*, while interested in their children's welfare, tend to see schools as broadly similar, and often will leave the final choice to the child. They have less capacity to get involved with the education market and will often choose the closest school. This choice might be the only feasible one if the parents do not have a car and public transport is inadequate.

Education policy under New Labour, 1997–

To the surprise of some, including teachers' unions, some elements of the Conservatives' education reforms have remained intact under New Labour. For example, the remaining grammar schools have been left untouched, a decision that has raised questions among scholars and educators who see grammar schools as substantially lowering the performance of local comprehensive schools by siphoning off the most able students. Also, New Labour has agreed with the Conservatives that mixed ability teaching within schools should be abandoned in favour of streaming or setting. (Schools that use streaming split pupils into several hierarchical groups according to ability, which then stay together for all lessons. Setting means putting pupils of a similar ability together for certain lessons – so that there can be different top and lower sets for maths and for English, for example.) The theory is that children of different abilities can progress at the quickest possible rate for them (see Gillborn and Youndell's discussion of 'the new IQism' below, pp. 723–8, for a critical view of this). Under New Labour, grant-maintained schools, originally set up by the Conservatives, have now become Foundation Schools, and are back under the control of their Local Education Authorities. However, these schools retain a large degree of the independence which they had previously had from central and local government.

On becoming Prime Minister in 1997, Tony Blair claimed that 'education, education and education' would top his political agenda. Blair acknowledged that standards of British schooling, as measured by international comparisons (see pp. 701–3 below), were not high and that further educational reform is a necessary priority. In a White Paper, *Excellence in Schools*, published soon after arriving in office in 1997, New Labour committed itself to defending and modernizing comprehensive schools. The White Paper called for intervention to be limited in schools that succeed and creative ways to attain good results, but acknowledged the need for government intervention in the case of schools with chronically sub-standard performance.

New Labour has introduced a number

of new and often controversial initiatives aimed at improving the performance of British state schools. Although state funding on education has risen since 1997 (see figure 17.1), New Labour has rejected many of the conventional arguments from teachers' unions and commentators on the left that poor educational performance is straightforwardly an outcome of inadequate spending and high concentra-

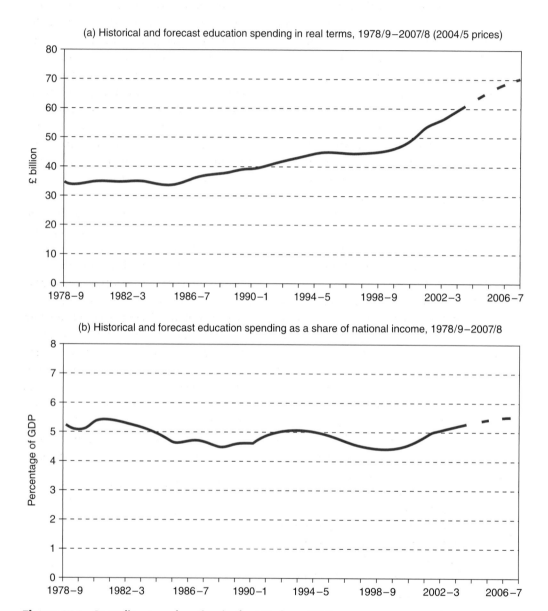

(a) Historical and forecast education spending in real terms, 1978/9–2007/8 (2004/5 prices)

(b) Historical and forecast education spending as a share of national income, 1978/9–2007/8

Figure 17.1   Spending on education in the UK since 1979

Source: Social Trends 35 (2005), p. 37

tions of disadvantaged students in certain schools. A variety of approaches has been used to raise educational standards. New Labour has emphasized the importance of good teaching methods and strong leadership by head teachers as the keys to educational reform. A National College for School Leadership was officially launched in November 2000, aimed at providing career development and support for existing and aspiring school leaders.

In primary schools, Literacy and Numeracy Strategies were introduced, to ensure that all children gained a solid grounding in core subjects. The introduction of daily literacy and numeracy hours was an important part of this, dedicating time to the developing of skills in reading and maths. The Literacy and Numeracy Strategies have now been expanded to form a Primary Strategy, which sets out standards in English, mathematics and science.

There has been a move towards encouraging competition and diversity amongst schools in order to drive up standards. Grant-maintained schools, as we saw above, have become Foundation Schools and have retained a high degree of independence. Specialist schools have been introduced which focus on particular areas of the curriculum, technology, arts or maths, for example. These schools are allowed to select up to 10 per cent of their intake according to a pupil's ability in these specialist areas.

City Academies have also been created in deprived areas and are heavily oversubscribed. At the start of 2004/5 there were seventeen of them across England. Sponsors from the private or charitable sector provide 20 per cent of the start-up costs of an academy, up to a maximum of two million pounds. The state then pays the rest. The sponsors then run the academy, which is funded by the taxpayer. Several companies, including private schools and religious groups, have shown an interest in running academies. The schools are free for pupils, who must be chosen from the local community. However, critics claim that the government's generous funding of academies drains resources from other schools. New Labour has also been rigorous in its policy of school inspections. Where schools are deemed to be failing, government agencies are able to intervene directly to take over the running of the school. In some cases, failing schools have reopened as City Academies.

Several measures designed to end poverty have an effect on education. For example, Education Action Zones were created in areas of high deprivation. Under this scheme, schools, local authorities and local businesses were asked to get together to discuss ways of tackling the problems of under-achievement in deprived areas. In these zones, money from government and the private sector could be used to attract more teachers through offers of higher pay, and tackle wider problems associated with social exclusion. By 2004 there were forty-seven Education Action Zones across England.

Social exclusion and education are discussed in more detail below, on pp. 721–3. Social exclusion is also a theme of chapter 10.

Higher education

There are large differences between societies in the organization of higher education (education after school, usually at

A new City Academy, part of New Labour's policy for schools.

Globalization and everyday life: lifelong learning

New technologies and the rise of the knowledge economy are transforming traditional ideas about work and education. The sheer pace of technological change is creating a much more rapid turnover of jobs than once was the case. As we have seen in this chapter, and will see again in chapter 18 ('Work and Economic Life'), training and the attainment of qualifications is now occurring throughout people's lives, rather than just once early in life. Mid-career professionals are choosing to update their skills through continuing education programmes and Internet-based learning. Many employers now allow workers to participate in on-the-job training as a way of enhancing loyalty and improving the company skills base.

As our society continues to transform, the traditional beliefs and institutions that underpin it are also undergoing change. The idea of education – implying the structured transmission of knowledge within a formal institution – is giving way to a broader notion of 'learning' that takes place in a diversity of settings. The shift from 'education' to 'learning' is not an inconsequential one. Learners are active, curious social actors who can derive insights from a multiplicity of sources, not just within an institutional setting. Emphasis on learning acknowledges that skills and knowledge can be gained through all types of encounters – with friends and neighbours, at seminars and museums, in conversations at the local pub, through the Internet and other media, and so forth.

The shift in emphasis towards lifelong learning can already be seen within schools themselves, where there is a growing number of opportunities for pupils to learn outside the confines of the classroom. The boundaries between schools and the outside world are breaking down, not only via cyberspace, but in the physical world as well. 'Service learning', for example, has become a mainstay of many American secondary schools. As part of their graduation requirements, pupils devote a certain amount of time to volunteer work in the community. Partnerships with local businesses have also become commonplace in the UK and USA, fostering interaction and mentor relationships between adult professionals and pupils.

Lifelong learning should and must play a role in the move towards a knowledge society. Not only is it essential to a well-trained, motivated workforce, but learning should also be seen in relation to wider human values. Learning is both a means and an end to the development of a rounded and autonomous self-education in the service of self-development and self-understanding. There is nothing utopian in this idea; indeed, it reflects the humanistic ideals of education developed by educational philosophers. An example already in existence is the 'university of the third age', which provides retired people with the opportunity to educate themselves as they choose, developing whatever interests they care to follow.

university or college). In some countries, all universities and colleges are public agencies, receiving their funding directly from government sources. Higher education in France, for instance, is organized nationally, with centralized control being almost as marked as in primary and secondary education. All course structures have to be validated by a national regulatory body responsible to the Minister of Higher Education. Two types of degree can be gained, one awarded by the individual university, the other by the state. National degrees are generally regarded as more prestigious and valuable than those of specific universities, since they are supposed to conform to guaranteed uniform standards. A certain range of occupations in government are only open to the holders of national degrees, which are also favoured by most industrial employers. Virtually all teachers in schools, colleges and universities in France are themselves state employees. Rates of pay and the broad framework of teaching duties are fixed centrally.

The United States is distinctive among developed countries in terms of the high proportion of colleges and universities that are in the private sector. Private organizations make up 54 per cent of organizations of higher education in the United States. These include some of the most prestigious universities, such as Harvard, Princeton and Yale. The distinction between public and private in American higher education, however, is not as clear-cut as is the case in other countries. Students at private universities are eligible for public grants and loans, and these universities receive public research funding. Public universities often possess substantial endowments, and may be given donations by private firms. They also often obtain research grants from private industrial sources.

The system in Britain

The British system of higher education is considerably more decentralized than that of France, but more unitary than that of the USA. Universities and colleges are government financed, and teachers at all levels of the educational system have their salaries determined according to national wage scales. Yet there is considerable diversity in the organization of institutions and curricula.

There were twenty-one universities in Britain in the immediate pre-war period. Most of the universities at this time were very small by today's standards. In 1937, the total number of undergraduates in British universities was only slightly greater than the number of full-time university academic staff in 1981 (Halsey 2000). Between 1945 and 1970 the higher education system in Britain grew to be four times as large. The older universities were expanded, and new universities – labelled 'red-brick' – were built (such as Sussex, Kent, Stirling and York). A binary system was set up with the creation of polytechnics. This second layer of higher education became relatively large, comprising some four hundred colleges offering a wide range of courses. The polytechnics concentrated more on vocational courses than the universities. The Council for National Academic Awards was created as a validating body to ensure that their degrees were of a uniform standard.

Today, British institutions of higher education have what has sometimes been called a 'standard coinage'. This means that a degree from Leicester or Leeds, at

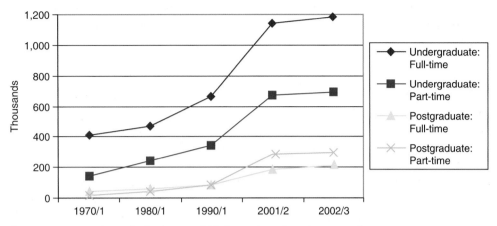

Figure 17.2 Students in further and higher education: by type of course, 1970–2003

Source: Social Trends 34 (2004), p. 44

least in theory, is of the same standard as one from Cambridge, Oxford or London. Yet Oxford and Cambridge are noted for a highly selective intake, about half of whom come from fee-paying schools. An Oxford or Cambridge degree confers a greater chance of a profitable career than a qualification from most other universities. The number of British students in higher education has grown significantly from a century ago. In 1900/1 there were a mere 25,000 students in full-time higher education. By 1971 the number had increased more than eighteen times to 457,000, and this figure has continued to grow substantially since (as figure 17.2 shows). By 2001/2 there were almost 1.2 million full-time undergraduate students in higher education in the UK. The number of students enrolled in part-time undergraduate and postgraduate courses at higher education institutions has also increased enormously.

Social class background influences the likelihood of a person carrying on into higher education. Despite increasing from a participation rate of 11 per cent in 1991/2 to 19 per cent in 2001/2, participation from the working class remains well below that of students from non-manual classes. Participation rates for the non-manual social classes increased from 35 per cent to 50 per cent over the same period (see figure 17.3). The debate about access to education for the children of working-class parents has been central to the debates about how higher education is funded.

The debate about funding

While the number of students in higher education has expanded massively, government spending has not grown at the same rate. The result has been a crisis in funding for higher education (see figure 17.4). Funding in British universities per student fell by 29 per cent in real terms between 1976 and 1989, and by a further 38 per cent between 1989 and 1999. A report issued in 1997 by the National

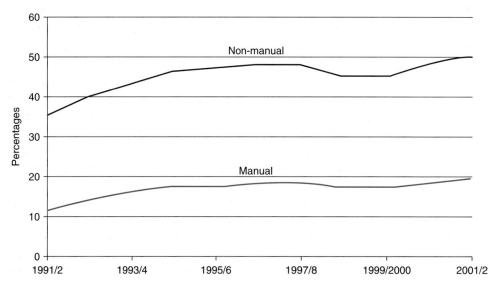

Figure 17.3 Participation rates in higher education in Britain: by social class, 1991–2002

Source: Social Trends 34 (2004), p. 45

Committee of Inquiry into Higher Education concluded that the expansion and improvement of higher education would be impossible under existing funding arrangements.

At the heart of the debate about higher education funding is the question of who pays. The two main possible sources of large-scale investment into universities are the general taxpayer and those who experience and benefit from higher education: the students. Some argue that, given the social and economic benefits that higher education provides society with, the gap in university funding should be met by the taxpayer. Where would we be without university-trained medical professionals and teachers, for example?

Others counter that there should be a limit to which those taxpayers who do not go to university should have to pay for those who do. Graduates enjoy many

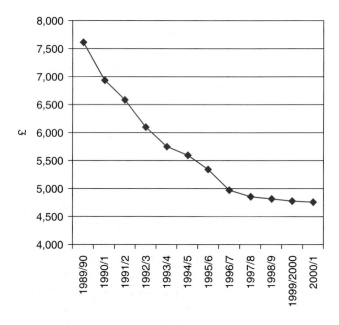

Figure 17.4 Publicly planned funding per FTE HE student in England, 1989–2001 (at 1999–2000 prices)

Source: <www.planning.ed.uk/pub/English_public_funding.htm>

career advantages – financial and non-financial – that non-graduates do not. A recent survey found that British graduates earn 59 per cent more than non-graduates, one of the highest premiums for gaining a degree in developed countries (OECD, 2004). Although the New Labour administration has increased funding for higher education from the general taxpayer it has largely accepted the argument that students, as the primary beneficiaries of a university education, must pay a greater share of their university costs.

A decision was made that from the 1998/9 academic year, students enrolling in higher education institutions in the UK were required to contribute a fee (set at £1,000 a term at the time) towards their tuition costs. However, many people argued that having to pay fees as they entered university would deter students from poor backgrounds from applying, as well as alienate many middle-class parents, who resented having to pay out such large sums of money in one lump sum.

As a result, up-front payment of tuition fees has now been abolished in the UK. From 2006, universities are allowed to charge up to £3,000 a year in 'top-up fees' for undergraduate courses. Students will repay the money, on a zero-rate of real interest loan, after they graduate and are earning more than a set amount, currently set at £15,000. Students are still able to take out loans to cover living expenses, and these will be repaid along with the loan for the fees. A graduate's debt will be written off after twenty-five years if it is not repaid, in order to safeguard people who don't work or who go into low-paid professions.

Some people have criticized the idea that some universities are free to charge higher fees than others. They argue that prestigious universities will be able to charge more, attract better staff and get better facilities, and they fear that a two-tier system will develop. They argue that students from low-income families would opt for the cheaper universities and courses. Many critics of the policy don't believe that fees at the most prestigious universities will stay at £3,000 for long.

Ministers have responded to this criticism by making a commitment not to raise the £3,000 limit on annual fees until 2009 at the earliest, and even then it will require a vote in both houses of parliament. The government has also created the Office for Fair Access (Offa), to make sure that no university can charge high fees without widening access for working-class and ethnic minority students. Grants have also been reinstated for the poorest third of students and a substantial proportion of their fees have been waived. The government has also promised that an independent review of top-up fees will be held after three years.

Comparative perspectives on British education

How does the British education system compare to that overseas? It is difficult to draw direct comparisons internationally, for there are wide differences between countries, both in the number of years children are expected to be in school and in ways of organizing educational systems.

Compared with the other wealthy countries that form the Organization of Economic Cooperation and Development (OECD), the UK has a high proportion of young children in education (81 per cent of 3–4-year-olds). The UK also ranks highly in terms of spending per pre-primary school child (US$7,595 per pupil per year compared with an OECD average of US$4,187). However, the ratio of pupils to teaching staff at the pre-primary level in the United Kingdom is, at 27:1, the highest among OECD countries (which have an average of just 15:1).

At primary school, expenditure per pupil is slightly below the OECD average. On the other hand, pupils spend longer in school than in other countries (889 hours in England and 1,000 hours in Scotland for 9–11-year-olds for example, well above the OECD average of 752 and 816 hours respectively). There are also reasonably high ratios of pupils to teaching staff in the UK system (20:1 in the United Kingdom compared with 17:1 at the OECD average level).

At secondary school, expenditure per student is again below the OECD average (US$5,933 compared to US$6,510). Here, unlike in primary schools, the pupil to teaching staff ratio is, at 15:1, only slightly above the OECD average of 14:1.

In line with the policies of both the Conservative government after 1979 and New Labour after 1997, discussed above (pp. 693–5), schools in England have a comparatively strong role in decision-making. It has been calculated that 85 per cent of all decisions analysed by the surveyors were taken at school level, compared to a much lower OECD average of 42 per cent (OECD 2004).

How do these statistics relate to educational achievement when compared with similar countries? A large-scale survey of 15-year-olds in OECD countries carried out by the Programme for International Student Assessment has found that UK teenagers compare reasonably well with those from other countries in terms of proficiency in reading, maths and science (see table 17.1). In reading, English students achieved similarly to those in Australia, Japan and Sweden, for example, and scored significantly better than France and Germany. In only two countries, Finland and Canada, did 15-year-olds do significantly better than in England (PISA, 2000).

English students also did significantly better than the OECD average in both mathematical and scientific literacy, averaging 529 and 533 points respectively – similar to the scores from Australia, Canada, Finland and New Zealand. Only Japan and Korea did significantly better in both mathematical and scientific literacy and only Korea in scientific literacy. English students did much better in both maths and science than students in, for example, Denmark, Ireland, the USA and Germany.

In England, girls scored significantly higher than boys in reading literacy – a finding that was repeated in all the participating countries (differences in gender achievement in the UK are discussed in more detail below, pp. 715–20). The relative disadvantage of boys was smaller in England than in most other countries. Gender differences were not indicative of a country's good or poor performance in the assessment overall. The two countries with the smallest differences between boys and girls were Korea and Mexico; the former had a similar score to that of England, whereas the latter had the lowest literacy score of all the participating countries. In both maths and science gender differences were much less marked than in reading. In England, boys scored slightly higher than girls, on average, but the differences were minor (PISA, 2000).

Table 17.1   Ranking in reading, maths and science amongst teenagers: by country (2002)

Countries in descending order of their mean score in reading literacy	Mean score	Countries in descending order of their mean score in mathematical literacy	Mean score	Countries in descending order of their mean score in scientific literacy	Mean score
Finland	546	Japan	557	Korea	552
Canada	534	Korea	547	Japan	550
New Zealand	529	New Zealand	537	Finland	538
Australia	528	Finland	536	England	533
Republic of Ireland	527	Australia	533	United Kingdom	532
Korea	525	Canada	533	Canada	529
United Kingdom	523	Switzerland	529	New Zealand	528
England	523	United Kingdom	529	Australia	528
Japan	522	England	529	Austria	519
Sweden	516	Belgium	520	Republic of Ireland	513
Austria	507	France	517	Sweden	512
Belgium	507	Austria	515	Czech Republic	511
Iceland	507	Denmark	514	France	500
Norway	505	Iceland	514	Norway	500
France	505	Sweden	510	United States	499
United States	504	Republic of Ireland	503	Hungary	496
Denmark	497	Norway	499	Iceland	496
Switzerland	494	Czech Republic	498	Belgium	496
Spain	493	United States	493	Switzerland	496
Czech Republic	492	Germany	490	Spain	491
Italy	487	Hungary	488	Germany	487
Germany	484	Spain	476	Poland	483
Hungary	480	Poland	470	Denmark	481
Poland	479	Italy	457	Italy	478
Greece	474	Portugal	454	Greece	461
Portugal	470	Greece	447	Portugal	459
Luxembourg	441	Luxembourg	446	Luxembourg	443
Mexico	422	Mexico	387	Mexico	422
OECD country average	500	OECD country average	500	OECD country average	500

Source: PISA (2000)

Theories of schooling and inequality

As we saw from Shaun's story at the start of this chapter, education and inequality are related. Shaun came from a poor background, and didn't get into the school his mother wanted him to. He then had to struggle to get on in class, when most of his friends were uninterested or even hostile to academic achievement. This section reviews a number of different ways in which sociological theorists have attempted to account for social inequalities in education. They can all be seen as concerned with 'social reproduction' in and through education, but in rather different ways. Ivan Illich stresses the effects informal processes at work through, what he calls, 'the hidden curriculum'; Basil Bernstein emphasizes the significance of language; Pierre Bourdieu examines the relationship between the cultures of school and home; and Paul Willis looks at the effects of cultural values in shaping pupil attitudes to education and labour. The later thinkers discussed in this section, Robin Usher and Richard Edwards, draw upon all these ideas in various ways, but develop them further in terms of culture and the complexities of identity construction (including sexuality and ethnicity) in the modern world. It should be noted how strongly cultural issues are focused upon these different approaches.

Ivan Illich: the hidden curriculum

One of the most controversial writers on educational theory was Ivan Illich (1926–2002). He is noted for his criticisms of modern economic development, which he described as a process whereby previously self-sufficient people are dispossessed of their traditional skills and made to rely on doctors for their health, teachers for their schooling, television for their entertainment and employers for their subsistence.

> Illich's views on health were discussed in chapter 8, 'Health, Illness and Disability', p. 262.

Illich (1973) argued that the very notion of compulsory schooling – now accepted throughout the world – should be questioned. He stressed the connection between the development of education and the requirements of the economy for discipline and hierarchy. He argued that schools have developed to cope with four basic tasks: the provision of custodial care, the distribution of people among occupational roles, the learning of dominant values and the acquisition of socially approved skills and knowledge. In relation to the first, the school has become a custodial organization because attendance is obligatory, and children are 'kept off the streets' between early childhood and their entry into work.

Much is learnt in school which has nothing to do with the formal content of lessons. Schools tend to inculcate what Illich called 'passive consumption' – an uncritical acceptance of the existing social order – by the nature of the discipline and regimentation they involve. These lessons are not consciously taught; they are implicit in school procedures and organization. The hidden curriculum teaches children that their role in life is 'to know their place and to sit still in it' (Illich 1973).

Illich advocated deschooling society.

Literacy in global focus

Literacy is the 'baseline' of education. Without it, schooling cannot proceed. We take it for granted in the West that the majority of people are literate, but, as has been mentioned, this is only a recent development in Western history, and in previous times no more than a tiny proportion of the population had any literacy skills.

In some countries only a small minority of the population have any reading or writing skills. This can be partially explained by the absence of universal education in some countries. Yet even if the provision of primary schooling were to increase with the level of population growth, illiteracy will not be much reduced for many years, because a high proportion of illiterates are adults. The absolute number of those who cannot read or write is actually rising.

Illiteracy has a strong gender dimension, especially in the poorest countries of the world. High rates of female illiteracy are linked strongly to poverty, infant mortality, high fertility rates and low levels of economic development. A combination of traditional culture and economic pressures keep many girls out of school: rural families tend to be more traditional and less supportive of women's education. But in large families, it is expensive to educate all the children, so girls are often sacrificed in favour of educating boys.

Although many countries have instituted literacy programmes, these have made only a small contribution to a problem of large-scale dimensions. Television, radio and the other electronic media can be used, where they are available, to skip the stage of learning literacy skills and convey educational programmes directly to adults. But educational programmes are usually less popular than commercialized entertainment.

During the period of colonialism, the colonial governments regarded education with some trepidation. Until the twentieth century, most believed indigenous populations to be too primitive to be worthy of educating. Later, education was seen as a way of making local elites responsive to European interests and ways of life. But to some extent, the result was to foment discontent and rebellion, since the majority of those who led anti-colonial and nationalist movements were from educated elites who had attended schools or colleges in Europe. They were able to compare first-hand the democratic institutions of the European countries with the absence of democracy in their lands of origin.

The education that the colonizers introduced usually pertained to Europe, not to the colonial areas themselves. Educated Africans in the British colonies knew about the kings and queens of England, read Shakespeare, Milton and the English poets, but knew next to nothing about their own countries' history or past cultural achievements. Policies of educational reform since the end of colonialism have not completely altered the situation even today.

Partly as a result of the legacy of colonial education, which was not directed towards the majority of the population, the educational system in many developing countries is top-heavy: higher education is disproportionately developed, relative to primary and secondary education. The result is a correspondingly overqualified group who, having attended colleges and universities, cannot find white-collar or professional jobs. Given the low level of industrial development, most of the better-paid positions are in government, and there are not enough of those to go around.

In recent years, some developing countries, recognizing the shortcomings of the curricula inherited from colonialism, have tried to redirect their educational programmes towards the rural poor. They have had limited success, because usually there is insufficient funding to pay for the scale of the necessary innovations. As a result, countries such as India have begun programmes of self-help education. Communities draw on existing resources without creating demands for high levels of finance. Those who can read and write and who perhaps possess job skills are encouraged to take others on as apprentices, whom they coach in their spare time.

The links between literacy and development are also discussed in chapter 11, 'Global Inequality', pp. 398–400.

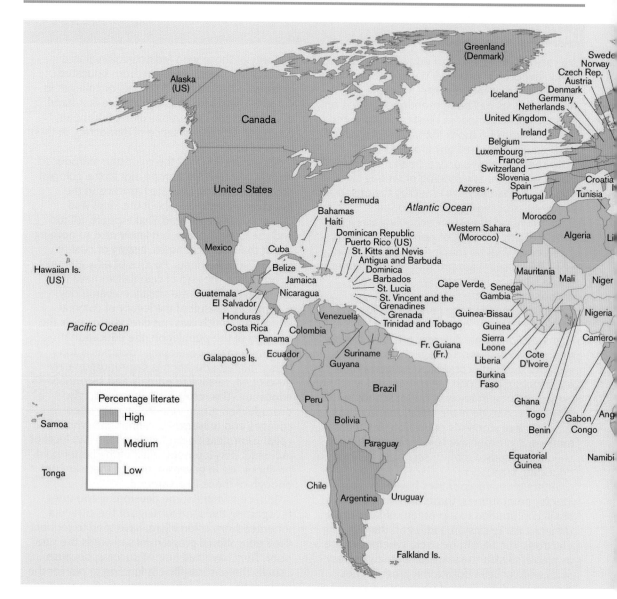

Figure 17.5 Adult literacy rates worldwide (15 years and older)

Source: UNDP (2003) (2001 data)

Compulsory schooling is a relatively recent invention, he pointed out; there is no reason why it should be accepted as somehow inevitable. Since schools do not promote equality or the development of individual creative abilities, why not do away with them in their current form? Illich did not mean by this that all forms of educational organization should be abolished. Everyone who wants to learn

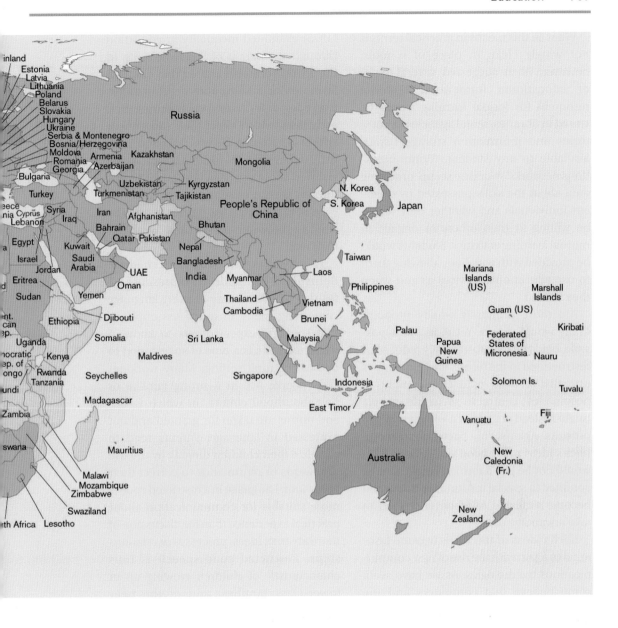

inland
Estonia
Latvia
Lithuania
Poland
Belarus
Slovakia
Hungary
Ukraine
Serbia & Montenegro
Bosnia/Herzegovina
Moldova
Romania   Armenia   Kazakhstan
Georgia   Azerbaijan
Bulgaria

Russia

Mongolia

Uzbekistan   Kyrgyzstan
Turkmenistan   Tajikistan

N. Korea
S. Korea   Japan

Turkey

eece
nia Cyprus   Syria
Lebanon   Iraq   Iran   Afghanistan

People's Republic of
China

a   Egypt
Israel   Saudi
Jordan   Arabia   UAE
Eritrea   Oman
Sudan   Yemen

Kuwait
Bahrain
Qatar Pakistan

Bhutan
Nepal
Bangladesh
India   Myanmar   Laos

Taiwan

Philippines

Mariana
Islands
(US)

Marshall
Islands

Guam (US)

nt.
can
ep.
Uganda
nocratic
ep. of
ongo
undi

Ethiopia   Djibouti

Somalia

Kenya
Rwanda
Tanzania

Madagascar

Thailand
Cambodia   Vietnam
Brunei

Sri Lanka   Malaysia

Maldives

Seychelles

Singapore

Kiribati

Palau   Federated
States of
Micronesia   Nauru

Papua
New
Guinea

Indonesia   Solomon Is.
Tuvalu

East Timor

Vanuatu   Fiji

Zambia

swana

Mauritius

Malawi
Mozambique
Zimbabwe
Swaziland
th Africa   Lesotho

Australia

New
Caledonia
(Fr.)

New
Zealand

should be provided with access to available resources – at any time in their lives, not just in their childhood or adolescent years. Such a system should make it possible for knowledge to be widely diffused and shared, not confined to specialists. Learners should not have to submit to a standard curriculum, and they should have personal choice over what they study.

What all this means in practical terms is not wholly clear. In place of schools, however, Illich suggested several types of educational framework. Material resources for formal learning would be stored in libraries, rental agencies, laboratories and information storage banks, available to any student. 'Communications networks' would be set up, providing data about the skills possessed by different individuals and whether they would be willing to train others or engage in mutual learning activities. Students would be provided with vouchers, allowing them to use educational services as and when they wished.

Are these proposals wholly utopian? Many would say so. Yet if, as looks possible, paid work is substantially reduced or restructured in the future, they appear less unrealistic. Were paid employment to become less central to social life, people might instead engage in a wider variety of pursuits. Against this backdrop, some of Illich's ideas make good sense. Education would not be just a form of early training, confined to special institutions, but would become available to whoever wished to take advantage of it.

Illich's ideas of the 1970s became fashionable again with the rise of new communications technologies. As we have seen, some believe that computers and the Internet can revolutionize education and reduce inequalities.

Basil Bernstein: language codes

Like Illich, the sociologist Basil Bernstein (1924–2000) was interested in the way in which education reproduces inequalities in society. Drawing on conflict theory (introduced on pp. 14–17) Bernstein (1975) examined inequality in education through an analysis of linguistic skills. In the 1970s Bernstein argued that children from varying backgrounds develop different codes, or forms of speech, during their early lives, which affect their subsequent school experience. He was not concerned with differences in vocabulary or verbal skills, as these are usually thought of; his interest was in systematic differences in ways of using language, particularly in the contrast between poorer and wealthier children.

The speech of working-class children, Bernstein contended, represents a restricted code – a way of using language containing many unstated assumptions that speakers expect others to know. A restricted code is a type of speech tied to its own cultural setting. Many working-class people live in a strong familial or neighbourhood culture, in which values and norms are taken for granted and not expressed in language. Parents tend to socialize their children directly by the use of rewards or reprimands to correct their behaviour. Language in a restricted code is more suitable for communication about practical experience than for discussion of more abstract ideas, processes or relationships. Restricted code speech is thus characteristic of children growing up in lower-class families, and of the peer groups in which they spend their time. Speech is oriented to the norms of the group, without anyone easily being able to explain why they follow the patterns of behaviour they do.

The language development of middle-class children, by contrast, according to Bernstein, involves the acquisition of an elaborated code – a style of speaking in which the meanings of words can be indi-

Children who have been given reasons and explanations for their behaviour are more likely to be able to master the elaborate language codes used in school, which is the key to academic success.

vidualized to suit the demands of particular situations. The ways in which children from middle-class backgrounds learn to use language are less bound to particular contexts; the child is able more easily to generalize and express abstract ideas. Thus middle-class mothers, when controlling their children, frequently explain the reasons and principles that underlie their reactions to the child's behaviour. While a working-class mother might tell a child off for wanting to eat too many sweets by simply saying 'No more sweets for you!', a middle-class mother is more likely to explain that eating too many sweets is bad for one's health and the state of one's teeth.

Children who have acquired elaborated codes of speech, Bernstein proposes, are more able to deal with the demands of formal academic education than those confined to restricted codes. This does not imply that working-class children have an 'inferior' type of speech, or that their codes of language are 'deprived'. Rather, the way in which they use speech clashes with the academic culture of the school. Those who have mastered elaborated codes fit much more easily into the school environment.

There is evidence to back up Bernstein's theory, although its validity is still debated. Joan Tough (1976) studied the language of working-class and middle-class children, finding systematic differences. She backs up Bernstein's thesis that working-class children generally have less experience of having their questions answered, or of being offered explanations about the reasoning of others. The same conclusion was reached in subsequent research by Barbara Tizard and Martin Hughes (1984).

Bernstein's ideas help us understand why those from certain socio-economic backgrounds tend to be 'under-achievers' at school. The following traits have been associated with restricted code speech, all of them inhibiting a child's educational chances:

1 The child probably receives limited responses to questions asked at home, and therefore is likely to be both less well informed and less curious about the wider world than those mastering elaborated codes.

2 The child will find it difficult to respond to the unemotional and abstract language used in teaching, as well as to appeals to general principles of school discipline.

3 Much of what the teacher says is likely to be incomprehensible, in language used in a way the child is not accustomed to. The child may attempt to cope with this by translating the teacher's language into something she or he is familiar with – but then could fail to grasp the very principles the teacher intends to convey.

4 While the child will experience little difficulty with rote or 'drill' learning, she or he may have major difficulties in grasping conceptual distinctions involving generalization and abstraction.

Pierre Bourdieu: education and cultural reproduction

Perhaps the most illuminating way of connecting some of the themes of these theoretical perspectives is through the concept of **cultural reproduction** (Bourdieu and Passeron 1977; Bourdieu 1986, 1988). Cultural reproduction refers to the ways in which schools, in conjunction with other social institutions, help perpetuate social and economic inequalities across the generations. The concept directs our attention to the means whereby, via what Illich called 'the hidden curriculum' (see above), schools influence the learning of values, attitudes and habits. Schools reinforce variations in cultural values and outlooks picked up early in life; when children leave school, these have the effect of limiting the opportunities of some, while facilitating those of others.

> Bourdieu's view on class and social capital are discussed in more detail in chapter 9, 'Stratification and Class', pp. 321–4.

The modes of language use identified by Bernstein no doubt connect with such broad cultural differences, which underlie variations in interests and tastes. Children from lower-class backgrounds, and often from minority groups, develop ways of talking and acting which clash with those dominant in the school. Schools impose rules of discipline on pupils, the authority of teachers being oriented towards academic learning. Working-class children experience a much greater cultural clash when they enter school than those from more privileged homes. The former find themselves in effect in a foreign cultural environment. Not only are they less likely to be motivated towards high academic performance; their habitual modes of speech and action, as Bernstein holds, do not mesh with those of the teachers, even if each is trying their best to communicate.

Children spend long hours in school. As Illich stresses, they learn much more there than is contained in the lessons they are officially taught. Children get an early taste of what the world of work will be like, learning that they are expected to be punctual and apply themselves diligently to the tasks which those in authority set for them (Webb and Westergaard 1991).

Learning to labour: Paul Willis's analysis of cultural reproduction

A celebrated discussion of cultural reproduction is provided in the report of a fieldwork study carried out by Paul Willis in a school in Birmingham (1977). Although the study was conducted three decades ago, it remains a classic sociological investigation.

The question Willis set out to investigate was how cultural reproduction occurs – or, as he put it, 'how working-class kids get working-class jobs'. It is often thought that, during the process of schooling, children from lower-class or minority backgrounds simply come to see that they 'are not clever enough' to expect to get highly paid or high-status jobs in their future work lives. In other words, the experience of academic failure teaches them to recognize their intellectual limitations; having accepted their 'inferiority', they move into occupations with limited career prospects.

As Willis pointed out, this interpretation does not conform at all to the reality of people's lives and experiences. The 'street wisdom' of those from poor neighbourhoods may be of little or no relevance to academic success, but involves as subtle, skilful and complex a set of abilities as any of the intellectual skills taught in school. Few if any children leave school thinking, 'I'm so stupid that it's fair and proper for me to be stacking boxes in a factory all day.' If children from less privileged backgrounds accept menial jobs, without feeling themselves throughout life to be failures, there must be other factors involved.

Willis concentrated on a particular boys' group in the school, spending a lot of time with them. The members of the gang, who called themselves 'the lads', were white; the school also contained many children from West Indian and Asian backgrounds. Willis found that the lads had an acute and perceptive understanding of the school's authority system – but used this to fight that system rather than work with it. They saw the school as an alien environment, but one they could manipulate to their own ends. They derived positive pleasure from the constant conflict – which they kept mostly to minor skirmishes – they carried on with teachers. They were adept at seeing the weak points of the teachers' claims to authority, as well as where they were vulnerable as individuals.

In class, for instance, the children were expected to sit still, be quiet and get on with their work. But the lads were all movement, save when the teacher's stare might freeze one of them momentarily; they would gossip surreptitiously, or pass open remarks that were on the verge of direct insubordination but could be explained away if challenged.

The lads recognized that work would be much like school, but they actively looked forward to it. They expected to gain no direct satisfaction from the work environment, but were impatient for wages. Far from taking the jobs they did – in tyre-fitting, carpet-laying, plumbing, painting and decorating – from feelings of inferiority, they held an attitude of dismissive superiority towards work, as they had towards school. They enjoyed the adult status that came from working, but were not interested in 'making a career' for themselves. As Willis points out, work in blue-collar settings often involves quite similar cultural features to those the lads created in their counter-school culture – banter, quick wit and the skill to subvert the demands of authority figures when necessary. Only later in their lives might they come to see themselves as trapped in arduous, unrewarding labour. When they have families, they might perhaps look back on education retrospectively, and see it – hopelessly – as having been the only escape. Yet if they try to pass this view on to their own children, they are likely to have no more success than their own parents did.

Learning not to labour: 'macho lads'

More than two decades after Willis conducted his study on 'the lads' in Birmingham, another sociologist, Máirtín Mac an Ghaill, investigated the experiences of young working-class men at the Parnell School in the West Midlands (1994). Mac an Ghaill was particularly interested in how male students develop specific forms of masculinity in school as part of their passage to manhood. His account was influential on Diane Reay, whose account of Shaun's transition from primary to secondary school began this chapter. Mac an Ghaill was intent on understanding how working-class boys in the early 1990s viewed their own transitions to adult life and prospects for the future. Unlike Willis's lads, the boys at the Parnell School were growing up in the shadow of high unemployment, the collapse of the manufacturing base in the region, and cutbacks in government benefits for young people.

Mac an Ghaill found that the transition to adulthood for young men at the Parnell School was much more fragmented than that experienced by Willis's lads twenty-five years earlier. There was no longer a clear trajectory stretching from school into wage labour. Many of the boys in the school saw the post-school years as characterized by dependency (on family in particular), 'useless' government training schemes, and an insecure labour market not favourable to young manual workers. There was widespread confusion among many of the students as to how education was relevant to their futures. This confusion manifested itself in very different responses to schooling – while some of the male peer groups tried to chart upwardly mobile paths for themselves as academic achievers or 'new enterprisers', others were openly hostile to schooling altogether.

Of the four peer groups Mac an Ghaill identified at the school, the 'macho lads' were the most traditionally working-class group in the school. The macho lads had coalesced as a group by the time they became teenagers; the group's members were in the bottom two academic 'sets' for all subjects. Their attitudes towards education were openly hostile – they shared a common view that the school was part of an authoritarian system that placed meaningless study demands on its captive students. Where Willis's 'lads' had found ways to manipulate the school environment to their advantage, the macho lads were defiant about their role within it.

The macho lads were seen by the school administration as the most 'dangerous' anti-school peer group at Parnell School. Teachers were encouraged to deal with them using more overtly authoritarian means than they might

with other students. The macho lads' symbolic displays of working-class masculinity – such as certain clothing, hairstyles and earrings – were banned by the school administration. Teachers were involved in the 'surveillance' of students, by constantly monitoring them in the hallways, instructing them to 'look at me when I'm talking to you' and telling them to 'walk properly down the corridor'.

Secondary school for the macho lads was their 'apprenticeship' in learning to be tough. School was not about the 3 R's (reading, writing and arithmetic), but about the 3 F's (fighting, fucking and football). 'Looking after your mates' and 'sticking together' were key values in the macho lads' social world. School became a contested territory, much like the streets. The macho lads regarded teachers in the same way they did law enforcement (with open disdain) and believed that they were the main source of conflict within the school. They refused to affirm the teachers' authority within the school setting, and were convinced that they were constantly being 'set up' to be punished, disciplined or humiliated.

Like Willis's 'lads', the macho lads also associated academic work and achievement with something inferior and effeminate. The students who excelled scholastically were labelled 'dickhead achievers'. Schoolwork was rejected out of hand as inappropriate for men. As one macho lad, Leon, commented: 'The work you do here is girls' work. It's not real work. It's just for kids. They [the teachers] try to make you write down things about how you feel. It's none of their fucking business' (Mac an Ghaill 1994, p. 59).

Mac an Ghaill's work demonstrates how the 'macho lads', more than other male peer groups, were undergoing a particular 'crisis of masculinity'. This is because they were actively developing an 'outdated' working-class masculinity that centred around manual waged labour – at a time when a secure future in manual labour had all but disappeared. According to Mac an Ghaill, the macho lads continued to fantasize about the 'full employment' society which their fathers and uncles had inhabited. Although some of their behaviours came across as hypermasculine and therefore defensive, they were grounded squarely in a working-class world-view which had been inherited from older generations.

The formation of masculinity is discussed in chapter 12, 'Sexuality and Gender', pp. 462–7.

Postmodern approaches to education

By the 1990s many sociologists had begun to turn away from social conflict theories towards postmodernism. (Some of the main ideas behind postmodernism were introduced in chapter 4, pp. 114–17.) One important account of what postmodernism means for education is found in the work of the British sociologists Robin Usher and Richard Edwards. To Usher and Edwards, theories of education that are based on functionalist or conflict theory are 'modernist'. They accept a 'meta-narrative' that education spreads rational beliefs in place of pre-modern superstitions. Implicit in this view of education is a view of progress. Education enables individuals to think freely and rationally, which makes social progress and innovation possible. As postmodernists, Usher and Edwards reject this meta-narrative. They are sceptical of the claim that science and reason can answer all human problems or that there is any one truth. They see no reason why one curriculum should be taught rather than any other, or why some subjects are more important than others.

Usher and Edwards's critique of modern education leads to the question, 'What would a postmodern education system look like?' Although they discuss several possibilities, the one that they are most sympathetic to is the development of a system that accepts the cultural pluralism and diversity that are central to the concerns of postmodernist thinkers. This system would give individuals the freedom to shape their own educational programmes, though lifelong learning or the exploration of cultural difference for example (Usher and Edwards 1994).

We now move on to discuss inequality in education – including gender, ethnicity and class – going on from there to analyse some further theories about performance.

Inequality and education

The formal curriculum in schools, apart from participation in games, no longer distinguishes in any systematic way between boys and girls. However, there are various other 'points of entry' for the development of gender differences in education. These include teacher expectations, school rituals and other aspects of a hidden curriculum, as noted by Illich above. Although rules are gradually loosening, regulations which compel girls to wear dresses or skirts in school form one of the most obvious ways in which gender-typing occurs. The consequences go beyond mere appearance. As a result of the clothes she wears, a girl lacks the freedom to sit casually, to join in rough and tumble games, or sometimes to run as fast as she is able.

Although this again is changing, school textbooks also help to perpetuate gender images. Until recently it was common for storybooks in primary schools to portray boys as showing initiative and independence, while girls, if they appeared at all, were more passive and watched their brothers. Stories written especially for girls often have an element of adventure in them, but this usually takes the form of intrigues or mysteries in a domestic or school setting. Boys' adventure stories are more wide-ranging, having heroes who travel off to distant places or are sturdily independent in other ways. At the secondary level, females have tended to be

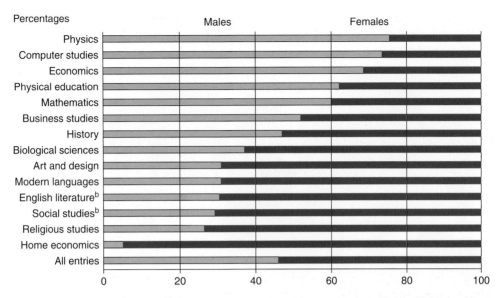

Figure 17.6   GCE A-level or equivalent entries for young people in the UK:[a] by selected subject, 2001/2 (%)

[a] Pupils in schools and students in further education institutions aged 16–18 at the start of the academic year in England and in Northern Ireland, and aged 17 in Wales. Pupils in Scotland generally sit Highers one year earlier and the figures relate to the result of pupils in Year S5/S6
[b] England and Wales only

Source: *Social Trends* 34 (2004), p. 44

'invisible' in most science and maths textbooks, perpetuating the view that these are 'male subjects'.

Gender differences in education are also very obvious when one looks at subject choice in schools. The view that some subjects are more suitable for boys or for girls is a common one. The sociologist Becky Francis has argued that girls are more likely to be encouraged into less academically prestigious subjects than boys (2000). There is certainly a marked difference in the subjects they chose to pursue. In 2001/2, around 75 per cent of young people aged sixteen to eighteen who entered for an A-level (or equivalent) in physics and in computer studies in the UK, and 60 per cent of those entered for maths, were male. By comparison, around

70 per cent of entries for social studies and English literature, and 95 per cent of entries for home economics, were female. The differences are shown in figure 17.6.

Gender and achievement in school

For many years, girls on average did better than boys in terms of school results until they reached the middle years of secondary education. They then fell behind: boys did better in exams at the ages of sixteen and eighteen, and at university. Until the late 1980s, girls were less likely than boys to attain the three A levels necessary for admission to university and were entering higher education in smaller numbers than boys. Concerned about

Girls are now outperforming boys at every level of education, and in most subjects.

such inequalities, feminist researchers conducted a number of important studies into how gender influences the learning process. They found that school curricula were often male-dominated and that teachers were devoting more attention to boys than to girls in the classroom.

In recent years, however, the debate over gender in schools has undergone a dramatic reversal. 'Under-achieving boys' are now one of the main subjects of conversation among educators and policy-makers alike. Beginning in the early 1990s, girls began consistently to outperform boys in all areas and at all levels of the British educational system (as table 17.2 and figure 17.7 show). Similar findings have been reported from America. Young women in the USA are more likely than young men to go further in school, get a college education and go on to do a postgraduate degree (as figure 17.8 on p. 718 shows).

The problem of 'failing boys' has been seized on with great concern because it is seen to be linked to a host of larger social problems such as crime, unemployment, drugs and lone parenthood. In combination, these factors have amounted to what has been described as the 'crisis in masculinity' (discussed in chapter 12, pp. 462–7) and explored above by Máirtín Mac an Ghaill. Boys who leave school early, or with poor educational results, are less likely to find good jobs and create stable families. As Britain's economic profile continues to change, fewer

Table 17.2   Pupils reaching or exceeding expected standards: by Key Stage and sex, England, 2004 (%)

	Teacher assessment		Tests	
	Boys	Girls	Boys	Girls
Key Stage 1				
English				
Reading	81	89	81	89
Writing	78	88	76	87
Mathematics	88	91	89	92
Science	88	91		
Key Stage 2				
English	69	80	72	83
Mathematics	75	76	74	74
Science	82	84	86	86
Key Stage 3				
English	62	77	64	77
Mathematics	72	76	72	74
Science	69	72	65	67

Source: *Social Trends* 35(2005), p. 38

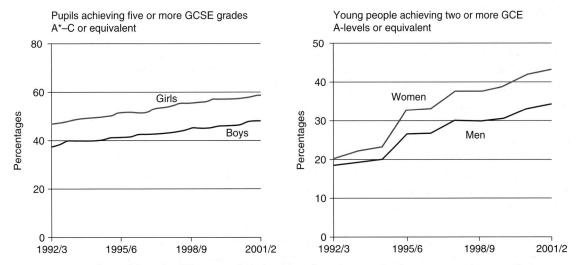

Figure 17.7   Male and female differences in educational attainment in the UK, 1992/3–2002/3

Source: ONS (2004c), p. 5

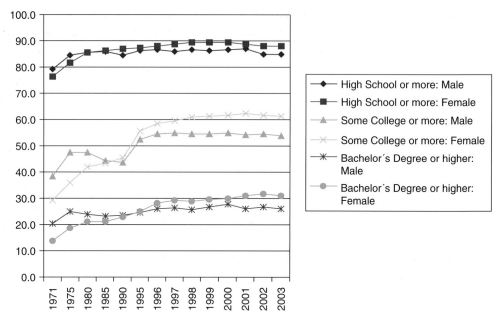

Figure 17.8   Percentage of 25–29-year-olds by level of education completed in the USA by gender, selected years, 1971–2003

Source: *Child Trends* (<www.childtrendsdatabank.org/pdf/6_PDF.pdf>)

unskilled manual jobs are available for young men with weak educational backgrounds. Meanwhile, a large proportion – up to 70 per cent – of jobs that are being created in the rapidly growing service sector are being filled by women.

Explaining the gender gap

A variety of explanations have been advanced to account for the turnaround in gender performance over the past decade. One factor that must be taken into account in explaining girls' achievement in school is the influence of the women's movement on their self-esteem and expectations. Many girls presently in school have grown up surrounded by examples of working women – indeed many of their own mothers work outside the home. Exposure to these positive role

models increases girls' awareness of career opportunities and challenges traditional stereotypes of women as housewives. Another result of feminism is that teachers and educationalists have become more aware of gender discrimination within the educational system. In recent years, many schools have taken steps to avoid gender stereotyping in the classroom, to encourage girls to explore traditionally 'male' subjects, and to promote educational materials that are free of gender bias.

Some theories to explain the gender gap in schools centre on the difference in learning styles between boys and girls. Girls are often regarded as better organized and more motivated than boys; they are also seen as maturing earlier. One manifestation of this is that girls tend to relate to one another by talking and using verbal skills. Boys, on the other hand, socialize in a more active manner – through sport, computer games and hanging out in the school playground – and tend to be more disruptive in the classroom. These broad patterns of behaviour seem to be reaffirmed by teachers in the classroom, who may have lower expectations for boys than for girls, and indulge boys' disruptions by paying more attention to them.

Another line of reasoning focuses on 'laddism' – a set of attitudes and outlooks shared by many boys that is anti-education and anti-learning (the studies carried out by Paul Willis and Máirtín Mac an Ghaill, discussed on pp. 711–13 above, provide evidence for these theories). Many see high rates of exclusion and truancy among boys as rooted in the belief that learning is 'uncool'. The then schools minister, Stephen Byers, commented in 1998 that 'we must challenge the laddish, anti-learning culture which has been allowed to develop over recent years and should not simply accept with a shrug of the shoulders that boys will be boys'.

Is underachievement really about gender?

Some scholars question the enormous amount of attention – and resources – being directed at under-achieving boys. They argue that the gender gap in language skills is one that can be found the world over. Differences that used to be ascribed to boys' 'healthy idleness' are now provoking a firestorm of controversy and frantic attempts to improve boys' results. As national performance targets, league tables and international literacy comparisons proliferate – drawing differences out into the open for all to see – 'equal outcomes' in education have become a top priority.

All this attention to boys, critics argue, serves to hide other forms of inequality within education. Although girls have forged ahead in many areas, they are still less likely than boys to choose subjects in school leading to careers in technology, science and engineering. Boys pull ahead in science by about the age of eleven and continue to outperform girls through to university: in subjects such as chemistry and computer science, which are central to economic growth in the present economy, they continue to dominate. Although women may be entering higher education in greater numbers, they continue to be disadvantaged in the job market in comparison with men who hold the same levels of qualification (Epstein 1998).

More than gender, some scholars argue, factors such as class and ethnicity produce the greatest inequalities within the educational system. For example, comparisons in achievement by pupils across social class reveal that 70 per cent of children from the top professional class receive five or more pass grades, compared with only 14 per cent from working-class backgrounds. Concentrating upon 'failing boys' is misleading, critics contend, since men continue to dominate positions of power in society. The underachievement of working-class boys, they argue, may have less to do with their gender than with the disadvantages of their social class.

Gender and higher education

As we saw above (pp. 695–701), there have been substantial increases in the number of students in higher education in recent decades. One significant aspect of the expansion in higher education is the increase in the number of female students. In 2001/2, 56 per cent of full-time and part-time students in higher education were female. This is a reversal of the position just a few decades ago, when there were far more male students than female (as figure 17.9 shows). By 2001/2 there were six times as many female students in higher education than in 1970/1, but only two and a half times as many male students.

Women's organizations in Britain and elsewhere have often attacked sex discrimination in school and higher education. Women still find themselves heavily under-represented among the teaching staff in colleges and universities, especially in senior posts. In 2002/3, although women made up 39 per cent of academic staff, only 26 per cent of senior lecturers and researchers were women and there were 1,860 women professors, accounting for just over 14 per cent of the total. However, there is a trend towards greater gender equality in higher education. The figures quoted here mark a 5.7 per cent rise in the number of female academics, and a 10.4 per cent leap in the number of female professors, over the year before (HESA 2004).

With men occupying more of the senior positions in higher education institutions, women, on average, are paid significantly less. A recent survey found that average pay for women is lower than for men at every university in the UK. Across the university sector as a whole, women earn on average more than £5,000 less than men, and the gender difference in pay is significantly larger at some institutions (*THES*, 3 September 2004).

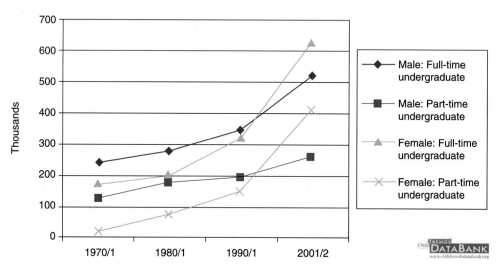

Figure 17.9 Students in higher education: by sex, 1970/1–2001/2

Source: Social Trends 34 (2004), p. 44

Ethnicity and education

Sociologists have carried out a good deal of research into the educational fortunes of ethnic minorities in Britain. Governments have also sponsored a series of investigations; an important earlier account was *Education for All*, the report of the Swann Committee in 1985. The Swann Report found significant differences in average levels of educational success between groups from different ethnic backgrounds. Children from Black Caribbean families tended to fare worst in school, as measured by formal academic attainments. They had improved from ten years earlier, however. Asian children did as well as white children, in spite of the fact that on average the families from which they came were economically worse off than white families (Swann Committee 1985).

Subsequent research indicates that the picture has shifted, however. Trevor Jones carried out research which indicated that children from all minority group backgrounds were more likely than white children to continue in full-time education from the age of sixteen to nineteen. Only 37 per cent of white children stayed on in education in 1988–90, compared to 43 per cent from West Indian backgrounds, 50 per cent of South Asians and 77 per cent of Chinese. In spite of this apparently positive picture, Jones suggested something of a negative reason. Many members of ethnic minority groups might stay on in education because of the problem of finding a job. (Jones 1993)

On the whole, members of ethnic minority groups are not under-represented in British higher education. People from Indian and Chinese backgrounds are, on average, significantly more likely to have a degree qualification or higher than those from other ethnic backgrounds. Men who defined themselves as 'Mixed Race' and women who defined themselves as 'Black/Black British' and 'Asian/Asian British' were slightly less likely to have gained a degree or higher qualification than the national average (HMSO 2004).

Social exclusion and schooling

As we have seen elsewhere in this book, social exclusion has become a topic of great interest for sociologists over the past decade. There has been growing awareness and concern over the number of children outside the education system. Within the sociology of education, connections are often drawn between the exclusion of students from school and other phenomena such as truancy, delinquency, poverty, limited parental supervision and weak commitments to education.

Exclusion rates have been increasing in recent years. In 2001/2, more than 10,000 children in Great Britain were permanently excluded from schools, (this marked a decline from 1996/7 when more than 13,000 children were permanently excluded). The number of boys permanently excluded outnumbered girls by nearly five to one in 2001/2. Exclusion rates also differ according to ethnicity (see figure 17.10). In 2002/3 the highest permanent exclusion rates in England were among black Caribbean and other black pupils, with rates of thirty-seven and thirty-two exclusions per ten thousand pupils of compulsory school age, respectively. (However, these figures were nearly half the rates of 1996/7 when seventy-eight and seventy-one pupils per ten thousand

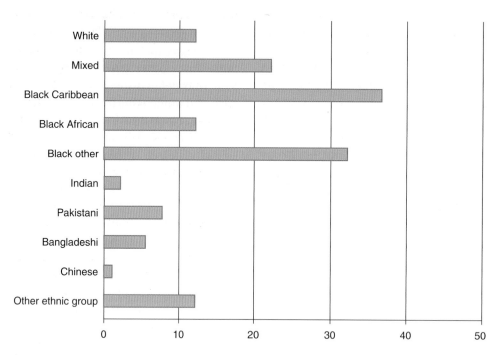

Figure 17.10   Permanent exclusion rates: by ethnic group, England, 2002/3[a]

[a] The number of permanent exclusions per 10,000 pupils (headcount) in each ethnic group in primary, secondary and special schools (excluding dually registered pupils in special schools) for compulsory school age

Source: Social Trends 34 (2004), p. 42

were excluded, respectively.) Rates of permanent exclusion were lowest for Indian and Chinese pupils. Findings from American spchools reflect a similar disparity in exclusion rates between black pupils and students from other ethnic backgrounds.

In the USA, more than 80 per cent of American schools have adopted 'zero tolerance' policies towards disruptive students, following a series of school shootings. A nationwide investigation into the results of such policies has revealed that black students are being excluded from schools at rates disproportionate to their representation within student bodies – and at a rate unlikely to be due simply to disruptiveness

in school. In San Francisco, black students account for 52 per cent of exclusions, yet make up only 16 per cent of school enrolment. In Phoenix, where the black population is 4 per cent, black students make up 21 per cent of exclusions. How can the high rate of exclusions among black male pupils be explained? A number of factors are likely to be involved. It is possible that in individual settings, exclusion policies are applied in a racially discriminatory way.

The links between social exclusion and ethnicity are discussed in more detail in chapter 10, 'Poverty, Social Exclusion and Welfare', pp. 350–1.

It is important also to consider how rates of school exclusion may reflect much broader patterns of exclusion and disadvantage within society. As we have seen elsewhere, many young people are growing up under challenging conditions, with a lack of adult guidance and support. Traditional notions of masculinity are under threat and there is no stable vision of the future. For young people growing up against this turbulent backdrop, schools may appear irrelevant or too authoritative – rather than a site for opportunity and advancement.

IQ and education

The discussion so far has not considered the issue of inherited differences in ability, and the assertion by some that variations in educational attainment and in subsequent occupational position and income directly reflect differential intelligence. In such circumstances, it is argued, there might in fact be equality of opportunity in the school system, with people finding a level equivalent to their innate potential.

What is intelligence?

For many years psychologists have debated whether there exists a single human ability which can be called intelligence, and, if so, how far it rests on innately determined differences. Intelligence is difficult to define, because it covers many different, often unrelated, qualities. We might suppose, for example, that the 'purest' form of intelligence is the ability to solve abstract mathematical puzzles. However, people who are very good at such puzzles sometimes have low abilities in other areas, such as grasping the narrative of history or understanding art. Since the concept has proved to be so resistant to accepted definition, some psychologists have proposed (and many educators have by default accepted) that intelligence can simply be regarded as 'what IQ tests measure' (IQ, intelligence quotient, meaning a measure of intelligence). The unsatisfactory nature of this is obvious enough, because the definition of intelligence becomes wholly circular.

Most IQ tests consist of a mixture of conceptual and computational problems. The tests are constructed so that the average score is 100 points: anyone scoring below is thus labelled as having 'below-average intelligence', and anyone scoring above has 'above-average intelligence'. In spite of the fundamental difficulty in measuring intelligence, IQ tests are widely used in research studies, as well as in schools and businesses.

IQ and genetic factors

Scores on IQ tests do in fact correlate highly with academic performance (which is not surprising, since the tests were originally developed to predict success in school). They therefore also correlate closely with social, economic and ethnic differences, since these are associated with variations in levels of educational attainment. White students score better, on average, than blacks or members of other disadvantaged minorities. An article published by Arthur Jensen in the 1960s caused a furore by attributing IQ differences between blacks and whites in part to genetic variations (Jensen 1967, 1979).

More recently, psychologist Richard J. Herrnstein and sociologist Charles Murray have reopened the debate about IQ and education in a controversial way.

They argue in their book *The Bell Curve: Intelligence and Class Structure in American Life* (1994) that the accumulated evidence linking IQ to genetic inheritance has now become overwhelming. The significant differences in intelligence between various racial and ethnic groups, they say, must in part be explained in terms of heredity. Most of the evidence they quote comes from studies carried out in the USA. According to Herrnstein and Murray, such evidence indicates that some ethnic groups on average have higher IQs than other groups. Asian Americans, particularly Japanese Americans and Chinese Americans, on average possess higher IQs than whites, though the difference is not large. The average IQs of Asians and whites, however, are substantially higher than those of blacks. Summarizing the findings of 156 studies, Herrnstein and Murray find an average difference of sixteen IQ points between these two racial groups. The authors argue that such differences in inherited intelligence contribute in an important way to social divisions in American society. The more clever an individual is, the greater the chance that she or he will rise in the social scale. Those at the top are there partly because they are cleverer than the rest of the population – from which it follows that those at the bottom remain there because, on average, they are not so clever.

Critics of Herrnstein and Murray deny that IQ differences between racial and ethnic groups are genetic in origin. They argue that differences in IQ result from social and cultural differences. IQ tests, they point out, pose questions – to do with abstract reasoning, for example – more likely to be part of the experience of more affluent white students than of blacks and ethnic minorities. Scores on IQ tests may also be influenced by factors that have nothing to do with the abilities supposedly being measured, such as whether the testing is experienced as stressful. Research has demonstrated that African-Americans score six points lower on IQ tests when the tester is white than when the tester is black (Kamin 1977).

Observations of deprived ethnic minority groups in other countries – such as the 'untouchables' in India, the Maoris in New Zealand and Burakumin of Japan – strongly suggest that the IQ variations between African-Americans and whites in the United States result from social and cultural differences. Children in all of these groups score an average of ten to fifteen IQ points below children belonging to the ethnic majority. This conclusion receives further support from a comparative study of fourteen nations (including the United States) showing that average IQ scores have risen substantially over the past half century for the population as a whole. IQ tests are regularly updated. When old and new versions of the tests are given to the same group of people, they score significantly higher on the old tests. Present-day children taking IQ tests from the 1930s outscored 1930s groups by an average of fifteen points – just the kind of average difference that currently separates blacks and whites. Children today are not innately superior in intelligence to their parents or grandparents; the shift presumably derives from increasing prosperity and social advantages. The average social and economic gap between whites and African-Americans is at least as great as that between the different generations, and is sufficient to explain the variation in

IQ scores. At the same time, average scores for whole groups do nothing to predict the level of intelligence of any particular member of that group. While the variations between individuals that influence scores on IQ tests may in part be genetic, that some races are on average cleverer than others remains unproven and improbable.

The Bell Curve Wars

In *The Bell Curve Wars* (Fraser 1995), a number of noted scholars got together to examine the ideas of Herrnstein and Murray. The editor of the volume describes *The Bell Curve* as 'the most incendiary piece of social science to appear in the last decade or more'. The claims and assertions in the work 'have generated flash floods of letters to the editor in every major magazine and newspaper, not to mention the over-the-air commentary on scores of radio and television shows' (Fraser 1995, p. 3).

The biologist Stephen Jay Gould (1941–2002), contributor to *The Bell Curve Wars*, argued that Herrnstein and Murray are wrong on four major counts. He disputed their claims that intelligence can be described by a single IQ number, that people can be meaningfully ranked along a single scale of intelligence, that intelligence derives substantially from genetic inheritance and that it cannot be altered. He showed that each of these assumptions is questionable.

Howard Gardner, another contributor, argues that a century of research has dispelled the notion of 'intelligence' as a general category. There are only 'multiple intelligences' – practical, musical, spatial, mathematical and so forth. Other contributors to *The Bell Curve Wars* claim that

there is no systematic relation between IQ scores and later job performance. 'Racist pseudoscience', is their common reaction. Gould concludes:

> We must fight the doctrine of *The Bell Curve* both because it is wrong and because it will, if activated, cut off all possibility of proper nurturance for everyone's intelligence. Of course, we cannot all be rocket scientists or brain surgeons, but those who can't might be rock musicians or professional athletes (and gain far more social prestige and salary thereby). (ibid., p. 22)

The New IQism

In their article 'The New IQism: Intelligence, "Ability" and the Rationing of Education' (2001) David Gillborn and Deborah Youndell argue that although measures of IQ are rarely used explicitly in education these days, educationalists now use the term 'ability' in a very similar way. Gillborn and Youndell argue that the use of the term 'ability' systematically disadvantages black and working-class students in schools

The authors carried out surveys in two London schools over two years in the mid-1990s. They interviewed and observed teachers, and pupils in their third and final years at secondary school. At both schools they surveyed, the authors found teaching was heavily shaped around 'the A-to-C economy'. By this phrase, they meant that schools were aiming to get as high a proportion of pupils as possible to obtain five or more grades A to C at GCSE. This is the case because the proportion of pupils meeting this benchmark is one of the key criteria on which schools are rated in the government's annually published official league tables. As the headmaster of one school noted in a memo to staff: 'The best thing we can do is to get the greatest possible proportion achieving the five high-grade benchmark.'

Although this seems a praiseworthy aim, Gillborn and Youndell found that it put teachers under pressure to spend more time on those pupils they think are able to achieve five or more GCSEs at grade C or above. The effect of this was that 'both schools are increasingly rationing the time and effort they expend on different groups of pupils'. Teachers had to make a choice over which pupils have the ability to get the five good GCSE grades – and they gave these pupils most attention. The authors found that in both schools teachers' notions of a pupils 'ability' determined whether they saw that pupil as a likely candidate to gain five or more GCSEs. From their interviews and observations of teachers and pupils, Gillborn and Youndell gained a clearer idea of what teachers meant by this term. They found that 'ability' was viewed as something fixed and which determined the potential of different pupils (as one headteacher remarked: 'You can't give someone ability can you? You can't achieve more than you're capable of can you?'). It was also found that teachers often believed that ability could be measured objectively. At one school, pupils were given a 'cognitive ability' test when they arrived, which teachers took as a good indication of GCSE performance later on.

Gillborn and Youndell found that in both the schools they studied, pupils complained that 'certain peers are favoured over others'. These are the pupils who are deemed to have ability. They tended to be white and middle class. Gillborn and Youndell interviewed one teacher who commented that poorer, out-of-work parents 'do not have the same expectations for their kids from education that "middle class" or your upwardly mobile working class parents are going to have'. Thus, class and parental expectation add to a teacher's assessment of a pupil's 'ability'. The authors also noted that they 'observed many occasions when Black pupils seemed to be dealt with more harshly or to face lower expectations than their peers of other ethnic backgrounds'. These beliefs about which pupils had ability, the authors argued, constituted an unwitting discrimination against black and working-class children.

The unofficial assessments by teachers of which pupils had ability meant that black and working-class children were less likely than white and middle-class children to be entered for higher-level GCSEs (in which the top marks are awarded.) The teacher's view of the pupil's ability also played an important role in determining which set they ended up in, with black and working-class children, who had been doing work of the same standard as their white, middle-class peers, more likely to end up in lower sets. The result, unsurprisingly, is that fewer black and working-class pupils get five GCSEs above grade C, thus reinforcing the teacher's assessment of their ability. In one of the schools, for example, 16 per cent of black pupils attained five or more GCSEs above C level, compared to 35 per cent of white pupils. These results are typical of the national pattern, which sees black and working-class pupils do worse academically than the average.

In this way, argue Gillborn and Youndell, the assumptions about 'ability' are the same as the beliefs about intelligence which saw a 'tripartite' division of British secondary schools (into grammar, technical and secondary modern) in earlier generations. The authors also argue that such beliefs have informed New Labour's thinking on education. Since Labour was elected in 1997, it has continued to support 'setting' in schools to group pupils according to ability. The authors argue that it is these assumptions about ability that play a significant role in the big differences in levels of achievement between different classes and ethnic groups.

Gillborn and Youndell conclude that their studies show that although most educationalists would disagree strongly with the idea that intelligence is largely inherited, put forward in books like *The Bell Curve*, 'in one sense at least, the hereditarians have won. Without any genuine debate the British education system is increasingly returning to policy and practice that takes for granted the assumptions proposed by IQists like Herrnstein and Murray.' To Gillborn and Youndell, the familiar social divisions (especially those of race and class) are reappearing through language that appears to stress the individual 'ability' of pupils, but actually relies on unstated prejudices about group identities.

Emotional and interpersonal intelligence

In his book *Emotional Intelligence* (1996) Daniel Goleman has tried to move the discussion away from the debate about IQ. Goleman has argued that 'emotional intelligence' might be at least as important as IQ in determining how we fare in our lives. Emotional intelligence refers to how people use their emotions – the ability to motivate oneself, to have self-control, enthusiasm and persistence. By and large,

these qualities aren't inherited and the more children can be taught them, the more chance they have of making use of their intellectual capabilities. According to Goleman, 'The brightest among us can founder on shoals of unbridled passion and unruly impulses; people with high IQs can be stunningly poor pilots of their private lives' (ibid, p. 34). This is one reason why measures of ordinary intelligence don't correlate very well with subsequent achievement.

Thus one research study followed ninety-five Harvard students who graduated in the 1940s. By the time they reached middle age, those who had achieved high IQ test scores in college were only slightly more successful than lower-scoring students in terms of their careers. Another piece of research looked at the other end of the IQ scale. Four hundred and fifty boys, two-thirds from families on welfare, and all from a slum area near Harvard, were studied. A third of the group had IQs below 90. Again, IQ had only a small connection with their subsequent careers. For example, 7 per cent of men with an IQ of less than 80 were unemployed, but so were 7 per cent with an IQ over 100. Childhood abilities such as handling emotions and getting on well with others were better predictors. As Howard Gardner has put it:

> Interpersonal intelligence is the ability to understand other people: what motivates them, how they work, how to work cooperatively with them. Successful salespeople, politicians, teachers, clinicians and religious leaders are all likely to be individuals with high degrees of interpersonal intelligence. Intrapersonal intelligence . . . is a capacity to form an accurate, veridical model of oneself and to be able to use that model to operate effectively in life. (1993, p. 9)

We have to revise our ideas of intelligence to include the diversity of factors that make for success in life. Something similar can be said of education itself. Education is a broader notion than that of formal schooling. It can also no longer be regarded as a stage of preparation before an individual enters work. As technology changes, necessary skills change, and even if education is seen from a purely vocational point of view – as providing skills relevant to work – most observers agree that lifelong exposure to education will be needed in the future.

Education and new communications technology

The spread of information technology is already influencing education in schools in a number of different ways. The knowledge economy demands a computer literate workforce and it is increasingly clear that education can, and must, play a critical role in meeting this need. While household computer ownership has risen sharply in recent years, many children still do not have access to a computer at home. For this reason, schools are a crucial forum for young people to learn about and become comfortable with the capabilities of computers and online technology.

Technology in the classroom

As we saw earlier in this chapter, the rise of education in its modern sense was connected with a number of other major changes happening in the nineteenth century. One was the development of printing and the arrival of 'book culture'.

The mass distribution of books, newspapers and other printed media was as distinctive a feature of the development of industrial society as were machines and factories. Education provided the skills of literacy and numeracy, giving access to the world of printed media. Nothing is more characteristic of the school than the schoolbook or textbook.

In the eyes of many, all this is set to change with the growing use of computers and multimedia technologies in education. Will the digital media increasingly replace the schoolbook? And will schools still exist in anything like the form in which they do today if children turn on their computers in order to learn, rather than listening to a teacher? The new technologies, it is said, will not just add to the existing curriculum; they will undermine and transform it. For young people now are already growing up in an information- and media-related society and are much more familiar with its technologies than most adults are – including their teachers.

Over recent years, the use of technology in education has been utterly transformed. In the UK there has been a series of national initiatives aimed at modernizing and computerizing British schools. Figures 17.11 to 17.14 show the dramatic rise in information and communication technology in schools in England, which meant that by 2002 practically all schools were connected to the Internet.

Some observers speak of a 'classroom revolution' – the arrival of 'desk-top virtual reality' and the classroom without walls. There is little question that computers have expanded opportunities in education. They provide the chance for children to work independently, to research topics with the help of online resources, and to

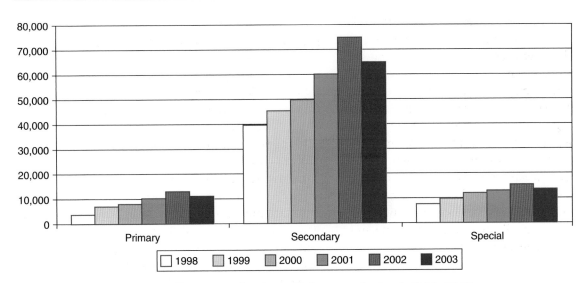

Figure 17.11   Average expenditure per school on ICT: by type of school, 1998–2003

*Source:*Department for Education and Skills (2003), pp. 5–7

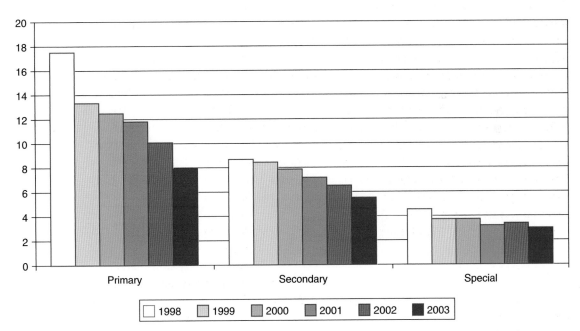

Figure 17.12   Average number of pupils per computer per school: by type of school (England), 1998–2003

Source: Department for Education and Skills (2003), pp. 5–7

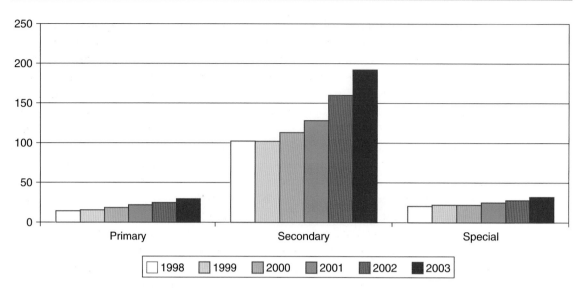

Figure 17.13 Average number of computers used mainly or solely for teaching and learning purposes per school (England), 1998–2003

Source: Department for Education and Skills (2003), pp. 5–7

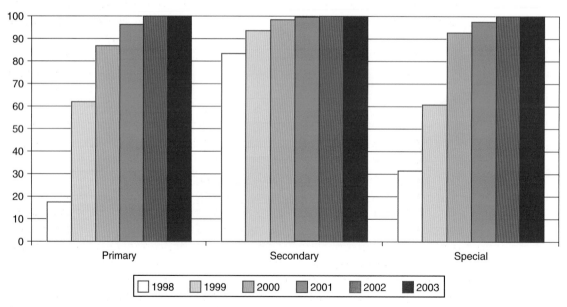

Figure 17.14 Percentage of schools with access to the Internet (England), 1998–2003

Source: Department for Education and Skills (2003), pp. 5–7

benefit from educational software that allows them to progress at their own pace. Yet the vision (or nightmare) of classrooms of children learning exclusively through individual computers has not yet come to pass. In fact, the 'classroom without walls' looks some way off.

Even if there were enough computers to go around at school or in the home (and although the number of pupils per computer is falling dramatically, this is still not the case – see figure 17.12), most teachers see computers as a supplement to traditional lessons, rather than as a replacement for them. Pupils can use computers to complete tasks within the standard curriculum, such as producing a research project or investigating current events. But few educators see information technology as a medium that can substitute for learning from and interacting with human teachers. The challenge for teachers is learning to integrate new information technologies into lessons in a way that is meaningful and educationally sound.

The arrival of e-universities?

Back in 1971, Britain's Open University pioneered the use of television in distance learning in higher education. Its programmes are broadcast by the BBC early in the morning and late at night. Students combine these with written materials, work by correspondence, meetings with a personal tutor and summer courses with other students. In this way they can take high-quality degree courses from home – and often while still doing a job. The OU has become the UK's largest university, and increasingly it is adding the Internet to its range – but it remains committed to a mix of encounters with its students.

The Internet now appears to be transforming education in an even more profound way than television did more than three decades ago. This approach was, and is, being pioneered by the University of Phoenix in the United States. Founded in 1989, it is the largest accredited university in the USA. Yet, unlike most large American universities, it cannot boast a grassy campus, a sprawling library, a football team or a student centre. The 68,000 students enrolled at the university meet and interact predominantly across the Internet – the University of Phoenix's 'online campus' – or at one of more than fifty 'learning centres' located in large cities throughout North America.

The University of Phoenix offers more than a dozen degree programmes which can be completed entirely online, making students' actual geographical location irrelevant. Online 'group mailboxes' substitute for physical classrooms: rather than making presentations or discussing ideas in person, students post their work in the electronic classroom for other students and the instructor to read. An electronic library is available for students to complete their research and reading assignments. At the start of each week, the course instructor distributes the week's reading list and discussion topics electronically. Students complete the required work according to their own schedules – they can access the 'electronic classroom' at any hour of day or night – and instructors mark assignments and return them to students with comments.

It is not simply the medium of learning that is distinctive at the University of Phoenix. The university only admits students who are over twenty-three years of age and who are employed at a workplace.

Both the structure and the content of the university's offerings are aimed at adult professionals who want new skills and qualifications, but need to complete this continuing education in a way that does not conflict with their busy personal and professional lives. For this reason, courses are taught in intensive five-to eight-week blocks and are run continuously throughout the year, rather than according to an academic calendar.

There is one more important way in which the University of Phoenix is different from traditional universities – it is a for-profit institution owned by a corporation called Apollo Communications. A decade after its creation, the University of Phoenix was making an average profit of $12.8 million a quarter. As we saw in our discussion of City Academies above (p. 695), a growing number of educational institutions in Britain as well as the United States are drawing on private rather than public management. Outside organizations with expertise in management, or in the production and distribution of technology, are becoming involved in the educational system as consultants or administrators.

The flexibility and convenience of Internet-based learning cannot be denied, but the approach is not without its critics. Many argue that there is no substitute for face-to-face learning in a truly interactive environment. Will future generations of learners be little more than networks of anonymous students known only by their online user names? Will skills-oriented, practical studies undermine the importance of abstract reasoning and learning 'for learning's sake'?

Globalization and technological advance have also enabled the creation of a global market in higher education. Although higher education has always had an international dimension – thanks to overseas students, cross-national research projects and international scholarly conferences – radically new opportunities are emerging for collaboration among students, academics and educational institutions scattered round the globe. Through Internet-based learning and the formation of 'e-universities', education and qualifications are becoming more accessible to a global audience. Credentials, certificates and degrees can now be acquired outside the world of physical classrooms and traditional educational establishments. A range of competing institutions and companies – some commercially based – are rapidly entering the global education market. More than ever before, knowledge and learning are 'up for grabs'.

Even conventional universities are taking steps to become 'e-universities' as well – consortia of institutions are sharing their academic resources, research facilities, teaching staff and students online. Universities around the world are acknowledging the benefits of these partnerships with other institutions whose offerings complement their own. As scholarship and technological innovation proliferate, it is impossible for even the most elite institutions to stay on top of advances in all disciplines. Through online partnerships, they can pool their expertise and make it available to students and researchers within the consortium. Students in London, for example, can access online libraries in San Francisco, email specialized academic staff elsewhere to have questions clarified and collaborate on research projects.

Conclusion: the future of education

New communication technologies create enormous new possibilities in education. They allow the possibility that formal education can escape the confines of the classroom or lecture hall and reach new students anywhere in the world, regardless of age, gender or class. However, rather than being a liberating and egalitar-

Is a new 'computer underclass' emerging in poorer countries?

ian force critics have pointed out that new information and communication technologies may act to reinforce educational inequalities. Information poverty might be added to the material deprivations and inequalities that education can serve to reproduce, and discussed in this chapter. The sheer pace of technological change and the demand of employers for computer-literate workers may mean that those who are technologically competent 'leapfrog' over people who have little experience with computers. This threat of a divide between those who are technologically qualified and those who are not reinforces the importance of lifelong learning (discussed on pp. 698–9) to cope with the new challenges of life in the information age.

Some already fear the emergence of a 'computer underclass' within Western societies. As the global economy becomes increasingly knowledge-based, there is a real danger that poorer countries will become even more marginalized because of the gap between the information rich and information poor.

Some have argued that Internet access has become the new line of demarcation between the rich and the poor. Internet users made up less than 4 per cent of the population of Latin America, East Asia, Eastern Europe, the Arab states and sub-Saharan Africa in 2000. In the same year, 54 per cent of the US population were Internet users (UNDP 2001).

Information technology enthusiasts argue that computers need not result in greater national and global inequalities – that their very strength lies in their ability to draw people together and to open up new opportunities. Schools in Asia and Africa that are lacking textbooks and qualified teachers can benefit from the Internet, it is claimed. Distance learning programmes and collaboration with colleagues overseas could be the key to overcoming poverty and disadvantage. When technology is put in the hands of smart, creative people, they argue, the potential is limitless.

While technology can be breathtaking and open important doors, it has to be recognized that there is no such thing as an easy 'techno-fix'. Underdeveloped regions struggling with mass illiteracy and lacking telephone lines and electricity need an improved educational infrastructure before they can truly benefit from new technologies that enable distance learning programmes. As we have seen throughout this chapter, education systems can reproduce inequalities, such as class and gender. New information and communication technologies may serve to exacerbate these divisions whilst creating new ones; however, if managed properly, new technologies offer exciting liberating and egalitarian possibilities for education systems around the world.

Summary points

1   Education in its modern form, involving the instruction of pupils in specially designated school premises, began to emerge with the spread of printed materials and higher levels of literacy. Knowledge could be retained, reproduced and consumed by more people in more places. With industrialization, work became more specialized, and more people acquired abstract knowledge in addition to the practical skills of reading, writing and calculating.

2   The expansion of education in the twentieth century was closely tied to perceived needs for a literate and disciplined workforce. With the move to a knowledge economy, education will become even more important. As opportunities for unskilled manual workers decrease, the labour market will require workers who are comfortable with new technology, can acquire new skills and are able to work creatively.

3   Following the 1944 Education Act, everyone in the UK had the opportunity for free secondary education, and the school-leaving age was raised to fifteen. State secondary education was shared among grammar schools, secondary modern schools and a small number of technical schools. The eleven-plus examination became the means of separating pupils between types of state schools according to ability.

4   In the 1960s the comprehensive school system for secondary education was introduced. The eleven-plus exam was abolished, along with most grammar schools and all secondary moderns. In recent years, the comprehensive system has itself come under much attack. Critics feel that the comprehensives have not achieved the educational standards their initiators hoped for.

5   Higher education has expanded significantly in Britain since the Second World War: new institutions have been built ('red brick' universities) and student enrolment has risen, particularly among women. Higher education in Britain is undergoing a funding crisis, however. Many students now take out loans in order to fund their higher education costs.

6 Various sociological theories have had an impact on interpretations of education and schooling. According to Bernstein's theory, children who have acquired elaborated codes of speech are more able to deal with the demands of formal education than those confined to restricted codes.

7 The formal school curriculum is only one part of a more general process of cultural reproduction influenced by many informal aspects of learning, education and school settings. The 'hidden curriculum' plays a significant role in cultural reproduction.

8 The organization of and teaching within schools have tended to sustain gender inequalities. Rules specifying distinct dress for girls and boys encourage sex-typing, as do texts containing established gender images. Despite these lingering tendencies, girls have been consistently outperforming boys in all levels of the educational system for the past decade. Concern about 'failing boys' has been linked to larger social issues such as crime, unemployment and absent fathers – although some believe that the attention is misleading.

9 Because intelligence is difficult to define, there has been a great deal of controversy about the subject. Some argue that genes determine the average IQs of groups; others believe that social influences determine them. The weight of evidence appears to be on the side of those arguing for social and cultural influences.

10 New technologies and the knowledge economy are changing our understandings of education and schooling: formal education is giving way to the notion of lifelong learning. There are growing opportunities for individuals, throughout their lifetimes, to engage in learning activities and training outside the traditional classroom.

11 Information technology is being integrated into educational processes – in the classroom, through the establishment of 'e-universities' and with the expansion of Internet-based learning. There are concerns that those who are not computer literate, or who do not have access to new technology, may suffer from a form of 'information poverty'.

Questions for further thought

1 What is education for?

2 Can education overcome social inequalities?

3 What policies should be adopted to encourage wider participation in higher education?

4 Do modern technologies make the deschooling of society either likely or desirable?

5 How might the 'hidden curriculum' appear in the electronic classroom?

6 Should schools and colleges place more emphasis on the development of emotional intelligence?

Further reading

Caroline Benn and Clyde Chitty, *Thirty Years On: Is Comprehensive Education Alive and Well or Struggling to Survive?* (London: David Fulton, 1996).

Ken Jones, *Education in Britain: 1944 to the Present* (Cambridge: Polity, 2002).

R. Moore, *Education and Society: Issues and Explanations in the Sociology of Education* (Cambridge: Polity, 2004).

A. H. Halsey et al., *Education: Culture, Economy and Society* (Oxford: Oxford University Press, 1997).

Internet links

21st Century Learning Initiative
http://www.21learn.org

Department for Education and Skills (UK)
http://www.dfes.gov.uk

Encyclopedia of Philosophy of Education
http://www.educacao.pro.br/

UNESCO Education Homepage
http://www.unesco.org/education

The University of the Third Age
http://www.u3a.org.uk/

DfES – Lifelong learning
http://www.lifelonglearning.co.uk/

Contents

18 Work and Economic Life

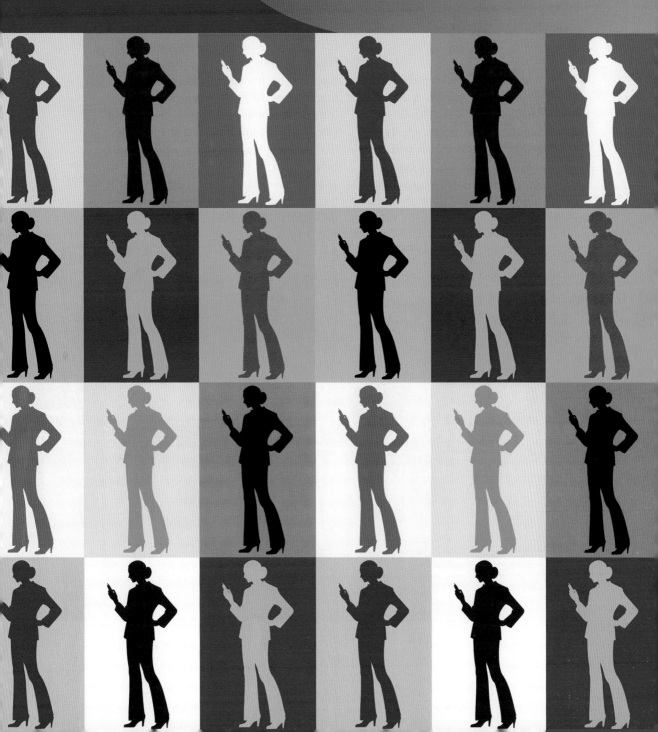

JOCKEY MADE his first bronze mush-room at five past six on a Monday morning in January 1885. The foreman showed him how: 'Now get thee belly well set up against t'lathe bed,' he said, 'feet planted solid on t'floor, an' rip into 'em.' Jockey ripped into them. The machinery sparked and screeched and a bronze mushroom valve for a steam-driven engine dropped into a box. ''Ow many do I 'ave to do?' Jockey asked innocently. ''Ow many stars in 'eaven' said the foreman, and walked away.

Jockey was fifteen then. The job was a promotion – a step up from making tea and running errands round the factory in Salford, near Manchester. Jockey never did another job for sixty-one years. After his first few years he joined the trade union. When he was twenty-five his feet went through the floorboards below him. The joiner came to fix them. Jockey excused himself: 'I gotta press down yer see – it wears.' 'Don't apologize', said the joiner. 'It's not my bleedin' floor.' The boards broke again in 1907 and then in 1916. In 1918 Jockey had three days off – 'Spanish 'flu', he apologized; 'couldn't 'old my 'ead up' – and he took two more in 1935, when

his wife died. During sixty-one years with the company, he missed five days of work.

When he was seventy-six, shortly after the end of the Second World War, and a week after making his millionth valve, the worn out floor collapsed under him once more. 'That's all I was waiting for', he said. He flicked off the lathe and went over to the foreman, a man young enough to be his grandson. 'I'm finishin' up at the weekend, George', he called over the noise of the machinery. The men bought him an armchair when he left: 'An' when you've worn t'seat out o' that,' they said, 'we'll send the joiner to put some boards in!' Late Friday afternoon the foreman introduced him to the new apprentice: 'Just put him in the way of it, will yer?' he asked. Jockey smiled: 'Sithee,' he said to the boy, 'there's not much to it. Get thee belly well set against t'lathe bed now, feet solid on t'floor, an' rip into 'em!'

The nature of work has changed massively since Robert Roberts described Jockey's working life in his classic, first-hand account of life in a Salford slum during the first quarter of the twentieth century (1971). For many of us, Jockey's work life is unrecognizably different from our own. This chapter explores the development of work in modern society and looks at the structure of modern economies. From here, we examine some more recent trends in work. First, however, we must look more closely at what is actually understood when we use the term 'work'.

What is work? Paid and unpaid work

We often tend to think of work as equivalent to having a paid job, as the notion of being 'out of work' implies, but in fact this is an oversimplified view. Non-paid labour (such as housework or repairing one's own car) looms large in many people's lives. Many types of work do not conform to orthodox categories of paid employment. Much of the work done in the informal economy, for example, is not recorded in any direct way in the official employment statistics. The term **informal economy** refers to transactions outside the sphere of regular employment, sometimes involving the exchange of cash for services provided, but also often involving the direct exchange of goods or services.

Someone who comes round to mend a leaking pipe, for example, may be paid in cash, without any receipt being given or details of the job recorded. People exchange 'cheap' – that is to say pilfered or stolen – goods with friends or associates in return for other favours. The informal economy includes not only 'hidden' cash transactions, but many forms of self-provisioning which people carry on inside and outside the home. Do-it-yourself activities, domestic machinery and household tools, for instance, provide goods and services which would otherwise have to be purchased (Gershuny and Miles 1983). Housework, which has traditionally been carried out mostly by women, is usually unpaid. But it is work, nevertheless – often very hard and exhausting work (see box). Voluntary work, for charities or other organizations, has an important social role. Having a paid job is important for all the reasons listed above – but the category of 'work' stretches more widely.

We can define **work**, whether paid or unpaid, as being the carrying out of tasks requiring the expenditure of mental and physical effort, which has as its objective the production of goods and services that cater to human needs. An **occupation**, or job, is work that is done in exchange for a regular wage or salary. In all cultures, work is the basis of the **economy**. The economic system consists of institutions that provide for the production and distribution of goods and services.

Housework

Housework in its current form came into existence with the separation of the home and workplace (Oakley 1974). With industrialization, home became a place of consumption rather than production of goods. Domestic work became 'invisible' as 'real work' was defined increasingly as that which receives a direct wage. Housework has traditionally been seen as the domain of women, while the realm of 'real work' outside the home was reserved for men. In this conventional model, the domestic division of labour – the way in which responsibilities at home are shared by household members – was quite straightforward. Women shouldered most, if not all, of the domestic tasks, while men 'provided' for the family by earning a wage.

The period of the development of a separate 'home' also saw other changes. Before the inventions and facilities provided by industrialization influenced the domestic sphere, work in the household was hard and exacting. The weekly wash, for example, was a heavy and demanding task. The introduction of hot and cold running water into homes eliminated many time-consuming tasks; previously, water had to be carried to the home and heated there, as it still is in much of the developing world. The piping of electricity and gas made coal and wood stoves obsolete, and chores such as the regular chopping of wood, carrying of coal and constant cleaning of the stove were largely eliminated.

Yet, surprisingly, the average amount of time spent on domestic work by women has not declined very markedly, even since the introduction of labour-saving equipment such as vacuum cleaners, washing

Women often work a 'double shift', at home and in paid employment.

machines and dishwashers. The amount of time British women not in paid employment spend on housework has remained quite constant over the past half-century. Household appliances eliminated some of the heavier chores, but new tasks were created in their place. Time spent on child care, stocking up the home with purchases and meal preparation all increased.

Unpaid domestic labour is of enormous significance to the economy. It has been estimated that housework accounts for between 25 and 40 per cent of the wealth created in the industrialized countries. The findings of a national survey of time-use published in 2002 estimated that if housework in the UK was paid, it would be worth £700 billion to the UK economy (Office of National Statistics 2002). Domestic work props up the rest of the economy by providing free services on which many of the population in paid work depend.

Yet housework itself has problematic dimensions. Anne Oakley's (1974) classic investigation into housework as a form of work showed that full-time devotion to domestic tasks can be isolating, alienating and lacking in intrinsic satisfaction. Housewives in her study found domestic tasks highly monotonous and had difficulty escaping self-imposed psychological pressure to meet certain standards which they established for their work.

Forms of paid and unpaid work are closely interrelated, as housework's contribution to the overall economy demonstrates. One of the main questions of interest to sociologists is how the growing involvement of women in the labour market has affected the domestic division of labour. If the quantity of domestic work has not diminished but fewer women are now full-time housewives, it follows that the domestic affairs of households must be arranged rather differently today.

The social organization of work

One of the most distinctive characteristics of the economic system of modern societies is the existence of a highly complex **division of labour**: work has become divided into an enormous number of different occupations in which people specialize. In traditional societies, non-agricultural work entailed the mastery of a craft. Craft skills were learned through a lengthy period of apprenticeship, and the worker normally carried out all aspects of the production process from beginning to end. For example, a metalworker making a plough would forge the iron, shape it and assemble the implement itself. With the rise of modern industrial production, most traditional crafts have disappeared altogether, replaced by skills that form part of larger-scale production processes. Jockey, whose life story we discussed at the beginning of this chapter, is an example. He spent his whole working career on one highly specialized task; other people in the factory dealt with other specific tasks.

Modern society has also witnessed a shift in the location of work. Before industrialization, most work took place at home and was completed collectively by all the members of the household. Advances in industrial technology, such as machinery operating on electricity and coal, contributed to the separation of work and home. Factories owned by entrepreneurs became the focal points of industrial development: machinery and equipment were concentrated within them and the **mass production** of goods began to eclipse small-scale artisanship based in the home. People seeking jobs in factories, like Jockey, would be trained to perform a specialized task and would receive a wage for this work. Employee performance was overseen by managers, who concerned themselves with implementing techniques for enhancing worker productivity and discipline.

The contrast in the division of labour between traditional and modern societies is truly extraordinary. Even in the largest traditional societies, there usually existed no more than twenty or thirty major craft trades, together with such specialized roles as merchant, soldier and priest. In a modern industrial system, there are literally thousands of distinct occupations. The UK Census lists some 20,000 distinct jobs in the British economy. In traditional communities, most of the population worked on farms and were economically self-sufficient. They produced their own food, clothes and other necessities of life. One of the main features of modern societies, by contrast, is an enormous expansion of **economic interdependence**. We are all dependent on an immense number of other workers – today stretching right across the world – for the products and services that sustain our lives. With few exceptions, the vast majority of people in modern societies do not produce the food they eat, the houses they live in or the material goods they consume.

Early sociologists wrote extensively about the potential consequences of the division of labour – both for individual workers and for society as a whole. Karl Marx was one of the first writers to speculate that the development of modern industry would reduce many people's work to dull, uninteresting tasks. According to Marx, the division of labour alienates human beings from their work. For Marx, **alienation** refers to feelings of indifference or hostility not only to work, but to the overall framework of industrial production within a capitalist setting. In traditional societies, he pointed out, work was often exhausting – peasant farmers sometimes had to toil from dawn to dusk. Yet peasants held a real measure of control over their work, which required much knowledge and skill. Many industrial workers, by contrast, have little control over their jobs, only contributing a fraction to the creation of the overall product, and they have no influence over how or to whom it is eventually sold. Marxists would argue that for workers like Jockey, work appears as something alien, a task that must be carried out in order to earn an income but that is intrinsically unsatisfying.

Durkheim had a more optimistic outlook about the division of labour, although he too acknowledged its potentially harmful effects. According to Durkheim, the specialization of roles would strengthen social solidarity within communities. Rather than living as isolated, self-sufficient units, people would be linked together through their mutual dependency. Solidarity would be enhanced through multidirectional relationships of production and consumption. Durkheim saw this arrangement as a highly functional one, although he was also aware that social solidarity could be disrupted if change occurred too rapidly. He referred to this resulting sense of normlessness as anomie.

You may find it useful to look at the overview of Durkheim and Marx's writings in chapter 1, 'What is Sociology?' pp. 12–17.

Taylorism and Fordism

Writing some two centuries ago, Adam Smith, one of the founders of modern economics, identified advantages that the division of labour provides in terms of increasing productivity. His most famous work, *The Wealth of Nations* (1776), opens with a description of the division of labour in a pin factory. A person working alone could perhaps make 20 pins per day. By breaking down that worker's task into a number of simple operations, however, ten workers carrying out specialized jobs in collaboration with one another could collectively produce 48,000 pins per day. The rate of production per worker, in other words, is increased from 20 to 4,800 pins, each specialist operator producing 240 times more than when working alone.

More than a century later, these ideas reached their most developed expression in the writings of Frederick Winslow Taylor (1865–1915), an American management consultant. Taylor's approach to what he called 'scientific management' involved the detailed study of industrial processes in order to break them down into simple operations that could be precisely timed and organized. **Taylorism,** as scientific management came to be called, was not merely an academic study. It was a system of production designed to maximize industrial output, and it had a widespread impact not only on the organization of industrial production and technology, but also on workplace politics as well. In particular, Taylor's time-and-motion studies wrested control over knowledge of the productions process from the worker and placed such knowledge firmly in the hands of management, eroding the basis

on which craft workers maintained autonomy from their employers (Braverman 1974). As such, Taylorism has been widely associated with the deskilling and degradation of labour.

The principles of Taylorism were appropriated by the industrialist Henry Ford (1863–1947). Ford designed his first auto plant at Highland Park, Michigan, in 1908 to manufacture only one product – the Model T Ford – involving the introduction of specialized tools and machinery designed for speed, precision and simplicity of operation. One of Ford's most significant innovations was the introduction of the assembly line, said to have been inspired by Chicago slaughterhouses, in which animals were disassembled section by section on a moving line. Each worker on Ford's assembly line was assigned a specialized task, such as fitting the left-side door handles as the car bodies moved along the line. By 1929, when production of the Model T ceased, more than 15 million cars had been produced.

Ford was among the first to realize that mass production requires mass markets. He reasoned that if standardized commodities such as the automobile were to be produced on an ever-greater scale, the presence of consumers who were able to buy those commodities must also be assured. In 1914, Ford took the unprecedented step of unilaterally raising wages at his Dearborn, Michigan, plant to $5 for an eight-hour day – a very generous wage at the time and one that ensured a working-class lifestyle that included owning such an automobile. As Harvey remarks: 'The purpose of the five-dollar, eight-hour day was only in part to secure worker compliance with the discipline required to work the highly productive assembly-line

The Ford production line was designed to increase efficiency.

system. It was coincidentally meant to provide workers with sufficient income to consume the mass-produced products the corporations were about to turn out in ever vaster quantities' (Harvey 1989). Ford also enlisted the services of a small army of social workers who were sent into the homes of workers in order to educate them in the proper habits of consumption.

Fordism is the name given to designate the system of mass production tied to the cultivation of mass markets. In certain contexts, the term has a more specific meaning, referring to a historical period in the development of post-Second World War capitalism, in which mass production was associated with stability in labour relations and a high degree of unionization. Under Fordism, firms made long-term commitments to workers, and wages were tightly linked to productivity growth. As such, *collective bargaining agreements* – formal agreements negotiated between firms and unions that specified working conditions such as wages, seniority rights, benefits and so on – closed a virtuous circle that ensured worker consent to automated work regimes *and* sufficient demand for mass-produced commodities. The system is generally understood to have broken down in the 1970s, giving rise to greater flexibility and insecurity in working conditions.

The limitations of Taylorism and Fordism

The reasons for the demise of Fordism are complex and intensely debated. As firms in a variety of industries adopted Fordist production methods, the system encountered certain limitations. At one time, it looked as though Fordism represented the likely future of industrial production as a whole. But this has not proved to be the case. The system can only be applied successfully in those industries, such as car manufacture, that produce standardized products for large markets. To set up mechanized production lines is enormously expensive, and once a Fordist system is established, it is quite rigid; to alter a product, for example, substantial reinvestment is needed. Fordist production is easy to copy if sufficient funding is available to set up the plant. But firms in countries where labour power is expensive find it difficult to compete with those where wages are cheaper. This was one of the factors originally leading to the rise of the Japanese car industry (although Japanese wage levels today are no longer low) and subsequently that of South Korea.

The difficulties with Fordism and Taylorism extend beyond the need for expensive equipment, however. Fordism and Taylorism are what some industrial sociologists call **low-trust systems**. Jobs are set by management and are geared to machines. Those who carry out the work tasks are closely supervised and are allowed little autonomy of action. In order to maintain discipline and high-quality production standards, employees are continuously monitored through various surveillance systems.

> Surveillance within work and other organizations is discussed in chapter 16, 'Organizations and Networks', pp. 648–51.

This constant supervision, however, tends to produce the opposite of its intended result: the commitment and morale of workers is often eroded because they have little say in the nature of their jobs or in how they are carried out. In workplaces with many low-trust positions, the level of worker dissatisfaction and absenteeism is high, and industrial conflict is common.

A **high-trust system**, by contrast, is one in which workers are permitted to control the pace, and even the content, of their work, within overall guidelines. Such systems are usually concentrated at the higher levels of industrial organizations. As we shall see, **high-trust systems** have become more common in many workplaces in recent decades, transforming the very way we think about the organization and execution of work.

The changing nature of work and working

The globalizing of economic production, together with the spread of information technology, is altering the nature of the jobs most people do. As discussed in chapter 9, the proportion of people working in blue-collar jobs in industrial countries has progressively fallen. Fewer people work in factories than before. New jobs have been created in offices and in service centres such as supermarkets and airports. Many of these new jobs are filled by women.

Industrial conflict

There have long been conflicts between workers and those in economic and political authority over them. Riots against conscription and high taxes and food riots at periods of harvest failure were common in urban areas of Europe in the eighteenth century. These 'pre-modern' forms of labour conflict continued up to not much more than a century ago in some countries. For example, there were food riots in several large Italian towns in 1868 (Geary 1981). Such traditional forms of confrontation were not just sporadic, irrational outbursts of violence: the threat or use of violence had the effect of limiting the price of grain and other essential foodstuffs (Rudé 1964; Booth 1977).

Industrial conflict between workers and employers at first tended to follow these older patterns. In situations of confrontation, workers would quite often leave their places of employment and form crowds in the streets; they would make their grievances known through their unruly behaviour or by engaging in acts of violence against the authorities. Workers in some parts of France in the late nineteenth century would threaten disliked employers with hanging (Holton 1978). Use of the *strike* as a weapon, today commonly associated with organized bargaining between workers and management, developed only slowly and sporadically.

Strikes

We can define a **strike** as a temporary stoppage of work by a group of employees in order to express a grievance or enforce a demand (Hyman 1984). All the components of this definition are important in separating strikes from other forms of opposition and conflict. A strike is *temporary*, since workers intend to return to the same job with the same employer; where workers quit altogether, the term *strike* is not appropriate. As a *stoppage of work*, a strike is distinguishable from an overtime ban or 'slowdown'. A *group* of workers has to be involved, because a strike involves collective action, not the response of one individual worker. That those involved are *employees* serves to separate strikes from protests such as

may be conducted by tenants or students. Finally, a strike involves seeking to make known a grievance or press a demand; workers who miss work to go to a soccer match could not be said to be on strike.

Strikes represent only one aspect or type of conflict in which workers and management may become involved. Other closely related expressions of organized conflict are lock-outs (where the employers rather than the workers bring about a stoppage of work), output restrictions and clashes in contract negotiations. Less-organized expressions of conflict may include high labour turnover (where employers regularly replace old staff with new), absenteeism and interference with production machinery.

Workers choose to go out on strike for many specific reasons. They may be seeking to gain higher wages, forestall a proposed reduction in their earnings, protest against technological changes that make their work duller or lead to lay-offs, or obtain greater security of employment. However, in all these circumstances the strike is essentially a mechanism of power: a weapon of people who are relatively powerless in the workplace and whose working lives are affected by managerial decisions over which they have little or no control. It is usually a weapon of 'last resort', to be used when other negotiations have failed, because workers on strike either receive no income or depend on union funds, which might be limited.

Trade unions

Although their levels of membership and the extent of their power vary widely, union organizations exist in all Western countries, which also all legally recognize the right of workers to strike in pursuit of economic objectives. Why have unions become a basic feature of Western societies? Why does union-management conflict seem to be a more or less ever-present possibility in industrial settings?

In the early development of modern industry, workers in most countries had no political rights and little influence over the conditions of work

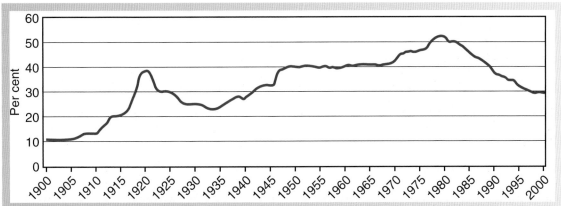

Figure 18.1 Proportion of people in employment who are members of a trade union, UK,[a] 1900–2000

[a] Data since 1975 from the Certification Officer's Annual Reports are for Great Britain only. See technical note for further information about the data souces. Note: Data have not been adjusted to reflect the post-2001 Census population estimates

Source: ONS (2003c), p. 139

in which they found themselves. Unions developed as a means of redressing the imbalance of power between workers and employers. Whereas workers had virtually no power as individuals, through collective organization their influence was considerably increased. An employer can do without the labour of any particular worker, but not without that of all or most of the workers in a factory or plant. Unions were originally mainly 'defensive' organizations, providing the means whereby workers could counter the overwhelming power that employers wielded over their lives.

Workers today have voting rights in the political sphere, and there are established forms of negotiation with employers, by means of which economic benefits can be pressed for and grievances expressed. However, union influence exists primarily in the form of a *veto power*, both at the level of the local plant and nationally. In other words, using the resources at their disposal, including the right to strike, unions can only *block* employers' policies or initiatives, not help formulate them in the first place. There are exceptions to this, for instance where unions and employers negotiate periodic contracts covering conditions of work.

The post-Second World War period witnessed a dramatic reversal in the positions of unions in advanced industrial societies. In most developed countries, the period from 1950 to 1980 was a time of steady growth in union density, a statistic that represents the number of union members as a percentage of the number of people who could potentially be union members. In the late 1970s and early '80s over 50 per cent of the British workforce were unionized. High union density was common in Western countries for several reasons. First, strong working-class political parties created favourable conditions for labour organization. Second, bargaining between firms and trade unions was coordinated at the national level rather than occurring in decentralized fashion at sectoral or local levels. Third, unions rather than the state directly administered unemployment insurance, ensuring that workers who lost their jobs did not leave the labour movement. Countries in which some combination but not all three of these factors were present had lower rates of union density, ranging from between two-fifths to two-thirds of the working population (figure 18.1 shows the rise and fall of trade union membership during the twentieth century).

From a peak in the 1970s, unions began to suffer a decline across the advanced industrial countries, including in the UK. There are several prominent explanations for the difficulties confronted by unions since 1980. Perhaps the most common is the decline of the older manufacturing industries and the rise of the service sector. Traditionally, manufacturing has been a stronghold for labour, whereas jobs in services are more resistant to unionization.

However, this explanation has come under scrutiny. Sociologist Bruce Western (Western 1997) argued that such an explanation cannot account for the experience of the 1970s, which was generally a good period for unions (although not in the United States) and yet was also characterized by a structural shift from manufacturing to services. Similarly, a significant share of growth in service sector employment has occurred in social services – typically public sector union jobs. As such, Western argued that declines in unionization *within* manufacturing may be more significant than declines across sectors.

Several explanations are consistent with the fall in union density within, as well as between, industries. First, the recession in world economic activity, associated with high levels of unemployment, particularly during the 1980s, weakens the bargaining position of labour. Second, the increasing intensity of international competition, particularly from Far Eastern countries, where wages are often lower than in the West, also weakens unions' bargaining powers. Third, the rise to power in many countries of right-wing governments, such as the British Conservatives led by Margaret Thatcher, who came to office in 1979 and launched an aggressive assault on unions in the 1980s. The unions came out second-best in several major strikes, notably the crushing of the National Union of Miners in the UK in 1984. Union-protected working conditions and wages have been eroded in several major industries over the past twenty-five years.

In 1984, British miners embarked on a protracted fight over pit closures.

Decline in union membership and influence is something of a general phenomenon in the industrialized countries and is not to be explained wholly in terms of political pressure applied by right-wing governments against the unions. Unions usually become weakened during periods when unemployment is high, as was the case in the UK for much of the 1980s and 1990s; trade union membership for both men and women stood at 29 per cent in June 2003 (*Social Trends* 35, 2005). Trends towards more flexible production tend to diminish the force of unionism, which flourishes more extensively where there are many people working together in large factories. Still, trade unionism remains a powerful force in most Western countries. The power of the unions to drive a hard bargain for their members was seen in the UK during the strikes by fire-fighters in 2002 and 2003. In that dispute, a demand for increased pay by the Fire Brigades Union was met by an equally strong demand for more flexibility in working practices by the New Labour government. (The flexibility of working practices is a key theme in the second half of this chapter.)

Gender inequality in the workplace is discussed further in chapter 16, 'Organizations and Networks', pp. 756–9.

Women and work

Throughout history, men and women have contributed to producing and reproducing the social world around them, both on a day-to-day basis and over long periods of time. Yet the nature of this partnership and the distribution of responsibilities within it has taken different forms over time. Until recently, paid work in Western countries was predominantly the sphere of men. Over the past few decades this situation has changed radically: more and more women have moved into the labour force. In most western countries, Russia and China, women are now around a quarter less likely to work outside the home than men (see figure 18.2). However, reports in the UK suggest that three-quarters of the working female population are engaged in part-time, low-paid work: clerical, cleaning, cashiering and catering (Women in the Workplace 2004).

In the following sections, we look at the origins and implications of this phenomenon – one of the most important transformations happening in modern society at the present time. We also consider some of the changes in the world of work that have taken place with the decline of Fordism and Taylorism, before examining some of the most important contemporary issues in the sociology of work.

Women and the workplace: the historical view

For the vast majority of the population in pre-industrial societies (and many people in the developing world), productive activities and the activities of the household were not separate. Production was carried on either in the home or nearby, and all members of the family participated in work on the land or in handicrafts. Women often had considerable influence within the household as a result of their importance in economic processes, even if they were excluded from the male realms of politics and warfare. Wives of craftsmen and farmers often kept business accounts and widows quite commonly owned and managed businesses.

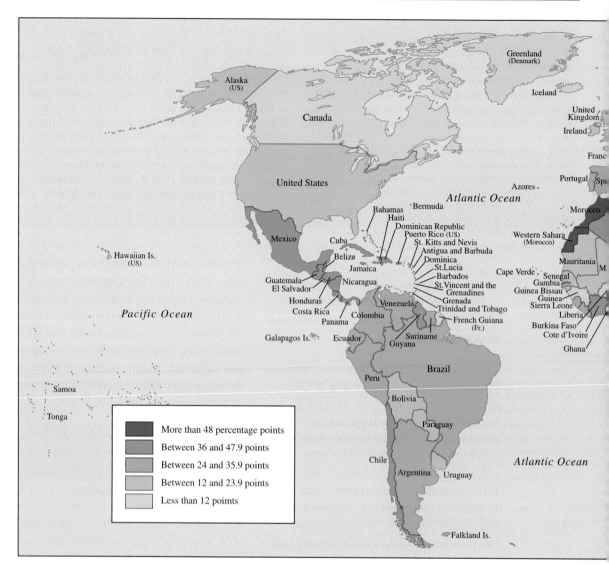

Figure 18.2 Women in the labour force worldwide

Source: World Bank, *World Development Indicators*, 1998

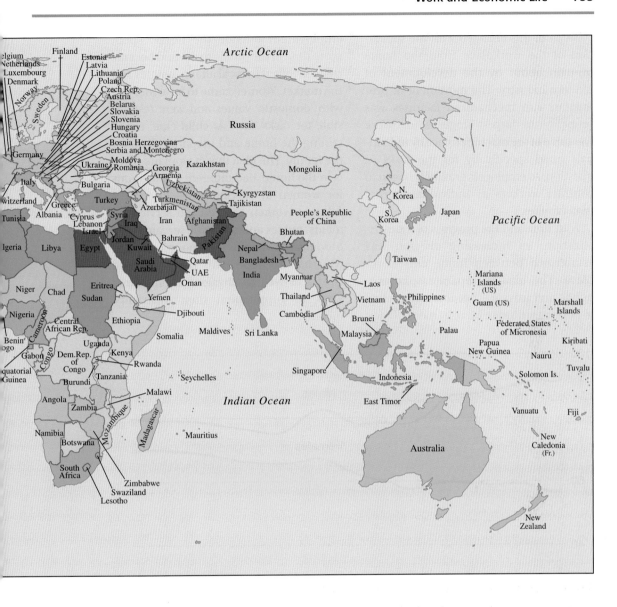

Arctic Ocean

Finland
Estonia
Latvia
Lithuania
Poland
Czech Rep.
Austria
Belarus
Slovakia
Slovenia
Hungary
Croatia
Bosnia Herzegovina
Serbia and Montenegro
Belgium
Netherlands
Luxembourg
Denmark
Norway
Sweden
Germany
Italy
Switzerland
Greece
Albania
Tunisia
Cyprus
Lebanon
Israel
Igeria
Libya
Egypt
Ukraine
Moldova
Romania
Bulgaria
Turkey
Georgia
Armenia
Azerbaijan
Syria
Iraq
Jordan
Kuwait
Bahrain
Qatar
UAE
Oman
Saudi Arabia
Yemen
Iran
Turkmenistan
Uzbekistan
Kyrgyzstan
Tajikistan
Afghanistan
Pakistan
Nepal
Bangladesh
India
Bhutan
Kazakhstan

Russia

Mongolia

People's Republic
of China

N. Korea
S. Korea
Japan

Pacific Ocean

Taiwan

Myanmar
Thailand
Cambodia
Vietnam
Laos
Philippines

Mariana Islands (US)
Guam (US)
Marshall Islands
Federated States of Micronesia
Palau
Papua New Guinea
Kiribati
Nauru
Tuvalu
Solomon Is.

Niger
Chad
Eritrea
Sudan
Nigeria
Central African Rep.
Cameroon
Benin
Togo
Gabon
Congo
Equatorial Guinea
Ethiopia
Uganda
Dem.Rep. of Congo
Kenya
Rwanda
Burundi
Tanzania
Somalia
Djibouti
Maldives
Sri Lanka
Seychelles
Brunei
Malaysia
Singapore
Indonesia
East Timor

Indian Ocean

Angola
Zambia
Namibia
Botswana
South Africa
Zimbabwe
Swaziland
Lesotho
Malawi
Mozambique
Madagascar
Mauritius

Vanuatu
Fiji
New Caledonia (Fr.)

Australia

New Zealand

Much of this changed with the separation of the workplace from the home brought about by the development of modern industry. The movement of production into mechanized factories was probably the largest single factor. Work was done at the machine's pace by individuals hired specifically for the tasks in question, so employers gradually began to contract workers as individuals rather than families.

With time and the progress of industrialization, an increasing division was established between home and workplace. The idea of separate spheres – public and private – became entrenched in popular attitudes. Men, by merit of their employment outside the home, spent more time in the public realm and became more involved in local affairs, politics and the market. Women came to be associated with 'domestic' values and were responsible for tasks such as child care, maintaining the home and preparing food for the family. The idea that 'a woman's place is in the home' had different implications for women at varying levels in society. Affluent women enjoyed the services of maids, nurses and domestic servants. The burdens were harshest for poorer women, who had to cope with the household chores as well as engaging in industrial work to supplement their husbands' income.

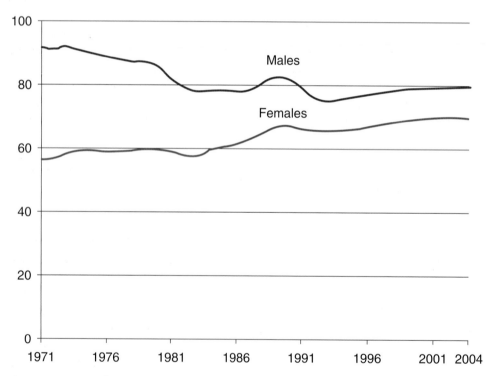

Figure 18.3   Employment rates in the UK: by sex (%)

Source: Social Trends 35 (2005), p. 4

Rates of employment of women outside the home, for all classes, were quite low until well into the twentieth century. Even as late as 1910, in Britain, more than a third of gainfully employed women were maids or house servants. The female labour force consisted mainly of young single women, whose wages, when they worked in factories or offices, were often sent by their employers direct to their parents. Once married, they generally withdrew from the labour force and concentrated on family obligations.

The growth in women's economic activity

Women's participation in the paid labour force has risen more or less continuously over the last century. One major influence was the labour shortage experienced during the First World War. During the war years, women carried out many jobs previously regarded as the exclusive province of men. On returning from the war, men again took over most of those jobs, but the pre-established pattern had been broken.

In the years since the Second World War, the gender division of labour has changed dramatically. The UK employment rate – that is, the proportion of working-age people who are in employment – rose from 56 per cent to 70 per cent for women between 1971 and 2004. In contrast the UK employment rate for men fell from 92 per cent to 79 per cent in the same period. Thus the gap between men's and women's employment rates fell from 35 per cent in 1971 to just 9 per cent in 2004 (this is shown in figure 18.3). This narrowing of the gender gap looks likely to continue to rise even more in the years to come. As we will see below (pp. 757–8), much of the increase in women's economic activity has been in part-time work.

There are a number of reasons why the gap in economic activity rates between men and women have been closing in recent decades. First, there have been changes in the scope and nature of the tasks that have traditionally been associated with women and the 'domestic sphere'. As the birth rate has declined and the average age of childbirth has increased, many women now take on paid work before having children and return to work afterwards. Smaller families have meant that the time many women previously spent at home caring for young children has been reduced. The mechanization of many domestic tasks has also helped to cut down the amount of time that needs to be spent to maintain the home. Automatic dishwashers, vacuum cleaners and washing machines have made the domestic workload less labour-intensive. There is also evidence that the domestic division of labour between men and women is being steadily eroded over time, although women certainly still carry out more domestic tasks than men (see below).

There are also financial reasons why a growing number of women have entered the labour market. The traditional nuclear family model – composed of a male breadwinner, female housewife and dependent children – now accounts for only a quarter of families in Britain. Economic pressures on the household, including a rise in male unemployment, have led more women to seek paid work. Many households find that two incomes are required in order to sustain a desired lifestyle. Other changes in household structure, including high rates of singlehood and childlessness as well as a growth in lone-mother households, has meant that women outside traditional families have also been entering the labour market – either out of choice or necessity. Additionally, recent efforts to reform welfare policies, both in Britain and the United States, have aimed to support women – including lone mothers and married women with small children – in entering paid work.

Finally, it is important to note that many women have chosen to enter the labour market out of a desire for personal fulfilment and in response to the drive for equality propelled forward by the women's movement of the 1960s and 1970s. Having gained legal equality with men, many women have seized on opportunities to realize these rights in their own lives. As we have already noted, work is central in contemporary society and employment is almost always a prerequisite for living an independent life. In recent decades women have made great strides towards parity with men; increased economic activity has been central to this process (Crompton 1997).

Gender and inequalities at work

Despite possessing formal equality with men, women still experience a number of inequalities in the labour market. In this section we will look at three of the main inequalities for women at work: occupational segregation, concentration in part-time employment, and the wage gap.

Occupational segregation

Women workers have traditionally been concentrated in poorly paid, routine occupations. Many of these jobs are highly gendered – that is, they are commonly seen as 'women's work'. Secretarial and caring jobs (such as nursing, social work and child care) are overwhelmingly held by women and are generally regarded as 'feminine' occupations. Occupational gender segregation refers to the fact that men and women are concentrated in different types of jobs, based on prevailing understandings of what is appropriate 'male' and 'female' work.

Occupations dominated by women tend to be the lowest paid.

Occupational segregation has been seen to possess vertical and horizontal components. Vertical segregation refers to the tendency for women to be concentrated in jobs with little authority and room for advancement, while men occupy more powerful and influential positions. Horizontal segregation refers to the tendency for men and women to occupy different categories of job. For example, women largely dominate in domestic and routine clerical positions, while men are clustered in semi-skilled and skilled manual positions. Horizontal segregation can be pronounced. More than 50 per cent of women's employment (compared to 17 per cent of men's) in the UK in 1991 fell into four occupational categories: clerical, secretarial, personal services and 'other elementary' (Crompton 1997). In 1998, 26 per cent of women were in routine white-collar work, compared with only 8 per cent of men, while 17 per cent of men were in skilled manual work, compared with only 2 per cent of women (HMSO 1999).

Changes in the organization of employment as well as sex-role stereotyping have contributed to occupational segregation. Alterations in the prestige and the work tasks of 'clerks' provide a good example. In 1850, in the UK, 99 per cent of clerks were men. To be a clerk was often to have a responsible position, involving knowledge of accountancy skills and sometimes carrying managerial responsibilities. Even the lowliest clerk had a certain status in the outside world. The twentieth century has seen a general mechanization of office work (starting with the introduction of the typewriter in the late nineteenth century), accompanied by a marked downgrading of the skills and status of 'clerk' – together with another related occupation, that of

'secretary' – into a low-status, low-paid occupation. Women came to fill these occupations as the pay and prestige associated with them declined. In 1998 nearly 90 per cent of clerical workers and 98 per cent of all secretaries in the UK were women. However, the proportion of people working as secretaries has fallen over the past two decades. Computers have replaced typewriters and many managers now do much of their letter-writing and other tasks directly onto the computer.

Concentration in part-time work

Although increasing numbers of women now work full time outside the home, a large number are concentrated in part-time employment. In recent decades, opportunities for part-time work have grown enormously, partly as a result of labour market reforms to encourage flexible employment policies and partly due to the expansion of the service sector (Crompton 1997).

Part-time jobs are seen as offering much greater flexibility for employees than full-time work. For this reason they are often favoured by women who are attempting to balance work and family obligations. In many cases this can be done successfully, and women who might otherwise forgo employment become economically active. Yet part-time work carries certain disadvantages, such as low pay, job insecurity and limited opportunities for advancement.

Part-time work is attractive to many women and much of the growth in women's economic activity in the post-war period can be attributed to this. By 2004 there were 5.2 million women in the UK in part-time employment, compared to just 1.2 million men (HMSO 2005). In this respect Britain is somewhat distinctive: among industrialized nations, the UK has one of the highest rates of female part-time employment.

Sociologists have long debated the phenomenon of women's part-time employment and sought to explain the strength of this pattern in Britain compared to other countries. Surveys have revealed that part-time jobs are poorly paid, insecure and often more flexible for the employer than for the employee. Yet, when asked, most female part-time workers say they are satisfied with part-time employment. The main reason given for working part time by those questioned is the fact that they prefer not to work full time.

Some scholars have argued that there are different 'types' of women – those who are committed to work outside the home and those who are uncommitted to work, viewing the traditional sexual division of labour as unobjectionable (Hakim 1996). According to such an approach, many women happily choose to work part time in order to fulfil traditional domestic obligations. However, there is an important sense in which women have little choice. Men, by and large, do not assume prime responsibility for the rearing of children. Women who have that responsibility (as well as other domestic obligations, as we saw in the box above, pp. 742–3) but still want, or need, to work in paid jobs inevitably find part-time work a more feasible option.

The wage gap

The average pay of employed women in Britain is well below that of men, although the difference has narrowed somewhat over the past thirty years. In 1970 women in full-time employment earned 63 pence for every pound earned by a man working full-time; by 1999 it had risen to 84 pence. Among women working part-time, the gap reduced from 51 pence to 58 pence over the same period of time. This general tendency towards closing the 'wage gap' has rightly been seen as a significant step in the move towards equality with men.

Several processes have affected these trends. One significant factor is that more women are moving into higher-paying professional positions than was earlier the case. Young women with good qualifications are now as likely as their male counterparts to land lucrative jobs. Yet this progress at the top of the occupational structure is offset by the enormous increase in the number of women in low-paid part-time jobs within the rapidly expanding service sector.

Occupational segregation by gender is one of the main factors in the persistence of a wage gap between men and women. Women are over-represented in the more poorly paid job sectors: more than 45 per cent of women earn less than £100 pounds per week, compared to just over 20 per cent of men. Despite some gains, women also remain under-represented at the top of the income distribution: 10 per cent of men earn more than £500 per week, compared to only 2 per cent of women (Rake 2000).

The introduction of a national minimum wage in 1999 (of £3.60 per hour for workers over the age of twenty-two) also helped to narrow the pay gap between men and women, since many women are concentrated in occupations such as hairdressing and waitressing, which for a long time have paid below the level at which the minimum wage was set. It was estimated that nearly 2 million people enjoyed a pay raise of approximately 30 per cent after the minimum wage was first introduced. Regular rises to the minimum wage since its introduction (which is set to reach £5.35 per hour for workers over the age of twenty-two from October 2006) have further benefited women in low-paid jobs. The benefits of the minimum wage, however, do not negate the fact that a large proportion of women still work in jobs which pay at or slightly above the minimum wage, and there are still many men and women who are employed (illegally) to work for less than the minimum wage – earnings on which it is exceedingly difficult to live, especially with dependent children.

One manifestation of this is the fact that a substantial proportion of women in the UK live in poverty. This is particularly true of women who are heads of households. The percentage of women among the poor has risen steadily in recent years. Poverty tends to be especially acute for women with very small children who need constant care. There is a vicious circle here: a woman who can obtain a reasonably well-paid job may be financially crippled by having to pay for child care, yet if she starts working part time, her earnings drop, whatever career prospects she may have had disappear, and she also loses other economic benefits – such as pension rights – which full-time workers receive.

Taken over a woman's lifetime, the wage gap produces striking differences in overall earnings. A recent study carried out in the 1990s (Rake 2000) found that a mid-skilled woman, for example, would experience a 'female forfeit' of more than £240,000 over her lifetime. The female forfeit refers to how much less a woman will earn over a lifetime than a man with similar qualifications, even if she has no children. The amount a woman will earn varies with her qualifications. For example, a childless women with no qualifications can be expected to earn £518,000 during her working life; if she is a graduate, she can expect to earn more than double that amount – her 'female forfeit' will be relatively low and she will not suffer the 'mother gap', the gap between the earnings of a woman with no children and a woman with children (see figure 18.4). By contrast, a low-skilled mother of two will be likely to have a 'mother gap' of approximately £285,000 (compared with what an equivalent man would earn), as against £140,000 for a mid-skilled woman and £19,000 for a high-skilled woman – to add to her 'female forfeit'. Women in the last two categories are more likely to return to work quickly and to use day-care facilities when the children are young (Rake 2000).

Changes in the domestic division of labour

One of the results of more women entering paid work is that certain traditional family patterns are being renegotiated. The 'male breadwinner' model has become the exception rather than the rule, and women's growing economic independence has meant that they are better placed to move out of gendered roles at home if they choose to do so. Both in terms of housework and financial decision-making, women's traditional domestic roles are undergoing significant changes. There appears to be a move towards more egalitarian relationships in many households, although women continue to shoulder the main responsibility

| The pay divide

The three categories of 'typical women'

Earnings forgone in three categories | Mrs Low-skill
left school with no qualifications, works as a shop assistant. Marries at 21 and has first child at 23 and second at 26. Takes nine years in all out of the labour market and works part-time for a further 28 years. | Mrs Mid-skill
has O levels/GCSEs and works in a clerical job, e.g. as a secretary. Marries at 26 and has first child at 28 and second at 31. Out of the labour market altogether for just two years and works part-time for a further 12. | Mrs High-skill
is a graduate and a professional, e.g. a teacher. Marries at 28, has first child at 30 and second at 33. Works part-time for just a year, working full-time for the rest of her working life. |
|---|---|---|---|
| The female forfeit – how much less the woman would earn in a lifetime than a man with similar qualifications, even if she had no children. | £197,000 | £241,000 | £143,000 |
| The mother gap – how much less the woman would earn in a life time than a woman with similar qualifications but no children. | £285,000 | £140,000 | £19,000 |
| The parent gap – how much less the woman would earn than a man with similar qualifications, i.e. the female forfeit and mother gap combined. | £482,000 | £381,000 | £162,000 |

Figure 18.4   The 'female forfeit', the 'mother gap' and the 'parent gap' in women's lifetime earnings

Sources: *Guardian* (21 February 2000); Rake (2000)

for most housework. The exception to this seems to be small household repairs, which men are more likely to carry out. Surveys have found that women still spend nearly 3 hours a day on average on housework (excluding shopping and child care). This compares with the 1 hour 40 minutes spent by men (Office of National Statistics 2003).

Studies show that married women employed outside the home do less domestic work than others, although they almost always bear the main responsibility for care of the home. The pattern of their activities is of course rather different. They do more housework in the early evenings and for longer hours at weekends than do those who are full-time housewives.

This issue is examined in more detail in chapter 7, 'Families and Intimate Relationships', pp. 218–19.

There is evidence that even this pattern may be changing, however. Men are contributing more to domestic work than they

have in the past, although scholars who have investigated the phenomenon argue that the process is one of 'lagged adaptation' (Gershuny 1994). By this it is meant that the renegotiation of domestic tasks between men and women is proceeding more slowly than women's entry into the labour market. Research has found that the division of labour within households varies according to factors such as class and the amount of time the woman spends in paid work. Couples from higher social classes tend to have a more egalitarian division of labour, as do households in which the woman is working full time. On the whole, men are taking on a greater amount of responsibility around the home, but the burden is still not equally shared.

A survey conducted by Warde and Heatherington (1993) in Manchester revealed that the domestic division of labour was more egalitarian among young couples than among those of older generations. The authors concluded that over time, gender stereotypes are loosening. Young people who were raised in households with parents who attempted to share domestic tasks were more likely to implement such practices in their own lives.

Vogler and Pahl (1994) examined a different aspect of the domestic division of labour – that of household financial 'management' systems. Their study sought to understand whether women's access to money and to control over spending decisions had become more egalitarian with the increase in female employment. Through interviews with couples in six different British communities, they found the distribution of financial resources to be, on the whole, done more fairly than in the past, but that it remained interlinked with class issues. Among higher income couples, 'pooled' finances tended to be managed jointly and there was a greater degree of equality in accessing money and making spending decisions. The more a woman contributes to the household financially, the greater the level of control she exercises over financial decisions.

In families with lower income, women were often responsible for the day-to-day management of household finances, but were not necessarily in charge of strategic decisions about budgeting and spending. In these cases, Vogler and Pahl noted a tendency for women to protect their husbands' access to spending money while depriving themselves of the same right. In other words, there appeared to be a disjunction between women's everyday control over finances and their access to money.

Post-Fordism

In recent decades, flexible practices have been introduced in a number of spheres, including product development, production techniques, management style, the working environment, employee involvement and marketing. Group production, problem-solving teams, multi-tasking and niche marketing are just some of the strategies that have been adopted by companies attempting to restructure themselves under shifting conditions. Some commentators have suggested that, taken collectively, these changes represent a radical departure from the principles of Fordism; they contend that we are now operating in a period that can best be understood as **post-Fordism**. The phrase was popularized by Michael Piore and Charles Sabel in *The Second Industrial Divide* (1984), and describes a new era of capitalist economic production in which flexibility and innovation are maximized in order to meet market demands for diverse, customized products.

The idea of post-Fordism is somewhat problematic, however. The term is used to refer to a set of overlapping changes that are occurring not only in the realm of work and economic life, but throughout society as a whole. Some writers argue that the tendency towards post-Fordism can be seen in spheres as diverse as party politics, welfare programmes and consumer and lifestyle choices. While observers of contemporary society often point to many of the same changes, there is no consensus about the precise meaning of post-Fordism or, indeed, if this is even the best way of understanding the phenomenon we are witnessing.

Despite the confusion surrounding the term, several distinctive trends within the world of work have emerged in recent decades that seem to represent a clear departure from earlier Fordist practices. These include the decentralization of work into non-hierarchical team groups, the idea of flexible production and mass customization, the spread of global production and the introduction of a more flexible occupational structure. We shall first consider examples of the first three of these trends, before looking at some criticisms of the post-Fordist thesis. Flexible working patterns will then be addressed in the section 'Current trends in the occupational structure'.

Group production

Group production – collaborative work groups in place of assembly lines – has sometimes been used in conjunction with automation as a way of reorganizing work. The underlying idea is to increase worker motivation by letting groups of workers collaborate in team production processes rather than requiring each worker to spend the whole day doing a single repetitive task, like inserting the screws in the door handle of a car.

An example of group production is **quality circles** (QCs), groups of between five and twenty workers who meet regularly to study and resolve production problems. Workers who belong to QCs receive extra training, enabling them to contribute technical knowledge to the discussion of production issues. QCs were initiated in the United States, taken up by a number of Japanese companies, then repopularized in Western economies in the 1980s. They represent a break from the assumptions of Taylorism, since they recognize that workers possess the expertise to contribute towards the definition and method of the tasks they carry out.

The positive effects of group production on workers can include the acquisition of new skills, increased autonomy, reduced managerial supervision and growing pride in the goods and services that they produce. However, studies have identified a number of negative consequences of team production. Although direct managerial authority is less apparent in a team process, other forms of monitoring exist,

such as supervision by other team workers. The American sociologist Laurie Graham went to work on the assembly line at the Japanese-owned Subaru-Isuzu car plant based in Indiana, in the USA, and found that peer pressure from other workers to achieve greater productivity was relentless.

> For more on Japanese models of business organization, see chapter 16, 'Organizations and Networks', pp. 665–6.

One co-worker told her that after initially being enthusiastic about the team concept, she found that peer supervision was just a new means of management trying to work people 'to death'. Graham (1995) also found that Subaru-Isuzu used the group-production concept as a means of resisting trade unions, their argument being that if management and workers were on the same 'team', then there should be no conflict between the two. In other words, the good 'team player' doesn't complain. At the Subaru-Isuzu plant that Graham worked in, demands for higher pay or reduced responsibilities were viewed as a lack of employee cooperativeness. Studies like Graham's have led sociologists to conclude that while team-based production processes provide workers with opportunities for less monotonous forms of work, systems of power and control remain the same in the workplace.

Flexible production and mass customisation

One of the most important changes in worldwide production processes over the past few years has been the introduction of computer-aided design and **flexible production**. While Taylorism and Fordism

Even where production has become customized, elements of the production line can still exist.

were successful at producing mass products (that were all the same) for mass markets, they were unable to produce small orders of goods, let alone goods specifically made for an individual customer. The limited ability of Taylorist and Fordist systems to customize their products is reflected in Henry Ford's famous quip about the first mass-produced car: 'People can have the Model T in any colour – so long as it's black.' Computer-aided designs, coupled to other types of computer-based technology, have altered this situation in a radical way. Stanley Davis speaks of the emergence of 'mass customizing': the new technologies allow the large-scale production of items designed for particular customers. Five thousand shirts might be produced on an assembly line each day. It is now possible to customize every one of the shirts just as quickly as, and at no greater expense than, producing five thousand identical shirts (Davis 1988).

While flexible production has produced benefits for consumers and the economy as a whole, the effect on workers has not been wholly positive. Though workers do learn new skills and have less monotonous jobs, flexible production can create a completely new set of pressures which result from the need to coordinate the complex production process carefully and to produce the results quickly. Laurie

Graham's study of the Subaru-Isuzu factory documented instances when workers were left waiting until the last minute for critical parts in the production process. As a result, employees were forced to work longer and more intensely to keep up with the production schedule, without additional compensation.

Technology such as the Internet can be used to solicit information about individual consumers and then manufacture products to their precise specifications. Enthusiastic proponents argue that **mass customization** offers nothing short of a new Industrial Revolution, a development as momentous as the introduction of mass production techniques in the previous century. Sceptics, however, are quick to point out that as currently practised, mass customization only creates the illusion of choice – in reality, the options available to the Internet customer are no greater than those offered by a typical mail-order catalogue (Collins 2000).

One of the manufacturers that has taken mass customization the farthest is Dell Computer. Consumers who want to purchase a computer from the manufacturer must go online – the company does not maintain retail outlets – and navigate Dell's website. Customers can select the precise mix of features they desire. After the order is placed, a computer is custom built according to specifications and then shipped – typically within days. In effect, Dell has turned traditional ways of doing business upside down: firms used to build a product first, then worry about selling it; now, mass customizers like Dell sell first and build second. Such a shift has important consequences for industry. The need to hold stocks of parts on hand – a major cost for manufacturers – has been dramat-ically reduced. In addition, an increasing share of production is outsourced. Thus, the rapid transfer of information between manufacturers and suppliers – also facilitated by Internet technology – is essential to the successful implementation of mass customization.

Global production

Changes in industrial production include not only *how* products are manufactured, but also *where* products are manufactured, as we saw with the example of the Barbie doll (chapter 2, pp. 57–8). For much of the twentieth century, the most important business organizations were large manufacturing firms that controlled both the making of goods and their final sales. Giant automobile companies such as Ford and General Motors in the USA typify this approach. Such companies employ tens of thousands of factory workers, making everything from individual components to the final cars, which are then sold in the manufacturers' showrooms. Such manufacture-dominated production processes are organized as large bureaucracies, often controlled by a single firm.

During the past twenty or thirty years, however, another form of production has become important – one that is controlled by giant retailers. In retailer-dominated production, firms such as the American retailer Wal-Mart – which in 2000 was the world's second largest corporation – buy products from manufacturers, who in turn arrange to have their products made by independently owned factories.

The American sociologists Edna Bonacich and Richard Appelbaum (2000) show that in clothing manufacturing, most manufacturers actually employ no garment workers at all. Instead, they rely on thousands of factories around the world to make their clothing, which they then sell in department stores and other retail outlets. Clothing manufacturers do not own any of these factories and therefore are not responsible for the conditions under which the clothing is made. Two-thirds of all clothing sold in America is made in factories outside the United States, where workers are paid a fraction of US wages. (In China, workers are lucky to make $40 – just over £20 – a month.) Bonacich and Appelbaum argue that such competition has resulted in a global 'race to the bottom', in which retailers and manufacturers will go to any place on earth where they can pay the lowest wages possible. One result is that much of the clothing we buy today is likely to have been made in **sweatshops** by young workers – probably teenage girls – who get paid mere pennies for making clothing or athletic shoes that sell for tens, if not hundreds, of pounds.

> The globalization of production is discussed in chapter 2, pp. 57–8, and global inequality is discussed in chapter 10.

Criticisms of post-Fordism

While acknowledging that transformations are occurring in the world of work, some commentators reject the label 'post-Fordism'. One common criticism is that post-Fordist analysts are exaggerating the extent to which Fordist practices have been abandoned. What we are witnessing is not a wholesale transformation, as advocates of post-Fordism would have us believe, but the integration of some new approaches into traditional Fordist techniques. This argument has been adopted by those who claim we are actually experiencing a period of 'neo-Fordism' – that is, modifications to the traditional Fordist techniques (Wood 1989).

It has been suggested that the idea of a smooth linear transition from Fordist to post-Fordist techniques overstates the true nature of work at both ends. Anna Pollert (1988) has argued that Fordist techniques were never as entrenched as some would have us believe. It is also an exaggeration, she contends, that the age of mass production has passed in favour of total flexibility. She points out that mass production techniques still dominate in many industries, especially those that are aimed at consumer markets. According to Pollert, economic production has always been characterized by a diversity of techniques rather than a standard, unified approach.

Current trends in the occupational structure

The occupational structure across all industrialized countries has changed very substantially since the beginning of the twentieth century. At the start of the twentieth century the labour market was dominated by blue-collar manufacturing jobs, but over time the balance has shifted towards white-collar positions in the service sector. Figure 18.5 (p. 770) shows the gradual decline of manufacturing work and the rise of service industries in the UK since the late 1970s. In the UK in 1900, more than three-quarters of the employed population was in manual (blue-collar) work. Some 28 per cent of these were skilled workers, 35 per cent semi-skilled and 10 per cent unskilled. White-collar and professional jobs were

Work and technology

The relationship between technology and work has long been of interest to sociologists. How is our experience of work affected by the type of technology that is involved? As industrialization has progressed, technology has assumed an ever-greater role at the workplace – from factory automation to the computerization of office work. The current information technology revolution has attracted renewed interest in this question. Technology can lead to greater efficiency and productivity, but how does it affect the way work is experienced by those who carry it out? For sociologists, one of the main questions is how the move to more complex systems influences the nature of work and the institutions in which it is performed.

Automation and the skill debate

The concept of **automation**, or programmable machinery, was introduced in the mid-1800s, when Christopher Spencer, an American, invented the Automat, a programmable lathe that made screws, nuts and gears. Automation has thus far affected relatively few industries, but with advances in the design of industrial robots, its impact is certain to become greater. A robot is an automatic device that can perform functions ordinarily done by human workers. The term 'robot' comes from the Czech word *robota*, or serf, popularized about fifty years ago by the playwright Karel apek.

The majority of the robots used in industry worldwide are to be found in automobile manufacture. The usefulness of robots in production thus far is relatively limited, because their capacity to recognize different objects and manipulate awkward shapes is still at a rudimentary level. Yet it is certain that automated production will spread rapidly in coming years; robots are becoming more sophisticated, while their costs are decreasing.

The spread of automation provoked a heated debate among sociologists and experts in industrial relations over the impact of the new technology on workers, their skills and their level of commitment to their work. In his influential *Alienation and Freedom* (1964), Robert Blauner examined the experience of workers in four different industries with varying levels of technology. Using the ideas of Durkheim and Marx, Blauner operationalized the concept of *alienation* and measured the extent to which workers in each industry experienced it in the form of powerlessness, meaninglessness, isolation and self-estrangement. He concluded that workers on assembly lines were the most alienated of all, but that levels of alienation were somewhat lower at workplaces using automation. In other words, Blauner argued that the introduction of automation to factories was responsible for *reversing* the otherwise steady trend towards increased worker alienation. Automation helped to integrate the workforce and gave workers a sense of control over their work that had been lacking with other forms of technology.

A very different thesis was set forth by Harry Braverman in his famous *Labor and Monopoly Capital* (1974). In Braverman's eyes, automation was part of the overall 'deskilling' of the industrial labour force. By imposing Taylorist organizational techniques and breaking up the labour process into specialized tasks, managers were able to exert control over the workforce. In both industrial settings and modern offices, the introduction of technology contributed to this overall degradation of work by limiting the need for creative human input. Instead, all that was required was an unthinking, unreflective body capable of endlessly carrying out the same unskilled task.

Braverman's work on deskilling of labour is echoed in George Ritzer's account of low-skill 'McJobs' discussed in chapter 16, 'Organizations and Networks', pp. 636–7.

A newer study sheds some more light on this debate. The sociologist Richard Sennett (1998) studied the people who worked in a bakery that had been bought by a large food conglomerate and automated with the introduction of high-tech machinery. Computerized baking radically altered the way that bread was made. Instead of using their hands to mix the ingredients and knead the dough, and their noses and eyes to judge when the bread was baked, the bakery's workers had no physical contact with the materials or the loaves of bread. In fact, the entire process was controlled and monitored via computer screen. Computers decided the temperature and baking time of the ovens. While at times the machines produced excellent-quality bread, at other times the results were burnt, blackened loaves. The workers at this bakery (it would be erroneous to call them bakers) were hired because they were skilled with computers, not because they knew how to bake bread. Ironically, these workers used very few of their computer skills. The production process involved little more than pushing buttons on a computer. In fact, when at one point the computerized machinery broke down, the entire production process was halted because none of the bakery's 'skilled' workers was trained or empowered to repair the problem. The workers whom Sennett observed wanted to be helpful, to make things work again, but they could not, because automation had diminished their autonomy. The introduction of computerized technology in the workplace has led to a general increase in all workers' skills, but has also led to a bifurcated workforce composed of a small group of highly skilled professionals with high degrees of flexibility and autonomy in their jobs and a larger group of clerical, service and production workers who lack autonomy in their jobs.

The skill debate is very difficult to resolve, however. Both the conceptualization and measurement of skill are problematic. As feminist researchers have argued, what constitutes 'skill' is socially constructed (Steinberg 1990). As such, conventional understandings of 'skilled' work tend to reflect the social status of the typical incumbent of the job, rather than the difficulty of the task in an objective sense. The history of occupations is rife with examples of jobs in which the very same task was assigned a different skill level (and even renamed) once women entered the field (Reskin and Roos 1990). The same, of course, holds for other low-status workers, such as racial minorities. Even where gender and racial biases

are not in operation, skill has multiple dimensions; the same job may be downgraded on one dimension while simultaneously upgraded on another (Block 1990). Thus, opinions as to whether automation has deskilled work depend on which dimension of skill is examined. In his comprehensive review of the skill debate, Spenner (1983) notes that studies that have examined skill in terms of the substantive complexity of tasks have tended to support the 'upskilling' position, whereas those that have examined skill in terms of the autonomy and/or control exercised by the worker have tended to find that work has in fact been 'deskilled' through automation (Zuboff 1988; Vallas and Beck 1996).

Information technology

The opposing perspectives of Blauner and Braverman, discussed above, on the effects of automation are echoed today in debates over the impact of information technology (IT) in the workplace. Certainly there is little question that the Internet, email, teleconferencing and e-commerce are changing the way in which companies do business. But they are also affecting the way in which employees work on a daily basis. Those who take an optimistic approach, as Blauner did, argue that information technology will revolutionize the world of work by allowing new, more flexible ways of working to emerge. These opportunities will permit us to move beyond the routine and alienating aspects of industrial work into a more liberating informational age, giving workers greater control over and input into the work process. Enthusiastic advocates of technological advances are sometimes referred to as 'technological determinists', because they believe in the power of technology to determine the nature and shape of work itself.

Others are not convinced that information technology will bring about an entirely positive transformation of work. As Shoshana Zuboff (1988) concluded in her research into the use of IT in firms, management can choose to use IT towards very different ends. When embraced as a creative, decentralizing force, information technology can help to break down rigid hierarchies, engage more employees in decision-making and involve workers more closely in the day-to-day affairs of the company. On the other hand, it can just as easily be used as a way to strengthen hierarchies and surveillance practices. The adoption of IT in the workplace can cut down on face-to-face interactions, block channels of accountability and transform an office into a network of self-contained and isolated modules. Such an approach sees the impact of information technology as influenced by the uses to which it is put and the way in which those using the technology understand its role.

The spread of information technology will certainly produce exciting and heightened opportunities for some segments of the labour force. In the fields of media, advertising and design, for example, IT both enhances creativity in the professional realm and introduces flexibility into personal work styles. It is qualified, valued employees in responsible positions for whom the vision of wired workers and telecommuting comes closest to being realized. Yet at the other end of the spectrum there are thousands of low-paid unskilled individuals working in call centres and data-entry companies. These positions, which are largely a product of the telecommunications explosion in recent years, are characterized by degrees of isolation and alienation that rival those of Braverman's deskilled workers. Employees at call centres that process travel bookings and financial transactions work according to strictly standardized formats where there is little or no room for employee discretion or creative input. Employees are closely monitored and their interactions with customers are tape-recorded for 'quality assurance'. The information revolution seems to have produced a large number of routine, unskilled jobs on a par with those of the industrial economy.

Has the adoption of IT in the workplace in fact deskilled employees such as these call centre workers?

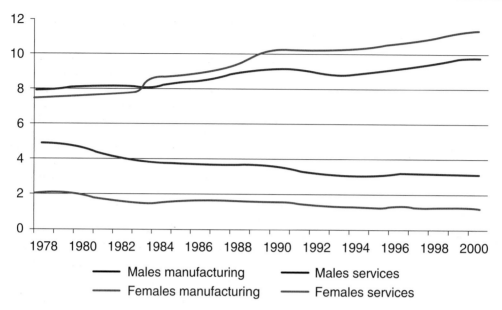

Figure 18.5 Employee jobs: by industry and sex at June each year, 1978–2000 (millions)

Source: ONS (2002a)

relatively few in number. By the middle of the century, manual workers made up less than two-thirds of the population in paid labour, and non-manual work had expanded correspondingly.

There is considerable debate over why such changes have occurred. The reasons seem to be several. One is the continuous introduction of labour-saving machinery, culminating in the spread of information technology in industry in recent years. Another is the rise of manufacturing industry outside the West, particularly in the Far East. The older industries in Western societies have experienced major cutbacks because of their inability to compete with the more efficient Far Eastern producers, whose labour costs are lower.

Economic growth and development are discussed in chapter 10, 'Poverty, Social Exclusion and Welfare', pp. 402–13

The knowledge economy

Taking these figures into account, some observers have suggested that what is occurring today is a transition to a new type of society that is no longer based primarily on industrialism. We are entering, they claim, a phase of development beyond the industrial era altogether. A variety of terms have been coined to describe this new social order, such as the *post-industrial society*, the *information age* and the *new economy*. The term that has come into most common usage, however, is the **knowledge economy**.

A precise definition of the knowledge economy is difficult to formulate, but in

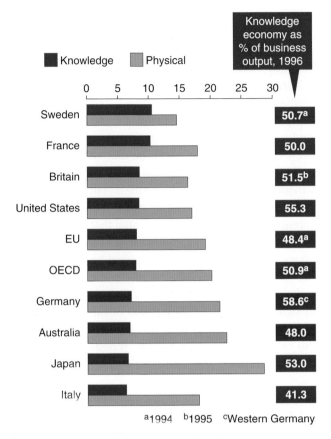

Figure 18.6 Business output in OECD countries: investment as % of GDP, 1995

Source: *The Economist* (14 October 1999)

general terms, it refers to an economy in which ideas, information and forms of knowledge underpin innovation and economic growth. A knowledge economy is one in which much of the workforce is involved not in the physical production or distribution of material goods, but in their design, development, technology, marketing, sale and servicing. These employees can be termed *knowledge workers*. The knowledge economy is dominated by the constant flow of information and opinions, and by the powerful potentials of science and technology. As Charles Leadbeater has observed:

> Most of us make our money from thin air: we produce nothing that can be weighed, touched or easily measured. Our output is not stockpiled at harbours, stored in warehouses or shipped in railway cars. Most of us earn our livings providing service, judgement, information and analysis, whether in a telephone call centre, a lawyer's office, a government department or a scientific laboratory. We are all in the thin-air business. (1999, p. vii)

How widespread is the knowledge economy at the start of the twenty-first century? A recent study by the Organization for Economic Cooperation and Development has attempted to gauge the extent of the knowledge economy among developed nations by measuring the percentage of each country's overall business output that can be attributed to knowledge-based industries (see figure 18.6). Knowledge-based industries are understood broadly to include high technology, education and training, research and development, and the financial and investment sector. Among OECD countries as a whole, knowledge-based industries accounted for more than half of all business output in the mid-1990s. Western Germany had a high figure of 58.6 per cent, and the United States, Japan, Britain, Sweden and France were all over 50 per cent.

Investments into the knowledge economy – in the form of public education, spending on software development, and research and development – now comprise a significant part of many countries' budgets. Sweden, for example, invested 10.6 per cent of its overall gross domestic product into the knowledge economy in 1995. France was a close second because of its extensive spending on public education.

Admittedly, the knowledge economy remains a difficult phenomenon to investigate – both quantitatively and qualitatively. It is easier to measure the value of physical things than 'weightless' ideas. Yet it is undeniable that the generation and application of knowledge is becoming increasingly central to the economies of Western societies.

Multi-skilling

One of the beliefs of post-Fordist commentators is that new forms of work allow employees to increase the breadth of their skills by engaging in a variety of tasks, rather than performing one specific task over and over again. Group production and teamwork are seen as promoting a 'multi-skilled' workforce capable of carrying out a broader set of responsibilities. This in turn leads to higher productivity and better quality goods and services; employees who are able to contribute to their jobs in multiple ways will be more successful in solving problems and coming up with creative approaches.

The move towards 'multi-skilling' has implications for the hiring process. If at one time these were made largely on the basis of education and qualifications, many employers now look for individuals who are adaptable and can learn new skills quickly. Thus, expert knowledge of a particular software application might not be as valuable as a demonstrable ability to pick up ideas easily. Specializations are often assets, but if employees have difficulty in applying narrow skills creatively in new contexts, they may not be seen as a benefit in a flexible, innovative workplace.

A Joseph Rowntree Foundation study on *The Future of Work* (Meadows 1996) investigated the types of skill which are now sought by employers. The authors of the study concluded that in both skilled and unskilled occupational sectors, 'personal skills' are increasingly valued. The ability to collaborate and to work independently, to take the initiative and to adopt creative approaches in the face of challenges are among the best skills an individual can bring to a job. In a market in which consumers' individual needs are increasingly catered for, it is essential that employees in a range of settings from the service sector to financial consulting be able to draw on 'personal skills' at the workplace. This 'downgrading' of technical skills, according to the authors of the study, may be most difficult for workers who have long worked in routine, repetitive work in which 'personal skills' had no place.

Training on the job

Multi-skilling is closely tied up with the idea of employee training and retraining. Rather than employing narrow specialists, many companies would prefer to hire capable non-specialists who are able to develop new skills on the job. As technology and market demands change, companies retrain their own employees as needed instead of bringing in expensive consultants or replacing existing staff with new employees. Investing in a core of employees who may become valuable lifelong workers is seen as a strategic way to keep up with rapidly changing times.

Some companies organize on-the-job training through job-sharing teams. This technique allows skills training and mentoring to take place at the same time as work is getting done: an IT specialist

The Internet, laptops and home computing have made working from home possible for some workers, but bringing the office into the home has its drawbacks. For example, some employees feel under pressure to work longer hours than before, while some employers are not convinced that their employees are working hard enough, and undervalue their performance.

might be paired for several weeks with a company manager in order for each to learn some of the other's skills. This form of training is cost-effective, as it does not significantly lessen working hours and allows all employees involved to broaden their skills base.

Training on the job can be an important way for workers to develop their skills and career prospects. But it is important to note that training opportunities are not equally available to all workers. The Economic and Social Research Council (ESRC) cohort studies of young people born in 1958 and 1970 found that employees already possessing qualifications were much more likely to receive training on the job than their counterparts who were without qualifications (ESRC 1997). Such studies suggest that there is more continuing investment in those who are already the most highly qualified, while those without qualifications suffer from fewer opportunities. Training also has an impact on wage levels: among the 1970 cohort, work-based training increased employee earnings by an average of 12 per cent.

Homeworking

Homeworking allows employees to perform some or all of their responsibilities from home, often via a computer connected to the Internet. In jobs which do not require regular contact with clients or co-workers, such as computer-based graphic design work or copy-writing for advertisements, employees find that working from home allows them to balance non-work responsibilities and perform more productively. The phenomenon of 'wired workers' seems sure to grow in the years to come as technology radically changes the way we work.

One example of these changes in practice is the Helsinki Virtual Village discussed in chapter 21, 'Cities and Urban Spaces', pp. 924–5.

Although working at home has become more accepted in recent years, it is not necessarily favoured by all employers. It is much more difficult to monitor an employee's work when they are out of the office; for this reason, new types of control are often placed on homeworkers in order to ensure that they do not abuse their 'freedom'. Workers might be expected to check in regularly with the office, for example, or to submit updates on their work more frequently than other employees.

For more discussion of surveillance in the work place, see chapter 16, 'Organizations and Networks', pp. 648–51.

While there is great enthusiasm about the potential of 'home offices', some scholars have cautioned that a significant polarization is likely to emerge between professional homeworkers who pursue challenging, creative projects from home, and largely unskilled homeworkers who perform routine jobs such as typing or data entry from home. Were such a schism to develop, women would be most likely to be concentrated among the lower ranks of homeworkers (Phizacklea and Wolkowitz 1995).

The end of the career for life and the rise of the portfolio worker

In light of the impact of the global economy and the demand for a 'flexible' labour force, some sociologists and economists have argued that more and more people in the future will become **portfolio workers**. They will have a 'skill portfolio' – a number of different job skills and credentials – which they will use to move between several jobs and kinds of job during the course of their working lives. Only a relatively small proportion of workers will have continuous 'careers' in the current sense. Indeed, proponents argue, the idea of a 'job for life' is becoming a thing of the past.

Some see this move to the portfolio worker in a positive light: workers will not be stuck in the same job for years on end and will be able to plan their work lives in a creative way (Handy 1994). Others hold that 'flexibility' in practice means that organizations can hire and fire more or less at will, undermining any sense of security their workers might have. Employers will only have a short-term commitment to their workforces and will be able to minimize the paying of extra benefits or pension rights.

A recent study of Silicon Valley, California, claims that the economic success of the area is already founded on the portfolio skills of its workforce. The failure rate of firms in Silicon Valley is very high: about three hundred new companies are established every year, but an equivalent number also go bust. The workforce, which has a very high proportion of professional and technical workers, has learned to adjust to this. The result, the authors say, is that talents and skills migrate rapidly from one firm to another, becoming more adaptable on the way. Technical specialists become consultants, consultants become managers, employees become venture capitalists – and back again (Bahrami and Evans 1995).

Among young people, especially consultants and specialists in information technology, there does seem to be a growing tendency towards portfolio work. By some estimates, young graduates in the UK can expect to work in eleven different jobs using three different skill bases over the course of their working lives. Yet such a situation still remains the exception rather than the rule. Employment statistics have not shown the great rise in employee turnover that one would expect with a large-scale shift towards portfolio work. Surveys carried out in the 1990s revealed that full-time workers in Britain and the USA – which have the most deregulated labour markets among industrial countries – spent as long in each job as they were doing ten years before (*The Economist*, 21 May 1995). The reasons seem to be that managers recognize that a high degree of turnover among workers is costly and bad for morale, and that they prefer to retrain their own employees rather than bring in new ones, even if this means paying above the market rate. In their book, *Built to Last* (1994), James Collins and Jerry Porras analysed eighteen American companies which had continuously outperformed the stock-market average since 1926. They found that these companies, far from hiring and firing at will, had followed highly protective policies towards their staff. Only two of these companies over the period studied brought in a chief executive from the outside, compared to thirteen of the less successful corporations included in the research.

These findings do not disprove the ideas of those who speak of the arrival of the portfolio worker. Organizational downsizing is a reality, throwing many thousands of workers who may have thought they had a lifetime job onto the labour market. To find work again, they may be forced to develop and diversify their skills. Many, particularly

older people, might never be able to find jobs comparable to those they held before, or perhaps even paid work at all.

Other aspects of modern work are discussed in chapter 16, 'Organizations and Networks', including issues to do with management of modern business organizations, such as the development of human resource management and concentration on corporate culture.

Job insecurity, unemployment and the social significance of work

While new ways of working present exciting opportunities for many people, they can also produce deep ambivalence on the part of others who feel that they are caught up in a runaway world. As we have seen in this chapter, the labour market is undergoing profound change as part of the shift from a manufacturing to a service-oriented economy. The widespread introduction of information technology is also provoking transformations in the way organizations structure themselves, the type of management style that is used and the manner in which work tasks are delegated and carried out. Rapid change can be destabilizing; workers in many different types of occupation now experience job insecurity and a sense of apprehension about both the future safety of their work position and their role within the workplace.

In recent decades, the phenomenon of job insecurity has become an important topic of debate within the sociology of work. Many commentators and media sources have suggested that there has been

The declining importance of work?

Persistent unemployment, job insecurity, downsizing, portfolio careers, part-time work, flexible employment patterns, job sharing: it seems that more than ever people are working in non-standard ways, or are not in paid work at all! Perhaps it is time to rethink the nature of work and in particular the dominant position it often has in people's lives.

Because we so closely associate 'work' and 'paid employment', it is sometimes difficult to see what options might exist outside this view. The French sociologist and social critic André Gorz is one analyst who has argued that in the future paid work will play a less and less important part in people's lives. Gorz bases his views on a critical assessment of Marx's writings. Marx believed that the working class – to which more and more people would supposedly belong – would lead a revolution that would bring about a more humane type of society, in which work would be central to the satisfactions life has to offer. Although writing as a leftist, Gorz rejects this view. Rather than the working class becoming the largest grouping in society (as Marx suggested) and leading a successful revolution, it is actually shrinking. Blue-collar workers have now become a minority – and a declining minority – of the labour force.

It no longer makes much sense, in Gorz's view, to suppose that workers can take over the enterprises of which they are a part, let alone seize state power. There is no real hope of transforming the nature of paid work, because it is organized according to technical considerations which are unavoidable if an economy is to be efficient. 'The point now', as Gorz puts it, 'is to free oneself from work' (1982, p. 67). This is particularly necessary where work is organized along Taylorist lines, or is otherwise oppressive or dull.

Rising unemployment, together with the spread of part-time work, Gorz argues, has already created what he calls a 'non-class of non-workers', alongside those in stable employment. Most people, in fact, are in this 'non-class', because the proportion of the population in stable paid jobs at any one time is relatively small – if we exclude the young, the retired, the ill and housewives, together with people who are in part-time work or unemployed. The spread of information technology, Gorz believes, will further reduce the numbers of full-time jobs available. The result is likely to be a swing towards rejecting the 'productivist' outlook of Western society, with its emphasis on wealth, economic growth and material goods. A diversity of lifestyles, followed outside the sphere of permanent, paid work, will be pursued by the majority of the population in coming years.

According to Gorz, we are moving towards a 'dual society'. In one sector, production and political administration will be organized to maximize efficiency. The other sector will be a sphere in which individuals occupy themselves with a variety of non-work pursuits offering enjoyment or personal fulfilment. Perhaps more and more individuals will engage in life planning, by which they arrange to work in different ways at different stages of their lives.

How valid is this viewpoint? That there are major changes going on in the nature and organization of work in the industrialized countries is beyond dispute. It does seem possible that more and more people will become disenchanted with 'productivism' – the stress on constant economic growth and the accumulation of material possessions. It is surely valuable, as Gorz has suggested, to see unemployment not wholly in a negative light, but as offering opportunities for individuals to pursue their interests and develop their talents. Yet, thus far at least, progress in this direction has been slight; we seem to be far from the situation Gorz envisages. With women pressing for greater job opportunities, there has been a rise, not a fall, in the numbers of people actively interested in securing paid employment. Paid work remains for many the key to generating the material resources necessary to sustain a varied life.

a steady increase in job insecurity for some thirty or more years and that this insecurity has now reached unprecedented heights in industrialized countries. Young people can no longer count on a secure career with one employer, they claim, because the rapidly globalizing economy is leading to ever more corporate mergers and corporate 'downsizings', where employees are laid off. The drive for efficiency and profit means that those with few skills – or the 'wrong' skills – are relegated to insecure, marginal jobs that are vulnerable to shifts in the global markets. Despite the benefits of flexibility at the workplace, the argument continues, we now live in a 'hire-and-fire' culture where the idea of a 'job for life' no longer applies.

The social significance of work

For most of us, work occupies a larger part of our lives than any other single type of activity. We often associate the notion of work with drudgery – with a set of tasks that we want to minimize and, if possible, escape from altogether. Work has more going for it than drudgery, however, or people would not feel so lost and disoriented when they become unemployed. How would you feel if you thought you would never get a job? In modern societies, having a job is important for maintaining self-esteem. Even where work conditions are relatively unpleasant, and the tasks dull, work tends to be a structuring element in people's psychological make-up and the cycle of their daily activities. Several characteristics of work are relevant here.

1 *Money* A wage or salary is the main resource many people depend on to meet their needs. Without an income,

anxieties about coping with day-to-day life multiply.

2 *Activity level* Work often provides a basis for the acquisition and exercise of skills and capacities. Even where work is routine, it offers a structured environment in which a person's energies may be absorbed. Without it, the opportunity to exercise such skills and capacities may be reduced.

3 *Variety* Work provides access to contexts that contrast with domestic surroundings. In the working environment, even when the tasks are relatively dull, people may enjoy doing something different from home chores.

4 *Temporal structure* For people in regular employment, the day is usually organized around the rhythm of work. While this may sometimes be oppressive, it provides a sense of direction in daily activities. Those who are out of work frequently find boredom a major problem and develop a sense of apathy about time.

5 *Social contacts* The work environment often provides friendships and opportunities to participate in shared activities with others. Separated from the work setting, a person's circle of possible friends and acquaintances is likely to dwindle.

6 *Personal identity* Work is usually valued for the sense of stable social identity it offers. For men in particular, self-esteem is often bound up with the economic contribution they make to the maintenance of the household.

Against the backdrop of this formidable list, it is not difficult to see why being without work may undermine individuals' confidence in their social value.

The rise in job insecurity

In 1999 the Joseph Rowntree Foundation published the results of the *Job Insecurity and Work Intensification Survey* (JIWIS), which drew on in-depth interviews with 340 working Britons from shopfloor workers to senior managers. The study was designed to assess the extent of job insecurity and to gauge its impact both in the workplace and in families and communities. The authors of the study found that job insecurity had been on the rise in Britain since 1966, with the most intensive period of growth occurring among blue-collar workers in the late 1970s and 1980s. Despite a general economic recovery beginning in the mid-1980s, however, job insecurity continued to grow. The study concluded that job insecurity had reached its highest point since the Second World War (Burchell 1999).

The survey also examined the types of worker who had experienced greater or lesser levels of insecurity with the passing of time. The authors found that in the mid-1990s the greatest increase in job insecurity occurred among non-manual workers. From 1986 to 1999, professionals shifted from the most secure occupational group to the least secure, while manual workers experienced somewhat lower levels of job insecurity. One of the main sources of this insecurity appeared to be a lack of trust in management. When asked if management looked out for the employees' best interests, 44 per cent of respondents claimed that they did so 'only a little' or 'not at all' (Burchell 1999).

Most scholars agree that job insecurity is not a new phenomenon. The disagreement surrounds the extent to which it has become more pronounced in recent years and, more importantly, which segments of the working population experience job insecurity most acutely. Some critics argue that studies like the JIWIS project are nothing more than an unwarranted response to perceived job insecurity among the middle classes.

The 'insecure middle': is job insecurity exaggerated?

In the late 1970s and 1980s Britain experienced an economic recession that proved to be particularly harmful to traditional manufacturing industries. Roughly one million jobs were lost during this time in sectors such as steel, shipbuilding and coal-mining. It wasn't until the 1980s and into the 1990s that professional and managerial workers had their first large-scale exposure to job insecurity. Corporate takeovers and lay-offs have affected the banking and finance sector; the spread of the information age has cost many civil servants their jobs, as systems are streamlined through the use of computer technology.

If manufacturing workers had become accustomed to living with the threat of redundancy, white-collar workers were less prepared for the changes affecting their occupations. This anxiety among professionals led some to speak of 'the insecure middle'. The term was used to describe white-collar workers whose faith in the stability of their jobs meant that they had taken on significant financial commitments such as sizeable mortgages, private education for children or expensive hobbies. Because redundancy had never crossed their minds before, the sudden spectre of unemployment caused them to experience enormous anxiety and insecurity. Job insecurity soon became a 'buzz' topic in the media and in profes-

The idea of a 'job for life' proved to be a myth to this unemployed worker.

sional circles – although some believe this was an overreaction when compared to the more chronic insecurity experienced by the working classes.

The harmful effects of job insecurity

The *Job Insecurity and Work Intensification* survey (Burchell et al. 1999) found that for many workers job insecurity is much more than a fear of redundancy. It also encompasses anxieties about the transformation of work itself, and the effects of that transformation on employees' health and personal life.

The study revealed that workers are being asked to take on more and more responsibility at work as organizational structures become less bureaucratic and decision-making is spread throughout the workplace. Yet at the same time that the demands on them are increasing, many workers see their chances of promotion decreasing (see figure 18.7). This combination leads workers to feel that they are 'losing control' over important features of their job, such as the pace of work and confidence in their overall career progression.

The sociologist Paul du Gay argues for the importance of bureaucracy in providing accountability and moral responsibility against increasingly entrepreneurial and flexile work practices. His argument is discussed in more detail in chapter 16, 'Organizations and Networks', pp. 645–6.

Living to work or working to live?

For some analysts, the end of the millennium should have witnessed a colossal change in patterns of work – or rather the lack of work – to the point where there would be no economic stimulus to immigration. As Jenkins and Sherman insisted in 1979: 'It is impossible to over-dramatize the forthcoming crisis. . . . Now we have inflation, a slump and rising unemployment. In fifteen or twenty years time we shall have a boom, minimal inflation, high growth and the largest unemployment in our history . . . a jobs holocaust' (1979, p. 182) . . .

Well we certainly have not reached the workerless economy – but have we instead arrived in a place where the kind of relationship we have to work has changed beyond all recognition? . . .

While it is easy to scoff at the pessimism of [authors such as Jenkins and Sherman] it remains the case that the contemporary *perception* of job insecurity appears to be almost as high as the *unreality* of job insecurity they predicted. D. Smith (1997, p. 39), for instance, compared the relative insignificance of newspaper stories about insecurity in 1986 (when unemployment in Britain was much

higher than a decade later) with its preponderant presence in 1996, by which time stories about job insecurity had increased 100-fold. According to the *Observer* (16 June 1996), 40 per cent of British employees feared for their jobs, while 60 per cent argued that insecurity had been rising. . . .

Yet, despite claims to the contrary, job tenure in Britain only marginally decreased between 1975 and 2000 (from 6 to 5.5 years), with women's tenure actually increasing (Gregg and Wadsworth, 1999; Nolan, 2000: 3; Green (2000) suggests that in the 1970s the average job tenure was 10 years and it remained stuck at 9.5 in 2000). Indeed, in the allegedly worst period of the 'neurotic nineties', tenure actually increased over the rate of the 'erratic eighties'. . . . 80 per cent of British employees remain in permanent jobs, and 28 per cent of employees have remained with the same employer for more than ten years. Indeed, most people can probably look forward to staying with the same employer for, at the very least, four or five years.

Source: Grint (2005), pp. 325–7

A second harmful dimension to job security can be seen in workers' personal lives. The study found a strong correlation between job insecurity and poor overall health. This link is substantiated by data from the British Household Panel Survey, which showed that people's mental and physical health continues to deteriorate with episodes of prolonged job insecurity. Rather than adjusting to the insecure conditions, workers remain anxious and under constant stress. This pressure from work seems to transfer into the home environment: those workers reporting high levels of job insecurity also tended to experience tensions at home (Burchell et al. 1999).

Unemployment

Rates of **unemployment** have fluctuated considerably over the course of this century. In Western countries, unemployment reached a peak in the early 1930s, with some 20 per cent of the labour force being out of work in Britain. The ideas of the economist John Maynard Keynes (1883–1946) strongly influenced public policy in Europe and the United States during the post-war period. Keynes believed that unemployment results from a lack of sufficient purchasing power to buy goods, so that production is not

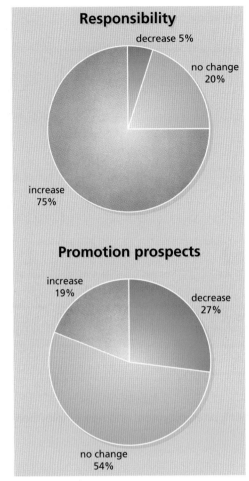

Responsibility

decrease 5%

no change 20%

increase 75%

Promotion prospects

increase 19%

decrease 27%

no change 54%

Figure 18.7 Employees experiencing a change in responsibilities and promotion prospects at work

Sources: Burchell et al. (1999)

stimulated and fewer workers are needed; governments can intervene to increase the level of demand in an economy, leading to the creation of new jobs. State management of economic life, many came to believe, meant that high rates of unemployment belonged to the past. Commitment to full employment became part of government policy in virtually all Western societies. Until the 1970s, these policies seemed successful and economic growth was more or less continuous.

During the 1970s and 1980s, unemployment rates proved difficult to control in many countries, and Keynesianism was largely abandoned as a means of trying to regulate economic activity. For about a quarter of a century after the Second World War, the British unemployment rate was less than 2 per cent. It rose as high as 12 per cent in the early 1980s, then fell, increasing again at the end of the decade. From the mid- to late-1990s, unemployment in Britain once again began to decline; by 2005 it stood at just under 5 per cent.

Analysing unemployment

Interpreting official unemployment statistics, however, is not straightforward (see figure 18.8). Unemployment is not easy to define. It means 'being out of work'. But 'work' here means 'paid work', and 'work in a recognized occupation'. People who are properly registered as unemployed may engage in many forms of productive activity, like painting the house or tending the garden. Many people are in part-time paid work, or only in paid jobs sporadically; the retired are not counted as 'unemployed'.

Many official statistics are calculated according to the definition of unemployment used by the International Labour Organization (ILO). The ILO's measure of unemployment refers to individuals who are without a job, who are available to start work within two weeks and who have attempted to look for a job within the previous month. Many economists think this standard unemployment rate should be supplemented by two other measures.

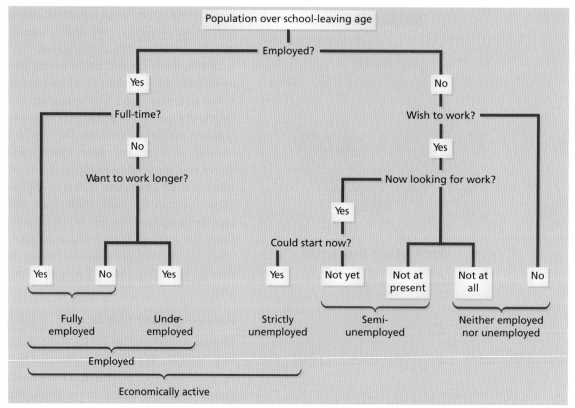

Figure 18.8   A taxonomy of possible employment, unemployment and non-employment states
Source: Sinclair (1987), p. 2

'Discouraged workers' are those who would like a job, but who despair of getting one and thus have given up looking. 'Involuntary part-time workers' are people who cannot find a full-time job even though they want one.

General unemployment statistics are also complicated by the fact that they encompass two different 'types' of unemployment. Frictional unemployment, sometimes called 'temporary unemployment', refers to the natural, short-term entry and exit of individuals into and out of the labour market for reasons such as switching jobs, searching for a position after graduation, or a period of poor health. Structural unemployment, by contrast, describes joblessness, which results from large shifts in the economy, rather than circumstances affecting particular individuals. The decline of heavy industry in Britain, for example, contributed to a higher level of structural unemployment.

Trends in unemployment in the UK

Variations in the distribution of government-defined unemployment within Britain are well documented. Unemployment is higher for men than for women. At

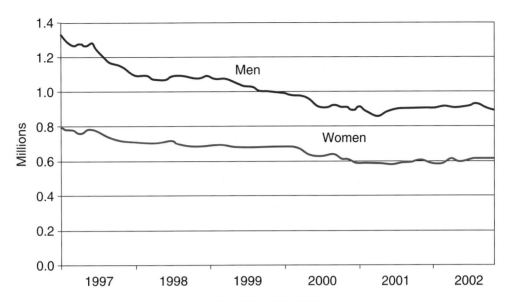

Figure 18.9 Unemployment: by gender, UK, 1997–2002

Source: ONS (2004a)

the end of 2002 there were 892,000 men unemployed, compared to 622,000 women, as figure 18.9 shows. Unemployed men were almost twice as likely as women to have previously been in work. Women registering for unemployment were ten times more likely than men to have been at home caring for children or the household.

On average, ethnic minorities have higher unemployment rates than whites. Ethnic minorities also have much higher rates of long-term unemployment than the rest of the population. However, these general trends hide a large amount of diversity in unemployment rates among ethnic minority groups (see figure 18.10). Unemployment among the white population stood at under 5 per cent in 2003/4, with the lowest rate of 3.8 per cent recorded in the south. For Indians, the rate was only slightly higher than this at around 7 per cent – one of the factors which leads some to suggest that the British Indian population has nearly attained socio-economic parity with the white population. For all other minority ethnic groups, unemployment rates were between two and three times higher than those for white men. The unemployment rate among Bangladeshis was the highest, at 20 per cent for men and 24 per cent for women.

Young people, particularly in minority ethnic groups, are especially affected by unemployment. Over 40 per cent of Bangladeshi men in the UK under the age of twenty-five were unemployed in 2001/2. Amongst the other ethnic minority groups, the unemployment rate for young men ranged between 25 and 31 per cent. This compared with a rate of 12 per cent for white men of the same age.

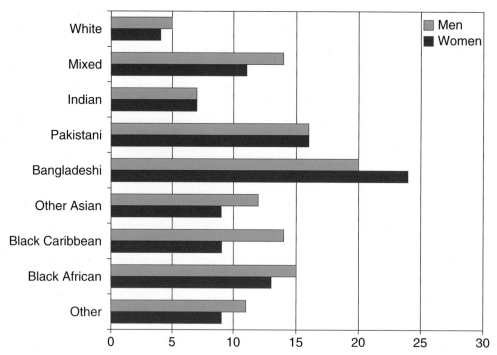

Figure 18.10   Unemployment rates: by ethnic group and sex, UK, 2001/2 (%)

Source: ONS (2004d)

A substantial proportion of young people are among the long-term unemployed, especially members of minority groups; and more than half the male teenage unemployment involves those out of work for six months or more. New government initiatives are targeted at young people aged eighteen to twenty-four who have been claiming job-seekers' allowance for more than six months. The long-term unemployed are now offered skills training, assistance in searching for jobs and opportunities for subsidized work.

Social class and unemployment rates are correlated. According to the ESRC cohort study for young people born in 1970, those people whose fathers were from social classes I or II experienced the lowest rates of unemployment. Those whose fathers were from social class V, or who were raised by lone mothers, had the highest rates of unemployment, including a high proportion of people who had never been in work at all (ESRC 1997).

Unemployment rates are also linked to educational qualifications. Surveys in the UK have shown that the higher the level of qualification, the lower the unemployment rate. In spring 2003 the unemployment rate among those with no qualifications was over three times that of those with a degree or equivalent (*Regional Trends* 38, 2003).

The experience of unemployment

The experience of unemployment can be very disturbing to those accustomed to having secure jobs. Obviously, the immediate consequence is a loss of income. The effects of this vary between countries, because of contrasts in the level of unemployment benefits. In countries where there is guaranteed access to healthcare and other welfare benefits, unemployed individuals may experience acute financial difficulties but remain protected by the state. In some Western countries, such as the United States, unemployment benefits last a shorter time and healthcare is not universal, making the economic strain on those without work correspondingly greater.

Studies of the emotional effects of unemployment have noted that people who are unemployed often pass through a series of stages as they adjust to their new status. While the experience is of course an individual one, the newly unemployed often experience a sense of shock, followed by optimism about new opportunities. When that optimism is not rewarded, as is often the case, individuals can slip into periods of depression and deep pessimism about themselves and their employment prospects. If the period of unemployment stretches on, the process of adjustment is eventually completed, with individuals resigning themselves to the realities of their situation (Ashton 1986).

The strength of communities and social ties can be undermined by high levels of unemployment. In a classic sociological study in the 1930s, Marie Jahoda and her colleagues investigated the case of Marienthal, a small town in Austria experiencing mass unemployment after the closure of the local factory (Jahoda et al. 1972). The researchers noted how the long-term experience of unemployment eventually undermined many of the community's social structures and networks. People were less active in civic affairs, spent less time socially with one another and even visited the town library less frequently.

It is important to note that the experience of unemployment also varies by social class. For those at the lower end of the income scale, the consequences of unemployment may be felt mostly financially. It has been suggested that middle-class individuals find unemployment damaging primarily in terms of their social, rather than their financial, status. A forty-five-year-old lecturer who is made redundant may have acquired enough assets to get by comfortably during the initial phases of unemployment, but may struggle to make sense of what unemployment means for their future career and worth as a professional.

Conclusion: the 'corrosion of character'?

Thirty years ago, in a study of blue-collar workers in Boston, USA, the sociologist Richard Sennett drew up a profile of Enrico, an Italian immigrant who spent his working years as a janitor in a downtown office building. Although Enrico did not enjoy the poor conditions and meagre pay, his job provided him with a sense of self-respect and an 'honest' way to provide for his wife and children. He cleaned toilets and mopped floors day in and day out for fifteen years before being able to afford a house in a suburb of the city. Although it was not glamorous, his work was secure, his job was protected by a union and Enrico and his wife could confidently plan their future and that of their children. Enrico knew well in advance exactly when he would retire and how much money he would have at his disposal. As Sennett noted, Enrico's work 'had one single and durable purpose, the service of his family'. Although Enrico was proud of his honest hard work, he did not want the same future for his children. It was important to Enrico that he create the conditions for his children to be upwardly mobile.

As Sennett discovered fifteen years later in a chance meeting with Enrico's son Rico, the children did become more mobile. Rico finished his first degree in engineering before going on to business school in New York. In the fourteen years following his graduation, Rico built up a highly lucrative career and rose to within the top 5 per cent of the wage scale. Rico and his wife Jeanette have moved no fewer than four times during their marriage in order to advance their respective careers. In taking risks and being open to change, Rico and Jeanette have adapted to the turbulent times and have become affluent as a result. Yet, despite their success, the story is not an entirely happy one. Rico and his wife worry that they are close to 'losing control of their lives'. As a consultant, Rico feels a lack of control over time and his work: contracts are vague and always changing, he has no fixed role, and his fate is largely dependent on the fortunes and pitfalls of networking. Jeanette similarly feels that she has only a tenuous hold on her job. She manages a team of accountants who are geographically divided: some work at home, some at the office and some thousands of miles away in a different branch of the company. In managing this 'flexible' team, Jeanette cannot rely on face-to-face interactions and personal knowledge of an individual's work. Instead, she manages from afar, using email and phone calls.

In moving around the country, Rico and Jeanette's meaningful friendships have fallen by the wayside; new neighbours and communities know nothing about their pasts, where they come from or who they are as people. As Sennett writes: 'The fugitive quality of friendship and local community form the background to the most important of Rico's inner worries, his family.' At home Rico and Jeannette find that their work lives interfere with their ability to fulfil their goals as parents. Hours are long and they worry that they neglect their children. But more troublesome than juggling time and schedules, however, is the concern that they are setting a disorienting example. While trying to teach their children the value of hard work, commitment and long-term goals, they fear that their own lives tell a different story. Rico and Jeanette are examples of the short-term, flexible approach to work that is increasingly favoured in contemporary society. Their work histories are characterized by constant movement, temporary commitments and short-term investments in what they are doing. The couple realizes that, in our current runaway society, 'the qualities of good work are not the qualities of good character'.

To Sennett, the experiences of Rico and his wife Jeannette illustrate some of the consequences of the flexible approach to work for employees' personal lives and characters. In his book *The Corrosion of Character* (1998), he argues that the growing emphasis on flexible behaviour and working styles can produce successful results, but inevitably leads also to both confusion and harm. This is because the expectations placed on workers today – to be flexible, adaptable, mobile and willing to take risks – directly contradict many of the core features of strong character: loyalty, pursuit of long-term goals, commitment, trust and purpose.

Sennett suggests that these types of tension are inevitable in the new era of flexibility; although flexibility is praised for giving workers more freedom to shape their individual life trajectories, Sennett argues that it also imposes rigid new constraints. Rather than committing to a life career, workers are now expected to work fluidly in teams, entering and exiting, moving from task to task. Loyalty becomes a liability rather than an asset. When life becomes a series of discrete jobs rather than a coherent career, long-term goals are eroded, social bonds fail to develop and trust is fleeting. People can no longer judge which risks will pay off in the end and the old 'rules' for promotions, dismissals and reward no longer seem to apply. For Sennett, the central challenge for adults in the present era is how to lead a life with long-term goals in a society which emphasizes the short term. In his eyes, features of the 'new capitalism' corrode elements of personal character which bind people together.

Summary points

1 Work is the carrying out of tasks, involving the expenditure of mental and physical effort, which have as their objective the production of goods and services catering for human needs. Many important kinds of work – like housework or voluntary work – are unpaid. An occupation is work which is done in exchange for a regular wage. Work is in all cultures the basis of the economic system.

2 A distinctive characteristic of the economic system of modern societies is the development of a highly complex and diverse division of labour. The division of labour means that work is divided into different occupations requiring specialization. One result is economic interdependence: we are all dependent on each other to maintain our livelihoods.

3 Industrial production was made more efficient with the introduction of Taylorism, or scientific management – the belief that all industrial processes can be divided into simple tasks that can be timed and organized. Fordism extended the principles of scientific management to mass production tied to mass markets. Fordism and Taylorism can be seen as low-trust systems that increase worker alienation. A high-trust system allows workers control over the pace and content of their work.

4 Union organizations, together with recognition of the right to strike, are characteristic features of economic life in all Western countries. Unions emerged as defensive organizations, concerned to provide a measure of control for workers over their conditions of labour. Today, union leaders quite often play an important role in formulating national economic policies.

5   In recent years Fordist practices have been replaced by more flexible operating techniques in many industrialized countries. The term 'post-Fordism' is favoured by some to describe the current period of economic production in which flexibility and innovation are maximized in order to meet market demands for diverse, customized products.

6   Some speak of the 'death of the career' and the arrival of the 'portfolio' worker – the worker who has a portfolio of different skills and will be able to move readily from job to job. Such workers do exist, but for many people in the workforce, 'flexibility' is more likely to be associated with poorly paid jobs with few career prospects.

7   Unemployment is a recurrent problem in the industrialized countries. As work is a structuring element in a person's life, the psychological experience of unemployment is often disorienting.

8   The effects of job insecurity can be as debilitating as the actual experience of being unemployed. Job insecurity is a sense of apprehension an employee feels about the future safety of his or her job and role at the workplace. Job insecurity has risen sharply among the middle classes, although some believe that anxiety over job insecurity is greatly exaggerated.

Questions for further thought

1   Could modern societies operate without a division of labour?

2   Why are some activities deemed to be work and others not?

3   If Taylorism and Fordism were so efficient, why have they recently been in decline?

4   If you were a portfolio worker, would your portfolio be large enough to keep you in work?

5   Why does Rico's life differ so much from that of Enrico?

Further reading

Keith Grint, *The Sociology of Work: An Introduction*, 3rd edn (Cambridge: Polity, 2005).

Keith Grint, *Work and Society: A Reader* (Cambridge: Polity, 2000).

Neil J. Smelser and Richard Swedberg (eds), *The Handbook of Economic Sociology* (Princeton: Princeton University Press, 1994).

P. Thompson and C. Warhurst (eds), *Workplaces of the Future* (Houndmills, Basingstoke: Macmillan Business, 1998).

Internet links

International Labour Organization
http://www.ilo.org

The Work Foundation
http://theworkfoundation.com/

SOSIG Sociology of Work
http://www.sosig.ac.uk/roads/subject-listing/world-cat/sociowork.html

University of Zurich Sociology of Works Links
http://socio.ch/arbeit/index_arbeit.htm

Contents

19 Crime and Deviance

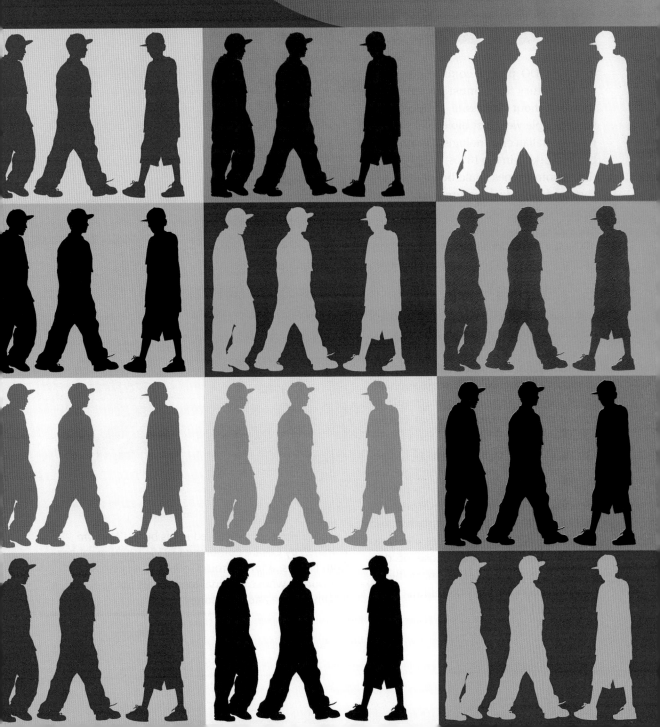

WHY DO people commit crimes? A century ago, most people who thought about the issue believed that some people were just biologically criminal. The Italian criminologist Cesare Lombroso, working in the 1870s, even believed that criminal types could be identified by certain anatomical features. He investigated the appearance and physical characteristics of criminals, such as the shape of the skull and forehead, jaw size and arm length, and concluded that they displayed traits held over from earlier stages of human evolution. Lombroso's pictures showing the physical characteristics of criminals are shown here.

Lombroso's ideas became thoroughly discredited, and seem almost comical to us today, although slightly more sophisticated variants on his biological explanation of crime have resurfaced at various points over the last century. A later theory distinguished three main types of human physique and claimed that one type was directly associated with delinquency. Muscular, active types (mesomorphs), the theory went, are more aggressive and physical, and therefore more likely to become delinquent than those of thin physique (ectomorphs) or more fleshy people (endomorphs) (Sheldon 1949; Glueck and Glueck 1956).

Again, such views have also been widely criticized. Even if there were an overall relationship between bodily type and delinquency, this would show nothing about the influence of heredity. People of the muscular type may be drawn towards

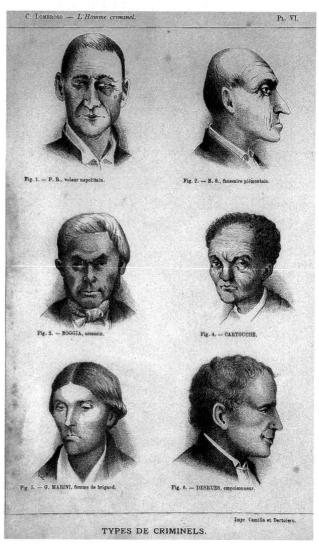

Criminal types, as presented in his book *L'Homme criminel*, by Cesare Lombroso (1836–1909): a robber from Naples, a forger from Piedmont, an assassin, Cartouche, whose criminal tendency is not specified, a brigand's wife and a poisoner.

criminal activities because these offer opportunities for the physical display of athleticism. Moreover, nearly all studies in this field have been restricted to delinquents in reform schools, and it may be that the tougher, athletic-looking delinquents are more liable to be sent to such schools than fragile-looking, skinny ones. Some individuals might be inclined towards irritability and aggressiveness, and this could be reflected in crimes of physical assault on others. Yet there is no decisive evidence that any traits of personality are inherited in this way, and, even if they were, their connection to criminality would at most be only a distant one.

If biological approaches to criminology do not satisfactorily answer our question: 'Why do people commit crimes?' is psychology more successful? Psychological approaches to criminality have searched for explanations of deviance within the individual, not society. But where biological approaches focus on physical features which predispose individuals to crime, psychological views concentrate on personality types. Much early criminological research was carried out in prisons and other institutions, such as asylums. In these settings, ideas about psychiatry were influential. Emphasis was placed on the distinctive traits of criminals – including 'feeble-mindedness' and 'moral degeneracy'. Hans Eysenck (1964), for example, has suggested that abnormal mental states are inherited; these can either predispose an individual to crime or create problems in the process of socialization.

Some have suggested that in a minority of individuals, an amoral, or psychopathic, personality develops. Psychopaths are withdrawn, emotionless characters who act impulsively and rarely experience sensations of guilt. Some psychopaths delight in violence for its own sake. Individuals with psychopathic traits do sometimes commit violent crimes, but there are major problems with the concept of the psychopath. It isn't at all clear that psychopathic traits are inevitably criminal. Nearly all studies of people said to possess these characteristics have been of convicted prisoners, and their personalities inevitably tend to be presented negatively. If we describe the same traits positively, the personality type sounds quite different, and there seems no reason why people of this sort should be inherently criminal.

Psychological theories of criminality can at best explain only some aspects of crime. While some criminals may possess personality characteristics distinct from the remainder of the population, it is highly improbable that the majority of criminals do so. There are all kinds of crime, and it is implausible to suppose that those who commit them share some specific psychological characteristics.

Both biological and psychological approaches to criminality presume that deviance is a sign of something 'wrong' with the individual, rather than with society. They see crime as caused by factors outside an individual's control, embedded either in the body or the mind. Therefore, if scientific criminology could successfully identify the causes of crime, it would be possible to treat those causes. In this respect, both biological and psychological theories of crime are *positivist* in nature. As we learned in our discussion of Auguste Comte in chapter 1, positivism is the belief that applying natural scientific methods to the study of the social world can reveal its basic truths. In the case of positivist criminology, this led to the belief that empirical research could pinpoint the causes of crime and in turn make recommendations about how to eradicate it.

Early positivist criminology came under great criticism from later generations of scholars. They argued that any satisfactory account of the nature of crime must be sociological, for what crime is depends on the social institutions of a society. Over time, attention shifted away from individualistic explanations of crime, of the kind we have looked at above, to sociological theories that stress the social and cultural context in which crime and deviance takes place. Any full answer to our question: 'Why do people commit crimes?' must be sociological, and it is most likely to start by questioning the terms implicit in the question. What do we mean by crime and deviance?

In this chapter we look at several sociological explanations for crime and deviant behaviour. First, however, we look more closely at what we mean by terms such as 'deviance' and 'crime'. Later in the chapter we examine crime in the UK, before turning to some of the important issues concerning the victims and perpetrators of crime.

Basic concepts

Deviance may be defined as non-conformity to a given set of norms that are accepted by a significant number of people in a community or society. No society, as has already been stressed, can be divided up in a simple way between those who deviate from norms and those who conform to them. Most of us on some occasions transgress generally accepted rules of behaviour. We may, for example, have at some point committed minor acts of theft, like shoplifting or taking small items from work – such as office notepaper and pens – for personal use. At some point in our lives, we may have exceeded the speed limit, made prank phone calls or smoked marijuana.

Deviance and crime are not synonymous, although in many cases they overlap. The concept of deviance is much broader than that of crime, which refers only to non-conformist conduct that breaks a law. Many forms of deviant behaviour are not sanctioned by law. Thus, studies of deviance might examine phenomena as diverse as naturalists (nudists), rave culture and New Age travellers.

The concept of deviance can be applied both to individual behaviour and to the activity of groups. An illustration is the Hare Krishna cult, a religious group whose beliefs and mode of life are different from those of the majority of people in Britain. The cult was first established in the 1960s when Sril Prabhupada came to the West from India to spread the word of Krishna consciousness. He aimed his message particularly at young people who were drug users, proclaiming that one could 'stay high all the time, discover eternal bliss' by following his teachings. The Hare Krishnas became a familiar sight, dancing and chanting in the streets, running vegetarian cafés and distributing literature about their beliefs to passers-by. They are generally regarded in a tolerant light by most of the population, even if their views seem somewhat eccentric.

Hare Krishna devotees dancing and singing in the streets of London.

The Hare Krishnas represent an example of a **deviant subculture**. Although their membership today has declined from its peak some years ago, they have been able to survive fairly easily within the wider society. The organization is wealthy, financed by donations from members and sympathizers. Their position diverges from that of another deviant subculture, which might be mentioned here by way of contrast: that of the permanently homeless. People who are down-and-out live on the streets by day, spending their time in parks or in public buildings. They may sleep outside or find refuge in shelters. Most of the permanently homeless eke out a difficult existence on the fringes of the wider society.

Two distinct, but related disciplines are engaged in the study of crime and deviance. **Criminology** concerns itself with forms of behaviour that are sanctioned by criminal law. Criminologists are often interested in techniques for measuring crime, trends in crime rates and policies aimed at reducing crime within communities. The **sociology of deviance** draws on criminological research, but also investigates conduct which lies beyond the realm of criminal law. Sociologists studying deviant behaviour seek to understand why certain behaviours are widely regarded as deviant and how these notions of deviance are applied differentially to people within society.

The study of deviance, therefore, directs

our attention to social *power*, as well as to the influence of social class – the divisions between rich and poor. When we look at deviance from or conformity to social rules or norms, we always have to bear in mind the question, *whose* rules? As we shall see, social norms are strongly influenced by divisions of power and class.

Explaining crime and deviance: sociological theories

In contrast to some areas of sociology in which a particular theoretical perspective has emerged over time as pre-eminent, many theoretical strands remain relevant to the study of deviance. Having looked briefly at biological and psychological explanations, we will now turn to the four sociological approaches that have been influential within the sociology of deviance: *functionalist theories, interactionist theories, conflict theories* and *control theories*.

Functionalist theories

Functionalist theories see crime and deviance resulting from structural tensions and a lack of moral regulation within society. If the aspirations held by individuals and groups in society do not coincide with available rewards, this disparity between desires and fulfilment will be felt in the deviant motivations of some of its members.

Crime and anomie: Durkheim and Merton

As we saw in chapter 1, the notion of *anomie* was first introduced by Emile

---

Norms and sanctions

We follow social norms mostly because, as a result of socialization, we are used to doing so. All social norms are accompanied by sanctions that promote conformity and protect against non-conformity. A sanction is any reaction from others to the behaviour of an individual or group that is meant to ensure compliance with a given norm. Sanctions may be positive (the offering of rewards for conformity) or negative (punishment for behaviour that does not conform). Sanctions can be levied formally or informally. Formal sanctions are applied by a specific body of people or an agency to ensure that a particular set of norms is followed. The main types of formal sanction in modern societies are those represented by the courts and prisons. A law is a formal sanction defined by government as a rule or principle that its citizens must follow; it is used against people who do not conform.

Informal sanctions are less organized and more spontaneous reactions to non-conformity. A studious pupil who is teased by classmates for working too hard, or who is accused of being a 'nerd' when he or she refuses to go out in the evenings, experiences a type of informal sanctioning. Informal sanctioning might also occur, for example, when an individual who makes a sexist or racist comment is met with disapproving responses from friends or co-workers.

Durkheim, who suggested that in modern societies traditional norms and standards become undermined without being replaced by new ones. Anomie exists when there are no clear standards to guide behaviour in a given area of social life. Under such circumstances, Durkheim believed, people feel disoriented and anxious; anomie is therefore one of the social factors influencing dispositions to suicide.

Durkheim saw crime and deviance as social facts; he believed both of them to be inevitable and necessary elements in modern societies. According to Durkheim, people in the modern age are less constrained than they were in traditional societies. Because there is more room for individual choice in the modern world, it is inevitable that there will be some nonconformity. Durkheim recognized that there would never be a complete consensus in any society about the norms and values which govern it.

Deviance is also necessary for society, according to Durkheim; it fulfils two important functions. First, deviance has an *adaptive* function. By introducing new ideas and challenges into society, deviance is an innovative force. It brings about change. Second, deviance promotes boundary *maintenance* between 'good' and 'bad' behaviours in society. A criminal event can provoke a collective response that heightens group solidarity and clarifies social norms. For example, residents of a neighbourhood facing a problem with drug dealers might join together in the aftermath of a drug-related shooting and commit themselves to maintaining the area as a drug-free zone.

Durkheim's ideas on crime and deviance were influential in shifting attention from individual explanations to social forces. His notion of anomie was drawn on by the American sociologist Robert K. Merton, who constructed a highly influential theory of deviance that located the source of crime within the very structure of American society (Merton 1957).

Merton modified the concept of anomie to refer to the *strain* put on individuals' behaviour when accepted norms conflict with social reality. In American society – and to some degree in other industrial societies – generally held values emphasize material success, and the means of achieving success are supposed to be self-discipline and hard work. Accordingly,

people who really work hard can succeed, no matter what their starting point in life. This idea is not in fact valid, because most of the disadvantaged are given only limited conventional opportunities for advancement, or none at all. Yet those who do not 'succeed' find themselves condemned for their apparent inability to make material progress. In this situation, there is great pressure to try to get ahead by any means, legitimate or illegitimate. According to Merton, then, deviance is a by-product of economic inequalities and the lack of equal opportunities.

Merton identifies five possible reactions to the tensions between socially endorsed values and the limited means of achieving them. *Conformists* accept both generally held values and the conventional means of realizing them, whether or not they meet with success. The majority of the population fall into this category. *Innovators* continue to accept socially approved values but use illegitimate or illegal means to follow them. Criminals who acquire wealth through illegal activities exemplify this type.

Ritualists conform to socially accepted standards, although they have lost sight of the values behind these standards. The rules are followed for their own sake without a wider end in view, in a compulsive way. A ritualist would be someone who dedicates herself to a boring job, even though it has no career prospects and provides few rewards. *Retreatists* have abandoned the competitive outlook altogether, thus rejecting both the dominant values and the approved means of achieving them. An example would be the members of a self-supporting commune. Finally, *rebels* reject both the existing values and the means but wish actively to substitute new ones and reconstruct the social system. The members of radical political groups fall into this category.

Merton's writings addressed one of the main puzzles in the study of criminology: at a time when society as a whole is becoming more affluent, why do crime rates continue to rise? By emphasizing the contrast between rising aspirations and persistent inequalities, Merton points to a sense of *relative deprivation* as an important element in deviant behaviour.

> The idea of relative deprivation was discussed in chapter 10, 'Poverty, Social Exclusion and Welfare', pp. 341–3.

Subcultural explanations

Later researchers located deviance in terms of subcultural groups that adopt norms that encourage or reward criminal behaviour. Like Merton, Albert Cohen saw the contradictions within American society as the main cause of crime. But while Merton emphasized individual deviant responses to the tension between values and means, Cohen saw the responses occurring collectively through subcultures. In *Delinquent Boys* (1955), Cohen argued that boys in the lower working class who are frustrated with their positions in life often join together in delinquent subcultures, such as gangs. These subcultures reject middle-class values and replace them with norms that celebrate defiance, such as delinquency and other acts of non-conformity.

Richard A. Cloward and Lloyd E. Ohlin (1960) agreed with Cohen that most delinquent youths emerge from the lower working class. But they argue that the boys most at 'risk' are those who have nevertheless internalized middle-class values and

have been encouraged, on the basis of their ability, to aspire towards a middle-class future. When such boys are unable to realize their goals, they are particularly prone to delinquent activity. In their study of boys' gangs, Cloward and Ohlin found that delinquent gangs arise in subcultural communities where the chances of achieving success legitimately are small, such as among deprived ethnic minorities.

Defining deviance

Many people take it for granted that a well-structured society is designed to prevent deviant behavior from occurring. But, as we have seen, functionalists following Emile Durkheim argued otherwise. Durkheim believed that deviance has an important part to play in a well-ordered society. He argued that by defining what is deviant, we become aware of what is not deviant and thereby become aware of the standards we share as members of a society. It is not necessarily the case, then, that we should aim to eliminate deviance completely. It is more likely that society needs to keep it within acceptable limits.

Seventy years after Durkheim's work appeared, the sociologist Kai Erikson published *Wayward Puritans*, a study of deviance in New England in the United States during the seventeenth century. Erikson sought 'to test [Durkheim's] notion that the number of deviant offenders a community can afford to recognize is likely to remain stable over time'. His research led him to conclude that:

> a community's capacity for handling deviance, let us say, can be roughly estimated by counting its prison cells and hospital beds, its policemen and psychiatrists, its courts and clinics. . . . The agencies of control

often seem to define their job as that of keeping deviance within bounds rather than obliterating it altogether. (1966)

Erikson advanced the hypothesis that societies need their quotas of deviance and that they function in such a way as to keep them intact.

What does a society do when the amount of deviant behaviour gets out of hand? In 'Defining Deviance Down', a controversial article written in 1993, ten years before his death, the American academic and politician Daniel Patrick Moynihan argued that the levels of deviance in US society had increased beyond the point that it could afford to recognize. As a result, we have been 'redefining deviance so as to exempt much conduct previously stigmatised', and also quietly raising the 'normal' level so that behaviour seen as abnormal by an earlier standard is no longer considered to be so.

How has American society gone about this? One example that Moynihan gave was the deinstitutionalization movement within the mental health profession that began in the 1950s. Instead of being forced into institutions, the mentally ill were treated with tranquillizers and released. As a result, the number of psychiatric patients in New York dropped from 93,000 in 1955 to 11,000 by 1992.

What happened to all of those psychiatric patients? Many of them became the homeless people who we see sleeping rough in New York. In 'defining deviance down', people sleeping on the street are defined not as insane, but as persons lacking affordable housing. At the same time, the 'normal' acceptable level of crime has risen. Moynihan points out that after the St Valentine's Day massacre in 1929, in which seven gangsters were mur-

dered, America was outraged. Today, violent gang murders are so common that there is hardly a reaction. Moynihan also sees the under-reporting of crime as another form of 'normalizing' it. As he concludes: 'We are getting used to a lot of behaviour that is not good for us.'

Evaluation

Functionalist theories rightly emphasize connections between conformity and deviance in different social contexts. Lack of opportunity for success in the terms of the wider society is the main differentiating factor between those who engage in criminal behaviour and those who do not. We should be cautious, however, about the idea that people in poorer communities aspire to the same level of success as more affluent people. Most tend to adjust their aspirations to what they see as the reality of their situation. Merton, Cohen and Cloward and Ohlin can all be criticized for presuming that middle-class values have been accepted throughout society. It would also be wrong to suppose that a mismatch of aspirations and opportunities is confined to the less privileged. There are pressures towards criminal activity among other groups too, as indicated by the so-called white-collar crimes of embezzlement, fraud and tax evasion, which we will study later.

Interactionist theory

Sociologists studying crime and deviance in the interactionist tradition focus on deviance as a socially constructed phenomenon. They reject the idea that there are types of conduct that are inherently 'deviant'. Rather, interactionists ask how behaviours initially come to be defined as deviant and why certain groups and not others are labelled as deviant.

Labelling theory

One of the most important approaches to the understanding of criminality is called **labelling theory**. Labelling theorists interpret deviance not as a set of characteristics of individuals or groups, but as a process of interaction between deviants and non-deviants. In their view, we must discover why some people come to be tagged with a 'deviant' label in order to understand the nature of deviance itself.

People who represent the forces of law and order, or are able to impose definitions of conventional morality on others, do most of the labelling. The labels that create categories of deviance thus express the power structure of society. By and large, the rules in terms of which deviance is defined are framed by the wealthy for the poor, by men for women, by older people for younger people, and by ethnic majorities for minority groups. For example, many children wander into other people's gardens, steal fruit or play truant. In an affluent neighbourhood, these might be regarded by parents, teachers and police alike as innocent pastimes of childhood. In poor areas, they might be seen as evidence of tendencies towards juvenile delinquency. Once a child is labelled a delinquent, he or she is stigmatized as a criminal and is likely to be considered untrustworthy by teachers and prospective employers. In both instances the acts are the same, but they are assigned different meanings.

Howard Becker is one of the sociologists most closely associated with labelling theory. He was concerned to show how deviant identities are produced through labelling rather than through deviant motivations or behaviours. According to Becker, 'deviant behaviour is behaviour that people so label'. He was highly critical of criminological approaches which claimed a clear division between 'normal' and 'deviant'. For Becker, deviant behaviour is not the determining factor in becoming 'deviant'. Rather there are processes unrelated to the behaviour itself which exercise a great influence on whether or not a person is labelled as deviant. A person's dress, manner of speaking, or country of origin could be the key factors that determine whether or not the deviant label is applied.

Labelling theory came to be associated with Becker's studies of marijuana smokers (Becker 1963). In the early 1960s, smoking marijuana was a marginal activity within subcultures rather than the lifestyle choice it is today. Becker found that becoming a marijuana smoker depended on one's acceptance into the subculture, close association with experienced users and one's attitudes towards non-users.

Labelling not only affects how others see an individual, but also influences the individual's sense of self. Edwin Lemert (1972) advanced a model for understanding how deviance can either coexist with or become central to one's identity. Lemert argued that, contrary to what we might think, deviance is actually quite commonplace and people usually get away with it. For example, some deviant acts, such as traffic violations, rarely come to light, while others, such as small-scale theft from the workplace, are often 'overlooked'. Lemert called the initial act of transgression **primary deviance**. In most cases, these acts remain 'marginal' to the person's self-identity – a process occurs by

Is this unconventional dresser more likely to be labelled 'deviant' than the bungee jumper?

which the deviant act is *normalized*. In some cases, however, normalization does not occur and the person is labelled as a criminal or delinquent. Lemert used the term **secondary deviance** to describe cases where individuals come to accept the label and see themselves as deviant. In such instances, the label can become central to a person's identity and lead to a continuation or intensification of the deviant behaviour.

Take, for example, Luke, who smashes a shop window while spending a Saturday night out on the town with his friends. The act may perhaps be called the accidental result of over-boisterous behaviour, an excusable characteristic of young men. Luke might escape with a reprimand and a small fine. If he is from a 'respectable' background, this is a likely outcome. And the smashing of the window stays at the level of primary deviance if the youth is seen as someone of good character who on this occasion became too rowdy. If, on the other hand, the police and courts hand out a suspended sentence and make Luke report to a social worker, the incident could become the first step on the road to secondary deviance. The process of 'learning to be deviant' tends to be accentuated by the very organizations supposedly set up to correct deviant behaviour – prisons and social agencies. (Lemert's studies on 'The Saints and the Roughnecks' are discussed further in the box on p. 810)

Evaluation

Labelling theory is important because it begins from the assumption that no act is intrinsically criminal. Definitions of criminality are established by the powerful, through the formulation of laws and their interpretation by police, courts and correctional institutions. Critics of labelling theory have sometimes argued that there are certain acts that are consistently prohibited across virtually all cultures, such as murder, rape and robbery. This view is surely incorrect; in Britain, for instance, killing is not always regarded as murder. In times of war, killing of the enemy is positively approved; until recently, the laws in Britain did not recognize sexual intercourse forced on a woman by her husband as rape, which also shows that labelling changes over time.

We can criticize labelling theory even more convincingly on other grounds. First, in emphasizing the active process of labelling, labelling theorists neglect the processes that lead to acts defined as deviant. For labelling certain activities as deviant is not completely arbitrary; differences in socialization, attitudes and opportunities influence how far people engage in behaviour likely to be labelled deviant. For instance, children from deprived backgrounds are more likely than richer children to steal from shops. It is not the labelling that leads them to steal in the first place so much as the background from which they come.

Second, it is not clear whether labelling actually does have the effect of increasing deviant conduct. Delinquent behaviour tends to increase following a conviction, but is this the result of the labelling itself? Other factors, such as increased interaction with other delinquents or learning about new criminal opportunities, may be involved.

Deviancy amplification

Leslie Wilkins (1964) was interested in the ramifications of 'managing' a deviant identity and integrating it into one's daily life. He suggested that the outcome of this process is often **deviancy amplification**. This refers to the unintended consequences that can result when, by labelling a behaviour as deviant, an agency of control actually provokes more of that same deviant behaviour. If the labelled person incorporates the label into his or her identity through secondary deviance, this is likely to provoke more responses from agencies of control. In other words, the very behaviour that was seen as undesirable becomes more prevalent, and those labelled as deviant become even more resistant to change.

The broad effects of deviancy amplification have been illustrated in an important work by Stanley Cohen called *Folk Devils and Moral Panics* (1980). In this classic study, Cohen examined how police attempts to control certain youth subcultures in the UK during the 1960s – the so-called Mods and Rockers – only succeeded in drawing additional attention to them and making them more popular among youth. The process of labelling a group as outsiders and troublemakers – in an attempt to control them – backfired and created even larger problems for law enforcement. Excessive and sensationalistic media coverage of the Mods and Rockers led to a **moral panic** – a term used by sociologists to describe a media-inspired over-reaction towards a certain group or type of behaviour. Moral panics often emerge around public issues that are taken as symptomatic of general social disorder; moral panics have arisen in recent years over topics such as youth crime and 'bogus' asylum-seekers.

Conflict theories: 'the new criminology'

The publication of *The New Criminology* by Taylor, Walton and Young in 1973 marked an important break with earlier theories of deviance. Its authors drew on elements of Marxist thought to argue that deviance is deliberately chosen and often political in nature. They rejected the idea that deviance is 'determined' by factors such as biology, personality, anomie, social disorganization or labels. Rather, they argued, individuals actively choose to engage in deviant behaviour in response to the inequalities of the capitalist system. Thus, members of countercultural groups regarded as 'deviant' – such as supporters of the Black Power or gay liberation movements – were engaging in distinctly political acts which challenged the social order. Theorists of **new criminology** framed their analysis of crime and deviance in terms of the structure of society and the preservation of power among the ruling class.

The broad perspective set forth in *The New Criminology* was developed in specific directions by other scholars. Stuart Hall and others at the Birmingham Centre for Contemporary Cultural Studies conducted an important study on a phenomenon which attracted enormous attention in the early 1970s in Britain – the crime of 'mugging'. Several high-profile muggings were broadly publicized and fuelled widespread popular concern about an explosion in street crime. Muggers were overwhelming portrayed as black, contributing to the view that immigrants were primarily responsible for the breakdown of society. In *Policing the Crisis* (1978), Hall and his colleagues argued that the moral panic about muggings was encouraged by both the state and the media as a way of deflecting attention away from growing unemployment, declining wages and other deep structural flaws within society.

Around the same time, other criminologists examined the formation and use of laws in society and argued that laws are tools used by the powerful to maintain their own privileged positions. They rejected the idea that laws are 'neutral' and are applied evenly across the population. Instead, they claimed that as inequalities increase between the ruling class and the working class, law becomes an ever more important instrument for the powerful to maintain order. This dynamic can be seen in the workings of the criminal justice system, which had become increasingly oppressive towards working-class 'offenders'; or in tax legislation which disproportionately favoured the wealthy. This power imbalance is not restricted to the creation of laws, however. The powerful also break laws, scholars have argued, but are rarely caught. These crimes on the whole are much more significant than the everyday crime and delinquency which attracts the most attention. But fearful of the implications of pursuing 'white-collar' criminals, law enforcement instead focuses its efforts on less powerful members of society, such as prostitutes, drug users and petty thieves (Pearce 1976; Chambliss 1978).

These studies and others associated with 'new criminology' were important in widening the debate about crime and deviance to include questions of social justice, power and politics. They emphasized that crime occurs at all levels of society and must be understood in the context of inequalities and competing interests between social groups.

Left Realism

In the 1980s, a new strain of criminology emerged. Known as New Left or **Left Realism**, it drew on some of the neo-Marxist ideas of the new criminologists discussed above, but distanced itself from 'left idealists' whom they saw as romanticizing deviance and downplaying the real fear of crime felt by much of the population. For a long while, many criminologists tended to minimize the importance of rises in official crime rates. They sought to show that the media created unnecessary public disquiet about the issue, or argued that most crime was a disguised form of protest against inequality. Left Realism moved away from this position, emphasizing that the increases in crime had actually occurred, and that the public was right to be worried by them. Left Realists argued that criminology needed to engage more with the actual issues of crime control and social policy, rather than debate them abstractly (Lea and Young 1984; Matthews and Young 1986).

Left Realism drew attention to the victims of crime and argued that victim surveys provide a more valid picture of the extent of crime than official statistics (Evans 1992). Such surveys revealed that crime was a serious problem, particularly in impoverished inner-city areas. Left Realists pointed out that rates of crime and victimization were concentrated in marginalized neighbourhoods – deprived groups in society were at a much greater risk of crime than others. The approach draws on Merton and Cloward and Ohlin and others to suggest that, in the inner cities, criminal subcultures develop. Such subcultures do not derive from poverty as such, but from their exclusion from the wider community. Criminalized youth groups, for example, operate at the margins of 'respectable society' and pit themselves against it. The fact that rates of crime carried out by blacks have risen over recent years is attributed to the fact that policies of racial integration have failed.

The ideas of relative deprivation and social exclusion, discussed in chapter 10, provide some of the important theoretical underpinning Left Realism.

To address these trends in crime, Left Realism advanced 'realistic' proposals for changes in policing procedures. Law enforcement needs to become more responsive to communities, it is claimed, rather than relying on 'military policing' techniques which alienate public support. Left Realists have proposed 'minimal policing' whereby locally elected police authorities would be accountable to citizens, who would have a larger say in setting the policing priorities for their area. Furthermore, by spending more time investigating and clearing up crimes, and less time on routine or administrative work, the police can regain the trust of local communities. On the whole, Left Realism represents a more pragmatic and policy-oriented approach than many of the criminological perspectives which preceded it.

Critics of Left Realism accept the importance of the stress on victimization. But they argue that Left Realism focused on individual victims only within the narrow confines of the political and media-driven discussions of the 'crime problem'. These narrow definitions of crime focus on the most visible forms of criminality, such as

Left Realists accept that the way crime is constructed may be the product of unequal power relations in society, but emphasize its very real and harmful effects, often for the very poorest people and communities.

street crimes, whilst neglecting other offences, such as those carried out by the state or corporations (Walton and Young 1998).

Control theories

Control theory posits that crime occurs as a result of an imbalance between impulses towards criminal activity and the social or physical controls that deter it. It is less interested in individuals' motivations for carrying out crimes; rather, it is assumed that people act rationally and that, given the opportunity, everyone would engage in deviant acts. Many types of crime, it is argued, are a result of 'situational decisions' – a person sees an opportunity and is motivated to act.

One of the most well-known control theorists, Travis Hirschi, has argued that humans are fundamentally selfish beings who make calculated decisions about whether or not to engage in criminal activity by weighing the potential benefits and risks of doing so. In *Causes of Delinquency* (1969), Hirschi claimed that there are four types of bond which link people to society and law-abiding behaviour: attachment, commitment, involvement and belief. When sufficiently strong, these elements help to maintain social control and conformity by rendering people unfree to break rules. If these bonds with society are weak, however, delinquency and deviance may result. Hirschi's approach suggests that delinquents are often individuals whose low levels of self-control are a result of inadequate socialization at home or at school (Gottfredson and Hirschi 1990).

Right Realism

The rise to power of Margaret Thatcher in Britain and Ronald Reagan in the United States in the late 1970s led to vigorous 'law-and-order' approaches to crime in both countries, often described as **Right**

Realism. This approach to the study of crime is still influential, particularly in the USA under the Presidency of George Bush Junior. The perceived escalation of crime and delinquency were linked to moral degeneracy, the decline of individual responsibility derived from dependence on the welfare state and permissive education, the collapse of the family and communities and the wider erosion of traditional values (Wilson 1975). Public debates and extensive media coverage centred on the crisis of violence and lawlessness which was threatening to grip society.

To Right Realists, deviance was portrayed as an individual pathology – a set of destructive lawless behaviours actively chosen and perpetrated by individual selfishness, a lack of self-control and morality. They were dismissive of the 'theoretical' approaches to the study of crime discussed elsewhere in this chapter, especially those that linked crime to poverty. Conservative governments in the UK and USA, influenced by Right Realism, began to intensify law enforcement activities. Police powers were extended, funding for the criminal justice system was expanded, and long prison sentences were increasingly relied on as the most effective deterrent against crime.

'Situational' crime prevention – such as target hardening and surveillance systems – has been a popular approach to 'managing' the risk of crime (Vold et al. 2002). Such techniques are often favoured by policy-makers because they are relatively simple to introduce alongside existing policing techniques, and they reassure citizens by giving the impression that decisive action against crime is being taken. Yet critics argue that because such techniques do not engage with the underlying causes of crime – such as social inequalities, unemployment and poverty – their greatest success lies in protecting certain segments of the population against crime and displacing delinquency into other realms.

One illustration of this dynamic can be seen in the physical exclusion of certain categories of people from common spaces in an attempt to reduce crime and the perceived risk of crime. In response to feelings of insecurity among the population at large, public spaces in society – such as libraries, parks and even street corners – are increasingly being transformed into 'security bubbles'. Risk-management practices, such as police monitoring, private security teams and surveillance systems, are aimed at protecting the public against potential risks. In shopping precincts, for example, security measures are becoming more prominent as part of a 'contractual bargain' between businesses and consumers. In order to attract and maintain a customer base, businesses must ensure the safety and comfort of their clients. Young people tend to be excluded from such spaces disproportionately because they are perceived as a greater threat to security and are statistically more likely to offend than adults. As part of creating 'locations of trust' for consumers, young people find that the public spaces open to them are shrinking.

Police forces have also been expanded in response to growing crime. When crime rates are on the rise, there is almost inevitably public clamour for putting more police 'on the street'. Governments eager to appear decisive on crime tend to favour increasing the number and resources of the police in an attempt to deter crime.

The popularly held view of policing is that it is the cornerstone of maintaining law and order. But what is the role of the police in actually controlling crime? It is not clear that a greater number of police necessarily translates into lower crime rates. In the United Kingdom, official statistics on the crime rate and number of police cast doubt on the link between the two. This raises several puzzling questions. If increased policing does not prevent offending, why do the public demand a visible police presence? What role does policing play in our society?

Controlling crime

Some control theorists see the growth of crime as an outcome of the increasing number of opportunities and targets for crime in modern society. As the population grows more affluent and consumerism becomes more central to people's lives, goods such as televisions, video equipment, computers, cars and designer clothing – favourite targets for thieves – are owned by more and more people. Residential homes are increasingly left empty during the daytime as more and more women take on employment outside the home. 'Motivated offenders' interested in committing crimes can select from a broad range of 'suitable targets'.

Responding to such shifts, many official approaches to crime prevention in recent years have focused on limiting the opportunities for crime to occur. Central to such policies is the idea of **target hardening** – making it more difficult for crimes to take place by intervening directly into potential 'crime situations'. For example, laws requiring steering locks in all new cars are intended to reduce opportunities for car thieves. In some areas, public telephones have been fitted with tougher coin boxes to deter opportunistic vandals. The installation of closed circuit television (CCTV) systems in city centres and public spaces is another attempt to deter criminal activity. Control theorists argue that, rather than changing the criminal, the best policy is to take practical measures to control the criminal's ability to commit crime.

Target hardening techniques, combined with **zero tolerance policing**, have gained favour among politicians in recent years and appear to have been successful in some contexts in curtailing crime. Zero tolerance policing targets petty crime and forms of disruptive conduct, such as vandalism, loitering, accosting people for money and public drunkenness. Police crackdowns on low-level deviance are thought to produce a positive effect in reducing more serious forms of crime (as we see below in the discussion of the 'broken windows' theory). But criticisms of such an approach can also be made. Target hardening and zero tolerance policing do not address the underlying causes of crime, but are aimed at protecting and defending certain elements of society from its reach. The growing popularity of private security services, car alarms, house alarms, guard dogs and gated communities has led some people to believe that we are living in an 'armoured society', where segments of the population feel compelled to defend themselves against others. This tendency is occurring not only in Britain and the United States as the gap between the wealthiest and the most deprived widens, but is particularly marked in countries such as the former Soviet Union, South Africa and Brazil, where a 'fortress mentality' has emerged among the privileged.

There is another unintended consequence of such policies: as popular crime targets are 'hardened', patterns of crime may simply shift from one domain to another. For example, the steering locks that were made compulsory for all new cars in the UK were not required on older cars. The result was that car thefts shifted primarily from newer models to older ones. Target hardening and zero tolerance approaches run the risk of displacing criminal offences from better protected areas into more vulnerable ones. Neighbourhoods that are poor or lacking in social cohesion may well experience a growth in crime and delinquency as affluent regions increase their defences.

The theory of 'broken windows'

Target hardening and zero tolerance policing are based on a theory known as 'broken windows' (Wilson and Kelling 1982). The theory is based on a study made in the 1960s by the American social psychologist Philip Zimbardo, who abandoned cars without licence plates and with their hoods up in two entirely different social settings: the wealthy community of Palo Alto, California, and a poor neighbourhood in the Bronx, New York. In both places, as soon as passers-by, regardless of class or race, sensed that the cars were abandoned and that 'no one cared', the cars were vandalized (Zimbardo 1969).

Physical signs of social disorder can lead to more serious crime, according to the 'broken windows' thesis.

Extrapolating from this study, the authors of the 'broken windows' theory argued that any sign of social disorder in a community, even the appearance of a broken window, encourages more serious crime to flourish. One unrepaired broken window is a sign that no one cares, so breaking more windows – that is, committing more serious crimes – is a rational response by criminals to this situation of social disorder. As a result, minor acts of deviance can lead to a spiral of crime and social decay (Felson 1994).

Since the late 1980s, the 'broken windows' theory has served as the basis for new policing strategies that aggressively focused on 'minor' crimes such as drinking or using drugs in public, and traffic violations. Zero tolerance policing has been widely introduced in large American cities, following its success in reducing crime in New York City, when it was pioneered by Mayor Rudolph Giuliani during his term in office between 1994 and 2001. Starting with an aggressive campaign to restore order in the city subway (underground), the New York Police Department expanded its zero tolerance approach to the streets, tightening restrictions on beggars, the homeless, street vendors and the owners of adult bookshops and clubs. Not only did rates for standard crimes (such as muggings and theft) decline dramatically, but the homicide rate fell to its lowest level in almost a century.

One important flaw of the 'broken windows' theory is that the police are left to identify 'social disorder' however they want. Without a systematic definition of disorder, the police are authorized to see almost anything as a sign of disorder and anyone as a threat. In fact, as crime rates fell throughout the 1990s, the number of complaints of police abuse and harassment went up, particularly by young, urban, black men who fit the 'profile' of a potential criminal.

Theoretical conclusions

What should we conclude from this survey of theories of crime? We must first recall a point made earlier: even though crime is only one subcategory of deviant behaviour as a whole, it covers such a variety of forms of activity – from shoplifting a bar of chocolate to mass murder – that it is unlikely that we could produce a single theory that would account for all forms of criminal conduct.

The contributions of the sociological theories of crime are twofold. First, these theories correctly emphasize the continuities between criminal and 'respectable' behaviour. The contexts in which particular types of activity are seen as criminal and punishable by law vary widely. This is almost certainly linked to questions of power and inequality within society. Second, all agree that context is important in criminal activities. Whether someone engages in a criminal act or comes to be regarded as a criminal is influenced fundamentally by social learning and social surroundings.

In spite of its deficiencies, labelling theory is perhaps the most widely used approach to understanding crime and deviant behaviour. This theory sensitizes us to the ways in which some activities come to be defined as punishable in law, and the power relations that form such definitions, as well as to the circumstances in which particular individuals fall foul of the law.

The way in which crime is understood directly affects the policies developed to combat it. For example, if crime is seen as the product of deprivation or social disorganization, policies might be aimed at reducing poverty and strengthening social services. If criminality is seen as voluntaristic, or freely chosen by individuals, attempts to counter it will take a different form. We shall now examine recent crime trends in the UK and consider some of the policy responses to them.

"We find that all of us, as a society, are to blame, but only the defendant is guilty."

Linking micro- and macrosociology: 'The Saints and the Roughnecks'

The connections between the processes by which deviant behaviour occurs and the larger class structure were noted by William Chambliss in a famous study, 'The Saints and the Roughnecks' (1973). Chambliss studied two groups of delinquents in an American school, one from upper-middle-class families ('the Saints') and the other from poor families ('the Roughnecks'). While the Saints were constantly involved in petty crimes such as drinking, vandalism, truancy, and theft, none of their members was ever arrested. The Roughnecks were involved in similar criminal activities, yet they were constantly in trouble with the police. After Chambliss concluded that neither group was more delinquent than the other, he looked to other factors that could explain the different reaction of the police and the broader community to these two groups.

Chambliss found, for example, that the upper-class gang had cars and thus were able to remove themselves from the eyes of the community. The lower-class boys, through necessity, congregated in an area where everyone in the community frequently saw them. Chambliss concluded that differences of this sort were indicative of the class structure of society, which gave certain wealthier groups advantages when it came to being labelled as deviant. For instance, the parents of the Saints saw their sons' crimes as harmless pranks, while the parents of the Roughnecks acquiesced to the police's labelling of their sons' behaviour as criminal. The community as a whole also seemed to agree with these different labels.

These boys went on to have lives consistent with this labelling, with the Saints living conventional middle-class lives and the Roughnecks having continual problems with the law. As we saw earlier in the chapter (p. 801), this outcome is linked to what Lemert called 'secondary deviance', because it is thought to result from the inability of a person to carry on as 'normal' once he has been labelled as 'deviant'.

Chambliss's study is widely cited by sociologists for showing the connection between macrosociological factors like social class and microsociological phenomena such as how people become labelled as deviant. This study provides an example of how difficult it is to isolate micro- and macro-level factors in the social construction of deviance.

Patterns of crime in the United Kingdom

As measured by statistics of crimes reported to the police, rates of crime in the UK increased enormously over the twentieth century. Prior to the 1920s there were fewer than 100,000 offences recorded each year in England and Wales; this number had reached 500,000 by 1950, and peaked at 5.6 million by 1992. Levels of recorded crime more than doubled between 1977 and 1992.

Since the mid-1990s overall the number of crimes committed in the UK appears to have levelled off. Measures such as the British Crime Survey (discussed on pp. 812–15), have shown a considerable fall in the overall amount of crime (see figure 19.1). According to recent data, the risk of becoming a victim of crime is at its lowest for more than twenty years (Clegg et al. 2005). The end to rising crime figures has taken many experts by surprise. The causes behind it, and whether this trend is sustainable, are still uncertain.

Despite recent falls shown in the statistics on crime, there remains a widespread perception amongst the population that, over time, crime has grown more prevalent and serious (Nicholas et al. 2005). Recently, it has been reported that levels of worry about the main types of crime have been falling, although anxiety about anti-social behaviour remains more stable (Clegg et al. 2005). If at one time crime was seen as something marginal or exceptional, in recent decades it has become a more prominent concern in many people's lives. Surveys show that people are now much more fearful of crime than in earlier times and are experiencing heightened anxiety about going out after

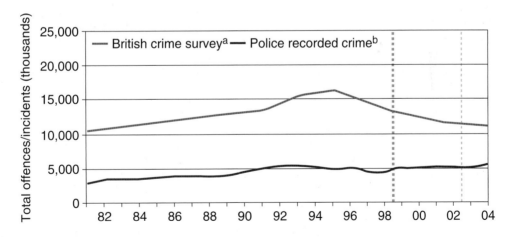

Figure 19.1   Recorded crime in England and Wales, 1981–2004

[a] BCS records number of incidents mentioned in interviews with public
[b] Recorded crime is total reported offences recorded by police
▪▪▪▪   Change in Home Office counting rules in 1998/9
- - - -   New Crime recording standard imposed in 2002

Source: BBC (2005)

dark, about their homes being burgled and about becoming the victims of violence. People are reportedly also more worried about more low-level kinds of disorder, such as graffiti, drunken rowdiness and groups of teenagers hanging about on the streets.

How much crime actually exists and how vulnerable is the population to it? What is being done to curb crime? These questions have become highly contested in the last few decades as media coverage of crime has risen along with public outrage, and as successive governments have promised to 'get tough on crime'. But untangling the nature and distribution of crime, let alone policies to address it, have proved to be far from straightforward.

Crime and crime statistics

To determine the extent of crime and the most common forms of criminal offence, one approach is to examine the official statistics on the number of crimes which the police actually record. Since such statistics are published regularly, there would seem to be no difficulty in assessing crime rates – but this assumption is quite erroneous. Statistics about crime and delinquency are probably the least reliable of all officially published figures on social issues. Criminologists have emphasized that we cannot take statistics on crime at face value.

First, the most basic limitation of statistics based on *reported* crime is that the majority of crimes never get passed on to the police at all. There are many reasons that people decide not to report a crime (as table 19.1 shows). Even in cases where a victim is wounded, more than half the cases are not reported to the police;

victims claim, for example, that it is a private affair or something they have dealt with themselves. Crime may go unreported for other reasons. Some forms of criminal violence, for example, are more 'hidden' than others. Physical and sexual abuse often takes place behind closed doors in the home, or in care institutions or prisons. Victims may fear that they won't be believed by the police, or that the abuse will get worse. As we will see below, the victims of domestic violence, for example, are often extremely reluctant to report the crime to police. Some people assume that the crime is too trivial to be taken to the police, or think that the police wouldn't be able to do anything about it anyway. A large proportion of car theft is reported, however, because the owner needs to have done so in order to claim on insurance policies.

Second, of the crimes that are reported to the police, many are not recorded in the statistics. It has been estimated that although 43 per cent of crimes do get reported to the police, just 29 per cent are recorded; this figure does, however, vary depending on the crime (BCS 2002/3). This can occur for a number of reasons. The police may be sceptical of the validity of some information about purported crimes that comes their way, or the victim may not want to lodge a formal complaint.

The overall effect of partial reporting and partial recording of crimes is that the official crime statistics reflect only a portion of overall criminal offences. The offences not captured in official statistics are referred to as the *hidden figure* of unrecorded crime.

Perhaps a more accurate picture of crime in the United Kingdom comes from

Table 19.1: Reasons for not reporting crime to the police 2003/4 (%)[a]

	Vandalism	Burglary	Thefts from vehicles & attempts[b]	Other household theft	Other personal theft	BCS violence	Comparable subset[c]	All BCS
Trivial/no loss/police would not/could not do anything[d]	82	72	85	78	71	47	71	72
Private/dealt with ourselves	16	20	12	19	16	46	24	22
Inconvenient to report	5	4	8	6	9	5	6	6
Reported to other authorities	2	4	1	2	17	8	4	5
Police-related reasons[e]	3	3	3	2	1	3	3	2
Fear of reprisal	2	4	1	1	0	6	3	2
Other	1	2	1	1	1	2	2	2
Unweighted base	*1,377*	*284*	*926*	*818*	*377*	*545*	*3,544*	*4,739*

[a] More than one reason could be given

[b] Thefts of vehicles not shown as very few incidents were not reported

[c] The comparable crime subset includes vandalism, burglary, vehicle theft, bicycle theft, wounding, common assault, robbery, snatch and stealth theft

[d] Too trivial/no loss/would not have been interested/attempt at offence was unsuccessful are merged due to the similarity in their definition

[e] Police-related reasons include: dislike or fear of the police and previous bad experience with the police or courts

Source: Nicholas et al. (2005)

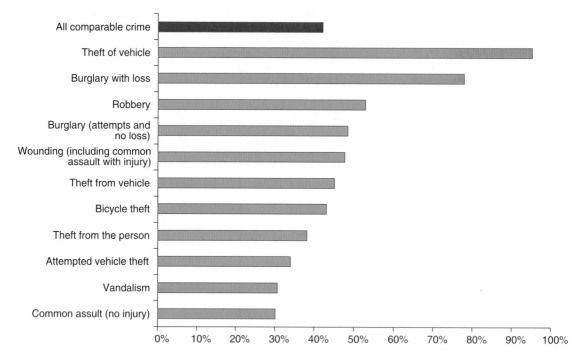

Figure 19.2 Estimate of percentage of crimes committed that are actually reported to the police

Source: Nicholas et al. (2005)

the annual British Crime Survey (BCS), which measures levels of crime in England and Wales by asking people about crimes which they have experienced over the last year. As a result, the BCS includes crimes which are not reported to or recorded by the police, and it can be seen as an important alternative to police records. The survey is based on interviews with people living in private households, who are asked about their experiences of crime in the last twelve months. Each year, the survey involves a representative survey of about 40,000 adults across the UK (see figure 19.2). Although there are differences in the rates of growth and decline for varying types of offences, with some

figures suggesting a recent rise in violent crime, the overall trend in both the BCS and the figures for recorded crimes has been downwards since the mid-1990s.

Surveys such as the BCS are known as **victimization studies**. While they are valuable indicators, the data from victimization studies must also be treated with caution. In certain instances the methodology of the study itself may result in significant under-reporting. The BCS is conducted through interviews in respondents' homes. This might mean that a victim of domestic violence, for example, would not report violent incidents in the presence of the abuser, or where the abuse has taken place. What is more, the survey does not include people under the age of sixteen, or who are homeless or live in some kind of institution, such as a care home. This is particularly important, as other research has shown that these groups can be particularly prone to being victims of crime, as we discover below.

Another important source of information about crime are self-report studies, in which people are asked to admit anonymously if they have ever committed an offence. Of course, these studies could also suffer from under-reporting, as participants might be unwilling to report an offence for fear of the consequences. Over-reporting could also take place, perhaps because of a bad memory or through a desire to show off.

Victims and perpetrators of crime

Are some individuals or groups more likely to commit crimes, or to become the victims of crime? Criminologists say 'yes' – research and crime statistics show that crime and victimization are not randomly distributed among the population. Men are more likely than women, for example, to commit crimes; the young are more often involved in crime than older people.

The likelihood of someone becoming a victim of crime is closely linked to the area where they live. Areas suffering from greater material deprivation generally have higher crime rates. Individuals living in inner-city neighbourhoods run a much greater risk of becoming victims of crime than do residents of more affluent suburban areas. That ethnic minorities are concentrated disproportionately in inner-city

regions appears to be a significant factor in their higher rates of victimization.

Gender and crime

Like other areas of sociology, criminological studies have traditionally ignored half the population. Feminists have been correct in criticizing criminology for being a male-dominated discipline in which women are largely 'invisible' in both theoretical considerations and empirical studies. Since the 1970s many important feminist works have drawn attention to the way in which criminal transgressions by women occur in different contexts from those of men, and how women's experiences with the criminal justice system are influenced by certain gendered assumptions about appropriate male and female roles. Feminists have also played a critical role in highlighting the prevalence of violence against women, both at home and in public.

Male and female crime rates

The statistics on gender and crime are startling. According to recent data, only about 19 per cent of all known offenders in England and Wales are female (Home Office 2003). There is also an enormous imbalance in the ratio of men to women in prison, not only in Britain but in all the industrialized countries. Although the number of women in custody in England and Wales has risen in recent years, by 173 per cent between 1992 and 2002, women still constitute only a tiny percentage of prisoners overall: around 6 per cent of the total prison population (Home Office 2003). There are also sharp contrasts between the types of crime that men and women commit. As figure 19.3 illustrates, women are much more likely to commit

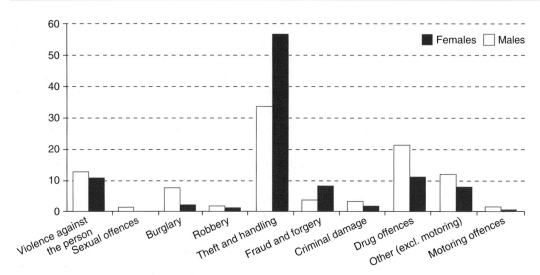

Figure 19.3 Offenders found guilty at all courts or cautioned for indictable offences, 2002 (%)
Source: Home Office (2004)

theft, usually from shops, than violent crimes.

Of course, it may be that the real gender difference in crime rates is less than the official statistics show. Otto Pollak (1950) suggested as much, contending that certain crimes perpetrated by women tend to go unreported. He saw women's predominantly domestic role as providing them with the opportunity to commit crimes at home and in the private sphere. Pollak regarded women as naturally deceitful and highly skilled at covering up their crimes. This, he argued, was grounded in biology, as women had learned to hide the pain and discomfort of menstruation from men and were also able to fake interest in sexual intercourse in a way that men could not. Pollak also argued that female offenders are treated more leniently because male police officers tend to adopt a 'chivalrous' attitude towards them (Pollak 1950).

Pollak's portrayal of women as conniving and deceptive is based in groundless stereotypes, yet the suggestion that women are treated more leniently by the criminal justice system has prompted much debate and examination. The chivalry thesis has been applied in two ways. First, it is possible that police and other officials may regard female offenders as less dangerous than men, and let pass activities for which males would be arrested. Second, in sentencing for criminal offences, women tend to be much less likely to be imprisoned than are male offenders. A number of empirical studies have been undertaken to test the chivalry thesis, but the results remain inconclusive. One of the main difficulties is assessing the relative influence of gender compared to other factors such as age, class and race. For example, it appears that older women offenders tend to be treated less aggressively than their male counterparts. Other studies have shown that black women receive worse treatment than white women at the hands of the police.

Another perspective that has been adopted by feminists examines how social understandings about 'femininity' affect women's experiences in the criminal justice system. Frances Heidensohn (1995) has argued that women are treated more harshly in cases where they have allegedly deviated from the norms of female sexuality. For example, young girls who are perceived to be sexually promiscuous are more often taken into custody than boys. In such cases, women are seen as 'doubly deviant' – not only have they broken the law, but they have also flouted 'appropriate' female behaviour. In such cases they are judged less on the nature of the offence and more on their 'deviant' lifestyle choice. Heidensohn and others have pointed out the double standard within the criminal justice system: where male aggression and violence is seen as a natural phenomenon, explanations for female offences are sought in 'psychological' imbalances.

In an effort to make female crime more 'visible', feminists have conducted a number of detailed investigations on female criminals – from girl gangs to female terrorists to women in prison. Such studies have shown that violence is not exclusively a characteristic of male criminality. Women are much less likely than men to participate in violent crime, but women do commit similar acts of violence.

Why, then, are female rates of criminality so much lower than those of men? There is some evidence that female lawbreakers are quite often able to escape coming before the courts because they are able to persuade the police or other authorities to see their actions in a particular light. They invoke what has been called the 'gender contract' – the implicit contract between men and women whereby to be a woman is to be erratic and impulsive, on the one hand, and in need of protection, on the other (Worrall 1990). According to this view, it is argued that the police and courts act chivalrously, and do not seek to punish women for behaviour which would be considered unacceptable in men. Other research suggests that particular women, such as those who do not live up to the norms of femininity, may end up being treated more harshly. Women perceived as 'bad mothers', for example, may receive more severe penalties from the courts (Carlen 1983).

Yet differential treatment could hardly account for the vast difference between male and female rates of crime. The reasons are almost certainly the same as those that explain gender differences in other spheres. There are, of course, certain specifically 'female crimes' – most notably, prostitution, for which women are convicted while their male clients are not. 'Male crimes' remain 'male' because of differences in socialization and because men's activities and involvements are still more non-domestic than those of most women. As we saw with Pollak's approach, gender difference in crime often used to be explained by supposedly innate biological or psychological differences – in terms of differential strength, passivity or preoccupation with reproduction. Nowadays 'womanly' qualities are seen as largely socially generated, in common with the traits of 'masculinity'. Many women are socialized to value different qualities in social life (caring for others and the fostering of personal relationships) from those valued by males. Equally important, through the influence of ideology and other factors – such as the idea of the 'nice girl' – women's behaviour is often kept confined and controlled in ways that male activities are not.

Ever since the late nineteenth century criminologists have predicted that gender equalization would reduce or eliminate the differences in criminality between men and women, but as yet crime remains a gendered phenomenon. Whether or not the variations between female and male crime rates will one day disappear, we still cannot say with any certainty.

Crime and the 'crisis of masculinity'

The high levels of crime found in poorer areas of large cities are associated particularly with the activities of young men. Why should so many young men in these areas turn to crime? Some answers we have already touched on. Boys are often part of gangs from an early age, a subculture in which some forms of crime are a way of life. And once gang members are labelled as criminals by the authorities, they embark on regular criminal activities. In spite of the existence today of girl gangs, such subcultures are fundamentally masculine and infused with male values of adventure, excitement and comradeship.

In chapter 12 ('Sexuality and Gender'), we discussed the notion that modern societies are witnessing a 'crisis of masculinity'. If at one time young men could look forward confidently to lifetime careers and a stable role as the family breadwinner, this role has become much more elusive for many men. Shifts in the labour market have made unemployment and job insecurity a tangible threat, while women are growing increasingly indepen-

dent financially, professionally and otherwise. Connell's ideas about 'hegemonic masculinity' (see pp. 462–7) have been drawn on by many sociologists and criminologists to explain how violence and aggression can be seen as an acceptable facet of masculine identity.

Crimes against women

There are certain categories of crime where men are overwhelmingly the aggressors and women the victims. Domestic violence, sexual harassment, sexual assault and rape are crimes in which males use their superior social or physical power against women. While each of these has been practised by women against men, they remain almost exclusively crimes carried out against women. It is estimated that 25 per cent of women are victims of violence at some point in their lives, but all women face the threat of such crimes either directly or indirectly.

For many years, these offences were ignored by the criminal justice system; victims had to persevere tirelessly to gain legal recourse against an offender. Even today, the prosecution of crimes against women remains far from straightforward. Yet feminist criminology has done much to raise awareness of crimes against women and to integrate such offences into mainstream debates on crime. In this section we shall examine the crime of rape, leaving discussions of domestic violence and sexual harassment to other chapters (see chapter 7, 'Families and Intimate Relationships', and chapter 18, 'Work and Economic Life').

The extent of rape is very difficult to assess with any accuracy. Only a small proportion of rapes actually come to the attention of the police and are recorded in the statistics. In 1999 the police recorded 7,809 offences as rape. The British Crime Survey estimates that the real figure is in fact much higher, but for the reasons discussed above, it is likely that the BCS also fails to count accurately incidences of rape.

Until 1991, as we have already noted, rape within marriage was not recognized in Britain. In a ruling delivered in 1736, Sir Matthew Hale declared that a husband 'cannot be guilty of rape committed by himself upon his lawful wife, for by their mutual matrimonial consent and contract the wife hath given up herself in this kind unto her husband which she cannot retract' (quoted in Hall et al. 1984, p. 20). This formulation remained the law in England and Wales until a decade ago when the House of Lords ruled that in modern times, the notion that a husband has the right to force himself on his wife is unacceptable.

There are many reasons why a woman might choose not to report sexual violence to the police. The majority of women who are raped either wish to put the incident out of their minds, or are unwilling to participate in what can be a humiliating process of medical examination, police interrogation and courtroom cross-examination. The legal process often takes a long time and can be intimidating. Courtroom procedure is public and the victim must come face to face with the accused. Proof of penetration, the identity of the rapist and the fact that the act occurred without the woman's consent all have to be forthcoming. A woman may feel that she is the one on trial, particularly if her own sexual history is examined publicly, as is often the case.

Over the last few years, women's groups have pressed for change in both legal and public thinking about rape. They have stressed that rape should not be seen as a sexual offence, but as a type of violent crime. It is not just a physical attack but an assault on an individual's integrity and dignity. Rape is clearly related to the association of masculinity with power, dominance and toughness. It is not for the most part the result of overwhelming sexual desire, but of the ties between sexuality and feelings of power and superiority. The sexual act itself is less significant than the debasement of the woman. The campaign has had some real results in changing legislation, and rape is today generally recognized in law to be a specific type of criminal violence.

There is a sense in which all women are victims of rape. Women who have never been raped often experience anxieties similar to those who have. They may be afraid to go out alone at night, even on crowded streets, and may be almost equally fearful of being on their own in a house or flat. Emphasizing the close connection between rape and orthodox male sexuality, Susan Brownmiller (1975) has argued that rape is part of a system of male intimidation that keeps all women in fear. Those who are not raped are affected by the anxieties thus provoked, and by the need to be much more cautious in everyday aspects of life than men have to be.

Crimes against homosexuals

Feminists have pointed out that understandings of violence are highly gendered and are influenced by 'common-sense' perceptions about risk and responsibility. Because women are generally seen as less able to defend themselves against violent attack, common sense holds that they should modify their behaviour in order to reduce the risk of becoming a victim of violence. For example, not only should women avoid walking in unsafe neighbourhoods alone and at night, but they should be careful not to dress provocatively or to behave in a manner that could be misinterpreted. Women who fail to do so can be accused of 'asking for trouble'. In a court setting, their behaviour can be taken as a mitigating factor in considering the perpetrator's act of violence (Dobash and Dobash 1992; Richardson and May 1999).

It has been suggested that a similar 'common-sense' logic applies in the case of violent acts against gay men and lesbians. Victimization studies reveal that homosexuals experience a high incidence of violent crime and harassment. A national survey of 4,000 gay men and women found that in the previous five years, 33 per cent of gay men and 25 per cent of lesbians had been the victim of at least one violent attack. In all, a third had experienced some form of harassment, including threats or vandalism, and an overwhelming 73 per cent had been verbally abused in public (Mason and Palmer 1996; Richardson and May 1999).

Diane Richardson and Hazel May have argued that because homosexuals remain stigmatized and marginalized in many societies, there is a greater tendency for them to be treated as 'deserving' of crime, rather than as innocent victims. Homosexual relationships are still seen as belonging to the private realm, while heterosexuality is the overwhelming norm in public spaces. According to Richardson and May, lesbians and gay men who deviate from this private–public contract by displaying their homosexual identities in public are often blamed for making

themselves vulnerable to crime. There is a sense that introducing homosexuality into the public sphere represents a form of provocation. Crimes against homosexuals led to calls by many social groups for the adoption of 'hate crime' legislation to protect the human rights of groups that remain stigmatized in society. These calls were enacted upon in the Criminal Justice Act of 2003, which allowed judges in England and Wales to increase a sentence if an assault was motivated by homophobia. Similar legislation has been introduced in Scotland and Northern Ireland.

Youth and crime

Popular fear about crime centres on offences such as theft, burglary, assault and rape – 'street crimes' that are largely seen as the domain of young working-class males. Media coverage of rising crime rates often focuses on 'moral breakdown' among young people and highlights such issues as vandalism, school truancy and drug use to illustrate the increasing 'permissiveness' in society. This equation of youth with criminal activity is not a new one, according to some sociologists. Young people are often taken as an indicator of the health and welfare of society itself.

Official statistics about crime rates do reveal high rates of offending among young people. According to self-report studies, fewer girls than boys admit to ever having committed an offence, as figure 19.4 illustrates. (As we saw on p. 815, studies based on self-reported data can be unreliable.) For boys, the peak age of offending tends to be around 18. For girls, this is lower, tending to peak around 15 (see figure 19.5).

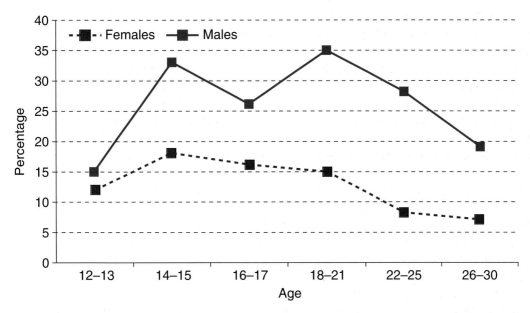

Figure 19.4   Prevalence of offending by age and sex (%)

Source: Home Office (2004)

According to this data, it might seem that offending by young people is a big problem. Yet we must approach assumptions about youth and crime with some caution, as John Muncie has noted (1999). He argues that 'moral panics' about youth criminality may not accurately reflect social reality. An isolated event involving young people and crime can be transformed symbolically into a full-blown 'crisis of childhood' demanding tough 'law and order' responses. The high-profile murder of two-year-old James Bulger in 1993 by a pair of ten-year-old boys is an example of how moral outrage can deflect attention away from larger social issues. In the Bulger case, closed circuit video cameras in a shopping centre captured the image of the older boys leading the small child by the hand, which etched the case into the public conscious-

ness. According to Muncie, the brutal murder was a watershed event in political and media portrayals of youth crime. Even young children were seen as potentially violent threats. The ten-year-old boys were labelled 'demons', 'monsters' and 'animals'. Less attention was paid to the personal histories of the offenders or to the fact that, despite early indications of a propensity to violence and self-aggression in one of the boys, no interventions had been made (Muncie 1999).

Similar caution can be expressed about the popular view that most youth crime is drug-related. Muncie has noted the common assumption that robberies, for example, are committed by young people in order to finance drug habits. Recent studies reveal that drug and alcohol use among young people has become relatively 'normalized' (Parker et al. 1998).

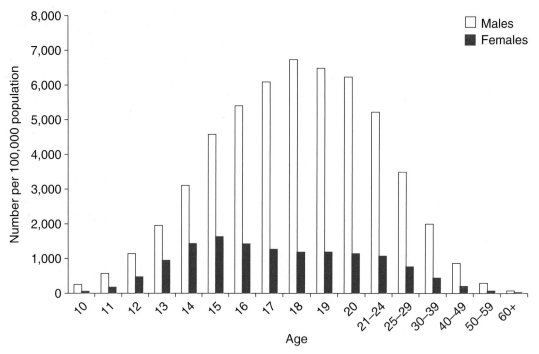

Figure 19.5 Persons found guilty of, or cautioned for, indictable offences per 100,000 population by age group 2003

Source: Home Office (2004)

A 2003 survey of more than 10,000 school children aged between eleven and fifteen for the Department of Health revealed that 9 per cent were regular smokers, 25 per cent had drunk alcohol in the last week, 21 per cent had taken drugs in the last year, and 4 per cent had used 'Class A' drugs, such as cocaine or heroin (DoH 2003).

Trends in drug use have shifted away from 'hard' drugs such as heroin, and towards combinations of substances such as amphetamines, alcohol and Ecstasy. Ecstasy in particular has become a 'lifestyle' drug associated with the rave and club subcultures, rather than the basis of an expensive, addictive habit. The 'war on drugs', Muncie argues, serves to criminalize large segments of the youth population who are generally law-abiding (Muncie 1999).

Analysis of youth criminality is rarely straightforward. Where crime implies a transgression of law, youth criminality is often associated with activities that, strictly speaking, are not crimes. Anti-social behaviour, subcultures and non-conformity in young people may be regarded as delinquency, but they are not in fact criminal conduct. Critics argue that the recent introduction of Anti-Social Behaviour Orders (ASBOs) will criminalize ordinary, borderline nuisance behaviour that for many is a normal part of growing up.

White-collar crime

Although there is a tendency to associate crime with young people, especially males in the lower classes, involvement in criminal activities is by no means confined to this segment of the population. The world's largest energy trading company Enron collapsed in 2001 after the discovery that false accounting was disguising huge debts. The company's bankruptcy caused the loss of thousands of jobs around the world. Several of its senior staff, including the company's founder Kenneth Lay, were arrested. A similar scandal at communications giant World-Com, in 2002, shows that wealthy and powerful people carry out crimes whose consequences can be much more far-reaching than the often petty crimes of the poor.

The term **white-collar crime** was first introduced by Edwin Sutherland (1949), and refers to crime that is carried out by those in the more affluent sectors of

Powerful men like Kenneth Lay, founder of Enron, rarely find themselves in the dock, even though their actions potentially have much more serious consequences than the types of crime usually dealt with by the courts.

society. The term covers many types of criminal activity, including tax frauds, illegal sales practices, securities and land frauds, embezzlement, the manufacture or sale of dangerous products, as well as straightforward theft. Of course most white-collar crime is not as grand as that which occurred at Enron or WorldCom. The distribution of white-collar crimes is even harder to measure than that of other types of crime; most forms of this crime do not appear in the official statistics at all. We can distinguish between white-collar crime and crimes of the powerful. White-collar crime mainly involves the use of a middle-class or professional position to engage in illegal activities. Crimes of the powerful are those in which the authority conferred by a position is used in criminal ways – as when an official accepts a bribe to favour a particular policy.

Although it is regarded by the authorities in a much more tolerant light than crimes of the less privileged (several of those convicted in the Enron scandal avoided serving time in jail), the cost of white-collar crime is enormous. Far more research has been carried out on white-collar crime in the United States than in Britain. In America, it has been calculated that the amount of money involved in white-collar crime (defined as tax fraud, insurance frauds, home improvement frauds and car repair frauds) is forty times as great as that in ordinary crimes against property (robberies, burglaries, larceny, forgeries and car thefts) (President's Commission on Organized Crime 1986).

Corporate crime

Some criminologists have referred to corporate crime to describe the types of offence which are committed by large cor-

'Kickbacks, embezzlement, price fixing, bribery . . . this is an extremely high-crime area.'
Reproduced by permission of Sidney Harris.

porations in society. Pollution, mislabelling and violations of health and safety regulations affect much larger numbers of people than does petty criminality. The increasing power and influence of large corporations, and their rapidly growing global reach, means that our lives are touched by them in many ways. Corporations are involved in producing the cars we drive and the food we eat. They also have an enormous impact on the natural environment and financial markets, aspects of life which affect all of us.

Gary Slapper and Steve Tombs (1999) have reviewed both quantitative and qualitative studies of corporate crime and have concluded that a large number of corporations do not adhere to the legal regulations which apply to them. Corporate crime is not confined to a few 'bad apples', they claim, but is pervasive and widespread. Studies have revealed six types of violation linked to large corporations: administrative (paperwork or non-compliance), environmental (pollution, permits violations), financial (tax violations, illegal payments), labour (working conditions, hiring practices), manufacturing (product safety, labelling) and unfair trade practices (anti-competition, false advertising).

Victimization patterns in corporate crime are not straightforward. Sometimes there are 'obvious' victims, as in cases of environmental disasters like the spill at the Bhopal chemical plant in India, or the health dangers posed to women by silicone breast implants. Recently, those injured in rail crashes or relatives of those who were killed have called for the executives of the companies responsible for the track and trains to be brought to trial where the companies have shown negligence. But very often victims of corporate crime do not see themselves as such. This is because in 'traditional' crimes the proximity between victim and offender is much closer – it is difficult not to recognize that you have been mugged! In the case of corporate crime, greater distances in time and space mean that victims may not realize they have been victimized, or may not know how to seek redress for the crime.

The effects of corporate crime are often experienced unevenly within society. Those who are disadvantaged by other types of socio-economic inequalities tend to suffer disproportionately. For example, safety and health risks in the workplace tend to be concentrated most heavily in low-paying occupations. Many of the risks from health-care products and pharma-ceuticals have had a greater impact on women than on men, as is the case with contraceptives or fertility treatments with harmful side-effects (Slapper and Tombs 1999).

Violent aspects of corporate crime are less visible than in cases of homicide or assault, but are just as real – and may on occasion be much more serious in their consequences. For example, flouting regulations concerning the preparation of new drugs, safety in the workplace or pollution may cause physical harm or death to large numbers of people. Deaths from hazards at work far outnumber murders, although precise statistics about job accidents are difficult to obtain. Of course, we cannot assume that all, or even the majority, of these deaths and injuries are the result of employer negligence in relation to safety factors for which they are legally liable. Nevertheless, there is some basis for supposing that many are due to the neglect of legally binding safety regulations by employers or managers.

Organized crime

Organized crime refers to forms of activity that have many of the characteristics of orthodox business, but are illegal. Organized crime embraces smuggling, illegal gambling, the drug trade, prostitution, large-scale theft and protection rackets, among other activities. It often relies on violence or the threat of violence to conduct its activities. While organized crime has traditionally developed within individual countries in culturally specific ways, it has become increasingly transnational in scope.

The reach of organized crime is now felt in many countries throughout the world,

Globalization and everyday life: drug-trafficking

How easy is it to purchase marijuana? Is there ever a drug-free pop festival? Lamentable as it may seem to some, most young people in Britain have relatively easy access to illegal drugs.

What factors determine the availability of illegal drugs in your community? The level of police enforcement is important, of course, as is the extent of local demand. But no less important is the existence of networks of traffickers able to transport the drugs from the countries where they are grown to your home town. These networks have been able to flourish, in part, because of globalization.

While the cultivation of marijuana may be just a matter of someone's back garden, almost all of the world's coca plants and opium poppies are grown in the Third World. Billions are spent each year to assist Third World nations with eradication efforts, but, despite this massive expenditure, there is little evidence that eradication or interdiction efforts have significantly decreased the supply of illegal drugs in Britain and other European countries. Why have these efforts failed?

One answer is that the profit motive is simply too great. Farmers struggling to scratch out a living for themselves in Bolivia or Peru, members of the Colombian drug cartels and low-level dealers on our streets and in our clubs all receive substantial monetary rewards for their illegal activities. These rewards create a strong incentive to devise ways around anti-drug efforts, and to run the risk of getting caught.

Another answer – one recently discussed at a summit attended by leaders of the eight major industrial powers – is that drug-traffickers have been able to take advantage of globalization. First, in their attempts to evade the authorities, traffickers make use of all the communications technologies that are available in a global age. As one commentator put it, drug traffickers 'now use sophisticated technology, such as signal interceptors, to plot radar and avoid monitoring . . . [and] they can use faxes, computers and cellular phones to coordinate their activities and make their business run smoothly'. Second, the globalization of the financial sector has helped create an infrastructure in which large sums of money can be moved around the world electronically in a matter of seconds, making it relatively easy to 'launder' drug money (that is, to make it appear to have come from a legitimate business venture). Third, recent changes in the policies of governments designed to allow the freer flow of persons and legitimate goods across international borders have increased the opportunities for smuggling.

At the same time, globalization may create new opportunities for governments to work together to combat drug-trafficking. Indeed, world leaders recently called for greater international cooperation in narcotics enforcement, stressing the need for information sharing and coordinated enforcement efforts.

but historically it has been particularly strong in a handful of nations. In America, for example, organized crime is a massive business, rivalling any of the major orthodox sectors of economic enterprise, such as the car industry. National and local criminal organizations provide illegal goods and services to mass consumers. Illicit gambling on horse races, lotteries and sporting events represents the greatest source of income generated by organized crime in the United States. Organized crime has probably become so significant in American society because of an early association with – and in part a modelling on – the activities of the industrial 'robber barons' of the late nineteenth century. Many of the early industrialists made fortunes by exploiting immigrant labour, largely ignoring legal regulations on working conditions and often using a mixture of corruption and violence to build their industrial empires.

Although we have little systematic information on organized crime in the United Kingdom, it is known that extensive criminal networks exist in areas of London and other large cities. Some of these have international connections. London in particular is a centre for criminal operations based in the United States and elsewhere. 'Triads' (Chinese gangsters, originally from Hong Kong and Southeast Asia) and 'Yardies' (drug dealers with links to the Caribbean) are two of the largest criminal networks, but other organized crime groups from Eastern Europe, South America and West Africa are involved in money-laundering, drug-trafficking, and fraud schemes.

Organized crime in Britain is more complex than it was some years ago. There is no single national organization linking different criminal groups, but such crime has become more sophisticated than ever before. For example, some of the larger criminal organizations find ways of laundering money through the big clearing banks, in spite of the procedures intended to foil them; using their 'clean' money, they then invest in legitimate businesses. Police believe that between £2.5 and £4 billion of criminally generated money passes through UK banks each year.

The changing face of organized crime

In *End of Millennium* (1998), Manuel Castells argues that the activities of organized crime groups are becoming increasingly international in scope. He notes that the coordination of criminal activities across borders – with the help of new information technologies – is becoming a central feature of the new global economy. Involved in activities ranging from the narcotics trade to counterfeiting to smuggling immigrants and human organs, organized crime groups are now operating in flexible international networks rather than within their own territorial realms.

According to Castells, criminal groups set up strategic alliances with one another. The international narcotics trade, weapons-trafficking, the sale of nuclear material and money-laundering have all become 'linked' across borders and crime groups. Criminal organizations tend to base their operations in 'low-risk' countries where there are fewer threats to their activities. In recent years, the former Soviet Union has been one of the main points of convergence for international organized crime. The flexible nature of this networked crime makes it relatively easy for crime groups to evade the reach of law enforcement initiatives. If one criminal 'safe haven' becomes more risky, the 'organizational geometry' can shift to form a new pattern.

The international nature of crime has been felt in the United Kingdom. Japanese Yakuza gangs and Italian and American mafia operators have established themselves in Britain. Among the newest arrivals are criminals from the former Soviet Union. Some commentators believe that the new Russian mafia is the world's most dangerous organized crime syndicate. The Russian criminal networks are deeply involved in money-laundering, linking up their activities with Russia's largely unregulated banks. Some think the Russian groups may come to be the world's largest criminal networks. They have their basis in a mafia-riddled Russian state, where underworld 'protection' is now routine for many businesses. The most worrying possibility is that Russia's new mobsters are smuggling nuclear materials on an international scale, materials taken from the Soviet nuclear arsenal.

Despite numerous campaigns by the government and the police, the narcotics trade is one of the most rapidly expanding international criminal industries, having an annual growth rate of more than 10 per cent in the 1980s and early 1990s and an extremely high level of profit. Heroin networks stretch across the Far East, particularly South Asia, and are also located in North Africa, the Middle East and Latin America. Supply lines also pass through Paris and Amsterdam, from where drugs are commonly supplied to Britain.

Cybercrime

Not only is international organized crime greatly facilitated by recent advances in information technology, it also seems certain that the information and tele-communications revolution will change the face of crime in fundamental ways. Advances in technology have provided exciting new opportunities and benefits, but they also heighten vulnerability to crime. While it is difficult to quantify the extent of **cybercrime** – criminal acts committed with the help of information technology – it is possible to outline some of the major forms it appears to be taking. P. N. Grabosky and Russell Smith (1998) have identified nine main types of technology-based crime:

1 Illegal interception of telecommunications systems means that eavesdropping has become easier. This has implications ranging from 'spouse-monitoring' to espionage.

2 There is heightened vulnerability to electronic vandalism and terrorism. Western societies are increasingly reliant on computerized systems; interference with such systems – from hackers or human-made computer viruses, for example – could pose serious security hazards.

3 The ability to steal telecommunications services means that people can conduct illicit business without being detected, or simply manipulate telecom and mobile phone services in order to receive free or discounted telephone calls.

4 Telecom privacy is a growing problem. It has become relatively easy to violate copyright rules by copying materials, software, films and CDs.

5 It is difficult to control pornography and offensive content in cyberspace. Sexually explicit material, racist propaganda and instructions for building incendiary devices can all be placed on, and downloaded from, the Internet. 'Cyberstalking' can pose not only virtual, but also real threats to online users.

6 A growth in telemarketing fraud has been noted. Fraudulent charity schemes and investment opportunities are difficult to regulate.

7 There is an enhanced risk of electronic funds-transfer crimes. The widespread use of cash machines, e-commerce and 'electronic money' on the Internet heightens the possibility that some transactions will be intercepted.

8 Electronic money-laundering can be used to 'move' the illegal proceeds from a crime in order to conceal their origins.

9 Telecommunications can be used to further criminal conspiracies. Because of sophisticated encryption systems

and high-speed data transfers, it is difficult for law enforcement agencies to intercept information about criminal activities. This has particular relevance to new international criminal activities.

There are indications that cybercrime is already on the rise. Internet-based fraud was the fastest growing category of crime in Britain in the late 1990s. In the year up to September 1999, fraud and forgery rose by 29 per cent – an increase of 70,000 offences over the course of one year. The increase has been attributed to the growth in Internet-based crime.

The global reach of telecommunications crime poses particular challenges for law enforcement. Criminal acts perpetrated in one country have the power to affect victims across the globe. As Grabosky and Smith (1998) note, this has troubling implications for detecting and prosecuting crimes. It becomes necessary for police from the countries involved to determine the jurisdiction in which the act occurred and to agree on extraditing the offenders and providing the necessary evidence for prosecution. Although police cooperation across national borders may improve with the growth of cybercrime, at present cybercriminals have a great deal of room to manoeuvre.

At a time when financial, commercial and production systems in countries around the world are being integrated electronically, rising levels of Internet fraud and unauthorized electronic intrusions and the constant threat of computer viruses are serving as potent warnings of the vulnerability of existing computer security systems. From the US Federal Bureau of Investigation (FBI) to the Japanese government's new anti-hacker policeforce, governments are scrambling to contend with new and elusive forms of cross-national computer activity.

Crimes of the future

Imagine a world in which physical cash no longer exists, all personal possessions are tagged with electronic chips and your personal identity is your most valuable asset. According to a report entitled *Just around the Corner*, published by the Department of Trade and Industry (DTI 2000), crime will soon be thoroughly transformed by advances in technology. Within two decades, the report suggests, many goods such as cars, cameras and computers will become less attractive targets for theft because they will be programmed to operate only in the hands of their legal owners. Personalized 'identities' – such as computer chips, PIN numbers and security codes – will become ubiquitous. They will be essential for conducting online transactions, using 'smart cards' (virtual cash) and passing through security systems. According to the report, cases of 'identity fraud' and thefts of personal identities will proliferate as more and more aspects of life become based in high technology.

Prisons: the answer to crime?

The underlying principle of modern prisons is to 'improve' individuals and prepare them to play a fit and proper part in society once released. Prison, and a reliance on long prison sentences, is also seen as a powerful deterrent to crime. For this reason, many politicians eager to 'get tough' on rising crime rates have favoured a more punitive justice system and the expansion of prison facilities. Do prisons have the intended effect of 'reforming' convicted criminals and preventing new crimes from being committed? It is a complex question, as we shall see, but evidence seems to suggest that they do not.

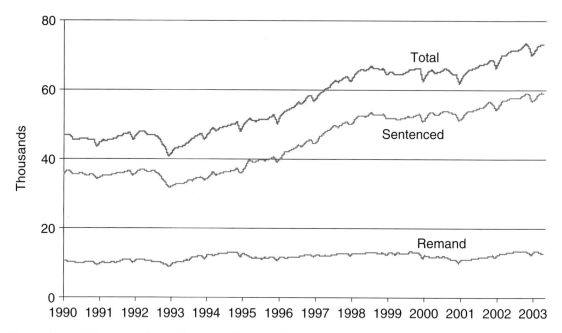

Figure 19.6 Prison population in England and Wales, 1990–2003

Source: Social Trends 34 (2004), p. 144

The British criminal justice system has become more punitive in recent years. As figure 19.6 shows, the prison population has been rising steadily; in 2003 there were 73,000 people in prison service facilities in England and Wales, an increase of more than 25,000 since 1990. England and Wales had a greater proportion of its population imprisoned (139 per 100,000) than any other country in the European Union, before ten new countries were admitted in 2004. (The figures for Scotland and Northern Ireland are measured separately and are both lower than for England and Wales.) In contrast to the figure for England and Wales, Germany has a prison population of just 96 per 100,000 and France 85 per 100,000 (Home Office 2003). English and Welsh courts also tend to assign longer prison sentences to offenders than do courts in other European countries. Some critics fear that Britain is following too closely in the path of the United States – by far the most punitive nation among industrial countries (see box on pp. 831–2).

Prisoners are no longer generally physically maltreated, as was once common practice, but they do suffer many other types of deprivation. They are deprived not only of their freedom, but also of a proper income, the company of their families and previous friends, heterosexual relationships, their own clothing and other personal items. They frequently live in overcrowded conditions, and have to accept strict disciplinary procedures and the regimentation of their daily lives (Stern 1989).

Living in these conditions tends to drive a wedge between prison inmates and the outside society; they cannot adjust their behaviour to the norms of that society. Prisoners have to come to terms with an environment quite distinct from 'the outside', and the habits and attitudes they learn in prison are quite often exactly the opposite of those they are supposed to acquire. For instance, they may develop a grudge against ordinary citizenry, learn to accept violence as normal, gain contacts with seasoned criminals which they maintain when freed, and acquire criminal skills about which they previously knew little. For this reason prisons are sometimes referred to as 'universities of crime'. It is therefore not surprising that rates of **recidivism** – repeat offending by those who have been in prison before – are disturbingly high. Over 60 per cent of all men set free after serving prison sentences in the UK are rearrested within four years of their original crimes.

While the evidence seems to show that prisons do not succeed in rehabilitating prisoners, there remains enormous pressure to increase the number of prisons and to toughen prison sentences for many crimes. The prison system is overcrowded, prompting calls for the construction of new facilities. Yet critics argue that not only are prison-building programmes an unreasonably expensive burden for taxpayers to bear, in addition they will have little impact on the crime rate.

Punitive justice: the case of the United States

The United States has by far the most punitive justice system in the world. The world's total prison population is around 8.75 million, almost 2 million of whom are presently incarcerated in American prisons. In the USA, for every 100,000 of the population 686 people are in prison (Home Office 2003).

The American prison system employs more

A prisoner on death row in California.

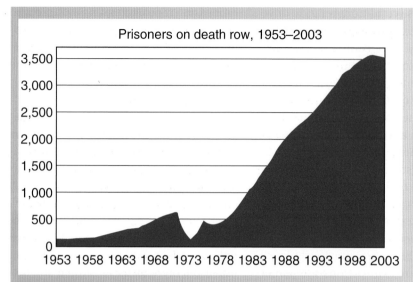

Prisoners on death row, 1953–2003

Figure 19.7   Number of people under sentence of death in the USA, 1953–2003

Source: US Bureau of Justice (2004)

from 1966, when 42 per cent of those surveyed supported the death penalty and 47 per cent were opposed (Gallup). The number of individuals awaiting execution has climbed steadily since 1977 when the Supreme Court upheld state capital punishment laws (see figure 19.7). At the end of 2003, more than 3,300 prisoners were on 'death row'. Of these, 99 per cent were men, 56 per cent were white and 42 per cent were black (US Bureau of Justice 1998).

Proponents of tough sentencing point to the overall drop in crime in the United States over the past decade as proof that prisons work. Critics disagree, claiming that the reduction in crime can be explained by other factors, such as the strong economy and low unemployment. They argue that high rates of incarceration are breaking up families and communities unnecessarily. More than a quarter of African-American men are either in prison or under the control of the penal system. Some 60 per cent of individuals imprisoned in the United States are serving sentences for non-violent drug-related crimes. Critics charge that such gross imbalances prove that incarceration is no longer a measure of 'last resort' – prison is now turned to as the solution for all social problems.

than 500,000 people and costs $35 billion annually to maintain. It has also become partially privatized, with private companies now able to win government contracts to build and administer prisons to accommodate the growing inmate population. Critics charge that a 'prison-industrial complex' has emerged: large numbers of people – including bureaucrats, politicians and prison employees – have vested interests in the existence and further expansion of the prison system.

Support for capital punishment (the 'death penalty') is high in the United States. In 2004, 71 per cent of adults surveyed said that they believed in capital punishment; 26 per cent opposed it. This represents a significant shift

Some campaigners for penal reform argue that there should be a shift away from punitive justice towards forms of **restorative justice**. 'Restorative justice' seeks to raise awareness among offenders of the effects of their crimes through 'sentences' served within the community. Offenders might be required to contribute to commu-

nity service projects or to engage in mediated reconciliation sessions with victims. Rather than being separated from society and shielded from the aftermath of their criminal acts, criminals need to be exposed to the costs of crime in a meaningful way.

There are no easy answers to the debate over whether or not prisons 'work'.

Although prisons do not seem to succeed in rehabilitating prisoners, it is possible that they deter people from committing crimes. While those who are actually imprisoned have not been deterred, the unpleasantness of prison life might well deter others. There is an almost intractable problem here for prison reformers. Making prisons thoroughly unpleasant places to be in probably helps deter potential offenders, but it makes the rehabilitating goals of prisons extremely difficult to achieve. (The harshness of prison life can also have unintended consequences, like the tragic death of Joseph Scholes discussed in the box below.) But the less harsh that prison conditions are, the more imprisonment loses its deterrent effect.

While prisons do keep some dangerous individuals off the streets, evidence suggests that we need to find other means to deter crime. A sociological interpretation of crime makes it clear that there are no quick fixes. The causes of crime are bound up with structural conditions of society, including poverty, the condition of the inner cities and the deteriorating life circumstances of many young men. While short-term measures, such as reforms that make prisons places of rehabilitation rather than simply incarceration, and experiments with alternatives to prison, such as community work schemes, need to be further explored, for solutions to be effective they must address the long term (Currie 1998).

Self-harm and suicide in prison: the death of Joseph Scholes

Joseph had an unsettled childhood and became a disturbed young boy. He had allegedly been sexually abused from an early age and was seeing a psychiatrist and taking medication at the time of his arrest. Joseph was depressed, had begun to self-harm and have periodic suicidal thoughts.

On 30 November 2001 he was voluntarily taken into the care of social services and placed in a children's home. Six days later, he went out with a group of children from the home and was involved in a series of mobile phone robberies. He was subsequently arrested and charged with robbery. Both victims and other witnesses accepted that Joseph's involvement in these incidents was peripheral; there was no suggestion that he had used or threatened violence.

As the robbery trial date drew nearer, Joseph became more depressed and agitated. Two weeks before his court appearance he slashed his face with a knife more than 30 times. The deepest wound, across his nose, cut right down to the bone. The walls in his room had to be completely repainted as they were covered in blood.

Prior to Joseph's sentencing, the judge at Manchester Crown Court was alerted to Joseph's vulnerability, his experience of sexual abuse and history of suicidal and self-harming behaviour.

Joseph was unfortunate to be tried at a time of heightened public anxiety over street crime. The Lord Chief Justice had issued sentencing guidelines which were widely interpreted as requiring an automatic custodial sentence for such crimes. On 15 March 2002 Joseph was sentenced to a two-year detention and training order. The judge stated in open court that he wanted the warnings about Joseph's self-harming and history of sexual abuse 'most expressly drawn to the attention of the authorities'.

After sentencing, the responsibility for Joseph's care transferred to the Youth Justice Board (YJB), which was informed of Joseph's history – most notably, his suicide attempt and self-harming behaviour. People involved in Joseph's care urged the YJB to place him in local authority secure accommodation where he would have access to the necessary intensive care and support. Despite his vulnerability, the

YJB placed him in Prison Service accommodation at Stoke Heath Young Offender Institution (YOI), claiming that no suitable alternative placement was available. Joseph's mother Yvonne subsequently telephoned Stoke Heath YOI to inform them that he had been a victim of sexual abuse, was depressed and unstable with a history of self-harm and suicidal behaviour.

On arrival at Stoke Heath YOI, Joseph was stripped of his clothing, including his underwear, and placed in a garment like a horse blanket with stiff Velcro fastenings. At the inquest, members of the jury and the coroner were visibly shocked when the garment was shown in court and the strip of clothing was described by a child care expert as 'dehumanizing'.

During his short time in Stoke Heath YOI he was kept in virtual seclusion and was not offered any meaningful activity. He was told that he would later be put on the main wing with other prisoners, a prospect that horrified him because of his history of sexual abuse. Joseph took his own life in March 2002.

A lack of close observation and unsafe conditions in Joseph's cell meant that he was able to hang himself from a sheet tied to the bars of his window. He was just nine days into his prison sentence . . .

A two-week inquest into Joseph's death was held in April 2004 . . . [Investigators] into Joseph's death were unanimous in their opinion that prison service accommodation was completely unsuitable for Joseph as it did not have the resources and facilities to cope with someone so vulnerable.

Source: Inquest, November 2004 (<http://inquest.gn.apc.org/pdf/Joseph%20 Scholes%20inquiry%20briefing%202004.pdf>)

The Howard League for Penal Reform, a pressure group working for the reform of the penal system, carries out research on criminal justice issues, including analysis of prison conditions. During 2003 it found that ninety-four men and women took their own lives in prison in England and Wales:

- fourteen women killed themselves: the highest number of women ever to take their lives in a single year;
- thirty-one young prisoners aged twenty-five years and under killed themselves; a third of the prisoners were on remand and 3 per cent were immigration detainees;
- five prisons experienced more than four deaths during 2003: Birmingham (4); Blakenhurst (5); Nottingham (4); Winchester (4); and Styal (4).

Anita Dockley, the Assistant Director at the Howard League said:

It is shameful that so many men and women in prison take their own lives. Yet sadly the Howard League does not anticipate the numbers falling while the prison population continues to surge and the system remains under such stress. The number of prison suicides will only fall when the numbers in prison are radically reduced and the strategies for dealing with suicide and self-harm are properly realized. We call on the government to act immediately to reduce the number of people behind bars.

The ability to implement prevention measures in prison must surely be given even greater prominence, especially when there is evidence of a national decline in suicide rates and among vulnerable psychiatric patients where prevention measures are starting to take effect.

Source: Howard League for Penal Reform (2004)

Questions

1 Is prison ever a suitable place for the punishment of young offenders?
2 How should society deal with minor crimes?
3 Why has the number of prisoners risen in recent years in the UK?

Conclusion: crime, deviance and social order

It would be a mistake to regard crime and deviance wholly in a negative light. Any society which recognizes that human beings have diverse values and concerns must find space for individuals or groups whose activities do not conform to the norms followed by the majority. People who develop new ideas, in politics, science, art or other fields, are often regarded with suspicion or hostility by those who follow orthodox ways. The political ideals developed in the American Revolution, for example – freedom of the individual and equality of opportunity – were fiercely resisted by many people at the time, yet they have now become accepted across the world. To deviate from the dominant norms of a society takes courage and resolution, but it is often crucial in securing processes of change which are later seen to be in the general interest.

Is 'harmful deviance' the price a society must pay when it allows considerable leeway for people to engage in non-conformist pursuits? For example, are high rates of criminal violence a cost which is exacted in a society in exchange for the individual liberties its citizens enjoy? Some have certainly suggested as much, arguing that crimes of violence are inevitable in a society where rigid definitions of conformity do not apply. But this view does not hold much water when examined closely. In some societies that recognize a wide range of individual freedoms and tolerate deviant activities (such as Holland), rates of violent crime are low. Conversely, countries where the scope of individual freedom is restricted (like some Latin American societies) may show high levels of violence.

A society that is tolerant towards deviant behaviour need not suffer social disruption. A good outcome can probably only be achieved, however, where individual liberties are joined to social justice – in a social order where inequalities are not glaringly large and in which everyone has a chance to lead a full and satisfying life. If freedom is not balanced with equality, and if many people find their lives largely devoid of self-fulfilment, deviant behaviour is likely to be channelled towards socially destructive ends.

Summary points

1 Deviant behaviour refers to actions which transgress commonly held norms. What is regarded as deviant can shift from time to time and place to place; 'normal' behaviour in one cultural setting may be labelled 'deviant' in another. The concept of deviance is broader than that of crime, which refers only to non-conformist conduct that breaks a law.

2 Sanctions, formal or informal, are applied by society to reinforce social norms. Laws are norms defined and enforced by governments.

3 Biological and physical theories have been developed claiming to show that crime and other forms of deviance are genetically determined; but these have been largely discredited. Sociologists argue that conformity and deviance are differently

defined in different social contexts. Divergences of wealth and power in society strongly influence what opportunities are open to different groups of individuals and what kinds of activities are regarded as criminal. Criminal activities are learned in much the same way as law-abiding ones, and in general are directed towards the same needs.

4   Functionalist theories see crime and deviance as produced by structural tensions and a lack of moral regulation within society. Durkheim introduced the term 'anomie' to refer to a feeling of anxiety and disorientation that comes with the breakdown of traditional life in modern society. Robert K. Merton extended the concept to include the strain felt by individuals whenever norms conflict with social reality. Subcultural explanations draw attention to groups, such as gangs, that reject mainstream values and replace them with norms celebrating defiance, delinquency or non-conformity.

5   Labelling theory (which assumes that labelling someone as deviant will reinforce their deviant behaviour) is important because it starts from the assumption that no act is intrinsically criminal (or normal). Labelling theorists are interested in how some behaviours come to be defined as deviant and why certain groups, but not others, are labelled as deviant.

6   Conflict theories analyse crime and deviance in terms of the structure of society, competing interests between social groups, and the preservation of power among elites.

7   Control theories posit that crime occurs when there are inadequate social or physical controls to deter it from happening. The growth of crime is linked to the growing number of opportunities and targets for crime in modern societies. The theory of broken windows suggests that there is a direct connection between the appearance of disorder and actual crime.

8   The extent of crime in any society is difficult to assess, as not all crimes are reported. The 'hidden figure' of unrecorded crime refers to offences not captured in official statistics. Victimization studies (surveys which ask respondents if they have been the victims of any crime during the previous year) reveal the discrepancy between official crime rates and people's actual experiences.

9   Rates of criminality are much lower for women than for men, probably because of general socialization differences between men and women, plus the greater involvement of men in non-domestic spheres. Unemployment and the 'crisis of masculinity' have been linked to male crime rates. In some types of crime, women are overwhelmingly the victims. Rape is almost certainly much more common than the official statistics reveal. There is a sense in which all women are victims of rape, since they have to take special precautions for their protection and live in fear of rape. Homosexual men and women experience high levels of criminal victimization and harassment, yet they are often seen as 'deserving' of crime rather than innocent victims because of their marginalized position in society.

10 Popular fear about crime often focuses on street crimes, such as theft, burglary and assault, that are largely the domain of young, working-class males. Official statistics reveal

high rates of offence among young people, yet we should be wary of moral panics about youth crime. Much deviant behaviour among youth, such as anti-social behaviour and non-conformity, is not in fact criminal.

11 White-collar crime and corporate crime refer to crimes carried out by those in the more affluent sectors of society. The consequences of such crime can be more far-reaching than the petty crimes of the poor, but there is less attention paid to them by law enforcement. Organized crime refers to institutionalized forms of criminal activity, in which many of the characteristics of orthodox organizations appear, but the activities engaged in are systematically illegal. Cybercrime describes criminal activity that is carried out with the help of information technology, such as electronic money-laundering and Internet fraud.

12 Prisons have developed partly to protect society and partly with the intention of 'reforming' the criminal. Prisons do not seem to deter crime, and the degree to which they rehabilitate prisoners to face the outside world without relapsing into criminality is dubious. Recidivism refers to repeat offending by individuals who have been in prison before. Alternatives to prison have been suggested, such as community-based sentencing.

Questions for further thought

1 How might the actions of someone labelled as 'deviant' be interpreted differently from the actions of a 'normal' person?

2 Why might victim surveys provide a more valid picture of the extent of crime than official statistics?

3 As women increasingly enter the public sphere, are changes in female criminality inevitable?

4 Is the corporate executive a more typical criminal than an unemployed youth?

5 How is crime affected by processes of globalization?

Further reading

H. Croall, *Crime and Society in Britain* (New York: Longman, 1998).

Erich Goode, *Deviant Behaviour* (Upper Saddle River, NJ: Prentice Hall, 1997).

Simon Holdaway and Paul Rock (eds), *Thinking about Criminology* (London: UCL Press, 1998).

J. Muncie and E. McLaughlin (eds), *Controlling Crime*, 2nd edn (London: SAGE, in association with The Open University, 2001).

J. Muncie and E. McLaughlin (eds), *The Problem of Crime*, 2nd edn (London: SAGE, in association with The Open University, 2001).

Paul Walton and Jock Young (eds), *The New Criminology Revisited* (London: Macmillan, 1998).

Robert Reiner, *The Politics of the Police* (Oxford: Oxford University Press, 1999).

Internet links

Amnesty International
http://www.amnesty.org

British Journal of Criminology
http://www3.oup.co.uk/crimin

Home Office (UK)
http://www.homeoffice.gov.uk

Howard League for Penal Reform
http://www.howardleague.org

NACRO – concerned with the prevention of crime and the welfare of offenders
http://www.nacro.org.uk

United Nations Crime and Justice Information Network
http://www.uncjin.org/

Contents

20 Politics, Government and Terrorism

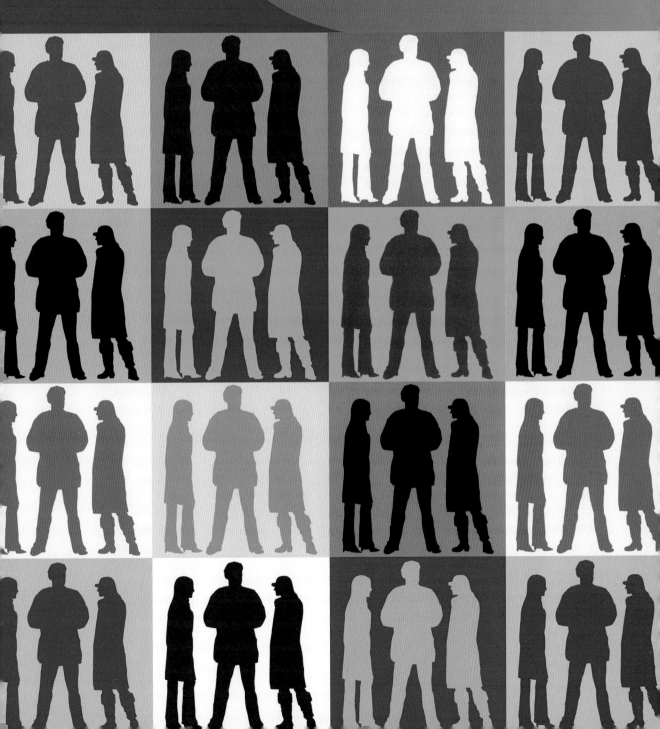

IN FEBRUARY 2003, global protests took place against the impending war in Iraq (see box on pp. 861–2). In London, more than one million people took to the streets: the country's largest ever demonstration. Similar size demonstrations took place in Rome and Barcelona, with smaller marches taking place in cities around the world from New York to Bangladesh. Rough estimates put the total number of protestors globally at up to ten million, in sixty countries (*Guardian*, 13 February 2003).

What made the coordination of millions of people marching on the same day in cities all over the world possible was the development of the media. Discussion of the likelihood of war dominated the television and newspapers for months before the event, and plans of the anti-war demonstration were circulated by the media in advance. Anti-war groups were able to mobilize supporters from a range of different backgrounds through emails and announcements on websites.

The people who marched in February 2003 were brought together by a variety of concerns. Some argued that, although democracy is the best model, exporting Western-style democracy to the Middle East by force contradicted its basic values. Others saw the war in the Middle East as a thinly veiled excuse for the West to get hold of a stable source of oil. In the UK, many feared that involvement in a US-led war would make Britain more, not less, likely to be the target of terrorist attacks like the ones suffered by Londoners on 7 July 2005 (see pp. 879–81). Another issue that mobilized support against the war was the failure of the pro-war governments to persuade the United Nations to pass a resolution explicitly allowing them to use force against Iraq for its non-compliance with earlier UN resolutions. When war with Iraq eventually began in March 2003, without explicit authorization from the United Nations, critics argued that it was illegitimate.

This chapter discusses many of the themes that emerged out of these protests and the subsequent war. We begin with a discussion of important, but contested, concepts in political sociology; in particular we examine the concept of power. We then look at the remarkable global spread of democracy over the last two decades and at issues of global governance. Next we highlight some of the crucial changes in British party politics in recent decades, including the rise of Thatcherism and of New Labour. From party politics we move on to politics in a wider sense, with a discussion of social movements, such as those behind the anti-war protests discussed above, and we look at some of the ways in which these movements are affected by globalization and changing technology. In many cases pressure for increased democracy has been tied to nationalist movements to create a powerful political force, so next we examine the rise of nationalism. We conclude with a discussion of one of the major issues in political sociology today: terrorism.

In February 2003 hundreds of thousands of people took to the streets to protest against the impending war in Iraq.

Debating basic concepts in political sociology

Politics, government and the state

Many people find politics remote and uninteresting, viewing it as the preserve, most often, of middle-aged men in Westminster, Brussels or Washington. Under this view, **politics** concerns the means whereby power is used to affect the scope and content of governmental activities. Yet politics is a contested concept and the sphere of the political may range well beyond that of government itself. The anti-war movement, with which we began this chapter, is a political movement, as are many of the groups, networks and organizations (such as those composed of environmentalists or feminists) that are discussed elsewhere in this book.

Whether we like it or not, however, all of our lives are touched by what happens in the political sphere – even in the narrow sense of governmental activity. Governments influence quite personal activities and, in times of war, can even order us to lay down our lives for aims they deem necessary. The sphere of **government** is the sphere of political power. All political life is about power: who holds it, how they achieve it and what they do with it. Below, the concept of power is examined more closely.

Where there is a political apparatus of government (institutions like a parliament or congress, plus civil service officials) ruling over a given territory, whose authority is backed by a legal system and by the capacity to use military force to implement its policies, we can say

that a **state** exists. All modern societies are **nation-states**. That is, they are states in which the great mass of the population consists of citizens who regard themselves as part of a single nation. Nation-states have come into existence at various times in different parts of the world (for example, the United States in 1776 and the Czech Republic in 1993). Their main characteristics contrast rather sharply with those of non-industrial or traditional civilizations, such as those described in chapter 2 ('Globalization and the Changing World'). They are:

- *Sovereignty* The territories ruled by traditional states were always poorly defined, the level of control wielded by the central government being quite weak. The notion of sovereignty – that a government possesses authority over an area with a clear-cut border, within which it is the supreme power – had little relevance. All nation-states, by contrast, are sovereign states.
- *Citizenship* In traditional states, most of the population ruled by the king or emperor showed little awareness of, or interest in, those who governed them. Neither did they have any political rights or influence. Normally only the dominant classes or more affluent groups felt a sense of belonging to an overall political community. In modern societies, by contrast, most people living within the borders of a political system are citizens, having common rights and duties and regarding themselves as part of a nation. While there are some people who are political refugees or are 'stateless', almost everyone in the world today is a member of a definite national political order.

- *Nationalism* Nation-states are associated with the rise of nationalism, which can be defined as a set of symbols and beliefs providing the sense of being part of a single political community. Thus, individuals feel a sense of pride and belonging in being British, American, Canadian, Russian, or whatever. These are the feelings that gave impetus to the quest of the East Timorese for independence. Probably people have always felt some kind of identity with social groups of one form or another – their family, village or religious community. Nationalism, however, made its appearance only with the development of the modern state. It is the main expression of feelings of identity with a distinct sovereign community. We will explore the phenomenon of nationalism in greater detail towards the end of this chapter.

Power

The meaning, nature and distribution of **power** are central issues for political sociologists. One of sociology's founding figures, Max Weber (whose work we looked at in chapter 1, pp. 17–19), gave a general definition of power as 'the chance of a man or a number of men to realize their own will in a command action even against the resistance of others who are participating in the action' (Gerth and Mills 1948). To Weber, power is about getting your own way, even when others don't want you to.

Many sociologists have followed Weber in making a distinction between forms of power that are *coercive* and those that have *authority*. Sceptics about the 2003 war in Iraq, for example, often criticized

the American-led invasion because it did not have explicit authority from the United Nations, so they viewed the war as illegitimate – a coercive use of power. Most forms of power are not based solely on force, but are legitimated by some form of authority.

Max Weber's discussion of power focused on distinguishing between different categories – or 'ideal types' – of authority. For Weber, there were three sources of authority: traditional, charismatic and rational-legal. *Traditional authority* is power legitimized through respect for long-established cultural patterns. Weber gives the example of hereditary family rule of nobles in medieval Europe.

By contrast, *charismatic authority* tends to disrupt tradition. It is drawn from the devotion felt towards a leader by his or her subordinates who believe that the leader possesses exceptional qualities that inspire devotion. 'Charisma', to Weber, is a trait of personality. Jesus Christ and Adolf Hitler are often given as examples of individuals with charismatic authority. Yet charismatic authority can be exercised in more mundane ways too: the authority of certain teachers, for example, may be in part charismatic. In Weber's view, most societies in the past were characterized by traditional authority structures which were periodically punctuated by bursts of charisma.

In the modern world, Weber argued, traditional authority was increasingly being replaced by *rational-legal authority*. This is power that is legitimated through legally enacted rules and regulations. It is found in modern organizations and bureaucracies (discussed in chapter 16), and in government, which Weber described as the formal organizations that direct the political life of a society (Gerth and Mills 1948).

Stephen Lukes: radical alternatives

An alternative and radical view of power has been proposed by the sociologist Stephen Lukes (1974). In his classic account Lukes offers a 'three-dimensional view' of power. The first dimension sees power in terms of the ability to make decisions to go one's own way in observable conflicts: for example, if the government had changed its support for military intervention in Iraq in response to the anti-war protests in February 2003, it would be evidence that the protestors had power. However, Lukes argues, the concept of power is much wider than this.

A second dimension to power concerns the ability to control what issues are decided upon. By this, Lukes means that groups or individuals with power can exercise it, not by making a decision, but by limiting the alternatives available to others. For example, one way in which authoritarian governments (such as in the Asian nation of Singapore: see p. 848) exert their power is by placing restrictions on what the press can report. In doing so, they are often able to prevent certain grievances – such as international condemnation of their use of judicial corporal punishment – from becoming issues within the political process.

Lukes argues that there is also a third dimension of power, which he calls the 'manipulation of desires'. He asks: 'Is it not the supreme exercise of power to get another or others to have the desires you want them to have – that is, to secure their compliance by controlling their thoughts and desires?' (1974). He points out that this does not necessarily mean brain-washing. Our desires can also be manipulated in more subtle ways. Marxists have sometimes argued, for example, that capitalists exercise power over workers by shaping their desires, through the media and other means of socialization, to take on the role of worker and mass consumer.

Drawing a distinction between the different dimensions of power, Lukes is able to present a wider definition of that than offered by Weber. For Lukes: '*A* exercises power over *B* when *A* affects *B* in a manner contrary to *B*'s interests' (ibid.). This still leaves the question, how do we know what *B*'s interests are? Lukes admits that this is ultimately a matter of opinion. Still, his conception of power has been influential in alerting sociologists to the different dimensions that the exercise of power involves.

Foucault and power

The French sociologist Michel Foucault (1926–84) has also developed a highly influential account of power, far removed from Weber's more formal definition. Foucault argued that power was not concentrated in one institution, such as the state, or held by any one group of individuals. He argued that these older models of power, including that of Stephen Lukes, relied on fixed identities. Power was held by groups that were easily identifiable: for example, the ruling class (for Marxists) or men (for feminists). Instead, Foucault argued power operates at all levels of social interaction, in all social institutions, by all people.

Foucault's thought was introduced in chapter 4, 'Theoretical Thinking in Sociology', pp. 116–17, and his account of power in organizations is discussed in chapter 16, 'Organizations and Networks', pp. 647–52.

To Foucault, power and knowledge are closely tied together, and serve to reinforce one another. The claims to knowledge of a doctor, for example, are also claims to power as they are put into practice in an institutional context, such as a hospital. The increase in knowledge about health and illness gave power to doctors who could claim authority over patients. Foucault describes the development of 'discourses', which provide ways of discussing power and knowledge – a 'Foucauldian' (someone who supports Foucault's arguments) might talk about 'medical discourses', for example (see p. 260).

Foucault's ideas have gained popularity as political sociology has shifted away from straightforward conflict theories (see p. 22), especially economic interpretations of Marxism, towards forms of political struggle based on identity, such as gender or sexuality (Foucault 1967, 1978). Foucault's account breaks down the simple division introduced above between authoritative and coercive forms of power (see p. 845), as power is understood as something found in all social relations rather than something exercised by dominant groups. Foucault's conception of power therefore widens the conception of the political. Critics of Foucault, however, argue that whilst he provided a highly subtle account of the way in which power operates in everyday social interactions, his hazy conception of the term underestimates the concentration of power in structures such as the military or social class.

Having looked at rival conceptions of power, we now concentrate in this chapter on the way in which power is exercised in formal politics. In the next section we turn from discussions of political power to their exercise, by examining two forms of political system.

Authoritarianism and democracy

Throughout history, societies have relied on a variety of political systems. Even today, at the start of the twenty-first century, countries around the world continue to organize themselves according to different patterns and configurations. While most societies now claim to be democratic – that is to say, they are ruled by the people – other forms of political rule continue to exist. In this section we shall profile democracy and authoritarianism, two of the basic types of political system.

Authoritarianism

If democracy, which we examine below, encourages the active involvement of citizens in political affairs, in **authoritarian states** popular participation is denied or severely curtailed. In such societies, the needs and interests of the state are prioritized over those of average citizens and no legal mechanisms have been established for opposing government or for removing a leader from power.

Authoritarian governments exist today in many countries, some of which profess to be democratic. Iraq, under the leadership of Saddam Hussein until 2003, was an example of an authoritarian state where dissent was smothered and an inordinate share of national resources was diverted for the benefit of a select few. The powerful monarchies in Saudi Arabia and Kuwait and the leadership of Myanmar (Burma) strictly curtail citizens' civil liberties and deny them meaningful participation in government affairs.

The Asian nation of Singapore is often cited as an example of so-called 'soft authoritarianism'. This is because the ruling People's Action Party maintains a tight grip on power but ensures a high quality of life for its citizens by intervening in almost all aspects of society. Singapore is notable for its safety, its civil order and the social inclusion of all citizens. Singapore's economy is successful, the streets are clean, people are employed and poverty is virtually unknown. However, despite the high standard of living in material terms, even minor transgressions such as dropping litter or smoking in public are punishable by stiff fines; there is tight regulation of the media, access to the Internet and on the ownership of satellite dishes; the police possess extraordinary powers to detain citizens for suspected offences and the use of corporal and capital judicial punishments is common. Despite this authoritarian control, popular satisfaction with the government has been high and social inequalities are minimal in comparison with many other countries. While Singapore may be lacking in democratic freedoms, the country's brand of authoritarianism is different from those of more dictatorial regimes, leading the writer William Gibson to describe the island as 'Disneyland with the death penalty'.

Democracy

The word **democracy** has its roots in the Greek term *demokratia*, the individual parts of which are *demos* ('people') and *kratos* ('rule'). Democracy in its basic meaning is therefore a political system in which the people, not monarchs or aristocracies, rule. This sounds straightforward enough, but it is not. Democratic rule has taken contrasting forms at varying periods and in different societies, depending on how the concept is interpreted. For example, 'the people' has been variously understood to mean all men, owners of property, white men, educated men, and adult men and women. In some societies the officially accepted version of democracy is limited to the political sphere, whereas in others it is extended to broader areas of social life.

The form that democracy takes in a given context is largely an outcome of how its values and goals are understood and prioritized. Democracy is generally seen as the political system which is most able to ensure political equality, protect liberty and freedom, defend the common interest, meet citizens' needs, promote moral self-development and enable effective decision-making which takes everyone's interests into account (Held 1996). The weight that is granted to these various goals may influence whether democracy is regarded first and foremost as a form of popular power (self-government and self-regulation) or whether it is seen as a framework for supporting decision-making by others (such as a group of elected representatives).

Participatory democracy

In **participatory democracy** (or direct democracy), decisions are made communally by those affected by them. This was the original type of democracy practised in ancient Greece. Those who were citizens, a small minority of the society, regularly assembled to consider policies and

A show of military strength at a May Day parade in North Korea. The country is perhaps the most politically isolated in the world, and its leader one of the most authoritarian. Head of State Kim Jong-il has recently decreed that men's hair may be no more than five centimetres in length. Balding men over the age of fifty are allowed an additional two centimetres for a 'comb-over'.

make major decisions. Participatory democracy is of limited importance in modern societies, where the mass of the population have political rights, and it would be impossible for everyone actively to participate in the making of all the decisions that affect them.

Yet some aspects of participatory democracy do play a part in modern societies. Small communities in New England, in the north-eastern part of the United States, continue the traditional practice of annual 'town meetings'. On these designated days, all the residents of the town gather together to discuss and vote on local issues that do not fall under state or federal government jurisdiction. Another example of participatory democracy is the holding of referenda, when the people express their views on a particular issue. Direct consultation of large numbers of people is made possible by simplifying the issue down to one or two questions to be answered. Referenda are regularly used at the national level in some European countries to inform important policy decisions. There were referenda in several European countries in 2005 over whether they should sign up to the proposed European Constitution. The UK also agreed to hold a vote, but the defeat of the proposal in France and the Netherlands in May 2005 destroyed any immediate hopes of the treaty being adopted and led to the suspension of plans for a British referendum. They have also been used to decide contentious issues of secession in ethnic nationalist regions such as Quebec, the predominantly French-speaking province of Canada.

Representative democracy

Practicalities render participatory democracy unwieldy on a large scale, except in specific instances such as a special referendum. More common today is **representative democracy**, political systems in which decisions affecting a community are taken, not by its members as a whole, but by people they have elected for this purpose. In the area of national government, representative democracy takes the form of elections to congresses, parliaments or similar national bodies. Representative democracy also exists at other levels where collective decisions are taken, such as in provinces or states within an overall national community, cities, counties, boroughs and other regions. Many large organizations choose to run their affairs using representative democracy by electing a small executive committee to take key decisions.

Countries in which voters can choose between two or more parties and in which the mass of the adult population has the right to vote are usually called liberal democracies. Britain and the other Western European countries, the USA, Japan, Australia and New Zealand all fall into this category. Many countries in the developing world, such as India, also have liberal democratic systems, and, as we shall see, this number is growing.

The global spread of democracy

When political sociologists of the future look back on the 1980s and 1990s, one historical development in particular is likely to stand out: the democratization of many of the world's nations. Since the early 1980s, a number of countries in Latin America, such as Chile, Bolivia and Argentina, have undergone the transition from authoritarian military rule to a thriving democracy. Similarly, with the collapse of the Communist bloc in 1989, many East European states – Russia, Poland and Czechoslovakia, for example – have become democratic. And in Africa, a number of previously undemocratic nations – including Benin, Ghana, Mozambique and South Africa – have come to embrace democratic ideals.

In the mid-1970s, more than two-thirds of all societies in the world could be considered authoritarian. Since that time, the situation has shifted markedly – now less than a third of societies are authoritarian in nature. Democracy is no longer concentrated primarily in Western countries, but is now endorsed, at least in principle, as the desired form of government in many areas of the world. As David Held (1996) has noted, 'democracy has become the fundamental standard of political legitimacy in the current era'.

The tearing down of the Berlin Wall in 1989 was a symbolic moment in the rapid dismantling of Communism in the East, giving way to an unprecedented spread of liberal democratic institutions.

In this section we will consider the global spread of liberal democracy and advance some possible explanations for its popularity. We will then move on to examine some of the main problems democracy faces in the contemporary world.

The fall of Communism

For a long while, the political systems of the world were divided between liberal democracy and communism, as found in the former Soviet Union and Eastern Europe (and which still exists in China and a few other countries). For much of the twentieth century, a large proportion of the world's population lived under political systems that were communist or socialist in orientation. The hundred years following Marx's death in 1883 seemed to bear out his prognosis of the spread of socialism and workers' revolutions around the globe.

Communist states regarded themselves as democracies, although the systems in these countries differed greatly from what people in the West understand by democracy. Communism was essentially a system of one-party rule. Voters were given a choice not between different parties but between different candidates of the same party – the Communist Party; there was often only one candidate running. There was thus no real choice at all. The Communist Party was easily the most dominant power in Soviet-style societies: it controlled not just the political system but the economy as well.

Almost everyone in the West, from trained scholars to average citizens, believed that the communist systems were deeply entrenched and had become a permanent feature of global politics. Few people, if any, predicted the dramatic course of events that began to unfold in 1989 as one communist regime after the other collapsed in a series of 'velvet revolutions'. What had seemed like a solid and pervasively established system of rule throughout Eastern Europe was thrown off almost overnight. The Communists lost power in an accelerating sequence in the countries they had dominated for half a century: Hungary, Poland, Bulgaria, East Germany, Czechoslovakia and Romania. Eventually, the Communist Party within the Soviet Union itself lost control of power. When the fifteen constituent republics of the USSR declared their independence in 1991, Mikhail Gorbachev, the last Soviet leader, was rendered a 'president without a state'. Even in China, the students and others protesting in Tiananmen Square in 1989 seemed to shake the Communist Party's grip on power until they were brutally dispersed by the army.

Since the fall of the Soviet Union, processes of democratization have continued to spread. Even among what were some of the world's most authoritarian states,

signs of democratization can be detected. Afghanistan was controlled by the Soviet Union after their troops invaded in 1979. The USSR occupation ended ten years later, after fierce resistance from the mujahidin (Muslim guerrilla warriors). During the early 1990s the country was the site of infighting between warlords composed of mujahidin factions. By 1996 the **Taliban** had seized control of most of the country and began the creation of a 'pure Islamic state'. They introduced an extreme interpretation of Islamic law, bringing in public executions and amputations, forbidding girls from going to school and women from working and banning 'frivolous' entertainment. Following the events of 9/11, the USA successfully led efforts to topple the Taliban, which it linked to the terrorist attacks. In late 2001, Hamid Karzai was chosen as Chairman of the Afghan Interim Authority, becoming President in June 2002, and he set about gaining approval for a new constitution. The constitution was signed in January 2004 and provides a strong executive branch, a moderate role for Islam and basic protections for human rights. The first elections in Afghanistan were held in October 2004 and resulted in Karzai winning a five-year mandate as President.

In China, which contains about a fifth of the world's population, the communist government is facing strong pressures to become more democratic. Thousands of people remain in prison in China for the non-violent expression of their desire for democracy (see box on the Internet and democratization, p. 855). But there are still groups, resisted by the Communist government, working actively to secure a transition to a democratic system. In recent years, other authoritarian Asian

The triumph of democracy: the end of history?

The writer whose name has come to be synonymous with the phrase 'the end of history' is Francis Fukuyama (1989). Fukuyama's classic and highly contested conception of the end of history is based on the worldwide triumph of capitalism and liberal democracy. In the wake of the 1989 revolutions in Eastern Europe, the dissolution of the Soviet Union and a movement towards multiparty democracy in other regions, Fukuyama argued, the ideological battles of earlier eras are over. The end of history is the end of alternatives. No one any longer defends monarchism, and fascism is a phenomenon of the past. So is communism, for so long the major rival of Western democracy. Capitalism has won in its long struggle with socialism, contrary to Marx's prediction, and liberal democracy now stands unchallenged. We have reached, Fukuyama asserts, 'the end point of mankind's ideological evolution and [the] universalisation of Western democracy as the final form of human government'.

Fukuyama's thesis has provoked critical responses, yet in some sense he has highlighted a key phenomenon of our time. At present, there is no sizeable electorate or mass movement able to envisage forms of economic and political organization beyond that of the market and liberal democracy. Although this currently seems to be the case, however, it seems very doubtful that history has come to a stop in the sense that we have exhausted all alternatives open to us. Who can say what new forms of economic, political or cultural order may emerge in the future? Just as the thinkers of medieval times had no inkling of the industrial society that was to emerge with the decline of feudalism, so we can't at the moment anticipate how the world will change over the coming century.

Questions

1 What did Fukuyama mean by his phrase 'the end of history'?
2 Was Fukuyama right to argue that we had reached 'the end of history'?
3 If we are now in a post-communist era, what political alternatives are open to us?

states, such as Myanmar, Indonesia and Malaysia, have also witnessed growing democratic movements. Some of these calls for greater freedoms have been met with violent responses. Nonetheless, the 'globalization of democracy' continues apace around the world.

This general trend towards democracy is not fixed in stone. For some countries in the former Soviet bloc, such as Poland, the Czech Republic, Hungary and the Baltic states, liberal democracy appears to be taking a firm hold, while in others, such as the former Central Asian republics of the Soviet Union, Yugoslavia and even Russia, democracy remains fragile. Indeed, democratic political institutions have been shown to be fragile and vulnerable at various points in history. In Iran, for example, one of the world's most militant Islamic states, popular discontent with the powerful mullahs (religious leaders) led to the election of reformist President Mohammed Khatami in 1997 with over 70 per cent of the vote. It seemed as if democracy was coming to Iran. Khatami was likened to Mikhail Gorbachev, as a leader who recognizes that popular yearnings for democracy – if left unaddressed – will result in the collapse of the system itself. However, Khatami only succeeded in introducing limited reforms after religious conservatives regained control of parliament, and in June 2005 one of their member, Mahmoud Ahmadinejad, was elected President, leaving prospects for further democratic reform highly unlikely. The recent history of Iran shows that we should not assume that democratization is an irreversible process. Yet the fact that democratization is tied to larger globalizing forces is reason for optimism about the future of democracy.

For more on the Taliban, terrorism and the risks that it creates for democracies, see pp. 879–88

Explaining the popularity of democracy

Why has democracy become so popular? One frequently cited explanation is that other types of political rule have been attempted and have failed – that democracy has proved itself to be the 'best' political system. It seems clear that democracy is a better form of political organization than authoritarianism, but this alone does not adequately explain the recent waves of democratization. While a full explanation for these developments would require a detailed analysis of the social and political situations in each country that led up to the transition to democracy, there can be little doubt but that globalizing processes have played an important role in this trend.

First, the growing number of cross-national cultural contacts that globalization has brought with it has invigorated democratic movements in many countries. A globalized media, along with advances in communications technology, has exposed inhabitants of many non-democratic nations to democratic ideals, increasing internal pressure on political elites to hold elections (see the box on democratization and the Internet opposite. Of course, such pressure does not automatically result from the diffusion of the notion of popular sovereignty. More important is that with globalization, news of democratic revolutions and accounts of the mobilizing processes that lead to them are quickly spread on a regional level. News of the revolution in Poland in 1989, for example, took little time to travel to Hungary, providing pro-democracy activists there with a useful, regionally appropriate model around which to orient their work.

Second, international organizations such as the United Nations and the European Union – which, in a globalized world, come to play an increasingly important role – have put external pressure on non-democratic states to move in democratic directions. (The European Union is profiled in the box on pp. 858–9.) In some cases, these organizations have been able to use trade embargoes, the conditional provision of loans for economic development and stabilization, and diplomatic manoeuvres of various kinds to encourage the dismantling of authoritarian regimes.

Third, democratization has been facilitated by the expansion of world capitalism. Although transnational corporations are notorious for striking deals with dictators, corporations generally prefer to do business in democratic states – not because of an inherent philosophical preference for political freedom and equality, but because democracies tend to be more stable than other kinds of states, and stability and predictability are essential for maximizing profits. Because political, economic and military elites, particularly in the developing world and in the former Soviet Union, are often anxious to increase levels of international trade and to encourage transnationals to set up shop in their countries, they have sometimes pursued a democratic agenda of their own, leading to what the political sociologist Barrington Moore (1966), once called 'revolutions from above'.

It is true that if globalization were the sole cause of the most recent wave of democratization, all countries today would be democratic. The persistence of authoritarian regimes in such countries as China, Cuba and Nigeria suggests that globalizing forces are not always sufficient to force a transition to democracy.

But democratic moves are afoot even in several of these countries, leading some sociologists to argue that under the influence of globalization, many more nations will become democratic in the years to come.

Globalization and everyday life: the Internet and democratization

The Internet is a powerful democratizing force. It transcends national and cultural borders, facilitates the spread of ideas around the globe and allows like-minded people to find one another in the realm of cyberspace. More and more people in countries around the world access the Internet regularly and consider it to be important to their lifestyles. Yet the dynamic spread of the Internet is perceived as a threat by governments – especially authoritarian ones – that recognize the potential of online activity to subvert state authority. Although the Internet has been allowed to exist more or less freely in most countries, some states have begun to take steps to curb its usage by citizens.

By the end of 2003, just eight years after the Internet became commercially available, the number of Internet users in China had reached 79.5 million, and this total continues to rise rapidly. In the eyes of the Chinese Communist leadership, the Internet presents a dangerous threat to state security by allowing political opposition groups to coordinate their activities.

In response to the rapid growth of the Internet, the Chinese government has introduced scores of regulations, closed thousands of Internet cafés, blocked emails, search engines, foreign news and politically sensitive websites, and introduced a filtering system for web searches on a list of prohibited key words and terms. Nevertheless, it appears that Internet activism is continuing to grow in China as fast as the controls are tightened.

In 2004 Amnesty International reported:

Signing online petitions, calling for reform and an end to corruption, planning to set up a pro-democracy party, publishing 'rumours about [the disease] SARS', communicating with groups abroad, opposing the persecution of the [religious movement] Falun Gong and calling for a review of the 1989 crackdown on the democracy protests are all examples of activities considered by the authorities to be 'subversive' or to 'endanger state security'. Such charges almost always result in prison sentences.

In an earlier report Amnesty estimated that '30,000 state security personnel are reportedly monitoring websites, chat rooms and private email messages' (2002).

Other governments have reached similar conclusions. The Burmese government has announced a ban on the dissemination of information 'detrimental to government' through the Internet or email. The Malaysian authorities demanded that cybercafés keep lists of all individuals who use their computers. Religious conservatives in the Iranian government forced the closure of hundreds of Internet cafés in late 2003 and introduced new rules requiring proprietors to restrict customers' access to a long list of 'immoral and anti-Islamic sites'.

Questions

1 How does the Internet differ from older forms of technology in acting as a democratizing force?
2 If the Internet is promoting the spread of global democracy, is it also promoting a global culture?

What explains increasing voter apathy?

Democracy in trouble?

As democracy is becoming so widespread, we might expect it to be working in a highly successful way. Yet such is not the case. Almost everywhere, democracy is in some difficulty. This is not only because it is proving difficult to set up a stable democratic order in Russia and other former communist societies. Democracy seems to be in trouble in its main countries of origin – the UK is a good example. In Britain, like other Western countries, the number of people who vote in European, general and local elections has declined considerably since the early 1990s (see table 20.1).

It has been argued that the decline in voting shows that people in the West seem have lost trust in those in power: some academics and politicians have talked about a wider 'crisis of trust' in society. The philosopher Onora O'Neil (2002) sums up this view:

> Mistrust and suspicion have spread across all areas of life, and supposedly with good reason. Citizens, it is said, no longer trust governments, or politicians, or ministers, or the police, or the courts, or the prison service. Consumers, it is said, no longer trust business, especially big business, or their products. None of us, it is said, trusts banks, or insurers, or pension providers. Patients, it is said, no longer trust doctors . . . and in particular no longer trust hospitals or hospital consultants. 'Loss of trust' is, in short, a cliché of our times.

Table 20.1   UK general elections: electorates and turnout, 1945–2005

Year	Turnouts %[a]
1945	72.8
1950	83.9
1951	82.6
1955	76.8
1959	78.7
1964	77.1
1966	75.8
1970	72.0
Feb 1974	78.8
Oct 1974	72.8
1979	76.0
1983	72.7
1987	75.3
1992	77.7
1997	71.5
2001	59.4
2005	61.3

[a] Total valid vote as a percentage of the electorate

Source: <http://www.electoral-reform.org.uk/publications/statistics/turnouts.htm> accessed 30.6.05

Evidence seems to confirm a loss of trust, at least when it comes to party politics. In the UK, for example, surveys have been carried out in general election years that ask voters if they trust the government to put national interests above party interests, 'all or most of the time'; the number of people who said they did not trust the government on this issue fell from 47 per cent in 1987, to 33 per cent in 1992 to 28 per cent in 2001 (cited in Skidmore and Harkin 2003).

Some have argued that trends like these indicate that people are increasingly sceptical of traditional forms of authority. Con-nected to this has been a shift in political values in democratic nations from 'scarcity values' to 'post-materialist values' (Inglehart 1997). This means that after a certain level of economic prosperity has been reached, voters become concerned less with economic issues than with the quality of their individual (as opposed to collective) lifestyles, such as the desire for meaningful work. As a result, voters are generally less interested in national politics, except for issues involving personal liberty.

The last few decades have also been a period in which, in several Western countries, the welfare state has come under attack. Rights and benefits, fought for over long periods, have been contested and cut back. Right-wing parties, such as the Conservatives in the UK or the Republicans in the USA, have attempted to reduce levels of welfare expenditure in their countries. One reason for this governmental retrenchment is the declining revenues available to governments as a result of the general world recession that began in the early 1970s. Yet there also seems to have developed an increasing scepticism, shared not only by some governments but by many of their citizens, about the effectiveness of relying on the state for the provision of many essential goods and services. This scepticism is based on the belief that the welfare state is bureaucratic, alienating and inefficient, and that welfare benefits can create perverse consequences that undermine what they were designed to achieve.

Global governance

As the American sociologist Daniel Bell has observed, national government is too small to respond to the big questions, such as the influence of global economic competition or the destruction of the world's environment; but it has become too big to deal with the small questions, issues that affect particular cities or regions (Bell 1997). Governments have little power, for instance, over the activities of giant business corporations, the main actors within the global economy. A British corporation may decide to shut down its production plants in the UK and shift production to Malaysia, as vacuum-cleaner manufacturer Dyson did in 2002 for example, in order to lower costs and compete more effectively with other corporations. The result is that British workers lose their jobs. They are likely to want the government to do something, but national governments are unable to control processes bound up with the world economy. All the government can do is try to soften the blow, for example, by providing unemployment benefits or job retraining.

Globalization has created new risks: the spread of weapons of mass destruction, pollution, terrorism and international financial crises, for example. These issues cannot be managed by nation-states alone and international governmental organizations (IGOs), like the World Bank, World Trade Organization and the United Nations, have been created as a way of pooling global risks. These organizations form the basis for discussions about **global governance**. Global governance is not about creating government on a global level. Instead it is concerned with the framework of rules needed to tackle global problems, and the diverse set of institutions (including both international organizations and national governments) needed to guarantee this framework of rules. Many of the global organizations already in place to tackle these problems lack democratic accountability. For example, the UN Security Council has fifteen members, of which five are permanent: the USA, Britain, France, China and Russia – several of the world's most powerful countries. For any resolution to be passed the Council requires nine votes, including the votes of all five permanent members. The UN did not back a

The European Union

The historical roots of the European Union lie in the Second World War. The idea of European integration was conceived to prevent such destruction from ever happening again. The British wartime Prime Minister Winston Churchill called for a 'United States of Europe' in 1946. The first practical moves towards European unity were proposed by the French Foreign Minister Robert Schuman in a speech on 9 May 1950. This date, the 'birthday' of what is now the EU, is celebrated annually as 'Europe Day'.

Initially, the European Union (EU) consisted of just six countries: Belgium, Germany, France, Italy, Luxembourg and the Netherlands.

Denmark, Ireland and the United Kingdom joined in 1973, Greece in 1981, Spain and Portugal in 1986, Austria, Finland and Sweden in 1995. In 2004 the biggest ever enlargement took place with ten new countries joining, mainly from Eastern Europe. Bulgaria and Romania are also expected join the EU in the next few years, and membership talks are beginning with Turkey.

In the early years, much of the cooperation between EU countries was about trade and the economy, but now the EU also deals with many other subjects of direct importance for our everyday life. EU agencies deal with areas as diverse as citizens' rights, security, job creation, regional development and environmental protection. EU member countries are democratic, and must be committed to working together for peace and prosperity.

Some people, especially in the UK, are concerned that membership of the EU undermines national sovereignty – that is, the independence and ability for self-government – of existing states, while others argue that the EU is not much more than another international body like the United Nations or the World Trade Organization.

Defenders of the EU argue that both the accounts above are inaccurate. They argue that the EU is an organization whose Member States have set up common institutions to which they delegate some of their power so that decisions on specific matters of joint interest can be made democratically at European level. All EU decisions and procedures are based on the Treaties, which are agreed by all the EU countries. This pooling of sovereignty is also called 'European integration'.

There are five EU institutions, each playing a specific role:

- European Parliament (elected by the peoples of the Member States);
- Council of the European Union (representing the governments of the Member States);
- European Commission (driving force and executive body);
- Court of Justice (ensuring compliance with the law);
- Court of Auditors (controlling sound and lawful management of the EU budget).

These are flanked by five other important bodies:

- European Economic and Social Committee (expresses the opinions of organized civil society on economic and social issues);
- Committee of the Regions (expresses the opinions of regional and local authorities);
- European Central Bank (responsible for monetary policy and managing the euro);
- European Ombudsman (deals with citizens' complaints about maladministration by any EU institution or body);

- European Investment Bank (helps achieve EU objectives by financing investment projects).

A number of agencies and other bodies complete the system.

The growth of the EU gave European leaders the opportunity to overhaul the organization's basic documents. In 2002 a constitutional convention was launched, chaired by former French President Valéry Giscard d'Estaing. The EU constitution, or 'constitutional treaty' which it produced, pulled together various treaties into a single document and committed members to closer cooperation on defence and immigration, amongst others things, and to stewardship under a single EU president. Defeat of the constitution in referenda in France and the Netherlands in 2005 (see p. 850) seems to have ended the hopes of those in favour of closer European political integration for the time being.

Supporters of the European Union argue that it has delivered half a century of stability, peace and prosperity. It has helped to raise living standards, built a single Europe-wide market, launched the single European currency, the euro, and strengthened Europe's voice in the world. The EU fosters co-operation among the peoples of Europe, promoting unity while preserving diversity and ensuring that decisions are taken as close as possible to the citizens. In the increasingly interdependent world of the twenty-first century, it will be even more necessary for every European citizen to cooperate with people from other countries in a spirit of curiosity, tolerance and solidarity.

Sources: 'The European Union at a Glance': *The Economist* (3 June 2005, 23 June 2005)

Questions

1 Is the European Union better equipped to deal with politics in a global age than the nation-state?
2 Does the EU have a 'democratic deficit' as some critics have claimed?
3 Does membership of the EU challenge national identity?
4 Is the UK's membership of the EU beneficial?

resolution explicitly allowing force against Iraq in 2003, because France threatened to veto it. This was one of the main grounds cited by critics of the war, who condemned it as an illegitimate use of power, as we saw at the start of this chapter. The views of the vast majority of the world's poorer countries were largely irrelevant to the debate.

We discuss the emergence of IGOs in chapter 16, 'Organizations and Networks', pp. 652–5.

What, then, is the fate of democracy in an age when democratic governance on a state level seems ill-equipped to deal with the flow of events? Some observers suggest that there is little to be done, that government cannot hope to control the rapid changes occurring around us, and that the most prudent course of action is to reduce the role of government and allow market forces to guide the way.

The British sociologist David Held contests this view. Held (2004) argues that in a global age we are in need of more, not less, government. Yet effective governing in our present era demands a deepening of democracy, at the level of the nation-state as well as above and below it. Held maintains that a **global social democracy** is needed to face the new challenges that globalization brings. This involves making global organizations accountable, in the same way that democratically elected governments are accountable to their electorate in national elections. Held argues that the foundations are already in place for a global social democracy. The International Criminal Court, which was set up to prosecute and bring to justice those responsible for the worst global crimes (such as genocide, crimes against humanity and war crimes), and the United

Nations both provide good foundations, although the latter needs to be made more democratically accountable. These institutions foster a vision of a world in which basic human rights are protected and a peaceful process for resolution of difference is agreed upon. The existence of these organizations marks the entrenchment of the values of the equal dignity and worth of all humans.

In Held's view, global social democracy will be achieved through multi-layer governance in which many organizations operate together at different levels: local, national and global. Whilst states were once the main actors in international politics, through their heads and foreign ministers, the primary actors now include administrative agencies, courts and legislatures as well. Think of how crucial the Secretary-General of the UN, Kofi Annan, has been in international politics, for example. Held also argues that non-governmental organizations, such as Oxfam and Amnesty International, as well as new social movements can also play an important role in the creation of global social democracy. Below, we turn from global questions to look at party politics in the UK, and we examine some of the major changes in British politics in recent decades.

Party politics in the UK

British electoral politics have changed significantly over the past three decades. The Labour and Conservative parties have each come under increasing pressure from dwindling membership rates, lower resources and a loss of voting support. The Labour Party managed successfully to

The Iraq War and after

After the Gulf War in 1991, Iraq was subjected to UN-imposed sanctions and weapons inspections. But Saddam Hussein rebuffed UN inspectors in November 1998, leading to a four-day bombardment of Iraq by American and British forces. The Allies – who were already patrolling 'no-fly zones' over northern and southern Iraq to stop attacks on dissident minorities – maintained a low-level air battery to stifle Iraq's anti-aircraft fire.

Sanctions ultimately failed to dislodge Saddam Hussein, whose resilience sowed confusion in the West. They were instead disastrous for ordinary Iraqis, even after a mitigating oil-for-food programme was introduced in 1996 (and especially since [the terrorist attacks on New York and Washington on] September 11th 2001). America and Britain tried to impose 'smart sanctions' on Iraq, but these efforts failed, and in May 2002, the UN slightly eased sanctions on Iraq.

The September 11th terrorist attacks changed America's thinking about Saddam. [The US President] George Bush [who took office in early 2001] . . . pushed for Saddam's ejection, and he vowed to act if the UN did not. After much diplomatic wrangling, the UN Security Council approved a strongly worded resolution calling on Saddam to allow unconditional weapons inspections. Saddam accepted, and inspectors began work in November 2002. But America and Britain concluded that he was defying the Security Council (though after the war it turned out that he had no active illegal weapons

George W. Bush with American troops in Iraq at Thanksgiving, 2004.

programme) and despite objections from France and others, launched a war on March 20th 2003. Three and a half weeks later, coalition forces had won, and Mr Bush was turning his attention to the long and expensive task of reconstruction.

Coalition forces have struggled to restore order to Iraq since ousting Saddam Hussein . . . Hopes that Saddam's capture and the killing of his sons would bring calm have proved ill-founded. Evidence of torture by American troops has led many to wonder if their presence is the problem rather than the solution. But Iraqi troops are still not ready to shoulder the burden of providing security.

In June 2004 control of Iraq's sovereignty passed from the Coalition Provisional Authority to an interim government led by Iyad Allawi. This struggled to improve Iraq's security, despite being able to call upon foreign military muscle and financial aid. Iraq's general election in January 2005 was a huge, and largely peaceful, step towards building the Arab world's first democracy. The new government will be dominated by the Shia majority – though to

legislate it will need to work with the Kurds and even the Sunni minority. It has one year to write a constitution that knits the country together before new elections are held.

Meanwhile, the country's infrastructure is being repaired and improved, and plans are afoot to privatize its moribund state-owned industries. But private investors are unlikely to open their purses until violence abates and a secure legal framework is in place. International lenders are holding off until questions about Iraq's responsibility for debts are answered.

Sources: *The Economist*
(18 October 2004, 10 March 2005)

Questions

1 What policies should the West have on 'rogue states' like Iraq?
2 Was a pre-emptive attack on Iraq justifiable?
3 Did the war in Iraq make terrorism more or less likely?
4 Is it possible to fight terrorism through conventional war?

reinvent itself and returned to power in 1997, repeating its general election success in 2001 and 2005, while the Conservative Party continues to face record lows in membership levels and an ageing base of supporters.

Several factors are important for understanding the experience of the main parties over the past three decades. The first factor is structural: the proportion of the economically active population involved in traditional blue-collar occupations has dropped considerably. There is little doubt that this has eroded some traditional sources of support for Labour, such as working-class communities and trade unions.

A second factor is the split that occurred in the Labour Party at the beginning of the

1980s, which led to the founding of the Social Democratic Party (SDP), which merged with the Liberal Party in 1988 to form the Liberal Democrats. In recent general elections, Britain's 'third party' has achieved significant support and drawn votes away from the two main parties. For much of the post-war period, the Liberal Party had only a small number of seats in Parliament (ranging from a low of 6 to a peak of 23 in 1983). Since 1997 this figure has risen. In the general election of 2005 the Liberal Democrats won 62 seats in the House of Commons (out of a total of 646) and gained over 21 per cent of the popular vote.

A third influence was that of the Conservative Prime Minister Margaret Thatcher, in post from 1979 to 1990. The vigorous programme of change initiated by Thatcher and her cabinets expressed a significant move from earlier Tory philosophy. 'Thatcherism' gave prime emphasis to restricting the role of the state in economic life, and made faith in market forces the basis of both individual liberties and economic growth. One way in which the state withdrew from the economy was through the privatization of public companies, many of which had been nationalized after the Second World War. The sale of shares in British Telecom, British Gas, British Steel, British Airways and British Petroleum drew a wide response. The advantages of privatization of this sort are claimed to be several. It is held to reintroduce healthy economic competition in place of unwieldy and ineffective public bureaucracies, reduce public expenditure and end political interference in managerial decisions. The privatization policies begun by Thatcher have had an enduring impact. At first, they were hotly constested by the Labour Party. Later, however, Labour abandoned its hostile stance and came to accept that much of this trend was irreversible.

However, after she had won a crushing victory in the election of 1987, Thatcher's popularity among the electorate began to decline sharply. Key factors were the unpopularity of the 'poll tax' (officially called the Community Charge, a tax not based on income or property but 'per head') and the slide of the economy into recession. In 1990 Thatcher was succeeded as Prime Minister by John Major, who himself resigned when the Conservatives were finally beaten by Labour in the 1997 general election. Under Major, the Conservatives continued to privatize state enterprises, even where such plans were less

than popular with the electorate. British Rail was divided and sold off by private tender, for example, although surveys showed that the majority of the population did not support such a programme.

A fourth factor in understanding the experience of the main parties over the past three decades was the emergence of 'New Labour' during the mid-1990s. New Labour has marked a substantively new approach to British politics, as we shall see below.

New Labour

Partly in response to the impact of Thatcherism, and partly as a reaction to wider global events, including the intensifying of global economic competition, the Labour Party began to shift its ideological outlook. This process was initiated under Neil Kinnock, who resigned from the Labour leadership after the party lost the election of 1992, and continued under John Smith, until his premature death. Tony Blair became leader of the party in 1994 and immediately embarked on further far-reaching internal reforms. Christening his reformed party **New Labour**, Blair led a successful campaign within the party to abolish Clause 4 – a clause in the party's constitution which committed it to widespread public ownership of industry.

Labour thus gave formal recognition to the central importance of the market economy, which Thatcher had been so determined to expand. In so doing, the party made changes similar to those which have happened in most other socialist parties in Western Europe. A decisive influence here has been the dissolution of communism in the Soviet Union and Eastern Europe. The outlook of the Labour Party has always been quite different from that of communism – the level of state ownership of industrial enterprise in the communist societies was much greater than anything the Labour Party ever envisaged. Yet most people accepted that the disintegration of communism was also a signal that less extreme ideas of socialism also needed to be radically overhauled. The idea that a modern economy can be 'managed' by direct state control – an idea central both to communism and 'Old Labour' socialism – now appears obsolete.

The election of 1997 which brought New Labour to power represented one of the largest electoral shifts in Britain in the twentieth century – a 10.3 per cent swing from Conservative to Labour – and put an end to eighteen years of Conservative Party rule. The Labour Party captured 419 parliamentary seats (compared to 165 for the Conservatives), giving them their largest ever majority of 179 seats. The Tories' share of the total UK vote (30.7 per cent) was their lowest since 1832. It marked a steep drop from the fairly stable levels of support enjoyed by Conservatives even earlier in the decade. In 1992, for example, the Tories won 41.9 per cent of the vote. Labour's continued electoral success in the general elections of 2001 and 2005 is due, in part, to the Conservatives' failure to raise their share of the vote to the levels they had previously enjoyed.

The 2001 general election saw Labour returned to power with another landslide majority of 166 seats. Perhaps the most significant difference compared with the 1997 general election was the lower turnout – just 59.4 per cent of those eligible to vote (Young 2001; see also figure 20.1). Tony Blair immediately pledged to con-

tinue the programme of revitalization of public services that New Labour had begun in 1997. Despite his desire to focus on investment in the UK, much of the debate during the 2001 Parliament revolved around the controversial decision to support the US-led invasion of Iraq, a policy with which Tony Blair was strongly associated. Partly as a result of the debate surrounding the reasons for the invasion, the popularity of Blair and New Labour fell during this term.

See pp. 861–2 for more on the war in Iraq. Terrorism and the 2001 attacks on the USA are discussed on pp. 879–88.

Labour was returned to power a third time in the general election of May 2005, but with a reduced majority of 65. Turnout remained low, at just 61.5 per cent. There were signs that opposition to the war in Iraq had cost Labour many seats. The party's share of the vote fell significantly in constituencies with high Muslim populations, who, as a group, were particularly opposed to the war. Often these votes went to the Liberal Democrats who, in contrast to the main parties, had opposed military action in Iraq. In Bethnal Green and Bow, a former Labour MP, George Galloway, overturned a large Labour majority to win the seat on an anti-war ticket for the newly formed Respect Party. The Conservative Party polled just 32.3 per cent of the UK vote, well short of the figures that they had commanded whilst in power. Following the election, the Conservative leader Michael Howard resigned to be replaced in December 2005 by David Cameron (the party's fourth leader in just over eight years). Labour's vote also fell in nine out of the ten constituencies with the highest student populations, reflecting opposition

'Are you satisfied or dissatisfied with the way Mr Blair is doing his job as
Leader of the Opposition/Prime Minister?'

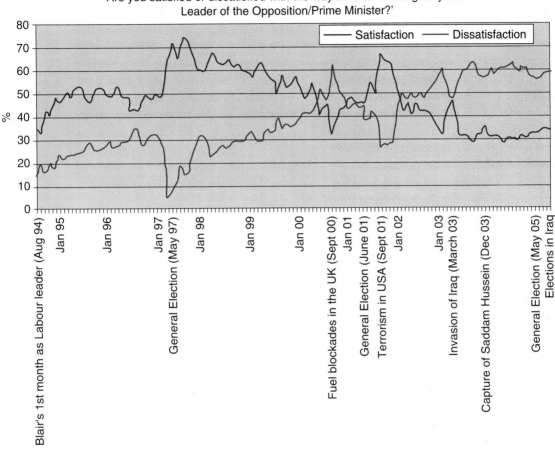

Figure 20.1   Satisfaction with Tony Blair and key events, 1994–2004

Source: MORI Political Monitor: Satisfaction Ratings 1979–2005

amongst many students to tuition fees (see chapter 17, pp. 699–701), with the Liberal Democrat vote gaining significantly in all of those seats (Mellows-Facer et al. 2005). However, in winning a third general election, Tony Blair had equalled Margaret Thatcher's three election victories – a feat never previously achieved by the Labour Party – and he promised that his third term would be his last as Prime Minister.

Some commentators, including myself, have described New Labour's project as part of a 'third way' (Giddens 1998). We will look at some of the key ideas behind the third way below.

Third way politics

After coming to power, New Labour embarked on an ambitious course of political reform and modernization. While maintaining a commitment to the values of social justice and solidarity, the government sought to engage with the realities of the new global order. It recognized that the old politics was out of line with the challenges of the new era. Like more than a dozen other European governments, New Labour wanted to move beyond the traditional political categories of left and right and embark on a new brand of centre-left politics. Because this approach tries to avoid customary political divides, it is often referred to as **third way politics**.

There are six main dimensions to third way politics:

1 *Reconstruction of government*   Active government is required to meet the needs of a rapidly changing world, yet government should not be exclusively associated with top-down bureaucracies and national policies. Dynamic forms of management and administration, such as those sometimes found in the business sector, can work with government in defending and revitalizing the public sphere.

2 *The cultivating of civil society*   Government and the market alone are not enough to solve the many challenges in late modern societies. **Civil society** – the realm outside the state and market – must be strengthened and joined up with government and business. Voluntary groups, families and civic associations can play vital roles in addressing community issues from crime to education.

3 *Reconstruction of the economy*   The third way envisages a new mixed economy characterized by a balance between government regulation and deregulation. It rejects the neo-liberal view that deregulation is the only way to ensure freedom and growth.

4 *Reform of the welfare state*   While it is essential to protect the vulnerable through the provision of effective welfare services, the welfare state must be reformed in order to become more efficient. Third way politics looks towards a 'society of care', while acknowledging that old forms of welfare were often unsuccessful in reducing inequalities, and controlled, rather than empowered, the poor.

5 *Ecological modernization*   Third way politics rejects the view that environmental protection and economic growth are incompatible. There are many ways that a commitment to defending the environment can generate jobs and stimulate economic development.

6 *Reform of the global system*   In an era of globalization, third way politics looks to new forms of global governance. Transnational associations can lead to democracy above the level of the nation-state and can allow greater governance of the volatile international economy.

Third way politics emerged against the backdrop of a double political crisis. As was noted earlier, the revolutions of 1989 revealed that socialism was not a viable approach to economic organization, yet the unchecked enthusiasm for the free market favoured by neo-liberal conservatives was also flawed. The modernizing agenda of third way politics adopted in Britain and elsewhere was an attempt to renew social democracy by responding creatively to the forces of globalization. It sought to harness the energy behind these transformations to revitalize the workings of government and democracy.

Supporters of third way politics have argued that it has now moved beyond the double political crisis from which it originally emerged. Many of its supporters see it as the main challenge to the conservative agenda of President Bush and the Republican Party in the United States, and the only way to negotiate successfully the processes of globalization that are radically changing our world.

This idea of finding a third way in politics, however, has been widely criticized. Many Conservatives see the new politics as largely empty of content – political posturing rather than a policy programme with real bite. Some on the more traditional left, on the other hand, argue that the third way does too little to deal with problems of inequality and insecurity. They hold that 'Old Labour' is still superior to the new version. (For an account of the third way, see Giddens 1998, 2001, 2002.)

Political and social change

Political life, as the above discussion shows, is by no means carried on only within the orthodox framework of political parties, voting and representation in legislative and governmental bodies. It often happens that groups find that their objectives or ideals cannot be achieved within, or are actively blocked by, this framework. Despite the spread of democracy described above, the persistence of authoritarian regimes in many countries – such as China, Turkmenistan and Cuba – reminds us that effecting change within existing political structures is not always possible. Sometimes political and social change can only be brought about through recourse to non-orthodox forms of political action.

The most dramatic and far-reaching example of non-orthodox political action is revolution – the overthrow of an existing political order by means of a mass movement, using violence. Revolutions are tense, exciting and fascinating events; understandably, they attract great attention. Yet for all of their high drama, revolutions occur relatively infrequently. The most common type of non-orthodox political activity takes place through social movements – collective attempts to further a common interest or secure a common goal through action outside the sphere of established institutions. A wide variety of social movements besides those leading to revolution, some enduring, some transient, have existed in modern societies. They are as evident a feature of the contemporary world as are the formal, bureaucratic organizations they often oppose. Many contemporary social movements are international in scope, and rely heavily on the use of information technology in linking local campaigners to global issues.

Globalization and social movements

Social movements come in all shapes and sizes. Some are very small, numbering no more than a few dozen members; others may include thousands or even millions of people. While some social movements carry on their activities within the laws of the society in which they exist, others operate as illegal or underground groups.

It is characteristic of protest movements, however, that they operate near the margins of what is defined as legally permissible by governments at any particular time or place.

Social movements often arise with the aim of bringing about change on a public issue, such as expanding civil rights for a segment of the population. In response to social movements, countermovements sometimes arise in defence of the status quo. The campaign for women's right to abortion, for example, has been vociferously challenged by anti-abortion ('pro-life') activists, who argue that abortion should be illegal.

Often, laws or policies are altered as a result of the action of social movements. These changes in legislation can have far-reaching effects. For example, it used to be illegal for groups of workers to call their members out on strike, and striking was punished with varying degrees of severity in different countries. Eventually, however, the laws were amended, making the strike a permissible tactic of industrial conflict.

Social movements are among the most powerful forms of collective action. Well-organized, persistent campaigns can bring about dramatic results. The American civil rights movement, for example, succeeded in pushing through important pieces of legislation outlawing racial segregation in schools and public places. The feminist movement scored important gains for women in terms of economic and political equality. In recent years, environmental activists have won important concessions from governments and corporations, as in the case of the Brent Spar oil installation (profiled in chapter 22, 'The Environment and Risk', pp. 947).

New social movements

Over the last four decades there has been an explosion of social movements in countries around the globe. These various movements – ranging from the civil rights and feminist movements of the 1960s and 1970s to the anti-nuclear and ecological movements of the 1980s to the gay rights campaign of the 1990s and later – are often referred to by commentators as **new social movements** (NSMs). This description seeks to differentiate contemporary social movements from those that preceded them in earlier decades. Many observers argue that NSMs are a unique product of late modern society and are profoundly different in their methods, motivations and orientations from forms of collective action in earlier times.

The rise of new social movements in recent decades is a reflection of the changing risks now facing human societies. The conditions are ripe for social movements, as increasingly traditional political institutions find it harder to cope with the challenges before them. They find it impossible to respond creatively to the negative risks facing the natural environment from nuclear energy, the burning of fossil fuels or experimentation in bio- or nanotechnology. These new problems and challenges are ones which existing democratic political institutions cannot hope to fix, and as a result they are frequently ignored or avoided until it is too late and a full-blown crisis is at hand.

The cumulative effects of these new challenges and risks is a sense that people are 'losing control' of their lives in the midst of rapid change. Individuals feel less secure and more isolated – a combination which leads to a sense of powerlessness.

A number of social movements have gained prominence in recent years, such as this protest in Seattle in 1999 against the World Trade Organization.

By contrast, corporations, governments and the media appear to be dominating more and more aspects of people's lives, heightening the sensation of a runaway world. There is a growing sense that, left to its own logic, globalization will present ever greater risks to citizens' lives.

> See the discussion of globalization and risk in chapter 22, 'The Environment and Risk', pp. 963–7

We can view new social movements in terms of a 'paradox of democracy'. While faith in traditional politics seems to be waning, the growth of NSMs is evidence that citizens in late modern societies are not apathetic or uninterested in politics, as is sometimes claimed. Rather there is a belief that direct action and participation is more useful than reliance on politicians and political systems. More than ever before, people are supporting social movements as a way of highlighting complex moral issues and putting them at the centre of social life. In this respect, NSMs are helping to revitalize democracy in many countries. They are at the heart of a strong civic culture or civil society – the sphere between the state and the marketplace occupied by family, community associations and other non-economic institutions.

Technology and social movements

In recent years, two of the most influential forces in late modern societies – information technology and social movements – have come together, with astonishing results. In our current information age, social movements around the globe are able to join together in huge regional and international networks comprising nongovernmental organizations, religious and humanitarian groups, human rights associations, consumer protection advocates, environmental activists and others who campaign in the public interest. These electronic networks now have the unprecedented ability to respond immediately to events as they occur, to access and share sources of information, and to put pressure on corporations, governments and international bodies as part of their campaigning strategies. The enormous protests against the war in Iraq in cities around the world in February 2003, for example, were organized in large part through Internet-based networks, as were the protests outside the meeting of world leaders in Genoa in 2001, and the protests that took place in Seattle in 1999 against the World Trade Organization (see box on the Internet and democratization above on pp. 855).

The Internet has been at the forefront of these changes, although mobile phones, fax machines and satellite broadcasting have also hastened their evolution. With the press of a button, local stories are disseminated internationally. Grass-roots activists from Japan to Bolivia can meet online to share informational resources, exchange experiences and coordinate joint action.

This last dimension – the ability to coordinate international political campaigns – is the one which is the most worrying for governments and the most inspiring to participants in social movements. In the last two decades, the number of 'international social movements' has grown steadily with the spread of the Internet. From global protests in favour of cancelling Third World debt to the international campaign to ban landmines (which culminated in a Nobel Peace Prize), the Internet has proved its ability to unite campaigners across national and cultural borders. Some observers argue that the information age is witnessing a 'migration' of power away from nation-states into new nongovernmental alliances and coalitions.

Policy advisers in think-tanks such as the RAND Corporation (in the United States) have spoken of 'netwars' – large-scale international conflicts in which it is information and public opinion that are the stakes in the contest, rather than resources or territory. Participants in netwars use the media and online resources to shape what certain populations know about the social world. These online movements are often aimed at spreading information about corporations, government policies or the effects of international agreements to audiences who may otherwise be unaware of them. For many governments – even democratic ones – netwars are a frightening and elusive threat. As a US Army report has warned: 'A new generation of revolutionaries, radicals and activists are beginning to create informationage ideologies in which identities and loyalties may shift from the nation state to the transnational level of global civic society' (quoted in the *Guardian*, 19 January 2000).

Are such fears misplaced? There are reasons to think that social movements have indeed been radically transformed in recent years. In *The Power of Identity* (1997), Manuel Castells examines the cases of three social movements which, while completely dissimilar in their concerns and objectives, have all attracted international attention to their cause through the effective use of information technology. The Mexican Zapatista rebels, the American 'militia' movement and the Japanese Aum Shinrikyo cult have all used media skills in order to spread their message of opposition to the effects of globalization and to express their anger at losing control over their own destinies.

According to Castells, each of these movements relies on information technologies as its organizational infrastructure. Without the Internet, for example, the Zapatista rebels would have remained an isolated guerrilla movement in southern Mexico. Instead, within hours of their armed uprising in January 1994, local, national and international support groups had emerged online to promote the cause of the rebels and to condemn the Mexican government's brutal repression of the rebellion. The Zapatistas used telecommunications, videos and media interviews to voice their objections to trade policies, such as the North American Free Trade Agreement (NAFTA), which further exclude impoverished Indians of the Oaxaca and Chiapas areas from the benefits of globalization. Because their cause was thrust to the forefront of the online networks of social campaigners, the Zapatistas were able to force negotiations with the Mexican government and to draw international attention to the harmful effects of free trade on indigenous populations.

Theories of nationalism and the nation

Some of the most important social movements in the contemporary world are nationalist movements. The sociological thinkers of the nineteenth and early twentieth centuries displayed little interest in or concern with nationalism. Marx and Durkheim saw nationalism as above all a destructive tendency and argued that the increasing economic integration produced by modern industry would cause its rapid decline. Only Max Weber spent much time analysing nationalism or was prepared to declare himself a nationalist. But even Weber failed to estimate the importance that nationalism and the idea of the nation would have in the twentieth century.

At the start of the twenty-first century, nationalism is not only alive, but – in some parts of the world, at least – flourishing. Although the world has become more interdependent, especially over the past thirty or forty years, this interdependence has not spelled the end of nationalism. In some respects, it has probably even helped to intensify it.

The resurgence of nationalism in the former Yugoslavia is described in chapter 13, 'Race Ethnicity and Migration', pp. 498–500.

Recent thinkers have come up with contrasting ideas about why this is so. There are also disagreements about the stage of history at which nationalism, the nation and the nation-state came into being. Some say they have much earlier origins than others.

Nationalism and modern society

Perhaps the leading theorist of nationalism is Ernest Gellner (1925–95). Gellner
(1983) argued that nationalism, the nation
and nation-state are all products of
modern civilization, whose origins lie in
the Industrial Revolution of the late eighteenth century. Nationalism, and the feelings or sentiments associated with it, do
not have deep roots in human nature.
They are the products of the new large-
scale society that industrialism creates.
According to Gellner, nationalism as such
is unknown in traditional societies, as is
the idea of the nation.

There are several features of modern
societies that have led to the emergence of
these phenomena. First, a modern industrial society is associated with rapid
economic development and a complex
division of labour. Gellner points out that
modern industrialism creates the need for
a much more effective system of state and
government than existed before. Second,
in the modern state, individuals must
interact all the time with strangers, since
the basis of society is no longer the local
village or town, but a very much larger
unit. Mass education, based on an 'official
language' taught in the schools, is the
main means whereby a large-scale society
can be organized and kept unified.

Gellner's theory has been criticized in
more than one respect. It is a functionalist
theory, critics say, which argues that education functions to produce social unity.
As with the functionalist approach more
generally, this view tends to underestimate the role of education in producing
conflict and division. Gellner's theory
does not really explain the passions that

nationalism can, and often does, arouse.
The power of nationalism is probably
related not just to education but also to its
capacity to create an *identity* for people –
something that individuals cannot live
without.

The need for identity is certainly not
just born with the emergence of modern
industrial society. Critics therefore argue
that Gellner is wrong to separate nationalism and the nation so strongly from pre-
modern times. Nationalism is in some
ways quite modern, but it also draws on
sentiments and forms of symbolism that
go back much further into the past.
According to one of the best-known
current scholars of nationalism, Anthony
Smith (1986), nations tend to have direct
lines of continuity with earlier ethnic
communities, or what he calls **ethnies**. An
ethnie is a group that shares ideas of
common ancestry, a common cultural
identity and a link with a specific homeland.

Many nations, Smith points out, do
have pre-modern continuities, and at
previous periods of history there have
been ethnic communities that resemble nations. The Jews, for example, have
formed a distinct ethnie for more than
2,000 years. At certain periods, Jews clustered in communities that had some of the
characteristics of nations. In 1948, following the genocide of Jews during the
Second World War, the state of Israel was
founded, marking the culmination of the
Zionist movement, whose aim was to
create a homeland for Jews scattered
around the world. Like most other nation-
states, Israel was not formed from just a
single ethnie. The Palestinian minority in
Israel traces its origins to a quite different
ethnic background and claims that the

creation of the Israeli state has displaced the Palestinians from their ancient homelands – hence their persistent tensions with Jews in Israel and the tensions between Israel and most surrounding Arab states.

Different nations have followed divergent patterns of development in relation to ethnies. In some, including most of the nations of Western Europe, a single ethnie expanded so as to push out earlier rivals. Thus in France in the seventeenth century, several other languages were spoken and different ethnic histories were linked to them. As French became the dominant language, most of these rivals subsequently disappeared. Yet remnants of them persist in a few areas. One is the Basque country overlapping the French and Spanish frontiers. The Basque language is quite different from either French or Spanish, and the Basques claim a separate cultural history of their own. Some Basques want their own nation-state, completely separate from France and Spain. While there has been nothing like the level of violence seen in other areas – such as East Timor, or Chechnya in southern Russia – separatist groups in the Basque country have sporadically used bombing campaigns to further their goal of independence.

Nations without states

The persistence of well-defined ethnies within established nations leads to the phenomenon of **nations without states**. In these situations, many of the essential characteristics of the nation are present, but those who comprise the nation lack an independent political community. Separatist movements like those in Chechnya and the Basque country, as well as those in many other areas of the world – such as in Kashmir in northern India – are driven by the desire to set up an autonomous, self-governing state.

Several different types of nations without states can be recognized, depending on the relationship between the ethnie and the larger nation-state in which it exists (Guibernau 1999). First, in some situations, a nation-state may accept the cultural differences found among its minority or minorities and allow them a certain amount of active development. Thus in Britain, Scotland and Wales are recognized as having histories and cultural features partly divergent from the rest of the UK, and to some extent have their own institutions. The majority of Scots, for instance, are Presbyterians, and Scotland has long had a separate educational system from that of England and Wales. Scotland and Wales achieved further autonomy within the UK as a whole with the setting up of a Scottish Parliament and a Welsh Assembly in 1999. Similarly, the Basque country and Catalonia (the area around Barcelona in northern Spain) are both recognized as 'autonomous communities' within Spain. They possess their own parliaments, which have a certain number of rights and powers. In both Britain and Spain, however, much power still remains in the hands of the national governments and parliaments, located in London and Madrid respectively.

A second type of nations without states consists of those that have a higher degree of autonomy. In Quebec (the French-speaking province of Canada) and Flanders (the Dutch-speaking area in the north of the Netherlands), regional political

Chechen rebels were responsible for the hostage siege at the school in Beslan, in Russia, which resulted in massive loss of life.

bodies have the power to take major decisions, without actually being fully independent. As in the cases mentioned under the first type, they also contain nationalist movements agitating for complete independence.

Thirdly, there are some nations which more or less completely lack recognition from the state that contains them. In such cases, the larger nation-state uses force in order to deny recognition to the minority. The fate of the Palestinians is one example of such a group. Others include the Tibetans in China and the Kurds, whose home-

land overlaps parts of Turkey, Syria, Iran and Iraq.

The Tibetans and Kurds date their cultural history back over many centuries. The history of Tibet is strongly bound up with particular forms of Buddhism that have flourished there. The Tibetan leader in exile, the Dalai Lama, is at the centre of movements outside Tibet which aim to achieve a separate Tibetan state through non-violent means. Among the Kurds, on the other hand, several independence movements, mostly also located abroad, proclaim violence as the means of achieving their ends. The Kurds have a 'parliament in exile' in Brussels, but this does not have the support of all of the separatist movements.

In the case of the Tibetans and Kurds, there is little chance of achieving even limited autonomy unless the governments of the nation-states involved decide at some point to change their existing policies. But in other instances it is possible that national minorities might opt for autonomy within, rather than complete independence from, the states in which they are located. In the Basque country, Catalonia and Scotland, for example, only a minority of the population currently supports complete independence. In Quebec, a provincial referendum in 1995 on independence from Canada was defeated when it failed to gain the necessary popular votes.

National minorities and the European Union

In the case of national minorities in Europe, the European Union has a significant part to play. The European Union was formed through allegiances created by the major nations of Western Europe. Yet a key element of the philosophy of the EU is the devolution of power to localities and regions. One of its explicit goals is to create a 'Europe of the regions'. This emphasis is strongly supported by most Basques, Scots, Catalans and other national minority groups. Members of these groups often feel resentment about the ways in which parts of their culture or institutions have been lost, and they wish to retrieve them. They look to the EU as a means of fostering their distinct identities. Their right to relate directly to EU organizations, such as

the European Parliament or European courts of law, might give them sufficient autonomy to be satisfied that they are in control of their own destinies. Hence it is at least conceivable that the existence of the EU will mean that national minorities might give up on the ideal of complete independence in favour of a cooperative relationship both with the larger nations of which they are a part and with the EU. (The basic roles and functions of the EU are introduced above, pp. 858–9.)

Nations and nationalism in developing countries

In most of the countries of the developing world, the course followed by nationalism, the nation and the nation-state has been different compared with that of the industrial societies. Most less developed countries were once colonized by Europeans and achieved independence at some point in the second half of the twentieth century. In many of these countries, boundaries between colonial administrations were agreed arbitrarily in Europe and did not take into account existing economic, cultural or ethnic divisions among the population. The colonial powers defeated or subjugated the kingdoms and tribal groupings existing on the African subcontinent, in India and other parts of Asia, and set up their own colonial administrations or protectorates. As a consequence, each colony was 'a collection of peoples and old states, or fragments of these, brought together within the same boundaries' (Akintoye 1976, p. 3). Most colonized areas contained a mosaic of ethnies and other groups.

When erstwhile colonies achieved their independence, they often found it difficult to create a sense of nationhood and national belonging. Although nationalism played a great part in securing the independence of colonized areas, it was largely confined to small groups of activists. Nationalist ideas did not influence the majority of the population. Even today many postcolonial states are continually threatened by internal rivalries and competing claims to political authority.

The continent that was most completely colonized was Africa. Nationalist movements promoting independence in Africa following the Second World War sought to free the colonized areas from European domination. Once this had been achieved, the new leaders everywhere faced the challenge of trying to create national unity. Many of the leaders in the 1950s and 1960s had been educated in Europe or the USA, and there was a vast gulf between them and their citizens, most of whom were illiterate, poor and unfamiliar with the rights and obligations of democracy. Under colonialism, some ethnic groups had prospered more than others; these groups had different interests and goals and legitimately saw each other as enemies.

Civil wars broke out in a number of postcolonial states in Africa, such as Sudan, Zaire and Nigeria, while ethnic rivalries and antagonisms characterized many others both in Africa and Asia. In the case of Sudan, about 40 per cent of the population claimed Arabic ethnic origins, whilst in other regions of the country, particularly in the south, most of the population were black, and Christian or animist in their religious beliefs. Once the nationalists took power, they set up a programme for national integration based on Arabic as the national language. The attempt was only partly successful, and

the stresses and strains it produced are still visible (as we saw in our discussion of ethnic conflicts, such as those in Rwanda or Darfur in Western Sudan, in chapter 13, pp. 498–500). Many of the wars that have taken place on the African continent since independence are a direct result of difficulties like these.

Nigeria is another example of the issues involved. The country has a population of some 120 million people: roughly one out of every four Africans is a Nigerian. Nigeria was formerly a British colony and achieved its independence on 1 October 1960. The country is made up of three main ethnic groups: Yoruba, Ibo and Hausa. Soon after independence in 1966, armed struggles developed in the country between different ethnic groups. A military government was set up and since then periods of civilian government have alternated with phases of military rule. In 1967 a civil war broke out in which one area, Biafra, sought independence from the rest of the country. The separatist movement was suppressed by the use of military force, with much loss of life. Successive governments have attempted to build up a clearer sense of national identity around the theme of 'motherland Nigeria', but creating a sense of national unity and purpose remains difficult. The country possesses large reserves of oil and petroleum, but remains largely mired in poverty and still in the grip of authoritarian rule.

In summary, most states in the developing world came into being as a result of different processes of nation formation from those that occurred in the industrialized world. States were imposed externally on areas that often had no prior cultural or ethnic unity, sometimes resulting in civil war after independence. Modern nations

Amy Chua: 'How Exporting Free Market Democracy Breeds Ethnic Hatred and Global Instability'

Many commentators have argued that the best way to reduce ethnic conflicts, like those discussed above, is to establish democracy and a free market. They argue that this would promote peace by giving everyone a say in running the country and by giving them access to the prosperity that comes from trading with others. In an influential book, *World on Fire: How Exporting Free Market Democracy Breeds Ethnic Hatred and Global Instability* (2003), Amy Chua, a professor at Yale University in the United States, contests this view.

Chua's starting point is that in many developing countries a small ethnic minority enjoys disproportionate economic power. One obvious example is the white minority that exploited the non-white ethnic groups in apartheid South Africa. Chua argues that the massacre of Tutsis by Hutus in Rwanda in 1994 and the hatred felt by Serbs towards Croats in former Yugoslavia were also partly related to the economic advantage enjoyed by the Tutsis and the Croats in their respective countries. Another example that Chua often uses concerns the Chinese ethnic minority in Indonesia.

The pro-market reforms of the former Indonesian dictator, General Suharto, particularly benefited the country's small Chinese minority. In turn, Chinese-Indonesians tended to support the Suharto dictatorship. In 1998, the year that mass pro-democracy demonstrations forced Suharto out of office, Chinese-Indonesians controlled 70 per cent of Indonesia's private economy, but made up just 3 per cent of its population. The end of Suharto's regime was accompanied by violent attacks against the Chinese minority, who were perceived as 'stealing' the country's indigenous wealth. Chua writes: 'The prevailing view among the *pribumi* [ethnic] majority was that it was "worthwhile to lose 10 years of growth to get rid of the Chinese problem once and for all".'

As General Suharto's dictatorship collapsed, the USA and other Western countries called for the introduction of democratic elections. Yet, Chua argues that introducing democracy to countries with what she calls 'market dominant minorities', such as the Chinese in Indonesia, is not likely to bring peace. Instead, Chua argues that the competition for votes in a democracy is likely to lead to a backlash from the country's ethnic majority. Political leaders will emerge who seek to scapegoat the resented minority and encourage the ethnic majority to 'reclaim' the country's wealth for the 'true' owners of the nation, as the *pribumi* majority in Indonesia did against the Chinese minority.

Chua's account shows us that although democracy and the market economy are in principle beneficent forces, they must be grounded in an effective system of law and civil society. Where they are not, as in many parts of the developing world, new and acute ethnic conflicts can emerge.

have arisen most effectively either in areas that were never fully colonized, or where there was already a great deal of cultural unity – such as Japan, Korea or Thailand.

Nationalism and globalization

How does globalization affect nationalism and national identity? The sociologist Andrew Pilkington has examined this question (2002). He argues that nationalism is actually quite a new phenomenon, despite the fact that many of its supporters claim to be members of nations with histories stretching back into the mists of time. Until relatively recently in historical terms, humans survived in small settlements, largely unaware of what goes on outside their own groups, and the idea of being members of a larger nation would have seemed alien to them. Pilkington has argued that it was only later, from the eighteenth century onwards, with the development of mass communications and media, that the idea of a national community developed and spread.

To Pilkington it was during this period that national identities were 'constructed'.

Social constructionism is discussed in chapter 5, 'Social Interaction and Everyday Life', pp. 152–4.

Crucial in developing a sense of nationhood, for Pilkington, was the existence of some 'Other', against which national identity was formed. Central in shaping a (Protestant) British identity, Pilkington argued, was the existence of (Catholic) France. Pilkington documents how a sense of Britishness spread downwards from the country's elite to the rest of society as levels of literacy spread throughout the whole population and as communications technology enabled the spread of ideas.

If national identity is socially constructed, as Pilkington argues, then it is possible that it will change and develop. One of the main factors in changing national identity today, Pilkington contends, is globalization. In his view, globalization creates conflicting pressures between centralization and decentralization. On the one hand, the powers of some business organizations and political units (such as multinational corporations or transnational organizations like the EU) become more concentrated, whilst on the other, there is pressure for decentralization (think of the collapse and fragmentation of the Soviet Union or the desire for a separate Basque nation in Spain, for example). As a result, Pilkington argues, globalization creates a dual threat to national identity: centralization creates pressures from above, particularly with the growing powers of the European Union, and decentralization creates pres-

sures from below, through the strengthening of ethnic minority identities. In the UK, one response to this has been to reassert a narrow understanding of Britishness. Pilkington cites the example of John Townsend, a former Conservative Party MP, who advanced a strongly anti-European, white, English-speaking, view of English national identity. Pilkington argues that a parallel response is also found amongst some members of ethnic minority groups within the UK, who, feeling excluded from a British identity, have strengthened their local identities and asserted their differences from other ethnic groups.

A second response to globalization, which Pilkington clearly believes to be a healthier one, is to accept that there are multiple identities – to argue, for example, that it is possible to be English, British and European at the same time. Pilkington sees evidence of this approach in the new 'hybrid identities' of ethnic minority groups in the UK, whose identities merge different cultures. For Pilkington, we must challenge the first nationalist response to globalization – which often leads to the retreat into religious fundamentalism or cultural racism – by representing the nation in an ethnically inclusive way and encouraging hyphenated identities, such as British-Asian. To Pilkington, globalization leads to contradictory pressures and contradictory responses for national identity.

The nation-state, national identity and globalization

In some parts of Africa, nations and nation-states are not fully formed. Yet in other areas of the world some writers are already speaking of the 'end of the nation-state' in the face of globalization. According to the Japanese writer Kenichi Ohmae, as a result of globalization we increasingly live in a 'borderless world' in which national identity is becoming weaker (Ohmae 1995; see also p. 61).

How valid is this point of view? All states are certainly being affected by globalizing processes. The very rise of 'nations without states', as discussed above, is probably bound up with globalization. As globalization progresses, people often react by reviving local identities, in an effort to achieve security in a rapidly changing world. Nations have less economic power of their own than they used to have, as a result of the spread of the global marketplace.

Yet it wouldn't be accurate to say that we are witnessing the end of the nation-state. In some ways, the opposite is the case. Today, every country in the world is a nation-state or aspires to be one – the nation-state has become a universal political form. Until quite recently, it still had rivals. For most of the twentieth century, colonized areas and empires existed alongside nation-states. Many sociologists have argued that the last empire only disappeared in 1990 with the collapse of Soviet communism, and others still see the United States as an empire (Ferguson 2004). The Soviet Union was effectively at the centre of an empire embracing its satellite states in Eastern Europe. Now all of these have become independent nations, as have many areas inside what was formerly the Soviet Union. There are actually far more sovereign nations in the world today than there were twenty years ago.

During much of the last century, nationalism and issues surrounding nations without states were often associated with the use of terrorism as a politi-cal weapon. Below we discuss terrorism, and look at how the concept has changed in recent years.

Terrorism

At around 8:45 a.m. on 11 September 2001 a passenger plane on a routine flight across the United States was hijacked by terrorists and flown into the North Tower of the World Trade Center in New York. Minutes later, another hijacked plane hit the South Tower, within an hour causing both buildings to collapse and killing thousands of people beginning their working day. Approximately an hour later a third plane was flown into the Pentagon, the headquarters of the US military, killing hundreds more people. A fourth plane, believed to be heading for the White House in Washington, DC, the seat of executive power in the USA, crashed into a field in rural Pennsylvania after passengers took on their hijackers. All the planes hijacked on 11 September were owned by one of two American companies: United or American Airlines. The targets selected by the hijackers – the World Trade Center, the Pentagon and the White House – were chosen for a purpose: to strike at the heart of American economic, military and political power.

President George W. Bush's response to the attacks was to declare a 'war on terror'. A month later came the first major military response in this 'war': an attack by a coalition of countries on Afghanistan in Asia in October 2001. Afghanistan, as we have seen above, was at the time ruled by a fundamentalist Islamic government, the Taliban, which had often supported the actions of **al-Qaeda**, the terrorist organization that carried out the 11 September

Al-Qaeda claimed responsibility for the terrorist attacks on London in July 2005

attacks and where many of its members had trained.

The years following the attacks on New York and Washington saw several further brutal acts of terrorism for which al-Qaeda claimed responsibility. An attack on a nightclub on the Indonesian island of Bali in October 2002 killed more than 200 people, many of them young tourists on holiday from nearby Australia. Bombs on a train in Madrid, Spain, during the morning rush hour killed around 200 commuters in March 2004. In London, 52 people died and several hundred more were injured after a coordinated series of explosions occurred on three underground trains and a bus in July 2005. Terrorism after 11 September 2001 reflects a new security environment in which a new form of terrorism, potentially more deadly than any before, became possible. It is to the concept of 'terrorism' that we now turn.

The origins of terror and terrorism

The word *terrorism* has its origins in the French Revolution of 1789. Thousands of people – originally aristocrats, but later many more ordinary citizens – were hunted down by the political authorities and executed by the guillotine. The term 'terror' was not invented by the revolutionaries themselves, but by the counter-revolutionaries: the people who despised the French Revolution and what it stood for, and who believed that the blood-letting which went on was a form of terrorizing the population (Laqueur 2003). 'Terror', in the sense of the use of violence to intimidate, was used extensively in the twentieth century, for example by the Nazis in Germany or the Russian secret police under Stalin. However, this kind of use of violence predates the origins of the term in the French Revolution.

Although the term 'terror' was not coined until the eighteenth century, the phenomenon of terrorizing people through violence is a very old one. In ancient civilizations, when one army invaded a city held by the enemy, it was not at all uncommon for them to raze the entire city to the ground and kill all the men, women and children in the city. The point of this was not just physically to destroy the enemy, but also to create terror in those living in other cities and demonstrate the power which that terror represented. So the phenomenon of using violence with the idea of terrifying populations, especially civilian populations, is obviously older than the term.

Social scientists disagree over whether the term 'terrorism' can be a useful concept – that is, whether it can be used in a reasonably objective way; it is a notoriously difficult term to define. One issue concerns the shifting moral assessments people make of terrorism and terrorists. It is often said that 'one person's terrorist is another person's freedom fighter'. It is also well known that people who were terrorists at one point themselves can later come to condemn terror just as violently as they practised it. It could be said, with some reservations, that the early history of the state of Israel, for example, was punc-

tuated by terrorist activity, but in the twenty-first century the Israeli leadership is self-declaredly part and parcel of the 'war on terror', and regards terrorism as its primary enemy. It is only a few decades since the former South African leader Nelson Mandela was wildly reviled as potential terrorist, but he is now one of the most revered political figures of recent times. For terrorism to be a useful term, it must be freed as far as possible from moral valuation that shifts across time or the perspective of the observer.

A second issue in looking for a useful conception of terrorism concerns the role of the state. Can states be said to practise terrorism? States have been responsible for far more deaths in human history than any other type of organization. States have brutally murdered civilian populations; in modern times, states have carried out something comparable to the razing of cities that occurred in traditional civilizations. For example, towards the end of the Second World War, the Allied fire bombs largely destroyed the German city of Dresden: hundreds of thousands of people died. Many historians argue that the attack on Dresden happened at a point in the war, when it was of no strategic advantage to the Allies. Critics of the Allies' action argue that the purpose of the destruction of Dresden was to create terror and fear in German society and thereby weaken the resolve of its citizens to carry on the war.

It is sensible to restrict the notion of terrorism to groups and organizations working outside the state. Otherwise, the concept becomes too close to that of war more generally. In spite of the problems noted above, many argue that a neutral definition can be found. We can define

Heavy concrete blocks have been placed in front of the Houses of Parliament to try to protect it from terrorist attacks.

terrorism as 'any action [by a non-state organization] . . . that is intended to cause death or serious bodily harm to civilians or non-combatants, when the purpose of such an act, by its nature or context, is to intimidate a population, or to compel a government or an international organization to do or to abstain from doing any act' (Anand Panyarachun et al. 2004). In other words, terrorism concerns attacks on civilians designed to persuade a government to alter its policies, or to damage its standing in the world.

Old- and new-style terrorism

Terrorism, as it has been described above, can be distinguished from acts of violence designed to terrorize in previous periods of history, such as the ancient razing of cities. Terrorism is connected to changes in communications technology. To terrorize populations on a fairly wide spectrum, information about the violence has to reach those populations affected quite quickly. It wasn't until the rise of modern communications in the late nineteenth century that this became possible. With the invention of the electronic telegraph, instantaneous communication became possible, transcending time and space. Before this time, information could take days or even months to spread. For example, as we saw in the introduction to chapter 15, news of Abraham Lincoln's assassination took many days to reach the UK. Once instantaneous communication is possible, symbolic acts of terrorist violence can occur that can be projected at distance – it is not only the local population that knows about them.

Old-style terroism

We can draw a distinction between old- and new-style terrorism. Old-style terrorism was dominant for most of the twentieth century and still exists today. This kind of terrorism is largely associated with the rise of nationalism and with the establishment of nations as sovereign, territorially bonded entities, which predominantly occurred from the late eighteenth century onwards in Europe, as we discussed above (pp. 877–8).

In all nations, boundaries are fixed somewhat arbitrarily, either as lines on a map, as they were by Western colonizers in Africa and Asia, or through conquest, battle and struggle. Ireland, for example, was brought into the United Kingdom in 1800, leading to independence struggles, which resulted in the partition of the country into North and South in the early 1920s. A patchwork of nations mapped out by colonial administrators, or founded on force, has led in various cases to nations that do not have their own state – that is, nations with a claim to having a common cultural identity, but without the territorial and state apparatus which normally belongs to a nation. Most forms of old-style terrorism are linked to nations without states.

The point of old-style terrorism is to establish states in areas where nations do not have control of the territory's state apparatus. This is true, for example, of Irish nationalists, such as the Irish Republican Army (IRA), and Basque nationalists, such as ETA, in Spain. The main issues are territorial integrity and identity in the formation of a state. Old-style terrorism is found where there are nations without states and where terrorists are prepared to use violence to achieve their ends. Old-style terrorism is fundamentally local because its ambitions are local. It wants to establish a state in a specific national area.

In recent years, old-style terrorism has also often had an international component to it as it draws on support from outside countries. For example, Libya, Syria and some Eastern European countries, as well as groups within the United States, have, in varying degrees, supported the terrorist acts of the IRA in Northern Ireland and Basque separatists in Spain. But although old-style terrorism might involve a wider global network of supporters for its funding or in filtering arms or drugs to buy weaponry, its ambitions are local.

As well as being limited in its ambitions, old-style terrorism is also limited in its use of violence. For example, although many people have lost their lives as the result of the conflict in Northern Ireland, the proportion of people killed as a result of terrorism since the 'Troubles' recommenced in the 1970s, including British soldiers, is on average less than those who have died in road accidents. With old-style terrorism, although the numbers of people maimed and killed are significant, the use of violence is limited, because the aims of this kind of terrorism are also relatively limited (fearsome and horrific though this violence still is).

In addition, the strong moral compulsion generated by national identity makes old-style terrorism difficult to combat, as British governments have found in recent decades in Northern Ireland. Nationalism, as we have seen, has a strong energizing component to it. The myth of national identity can continue to fuel devotees of a movement that seeks to establish a state in cases where a nation exists without one. In cases where there are contested claims on the same territory, historical experience reveals that a settlement is often especially difficult

to reach. This has been true of the long struggle in Northern Ireland, where there is conflicting pressure from unionists who want to remain part of the UK and nationalist groups that want to be part of Ireland.

A fundamental distinction can be drawn between old- and new-style terrorism (Tan and Ramakrishna 2002). New-style terrorism is made possible by the changes in communications technology that are driving globalization, and it has a global spread. This type of terrorism is most famously associated with the Islamic fundamentalism of al-Qaeda (see box), although it is by no means limited to it. It is to a discussion of new-style terrorism that we now turn.

Al-Qaeda's origins and links

Al-Qaeda, meaning 'the base', was created in 1989 as Soviet forces withdrew from Afghanistan and Osama Bin Laden and his colleagues began looking for new jihads [a term loosely translated as holy struggle or war]. The organization grew out of the network of Arab volunteers who had gone to Afghanistan in the 1980s to fight under the banner of Islam against Soviet communism. During the anti-Soviet jihad, Bin Laden and his fighters received American and Saudi funding. Some analysts believe Bin Laden himself had security training from the CIA. The 'Arab Afghans', as they became known, were battle-hardened and highly motivated.

In the early 1990s, al-Qaeda operated in Sudan. After 1996, its headquarters and about a dozen training camps moved to Afghanistan, where Bin Laden forged a close relationship with the Taliban. The US campaign in Afghanistan, which started in late 2001, dispersed the organization and drove it underground as its personnel were attacked and its bases and training camps destroyed.

Cells across the world

The organization is thought to operate in forty to fifty countries, not only in the Middle East and Asia but also in North America and Europe. In Western Europe there have been known or suspected cells in London, Hamburg, Milan and Madrid. These have been important centres for recruitment, fundraising and planning operations.

For training, the group favours lawless areas where it can operate freely and in secret. These are believed to have included Somalia, Yemen and Chechnya, as well as mountainous areas of Afghanistan. There have also been reports of a secret training camp on one of the islands of Indonesia.

Unlike the tightly-knit groups of the past, such as the Red Brigades in Italy or the Abu Nidal group in the Middle East, al-Qaeda is loosely knit. It operates across continents as a chain of interlocking networks. Individual groups or cells appear to have a high degree of autonomy, raising their own money, often through petty crime, and making contact with other groups only when necessary.

Defining al-Qaeda?

This loose connection between groups has raised a question of definition. When we talk about al-Qaeda, do we refer to an actual organization or are we now talking about something closer to an idea?

Attacks like the May 2003 bombings in Riyadh and the attack on Israeli tourists in Mombasa in 2002 are widely attributed to al-Qaeda. But were these attacks in any way planned or financed or organized by Bin Laden or the organization he is still believed to lead?

Some analysts have suggested that the word al-Qaeda is now used to refer to a variety of groups connected by little more than shared aims, ideals and methods. We do, however, know that several radical groups are or have been formally affiliated with al-Qaeda. The most important is the radical wing of the Egyptian group Islamic Jihad, whose members took refuge in Afghanistan and merged with al-Qaeda. Its leader is Ayman al-Zawahri, a ruthless Egyptian believed to be the brains behind al-Qaeda and the mastermind of many of its most infamous operations. These include the attacks on two US embassies in Africa in 1998 and the 9/11 attacks in New York and Washington.

There are also believed to be links with militant Kashmiri groups; the Islamic Movement of Uzbekistan, or IMU; the Abu Sayyaf group in the Philippines; and the GIA, or Armed Islamic Group, in Algeria and its radical offshoot known as the Salafist group, or GSPC.

'War on terror'

Western policeforces and intelligence agencies have had some successes in breaking up al-Qaeda cells, closing down front companies and freezing assets as part of the 'war on terror'. Some of its top leaders have been killed or captured, and interrogations of some members at Guantanamo Bay have further weakened the organization. However, uprooting the organization in its entirety is a highly complex and frustrating task.

In a recent report on Iraq and the war on terror, the Oxford Research Group noted that despite the detention of many of its members, al-Qaeda 'remains vibrant and effective'. Most frustratingly, the fate and whereabouts of Osama Bin Laden himself is still a deep mystery.

Source: BBC (20 July 2004)

New-style terrorism

New-style terrorism differs from old-style terrorism in several ways, first, in respect of the scope of its claims. One of the distinguishing features of al-Qaeda's view of the world, for example, is that it has global geopolitical aims: it seeks to restructure world society. Parts of the al-Qaeda leadership have wanted to reconstruct an Islamic society stretching from the Indian subcontinent into Europe. This would involve establishing Islamic governments throughout the Middle East and the recapture of North Africa. Al-Qaeda's supporters argue that over the last millennium the West has expelled Islamic groups from those areas to which it has a legitimate claim. These areas include the Balkans and those parts of Spain that were previously ruled by the Moors (Muslims originally from North Africa who controlled much of Spain between the eighth century and the fifteenth century). Large expanses of what we now regard as Europe were previously Islamic, ruled either by the Ottoman Empire or from North Africa. Al-Qaeda aims to re-establish the global role of Islam in these regions and areas. So whereas old-style nationalism is local and linked to particular states – normally quite small states – new-style terrorism is global in its ambitions. It wants to reverse the tide of world power.

There is a characteristic tension between modernism and anti-modernism in the world-view of al-Qaeda and similar terrorist organizations. In attempting to re-establish the Islamic dominance of large parts of Europe, the Middle East and Asia that existed in an earlier age, they make great use of modern communications in order to criticize modernity, and attempt to reverse what they see as the moral degeneracy of modern Western society (Gray 2003).

Second, new-style terrorism differs from old-style terrorism in terms of its organizational structure. Although careful not to take this parallel too far, the sociologist Mary Kaldor has pointed out several similarities between the infrastructure of new terrorist groups, notably al-Qaeda, and international non-governmental organizations (NGOs), such as Oxfam or Friends of the Earth.

NGOs are discussed in more detail in chapter 16, 'Organizations and Networks', pp. 652–5.

In its organizational structure, al-Qaeda deploys the same global forms of organization as do many NGOs. Both new terrorist organizations and NGOs like Friends of the Earth are driven by a sense of mission and commitment. This sense of mission and commitment allows a fairly loose global organization to flourish (Glasius et al. 2002).

Both NGOs and new terrorist organizations are based on networks, of the kinds discussed by Manuel Castells (see chapter 16, pp. 671–3). They are highly decentralized structures. There is a lot of autonomy in local cells and these can reproduce without necessarily having any strong direction from the centre. The American attacks on

Afghanistan in 2001 substantially weakened al-Qaeda's leadership, but the organization remains strong because of its moral conviction. This drives a sense of mission that can keep cells functioning even when some aspects of the overall organization have been weakened or broken.

Terrorist organization and NGOs both also have a global spread of supporters in many countries. Experts on terrorism disagree over the extent to which al-Qaeda survived the American-led attack on Afghanistan in 2001, but it has been estimated that there are still al-Qaeda cells in around sixty countries, drawing on approximately 20,000 people who are willing to die violently for the cause, most of whom exist semi-autonomously from the centre.

It can also be noted that new terrorist groups and NGOs both work with states. No NGO could flourish completely as a non-state organization. They all have some contacts and support from states and this is true, Kaldor argues, of new-style terrorist organizations too. The Libyan involvement in the bombing of a passenger plane that landed on the Scottish village of Lockerbie in 1988 provides one example of this. Of course, the analogy between new terrorist organization and NGOs cannot be taken too far; but in their organizational structures and shared sense of admittedly very different missions, al-Qaeda could be seen as a malign kind of NGO.

The third and last way in which old- and new-style terrorism differ is over means. Old-style terrorism, as we saw above, had relatively limited objectives, and as a result the violence involved was normally fairly limited too. New-style terrorism seems much more ruthless in the means it is prepared to use. Al-Qaeda websites, for example, talk in extremely destructive language of 'the enemy' – that is, principally the United States, but to some extent the West as a whole. These will often explicitly say that terrorist acts should be carried out that kill as many people as possible. This ruthlessness is evident, for example, in the founding statement of al-Qaeda from 1998, which claims:

> The ruling to kill the Americans and their allies – civilians and military – is an individual duty for every Muslim who can do it in any country in which it is possible to do it, in order to liberate the [Muslim holy sites of the] al-Aqsa Mosque and the Holy Mosque [Mecca] from their grip, and in order for their armies to move out of all the lands of Islam, defeated and unable to threaten any Muslim.
>
> (Cited in Halliday 2002, p. 219)

This is very different from the more limited use of violent means characteristic of old-style terrorism. There are some cases where the two overlap, as in Chechnya in the former Soviet Union, for example, which turned from a separatist struggle to a recruiting ground for newer forms of terrorism.

Terrorism and war

How should we respond to the threat of new-style terrorism? Terrorism of the kind seen on 11 September 2001 raises difficult questions for political sociologists. Can terrorism be fought like conventional wars? The coalition that attacked Afghanistan in 2001 did destroy at least some of the al-Qaeda terrorist networks. Yet despite some successes against new-style terrorism through conventional warfare, critics are surely right to argue that in many cases the levels of violence, aims and organizational structure of new-style terrorist groups differentiate them from conventional enemies such as hostile nation-states. This has led some sociologists and political scientists to question the concept of a 'war on terrorism'. The war on Iraq launched in 2003 (see box on pp. 861–2) was in part justified, especially in the USA, by concerns that Iraq was developing weapons that would be used to supply terrorist organizations. The debate about whether terrorism can be tackled through conventional warfare raises further difficult questions regarding the relationship between terrorism and nation-states, like Afghanistan, that have supported it. In turn, this leads to questions about global governance. In a global age, what international support and proof is needed in order to act to prevent a perceived threat? And what are the best institutions to deal with a global terrorist threat?

Summary points

1 The term 'government' refers to a political apparatus in which officials enact policies and make decisions. 'Politics' is the means by which power is used and contested to affect the scope and content of government activities.

2 A state exists where there is a political apparatus, ruling over a given territory, whose authority is backed by a legal system and by the ability to use force to implement its policies. Modern states are nation-states, characterized by the idea of citizenship, the recognition that people have common rights and duties and are aware of their part in the state, and nationalism, the sense of being part of a broader, unifying political community.

3 Power, according to Max Weber, is the capacity to achieve one's aims even against the resistance of others, and often involves the use of force. Since Weber, several alternative understandings of the concept have also been advanced. A government is said to have authority when its use of power is legitimate. Such legitimacy derives from the consent of those being governed. The most common form of legitimate government is democratic, but other legitimate forms are also possible.

4 In authoritarian states, popular participation is denied or severely curtailed. The needs and interests of the state are prioritized over those of average citizens and there are no legal mechanisms in place for opposing government or for removing a leader from power.

5 Democracy is a political system in which the people rule. In participatory democracy (or

direct democracy), decisions are made by those affected by them. A liberal democracy is a representative democracy where all citizens have the vote and can choose between at least two parties.

6 The number of countries with democratic governments has rapidly increased in recent years, due in large part to the effects of globalization, mass communications and competitive capitalism. But democracy is not without its problems: people everywhere have begun to lose faith in the capacity of politicians and governments to solve problems and to manage economies, and political participation in the electoral system is decreasing.

7 British politics was profoundly changed by the impact of Thatcherism – a set of doctrines associated with Margaret Thatcher, the Conservative Prime Minister from 1979 until 1990. Thatcherism involved a belief in the desirability of cutting back on the role of the state and of encouraging free market enterprise.

8 The Labour Party has undergone major changes over the past twenty-five years. Under the leadership of Tony Blair in particular, 'New Labour' has moved away from older socialist notions, including nationalization and planned economic enterprise. After coming to power in 1997, New Labour pursued a course of political reform and modernization that moves beyond traditional 'left–right' politics. This new brand of centre-left politics is often referred to as 'third way' politics. New Labour was re-elected in 2001 with a large majority, and again in 2005, but with a reduced majority.

9 Social movements involve a collective attempt to further common interests through collaborative action outside the sphere of established institutions. The term 'new social movements' is applied to a set of social movements that have arisen in Western countries since the 1960s in response to the changing risks facing human societies. Unlike earlier social movements, NSMs are single-issue campaigns oriented to non-material ends and they draw support from across class lines. Information technology has become a powerful organizing tool for many new social movements.

10 Nationalism refers to a set of symbols and beliefs that provide the sense of being part of a single political community. It emerged alongside the development of the modern state. Although the founders of sociology believed that nationalism would disappear in industrial societies, at the start of the twenty-first century it seems to be flourishing. 'Nations without states' refer to cases in which a national group lacks political sovereignty over the area it claims as its own.

11 Old-style terrorism is most often associated with nations without states. New-style terrorism draws on globalization and differs from old-style terrorism in its scope, organization structure and means.

Questions for further thought

1 Why should sociology concern itself with the study of politics?

2 Why are liberal democracy and capitalism so often found together?

3 If Western nations are so committed to democracy, why in many countries do such low numbers turn out to vote?

4 What is 'new' about 'New Labour'?

5 How do social movements make use of existing social and political institutions?

6 Are nation-states becoming unimportant with the advance of globalization?

7 What is the relationship between globalization and terrorism?

Further reading

Robert A. Dahl, *On Democracy* (New Haven: Yale University Press, 1998).

Elaine Ciulla Kamarck and Joseph S. Nye (eds), *Democracy.com? Governance in a Networked World* (Hollis, NH: Hollis, 1999).

F. Halliday, *Two Hours that Shook the World: September 11, 2001: Causes and Consequences* (Saqi Books: London, 2002).

P. Griset and S. Mahan, *Terrorism in Perspective* (Thousand Oaks, CA: Sage, 2003).

M. Kaldor, *New and Old Wars: Organized Violence in a Global Era*, 2nd edn (Cambridge: Polity, 2001).

Alberto Melucci, *Nomads of the Present: Social Movements and Individual Needs in Contemporary Society* (London: Hutchinson Radius, 1989).

Cornelia Navari, *Internationalism and the State in the Twentieth Century* (New York: Routledge, 2000).

A. Tan and K. Ramakrishna (eds), *The New Terrorism: Anatomy, Trends and Counter Strategies* (Times Media: Singapore, 2002).

Internet links

Bulletin of the Atomic Scientists
http://www.thebulletin.org/index.htm

International Institute for Democracy and Electoral Assistance
http://www.idea.int/

Internet Modern History Sourcebook: nationalism
http://www.fordham.edu/halsall/mod/modsbook17.html

Oxford Research Group
http://www.oxfordresearchgroup.org.uk/

Foreign Policy
http://www.foreignpolicy.com/

International Institute for Strategic Studies
http://www.iiss.org/

Contents

21 Cities and Urban Spaces

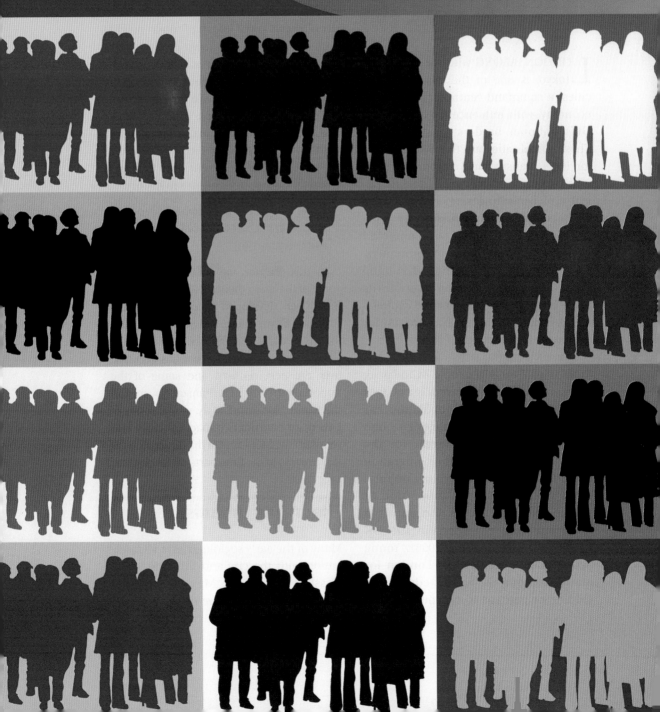

LONDON, ALONG with New York and Tokyo, is one of the world's 'global cities', a command centre for the world's economy, with influence far beyond the UK's national borders (Sassen 2001). These global cities are the headquarters for large, transnational corporations, as well as a profusion of financial, technological and consulting services. The UK's capital has a resident workforce of some 3.4 million, which is supplemented further by a large number of commuters. London also has an unrivalled cultural and artistic heritage, helping to confirm its place as a vibrant and dynamic capital – almost 30 million tourists come to stay for a night or more each year.

The UK's capital city is also home to more than 7 million people, who speak more than three hundred languages between them, and its population has been increasing by an average of around nineteen thousand each year for the past twenty years. London's migration levels have resulted in a young population, with a far greater proportion of people between the ages of twenty and forty-four than elsewhere in the UK (ONS, *Focus on London*, 2003). Young people move to cities like London for many reasons – work, education, culture, or perhaps to escape from the conformity and provincialism of life outside the city.

Yet, despite the rich opportunities that big cities offer, many people find them lonely or unfriendly places. One distinctive characteristic of modern urban life is the frequency of interactions between strangers. Even within the same neighbourhood or block of flats, it's unlikely that people will know most of their neighbours. If you live in a town or city, think about the number of times that you interact with people who you don't know every day. The list might include the bus driver, people working in shops, other students and even people you exchange glances with in the street. This fact alone makes life in cities today different from life elsewhere or during earlier times in history.

Social interaction in modern societies is studied in chapter 5, 'Social Interaction and Everyday Life'.

In this chapter, we shall first consider some of the main theories of urbanism that have been developed to understand this process. From there, we will study the origins of cities and the vast growth in the numbers of city dwellers that has occurred over the past century, and some of the important trends in urbanization around the world. Not surprisingly, globalization is having an enormous impact on cities and we shall consider some of the dimensions of this process in the final parts of the chapter.

Theorizing urbanism

Many of the early sociologists had a fascination with the city and urban life. The classical sociologist Max Weber even wrote a book called *The City* (published

Everyday life in the city bombards the individual with new images, impressions and sensations.

posthumously in 1921) in which he traced the conditions that made modern capitalism possible back to the medieval, Western city. Other early theorists were more concerned with the way in which the development of the city changed the social as well as the physical environment. The work of Georg Simmel and Ferdinand Tönnies provided two of the most important early contributions to urban sociology, and is discussed in the box on p. 896. These thinkers deeply influenced later urban sociologists. Robert Park, for

example, a key member of the Chicago School, to which we turn below, studied under Simmel in Germany at the turn of the twentieth century.

The Chicago School

A number of writers associated with the University of Chicago from the 1920s to the 1940s, especially Robert Park, Ernest Burgess and Louis Wirth, developed ideas which were for many years the chief basis of theory and research in urban sociology. Two concepts developed by the Chicago School are worthy of special attention. One is the so-called ecological approach in urban analysis; the other is the characterization of urbanism as a way of life, developed by Wirth (Wirth 1938; Park 1952).

Urban ecology

Ecology is a term taken from a physical science: the study of the adaptation of plant and animal organisms to their environment. This is the sense in which 'ecology' is used in the context of problems of the environment in general (see chapter 22, 'The Environment and Risk'). In the natural world, organisms tend to be distributed in systematic ways over the terrain, such that a balance or equilibrium between different species is achieved. The Chicago School believed that the siting of major urban settlements and the distribution of different types of neighbourhood within them can be understood in terms of similar principles. Cities do not grow up at random, but in response to advantageous features of the environment. For example, large urban areas in modern societies tend to develop along the shores of rivers, on fertile plains or at the intersection of trading routes or railways.

Early theorists of urban life

Georg Simmel and the 'mental life of the city'

One of the earliest theorists of city life was the German sociologist Georg Simmel, who provided an account of how the city shapes its inhabitants' 'mental life'. In *The Metropolis and Modern Life* (1903) Simmel argued that city life bombards the mind with images and impressions, sensations and activity. This is 'a deep contrast with the slower, more habitual, more smoothly flowing rhythm' of the small town or village. Simmel believed that city dwellers protect themselves from 'the unexpectedness of violent stimuli' and the assault of 'changing images' by becoming become blasé and disinterested. They tune out much of the buzz that surrounds them, focusing on whatever they need to, in order to get by. The result of this blasé attitude, thought Simmel, is that although city dwellers are part of the 'metropolitan crush', they distance themselves from one another emotionally. With his account of life in the modern metropolis, Simmel provides a sociological explanation to those who complain about the unfriendliness or loneliness of city living.

Ferdinand Tönnies: from *Gemeinschaft* to *Gesellschaft*

Ferdinand Tönnies, a contemporary of Simmel, was also concerned with the effect of city life on the individual. He argued that urbanization, which occurred with the Industrial Revolution, irredeemably changed social life. He charted with sadness the gradual loss of what he called *Gemeinschaft* or community (1887), which he characterized as based on traditional, close-knit ties, personal and steady relationships between neighbours and friends, and a clear understanding of one's social position.

Gemeinschaft, Tönnies argued, was being replaced by *Gesellschaft*. He characterized this as a kind of society or association based on transitory and instrumental relationships. The transformation of social life built around community to one built around association is part of the modern shift to a more individualist society. In this society, relationships are generally specific to a particular setting and purpose, and only take into account a part of the person. For example, if we take a bus in the city, our interaction with the driver is likely to be limited to a brief exchange at the door of the bus as we pay, and our use for him will be limited to his ability to get us to our destination. To Tönnies, as well as to Simmel, the city is a place full of strangers.

'Once set up,' in Park's words, 'a city is, it seems, a great sorting mechanism which . . . infallibly selects out of the population as a whole the individuals best suited to live in a particular region or a particular milieu' (1952, p. 79). Cities become ordered into 'natural areas', through processes of competition, invasion and succession – all of which occur in biological ecology. If we look at the ecology of a lake in the natural environment, we find that competition between various species of fish, insects and other organisms operates to reach a fairly stable distribution between them. This balance is disturbed if new species 'invade' – try to make the lake their home. Some of the organisms which used to proliferate in the central area of the lake are driven out to suffer a more precarious existence around its fringes. The invading species are their successors in the central sections.

Patterns of location, movement and relocation in cities, according to the ecological view, have a similar form. Different neighbourhoods develop through the adjustments made by inhabitants as they struggle to gain their livelihoods. A city can be pictured as a map of areas with distinct and contrasting social characteristics. In the initial stages of the growth of modern cities, industries congregate at sites suitable for the raw materials they need, close to supply lines. Populations cluster around these workplaces, which come to be increasingly diversified as the number of the city's inhabitants grows. The amenities thus developed become correspondingly more attractive, and greater competition develops for their acquisition. Land values and property taxes rise, making it difficult for families to carry on living in the central neighbourhood,

"We love the view. It helps to remind us that we're part of a larger community."

except in cramped conditions or in decaying housing where rents are still low. The centre becomes dominated by businesses and entertainment, with the more affluent private residents moving out to newly forming suburbs around the perimeter. This process follows transport routes, since these minimize the time taken in travelling to work; the areas between these routes develop more slowly.

Cities can be seen as formed in concentric rings, broken up into segments. In the centre are the inner-city areas, a mixture of big business prosperity and decaying private houses. Beyond these are longer established neighbourhoods, housing workers employed in stable manual occupations. Further out still are the suburbs in which higher income groups tend to live. Processes of invasion and succession occur within the segments of the concentric rings. Thus, as property decays in a central or near-central area, ethnic minority groups might start to move into it. As they do so, more of the pre-existing population start to leave, precipitating a wholesale flight to neighbourhoods elsewhere in the city or out to the suburbs.

Although for a period the **urban ecology** approach fell into disrepute, it was later revived and elaborated in the writings of a number of authors, particularly Amos Hawley (1950, 1968). Rather than concentrating on competition for scarce resources, as his predecessors had done, Hawley emphasized the *interdependence* of different city areas. *Differentiation* – the specialization of groups and occupational roles – is the main way in which human beings adapt to their environment. Groups on which many others depend will have a dominant role, often reflected in their central geographical position. Business groups, for example, like large banks or insurance companies, provide key services for many in a community, and hence are usually to be found in the central areas of settlements. But the zones which develop in urban areas, Hawley points out, arise from relationships not just of space, but of time. Business dominance, for example, is expressed not only in patterns of land use, but also in the rhythm of activities in daily life – an illustration being the rush hour. The ordering in time of people's daily lives reflects the hierarchy of neighbourhoods in the city.

The ecological approach has been as important for the empirical research it has helped to promote as for its value as a theoretical perspective. Many studies, both of cities and of particular neighbour-hoods, have been prompted by ecological thinking, concerned, for example, with the processes of 'invasion' and 'succession' mentioned above. However, various criti-cisms can justifiably be made. The ecolog-ical perspective tends to underemphasize the importance of conscious design and planning in city organization, regarding urban development as a 'natural' process. The models of spatial organization devel-oped by Park, Burgess and their colleagues were drawn from American experience, and fit only some types of city in the United States, let alone cities in Europe, Japan or the developing world.

Urbanism as a way of life

Wirth's thesis of **urbanism** as *a way of life* is concerned less with the internal differen-tiation of cities than with what urbanism is as a form of social existence. Wirth observes:

> The degree to which the contemporary world may be said to be 'urban' is not fully or accurately measured by the proportion of the total population living in cities. The infl-uences which cities exert on the social life of man are greater than the ratio of the urban population would indicate; for the city is not only increasingly the dwelling-place and the workshop of modern man, but it is the initiating and controlling centre of eco-nomic, political and cultural life that has drawn the most remote communities of the world into its orbit and woven diverse areas, peoples and activities into a cosmos. (1938, p. 342)

In cities, Wirth points out, large numbers of people live in close proximity to one another, without knowing most of the others personally – a fundamental con-trast to small, traditional villages. Most contacts between city dwellers are fleeting and partial, and are means to other ends, rather than being satisfying relationships in themselves. Interactions with salespeo-ple in shops, cashiers in banks or ticket collectors on trains are passing encoun-ters, entered into not for their own sake but as means to other aims.

Since those who live in urban areas tend to be highly mobile, there are relatively weak bonds between them. People are involved in many different activities and situations each day – the 'pace of life' is faster than in rural areas. Competition pre-vails over cooperation. Wirth accepts that the density of social life in cities leads to the formation of neighbourhoods having distinct characteristics, some of which may preserve the characteristics of small communities. In immigrant areas, for example, traditional types of connections between families are found, with most people knowing most others on a personal basis. The more such areas are absorbed into wider patterns of city life, however, the less these characteristics survive.

Wirth's ideas have deservedly enjoyed wide currency. The impersonality of many day-to-day contacts in modern cities is undeniable – and, to some degree, this is true of social life in general in modern societies. Wirth's theory is important for its recognition that urbanism is not just part of a society, but expresses and influences the nature of the wider social system. Aspects of the urban way of life are characteristic of social life in modern societies as a whole, not just the activities of those who happen to live in big cities. Yet Wirth's ideas also have marked limitations. Like the ecological perspective, with which it has much in common, Wirth's theory is based mainly on observations of American cities, yet generalized to urbanism everywhere. Urbanism is not the same at all times and places. As has been mentioned, for example, ancient cities were in many respects quite different from those found in modern societies. Life for most people in the early cities was not much more anonymous or impersonal than for those living in village communities.

Wirth also exaggerates the impersonality of modern cities. Communities involving close friendship or kinship links are more persistent within modern urban communities than he supposed. Everett Hughes, a colleague of Wirth's at the University of Chicago, wrote of his associate: 'Louis used to say all those things about how the city is impersonal – while living with a whole clan of kin and friends on a very personal basis' (quoted in Kasarda and Janowitz 1974). Groups such as those Herbert Gans (1962) calls 'the urban villagers' are common in modern cities. His 'urban villagers' are Italian-Americans living in an inner-city Boston neighbourhood. Such 'white ethnic' areas are probably becoming less significant in American cities than they once were, but they are being replaced by inner-city communities involving newer immigrants.

More importantly, neighbourhoods involving close kinship and personal ties seem often to be actively created by city life; they are not just remnants of a pre-existing way of life which survive for a period in the city. Claude Fischer (1984) has put forward an interpretation of why large-scale urbanism tends actually to promote diverse subcultures, rather than swamp everyone within an anonymous mass. Those who live in cities, he points out, are able to collaborate with others of similar backgrounds or interests to develop local connections; and they can join distinctive religious, ethnic, political and other subcultural groups. A small town or village does not allow the development of such subcultural diversity. Those who form ethnic communities within cities, for instance, might have little or no knowledge of one another in their land of origin. When they arrive, they gravitate to areas where others from a similar linguistic and cultural background are living, and new sub-community structures are formed. An artist might find few others to associate with in a village or small town, but in a large city he or she might become part of a significant artistic and intellectual subculture.

A large city is a 'world of strangers', yet it supports and creates personal relationships. This is not paradoxical. We have to separate urban experience into the public sphere of encounters with strangers and the more private world of family, friends and work colleagues. It may be difficult to 'meet people' when one first moves to a large city. But anyone moving to a small, established rural community may find the friendliness of the inhabitants largely a matter of public politeness – it may take years to become 'accepted'. This is not so in the city. As Edward Krupat has commented:

> The urban egg . . . has a harder shell to crack. Lacking the occasion and circumstances for making an entrée, many persons who see each other day after day at a bus or railroad station, in a cafeteria or passing in the hallways at work, never become anything more than 'familiar strangers'. Also, some people may remain totally on the outside because they lack social skills or initiative. Yet the overwhelming evidence is that because of the diversity of strangers – each one is a potential friend – and the wide range of lifestyles and interests in the city, people do move from the outside in. And once they are on the inside of one group or network, the possibilities for expanding their connections multiply greatly. As a result, the evidence indicates that the positive opportunities in the city often seem to outweigh the constraining forces, allowing people to develop and maintain satisfying relationships. (1985, p. 36)

Wirth's ideas retain some validity, but in the light of subsequent contributions it is clear that they are over-generalized. Modern cities frequently involve impersonal, anonymous social relationships, but they are also sources of diversity – and, sometimes, intimacy.

Urbanism and the created environment

More recent theories of urbanism have stressed that it is not an autonomous process, but has to be analysed in relation to major patterns of political and economic change. The two leading writers in urban analysis, David Harvey (1973, 1982,

1985) and Manuel Castells (1977, 1983), have both been strongly influenced by Marx.

Harvey: the restructuring of space

Drawing on broadly Marxist ideas, David Harvey has argued that urbanism is one

The modern city may seem paradoxical, with contradictory potential to be impersonal yet also highly sociable. London's China Town is one example of how a tight-knit ethnic community can create intimacy in a city, and also contribute to its diversity.

aspect of the **created environment** brought about by the spread of industrial capitalism. In traditional societies, city and countryside were clearly differentiated. In the modern world, industry blurs the division between city and countryside. Agriculture becomes mechanized and is run simply according to considerations of price and profit, just like industrial work, and this process lessens the differences in modes of social life between urban and rural people.

In modern urbanism, Harvey points out, space is continually *restructured*. The process is determined by where large firms choose to place their factories, research and development centres and so forth; by the controls asserted by governments over both land and industrial production; and by the activities of private investors, buying and selling houses and land. Business firms, for example, are constantly weighing up the relative advantages of new locations against existing ones. As production becomes cheaper in one area than in another, or as the firm moves from one product to another, offices and factories will be closed down in one place and opened up elsewhere. Thus at one period, when there are considerable profits to be made, there may be a spate of office-block building in the centre of large cities. Once the offices have been built, and the central area 'redeveloped', investors look for potential for further speculative building elsewhere. Often what is profitable in one period will not be so in another, when the financial climate changes.

The activities of private home buyers are strongly influenced by how far, and where, business interests buy up land, as well as by rates of loans and taxes fixed by local and central government. After the Second World War, for instance, there was a vast expansion of suburban development in major cities in the United States. This was partly due to ethnic discrimination and the tendency of whites to move away from inner-city areas. However, it was only made possible, Harvey argues, because of government decisions to provide tax concessions to home buyers and construction firms, and by the setting up of special credit arrangements by financial organizations. These provided the basis for the building and buying of new homes on the peripheries of cities, and at the same time promoted demand for industrial products such as the motorcar. In England, the growth in size and prosperity of towns and cities in the south in the post-war period is directly connected to the decline of older industries in the north, and the consequent movement of investment to new industrial opportunities.

Castells: urbanism and social movements

Like Harvey, Castells stresses that the spatial form of a society is closely linked to the overall mechanisms of its development. To understand cities, we have to grasp the processes whereby spatial forms are created and transformed. The layout and architectural features of cities and neighbourhoods express struggles and conflicts between different groups in society. In other words, urban environments represent symbolic and spatial manifestations of broader social forces. For example, skyscrapers may be built because they are expected to provide profit, but the giant buildings also 'symbolise the power of money over the city through technology and self-confidence and are the cathedrals of the period of rising corporate capitalism' (Castells 1983, p. 103).

In contrast to the Chicago sociologists, Castells sees the city not only as a distinct location – the urban area – but as an integral part of processes of **collective consumption**, which in turn are an inherent aspect of industrial capitalism. Schools, transport services and leisure amenities are ways in which people collectively 'consume' the products of modern industry. The taxation system influences who is able to buy or rent where, and who builds where. Large corporations, banks and insurance companies, which provide capital for building projects, have a great deal of power over these processes. But government agencies also directly affect many aspects of city life, by building roads and public housing, planning green belts, on which new development cannot encroach, and so forth. The physical shape of cities is thus a product of both market forces and the power of government.

But the nature of the created environment is not just the result of the activities of wealthy and powerful people. Castells stresses the importance of the struggles of underprivileged groups to alter their living conditions. Urban problems stimulate a range of social movements, concerned with improving housing conditions, protesting against air pollution, defending parks and green belts and combating building development that changes the nature of an area. For example, Castells studied the gay movement in San Francisco, which succeeded in restructuring neighbourhoods around its own cultural values – allowing many gay organizations, clubs and bars to flourish – and

gained a prominent position in local politics.

Cities, Harvey and Castells both emphasize, are almost wholly artificial environments, constructed by people. Even most rural areas do not escape the influence of human intervention and modern technology, for human activity has reshaped and reordered the world of nature. Food is not produced for local inhabitants, but for national and international markets; and in mechanized farming, land is rigorously subdivided and specialized in its use, ordered into physical patterns which have little relationship to natural features of the environment. Those who live on farms and in isolated rural areas are economically, politically and culturally tied to the larger society, however, different some of their modes of behaviour may be from those of city dwellers.

Evaluation

The views of Harvey and Castells have been widely debated, and their work has been important in redirecting urban analysis. In contrast to the ecologists' approach, it puts emphasis not on 'natural' spatial processes, but on how land and the created environment reflect social and economic systems of power. This marks a significant shift of emphasis. Yet the ideas of Harvey and Castells are often stated in a highly abstract way, and have not stimulated such a large variety of research studies compared with the work of the Chicago School.

In some ways, the views set out by Harvey and Castells and those of the Chicago School usefully complement each other, and can be combined to give a comprehensive picture of urban pro-

Like anything else, land and property can be bought and sold, reflecting social and economic systems of power.

cesses. The contrasts between city areas described in urban ecology do exist, as does the overall impersonality of city life. But these are more variable than the members of the Chicago School believed, and are primarily governed by the social and economic influences analysed by Harvey and Castells. John Logan and Harvey Molotch (1987) have suggested an approach that directly connects the perspectives of authors like Harvey and Castells with some features of the ecological standpoint. They agree with Harvey and Castells that broad features of economic development, stretching nationally and internationally, affect urban life in quite a direct way. But these wide-ranging economic factors, they argue, are focused through local organizations, including neighbourhood businesses, banks and government agencies, together with the activities of individual house buyers.

Places – land and buildings – are bought and sold, according to Logan and Molotch, just like other goods in modern societies, but the markets which structure city environments are influenced by how different groups of people want to use the property they buy and sell. Many tensions and conflicts arise as a result of this process – and these are the key factors structuring city neighbourhoods. For instance, in modern cities, Logan and Molotch point out, large financial and business firms continually try to intensify land use in specific areas. The more they can do so, the more there are opportunities for land speculation and for the profitable construction of new buildings. These companies have little concern with the social and physical effects of their activities on a given neighbourhood – with whether or not, for example, attractive older residences are destroyed to make room for large new office blocks. The growth processes fostered by big firms involved in property development often go against the interests of local businesses or residents, who may attempt actively to resist them. People come together in neighbourhood groups in order to defend their interests as residents. Such local associations may campaign for the extension of zoning restrictions, block new building encroaching on parks, or press for more favourable rent regulations.

The development of the city

Although there were great cities in the ancient world, like Athens and Rome in Europe, city life, as we now know it, is very different from that experienced in previous ages. As early sociologists like Simmel and Tönnies showed, the development of the modern city changed the way in which humans felt and thought about the world and the ways in which they interacted with one another. In this section we look at the advance of the city from its beginnings in traditional societies to the most recent trends in urban development, both in the West and globally.

Cities in traditional societies

The world's first cities appeared about 3500 BCE, in the river valleys of the Nile in Egypt, the Tigris and Euphrates in what is now Iraq, and the Indus in what is today Pakistan. Cities in traditional societies were very small by modern standards. Babylon, for example, one of the largest ancient Near Eastern cities, extended over an area of only 3.2 square miles and at its height, around 2000 BCE, probably numbered no more that 15,000–20,000 people. Rome under Emperor Augustus in the first century BCE was easily the largest premodern city outside China, with some 300,000 inhabitants – roughly the population of Coventry or Doncaster in the UK today.

Most cities of the ancient world shared certain common features. They were usually surrounded by high walls that served as a military defence and emphasized the separation of the urban community from the countryside. The central area of the city was usually occupied by a religious temple, a royal palace, government and commercial buildings and a public square. This ceremonial, commercial and political centre was sometimes enclosed within a second, inner wall and was usually too small to hold more than a minority of the citizens. Although it usually contained a market, the centre was different from the business districts found at the core of modern cities, because the main buildings were nearly always religious and political (Sjoberg 1960, 1963; Fox 1964; Wheatley 1971).

The dwellings of the ruling class or elite tended to be concentrated near the centre. The less privileged groups lived towards the perimeter of the city or outside the walls, moving inside if the city came under attack. Different ethnic and religious communities were often allocated to separate neighbourhoods, where their members both lived and worked. Sometimes these neighbourhoods were also surrounded by walls. Communications among city dwellers were erratic. Lacking any form of printing press, public officials had to shout at the tops of their voices to deliver pronouncements. 'Streets' were usually strips of land on which no one had yet built. A few traditional civilizations boasted sophisticated road systems linking various cities, but these existed mainly for military purposes, and transportation for the most part was slow and limited. Merchants and soldiers were the only people who regularly travelled over long distances.

While cities were the main centres for science, the arts and cosmopolitan culture, their influence over the rest of the country was always weak. No more than a tiny proportion of the population lived in the cities, and the division between cities and countryside was pronounced. By far the majority of people lived in small rural communities and rarely encountered more than the occasional state official or merchant from the towns.

Industrialization and urbanization

The contrast between the largest modern cities and those of pre-modern civilizations is extraordinary. The most populous cities in the industrialized countries number almost 20 million inhabitants. A **conurbation** – a cluster of cities and towns forming a continuous network – may include even larger numbers of people. The peak of urban life today is represented by what is called the **megalopolis**, the 'city of cities'. The term was originally coined in ancient Greece to refer to a city-state that was planned to be the envy of all civilizations, but in current usage it bears little relation to that utopia. The term was first applied in relation to the north-eastern seaboard of the United States, a conurbation covering some 450 miles from north of Boston to below Washington, DC. In this region, about 40 million people live at a density of more than 700 persons per square mile.

Britain was the first society to undergo industrialization, a process that began in the mid-eighteenth century. The process of industrialization generated increasing **urbanization** – the movement of the population into towns and cities, and away from the land. In 1800, fewer than 20 per cent of the British population lived in towns or cities of more than 10,000 inhabitants. By 1900, this proportion had risen to 74 per cent. The capital city, London, was home to about 1.1 million people in 1800; by the beginning of the twentieth century, it had increased in size to a population of more than 7 million. London was then by far the largest city ever seen in the world. It was a vast manufacturing, commercial and financial centre at the heart of a still-expanding British Empire.

The urbanization of most other European countries and the United States took place somewhat later – but in some cases, once under way, accelerated even faster. In 1800, the United States was a more rural

The modern megalopolis – heaven or hell?

society than the leading European countries at the same date. Less than 10 per cent of the population lived in communities with populations of more than 2,500 people. Today well over three-quarters of Americans do so. Between 1800 and 1900, the population of New York leapt from 60,000 people to 4.8 million.

Urbanization is now a global process, into which developing countries are increasingly being drawn. In 1950, only 30 per cent of the world's population were urban dwellers; by 2000, this had reached 47 per cent – 2.9 billion people – and by 2030 it is expected to reach 60 per cent – 5 billion people. At current rates of change, the number of people living in urban areas will overtake the number of people in rural areas by 2007. Most urbanization is now taking place in the developing world. The urban population of the less developed regions is expected to rise by more than 2 billion people between 2000 and 2030 from around 2 to 4 billion. By contrast, as table 21.1 shows, the urban population of developed regions is expected to increase much more slowly, from 0.9 billion in 2000 to 1 billion in 2030 (UN 2001).

The development of the modern city

Only at the turn of the twentieth century did statisticians and social observers

Table 21.1   Urbanization of regions of the world by levels of development, 1950, 1975, 2000 and 2030 (projected)

	Population (billions)			
	1950	1975	2000	2030
Total population				
World	2.52	4.07	6.06	8.27
More developed regions	0.81	1.05	1.19	1.22
Less developed regions	1.71	3.02	4.87	7.05
Urban population				
World	0.75	1.54	2.86	4.98
More developed regions	0.45	0.73	0.90	1.00
Less developed regions	0.30	0.81	1.96	3.98
Rural population				
World	1.77	2.52	3.19	3.29
More developed regions	0.37	0.31	0.29	0.21
Less developed regions	1.40	2.21	2.90	3.08

Source: UN (2001)

begin to distinguish between the town and the city. Cities with large populations were recognized to be usually more cosmopolitan than smaller centres, with their influence extending beyond the national society of which they were a part.

The expansion of cities came about because of population increase, plus the migration of outsiders from farms, villages and small towns. This migration was often international, with people moving from peasant backgrounds directly into cities in the other countries. The immigration of very large numbers of Europeans from poor farming backgrounds to the United States is the most obvious example.

Cross-national immigration into cities was also widespread between countries in Europe itself. Peasants and villagers migrated to the towns (as they are doing on a massive scale in developing countries today) because of lack of opportunities in the rural areas, coupled with the apparent advantages and attractions of cities, where it was rumoured that the streets were 'paved with gold' (jobs, wealth, a wide range of goods and services). Cities, moreover, became concentrated centres of financial and industrial power, entrepreneurs sometimes creating new urban areas almost from scratch.

The development of modern cities has had an enormous impact, not only on habits and modes of behaviour, but on patterns of thought and feeling. From the time when large urban agglomerations first formed, in the eighteenth century, views about the effects of cities on social life have been polarized. Some saw cities as representing 'civilized virtue', the fount of dynamism and cultural creativity. For these authors, cities maximize opportunities for economic and cultural development, and provide the means of living a comfortable and satisfying existence. Others have branded the city as a smoking inferno thronged with aggressive and mutually distrustful crowds, riddled with crime, violence, corruption and poverty.

As cities mushroomed in size, many people were horrified to see that inequalities and urban poverty seemed to intensify correspondingly. The extent of urban poverty and the vast differences between city neighbourhoods were among the main factors that prompted early sociological analyses of urban life. Unsurprisingly, the first major sociological studies of, and theories about, modern urban conditions originated in Chicago, a city marked by a phenomenal rate of development – it grew from a virtually uninhabited area in the 1830s to a population of well over 2 million by 1900 – and by very pronounced inequalities.

Recent urban trends in Britain and the USA

In this section, we consider some of the main patterns in Western urban development in the post-war era, using Britain and the United States as examples. Attention will focus on the rise of suburban areas, the decline of inner-city areas and strategies aimed at urban renewal.

Suburbanization

In the USA, the process of **suburbanization** reached its peak in the 1950s and 1960s. The centres of cities during those decades had a 10 per cent growth rate, while that of the suburban areas was 48 per cent. Most of the early movement to the suburbs involved white families. The enforcement of racial mixing in schools can be seen as a major factor in the deci-sion of many whites to decamp from inner-city areas. Moving to the suburbs was an attractive option for families who wished to put their children in all-white schools. Even today, American suburbs remain mostly white.

However, the white domination of suburbia in the United States is being eroded as more and more members of ethnic minorities move there. An analysis of data from the US 2000 Census showed that racial and ethnic minorities make up 27 per cent of suburban populations, up from 19 per cent in 1990. Like the people who began the exodus to suburbia in the 1950s, members of minority ethnic groups who move to the suburbs are mostly middle-class professionals. They move in search of better housing, schools and amenities. According to the chairman of the Chicago Housing Authority, 'suburbanization isn't about race now; it's about class. Nobody wants to be around poor people because of all the problems that go along with poor people: poor schools, unsafe streets, gangs' (quoted in De Witt 1994).

In the UK, many of the suburbs around London grew up between the two world wars, and clustered round new roads and links by underground trains that could bring commuters into the centre. Some converts to the big city life have looked with disdain on the large expanses of suburbia, with its semi-detached villas and well-tended gardens blanketing the fringes of English cities. Others, like the poet John Betjeman (1906–84), have celebrated the modest eccentricity of the architecture of the suburbs, and the impulse to combine the employment opportunities of the city with a mode of life connected in practical terms with

Many Victorians saw the newly industrializing cities such as Manchester and Leeds as sewers of degeneration and vice.

owner-occupation and car ownership, and in terms of values with traditional family life.

In Britain, the migration of the residential population from central city areas to outlying suburbs and dormitory towns (towns outside the city boundaries lived in mainly by people who work in the city) or villages in the 1970s and early 1980s meant that the population of Greater London dropped by about half a million over the period. In the industrial towns of the North, the rapid loss of manufacturing industry during this period also reduced the population of inner-city areas. At the same time, many smaller cities and towns grew quickly – for example, Cambridge, Ipswich, Norwich, Oxford and Leicester. The 'flight to the suburbs' has had dramatic implications for the health and vitality of both British and American urban centres, as we shall see. Suburbanization has also affected men and women differently as we see in the box overleaf.

'Engendering' the city

Writing from a feminist perspective, several authors have examined how the city reflects the unequal gender relations in society, and have looked at ways to overcome this.

Jo Beall (1998) has noted that if social relations, in this case between men and women, are underpinned by power, then cities demonstrate the correlation between power and space in terms of what gets built, where it is built, how and for whom. Beall writes that 'Cities are literally concrete manifestations of ideas on how society was, is and how it should be'.

The growth of the city in the nineteenth century is associated with gender separation. Public life and space was dominated by men, who were free to travel through the city as they wanted. Women were not expected to be seen in most public places, and those that were, were likely to be regarded as prostitutes or 'street walkers'.

As the process of suburbanization began, the gender separation grew even clearer. Whilst the male head of the family commuted into the city on a daily basis, the women (wives) were expected to remain at home to care for the family. Transport links were built for travel between the suburbs and the city centre, but little thought was given by their male designers to transportation within the suburbs, as a result of which it was more difficult for women to leave home (Greed 1994).

Elizabeth Wilson has argued, however, that the development of the city was not all bad for women. She believes that some feminists have reduced the role of women in the city to that of victims. In fact, Wilson contests, the development of the city provided opportunities that non-urban forms of life could not give. With the emergence of female white-collar work in the city and later the expansion of the service industry, women increasingly entered the workforce. The city offered women employment as an escape from unpaid labour in the house that did not exist outside urban life (Wilson 2002).

Inner-city decay

In the USA, the severe inner-city decay, which has marked all large cities over the past few decades, is a direct consequence of the growth of the suburbs. The movement of high-income groups away from the city has meant a loss of their local tax revenues. Since those that remain, or replace them, include many living in poverty, there is little scope for replacing that lost income. If rates are raised in the central city, wealthier groups and businesses tend to move further out.

This situation is worsened by the fact that the building stock in central cities becomes more run-down than in the suburbs, crime rates rise and there is higher unemployment. More must therefore be spent on welfare services, schools, the upkeep of buildings and police and fire services. A cycle of deterioration develops in which the more suburbia expands, the greater become the problems of the city centres. In many American urban areas, the effect has been dramatic – particularly in the older cities, such as New York, Boston or Washington, DC. In some neighbourhoods in these cities, the deterioration of property is probably worse than in large urban areas anywhere else in the industrialized world. Decaying tenement blocks and boarded-up and burnt-out buildings alternate with empty areas of land covered in rubble.

In Britain, inner-city decay has been less marked than in the United States. Yet, some inner-city areas are as dilapidated as many neighbourhoods in American cities. An important Church of England report,

Faith in the City (1985), described the inner-city areas in bleak terms:

> Grey walls, littered streets, boarded-up windows, graffiti, demolition and debris are the drearily standard features of the districts and parishes with which we are concerned . . . the dwellings in the inner cities are older than elsewhere. Roughly one-quarter of England's houses were built before 1919, but the proportion in the inner areas ranged from 40 to 60 per cent.

One reason for the decay in Britain's inner cities is the financial crises that have affected many of these areas. From the late 1970s onwards, central government put strong pressure on local authorities to limit their budgets and to cut local services, even in inner-city areas most subject to decay. Local authorities that exceeded nationally set expenditure levels could be penalized. This led to intense conflicts between the government and many of the councils that ran distressed inner-city areas, when they could not meet their set budgets. The introduction of the Poll Tax (officially called the Community Charge) under Mrs Thatcher's Conservative government further affected local government finances. Although the Poll Tax was finally repealed because of widespread opposition, including large demonstrations in several cities during 1990, many city councils found themselves with less revenue than before and were compelled to cut back on what were largely regarded as essential services.

Inner-city decay in the UK is also related to changes in the global economy. Recently industrialized countries such as Singapore, Taiwan or Mexico often have much cheaper labour costs than countries like the UK, which can make them an attractive location for manufacturing industry. In response to this, over the last few decades, some already industrialized nations, for example, Japan and (West) Germany, shifted their economies to the kinds of activity that require a high level of capital investment and a highly skilled, well-educated workforce. In his classic study, *Inside the Inner-City* (1983), Paul Harrison has examined the impact of these global changes upon Hackney, still one of London's poorest boroughs. The 1970s saw a dramatic decline in Hackney's manufacturing sector, paralleling a national decline. The number of manufacturing jobs in the borough dropped from 45,500 in 1973 to 27,400 in 1981 – a fall of 40 per cent. Until the mid-1970s Hackney's male unemployment rate was roughly level with the national average; by 1981 it had risen to 17.1 per cent (50 per cent above the average). As the number of people out of work increased, so too did the number of people living in poverty. Harrison summarizes the effects of such a concentration of disadvantaged people:

> [L]ocal government poor in resources and sometimes in the quality of staffing; a poor health service, since doctors cannot find a decent accommodation or much in the way of private practice; a low level of educational attainment due primarily to poor home backgrounds and the low average ability in schools; and, finally, high levels of crime, vandalism and family breakdown, and, wherever communities of divergent cultures live together, conflicts based on religion or race.

Sometimes these multiple disadvantages overlap to such an extent that they burst forth openly in the form of urban conflict and riots.

For more on the problems arising from inner-city decay, see pp. 317–21, on the 'underclass' and pp. 356–65 on social exclusion.

Riots

In an era of globalization, population movement and rapid change, large cities have become concentrated and intensified expressions of the social problems that afflict society as a whole. All too often, the 'invisible' fault-lines within cities, generally created by unemployment and racial tension, undergo the equivalent of social earthquakes. Simmering tensions flare to the surface, sometimes violently in the form of riots, looting and widespread destruction.

This occurred in the USA, in the spring of 1992 when riots engulfed parts of Los Angeles. Henry Cisneros, then Secretary of the Department of Housing and Urban Development, flew out to the city to investigate at first hand what was going on:

> What I saw was a city in which smoke was everywhere. It smelled of burning wire and plastic. The smoke was so thick that it obscured the lights of a helicopter circling directly overhead. Sirens screamed every few seconds, as strike teams of fire engines escorted by California highway patrol cars – literally convoys of twenty vehicles, the patrol cars to protect the firefighters – raced from one fire to the next. . . . Los Angeles that Thursday night was truly the urban apocalypse in a kind of smoky orange, an assault on all of the senses, people wide-eyed, all-out panic just one loud sound away. (1993)

Riots have afflicted British neighbourhoods as well; for example, Brixton in South London in 1981, 1985 and 1995; Ely

Rioting in Bradford in July 2001 was sparked by local tensions between white and ethnic minority communities.

in Cardiff in 1991; and Oldham, Burnley and Lidget Green in Bradford in 2001. The 2001 riots involved clashes between members of different cultural and ethnic backgrounds, attacks upon the police and the destruction of property.

Following the riots in 2001, the government set up a Community Cohesion Review Team, chaired by Ted Cantle, to produce a report into the causes of the riots. The report found a deep polarization between different ethnic communities in Britain's urban areas. It argued that many aspects of people's everyday lives compounded this split; for example, having separate educational arrangements, voluntary bodies, employment patterns, places of worship and language. A Muslim of Pakistani origin, interviewed for the

report, summed this up, saying: 'When I leave this meeting with you I will go home and not see another white face until I come back here next week.' The report argued:

In such a climate, there has been little attempt to develop clear values which focus on what it means to be a citizen of a modern multi-racial Britain and many still look backwards to some supposedly halcyon days of a mono-cultural society, or alternatively look to their country of origin for some form of identity.

The report suggested that greater community cohesion is needed, based upon knowledge of, contact between, and respect for, the various cultures that make up the UK. To do this it 'is also essential to establish a greater sense of citizenship, based on (a few) common principles which are shared and observed by all sections of the community. This concept of citizenship would also place a higher value on cultural differences.' To achieve these aims, the report called for a well-resourced national debate, heavily influenced by younger people, and expressed the hope that this debate would lead to a new conception of citizenship, creating a more coherent approach to issues like education, housing, regeneration and employment. There were also suggestions for the preparation of local 'community cohesion plans', the promotion of cross-cultural contact in order to foster respect and explode cultural myths and the establishment of a new Community Cohesion Task Force to oversee these developments (Independent Report of the Community Cohesion Review Team 2001). Ethnic tensions fuelled by decaying infrastructure and housing led to rioting in many French cities in late 2005, reigniting debates across Europe on immigration and relations between ethnic groups (see pp. 497–8).

Urban renewal

What kind of approach should local, regional and national governments take in addressing the complex problems crippling inner cities? How can the rapid expansion of outlying suburban areas be checked to prevent the erosion of green areas and countryside? A successful **urban renewal** policy is particularly challenging because it demands simultaneous action on multiple fronts.

In the UK, a range of national schemes – involving, for example, grants for the rehabilitation of houses by their owners or tax incentives to attract business – have been introduced to try to revive the fortunes of the inner cities. Over the last few decades a range of government programmes has been launched that pursue different methods of urban regeneration. The Conservative government's *Action for Cities* programme of 1988, for example, looked more to private investment and free market forces to generate improvement than to state intervention. However, the response from business was much weaker than had been anticipated. Because of the seeming intractability of many of the problems facing the inner cities, there has been a tendency for programmes to be frequently dropped or replaced when results are not quick to arrive.

Studies indicate that, apart from the odd showpiece project, providing incentives and expecting private enterprise to do the job is ineffective as a way of tackling the fundamental social problems generated by the central cities. So many oppressive circumstances come together in the inner-city, that reversing processes of decay once they have got under way is in any case exceedingly difficult. Investigations into inner-city decay, such as the Scarman Report on the 1981 Brixton riots, have noted the lack of a coordinated approach to inner-city problems (Scarman 1982). Without major public expenditure – which is unlikely to be forthcoming from government – the prospects for radical improvement are slender indeed (Macgregor and Pimlott 1991).

The Labour government elected in 1997 has launched two main regeneration funds: the new deal for communities and the neighbourhood renewal fund. Other sources of funding focused on specific activities are also important in aiding urban renewal, including money from the National Lottery, funding for action zones in health, employment and education, and Housing Corporation cash for new social housing, 60 per cent of which has to support regeneration schemes. An important difference between current programmes and earlier schemes is that the earlier projects tended to focus on physical aspects of regeneration, particularly housing, whereas later programmes have tried to stimulate both social and economic regeneration.

The new deal for communities is the Labour government's flagship regeneration scheme. It was launched in 1998 and there are currently thirty-nine communities with projects across the UK. So far, around £2 billion has been committed to these projects over a period of ten years. The main goal of the programme is to reduce disadvantages in the poorest areas by focusing on five specific issues: poor job prospects, high levels of crime, educational under-achievement, poor health, and problems with housing and the physical environment.

The Neighbourhood Renewal Fund, which began in 2001, will be targeted at the most deprived areas. By 2005, around £1.875 billion had been committed to the Fund. Money is given as extra help to meet government targets for reducing inequality. The Neighbourhood Renewal Fund aims to enable the eighty-eight most deprived authorities, in collaboration with their Local Strategic Partnership, to improve services, narrowing the gap between deprived areas and the rest of England (Neighbourhood Renewal Unit 2004).

A number of questions remain about the effectiveness of regeneration schemes. How can top-down government programmes gain the backing and involvement of local people that is usually crucial to their success? Can public cash really stimulate local economies and create jobs? How can regeneration schemes prevent displacing problems from one area to another (Weaver 2001)?

Gentrification and 'urban recycling'

Urban recycling – the refurbishing or replacement of old buildings and new uses for previously developed land – has become common in large cities. Occasionally this has been attempted as part of planning programmes, but more often it is the result of **gentrification** – the renovation of buildings in dilapidated city neighbourhoods for use by those in higher income groups, plus the provision of amenities like shops and restaurants to serve them. The gentrification of inner-city areas has occurred in many cities in Britain, the USA and other developed nations, and seems set to continue in years to come.

In the USA, the sociologist Elijah Anderson analysed the impact of gentrification in his book, *Streetwise: Race, Class, and Change in an Urban Community* (1990). While the renovation of a neighbourhood generally increases its value, it rarely improves the living standards of its current low-income residents, who are usually forced to move out. In the Philadelphia neighbourhood that Anderson studied, many black residences were condemned, forcing more than a thousand people to leave. Although they were told that their property would be used to build low-cost housing that they would be given the first opportunity to buy, large businesses and a high school now stand there.

The poor residents who continued to live in the neighbourhood received some benefits in the form of improved schools and police protection, but the resulting increase in taxes and rents finally forced them to leave for a more affordable neighbourhood, most often into areas of greater social exclusion. Black residents interviewed by Anderson expressed resentment at the influx of 'yuppies', whom they held responsible for the changes that drove the poorer people away.

The white newcomers had come to the city in search of cheap 'antique' housing, closer access to their city-based jobs, and a trendy urban lifestyle. They professed to be 'open-minded' about racial and ethnic differences; in reality, however, little fraternizing took place between the new and old residents unless they were of the same social class. Since the black residents were mostly poor and the white residents were middle class, class differences were compounded by ethnic ones. While some middle-class blacks lived in the area, most who could afford to do so chose a more suburban lifestyle, fearing that they would otherwise receive from whites the same treatment that was reserved for the black underclass. Over time, the neighbourhood was gradually transformed into a white middle-class enclave.

One reason behind gentrification is demographic. Young professional people are choosing to marry and start families later in life; as a result, more housing is needed for individuals and couples, rather than families. In the UK, the government predicts that an additional 3.8 million households will form between 1996 and 2021 (Urban Task Force 1999). Because young people are having families later and their careers often demand long hours in inner-city office buildings, life in suburbia

becomes more of an inconvenience than an asset. Affluent childless couples are able to afford expensive housing in refurbished inner-city areas and may even prefer to build lifestyles around the high-quality cultural, culinary and entertainment options available in city centres. Older couples whose children have left home may also be tempted back into inner-city areas for similar reasons.

It is important to note that the process of gentrification parallels another trend discussed earlier: the transformation of the urban economy from a manufacturing to a service-industries base. Addressing the concerns of the victims of these economic changes is critical for the survival of the cities.

In London, Docklands has been a notable example of 'urban recycling'. The

London's Docklands has become a prime example of 'urban recycling'.

Docklands area in East London occupies some eight and a half square miles of territory adjoining the Thames – deprived of its economic function by dock closures and industrial decline. Docklands is close to the financial district of the City of London, but also adjoins poor, working-class areas on the other side. From the 1960s onwards there were intense battles – which continue today – about what should happen to the area. Many living in or close to Docklands favoured redevelopment by means of community development projects, which would protect the interests of poorer residents. In the event, with the setting up of the Docklands Development Corporation in 1981, the region became a central part of the Conservative government's strategy of encouraging private enterprise to play the prime part in urban regeneration. The constraints of planning requirements and regulations were deliberately relaxed. The area today is covered in modern buildings, often adventurous in design. Warehouses have been converted into luxury flats, and new blocks have been constructed alongside them. A very large office development, visible from many other parts of London, has been constructed at Canary Wharf. Yet amid the glitter there are still dilapidated buildings and empty stretches of wasteland. Office space quite often lies empty, as do some of the new dwellings which have proved unsaleable at the prices they were originally projected to fetch. The boroughs of the Docklands have some of the poorest housing in the country, but many people living in such housing argue that they have benefited little from the construction that has gone on around them.

On pp. 929–31 we look at the role of sport in urban regeneration, through the example of Manchester's 2002 Commonwealth Games.

In the USA, developers are buying up abandoned industrial warehouses in cities from Milwaukee to Philadelphia and converting them into expensive residential lofts and studio apartments. The creation of vibrant public spaces within the blighted urban centres of Baltimore and Pittsburgh has been heralded as a triumph of urban renewal. Yet, it is difficult to conceal the deprivation that remains in neighbourhoods just blocks away from these revitalized city centres.

Arguing against developments such as Docklands in his book about the history of the city, *The Conscience of the Eye* (1993), Richard Sennett has argued that attempts should be made by urban planners to preserve, or to return to, what he calls 'the humane city'. The large, impersonal buildings in many cities turn people inwards, away from one another. But cities can turn people outwards, putting them into contact with a variety of cultures and ways of life. We should seek to create city streets that are not only unthreatening but also 'full of life', in a way that 'traffic arteries, for all their rushing vehicular motion, are not'. The suburban shopping mall with its standardized walkways and shops is just as remote from 'the humane city' as is the traffic highway. Sennett argues that we should instead draw our inspiration from older city areas, like those found in many Italian city centres, which are on a human scale and mix diversity with elegance of design.

Urbanization in the developing world

The world's urban population could reach almost 5 billion people by 2030. As table 21.1, on p. 907, shows, the United Nations estimates that almost 4 billion of these urban dwellers will be residents of cities in the developing world. As the map of the world's 'megacities' shows (see figure 21.1), most of the twenty-two cities projected to have more than 10 million residents in 2015 are located in the developing world.

Manuel Castells (1996) refers to **megacities** as one of the main features of third millennium urbanization. They are not defined by their size alone – although they are vast agglomerations of people – but also by their role as connection points between enormous human populations and the global economy. Megacities are intensely concentrated pockets of activity through which politics, media, communications, finances and production flow. According to Castells, megacities function as magnets for the countries or regions in which they are located. People are drawn towards large urban areas for various reasons; within megacities are those who succeed in tapping into the global system and those who do not. Besides serving as nodes in the global economy, megacities also become 'depositories of all these segments of the population who fight to survive'.

Figure 21.1   The 22 cities expected to have 10 million or more inhabitants by 2015

Source: UN (2003)

Why is the rate of urban growth in the world's lesser developed regions so much higher than elsewhere? Two factors in particular must be taken into account. First, rates of population growth are higher in developing countries than they are in industrialized nations (see chapter 22, 'The Environment and Risk'). Urban growth is fuelled by high fertility rates among people already living in cities.

Second, there is widespread internal migration from rural areas to urban ones – as in the case of the developing Hong Kong–Guangdong megacity profiled in the box. People are drawn to cities in the developing world either because their traditional systems of rural production have disintegrated, or because the urban areas offer superior job opportunities. Rural poverty prompts many people to try their hand at city life. They may intend to migrate to the city only for a relatively short time, aiming to return to their villages once they have earned enough money. Some actually do return, but most find themselves forced to stay, having for one reason or another lost their position in their previous communities.

Challenges of urbanization in the developing world

Economic implications

As a growing number of unskilled and agricultural workers migrate to urban centres, the formal economy often struggles to absorb the influx into the workforce. In most cities in the developing world, it is the informal economy that allows those who cannot find formal work to make ends meet. From casual work in manufacturing and construction to small-scale trading activities, the unregulated informal sector offers earning opportunities to poor or unskilled workers.

Informal economic opportunities are important in helping thousands of families to survive in urban conditions, but they have problematic aspects as well. The informal economy is untaxed and unregulated. It is also less productive than the formal economy. Countries where economic activity is concentrated in this sector fail to collect much-needed revenue through taxation. The low level of productivity also hurts the general economy – the proportion of the GDP generated by informal economic activity is much lower than the percentage of the population involved in the sector.

The OECD (Organization of Economic Cooperation and Development) estimates that a billion new jobs will be needed by 2025 to sustain the estimated population growth in cities in the developing world. It is unlikely that all of these jobs will be created within the formal economy. Some development analysts argue that attention should be paid to formalizing or regulating the large informal economy, where much of the 'excess' workforce is likely to cluster in the years to come.

Environmental challenges

The rapidly expanding urban areas in developing countries differ dramatically from cities in the industrialized world. Although cities everywhere are faced with environmental problems, those in developing countries are confronted by particularly severe risks. Pollution, housing shortages, inadequate sanitation and unsafe water supplies are chronic problems for cities in less developed countries.

Housing is one of the most acute problems in many urban areas. Cities such as

Calcutta and São Paulo are massively congested; the rate of internal migration is much too high for the provision of permanent housing. Migrants crowd into squatters' zones, which mushroom around the edges of cities. In urban areas in the West, newcomers are most likely to settle close to the central parts of the city, but the reverse tends to happen in developing countries, where migrants populate what has been called the 'septic fringe' of the urban areas. Shanty dwellings made of sacking or cardboard are set up around the edges of the city wherever there is a little space.

In São Paulo, it is estimated that there was a 5.4 million shortfall in habitable homes in 1996. Some scholars estimate that the shortage is as high as 20 million, if the definition of 'habitable housing' is interpreted more strictly. Since the 1980s, the chronic deficit of housing in São Paulo has produced a wave of unofficial 'occupations' of empty buildings. Groups of unhoused families initiate 'mass squats' in abandoned hotels, offices and government buildings. Many families believe that it is better to share limited kitchen and toilet facilities with hundreds of others than to live on the streets or in *favelas* – the makeshift shantytowns on the edges of the city.

City and regional governments in less developed countries are hard-pressed to keep up with the spiralling demand for housing. In cities such as São Paulo there are disagreements among housing authorities and local governments about how to address the housing problem. Some argue that the most feasible route is to improve conditions within the *favelas* – to provide electricity and running water, pave the streets and assign postal

The making of a megacity

One of the largest urban settlements in history is currently being formed in Asia in an area of 50,000 square kilometres reaching from Hong Kong to mainland China, the Pearl River Delta and Macao. Although the region has no formal name or administrative structure, by 1995 it had already encompassed a population of 50 million people. According to Manuel Castells, it is poised to become one of the most significant industrial, business and cultural centres of the century.

Castells points to several interrelated factors that help to explain the emergence of this enormous conurbation. First, China is undergoing an economic transformation, and Hong Kong is one of the most important 'nodal points' linking China into the global economy. Next, Hong Kong's role as a global business and financial centre has been growing as its economic base shifts away from manufacturing towards services. Finally, between the mid-1980s and the mid-1990s, Hong Kong industrialists initiated a dramatic process of industrialization within the Pearl River Delta. More than 6 million people are employed in 20,000 factories and 10,000 firms. The result of these overlapping processes has been an 'unprecedented urban explosion' (Castells 1996).

addresses. Others fear that makeshift shantytowns are fundamentally uninhabitable and should be demolished to make way for proper housing for poor families.

Congestion and over-development in city centres lead to serious environmental problems in many urban areas. Mexico City is a prime example. There, 94 per cent of the city consists of built-up areas, with only 6 per cent of land being open space. The area of 'green spaces' – parks and open stretches of green land – is far below that found in even the most densely populated North American or European cities. Pollution is a major problem, coming mostly from the cars, buses and trucks which pack the inadequate roads of the city, the rest deriving from industrial pol-

Pollution makes city living increasingly dangerous, especially for the world's poorest people.

lutants. It has been estimated that living in Mexico City is equivalent to smoking forty cigarettes a day. In March 1992, pollution reached one of its highest levels ever. Whereas an ozone level of just under 100 points was deemed 'satisfactory' for health, in that month the level climbed to 398 points. The government had to order factories to close down for a period, schools were shut and 40 per cent of cars were banned from the streets on any one day.

Social effects

Many urban areas in the developing world are overcrowded and under-resourced. Poverty is widespread and existing social services cannot meet the demands for healthcare, family planning advice, education and training. The unbalanced age distribution in developing countries adds to their social and economic difficulties. Compared to industrialized countries, a much larger proportion of the population in the developing world is under the age of fifteen. A youthful population needs support and education, but many developing countries lack the resources to provide universal education. When their families are poor, many children must work full time, and others have to scratch a living as street children, begging for whatever they can. When the street children mature, most become unemployed, homeless or both.

The future of urbanization in the developing world

In considering the scope of the challenges facing urban areas in developing countries, it can be difficult to see prospects for change and development. Conditions of life in many of the world's largest cities seem likely to decline even further in the years to come. But the picture is not entirely negative.

First, although birth rates remain high in many countries, they are likely to drop in the years to come as urbanization proceeds. This in turn will feed into a gradual decrease in the rate of urbanization itself. In West Africa, for example, the rate of urbanization should drop to 4.2 per cent per year by 2020, down from an annual rate of 6.3 per cent growth over the previous three decades.

> Population growth is discussed further in chapter 11, 'Global Inequality', pp. 418–28.

Second, globalization is presenting important opportunities for urban areas in developing countries. With economic integration, cities around the world are able to enter international markets, to promote themselves as locations for investment and development, and to create economic links across the borders of nation-states. Globalization presents one of the most dynamic openings for growing urban centres to become major forces in economic development and innovation. Indeed, many cities in the developing world are already joining the ranks of the world's 'global cities', as we shall see shortly.

Cities and globalization

In pre-modern times, cities were self-contained entities that stood apart from the predominantly rural areas in which they were located. Road systems sometimes linked major urban areas, but travel was a specialized affair for merchants, soldiers and others who needed to cross distances with any regularity. Communication between cities was limited. The picture in the first decade of the twenty-first century could hardly be more different. Globalization has had a profound effect on cities by making them more interdependent and encouraging the proliferation of horizontal links between cities across national borders. Physical and virtual ties between cities now abound, and global networks of cities are emerging.

Some people have predicted that globalization and new communications technology might lead to the demise of cities as we know them – the Helsinki Virtual Village profiled in the box provides one possibility. This is because many of the traditional functions of cities can now be carried out in cyberspace rather than in dense and congested urban areas. For example, financial markets have gone electronic, e-commerce reduces the need for both producers and consumers to rely on city centres and 'e-commuting' permits a growing number of employees to work from home rather than in an office building.

Yet, thus far, such predictions have not been borne out. Rather than undermining cities, globalization is transforming them into vital hubs within the global economy. Urban centres have become critical in coordinating information flows, managing business activities and innovating new services and technologies. There has been a simultaneous dispersion and concentration of activity and power within a set of cities around the globe (Castells 1996).

Global cities

The role of cities in the new global order has been attracting a great deal of attention from sociologists. Globalization is often thought of in terms of a duality between the national level and the global, yet it is the largest cities of the world that comprise the main circuits through which globalization occurs (Sassen 1998). The functioning of the new global economy is dependent on a set of central locations with developed informational infrastructures and a 'hyper-concentration' of facilities. It is in such points that the 'work' of globalization is performed and directed. As business, production, advertising and marketing assume a global scale, there is an enormous amount of organizational activity that must be done in order to maintain and develop these global networks.

Saskia Sassen has been one of the leading contributors to the debate on cities and globalization. She uses the term **global city** to refer to urban centres that are home to the headquarters of large, transnational corporations and a superabundance of financial, technological and consulting services. In *The Global City* (1991), Sassen based her work on the study of three such cities: New York, London and Tokyo. The contemporary development of the world economy, she argued, has created a novel strategic role for major cities. Most such cities have long been centres of international trade, but they now have four new traits:

1 They have developed into 'command posts' – centres of direction and policy-making – for the global economy.
2 Such cities are the key locations for financial and specialized service firms, which have become more important in influencing economic development than is manufacturing.
3 They are the sites of production and innovation in these newly expanded industries.
4 These cities are markets on which the 'products' of financial and service industries are bought, sold or otherwise disposed of.

New York, London and Tokyo have very different histories, yet we can trace comparable changes in their nature over the past two or three decades. Within the highly dispersed world economy of today, cities like these provide for central control of crucial operations. Global cities are much more than simply places of coordination, however; they are also contexts of production. What is important here is not the production of material goods, but the production of the specialized services required by business organizations for administering offices and factories scattered across the world, and the production of financial innovations and markets. Services and financial goods are the 'things' the global city makes.

The downtown areas of global cities provide concentrated sites within which whole clusters of 'producers' can work in

Using your sociological imagination: the Helsinki Virtual Village

Jari Mielonen and his colleagues have a motto: *Sanoista tekoihin*, which loosely translates to 'Don't talk – make it happen.' Mielonen is Chief Technology Officer of Sonera, Finland's leading telecommunications company and one of Europe's most aggressive players in the wireless market. 'Everyone's been talking about possibilities', he says. 'Nobody's been saying, "This is it. Touch and feel. Try it."'

That's why he and a group of businesspeople, academics and city planners are collaborating to turn a new development on the tussocky shore of the Gulf of Finland into the world's first wireless community. It's a simple but intriguing idea: give the workers and residents of a new Helsinki suburb a state-of-the-art wireless infrastructure and the very latest wireless services; to log on, locals won't even need a PC – just a mobile phone. Then stand back and watch how the info-age town of the future actually functions.

The site, known as Arabianranta (Arabia shore), is a flat, windswept, mostly barren expanse named for the pottery works that once stood there. Even before Mielonen and his colleagues started hatching plans to turn the area into a wireless wonderland, it has been earmarked by the city of Helsinki for development as a tech hub. If all goes as planned, by 2010 the location will be home to about 12,000 residents and 700 IT companies with some 8,000 employees, along with 4,000 students enrolled at local universities. It will also be home to a real-world experiment in community networking that will untangle some of the most pressing questions about the social effects of pervasive connectivity. Will the constant availability of wireless connection make communities more cohesive, or more isolated? How will people balance privacy concerns with the obvious advantages of extended wireless reach? And how much connectivity – once it becomes the status quo – will people really want?

Construction has already begun on the first wave of new office buildings and homes . . . Alongside the concrete and steel pilings, another, less visible, framework is being built here by Sonera and its partners – IBM, local software producer Digia, and the European-based Symbian Alliance, a joint effort involving Ericsson, Motorola, Nokia, Matsushita and Psion. They are creating what they call Helsinki Virtual Village, a wireless interactive community for the entire suburb of Arabianranta. HVV will include a local area network and a wide range of services available through broadband fiber-optic cable and wireless links, which will be accessible anytime, anywhere. Users will be able to participate in HVV via any wireless handset, as well as by PC and digital TV.

For instance, residents could consult their personal calendar wherever they happen to be – in front of a computer at the office, watching TV at home, or using a mobile phone on the go. The envisioned menu of offerings will let them create their own social organizations, office networks, or mobile commerce opportunities, and a profiling system will let them control and update their personal data minute by minute . . .

Now HVV is throwing mobility into the mix, making communication casual and unobtrusive. IBM Nordic's Kurt Lönnqvist, who has watched his children grow up in a mobile-tech world, believes Finnish society has changed forever. Young people can be spontaneous about making social plans, he says. On the streets, they're continually sending a stream of messages back and forth to their friends: 'Where R U?' 'Let's meet.' 'C U at the bar.' Lönnqvist believes his children have become freer about the way they lead their lives than his generation is. 'They live with mobility every day. It's a way of life.'

At the Helsinki University of Technology, sociologist Timo Kopomaa has tried to track these changes in Finnish society. 'Spontaneity is something that is going to stay', he says. 'It's a new generation that has grown up with these devices, and their lives are bound up with them.' He studied groups of young phone users and noted several differences in lifestyle. Today's society may be more casual, but that doesn't mean social ties are disappearing. In fact, he found that phones are drawing people together in new ways. Young 'telesurfers' often have larger social circles than non-phone-users. Close friends or relatives are in almost constant contact with each other, tending to share

Is mobile phone use an integral part of modern city living?

experiences as they happen. For friends, this has brought a new sense of tele-intimacy; for parents, reassurance.

Kopomaa believes the new wireless intimacy affects the workplace as well. 'The mobile phone softens the structure of the working day', he says. 'Workers don't have to plan so rigidly anymore – each day can unfold as meetings are set up when needed.'

Source: Shaw (2001)

Questions

1 The planners of Helsinki Virtual Village describe the town as a technological utopia. Do you think mobile phone connectivity will drastically change life in the ways they describe? What effects have mobile phones already had on our society?

2 What might be the unintended consequences of mobile phone usage?

3 Are people really more connected because of mobile phones? How could mobile phone technology make people more isolated?

close interaction, often including personal contact, with one another. In the global city, local firms mingle with national and multinational organizations, including a multiplicity of foreign companies. Thus 350 foreign banks have offices in New York City, plus 2,500 other foreign financial corporations; one out of every four bank employees in the city works for a foreign bank. Global cities compete with one another, but they also constitute an interdependent system, partly separate from the nations in which they are located.

Other authors have built on Sassen's work, noting that as globalization progresses, more and more cities are joining New York, London and Tokyo in the ranks of the 'global city'. Castells has described the creation of a tiered hierarchy of world cities – with places such as Hong Kong, Singapore, Chicago, Frankfurt, Los Angeles, Milan, Zurich and Osaka serving as major global centres for business and financial services. Beneath these, a new set of 'regional centres' is developing as key nodes within the global economy. Cities such as Madrid, São Paulo, Moscow, Seoul, Jakarta and Buenos Aires are becoming important hubs for activity within the so-called 'emerging markets'.

Inequality and the global city

The new global economy is highly problematic in many ways. Nowhere can this be seen more clearly than in the new dynamics of inequality visible within the global city. The juxtaposition between the central business district and impoverished inner-city areas of many global cities should be seen as interrelated phenomena, as Sassen and others remind us. The 'growth sectors' of the new economy – financial services, marketing, high technology – are reaping profits far greater than any found within traditional economic sectors. As the salaries and bonuses of the very affluent continue to climb, the wages of those employed to clean and guard their offices are dropping. Sassen argues that we are witnessing the 'valorization' of work located at the forefront of the new global economy, and the 'devalorization' of work which occurs behind the scenes.

Deprivation and social exclusion are discussed in chapter 10, 'Poverty, Social Exclusion and Welfare', and inequality in chapter 11, 'Global Inequality'.

Disparities in profit-making capabilities are expected in market economies, but the magnitude of the disparities in the new global economy is having a negative effect on many aspects of the social world, from housing to the labour market. Those who work in finance and global services receive high salaries, and the areas where they live become gentrified. At the same time, orthodox manufacturing jobs are lost, and the very process of gentrification creates a vast supply of low-wage jobs – in restaurants, hotels and boutiques. Affordable housing is scarce in gentrified areas, forcing an expansion of low-income neighbourhoods. While central business districts are the recipients of massive influxes of investment in real estate, development and telecommunications, marginalized areas are left with few resources.

Within global cities, a geography of 'centrality and marginality' is taking shape. Alongside resplendent affluence, there is acute poverty. Yet although these two worlds coexist side by side, the actual contact between them can be surprisingly minimal. As Mike Davis has noted in his study of Los Angeles, there has been a 'conscious hardening' of the city surface against the poor (Davis 1990, p. 232). Accessible public spaces have been replaced by walled compounds, neighbourhoods guarded by electronic surveillance, and 'corporate citadels'. In Davis's words:

> To reduce contact with untouchables, urban redevelopment has converted once vital pedestrian streets into traffic sewers and transformed public parks into temporary receptacles for the homeless and wretched. The American city . . . is being systematically turned inside out – or, rather, outside in. The valorized spaces of the new mega-structures and super-malls are concentrated in the center, street frontage is denuded, public activity is sorted into strictly functional compartments, and circulation is internalized in corridors under the gaze of private police.

According to Davis, life is made as 'unliveable' as possible for the poorest and most marginalized residents of Los Angeles. Benches at bus stops are barrel-shaped to prevent people from sleeping on them, the number of public toilets is fewer than in any other North American city, and sprinkler systems have been installed in many parks to deter the homeless from living in them. Police and city planners have attempted to contain the homeless population within certain regions of the city, but in periodically sweeping through and confiscating makeshift shelters, they have effectively created a population of 'urban bedouins'.

Governing cities in a global age

Like globalization, urbanization is double-edged and contradictory. It has both creative and destructive effects on cities. On one hand, it allows for the concentration of people, goods, services and opportunities. But at the same time, it fragments and weakens the coherence of places, traditions and existing networks. Alongside the new potentials created by centralization and economic growth are the dangerous effects of marginalization. Not only in developing countries, but in industrialized ones as well, many city dwellers operate on the periphery, outside the realm of formal employment, the rule of law and civic culture (Borja and Castells 1997).

Managing the global

Although globalization is aggravating many of the challenges facing cities around the world, it is also making room for cities and local governments to play a revitalized political role. Cities have become more important than ever before as nation-states are increasingly unable to manage global trends. Issues such as ecological risk and volatile financial markets are operating at levels far above that of the nation-state; individual countries – even the most powerful – are too 'small' to counter such forces. Yet nation-states also remain too 'large' to address adequately the rich diversity of needs found within cosmopolitan urban areas. Where the nation-state is unable to act effectively, local and city governments may be more 'agile forms for managing the global' (Borja and Castells 1997).

See also the rise of social movements in response to political and social change in chapter 20, 'Politics, Government and Terrorism', pp. 867–71.

Jordi Borja and Manuel Castells (1997) argue that there are three main realms in which local authorities can act effectively to manage global forces. First, cities can contribute to economic productivity and competitiveness by managing the local 'habitat' – the conditions and facilities that form the social base for economic productivity. Economic competitiveness in the new economy depends on a productive qualified workforce; to be productive, that workforce needs a strong educational system for its children, good public transport, adequate and affordable housing, capable law enforcement, effective emergency services and vibrant cultural resources.

Second, cities play an important role in ensuring socio-cultural integration within diverse multi-ethnic populations. Global cities bring together individuals from dozens of countries, varying religious and linguistic backgrounds, and different socio-economic levels. If the intense pluralism found within cosmopolitan cities is not countered by forces of integration, fragmentation and intolerance can result. Especially in cases where the effectiveness of the nation-states for promoting social cohesion is compromised for historic, linguistic or other reasons, individual cities can be positive forces for social integration.

Third, cities are important venues for political representation and management. Local authorities have two inherent advantages over the nation-state in managing global issues: they enjoy greater legitimacy with those they represent, and they have more flexibility and room for manoeuvre than national structures. As we saw see in chapter 20 ('Politics, Government and Terrorism'), many citizens feel that national political systems do not adequately represent their interests and concerns. In cases where the nation-state is too distant to represent specific

cultural or regional interests, city and local authorities are more accessible forums for political activity.

Cities as political, economic and social agents

A great many organizations, institutions and groups cross paths within cities. Domestic and international businesses, potential investors, government bodies, civic associations, professional groups, trade unions and others meet and form links in urban areas. These links can lead to collective and joint actions in which cities act as social agents in political, economic, cultural and media spheres.

Examples of cities as economic actors have been increasing in recent years. In Europe, beginning with the recession of the 1970s, cities have banded together to promote investment and generate new forms of employment. The Eurocities movement which now encompasses Europe's fifty largest cities was formed in 1989. Asian cities such as Seoul, Singapore and Bangkok have been particularly effective as economic actors, acknowledging the importance of speed of information about international markets and the need for flexible productive and commercial structures.

Some cities construct medium- and long-term strategic plans to address the complex challenges before them. Under such plans, local government authorities, civic groups and private economic agents can work together to refurbish the urban infrastructure, organize a world-class event or shift the employment base away from industrial enterprises to knowledge-based ones. Birmingham, Amsterdam, Lyon, Lisbon, Glasgow and Barcelona are examples of European cities that have carried out successful urban renewal projects with the help of strategic plans.

The case of Barcelona is particularly noteworthy. Launched in 1988, the Barcelona 2000 Economic and Social Strategic Plan brought together public and private organizations under a shared vision and action plan for transforming the city. The Barcelona municipal government and ten additional bodies (including the chamber of commerce, the university, the city port authority and trade unions) have been overseeing the implementation of the plan's three main objectives: to connect Barcelona into a network of European cities by improving the communication and transport infrastructure, to improve the quality of life of Barcelona's inhabitants and to make the industrial and service sector more competitive, while promoting promising new economic sectors.

One of the cornerstones of the Barcelona 2000 plan took place in 1992 when the city hosted the Olympic Games. Staging the Olympics allowed Barcelona to 'internationalize' itself; the city's assets and vision were on display for the whole world to see. In the case of Barcelona, organizing a world-class event was crucial on two fronts: it enhanced the profile of the city in the eyes of the world and it generated additional enthusiasm within the city for completing the urban transformation (Borja and Castells 1997). Sport can now play an important part in urban regeneration (Taylor et al. 1996). Member of the International Olympic Committee were impressed by the importance placed on regeneration in London's successful bid for the 2012 Olympic Games. London's plan for 2012 focuses on the regeneration of around 500 acres of land in the Stratford area of East London, one of the most deprived areas in the UK. In the box below, we look at the 2002 Commonwealth Games as a catalyst for urban regeneration in Manchester.

Using your sociological imagination: sport and urban regeneration

Why Manchester may rue the day it won the Commonwealth Games

The Commonwealth Games, first staged in 1930 to celebrate the pride of the British Empire, are extracting an unwelcome modern cost on the citizens of Manchester who now face increased council tax bills and cuts in services as the city attempts to make up a £45m funding shortfall for the event it hosts next summer.

While organizers mark the one-year countdown to the opening of the games today – proclaiming they will regenerate Manchester and leave a sporting legacy that includes state-of-the art facilities – residents and councillors are protesting that they are paying the ultimate price with grass-roots facilities and services facing closure.

Residents' groups and opposition politicians in Labour-controlled Manchester city council claim that cuts have already started to bite, leading to at least 14 offices of the housing department being shut and a number of redundancies among council staff. Two swimming pools are to be closed in east Manchester while a boxing club in Withenshaw is having to move after having its funds withdrawn as concern mounts that the council is taking a massive financial risk in underwriting the entire cost of the games.

Manchester council has confirmed that it is to take out a £10m commercial loan and use valuable financial reserves as a way to fund the games and make up any shortfall. According to some reports, any profits from Manchester Airport, which is owned by the local authority, could also be diverted towards funding the games.

Councillors and residents claim that council taxes could eventually be increased because of the huge financial commitment taken on by the city council. In total, the council is to spend £80m on running the Commonwealth Games. Originally it was only committed to spending £35m. However, last month it was ordered by the government to contribute an extra £45m after it became apparent that there would be a massive shortfall.

A government-backed report by the millionaire businessman Patrick Carter, who was commissioned to examine the finances of the games, found that there was a £110m funding gap. It was eventually decided that the government would contribute £30m, Sport England – which distributes sports lottery money – another £30m and £45m would be provided by Manchester city council.

Simon Ashley, leader of the Liberal Democrats on Manchester city council said: 'We were promised that the Commonwealth Games would not affect services or council tax but this is not true. We are very concerned at the financial management of the games and the impact this is going to have on the city'.

'The council has to find an extra £45m and this has to come from somewhere and in total is going to spend £80m. This is a massive financial risk for the council to take but it should be up to central government to fund large sports projects'.

'Swimming pools and housing offices are being closed and services are being cut. If you are spending millions on the games it means you are not able to spend it on anything else.' . . .

Source: Vivek Chaudhary, *Guardian* (25 July 2001)

Will the Manchester Commonwealth Games be remembered as the 'Regeneration Games'?

The pros and cons of Manchester staging the Commonwealth Games

- regeneration of east Manchester;
- increase in tourism – possibly 1 million visitors during Games;
- £170 million be spent on new venues, including new stadium for Manchester City FC and new pool in east Manchester;
- £5m to be spent on cosmetic improvements of city;
- 5,000 new jobs, most of them temporary;
- enhanced image of city throughout world;
- increase in council tax;
- £10m commercial loan;
- two swimming pools and one boxing club to close;
- 14 offices in housing department to close;
- 56 staff to be made redundant;
- profits from Manchester airport could be diverted to fund games;
- council cuts likely in future.

The regeneration games?

Around the corner from Manchester's impressive Commonwealth Games stadium, lies a row of terraced houses. Red brick shining out against the mid-summer gloom, they were once the epitome of a northern inner-city community - classic Coronation Street, in fact. But now Ben Street's main features are the grim metal shutters over windows and an eerie, ghost-town like silence.

The contrast with the Sports City complex just half a mile away, where much of the Commonwealth Games events were staged, is striking. Now many residents are wondering whether the Games – hailed as a success when they were staged a year ago – will prove equally as successful in improving their lives in the long term.

The city council certainly seems to think so. Only last week it announced the Games had created 6,300 new full-time jobs, an annual boost of £18m in tourist income and £570m regeneration money for east Manchester. But for Bill Booth, who has lived in the suburb of Clayton for 27 years, questions remain . . .

A brand new canalside apartment block is also currently being built – but Mr Booth says they are not the answer. He said: 'The new jobs are 100 per cent welcome and I don't mind the new apartments being built, which will bring new people into the area. But my big fear is that these new properties will be too expensive for the locals. All of this regeneration, is it for the people who have lived here most of their lives?'

Jim Larkin, who lives in Bank Street, Clayton, has similar fears. He said: 'I could see poorer people being forced out into poorer areas and the problems we've had here being replicated elsewhere. I just hope that the whole feeling that came from the games keeps on expanding.'

Both men cite the Games as the best thing to happen to east Manchester in decades. And in nearby Beswick, people like Barbara Taylor, who runs a Homewatch group, have mainly positive things to say. She said: 'It's put Beswick on the map and made people realize that we aren't bandit country anymore. There's been a lot of money spent on the private and council properties which will be transferred to a social landlord. Also, while I'm not too sure people feel a sense of pride at this time, they aren't talking about moving away anymore. They can see a future for themselves and for their children.'

Veronica Powell, 74, who has lived in Beswick all of her life, is equally optimistic. She said: 'It was absolutely wonderful that we got the Commonwealth Games, it's the beginning of what's going to continue for this area. Ten years ago we had a really bad time because we had horrible flats and maisonettes, and a big fear of crime. The rebuilding that they are doing and the hotels that are going to spring up will bring a different kind of people in, but it's going to bring money into the area. Once we get the Metro [trams] here, going into Manchester for work will be easy-peasy. It's going to be quite profitable for us, I think.'

Source: David Green, *BBC News Online*, Manchester (28 July 2003)

Questions

1. What role should existing residents have in urban regeneration?
2. Who should pay for urban regeneration?
3. Was Manchester right to bid for the Commonwealth Games in 2002?

The role of mayors

As cities assume new importance in the global system, the role of city mayors is also changing. Mayors of large cities are able to provide a type of personalized leadership that can be crucial in promoting urban agendas and raising a city's international profile. In several prominent cases in which cities have successfully transformed their image, the role of the city mayor has been decisive. The mayors of Lisbon and Barcelona, for example, were driving forces behind efforts to elevate their cities to the ranks of the world's major urban centres. Likewise, mayors in smaller cities can play a crucial role in making the city known internationally and in attracting new economic investment.

The growing importance of city mayors can also be seen in the UK. After it came to power in 1997, the Labour government announced its intention to devolve authority over London's affairs to an elected mayor. Since the abolition of the Greater London Council by Mrs Thatcher in 1986, the city had not had its own local administration. Ken Livingstone became London's first elected mayor in May 2000. He has since pursued a distinctive set of policies which include investment in public transport (paid for in part through a congestion charge against most vehicles entering central London during weekday working hours) and an increase in affordable housing for 'key workers' such as teachers and nurses. Livingstone strongly supported London's successful bid to host the 2012 Olympic Games. He believes the Games will 'provide a major catalyst for change and regeneration' in the city. Regeneration was a central issue in the Barcelona Olympics in 1992 and the 2002 Manchester Commonwealth Games (London Plan 2004). The success of the Manchester Commonwealth Games in regeneration was debated in the box on pp. 929–31.

In the United States, city mayors have become a powerful economic and political force in recent decades. As gun-related violence has soared in American cities, more than twenty city mayors have abandoned reliance on federal attempts to pass gun control legislation and have filed lawsuits against the gun manufacturers on behalf of their cities. New York mayor Rudolph Giuliani generated a firestorm of controversy – but grudging respect from many – by implementing tough 'law and order' policies aimed at lowering crime rates. New York's violent crime rate dropped dramatically during the 1990s; strict 'quality of life' policies aimed at the homeless population transformed the face of New York's busy streets. After the terrorist attacks on 11 September 2001, Giuliani's determined leadership set the tone for the world's media, and he was named *Time* magazine's Person of the Year for 2001.

In Britain and other countries, mayors are enjoying increased influence as spokespeople for their cities and regions. City mayors are often able to shape the policy agenda for areas that lie outside the city limits by entering into agreements with communities in the general metropolitan area. These types of partnerships can be drawn on in attracting foreign investment, for example, or in bidding to play host to a world-class event.

Conclusion: cities and global governance

Cooperation between cities is not restricted to the regional level. There is a growing acknowledgement that cities can and should play a significant role in addressing international political, economic and social issues. Informal and formal networks of cities are emerging as globalizing forces draw disparate parts of the world more closely together. The problems facing the world's largest cities are not isolated ones; they are embedded in the larger context of a global economy, international migration, new trade patterns and the power of information technology.

We have noted elsewhere that the complexities of our changing world are demanding new forms of democratic international governance. Networks of cities should figure prominently among these new mechanisms. One such structure already exists – a World Assembly of Cities and Local Authorities is convened in parallel to the UN's Habitat conference. Bodies such as the World Assembly promise to allow the gradual integration of city organizations into structures presently composed of national governments.

The heightened involvement of cities has the potential to democratize international relations; it may also make them more efficient. As the world's urban population continues to grow, more and more policies and reforms will need to be targeted at populations living in urban areas. City governments will be necessary and vital partners in these processes.

Summary points

1   Early approaches to urban sociology were dominated by the work of the Chicago School, whose members saw urban processes in terms of ecological models derived from biology. Louis Wirth developed the concept of urbanism as a way of life, arguing that city life breeds impersonality and social distance. These approaches have been challenged, without being discarded altogether. Critics have pointed out that city life isn't always impersonal: many close, personal ties can be formed and sustained in urban neighbourhoods.

2   The more recent work of David Harvey and Manuel Castells connects patterns of urbanism to the wider society, rather than treating urban processes as self-contained. The modes of life people develop in cities, as well as the physical lay-out of different neighbourhoods, express broad features of the development of industrial capitalism.

3   In traditional societies, only a small minority of the population lived in urban areas. In the industrialized countries today, between 60 and 90 per cent do so. Urbanism is developing very rapidly in the developing world as well.

4   The expansion of suburbs and dormitory towns has contributed to inner-city decay. Wealthier groups tend to move out of the centre of the city to live in low-rise housing and more homogeneous neighbourhoods. A cycle of deterioration is set under way, so that the more suburbia expands, the greater are the problems faced by those living in the inner cities. Urban recycling – including the refurbishing of old buildings to put them to

new uses – has become common in many large cities.

5   Massive processes of urban development are occurring in developing countries. Cities in these societies differ in major respects from those of the West, and are often dominated by makeshift illegal housing, where conditions of life are extremely impoverished. The informal economy is pronounced in many cities in the developing world. Governments often cannot meet the growing demands of the population for education, healthcare and family planning.

6   Cities are being strongly influenced by globalization. Global cities are urban centres, such as New York, London and Hong Kong, that are home to the headquarters of large corporations and a superabundance of financial, technological and consulting services. A set of regional cities, such as Seoul, Moscow and São Paulo, are developing as key nodes of the global economy.

7   As cities become more important within the global economy, their relationship with outlying regions is altered. Cities become disconnected from the region and nation in which they are located and horizontal links with other global cities take on greater significance. Global cities are characterized by high levels of inequality. Great affluence and abject poverty coexist side by side, but contact between the two worlds can be minimal.

8   The role of cities as political and economic agents is increasing. City governments are positioned to manage the effects of some global issues better than national governments. Cities can contribute to economic productivity and competitiveness, promote social and cultural integration, and serve as accessible venues for political activity. Some cities construct strategic plans to promote the city's profile by hosting a world-class event or carrying out urban renewal and economic development programmes. City mayors are becoming important political forces for advancing urban agendas.

9   As globalization progresses, the role of cities in addressing international issues is likely to grow. This is because many of the problems facing large cities are linked to global issues such as economic integration, migration, trade, public health and information technology. Regional and international networks of cities are emerging and may become more actively involved in forms of global governance currently composed of nation-states.

Questions for further thought

1 Is the city a place of strangers?
2 What is the influence of the Chicago School on more recent thinking about urban life?
3 Why do groups come into conflict over resources in cities?
4 Have attempts at urban renewal in the UK been successful?
5 Should the Third World's 'megacities' stop urbanizing because of the oppressive social conditions this process creates?
6 Why has there been so much recent enthusiasm for the concept of elected city mayors?

Further reading

Marshall Berman, *All That is Solid Melts into Air* (London: Verso, 1982).
Roger Bocock and Kenneth Thompson (eds), S*ocial and Cultural Forms of Modernity* (Cambridge: Polity, 1992).
James Donald, *Imagining the Modern City* (London: Athlone, 1999).
Nan Ellin, *Postmodern Urbanism* (Oxford: Blackwell, 1995).
David Frisby, *Cityscapes of Modernity: Critical Explorations* (Cambridge: Polity, 2001).
Richard Le Gates and Frederic Stout (eds), *The City Reader* (London: Routledge, 2003).
Philip Kasinitz (ed.), *Metropolis: Centre and Symbol of our Times* (Basingstoke: Macmillan, 1995).
Peter Marcuse and Ronald van Kempen (eds), *Globalizing Cities: A New Spatial Order?* (Oxford: Blackwell, 2000).
Mike Savage and Allan Warde (eds), *Urban Sociology, Capitalism and Modernity* (Basingstoke: Macmillan, 1993).
John Rennie Short, *The Urban Order: An Introduction to Cities, Culture and Power* (Oxford: Blackwell, 1996).
Fran Tonkiss, *Space, the City and Social Theory* (Cambridge: Polity, 2005).

Internet links

Sustainable architecture, building and culture: http://www.sustainableabc.com

University of Leicester, Centre for Urban History: http://www.le.ac.uk/urbanhist/index.html

The Government's Neighbourhood Renewal Unit: http://www.neighbourhood.gov.uk/

City Mayors: http://www.citymayors.com/features/euro_cities.html

H-Urban Discussion Site: http://h-net.msu.edu/~urban/

Radical Urban Theory: http://www.rut.com/

Virtual Cities Resource Centre: http://www.casa.ucl.ac.uk/vc/welcome.htm

Contents

22 The Environment and Risk

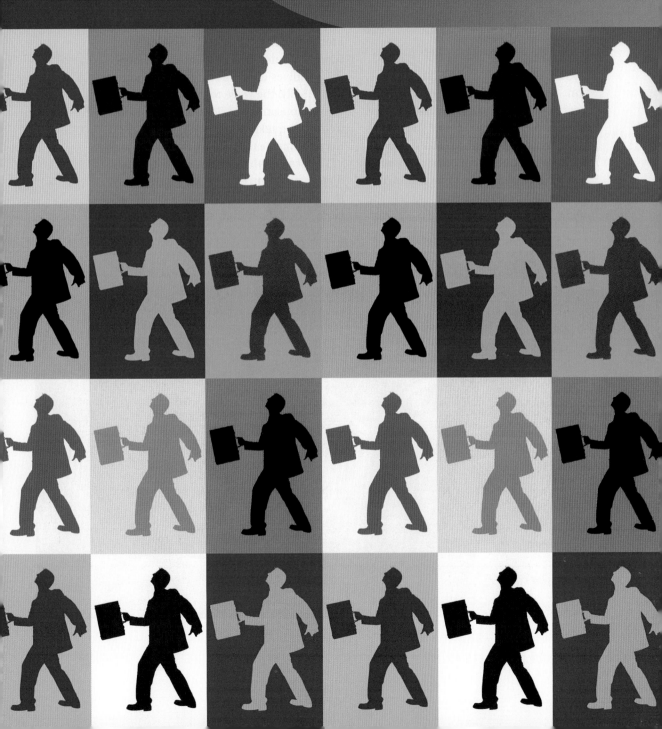

JUST BEFORE one o'clock, British time, on Boxing Day morning 2004, the largest earthquake in forty years occurred beneath the Indian Ocean. The earthquake shifted the seabed and displaced hundreds of cubic kilometres of water. A large wave caused by the tremor, known as a tsunami, began moving across the Indian Ocean away from the quake's epi-

centre at a speed of around five hundred miles an hour. As it neared the coast, the tsunami slowed dramatically to just thirty miles per hour and began to increase in height. The tsunami reached the nearest landmass, Aceh in northern Indonesia, just fifteen minutes after the initial quake, in many places destroying everything in its path and sweeping debris hundreds of metres inland. Thailand was hit after ninety minutes, Sri Lanka after two hours, the Maldives after three and a half hours and, finally, the wave reached the African coast, thousands of miles from the epicentre of the quake, some seven hours after the earthquake that caused it.

The scale of the tragedy was not immediately apparent. By the end of Boxing Day it was reported that 12,000 people had been killed, including several holidaying

Westerners. A few weeks later the United Nations estimated that more than 175,000 people had died. Most deaths were in Indonesia, where it is thought that around 160,000 people lost their lives. Figures for the total number of people killed around the Indian Ocean vary hugely, but the British Red Cross has estimated a death toll closer to the region of a staggering 1 million. In Sri Lanka more than 30,000 people were killed, more than a thousand of whom drowned when an 80-tonne train was lifted off its tracks and submerged under water. In India just under 10,000 people are thought to have died. Travelling west, the wave caused devastation as far away as Africa, killing around 140 people along the continent's east coast. Many millions of people around the Indian Ocean were left homeless.

The Boxing Day tsunami was a global disaster, and shows how, in a globalized world, events thousands of miles away have a great impact on our lives. Although the vast majority of people killed in the tsunami were locals, several thousand were Westerners, many of whom had been enjoying an idyllic Christmas break in the region. The tsunami claimed the lives of 149 people who were British citizens or had close links with the UK: the greatest loss of British lives in any one incident since the Second World War and far greater than the number of Britons who died in the terrorist attacks in New York and Washington in 2001. The high loss of life amongst Westerners reflects the processes of globalization. Thailand, where most holiday-makers were killed, has only became a destination for mass tourism in the last two decades, as people from the rich world become increasingly prepared to travel further afield for their holidays.

The relief effort was also global in scope. In the days after the catastrophe the world's news stations beamed pictures and reports of the suffering around the planet. In rich countries millions of dollars were donated by the general public and by governments, which also agreed that debt repayments from the worst hit countries should be suspended, and which sent offers of troops and expertise to the region. In early January 2005, millions of people across Europe stopped what they were doing to take part in a three-minute silence in memory of those killed.

The environment as a sociological issue

Why should sociologists be interested in episodes such as this? Surely the tsunami was a wholly natural event, an example of the massive power of nature? Yet sociologists can and must take a direct interest in our relation to nature – to the physical environment in which we live. First, sociology can help us to understand how environmental threats are distributed. Although the tsunami in Asia killed people from all over the globe, as we saw above, most of the people who died were native to the coastal regions around the Indian Ocean. If it had occurred in the richer countries of the Pacific Ocean, the Pacific Tsunami Warning System based in the American state of Hawaii would have quickly alerted the emergency authorities in the endangered countries where the infrastructure should be in place to move people away from the coast before a wave strikes. (An early warning system will now be built for the Indian Ocean, with money from Western donors.) The distribution of risk from the environment varies with other types of environmental threats too. Although global warming, for example, will affect everyone on the planet, it will do so in different ways. (Global warming and its likely affects are discussed on pp. 953–9) Flooding kills many more people in low-lying, poor countries, such as Bangladesh, where housing and emergency infrastructure are less able to cope with severe weather than in the UK, for example. In richer countries, such as the USA, the issues raised by global warming for policy-makers are likely to concern indirect effects, such as rising levels of immigration as people try to enter the country from areas more directly affected.

Second, sociologists can provide an account of how patterns of human behaviour create pressure on the natural environment (Cylke 1993). Although the Boxing Day tsunami was not a result of human action, many environmental challenges we discuss in this chapter are. For example, the levels of pollution produced by industrialized countries would cause catastrophe if repeated in the world's poorer, non-industrial nations. (We look at this issue in more detail in our discussion of the limits to growth and sustainable development below.) If the impoverished sectors of the world are to catch up with the richer ones, then citizens of the rich world are going to have to revise their expectations about constant economic growth. Some 'green' (environmentalist) authors argue that people in the rich countries must react against consumerism and return to simpler ways of life if global ecological disaster is to be avoided (see, for example, Schumacher 1977; Stead and Stead 1996). They argue that rescuing the global environment will thus mean social as well as technological change. Given the vast global inequalities that exist, there is little chance that the poor countries of the developing world will sacrifice their own economic growth because of environmental problems created largely by the rich ones. Sociology enables us to study how environmental problems are linked to changing social trends.

In this chapter, we look at some of the wider threats to the natural environment – most of them, unlike the tsunami, come from human beings themselves. We ask whether current levels of consumption are sustainable, and examine some of the major threats to our environment, including pollution, waste and resource depletion. We then look at some of the major environmental risks that we face today.

Our common environment

Questions about the harmful impact of human beings on the natural world, such as global warming and the destruction of the world's rainforests, have come to be known as **environmental ecology**. Public concern about the environment has led to the formation of 'green' parties and non-governmental organizations, like Friends of the Earth and Greenpeace, which campaign around environmental issues. While there are varied green philosophies, a common thread is the concern to take action to protect the world's environment, conserve rather than exhaust its resources and protect the remaining animal species.

Are there limits to growth?

One important influence on the rise of green movements, and on public concern about environmental problems, can be traced back to a famous report first published in the early 1970s – *The Limits to Growth*, published by the Club of Rome (Meadows et al. 1972). The Club of Rome was a group of industrialists, business advisers and civil servants formed in the Italian capital. It commissioned a study that used computer modelling techniques to make predictions about the consequences of continued economic growth, population growth, pollution and the depletion of natural resources. The computer model showed what would happen if the trends that were established between 1900 and 1970 continued to the year 2100. The computer projections were altered to generate a variety of possible consequences, depending on different rates of growth of the factors considered. The researchers found that each time they altered one variable, there would eventually be an environmental crisis. The main conclusion of the Club of Rome report was that rates of industrial growth are not compatible with the finite nature of the earth's resources and the capability of the planet to carry population growth and absorb pollution. The report pointed to the unsustainability of current levels of growth in 'population, industrialization, pollution, food production and resource depletion'.

The Club of Rome report was widely criticized, and even the original authors later came to accept that some of the criticisms were justified. The method used by the researchers focused on physical limits and assumed existing rates of growth and technological innovation. The report did not sufficiently take into account the capacity of human beings to respond to environmental challenges through tech-

nological advances or by political means. Moreover, the critics pointed out, market forces can act to limit the over-exploitation of resources. As an example, if a mineral like magnesium starts to become scarce, its price will rise. As its price rises, it will be used less, and producers might even find a way of dispensing with it altogether should costs rise too steeply. Whatever its limitations, the report made a strong impact on public consciousness. It served to make many people aware of the damaging consequences which industrial development and technology can have, as well as warning about the perils of allowing different forms of pollution to develop unchecked. The report served as a catalyst for the burgeoning environmental movements, discussed in chapter 20, pp. 867–71.

The basic idea of *The Limits to Growth* was that there are both social and natural influences limiting how far the earth can absorb continuing economic development and population growth. The findings of the Club of Rome report were used by many groups to suggest that economic development should be severely curtailed in order to protect the environment. Yet such a view was criticized by others as implausible and unnecessary. Economic development can be and should be promoted, they argued, because it is the means of increasing the world's wealth. The less developed countries can never hope to catch up with the richer ones if they are somehow barred from their own processes of industrial growth.

Sustainable development

Rather than calling for economic growth to be reined in, more recent developments turn on the notion of **sustainable development**. The term was first introduced in a 1987 report commissioned by the United Nations, *Our Common Future*. This is also known as the Brundtland Report, since the organizing committee that produced the report was chaired by Gro Harlem Brundtland, at that time Prime Minister of Norway. The authors of the report argued that the use of the Earth's resources by the present generation was unsustainable:

> Over the course of the twentieth century the relationship between the human world and the planet that sustains it has undergone a profound change . . . major, unintended changes are occurring in the atmosphere, in soils, in waters, among plants and animals, and in the relationships among all of these. The rate of change is outstripping the ability of scientific disciplines and our current capabilities to assess and advise. It is frustrating the attempts of political and economic institutions, which evolved in a different, more fragmented world, to adapt and cope. . . . To keep options open for future generations, the present generation must begin now, and begin together, nationally and internationally.

Sustainable development was defined as the use of renewable resources to promote economic growth, the protection of animal species and biodiversity, and the commitment to maintaining clean air, water and land. The Brundtland Commission regarded sustainable development as 'meeting the needs of the present, without compromising the ability of future generations to meet their own needs'. Sustainable development means that growth should, at least ideally, be carried on in such a way as to recycle physical resources rather than deplete them, and to keep levels of pollution to a minimum.

Following the publication of *Our Common Future*, the phrase 'sustainable development' came to be widely used both by environmentalists and by governments. It was employed at the UN Earth Summit in Rio de Janeiro in 1992 and has subsequently appeared in other ecological summit meetings organized by the UN, such as the World Summit on Sustainable Development in Johannesburg in 2002. Sustainable development is also one of the Millennium Development Goals (MDGs) which have been agreed by 191 states around the world as they aim to reduce many forms of poverty in the coming decades. The relevant MDGs include the integration of the principles of sustainable development into country policies and programmes, the reversal of the loss of environmental resources, the reduction by half of the proportion of people without sustainable access to safe drinking water and achieving a significant improvement in the lives of at least 100 million slum dwellers – all by 2020.

For more on the Millennium Development Goals, see chapter 11, 'Global Inequality', p. 415.

The Brundtland Report attracted much criticism, just as the report of the Club of Rome had done some quarter of a century earlier. Critics see the notion of sustainable development as too vague and as neglecting the specific needs of poorer countries. According to the critics, the idea of sustainable development tends to focus attention only on the needs of richer countries; it does not consider the ways in which the high levels of consumption in the more affluent countries are satisfied at the expense of other people. For instance, demands on Indonesia to conserve its rainforests could be seen as unfair, because Indonesia has a greater need than the industrialized countries for the revenue it must forgo by accepting conservation.

Consumption, poverty and the environment

Much of the debate surrounding the environment and economic development hinges on the issue of consumption patterns. Consumption refers to the goods, services, energy and resources that are used up by people, institutions and societies. It is a phenomenon with both positive and negative dimensions. On the one hand, rising levels of consumption around the world mean that people are living under better conditions than in times past. Consumption is linked to economic development – as living standards rise, people are able to afford more food, clothing, personal items, leisure time, holidays, cars and so forth. On the other hand, consumption can have negative impacts as well. Consumption patterns can damage the environmental resource base and exacerbate patterns of inequality.

The trends in world consumption over the course of the twentieth century are startling. By the end of the century private and public consumption expenditures amounted to around 24 trillion dollars – twice the level of 1975 and six times that of 1950. In 1900, world consumption levels were just over 1.5 trillion dollars (UNDP 1998). Consumption rates have been growing extremely rapidly over the past thirty years. In industrialized countries, consumption per head has been growing at a rate of 2.3 per cent annually; in East Asia growth has been even faster – 6.1 per cent annually. By contrast, the average

African household consumes 20 per cent less today than it did thirty years ago. There is widespread concern that the consumption explosion has passed by the poorest fifth of the world's population.

The inequalities in consumption between the world's rich and poor are significant. North America and Western Europe contain only around 12 per cent of the world's population, but their private consumption – the amount spent on goods and services at the household level – is over 60 per cent of the world's total. In contrast, the world's poorest region – sub-Saharan Africa, which contains around 11 per cent of the total global population – has just a 1.2 per cent share of the world's total private consumption (see table 22.1).

Environmentalists argue that current consumption patterns are not only highly unequal, but they also are having a severe impact on the environment. For example, the consumption of fresh water has doubled since 1960, the burning of fossil fuels, which is the main contributor to global warming discussed below, has almost quintupled in the past fifty years and the consumption of wood is up by 40 per cent from twenty-five years ago. Fish stocks are declining, wild species are becoming extinct, water supplies are diminishing and wooded areas are shrinking in size. Patterns of consumption are not only depleting existing natural elements, but are also contributing to their degradation through waste products and harmful emissions (UNDP 1998).

Finally, although the rich are the world's main consumers, the environmental damage that is caused by growing consumption has the heaviest impact on the poor. As we will see when we discuss global warming (pp. 953–9), the wealthy

Table 22.1   Consumer spending and population: by region, 2000 (%)

Region	Share of world population	Share of world private consumption expenditures
United States and Canada	5.2	31.5
Western Europe	6.4	28.7
East Asia and Pacific	32.9	21.4
Latin America and the Caribbean	8.5	6.7
Eastern Europe and Central Asia	7.9	3.3
South Asia	22.4	2.0
Australia and New Zealand	0.4	1.5
Middle East and North Africa	4.1	1.4
Sub-Saharan Africa	10.9	1.2

Source: Worldwatch Institute (2004)

are in a better position to enjoy the many benefits of consumption without having to deal with its negative effects. On a local level, affluent groups can usually afford to move away from problem areas, leaving the poor to bear most of the costs. Chemical plants, power stations, major roads, railways and airports are often sited close to low-income areas. On a global level, we can see a similar process at work: soil degradation, deforestation, water shortages, lead emissions and air pollution are all concentrated within the developing world. Poverty also intensifies these environmental threats. People with few resources have little choice but to maximize the resources that are available to them. As a result, more and more pressures are put on a shrinking resource base as the human population increases.

Sources of threat

As we have seen, there are many different global environmental threats confronting the contemporary world. These can be roughly divided into two basic sorts: pollution and waste products that are released into the environment and the depletion of renewable resources.

Pollution and waste

Air pollution

Air pollution, caused by toxic emissions into the atmosphere, is thought to claim more than 2.7 million lives per year. It is possible to make a distinction between two types of air pollution: 'outdoor pollution' – produced mainly by industrial pollutants and automobile emissions – and 'indoor pollution', which is caused by burning fuels in the home for heating and cooking. Traditionally, air pollution has been seen as a problem that afflicts industrialized countries, with their greater numbers of factories and motorized vehicles. In recent years, however, attention has been drawn to the dangers of 'indoor pollution' in the developing world. It is believed that more than 90 per cent of deaths linked to air pollution occur in the developing world. This is because many of the fuels that are burned by people in developing countries, such as wood and dung, are not as clean as modern fuels such as kerosene and propane.

Until the middle of the twentieth century, air pollution in Britain was caused primarily by the widespread burning of coal, which emits sulphur dioxide and thick black smoke into the atmosphere. Coal was used extensively to heat homes, and to a somewhat lesser extent in factories. In 1956, in an attempt to reduce smog, a Clean Air Act was passed to regulate emissions from chimneys. Smokeless types of fuels, such as kerosene, propane and natural gas, were promoted and are now used widely in Britain and other industrialized countries.

Since the 1960s the main source of air pollution has been the growth in the use of motorized vehicles. Vehicle emissions are particularly harmful because they enter the atmosphere at a much lower level than emissions from chimneys. As figure 22.1 shows, the range of emissions that are produced by different types of vehicle is quite large. Cars, which account for some 80 per cent of travel in Europe, have a particularly harmful impact on the environment.

For this reason, attempts to reduce air pollution in many industrialized countries have focused on the use of low-emission travel alternatives such as passenger trains, high occupancy buses and the pooling of cars.

Air pollution has been linked to a number of health problems among humans, including respiratory difficulties, cancers and lung disease. Although outdoor pollution has long been associated with industrialized countries, it is growing rapidly in the developing world. As countries undergo rapid processes of industrialization, factory emissions increase and the number of vehicles on the roads also grows. In many developing countries, leaded petrol is still in use, although it has been phased out in much of the developed world. Levels of air pollution are particularly high in many areas of Eastern Europe and the former Soviet Union.

Air pollution does not only affect the health of human and animal populations;

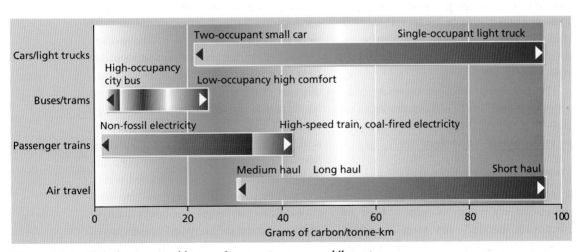

Figure 22.1 Emissions caused by moving one tonne, one kilometre

Sources: IPPC. From *Guardian Education* (25 January 2000), p. 11; *Graphic*: Michael Agar, Jenny Ridley, Graphic News.

it also has a damaging impact on other elements of the ecosystem. One harmful consequence of air pollution is acid rain, a phenomenon which occurs when sulphur and nitrogen oxide emissions in one country drift across borders and produce acidic rainfalls in another. Acid rain is harmful to forests, crops and animal life, and leads to the acidification of lakes. Canada, Poland and the Nordic countries have been particularly hard hit by acid rain. In Sweden, for example, 20,000 lakes out of a total of 90,000 have been acidified.

Like many environmental threats, acid rain is difficult to counteract because it is transnational in its origins and consequences. Much of the acid rain in eastern Canada, for example, is believed to be linked to industrial production in the state of New York, across the US–Canadian border. Other countries suffering from acid rain have similarly found that it is not within their control to tackle the problem, since its origins lie across national borders. In some instances, bilateral or regional agreements have been concluded in an attempt to reduce the severity of acid rain. Yet emissions remain high in some areas and are growing quickly in the developing world.

The box on Brent Spar opposite provides one case study of how practices of polluting can be challenged and changed by environmental activism.

Water pollution

Throughout history, people have depended on water to fulfil a host of important needs – drinking, cooking, washing, irrigating crops, fishing and many other pursuits. Although water is one of the most valuable and essential natural resources, it has also suffered enormous abuse at the hands of human beings. For many years, waste products – both human and manufactured – were dumped directly into rivers and oceans with barely a second thought. Only in the last half century or so have concerted efforts been made in many countries to protect the quality of water, to preserve the fish and wildlife that depend on it, and ensure access to clean water for the human population. Regardless of these efforts, water pollution remains a serious problem in many parts of the world.

One of the Millennium Development Goals set by the United Nations is to 'reduce by half the proportion of people without access to safe drinking water' by 2015. Water pollution can be understood broadly to refer to the contamination of the water supply by elements such as toxic chemicals and minerals, pesticides or untreated sewage. It poses the greatest threat to people in the developing world. Currently, more than one billion people around the world lack access to safe drinking water and more than two billion lack sanitation. Sanitation systems remain underdeveloped in many of the world's poorest countries and human waste products are often emptied directly into streams, rivers and lakes. The high levels of bacteria that result from untreated sewage lead to a variety of water-borne diseases, such as diarrhoea, dysentery and hepatitis. Some two billion cases of diarrhoea are caused annually by contaminated water; five million people die each year from diarrhoeal diseases. Progress is being made to improve access to the world's resources of water. During the 1990s, nearly one billion people gained access to safe water and the same number to sanitation (UNDP 2002; see also figure 22.2).

Environmental activism: Greenpeace, Shell and the Brent Spar

Environmental groups have been involved in many high-profile campaigns in recent years. A notable success was *Greenpeace*'s campaign against the plans of the oil multinational Shell to dump its Brent Spar oil installation on the seabed in 1998.

Three years after an 11th-hour reprieve as she was towed toward a watery grave, the end finally came yesterday for Brent Spar, the oil installation that was the battlesite for an environmental war. It had been destined to be sunk in the Atlantic, until a massive and successful campaign by Greenpeace to stop the dumping.

Yesterday, however, the first moves were made to take it apart to allow it to be recycled and, after 22 years as a North Sea loading and storage buoy, become a quayside for ferries in Norway. The 1600-tonne 'topsides', the section of the installation visible above the water, was lifted off by one of the largest floating cranes in the world, the Thialf. It will be taken ashore to be dismantled and scrapped at Vikaneset, near Hjelmeland, north-east of Stavanger.

Over the next six months, the Spar will be raised in the water and its hull, longer than a football pitch floating on its end, will be cut into rings. They will be cleaned and placed on the seabed at Mekjarvik, filled with ballast, and completed with a concrete surface to form the new quay.

The environmentally friendly destruction of the rig will cost Shell £43m, compared to £4.5m for dumping.

Greenpeace oil expert Jan Rispens said they were delighted the work had finally begun: 'This is the best possible solution. It protects the oceans, it creates jobs, and it reuses the material.'

Greenpeace activists occupied the redundant rig in 1995 when it was moored in the North Sea awaiting a tow to the Atlantic. They were removed but boarded it again during the journey to the intended destination. Mass public support was generated by the Greenpeace campaign across Europe, and Shell eventually abandoned their plans after petrol stations were boycotted and, on the Continent, attacked with firebombs and bullets [an act Greenpeace strongly condemned]. . . .

Early next year, a specially adapted barge, the H851, also operated by Heerema, will go to Vats to lift the Spar vertically for slicing and for the rings to be transported to Mekjarvik, where the Thialf will position them for the new quay foundation. The quay is scheduled to be complete by the end of next year.

Source: Graeme Smith, 'Beginning of end for Brent Spar; Eco-battleground to be ferry terminal', *The Herald* (Glasgow), 26 November 1998

Questions

1 Can new social movements make a difference to the actions of multinational corporations, or are cases like the Brent Spar decisions of minor importance?
2 To whom do multinational corporations owe responsibility?

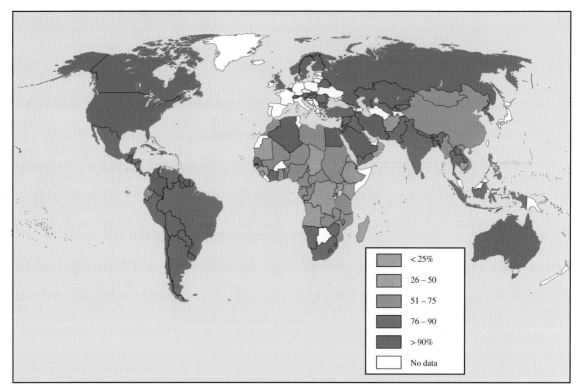

Figure 22.2 Percentage of population with access to safe water: by country, 2000

Source: *Nature*, <http://www.nature.com/nature/focus/water/map.html>

In industrialized countries, cases of water pollution are often caused by the overuse of fertilizers in agricultural areas. Over a period of years, nitrates from chemical pesticides seep into the groundwater supply; nearly 25 per cent of groundwater in Europe shows levels of contamination higher than that deemed permissible by the European Union (UNDP 1998). Some of the most polluted water can be found near former industrial areas, where traces of mercury, lead and other metals have lodged in the sediments and continue slowly to emit pollutants into the water supply over a period of years.

The quality of rivers in most Western industrialized countries has been improving in recent years. In Eastern Europe and the former Soviet Union, however, river pollution remains a very real threat. Four-fifths of the water samples taken from two hundred rivers in the former Soviet Union revealed levels of contamination that were dangerously high.

Solid waste

Next time you visit a supermarket, toy store or fast-food restaurant, pay attention to the amount of packaging that accompanies the products you see there. There are few things you can buy without packaging in our present age. Although there are clear benefits to packaging in terms of displaying goods attractively and guaranteeing the safety of products, there are enormous drawbacks as well. One of the clearest indicators of increasing consumption is the growing amount of domestic waste – what goes into our rubbish bins – being produced worldwide. Where the developing countries generated 100–330 kilograms of domestic solid waste per capita in the early 1990s, the figure was 414 kilograms for the European Union and 720 for North America (UNDP 1998). There have been increases in both the absolute amount of waste produced, and the amount produced per person, in countries around the world.

The industrialized societies have sometimes been called 'throw-away societies' because the volume of items discarded as a matter of course is so large. According to government statistics, households in England and Wales each produce 22 kilograms of waste per week. In 1997–8, of the 27 million tonnes of waste that were produced, 90 per cent was domestic. Approximately 85 per cent of solid waste was sent to landfills (HMSO 2000). In most countries of the industrialized world, waste collection services are almost universal, but it is becoming increasingly difficult to dispose of the enormous amounts of refuse. Landfills are quickly filling up, and many urban areas have run out of disposal room for domestic waste.

In the UK, the government set a target of recycling 40 per cent of municipal waste by 2005. However, in 2001–2 just 12 per cent of household waste was recycled, compared with 7 per cent in 1996–7. During the same period, the amount of waste produced by each household in England increased by 17 per cent (HMSO 2004). Although this amount of recycling may seem low compared to the overall amount of domestic waste that is produced, a large proportion of what is thrown away cannot be easily reprocessed or reused. Many kinds of plastics widely employed in food packaging simply become unusable waste; there is no way of recycling it, and it has to be buried in refuse tips where it remains for centuries. Table 22.2 shows how waste is managed in England.

In the developing world, the greatest problem with domestic waste at the present time is the lack of refuse collection services. It has been estimated that 20 to 50 per cent of domestic waste in the developing world goes uncollected. Poorly managed waste systems mean that refuse piles up in the streets, contributing to the spread of disease. With the passing of time, it is very likely that the developing world will face problems with waste disposal that are even more acute than the current situation in the industrialized countries. As societies become richer, there is a gradual shift from organic waste, such as food remains, to plastic and synthetic materials, like packaging, that take much longer to decompose.

Depletion of resources

Human societies depend on very many resources from the natural world – for example, water, wood, fish, animals and

Table 22.2   Management of municipal waste, England: by method

	1996/7	1998/9	2000/1	2001/2
Landfill	20,631	21,534	22,039	22,317
Incineration with energy from waste	1,446	2,117	2,391	2,459
Recycled/composted[a]	1,750	2,525	3,446	3,907
Other[b]	761	160	182	140
Total	*24,588*	*26,337*	*28,057*	*28,823*

[a] Includes household and non-household sources collected for recycling or for centralized composting; home composting estimates are not included in this total

[b] Includes incineration without energy from waste and refuse derived fuel manufacture. Excludes any processing prior to landfilling and materials sent to materials reclamation facilities (MRFs)

Source: HMSO (2004)

plant life. These elements are often termed renewable resources, because in a healthy ecosystem they replace themselves automatically with the passing of time. Yet if the consumption of renewable resources gets out of balance or too extreme, there is a danger that they will be depleted altogether. Some evidence suggests that such a process may be occurring. The deterioration of renewable resources is of great concern to many environmentalists.

Water

You may not think of water as a depletable resource – after all, it constantly replenishes itself through rainfall. If you live in Europe or North America, you probably don't give much thought to your water supply at all, except occasionally when restrictions are put on its use in the summer months. Yet for people in many parts of the world, access to a constant water supply is a more chronic and severe problem. In some densely populated regions, the high demand for water cannot be met by available water resources. In the arid climates of North Africa and the Middle East, for example, the pressure on

water supply is acute and shortages have become commonplace. This trend is almost sure to intensify in the years to come.

There are several reasons why this is so. The first is that much of the projected world population growth over the next quarter-century (discussed further in chapter 11, pp. 48–28) is likely to be concentrated in areas that are already experiencing problems with water shortages. Furthermore, much of this growth will occur in urban areas, where the infrastructure will struggle to accommodate the water and sanitation needs of this expanded population.

Global warming also has a potential impact on the depletion of the water supply. As temperatures rise, more water will be needed for drinking and irrigation. Yet it is also likely that groundwater may not replenish itself as rapidly as before and that rates of evaporation may also increase. Finally, changes in climate patterns which may accompany global warming will be likely to affect existing patterns of precipitation, altering access to water supplies in ways that are quite unpredictable.

Soil degradation and desertification

According to the 1998 UN Human Development Report, a third of the world's population lives more or less directly from the land – on the food they can grow or gather, and the game they can catch. Because they are largely dependent on the earth, they are particularly vulnerable to changes affecting their ability to live off the land. In many areas of Asia and Africa that are experiencing rapid population growth, the problem of soil degradation threatens to impoverish millions of people. **Soil degradation** is the process by which the quality of the earth is worsened and its valuable natural elements are stripped away through over-use, drought or inadequate fertilization.

The long-term effects of soil degradation are extremely severe and difficult to reverse. In areas where the soil has been degraded, agricultural productivity declines and there is less arable land available per head. It becomes difficult or impossible to keep cattle or other livestock because of a lack of fodder. In many instances, people are forced to migrate in search of more fertile land. **Desertification** refers to instances of intense land degradation which result in desert-like conditions over large areas. This phenomenon has already affected territory adding up to the size of Russia and Indonesia combined (see figure 22.3) – putting more than 110 countries at risk.

Deforestation

Forests are an essential element of the ecosystem: they help to regulate water supplies, release oxygen into the atmosphere and prevent soil erosion. They also contribute to many people's livelihoods as sources of fuel, food, wood, oils, dyes, herbs and medicines. Yet despite their crucial importance, more than a third of the earth's original forests have now disappeared. **Deforestation** describes the destruction of forested land, usually through commercial logging. Deforestation claimed 15 million hectares of land in the 1980s, with the largest amounts occurring in Latin America and the Caribbean (losing 7.4 million hectares) and sub-Saharan Africa (losing 4.1 million hectares).

Although many types of forest are involved in the process of deforestation,

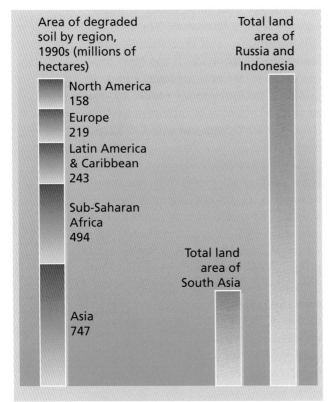

Figure 22.3 The magnitude of soil degradation

Source: UNDP (1998), p. 74

the fate of tropical rainforests has attracted the greatest attention. Tropical rainforests, which cover some 7 per cent of the earth's surface, are home to a great number of plant and animal species that contribute to the earth's biodiversity – the diversity of species of life forms. They are also home to many of the plants and oils from which medicines are developed. Tropical rainforests are currently shrinking at a rate of approximately 1 per cent a year, and may well disappear altogether by the end of this century if current trends are not halted. In many areas of South America where tropical rainforests are most extensive, rainforests have been burned to make room for more land to graze cattle. In other areas of the world, such as West Africa and the South Pacific, the international demand for exotic hardwoods has fuelled the destruction of rainforests. Trends in increasing consumption therefore encourage developing countries to export their natural commodities – a process which results in both environmental destruction and a loss of biodiversity.

Deforestation has both human and environmental costs. In terms of human costs, some poor communities which were previously able to sustain or supplement their livelihoods through forests are no longer able to do so. Deforestation can further impoverish marginalized populations, who rarely share in the enormous revenues generated from the granting of logging rights and the sale of timber. The environmental costs of deforestation include soil erosion and floods: when they are intact, mountainous forests perform the important function of absorbing and recycling much of the water from rainfall. Once the forests are missing, rain cascades off the slopes, causing floods and then droughts.

Risk, technology and the environment

'Humanity, get down on your knees', yell the hoardings advertising *Prey*, the 2002 novel by Michael Crichton, author of bestsellers such as *Jurassic Park* and creator of the popular TV series *ER* (*The Economist*, 5 December 2002). In *Prey*, Crichton creates a world in which the unintended effects of a scientific experiment cause catastrophe. A cloud of nanoparticles – tiny robots, each smaller than most grains of dust – escapes from a laboratory. The cloud is self-sustaining, self-reproducing, and learns from experience. It has been programmed to act as a predator, and as it grows, it becomes more deadly by the minute. All attempts to capture or destroy the cloud are failing, and worse, humans are its prey.

Crichton's novel about miniscule robots is the stuff of science-fiction. But **nanotechnology** is an exciting new area in science and technology. A nanometre is one-billionth of a metre, and a broad definition of nanotechnology involves anything that can be precisely fabricated with dimensions of less than 100 nanometres (a single human hair is around 80,000 nanometres wide). So far, nanotechnology's impact has been modest. It is currently used, for example, to make skin creams more transparent and ski wax more slippery.

Some writers have worried about the negative risks associated with nanotechnology. Besides the alarms raised by science-fiction writers like Michael Crichton, some scientists have worried that if the technology could be made for nano-size particles to self-replicate, they 'could spread like blowing pollen, replicate swiftly, and reduce the biosphere to dust in a matter of days. Dangerous replicators could easily be too tough, small, and rapidly spreading to stop – at least if we make no preparation.' This threat has become known as the 'grey goo problem' (Drexler 1992). Others have worried that nanotechnology could be used for military or terrorist uses. Nanotechnology devices could perhaps one day be built that selectively target only certain geographical areas or groups of people with certain genes (Joy 2000). Another concern is that nanosize particles could be breathed in, causing damage to the body, perhaps accumulating in the lungs like asbestos.

If these disasters were likely, then it would seem that the negative risks of further development in nanotechnology would far outweigh the positives. However, enthusiasts for nanotechnology are investigating whether it could be used to improve the delivery of cancer-fighting drugs or whether nanoscale carbon could be used to increase the speed and power of computer circuits. Richard Smalley, a Nobel prize-winning chemist, has even suggested that one day nanotechnology could be used in solar panels to solve the world's energy problems.

Discussions of nanotechnology and other innovations in science and technology raise important questions for sociologists. As we have seen above, scientific and technological change increasingly present us with different risks – bad, good and in-between, from grey goo to unlimited and safe energy.

Humans have always had to face risks of one kind or another, but today's risks are qualitatively different from those that came in earlier times. Until quite recently, human societies were threatened by **external risk** – dangers such as drought, earthquakes, famines and storms that spring from the natural world and are unrelated to the actions of humans. Today, however, we are increasingly confronted with various types of **manufactured risk** – risks that are created by the impact of our own knowledge and technology on the natural world. As we shall see, many environmental and health risks facing contemporary societies are instances of manufactured risk: they are the outcomes of our own interventions into nature. The advent of nanotechnology which we looked at above is one example of how manufactured risk has spread; below, we look at two more cases – the controversies surrounding global warming and genetically modified food.

Global warming

August 2003 was the hottest August on record in the Northern hemisphere. Many people argued that the hot weather was an example of how global warming was affecting the Earth's climate. The effects of the heat were catastrophic. The Earth Policy Institute, an environmental think-tank, has estimated that the heat wave killed more than 35,000 people in Europe. France suffered the worst losses. It was estimated that 14,802 people died from causes attributable to the high temperatures – with older people being particularly vulnerable (*New Scientist*, 10 October 2003). Scientists have recently estimated that global warming kills about

160,000 people every year, with children in developing countries being most at risk. It has been estimated that the numbers dying from the 'side-effects' of climate change, such as malaria and malnutrition, could almost double by 2020 (*New Scientist*, 1 October 2003). The British Prime Minister, Tony Blair, has argued that climate change is in the 'long term, the single most important issue that we face as a global community' (speech at the launch of the Climate Group, 27 April 2004). Here we look at the causes behind global warming and examine its likely consequences in more detail.

What is global warming?

Global warming is regarded by many people to be the most serious environmental challenge of our time. If many scientific predictions are true, it has the potential to alter irreversibly the functioning of the earth's climate and to produce a series of devastating environmental consequences which will be felt worldwide. Global warming refers to the gradual rise in the earth's average temperature due to changes in the chemical composition of the atmosphere. It is believed to be caused in large part by humans, because the gases that have built up and altered the earth's atmosphere are ones that are produced in great quantities by human activities.

The process of global warming is closely related to the idea of the **greenhouse effect** – the build-up of heat-trapping greenhouse gases within the earth's atmosphere. The principle is a simple one. Energy from the sun passes through the atmosphere and heats the earth's surface. Although most of the solar radiation is absorbed directly by the earth, some of it is reflected back. The greenhouse gases act

as a barrier to this outgoing energy, trapping heat within the earth's atmosphere much like the glass panels of a greenhouse (see figure 22.4). This natural greenhouse effect is what keeps the earth's temperatures at reasonably comfortable temperatures – at about 60 degrees Fahrenheit. If it were not for the role of greenhouse gases in retaining heat, the earth would be a much colder place, with an average temperature of around 0 degrees Fahrenheit.

When concentrations of atmospheric greenhouse gases rise, however, the greenhouse effect is intensified and much warmer temperatures are produced. Since the start of industrialization, the concentration of greenhouse gases has risen significantly. Carbon dioxide, the main greenhouse gas, has seen its concentrations increase the most – by around 30 per cent since 1880. Methane concentrations have doubled, nitrous oxide concentrations are up by about 15 per cent and greenhouse gases that are not naturally occurring (see box opposite) have been generated by human industrial development. Most scientists agree that the large increase in carbon dioxide in the atmosphere can be attributed to the burning of fossil fuels and other human activities, such as industrial production, large-scale agriculture, deforestation, mining, landfills and vehicle emissions.

Figure 22.5 (on p. 956) shows the upward trend in surface temperatures since the late nineteenth century by charting them against the average temperature in the period 1961–90 in Central England and globally. During the whole of the twentieth century, seven out of the ten hottest years on record occurred during the 1990s – with 1998 being the warmest year ever recorded.

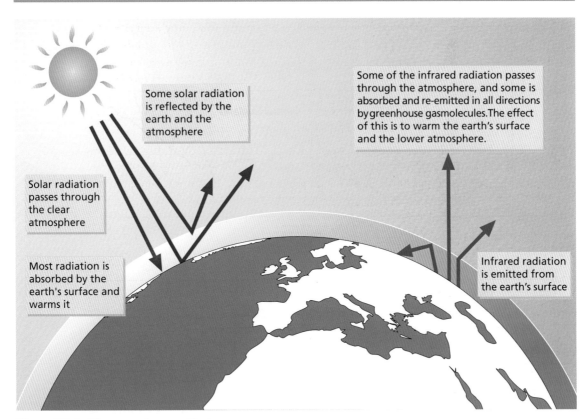

Some solar radiation is reflected by the earth and the atmosphere

Some of the infrared radiation passes through the atmosphere, and some is absorbed and re-emitted in all directions by greenhouse gasmolecules. The effect of this is to warm the earth's surface and the lower atmosphere.

Solar radiation passes through the clear atmosphere

Most radiation is absorbed by the earth's surface and warms it

Infrared radiation is emitted from the earth's surface

Figure 22.4   The greenhouse effect

Source: Environmental Protection Agency website

What are greenhouse gases?

Some greenhouse gases occur naturally in the atmosphere, while others result from human activities. Naturally occurring greenhouse gases include water vapour, carbon dioxide, methane, nitrous oxide and ozone. Certain human activities, however, add to the levels of most of these naturally occurring gases.

Carbon dioxide is released to the atmosphere when solid waste, fossil fuels (oil, natural gas and coal), and wood and wood products are burned.

Methane is emitted during the production and transport of coal, natural gas and oil. Methane emissions also result from the decomposition of organic wastes in solid waste landfills, and the raising of livestock.

Nitrous oxide is emitted during agricultural and industrial activities, as well as during combustion of solid waste and fossil fuels.

Greenhouse gases that are not naturally occurring include byproducts of foam production, refrigeration and air conditioning called chlorofluorocarbons (CFCs), as well as hydrofluorocarbons (HFCs) and perfluorocarbons (PFCs) generated by industrial processes.

Source: Environmental Protection Agency (EPA)
Global Warming Site
http://www.epa.gov/globalwarming/climate/index.htm

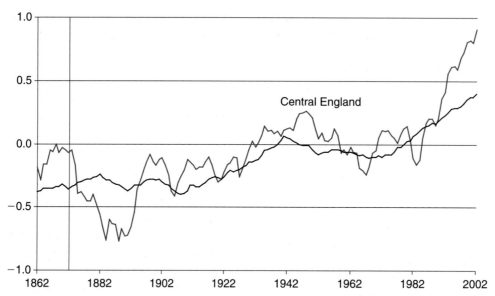

Figure 22.5   Difference in average surface temperature 1861–2002: comparison with 1961–90 average, global and central England, (degrees centigrade)

Source: ONS

The potential consequences of global warming

If global warming is indeed taking place, the consequences are likely to be devastating. The local effects, on the UK for example, are difficult to predict, as global weather patterns change. However, some of the potentially harmful effects worldwide include:

1 *Rising sea levels*   Global warming may cause the polar ice caps to melt and the oceans to warm and expand. As glaciers and other forms of land ice melt, sea levels will rise. Cities that are near the coasts or in low-lying areas will be flooded and become uninhabitable. If sea levels were to rise by one metre, Bangladesh would lose 17 per cent of its total land area, Egypt would lose 12 per cent and the Netherlands would lose 6 per cent (UNDP 1998). The Indian Ocean tsunami, which we discussed at the beginning of this chapter, would

have caused considerably more devastation if sea levels were higher than they are today.

2 *Desertification*   Global warming may contribute to large tracts of fertile land becoming desert. Sub-Saharan Africa, the Middle East and South Asia will be further affected by desertification and intense soil erosion.

3 *The spread of disease*   Global warming may extend the geographical range and the seasonality for organisms, such as mosquitoes, which spread diseases like malaria and yellow fever. If temperatures were to rise by 3–5 degrees Celsius, the number of malaria cases could increase by 50 to 80 million per year.

4 *Poor harvests*   Agricultural yields may fall in many of the poorest areas of the world if global warming progresses. Populations in Southeast Asia, Africa and Latin America would be likely to be most affected.

5 *Changing climate patterns*   Climate patterns that have been relatively stable for thousands of years may undergo rapid disruptions because of global warming. Forty-six million people currently live in areas that could be destroyed by sea storms, while many others may suffer from floods and hurricanes.

6 *Geopolitical instability*   A report published for the US Department of Defence warned that, at their most abrupt, the effects of climate change discussed above could lead to disputes or even wars between nations as they attempt to protect their increasingly limited agricultural, fresh water and energy resources. The report cautions that mass migration could occur as people attempt to move to those regions which posses the resources to adapt to climate change (Schwartz and Randall 2003).

Some trends associated with global warming seem to be moving much faster than scientists originally predicted. In December 1999, for example, a study by satellite showed that the Arctic ice-cap is shrinking much more rapidly than scientists previously believed – a process that could have dramatic effects on the world climate in coming years. Similarly, in early 2002 two huge ice shelves – Larsen B and Thwaites glacier tongue – collapsed in Antarctica, shattering into thousands of icebergs within days. It is possible that the reduction in ice is the result of natural changes, but whatever its origins the ice seems to be melting at an extraordinary pace. Measurements show that the North Pole sea-ice has thinned by 40 per cent in recent decades in the summer and autumn, and decreased by 10–15 per cent since the 1950s in the spring and summer. Global snow cover has shrunk by 10 per cent since the 1960s, and mountain glaciers have sharply retreated.

Responses to the risk of global warming

For a long time the thesis of global warming was disputed. Some scientists doubted whether the claimed effects were real, while others held that changes in the world's climate could be the result of natural trends, rather than the outcome of human intervention. However, there is now a strong consensus behind the view that global warming is indeed occurring and that the greenhouse effect is to blame. In January 2000 a panel of eleven climate experts from diverse scientific fields released one of the most extensive reports yet produced on the subject. All were in agreement that global warming is a real phenomenon. They concluded that the surface temperature of the earth has risen between 0.7 and 1.4 degrees Fahrenheit (0.4 to 0.8 degrees Celsius) in the last century. The increase in temperature has been particularly high over the past twenty years.

As figure 22.6 shows, global emissions of carbon dioxide have been increasing at an alarming rate. The industrial countries currently produce far more greenhouse gases than the developing world, with the United States emitting more carbon dioxide than any other single country. The production of greenhouse gases is not limited to the developed world, however. Emissions from the developing world are also increasingly rapidly, particularly in countries that are undergoing rapid industrialization and are expected to equal those of industrialized countries until 2035.

At a world ecological summit held in 1997 in Kyoto, in Japan, agreement was reached to cut greenhouse gas emissions significantly by 2010. Under the terms of the protocol, industrialized nations committed themselves to a range of targets to reduce emissions between 1990, the base year, and 2010. World targets range from an average 8 per cent cut for most of Europe to a maximum 10 per cent increase for Iceland and an 8 per cent increase for Australia. (The USA originally committed itself to a 7 per cent cut.) Many scientists claim that this target was too modest, and argue that emissions must be cut by as much as 70 or 80 per cent if serious climatic consequences are to be avoided. Whatever governments do to cut

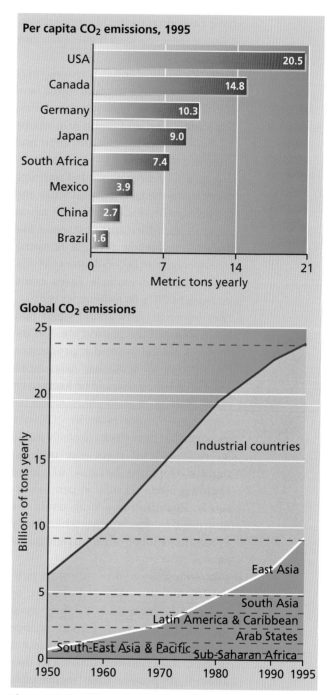

Figure 22.6 CO_2 emissions in industrialized and less developed areas of the world

Source: UNDP (1998), p. 3

emissions, it will be some time before the effects of global warming are altered. It takes more than a century for carbon dioxide to be removed from the atmosphere through natural processes.

In 2001, the new US President, George W. Bush, refused to ratify the Kyoto Protocol, arguing that it would damage the US economy. After some debate, most other nations agreed to go ahead without the United States, in spite of it being the world's largest producer of greenhouse gases. Talks in Bonn in Germany and Marrakech in Morocco later in 2001 finally agreed the increasingly complicated fine print of the protocol and signatory nations were urged to ratify the deal in their national legislatures by the end of 2002. In recent years, several of the largest producers of greenhouse gases have successfully cut emissions, including the UK, Germany, China and Russia – although Russia's cuts can largely be explained by the decline in its economy.

As with many new forms of manufactured risk, no one can be sure what the effects of global warming will be. Its causes are so diffuse and its precise consequences are difficult to calculate. Would a 'high' emissions scenario truly result in widespread natural disasters? Will stabilizing the level of carbon dioxide emissions protect most people in the world from the negative effects of climate changes? Is it possible that current processes of global warming have already triggered a series of further climatic disturbances? We cannot answer these questions with any certainty. The earth's climate is extremely complex and a variety of factors will interact to produce different consequences in individual countries at varying points across the earth.

Genetically modified foods

As we saw in chapter 11 (p. 428), 830 million people around the globe go hungry each day. The process of global warming may contribute to increased desertification and poor harvests and has lead to fears that food shortages may become even more widespread. In some of the world's most densely populated areas, people are highly dependent on staple food crops – such as rice – whose stocks are dwindling. Many worry that present farming techniques will not be able to produce rice yields sufficient to support the growing population. As with many environmental challenges, the threat of famine is not evenly distributed. The industrialized countries have extensive surpluses of grain. It is the poorer countries, where the population growth is projected to be greatest, that grain shortfalls are likely to be a chronic problem.

Some people believe that the key to averting a potential food crisis may lie in recent advances in science and biotechnology. By manipulating the genetic composition of basic crops, such as rice, it is now possible to boost a plant's rate of photosynthesis and to produce bigger crop yields. This process is known as genetic modification; plants that are produced in such a way are called **genetically modified organisms** (GMOs). Genetic modification can be carried out for a variety of purposes – not only to enhance the crop yield. Scientists have produced GMOs with higher than normal vitamin content, for example; other genetically modified crops are resistant to commonly used agricultural herbicides that are used to kill the weeds round them, as well as insects and fungal and viral pests. Food products that are made from, or contain traces of, genetically modified organisms are known as GM foods.

GM crops are different from anything that has existed before, because they involve transplanting genes between different organisms. This is a much more radical intervention into nature than the older methods of cross-breeding that have been used for many years. GMOs are produced by techniques of gene splicing that can be used to transplant genes between animals as well as plants. For instance, in recent experiments human genes have been introduced into farm animals, such as pigs, with a view to eventually providing replacement parts for human transplants. Human genes have even been spliced into plants, although the GM crops that have been marketed so far do not involve this kind of radical bioengineering.

Scientists claim that a GM strain of 'super-rice' could boost rice yields by as much as 35 per cent. Another strain called 'golden rice' – which contains added amounts of vitamin A – could reduce vitamin A deficiency in more than 120 million children worldwide. You might think that such advances in biotechnology would be welcomed enthusiastically by people around the world. But, in fact, the issue of genetic modification has become one of the most controversial issues of our age. For many people, it highlights the fine line that exists between the benefits of technology and scientific innovation, on the one hand, and the risks of environmental destruction, on the other.

Controversy over GM foods

The saga of GM foods began only a few years ago when some of the world's leading chemical and agricultural firms decided that new knowledge about the workings of genes could transform the world's food supply. These companies had been making pesticides and herbicides, but wanted to move into what they saw as a major market for the future. The American firm Monsanto was the leader in developing much of the new technology. Monsanto bought up seed companies, sold off its chemical division and devoted much of its energies to bringing the new crops to the market. Led by its then Chief Executive Robert Shapiro, Monsanto launched a gigantic advertising campaign promoting the benefits of its GM crops to farmers and to consumers. The early responses were just as the company had confidently anticipated. By early 1999, 55 per cent of the soya beans and 35 per cent of the maize produced in the United States contained genetic alterations. Genetically modified crops at that point were already growing on 35 million hectares of land across the world – an area one and a half times the size of Britain. In addition to North America, GM crops were being widely grown in China.

Monsanto's sales campaign stressed a number of positive virtues of GM foods. The company claimed that GM crops could help feed the world's poor and could help reduce the use of chemical pollutants, especially the chemicals used in pesticides and herbicides. It is claimed, for example, that GM potatoes need 40 per cent less chemical insecticide than would be required using traditional farming techniques. Biotechnology, according to Monsanto, will allow us to grow better-quality crops with higher yields while at the same time sustaining and protecting the environment.

Greenpeace has led some of the anti-GM protests in recent years, such as this attack on a field of genetically modified corn in Norfolk.

Since GM crops are essentially quite new, no one can be certain about what their effects will be once they are introduced into the environment. Many ecological and consumer groups became concerned about the potential risks involved with the adoption of this largely untested technology. Concern about GM foods was especially widespread in Europe. In Britain, hostility to the commercial growing of GM crops was stimulated by the findings of Dr Arpad Pusztai, an internationally renowned geneticist working in a government laboratory in Scotland. In his research, Dr Pusztai had tested potatoes with a gene for a particular

natural insecticide inserted – a protein known as lectin, extracted from a certain type of flower. The results indicated that rats which ate the GM potatoes experienced significant damage to their immune systems and reduced organ growth. Dr Pusztai's findings were criticized by other leading scientists and he was dismissed from his post at the government laboratory after speaking on television about his worries concerning GM foods.

By this time, GM foods had become a front-page story in the news almost every day. Numerous TV and radio debates, chat shows and phone-ins were organized to discuss the issue. Many members of the British public registered their antagonism to GM crops; some even engaged in 'direct action', pulling GM crops out of the ground at official trial sites across the country. Similar responses occurred in a range of other European countries. These eventually spread back to the USA, where there had previously been little debate. In the UK, seven out of the eight major supermarket chains changed their policy on GM foods. Five of them imposed a complete ban on GM ingredients in their own-brand products, which is still in place, and all of them insisted on better labelling in their stores. Two large companies, Unilever and Nestlé, announced that they would withdraw their acceptance of genetically modified foodstuffs. Some farmers in the USA who had been engaged in the large-scale cultivation of GM crops changed back to conventional crop production. A survey in 2003 showed that 59 per cent of the UK population strongly agreed that genetically modified foods should be banned (HMSO 2005).

The protests of environmentalists and consumer groups had a major impact on the fate of Monsanto, and caused a serious decline in its share value. Robert Shapiro appeared on television to admit that his company had made major mistakes: 'We have probably irritated and antagonized more people than we have persuaded', he said. 'Our confidence in this technology and our enthusiasm for it has, I think, been widely seen – and understandably so – as condescension or indeed arrogance.' It was an extraordinary turnaround from the world-beating confidence with which he had spoken only a few months before. Monsanto was forced to drop altogether one of its most controversial plans – the

idea of using a gene called 'the terminator'. This gene would have ensured that seeds which Monsanto sold to farmers would be sterile after one generation. The farmers would have had to order seeds each year from the company. Critics of Monsanto claimed that the company was trying to lure farmers into a form of 'bioslavery'.

Genetically modified food continues to generate controversy in Europe and large parts of Africa. The European Union refused patents of new GM crops between 1998 and 2004. The complete moratorium was raised in 2004 when imports of a further GM maize crop were approved, and a scheme was introduced to label foods containing GM products. However, the EU's actions were too slow for the big GM producers, particularly in the United States, who filed a complaint against the EU's failure to authorize the commercialization of GM crops with the World Trade Organization in May 2003, claiming that the European position had no scientific basis and broke free trade laws (Toke 2004).

In Africa, GM food aid has run into trouble. In 2002, Zambia refused to accept American food aid donations of corn and soya because much of it was genetically modified. Zambia's president, Levy Mwanawasa, called the imports 'poison'. By 2004 Zambia had been joined by Zimbabwe, Malawi, Mozambique, Lesotho and Angola in refusing genetically modified food aid.

Evaluating the risks of GM foods

Despite the assertions of the GM producers, no one can possibly say with certainty that genetically modified crops are risk-free. The genetic code is highly complicated – adding new genes into plants or organisms could produce as yet unpredicted diseases or other harmful consequences. Because the technology is so unknown, new findings and discoveries are being uncovered with startling frequency. In May 2000, the British government admitted that thousands of acres of conventional oilseed rape that had been planted by farmers had in fact been 'contaminated' as GM crops pollinated those nearby. German research published just weeks later claimed that a gene commonly used to modify oilseed rape had jumped the species barrier into the guts of bees. In the short period between these two startling revelations, Monsanto itself acknowledged that its modified soybeans – the GMO that has been cultivated most extensively for commercial purposes – contain unexpected gene fragments that had previously gone undetected.

Such findings reinforce what many environmental activists have been warning for some time. Although genetic modification may have enormous potential benefits, the risks involved are unpredictable and difficult to calculate. Once released into the environment, GMOs may set off a string of knock-on effects that will be difficult to monitor and control. In the face of this dilemma, many environmentalists favour what is often termed the **precautionary principle**. This principle proposes that where there is sufficient doubt about the possible risks of new departures, it is better to stick to existing practices than to change them. Despite the concerns of environmentalists, the amount of land given over to growing GM crops has continued to increase dramatically in recent years, particularly in the developing world, where the environmental movement is not as strongly established and laws restricting the growth of GM crops are generally less strict (see figure 22.7 overleaf).

Some writers have pointed out the parallels between GM foods and nanotechnology (discussed earlier in this chapter). Jeffrey Matsuura, an American academic, has argued that the nanotechnology industry should learn from the public backlash surrounding GM foods. Assessing the debate about GM foods, Matsuura (2004) argues that in the early days the biotechnology industry made two mistakes: first it tried to ignore public concerns and then it attempted to address them through purely rational arguments. Matsuura argues that the nanotechnology industry is currently following a similar path. Instead of this, he believes, nanotechnology's proponents should launch an aggressive public relations campaign, based on both rational *and* emotional arguments to win support. He argues that immediate action to promote nanotechnology is necessary in order to avoid the type of public backlash that could impede the development of the technology and lead to significant economic losses. However, Matsuura's argument ignores the negative risks that new technologies can bring and focuses narrowly on their potential, largely economic, benefits. In the next section, we look at a broader approach to the idea of risk, taken by the German sociologist Ulrich Beck.

The global 'risk society'

Nanotechnology, the debate over genetically modified foods, global warming and other manufactured risks, have presented individuals with new choices and challenges in their everyday lives. Because

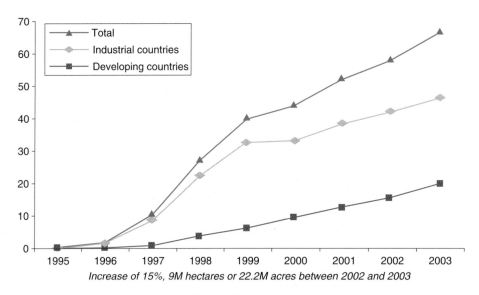

Increase of 15%, 9M hectares or 22.2M acres between 2002 and 2003

Figure 22.7   Global area of genetically modified crops

Source: ISAAA (2003)

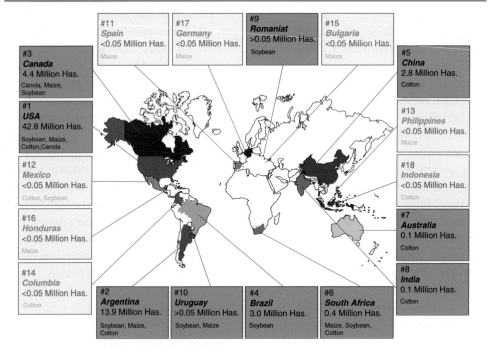

■ Ten countries growing 50,000 hectares or more of GM crops.

Figure 22.8   GM crop countries, 2003

Source: ISAAA (2003)

Manufactured risk and the survival of humanity

In 2003 Martin Rees, the British Astronomer Royal, published a book provocatively called *Our Final Century*, subtitled with the question: 'Will the human race survive the twenty-first century?' Rees argues that the explosive advances in science and technology, seen for example in bio-, cyber- and nanotechnology and in the exploration of space, do not just offer exhilarating prospects for the future, but also contain what he calls a dark side.

Scientific advancement can have unintended consequences, as we have seen, and Rees's book examines the likelihood of catastrophic scenarios where human civilization dies out. Rees describes some of the apocalyptic risks that could occur with the new science of the twenty-first century: these include nuclear holocaust, caused by terrorists or nations and terrorist use of biological weapons or laboratory errors that create new diseases.

Rees's conclusions are sobering. He separates the long term from the short term. In the short term, which he defines as the next twenty years, he is prepared to bet on a major catastrophe killing over a million people (though he fervently hopes that he will be wrong in his assessment). Returning to the subtitle of his book, Rees argues, over the next hundred years – which he calls the long term – he gives humanity a 50/50 chance of surviving the twenty-first century.

The prognosis may seem desperately pessimistic, but Rees argues he hopes his book will 'stimulate discussion on how to guard (as far as possible) against the worst risks, while deploying new knowledge optimally for human benefit'.

there is no road map to these new dangers, individuals, countries and transnational organizations must negotiate risks as they make choices about how lives are to be lived. Because there are no definitive answers about the causes and outcomes of such risks, each individual is forced to make decisions about which risks he or she is prepared to take. This can be a bewildering endeavour. Should we use food and raw materials if their production

or consumption might have a negative impact on our own health and on the natural environment? Even seemingly simple decisions about what to eat are now made in the context of conflicting information and opinions about the product's relative merits and drawbacks.

Ulrich Beck (1992) has written extensively about risk and globalization and sees these factors contributing to the formation of a global **risk society**. As technological change progresses more and more rapidly and produces new forms of risk, we must constantly respond and adjust to these changes. The risk society, he argues, is not limited to environmental and health risks alone; it includes a whole series of interrelated changes within contemporary social life: shifting employment patterns, heightened job insecurity, the declining influence of tradition and custom on self-identity, the erosion of traditional family patterns and the democratization of personal relationships. Because personal futures are much less fixed than they were in traditional societies, decisions of all kinds present risks for individuals. Getting married, for example, is a more risky endeavour today than it was at a time when marriage was a lifelong institution. Decisions about educational qualifications and career paths can also feel risky: it is difficult to predict what skills will be valuable in an economy that is changing as rapidly as ours is.

According to Beck (1995), an important aspect of the risk society is that its hazards are not restricted spatially, temporally or socially. Today's risks affect all countries and all social classes; they have global, not merely personal, consequences. As we saw above, many forms of manufactured risk, such as those concerning human health and the environment, cross national boundaries. The explosion at the Chernobyl nuclear power plant in Ukraine in 1986 provides a clear illustration of this point. Everyone living in the immediate vicinity of Chernobyl – regardless of age, class, gender or status – was exposed to dangerous levels of radiation. At the same time, the effects of the accident stretched far beyond Chernobyl itself – throughout Europe and beyond, abnormally high levels of radiation were detected long after the explosion.

Looking ahead

As we stand in the first decade of a new century, we cannot foresee whether the coming hundred years will be marked by peaceful social and economic development or by a multiplication of global problems – perhaps beyond the ability of humanity to solve. Unlike the sociologists writing two hundred years ago, we see clearly that modern industry, technology and science are by no means wholly beneficial in their consequences, as the discussion of Martin Rees's pessimistic predictions for the twenty-first century show (see box). Scientific and technological developments have created a world that contains risks that make possible huge gains and losses. Especially in the developed world, the population is wealthier than ever before, yet the whole world is closer to ecological disaster.

Should we resign ourselves to an attitude of despair? Certainly not. If there is one thing sociology offers us, it is a profound consciousness of the human authorship of social institutions. We see the possibility of controlling our destiny and shaping our lives for the better, unimaginable to previous generations.

The idea of sustainable development, which was discussed above, has helped promote some important innovations in the environmental field. These include in particular the concepts of eco-efficiency and ecological modernization. Eco-efficiency means developing technologies that are effective in generating economic growth, but which do so at minimal cost to the environment. Even as late as the 1980s, when the Brundtland Report appeared, it was widely assumed that most forms of industrial development and ecological protection are incompatible. The central idea involved in the thesis of ecological modernization is that this assumption is false. The use of eco-efficient technologies can produce forms of economic development that combine economic growth with positive policies for the environment.

The possibilities offered by ecological modernization can be illustrated by reference to the waste disposal industry – the industry that gets rid of the tonnes of waste products that industries and consumers generate every day. Until recently, as we saw above, most of this waste was simply processed and buried. Today, however, the whole industry is being transformed. Technological developments make it much cheaper to produce newsprint from recycled paper than from wood pulp, as used to be the case. Hence there are good economic reasons, as well as environmental ones, to use and reuse paper rather than endlessly cutting down trees. Not just individual companies, but whole industries are actively pursuing the goal of 'zero waste' – that is, the complete recycling of all waste products for future industrial use. The carmakers Toyota and Honda have already reached a level of 85 per cent recyclability for the car parts they use. In this context, waste is no longer just the harmful dumping of materials, but a resource for industry and, to some extent, a means of driving further technological innovation.

Significantly, some of the major contributions to recycling, and therefore to sustainable development, have come from areas with a heavy concentration of information technology industries, such as California's Silicon Valley. Information technology, unlike many older forms of industrial production, is environmentally clean. The more it plays a part in industrial production, the greater the likelihood that harmful environmental effects will be reduced. This consideration could have some bearing on the future development of the world's poorer societies. In some areas of production, at least, it might be possible for them to achieve rapid economic development without the pollution produced by the older industrial economies, because information technology will play a much greater role.

Even the strongest advocates of ecological modernization are forced to admit that rescuing the global environment is likely to require changes in the levels of inequality that now exist in the world. As we have seen, industrial countries currently account for only about one-fifth of the world's population. Yet they are responsible for over 75 per cent of the emissions that serve to pollute the atmosphere and hasten global warming. The average person in the developed world consumes natural resources at ten times the rate of the average individual in less developed countries. Poverty is itself a prime contributor to practices that lead to environmental damage in poor countries. People living in conditions of economic hardship have no choice but to make maximum use of the local resources available to them. Sustainable development therefore cannot be seen in separation from global inequalities.

Summary points

1   There are few aspects of the natural world that have not been affected by human activity. All societies are now faced by concerns over environmental ecology – how best to cope with and contain environmental damage in the face of the impact of modern industry and technology. The idea of 'limits to growth', popularized in the 1970s, is that industrial growth and development is not compatible with the finite nature of the earth's resources. Sustainable development, by contrast, holds that growth should occur, but in such a way as to recycle resources rather than to deplete them.

2   Rising worldwide consumption patterns are a reflection of economic growth, but they also damage environmental resources and exacerbate global inequality. Energy consumption and the consumption of raw materials are vastly higher in the Western countries than in other areas of the world. Yet the environmental damage caused by growing consumption has the most severe impact on the poor.

3   There are many sources of environmental threat. Some are linked to pollution and waste products released into the atmosphere: air pollution, acid rain, water

pollution and unrecyclable solid waste. Other environmental threats involve the depletion of renewable natural resources, such as water, soil and forests, reducing biodiversity.

4   Eco-efficiency refers to technologies that generate economic growth at minimal cost to the environment. Ecological modernization is the belief that industrial development and ecological protection are not incompatible.

5   Most environmental issues are closely connected with risk, because they are the result of the expansion of science and technology. Genetically modified crops are produced through the manipulation of a plant's genetic composition. Global warming refers to the gradual rise in the earth's temperature caused by rising levels of carbon dioxide and other gases in the atmosphere. The potential consequences of global warming are severe, including flooding, the spread of disease, extreme weather and rising sea levels. Global warming presents potential risks to all humankind, but efforts to counter it are difficult to organize because its causes and potential consequences are so diffuse.

6   GM foods are controversial: genetic modification may have enormous benefits for the relief of hunger and malnutrition, but the technology involved is new and may also carry risks for humans and the natural environment. The precautionary principle proposes that where there is sufficient doubt about possible risks, it is better to adhere to existing practices rather than to forge ahead.

Questions for further thought

1   Is science or society to blame for environmental damage?

2   Can the individual make a difference in an era of global risks?

3   Is it fair to impose 'limits to growth' on developing countries when the West has largely completed its industrialization?

4   Given the greenhouse effect, is a move to nuclear power a sensible risk to take?

Further reading

Bill Devall, *Simple in Means, Rich in Ends* (London: Green Print, 1990).

Andrew Dobson, *Green Political Thought*, 3rd edn (New York: Routledge, 2000).

Steve Hinchliffe and Kath Woodward (eds), *The Natural and the Social: Uncertainty, Risk, Change* (New York: Routledge, 2000).

David Pearce and Edward Barbier, *Blueprint for a Sustainable Economy* (London: Earthscan, 2000).

Jonathon Porritt, *Seeing Green: The Politics of Ecology Explained* (Oxford: Blackwell, 1984).

Mark J. Smith, *Ecologism: Towards Ecological Citizenship* (Buckingham: Open University Press, 1998).

G. Tyler Miller, Jr, *Living in the Environment: Principles, Connections and Solutions* (London: Brooks/Cole, 2000).

Steven Yearley, *The Green Case: A Sociology of Environmental Issues, Arguments and Politics* (London: Unwin Hyman, 1991).

Internet links

Department for Environment, Food and Rural Affairs
http://www.defra.gov.uk/environment/index.htm

Environmental Organization Web Directory
http://www.webdirectory.com

Friends of the Earth
http://www.foe.co.uk

Greenpeace
http://www.greenpeace.org.uk

United Nations Development Programme
http://www.undp.org

Bibliography

Abbott, D. (2001) 'The Death of Class?', *Sociology Review* 11 (November).

Abeles, R. P. and M. W. Riley (1987) 'Longevity, Social Structure, and Cognitive Aging', in C. Schooler and K. W. Schaie, eds, *Cognitive Functioning and Social Structure Over the Life Course* (Norwood, NJ: Ablex).

Abel-Smith, B. and P. Townsend (1965) *The Poor and the Poorest: A New Analysis of the Ministry of Labour's Family Expenditure Survey of 1953–54 and 1960* (London: Bell).

Ahmed, A. S. and H. Donnan (1994) 'Islam in the Age of Postmodernity', in A. S. Ahmed and D. Hastings, eds, *Islam, Globalization and Postmodernity* (London: Routledge).

Akintoye, S. (1976) *Emergent African States: Topics in Twentieth Century African History* (London: Longman).

Albrow, M. (1997) *The Global Age: State and Society Beyond Modernity* (Stanford, CA: Stanford University Press).

Aldrich, H. E. and P. V. Marsden (1988) 'Environments and Organizations', in N. J. Smelser, ed., *Handbook of Sociology* (Newbury Park, CA: Sage).

Alexander, Z. (1999) *The Department of Health Study of Black, Asian and Ethnic Minority Issues* (London, DoH).

Allen, M. P. (1981) 'Managerial Power and Tenure in the Large Corporation', *Social Forces* 60.

Amnesty International (2002) 'State Control of the Internet in China', 27 February.

Amnesty International (2004) 'People's Republic of China Controls Tighten as Internet Activism Grows', 28 January.

Amsden, A. H. (1989) *Asia's Next Giant: South Korea and Late Industrialization* (New York: Oxford University Press).

Amsden, A. H., J. Kochanowicz and L. Taylor (1994) *The Market Meets Its Match: Restructuring the Economies of Eastern Europe* (Cambridge, MA: Harvard University Press).

Anderson, E. (1990) *Streetwise: Race, Class, and Change in an Urban Community* (Chicago: University of Chicago Press).

Anderson, F. S. (1977) 'TV Violence and Viewer Aggression: Accumulation of Study Results 1956–1976', *Public Opinion Quarterly* 41.

Anderson, S. and J. Cavanagh (2000) *Top 200: The Rise of Corporate Global Power*, 4 December (Institute for Policy Studies).

Anheier, H., M. Glasius and M. Kaldor, eds (2002) *Global Civil Society 2002* (Oxford: Oxford University Press).

Annenberg Center (2003) 'Parents' Use of the V-Chip to Supervise Children's Television Use' (University of Pennsylvania).

Appadurai, A. (1986) 'Introduction: Commodities and the Politics of Value', in

A. Appadurai, ed., *The Social Life of Things* (Cambridge: Cambridge University Press).

Appelbaum, R. P. and B. Christerson (1997) 'Cheap Labor Strategies and Export-Oriented Industrialization: Some Lessons from the East Asia/Los Angeles Apparel Connection', *International Journal of Urban and Regional Research* 21(2).

Appelbaum, R. P. and J. Henderson, eds (1992) *States and Development in the Asian Pacific Rim* (Newbury Park, CA: Sage).

Apter, T. (1994) *Working Women Don't Have Wives: Professional Success in the 1990s* (New York: St Martin's Press).

Arber, S. and J. Ginn (2004) 'Ageing and Gender: Diversity and Change', *Social Trends 34* (London: HMSO).

Arber, S., K. Davidson and J. Ginn, eds (2003) *Gender and Ageing: Changing Roles and Relationships* (Buckingham: Open University Press).

Aries, P. (1965) *Centuries of Childhood* (New York: Random House).

ARIS (2001) *American Religious Identification Survey 2001* (The Graduate Center of the City University of New York).

Arrighi, G. (1994) *The Long Twentieth Century: Money, Power, and the Origin of Our Times* (New York: Verso).

Ashton, D. N. (1986) *Unemployment Under Capitalism: The Sociology of British and American Labour Markets* (London: Wheatsheaf).

Ashworth, A. E. (1980) *Trench Warfare, 1914–1918* (London: Macmillan).

Askwith, R. (2003) 'Contender', *Observer*, 6 April.

Atchley, R. C. (2000) *Social Forces and Aging: An Introduction to Social Gerontology* (Belmont, CA: Wadsworth).

Back, L. (1995) *Ethnicities, Multiple Racisms: Race and Nation in the Lives of Young People* (London: UCL Press).

Bahrami, H. and S. Evans (1995) 'Flexible Recycling and High-Technology Entrepreneurship', *California Management Review* 22.

Bailey, J. M. (1993) 'Heritable Factors Influence Sexual Orientation in Women', *Archives of General Psychiatry* 50.

Bailey, J. M. and R. C. Pillard (1991) 'A Genetic Study of Male Sexual Orientation', *Archives of General Psychiatry* 48.

Baker, D. and M. Weisbrot (1999) *Social Security: The Phony Crisis* (Chicago: University of Chicago Press).

Balmer, R. (1989) *Mine Eyes Have Seen the Glory: A Journey into the Evangelical Subculture in America* (New York: Oxford University Press).

Balswick, J. O. (1983) 'Male Inexpressiveness', in K. Soloman and N. B. Levy, eds, *Men in Transition: Theory and Therapy* (New York: Plenum Press).

Baltes, P. B. and K. W. Schaie (1977) 'The Myth of the Twilight Years', in S. Zarit, ed., *Readings in Aging and Death: Contemporary Perspectives* (New York: Harper and Row).

Bamforth, A. (1999) 'The Restive Season', *Guardian*, 15 December.

Barash, D. (1979) *The Whisperings Within* (New York: Harper and Row).

Barker, M. (1981) *The New Racism: Conservatives and the Ideology of the Tribe* (Frederick MD: University Publications of America).

Barker, R. (1997) *Political Ideas in Modern Britain* (London and New York: Routledge).

Barnes, C. (1991) *Disabled People in Britain and Discrimination* (London: Hurst and Co).

Barnes, C. (2002) *Disability Studies* (Cambridge: Polity).

Barnes, C. (2003) *Disability Studies: What's the Point?* (University of Lancaster).

Barnet, R. J. and J. Cavanagh (1994) *Global Dreams: Imperial Corporations and the New World Order* (New York: Simon and Schuster).

Barret-Ducrocq, F. (1992) *Love in the Time of Victoria: Sexuality and Desire Among Working-Class Men and Women in Nineteenth-Century London* (Harmondsworth: Penguin).

Barth, F. (1969) *Ethnic Groups and Boundaries* (London: Allen and Unwin).

Basu, A., ed. (1995) *The Challenge of Local Feminisms: Women's Movements in Global Perspective* (Boulder, CO: Westview).

Baudrillard, J. (1988) *Selected Writings* (Cambridge: Polity).

Bauman, Z. (1989) *Modernity and the Holocaust* (Cambridge: Polity).

Bauman, Z. (2003) *Liquid Love: On the Frailty of Human Bonds* (Cambridge: Polity).

BBC (2001) *Murdoch Heads Media Power List*, 16 July. Available online at <http://news.bbc.co.uk/1/hi/entertainment/1441094.stm>.

BBC (2002) *Falwell 'Sorry' for Mohammed Remark*, 13 October. Available online at <http://news.bbc.co.uk/2/hi/americas/2323897.stm>.

BBC (2004) *Official Downloads Chart Launches*, 28 June. Available online at <http://news.bbc.co.uk/1/hi/entertainment/music/3846455.stm>.

BBC (2004) *Q&A: Will I Be Sued for Music-Swapping?*, 7 October. Available online at <http://news.bbc.co.uk/1/hi/entertainment/music/3722622.stm>.

BBC (2004) *UK Music to Sue Online 'Pirates'*, 7 October. Available online at <http://news.bbc.co.uk/1/hi/entertainment/music/3722428.stm>.

BBC (2005) *Violent Crime 'Rise' Sparks Row*, 21 April. Available online at <http://news.bbc.co.uk/1/hi/uk_politics/vote_2005/frontpage/4467569.stm>.

Beall, J. (1998) 'Why Gender Matters', *Habitat Debate* 4(4).

Beasley, C. (1999) *What Is Feminism?* (Thousand Oaks, CA, and London).

Beck, U. (1992) *Risk Society: Towards a New Modernity* (London: Sage).

Beck, U. (1995) *Ecological Politics in an Age of Risk* (Cambridge: Polity).

Beck, U. and E. Beck-Gernsheim (1995) *The Normal Chaos of Love* (Cambridge: Polity).

Becker, H. (1950) *Through Values to Social Interpretation*. (Durham, NC: Duke University Press).

Becker, H. S. (1963) *Outsiders: Studies in the Sociology of Deviance* (New York: Free Press).

Bell, A., M. Weinberg and S. Hammersmith (1981) *Sexual Preference: Its Development in Men and Women* (Bloomington: Indiana University Press).

Bell, D. (1997) 'The World and the United States in 2013', *Daedelus* 115 (Summer).

Beresford, P. and J. Wallcraft (1997) 'Psychiatric System Survivors and Emancipatory Research: Issues, Overlaps and Differences', in C. Barnes and G. Mercer, eds, *In Doing Disability Research* (Leeds: The Disability Press).

Berger, P. L. (1963) *Invitation to Sociology* (Garden City, NY: Anchor Books).

Berger, P. L. (1967) *The Sacred Canopy: Elements of a Sociological Theory of Religion* (Garden City, NY: Anchor Books).

Berger, P. L. (1986) *The Capitalist Revolution: Fifty Propositions about Prosperity, Equality, and Liberty* (New York: Basic Books).

Berger, P. L. and T. Luckmann (1966) *The Social Construction of Reality: A Treatise in the Sociology of Knowledge* (Garden City, NY: Doubleday).

Berle, A. and G. C. Means (1997) *The Modern Corporation and Private Property* (Buffalo, NY: Heim).

Bernstein, B. (1975) *Class, Codes and Control* (London: Routledge).

Bertelson, D. (1986) *Snowflakes and Snowdrifts: Individualism and Sexuality in America.* (Lanham, MD: University Press of America).

Berthoud, R. (1998) *The Incomes of Ethnic Minorities* (Colchester: University of Essex, Institute for Social and Economic Research).

Birren, J. E. and K. W. Schaie, eds (2001) *Handbook of the Psychology of Aging*, 5th edn (San Diego, CA, and London: Academic Press).

Blackburn, R. (2002) *Banking on Death* (London: Verso).

Blair, T. (2004) Speech by the Prime Minister at the Launch of the Climate Group, 1 August 2005 (<http://www.number-10.gov.uk/output/page5716.asp>).

Blanden, J., A. Goodman, P. Gregg, et al. (2002) *Changes in Intergenerational Mobility in Britain* (London: Centre for the Economics of Education, London School of Economics and Political Science).

Blankenhorn, D. (1995) *Fatherless America* (New York: Basic Books).

Blau, P. M. (1963) *The Dynamics of Bureaucracy* (Chicago: University of Chicago).

Blau, P. M. and O. D. Duncan (1967) *The American Occupational Structure* (New York: Wiley).

Blauner, R. (1964) *Alienation and Freedom* (Chicago: University of Chicago Press).

Block, F. (1990) *Postindustrial Possibilities: A Critique of Economic Discourse* (Berkeley: University of California Press).

Blondet, C. (1995) 'Out of the Kitchen and Onto the Streets: Women's Activism in Peru', in A. Basu, ed., *The Challenge of Local Feminisms* (Boulder, CO: Westview).

Bobak, L. (1996) 'India's Tiny Slaves', *Ottowa Sun*, 23 October.

Boden, D. and H. Molotch (1994) 'The Compulsion of Proximity', in D. Boden and R. Friedland, eds, *Nowhere Space, Time, and Modernity* (Berkeley: University of California Press).

Bonacich, E. and R. P. Appelbaum (2000) *Behind the Label: Inequality in the Los Angeles Garment Industry* (Berkeley: University of California Press).

Bonney, N. (1992) 'Theories of Social Class and Gender', *Sociology Review* 1.

Booth, A. (1977) 'Food Riots in the North-West of England, 1770–1801', *Past and Present* 77.

Borja, J. and M. Castells (1997) *Local and Global: The Management of Cities in the Information Age* (London: Earthscan).

Born, G. (2004) *Uncertain Vision: Birt, Dyke and the Reinvention of the BBC* (London: Secker & Warburg).

Boswell, J. (1995) *The Marriage of Likeness: Same-Sex Unions in Pre-Modern Europe* (London: Fontana).

Bourdieu, P. (1986) *Distinction: A Social Critique of Judgements of Taste* (London: Routledge and Kegan Paul).

Bourdieu, P. (1988) *Language and Symbolic Power* (Cambridge: Polity).

Bourdieu, P. (1990) *The Logic of Practice* (Cambridge: Polity).

Bourdieu, P. (1992) *An Invitation to Reflexive Sociology* (Chicago: University of Chicago Press).

Bourdieu, P. and J.-C. Passeron (1977) *Reproduction in Education, Society and Culture* (London: Sage).

Bowlby, J. (1953) *Child Care and the Growth of Love* (Harmondsworth: Penguin).

Boyer, R. and D. Drache (1996) *States against Markets: The Limits of Globalization* (London: Routledge).

Brannen, J. (2003) 'The Age of Beanpole Families', *Sociology Review* 13(1).

Brass, D. J. (1985) 'Men's and Women's Networks: A Study of Interaction Patterns and Influence in an Organization', *Academy of Management Journal* 28.

Braverman, H. (1974) *Labour and Monopoly Capital: The Degradation of Work in the Twentieth Century* (New York: Monthly Review Press).

Bread for the World Institute (2005) *Hunger Basics*. Available online at <http://www.bread.org/hunger basics/>.

Breen, R. and J. H. Goldthorpe (1999) 'Class Inequality and Meritocracy: A Critique of Saunders and an Alternative Analysis', *British Journal of Sociology* 50.

Brennan, T. (1988) 'Controversial Discussions and Feminist Debate', in N. Segal and E. Timms, eds, *The Origins and Evolution of Psychoanalysis New Haven* (New Haven, CT: Yale University Press).

Brewer, R. M. (1993) 'Theorizing Race, Class and Gender: The New Scholarship of Black Feminist Intellectuals and Black Women's Labor', in S. M. James and A. P. A. Busia, eds, *Theorizing Black Feminisms: The Visionary Pragmatism of Black Women* (New York: Routledge).

Brisenden, S. (2005) *Poems for Perfect People* (<http://www.leeds.ac.uk/disability-studies/archiveuk/brisenden/Poems.pdf>).

Brown, C. and K. Jasper, eds (1993) *Consuming Passions: Feminist Approaches to Eating Disorders and Weight Preoccupations* (Toronto: Second Story Press).

Browne, K. (2005) *An Introduction to Sociology*, 3rd edn (Cambridge: Polity).

Browne, K. and I. Bottrill (1999) 'Our Unequal, Unhealthy Nation', *Sociology Review* 9.

Brownmiller, S. (1975) *Against Our Will: Men, Women and Rape* (London: Secker and Warburg).

Brubaker, R. (1998) 'Migrations of Ethnic Unmixing in the "New Europe"', *International Migration Review* 32.

Bruce, S. (1990) *Pray TV: Televangelism in America* (New York: Routledge).

Bruce, S. (1996) *Religion in the Modern World from Cathedrals to Cults* (Oxford: Oxford University Press).

Brumberg, J. J. (1997) *The Body Project* (New York: Vintage).

Brundtland, C. (1987) *Our Common Future* (New York: United Nations).

Bryson, V. (1993) 'Feminism', in R. Eatwell and A. Wright, eds, *Contemporary Political Ideology* (London: Pinter).

Bull, P. (1983) *Body Movement and Interpersonal Communication* (New York: Wiley).

Burchell, B. et al. (1999) *Job Insecurity and Work Intensification: Flexibility and the Changing Boundaries of Work* (York: YPS).

Burgoon, J. et al. (1996) *Nonverbal Communication: The Unspoken Dialogue*, 2nd edn (New York: McGraw-Hill).

Burleigh, M. (1994) *Death and Deliverance* (Cambridge: Cambridge University Press).

Burns, T. and G. M. Stalker (1966) *The Management of Innovation* (London: Tavistock).

Butler, J. (1999) *Gender Trouble: Feminism and the Subversion of Identity* (London: Routledge).

Butler, J. (2004) *Undoing Gender* (London: Routledge).

Butler, T. and M. Savage (1995) *Social Change and the Middle Classes* (London: UCL Press).

Bytheway, B. (1995) *Ageism* (Buckingham and Bristol, PA: Open University Press).

Cabinet Office (1999) *Sharing the Nation's Prosperity. Variation in Economic and Social Conditions across the UK* (London: HMSO).

Cabinet Office (2003) *Ethnic Minorities and the Labour Market: Final Report, March* (London: HMSO).

Cahill, S. (2004) 'The Interaction Order of Public Bathrooms', in Cahill, ed., *Inside Social Life: Readings in Sociological Psychology and Microsociology*, 4th edn (Los Angeles: Roxbury Publishing Company).

Cantle, T. (2003) *Independent Report of the Community Cohesion Review Team* (London: Home Office).

Capps, W. H. (1990) *The New Religious Right: Piety, Patriotism, and Politics* (Columbia: University of South Carolina Press).

Cardoso, F. H. and E. Faletto (1979) *Dependency and Development in Latin America* (Berkeley: University of California Press).

Carlen, P. (1983) *Women's Imprisonment: A Study in Social Control* (London and Boston: Routledge & Kegan Paul).

Carrington, K. (1995) 'Postmodernism and Feminist Criminologies: Disconnecting Discourses', *International Journal of the Sociology of Law* 22.

Carrington, K. (1998) 'Postmodernism and Criminologies: Fragmenting the Criminological Subject', in P. Walton and J. Young, eds, *The New Criminology Revisited* (London: Macmillan).

Castells, M. (1977) *The Urban Question: A Marxist Approach* (London: Edward Arnold).

Castells, M. (1983) *The City and the Grass Roots: A Cross-Cultural Theory of Urban Social Movements* (London: Edward Arnold).

Castells, M. (1992) 'Four Asian Tigers with a Dragon Head: A Comparative Analysis of the State, Economy, and Society in the Asian Pacific Rim', in R. P. Appelbaum and J. Henderson, eds, *States and Development in the Asian Pacific Rim* (Newbury Park, CA: Sage).

Castells, M. (1996) *The Rise of the Network Society* (Oxford: Blackwell).

Castells, M. (1997) *The Power of Identity* (Oxford: Blackwell).

Castells, M. (1998) *End of Millennium* (Oxford: Blackwell).

Castells, M. (2000) 'Information Technology and Global Capitalism', in W. Hutton and A. Giddens, eds, *On the Edge: Living with Global Capitalism* (London: Cape).

Castells, M. (2001) *The Internet Galaxy: Reflections on the Internet, Business, and Society* (Oxford: Oxford University Press).

Castles, S. and M. J. Miller (1993) *The Age of Migration: International Population Movements in the Modern World* (London: Macmillan).

Chamberlain, M. (1999) 'Brothers and Sisters, Uncles and Aunts: A Lateral Perspective on Caribbean Families', in E. B. Silva and C. Smart, eds, *The New Family?* (London: Sage).

Chambliss, W. J. (1973) 'The Saints and the Roughnecks', *Society*, November.

Chambliss, W. J. (1978) *On the Take: From Petty Crooks to Presidents* (Bloomington: Indiana University Press).

Charlton, J. I. (1998) *Nothing About Us Without Us: Disability Oppression and Empowerment* (Berkeley: University of California Press).

Chase-Dunn, C. (1989) *Global Formation: Structures of the World Economy* (Oxford: Blackwell).

Cherlin, A. (1999) *Public and Private Families: An Introduction* (New York: McGraw Hill).

Chodorow, N. (1978) *The Reproduction of Mothering* (Berkeley: University of California Press).

Chodorow, N. (1988) *Psychoanalytic Theory and Feminism* (Cambridge: Polity).

Chomsky, N. (1991) *Media Control: The Spectacular Achievements of Propaganda* (New York: Seven Stories Press).

Chua, A. (2003) *World on Fire: How Exporting Free Market Democracy Breeds Ethnic Hatred and Global Instability* (New York: Doubleday).

Church of England (1985) *Faith in the City: The Report of the Archbishop of Canterbury's Commission on Urban Priority Areas* (London: Christian Action).

CIA (2000/4) *The World Factbook*. Available online at <www.cia.gov/cia/publications/factbook>.

Cicourel, A. V. (1968) *The Social Organization of Juvenile Justice* (New York: Wiley).

Cisneros, H. G. (1993) *Interwoven Destinies: Cities and the Nation* (New York: Norton).

Clark, K. and S. Drinkwater (1998) 'Self-Employment and Occupational Choice', in D. Leslie, ed., *An Investigation of Racial Disadvantage* (Manchester: Manchester University Press).

Clark, T. N. and V. Hoffman-Martinot (1998) *The New Political Culture Boulder* (Boulder, CO: Westview).

Clegg, M., A. Finney and K. Thorpe (2005) *Crime in England and Wales: Quarterly Update to December 2004* (London: Home Office).

Clegg, S. (1990) *Modern Organizations: Organization Studies in the Postmodern World* (London: Sage).

Cloward, R. and L. Ohlin (1960) *Delinquency and Opportunity* (New York: Free Press).

CNN (2001) *Falwell Apologizes to Gays, Feminists, Lesbians*, 14 September (<http://archives.cnn.com/2001/US/09/14/Falwell.apology/>).

Cohen, A. (1955) *Delinquent Boys* (London: Free Press).

Cohen, L. E., J. P. Broschak and H. A. Haveman (1998) 'And Then There Were More? The Effect of Organizational Sex Composition on the Hiring and Promotion of Managers', *American Sociological Review* 63(5).

Cohen, R. (1997) *Global Diasporas: An Introduction* (London: UCL Press).

Cohen, S. (1980) *Folk Devils and Moral Panics: The Creation of the Mods and Rockers* (Oxford: Martin Robertson).

Cole, T. R. (1992) *The Journey of Life: A Cultural History of Aging in America* (Cambridge: Cambridge university Press).

Collins, J. (2000) 'Quality by Other Means'. Unpublished manuscript, Department of Sociology, University of Wisconsin-Madison.

Collins, J. and J. Porras (1994) *Built to Last* (New York: Century).

Connell, R. W. (1987) *Gender and Power: Society, the Person and Sexual Politics* (Cambridge: Polity).

Connell, R. W. (2001) *The Men and the Boys* (Berkeley and Los Angeles: Allen and Unwin).

Connell, R. W. (2005) *Masculinities* (Cambridge: Polity).

Cook, R. (2001) Robin Cook's 'Chicken Tikka Masala Speech'. Extracts from a Speech by the Foreign Secretary to the Social Market Foundation in London, *Guardian*, Thursday 19 April.

Coontz, S. (1992) *The Way We Never Were: American Families and the Nostalgia Trap* (New York: Basic Books).

Corbin, J. and A. Strauss (1985) 'Managing Chronic Illness at Home: Three Lines of Work', *Qualitative Sociology* 8.

Corsaro, W. (1997) *The Sociology of Childhood* (Thousand Oaks, CA: Pine Forge Press).

Coward, R. (1984) *Female Desire: Women's Sexuality Today* (London: Paladin).

Cox, O. C. (1959) *Class, Caste and Race: A Study in Social Dynamics* (New York: Monthly Review Press).

Crick, B. (2004) *Is Britain Too Diverse? The Responses* (<http://www.prospect-magazine.co.uk/HtmlPages/replies.asp>).

Crompton, R. (1997) *Women and Work in Modern Britain* (Oxford, Oxford University Press).

Crompton, R. (1998) *Class and Stratification: An Introduction to Current Debates*, 2nd edn (Cambridge: Polity).

Crow, G. and M. Hardey (1992) 'Diversity and Ambiguity Among Lone-Parent Households in Modern Britain', in C. Marsh and S. Arber, eds, *Families and Households: Divisions and Change* (London: Macmillan).

Cumings, B. (1987) 'The Origins and Development of the Northeast Asian Political Economy: Industrial Sectors, Product Cycles, and Political Consequences', in F. C. Deyo, ed., *The Political Economy of the New Asian Industrialism* (Ithaca, NY: Cornell University Press).

Cumings, B. (1997) *Korea's Place in the Sun: A Modern History* (New York: Norton).

Cumming, E. and W. E. Henry (1961) *Growing Old: The Process of Disengagement* (New York: Basic Books).

Curran, J. and J. Seaton (2003) *Power Without Responsibility: The Press, Broadcasting and New Media in Britain* (London: Routledge).

Currie, D. and M. Siner (1999) 'The BBC Balancing Public and Commercial Purpose', in *Public Purpose in Broadcasting Funding the BBC* (Luton: University of Luton Press).

Currie, E. (1998) 'Crime and Market Society Lessons from the United States', in P. Walton and J. Young, eds, *The New Criminology Revisited* (London: Macmillan).

Cylke, F. K. (1993) *The Environment* (New York: Harper Collins).

Dahlburg, J.-T. (1995) 'Sweatshop Case Dismays Few in Thailand', *Los Angeles Times*, 27 August.

Dahrendorf, R. (1959) *Class and Class Conflict in Industrial Society* (London: Routledge).

Davie, G. (1994) *Religion in Britain Since 1945: Believing without Belonging* (Oxford: Blackwell).

Davie, G. (2000) *Religion in Modern Europe: A Memory Mutates* (Oxford: Oxford University Press).

Davies, B. (1991) *Frogs and Snails and Feminist Tales* (Sydney: Allen and Unwin).

Davis, M. (1990) *City of Quartz: Excavating the Future in Los Angeles* (London: Vintage).

Davis, S. M. (1987) *Future Perfect* (Reading, MA: Addison-Wesley).

Davis, S. M. (1988) *2001 Management: Managing the Future Now* (London: Simon and Schuster).

De Beauvoir, S. (1949) *Le Deuzième Sex* (Paris: Gallimard).

De Witt, K. (1994) 'Wave of Suburban Growth Is Being Fed by Minorities', *New York Times*, 15 August.

D'Emilio, J. (1983) *Sexual Politics, Sexual Communities: The Making of a Homosexual Minority in the United States, 1940–1970* (Chicago: University of Chicago Press).

Denney, D. (1998) 'Anti-Racism and the Limits of Equal Opportunities Policy in the Criminal Justice System', in C. J. Finer and M. Nellis. eds, *Crime and Social Exclusion* (Oxford: Blackwell).

Dennis, N. and G. Erdos (1992) *Families without Fatherhood* (London: IEA Health and Welfare Unit).

Department for Education and Skills (2003) *Survey of Information and Communications Technology in School* (London: HMSO).

Department for Work and Pensions (2002) *Disabled for Life? Attitudes Towards, and Experiences of, Disability in Britain* (London: HMSO).

Department of Economic and Social Affairs (2002) *International Migration Report 2002* (New York: United Nations).

Department of Social Security (1998) *New Ambitions for Our Country: A New Contract for Welfare* (London: HMSO).

Derrida, J. (1978) *Writing and Difference* (London: Routledge & Kegan Paul).

Derrida, J. (1981) *Positions* (London: Athlone Press).

Devault, M. L. (1991) *Feeding the Family: The Social Organization of Caring as Gendered Work* (Chicago: University of Chicago Press).

Deyo, F. C. (1989) *Beneath the Miracle: Labor Subordination in the New Asian Industrialism* (Berkeley: University of California Press).

DHSS (1980) *Inequalities in Health* (London: DHSS).

Dicken, P. (1992) *Global Shift: The Internationalization of Economic Activity* (London: Chapman).

Disability Rights Commission (2002) *Briefing*, October.

Dobash, R. E. and R. P. Dobash (1992) *Women, Violence and Social Change* (London: Routledge).

DoH (2003) *Smoking, Drinking and Drug Misuse among Young People in England* (London: Department of Health). Available online at <http://www.publications.doh.gov.uk/public/sddsurvey2003.pdf>.

Dore, R. (1973) *British Factory, Japanese Factory: The Origins of National Diversity in Industrial Relations* (London: Allen and Unwin).

Doyal, L. (1995) *What Makes Women Sick: Gender and the Political Economy of Health* (London: Macmillan).

Drentea, P. (1998) 'Consequences of Women's Formal and Informal Job Search Methods for Employment in Female-Dominated Jobs', *Gender and Society* 12.

Drexler, K. E. (1992) *Engines of Creation* (Oxford: Oxford University Press).

DTI (2000) *Just Around the Corner* (London: Department of Trade and Industry).

Du Gay, P. (2000) *In Praise of Bureaucracy: Weber, Organization, Ethics* (London: Sage).

Duncombe, J. and D. Marsden (1993) 'Love and Intimacy. The Gender Division of Emotion and "Emotion Work": A Neglected Aspect of Sociological Discussion of Heterosexual Relationships', *Sociology* 27.

Duneier, M. (1999) *Sidewalk* (New York: Farrar, Straus and Giroux).

Duneier, M. and H. Molotch (1999) 'Talking City Trouble: Interactional Vandalism, Social Inequality, and the "Urban Interaction Problem"', *American Journal of Sociology* 104.

Durkheim, E. (1952) *Suicide: A Study in Sociology* (London: Routledge and Kegan Paul).

Durkheim, E. (1961 [1925]) *L'Education morale* (Paris: Alcan).

Durkheim, E. (1976 [1912, 1965]) *The Elementary Forms of the Religious Life* (London: Allen and Unwin).

Durkheim, E. (1982 [1895]) *The Rules of Sociological Method* (London: Macmillan).

Durkheim, E. (1984 [1893]) *The Division of Labour in Society* (London: Macmillan).

Duster, T. (1990) *Backdoor to Eugenics* (New York: Routledge).

Dutt, M. (1996) 'Some Reflections on US Women of Color and the United Nations Fourth World Conference on Women and NGO Forum in Beijing, China', *Feminist Studies* 22.

Dworkin, R. M. (1993) *Life's Dominion: An Argument About Abortion, Euthanasia, and Individual Freedom* (New York: Knopf).

Dyer, C. (1999) 'Let's Stay Together', *Guardian*, 25 October.

Eating Disorders Association (2000) *Eating Disorders in the United Kingdom: Review of the Provision of Health Care Services for Men with Eating Disorders.* Available online at <http://www.edauk.com/sub_some_statistics.htm>.

The Economist (2000a) 'All-Clear?', 13 April.

The Economist (2000b) 'Paradise Regained', 21 December.

The Economist (2002) 'Trouble in Nanoland', 5 December.

The Economist (2004) 'The Kindness of Strangers?', 26 February.

The Economist (2005a) 'Backgrounder: The EU Constitution', 3 June.

The Economist (2005b) 'Backgrounder: EU Enlargement', 23 June.

The Economist (2005c) 'Backgrounder: The Iraq Dossier Row', 5 April.

Efron, S. (1997) 'Eating Disorders Go Global', *Los Angeles Times*, 18 October.

Ehrenreich, B. and J. Ehrenreich (1979) 'The Professional-Managerial Class', in P. Walker, ed., *Between Labour and Capital* (Hassocks: Harvester Press).

Eibl-Eibesfeldt, I. (1973) 'The Expressive Behaviour of the Deaf-and-Blind Born', in M. von Cranach and I. Vine, eds, *Social Communication and Movement* (New York: Academic Press).

Ekman, P. and W. V. Friesen (1978) *Facial Action Coding System* (New York: Consulting Psychologists Press).

Elder, G. H. J. (1974) *Children of the Great Depression: Social Change in Life Experience* (Chicago and London: University of Chicago Press).

Electoral Reform Society (2005) *UK General Elections: Electorates and Turnout 1945–2005*, 1 August.

Ell, K. (1996) 'Social Networks, Social Support and Coping with Serious

Illness: The Family Connection', *Social Science and Medicine* 42.

Elshtain, J. B. (1987) *Women and War* (New York: Basic Books).

Elstein, D., D. Cox, B. Donoghue, et al. (2004) *Beyond the Charter: The BBC after 2006* (London: The Conservative Party).

Emmanuel, A. (1972) *Unequal Exchange: A Study of the Imperialism of Trade* (New York: Monthly Review Press).

Employers' Forum on Disability (2003) *Briefing for CSR Practitioners*. Available online at <http://www.employers-forum.co.uk/www/csr/sttn/labstandards/labstand1.htm>.

Epstein, D. (1998) *Failing Boys Issues in Gender and Achievement* (Buckingham: Open University Press).

Epstein, S. (2002) 'A Queer Encounter: Sociology and the Study of Sexuality', in C. L. Williams and A. Stein, eds, *Sexuality and Gender* (Oxford: Blackwell).

Erikson, K. (1966) *Wayward Puritans: A Study in the Sociology of Deviance* (New York: Wiley).

Erikson, R. and J. Goldthorpe (1993) *The Constant Flux: A Study of Class Mobility in Industrial Societies* (Oxford: Clarendon Press).

Esping-Andersen, G. (1990) *The Three Worlds of Welfare Capitalism* (Cambridge: Polity).

ESRC (1997) *Twenty-Something in the 1990s: Getting on, Getting by, Getting Nowhere*. Research briefing. (Swindon: Economic and Social Research Council).

Estes, C. L. and M. Minkler, eds. (1991) *Critical Perspectives on Aging: The Political and Moral Economy of Growing Old* (Amityville: Baywood).

Estes, C. L., E. A. Binney and R. A. Culbertson (1992) 'The Gerontological Imagination: Social Influences on the Development of Gerontology, 1945–Present', *Aging and Human Development* 35.

Estes, C., S. Biggs and C. Phillipson (2003) *Social Theory, Social Policy and Ageing* (Buckingham: Open University Press).

EU (2005) *The European Union at a Glance?* Available online at <http://europa.eu.int/abc/index_en.htm>.

Evans, D. J. (1992) 'Left Realism and the Spatial Study of Crime', in *Crime, Policing and Place: Essays in Environment Criminology* (London: Routledge).

Evans, M. (2000) 'Poor Show', *Guardian*, 6 March.

Evans, P. (1979) *Dependent Development* (Princeton: Princeton University Press).

Evans-Pritchard, E. E. (1956) *Nuer Religion* (Oxford: Oxford University Press).

Eysenck, H. (1964) *Crime and Personality* (London: Routledge & Kegan Paul).

Faludi, S. (1999) *Stiffed: The Betrayal of the Modern Man* (London: Chatto and Windus).

Featherstone, M and A. Renwick, eds (1995) *Images of Aging: Cultural Representations of Later Life* (London; New York: Routledge).

Felson, M. (1994) *Crime and Everyday Life: Insights and Implications for Society* (Thousand Oaks, CA: Pine Forge Press).

Ferguson, K. E. (1984) *The Feminist Case against Bureaucracy* (Philadelphia: Temple University Press).

Ferguson, N. (2004) *Colossus: The Rise and Fall of the American Empire* (London: Allen Lane).

Feuerbach, L. (1957) *The Essence of Christianity* (New York: Harper and Row).

Fielder, H. G. (1946) *Textual Studies of Goethe's Faust* (Oxford: Blackwell).

Finke, R. and R. Stark (1988) 'Religious Economies and Sacred Canopies:

Religious Mobilization in American Cities, 1906', *American Sociological Review* 53.

Finke, R. and R. Stark (1992) *The Churching of America, 1776–1990: Winners and Losers in Our Religious Economy* (New Brunswick, NJ: Rutgers University Press).

Finkelstein, V. (1980) *Attitudes and Disabled People* (New York: World Rehabilitation Fund).

Finkelstein, V. (1981) 'To Deny or Not to Deny Disability', in A. Brechin et al., eds, *Handicap in a Social World* (Sevenoaks: Hodder and Stoughton).

Firestone, S. (1971) *The Dialectic of Sex: The Case for Feminist Revolution* (London: Cape).

Fischer, C. S. (1984) *The Urban Experience*, 2nd edn (New York: Harcourt).

Fischer, S. (2004) 'Penn World Tables', *The Economist*, 11 March.

Fiske, J. (1989) *Reading the Popular* (London: Unwin Hyman).

Fitzgerald, M. (2001) 'Ethnic Minorities and Community Safety', in R. Matthews and J. Pitts, eds, *Crime, Disorder and Community Safety: A New Agenda* (London: Routledge).

Flaherty, J., J. Veit-Wilson and P. Dornan (2004) *Poverty: The Facts*, 5th edn (London: Child Poverty Action Group).

Flour Advisory Bureau (1998) *Pressure to Be Perfect Report: Bread for Life Campaign* (London: Flour Advisory Bureau).

Forbes (2000) 'The World's Richest People' (29 June).

Forbes (2004) *The World's Billionaires*. Available online at <http://www.forbes.com/billionaires/>.

Ford, C. S. and F. A. Beach (1951) *Patterns of Sexual Behaviour* (New York: Harper and Row).

Foucault, M. (1967) *Madness and Civilization: A History of Insanity in the Age of Reason* (London: Tavistock Publications).

Foucault, M. (1971) *The Order of Things: An Archaeology of the Human Sciences* (New York: Pantheon).

Foucault, M. (1973) *The Birth of the Clinic: An Archaeology of Medical Perception* (London: Tavistock Publications).

Foucault, M. (1978) *The History of Sexuality* (London: Penguin).

Foucault, M. (1979) *Discipline and Punish* (Harmondsworth: Penguin).

Foucault, M. (1988) 'Technologies of the Self', in L. H. Martin, H. Gutman and P. H. Hutton, eds, *Technologies of the Self: A Seminar with Michel Foucault* (Amherst: University of Massachusetts Press).

Fox, O. C. (1964) 'The Pre-Industrial City Reconsidered', *Sociological Quarterly* 5.

Francis, B. (2000) *Boys, Girls and Achievement: Addressing the Classroom Issues* (London: Routledge).

Frank, A. G. (1966) 'The Development of Underdevelopment', *Monthly Review* 18.

Frank, A. G. (1969) *Capitalism and Underdevelopment in Latin America: Historical Studies of Chile and Brazil* (New York: Monthly Review Press).

Frank, D. J. and E. H. McEneaney (1999) 'The Individualization of Society and the Liberalization of State Policies on Same-Sex Sexual Relations, 1984–1995', *Social Forces* 7(3).

Fraser, N. (1989) *Unruly Practices: Discourse and Gender in Contemporary Social Theory* (Cambridge: Polity).

Fraser, S. (1995) *The Bell Curve Wars Race, Intelligence and the Future of America* (New York: Basic Books).

Free the Children (1998) Available online at <http://www.freethechildren.org/aboutus/history_ftc.htm>.

Freedman, C., ed. (2001) *Economic Reform in Japan: Can the Japanese Change?* (Cheltenham: Edward Elgar).

Freidson, E. (1970) *Profession of Medicine: A Study of the Sociology of Applied Knowledge* (New York: Dodd, Mead).

Fremlin, J. H. (1964) 'How Many People Can The World Support?' *New Scientist.*

Friedan, B. (1963) *The Feminine Mystique* (London: Victor Gollancz).

Friedlander, D. and G. Burtless (1994) *Five Years After: The Long-Term Effects of Welfare-to-Work Programs* (New York: Russell Sage).

Fries, J. F. (1980) 'Aging, Natural Death, and the Compression of Morbidity', *New England Journal of Medicine* 303.

Fröbel, F., J. Heinrichs and O. Kreye (1979) *The New International Division of Labor* (New York: Cambridge University Press).

Fukuyama, F. (1989) 'The End of History?' *National Interest* 16.

Gagnon, J. H. and W. Simon (1973) *Sexual Conduct: The Social Sources of Human Sexuality* (Chicago: Aldine).

Gallie, D. (1994) 'Are the Unemployed an Underclass? Some Evidence from the Social Change and Economic Life Initiative', *Sociology* 28.

Gallup (2004) *Poll Topics and Trends: Religion*, 1 August.

Gamble, A. (1999) *Marxism after Communism: The Interregnum. Controversies in World Politics 1989–1999* (Cambridge: Cambridge University Press).

Gans, H. J. (1962) *The Urban Villagers: Group and Class in the Life of Italian-Americans*, 2nd edn (New York: Free Press).

Gardner, C. B. (1995) *Passing by Gender and Public Harassment* (Berkeley: University of California Press).

Garfinkel, H. (1963) 'A Conception of, and Experiments with, "Trust" as a Condition of Stable Concerted Actions', in O. J. Harvey, ed., *Motivation and Social Interaction* (New York: Ronald Press).

Geary, D. (1981) *European Labor Protest, 1848–1939* (New York: St Martin's Press).

Geertz, C. (1973) *The Interpretation of Cultures* (New York: Basic Books).

Gelder, L. van (1996) 'The Strange Case of the Electronic Lover', in R. Kling, ed., *Computerization and Controversy* (San Diego, CA: Academic Press, Inc.).

Gelles, R. and C. P. Cornell (1990) *Intimate Violence in Families* (Newbury Park, CA: Sage).

Gellner, E. (1983) *Nations and Nationalism* (Oxford: Blackwell).

Gerbner, G. (1979) 'The Demonstration of Power Violence, Profile No. 10', *Journal of Communication* 29.

Gerbner, G. (1980) 'The "Mainstreaming" of America: Violence Profile No. 11', *Journal of Communication* 30.

Gereffi, G. (1995) 'Contending Paradigms for Cross-Regional Comparison: Development Strategies and Commodity Chains in East Asia and Latin America', in P. H. Smith, ed., *Latin America in Comparative Perspective: New Approaches to Methods and Analysis* (Boulder, CO: Westview Press).

Gershuny, J. (1994) 'The Domestic Labour Revolution: A Process of Lagged Adaptation', in M. Anderson, F. Bechofer and J. Gershuny, eds, *The Social and Political Economy of the Household* (Oxford: Oxford University Press).

Gershuny, J. I. and I. D. Miles (1983) *The New Service Economy: The Transforma-*

tion of Employment in Industrial Societies (London: Frances Pinter).

Gerth, H. H. and C. W. Mills, eds. (1948) *From Max Weber: Essays in Sociology* (London: Routledge & Kegan Paul Ltd).

Gewirtz, S., S. Ball and R. Bowe (1995) *Markets, Choice, and Equity in Education* (Buckingham: Open University Press).

Gibbons, J. H. (1990) *Trading around the Clock Global Securities Markets and Information Technology* (Washington DC: US Congress).

Giddens, A. (1984) *The Constitution of Society* (Cambridge: Polity).

Giddens, A. (1993) *The Transformation of Intimacy: Love, Sexuality and Eroticism in Modern Societies* (Cambridge: Polity).

Giddens, A. (1998) *The Third Way: The Renewal of Social Democracy* (Cambridge: Polity).

Giddens, A., ed. (2001) *The Global Third Way Debate* (Cambridge: Polity).

Giddens, A. (2002) *Runaway World: How Globalisation Is Reshaping Our Lives* (London: Profile).

Gillan, A. (1999) 'Shelter Backs Rethink on Homeless', *Guardian*, 15 November.

Gillborn, D. and D. Youdell (2001) 'The New IQism: Intelligence, "Ability" and the Rationing of Education', in J. Demaine, ed., *Sociology of Education Today* (London: Palgrave).

Gilleard, C. and P. Higgs (2005) *Contexts of Ageing: Class, Cohort and Community* (Cambridge: Polity).

Gilligan, C. (1982) *In a Different Voice: Psychological Theory and Women's Development* (Cambridge, MA: Harvard University Press).

Ginn, J. and S. Arber (2000) 'Ethnic Inequality in Later Life: Variation in Financial Circumstances by Gender and Ethnic Group', *Education and Ageing* 15(1).

Ginzburg, C. (1980) *The Cheese and the Worms* (London: Routledge & Kegan Paul).

Gittings, D. (1999) 'Mickey Mouse Invasion', *Guardian*, 3 November.

Gittins, D. (1993) *The Family in Question: Changing Households and Familiar Ideologies* (Basingstoke: Macmillan).

Glasgow Media Group (1976) *Bad News* (London: Routledge).

Glasius, M., M. Kaldor and H. Anheier, eds (2002) *Global Civil Society 2002* (Oxford: Oxford University Press).

Glass, D. (1954) *Social Mobility in Britain* (London: Routledge & Kegan Paul).

Goffman, E. (1963) *Stigma* (Englewood Cliffs, NJ: Prentice-Hall).

Goffman, E. (1967) *Interaction Ritual* (New York: Doubleday/Anchor).

Goffman, E. (1968) *Asylums. Essays on the Social Situation of Mental Patients and Other Inmates* (Harmondsworth: Penguin).

Goffman, E. (1971) *Relations in Public: Microstudies of the Public Order* (London: Allen Lane).

Goffman, E. (1973) *The Presentation of Self in Everyday Life* (New York: Overlook Press).

Goffman, E. (1981) *Forms of Talk.* (Philadelphia: University of Pennsylvania Press).

Gold, T. (1986) *State and Society in the Taiwan Miracle.* (Armonk, NY: M. E. Sharpe).

Golding, P. and G. Murdock, eds (1997) *The Political Economy of the Media* (Cheltenham: Edward Elgar Ltd).

Goldscheider, F. K. and L. J. Waite (1991) *New Families, No Families? The Transformation of the American Home*

(Berkeley: University of California Press).

Goldthorpe, J. H. (1968–9) *The Affluent Worker in the Class Structure*, 3 vols (Cambridge: Cambridge University Press).

Goldthorpe, J. H. (1983) 'Women and Class Analysis in Defence of the Conventional View', *Sociology* 17.

Goldthorpe, J. H. and C. Payne (1986) 'Trends in Intergenerational Class Mobility in England and Wales 1972–1983', *Sociology* 20.

Goldthorpe, J. H. and G. Marshall (1992) 'The Promising Future of Class Analysis', *Sociology* 26.

Goldthorpe, J. H., C. Llewellyn and C. Payne (1980) *Social Mobility and Class Structure in Modern Britain* (Oxford: Clarendon Press; 2nd edn 1987).

Goleman, D. (1996) *Emotional Intelligence: Why It Can Matter More Than IQ* (London: Bloomsbury).

Goode, W. J. (1963) *World Revolution in Family Patterns* (New York: Free Press).

Goode, W. J. (1971) 'Force and Violence in the Family', *Journal of Marriage and the Family* 33.

Goodhart, D. (2004) 'Too Diverse? Is Britain Becoming Too Diverse to Sustain the Mutual Obligations Behind a Good Society and the Welfare State?' *Prospect Magazine*, February.

Gordon, D., R. Levitas, C. Pantazis, et al. (2000) *Poverty and Social Exclusion in Britain* (York: Joseph Rowntree Foundation).

Gorz, A. (1982) *Farewell to the Working Class* (London: Pluto Press).

Gottfredson, M. R. and T. Hirschi (1990) *A General Theory of Crime* (Stanford CA: Stanford University Press).

Grabosky, P. N. and R. G. Smith (1998) *Crime in the Digital Age: Controlling Telecommunications and Cyberspace Illegalities* (New Brunswick, NJ: Transaction).

Graef, R. (1989) *Talking Blues* (London: Collins).

Graham, H. (1987) 'Women's Smoking and Family Health', *Social Science and Medicine* 25.

Graham, H. (1994) 'Gender and Class as Dimensions of Smoking Behaviour in Britain: Insights from a Survey of Mothers', *Social Science and Medicine* 38.

Graham, L. (1995) *On the Line at Suburu-Isuzu* (Ithaca, NY: Cornell University Press).

Granovetter, M. (1973) 'The Strength of Weak Ties', *American Journal of Sociology* 78.

Gray, J. (2003) *Al Qaeda and What It Means to Be Modern* (Chatham, Kent: Faber and Faber).

Greed, C. (1994) *Women and Planning: Creating Gendered Realities* (London: Routledge).

Green, F., A. Felstead and B. Burchell (2000) 'Job Insecurity and the Difficulty of Regaining Employment: An Empirical Study of Unemployment Expectations', *Oxford Bulletin of Economics and Statistics* 62 (Special Issue).

Gregg, P. and J. Wadsworth (1999) 'Job Tenure, 1975–98', in P. Gregg and J. Wadsworth, eds, *The State of Working Britain* (Manchester: Manchester University Press).

Grint, K. (2005) *The Sociology of Work*, 3rd edn (Cambridge: Polity).

Grossberg, L., E. Wartella and D. C. Whitney (1998) *Mediamaking* (Thousand Oaks, CA: Sage Publications).

Grusky, D. B. and R. M. Hauser (1984) 'Comparative Social Mobility Revisited: Models of Convergence and Divergence in 16 Countries', *American Sociological Review* 49.

Guardian (2004) *Refugees in Britain*, 9 October. Available online at <http://www.guardian.co.uk/Refugees_in_Britain/Story/0,2763,1323311,00.html>.

Gubrium, J. (1986) *Oldtimers and Alzheimer's: The Descriptive Organization of Senility* (Greenwich, CT; London: Jai).

Guibernau, M. (1999) *Nations without States: Political Communities in a Global Age* (Cambridge: Polity).

Gunter, B. (1985) *Dimensions of Television Violence* (London: Gower).

Habermas, J. (1986–8) *The Theory of Communicative Action*, 2 vols (Cambridge: Polity).

Hadden, J. (1997) *New Religious Movements Mission Statement*. Available online at <http://religiousmovements.lib.virginia.edu/welcome/mission.htm>.

Hadden, J. and A. Shupe (1987) 'Televangelism in America', *Social Compass* 34(1).

Hakim, C. (1996) *Key Issues in Women's Work: Female Heterogeneity and the Polarisation of Women's Employment* (London: Athlone Press).

Hall, E. T. (1969) *The Hidden Dimension* (New York: Doubleday).

Hall, E. T. (1973) *The Silent Language* (New York: Doubleday).

Hall, R., S. James and J. Kertesz (1984) *The Rapist Who Pays the Rent*, 2nd edn (Bristol: Falling Wall Press).

Hall, S. (1980) *Culture, Media, Language: Working Papers in Cultural Studies, 1972–79* (London: Hutchinson, in association with the Centre for Contemporary Cultural Studies, University of Birmingham).

Hall, S. and M. Jacques (1988) 'New Times', *Marxism Today*.

Hall, S. et al. (1978) *Policing the Crisis: Mugging, the State, and Law and Order* (London: Macmillan).

Hall, S. et al. (1982) *The Empire Strikes Back* (London: Hutchinson).

Halliday, F. (2002) *Two Hours That Shook the World: September 11, 2001: Causes and Consequences* (London: Saqi Books).

Halloran, J. D., ed. (1970) *The Effects of Television* (London: Panther).

Halpern, C. T. (2000) 'Smart Teens Don't Have Sex (or Kiss Much Either)', *Journal of Adolescent Health* 26(3).

Halpern, D. (2005) *Social Capital* (Cambridge: Polity).

Halsey, A. H., ed. (1997) *Education: Culture, Economy, and Society* (Oxford: Oxford University Press).

Halsey, A. H. and J. Webb, eds (2000) *Twentieth-Century British Social Trends* (New York: Macmillan).

Hammond, P. E. (1992) *Religion and Personal Autonomy: The Third Disestablishment in America.* (Columbia, SC: University of South Carolina Press).

Handy, C. (1994) *The Empty Raincoat: Making Sense of the Future* (London: Hutchinson).

Harkin, J. and P. Skidmore (2003) *Grown up Trust* (London: Demos).

Harris, J. R. (1998) *The Nurture Assumption: Why Children Turn out the Way They Do* (New York: Free Press).

Harris, M. (1978) *Cannibals and Kings: The Origins of Cultures* (New York: Random House).

Harrison, M. (1985) *TV News: Whose Bias?* (Hermitage: Policy Journals).

Harrison, P. (1983) *Inside the Inner City: Life under the Cutting Edge* (Harmondsworth: Penguin).

Hartley-Brewer, J. (1999) 'Gay Couple Will Be Legal Parents', *Guardian*, 28 October.

Harvard Magazine (2000) 'The World's Poor: A Harvard Magazine Roundtable', *Harvard Magazine* 103(2).

Harvey, D. (1973) *Social Justice and the City* (Oxford: Blackwell).

Harvey, D. (1982) *The Limits to Capital* (Oxford: Blackwell).

Harvey, D. (1985) *Consciousness and the Urban Experience: Studies in the History and Theory of Capitalist Urbanization* (Oxford: Blackwell).

Harvey, D. (1989) *The Condition of Postmodernity* (Oxford: Blackwell).

Hasler, F. (1993) 'Developments in the Disabled People's Movement', in J. Swain, ed., *Disabling Barriers, Enabling Environments* (London: Sage).

Hatch, N. (1989) *The Democratization of American Christianity* (New Haven: Yale University Press).

Hawley, A. H. (1950) *Human Ecology: A Theory of Community Structure* (New York: Ronald Press).

Hawley, A. H. (1968) *Human Ecology* (Glencoe: Free Press).

Healy, M. (2001) 'Pieces of the Puzzle', *Los Angeles Times*, 21 May.

Heaphy, B., C. Donovan and J. Weeks (1999) 'Sex, Money and the Kitchen Sink: Power in Same-Sex Couple Relationships', in J. Seymour and P. Bagguley, eds, *Relating Intimacies: Power and Resistance* (Basingstoke: Macmillan).

Heath, A. (1981) *Social Mobility* (London: Fontana).

Hebdige, D. (1997) *Cut 'n' Mix: Culture, Identity, and Caribbean Music* (London: Methuen).

Heidensohn, F. (1985) *Women and Crime* (London: Macmillan).

Heise, D. R. (1987) 'Sociocultural Determination of Mental Aging', in C. Schooler and K. Warner Schaie, eds, *Cognitive Functioning and Social Structure over the Life-Course* (Norwood, NJ: Ablex).

Held, D. (1996) *Models of Democracy*, 2nd edn (Cambridge: Polity).

Held, D. (2004) *Global Covenant: The Social Democratic Alternative to the Washington Consensus* (Cambridge: Polity).

Held, D. et al. (1999) *Global Transformations: Politics, Economics and Culture* (Cambridge: Polity).

Henderson, J. and R. P. Appelbaum (1992) 'Situating the State in the Asian Development Process', in R. P. Appelbaum and J. Henderson, eds, *States and Development in the Asian Pacific Rim* (Newbury Park, CA: Sage).

Hendricks, J. (1992) 'Generation and the Generation of Theory in Social Gerontology', *Aging and Human Development* 35.

Henslin, J. M. and M. A. Biggs (1971) 'Dramaturgical Desexualization: The Sociology of the Vaginal Examination', in J. M. Henslin, ed., *Studies in the Sociology of Sex* (New York: Appleton-Century-Crofts).

Henslin, J. M. and M. A. Biggs (1997) 'Behaviour in Public Places: The Sociology of the Vaginal Examination', in J. M. Henslin, ed., *Down to Earth Sociology: Introductory Readings*, 9th edn (New York: Free Press).

Hepworth, M. (2000) *Stories of Ageing* (Buckingham: Open University Press).

Heritage, J. (1985) *Garfinkel and Ethnomethodology* (New York: Basil Blackwell).

Herman, E. (1998) 'Privatising Public Space', in D. K. Thussu, ed., *Electronic Empires Global Media and Local Resistance* (London: Arnold).

Herman, E. S. and R. W. McChesney (1997) *The Global Media the New Missionaries of Global Capitalism* (London: Cassell).

Herrnstein, R. J. and C. Murray (1994) *The Bell Curve Intelligence and Class Structure in American Life* (New York: Free Press).

HESA (2004) *Increase in Female Academics*, Higher Education Statistics Agency. Available online at <http://www.hesa.ac.uk/press/pr76/pr76.htm>.

Hexham, I. and K. Poewe (1997) *New Religions as Global Cultures* (Boulder, CO: Westview Press).

Hills, J. (1998) 'Does Income Mobility Mean That We Do Not Need to Worry About Poverty?' in A. B. Atkinson and J. Hills, eds, *Exclusion, Employment and Opportunity* (London: Centre for the Analysis of Social Exclusion).

Hirschi, T. (1969) *Causes of Delinquency* (Berkeley: University of California Press).

Hirst, P. (1997) 'The Global Economy: Myths and Realities', *International Affairs* 73.

Hirst, P. and G. Thompson (1992) 'The Problem of "Globalization": International Economic Relations, National Economic Management, and the Formation of Trading Blocs', *Economy and Society* 24.

Hirst, P. and G. Thompson (1999) *Globalization in Question: The International Economy and the Possibilities of Governance*, rev. edn (Cambridge: Polity).

Hite, S. (1994) *The Hite Report on the Family: Growing up under Patriarchy* (London: Bloomsbury).

HMSO (1992) *Social Trends 22* (London, HMSO).

HMSO (1999) *Social Trends 29* (London, HMSO).

HMSO (2000) *Social Trends 30* (London, HMSO).

HMSO (2004) *Social Trends 34* (London, HMSO).

HMSO (2005) *Social Trends 35* (London, HMSO).

Ho, S. Y. (1990) *Taiwan: After a Long Silence* (Hong Kong: Asia Monitor Resource Center).

Hobson, D. (2002) *Soap Opera* (Cambridge: Polity).

Hochschild, A. (1983) *The Managed Heart: Commercialization of Human Feeling* (Berkeley: University of California Press).

Hochschild, A. (1989) *The Second Shift: Working Parents and the Revolution at Home* (New York: Viking).

Hodge, R. and D. Tripp (1986) *Children and Television: A Semiotic Approach* (Cambridge: Polity).

Hogge, B. (2005) 'Great Firewall of China'. Available online at <www.opendemocracy.net/media-edemocracy/china_internet_2524.jsp>.

Holton, R. J. (1978) 'The Crowds in History: Some Problems of Theory and Method', *Social History* 3.

Homans, H. (1987) 'Man-Made Myth: The Reality of Being a Woman Scientist in the NHS', in A. Spencer and D. Podmore. *A Man's World: Essays on Women in Male-Dominated Professions* (London: Tavistock).

Home Office (2002) *Secure Borders, Safe Haven: Integration with Diversity in Modern Britain* (London: Home Office).

Home Office (2003) *World Prison Population List*, 4th edn (London: Home Office).

Home Office (2004) *Criminal Statistics: England and Wales 2003* (London: Home Office).

hooks, b. (1997) *Bone Black: Memories of Girlhood* (London: Women's Press).

Hopkins, T. H. and I. Wallerstein (1996*) The Age of Transition: Trajectory of the World-System, 1945–2025* (London: Zed Books).

Horkheimer, M. and T. W. Adorno (2002) *Dialectic of Enlightenment: Philosophical Fragments* (Stanford, CA: Stanford University Press; originally published in 1947).

Hotz, R. L. (1998) 'Boomers Firing Magic Bullets at Signs of Aging', *Los Angeles Times.*

Howard, J. H. (1986) 'Change in "Type A" Behaviour a Year after Retirement', *Gerontologist* 26.

Howard League for Penal Reform (2004). Available online at <http://www.howardleague.org/press/2004/060104a.htm>.

Hughes, E. C. (1945) 'Dilemmas and Contradictions of Status', *American Journal of Sociology* 50.

Hughes, G. (1991) 'Taking Crime Seriously? A Critical Analysis of New Left Realism', *Sociology Review* 1.

Humphreys, L. (1970) *Tearoom Trade: A Study of Homosexual Encounters in Public Places* (London: Duckworth).

Hunt, P., ed. (1966) *Stigma: The Experience of Disability* (London: Geoffrey Chapman).

Huntington, S. P. (1996) *The Clash of Civilizations and the Remaking of World Order* (New York: Simon and Schuster).

Huston, A. C., E. Donnerstein, H. Fairchild, et al. (1992) *Big World, Small Screen: The Role of Television in American Society* (Lincoln: University of Nebraska Press).

Hutton, W. (1995) *The State We're in* (London: Jonathan Cape).

Hyman, R. (1984) *Strikes*, 2nd edn (London: Fontana).

ICBL (2001) *International Campaign to Ban Land Mines.* Available online at <www.icbl.org>.

Iganski, P. and G. Payne (1999) 'Socio-Economic Restructuring and Employment: The Case of Minority Ethnic Groups', *British Journal of Sociology* 50.

Illich, I. (1975) *Medical Nemesis: The Expropriation of Health* (London: Calder and Boyars).

Illich, I. D. (1973) *Deschooling Society* (Harmondsworth: Penguin).

ILO (1999) *C182 Worst Forms of Child Labour Convention*, International Labour Organization. Available online at <www.ilo.org/public/English/standards/ipec/ratification/convention/text.htm>.

ILO (2000) *Statistical Information and Monitoring Programme on Child Labour (SIMPOC): Overview and Strategic Plan 2000–2002* (International Programme on the Elimination of Child Labour (IPEC) and Bureau of Statistics (STAT)).

ILO (2004) *Global Employment Trends for Women*, International Labour Office, March. Available online at <http://www.ilo.org/public/english/employment/strat/download/trendsw.pdf>.

Inglehart, R. (1997) *Modernization and Postmodernization: Cultural, Economic and Political Change in 43 Societies* (Princeton, NJ: Princeton University Press).

Innis, H. A. (1951) *The Bias of Communication* (Toronto: Toronto University Press).

Inquest (2004) *Why Are Children Dying in Custody? Call for a Public Inquiry into the Death of Joseph Scholes*. Available online at <http://inquest.gn.apc.org/pdf/Joseph%20Scholes%20inquiry%20briefing%2004.pdf>.

IPPR (1999) *Unsafe Streets: Street Homelessness and Crime* (London: Institute for Public Policy Research).

ISSA (2003) 'Global Status of Commercialized Transgenic Crops: 2003' (International Service for the Acquisition of Agri-Biotech Applications). Available online at <http://www.isaaa.org/kc/CBTNews/press_release/briefs30/es_b30.pdf>.

Jacoby, S. (1997) *Modern Manors: Welfare Capitalism Since the New Deal* (Princeton: Princeton University Press).

Jahoda, M., P. F. Lazarsfeld and H. Zeisel (1972 [1933]) *Marienthal: The Sociography of an Unemployed Community* (London: Tavistock).

James, C. (2003) *Global Status of Commercialized Transgenic Crops* (International Service for the Acquisition of Agri-Biotech Applications).

Jencks, C. (1994) *The Homeless Cambridge.* (Harvard, MA: Harvard University Press).

Jenkins, C. and B. Sherman (1979) *The Collapse of Work* (London: Eyre Methuen).

Jensen, A. (1967) 'How Much Can We Boost IQ and Scholastic Achievement?' *Harvard Educational Review* 29.

Jensen, A. (1979) *Bias in Mental Testing* (New York: Free Press).

Jobling, R. (1988) 'The Experience of Psoriasis Under Treatment', in M. Bury and R. Anderson, eds, *Living with Chronic Illness: The Experience of Patients and their Families* (London: Unwin Hyman).

John, M. T. (1988) *Geragogy: A Theory for Teaching the Elderly* (New York: Haworth).

Johnson, M. P. (1995) 'Patriarchal Terrorism and Common Couple Violence: Two Forms of Violence against Women in US Families', *Journal of Marriage and the Family* 57.

Johnston, C. (2004) 'Women Suffer £5k Pay Gap', *Times Higher Education Supplement*, 3 September.

Jones, D. E., S. Doty, C. Grammich, et al. (2002) *Religious Congregations & Membership in the United States 2000: An Enumeration by Region, State and the County Based on Data Reported for 149 Religious Bodies* (Nashville, TN: Glenmary Research Centre).

Jones, T. (1993) *Britain's Ethnic Minorities* (London: Policy Studies Institute).

Joy, B. (2000) 'Why the Future Doesn't Need Us', *Wired* 8(4).

Judge, K. (1995) 'Income Distribution and Life Expectancy: A Critical Appraisal', *British Medical Journal* 311.

Kamin, L. J. (1977) *The Science and Politics of IQ* (Harmondsworth: Penguin).

Kanter, R. M. (1977) *Men and Women of the Corporation* (New York: Basic Books).

Kasarda, J. D. and M. Janowitz (1974) 'Community Attachment in Mass Society', *American Sociological Review* 39.

Katz, E. (1959) 'The Functional Approach to the Study of Attitudes', *Public Opinion Quarterly* (24).

Katz, E. and P. Lazarsfeld (1955) *Personal Influence* (New York: The Free Press).

Katz, S. (1996) *Disciplining Old Age: The Formation of Gerontological Knowledge* (Charlottesville and London: University Press of Virginia).

Kautsky, J. (1982) *The Politics of Aristocratic Empires* (Chapel Hill: University of North Carolina Press).

Keith, M. (1993) *Race, Riots, and Policing: Lore and Disorder in a Multi-Racist Society* (London: UCL Press).

Kelly, M. P. (1992) *Colitis* (London: Tavistock).

Kemp, A. et al. (1995) 'The Dawn of a New Day: Redefining South African Feminism', in A. Basu, ed., *The Challenge of Local Feminisms* (Boulder, CO: Westview).

Kepel, G. (1994) *The Revenge of God: The Resurgence of Islam, Christianity and Judaism in the Modern World* (Cambridge: Polity).

Kerr, A. and T. Shakespeare (2002) *Genetic Politics: From Eugenics to Genome* (Cheltenham: New Clarion).

Kiecolt, K. J. and H. M. Nelson (1991) 'Evangelicals and Party Realignment, 1976–1988', *Social Science Quarterly* 72.

Kinsey, A. C. (1948) *Sexual Behaviour in the Human Male* (Philadelphia: W. B. Saunders).

Kinsey, A. C. (1953) *Sexual Behaviour in the Human Female* (Philadelphia: W. B. Saunders).

Kirkwood, T. (2001) *Ageing Vulnerability: Causes and Interventions* (Chichester: Wiley).

Knoke, D. (1990) *Political Networks: The Structural Perspective* (New York: Cambridge University Press).

Knorr-Cetina, K. and A. V. Cicourel (1981) *Advances in Social Theory and Methodology: Towards an Interpretation of Micro- and Macro-Sociologies* (London: Routledge & Kegan Paul).

Kohn, M. (1977) *Class and Conformity* (Homewood, IL: Dorsey Press).

Kollock, P. (1999) 'The Production of Trust in Online Markets', *Advances in Group Processes* (16).

Koser, K. and H. Lutz (1998) 'The New Migration in Europe: Contexts, Constructions and Realities', in K. Koser and H. Lutz, eds, *The New Migration in Europe: Social Constructions and Social Realities* (Basingstoke: Macmillan).

Koss, S. E. (1973) *Fleet Street Radical: A. G. Gardiner and the Daily News* (London: Allen Lane).

Krupat, E. (1985) *People in Cities: The Urban Environment and Its Effects* (Cambridge: Cambridge University Press).

Kulkarni, V. G. (1993) 'The Productivity Paradox: Rising Output, Stagnant Living Standards', *Business Week*, 8 February.

Kuznets, S. (1955) 'Economic Growth and Income Inequality', *Economic Review* XLV(1).

Lacan, J. (1995) *Lacan's Four Fundamental Concepts of Psychoanalysis* (New York: State University of New York Press).

Laming (Lord) (2003) *The Victoria Climbie Inquiry*, January.

Land, K. C., G. Deane and J. R. Blau (1991) 'Religious Pluralism and Church Membership', *American Sociological Review* 56.

Landes, D. S. (1969) *The Unbound Prometheus* (New York: Cambridge University Press).

Lappe, F. M. (1998.) *World Hunger: 12 Myths* (New York: Grove Press).

Laqueur, W. (2003) *No End to War: Terrorism in the Twenty-First Century Terrorism in the 21st Century* (New York: Continuum).

Laslett, P. (1996) *A Fresh Map of Life: The Emergence of the Third Age* (Basingstoke: Macmillan).

Laswell, H. (1948) *The Structure and Function of Communication and Society* (New York: Harper & Brothers).

Laumann, E. O. (1994) *The Social Organization of Sexuality: Sexual Practices in the United States* (Chicago: University of Chicago Press).

Lazarsfeld, P. F., B. Berelson and H. Gaudet (1948) *The People's Choice?* (New York: Columbia University Press).

Lea, J. and J. Young (1984) *What Is To Be Done about Law and Order?* (London: Penguin).

Leadbeater, C. (1999) *Living on Thin Air: The New Economy* (London: Viking).

Lee, R. B. (1968) 'What Hunters Do for a Living, or How to Make out on Scarce Resources', in R. B. Lee and I. De Vore, eds, *Man the Hunter* (Chicago: Aldine Press).

Lee, R. B. (1969) '!Kung Bushman Subsistence: An Input-Output Analysis', in A. P. Vayda, ed., *Environment and Cultural Behavior* (New York: Natural History Press).

Lee, R. B. and I. De Vore, eds (1968) *Man the Hunter* (Chicago: Aldine Press).

Leisering, L. and S. Leibfried (1999) *Time and Poverty in Western Welfare States* (Cambridge: Cambridge University Press).

Lemert, E. (1972) *Human Deviance, Social Problems and Social Control* (Englewood Cliffs, NJ: Prentice Hall).

Levin, W. C. (1988) 'Age Stereotyping: College Student Evaluations', *Research on Aging* 10.

Liebert, R. M., J. N. Sprafkin and M. A. S. Davidson (1982) *The Early Window Effects of Television on Children and Youth* (London: Pergamon Press).

Lim, L. L. (1998) *The Sex Sector: The Economic and Social Bases of Prostitution in Southeast Asia* (Geneva: International Labour Organization).

Lipset, S. M. (1991) 'Comments on Luckmann', in P. Bourdieu and J. S. Coleman, eds, *Social Theory in a Changing Society* (Boulder, CO: Westview).

Lipset, S. M. and R. Bendix (1959) *Social Mobility in Industrial Society* (Berkeley: University of California Press).

Lister, R., ed. (1996) *Charles Murray and the Underclass: The Developing Debate* (London: IEA Health and Welfare Unit, in association with *The Sunday Times*).

Lloyd-Sherlock, P. (2004) *Living Longer* (London: Zed Books).

Locke, J. and E. Pascoe (2000) 'Can a Sense of Community Flourish in Cyberspace?' *Guardian*, 11 March.

Logan, J. R. and H. L. Molotch (1987) *Urban Fortunes: The Political Economy of Place* (Berkeley: University of California Press).

The London Plan (2004) *Spatial Development Strategy* (London: Mayor of London).

Lorber, J. (1994) *Paradoxes of Gender* (New Haven, CO: Yale University Press).

Lukes, S. (1974) *Power: A Radical View* (London: Macmillan).

Lull, J. (1997) 'China Turned on Revisited Television, Reform and Resistance', in A. Sreberny-Mohammadi, ed., *Media in Global Context: A Reader* (London: Arnold).

Lull, J. (1980) *Inside Family Viewing: Ethnographic Research on Television's Audiences* (London: Routledge).

Lyon, C. and P. de Cruz (1993) *Child Abuse* (London: Family Law).

Lyon, D. (1994) *The Electronic Eye: The Rise of Surveillance Society* (Cambridge: Polity).

Lyotard, J.-F. (1985) *The Postmodern Condition* (Minneapolis: University of Minnesota Press).

Mac an Ghaill, M. (1994) *The Making of Men: Masculinities, Sexualities and Schooling* (Buckingham: Open University Press).

Macgregor, S. and B. Pimlott (1991) 'Action and Inaction in the Cities', in *Tackling the Inner Cities: The 1980s Reviewed. Prospects for the 1990s* (Oxford: Clarendon Press).

Mack, J. and S. Lansley (1985) *Poor Britain* (London: George Allen and Unwin).

Mack, J. and S. Lansley (1992) *Breadline Britain 1990s: The Findings of the Television Series* (London: London Weekend Television).

McKeown, T. (1979) *The Role of Medicine Dream, Mirage or Nemesis?* (Oxford: Blackwell).

McKnight, A. (2000) 'Earnings Inequality and Earnings Mobility, 1977–1997: The Impact of Mobility on Long Term Inequality', *Employment Relations Research Series No. 8* (London: Department of Trade and Industry).

McLuhan, M. (1964) *Understanding Media* (London: Routledge & Kegan Paul).

McMichael, P. (1996) *Development and Social Change: A Global Perspective* (Thousand Oaks, CA: Pine Forge).

McNeely, C. L. (1995) *Constructing the Nation-State: International Organization and Prescriptive Action* (Westport, CT: Greenwood).

Macpherson, S. W. (1999) *The Stephen Lawrence Inquiry* (London: HMSO).

McQuail, D. (2000) *Mcquail's Mass Communication Theory* (London: Sage).

Makino, M., K. Tsuboi and L. Dennerstein (2004) 'Prevalence of Eating Disorders: A Comparison of Western and Non-Western Countries', *Medscape General Medicine* 6(3).

Malthus, T. (1976 [1798]) *Essay on the Principle of Population* (New York: Norton).

Marcuse, H. (1964) *One Dimensional Man: Studies in the Ideology of Advanced Industrial Society* (London: Routledge & Kegan Paul).

Marsden, P. (1987) 'Core Discussion Networks of Americans', *American Sociological Review* 52.

Marsden, P. and N. Lin (1982) *Social Structure and Network Analysis* (Beverly Hills, CA: Sage).

Marshall, G. (1988) *Social Class in Modern Britain* (London: Hutchinson).

Marshall, G. and D. Firth (1999) 'Social Mobility and Personal Satisfaction Evidence from Ten Countries', *British Journal of Sociology* 50.

Marshall, T. H. (1973) *Class, Citizenship and Social Development* (Westport, CN: Greenwood).

Martin, D. (1990) *Tongues of Fire: The Explosion of Protestantism in Latin America* (Oxford: Blackwell).

Martineau, H. (1962 [1837]) *Society in America Garden City* (New York: Doubleday).

Marx, K. and F. Engels (2001 [1848]) *The Communist Manifesto* (London: Electric Book Co.).

Mason, A. and A. Palmer (1996) *Queer Bashing: A National Survey of Hate Crimes against Lesbian and Gay Men* (London: Stonewall).

Mason, D. (1995) *Race and Ethnicity in Modern Britain* Oxford: Oxford University Press).

Matsuura, J. H. (2004) 'Commercial Tools, Processes and Materials Anticipating the Public Backlash: Public Relations Lessons for Nanotechnology from the

Biotechnology Experience', *Nanotech 2004* 3.

Matthews, R. and J. Young (1986) *Confronting Crime* (London: Sage).

Maugh, T. H. and N. Zamichow (1991) 'Medicine: San Diego's Researcher's Findings Offer First Evidence of a Biological Cause for Homosexuality', *Los Angeles Times*, 30 August.

McFadden, D. and C. A. Champlin (2000) 'Comparison of Auditory Evoked Potentials in Heterosexual, Homosexual, and Bisexual Males and Females', *Journal of the Association for Research in Otolaryngology* 1.

Meadows, D. H. (1972) *The Limits to Growth* (New York: Universe Books).

Meadows, P. (1996) *The Future of Work: Contributions to the Debate* (York: YPS).

Mellows-Facer, A., R. Young and R. Cracknell (2005) *General Election 2005*, 17 May (London: House of Commons Library).

Melton, J. G. (1989) *The Encyclopedia of American Religions* (Detroit: Gale Research).

Merton, R. K. (1957) *Social Theory and Social Structure*, rev. edn (Glencoe: Free Press).

Metropolitan Police Authority (2004) *Report of the MPA Scrutiny on MPS Stop and Search Practice*, May (London: MPA).

Meyer, J. W. and B. Rowan (1977) 'Institutionalized Organizations: Formal Structure as Myth and Ceremony', *American Journal of Sociology* 83.

Michels, R. (1967 [1911]) *Political Parties* (New York: Free Press).

Miles, R. (1993) *Racism after 'Race Relations'* (London: Routledge).

Mills, C. W. (1970) *The Sociological Imagination* (Harmondsworth: Penguin).

Milne, A. E. H. and T. Harding (1999) *Later Lifestyles: A Survey by Help the Aged and Yours Magazine* (London: Help the Aged).

Mirza, H. (1986) *Multinationals and the Growth of the Singapore Economy* (New York: St Martin's Press).

Mission Frontiers (2000) *An Overview of the World by Religious Adherents*. Available online at <http://www.mission frontiers.org/2000/03/overview.htm>.

Mitchell, J. (1966) *Women: The Longest Revolution. Essays in Feminism and Psychoanalysis* (London: Virago).

Mitchell, J. (1975) *Psychoanalysis and Feminism* (New York: Random House).

Modood, T. (1991) 'The Indian Economic Success', *Policy and Politics* 19.

Modood, T. (1994) 'Political Blackness and British Asians', *Sociology* 28.

Modood, T. et al. (1997) *Ethnic Minorities in Britain: Diversity and Disadvantage* (London: Policy Studies Institute).

Mohammadi, A. (1998) 'Electronic Empires an Islamic Perspective', in D. K. Thussu, ed., *Electronic Empires Global Media and Local Resistance* (London: Arnold).

Moore, B. (1966) *Social Origins of Dictatorship and Democracy: Lord and Peasant in the Making of the Modern World* (Boston, MA: Beacon Press).

Moore, G. (1990) 'Structural Determinants of Men's and Women's Personal Networks', *American Sociological Review* 55.

Moore, L. R. (1994) *Selling God: American Religion in the Marketplace of Culture* (New York: Oxford University Press).

Moore, R. (1995) *Ethnic Statistics and the 1991 Census* (London: Runnymede Trust).

Morgan, R. (1994) *The Word of a Woman: Feminist Dispatches* (New York: Norton).

MORI (2000) *Britain Today: Are We An Intolerant Nation?* 23 October. Available online at <http://www.mori.com/polls/2002/refugee.shtml>.

MORI (2002) *Attitudes Towards Asylum Seekers for 'Refugee Week'*, 17 June. Available online at <http://www.mori.com/polls/2002/refugee.shtml>.

MORI (2004) *Can We Have Trust and Diversity?* 19 January. Available online at <http://www.mori.com/polls/2003/community.shtml>.

Morris, L. (1993) *Dangerous Classes: The Underclass and Social Citizenship* (London: Routledge).

Mullan, P. (2002) *The Imaginary Time Bomb: Why an Ageing Population Is Not a Social Problem* (London: I. B. Tauris).

Mumford, L. (1973) *Interpretations and Forecasts* (London: Secker and Warburg).

Muncie, J. (1999) *Youth and Crime: A Critical Introduction* (London: Sage).

Murdoch, R. (1994) 'The Century of Networking'. Eleventh Annual John Bonython Lecture. Australia, Centre for Independent Studies.

Murray, C. (1990) *The Emerging British Underclass* (London: Institute of Economic Affairs).

Murray, C. A. (1984) *Losing Ground: American Social Policy 1950–1980* (New York: Basic Books).

Narayan, D. (1999) *Can Anyone Hear Us? Voices from 47 Countries*, December (Washington, DC: World Bank Poverty Group, PREM).

National Statistics Online (2004) *Internet Access*. Available online at <http://www.statistics.gov.uk/cci/nugget.asp?id=8>.

National Survey of Family Growth (1995), 'Centers for Disease Control and Prevention', National Center for Health Statistics (Washington, DC: Government Printing Office).

Nature (2000) *Atlas of a Thirsty Planet: Percentage of Population with Access to Safe Water by Country 2000*. Available online at <http://www.nature.com/nature/focus/water/map.html>.

Negroponte, N. (1995) *Being Digital* (London: Hodder and Stoughton).

Neighbourhood Renewal Unit (2004) Available online at <http://www.neighbourhood.gov.uk/ourprogs.asp?pageid=4>.

Nettleton, S. (2006) *The Sociology of Health and Illness*, 2nd edn (Cambridge: Polity).

New Internationalist (2000) 'Love, Hate and the Law', *New Internationalist* 328.

Newman, K. S. (2000) *No Shame in My Game: The Working Poor in the Inner City* (New York: Vintage).

Nicholas, S., D. Povey, A. Walker, et al. (2005) *Crime in England and Wales 2004/2005* (London: Home Office).

Nielsen, F. (1994) 'Income Inequality and Industrial Development: Dualism Revisited', *American Sociological Review* 59 (October).

Nolan, P. (2000) 'Labouring Under an Illusion', *THES Millennium Magazine* 22(29), December.

Oakley, A. (1974) *The Sociology of Housework* (Oxford: Martin Robertson).

Oakley, A. et al, (1994) 'Life Stress, Support and Class Inequality: Explaining the Health of Women and Children', *European Journal of Public Health* 4.

OFCOM (2003) *Hours Viewed Per Household Per Day by Age, Social Class and Platform*. Available online at <http://www.ofcom.org.uk/research/

industry_market_research/m_i_index/ tv_radio_region/itc_market_info/tv_ overview/industry_info_june03.pdf>.

Ohmae, K. (1990) *The Borderless World: Power and Strategy in the Industrial Economy* (London: Collins).

Ohmae, K. (1995) *The End of the Nation State: The Rise of Regional Economies* (London: Free Press).

Oliver, M. (1983) *Social Work with Disabled People* (Basingstoke: Macmillan).

Oliver, M. (1990) *The Politics of Disablement* (Basingstoke: Macmillan).

Oliver, M. (1996) *Understanding Disability: From Theory to Practice* (Basingstoke: Macmillan).

Oliver, M. and G. Zarb (1989) 'The Politics of Disability: A New Approach', *Disability, Handicap & Society* 4.

Omi, M. and H. Winant (1994) *Racial Formation in the United States from the 1960s to the 1990s*, 2nd edn (New York: Routledge).

O'Neill, O. (2002) *The Reith Lectures: A Question of Trust*. Available online at <http://www.bbc.co.uk/radio4/reith20 02/>.

O'Neill, R. (2002) *Experiments in Living: The Fatherless Family*, September (London: Civitas).

ONS (2001) *Geographic Variations in Health – Decennial Supplement* (London: Office of National Statistics). Available online at <http://www.statis tics.gov.uk/downloads/theme_health/ DS16/DS16_cap12.pdf>.

ONS (2002a) *Labour Force Survey*, Spring (London: Office of National Statistics). Available online at <http://www.statis tics.gov.uk/cci/nugget.asp?id=11>.

ONS (2002b) *Focus on Ethnicity and Identity* (London, Office of National Statistics). Available online at <http://www.

statistics.gov.uk/downloads/theme_ compendia/foe2004/Ethnicity.pdf>.

ONS (2003a) *Ethnicity: Population Size: 7.9% from a Minority Ethnic Group* (London, Office of National Statistics). Available online at http://www.statis tics.gov.uk/cci/nugget.asp?id=273>.

ONS (2003b) *Focus on London* (London: Office of National Statistics).

ONS (2003c) *A Century of Labour Market Change* (Office of National Statistics). Available online at <http://www. nationalstatistics.org.uk/articles/ labour_market_trends/century_labour _market_change_mar2003.pdf>.

ONS (2004a) *Focus on the Labour Market 2002* (London: Office of National Statistics). Available online at <http://www .statistics.gov.uk/CCI/nugget.asp?ID =697&Pos=2&ColRank=1&Rank=310>.

ONS (2004b) *Travel Trends*, 17 December (London: Office of National Statistics).

ONS (2004c) *Focus on Gender* (London: Office of National Statistics).

ONS (2004d) *Social Focus in Brief: Ethnicity 2002* (London: Office of National Statistics). Available online at <http:// www.statistics.gov.uk/downloads/ theme_social/social_focus_in_brief/ ethnicity/ethnicity.pdf>.

ONS (2005) *Focus on Ethnicity and Identity*, March (London: Office of National Statistics).

Pahl, J. (1989) *Money and Marriage* (Basingstoke: Macmillan).

Pakulski, J. and M. Waters (1996) *The Death of Class* (London: Sage).

Palmore, E. B. (1985) *Retirement: Causes and Consequences* (New York: Springer).

Panyarachun, A. (2004) *A More Secure World: Our Shared Responsibility: Report of the High-Level Panel on*

Threats, Challenges and Change (New York: United Nations).

Parekh, B. (2004) *Is Britain Too Diverse? The Responses* (<http://www.prospect-magazine.co.uk/HtmlPages/replies.asp>).

Park, R. E. (1952) *Human Communities: The City and Human Ecology* (New York: Free Press).

Parker, H., J. Aldridge and F. Measham (1998) *Illegal Leisure: The Normalization of Adolescent Recreational Drug Use* (London; New York: Routledge).

Parry, N. and J. Parry (1976) *The Rise of the Medical Profession* (London: Croom Helm).

Parsons, T. (1952) *The Social System* (London: Tavistock).

Parsons, T. (1960) 'Towards a Healthy Maturity', *Journal of Health and Social Behavior* 1.

Parsons, T. and R. F. Bales (1956) *Family Socialization and Interaction Process* (London: Routledge & Kegan Paul).

Pearce, F. (1976) *Crimes of the Powerful: Marxism, Crime and Deviance* (London: Pluto Press).

Perlmutter, H. V. (1972) 'Towards Research on and Development of Nations, Unions, and Firms as Worldwide Institutions', in H. Gunter, ed., *Transnational Industrial Relations* (New York: St Martin's Press).

Peterson, P. G. (1999) *Gray Dawn: How the Coming Age Wave will Transform America – and the World* (New York: Random House).

Pew Forum on Religion and Public Life (2002) *Americans Struggle with Religion's Role at Home and Abroad*, 20 March (Washington, DC: The Pew Research Center).

Philo, G. and M. Berry (2004) *Bad News From Israel* (London: Pluto Press).

Phizacklea, A. and C. Wolkowitz (1995) *Homeworking Women: Gender, Racism and Class at Work* (London: Sage).

Piachaud, D. (1987) 'Problems in the Definition and Measurement of Poverty', *Journal of Social Policy* 16(2).

Piachaud, D. and H. Sutherland (2002) *Changing Poverty Post-1997* (London: Centre for Analysis of Social Exclusion, London School of Economics).

Pierson, C. (1994) *Dismantling the Welfare State? Reagan, Thatcher and the Politics of Retrenchment* (Cambridge: Cambridge University Press).

Pilkington, A. (2002) 'Cultural Representations and Changing Ethnic Identities in a Global Age', in M. Holborn, ed., *Developments in Sociology* (Ormskirk: Causeway Press).

PISA (2000) *Student Achievement in England: Results in Reading, Mathematical and Scientific Literacy among 15-Year-Olds* (London: Programme for International Student Assessment. OECD).

Pollak, O. (1950) *The Criminality of Women* (Philadelphia: University of Pennsylvania Press).

Pollert, A. (1988) 'Dismantling Flexibility', *Capital and Class* 34.

Postman, N. (1986) *Amusing Ourselves to Death: Public Discourse in the Age of Show Business* (London: Heinemann).

President's Commission on Organized Crime (1986) *Records of Hearings, June 24–26, 1985* (Washington, DC: US Government Printing Office).

Putnam, R. (1993) 'The Prosperous Community: Social Capital and Public Life', *American Prospect* 13.

Putnam, R. (1995) 'Bowling Alone: America's Declining Social Capital', *Journal of Democracy* 6.

Putnam, R. (1996) 'The Strange Disappearance of Civic America', *American Prospect* 7(24).

Putnam, R. (2000) *Bowling Alone: The Collapse and Revival of American Community* (New York: Simon and Schuster).

Quah, D. (1999) *The Weightless Economy in Economic Development* (London: Centre for Economic Performance).

Radway, J. A. (1984) *Reading the Romance* (Chapel Hill: University of North Carolina Press).

Rake, K. ed. (2000) *Women's Incomes over the Lifetime* (London: HMSO).

Ranis, G. (1996) *Will Latin America Now Put a Stop to 'Stop-and-Go?'* (New Haven, CT: Yale University, Economic Growth Center).

Rapoport, R. N., M. P. Fogarty and R. Rapoport, eds, (1982) *Families in Britain* (London: Routledge & Kegan Paul).

Ratcliffe, P. (1999) 'Housing Inequality and "Race": Some Critical Reflections on the Concept of "Social Exclusion"', *Ethnic and Racial Studies* 22.

Rawstorne, S. (2002) 'England and Wales', in R. W. Summers and A. M. Hoffman, eds, *Domestic Violence: A Global View* (Westport, CT: Greenwood Press).

Reay, D. (2002) 'Shaun's Story: Troubling Discourses of White Working-Class Masculinities', *Gender & Education* 14.

Redman, P. (1996) 'Empowering Men to Disempower Themselves: Heterosexual Masculinities, HIV and the Contradictions of Anti-Oppressive Education', in M. Mac an Ghaill, ed., *Understanding Masculinities* (Buckingham: Open University Press).

Rees, M. (2003) *Our Final Century: Will the Human Race Survive the Twenty-First Century?* (London: William Heinemann).

Regional Trends 38 (2003) *Unemployment: By Highest Qualification*. Available online at <http://www.statistics.gov.uk/StatBase/ssdataset.asp?vlnk=7705&More=Y>.

Reich, R. (1991) *The Work of Nations: Preparing Ourselves for 21st-Century Capitalism* (New York: Knopf).

Reid, I. (1991) 'The Education of the Elite', in G. Walford, ed., *Private Schooling Tradition, Change and Diversity* (Oxford: Chapman).

Reisman, D. (1961) *The Lonely Crowd. A Study of the Changing American Character* (New Haven: Yale University Press).

Reskin, B. and P. A. Roos (1990) *Job Queues, Gender Queues: Explaining Women's Inroads into Male Occupations.* (Philadelphia: Temple University Press).

Rex, J. and R. Moore (1967) *Race, Community and Conflict: A Study of Sparkbrook* (Oxford: Oxford University Press).

Rich, A. (1981) *Compulsory Heterosexuality and Lesbian Existence* (London: Onlywomen Press).

Richardson, D. and H. May (1999) 'Deserving Victims? Sexual Status and the Social Construction of Violence', *Sociological Review* 47.

Riley, M. W., A. Foner and J. Waring (1988) 'Sociology of Age', in N. J. Smelser, ed., *Handbook of Sociology* (Newbury Park, CA: Sage).

Riley, M. W., R. L. Kahn and A. Foner (1994) *Age and Structural Lag: Changes in Work, Family, and Retirement* (Chichester: J. Wiley).

Ritzer, G. (1983) 'The McDonaldization of Society', *Journal of American Culture* 6(1).

Ritzer, G. (1993) *The McDonaldization of Society* (Newbury Park, CA: Pine Forge Press).

Ritzer, G. (1998) *The McDonaldization Thesis: Explorations and Extensions* (London: Sage).

Roberts, R. (1971) *The Classic Slum: Salford Life in the First Quarter of the Century* (Manchester: Manchester University Press).

Roof, W. C. (1993) *A Generation of Seekers: The Spiritual Journeys of the Baby Boom Generation* (San Francisco: Harper San Francisco).

Roof, W. C. and W. McKinney (1990) *American Mainline Religion: Its Changing Shape and Future Prospects* (New Brunswick, NJ) Rutgers University Press).

Rose, S., L. Kamin and R. C. Lewontin (1984) *Not in Our Genes: Biology, Ideology and Human Nature* (Harmondsworth: Penguin).

Rosenau, J. N. (1997) *Along the Domestic-Foreign Frontier: Exploring Governance in a Turbulent World* (Cambridge: Cambridge University Press).

Ross, P. and B. Reskin (1992) 'Occupational Desegregation in the 1970s: Integration and Economic Equity', *Sociological Perspectives* 35.

Rossi, A. (1973) 'The First Woman Sociologist: Harriet Martineau', in *The Feminist Papers: From Adams to De Beauvoir* (New York: Columbia University Press).

Rostow, W. W. (1961) *The Stages of Economic Growth* (Cambridge: Cambridge University Press).

Rowling, J. K. (1998) *Harry Potter and the Philosopher's Stone* (London: Bloomsbury).

Rubin, L. (1990) *The Erotic Wars: What Happened to the Sexual Revolution?* (New York: Farrar).

Rubin, L. B. (1994) *Families on the Fault Line* (New York: Harper Collins).

Rudé, G. (1964) *The Crowd in History: A Study of Popular Disturbances in France and England, 1730–1848* (New York: Wiley).

Ruspini, E. (2000) 'Longitudinal Research in the Social Sciences', *Social Research Update* 28.

Rusting, R. L. (1992) 'Why Do We Age?' *Scientific American* 267.

Rutherford, J. and R. Chapman (1988) 'The Forward March of Men Halted', in R. Chapman and J. Rutherford, eds, *Male Order: Unwrapping Masculinity* (London: Lawrence and Wishart).

Sabel, C. F. (1982) *Work and Politics: The Division of Labour in Industry* (Cambridge: Cambridge University Press).

Sachs, J. (2000) 'A New Map of the World', *The Economist*, 22 June.

Saks, M. (1992) *Alternative Medicine in Britain* (Oxford: Clarendon Press).

Salter, H. (1998) 'Making a World of Difference: Celebrating 30 Years of Development Progress', 25 June, US AID Press Release.

Sassen, S. (1991) *The Global City: New York, London, Tokyo.* (Princeton: Princeton University Press).

Sassen, S. (1998) *Globalization and Its Discontents: Essays on the Mobility of People and Money* (New York: New Press).

Sassen, S. (2001) *The Global City: New York, London, Tokyo.* (Princeton: Princeton University Press).

Sassen, S. (2004) *Is Britain Too Diverse? The Responses*, 23 November (<http://www.prospect-magazine.co.uk/HtmlPages/replies.asp>).

Saunders, P. (1990) *Social Class and Stratification* (London: Routledge).

Saunders, P. (1996) *Unequal But Fair? A Study of Class Barriers in Britain* (London: IEA Health and Welfare Unit).

Savage, M. et al. (1992) *Property, Bureaucracy and Culture: Middle Class Formation in Contemporary Britain* (London: Routledge).

Sayers, J. (1986) *Sexual Contradiction: Psychology, Psychoanalysis and Feminism* (London: Tavistock).

Scarman, L. G. (1982) *The Scarman Report* (Harmondsworth: Penguin).

Schaie, K. W. (1979) 'The Primary Mental Abilities in Adulthood: An Exploration in the Development of Psychometric Intelligence', in P. B. Baltes and O. G. Brim, eds, *Lifespan Development and Behavior*, vol. 2 (New York: Academic Press).

Schaie, K. W. (1990) 'Handbook of the Psychology of Aging', in J. E. Birren and K. W. Schaie, eds, *Handbook of the Psychology of Aging*, 5th edn (San Diego, CA, and London: Academic Press, 2001).

Schumacher, E. F. (1977) *Small Is Beautiful: A Study of Economics As If People Mattered* (London: Abacus).

Schwartz, G. (1970) *Sect Ideologies and Social Status* (Chicago: University of Chicago Press).

Schwartz, P. and D. Randall (2003) *An Abrupt Climate Change Scenario and Its Implications for United States National Security, October* (New York: Pentagon).

Schwarz, J. and T. Volgy (1992) *The Forgotten Americans* (New York: Norton).

Scott, J. (1991) *Who Rules Britain?* (Cambridge: Polity).

Scott, S. and D. Morgan (1993) 'Bodies in a Social Landscape', in S. Scott and D. Morgan, eds, *Body Matters: Essays on the Sociology of the Body* (London: Falmer Press).

Scott, W. R. and J. W. Meyer (1994) *Institutional Environments and Organizations: Structural Complexity and Individualism* (Thousand Oaks, CA: Sage).

Sedlak, A. and D. Broadhurst (1996) *Third National Incidence Study of Child Abuse and Neglect.* (Washington, DC: US Department of Health and Human Services).

Segura, D. A. and J. L. Pierce (1993) 'Chicana/o Family Structure and Gender Personality: Chodorow, Familism, and Psychoanalytic Sociology Revisited', *Signs* 19.

Seidman, S. (1997) *Difference Troubles: Queering Social Theory and Sexual Politics* (Cambridge: Cambridge University Press).

Sennett, R. (1993) *The Conscience of the Eye: The Design and Social Life of Cities* (London: Faber and Faber).

Sennett, R. (1998) *The Corrosion of Character: The Personal Consequences of Work in the New Capitalism* (London: Norton).

Seymour-Ure, C. (1998) 'Leaders and Leading Articles Characterization of John Major and Tony Blair in the Editorials of the National Daily Press', in I. Crewe, B. Gosschalk and J. Bartle, eds, *Political Communications: Why Labour Won the General Election of 1997* (London: Frank Cass).

Shakespeare, T. and N. Watson (2002) 'The Social Model of Disability: An Outdated Ideology?' *Research in Social Science and Disability* 2.

Sharma, U. (1992) *Complementary Medicine Today: Practitioners and Patients* (London: Routledge).

Shaw, W. (2001) 'In Helsinki: Virtual Village', *Wired*, March.

Sheldon, W. A. (1949) *Varieties of Delinquent Youth* (New York: Harper).

Shelton, B. A. (1992) *Women, Men, and Time: Gender Differences in Paid Work, Housework, and Leisure* (Westport, CT: Greenwood).

Shelton, B. A. and D. John (1993) 'Does Marital Status Make a Difference?: Housework among Married and Cohabiting Men and Women', *Journal of Family Issues* 14(3).

Signorielli, N. (2003) 'Prime-Time Violence 1993–2001: Has the Picture Really Changed?' *Journal of Broadcasting & Electronic Media* 47.

Simmel, G. (1971 [1903]) 'The Metropolis and Mental Life', in D. N. Levine, ed., *On Individuality and Social Forms: Selected Writings of Georg Simmel* (Chicago: University of Chicago Press).

Simpson, G. E. and J. M. Yinger (1986) *Racial and Cultural Minorities: An Analysis of Prejudice and Discrimination* (New York: Plenum Press).

Simpson, J. H. (1985) 'Socio-Moral Issues and Recent Presidential Elections', *Review of Religious Research* 27.

Sinclair, P. (1987) *Unemployment: Economic Theory and Evidence* (Oxford: Blackwell).

Sjoberg, G. (1960) *The Pre-Industrial City: Past and Present* (New York: Free Press).

Sjoberg, G. (1963) 'The Rise and Fall of Cities: A Theoretical Perspective', *International Journal of Comparative Sociology* 4.

Skeggs, B. (1997) *Formations of Class and Gender: Becoming Respectable* (London: Sage).

Skocpol, T. (1979) *States and Social Revolutions: A Comparative Analysis of France, Russia and China* (Cambridge: Cambridge University Press).

Slapper, G. and S. Tombs (1999) *Corporate Crime* (Essex: Longman).

Smart, C. and B. Neale (1999) *Family Fragments?* (Cambridge: Polity).

Smith, A. (1991 [1776]) *The Wealth of Nations* (London: Everyman's Library).

Smith, A. D. (1986) *The Ethnic Origins of Nations* (Oxford: Blackwell).

Smith, D. (1990) *Stepmothering* (London: Harvester).

Smith, D. (1997) 'Job Insecurity and Other Myths', *Management Today*.

So, A. (1990) *Social Change and Development: Modernization, Dependency, and World-Systems Theories* (Newbury Park, CA: Sage).

Social Exclusion Unit (1998) *Rough Sleeping* (London: HMSO).

Sokolovsky, J. (1990) *The Cultural Context of Aging: Worldwide Perspectives* (New York: Bergin and Garvey).

Spenner, K. (1983) 'Deciphering Prometheus: Temporal Change in the Skill Level of Work', *American Sociological Review* 48.

Stanton, E. C. (1985 [1895]) *The Woman's Bible: The Original Feminist Attack on the Bible* (Edinburgh: Polygon Books).

Stanworth, M. (1984) 'Women and Class Analysis: A Reply to John Goldthorpe', *Sociology* 18.

Stark, R. and W. S. Bainbridge (1980) 'Towards a Theory of Religious Commitment', *Journal for the Scientific Study of Religion* 19.

Stark, R. and W. S. Bainbridge (1985) *The Future of Religion: Secularism, Revival, and Cult Formation* (Berkeley: University of California Press).

Stark, R. and W. S. Bainbridge (1987) *A Theory of Religion* (New Brunswick, NJ: Rutgers University Press).

Statham, J. (1986) *Daughters and Sons: Experiences of Non-Sexist Childraising* (Oxford: Blackwell).

Stead, W. E. and J. G. Stead (1996) *Management for a Small Planet: Strategic Decision Making and the Environ-*

ment (Thousand Oaks, CA, and London).

Stern, V. (1989) *Bricks of Shame: Britain's Prisons* (London: Penguin Books).

Stiglitz, J. E. (2002) *Globalization and Its Discontents* (London: Allen Lane).

Stone, L. (1980) *The Family, Sex, and Marriage in England, 1500–1800* (New York: Harper and Row).

Strategy Unit (2003) *Ethnic Minorities and the Labour Market*. Available online at: <www.number10.gov.uk/su/ethnic%20 minorities/report/downloads/ethnic_ minorities.pdf>.

Straus, M. A. and R. J. Gelles (1986) 'Societal Change and Change in Family Violence from 1975 to 1985 as Revealed by Two National Surveys', *Journal of Marriage and the Family* 48.

Sullivan, A. (1995) *Virtually Normal: An Argument About Homosexuality* (London: Picador).

Sullivan, O. (1997) 'Time Waits for No Woman: An Investigation of the Gendered Experience of Domestic Time', *Sociology* 31.

Sutherland, E. H. (1949) *Principles of Criminology* (Chicago: Lippincott).

Swann Committee (1985) *Education for All: Report of the Committee into the Education of Ethnic Minority Children* (London: HMSO).

Tan, A. and K. Ramakrishna, eds (2002) *The New Terrorism* (Singapore: Eastern Universities Press).

Taylor, I., K. Evans and P. Fraser (1996) *A Tale of Two Cities. Global Change, Local Feeling and Everyday Life in the North of England: A Study in Manchester and Sheffield* (London: Routledge).

Taylor, I., P. Walton and J. Young (1973) *The New Criminology for a Social Theory of Deviance* (London: Routledge & Kegan Paul).

Tempest, R. (1996) 'Barbie and the World Economy', *Los Angeles Times*, 22 September.

Thomas W. I. and F. Znaniecki (1966 [1918–20] *The Polish Peasant in Europe and America: Monograph of Our Immigrant Group*, 5 vols (New York: Dover).

Thomas, C. (1999) *Female Forms: Experiencing and Understanding Disability*. (Buckingham: Open University Press).

Thomas, C. (2002) 'Disability Theory: Key Ideas, Issues and Thinkers', in C. Barnes, L.Barton and M.Oliver, eds, *Disability Studies Today* (Cambridge: Polity).

Thomas, G. M. (1987) *Institutional Structure: Constituting State, Society and the Individual* (Newbury Park, CA: Sage).

Thompson, J. B. (1990) *Ideology and Modern Culture* (Cambridge: Polity).

Thompson, J. B. (1995) *The Media and Modernity: A Social Theory of the Media* (Cambridge: Polity).

Thompson, P. and P. Findlay (1999) 'Changing the People: Social Engineering in the Contemporary Workplace', in A. Sayer and L. Ray, eds, *Culture and Economy after the Cultural Turn* (London: Sage).

Thompson, W. S. (1929) 'Population', *American Journal of Sociology* 34.

Thorne, B. (1993) *Gender Play: Girls and Boys in School* (New Brunswick, NJ: Rutgers University Press).

Tilly, C. (1995) 'Globalization Threatens Labor's Rights', *International Labor and Working Class History* 47.

Tizard, B. and M. Hughes (1984) *Young Children Learning, Talking and Thinking at Home and at School* (London: Fontana).

Toke, D. (2004) *The Politics of GM Food: A Comparative Study of the UK, USA, and EU* (New York: Routledge).

Tonnies, F. (2001 [1887]) *Gemeinschaft Und Gesellschaft [Community and Civil Society]* (New York: Cambridge University Press).

Tough, J. (1976) *Listening to Children Talking* (London: Ward Lock Educational).

Townsend, I. (2002) 'The Burden of Taxation', 9 July, London, House of Commons Library: Research Paper 02/43.

Townsend, P. (1979) *Poverty in the United Kingdom* (Harmondsworth: Penguin).

Toynbee, P. (2003) *Hard Work: Life in Low Pay Britain* (London: Bloomsbury).

Treas, J. (1995) 'Older Americans in the 1990s and Beyond', *Population Bulletin* 5.

Troeltsch, E. (1981 [1931]) *The Social Teaching of the Christian Churches*, 2 vols (Chicago: University of Chicago Press).

UK Christian Handbook (2004) *Religious Trends No. 4*, Christian Research.

UK Film Council (2003) *Statistical Yearbook 2003*.

UN (2003a) *World Population Prospects: The 2002 Revision Highlights* (New York: UN Department of Economic and Social Affairs Population Division).

UN (2003b) *World Urbanisation Prospects: The 2001 Revision Highlights* (New York: UN Department of Economic and Social Affairs Population Division).

UNDP (1998) *Human Development Report* (New York: United Nations Development Programme).

UNDP (1999) *Human Development Report* (New York: United Nations Development Programme).

UNDP (2002) *Are the Millennium Development Goals Feasible?*, United Nations Development Programme. Available online at <http://www.undp.org/dpa/choices/2002/september/Choices0902p7.pdf>.

UNDP (2003) *Human Development Report* (New York: United Nations Development Programme).

UNDP (2004) *Human Development Report: Cultural Liberty in Today's Diverse World* (New York: United Nations Development Programme).

UNFAO (2001) *The Impact of HIV/AIDS on Food Security*. United Nations Food and Agricultural Organization, Conference on World Food Security.

UNFPA (2004) *State of the World Population 2004*. Available online at <http://www.unfpa.org/swp/2004/pdf/en_swp04.pdf>.

UNICEF (2000) *The State of the World's Children, 2000* (New York: United Nations Children's Fund).

Union of International Associations (1996–7) 'International Organizations by Year and by Type, 1909–1996', *Yearbook of International Organizations, 1996–97*.

Union, T. E. (2005) *The European Union at a Glance*. Available online at <http://europa.eu.int/abc/index_en.htm>.

UNWFP (2001) *News Release: WFP Head Releases World Hunger Map and Warns of Hunger 'Hot Spots' in 2001*, January 8 (New York: United Nations World Food Programme).

UPIAS (1976) *Fundamental Principles of Disability* (London: Union of Physically Impaired Against Segregation).

Urban Task Force (1999) *Towards an Urban Renaissance*. Final Report of the Urban Task Force, Chaired by Lord

Rogers of Riverside (London: Department of the Environment, Transport and the Regions).

Urry, J. (1990) *The Tourist Gaze: Leisure and Travel in Contemporary Societies* (London: Sage; 2nd edn 2001).

US Bureau of Justice (1998) *Capital Punishment 1997, Statistics Bulletin* (Washington DC: US Government Printing Office).

US Bureau of Justice (2004) *Capital Punishment 2003* (Washington, DC: Office of Justice Programs, Bureau of Justice Statistics). Available online at <http://www.ojp.usdoj.gov/bjs/glance.dr.htm>.

US Department of Health and Human Services (2000) *Child Maltreatment 1998: Reports from the States to the National Child Abuse and Neglect Data System* (Washington, DC: US Government Printing Office)

Usher, R. and R. Edwards (1994) *Postmodernism and Education* (New York: Routledge).

Vallas, S. and J. Beck (1996) 'The Transformation of Work Revisited: The Limits of Flexibility in American Manufacturing', *Social Problems* 43(3).

Van der Veer, P. (1994) *Religious Nationalism: Hindus and Muslims in India* (Berkeley: University of California Press).

van Gennep, A. (1977 [1908]) *The Rites of Passage* (London: Routledge & Kegan Paul).

Vatican (2004) *Letter to the Bishops of the Catholic Church on the Collaboration of Men and Women in the Church and in the World.* Available online at <http://www.vatican.va/roman_curia/congregations/cfaith/documents/rc_con_cfaith_doc_20040731_collaboration_en.html>.

Vaughan, D. (1990) *Uncoupling: Turning Points in Intimate Relationships* (New York: Vintage).

Vidal, J. (2003) '10 Million Join World Protest Rallies', *Guardian*, 13 February.

Vincent, J. (1999) *Politics, Power, and Old Age* (Buckingham: Open University Press).

Vincent, J. (2003) *Old Age* (London: Routledge).

Viorst, J. (1986) 'And the Prince Knelt Down and Tried to Put the Glass Slipper on Cinderella's Foot', in J. Zipes, ed., *Don't Bet on the Prince: Contemporary Feminist Fairy Tales in North America and England* (New York: Methuen).

Vogler, C. and J. Pahl (1994) 'Money, Power and Inequality in Marriage', *Sociological Review* 42.

Vold, G. B., T. J. Bernard and J. B. Snipes (2002) *Theoretical Criminology* (New York: Oxford University Press).

Wagar, W. (1992) *A Short History of the Future* (Chicago: University of Chicago Press).

Walby, S. (1990) *Theorizing Patriarchy* (Oxford: Blackwell).

Walby, S. A. (1986) 'Gender, Class and Stratification toward a New Approach', in R. Crompton and M. Mann, eds, *Gender and Stratification* (Oxford: Blackwell).

Walker, C. (1994) 'Managing Poverty', *Sociology Review* (April).

Wallerstein, I. (1974) *The Modern World-System* (New York: Academic Press).

Wallerstein, I. (1990) *The Modern World-System II* (New York: Academic Press).

Wallis, R. (1984) *The Elementary Forms of New Religious Life* (London: Routledge and Kegan Paul).

Warde, A. and K. Heatherington (1993) 'A Changing Domestic Division of

Labour? Issues of Measurement and Interpretation', *Work, Employment and Society* 7.

Warner, S. (1993) 'Work in Progress toward a New Paradigm for the Sociological Study of Religion in the United States', *American Journal of Sociology* 98.

Warren, B. (1980) *Imperialism: Pioneer of Capitalism* (London, Verso).

Watson, J. (2003) *Media Communication: An Introduction to Theory and Process* (Basingstoke: Palgrave Macmillan).

Weaver, M. (2001) 'Urban Regeneration - the Issue Explained', *Guardian*, 19 March.

Weber, M. (1958 [1921]) *The City* (Glencoe, IL: Free Press).

Weber, M. (1958) *The Religion of India* (New York: Free Press).

Weber, M. (1963) *The Sociology of Religion* (Boston, MA: Beacon).

Weber, M. (1976) *The Protestant Ethic and the Spirit of Capitalism* (London: Allen and Unwin).

Weber, M. (1979) *Economy and Society: An Outline of Interpretive Sociology* (Berkeley: University of California Press).

Weeks, J. (1977) *Coming Out: Homosexual Politics in Britain, from the Nineteenth Century to the Present* (New York: Quartet).

Weeks, J. (1986) *Sexuality* (London: Methuen).

Weitzman, L. (1972) 'Sexual Socialization in Picture Books for Preschool Children', *American Journal of Sociology* 77.

Wellman, B. S., P. J. Carrington and A. Hall (1988) 'Networks as Personal Communities', in B. Wellman and S. D. Berkowitz, eds, *Social Structures: A Network Approach* (New York: Cambridge University Press).

Westergaard, J. (1995) *Who Gets What? The Hardening of Class Inequality in the Late Twentieth Century* (Cambridge: Polity).

Western, B. (1997) *Between Class and Market: Postwar Unionization in the Capitalist Democracies* (Princeton: Princeton University Press).

Wheatley, P. (1971) *The Pivot of the Four Quarters* (Edinburgh: Edinburgh University Press).

Wheeler, D. L. (1998) 'Global Culture or Culture Clash: New Information Technologies in the Islamic World – a View from Kuwait', *Communication Research* 25(4).

White, M. and M. Trevor (1983) *Under Japanese Management: The Experience of British Workers* (London: Heinemann).

WHO (2001) *Rethinking Care from the Perspective of Disabled People.* World Health Organization Conference Report and Recommendations, August.

Wilde, O. (1960) *The Picture of Dorian Gray* (Brown, Watson: London).

Wilkins, L. T. (1964) *Social Deviance: Social Policy Action and Research* (London: Tavistock).

Wilkinson, H. (1994) *No Turning Back* (London: Demos).

Wilkinson, H. and G. Mulgan (1995) *Freedom's Children Work, Relationships and Politics for 18–34 Year Olds in Britain Today* (London: Demos).

Wilkinson, R. (1996) *Unhealthy Societies: The Afflictions of Inequality* (London: Routledge).

Will, J., P. Self and N. Datan (1976) 'Maternal Behavior and Perceived Sex of Infant', *American Journal of Orthopsychiatry* 46.

Williams, S. J. (1993) *Chronic Respiratory Illness* (London: Routledge).

Willis, P. (1977) *Learning to Labour: How Working-Class Kids Get Working-Class Jobs* (London: Saxon House).

Wilson, B. (1982) *Religion in Sociological Perspective* (Oxford: Oxford University Press).

Wilson, E. (2002) 'The Sphinx in the City: Urban Life, the Control of Disorder', in G. Bridge and S. Watson, eds, *The Blackwell City Reader* (Oxford: Blackwell).

Wilson, E. O. (1975) *Sociobiology: The New Synthesis* (Cambridge, MA: Harvard University Press).

Wilson, W. J. (1987) *The Truly Disadvantaged: The Inner City, the Underclass, and Public Policy* (Chicago: University of Chicago Press).

Wilson, W. J. (1996) *When Work Disappears: The World of the New Urban Poor* (New York: Knopf).

Wirth, L. (1938) 'Urbanism as a Way of Life', *American Journal of Sociology* 44.

Wood, S. (1989) *The Transformation of Work? Skills, Flexibility and the Labour Process* (London: Unwin Hyman).

Woodrum, E. (1988) 'Moral Conservatism and the 1984 Presidential Election', *Journal for the Scientific Study of Religion* 27.

Woolgar, S. and D. Pawluch (1985) 'Ontological Gerrymandering the Anatomy of Social Problems Explanations', *Social Problems* 32.

World Bank (1995) *Workers in an Integrating World* (New York: Oxford University Press).

World Bank (1996) *Poverty Reduction: The Most Urgent Task* (Washington, DC: World Bank).

World Bank (1997) *World Development Report 1997: The State in a Changing World* (New York: Oxford University Press).

World Bank (2000–1) 'World Development Indicators', in *World Development Report 2000-2001: Attacking Poverty* (New York: Oxford University Press).

World Bank (2001) *Povertynet: Topics Relevant to Social Capital* (New York: Oxford University Press).

World Bank (2003) *World Development Indicators* (New York: Oxford University Press).

World Bank (2004) *World Development Report: Making Services Work for Poor People* (New York: Oxford University Press).

World Bank Atlas (2003) *World Bank Atlas 2003* (Washington, DC: World Bank).

World Bank Group (2002) 'Disability in Developing Countries', World Bank Conference marks the International Day of Disabled.

Worldwatch Institute (2004) *State of the World 2004: Consumption by the Numbers*. Available online at <http://www.worldwatch.org/press/news/2004/01/07/>.

Worrall, A. (1990) *Offending Women: Female Law-Breakers and the Criminal Justice System* (London: Routledge).

Wright, E. O. (1978) *Class, Crisis and the State* (London: New Left Books).

Wright, E. O. (1985) *Classes* (London: Verso).

Wright, E. O. (1997) *Class Counts Comparative Studies in Class Analysis* (Cambridge: Cambridge University Press).

Wright, E. O. (2000) *Class Counts: Student Edition* (New York: Cambridge University Press).

Wright, C. R. (1940) 'Functional Analysis and Mass Communication', *Public Opinion Quarterly* 24.

Wrigley, E. A. (1968) *Population and History* (New York: McGraw-Hill).

Wuthnow, R. (1988) 'Sociology of Religion', in N. J. Smelser, ed., *Handbook of Sociology* (Newbury Park, CA: Sage).

Young, I. M. (1990) *Throwing Like a Girl and Other Essays in Feminist Philosophy and Social Theory* (Bloomington: Indiana University Press).

Young, J. (1998) 'Breaking Windows: Situating the New Criminology', in P. Walton and J. Young, eds, *The New Criminology Revisited* (London: Macmillan).

Young, J. (1999) *The Exclusive Society: Social Exclusion, Crime and Difference in Late Modernity* (London: Sage).

Young, M. and P. Willmott (1973) *The Symmetrical Family: A Study of Work and Leisure in the London Region* (London: Routledge and Kegan Paul).

Zammuner, V. L. (1986) 'Children's Sex-Role Stereotypes: A Cross-Cultural Analysis', in P. Shaver and C. Hendrick, eds, *Sex and Gender* (Beverly Hills, CA: Sage).

Zammuner, V. L. (1987) 'Children's Sex-Role Stereotypes: A Cross-Cultural Analysis', in P. S. C. Hendrick, eds, *Sex and Gender* (London: Sage).

Zeitlin, I. (1984) *Ancient Judaism: Biblical Criticism from Max Weber to the Present* (Cambridge: Polity).

Zeitlin, I. (1988) *The Historical Jesus* (Cambridge: Polity).

Zerubavel, E. (1979) *Patterns of Time in Hospital Life* (Chicago: University of Chicago Press).

Zerubavel, E. (1982) 'The Standardization of Time a Sociohistorical Perspective', *American Journal of Sociology* 88.

Zhang, N. and W. Xu (1995) 'Discovering the Positive within the Negative: The Women's Movement in a Changing China', in A. Basu, ed., *The Challenge of Local Feminisms* (Boulder, CO: Westview).

Zimbardo, P. G. (1969) 'The Human Choice: Individuation, Reason, and Order Versus Deindividuation, Impulse, and Chaos', in W. J. Arnold and D. Levine, eds, *Nebraska Symposium on Motivation* (Lincoln: University of Nebraska Press).

Zimbardo, P. G. (1972) 'Pathology of Imprisonment', *Society* 9.

Zubaida, S. (1996). 'How Successful is the Islamic Republic in Islamizing Iran?' in J. Beinen and J. Stork, eds, *Political Islam Essays from the Middle East Report* (Berkeley: University of California Press).

Zuboff, S. (1988) *In the Age of the Smart Machine: The Future of Work and Power* (New York: Basic Books).

Glossary

Absent father A father who, as a result of divorce or for other reasons, has little or no contact with his children.

Absolute poverty Poverty as defined in terms of the minimum requirements necessary to sustain a healthy existence.

Achieved status Social status based on an individual's effort, rather than traits assigned by biological factors. Examples of achieved status include 'veteran', 'graduate' or 'doctor'.

Affective individualism The belief in romantic attachment as a basis for contracting **marriage** ties.

Age-grade The system found in small traditional cultures according to which people belonging to a similar age group are categorized together and hold similar rights and obligations.

Ageing The combination of biological, psychological and social processes that affect people as they grow older.

Ageism Discrimination or prejudice against a person on the grounds of age.

Agencies of socialization Groups or social contexts within which processes of socialization take place. The family, peer groups, schools, the media and the workplace are all arenas in which cultural learning occurs.

Agrarian societies Societies whose means of subsistence is based on agricultural production (crop-growing).

Alienation The sense that our own abilities, as human beings, are taken over by other entities. The term was originally used by Marx to refer to the projection of human powers onto gods. Subsequently he employed the term to refer to the loss of control on the part of workers over the nature of the labour task, and over the products of their labour. Feuerbach used the term to refer to the establishing of gods or divine forces distinct from human beings.

Alternative medicine Also referred to as complementary medicine, this approach to the treatment and prevention of disease encompasses a wide range of healing techniques which lie outside of, or overlap with, orthodox medical practices. Alternative or complementary medicine embodies a holistic approach to health, addressing both physical and psychological elements of an individual's well-being.

Animism A belief that events in the world are mobilized by the activities of spirits.

Anomie A concept used by Durkheim to describe feelings of aimlessness and despair provoked by the processes of change in the modern world which result in social norms losing their hold over individual behaviour.

Apartheid The official system of racial segregation established in South Africa in 1948 and practised until 1994.

Ascribed status Social status based on biological factors, such as race, sex or age.

Assimilation The acceptance of a minority group by a majority population, in which the group takes on the values and norms of the dominant culture.

Asylum-seeker A person who has applied for refuge in a foreign country due to a fear of religious or political persecution in his or her country of origin.

Authoritarian states Political systems in which the needs and interests of the state take priority over those of average citizens, and popular participation in political affairs is severely limited or denied.

Authority Following Max Weber, many sociologists have argued that authority is the *legitimate* power which one person or a group holds over another. The element of legitimacy is vital to this understanding of authority and is the main means by which authority is distinguished from the more general concept of power. Power can be exerted by the use of force or violence. Authority, by contrast, depends on the acceptance by subordinates of the right of those above them to give them orders or directives.

Automation Production processes monitored and controlled by machines with only minimal supervision from people.

Back region An area away from 'front region' performances, characterized by Erving Goffman, where individuals are able to relax and behave in an informal way.

Bias Generally a preference or an inclination, especially one that inhibits impartial judgment. In statistical sampling or testing, an error caused by systematically favouring some outcomes over others.

Binuclear families A family structure in which a child has parents living in two different homes after separating, both of whom are involved in the child's upbringing.

Biodiversity The diversity of species of life forms.

Biomedical model of health The set of principles underpinning Western medical systems and practices. The biomedical model of health defines diseases objectively, in accordance with the presence of recognized symptoms, and believes that the healthy body can be restored through scientifically based medical treatment. The human body is likened to a machine that can be returned to working order with the proper repairs.

Bisexual An orientation of sexual activities or feelings towards other people of either sex.

Black feminism A strand of feminist thought which highlights the multiple disadvantages of gender, class and race that shape the experiences of non-white women. Black feminists reject the idea of a single unified gender oppression that is experienced evenly by all women, and argue that early feminist analysis reflected the specific concerns of white, middle-class women.

Bureaucracy An organization of a hierarchical sort, which takes the form of a pyramid of authority. The term 'bureaucracy' was popularized by Max Weber. According to Weber, bureaucracy is the most efficient type of large-scale human organization. As organizations grow in size, Weber argued, they inevitably tend to become more and more bureaucratized.

Capital punishment The state-sanctioned execution of a person who has been convicted of a crime that is punishable by death. Capital punishment is commonly known as the 'death penalty'.

Capitalism A system of economic enterprise based on market exchange. 'Capital' refers to any asset, including money, property and machines, which can be used to produce commodities for sale or invested in a market with the hope of achieving a profit. Nearly all industrial societies today are capitalist in orientation – their economic systems are based on free enterprise and on economic competition.

Capitalists Those who own companies, land or stocks and shares, using these to generate economic returns.

Caste A form of stratification in which an individual's social position is fixed at birth and cannot be changed. There is virtually no intermarriage between the members of different caste groups.

Causal relationship A relationship in which one state of affairs (the effect) is brought about by another (the cause).

Causation The causal influence of one factor on another. Causal factors in sociology include the reasons individuals give for what they do, as well as external influences on their behaviour.

Church A large body of people belonging to an established religious organization. Churches normally have a formal structure, with a hierarchy of religious officials, and the term is also used for the building where their religious ceremonials are held.

Citizen A member of a political community, having both rights and duties associated with that membership.

Civil inattention The process whereby individuals who are in the same physical setting of interaction demonstrate to one another that they are aware of each other's presence, without being either threatening or over-friendly.

Civil society The realm of activity which lies between the state and the market, including the family, schools, community associations and non-economic institutions. 'Civil society', or civic culture, is essential to vibrant democratic societies.

Class Although it is one of the most frequently used concepts in sociology, there is no clear agreement about how the notion should best be defined. For Marx a class was a group of people standing in a common relationship to the means of production. Weber also saw class as an economic category, but stressed its interaction with social status and the affinities of 'party'. In recent times, some social scientists have used occupation extensively as an indicator of social class, others have stressed ownership of property and other wealth; still others are looking to lifestyle choices.

Clock time Time as measured by the clock – that is, assessed in terms of hours, minutes and seconds. Before the invention of clocks, time reckoning was based on events in the natural world, such as the rising and setting of the sun.

Cognition Human thought processes involving perception, reasoning, and remembering.

Cohabitation Two people living together in a sexual relationship of some permanence, without being married to each other.

Cold War The situation of conflict between the United States and the Soviet Union, together with their allies, which existed from the late 1940s until 1990. It was a 'Cold War' because the two sides never actually engaged in military confrontation with each other.

Collective consumption A concept used by Manuel Castells to refer to processes of consumption of common goods promoted by the city, such as transport services and leisure amenities.

Colonialism The process whereby Western nations established their rule in parts of the world away from their home territories.

Communication The transmission of information from one individual or group to another. Communication is the necessary basis of all social interaction. In face-to-face contexts, communication is carried on by the use of language, but also by many bodily cues which individuals interpret in understanding what others say and do. With the development of writing and of electronic media like radio, television or computer transmission systems, communication becomes to varying degrees detached from immediate contexts of face-to-face social relationships.

Communism A set of political ideas associated with Marx, as developed particularly by Lenin, and institutionalized in China and, until 1990, in the Soviet Union and Eastern Europe.

Comparative questions Questions concerned with the drawing of comparisons between one context in a society and another, or contrasting examples from different societies, for the purposes of sociological theory or research.

Comparative research Research that compares one set of findings on one society with the same type of findings on other societies.

Complicit masculinity A term associated with R. W. Connell's writings on the gender hierarchy in society. Complicit masculinity is embodied by the many men in society who do not themselves live up to the ideal of hegemonic masculinity, yet benefit from its dominant position in the patriarchal order.

Compulsion of proximity The need felt by individuals to interact with others in face-to-face settings.

Concrete operational stage A stage of cognitive development, as formulated by Piaget, in which the child's thinking is based primarily on physical perception of the world. In this phase, the child is not yet capable of dealing with abstract concepts or hypothetical situations.

Conflict theories A sociological perspective that focuses on the tensions, divisions and competing interests present in human societies. Conflict theorists believe that the scarcity and value of resources in society produces conflict as groups struggle to gain access to and control those resources. Many conflict theorists have been strongly influenced by the writings of Marx.

Confluent love Active and contingent love, as opposed to the 'forever' qualities of **romantic love**.

Control theory A theory which sees crime as the outcome of an imbalance between impulses towards criminal activity and controls which deter it. Control theorists hold that criminals are rational beings who will act to maximize their own reward unless they are rendered unable to do so through either social or physical controls.

Controls A statistical or experimental means of holding some variables constant in order to examine the causal influence of others.

Conurbation A clustering of towns or cities into an unbroken urban environment.

Conversation analysis The empirical study of conversations, employing techniques drawn from ethnomethodology. Conversation analysis examines details of naturally occurring conversations to reveal the organizational principles of talk and its role in the production and reproduction of social order.

Core countries According to world-systems theory, the most advanced industrial countries, which take the lion's share of profits in the world economic system.

Corporate crime Offences committed by large corporations in society. Examples of corporate crime include pollution, false advertising, and violations of health and safety regulations.

Corporate culture A branch of management theory that seeks to increase productivity and competitiveness through the creation of a unique organizational culture involving all members of a firm. A dynamic corporate culture – involving company events, rituals and traditions – is thought to enhance employee loyalty and promote group solidarity.

Correlation A regular relationship between two dimensions or variables, often expressed in statistical terms. Correlations may be positive or negative. A positive correlation between two variables exists where a high rank on one variable is regularly associated with a high rank on the other. A negative correlation exists where a high rank on one variable is regularly associated with a low rank on the other.

Correlation coefficient A measure of the degree of correlation between two variables.

Cosmopolitan A term describing people or societies that share many social qualities as a result of constant exposure to new ideas and values.

Created environment Those aspects of the physical world deriving from the application of technology. Cities are created environments, featuring constructions established by human beings to serve their needs – including roads, railways, factories, offices, private homes and other buildings.

Crime Any action that contravenes the laws established by a political authority. Although we may tend to think of 'criminals' as a distinct subsection of the population, there are few people who have not broken the law in one way or another during the course of their lives. While laws are formulated by state authorities, it is by no means unknown for those authorities to engage in criminal behaviour in certain contexts.

Criminology The study of forms of behaviour that are sanctioned by criminal law.

Crisis of masculinity The belief, held by some, that traditional forms of masculinity are being undermined by a combination of contemporary influences, provoking a critical phase in which men are unsure of themselves and their role in society.

Crude birth rate A statistical measure representing the number of births within a given population per year, normally calculated in terms of the number of births per thousand members. Although the crude birth rate is a useful index, it is only a general measure, because it does not specify numbers of births in relation to age distribution.

Crude death rate A statistical measure representing the number of deaths that occur annually in a given population per year, normally calculated as the ratio of deaths per thousand members. Crude death rates give a general indication of the mortality levels of a community or society, but are limited in their usefulness because they do not take into account the age distribution.

Cult A fragmentary religious grouping, to which individuals are loosely affiliated, but which lacks any permanent structure. Cults quite often form round an inspirational leader.

Cultural pluralism The coexistence of several subcultures within a given society on equal terms.

Cultural reproduction The transmission of cultural values and norms from generation to generation. Cultural reproduction refers to the mechanisms by which continuity of cultural experience is sustained across time. The processes of schooling in modern societies are among the main mechanisms of cultural reproduction, and do not operate solely through what is taught in courses of formal instruction. Cultural reproduction occurs in a more profound way through the hidden curriculum – aspects of behaviour learnt by individuals in an informal way while at school.

Culture of poverty The thesis, popularized by Oscar Lewis, that poverty is not a result of individual inadequacies, but the outcome of a larger social and cultural atmosphere into which successive generations of children are socialized. The 'culture of poverty' refers to the values, beliefs, lifestyles, habits and traditions that are common among people living under conditions of material deprivation.

Culture The values, ceremonies and ways of life characteristic of a given group. Like the concept of society, the notion of culture is very widely used in sociology, as well as in the other social sciences (particularly anthropology). Culture is one of the most distinctive properties of human social association.

Cybercrime Criminal activities by means of electronic networks, or involving the use of new information technologies. Electronic money laundering, personal identity theft, electronic vandalism and monitoring electronic correspondence are all emergent forms of cybercrime.

Cyberspace Electronic networks of interaction between individuals at different computer terminals, linking people at a level – in a dimension – that has no regard for territorial boundaries or physical presence.

Debureaucratization Decline in the predominance of Weberian-style bureaucracies as the typical organizational form within modern society.

Decommodification In the context of welfare provision, the degree to which welfare services are free of the market. In a predominantly decommodified system, welfare services such as education and healthcare are provided to all and are not linked to market processes. In a commodified system, welfare services are treated as commodities to be sold on the market like other goods and services.

Deforestation The destruction of forested land, often by commercial logging.

Degree of dispersal The range or distribution of a set of figures.

Deinstitutionalization The process by which individuals cared for in state facilities are returned to their families or to community-based residences.

Democracy A political system providing for the participation of citizens in political decision-making, often by the election of representatives to governing bodies.

Demographic transition An interpretation of population change, which holds that a stable ratio of births to deaths is achieved once a certain level of economic prosperity has been reached. According to this notion, in pre-industrial societies there is a rough balance between births and deaths, because population increase is kept in check by a lack of available food, and by disease or war. In modern societies, by contrast, population equilibrium is achieved because families are moved by economic incentives to limit the number of children.

Demography The study of the characteristics of human populations, including their size, composition and dynamics.

Denomination A religious sect which has lost its revivalist dynamism, and has become an institutionalized body, commanding the adherence of significant numbers of people.

Dependency culture A term popularized by Charles Murray to describe individuals who rely on state welfare provision rather than entering the labour market. The dependency culture is seen as the outcome of the 'nanny state' which undermines individual ambition and people's capacity for self-help.

Dependency ratio The ratio of people of dependent ages (children and the elderly) to people of economically active ages.

Dependency theory Theory of economic development derived from Marxism arguing that the poverty of low-income countries stems directly from their exploitation by wealthy countries and the transnational corporations that are based in wealthy countries.

Dependent variable A variable, or factor, causally influenced by another (the independent variable).

Desertification Instances of intense land degradation resulting in desert-like conditions over large areas.

Developmental questions Questions posed by sociologists when looking at the origins and path of development of social institutions from the past to the present.

Deviance Modes of action which do not conform to the norms or values held by most of the members of a group or society. What is regarded as 'deviant' is as widely variable as the norms and values that distinguish different cultures and subcultures from one another. Many forms of behaviour which are highly esteemed in one context, or by one group, are regarded negatively by others.

Deviancy amplification The unintended consequences that can result when by labelling a behaviour as deviant, an agency of control actually provokes more of the same behaviour. For example, the reactions of police, the media and the public to perceived acts of deviance can 'amplify' the deviance itself, creating a 'spiral of deviancy'.

Deviant subculture A subculture whose members have values which differ substantially from those of the majority in a society.

Diaspora The dispersal of an ethnic population from an original homeland into foreign areas, often in a forced manner or under traumatic circumstances.

Discourses The frameworks of thinking in a particular area of social life. For instance, the discourse of criminality means how people in a given society think and talk about crime.

Discrimination Activities that deny to the members of a particular group resources or rewards which can be obtained by others. Discrimination has to be distinguished from prejudice, although the two are usually quite closely associated. It can be the case that individuals who are prejudiced against others do not engage in discriminatory practices against them; conversely, people may act in a discriminatory fashion even though they are not prejudiced against those subject to such discrimination.

Disengagement theory A functionalist theory of ageing that holds that it is functional for society to remove people from their traditional roles when they become elderly, thereby freeing up those roles for others.

Displacement The transferring of ideas or emotions from their true source to another object.

Division of labour The division of a production system into specialized work tasks or occupations, creating economic interdependence. All societies have at least a rudimentary form of division of labour, especially between the tasks allocated to men and those performed by women. With the development of industrialism, however, the division of labour became vastly more complex than in any prior type of production system. In the modern world, it is international in scope.

Doubling time The time it takes for a particular level of population to double.

Dramaturgical analysis An approach to the study of social interaction based on the use of metaphors derived from the theatre.

Dysfunction Features of social life that challenge or create tensions in a social system.

Eco-efficiency The development of technologies that generate economic growth, but which do so at minimal cost to the environment.

Ecological modernization Economic growth and development that incorporate positive policies for the environment. Supporters of ecological modernization believe that industrial development and ecological protection are not incompatible.

Economic interdependence The outcome of specialization and the division of labour, when self-sufficiency is superseded and individuals depend on others to produce many or most of the goods they need to sustain their lives.

Economy The system of production and exchange which provides for the material needs of individuals living in a given society. Economic institutions are of key importance in all social orders. What goes on in the economy usually influences many other aspects of social life. Modern economies differ very substantially from traditional ones, because the majority of the population is no longer engaged in agricultural production.

Education The transmission of knowledge from one generation to another by means of direct instruction. Although educational processes exist in all societies, it is only in the modern period that mass education has taken the form of schooling – that is, instruction in specialized educational environments in which individuals spend several years of their lives.

Egocentric According to Piaget, the characteristic quality of a child during the early years of her life. Egocentric thinking involves understanding objects and events in the environment solely in terms of the child's own position.

Elaborated code A form of speech involving the deliberate and constructed use of words to designate precise meanings, and adaptable to various cultural settings.

Embourgeoisement thesis The process by which bourgeois aspirations, and a bourgeois standard and style of life, becomes institutionalized in the working class. Marxists have argued that this phenomenon undermines working class consciousness and frustrates working class attempts to create social change.

Emigration The movement of people out of one country in order to settle in another.

Emotional intelligence The ability of individuals to use their emotions to develop qualities such as empathy, self-control, enthusiasm and persistence.

Emphasized femininity A term associated with R. W. Connell's writings on the gender hierarchy in society. Emphasized femininity forms an important complement to hegemonic masculinity, because it is oriented to accommodating the interests and needs of men. Many representations of women in the media and advertising embody emphasized femininity.

Empirical investigation Factual inquiry carried out in any given area of sociological study.

Encounter A meeting between two or more individuals in a situation of face-to-face interaction. Our day-to-day lives can be seen as a series of different encounters strung out across the course of the day. In modern societies, many of the encounters we have with others involve strangers rather than people we know well.

Endogamy The forbidding of marriage or sexual relations outside one's social group.

Environmental ecology A concern with preserving the integrity of the physical environment in the face of the impact of modern industry and technology.

Epidemiology The study of the distribution and incidence of disease and illness within the population.

Estate A form of stratification involving inequalities between groups of individuals established by law.

Ethical religions Religions which depend on the ethical appeal of a 'great teacher' (like Buddha or Confucius), rather than on a belief in supernatural beings.

Ethnic cleansing The creation of ethnically homogeneous territories through the mass expulsion of other ethnic populations.

Ethnicity Cultural values and norms which distinguish the members of a given group from others. An ethnic group is one whose members share a distinct awareness of a common cultural identity, separating them from other groups around them. In virtually all societies ethnic differences are associated with variations in power and material wealth. Where ethnic differences are also regarded as racial, such divisions are sometimes especially pronounced.

Ethnie A term used by Anthony Smith to describe a group that shares ideas of common ancestry, a common cultural identity and a link with a specific homeland.

Ethnocentric Understanding the ideas or practices of another culture in terms of those of one's own culture. Ethnocentric judgements fail to recognize the true qualities of other cultures. An ethnocentric individual is someone who is unable, or unwilling, to look at other cultures in their own terms.

Ethnography The study of people at first-hand using participant observation or interviewing.

Ethnomethodology The study of how people make sense of what others say and do in the course of day-to-day social interaction. Ethnomethodology is concerned with the 'ethnomethods' by means of which human beings sustain meaningful interchanges with one another.

Evangelicalism A form of Protestantism characterized by a belief in spiritual rebirth (being 'born again').

Experiment A research method in which a hypothesis can be tested in a controlled and systematic way, either in an artificial situation constructed by the researcher, or in naturally occurring settings.

Exploitation A social or institutional relationship in which one party benefits at the expense of the other through an imbalance in power.

Extended family A family group consisting of close relatives extending beyond a couple and their children living either within the same household or in a close and continuous relationship with one another.

External risk Dangers that spring from the natural world and are unrelated to the actions of humans. Examples of external risk include droughts, earthquakes, famines and storms.

Factual questions Questions that raise issues concerning matters of fact (rather than theoretical or moral issues).

Family A group of individuals related to one another by blood ties, marriage or adoption, who form an economic unit, the adult members of which are responsible for the upbringing of children. All known societies involve some form of family system, although the nature of family relationships is widely variable. While in modern societies the main family form is the nuclear family, a variety of extended family relationships are also often found.

Family capitalism Capitalistic enterprise owned and administered by entrepreneurial families.

Fecundity A measure of the number of children that it is biologically possible for a woman to produce.

Feminist theories A sociological perspective which emphasizes the centrality of gender in analysing the social world, and particularly the uniqueness of the experience of women. There are many strands of feminist theory, but they all share in common the desire to explain gender inequalities in society and to work to overcome them.

Fertility The average number of live-born children produced by women of child-bearing age in a particular society.

First World The group of nation-states that possesses mature industrialized economies, based on capitalistic production.

Flexible production Process in which computers design customized products for a mass market.

Focused interaction Interaction between individuals engaged in a common activity or a direct conversation with one another.

Fordism The system pioneered by Henry Ford, involving the introduction of the moving assembly line, and crucially linking methods of mass production to the cultivation of a mass market for the goods produced – in Ford's case particularly his famous Model T Ford car.

Formal operational stage According to Piaget's theory, a stage of cognitive development at which the growing child becomes capable of handling abstract concepts and hypothetical situations.

Formal relations Relations which exist in groups and organizations laid down by the norms or rules of the 'official' system of authority.

Front region A setting of social activity in which individuals seek to put on a definite 'performance' for others.

Functionalism A theoretical perspective based on the notion that social events can best be explained in terms of the functions they perform – that is, the contributions they make to the continuity of a society – and on a view of society as a complex system whose various parts work in a relationship to each other in a way that needs to be understood.

Fundamentalism A belief in returning to the literal meanings of scriptural texts.

Fundamentalism may arise as a response to modernization and rationalization, insisting on faith-based answers, and defending tradition by using traditional grounds.

Gender inequality The differences in the status, power and prestige women and men have in groups, collectivities and societies.

Gender order A term associated with the writings of R. W. Connell, the gender order represents patterns of power relations between masculinities and femininities that are widespread throughout society.

Gender regime The configuration of gender relations within a particular setting, such as a school, a family or a neighbourhood.

Gender relations The societally patterned interactions between men and women.

Gender roles Social roles assigned to each sex and labelled as masculine or feminine.

Gender Social expectations about behaviour regarded as appropriate for the members of each sex. Gender does not refer to the physical attributes in terms of which men and women differ, but to socially formed traits of masculinity and femininity. The study of gender relations has become one of the most important areas of sociology in recent years, although for a long time they received little attention.

Gender socialization How individuals develop different gender characteristics in the course of socialization processes.

Generalized other A concept in the theory of George Herbert Mead, according to which the individual takes over the general values of a given group or society during the socialization process.

Genetically modified organisms GMOs are plants or crops that have been produced through manipulation of the genes that compose them.

Genocide The systematic, planned destruction of a racial, political or cultural group.

Genre A concept applied in media studies to refer to a distinct type of media product or cultural item. In the world of television, for example, different genres include soap opera, comedy, news programmes, sport and drama.

Gentrification A process of urban renewal in which older, decaying housing is refurbished by affluent people moving into the area.

Global city A city, such as London, New York or Tokyo, which has become an organizing centre of the new global economy.

Global commodity chains A worldwide network of labour and production processes yielding a finished product.

Global governance The framework of rules needed to tackle global problems, and the diverse set of institutions (including both international governmental organizations and national governments) needed to guarantee this framework of rules.

Global village A notion associated with the Canadian writer Marshall McLuhan, who saw the spread of electronic communication as binding the world into a small community. Thus, people in many different parts of the world follow the same news events through television programming.

Global warming The gradual increase in temperature of the earth's atmosphere. Global warming, or the 'greenhouse effect', occurs as built-up carbon dioxide traps the sun's rays and heats up the earth. The effects of global warming are potentially devastating, including floods, droughts and other changes to the world climate.

Globalization Growing interdependence between different peoples, regions and countries in the world as social and economic relationships come to stretch worldwide.

Government The regular enactment of policies, decisions and matters of state by officials within a political apparatus. We can speak of 'government' as a process, or the government to refer to the political authorities overseeing the implementation of their policies by officials. While in the past virtually all governments were headed by monarchs or emperors, in most modern societies the political authorities are elected and their officials are appointed on the basis of expertise and qualifications.

Greenhouse effect The build-up of heat-trapping greenhouse gases within the earth's atmosphere. While a 'natural' greenhouse effect keeps the earth's temperatures at a comfortable level, the build-up of high concentrations of greenhouse gases through human activities has been linked to global warming.

Greying A term used to indicate that an increasing proportion of a society's population is becoming elderly.

Gross Domestic Product (GDP) All the goods and services on record as being produced by a country's economy in a particular year, regardless of who owns these factors.

Gross National Income (GNI) Gross Domestic Product plus net property income (interest, rent, dividends and profits) from abroad. (The term GNI is now used in preference to a Gross National Product, or GNP, an older but similar measure.)

Group closure The means whereby a group establishes a clear boundary for itself and thereby separates itself from other groups.

Group production Production organized by means of small groups rather than individuals.

Health transition The shift from acute, infectious diseases to chronic non-infectious diseases as the main cause of death in a society. In industrialized societies which have undergone the health transition, infectious diseases such as tuberculosis, cholera and malaria have been practically eradicated and chronic diseases such as cancer and heart disease have become the most common cause of death.

Hegemonic masculinity A term first introduced by R. W. Connell, hegemonic masculinity refers to the dominant form of masculinity within the gender hierarchy. Although hegemonic masculinity subordinates other masculinities and femininities, it can be challenged by them. In most Western societies today, hegemonic masculinity is associated with whiteness, heterosexuality, marriage, authority and physical toughness.

Heterosexuality An orientation in sexual activity or feelings towards people of the opposite sex.

Hidden curriculum Traits of behaviour or attitudes that are learned at school, but which are not included within the formal curriculum. The hidden curriculum is the 'unstated agenda' involved in schooling – conveying, for example, aspects of gender differences.

Higher education Education beyond school level, in colleges or universities.

High-trust systems Organizations, or work settings, in which individuals are permitted a great deal of autonomy and control over the work task.

Homeless People who have no place to sleep and either stay in free shelters or sleep in public places not meant for habitation.

Homophobia An irrational fear or disdain of homosexuals.

Homosexual masculinity According to R. W. Connell's model of gender relations, homosexual masculinity is stigmatized and located at the bottom of the gender hierarchy for men. In the prevailing gender order, homosexuals are seen as the opposite of the 'real man' embodied by hegemonic masculinity.

Homosexuality An orientation of sexual activities or feelings towards others of the same sex.

Housework (domestic labour): Unpaid work carried on, usually by women, in the home; domestic chores such as cooking, cleaning, and shopping.

Human resource management A branch of management theory that regards employee enthusiasm and commitment as essential to economic competitiveness. The human resource management (HRM) approach seeks to develop in workers the sense that they have an investment in company products and in the work process itself.

Hunting and gathering societies Societies whose mode of subsistence is gained from hunting animals, fishing and gathering edible plants.

Hyperreality An idea associated with the French author Jean Baudrillard. Baudrillard argues that, as a result of the spread of electronic communication, there is no longer a separate 'reality' to which TV programmes and other cultural products refer. Instead, what we take to be 'reality' is structured by such communication itself. So the items reported on the news are not just about a separate series of events, but actually themselves define and construct what those events are.

Hypothesis An idea, or an educated guess, about a given state of affairs, put forward as a basis for empirical testing.

Ideal type A 'pure type', constructed by emphasizing certain traits of a given social item into an analytical model which does not necessarily exist anywhere in reality. The traits are defining, not necessarily desirable, ones. An example is Max Weber's ideal type of bureaucratic organization.

Identity The distinctive characteristics of a person's character or the character of a group which relate to who they are and what is meaningful to them. Some of the main sources of identity include gender, sexual orientation, nationality or ethnicity, and social class. An important marker of an individual's identity is his or her name, and naming is also important for group identity.

Ideology Shared ideas or beliefs which serve to justify the interests of dominant groups. Ideologies are found in all societies in which there are systematic and ingrained inequalities between groups. The concept of ideology has a close connection with that of power, since ideological systems serve to legitimize the differential power held by groups.

Immigration The movement of people into one country from another for the purpose of settlement.

Impression management An idea associated with the American sociologist Erving Goffman. People 'manage' or control the impressions others have of them by choosing what to conceal and what to reveal when they meet other people.

Incest Sexual activity between close family members.

Independent variable A variable, or factor, that causally influences another (the dependent variable).

Individual model of disability A theory that holds that individual limitations are the main cause of the problems experienced by disabled people: bodily 'abnormality' is seen as causing some degree of 'disability' or functional limitation. This functional limitation is seen as the basis for a wider classification of an individual as 'an invalid'. The individual model of disability has been criticized by supporters of the social model of disability.

Industrial Revolution The broad spectrum of social and economic transformations that surrounded the development of modern forms of industry. The Industrial Revolution launched the process of industrialization.

Industrial societies Societies in which the vast majority of the labour force works in industrial production.

Industrialization The development of modern forms of industry – factories, machines and large-scale production processes. Industrialization has been one of the main sets of processes influencing the social world over the past two centuries. Those societies which are industrialized have characteristics quite different from those of the less developed countries. For instance, with the advance of industrialization only a tiny proportion of the population works in agriculture – a major contrast with pre-industrial countries.

Infant mortality rate The number of infants who die during the first year of life, per thousand live births.

Informal economy Economic transactions carried on outside the sphere of orthodox paid employment.

Informal relations Relations which exist in groups and organizations developed on the basis of personal connections; ways of doing things that depart from formally recognized modes of procedure.

Information poverty The 'information poor' are people who have little or no access to information technology, such as computers.

Information society A society no longer based primarily on the production of material goods but on the production of knowledge. The notion of the information society is closely bound up with the rise of information technology.

Information technology Forms of technology based on information processing and requiring microelectronic circuitry.

Institutional capitalism Capitalistic enterprise organized on the basis of institutional shareholding.

Institutional racism Patterns of discrimination based on ethnicity that have become structured into existing social institutions.

Intelligence Level of intellectual ability, particularly as measured by IQ (intelligence quotient) tests.

Interactional vandalism The deliberate subversion of the tacit rules of conversation.

Intergenerational mobility Movement up or down a social stratification hierarchy from one generation to another.

International governmental organization (IGO) An international organization established by treaties between governments for the purpose of conducting business between the nations making up its membership.

International non-governmental organizations (INGOs) An international organization established by agreements between the individuals or private organizations making up its membership.

Internet A global system of connections between computers allowing people to communicate with one another and find information on the World Wide Web by visuals, sounds and text in a way that escapes the time and space, and the cost, limitations of distance – and also the control of territorial governments.

Internet-based learning Educational activity connected through the medium of the internet.

Intragenerational mobility Movement up or down a social stratification hierarchy within the course of a personal career.

IQ Short for 'intelligence quotient', a score attained on tests consisting of a mixture of conceptual and computational problems.

Iron law of oligarchy A term coined by Weber's student Roberto Michels, meaning that large organizations tend towards the centralization of power in the hands of the few, making democracy difficult.

Job insecurity A sense of apprehension experienced by employees about both the stability of their work position and their role within the workplace.

Kinship A relation which links individuals through blood ties, marriage or adoption. Kinship relations are by definition involved in marriage and the family, but extend much more broadly than these institutions. While in most modern societies few social obligations are involved in kinship relations extending beyond the immediate family, in many other cultures kinship is of vital importance for most aspects of social life.

Knowledge economy A society no longer based primarily on the production of material goods but on the production of knowledge. Its emergence has been linked to the development of a broad base of consumers who are technologically literate and have made new advances in computing, entertainment and telecommunications part of their lives.

Knowledge society Another common term for information society – a society based on the production and consumption of knowledge and information.

Kuznets Curve A formula showing that inequality increases during the early stages of capitalist development, then declines, and eventually stabilizes at a relatively low level; advanced by the economist Simon Kuznets.

Labelling theory An approach to the study of deviance which suggests that people become 'deviant' because certain labels are attached to their behaviour by political authorities and others.

Latent functions Functional consequences that are not intended or recognized by the members of a social system in which they occur.

Lateral mobility Movement of individuals from one region of a country to another, or across countries.

Left Realism A strain of criminology, popularized in the 1980s by the work of Jock Young, that focused on the victims of crime and called for criminology to engage practically with issues of crime control and social policy.

Legitimacy A particular political order gains legitimacy if most of those governed by it recognize it as just and valid.

Lesbianism Homosexual activities or attachment between women.

Liberal democracy A system of democracy based on parliamentary institutions, coupled to the free market system in the area of economic production.

Liberal feminism A form of feminist theory that believes that gender inequality is produced by reduced access for women and girls to civil rights and certain social resources, such as education and employment. Liberal feminists tend to seek solutions through changes in legislation that ensure the rights of individuals are protected.

Life course The various transitions people experience during their lives.

Life expectancy The length of time people can on average expect to live when born. Specifically, the concept refers to the number of years a newborn infant can be expected to live if prevailing patterns of mortality at the time of its birth stay the same throughout its life, regardless of gender.

Life histories Studies of the overall lives of individuals, often based both on self-reporting and on documents such as letters.

Lifelong learning The idea that learning and the acquisition of skills should occur at all stages of an individual's life, not simply in the formal educational system early in life. Adult continuing education programmes, mid-career training, Internet-based learning opportunities and community-based 'learning banks' are all ways in which individuals can engage in lifelong learning.

Lifelong literacy The ability to read and write.

Life-span The maximum length of life that is biologically possible for a member of a given species.

Lifestyle choices Decisions made by individuals about their consumption of goods, services and culture. Lifestyle choices have been seen by many sociologists as important reflections of class positions.

Low-trust systems An organizational or work setting in which individuals are allowed little responsibility for, or control over, the work task.

Macrosociology The study of large-scale groups, organizations or social systems.

Male breadwinner Until recently in many industrialized societies, the traditional role of the man in providing for the family through employment outside the home. The 'male breadwinner model' has declined in significance with changes in family patterns and the steady growth in the numbers of women entering the labour market.

Male inexpressiveness The difficulties men have in expressing, or talking about, their feelings to others.

Malthusianism The idea, first advanced by Thomas Malthus two centuries ago, that population growth tends to outstrip the resources available to support it. Malthus argued that people must limit their frequency of sexual intercourse in order to avoid excessive population growth and a future of misery and starvation.

Managerial capitalism Capitalistic enterprises administered by managerial executives rather than by owners.

Manifest functions The functions of a type of social activity that are known to and intended by the individuals involved in the activity.

Manufactured risk Dangers that are created by the impact of human knowledge and technology upon the natural world. Examples of manufactured risk include global warming and genetically modified foods.

Market-oriented theories Theories about economic development that assume that the best possible economic consequences will result if individuals are free to make their own economic decisions, uninhibited by governmental constraint.

Marriage A socially approved sexual relationship between two individuals. Marriage almost always involves two persons of opposite sexes, but in some cultures types of homosexual marriage are tolerated. Marriage normally forms the basis of a family of procreation – that is, it is expected that the married couple will produce and bring up children. Many societies permit polygamy, in which an individual may have several spouses at the same time.

Mass customization The large-scale production of items designed for particular customers through the use of new technologies.

Mass media Forms of communication, such as newspapers, magazines, radio and television, designed to reach mass audiences.

Mass production The production of long runs of goods using machine power. Mass production was one outcome of the Industrial Revolution.

Master status The status or statuses that generally take priority over other indicators of social standing and determine a person's overall position in society.

Materialist conception of history The view developed by Marx according to which 'material' or economic factors have a prime role in determining historical change.

Maternal deprivation The absence of a stable and affectionate relationship between a child and its mother early in life. John Bowlby argued that maternal deprivation can lead to mental illness or deviant behaviour later in life.

Matrilineal Relating to, based on, or tracing ancestral descent through the maternal line.

Matrilocal Of family systems in which the husband is expected to live near the wife's parents.

Mean A statistical measure of central tendency, or average, based on dividing a total by the number of individual cases.

Means of production The means whereby the production of material goods is carried on in a society, including not just technology but the social relations between producers.

Means-tested benefits Welfare services that are available only to citizens who meet certain criteria based not only on need but on levels of income and savings.

Measures of central tendency These are ways of calculating averages, the three most common being the mean, the median and the mode.

Media imperialism A version of imperialism enabled by communications technology, claimed by some to have produced a cultural empire in which media content originating in the industrialized countries is imposed on less developed nations which lack the resources to maintain their cultural independence.

Media regulation The use of legal means to control media ownership and the content of media communications.

Median The number that falls halfway in a range of numbers – a way of calculating central tendency that is sometimes more useful than calculating a mean.

Medical gaze In modern medicine, the detached and value-free approach taken by medical specialists in viewing and treating a sick patient.

Megacities A term favoured by Manuel Castells to describe large, intensely concentrated urban spaces that serve as connection points for the global economy. It is projected that by 2015, there will be thirty-six 'megacities' with populations of more than eight million residents.

Megalopolis The 'city of all cities', a term coined in ancient Greece to refer to a city-state that was planned to be the envy of all civilizations, but used in modern times to refer to very large – or overlarge – conurbations.

Melting pot The idea that ethnic differences can be combined to create new patterns of behaviour drawing on diverse cultural sources.

Meritocracy A system in which social positions are filled on the basis of individual merit and achievement, rather than ascribed criteria such as inherited wealth, sex or social background.

Metanarratives Broad, overarching theories or beliefs about the operation of society and the nature of social change. Marxism and functionalism are examples of metanarratives that have been employed by sociologists to explain how the world works. Postmodernists reject such 'grand theories', arguing that it is impossible to identify any fundamental truths underpinning human society.

Microsociology The study of human behaviour in contexts of face-to-face interaction.

Middle class A broad spectrum of people working in many different occupations, from employees in the service industry to school teachers to medical professionals. Because of the expansion of professional, managerial and administrative occupations in advanced societies, the middle class may encompass the majority of the population in countries like Britain.

Minority group A group of people in a minority in a given society who, because of their distinct physical or cultural characteristics, find themselves in situations of inequality within that society. Such groups include ethnic minorities.

Mode of production Within Marxism, the constitutive characteristic of a society based on the socio-economic system predominant within it – for example, capitalism, feudalism or socialism.

Mode The number that appears most often in a given set of data. This can sometimes be a helpful way of portraying central tendency.

Modernization theory A version of market-oriented development theory that argues that low-income societies develop economically only if they give up their traditional ways and adopt modern economic institutions, technologies, and cultural values that emphasize savings and productive investment.

Monarchies Those political systems headed by a single person whose power is passed down through their family across generations.

Monogamy A form of marriage in which each married partner is allowed only one spouse at any given time.

Monopoly A situation in which a single firm dominates in a given industry.

Monotheism Belief in one, single God.

Moral panic A term popularized by Stanley Cohen to describe a media-inspired overreaction to a certain group or type of behaviour that is taken as symptomatic of general social disorder. Moral panics often arise around events that are in fact relatively trivial in terms of the nature of the act and the number of people involved.

Mortality The number of deaths in a population.

Multiculturalism Ethnic groups exist separately and share equally in economic and political life.

Multimedia The combination of what used to be different media requiring different technologies (for instance, visuals and sound) on a single medium, such as a CD-ROM, which can be played on a computer.

Nanotechnology The science and technology of building electronic circuits and devices with, according to a broad definition, dimensions of less than 100 nanometres (one nanometre is one-billionth of a metre).

Nationalism A set of beliefs and symbols expressing identification with a given national community.

Nations without states Instances in which the members of a nation lack political sovereignty over the area they claim as their own.

Nation-state A particular type of state, characteristic of the modern world, in which a government has sovereign power within a defined territorial area, and the mass of the population are citizens who know themselves to be part of a single nation. Nation-states are closely associated with the rise of nationalism, although nationalist loyalties do not always conform to the boundaries of specific states that exist today. Nation-states developed as part of an emerging nation-state system, originating in Europe, but in current times spanning the whole globe.

Neo-liberalism The economic belief that free market forces, achieved by minimizing government restrictions on business, provide the only route to economic growth.

Neo-local residence involves the creation of a new household each time a child marries or when she or he reaches adulthood and becomes economically active.

Network A set of informal and formal social ties that links people to each other.

New Age movement A general term to describe the diverse spectrum of beliefs and practices oriented on inner spirituality. Paganism, Eastern mysticism, shamanism, alternative forms of healing, and astrology are all examples of 'New Age' activities.

New criminology A branch of criminological thought, prominent in Britain in the 1970s, that regarded deviance as deliberately chosen and often political in nature. The 'new criminologists' argued that crime and deviance could only be understood in the context of power and inequality within society.

New Labour The reforms introduced by Tony Blair when he assumed leadership of the British Labour Party, and by means of which he sought to move the party in new directions, particularly in the early days by a successful campaign to abolish Clause 4, which committed the party to a policy of widespread public ownership of industry.

New migration A term referring to changes in patterns of migration in Europe in the years following 1989. The 'new migration' has been influenced by the end of the Cold War and the fall of the Berlin Wall, the prolonged ethnic conflict in the former Yugoslavia, and the process of European integration, altering the dynamics between traditional 'countries of origin' and 'countries of destination'.

New racism Racist outlooks, also referred to as cultural racism, that are predicated on cultural or religious differences, rather than biological ones.

New religious movements The broad range of religious and spiritual groups, cults and sects that have emerged alongside mainstream religions. NRMs range from spiritual and self-help groups within the New Age movement to exclusive sects such as the Hare Krishnas.

New social movements A set of social movements that have arisen in Western societies since the 1960s in response to the changing risks facing human societies. NSMs such as feminism, environmentalism, the anti-nuclear movement, protests against genetically modified food, and 'anti-globalization' demonstrations differ from earlier social movements in that they are single-issue campaigns oriented to non-material ends and draw support from across class lines.

Newly industrialized countries Third World economies which over the past two or three decades have begun to develop a strong industrial base, such as Brazil and Singapore.

Non-verbal communication Communication between individuals based on facial expression or bodily gesture, rather than on the use of language.

Norms Rules of behaviour which reflect or embody a culture's values, either prescribing a given type of behaviour, or forbidding it. Norms are always backed by sanctions of one kind or another, varying from informal disapproval to physical punishment or execution.

Nuclear family A family group consisting of mother, father (or one of these) and dependent children.

Occupation Any form of paid employment in which an individual works in a regular way.

Occupational gender segregation The way that men and women are concentrated in different types of jobs, based on prevailing understandings of what is appropriate 'male' and 'female' work.

Oligopoly The domination of a small number of firms in a given industry.

Oral history Interviews with people about events they witnessed or experienced earlier in their lives.

Organic solidarity According to Emile Durkheim, the social cohesion that results from the various parts of a society functioning as an integrated whole.

Organization A large group of individuals, involving a definite set of authority relations. Many types of organization exist in industrial societies, influencing most aspects of our lives. While not all organizations are bureaucratic in a formal sense, there are quite close links between the development of organizations and bureaucratic tendencies.

Participant observation A method of research widely used in sociology and anthropology, in which the researcher takes part in the activities of a group or community being studied.

Participatory democracy A system of democracy in which all members of a group or community participate collectively in the taking of major decisions.

Party A group of individuals who work together because they have common backgrounds, aims or interests. According to Weber, party is one of the factors, alongside class and status, that shape patterns of social stratification.

Pastoral societies Societies whose subsistence derives from the rearing of domesticated animals; there is often a need to migrate between different areas according to seasonal changes or to seek fresh grazing.

Pathologies Literally, the scientific study of the nature of diseases, their causes, processes, development and consequences.

Patriarchy The dominance of men over women. All known societies are patriarchal, although there are variations in the degree and nature of the power men exercise, as compared with women. One of the prime objectives of women's movements in modern societies is to combat existing patriarchal institutions.

Patrilineal Relating to, based on, or tracing ancestral descent through the paternal line.

Patrilocal Of family systems in which the wife is expected to live near the husband's parents.

Pauperization Literally, to make a pauper of, or impoverish. Marx used the term to describe the process by which the working class grows increasingly impoverished in relation to the capitalist class.

Peer group A friendship group composed of individuals of similar age and social **status.**

Peripheral countries Countries that have a marginal role in the world economy and are thus dependent on the core-producing societies for their trading relationships.

Personal space The physical space individuals maintain between themselves and others; it may vary between intimate distance for close relationships, social distance for formal encounters and public distance when confronted by an audience.

Personality stabilization According to functionalists, the family plays a crucial role in assisting its adult members emotionally. Marriage between adult men and women is the arrangement through which adult personalities are supported and kept healthy.

Pilot studies Trial runs in survey research.

Plastic sexuality Sexuality freed from the needs of reproduction and moulded by the individual.

Political party An organization established with the aim of achieving governmental power by electoral means and using that power to pursue a specific programme.

Politics The means by which power is employed and contested to influence the nature and content of governmental activities. The sphere of the 'political' includes the activities of those in government, but also the actions and competing interests of many other groups and individuals.

Polyandry A form of marriage in which a woman may simultaneously have two or more husbands.

Polycentric transnationals Transnational corporations whose administrative structure is global but whose corporate practices are adapted according to local circumstances.

Polygamy A form of marriage in which a person may have two or more spouses simultaneously.

Polygyny A form of marriage in which a man may have more than one wife at the same time.

Polytheism Belief in two or more gods.

Population In the context of social research, the people who are the focus of a study or survey.

Portfolio worker A worker who possesses a diversity of skills or qualifications and is therefore able to move easily from job to job.

Positivism In regard to sociology, the view that the study of the social world should be conducted according to the principles of natural science. A positivist approach to sociology holds that objective knowledge can be produced through careful observation, comparison and experimentation.

Post-Fordism A general term used to describe the transition from mass industrial production, characterized by Fordist methods, to more flexible forms of production favouring innovation and aimed at meeting market demands for customized products.

Post-industrial society A notion advocated by those who believe that processes of social change are taking us beyond the industrialized order. A post-industrial society is based on the production of information rather than material goods. According to post-industrialists, we are currently experiencing a series of social changes as profound as those that initiated the industrial era some two hundred years ago.

Postmodern feminism Postmodern feminism draws on the general features of postmodernism in rejecting the idea of single explanations or philosophies. Feminist postmodernism involves, amongst other things, opposition to essentialism (the belief that differences between men and women are innate rather than socially/experientially constructed), and a belief in more plural kinds of knowledge.

Postmodernism The belief that society is no longer governed by history or progress. Postmodern society is highly pluralistic and diverse, with no 'grand narrative' guiding its development.

Poverty line An official measure used by governments to define those living below this income level as living in poverty. Many states have an established poverty line, although Britain does not.

Power The ability of individuals, or the members of a group, to achieve aims or further the interests they hold. Power is a pervasive aspect of all human relationships. Many conflicts in society are struggles over power, because how much power an individual or group is able to achieve governs how far they are able to realize their own wishes at the expense of the wishes of others.

Precautionary principle The presumption that, where there is sufficient doubt about the possible risks of new departures, it is better to maintain existing practices than to change them.

Prejudice The holding of preconceived ideas about an individual or group, ideas that are resistant to change even in the face of new information. Prejudice may be either positive or negative.

Pre-operational stage A stage of cognitive development, in Piaget's theory, in which the child has advanced sufficiently to master basic modes of logical thought.

Primary deviance In the sociology of deviance, an initial act of crime or deviance. According to Edwin Lemert, acts at the level of primary deviance remain marginal to an individual's self-identity. A process usually occurs by which the deviant act is normalized.

Primary socialization The process by which children learn the cultural norms of the society into which they are born. Primary socialization occurs largely in the family.

Procreative technology Techniques of influencing the human reproductive process.

Profane That which belongs to the mundane, everyday world.

Proletariat To Marx, the working class under capitalism.

Prophets Religious leaders who mobilize followers through their interpretation of sacred texts.

Prostitution The sale of sexual favours.

Psychopathic A specific personality type. Such individuals lack the moral sense and concern for others that most normal people have.

Public sphere An idea associated with the German sociologist Jürgen Habermas. The public sphere is the arena of public debate and discussion in modern societies.

Pure relationship A relationship of sexual and emotional equality.

Push and pull factors In the early study of global migration, these were the internal and external forces believed to influence patterns of migration. 'Push factors' refer to dynamics within the country of origin, such as unemployment, war, famine or political persecution. 'Pull factors' describe features of destination countries, such as a buoyant labour market, lower population density and a high standard of living.

Quality circle (QC) Types of industrialized group production, where workers use their expertise to actively participate in decision-making.

Queer theory Queer theory argues that sociology and other disciplines are prejudiced towards heterosexuals, and that non-heterosexual voices must be brought to the fore in order to challenge the heterosexual assumptions that underlie much contemporary thinking.

Race A set of social relationships which allow individuals and groups to be located, and various attributes or competencies assigned, on the basis of biologically grounded features.

Racialization The process by which understandings of race are used to classify individuals or groups of people. Racial distinctions are more than ways of describing human differences: they are important factors in the reproduction of patterns of power and inequality.

Racism The attributing of characteristics of superiority or inferiority to a population sharing certain physically inherited characteristics. Racism is one specific form of prejudice, focusing on physical variations between people. Racist attitudes became entrenched during the period of colonial expansion by the West, but seem also to rest on mechanisms of prejudice and discrimination found in very many contexts of human societies.

Radical feminism Form of feminist theory that believes that gender inequality is the result of male domination in all aspects of social and economic life.

Random sampling A sampling method in which a sample is chosen so that every member of the population has the same probability of being included.

Rationalization A concept used by Weber to refer to the process by which modes of precise calculation and organization, involving abstract rules and procedures, increasingly come to dominate the social world.

Recidivism Reoffending by individuals previously found guilty of a crime.

Reconstituted family A family in which at least one of the adults has children from a previous union, either living in the home or nearby. Reconstituted families are also known as 'step-families'.

Reflexivity This describes the connections between knowledge and social life. The knowledge we gain about society can affect the way in which we act in it. For instance, reading a survey about the high level of support for a political party might lead an individual to express support for that party too.

Regionalization Divisions of time and space which may be used to 'zone' activities at a very local, domestic level; or the larger division of social and economic life into regional settings or zones at a scale either above or below that of the nation-state.

Reincarnation Rebirth of the soul in another body or form. This belief is most often associated with Hindus and Buddhists.

Relative poverty Poverty defined by reference to the overall standard of living in any given society.

Religion A set of beliefs adhered to by the members of a community, involving symbols regarded with a sense of awe or wonder, together with ritual practices in which members of the community engage. Religions do not universally involve a belief in supernatural entities. Although distinctions between religion and magic are difficult to draw, it is often held that magic is primarily practised by individuals rather than being the focus of community ritual.

Religious economy A theoretical framework within the sociology of religion, which argues that religions can be fruitfully understood as organizations in competition with one another for followers.

Representative democracy A political system in which decisions affecting a community are taken, not by its members as a whole, but by people they have elected for this purpose.

Representative sample A sample from a larger population that is statistically typical of that population.

Research methods The diverse methods of investigation used to gather empirical (factual) material. Numerous different research methods exist in sociology, but perhaps the most commonly used are fieldwork (or participant observation) and survey methods. For many purposes it is useful to combine two or more methods within a single research project.

Resistant femininity A term associated with R. W. Connell's writings on the gender hierarchy in society. Women embodying resistant femininity reject the conventional norms of femininity in society ('emphasized femininity') and adopt liberated lifestyles and identities. Feminism and lesbianism, for example, are forms of resistant femininity that are not subordinated to the dominant role of hegemonic masculinity.

Resource allocation How different social and material resources are shared out between and employed by social groups or other elements of society.

Response cries These seemingly involuntary exclamations individuals make when, for example, being taken by surprise, dropping something inadvertently or expressing pleasure may be part of our controlled management of the details of social life, studied by ethnomethodologists and conversation analysts.

Restorative justice A branch of criminal justice which rejects punitive measures in favour of community-based sentences that attempt to raise awareness among offenders of the effects of their actions.

Restricted code A mode of speech that rests on strongly developed cultural understandings, so that many ideas do not need to be – and are not – put into words.

Revolution A process of political change, involving the mobilizing of a mass social movement, which by the use of violence successfully overthrows an existing regime and forms a new government. A revolution is distinguished from a *coup d'état* because it involves a mass movement and the occurrence of major change in the political system as a whole. A *coup d'état* refers to the seizure of power through the use of arms by individuals who then replace the existing political leaders, but without otherwise radically transforming the governmental system. Revolutions can also be distinguished from rebellions, which involve challenges to the existing political authorities, but again aim at the replacement of personnel rather than the transformation of the political structure as such.

Right realism In criminology, right realism grew out of control theory and political conservatism. It links the perceived escalation of crime and delinquency to a decline in individual responsibility and moral degeneracy. To right realists, crime and deviance are an individual pathology – a set of destructive lawless behaviours actively chosen and perpetrated by individual selfishness, a lack of self-control and morality. Right realists are dismissive of the 'theoretical' approaches to the study of crime.

Risk society A notion associated with the German sociologist Ulrich Beck. Beck argues that industrial society has created many new dangers of risks unknown in previous ages. The risks associated with global warming are one example.

Rituals Formalized modes of behaviour in which the members of a group or community regularly engage. Religion represents one of the main contexts in which rituals are practised, but the scope of ritual behaviour extends well beyond this particular sphere. Most groups have ritual practices of some kind or another.

Romantic love As distinct from passionate love, the idea of romantic love emerged in the eighteenth century, and involves the idea that marriage is based on mutual attraction, rather than on economic reasons. It is a prelude to, but is also in tension with, the idea of a pure relationship.

Sacred That which inspires attitudes of awe or reverence among believers in a given set of religious ideas.

Sampling Studying a proportion of individuals or cases from a larger population as representative of that population as a whole.

Sanction A mode of reward or punishment that reinforces socially expected forms of behaviour.

Scapegoating Blaming an individual or group for wrongs that were not of their doing.

Science In the sense of physical science, the systematic study of the physical world. Science – and sociology as a scientific endeavour – involves the disciplined marshalling of empirical data, combined with the construction of theoretical approaches and theories which illuminate or explain those data. Scientific activity combines the creation of bold new modes of thought with the careful testing of hypotheses and ideas. One major feature which helps distinguish science from other types of idea system (such as that involved in religion) is the assumption that all scientific ideas are open to mutual criticism and revision by members of the scientific community.

Second World The industrialized, formerly communist societies of Eastern Europe and the Soviet Union.

Secondary deviance An idea associated with the American criminologist Edwin Lemert. Primary deviance refers to an initial act which contravenes a norm or law – for instance, stealing an item from a shop. Secondary deviance is where a label becomes attached to the individual who carried out the act, as where the person stealing from the shop is labelled a 'shoplifter'.

Sect A religious movement which breaks away from orthodoxy.

Secularization A process of decline in the influence of religion. Although modern societies have become increasingly secular, tracing the extent of secularization is a complex matter. Secularization can refer to levels of involvement with religious organizations (such as rates of church attendance), the social and material influence wielded by religious organizations, and the degree to which people hold religious beliefs.

Self-consciousness Awareness of one's distinct social identity, as a person separate from others. Human beings are not born with self-consciousness but acquire an awareness of self as a result of early socialization. The learning of language is of vital importance to the processes by which the child learns to become a self-conscious being.

Self-identity The ongoing process of self-development and definition of our personal identity through which we formulate a unique sense of ourselves and our relationship to the world around us.

Semi-peripheral countries Countries that supply sources of labour and raw materials to the core industrial countries and the world economy but are not themselves fully industrialized.

Sensorimotor stage According to Piaget, a stage of human cognitive development in which the child's awareness of its environment is dominated by perception and touch.

Service class A term adopted by John H. Goldthorpe to describe those whose employment is based on a code of service rather than a labour contract, and whose work therefore involves a high degree of trust and autonomy. In Goldthorpe's account, the service class (which he categorizes as Class I) refers to professional, senior administrative, and senior managerial employees. (Members of the service class are *not* those employed in the service industries.)

Sex The anatomical differences which separate men from women. Sociologists often contrast sex with gender. Sex refers to the physical characteristics of the body; gender concerns socially learned forms of behaviour. Sex and gender divisions are not the same. A transvestite, for example, is someone who is physically a man but sometimes assumes the gender of a woman.

Sex tourism The term used to describe international travel oriented on prostitution. It is most highly developed in the countries of the Far East, where groups of men from abroad travel for the opportunity to engage in inexpensive sexual liaisons with women and young children.

Sexual harassment Unwanted sexual advances, remarks or behaviour by one person towards another, persisted in even though it is made clear that the other person is resistant.

Sexual orientation The direction of one's sexual or romantic attraction.

Sexuality A broad term which refers to the sexual characteristics, and sexual behaviour, of human beings.

Shaman An individual believed to have special magical powers; a sorcerer or witch doctor.

Shared understandings The common assumptions which people hold and which allow them to interact in a systematic way with one another.

Sick role A term, associated with the American functionalist Talcott Parsons, to describe the patterns of behaviour which a sick person adopts in order to minimize the disruptive impact of his or her illness on others.

Simulacra In the world of hyperreality evoked by the French author Jean Baudrillard, simulacra are copies of items for which there is no original. For example, a 'mock Tudor' house looks nothing like original Tudor buildings.

Slavery A form of social stratification in which some individuals are literally owned by others as their property.

Social age The norms, values, and roles that are culturally associated with a particular chronological age.

Social capital The social knowledge and connections that enable people to accomplish their goals and extend their influence.

Social change Alteration in the basic structures of a social group or society. Social change is an ever-present phenomenon in social life, but has become especially intense in the modern era. The origins of modern sociology can be traced to attempts to understand the dramatic changes shattering the traditional world and promoting new forms of social order.

Social constraint A term referring to the fact that the groups and societies of which we are a part exert a conditioning influence on our behaviour. Social constraint was regarded by Durkheim as one of the distinctive properties of 'social facts'.

Social constructionism The theory that social reality is a creation of the interaction of individuals and groups.

Social exclusion The outcome of multiple deprivations which prevent individuals or groups from participating fully in the economic, social and political life of the society in which they are located.

Social facts According to Emile Durkheim, the aspects of social life that shape our actions as individuals. Durkheim believed that social facts could be studied scientifically.

Social gerontology The study of ageing and the elderly.

Social group Collection of individuals who interact in systematic ways with one another. Groups may range from very small associations to large-scale organizations or societies. Whatever their size, it is a defining feature of a group that its members have an awareness of a common identity. Most of our lives are spent in group contact; in modern societies, most people belong to groups of many different types.

Social interaction Any form of social encounter between individuals. Most of our lives are made up of social interaction of one type or another. Social interaction refers to both formal and informal situations in which people meet one another. An illustration of a formal situation of social interaction is a school classroom; an example of informal interaction is two people meeting in the street or at a party.

Social mobility Movement of individuals or groups between different socio-economic positions. Vertical mobility refers to movement up or down a hierarchy in a stratification system. Lateral mobility is physical movement of individuals or groups from one region to another. When analysing vertical mobility, sociologists distinguish between how far people are mobile in the course of their career, and how far the position they reach differs from that of their parents.

Social model of disability A theory that locates the cause of disability within society, rather than the individual. It is not individual limitations that cause disability but the barriers that society places in the way of full participation for disabled people.

Social movement A large grouping of people who have become involved in seeking to accomplish, or to block, a process of social change. Social movements normally exist in relations of conflict with organizations whose objectives and outlook they frequently oppose. However, movements which successfully challenge for power, once they become institutionalized, can develop into organizations.

Social position The social identity an individual has in a given group or society. Social positions may be general in nature (those associated with gender roles) or may be more specific (occupational positions).

Social role The expected behaviour of an individual occupying a particular social position. The idea of social role originally comes from the theatre, referring

to the parts which actors play in a stage production. In every society individuals play a number of different social roles, according to the varying contexts of their activities.

Social self The basis of self-consciousness in human individuals, according to the theory of G. H. Mead. The social self is the identity conferred upon an individual by the reactions of others. A person achieves self-consciousness by becoming aware of this social identity.

Social stratification The existence of structured inequalities between groups in society, in terms of their access to material or symbolic rewards. While all societies involve some forms of stratification, only with the development of state-based systems do wide differences in wealth and power arise. The most distinctive form of stratification in modern societies involves class divisions.

Social structure Patterns of interaction between individuals or groups. Social life does not happen in a random fashion. Most of our activities are structured: they are organized in a regular and repetitive way. Although the comparison can be misleading, it is handy to think of the social structure of a society as rather like the girders which underpin a building and hold it together.

Socialist feminism The beliefs that women are treated as second-class citizens in patriarchal capitalist societies and that both the ownership of the means of production *and* women's social experience need to be transformed because the roots of women's oppression lie in the total economic system of capitalism. Socialist feminists have criticized some socialists' gender-blind understanding of class.

Socialization The social processes through which children develop an awareness of social norms and values, and achieve a distinct sense of self. Although socialization processes are particularly significant in infancy and childhood, they continue to some degree throughout life. No human individuals are immune from the reactions of others around them, which influence and modify their behaviour at all phases of the life cycle.

Socialization of nature The process by which we control phenomena regarded as 'natural', such as reproduction.

Society The concept of society is one of the most important of all sociological notions. A society is a system of structured social relationships connecting people together according to a shared culture. Some societies, like those of hunters and gatherers, are very small, numbering no more than a few dozen people. Others are very large, involving many millions – modern Chinese society, for instance, has a population of more than a billion individuals.

Sociological imagination The application of imaginative thought to the asking and answering of sociological questions. The sociological imagination involves one in 'thinking oneself away' from the familiar routines of day-to-day life.

Sociology of the body The branch of sociology that focuses on how our bodies are affected by social influences. Health and illness, for instance, are determined by social and cultural influences.

Sociology of deviance The branch of sociology concerned with the study of deviant behaviour and with understanding why some behaviour is identified as deviant.

Sociology The study of human groups and societies, giving particular emphasis to the analysis of the industrialized world. Sociology is one of a group of social sciences, which also includes anthropology, economics, political science and human geography. The divisions between the various social sciences are not clear-cut, and all share a certain range of common interests, concepts and methods.

Soil degradation The process by which the quality of the earth is worsened and its valuable natural elements are stripped away through over-use, drought or inadequate fertilization.

Solidarity For Durkheim, the internal forces of social cohesion. More generally, a term often used by the left to describe the political consciousness of an emerging class struggling against oppression – e.g. working-class solidarity.

Source A publication, passage from a publication, or other information that is referred to.

Sovereignty The title to supreme power of a monarch, leader or government over an area with a clear-cut border.

Standard deviation A way of calculating the spread of a group of figures.

State A political apparatus (government institutions, plus civil service officials) ruling over a given territory, with an authority backed by law and the ability to use force. Not all societies are characterized by the existence of a state. Hunting and gathering cultures, and smaller agrarian societies, lack state institutions. The emergence of the state marks a distinctive transition in human history, because the centralization of political power involved in state formation introduces new dynamics into processes of social change.

State-centred theory Development theories that argue that appropriate government policies do not interfere with economic development, but rather can play a key role in bringing it about.

Status The social honour or prestige accorded to a person or a particular group by other members of a society. Status groups normally involve distinct styles of life – patterns of behaviour which the members of a group follow. Status privilege may be positive or negative. 'Pariah' status groups are regarded with disdain, or treated as outcasts, by the majority of the population.

Status set An individual's group of social statuses.

Stereotype A fixed and inflexible characterization of a group of people.

Stigma Any physical or social characteristic believed to be demeaning.

Structuration The two-way process by which we shape our social world through our individual actions and are ourselves reshaped by society.

Subculture Any segment of the population which is distinguishable from the wider society by its cultural pattern.

Suburbanization The development of suburbia, areas of low-rise housing outside inner cities.

Surplus value In Marxist theory, the value of an individual's labour power which is 'left over' when an employer has repaid the cost involved in hiring a worker.

Surveillance society A society in which individuals are regularly watched and their activities documented. The spread of video cameras on motorways, in streets and shopping centres is one aspect of the expansion of surveillance.

Surveillance The supervising of the activities of some individuals or groups by others in order to ensure compliant behaviour.

Survey A method of sociological research usually involving the administration of questionnaires to a population being studied, and the statistical analysis of their replies to find patterns or regularities.

Sustainable development The notion that economic growth should proceed only in so far as natural resources are recycled rather than depleted, biodiversity is maintained, and clean air, water and land are protected.

Sweatshop A derogatory term for a factory or shop in which employees work long hours for low pay under poor conditions.

Symbol One item used to stand for or represent another – as in the case of a flag which symbolizes a nation.

Symbolic interactionism A theoretical approach in sociology developed by Mead, which places strong emphasis on the role of symbols and language as core elements of all human interaction.

Taliban a fundamentalist Islamic militia; by 1996 the Taliban controlled Afghanistan and set up an Islamic government that enforced a strict Muslim code of behaviour. They were overthrown by an American-led international coalition in 2001 after being linked to groups responsible for the September 2001 attacks on New York and Washington.

Talk The carrying on of conversations or verbal exchanges in the course of day-to-day social life. Increasingly this has been seen as a subject for scrutiny by sociologists, particularly ethnomethodologists.

Target hardening Crime deterrence techniques that aim to make it more difficult for crime to take place through direct interventions into potential crime situations. Steering locks in cars, for example, are required in some areas in order to reduce the attractiveness of car theft.

Taylorism A set of ideas, also referred to as 'scientific management', developed by Frederick Winslow Taylor, according to which productivity could be immensely increased by breaking down industrial tasks into a series of simple operations that could be precisely timed and optimally coordinated.

Technology The application of knowledge to production from the material world. Technology involves the creation of material instruments (such as machines) used in human interaction with nature.

Telecommunications The communication of information, sounds or images at a distance through a technological medium.

Thatcherism The doctrines associated with the former British Prime Minister Margaret Thatcher. These doctrines emphasize the importance of economic enterprise coupled to a cutback in the reach of the state, while maintaining a core role for strong national government.

Theism A belief in a god or gods.

Theoretical questions Questions posed by the sociologist when seeking to explain a particular range of observed events. The asking of theoretical questions is crucial to allowing us to generalize about the nature of social life.

Theory An attempt to identify general properties that explain regularly observed events. Theories form an essential element of all sociological works. While theories tend to be linked to broader theoretical approaches, they are also strongly influenced by the research results they help generate.

Theory of broken windows The idea that there is a connection between the appearance of disorder, such as a broken window or vandalism, and actual crime.

Third age The years in later life when people are free from both parenting responsibilities and the labour market. In contemporary societies, the third age is longer than ever before, allowing older people to live active and independent lives.

Third way politics A political philosophy, pioneered by New Labour and favoured by other centrist democratic leaders, that is committed to preserving the values of socialism while endorsing market policies for generating wealth and dispelling economic inequality.

Third World The less developed societies, in which industrial production is either virtually non-existent or only developed to a limited degree. The majority of the world's population live in Third World countries.

Total institutions A term popularized by Erving Goffman to refer to facilities such as asylums, prisons and monasteries that impose on their residents a forcibly regulated system of existence in complete isolation from the outside world.

Totemism A system of religious belief which attributes divine properties to a particular type of animal or plant.

Transnational corporations Business corporations located in two or more countries. Even when TNCs have a clear national base, they are oriented to global markets and global profits.

Triangulation The use of multiple research methods as a way of producing more reliable empirical data than is available from any single method.

Underclass A class of individuals situated right at the bottom of the class system, often composed of people from ethnic minority backgrounds.

Unemployment Rates of unemployment measure the proportion of people who are 'economically active' and available for work but cannot get a paid job. A person who is 'out of work' is not necessarily unemployed in the sense of having nothing to do. Housewives, for instance, don't receive any pay, but they usually work very hard.

Unfocused interaction Interaction occurring among people present in the same setting but where they are not engaged in direct face-to-face communication.

Universal benefits Welfare benefits that are available equally to all citizens, regardless of level of income or economic status. Access to the National Health Service in Britain is an example of a universal benefit, as all Britons have the right to use it on an ongoing basis for regular healthcare.

Upper class A social class broadly composed of the more affluent members of society, especially those who have inherited wealth, own large businesses or hold large numbers of stocks and shares.

Urban ecology An approach to the study of urban life based on an analogy with the adjustment of plants and organisms to the physical environment. According to ecological theorists, the various neighbourhoods and zones within cities are formed as a result of natural processes of adjustment on the part of urban populations as they compete for resources.

Urban recycling The refurbishing of deteriorating neighbourhoods by encouraging the renewal of old buildings and the construction of new ones on previously developed land, rather than extending out to fresh sites.

Urban renewal Reviving deteriorating neighbourhoods by such processes as recycling land and existing buildings, improving the urban environment, managing local areas better and with the participation of local citizens, and using public funds both to regenerate the area and to attract further private investment.

Urbanism A term used by Louis Wirth to denote distinctive characteristics of urban social life, such as its impersonality.

Urbanization The development of towns and cities.

Values Ideas held by human individuals or groups about what is desirable, proper, good or bad. Differing values represent key aspects of variations in human culture. What individuals value is strongly influenced by the specific culture in which they happen to live.

Variable A dimension along which an object, individual or group may be categorized, such as income or height, allowing specific comparisons with others or over time.

Vertical mobility Movement up or down a hierarchy of positions in a social stratification system.

Victimization studies Surveys aimed at revealing the proportion of the population that has been victimized by crime during a certain period. Victim surveys attempt to compensate for the 'dark figure of unreported crime' by focusing directly on people's actual experience of crime.

Welfare capitalism Practice in which large corporations protect their employees from the vicissitudes of the market.

Welfare dependency A situation where people on welfare, such as those receiving unemployment benefit, treat this as a 'way of life' rather than attempting to secure a paid job.

Welfare state A political system that provides a wide range of welfare benefits for citizens.

White-collar crime Criminal activities carried out by those in white-collar or professional jobs.

Work The activity by which human beings produce from the natural world and so ensure their survival. Work should not be thought of exclusively as paid employment. In traditional cultures, there was only a rudimentary monetary system, and very few people worked for money payments. In modern societies, there remain many types of work, including housework, which do not involve direct payment of wages or salary.

Working class A social class broadly composed of people involved in blue-collar or manual occupations.

World-accommodating movement A religious movement that emphasizes the importance of inner religious life and spiritual purity over worldly concerns.

World-affirming movement A religious movement that seeks to enhance followers' ability to succeed in the outside world by helping them to unlock their human potential.

World-rejecting movement A religious movement that is exclusive in nature, highly critical of the outside world, and demanding of its members.

World-systems theory Pioneered by Immanuel Wallerstein, this theory emphasizes the interconnections among countries based on the expansion of a capitalist world economy. This economy is made up of core countries, semi-peripheral countries and peripheral countries.

Zero tolerance policing An approach to crime prevention and control that emphasizes the ongoing process of maintaining order as the key to reducing serious crime. In targeting petty crime and minor disturbances, zero tolerance policing reflects the principles underlying the theory of broken windows.

Credits

The publisher and author would like to thank the following for permission to reproduce copyright material:

5 © Corbis; 6 © (l) Corbis, (r) Mary Evans Picture Library; 9 © Staatliche Museen zu Berlin/BPK; 11 © Getty-Images; 12 © Corbis/Bettmann; 14 © Corbis/Bettmann; 17 © Topfoto; 20 © Corbis/Bettmann; 32 © Christopher Anderson; 34 © Powerstock; 36 © Panos Pictures/Paul Weinberg; 38 © Still Pictures/Fredrick Stark; 47 © Istockphotos; 51 © Rex Features; 53 © Panos Pictures/Dermot Tatlow; 55 © Emma Longstaff c/o Polity Press; 58 © Rex Features; 74 © Getty-Images; 79 © New Yorker Cartoonbank.com; 81 © UPS; 83 © United Media; 87 © AnthroPhoto/Edward Tronick.

102 © Getty-Images; 108 © ASA; 112 © Gezette; 116 © (t) Corbis, (b) © Corbis/ Bettmann; 118 © ASA; 119 © Isolde Ohlbaum; 122 © Nigel Stead/LSE; 128 © Rex Features; 129 © Magnum/Martin Parr; 132 © Paul Ekman; 140 © David Hoffman; 144 © New Yorker Cartoonbank.com; 151 © Alamy/Don Jon Red; 156 © Polity; 162 © Aquarius; 176 © Rex Features; 178 © Empics; 181 © Photofusion/Jackie Chapman; 183 © New Yorker Cartoonbank.com 188 © Photofusion/ Paul Baladesau 195 © Katherine Lamb 196 © Photofusion/Paule Solleway.

204 © Rex Features; 206 © BBC; 207 © Empics/ EPA; 210 © Panos Pictures/Gisele Wulfsohn; 214 © Magnum/David Hurn; 217 © Photofusion/Ulrike Preuss; 228 © Corbis/ Tim Graham; 231 © Empics; 237 © Corbis/ Peter M. Fisher; 252 © (l) Corbis/Viviane Moos, (r) Sally & Richard Greenhill; 253 © The Toilet of Venus, c. 1613 (oil on canvas) Rubens, Peter Paul (1577–1640), Private Collection, Giraudon/Bridgeman Art Library; 255 © Sally & Richard Greenhill; 257 © Photofusion/ Caroline Mardon; 261 © Getty-Images; 265 © Rex Features;

P.267 © New Yorker Cartoonbank.com 275 © Alamy/Janine Wiedel Photo Library; 284 © Empics; 285 © Vicky Lucas; 288 © Empics; 294 © Empics; 299 © Panos Pictures/Eric Miller.

313 © Empics; 321 (l) © Eddie Mulholland/Rex Features; (r)© Paul Grover/Rex Features; 326 © Corbis/Bettmann; 340 © Photofusion/ Ulrike Presse; 343 © (t) Panos Pictures/Chris Sattlberger, (b) Photofusion/Joanne O'Brien; 350 © Courtesy of Campaign for Racial Equality; 360 © Alamy/Photofusion; 362 © Corbis/Ashley Cooper; 364 © Rex Features; 369 © Popperfoto; 371 © Empics; 386 © (t)Rex Features, (b)United Media; 387 © Corbis/ Andrew Holbrooke; 398 © Corbis/Peter Turnley; 399 © Panos Pictures/Pietro Cenini.

400 © (l) Corbis/Dean Conger, (r) Corbis/ Danny Lehman; 417 © Panos Pictures/Sean Sprague; 422 © Still Pictures/Ron Gilling; 426 © Panos Pictures/Chris Sattlberger; 434 © Corbis/C J Gunther/Suma; 438 © Ancient Art & Architecture; 439 © Alamy/Frank Herbholdt; 444 © Mary Evans Picture Library; 452 © New Yorker Cartoonbank.com; 455 © Corbis/Lynn Goldsmith; 461 © Corbis/T & G Baldizzo; 472 © Roger Scruton; 482 © Corbis/ David Turnley; 484 © Empics/EPA; 486 © Empics/EPA 489 © Empics 491 © Rex Features; 492 © Empics/Associated Press; 498 © Food Features.

501 © Panos Pictures; 502 © Fabrica; 503 © Popperfoto; 510 © Alamy/Janine Wiedel Photo Library; 516 © Rex Features; 522 © Empics; 533 © Rex Features; 538 © Rex Features; 543 © Photofusion/Don Gray; 548 © Rex Features; 554 © Roger Scruton; 556 © Network Photographers/Barry Lewis; 568 © Rex Features; 573 © Empics/Associated Press; 576 © Empics/EPA; 584 © Corbis; 585 © Corbis/Reuters; 589 © Corbis; 593 © Rex Features.

Index

early merchant cities, 104
and European Union, 858
film industry, 622
gender learning, 170
illegal immigration, 520
migrants, 319
Milan, 926
and Mother Teresa, 532
protests against Iraq war, 842
Red Brigades, 885
religion, 558
secularization, 555
social mobility, 329

Jacoby, Sanford, 657
Jahoda, Marie, 785
Jamaica, 63
Janowitz, M, 899
Japan
    1950s development, 402, 404
    agrarian sector, 39
    Aum Shinrikyo, 551, 871
    and Barbie, 57
    Buddhism, 545
    car industry, 747
    colonial power, 403
    core country, 411
    eating disorders, 254
    economic shift, 911
    economic slowdown, 666
    education, 702
    effect of WWII, 49
    film industry, 622
    First World, 42
    global cities, 923, 926
    health level, 279
    high-income country, 390
    kamikaze pilots, 15
    knowledge economy, 771
    labour unrest, 404
    old age, 183, 198–9
    organizational model, 665–6
    role of state in economy, 412
    social capital, 677
    social mobility, 329
    sogo shosha, 660
    transnational corporations, 55, 658, 660
Jasper, K., 253
Jedi, 559
Jehovah's Witnesses, 562
Jencks, Christopher, 363
Jenkins, C., 780
Jensen, Arthur, 723

Jesus, 46, 549, 553
Jews, 297, **492**, 500, 542–3, 559, 560, 564, 565, 570
Jobling, R., 270
John, Jeffrey, 553
John, M. T., 182
John Paul II, Pope, 532, 553, 570
Jones, D. E., 567
Jones, Trevor, 721
Jordan, **55**, 628–9
Joy, B., 953
Judaism, 535, 542–3, 560
Judge, K., 280
Julius Caesar, 46

Kadish, Marcia, 434, 435
Kafka, Franz, 639
Kaldor, Mary, 887
kamikaze pilots, 15
Kamin, L. J., 724
Kanter, Rosabeth Moss, 663–4
Karzai, Hamid, 852
Kasada, J. D., 899
Kashmir, 873, 886
Katz, J. E., 154, 157, 192, 609
Kautsky, J., 39
Kazakhstan, 519
Keith, M., 518
Kelly, David, 615
Kemp, A., 476
Kemsley, Lord, 588
Kennedy, J. F., 405
Kenya, 42, 886
Kepel, G., 576, 577
Keynes, John Maynard, 780–1
Khamenei, Ayatollah Ali, **573**, 574
Khatami, Mohammad, 574, 853
Khomeini, Ayatollah, **573**, 573–4
Kiecolt, K. J., 576
Kim Il Sung, 48
Kim Jong Il, 48, 849
Kinsey, Alfred, 444–7, 448, 453
kinship, 206–7, 899
Kirkwood, T., 182, 183
Klu-Klux-Klan, 485
Knoke, D., 670
Knorr-Cetina, K., 25, 134
knowledge society, 54, 321, 770–2
Kochanowicz, J., 411–12
Kollock, Peter, 157
Kopomaa, Timo, 924–5
Koresh, David, 547, **548**
Koser, K., 519, 520
Kosovo, 54, 499, 575, 652